D1615347

THE LAY SUBSIDY
OF 1334

Particulars of Account for part of Repton hundred, Derbyshire, 1334.
(Public Record Office, London, E 179/91/7)

RECORDS OF SOCIAL AND ECONOMIC HISTORY
NEW SERIES · II

THE LAY SUBSIDY
OF 1334

EDITED BY

ROBIN E. GLASSCOCK

LONDON · *Published for* THE BRITISH ACADEMY
by OXFORD UNIVERSITY PRESS
1975

Oxford University Press, Ely House, London W. 1

GLASGOW NEW YORK TORONTO MELBOURNE WELLINGTON
CAPE TOWN IBADAN NAIROBI DAR ES SALAAM LUSAKA ADDIS ABABA
DELHI BOMBAY CALCUTTA MADRAS KARACHI LAHORE DACCA
KUALA LUMPUR SINGAPORE HONG KONG TOKYO

ISBN 0 19 725933 2

© *The British Academy 1975*

Printed in Great Britain
at the University Press, Oxford
by Vivian Ridler
Printer to the University

PREFACE

THE purpose of this volume is to publish under one cover the returns of the Lay Subsidy of 1334, a taxation on personal property for which coverage is available for almost the whole of England. The subsidy is of considerable value for the study of various aspects of medieval history, coming as it did shortly before the Black Death and before the full impact of the social and economic change that followed. Much use has already been made of these tax returns in the few counties for which they have already been published. The analysis and interpretation of the returns is not attempted in this volume except through some brief discussion in the Introduction.

This work began fifteen years ago as a thesis on the distribution of lay wealth in south-east England in 1334. Like so many theses it has lain dormant for some years but in a renewal of activity the basis of the original work has been expanded to cover England as a whole. It is a pleasure to record my thanks to those who have contributed to this work in various ways over many years. The guidance of Mr. E. K. Timings of the Public Record Office, London, has been invaluable throughout all stages of the work. For discussion of general problems and advice on particular matters I am indebted to Dr. K. J. Allison, Dr. R. S. Schofield, Dr. A. B. Scott, Dr. J. Sheail, Dr. J. Z. Titow, and Dr. M. Williams. For help in the identification and location of particular place-names in different counties I have made acknowledgement in the introduction to each county list in the text.

I am indebted to Mr. G. R. Versey, not only for drawing maps I and II but for many helpful discussions about the mapping of the tax returns. The burden of the typing has fallen at different times and in different places on Mrs. Betty Watt, Mrs. Laura Busbridge, Mrs. Velma Atcheson, Miss Elizabeth Knox, and Miss Pamela Martin. To them, and to other typists who have helped at critical moments of trying to meet deadlines, I am most grateful, as I am also to Mrs. Joan Kenny and to Mrs. Rosemary Logan who gave valuable assistance in the preparation of this material. My sincere thanks are also due to Mrs. Ann Warren who undertook the making of the index, and to the British Academy who gave a grant towards its preparation.

My thanks go to Professor H. C. Darby who, through his teaching and writing, aroused my interest in medieval England and who first encouraged me to work on the 1334 Lay Subsidy. I am indebted to him and to the Cambridge University Press for permission to reproduce the maps from my contribution to *A New Historical Geography of England* (1973), ed. H. C. Darby. Professor Maurice Beresford and Mr. John Hurst indirectly helped this work along by involving me in their work on medieval settlement and the depopulation of villages. Finally I wish to thank Professor E. M. Carus-Wilson for encouraging me to publish these lay subsidy returns, for her constructive editorial guidance, and for her patience in awaiting the final typescript. By endeavouring to prepare this material in Belfast during 1971–3 I feel that I have maintained the dramatic element referred to in the preface to the first volume of this new series.

For the errors that have crept through I bear sole responsibility. I hope that others, in using the volume, will fill the gaps, resolve some of the queries, and let me have a note of any corrections that need to be made. If the volume is found to be a useful aid in further historical inquiry it will have fulfilled the purpose for which it is designed.

ROBIN E. GLASSCOCK

Department of Geography
The Queen's University of Belfast
November 1973

INTRODUCTORY NOTE TO THE NEW SERIES

ONE of the earliest publishing ventures of the British Academy was the launching, in 1914, of the series entitled 'Records of the Social and Economic History of England and Wales' which reflected the pioneer work then being done in this field of study. The series was continued until the appearance, in 1935, of Volume IX, after which it lapsed. Since then, however, interest in social and economic history, far from abating, has greatly increased; more and more scholars have been drawn to research in the subject, and the teaching of it has so developed that it has become an integral part of the curriculum in most universities, whether in social science faculties or in departments of history. The Academy has therefore thought it appropriate to revive its original project, slightly expanding its scope, and in 1972 it issued the first volume of a new series of 'Records of Social and Economic History'. The title of the series has been thus abbreviated to permit the introduction of material other than that relating only to England and Wales, and in accordance with this policy the first volume—*Charters of the Honour of Mowbray 1107–1191*—covered the whole honour of Mowbray, thus including charters concerning lands in Normandy as well as in ten different counties of England. Similarly the fourth volume is planned to include surveys of both the Norman and the English estates of the Abbey of Caen. The creation in the last half-century of many new local record societies and the increasing activity of many old ones have opened up fresh opportunities for the publication of social and economic records relating to a particular locality, but it is hoped that this new series will prove especially valuable as a means of publishing material, such as that in this second volume, which does not fall within the scope of any one local record society.

E. M. CARUS-WILSON

Chairman
Records of Social and Economic
History Committee

CONTENTS

PREFACE — v

INTRODUCTORY NOTE — vii

LIST OF ILLUSTRATIONS — xi

A NOTE ON FOOTNOTE REFERENCES — xii

INTRODUCTION

    I. The lay subsidies of the early fourteenth century — xiii

    II. The fifteenth and tenth of 1334 — xv

    III. Exemptions from the lay subsidy of 1334 — xvii

    IV. The 1334 tax quotas: what they represent and their uses in historical inquiry — xxiv

EDITORIAL NOTES — xxxiii

ABBREVIATIONS — xxxviii

THE LAY SUBSIDY OF 1334

    Bedfordshire — 1

    Berkshire — 6

    Buckinghamshire — 15

    Cambridgeshire — 23

    Cornwall — 29

    Cumberland (1336) — 36

    Derbyshire — 42

    Devon — 49

    Dorset — 67

    Essex — 79

    Gloucestershire — 90

    Hampshire — 105

    Herefordshire — 122

    Hertfordshire — 131

    Huntingdonshire — 136

    Kent — 140

    Lancashire — 149

Leicestershire	157
Lincolnshire	167
City of London	187
Middlesex	189
Norfolk	192
Northamptonshire	209
Northumberland (1336)	219
Nottinghamshire	227
Oxfordshire	237
Rutland	246
Shropshire	249
Somerset	258
Staffordshire	276
Suffolk	284
Surrey	297
Sussex	304
Warwickshire	319
Westmorland (1336)	328
Wiltshire	332
Worcestershire	349
Yorkshire	356
East Riding	357
North Riding	371
West Riding	382
INDEX OF PLACE-NAMES	397

LIST OF ILLUSTRATIONS

Particulars of Account for part of Repton hundred, Derbyshire, 1334. (Public Record Office, London, E 179/91/77)   *frontispiece*

MAPS

I. Assessed lay wealth in 1334   *page* xxvii

II. Taxation boroughs in 1334   xxxi

A NOTE ON FOOTNOTE REFERENCES

All documents cited are in the Public Record Office, London, unless otherwise stated.

A number of references used in footnotes throughout the Introduction and text are abbreviated as follows:

C.C.R.	*Calendar of Close Rolls*
C.F.R.	*Calendar of Fine Rolls*
C.P.R.	*Calendar of Patent Rolls*
E.H.R.	*The English Historical Review*
Ec.H.R.	*The Economic History Review*
E.P.N.S.	The English Place-name Society
F.A.	*Feudal Aids, 1284–1431*, 6 vols., London, 1899–1920
K.R.M.R.	King's Remembrancer Memoranda Rolls, P.R.O.
P.R.O.	Public Record Office
V.C.H.	*The Victoria History of the Counties of England*

INTRODUCTION

1. *The lay subsidies of the early fourteenth century*

THROUGHOUT the early fourteenth century the continual trouble with France on the one hand and with Scotland on the other made extra demands upon the revenue of the Crown. With increasing frequency these special needs were met by subsidies granted by Parliament to the Crown in the form of taxes upon the personal wealth of the laity.[1] By this means of taxation, first used in the late twelfth century, people paid taxes based upon the value of their movable goods, principally on crops and stock (see pp. xxiii–xxiv), rather than on their land and buildings. The fraction of the value of goods that a man might pay in tax varied from one year to another, perhaps a ninth, perhaps a twentieth, but the principle remained the same. Such subsidies were regarded as additional sources of crown revenue over and above regular income and for this reason they were particularly useful in financing military operations, either already undertaken or planned. J. F. Willard, author of the standard monograph on these taxes, has shown that the majority of subsidies levied between 1290 and 1322 were in fact destined for purposes of war although this was not always specifically stated.[2]

The subsidies of the early part of the reign of Edward III (1327–77) continued what had by then become established practice. The threat of Scottish invasion prompted the tax of a twentieth in 1327 and, together with the troubles in Ireland, was the main motive behind the fifteenth and tenth of 1332. Despite successes over the Scots at Dupplin Moor (1332) and Halidon Hill (1333) the threat of invasion from the north was still a

---

[1] The taxes upon personal property of the laity are commonly termed lay subsidies, the name given to the class of documents in the Public Record Office, London, in which the tax rolls are included (class E 179). All documents to which reference is made in this volume are in the P.R.O., London, unless otherwise stated.

The typed county lists of the subsidy rolls available in the Public Record Office have now been photographically reproduced and published by The List & Index Society as follows:

Vol. 44 (part I, Bedford–Essex), 1969
Vol. 54 (part II, Gloucester–Lincoln), 1970
Vol. 63 (part III, London–Somerset), 1971
Vol. 75 (part IV, Stafford–Yorkshire), 1972
Vol. 87 (part V, Wales, . . . Diverse Counties, etc.), 1972.

[2] J. F. Willard, *Parliamentary Taxes on Personal Property 1290 to 1334*, Cambridge, Mass., 1934, 19–21. For shorter accounts of the lay subsidies see M. W. Beresford, 'The lay subsidies', *The Amateur Historian*, 3 (1958), 325–8, and 4 (1959), 101–9. These articles were expanded and published later as *Lay Subsidies and Poll Taxes*, 1963.

probability and as a precautionary measure Parliament, meeting at West-minster, granted a further tax upon personal property on 19 September 1334. The rate was to be the same as that in 1332, namely a fifteenth from rural areas and a tenth from boroughs (see p. xxvii) and ancient demesnes.[3] But while it was modelled on the same principle this tax differed in an important respect from its predecessors, for in 1334 the system of direct taxation on the wealth of individuals was replaced by one whereby every community agreed upon a sum which it was to pay. While the sum (or 'quota' as it has been aptly called by Beresford) was to be agreed by negotiation between the taxers and the community it was stipulated that the amount was to be not less than the collective sum paid by individuals to the fifteenth and tenth of 1332. This new departure is reflected in the changing format of the taxation documents of 1334 and after, when the lists of personal names and amounts that characterize the lay subsidy rolls before 1334 were replaced by comparatively brief statements showing only the total sums due from every township and borough.[4] In order therefore to understand the background to the 1334 lay subsidy it is necessary to draw upon the greater detail available in the surviving rolls of its immediate forerunners, the twentieth of 1327 and the fifteenth and tenth of 1332.

The general procedure for assessment used in the nine lay subsidies between 1307 and 1332 may be briefly summarized as follows. The assess-ment of the value of movables and the subsequent determination of the tax and its collection were supervised by two chief taxers in each county or other appointed district. These men, usually landowners, were selected on the basis of their status and because they had a working knowledge of the districts in which they were chosen to serve. Having received their com-missions and travelled to their assigned districts the chief taxers summoned before them a number of men from whom they selected four to six sub-taxers for each taxation unit. Having been sworn in, the sub-taxers went from house to house on the appointed day (usually Michaelmas, 29 September) valuing the relevant movable goods and recording the information of local rolls. The tax payments due were summarized and written on an indented roll, one half of which was used for the subsequent collection of money while the other was retained by the chief taxers.

---

[3] Ancient demesnes were, in general, rural manors which had been listed under the heading *Terra Regis* in Domesday Book. The terms *antiquum dominicum* and *dominici domini regis* are both found in the early fourteenth-century subsidies; for a full discussion of their meaning see R. S. Hoyt, *The Royal Demesne in English Constitutional History*, Ithaca, New York, 1950, 171–207.

[4] For an example of the contrast between the pre- and post-1334 rolls see the transcrip-tions of the Surrey rolls of 1332 and 1336 in *Surrey Taxation Returns*, eds. J. F. Willard and H. C. Johnson, Surrey Record Society, xviii (1922) and xxxiii (1932).

Until 1332 the responsibility for the valuation and collection lay squarely on the local men of each township; the chief taxers acted in a supervisory capacity and were the agents through whom the Exchequer received the money. But both local men and chief taxers were tempted to line their own pockets before the crown purse, and hardly a tax went by without justified charges of corruption being levelled at both chief and sub-taxers.[5] In respect of such accusations the twentieth of 1 Edward III (1327) had a better record than many of its predecessors, but the complaints which followed the fifteenth and tenth of 6 Edward III (1332) were so numerous that the government could no longer afford to ignore them. Indeed, a number of the abuses of 1332 only came to light when the taxers of 1334 were making their rounds two years later.[6] Government concern to protect the Exchequer, to allay discontent, and to protect people from the misdeeds of the collectors[7] resulted in the introduction of the new method of taxation in 1334 together with changes in the personnel concerned. These changes, although directly prompted by the abuses of 1332, were in fact, as Willard has remarked, 'the outcome of over forty years' experience with alleged and proved fraud',[8] and one cannot help but feel that action of this kind was long overdue.

11. *The fifteenth and tenth of 1334*

The chief taxers in 1334 were men above the ordinary run of suspicion. As before, two were chosen for each county or appointed district, but this time one was a leading ecclesiastic, usually an abbot or a prior, and the other an officer of the Crown.[9] In fact 1334 was the only year when the leading clergy were called upon in any number to supervise the collection of a lay subsidy. The commissions made it clear that only the ecclesiastic was answerable for the collection and delivery of the money. In addition the government sought to make the taxation more efficient, and thereby to increase its yield, by taking the assessment out of the hands of the ever-suspect sub-taxers. It ceased to concern itself directly with the wealth of individuals and instructed the chief taxers to negotiate and reach agreement with local people on how much each community should pay, a proviso being that the agreed amount should be no less than that paid in 1332.[10] If the sum could not be decided by negotiation then the chief taxers plus a clerk appointed by them were to carry out an assessment on the old lines.

[5] For examples, see Willard (1934), op. cit. in note 2, 205–29.   [6] Ibid. 224.
[7] Described in Patent Roll, 8 Edward III, *Rot. Parl.* ii. 447, as *oppressiones, extorsiones et gravamina huiusmodi.*
[8] Willard (1934), op. cit. in note 2, 219.
[9] For a list of the appointments see *C.P.R., 1334–1338*, 38–40.
[10] K.R.M.R., No. 111, m. 321.

This new method had its antecedents in earlier taxations when, in order to escape from the inconvenience of assessment, some boroughs paid an agreed sum or fine for exemption from the tax.[11]

Thus in 1334, with a few exceptions, notably Kent, the method of negotiation with communities replaced that of direct assessment on individuals. How each sum was apportioned and raised within each unit was left in the hands of local men. It does seem, however, that the sums agreed upon were considered a reasonable compromise by both taxers and taxed; the fact that agreement was reached in almost every case suggests that there was give and take on both sides. For the communities the slight increase over the sums paid in 1332 was probably a small price to pay to avoid a new and painstaking (and more honest?) assessment of the value of personal possessions. Unfortunately for the historian, however, the new method obviated the need for detailed rolls, so that it is impossible to see what processes went on at the local level in the lay subsidy of 1334.

Parliament and the King must have been pleased with the first fruits of the new method of taxation, for it certainly proved to be more efficient and, as a result, the total tax increased from £34,295. 17. 2½d. in 1332 to £37,429. 18. 0½d. in 1334. At the granting of the next fifteenth and tenth in 1336 a move towards further efficiency was made when the lengthy job of assessment was dispensed with altogether and the taxers were ordered to collect the same quotas as those agreed in 1334. To facilitate this they were issued with a copy of the 1334 details; some of the rolls of 1336 still have indentures of 1334 attached to them.

The fifteenth and tenth of 1336 proved to be the first of many lay subsidies which were based directly on the quotas agreed upon in 1334, and from this time onwards the fifteenth and tenth became a standard form of taxation, lasting on and off for almost three hundred years until 1623. Robbed of its original meaning it came to be recognized as a fixed sum of money, that of 1334, which could be raised whenever Parliament saw fit to make a grant. By this means the Crown was assured of a fixed income which would not be lessened as it might have been if there had been either a reassessment of movable wealth at every grant or an increase in corrupt practices such as under-valuation.[12] Within a very short time the tax ceased to bear any direct relationship to the lay wealth and taxable capacity of the country. The flexibility of the earlier taxes on movables was lost and the

---

[11] For example, London fined for £2,000 in the tax of 1306, and Bristol for £200 in 1332. There were occasions when smaller towns used the same method, as in 1319 when Taunton fined for £16. 13. 4 and Stafford for £20. 6. 8, and in 1332 when Melton Mowbray fined for £13. 10. 0 (Willard (1934), op. cit. in note 2, 131–5).

[12] Despite the improvements of 1334 it was not to be long before complaints against the collectors for illegal gains were heard again, for example in 1349 and 1351: B. H. Putnam, *The Enforcement of the Statute of Labourers* (1908), 102–3.

Crown had to resort to other means in order to meet its financial commitments and to adjust to the varying economic fortunes of local communities.
As it happened, with rapid social and economic change in the next century,
much of it consequent upon the Black Death, many communities found
themselves unable to raise the 1334 quota and had to apply for relief.[13]

The standardization of the taxes after 1336 takes away much of the
interest that they might have retained had there been a reassessment of
wealth at every grant. But an important consolation is that the few surviving
tax rolls of 1334 may be supplemented by later ones which give the same
information, and by this means it has been possible to obtain complete
coverage for all those parts of England which were liable to the fifteenth
and tenth of 1334. For this reason the 1334 subsidy is most valuable and is
very different from all other early fourteenth-century taxes on personal
property since from these only a patchy coverage is obtainable.

III. Exemptions from the lay subsidy of 1334

Before evaluating the 1334 tax returns and their uses for historical
inquiry it is as well to be clear on what was *not* taxable in the lay subsidy.
Certain types of property and particular areas not subject to the tax are
discussed under the following headings:

(i) Clerical property   (a) of the clergy
                        (b) of the villeins of the clergy.
(ii) The taxable minimum and the valuation of goods.
(iii) Counties and palatinates.
(iv) Local exemptions.

(i) Clerical property

(a) of the clergy

In the introduction to his transcription of the Suffolk lay subsidy roll
of 1327, S. H. A. Hervey wrote, 'The question of the taxation of the clergy
is complicated and I shall shirk it.'[14] His admirable honesty was under-
standable in 1906 when only a few workers, notably Dowell, Stubbs, and
Vincent, had touched upon the problem.[15] Such a statement would not be
acceptable today, for the works of Rose Graham, Lunt, and Willard,[16]

[13] For useful accounts of the subsequent history of the fifteenth and tenth see, *Surrey Taxation Returns* (1932), lv–lix, and Beresford (1963), op. cit. in note 2, 7–19.
[14] S. H. A. Hervey, 'Suffolk in 1327', *Suffolk Green Books*, 9 (1906), xv.
[15] S. Dowell, *A History of Taxation and Taxes in England*, 4 vols., 2nd edition, 1888. W. Stubbs, *The Constitutional History of England*, 3 vols., 1896. J. A. C. Vincent, 'Lancashire lay subsidies', *Record Society for Lancs. and Cheshire* (1893).
[16] Rose Graham, 'The Taxation of Pope Nicholas IV', *E.H.R.*, 23 (1908), 434–54. W. E. Lunt, *The Valuation of Norwich*, 1929. Willard (1934), op. cit. in note 2.

among others, have clarified many of the problems of clerical taxation. If we are to understand the 1334 figures then we have to face the same problem which bothered Hervey, namely, why was a certain part of the property of the church included in the lay subsidy and what did it comprise. It is only necessary here to restate the position as it affected the 1334 taxation and in doing this I have drawn heavily on the work of Willard with whose conclusions I absolutely agree.

The 1334 rolls show only the quotas for the townships and boroughs as agreed between the taxers and local communities. The main exception to this rule is the roll for Kent, a county in which the system of taxation remained the same as in 1332 and where the names of the individual taxpayers continued to be recorded.[17] Among the names on this roll are those of several clergy, and their mention on other county rolls of 1327 and 1332 leaves no doubt that some clerical property was liable for the lay subsidy.

Clerical incomes were principally derived from two main sources, i.e. Spiritualities or incomes from tithes, oblations, and glebe, and Temporalities or incomes from other land, manors, markets, burgages, etc., held by the clergy in a similar way to those held by the laity. In order to facilitate the assessment and collection of papal taxes two great schedules of clerical property had been drawn up in the second half of the thirteenth century, the Valuation of Norwich in 1254 and the Taxation of Pope Nicholas in 1291. The 1291 valuation included all the Spiritualities of the church and the greater part of the Temporalities[18] (subsequently referred to as Temporalities annexed to Spiritualities). All the property listed in 1291 was thereafter subject to clerical taxation and exempt from lay subsidies.

Even by 1307, the year of the first lay subsidy of Edward II, some confusion about the procedure had set in and instructions to the lay taxers were made more explicit. It was restated that all the property of the church listed in 1291 should be exempt but that personal property upon, or issuing from, land acquired by the clergy since 1291, or upon temporal property not listed in the papal schedule, was to be taxed whenever a subsidy upon movables was granted.[19] Furthermore, after deductions for rents and services the movable goods of the villeins of the clergy were to be liable to the lay subsidy. This general procedure was observed throughout the reign of Edward II, and although the specific clauses were omitted from the instructions issued under Edward III we may be certain that the same

[17] E 179/123/12; printed in H. A. Hanley, and C. W. Chalklin, eds., 'The Kent lay-subsidy roll of 1334–5', *Kent Records*, xviii (1964), 58–172.

[18] Rose Graham, op. cit. in note 16, 448–51.

[19] See J. F. Willard in *Surrey Taxation Returns*, 1922, op. cit. in note 4, xi.

precepts were followed in the taxations of 1327, 1332, and 1334. In other words, the clerical property subject to inclusion in these lay subsidies consisted of (i) movable goods on Temporalities not annexed to Spiritualities and therefore not listed in 1291, (ii) movable goods on Temporalities acquired by the church between 1291 and 1327 (a period in which acquisitions were minor compared with the preceding two centuries), and (iii) the movable goods of villeins of the clergy, allowance having been made for rents and services. We may conclude therefore that only a very small fraction of clerical property was taxed in the lay subsidies.

An examination of some county rolls of 1332 and the Kent roll of 1334 shows the system as it applied first to the clergy and, secondly, to their villeins.

Over thirty clergy are named on the Kent roll, the only county roll of 1334 which lists the individual taxpayers.[20] In addition to local clergy the list includes the bishops of London and Rochester, the abbots of Westminster, Lesnes, Boxley, Langdon, St. Augustine's Canterbury, and St. Radegund, the abbess of Malling, and the priors of Beaulieu, St. John, Southwark, and Rochester. This confirms that in 1334, as in 1327 and 1332, some clergy contributed to the lay subsidy. Although we do not have the names of the taxpayers in other counties in 1334 we can say with certainty that the clergy made tax contributions in many communities. Unfortunately we do not know, even for Kent, upon what goods the clerics paid nor precisely where their goods were assessed, since the tax unit in Kent was the hundred and not the vill as elsewhere. However, it is possible to show from an examination of the detailed roll of 1332 for Buckinghamshire[21] that the clergy were taxed on the same kind of goods as the laity.

On the Buckinghamshire roll one of the taxpayers was the prioress of Studley, Oxfordshire, who was charged 2s. 1¾d., being a fifteenth of goods valued at 32s. 2d. in Ilmer with Aston Sandford. The goods were as follows: 1 beast value 2s.; 1 ox value 6s.; 1 heifer value 4s.; 2 quarters wheat value 6s. 8d.; 3 quarters drage (mixed corn) value 7s. 6d.; 2 quarters beans value 5s.; hay and fodder value 1s. The prioress is also named on the Warwickshire roll of 1332 where she is taxed at 3s. 4d. in Compton Magna.[22] The goods on which she was taxed are similar to those of the laity.

[20] E 179/123/12. There are a few other instances of townships and boroughs where the taxpayers are named, for example, those of Salisbury, Ludgershall, and Hindon on the Wiltshire roll of 1334 (E 179/196/10), and for Northumberland on the roll of 1336 (E 179/158/7).

[21] E 179/242/4; printed in A. C. Chibnall, ed., 'Early taxation returns', *Bucks. Rec. Soc.* 14 (1966), 17.

[22] E 179/192/5; printed in W. F. Carter, ed., 'The lay subsidy roll for Warwickshire of 6 Edward III (1332)', *Dugdale Soc. Publications*, 6 (1926). It is not certain when Studley acquired its property in Ilmer with Aston Sandford and Long Compton. The priory was excused the tax of 1291, probably because of poverty, *V.C.H., Oxon.* II (1907), 78.

In Warwickshire, nineteen leading clergy are named on the roll of 1332. They include the bishops of Ely and Norwich, the abbots of Alcester and Stoneleigh, six priors, four prioresses, and five masters of hospitals. All are named once except the prior of Kenilworth whose goods were taxed in three places, and the master of the hospital of St. John in Coventry in two. Of the twenty-two charges against these clerics ten were cancelled *per breve* (by the King's writ) when they reached the correctors. The remaining twelve charges stood. The bishop of Ely, for example, paid 5*s.* in Austrey, the bishop of Norwich 12*s.* 1*d.* in Long Compton, and the abbot of Alcester 8*s.* in Exhall.[23] These charges were the highest in each vill.

These examples show the uncertainty of the local taxers in the field. Several of the above clergy claimed to be free of this imposition,[24] saying that the lands upon which their goods had been assessed were Temporalities annexed to Spiritualities and that the goods were liable to clerical taxation. At the Exchequer the claims of eight of the Warwickshire clerics, including the prior of Kenilworth, were upheld and the charges cancelled. When one considers the extent of the property of Kenilworth abbey in Warwickshire[25] and the fact that in the end none of it was charged, it may be better appreciated how much clerical property was excluded from lay subsidies. The same may be shown elsewhere.[26]

The tax charges against the Warwickshire clergy which were allowed to stand must have been on movable property on land which for some reason had not been taxed in 1291 or had been acquired after that date. A preliminary examination shows that most of the payments were in vills where the property had been acquired before 1291 and that the lay tax must therefore have been on Temporalities not annexed to Spiritualities. In none of the above examples has acquisition after 1291 been proved, but the topic calls for detailed studies combining the evidence of subsidy rolls and surviving cartularies. The best approach would probably be from the opposite angle, namely to identify monastic acquisitions after 1291 and then to see whether tax was paid on them.

(b) of the villeins of the clergy

The local taxers in Surrey in 1332 either forgot, or were not told of, the accepted procedure with regard to the taxation of the villeins of the

---

[23] Carter, op. cit. in note 22, 16 (Long Compton), 59 (Austrey), 81 (Exhall).

[24] See Willard (1934), op. cit. in note 2, 107.

[25] Dugdale, *Monasticon*, vi. 220–5, and *V.C.H.*, *Warwicks.* II (1908), 86.

[26] For example, the cartularies of the Bedfordshire houses of Chicksand (*Beds. Hist. Rec. Soc.* 1 (1913)), Old Warden (*B.H.R.S.* 13 (1930)), and Bushmead (*B.H.R.S.* 22 (1945)) show their extensive possessions in the county. Yet in 1332 the goods of the abbot of Chicksand were assessed in only three vills, those of the abbot of Warden in eight, and those of the prior of Bushmead in only one. All the tax charges were later cancelled.

clergy.[27] They overcharged many of them by valuing their goods and deciding upon the tax charge before services and goods due to the lord as payments had been deducted. In correcting this error the taxers promptly made another, for, forgetting that there was a minimum clause in 1332 (men in rural areas with movables valued at less than 10s. were exempt), they merely subtracted from the original charge the amount that had been wrongly included. What should have happened may be seen at Southease in Sussex where, after the valuation of the goods of the villeins of the prior of Lewes, the amounts due to the prior were allowed for when the tax charges were decided.[28] It was the error of procedure in Surrey which resulted in seventy-five villeins of the clergy being taxed at less than 8d., the usual minimum charge. What is of more interest is that the mistake brings to light seventy-five men who would in normal circumstances have escaped the tax.

On the Surrey roll of 1332 villeins of the clergy are included in sixteen vills. Of the 283 listed 196 were villeins of the abbot of Chertsey, a house which had thirteen demesne manors in the county.[29] Villeins paid tax in all of these except Horley, one of the abbey's least valuable possessions. In the twelve vills concerned the total number of taxpayers named was 410[30] of whom 196 or 47 per cent were villeins of the abbot. If the seventy-five who were included by mistake are deducted, the number of taxpayers would have been 335 of whom 121 or 36 per cent were villeins of the abbot. By a similar calculation 38 per cent of the taxpayers in the vills where the abbot of Westminster had manors were his villeins.

In Surrey, therefore, it is clear that while the clergy did not pay tax on certain possessions their villeins on Temporalities did. This explains why over the whole country almost every vill which contained a clerical manor is named in the lay subsidies. In Leicestershire, for example, sixteen of the seventeen places with demesne manors of Leicester abbey which were under cultivation in 1341 appear in the subsidy of 1334.[31] Similarly, Gaydon has shown that of the thirty-four clerical manors in three Bedfordshire hundreds only five were excluded from the tax of 1297.[32]

We are fortunate that the Surrey roll of 1332 differentiates the villeins on clerical property. On the rolls of other counties only a comparison of

[27] E 179/184/4; *Surrey Taxation Returns*, 1922 and 1932, op. cit. in note 4.

[28] L. F. Salzman, 'Early taxation in Sussex', *Sussex Arch. Coll.* 98 (1960), and 99 (1961), part II, 1961, 9 and table on p. 15.

[29] Chertsey Abbey Cartularies, 2, pt. 1, xl–l. *Surrey Rec. Soc.* xii (1958).

[30] Ibid. 337–44. Three additional villeins are named in Cobham who are not named on the 1332 roll. The figures given by Willard (1934), op. cit. in note 2, 176, are very different as he used only part of the 1332 roll.

[31] Named in R. H. Hilton, *The Economic Development of some Leicestershire Estates in the Fourteenth and Fifteenth Centuries* (1947), 50; only Stainton by Bagworth is not in 1334.

[32] A. T. Gaydon, 'The taxation of 1297', *Beds. Hist. Rec. Soc.* 39 (1959), xxvii.

the names of the taxpayers with those on the records of clerical manors will yield this information. This has been tried for three Hampshire manors of the bishop of Winchester. Dr. J. Z. Titow has kindly examined my transcriptions of the names of the taxpayers in the vills of Fareham, East Meon, and Bishop's Waltham in 1332[33] and I am greatly indebted to him for the information he has supplied. For all three manors he was able to show that the majority of taxpayers were the bishop's tenants. In Fareham three only of the nine taxpayers could not be traced in entry fines for the years around 1332, and in East Meon, only three of the thirteen. For Bishop's Waltham the task was made easier by a rental of *c.* 1331–2, and only one taxpayer could not be traced. Unfortunately we cannot tell upon which goods these people were assessed, since although the rental lists their possessions it does not specify movables. Of more importance, this exercise showed that only a small fraction of the total tenant population paid tax in 1332 (and presumably also in 1334). Even when allowance is made for the minimum clause the question of the inclusion of some tenants and not others is a problem upon which further work is needed.

(ii) *The taxable minimum and the valuation of goods*

The new method of taxation adopted in 1334 did not explicitly provide for the exemption from tax, as in 1332, of those with goods valued at less than ten shillings in rural areas and at less than six shillings in boroughs and ancient demesnes. But as the 1334 quotas were based directly upon what was collected in 1332 we might expect that those who escaped in 1332 were not expected to contribute in 1334. It is not known how local communities raised the sums agreed upon in 1334. In all probability the method varied from place to place, but we can say with certainty that in general the agreed quotas of 1334 were reached without taking into account the movable property of a large percentage of the people in every township and borough whose movable goods were valued at less than ten shillings.

We must also take into account that there were not only deliberate concealments of movable goods but more subtle types of evasion in the form of both conventional valuation and under-valuation by the taxers. The local rolls of subsidies before 1334 show that grain and stock were seldom valued at their market prices. For the taxers it was easier to undervalue than to risk juggling with the arithmetic and being subsequently discovered; no doubt this was the way by which local taxers kept at least on speaking terms with fellow villagers while ensuring that some money found its way to the Exchequer. The quotas of 1334 show that the tax charges were often only approximate. The opportunity was often taken by the 1334 taxers to

[33] E 179/242/15a, mm. 5, 7d, 8.

agree on quotas in round figures or in multiples of a quarter mark (3s. 4d.). Is it chance that 131 of the 140 quotas in Cambridgeshire end in a round shilling? In some counties, for example adjacent Essex, the taxers were either more meticulous or fearful of the consequences of rounding off the figures. While there are minor variations of this kind from one county to another there is no reason to think that any one locality was markedly more dishonest than any other. The basis of assessment remained the same over all and while evasion and dishonesty unquestionably affect the total amount of tax, thus making it impossible to think in terms of *absolute* wealth, they should not unduly distort the *relative* distribution of movable wealth.

(iii) *Counties and palatinates*

The palatinates of Chester and Durham were exempt from royal taxation and there is therefore no data for the modern counties of Cheshire and County Durham. Cumberland, Northumberland, and Westmorland were excused from the 1334 subsidy on account of recent devastation by the Scots.[34] But they were not exempted from the subsidy of 1336 and the returns for that year are included in this volume. It should be remembered, however, that the tax quotas are bound to reflect the unsettled condition of the north at this time. In Shropshire the hundreds of Oswestry and Clun were both exempt from English law and are not included in the returns for the county.

(iv) *Local exemptions*

Since men of the liberty of the Cinque Ports were exempt from the lay subsidies, several ports wholly within the liberty are nowhere mentioned in the 1334 returns even though they were boroughs. Among them are Dover, Sandwich, Hythe, and New Romney in Kent, and Hastings, Pevensey, Rye, and Winchelsea in Sussex. On the Kent 1334 roll, however, which lists individual taxpayers, individual charges on the men of the liberty for their movables both in the liberty and in other parts of the county are in fact included in the returns for each hundred, although there was never any intention of collecting the money. Tax charges against the moneyers of Canterbury are similarly included, although these men were also exempt (see p. 140). The Sussex roll of 1334 does not list individual taxpayers; hence we have no clue as to the extent of their movable possessions in the county.

In the south-west the stannary men, or tinners, of Devon and Cornwall were exempted (see introduction to the Devon list, p. 49). Other lesser

[34] *C.P.R., 1334–1338*, 38–40, for the appointed taxers for these counties, positions later vacated.

catagories of local exemption have been treated at length by Willard (1934, Chapter VI) and need not be elaborated upon here.

IV. *The 1334 tax quotas: what they represent and their uses in historical inquiry*

The subsidy rolls of 1334, and of subsequent grants of the fifteenth and tenth, are comparatively stark records which in most cases record only the names of the townships and boroughs and the quotas which they were to contribute to the lay subsidy. Unfortunately they give us no information as to what percentage of the population contributed or upon what goods they were taxed.

It is not possible to say how many people or what percentage of the population contributed to the lay subsidy of 1334. The apportionment of payments within each community was left at the discretion of local men and we have little idea how this was done either in 1334 or in subsequent levies of the fifteenth and tenth when there had been changes in personnel and in the economic status of individuals within each community.[35] As the 1334 quotas were based upon the direct assessment of the movable goods of individuals in 1332 the only answer to the question of how many were taxed must be sought from the rolls of that year. Yet the rolls of 1332, like those of 1327, name only the taxpayers in each unit; they tell us nothing of the total population nor should they be used to estimate it. All the evidence suggests that only a relatively small number of people in each community paid tax, so that at best the evidence of 1327 and 1332 may be used only to infer the relative size of places, and then only after the number of taxpayers, the size of the tax charges, and the area of the units have been taken into account. If possible the social structure of communities and the distribution of wealth within them must also be considered.

On the question of estimating total population from the lay subsidy rolls I will do no more than quote from the findings of Willard: 'After many attempts to discover a method of estimating population on the basis of the rolls of taxation of movables, I have given up the search. In my opinion, the greatest difficulty, that of determining the number of people whose taxable property was worth less than the minimum provided, is insurmountable. In comparison, the other difficulties are of minor importance. It is evident, however, that the names of a very large number of the people never appeared on the rolls of a fifteenth and tenth and that any estimates of the total population based on such rolls may be regarded as purely

---

[35] Some work has been done along these lines for Kent where the burden of paying the tax was re-examined at every grant (Hanley and Chalklin, op. cit. in note 17, 62).

conjectural and probably erroneous.'[36] If this is so for the rolls of 1327 and 1332 then it almost goes without saying that the rolls of 1334 are of absolutely no use in this respect.

On the question of which goods were taxable only local rolls of the period before 1334 (p. xxxiv) give details of the movable goods of the taxpayers, their value, and the resulting tax charges. Few such rolls have as yet been discovered and few have been published. The best examples for rural areas are those for the hundred of Blackbourne, Suffolk, in 1283, for three hundreds of Bedfordshire in 1297, for a part of Sussex in 1332, and for parts of Buckinghamshire in the same year.[37]

Examination of such local rolls shows that the movables in rural areas usually meant the larger domestic animals (horses, cattle, sheep, and pigs), grains (wheat, barley, oats, rye, and mixed corn), other crops (peas, beans), hay and fodder, and very occasionally carts and items of merchandise. Personal effects were officially exempt from taxation and there is rarely mention of household goods, utensils and farm implements, poultry or eggs, bread and drink, cheese and other foods. Since the instructions to the taxers stated that all goods in the hands of the people at Michaelmas were to be taxed this seems odd, but clearly it was customary practice for the taxers to ignore the essential goods which a household needed for day-to-day living.

From a detailed study of local rolls Willard concluded that invariably the amounts of movable goods listed, especially grain, were insufficient to carry a family through the following winter, let alone leave any surplus for sale.[38] It is unlikely that the small size of these amounts was due to concealment, for if it was we might expect to find considerable variations depending upon local production and the integrity of the taxers and the taxed. Nor could it be due to the arbitrary selection of goods as the amounts stated on local rolls are usually most precise. Gaydon postulated that perhaps only the threshed corn was liable to tax, but thinks that if this was so one would expect to find references to corn in sheaf.[39] My own feeling is that the most plausible explanation is that proposed by Willard, and since supported by Gaydon and Salzman, namely that the taxers were following much earlier precedent by not taxing either the food provided and ready for use (as instructed in 1283) or that which was not for sale (as instructed in 1225).[40] This would mean that the goods listed on local rolls are those over and

[36] Willard (1934), op. cit. in note 2, 181.
[37] E. Powell, *A Suffolk Hundred in 1283*, 1910. Gaydon (1959), op. cit. in note 32. Salzman (1960–1), op. cit. in note 28. A. C. Chibnall, 'Early taxation returns', *Bucks. Rec. Soc.* 14 (1966).
[38] Willard (1934), op. cit. in note 2, 73–7.
[39] Gaydon (1959), op. cit. in note 32, xxi.
[40] Willard (1934), op. cit. in note 2, 84–5.

above the everyday needs of the villager and his family, or in other words the surplus which was saleable.

Although this explanation is acceptable it has not yet been proved. In testing Willard's 'surplus' hypothesis Gaydon compared the movables on the Bedfordshire roll of 1297 with those on other documents but unfortunately there is not an exact coincidence of dates. If there was we might hope to compare total movable goods with those which were taxed, thereby isolating what was considered basic and what surplus. Gaydon's work has shown, however, that the movables taxed in 1297 were far fewer than those on near-contemporary extents and reeves' accounts. If we accept that movables taxed were surplus then many questions are consequent upon this. For example, did a number of people in many vills have hay and fodder in excess of their own needs? Does the mention of a cart imply that a man had more than one, that the cart was for sale, or that it was simply considered surplus to basic requirements? Much detailed research is needed into this whole question of surplus, but unfortunately the instances where local tax rolls may be compared with more detailed contemporary records will be found to be very few indeed.

Assuming that the movables taxed did represent surplus then light is thrown upon two important problems. First, this would help to explain why only a limited number of householders in every community paid tax. Second, it might help to resolve the puzzle of why men who from other sources are known to be fairly wealthy did not pay tax. A man with greater commitments or a larger family to support might not have paid, whereas a poorer man with fewer foods but lesser responsibilities might have had a small surplus for sale and was therefore taxed upon his goods.

If we accept, therefore, that the tax charges upon movables represent, for the most part, taxes upon goods over and above basic needs then the returns, when mapped, will in fact show the relative distribution of surplus on lay property, or what Buckatzsch has called 'important income-generating resources'.[41] Map I is such a map for the lay subsidy of 1334, the only year in the fourteenth century for which a detailed map of this kind may be compiled for almost the whole of England. Even so there are no data for Cheshire and Durham, and the figures included for Cumberland, Northumberland, and Westmorland are those of 1336. For the purpose of making the map the tax quotas for every place have been multiplied by ten or fifteen as the case may be to give the value at which the movable goods were assessed. These values have then been calculated

[41] E. J. Buckatzsch, 'The geographical distribution of wealth in England, 1086–1843', *Ec.H.R.*, 2nd series, 3 (1950), 180–202. See also the article critical of Buckatzsch's views by R. S. Schofield, 'The geographical distribution of wealth in England, 1334–1649', *Ec.H.R.*, 2nd series, 18 (1965), 483–510.

in averages per square mile. As the basis of assessment was the same over all and on the assumption that the payments reflect the ability of an area to pay, the resulting map may be regarded as a fair indicator of the relative

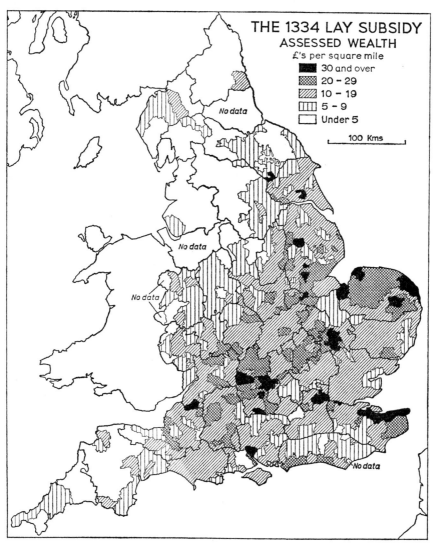

THE 1334 LAY SUBSIDY
ASSESSED WEALTH
£'s per square mile
■ 30 and over
▨ 20 – 29
▧ 10 – 19
▥ 5 – 9
□ Under 5

100 Kms

MAP I

distribution of lay wealth over the country. It is important to stress, how-ever, that the map represents only the assessed movable wealth included in the lay subsidy; it does not show total wealth. A serious drawback is the omission of most of the movable wealth of the church (cf. pp. xvii–xxii), but even if allowance were to be made for this and for other exemptions it is likely that the pattern of relative prosperity over the country as a whole would be refined rather than radically altered, as has been demonstrated by Schofield looking at it county by county.[42] In more detailed studies of smaller areas the exclusion of clerical property is more serious, as for example in marshland areas owned by monastic houses and grazed by their flocks.

Although the purpose of this volume is to make available the 1334 data rather than to attempt their analysis and interpretation some comments upon the general picture might be of help to those who wish to work on these figures for particular areas and to fit their findings into the pattern for the country as a whole. The map presents visually the same picture that emerges when the counties are ranked according to their average assessed wealth per thousand acres[43] or per square mile.[44] In general terms, a line drawn from York to Exeter would divide England in 1334 into the wealthier land of the south and east, with assessed wealth above £10 per square mile, and the poorer areas of the north and west, with values below £10. Within lowland England there was a noticeable zone of wealth running south-west to north-east across the country from Somerset and Wiltshire to Norfolk, Lincolnshire, and the East Riding. Within this belt many areas had assessed wealth well above average at over £20 per square mile. Outside it the only rural areas of comparable wealth were the Thames valley, east Kent, and the coastal plain of Hampshire and Sussex. All these areas carried twice, and in places three times, as much movable wealth as the west midlands and the north.

There was a scatter of very wealthy localities, some of which were linked to the wealth of towns, as for example to London, Bristol, Southampton, King's Lynn, and York. But a number of rural areas without large towns had values of over £30 per square mile, for example the marshland of east Norfolk, north-west Norfolk, north Kent, upland Cambridgeshire, parts of mid Oxfordshire, west Berkshire, and the Kesteven claylands of Lincolnshire. No common factor may be found to explain such a distribution; it is likely that these very high assessments reflect exceptional local agricultural prosperity. More detailed work suggests that the wealthiest parts of England in 1334 were intensively farmed, fertile, lowland areas associated especially with grain farming.[45] With the exception of Norfolk and Kent the more prosperous areas were situated within H. L. Gray's zone

[42] Schofield, op. cit., in note 41, 503–9, especially maps 1 and 2.
[43] Schofield, op. cit., table 2, column (2).
[44] Glasscock, in H. C. Darby, ed., *A New Historical Geography of England*, 1973, 137–43.
[45] R. E. Glasscock, 'The distribution of lay wealth in south-east England in the early fourteenth century', unpublished Ph.D. thesis, University of London, 1963, 63–76.

of the midland field system. One thing is clear, however, namely that very different amounts of movable wealth were found in areas of similar physical conditions and, on the other hand, there were very similar amounts on contrasting areas. For example, values of between £20 and £30 per square mile were to be found on the silts of the Lincolnshire fenlands, on the clays of western Cambridgeshire, and on the medium soils of much of Norfolk. While climate, relief, and soils exerted broad controls over differences in agriculture and underlay the marked contrast between the north-and-west and the south-and-east, the wealth of any particular locality can only be explained in terms of its local physical, economic, and social conditions.

To this end the 1334 figures have already been used in a number of studies of particular counties and regions[46] and it is to be hoped that there will be similar studies for other parts of England.

Whereas Map I is a composite picture of urban and rural wealth in 1334 it is possible to consider these separately. Most of the published studies referred to have been principally concerned with the rural areas, and as yet comparatively little work has been done on the towns. There is, for example, the intriguing question of the selection of taxation boroughs; this varied from one subsidy to the next and does not seem to have conformed to any consistent rules. Nor do the places selected correspond with places defined as boroughs by charter, burgage tenure, etc. Some places considered boroughs in 1334, and therefore taxed at the higher rate of the tenth, were not considered boroughs a few years earlier or later.[47] Conversely some towns which were considered boroughs in earlier taxations were not so in 1334. Many places which were taxed as boroughs had tax quotas smaller than many villages and could hardly have been thought of as truly urban

[46] F. W. Morgan, 'The Domesday geography of Devon', *Trans. Devon. Assn.* 72 (1940), 321. H. C. Darby, *The Medieval Fenland*, 1940. W. G. Hoskins, 'The wealth of medieval Devon' in W. G. Hoskins and H. P. R. Finberg, *Devonshire Studies*, 1952, 212–49. W. G. Hoskins and E. M. Jope, 'The medieval period', in A. F. Martin and R. W. Steel, eds., *The Oxford Region*, 1954, 109. C. T. Smith, 'Population. III. The thirteenth and fourteenth centuries' in *V.C.H., Leics.* III (1955), 132–6. B. Reynolds, 'Late medieval Dorset; three essays in historical geography', unpublished M.A. thesis, University of London, 1958. R. E. Glasscock, thesis, 1963, op. cit. in note 45 (includes brief studies of the distribution of lay wealth within twenty-five counties of midland and south-east England). R. E. Glasscock, 'The distribution of wealth in East Anglia in the early fourteenth century', *Trans. Institute of British Geographers*, 32 (1963), 113–23. R. E. Glasscock, 'The lay subsidy of 1334 for Lincolnshire', *Lincs. Architectural and Archaeological Soc. Reports and Papers*, 10, part 2 (1964), 115–33. R. E. Glasscock, 'The distribution of lay wealth in Kent, Surrey and Sussex, in the early fourteenth century', *Arch. Cantiana*, 80 (1965), 61–8. N. J. G. Pounds, 'Taxation and wealth in late medieval Cornwall', *Jnl. Royal Institution of Cornwall*, new series vi (1971), 154–67.

[47] J. F. Willard, 'Taxation boroughs and parliamentary boroughs, 1294–1336' in J. G. Edwards *et al.*, eds., *Historical Essays in Honour of James Tait*, 1933, 417–35 (this paper includes a very useful list of taxation boroughs for the period 1294–1336).

in function. On the other hand some large towns, notably London, Boston, and Coventry were not considered taxation boroughs and consequently escaped the higher rate of the tenth. Map II shows that except in Somerset and Wiltshire there were very few taxation boroughs in the wealthier zone of the south and east. They were more numerous in the south-west where they were clearly related either to the personal choice of the taxers or, more likely, to the profusion of new boroughs created there in the twelfth and thirteenth centuries.[48]

For many reasons, but particularly because of the problem of the inclusion or exclusion of suburbs in tax quotas, it is not easy to construct an entirely satisfactory list of towns ranked in the order of their taxed movable lay wealth.[49] There are no data for Chester and Durham, both of which would probably be fairly high on the list, and the Cinque Ports were excluded. Although a revised ranking has been produced[50] it has to be admitted that any list based on the 1334 returns must have its weaknesses and could only be used as a rough guide to the relative status of towns. As yet no work has been done on the ranking of lesser towns and villages in particular parts of the country.

Yet, despite their limitations, the tax quotas of 1334 are still very useful. Apart from their value in the study of medieval taxation and as indicators of relative wealth in 1334, subsidy returns may be used in many other ways. They provide, for instance, a fairly comprehensive list of settlements and place-names for the early fourteenth century. While many small places are not named in 1334 few sizeable places escaped mention; approximately 13,089 places are specifically named on the rolls apart from the numerous unspecified 'members'. Since additional names may be obtained from earlier subsidy rolls and from the *Nomina Villarum* of 1316[51] there is the nucleus here of a gazetteer of early fourteenth-century England. From the 1334 list it is also possible to reconstruct the outlines of the contemporary hundreds and wapentakes for each county.[52]

The place-names and tax quotas of 1334 may also be used in studies of change in particular areas. By looking backward, so to speak, from 1334 to the Domesday survey it is possible to see the relative growth of settlements recorded in 1086 and also to notice the new 'arrivals' of the twelfth- and thirteenth-century colonization period. With a view to the possibility of comparing maps of the 1334 lay subsidy with maps of population and other

[48] Maurice Beresford, *New Towns of the Middle Ages*, 1967, 399–402.

[49] W. G. Hoskins (*Local History in England*, 1959, 174–8) used the 1334 figures for the ranking of towns but unfortunately overlooked the problem of the different rates of taxation. [50] Glasscock, in Darby (1973), op. cit. in note 44, 184.

[51] Published in *Feudal Aids, 1284–1431*, 6 vols., London, 1899–1920.

[52] Maps for twenty-five counties of midland and south-east England are included in Glasscock, thesis, 1963, op. cit. in note 45.

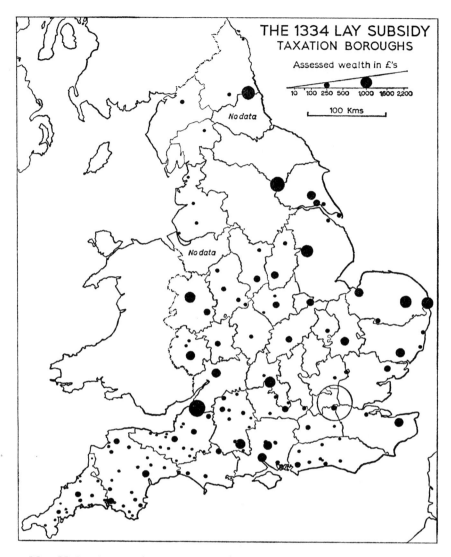

MAP II. London, taxed at a fifteenth, is shown by an outline circle for comparative
purposes in view of its great size.

features in 1086 the areal units used as a basis for the calculation of
assessed wealth per square mile (Map I) are identical to those used in H. C.
Darby's *Domesday Geography of England.*[53]

Looking forward in time the 1334 subsidy provides an especially
valuable base-line against which to measure later change. This is not only

[53] Glasscock, thesis, 1963, op. cit. in note 45.

because of its exceptional coverage but also because it comes at an oppor-
tune moment fourteen years before the Black Death and before the great
changes of the late fourteenth and fifteenth centuries. For areas where
the relevant records are extant, comparisons with the poll tax returns of
1377–81 and the fifteenth-century tax reliefs give indications of change
subsequent to the Black Death.[54] In this respect the 1334 subsidy returns
have played an important part in the study of the desertion of medieval
villages, for the identification and location of places listed in 1334 have
produced many examples additional to those discovered by map and field
evidence, and the comparative tax quotas and tax reliefs have been used to
great effect in the study of the location and chronology of village desertion.[55]

In every county of England there is need for detailed studies of medieval
social and economic life and settlement. If, by making the 1334 subsidy
returns more accessible, this volume can aid such work it will have served
the purpose for which it is designed.

[54] See part II of Beresford (1963), op. cit. in note 2, for the lay subsidies after 1334, the
poll taxes, and tax reliefs.
[55] As in M. W. Beresford, *The Lost Villages of England*, 1954, and M. W. Beresford and
J. G. Hurst, eds., *Deserted Medieval Villages: Studies*, 1971.

EDITORIAL NOTES

THE aim in the accompanying text has been to present the basic lists, county by county, of the places taxed in 1334 together with their tax quotas. The lists are *not* transcriptions of specific lay subsidy rolls. As has been explained in the Introduction (p. xvii) the exceptional coverage for almost the whole of England is possible only because the surviving rolls of 1334 may be supplemented from later rolls which give similar information. All of the accompanying county lists have in fact been compiled from the information in two or more subsidy rolls; for this reason membrane numbers of specific rolls are not included. It has been found in almost every case that the order of the lists of hundreds and wapentakes (in turn inherited from pre-1334 rolls) remains much the same in subsequent rolls of the fifteenth and tenth. Nevertheless where more than one roll is extant there are slight variations in the number of place-names included, in the spelling of place-names, and in the amounts of tax (due both to errors and to changes). In addition there are differences in marginal information, much of it added later, relating to exemptions, cancellations, and to the collection of the money, but except where these are relevant to the sums agreed upon in 1334 they are omitted.

This volume is not concerned with how money did or did not reach the Exchequer, nor with the related problems of collection, of deductions for expenses, of transport of cash to the Exchequer, nor with the procedures of accounting. For the period 1290 to 1334 these details have been dealt with by J. F. Willard in his major work on the taxation processes of the period. A similar detailed study of lay taxation after 1334 has still to be written. In one way the subject loses some fascination in that the quotas agreed upon in 1334 were used as the basis for all subsequent grants of the fifteenth and tenth. On the other hand there are new lines of inquiry to be explored such as the frequency and fraction of the grants (sometimes a double fifteenth and tenth), and the search for new forms of taxation which would augment the yield from the fifteenth and tenth. Of particular interest are the fifteenth-century reliefs and abatements to the basic 1334 quotas which gave some clues to the economic fortunes of particular communities. For a brief introduction to the problems and uses of taxation returns after 1334 the reader is referred to M. W. Beresford's *Lay Subsidies and Poll Taxes*, 1963.

Types of documents

The separate stages of assessment, collection, and auditing of the fifteenth and tenth are represented by different types of documents, the characteristics of which may be briefly summarized as follows:[56]

(a) Local rolls

Before 1334 detailed rolls were compiled in duplicate by sub-taxers, stating for particular boroughs and vills the names of the taxpayers and the movable possessions of each, with their value and the resulting tax assessment. These rolls are of great value for seeing the tax process at the local level and, in particular, for establishing which goods were considered taxable and what value was placed upon them (see pp. xxv–xxvi).

The usual practice throughout the early fourteenth century was that one copy of each local roll was retained by the sub-taxers and one by the chief taxers. The rolls were not sent to the Exchequer unless an official, when verifying the figures or investigating an irregularity, requested to see them. Consequently very few local rolls ever ended up in the Exchequer records; those that did were soon regarded as expendable and were later thrown away or sometimes cut up and used to tie up other medieval documents. Only a few survived.

The change in the method of taxation in 1334 obviated the need for such detailed local rolls showing possessions and valuations and thereafter local rolls show only the taxpayers and the amounts they contributed to the fixed quota for the borough or vill. No local rolls of 1334 are known but some later ones are extant and more may come to light in local records. One example is the Leicester record of the 1336 subsidy (Leicester borough records, Box 4, nos. 93 and 94) which shows the taxpayers, the amounts they paid, and the total sum sent to the Exchequer after the deduction of expenses.[57]

(b) County rolls (P.R.O., class E 179)

These are summaries, drawn up by the chief taxers for each county, of the information contained in the local rolls. For lay subsidies before 1334 they list for each township the names of those with movable goods liable for tax and the amount due from them. Personal names were omitted from the county rolls of the fifteenth and tenth of 1334 and later (see p. xiv), and

---

[56] For a full account of the taxation process see J. F. Willard (1934), op. cit. in note 2. A most useful summary of the main types of documents, with transcriptions, is contained in *Surrey Taxation Returns*, op. cit. in note 4 (1922, xii–xix, for before 1334, and 1932, lxiii–lxxvi, for 1334 and afterwards).

[57] Printed in *Records of the Borough of Leicester*, ed. Mary Bateson, ii (1901), 34–40.

under the headings of hundreds or wapentakes only place-names and the agreed sums due from each community are given. Boroughs and ancient demesnes taxed at a tenth are sometimes listed separately. Despite their comparative brevity these rolls were described in the Exchequer as rolls of *Particulars of Account*. The Particulars for 1334 take the form of an indenture (*indentura*) between an official of the Exchequer and the chief taxer setting out the amount due from each community (see frontispiece). All the place-names and tax quotas in the accompanying lists are taken from county rolls of Particulars.[58]

(*c*) *Accounts* (P.R.O., class E 179)

Accounts (*compoti*) are brief statements drawn up at the Exchequer after the first stage of audit, with the names of the Exchequer auditors, a baron and a clerk, always appearing at the top. Accounts for 1334 survive for almost all counties and they are useful, if brief, statements of the names of the taxers, the total sums due from each county at a fifteenth and at a tenth, and the names of places taxed as boroughs and ancient demesnes.[59] A line drawn through the Account from top to bottom denotes that the document is cancelled and that the information has been recorded elsewhere, usually on the Memoranda Roll of the Lord Treasurer's Remembrancer.

(*d*) *Enrolled Accounts* (P.R.O., class E 359)

After the final audit at the Exchequer the position was recorded on an Enrolled Account of the Lord Treasurer's Remembrancer of the subsidy for the whole country. All counties for which the collectors had accounted at the Exchequer are listed and the total sums received are included. Both Accounts and Enrolled Accounts are particularly useful sources of information about the collection of tax, deductions for expenses, etc., and amounts reaching the Exchequer. The 1334 information may be found in E 359/8. The county totals have already been published by J. F. Willard.[60]

The accompanying county lists

To the lists of places and tax charges as recorded on the original subsidy rolls have been added identifications and grid references. For each county there is a brief introduction noting from which documents the information

---

[58] For an example of a roll of Particulars see the Surrey roll of 1336 (E 179/184/6) in *Surrey Taxation Returns*, op. cit., 1932, lxv–lxix. A useful list of townships and their tax quotas for the whole country is a Book of Fifteenths and Tenths compiled from earlier Particulars sometime in the early fifteenth century (E 164/7). Despite its clarity (it can be of use in reading place-names) the book is full of errors and should be used with caution.

[59] For an example of this type see the Surrey Account of 1334 (E 179/184/5) in *Surrey Taxation Returns*, ibid., lxxiv.

[60] J. F. Willard, 'Taxes on movables in the reign of Edward III', *E.H.R.* 30 (1915), 69–74.

is derived (that marked with an asterisk being the principal one), the names of the taxers in 1334, the total tax yield expected according to the agreed assessments, notes on such matters as boroughs and ancient demesnes, the boundary of the county in the early fourteenth century, places in the modern county taxed elsewhere in 1334, and references to previous publications that are of particular help in work on the 1334 subsidy.

The accompanying lists consist of four columns:

(i) *Place-names as in 1334*

These are as they appear on the document marked * in the introduction to the county, unless otherwise stated. Contractions in the middle of names have been expanded but the terminal apostrophe left. Many names are difficult to transcribe with certainty both because of illegibility and because of the similarities between the letters u and n, c and t, e and o. Initial ff has been changed to F, and where v is the obvious form it has been used instead of u.

Where an entry refers to more than one place-name, the second name is indented in the accompanying text for the sake of clarity; the form of linked entries in the originals varies greatly according to the size of the writing and the space available on the document.

Where places are designated *burgus, villa*, etc., a symbol is added in the lists (see Abbreviations, p. xxxviii). Where places appear *cum membris* (c.m) suggestions are made in footnotes as to which places might be meant, especially if evidence is available from an earlier subsidy roll or from the *Nomina Villarum* of 1316 (published in *Feudal Aids*, i–vi).

(ii) *Modern names*

Identifications are inevitably more certain and complete in counties for which there are already volumes of the English Place-name Society. Even so there are many uncertainties and these are denoted by ?, and, where possible, likely identifications are explored in footnotes.

Modern place-name spellings are taken from the latest Ordnance Survey One Inch and Two-and-a-half Inch series. Although there are many variations of spelling on these maps, especially in hyphenated place-names, the same rule of following the Ordnance Survey maps has been observed throughout. For places which are no longer in the county in which they were taxed in 1334 their recent—as of 1960—county is stated.

(iii) *Grid references*

National grid references are given. These consist of letters denoting the 100 kilometre grid square followed by six-figure references. These national grid references are now applicable to all large-scale Ordnance Survey maps. The grid reference is usually to the church even if this is some distance from the settlement. If there is no church then the reference is to the main cluster of buildings carrying the name. In the case of deserted villages the reference given is either to a farm or single building which retains the name, or, in cases of total desertion, to the earthworks or to the approximate site of the village, using the references in the county gazetteers in M. W. Beresford and J. G. Hurst, eds., *Deserted Medieval Villages: Studies*, 1971, 182–212.

(iv) *Tax quotas*

The tax quota for each place, as listed, is normally the one that appears on the roll of Particulars marked by an asterisk. Sometimes, however, this is not so owing either to illegibility or to an error of some kind on the original. In such cases the correct figure (arrived at by cross-checking with other rolls) is given.

County totals are given from Accounts and Enrolled Accounts.

Roman numerals have been changed to Arabic figures, and the sums converted to £. *s. d.* from the original form on the documents (often in shillings only, sometimes in marks). (T) after a quota denotes that the tax was at the higher rate of the tenth.

ABBREVIATIONS

A.D	*antiquum dominicum*	ancient demesne
B	*burgus*	borough
Ba	*baronia*	barony
c.h	*cum hamelettis*	with hamlets
c.m	*cum membris*	with members
d	*decennaria*	tithing
Dm. hd.	*dimidium hundredum*	half-hundred
for'	*forinsecus*	foreign, or without
h	*hamelettus*	hamlet
H	*honor*	honor
Hd.	*hundredum*	hundred
int'	*intrinsecus*	within
La	*leucata*	lowy
Lib.	*libertas*	liberty
man.	*manerium*	manor
P	*parochia*	parish
p	*pars (parte de)*	part
[T]		taxed at a tenth
V	*villa*	town/township
va	*villata*	township
Wap.	*wapentagium*	wapentake

BEDFORDSHIRE

DOCUMENTS

8 Edward III: Account   E 179/71/14
8 Edward III: Particulars not extant
10 Edward III: Particulars E 179/71/15*

TAXERS

The prior of Dunstable and Hugh de Croft

TAX YIELD

15th	£654.	18.	9¾
10th	£ 19.	11.	7
	£674.	10.	4¾

Representing assessed movable wealth of

£10,019. 19. 0¼

NOTES

Bedford, a taxation borough in 1332 and 1336 but not in 1334, was the only place taxed at a tenth and is listed at the end of the roll. The outline of the county in 1334 was slightly different from that of the modern county. Holwell and Tilbrook, both taxed in Bedfordshire, have since been transferred to Hertfordshire and Huntingdonshire respectively. Kensworth, Barwythe hamlet in Studham, and parts of Meppershall and Caddington, now in Bedfordshire, were taxed in Hertfordshire in 1334.

REFERENCES

Hilary Jenkinson, 'Some Bedfordshire assessments for the taxation of a ninth (1297)', *Beds. Hist. Rec. Soc.* 8 (1924), 119–31.
S. H. A. Hervey, 'Two Bedfordshire subsidy lists, 1309 and 1322', *Suffolk Green Books*, 18 (1925).
A. T. Gaydon, 'The taxation of 1297', *Beds. Hist. Rec. Soc.* 39 (1959).

Hd. Bikeleswad [BIGGLESWADE HUNDRED]

Saundeye	Sandy	TL/174491	6.	8.	8
Dunton'	Dunton	TL/238442	3.	12.	6¼
Mulnho	Millow	TL/229433	4.	8.	8
Hattele	Cockayne Hatley	TL/256496	5.	12.	2
Langeford	Langford	TL/185413	4.	6.	3¾
Potton'	Potton	TL/223491	5.	8.	8
Edworth'	Edworth	TL/222406	2.	5.	0¾
Sutton'	Sutton	TL/222473	5.	14.	4
Bikeleswad	Biggleswade	TL/182446	5.	11.	2½

Holm cum Estwyk'	Holme with Astwick	TL/197426 TL/213385	3.	14.	8
Eyeworth'	Eyeworth	TL/250456	3.	2.	8
Berkford cum Everton'	Little Barford with Everton	TL/178570 TL/203513	3.	16.	6
Temeseford	Tempsford	TL/162530	3.	18.	0
Wrastlyngworth'	Wrestlingworth	TL/259473	5.	18.	9
Stratton'	Stratton	TL/204442	2.	13.	8½
			66.	11.	10¾

Hd. Bereford [BARFORD HUNDRED]

Eton'[1]	Eaton Socon	TL/171589	10.	12.	0
Wyboldeston'	Wyboston	TL/164566	8.	7.	1½
Chaluesterne	Chawston	TL/157562	5.	14.	7½
Colmord	Colmworth	TL/109586	7.	0.	2
Wilden'	Wilden	TL/094552	4.	19.	4
Rokkesdon'	Roxton	TL/153545	5.	4.	0
Goldyngton'	Goldington	TL/077510	3.	7.	4
Ronhal cum Ravenesden'	Renhold with Ravensden	TL/089529 TL/078543	6.	7.	8½
Bereford	Great Barford	TL/134517	5.	18.	8
			57.	10.	11½

Hd. Wylie [WILLEY HUNDRED]

La Lye	Thurleigh	TL/052585	3.	8.	6½
Bletnesho	Bletsoe	TL/023583	2.	11.	8
Turveye	Turvey	SP/940526	8.	10.	2
Podyngton'	Podington	SP/942627	5.	4.	8
Harewold	Harrold	SP/954567	3.	6.	1
Bromham cum Bidenham	Bromham with Biddenham	TL/014513 TL/014499	10.	8.	8
Carlton' cum Chelewyngton'	Carlton with Chellington	SP/954552 SP/961563	4.	15.	1
Pabenham	Pavenham	SP/992560	3.	15.	7
Stacheden'	Stagsden	SP/982491	6.	2.	6
Wodhulle	Odell	SP/967581	4.	9.	4
Stevyngton'	Stevington	SP/991536	5.	2.	8½
Felmersham	Felmersham	SP/992579	5.	17.	0
Sharnebrok'	Sharnbrook	SP/994596	7.	0.	0
Wemyngton'	Wymington	SP/955644	3.	17.	0
			74.	9.	0

Hd. Wixtonstr' [WIXAMTREE HUNDRED]

Wiliton'	Willington	TL/107498	3.	6.	11¼
Coupol	Cople	TL/103484	4.	12.	8
Blounham	Blunham	TL/153511	4.	19.	8

---

[1] Sudbury, in Eaton Socon, was taxed in Barford hundred in 1332 (E 179/71/13), but does not appear on subsequent rolls of the fifteenth and tenth until 1352 (E 179/71/25) when it was taxed at 7s. as in 1332.

Mogerhang'	Mogerhanger	TL/143493	4.	12.	9½
Southgiuel	Southill	TL/146422	5.	7.	4
Wardon'	Old Warden	TL/137433	3.	7.	9
Beeston'	Beeston	TL/169483	3.	16.	2¾
Kerdyngton'	Cardington	TL/086479	5.	18.	6
Estcotes	Eastcotts[1]	TL/085455	5.	17.	10.
Northgiuel	Northill	TL/149465	4.	8.	8
Staneforde	Stanford	TL/162411	2.	5.	5
			48.	13.	9½

Hd. Flitte [FLITT HUNDRED]

Siuelesho	Silsoe	TL/082355	9.	2.	4
Barton'	Barton le Clay	TL/085304	8.	19.	3
Stratle cum	Streatley with	TL/070286	5.	9.	3
Sharpenho	Sharpenhoe	TL/064305			
Luton'	Luton	TL/090212	23.	5.	4
Cadendon'[2]	Caddington	TL/063198	2.	4.	9
Pullokeshull'	Pulloxhill	TL/061338	5.	8.	7½
Heigham cum	Higham Gobion with	TL/103327	5.	6.	4½
Faldho	Faldo	TL/074318			
Clophulle cum	Clophill with	TL/092388	5.	12.	10½
Caynho	Cainhoe	TL/100367			
Haunes	Haynes	TL/081411	4.	12.	7
Sonyndon'	Sundon	TL/048269	4.	3.	4
Shutlyngdon'	Shillington	TL/123339	5.	10.	6
Eyen cum	Ion with	TL/104347	4.	12.	10½
Gravenhurst'	Gravenhurst[3]	TL/112360			
			84.	8.	1

Hd. Redebournestoke [REDBORNSTOKE HUNDRED]

Litlyngton'	Lidlington	SP/992388	7.	10.	0
Flitwyk' cum	Flitwick with	TL/028342	3.	13.	10
Stepyngle	Steppingley	TL/012354			
Elnestowe	Elstow	TL/049474	5.	6.	8
Houghton' Conquest'	Houghton Conquest	TL/043413	6.	7.	0¾
Wilshamsted	Wilshamstead	TL/062435	5.	0.	6¾
Craunfeld	Cranfield	SP/956420	10.	16.	11
Merston'	Marston Moretaine	SP/996411	12.	3.	2
Segenho cum	Segenhoe with	SP/981358	4.	2.	1½
Ruchemound	Ridgmont	SP/976361			
Wotton'	Wootton	TL/003451	10.	3.	4
Maldon'	Maulden	TL/058381	5.	8.	0
Ampthulle cum	Ampthill with	TL/037382	10.	12.	0
Mulbrok'	Millbrook	TL/013385			
Kempston'	Kempston	TL/027474	12.	10.	0
			93.	13.	8

[1] Grid ref. is to Cotton End, the probable identification of 'Estcotes' (E.P.N.S., III, Beds. & Hunts. (1926), 91). The present Eastcotts is the name of a civil parish created in 1894.
[2] Part of Caddington was taxed in Herts. (Dacorum hundred, p. 134).
[3] Grid ref. is to Upper Gravenhurst.

Hd. Mannesheued [MANSHEAD HUNDRED]

Todyngton'	Toddington	TL/010289	10.	13.	4¼
Hussebourn' Craule	Husborne Crawley	SP/956362	3.	4.	0½
Toternho	Totternhoe	SP/988209	2.	4.	0½
Chalgrave[1]	Chalgrave	TL/008274	3.	19.	3
Weston'	Westoning	TL/028328	4.	7.	10
Badelesdon'	Battlesden	SP/959291	1.	7.	10
Eyton'	Eaton Bray	SP/970208	8.	6.	2½
Everesholt'	Eversholt	SP/982325	4.	9.	8
Birchemor cum capella	Birchmoor with chapel[2]	SP/945344	4.	16.	8
Midelton Brian	Milton Bryan	SP/971308	1.	8.	8
Ting' cum	Tingrith with	TL/006324	4.	12.	8
Prestele	Priestley	TL/020332			
Tullesworth'	Tilsworth	SP/975243	2.	15.	2
Stanbrigge cum	Stanbridge with	SP/966242	8.	2.	11½
Stodham	Studham	TL/016160			
Pottesgrave	Potsgrove	SP/951299	2.	5.	4
Hoclive	Hockliffe	SP/966270	1.	10.	6
Aspele	Aspley Guise	SP/942363	4.	5.	5
Herlyngdon'	Harlington	TL/037305	5.	4.	2
Saleford cum	Salford with	SP/936391	2.	18.	8
Holecote	Holcot	SP/944388			
Dunstaple	Dunstable	TL/022219	14.	2.	2
Leyghton'	Leighton Buzzard	SP/920250	16.	12.	1
Houghton'	Houghton Regis	TL/018240	13.	15.	4½
			121.	2.	0¾

Hd. Clifton' [CLIFTON HUNDRED]

Alruchesleye	Arlesey	TL/192375	8.	15.	4
Holewelle	Holwell [in Herts.]	TL/165333	6.	2.	6
Shefforde cum	Shefford with	TL/143390	7.	3.	4
Cambelton'	Campton	TL/130381			
Henlowe	Henlow	TL/178387	6.	9.	1
Clifton'	Clifton	TL/164388	4.	3.	8½
Mepereshal[3]	Meppershall	TL/135359	5.	0.	8
Stotfold	Stotfold	TL/220366	6.	12.	10
			44.	7.	5½

Hd. Stodden' [STODDEN HUNDRED]

Melchebourn'	Melchbourne	TL/028653	6.	5.	5
Tilbrok'	Tilbrook [in Hunts.]	TL/081692	4.	11.	3
Rysle	Riseley	TL/039631	6.	11.	11
Yeuelden'	Yelden	TL/012672	2.	4.	8
Pertenhale	Pertenhall	TL/084654	6.	12.	0
Shelton'	Shelton	TL/033688	4.	10.	10½

[1] This entry probably includes Humbershoe, now in Hertfordshire, which is listed with Chalgrave on some later documents, e.g. in the Book of Fifteenths and Tenths of the early fifteenth century (E 164/7, fol. cclxix).

[2] The chapel is presumed to be Woburn chapel, which was included with Birchmoor in a valuation of the lands of Woburn Abbey in 1542 (*V.C.H., Beds.* i (1904), 370).

[3] Part of Meppershall was taxed in Herts. (Hitchin hundred, p. 133).

Dene	Dean[1]	TL/046676	5.	10.	0
Midelton' Erneys	Milton Ernest	TL/020562	2.	17.	10¼
Caysho	Keysoe	TL/073625	4.	10.	2
Knottynge	Knotting	TL/002635	4.	8.	8
Clopham cum	Clapham with	TL/034524	10.	9.	0
Okle	Oakley	TL/011530			
Bolnhurst'	Bolnhurst	TL/081587	5.	10.	0¾
			64.	1.	10¼
Bedeford [A.D]	Bedford	TL/049497	19.	11.	7 [T]

TOTAL: £674. 10. 4¾[2]

---

[1] Grid ref. is to Upper Dean.

[2] As on 1334 Account, E 179/71/14. The figures for the hundreds in the Particulars in fact add up to £674. 10. 4¼.

BERKSHIRE

DOCUMENTS

8 Edward III: Account   not extant
8 Edward III: Particulars E 179/73/9*
10 Edward III: Particulars E 179/73/10

TAXERS

The Abbot of Reading (after the death of the abbot of Abingdon) and Jacob de Wodestok

TAX YIELD

15th £864. 18. 2
10th £171.   5. 4¾

      £1,036. 3. 6¾

Representing assessed movable wealth of

      £14,686. 7. 8½

NOTES

Places are listed under the heading of twenty-four hundreds; three townships that comprise the late-created Wargrave hundred appear almost as an afterthought at the end of the roll. Ancient demesnes are listed within the hundreds but boroughs are listed separately; they were Reading, New Windsor, Wallingford, and Thatcham, the four which were regularly taxed as boroughs throughout the early fourteenth century.

From the places listed it is clear that the outline of the county in 1334 showed important differences from that of the modern county. Nine places taxed in Berkshire have since been transferred to neighbouring counties, viz. Shalbourne, Bagshot, and Inglesham to Wiltshire; Langford, Little Faringdon, Shilton, and Grandpont to Oxfordshire; Great Barrington to Gloucestershire; and Stratfield Saye to Hampshire. On the other hand, fifteen places in modern Berkshire were taxed elsewhere in 1334; twelve of these belonged to detached parts of Wiltshire and are listed in that county. The remaining three are Caversham (partly in Oxfordshire until 1911), Stratfield Mortimer (partly in Hampshire until 1844), and Combe (transferred from Hampshire in 1895).

Hd. Byenressch' [BEYNHURST HUNDRED]

Hurle	Hurley	su/826837	5.	5.	0
Schotesbrok'	Shottesbrooke	su/842771	2.	11.	0
Whytewaltham	White Waltham	su/854775	5.	15.	0
Remenham	Remenham	su/771842	3.	15.	0
Bustlesham	Bisham	su/848854	4.	1.	5½

Knyghtelynghton'	Elington[1]		1.	7.	6
Brassewell'	Cresswells	SU/888782	3.	2.	6
Cruchefeld	Cruchfield	SU/880740	2.	15.	0
			28.	12.	5½

Hd. Repplesmere [RIPPLESMERE HUNDRED]

Yasshamstede	Easthampstead	SU/863676	5.	14.	1¾
Wynkefeld	Winkfield	SU/904724	10.	14.	2½
Clywar'	Clewer	SU/955772	3.	14.	5¾
Dydeworth' for'	Dedworth [foreign]		5.	6.	3¼
Dydeworth' int'	Dedworth [within]	SU/942763	2.	3.	0 [T]
Vet' Wyndes [A.D]	Old Windsor	SU/992747	4.	0.	0 [T]
			31.	12.	1¼

Hd. Cherldon' [CHARLTON HUNDRED]

Berkham	Barkham	SU/784664	2.	12.	9¼
Fynghamstede	Finchampstead	SU/793637	4.	13.	0
Hurste	Hurst	SU/795729	5.	19.	3¼
Erle	Earley	SU/744720	7.	6.	8
Swalugfeld & Schenyngfeld	Swallowfield and Shinfield	SU/732648 SU/729682	6.	19.	2
			27.	10.	10½

Hd. Sunnyngg' [SONNING HUNDRED]

Sonnyng'	Sonning	SU/756756	3.	10.	11¼
Ressecomp'	Ruscombe	SU/798763	1.	2.	11¾
Byneressh'	Winnersh	SU/782705	1.	10.	1¼
Wokyngham	Wokingham	SU/815688	4.	9.	8
Erburghfeld	Arborfield	SU/758678	1.	13.	8
Sandhurst'	Sandhurst	SU/833618	2.	5.	7
			14.	12.	11¼

Hd. Reddyngg' [READING HUNDRED]

Henewyk'	Henwick	SU/497681	4.	19.	0
Benham	Beenham	SU/591684	3.	5.	6
Burghildebur'	Bucklebury	SU/553709	2.	19.	9
Crokham	Crookham	SU/539643	2.	15.	0¼
Tylhurst'	Tilehurst	SU/673729	10.	17.	8½
Colle	Coley	SU/705720		14.	5¼
Pankebourn'	Pangbourne	SU/634765	2.	14.	0½
Maydenhach'	Maidenhatch	SU/619742	1.	6.	5½
Whytele	Whitley	SU/717706	4.	5.	10½
Silhamstede Abb'	Sulhamstead Abbots	SU/645679	3.	0.	7½
Greysull'	Grazeley	SU/699669	2.	8.	2½

[1] This follows *V.C.H.*, *Berks.* iii (1923), 137 in identifying *Knyghtelynghton* as Elington, later known as Spencers, ibid. 126. Elington was probably the area upon which the town of Maidenhead grew up in the fourteenth century.

Stratfeld Say[1]	Stratfield Saye [in Hampshire]	su/695614	1.	9.	8¼
Underoure	Windsor Underoure[2] [in the borough of Windsor]	su/969772	2.	7.	7½
Blebur'[3]	Blewbury	su/531859	4.	10.	8
Eadem villa [A.D]	Blewbury		3.	12.	1¾ [T]
Henreth'[4]	East Hendred	su/459886	1.	13.	0
Choleseye	Cholsey	su/583870	5.	9.	3
			58.	9.	0

Hd. La Thele [THEALE HUNDRED]

Hertrug'	Hartridge	su/570778	1.	8.	4½
Porle Parva	Purley Parva [Westbury]	su/653768	1.	10.	2¾
Englefeld	Englefield	su/623720	3.	2.	11
Bradefeld	Bradfield	su/605726	7.	5.	0
Nonhide	Nunhide	su/646725		2.	3
Porle Maior	Purley	su/668761	2.	8.	4¾
Solham	Sulham	su/646743	2.	12.	11¾
Burghfeld	Burghfield	su/671684	3.	0.	7¾
Thudemerch'	Tidmarsh	su/635745		18.	10½
Aldermaston'	Aldermaston	su/596650	7.	6.	8
Welhampton'	Woolhampton	su/577677	2.	8.	3¾
Padeworth'	Padworth	su/613662	2.	6.	9½
Offton' Roberti'	Ufton Robert	su/632673	2.	7.	0½
Offton' Neyruitt'	Ufton Nervet	su/635675	1.	3.	7½
Silhamstede Banastr'	Sulhamstead Bannister	su/639685	1.	9.	1
Burghfeld Reg'	Burghfield Regis[5]	su/671684	2.	16.	8¾
Shefeld	Sheffield Bottom	su/649699	2.	13.	1½
Hertle	Hartley Dummer	su/703689	2.	18.	8½
Southcote	Southcote	su/691717	1.	4.	0
Trucwell'	Beech Hill	su/698644		8.	6¾
Woghfeld	Wokefield	su/673657	1.	17.	7½
Stratfeld Mortim'[6]	Stratfield Mortimer	su/669641	3.	13.	7
			55.	3.	6¼

Hd. Burghildebur' [BUCKLEBURY HUNDRED]

Hampstede	Hampstead Norris	su/529763	5.	13.	8
Elynge	Eling	su/523750		12.	0
Wyle	Wellhouse	su/519724	1.	0.	10¾
Markleston'	Marlston	su/529720	1.	18.	9¼
Yatyngden'	Yattendon	su/554745	3.	5.	0¾
Frydelesham	Frilsham	su/538732	2.	9.	4¼
Stanford	Stanford Dingley	su/576716	2.	16.	0
			17.	15.	9

---

[1] The rest of Stratfield Saye was taxed in Hampshire (Holdshot hundred, p. 117).
[2] *V.C.H., Berks.* iii (1923), 66 suggests that the manor of Windsor Underoure included the land lying between Windsor and Eton, north-west of the castle.
[3] Part of Blewbury was taxed in Moreton hundred.
[4] Part of East Hendred was taxed in Wantage hundred.
[5] Burghfield was divided into two parts, one of which was Burghfield Regis (*V.C.H., Berks.* iii (1923), 400).
[6] Part of Stratfield Mortimer was taxed in Hampshire (Holdshot hundred, p. 117).

Hd. Cotsetlefeld [COTTSETTLESFORD HUNDRED]

Migham	Midgham	su/556672	4.	16.	0
Colthrop	Colthrop	su/537666		16.	10
Wavesyng'	Wasing	su/576643	1.	8.	0¾
Brympton'	Brimpton	su/557647	2.	12.	3
Grenham	Greenham	su/483653	3.	10.	3¾
Wodespene	Woodspeen	su/444692	3.	6.	10¾
Spene	Speen	su/455678	4.	5.	3
Donynton'	Donnington	su/466687	2.	2.	5¼
Cosrug'	Curridge	su/490719	3.	10.	0
Saghe	Shaw	su/475684	2.	1.	11¾
Bagenor'	Bagnor	su/452695		5.	5¼
Spenhamlonde	Speenhamland	su/475677	1.	5.	0¼
Neubur' [v]	Newbury	su/470672	27.	9.	6
			57.	9.	11¾

Hd. Roubergh' [ROEBERG HUNDRED]

Wynterbourn'	Winterbourne	su/451719	4.	18.	11½
Boxor'	Boxford	su/428715	6.	17.	5½
Benham	Hoe Benham	su/409699	2.	8.	10¼
Wikham	Wickham	su/395715		6.	5¾
Weston'	Weston	su/399737	2.	5.	9¼
Weleford	Welford	su/409732	1.	7.	3
Eston'	Easton	su/416723	1.	10.	9
Lekhampstede	Leckhampstead	su/439760	3.	5.	6¼
Pesmere	Peasemore	su/458771	4.	14.	0
Beden'	Beedon	su/483782	3.	7.	5¼
Langele	Langley	su/498766	4.	6.	4
Chiuele	Chieveley	su/474741	3.	14.	6¾
			39.	3.	4½

Hd. Eggele [EAGLE HUNDRED]

Southfalle	South Fawley	su/391802	1.	7.	6
Woluele	Woolley	su/411801	1.	18.	2½
Est Schifford	East Shefford	su/391744	2.	6.	1
West Schifford	Great Shefford	su/380753	3.	6.	5½
Watecombe	Whatcombe	su/393789		9.	0
Kenetebur' Ambr'	Kintbury-Amesbury[1]	su/c.385652	3.	15.	10¾
Chadelworth'	Chaddleworth	su/412779	2.	5.	8¼
Valle	Fawley	su/391814	1.	3.	8
Chaulo	Challow[2]	su/381883	5.	1.	11½
Ledecombe Basset'	Letcombe Bassett	su/374849	3.	15.	4
Ledecombe Reg'	Letcombe Regis	su/380865	9.	12.	10
			35.	2.	7½

[1] Kintbury-Amesbury was a manor in the north of Kintbury township, held by the nuns of Amesbury (*V.C.H., Berks.* iv (1924), 206).

[2] Grid ref. is to East Challow.

Hd. Lambourn' [LAMBOURN HUNDRED]

Lambourn' [A.D]	Lambourn	SU/326790	11.	4.	5¾ [T]
Estgarston'	East Garston	SU/361771	5.	0.	8¾
Maydenecot'	Maidencourt	SU/373760	1.	17.	4
Estbur'	Eastbury	SU/347771	3.	6.	2
Bokhampton'	Bockhampton	SU/333781	4.	5.	7¼
Blakgrave	Blagrave[1]	lost			
Up Lambourn'	Upper Lambourn	SU/313803	5.	17.	7¼
			31.	11.	11

Hd. Kentebur' [KINTBURY HUNDRED]

Enebourn'	Enborne	SU/435658	5.	10.	4
Hampstede March'	Hamstead Marshall	SU/420668	3.	1.	10¼
Wodehaye	West Woodhay	SU/391631	2.	5.	0
Ingepenne	Inkpen	SU/359642	4.	13.	5½
Godyngflod	Anville's Farm[2]	SU/342652		6.	1
Ingelflod Balet	Inglewood	SU/365666	1.	4.	0
Shaldebourn'[3]	Shalbourne [in Wilts.]	SU/315635	2.	2.	0
Bugesgate	Bagshot [in Wilts.]	SU/317653	1.	14.	0
Leverton'	Leverton	SU/333701	1.	11.	0
Colcote	Calcot	SU/c.340698		15.	8
Denford	Denford	SU/360693	1.	18.	0
Avynton'	Avington	SU/372680	4.	11.	0
Benham Valence	Marsh Benham	SU/430674	6.	16.	5¾
Holte	Holt	SU/401645	3.	6.	0
Kuntebur'	Kintbury	SU/383670	2.	16.	4¾
Tytecombe [A.D]	Titcomb	SU/377653		13.	1¾ [T]
Templeton'	Templeton	SU/359663		10.	7¼
Sandon'	Sandon Fee[4]	SU/323663	1.	0.	3¼
Hudden'	Hidden	SU/352701	1.	13.	2¼
Hungerford	Hungerford	SU/333686	10.	1.	4½
			56.	9.	10¼

Hd. Shrivenham [SHRIVENHAM HUNDRED]

Kyngeston'	Kingston Lisle	SU/326876	3.	12.	3½
Fauler'	Fawler	SU/319882	1.	2.	9½
Badelkyng'	Baulking	SU/317906	4.	11.	7
Offinton'	Uffington	SU/302893	4.	1.	3¼
Compton'	Compton Beauchamp	SU/279869	1.	17.	1½
Ordeston'	Odstone	SU/271862	2.	10.	6
Beckote	Beckett	SU/247892	2.	6.	1½
Wolfricheston'	Woolstone	SU/294877	2.	6.	9½
Shryvenham	Shrivenham	SU/241891	1.	14.	4
Eadem villa [A.D]	Shrivenham		3.	13.	9 [T]
Bourghton'	Bourton	SU/232870	1.	19.	1
Eadem villa [A.D]	Bourton			18.	7 [T]

---

[1] The name Blagrave has not survived. The place was probably in the south of Lambourn parish (*V.C.H., Berks.* iv (1924), 252).

[2] Anville's Farm, until recently in a detached part of Kintbury parish, but now in Inkpen, was formerly known as *Godyngflod* (*V.C.H., Berks.* iv (1924), 211).

[3] See also p. 348.

[4] North Standen and Charnham Street, also in Hungerford, were assessed in Wilts. (*V.C.H., Wilts.* iv (1959), 300) (see note 2, p. 348).

Cotes [A.D]	Longcot	SU/274907	1.	13.	9	[T]
Fernham [A.D]	Fernham	SU/293919	3.	8.	5	[T]
Parva Worth'	Littleworth	SU/312972	2.	0.	3¾	
Eton'	Eaton Hastings	SU/260982	4.	4.	6¾	
Wachenesfeld	Watchfield	SU/245903	4.	3.	10½	
Borwardescote	Buscot	SU/226981	5.	7.	4¼	
Coleshull'	Coleshill	SU/236938	4.	15.	2¼	
Edwyneston' [A.D]	Idstone	SU/257843	4.	9.	10¾	[T]
Asshebur'	Ashbury	SU/265849	5.	3.	5¾	
			66.	1.	0¾	

Hd. Faryndon' [FARINGDON HUNDRED]

Faryndon' de X[a] & XV[a] [A.D][1]	Faringdon	SU/288957	15.	11.	11¼	[T]
Westbrok'	Westbrook	SU/286954	9.	16.	5	
Inglesham	Inglesham [in Wilts.]	SU/205984	3.	14.	8¼	
Langeford	Langford [in Oxon.]	SP/249026	7.	0.	0¼	
Parva Faryndon'	Little Faringdon [in Oxon.]	SP/226013	4.	11.	9½	[T]
Bernynton' [A.D][2]	Great Barrington [in Glos.]	SP/205134	4.	3.	8	[T]
Shulton' [A.D]	Shilton [in Oxon.]	SP/267083	6.	7.	9¼	[T]
Magna Cockeswelle	Great Coxwell	SU/270934	5.	6.	9	
Parva Cokkeswelle [A.D]	Little Coxwell	SU/283935	4.	2.	6	[T]
			60.	15.	6½	

Hd. Wanetyng' [WANTAGE HUNDRED]

Cherlton'	Charlton	SU/411885	3.	7.	9¼	
Westgenge	West Ginge	SU/443868	1.	10.	8¾	
Beterton'	Beterton	SU/431868	1.	3.	11	
Lakynge	Lockinge	SU/428872	2.	13.	7¾	
Archynton'	Ardington	SU/432883	6.	10.	7	
Wanetynge [A.D]	Wantage	SU/397879	7.	11.	3	[T]
Grove [A.D]	Grove	SU/401902	5.	10.	11¾	[T]
Southdenchesworth'	Denchworth	SU/381917	5.	7.	11	
Chelreye	Childrey	SU/360878	7.	12.	5¾	
Spersholt'	Sparsholt	SU/347875	12.	7.	3¼	
Weshanneye	West Hanney	SU/406928	6.	6.	10	
Esthanneye [p][3]	East Hanney [part of]	SU/419930	5.	6.	2	
Estgenge	East Ginge	SU/448866	1.	9.	8	
Westhanreth'	West Hendred	SU/447883	2.	2.	8	
Esthenreth' [p][4]	East Hendred [part of]	SU/459886	4.	0.	8	
			73.	2.	6½	

Hd. Gamenfelde [GANFIELD HUNDRED]

Stanford	Stanford in the Vale	SU/342935	7.	19.	9¼
Shalyngford	Shellingford	SU/319935	4.	17.	8

[1] The tax of Faringdon was included as Tenth entirely in the final total for the county.

[2] Great and Little Barrington were also taxed in Gloucestershire (Salmonsbury hundred, p. 103).

[3] Part of East Hanney was taxed in Ock hundred.

[4] See also Reading hundred.

Carsewell'	Carswell	SU/326977	2.	3.	2¼
Boklonde	Buckland	SU/342982	8.	10.	1¾
Pusye	Pusey	SU/360965	2.	10.	0
Heynton'	Hinton Waldrist	SU/375991	4.	13.	8¾
Worth'	Longworth	SU/384995	3.	3.	0¼
Charneye	Charney Bassett	SU/380946	2.	10.	11¼
Hautford	Hatford	SU/338948	1.	9.	8½
			37.	18.	2

Hd. Hornmere [HORMER HUNDRED]

Abyndon'	Abingdon	SU/497972	17.	18.	7½
Kenyngton'	Kennington	SP/523024	1.	8.	5¾
Northhenx'	North Hinksey	SP/495055	1.	18.	0
Southhenx'	South Hinksey	SP/509040	1.	16.	3½
Radele	Radley	SU/532993	3.	0.	9½
Throp	Thrupp	SU/518973		15.	4
Ricardi Bissop [d]	Bishops	SU/499973		12.	0
Wynyerd	Vineyards	SU/498972		9.	2¾
Northcote	Northcourt	SU/493982		18.	0
Sonnyngwell'	Sunningwell	SP/496005	3.	3.	0½
Grantpont'	Grandpont [in Oxford] [in Oxon.]	SP/513053		7.	8
Wotton'	Wootton	SP/476016	2.	4.	2¾
Whytele	Whitley[1]	SP/450047		12.	7¼
Botle	Botley	SP/486062	1.	0.	5
Strode [d]	Stroud	SP/444075	2.	4.	7
Swimeford	Swinford	SP/445085	1.	7.	7½
Hulle	Hillend	SP/466066	1.	8.	0½
Shupene	Shippon	SP/482981	2.	18.	6
Sandford	Dry Sandford	SP/468004	1.	19.	8
Leigh'	Bessels Leigh	SP/458018	1.	19.	1¼
Comenor	Cumnor	SP/462042	2.	4.	10¾
Chalueleye	Chawley	SP/472045	2.	0.	10
Seukworth'	Seacourt	SP/486075	1.	6.	9½
Wytham	Wytham	SP/475086	3.	16.	5
			57.	11.	2

Hd. Okke [OCK HUNDRED]

Goseye	Goosey	SU/357918	1.	5.	7¼
Draycotemor'	Draycott Moor	SU/400994	1.	3.	7¼
Garford	Garford	SU/429962	1.	13.	11
Hanneye [p][2]	East Hanney [part of]	SU/419930	2.	8.	9¾
Suthcote	Circourt[3]	SU/375910	2.	2.	9¼
Tubbeneye	Tubney	SU/436993	2.	2.	11
Appleton'	Appleton	SU/443016	3.	7.	1
Frileford	Frilford	SU/441972	2.	12.	5
Mercham	Marcham	SU/452968	5.	3.	6½
Kyngeston'	Kingston Bagpuize	SU/408981	3.	3.	11¼
Fifide	Fyfield	SU/423987	3.	19.	10¾
Lyfford	Lyford	SU/390943	1.	10.	0
			30.	14.	6

[1] Grid ref. is to Upper Whitley Farm.
[2] See also Wantage hundred.
[3] Grid ref. is to Upper Circourt Farm.

Hd. Sutton' [SUTTON HUNDRED]

Sutton' cum Wik'	Sutton Courtenay with Sutton Wick	SU/505942 SU/480948	13.	13.	5	
Wyttenham Com'	Long Wittenham	SU/548941	5.	17.	0	
Appelford	Appleford	SU/531937	3.	1.	8	
Styvynton' [A.D]	Steventon	SU/463914	3.	13.	8	[T]
Wittenham Abb'	Little Wittenham	SU/566935	2.	18.	2	
Drayton'	Drayton	SU/481941	5.	2.	0	
Middelton'	Milton	SU/486924	2.	11.	0	
			36.	16.	11	

Hd. Morton' [MORETON HUNDRED]

Dodecote	Didcot	SU/520905	4.	7.	5½
Foulescot'	Fulscot	SU/546888	2.	11.	4½
Clopcot'	Clapcot[1]	lost	1.	13.	0
Est Hakebourn'	East Hagbourne	SU/525881	8.	12.	2¼
West Hakebourn'	West Hagbourne	SU/513877	3.	7.	4
Makkeneye	Mackney	SU/580899	3.	17.	1
Bryttewell'	Brightwell	SU/578908	7.	4.	0¾
Harewell'	Harwell	SU/492891	8.	8.	8¼
Southmorton'	South Moreton	SU/560882	4.	17.	1¾
Northmorton'	North Moreton	SU/562895	4.	16.	6½
Aston'	Aston[2]	SU/557861	7.	7.	2
Uppton'	Upton	SU/513867	2.	18.	0
Blebur' [p][3]	Blewbury [part of]	SU/531859		18.	0
			60.	18.	0½

Hd. Slotesford' [ELETESFORD HUNDRED]

Bastelden'	Basildon	SU/612793	6.	15.	2¾
Stretle	Streatley	SU/594809	5.	6.	6¾
Molesford	Moulsford	SU/591841	4.	5.	11¾
Sotewell'	Sotwell	SU/586907	2.	19.	9¾
			19.	7.	7

Hd. Compton' [COMPTON HUNDRED]

Farnebourgh'	Farnborough	SU/435819	2.	11.	7½
West Ildesle	West Ilsley	SU/473825	2.	16.	11½
Catmere	Catmore	SU/453803	1.	10.	0
Estildesle	East Ilsley	SU/493809	2.	13.	4
Hodycote	Hodcott	SU/477817		13.	4
Chylton'	Chilton	SU/489860	2.	19.	4
Compton cum Asshedon'	Compton and West Compton	SU/526797 SU/520800	4.	6.	11½
Aldeworthe	Aldworth	SU/554794	2.	15.	0
			20.	6.	6½

Brytwalton'	Brightwalton	SU/427793	5.	2.	8¼

1 Site *c.* SU/605916.
2 Grid ref. is to Aston Tirrold.
3 See also Reading hundred.

Hd. Cokham [COOKHAM HUNDRED]

Cokham [A.D]	Cookham	su/896855	13.	12.	0 [T]
Benetfeld	Binfield	su/845722	7.	3.	10¾
Sonnynghull'	Sunninghill	su/939686	1.	15.	10¼
			22.	11.	9

Hd. Braye [BRAY HUNDRED]

Braye [A.D]	Bray	su/902796	16.	11.	2¼ [T]

[BOROUGHS]

Thacham [B]	Thatcham	su/516672	3.	3.	11½ [T]
Wyndes [B]	Windsor [New]	su/968768	11.	8.	11 [T]
Walyngford [B]	Wallingford	su/607893	9.	12.	5¾ [T]
Reddyng [B]	Reading	su/715735	29.	6.	1½ [T]
			53.	11.	5¾ [T]

Waregrave	Wargrave	su/783784			
Waltham Sti'	Waltham St.	su/829770			
Laurenc' &	Lawrence and				
Warefeld'	Warfield	su/880722	21.	0.	0

TOTAL: £1,036. 3. 6¾[1]

---

[1] As on E 179/73/9 and the hundred totals add up to this figure. £1036. 3. 5¾ is given on the Enrolled Account for 1334 (E 359/8 mm. 4–5).

BUCKINGHAMSHIRE

DOCUMENTS

8 Edward III: Account   E 179/77/3
8 Edward III: Particulars not extant
10 Edward III: Particulars E 179/77/4*

TAXERS

The abbot of Notley and John de Stonore

TAX YIELD

15th £638. 18. 8
10th £ 49. 6. 8
      ─────────────
      £688. 5. 4

Representing assessed movable wealth of

£10,077. 6. 8

NOTES

Nine places taxed at a tenth are listed separately at the end of the roll. Six of these, Amersham, Aylesbury, Brill, Marlow, Wendover, and High Wycombe, had been intermittently considered boroughs in previous subsidies (see Willard (1933), op. cit. 430), but none were named as such in 1334 or 1336.

Only along the border with Oxfordshire are there any significant differences between the boundary of the modern county and that of 1334. Three places then taxed in Buckinghamshire have since been transferred to Oxfordshire, viz. Caversfield in 1844, Towersey, and probably the site of the lost Little Eye, in 1932. Four places now in Buckinghamshire were taxed in Oxfordshire in 1334, viz. Stokenchurch (formerly a detached portion of Aston Rowant), Lillingstone Lovell, Boycott, and Tythrop.

REFERENCES

A. C. Chibnall and A. Vere Woodman, 'Subsidy roll for the county of Buckinghamshire, Anno 1524', *Bucks. Rec. Soc.* 8 (1944).
A. C. Chibnall, 'Early taxation returns: taxation of personal property in 1332 and later', *Bucks. Rec. Soc.* 14 (1966) (a most valuable recent work on the lay subsidies).[1]

---

[1] In which the 1334 quotas for the county, taken from E 179/77/4 (1336), have been published with an introduction, pp. 100–7. There are, however, a number of mistakes in this version. The hundred totals given on the roll are correct despite the assertion to the contrary on p. 100; this view has arisen because of errors in transcription of the quotas for a number of townships. Where there are errors I have made a footnote in the following list.

Hd. Buk' [BUCKINGHAM HUNDRED]

Buckyngham	Buckingham	sp/694338	4.	0.	0
Twyford	Twyford	sp/665266	5.	6.	0
Padebury	Padbury	sp/721309	3.	10.	0
Stepelclaydon'	Steeple Claydon	sp/706267	3.	3.	4
Thornbergh'	Thornborough	sp/743337	3.	5.	0
Mersch'	Marsh Gibbon	sp/648232	3.	0.	0
Thornton'	Thornton	sp/752362	1.	18.	0
Adynton'	Addington	sp/742285	2.	18.	0
Adestoke'	Adstock	sp/735301	2.	13.	0
Achecote'	Edgcott	sp/680229	2.	2.	0
			31.	15.	4

Hd. Stodefold [STODFOLD HUNDRED]

Lyllyngston	Lillingstone Dayrell	sp/705398	2.	10.	0
Stowelangeport	Stow and	sp/676373	2.	10.	0
	Lamport	sp/683375			
Schaldestone	Shalstone	sp/642364	1.	16.	8[1]
Westbury	Westbury	sp/623357	2.	13.	4[1]
Lechamsted	Leckhampstead	sp/726380	2.	10.	0
Weststaford	Water Stratford	sp/652343	2.	10.	0
Radeclyve cum	Radclive with	sp/676339	2.	5.	0
Chakemor	Chackmore	sp/685357			
Evereshawe	Evershaw	sp/636383		8.	0
Foxcote	Foxcote	sp/717358	1.	5.	0
Mortone	Maids' Moreton	sp/707352	1.	15.	0
Oclee	Akeley	sp/708378	1.	13.	4
Thoruestone	Turweston	sp/601377	1.	13.	4
			23.	9.	8

Hd. Rowelowe [ROWLEY HUNDRED]

Hyldesdone	Hillesden	sp/686287	4.	6.	8
Caveresfeld	Caversfield [in Oxon.]	sp/581252	1.	4.	0
Chetwode	Chetwode	sp/641298	2.	0.	0
Bartone	Barton Hartshorn	sp/641309		10.	0
Bourton'	Bourton	sp/709333	2.	8.	0[1]
Lethyngburgh'	Lenborough	sp/705300	3.	6.	8
Bechamptone	Beachampton	sp/771371	2.	10.	0
Prestone cum	Preston Bissett with	sp/658299	2.	13.	4
Couele	Cowley	sp/663281			
Tyngewyk'	Tingewick	sp/658331	3.	0.	0
			21.	18.	8[2]

Hd. Segelowe [SECKLOE HUNDRED]

Newport &	Newport Pagnell and	sp/878440	12.	0.	0
Tykeford cum	Tickford End with	sp/883436			
Marisco	Marsh[3]	sp/c.876434			

---

[1] Error in *Bucks. Rec. Soc.* 14 (1966), 102.　　　　　　[2] Ditto, 103.
[3] Marsh included most of the land to the south and west of Newport Pagnell, the south part of which is still known as Marsh End.

Calvertone cum Stratford [p]	Calverton with Stony Stratford [part of]¹	SP/791390 SP/787404	5.	0.	0
Wolvertone cum Stratford [p]	Wolverton with Stony Stratford [part of]	SP/803413 SP/787404	6.	0.	0
Wylyes cum Caldecote [p]	Willen with Caldecote [part of]	SP/879412 SP/879423	2.	3.	4
Etone c.m	Water Eaton [with members]	SP/879331	12.	0.	0
Seuenestone	Simpson	SP/883362	2.	15.	0
Loughtone cum Parva Schenle²	Loughton with ?	SP/838379	3.	5.	0
Stoke Hawmond	Stoke Hammond	SP/879298	2.	12.	0
Wolston Magna & Parva	Great Woolstone and Little Woolstone	SP/875385 SP/873393	4.	6.	8
Woketone	Woughton on the Green	SP/877376	2.	5.	0
Newentone Longeville	Newton Longville	SP/848313	2.	14.	0
Magna Lynford	Great Linford	SP/851423	2.	10.	0
Stontone cum Bradewelle	Stantonbury with Bradwell	SP/835428 SP/831394	2.	6.	8
			59.	17.	8

Hd. Molsho [MOULSOE HUNDRED]

Harmedene	Hardmead	SP/935476	2.	10.	0
Embertone	Emberton	SP/886495	3.	6.	8
Brychull' Magna & Parva	Great Brickhill and Little Brickhill	SP/901308 SP/911324	3.	13.	4
Chechelee cum Parva Crawle	Chicheley with Little Crawley	SP/904458 SP/922453	3.	13.	4
Crawlee Magna	North Crawley	SP/927447	5.	0.	0
Wavendone	Wavendon	SP/912373	3.	0.	0
Molsho	Moulsoe	SP/906417	4.	0.	0
Schyryngton'	Sherington	SP/891467	3.	6.	8
Broughton'	Broughton	SP/893401	2.	3.	4
Middelton' Kaynes	Milton Keynes	SP/888391	2.	10.	0
Estwode	Astwood	SP/951474	2.	6.	8
Clyfton' cum Newenton'	Clifton Reynes with Newton Blossomville	SP/899513 SP/926515	7.	0.	0
Bollebrychull' c.m	Bow Brickhill [with members]³	SP/912344	3.	13.	4
			46.	3.	4

Hd. Bunstowe [BUNSTY HUNDRED]

Hamslape	Hanslope	SP/803467	12.	4.	6
Ravenestone	Ravenstone	SP/851509	4.	0.	0
Haverysham	Haversham	SP/828428	5.	0.	0
Tyryngham cum Philegrave	Tyringham with Filgrave	SP/859467 SP/870482	3.	6.	8

¹ Part of Stony Stratford was taxed with Wolverton (next entry).

² *Parva Schenle* is difficult to identify. In *E.P.N.S., II, Bucks.* (1925), 24 Parva is identified as Shenley Brook End but this seems unlikely. Mrs. Betty Grant, to whom I am indebted for research into the identification of the Shenleys, concludes that Parva Shenley refers to the hamlet of Westbury (SP/826356) in Shenley parish.

³ Members of Bow Brickhill in 1316 included Coldecotte and Walton (*F.A.* i. 110).

Stokegoldyngton' cum Ickele	Stoke Goldington with Eakley	SP/832492 SP/826507	3.	0.	0
Cahurst cum Parva Lynford	Gayhurst with Little Linford	SP/847463 SP/843444	3.	10.	0
Olneye c.m	Olney [with members]	SP/890510	9.	0.	0
Westone	Weston Underwood	SP/863403	3.	10.	0
Lavendone cum Snellestone	Lavendon with Snelson	SP/916536 SP/937542	5.	0.	0
Lathebury	Lathbury	SP/875450	5.	4.	0
			53.	15.	2

Hd. Coteslowe [COTTESLOE HUNDRED]

Wenge	Wing	SP/881226	8.	3.	6
Mentemor	Mentmore	SP/903198	6.	0.	0
Herdewyk cum Wedone	Hardwick with Weedon	SP/806189 SP/814181	4.	10.	0
Wengrave	Wingrave	SP/869190	4.	2.	0
Kreselawe cum Luttelecote	Creslow with Littlecote	SP/812218 SP/832243	2.	10.	0
Solbury	Soulbury	SP/882271	5.	5.	0
Lynchelade	Linslade	SP/910269	2.	15.	0
Coblyntone	Cublington	SP/839222	2.	2.	0
Whytchyrche cum Bryddesthorn'	Whitchurch with Burston[1]	SP/802208 SP/839188	6.	0.	0
Astone Abbatis	Aston Abbots	SP/847203	1.	16.	8
Draytone Beauchamp cum Helpesthrop'	Drayton Beauchamp with Helsthorpe	SP/902118 SP/888192	2.	10.	0[2]
			45.	14.	2

Hd. Erle [YARDLEY HUNDRED]

Edlesburgh'	Edlesborough	SP/970191	9.	0.	0
Massewworth'	Marsworth	SP/920146	4.	0.	0
Pychelesthorne	Pitstone	SP/942149	5.	0.	0
Chetyndone	Cheddington	SP/922180	2.	16.	0
Shaptone	Slapton	SP/937206	5.	0.	0
Ivyngho	Ivinghoe	SP/946162	5.	0.	0
			30.	16.	0

Hd. Mersele [MURSLEY HUNDRED]

Hoggestone	Hoggeston	SP/808250	1.	16.	0
Wyncelawe cum Schipdon' & Parva Horwode	Winslow with Shipton and Little Horwood	SP/769276 SP/777273 SP/791309	3.	10.	0
Styuecle	Stewkley	SP/852261	2.	15.	0[2]
Shenle cum Totenho	Shenley[3] with Tattenhoe	SP/832367 SP/829339	2.	16.	0

[1] Grid ref. is to Lower Burston.

[2] Error in *Bucks. Rec. Soc.* 14 (1966), 103.

[3] It is not clear to which part of Shenley this refers. It is probably Brook End (SP/832367) but the assessment may include Church End (or Shenley Magna) which is not specifically named in the subsidy. Parva Shenley was assessed with Loughton in Seckloe hundred (p. 17).

			£.	s.	d.
Whaddon' cum Assche	Whaddon with Nash	SP/805341 SP/782340	3.	0.	0
Merselee	Mursley	SP/817286	2.	0.	0
Draytone Passelewe	Drayton Parslow	SP/837284	2.	6.	0[1]
Niclus Passelewe[2]			2.	0.	0
Dodyntone	Dunton	SP/823243	1.	14.	0
Horwode Magna cum Synkeborwe	Great Horwood with Singleborough	SP/771312 SP/767320	4.	13.	4
Swaneborne Superior & Inferior	Swanbourne[3]	SP/801273	3.	0.	0
			29.	10.	4

Hd. Esshedone [ASHENDON HUNDRED]

			£.	s.	d.
Esschedone cum Polycote	Ashendon with Pollicott[4]	SP/705142 SP/702130	4.	10.	0
Ovynge	Oving	SP/782213	1.	10.	0
Hoggeshawe cum Folebrok	Hogshaw with Fulbrook	SP/739228 SP/750225	2.	10.	0
Bychendon'	Beachendon	SP/759137	1.	0.	0
Cherdele	Chearsley	SP/720103	2.	13.	4
Grendone	Grendon Underwood	SP/677210	2.	6.	8
Lotegrashale cum Tochewyk	Ludgershall with Tetchwick	SP/660172 SP/679187	2.	6.	8
Dodreshulle cum La Lee	Doddershall with Shipton Lee	SP/721202 SP/731212	2.	10.	0
Wynchendone Inferior	Lower Winchendon	SP/733123	4.	10.	0
Wottone	Wotton Underwood	SP/689159	2.	10.	0
Wynchendone Superior	Upper Winchendon	SP/746145	3.	6.	8
Queyntone	Quainton	SP/750202	2.	10.	0
			32.	3.	4

Hd. Wottesdone [WADDESDON HUNDRED]

			£.	s.	d.
Wottesdone	Waddesdon	SP/741170	4.	15.	0
Estclaydone & Bottelclaydone	East Claydon and Botolph Claydon	SP/740255 SP/733245	2.	10.	0
Querndone	Quarrendon	SP/803158	2.	10.	0
Flettemerstone	Fleet Marston	SP/779159	1.	13.	4
Northmerstone	North Marston	SP/777227	2.	0.	0
Edrop c.m	Eythrope [with members][5]	SP/772142	2.	13.	4
Middelclaydone	Middle Claydon	SP/719253	2.	0.	0
Pychecote	Pitchcott	SP/776203	1.	5.	0
Greneburgh	Granborough	SP/768250	1.	13.	4
			21.	0.	0

[1] Error in *Bucks. Rec. Soc.* 14 (1966), 104.

[2] A personal tax charge on Nicholas Passelewe, lord of the manor of Drayton, who was assessed for 40s. in 1332 but exempt from payment as he was a collector for the county. The same thing seems to have happened in 1334 and 1336 as there is a marginal note *coll' exon' inde in comp'*; the figure was nevertheless included in the totals for the hundred and the county.

[3] Swanbourne consisted of two manors in 1334.

[4] Grid ref. is to Lower Pollicott.

[5] Members of Eythrope in 1316 included Cranwell and Blackgrove (*F.A.* i. 114).

Hd. Ikeshull' [IXHILL HUNDRED]

Crendone	Long Crendon	SP/698991	7.	10.	0
Ilmere cum	Ilmer with	SP/769054	1.	15.	0
Astone Bernard	Aston Mullins	SP/769083			
Wormenhale	Worminghall	SP/642081	3.	0.	0
Schobyntone	Shabbington	SP/667067	2.	0.	0
Tourseye cum	Towersey with	SP/736053	4.	0.	0
Parva Eye	Little Eye[1] [both in Oxon.]	lost			
Kyngeseye	Kingsey	SP/743067	3.	0.	0
Walderuge	Waldridge	SP/783073	1.	0.	0
Icforde	Ickford	SP/646073	2.	0.	0
Astone Sannford	Aston Sandford	SP/757079	1.	6.	8
Dortone	Dorton	SP/679139	2.	10.	0
Chyltone cum	Chilton with	SP/687116	5.	0.	0
Esyntone	Easington	SP/687102			
			33.	1.	8

Hd. Aylesbury [AYLESBURY HUNDRED]

Westone Turvill'	Weston Turville	SP/859103	6.	0.	0
Broughton' &	Broughton and	SP/845138	4.	6.	8
Huckote	Hulcott	SP/853167			
Astone Clyntone	Aston Clinton	SP/879119	6.	0.	0
Eselburgh'	Ellesborough	SP/836067	5.	6.	8
Messendene Magna	Great Missenden	SP/900010	4.	0.	0
Boclonde	Buckland	SP/888124	2.	6.	8
Hampdene	Great Hampden[2]	SP/848023	1.	0.	0
Stokemaundevill'	Stoke Mandeville	SP/834104	4.	6.	8[3]
Haltone	Halton	SP/874101	2.	0.	0
Messendene Parva	Little Missenden	SU/921989	1.	10.	0
			36.	16.	8

Hd. Stone [STONE HUNDRED]

Hadenham cum	Haddenham with	SP/741080	10.	0.	0
Codyntone	Cuddington	SP/737112			
Hertwelle cum	Hartwell with	SP/795125	3.	6.	8
Parva Hampdene	Little Hampden	SP/860036			
Donytone	Dinton	SP/767111	4.	13.	4
Kynebelle Magna	Great Kimble	SP/825060	6.	0.	0
Stone	Stone	SP/784123	5.	6.	8
Uptone	Upton	SP/773115	2.	13.	4
Kynebelle Parva	Little Kimble	SP/823070	2.	0.	0
			34.	0.	0

---

[1] *V.C.H.*, *Bucks.* iv (1927), 106. Little Eye, part of the vill of Towersey, cannot be separately distinguished after 1346, at which time it was listed in an aid (*F.A.* i. 120).
[2] Little Hampden was taxed in Stone hundred.
[3] Error in *Bucks. Rec. Soc.* 14 (1966), 105.

Hd. Ryseburgh' [RISBOROUGH HUNDRED]

Bledelawe	Bledlow	SP/778022	6.	0.	0
Ryseburgh Comitis	Princes Risborough	SP/806035	5.	0.	0
Ryseburgh Monachorum	Monks Risborough	SP/812043	5.	0.	0
Horsendone	Horsenden	SP/793029		13.	4
			16.	13.	4

Hd. Dusteburgh' [DESBOROUGH HUNDRED]

Merlawe for'	Marlow [foreign]	SU/852863	3.	6.	8
Wycombe for'	High Wycombe [foreign]	SU/866931	6.	0.	0
Parva Merlawe	Little Marlow with	SU/873878	4.	13.	4
cum Hedesore	Hedsor	SU/907862			
West Wycombe cum	West Wycombe with	SU/828950	4.	10.	0
Mortone	Moreton	SP/792096			
Wenbourne	Wooburn	SU/909878	3.	0.	0
Saundresdone	Saunderton	SP/796019	2.	10.	0
Huchendene	Hughendon	SU/863955	2.	0.	0
Medmenham	Medmenham	SU/804844	1.	13.	4
Hameldene	Hambleden	SU/783866	5.	0.	0
Tyrefeld cum	Turville with	SU/767912	2.	0.	0
Ippestan	Ibstone	SU/753935			
Bradenham	Bradenham	SU/828971	1.	6.	8
Tynghurst	Fingest	SU/776911		13.	4
Falle	Fawley	SU/753867	1.	10.	0
			38.	3.	4

Hd. Stoke [STOKE HUNDRED]

Evere	Iver	TQ/039812	8.	0.	0
Langele cum	Langley Marish with	TQ/005795	6.	6.	8
Wyrardesbury	Wraysbury	TQ/001739			
Uptone	Upton	SU/981791	2.	13.	4
Stokepogeys	Stoke Poges	SU/976827	2.	13.	4
Hortone	Horton	TQ/014758	3.	6.	8
Dachet cum	Datchet with	SU/988772	3.	13.	4
Fulmere	Fulmer	SU/999856			
Denham	Denham	TQ/043870	2.	13.	4
Etone c.m	Eton [with members][1]	SU/966775	5.	10.	0
			34.	16.	8

Hd. Burnham [BURNHAM HUNDRED]

Burnham	Burnham	SU/931823	8.	0.	0
Cyppenham	Cippenham	SU/943803	6.	0.	0
Chesham	Chesham	SP/957015	7.	0.	0
Teppelawe cum	Taplow with	SU/912822	3.	0.	0
Penna	Penn	SU/917933			
Farnham	Farnham Royal	SU/962827	3.	0.	0
Chalfhunte Sancti' Pet'	Chalfont St. Peter	TQ/001909	3.	10.	0
Chalfhunte Sancti Egidii	Chalfont St. Giles	SU/991935	3.	6.	8

---

[1] A member of Eton in 1316 was Hedgerley (*F.A.* i. 115).

Bekenesfeld	Beaconsfield	su/945900	3.	6.	8	
Dorneye cum	Dorney with	su/924790	3.	10.	o	
Hucham	Hitcham	su/920825				
Agmondesham for'	Amersham [foreign]	su/958973	3.	10.	o	
			44.	3.	4	
Berkhamstede [H]	Berkhamsted[1]		5.	0.	o	
Aylesbury c.m [A.D]	Aylesbury [with members]	sp/817139	12.	13.	4	[T]
Wendover' cum for' [A.D]	Wendover [with foreign]	sp/871073	9.	10.	o	[T]
Wycombe [A.D][2]	High Wycombe	su/866931	9.	0.	o	[T]
Brehull' c.m[3] [A.D]	Brill [with members]	sp/657138	8.	0.	o	[T]
Agmondesham [A.D][4]	Amersham	su/958973	2.	10.	o	[T]
Magna Merlawe [A.D][5]	Marlow	su/852863	2.	6.	8	[T]
Radenache [A.D]	Radnage	su/787979	2.	13.	4	[T]
Gauecote [A.D] cum	Gawcott with	sp/681319	2.	13.	4	[T]
Prebenda	Prebend End	sp/693335				
			49.	6.	8	[T]

TOTAL: £688. 5. 4[6]

[1] The exact number of places comprising the entry for the Honor of Berkhamsted is not known, but as an approximate guide twelve places were listed in the Honor in the aid of 1302–3 (*F.A.* i. 107). This entry is omitted from the list in *Bucks. Rec. Soc.* 14 (1966).

[2] High Wycombe foreign was taxed at a fifteenth (Desborough hundred).

[3] A member of Brill in 1316 was Boarstall (*F.A.* i. 114).

[4] Amersham foreign was taxed at a fifteenth (Burnham hundred).

[5] Marlow foreign was taxed at a fifteenth (Desborough hundred).

[6] As on 1334 Account, E 197/77/3.

CAMBRIDGESHIRE

DOCUMENTS

8 Edward III: Account E 179/81/11
8 Edward III: Particulars E 179/81/10*
10 Edward III: Particulars E 179/81/12

TAXERS

The prior of Ely and Henry de Carleton

TAX YIELD

15th £937. 11. 8¼
10th £ 73. 18. 10¼

—————————————
£1,011. 10. 6½

Representing assessed movable wealth of

£14,803. 3. 10¼

NOTES

The borough of Cambridge and three ancient demesnes taxed at a tenth are
listed at the beginning of the roll.

The boundary of the county in 1334 differed slightly from that of modern
Cambridgeshire. Newmarket (*Saxston' cum novo mercato*) and part of the village
of Kentford, both now in Suffolk, were then taxed in Cambridgeshire, as was
part of Royston, now in Herts., which remained in Cambridgeshire until 1897.
Some villages in modern Cambridgeshire were taxed elsewhere in 1334: Heydon
and Great and Little Chishill in Essex, and part of Papworth St. Agnes in
Huntingdonshire.

REFERENCES

J. B. Pearson, 'The assessments of Cambridgeshire, 1291–1889', *Cambs. Anti-
quarian Soc.* 8 (1891–4), 283–91 (includes the 1334 figures).
J. B. Pearson, 'On the Cambridgeshire subsidies', *Cambs. Antiquarian Soc.* 9
(1894–8), 120–37.
J. J. Muskett, 'Lay Subsidies, Cambridgeshire, 1 Edward III (1327)', *East
Anglian Notes and Queries*, x–xii (1903–8).

Cantebr' [B]	Cambridge	TL/448585			
Warda ultra pontem	Ward beyond the Bridge		3.	12.	0½ [T]
Warda citra pontem	Bridge Ward		7.	17.	0 [T]
Heyward	High Ward		3.	0.	0 [T]
Bernewelleward	Barnwell Ward		2.	0.	4 [T]
Warda de Foro	Market Ward		11.	10.	1¼ [T]
Warda de Trumpiton'	Trumpington Ward		8.	0.	6 [T]

Milleward cum Newenham	Milne Ward with Newnham		6.	12.	0¼ [T]
Religiosi	Clerics		4.	0.	2¼ [T]
			46.	12.	2¼ [T]

Dominica Domini Regis [ROYAL DEMESNES]

Cestretone [A.D]	Chesterton	TL/466600	12.	0.	0 [T]
Sahaam [A.D][1]	Soham	TL/593732	13.	0.	0 [T]
Wilburham Magna [A.D][2]	Great Wilbraham	TL/548578	2.	6.	8 [T]
			27.	6.	8 [T]

Hd. Stapilho [STAPLOE HUNDRED]

Saham[3]	Soham	TL/593732	3.	12.	0
Borewell	Burwell	TL/589660	7.	10.	0
Iselham	Isleham	TL/644744	7.	13.	4
Badelingham[4]	Badlingham	TL/678709	1.	16.	0
Kenet cum Kenteforth'[5]	Kennett with Kentford [in Suffolk]	TL/699681 TL/707668	2.	4.	4½
Chipenham	Chippenham	TL/663698	8.	0.	0
Wykes	Wicken	TL/578706	4.	10.	0
Landwade	Landwade	TL/623682	2.	0.	0
Snaylwelle	Snailwell	TL/642676	4.	13.	4
Fordham	Fordham	TL/633707	7.	0.	0
			48.	19.	0½

Hd. Stane [STAINE HUNDRED]

Swafham Priour	Swaffham Prior	TL/568639	7.	14.	0
Swafham Bulbek	Swaffham Bulbeck	TL/555622	7.	0.	0
Stouwe cum Qweye	Stow cum Quy	TL/516599	5.	0.	0
Bodekesham	Bottisham	TL/545605	11.	10.	0
Wilburham Parva	Little Wilbraham	TL/546586	5.	10.	0
Wilburham Magna[6]	Great Wilbraham	TL/548578	5.	0.	0
			41.	14.	0

Hd. Flemdich [FLEMDISH HUNDRED]

Fulbourne	Fulbourn	TL/521562	19.	10.	0
Theveresham	Teversham	TL/496585	6.	10.	0
Hyntone	Cherry Hinton	TL/489571	9.	5.	0
Ditton' cum Horningesey	Fen Ditton with Horningsea	TL/482603 TL/492626	15.	10.	0
			50.	15.	0

[1] Part of Soham was taxed at a fifteenth (Staploe hundred).
[2] Part of Great Wilbraham was taxed at a fifteenth (Staine hundred).
[3] See also Royal Demesnes, above.
[4] Badlingham was taxed with Kennet in 1327 (Muskett, op. cit. x. 369).
[5] Kentford is not mentioned on the 1327 roll, ibid. See also p. 294.
[6] See also Royal Demesnes, above.

Hd. Pappeworth [PAPWORTH HUNDRED]

Fendrayton'	Fen Drayton	TL/340681	3.	6.	o
Swavishethe	Swavesey	TL/362693	14.	o.	o
Knapwelle	Knapwell	TL/336630	2.	10.	o
Conigton'	Conington	TL/320660	4.	o.	o
Grauele	Graveley	TL/250640	6.	o.	o
Overe	Over	TL/372708	13.	o.	o
Ellesworth	Elsworth	TL/318635	7.	o.	o
Papworthe Everard	Papworth Everard	TL/283626	4.	10.	o
Papworthe Anneys[1]	Papworth St. Agnes	TL/269644	4.	o.	o
Wyuelingham	Willingham	TL/405705	7.	o.	o
Bokesworthe	Boxworth	TL/348645	6.	o.	o
			71.	6.	o

Hd. Northstouwe [NORTHSTOW HUNDRED]

Lolleworth'	Lolworth	TL/369642	5.	10.	o
Gryttone	Girton	TL/423623	5.	o.	o
Longestantone	Longstanton[2]	TL/399663	10.	o.	o
Maddingle	Madingley	TL/395603	4.	16.	o
Impingtone	Impington	TL/448632	3.	10.	o
Ramptone	Rampton	TL/429681	3.	10.	o
Hoketone	Oakington	TL/415648	7.	10.	o
Landbeche	Landbeach	TL/477653	4.	10.	o
Watirbeche	Waterbeach	TL/498651	7.	10.	o
Middiltone	Milton	TL/480629	7.	10.	o
			59.	6.	o

Hd. Cestreton' [CHESTERTON HUNDRED]

Cotingham cum Westwyk	Cottenham with Westwick	TL/455686 TL/421651	15.	10.	o
Childirle Magna & Parva	Great Childerley and Little Childerley	TL/359616 lost	3.	6.	o
Draytone	Dry Drayton	TL/380619	6.	6.	o
Histone	Histon	TL/436640	10.	10.	o
			35.	12.	o

Hd. Armingforth' [ARMINGFORD HUNDRED]

Bassingbourne	Bassingbourn	TL/338442	9.	10.	o
Melrethe[3]	Meldreth	TL/378468	8.	10.	o
Clopton' cum Hattele	Clopton with East Hatley	TL/302488 TL/285504	5.	5.	o
Tadelowe cum Pyncote	Tadlow with Pincote	TL/280476 TL/274500	5.	4.	o
Croudene	Croydon	TL/315496	5.	o.	o
Schemgeye' cum Wendeye[4]	Shingay with Wendy	TL/308471 TL/322476	8.	6.	o

[1] Part of Papworth St. Agnes was taxed in Huntingdonshire (Toseland hundred, p. 136).
[2] Grid ref. is to Longstanton All Saints.
[3] Meldreth is a later insertion on E 179/81/10.
[4] Shingay was taxed separately in 1327 (Muskett, op. cit. xi. 334).

Crux Roes'[1]	Royston [in Herts.]	TL/358407	2.	5.	o
Abyngtone	Abington Pigotts	TL/304446	3.	4.	o
Meldebourne	Melbourn	TL/382449	10.	10.	o
Stepilmordone	Steeple Morden	TL/285425	6.	15.	o
Gildenemordone	Guilden Morden	TL/280442	6.	10.	o
Litlingtone	Litlington	TL/310427	4.	8.	o
Knesworth'	Kneesworth	TL/338442	4.	4.	o
Waddone'	Whaddon	TL/349465	7.	0.	o
			86.	11.	o

Hd. Stouwe [LONGSTOW HUNDRED]

Eltisle	Eltisley	TL/268596	6.	16.	o
Grantisdene Parva	Little Gransden	TL/271552	5.	16.	o
Caldecote	Caldecote	TL/347563	2.	18.	o
Herdwyk	Hardwick	TL/372586	3.	16.	o
Kyngestone	Kingston	TL/346554	6.	10.	o
Caxstone	Caxton	TL/300578	6.	0.	o
Croxstone	Croxton	TL/252592	8.	10.	o
Bourne	Bourn	TL/324563	11.	6.	o
Gamelingeye	Gamlingay	TL/242523	9.	14.	o
Stouwe	Longstowe	TL/311554	5.	6.	o
Toft	Toft	TL/363558	3.	6.	8
Everesdene	Eversden[2]	TL/367533	10.	10.	o
Hungrihattele	Hatley St. George	TL/277511	2.	5.	o
			82.	13.	8

Hd. Wetherle [WETHERLEY HUNDRED]

Harletone	Harlton	TL/386525	7.	0.	o
Arningtone	Arrington	TL/324503	6.	12.	o
Wynepol	Wimpole	TL/337510	7.	5.	o
Orewell cum	Orwell with	TL/362505	9.	6.	o
Malketon'	Malton	TL/373483			
Berton' cum	Barton with	TL/408557	5.	10.	o
Quitewell	Whitwell	TL/402584			
Scheperethe	Shepreth	TL/393474	6.	15.	o
Cumbirtone	Comberton	TL/383555	6.	8.	o
Grancestre cum	Grantchester with	TL/433555	9.	0.	o
Cotes	Coton	TL/409589			
Haselingfeld	Haslingfield	TL/403522	7.	6.	o
Baringtone	Barrington	TL/396500	12.	0.	o
			77.	2.	o

Hd. Trippelawe [THRIPLOW HUNDRED]

Foxtone	Foxton	TL/412483	7.	0.	o
Trippelawe	Thriplow	TL/442470	7.	10.	o
Hardlestone	Harston	TL/418510	6.	10.	o
Neweton' cum	Newton with	TL/435492	8.	0.	o
Haukist'	Hauxton	TL/435522			
Trumpetone	Trumpington	TL/442549	9.	8.	o

[1] Part of Royston was taxed in Hertfordshire (Odsey hundred, p. 132).
[2] Grid ref. is to Great Eversden.

Stapilforth'	Stapleford	TL/471522	5.	5.	o
Schelforth' Magna	Great Shelford	TL/459519	8.	o.	o
Schelforth' Parva	Little Shelford	TL/453517	3.	16.	o
Foulmere	Fowlmere	TL/422459	5.	16.	o
			61.	5.	o

Hd. Chelesforth [CHILFORD HUNDRED]

Badburham	Babraham	TL/509505	7.	12.	o
Abytone Magna	Great Abington	TL/531489	4.	18.	o
Abytone Parva	Little Abington	TL/529492	5.	o.	o
Hildresham	Hildersham	TL/545489	1.	16.	o
Linton' Magna	Linton	TL/562467	8.	10.	o
Parva cum	Little Linton with	TL/556475			
Bergham	Barham	TL/573461			
Berkelowe	Bartlow	TL/586452	1.	10.	o
Schodicampes	Shudy Camps	TL/621444	3.	5.	o
Caumpes Magna	Castle Camps	TL/625425	6.	10.	o
Horsethe	Horseheath	TL/613473	5.	16.	o
Wykam	West Wickham	TL/612492	5.	o.	o
Strele cum	Streetly End with	TL/613481			
Enhale	Yen Hall	TL/616503			
Pampesworthe	Pampisford	TL/498483	6.	o.	o
			55.	17.	o

Hd. Wytlesforth' [WHITTLESFORD HUNDRED]

Saustone	Sawston	TL/487493	7.	10.	o
Wytlesforth'	Whittlesford	TL/474485	9.	10.	o
Hyngistone	Hinxton	TL/497452	5.	15.	o
Ikelingtone	Ickleton	TL/494439	5.	14.	o
Dokisworthe	Duxford	TL/478462	8.	12.	o
			37.	1.	o

Hd. Radefold [RADFIELD HUNDRED]

Balsham	Balsham	TL/588508	4.	13.	4
Wrattinge	West Wratting	TL/606523	3.	17.	o
Westone	Weston Colville	TL/616532	4.	8.	o
Brinkele	Brinkley	TL/629549	6.	12.	o
Carleton' &	Carlton and	TL/642530			
Willingham	Willingham	TL/625539			
Bourgh' cum	Burrough Green with	TL/635554	4.	10.	o
Westle	Westley Waterless	TL/620563			
Dullingham	Dullingham	TL/632577	7.	o.	o
Steuthesworth'	Stetchworth	TL/642590	3.	5.	o
			34.	5.	4

Hd. Chevele [CHEVELEY HUNDRED]

Critelinge	Kirtling	TL/687575	5.	6.	o
Aysschele cum	Ashley with	TL/697615	4.	6.	o
Silverle	Silverley	TL/704602			
Chevele	Cheveley	TL/684609	4.	13.	4

Dytton' Camoys	Camois	TL/655585	7.	0.	0
Dytton' Waleys	Woodditton	TL/659591			
Saxston' cum	Saxon	TL/675602			
novo mercato[1]	with Newmarket [in Suffolk]	TL/644633			
			21.	5.	4

Insula Elien' [ISLE OF ELY]

Ely c.m[2]	Ely [with members]	TL/538802	23.	16.	9¾
Litleport	Littleport	TL/566870	3.	3.	0
Dounham	Downham	TL/527842	2.	8.	0
			29.	7.	9¾

Hd. Wychforth' [WITCHFORD HUNDRED]

Sutton' cum Mephale	Sutton with Mepal	TL/448790 TL/442808	5.	5.	0
Dodingtone	Doddington	TL/400905	6.	4.	0
Wytleseye	Whittlesey	TL/270970	9.	2.	0
Stretham cum Theforth'	Stretham with Little Thetford	TL/512745 TL/532762	7.	10.	6
Wycham Coveneye & Maneye	Witcham Coveney and Manea	TL/465801 TL/489822 TL/480895	3.	14.	0
Hadinham	Haddenham	TL/464756	9.	2.	0
Wilbirtone	Wilburton	TL/480750	2.	8.	0
Chateritz	Chatteris	TL/395860	5.	12.	0
Wychforth' cum Wynteworth'	Witchford with Wentworth	TL/504788 TL/481786	6.	2.	0
			54.	19.	6

Hd. Wysebech' [WISBECH HUNDRED]

Wysebeche	Wisbech	TF/462096	27.	6.	0
Leveringtone	Leverington	TF/444114	24.	0.	0
Newetone	Newton	TF/441149	10.	10.	0
Tyd	Tydd St. Giles	TF/427164	11.	0.	0
Elm	Elm	TF/470069	12.	12.	0
Welle[3]	Upwell	TF/504028	2.	4.	0
			87.	12.	0

TOTAL: £1,011. 10. 6½[4]

---

[1] In 1327 *et Wick* is added to this entry (Muskett, op. cit. xi. 79).

[2] Stuntney, separately taxed in 1327 (ibid. xii. 136), was probably included in the Ely entry.

[3] *Welle* could refer either to Outwell or Upwell. Muskett identified *Welles* (1327) with Upwell, op. cit. xii. 268. See also Norfolk (Clackclose hundred, p. 203).

[4] As on 1334 Account, E 179/81/11.

CORNWALL

DOCUMENTS

8 Edward III: Account	not extant
8 Edward III: Particulars	E 179/87/9* (incomplete)
10 Edward III: Indenture of 1334	E 179/87/10 (incomplete)
13 Edward III: Particulars	E 179/87/15

Place-name spellings in the accompanying list are mainly from E 179/87/9, but where illegible on this roll they are taken from either 87/10 or 87/15.

TAXERS

The prior of Launceston and Silvester de Trefruthken

TAX YIELD

15th	£378.	19.	5
10th	£ 99.	18.	4
	£478.	17.	9

Representing assessed movable wealth of

£6,683. 14. 7

NOTES

The Cornish rolls are unusual in that for each entry they show the tax of 1332 and the *incrementum* which together give the 1334 quota. Most of the entries are described as *parochia*. There were eighteen taxation boroughs in the county in 1334, many with very small tax quotas. The proliferation of small boroughs in Cornwall, as in Devon, is of special interest; there is a brief summary of the problem in Maurice Beresford, *New Towns of the Middle Ages*, 1967, 399–402, and a number of the taxation boroughs are included in his gazetteer for the county, 402–14. As in Devon the tinners were exempt from the lay subsidy but the rolls, unlike those of Devon, give no details of the charges against these men.

The 1334 lay subsidy and subsequent tax reliefs of the fifteenth century are the subjects of a recent analysis by Professor N. J. G. Pounds. While there are some inaccuracies in his version of the subsidy his paper includes a valuable discussion of taxation in the county.

REFERENCES

N. J. G. Pounds, 'Taxation and wealth in late medieval Cornwall', *Jnl. Royal Institution of Cornwall*, new series, vi (1971), 154–67.

J. Hatcher, *Rural Economy and Society in the Duchy of Cornwall, 1300–1500*, 1970.

ACKNOWLEDGEMENTS

I am indebted to Professor N. J. G. Pounds for kindly sending me an offprint of his paper and to Mr. P. L. Hall, County Archivist, for help in the identification and location of some place-names.

Hd. Penewyth' [PENWITH HUNDRED]

Sancti Justi	St. Just	sw/372315	2.	11.	8[1]
Sancti Silvani'	St. Levan	sw/380222	2.	12.	5[1]
Sancte Senane	Sennen	sw/358255	3.	6.	0
Sancte Beriane	St. Buryan	sw/409258	8.	5.	2
Sancti Sancredi	Sancreed	sw/421293	1.	14.	0
Sancti Maderni'	Madron	sw/453318	4.	14.	0
Sancti Goythiani'	Gwithian	sw/586413	1.	15.	0
Sancte Ie	St. Ives	sw/518404	3.	6.	8
Sancti Tewynnoci	Towednack	sw/488381	2.	5.	0
Sancte Crewenne[2]	Crowan	sw/645345	2.	1.	2
Sancte Senare	Zennor	sw/454385	2.	11.	2
Sancte Felicitatis	Phillack	sw/566384	2.	12.	0
Sancti Michaelis	St. Michaels [Marazion]	sw/519306	2.	11.	3
Sancti Hillar'	St. Hilary	sw/551312	2.	18.	7
Reddruth'	Redruth	sw/699420	1.	12.	0
Sancti Illogani'	Illogan	sw/671440	4.	7.	10
Cambron	Camborne	sw/646401	4.	2.	0
Sancti Wynneri'	Gwinear	sw/595374	3.	6.	0
Sancti Erti'	St. Erth	sw/550350	3.	11.	8
Lananta	Lelant	sw/544372	6.	16.	5
Sancti Pauli'	Paul	sw/465271	6.	5.	10
Luduon	Ludgvan	sw/505331	2.	16.	6
Sancte Weluele	Gulval	sw/485317	3.	5.	0
Uthno	Perranuthnoe	sw/539295		12.	6
Morweth'	Morvah	sw/402354		17.	6
Germogh'	Germoe	sw/585294		10.	8
			81.	8.	0

Hd. Kerrier [KERRIER HUNDRED]

Sancte Weneppe	Gwennap	sw/739401	2.	8.	0	
Sancti Maunani	Mawnan	sw/787272	1.	8.	0	
Menster	Manaccan	sw/763250	1.	4.	6	
Dedynini'	St. Martin in Meneage	sw/735236		18.	8	
Sancte Stediane	Stithians	sw/735367	2.	19.	4	
Sancti Budoci Maior	Budock	sw/786324	2.	9.	0	
Sancti Glywyati'	St. Gluvias	sw/783347	2.	2.	10	
Penryn [B]	Penryn	sw/787345	2.	0.	0	[T]
Arworthel	Perranarworthal	sw/779390	1.	4.	9	
Sancti Constantini'	Constantine	sw/731291	3.	6.	4	
Sancti Laudi'	Mabe	sw/763341	1.	10.	4	
Sancti Melori'	Mylor	sw/820352	2.	4.	0	
Sancti Melani'	Mullion	sw/679192	2.	18.	4	
Sancti Maugani	Mawgan	sw/709251	1.	16.	0	
Sancti Kyerani'	St. Keverne	sw/791212	6.	13.	0	
Sancte Breace	Breage	sw/617285	2.	3.	0	
Sancti Rumoni' Magni'	Ruan Major	sw/703164	1.	2.	0	
Sancti Wynwolai'	Landewednack	sw/711126		10.	4	
Sancte Grade	Grade	sw/712143	1.	4.	6	
Sancti Antonini'	St. Anthony in Meneage	sw/c.778241		8.	0	

General note: unless denoted otherwise as *manerium* [man.], *burgus* [B], or *villa* [v], entries for this county are described as *parochia*.

[1] Slight error in Pounds, op. cit. 156.
[2] Part of Crowan was taxed in Kerrier hundred, p. 31.

			£	s.	d.	
Sancti Rumoni' Parvi	Ruan Minor	sw/721152		7.	2	
Wynyanton'	Winnianton	sw/660205		14.	10	
Sancti Corentini	Cury	sw/678213		15.	0	
Sancte Crewenne[1]	Crowan	sw/645345	1.	0.	10	
Sancti Sithnini	Sithney	sw/637290	2.	0.	0	
Helleston' [B]	Helston	sw/658277	4.	6.	8	[T]
Sancte Wendrone [A.D]	Wendron	sw/679311	3.	12.	0	[T]
Sancti Eunini	Merther Uny	sw/703293		15.	4	
			54.	2.	9[2]	

Hd. Poudresshire [POWDER HUNDRED]

			£	s.	d.	
Tywardrayth'	Tywardreath	sx/085543	2.	15.	11	
Grogyth	Grogoth	sw/916452		13.	4	
Sancti Ermetis	St. Erme	sw/847498	1.	14.	0	
Fawe Extra[3]	Fowey Extra	sx/c.125517	1.	4.	8	
Argalles	Arallas	sw/882539	1.	14.	4	
Fawe [B]	Fowey	sx/125517	3.	8.	4	[T]
Lanndege	Kea	sw/809427	2.	7.	0	
Sancti Sampsonis	St. Sampson	sx/120551	1.	15.	0	
Lausulyan	Luxulyan	sx/052581	1.	10.	6	
Roche	Roche	sw/988598	2.	8.	7	
Sancti Stephi'	St. Stephen in Brannel	sw/944533	3.	6.	3	
Sancti Aluny	St. Allen	sw/822506	2.	4.	6	
Keynewyn	Kenwyn	sw/c.780472	2.	19.	0	
Sancti Gerendi	Gerrans	sw/873352	2.	0.	0	
Lamoren	Lamorran	sw/878418		17.	0	
Sancte Feoce	Feock	sw/825384	1.	10.	0	
Eglosros	Philleigh	sw/871394	1.	16.	0	
Sancte Ladoce	Ladock	sw/894510	2.	14.	0	
Moresk' [A.D]	St. Clement	sw/850439	2.	0.	0	[T]
Caryhaes	Caerhays	sw/971415		11.	6	
Sancte Ewe	St. Ewe	sw/978461	1.	8.	3	
Sancti Austoli	St. Austell	sx/014525	6.	19.	11	
Tewynton' [man.][4]	Tewington		1.	14.	0	[T]
Sancti Dyonisii	St. Dennis	sw/951583	1.	16.	6	
Sancti Mewani	St. Mewan	sw/998518	1.	12.	1	
Penkeuel	St. Michael Penkevil	sw/858422		11.	8	
Elerky	Veryan	sw/917396	3.	6.	0	
Sancti Antonini'	St. Anthony in Roseland	sw/855320		12.	2	
Sancte Cride [A.D]	Creed	sw/935473	2.	1.	0	[T]
Sancti Kybii	Cuby	sw/928453	1.	2.	0	
Maudut [B]	St. Mawes	sw/845330		5.	6	[T]
Landrayth'	St. Blazey[5]	sx/068548		17.	8	
Tregony [B]	Tregoney	sw/925450	1.	15.	2	[T]
Sancti Goroni'	St. Goran	sw/999423	1.	16.	0	
Sancti Justi	St. Just in Roseland	sw/848357	1.	15.	0	
Eglosmerther	Merther	sw/862448		18.	0	
Granpount [B]	Grampound	sw/936483		14.	6	[T]
Sancti Probi	Probus	sw/899478	5.	6.	0	

[1] Part of Crowan was assessed in Penwith hundred, above, p. 30.

[2] Totals in error in Pounds, op. cit. 157.

[3] *Extra* not *ex X*^{am} as in Pounds, ibid.

[4] Tewington was a manor of the Duchy of Cornwall which lay in the parishes of St. Austell, St. Blazey, and Roche.

[5] Grid ref. is to modern St. Blazey; the medieval settlement was further south, near the estuary.

			£	s	d	
Lamorek'	Mevagissey	sx/015449	1.	10.	0	
Lostwithiel [B]	Lostwithiel	sx/103600	8.	13.	4	[T]
Lanyhorn'	Ruan Lanihorne	sw/894420	1.	14.	8[1]	
Truru [B]	Truro	sw/828448	12.	1.	10	[T]
Lanlyveri'	Lanlivery	sx/080591	1.	0.	8	
Penknegh' [man.] [A.D] &	Penknight and	sx/093596		3.	8	[T]
Rostormel [man.] [A.D]	Restormel	sx/103613		6.	8	[T]
			99.	12.	3[2]	

Hd. Pydresshir' [PYDER HUNDRED]

			£	s	d	
Lanhydrok'	Lanhydrock	sx/085636		17.	8	
Sancti Ermetis	St. Ervan	sw/892703	1.	2.	6	
Sancti Petroci Minoris	Little Petherick	sw/918722		6.	4	
Sancti Pyerani[3]	Perranzabuloe	sw/770520	2.	6.	8	
Sancti Enodri'	St. Enoder	sw/892570	3.	0.	0	
Laneveth	Lanivet	sx/039642	1.	10.	0	
Sancti Karentoci	Crantock	sw/790606	2.	13.	0	
Sancte Marine	St. Merryn	sw/887742	2.	1.	0	
Sancte Ide	St. Issey	sw/929718	1.	12.	0	
Sancti Uveli	St. Eval	sw/872692	1.	10.	0	
Wythiel	Withiel	sw/994654	1.	6.	8	
Sancti Brioci	St. Breock	sw/977717	2.	7.	0	
Sancte Agnetis	St. Agnes	sw/720507	1.	8.	10	
Medesshole [B]	Mitchell	sw/859545		8.	0	[T]
Sancte Newelyne	Newlyn	sw/829563	3.	17.	4	
Sancti Petroci Maioris [A.D]	Padstow [Rural]	sw/916754	2.	4.	10	[T]
Oldestowe[4]	Padstow	sw/916754	1.	19.	0	[T]
Sancti Colani'	Colan	sw/868613	1.	4.	6	
Sancte Columbe Maior	St. Columb Major	sw/912637	5.	13.	0	
Lanhern'	Lanherne	sw/873674	3.	0.	0	
Sancti Cutberti'	Cubert	sw/786578	2.	0.	0	
Sancte Wenne	St. Wenn	sw/968649	1.	18.	0	
Sancte Columbe Minor'	St. Columb Minor	sw/840624	4.	11.	0	
			48.	17.	4[5]	

Hd. Trigg' [TRIGG HUNDRED]

			£	s	d	
Sancte Tethe	St. Teath	sx/064805	2.	9.	6	
Sancte Mabene	St. Mabyn	sx/042732	1.	10.	11	
Lannou	St. Kew	sx/021769	1.	6.	0	
Sancte Menfrede	St. Minver	sw/965771	1.	15.	0	
Penmaen [man] [A.D]	Penmayne	sw/948760		4.	10	[T]
Sancte Endeliane	St. Endellion	sw/997787	1.	8.	0	
Bodmine' Extra[6]	Bodmin Extra		1.	16.	0	

---

[1] Error in Pounds, op. cit. 158 (the *incrementum* is 18*d*. not 18*s*.).

[2] The quotas for this hundred add up to £99. 12. 2; the 1*d*. discrepancy is somewhere in the fifteenths.

[3] Taxed at a tenth according to E 179/87/9 but the totals show this to be an error. Some later documents perpetuate the mistake.

[4] Padstow was taxed as a borough intermittently in the early fourteenth century; in 1334 it is not described as such but was still taxed at a tenth.

[5] Pounds, op. cit. 159, gives the totals for Trigg hundred here, in error.

[6] *Extra* not *e X^{am}* as in Pounds, op. cit. 159.

Eglosheyl	Egloshayle	sx/001719	2.	3.	8
Sancti Tudii	St. Tudy	sx/067763	1.	16.	8
Sancti Brueredi	St. Breward	sx/098773	1.	19.	5
Blyston'	Blisland	sx/101732	1.	17.	1
Hellaund	Helland	sx/075710		19.	0
Bodmine' [B]	Bodmin	sx/072670	20.	0.	0 [T]
Temple	Temple	sx/147733		5.	0
			39.	11.	1

Hd. Lysnewyth' [LESNEWTH HUNDRED]

Sancti Clederi	St. Clether	sx/205844	1.	13.	8
Alternon	Altarnun	sx/223813	1.	18.	6
Sancti Genesii'	St. Gennys	sx/149972	1.	14.	2
Sancte Warburge	Warbstow	sx/205903	1.	18.	4
Sancti Dauid	Davidstow	sx/151872	2.	6.	8
Lysnewyth	Lesnewth	sx/131903	1.	8.	0
Sancte Iulitte	St. Juliot	sx/129913		14.	8
Trevalga	Trevalga	sx/081900	1.	0.	0
Tynetagel [B]	Tintagel	sx/051884		13.	2 [T]
Tynetagel [man.] [A.D]	Tintagel		1.	7.	0 [T]
Castelboterell [B]	Boscastle	sx/096098		12.	0 [T]
Mynstr'	Minster	sx/101905	1.	4.	2
Poundystok'	Poundstock	sx/202995	4.	5.	2
Oterham	Otterham	sx/169908		19.	0
Treneglos	Treneglos	sx/208881	1.	6.	8
Mighelstawe [A.D]	Michaelstow	sx/081789		19.	0 [T]
Lanteglos [A.D]	Lanteglos by Camelford	sx/c.105836	1.	10.	0 [T]
Sancti Adweni	Advent	sx/105816	1.	0.	0
Camelford [B]	Camelford	sx/105836		9.	0 [T]
			26.	19.	2

Hd. Strattone [STRATTON HUNDRED]

Kylkamlonde	Kilkhampton [Rural][1]		3.	4.	4
Marwynchurch'	Marhamchurch	ss/223037	2.	0.	0
Boyton'	Boyton	sx/320920	1.	9.	0
Iacobstawe	Jacobstow	sx/198958	1.	15.	4
Wyteston'	Whitstone	sx/263986	1.	13.	0
Strattone	Stratton	ss/232065	2.	19.	6
Poghawille	Poughill	ss/222078		19.	0
Bruggerewal[2]	Bridgerule [in Devon]	ss/281031		12.	6
Wyke	Week St. Mary	sx/237977	1.	15.	0
Lanncels	Launcells	ss/243057	1.	8.	0
Tamerton'	North Tamerton	sx/312973	1.	10.	0
Moreinstawe	Morwenstow	ss/205153	3.	6.	0
Kylkampton' [B][3]	Kilkhampton	ss/252113	1.	0.	2 [T]
			23.	11.	10

[1] For Kilkhampton borough see below. Pounds, op. cit. 160, gives quota as £3. 5. 4, in error.

[2] This entry refers to West Bridgerule; East Bridgerule was taxed in Devon, p. 61.

[3] For Kilkhampton Rural see above.

Hd. Westweuel' [WEST HUNDRED]

Sancti Neoti	St. Neot	sx/186679	2.	7.	o	
Dulo	Duloe	sx/234581	1.	17.	6	
Botkonnic'	Boconnoc	sx/147606		12.	4[1]	
Cardynan	Cardinham	sx/123687	1.	18.	o	
Worlegan	Warleggan	sx/157692	1.	2.	o	
Lanraythou	Lanreath	sx/181569	1.	8.	6	
Morval	Morval	sx/260567	1.	17.	o	
Plenynt'	Pelynt	sx/203550	2.	7.	o	
Portpighan [v][2]	West Looe	sx/253532	1.	13.	o	[T]
Sancti Clari'	St. Cleer	sx/248682	2.	1.	7	
Lysk'	Liskeard [Rural][3]	sx/250646	1.	12.	o	
Sancti Martini de Lo	St. Martin	sx/260550	1.	10.	o	
Tallan	Talland	sx/228516	1.	12.	o	
Lanteglos	Lanteglos	sx/145515	5.	o.	o	
Brodek'	Braddock	sx/162622		18.	o	
Lansalwys	Lansallos	sx/172516	1.	9.	o	
Lysk' [B][4]	Liskeard	sx/250646	6.	14.	o	[T]
Sancte Keyne	St. Keyne	sx/242608		8.	4	
Sancti Uepi	St. Veep	sx/140550	1.	13.	4	
Sancti Wynnoci'	St. Winnow	sx/115570	2.	o.	o	
Sancti Pynnoci'	St. Pinnock	sx/200633		19.	o	
Lysk' [man.] [A.D][5]	Liskeard	sx/250646	1.	13.	o	[T]
Loo [B]	East Looe	sx/256533	1.	10.	o	[T]
Reprena	Respryn	sx/098636		8.	o	
			44.	11.	o[6]	

Hd. Estweuelisshire [EAST HUNDRED]

Anton'	Antony	sx/398546	1.	11.	o	
Lansant	Lezant	sx/339791	1.	18.	o	
Sancti Melani'	St. Mellion	sx/388655	1.	6.	o	
Lawyttatoni'	Lawhitton	sx/355823	1.	3.	o	
Sancti Johannis	St. John	sx/409536	1.	6.	11	
Rame	Rame	sx/426492	1.	11.	o	
Southhille	South Hill	sx/329726	2.	4.	o	
Sanct Stephi' de Laut'	St. Stephen by Launceston	sx/324856	4.	16.	o	
Sancti Yvonis	St. Ive	sx/309672	1.	19.	o	
Pyderwyn	South Petherwin	sx/309819	2.	3.	o	
Quedyk'	Quethiock	sx/312648	1.	7.	o	
Sancti Dominici	St. Dominick	sx/401678	1.	4.	o	
Landilp	Landulph	sx/431615		17.	6	
Northhille	North Hill	sx/272766	1.	15.	o	
Lawanek'	Lewannick	sx/276807	1.	10.	o	
Tremeton [man.] [A.D]	Trematon	sx/393598	2.	15.	4	[T]
Stoke [A.D]	Stoke Climsland	sx/360734	2.	9.	o	[T]
Lanrak'	Landrake	sx/374605	1.	19.	o	
Mehynyot'	Menheniot	sx/288628	4.	6.	o	

[1] Error in Pounds, op. cit. 160, where the 1332 figure should be 11s. 4d.
[2] Except in 1334 West Looe was taxed as a borough (see Willard (1933), op. cit. 430).
[3] For the manor and the borough of Liskeard see separate entries below.
[4] For the parish, see above; for the manor, see below.
[5] For the borough of Liskeard and the parish see separate entries above.
[6] The quotas for this hundred add up to £44. 10. 7; the 5d. discrepancy is somewhere in the fifteenths.

Lankynhorn'	Linkinhorne	sx/319735	2.	0.	0	
Saltesse [B]	Saltash	sx/428589	2.	0.	8	[T]
Egloskery	Egloskerry	sx/273865	2.	5.	0	
Sevyok'	Sheviock	sx/370551	1.	4.	0	
Pylaton'	Pillaton	sx/367643		15.	4	
Sancti Germani'	St. Germans	sx/359578	6.	10.	0	
Calystok' [A.D]	Calstock	sx/436686	3.	6.	0	[T]
Bodflemy' [A.D]	Botus Fleming	sx/404613		11.	0	[T]
Macre	Maker	sx/447520		14.	10	
Donnheued [B]	Launceston	sx/332846	2.	16.	8	[T]
			60.	4.	3	

TOTAL: £478. 17. 9[1]

---

[1] As on the 1334 Enrolled Account, E 359/8, mm. 4–5. The figures for the hundreds in the Particulars in fact add up to £478. 17. 8.

CUMBERLAND (1336)

DOCUMENTS

8 Edward III: Not taxed
10 Edward III: Account   not extant
10 Edward III: Particulars E 179/90/4*

TAXERS

1334 The prior of Carlisle and William de Werdale (vacated)
1336 Clement de Skelton and John de Hotonroef

TAX YIELD

1336 15th £434. 11. 10½
     10th £119. 16. 8¼

          £554. 8. 6¾

Representing assessed movable wealth of

          £7,717. 5. 0

NOTES

Cumberland, like Northumberland and Westmorland, was excused from the 1334 lay subsidy on account of recent devastation by the Scots. The following list is therefore that of the fifteenth and tenth of 1336. The tax quotas for the county were probably unduly low owing to the unsettled conditions. All the places taxed at a tenth are listed at the end of the roll; they comprise the city of Carlisle and a number of ancient demesnes including Penrith.

REFERENCES

J. P. Steel, *Cumberland Lay Subsidy* [6 Edward III], Kendal, 1912.
C. M. Fraser, 'The Cumberland and Westmorland lay subsidies for 1332', *Trans. Cumberland and Westmorland Antiq. and Arch. Soc.*, new series, 66 (1966), 131–58.

ACKNOWLEDGEMENTS

I am indebted to Mr. Kenneth Smith and Miss A. M. Armstrong for help in the identification of some place-names.

Wap. Lith' [LEATH WAPENTAKE]

Kirkosewald' [v]	Kirkoswald	NY/553412	10.	6.	1¼
Gamelesby [v]	Gamblesby	NY/610394	4.	6.	6
Melmerby [v]	Melmerby	NY/611374	4.	4.	1½
Graystok' [v]	Greystoke	NY/443307	3.	13.	11½
Graistokskales [h][1]	lost		1.	8.	8¼

[1] A lost place in Greystoke parish (*E.P.N.S.*, XX, *Cumberland*, part 1 (1950), 196).

Threlkeld [h]	Threlkeld	NY/322253	3.	3.	6½
Grisedale [h]	Mungrisdale	NY/363304	2.	8.	11½
Hoton' John'	Hutton John	NY/439269	2.	8.	3¼
Jonby [h]	Johnby	NY/433330	2.	0.	9½
Caterlen' [v]	Catterlen	NY/483333		19.	10
Dacre [h]	Dacre	NY/460266	1.	10.	7½
Berier [h]	Berrier	NY/400296	1.	11.	11
Mathirdale [h]	Matterdale	NY/396234	2.	11.	9½
Mothirby [h]	Motherby	NY/429283	2.	4.	7
Blencow [h]	Blencow[1]	NY/456325	1.	9.	10
Thistilthuait [h]	probably Thistlewood[2]	NY/396436	1.	5.	4
Staynton'	Stainton	NY/485283	2.	16.	9¼
Neubiggyng'	Newbiggin	NY/470294	2.	8.	3¾
Skelton'	Skelton	NY/440354	4.	19.	1½
Souleby [h]	Soulby	NY/462251	1.	6.	8
Aynstaplith' [v]	Ainstable	NY/530467	7.	1.	2½
Crogelyne [v]	Croglin	NY/574473	2.	4.	7
Rauenwik'	Renwick	NY/597435	2.	1.	4
Glassanby	Glassonby	NY/577390	1.	13.	4
Skirwith'	Skirwith	NY/618326	1.	19.	11
Blenkarn & Kirkland	Blencarn and Kirkland	NY/638312 NY/646325	3.	5.	9¼
Hoton' Roef' [h]	Hutton Roof	NY/373341	1.	9.	7¾
Edynhale	Edenhall	NY/569321	3.	5.	4
Laisyngby	Lazonby	NY/549398	4.	2.	1½
Neuton' Reny	Newton Reigny	NY/480316		7.	0
Dyrawe [h]	Dyrah	NY/597446	1.	11.	8¼
Sparkheued [h]	Sparket	NY/430257	1.	11.	7
Unthank' [h]	Unthank	NY/450363		13.	8
Lambenby [h]	Lamonby	NY/410358		15.	5
Culgaith'	Culgaith	NY/610297	5.	2.	8½
Hoton' in For'	Hutton in the Forest	NY/460358	4.	3.	1
Clementis de Skelton'				6.	8
John de Hoton' Roef'				6.	8
Midleskuogh'	Middlesceugh	NY/400418		14.	0
			100.	1.	5¾

Wap. Cumbr' [CUMBERLAND WAPENTAKE]

Burgh'	Burgh by Sands	NY/328591	11.	8.	9
Grynnesdale	Grinsdale	NY/373581	1.	8.	2¾
Whitrig'	Whitrigg	NY/227579	5.	11.	8½
Beaumont	Beaumont	NY/348593	2.	13.	4¼
Routheclif'	Rockcliffe	NY/358616	5.	17.	8¼
Bowneys	Bowness on Solway	NY/224627	5.	4.	9¾
Bampton'	Kirkbampton	NY/305564	5.	17.	8
Orreton'	Orton[3]	NY/329543	1.	18.	2
Thoresby	Thursby	NY/324503	1.	11.	3
Wyggeton'	Wigton	NY/256483	7.	14.	5¼
Waverton'	Waverton	NY/220473	2.	6.	2½
Blencogowe	Blencogo	NY/196480	1.	0.	3½
Dundrawe	Dundraw	NY/215498	1.	8.	5¼
Staynton'	Stainton	NY/380569	2.	3.	8¼
Kirkandres	Kirkandrews upon Eden	NY/354583	1.	11.	10

[1] Grid ref. is to Great Blencow.
[2] Identification suggested in *E.P.N.S., XX, Cumberland*, part 1 (1950), 246.
[3] Grid ref. is to Great Orton.

Langholm [h][1]		lost	1.	14.	1¾
Raghton'	Raughton	NY/390476	3.	15.	8
Kirkthuayt [h] & Scarthuait' [h]	East and West Curthwaite	NY/334487 NY/323489	1.	4.	6
Warthewyk'	Warwick	NY/465565	2.	7.	10¼
Blakhale	Blackhall [= Blackwell]	NY/402530	2.	16.	7½
Pertane [h]	Parton	NY/278508		12.	11½
Kirkebrid'	Kirkbride	NY/230566	1.	16.	0
Ulueton'	Oulton	NY/244508		14.	8
Ayketon'	Aikton	NY/274530	4.	4.	10¼
Comquintyne & Bochardby	Cumwhinton and Botcherby	NY/449525 NY/420559		14.	7½
Tenentibus Abbatis de Holmcoltrane	Tenants of the Abbot of Holm Cultram		4.	1.	3¼
Wederhale	Wetheral	NY/467544	1.	4.	11
Heyheued' [h]	High Head	NY/408438		14.	1
Ermytthuait' [h]	Armathwaite	NY/506460	1.	14.	6½
			85.	13.	2¾

Wap. Esk' [ESKDALE WAPENTAKE]

Brampton'	Brampton	NY/528610	6.	12.	2½
Walton' Wod	Walton Wood	NY/550661		16.	0¼
Northmore [h][2]		lost	1.	5.	8
Irthington'	Irthington	NY/499617	2.	13.	2
Halton'	Hayton	NY/508577	1.	6.	3¾
Trenirmane	Triermain	NY/593668	1.	16.	1¾
Torcrossk'	Tercrosset	NY/570682		14.	11½
Foulwod [h][3]		lost	1.	8.	3
Bothecastre	Bewcastle	NY/565746	2.	9.	10½
Walton' & Lanercost	Walton and Lanercost	NY/522645 NY/554638	3.	16.	1
Stapilton' & Cambok	Stapleton and Kirkcambeck	NY/503713 NY/533689		17.	6¾
Comrew & Castelcayrek	Cumrew and Castle Carrock	NY/551503 NY/543554	5.	15.	5½
Farlham'	Farlam	NY/555588	2.	6.	1¾
Foresta Nichi'	Nicholforest[4]	NY/455780	2.	7.	1½
Ascreton'	Askerton	NY/550693		18.	0
Skaleby	Scaleby	NY/447632	1.	15.	9
Comquittyngton'	Cumwhitton	NY/506522	2.	12.	4¼
Parva Corkeby	Little Corby	NY/479571		10.	1¼
Magna Corkeby	Great Corby	NY/472543	2.	12.	9
Hederesford[5]		lost	1.	13.	10½
Kirkleuyngton'	Kirklinton	NY/433670	2.	6.	5
Hoghton'	Houghton	NY/408598		11.	5½
Denton'	Denton	NY/578630	2.	15.	4
Artureth'	Arthuret	NY/379677	1.	11.	11
Stubhill[6]		lost		3.	9

1 A lost place in Sebergham parish, *E.P.N.S.*, *XX*, *Cumberland*, part 1 (1950), 151.
2 A lost place in Askerton parish, *E.P.N.S.*, *XX*, *Cumberland*, part 1 (1950), 56.
3 A lost place in Askerton parish, ibid.
4 Parish name only; grid ref. is to Kingfield.
5 A lost place in Kirklinton Middle parish, *E.P.N.S.*, *XX*, *Cumberland*, part 1 (1950), 102.
6 A lost place in Arthuret parish, *E.P.N.S.*, *XX*, *Cumberland*, part 1 (1950), 54.

Solperd cum Eston'	Solport with Easton	NY/473724 NY/430720	1.	0.	11½
Westleuyngton'	Westlinton	NY/393645		14.	0½
Fenton'	Fenton	NY/502562		13.	8
Lidel	Liddel	NY/c.403743		6.	8
			54.	12.	0¼

Wap. Allird [ALLERDALE WAPENTAKE]

Blencraik	Blindcrake	NY/148347	6.	10.	0
Gilcrouce	Gilcrux	NY/113380	2.	3.	8
Broughton'	Broughton[1]	NY/073314	2.	11.	8
Ribbeton'	Ribton	NY/047305	2.	15.	0
Uluedale	Uldale	NY/251370	6.	19.	4
Caldebek	Caldbeck	NY/324398	9.	0.	0
Bastenthuait'	Bassenthwaite	NY/230322	6.	3.	0
Blenerhaiset	Blennerhasset	NY/177414	3.	15.	4
Cambreton'	Camerton	NY/038309		16.	0
Seton'	Seaton	NY/018306	2.	11.	0
Askpaterik'	Aspatria	NY/148419	8.	16.	6
Thorpenhow	Torpenhow	NY/206398	4.	19.	4
Bowaldith'	Bewaldeth	NY/210347	1.	10.	0
Ukmanby	Upmanby	NY/190423		10.	0
Plumland	Plumbland	NY/152392	4.	0.	8
Bothil	Bothel	NY/182388	5.	5.	0
Alenburgh'	Ellenborough	NY/046258	2.	9.	4
Neuton'	Westnewton	NY/135442	4.	0.	8
Parsonby [h]	Parsonby	NY/142389		13.	4
Derham	Dearham	NY/072364	6.	9.	6½
Ireby	Ireby	NY/238390	6.	6.	8
Castelrig'[2]	Castlerigg	NY/282225	8.	0.	0
Papecastr'	Papcastle	NY/108313	5.	0.	0
Kirklandthorp' [h]	Kirkland	NY/192402	1.	10.	0
Skolitelgarth' [h]	probably Snittlegarth	NY/219378	1.	10.	0
Canounby [h]	Crosscanonby	NY/070390	1.	0.	0
Bolton'	Bolton[3]	NY/237443	5.	16.	8½
Bridekirk'	Bridekirk	NY/116336		16.	0¼
Bromfeld	Bromfield	NY/174470	7.	7.	1¼
John' ten' de Neuland			1.	0.	0
			120.	5.	10½

Lib. Cokermouth' [COCKERMOUTH LIBERTY]

Cokermouth'	Cockermouth	NY/123306	2.	17.	1¾
Brigham	Brigham	NY/085302	1.	1.	2
Craisothm'	Greysouthen	NY/071290		16.	8¼
Eglesfeld	Eaglesfield	NY/095281	1.	7.	0¾
Clifton'	Clifton[4]	NY/041295	1.	0.	6¾
Dene	Dean	NY/075252	1.	11.	3

[1] Grid ref. is to Great Broughton.
[2] This entry may include parts of Keswick. Keswick is not named on the tax rolls and it must be included either in Castlerigg or Braithwaite, below, p. 40.
[3] Grid ref. is to Bolton Low Houses.
[4] Grid ref. is to Great Clifton.

Whynfell'	Whinfell	NY/150253		15.	11
Braithuait'	Braithwaite	NY/230236	10.	17.	9¼[1]
			20.	7.	6¾

Lib. Egrem' [EGREMONT LIBERTY]

Wirkyngton'	Workington	NY/002288	2.	8.	4½
Lamplegh'	Lamplugh	NY/089209	1.	11.	0¼
Hauryngton'	Harrington	NX/994256		16.	2
Kelton'	Kelton	NY/069189	1.	5.	0
Murton'	Murton	NY/075202	1.	15.	5¾
Distington'	Distington	NY/006234		16.	4
Fresyngton'	Frizington	NY/033170	1.	3.	6¾
Cletergh'	Cleator	NY/013134		12.	0
Egremound	Egremont	NY/011105	7.	10.	4¾
Kirkeby	Kirkeby, now St. Bees	NX/971115	3.	13.	7¼
Wilton' &	Wilton and	NY/040111		18.	3¼
Hale	Haile	NY/033086			
Caldre	Calder	NY/040035		18.	4¼
Neuton'	Newton	NY/054029		15.	3
Goseford	Gosforth	NY/069035	1.	2.	5
Bolton'	Bolton	NY/086026	1.	1.	6
Santon'	Santon	NY/102017	1.	15.	2½
Dreg'	Drigg	SD/070992	1.	6.	11½
Mulcastr'	Muncaster	SD/103966	1.	0.	9¼
Bretteby	Birkby	SD/c.117963	1.	10.	0
Seton'	Seaton	SD/108900	1.	8.	1
Bolton'	?		1.	8.	8¾
Selecroft'	Silecroft	SD/130819	1.	6.	8¼
Kirksantane	Kirksanton	SD/140807	1.	10.	3¼
Milnholm'	Millom	SD/170803	1.	16.	4¼
			39.	10.	11¼

Lib. Prioris Karliol' [LIBERTY OF THE PRIOR OF CARLISLE]

Carleton'	Carleton	NY/430527	1.	12.	0
Bochardgat'	Botchergate	NY/406553	2.	3.	2½
Birschawe	Brisco	NY/420520	1.	4.	11½
Petrelwraa	Wreay	NY/435490	1.	0.	0
Seburgham	Sebergham	NY/363418		18.	0¾
Veteri Salkeld	Little Salkeld	NY/566362		13.	4
			7.	11.	6¾

Lib. Episcopi Karl' [LIBERTY OF THE BISHOP OF CARLISLE]

Dalston' [A.D][2]	Dalston	NY/369502	16.	1.	1¼ [T]
Linstok	Linstock	NY/429584	6.	9.	2½
Caldecote [A.D]	Caldecotes	NY/393559	5.	10.	10¼ [T]
			28.	1.	2

---

[1] This is an enormous quota for a small place. The entry probably includes assessments for a number of places in the liberty of Cockermouth, not mentioned separately, and possibly also Keswick (see footnote to Castlerigg, above).

[2] Steel, op. cit. 62, suggests that this entry includes all vills in the barony of Dalston.

Civitas Karl'	Carlisle	NY/399562	13.	6.	8 [T]
Staynwyg' [A.D]	Stanwix	NY/398570	1.	16.	10¼ [T]
Sokag' extra	Soke beyond		1.	15.	7 [T]
portam Ricardi	Rickergate [in Carlisle]				
Foukholm' [A.D][1]	lost			12.	5¼ [T]
Hobrightby [A.D]	Upperby	NY/412536		10.	6 [T]
Ulnesby [A.D]	Ousby	NY/626346	2.	8.	11 [T]
			7.	4.	3½ [T]

Lib. de Penreth' [PENRITH LIBERTY]

Penreth [A.D]	Penrith	NY/515302	39.	16.	3½ [T]
Carlaton' [A.D]	Carlatton	NY/523525	1.	5.	2 [T]
Scotteby [A.D]	Scotby	NY/441552	2.	3.	10¼ [T]
Carleton' iuxta Penreth'	Carleton	NY/530297	1.	8.	7¼ [T]
[A.D]					
Langwathby [A.D]	Langwathby	NY/569337	15.	1.	4½ [T]
Salkeld [A.D]	Great Salkeld	NY/551368	6.	0.	0½ [T]
Soureby [A.D]	Castle Sowerby	NY/c.370380	11.	18.	5¼ [T]
			77.	13.	9¼ [T]

TOTAL: £554. 8. 6¾[2]

---

[1] A lost place in St. Cuthbert Without parish, *E.P.N.S.*, *XX*, *Cumberland*, part 1 (1950), 150.

[2] As on Enrolled Account for 1336, E 359/14 m. 24.

DERBYSHIRE

DOCUMENTS

8 Edward III: Account E 179/91/8
8 Edward III: Particulars E 179/91/7*
10 Edward III: Particulars E 179/91/9
10 Edward III: Particulars E 179/91/31

TAXERS

The abbot of Darley and William de Hardeshull

TAX YIELD

15th	£407.	16.	11¼
10th	£ 63.	6.	5
	£471.	3.	4¼

Representing assessed movable wealth of

£6,750. 18. 2¾

NOTES

Chesterfield and Derby, the two taxation boroughs, are listed at the end of the roll, but ancient demesnes taxed at a tenth are included within the entries for the five wapentakes and two hundreds.

Since 1334 there have been changes in the boundary between Derbyshire and Leicestershire. The Derbyshire list includes nine places in modern Leicestershire while the villages of Over and Nether Seal, now in Derbyshire, were then taxed in Leicestershire. Parts of Packington and Ravenstone, both now in Leicestershire, were also then taxed in Derbyshire. In addition four places now in Staffordshire were taxed in Derbyshire in 1334.

REFERENCE

J. C. Cox, 'Subsidy roll (lay): Derbyshire in 1327–8 (a twentieth)', *Derbyshire Arch. and Nat. Hist. Soc. Jnl.* 30 (1908), 23–96.

Wap. Morleyston' [MORLEYSTON WAPENTAKE]

Ilkeston'	Ilkeston	SK/465417	1.	6.	10
Parva Eyton'	Little Eaton	SK/361415	1.	6.	6
Pentrich'	Pentrich	SK/389525	2.	0.	6
Smalleye	Smalley	SK/407445	1.	5.	9
Rippeleye	Ripley	SK/399505	2.	0.	1
Kydesleye	Kidsleypark	SK/416459		10.	2
Cruch'	Crich	SK/348546	1.	15.	0
Kyrkhalom	Kirk Hallam	SK/458405		16.	6
Breydessale	Breadsall	SK/371398	1.	18.	0
Westhalom	West Hallam	SK/432411	1.	13.	0
Staunton' iuxta la Dale	Stanton by Dale	SK/464381	1.	2.	1

Okebrok	Ockbrook	SK/423357	2.	10.	4	
Sandiacre	Sandiacre	SK/480363	1.	13.	4	
Henouer	Heanor	SK/435464	1.	5.	10	
Shippeleye	Shipley	SK/436443	2.	3.	7	
Stanleye	Stanley	SK/417403	1.	9.	0	
Beaurepeyr	Belper	SK/351476	1.	10.	0	
Duffeld	Duffield	SK/343436	1.	16.	1	
Wynleye	Windley	SK/306452		19.	8	
Parva Cestre	Little Chester	SK/356371		4.	4	
Spondone	Spondon	SK/398360	3.	15.	4	
Magister Hospital' de Burton' Sancti Lazari				13.	4	
Ryseleye	Risley	SK/461357		6.	8	
Holbrok' & Southwode	Holbrook and Southwood Manor [in Holbrook][1]	SK/363447		13.	6	
Chaddesdene	Chaddesden	SK/381369	2.	15.	0	
Deneby	Denby	SK/398464	1.	14.	9	
Parva Halom	Little Hallam	SK/466405	1.	5.	6	
Codenouere	Codnor	SK/420495	2.	4.	8	
Horseleye Wodehous' [A.D]	Horsley Woodhouse	SK/393449	2.	3.	4	[T]
Horseleye [A.D]	Horsley	SK/375445	1.	15.	6	[T]
Horeston [A.D.]	Horsley Castle	SK/377432		13.	10	[T]
Breydeston'	Breaston	SK/460334	2.	10.	1	
Kilburne[2]	Kilburn [part of]	SK/380457		13.	4	
Kylburne [A.D]	Kilburn [part of]	SK/380457		6.	0	[T]
Sallowe	Sawley	SK/472313		17.	3	
Draycote	Draycott	SK/443331	1.	2.	8	
Hopwelle	Hopwell	SK/440362		16.	8	
Wyuelesthorp'	Wilsthorpe	SK/475338		14.	4	
Morleye	Morley	SK/397410	1.	8.	6	
Heghegge	Heage	SK/370506	1.	0.	0	
Longa Eyton'	Long Eaton	SK/491338	2.	6.	3	
			59.	3.	1	

Wap. Lutch' [LITCHURCH WAPENTAKE]

Weston' super Trentam	Weston upon Trent	SK/402280	3.	4.	4	
Shardelowe	Shardlow	SK/438303	1.	3.	2	
Querndon'	Quarndon	SK/335410	1.	2.	0	
Magna Overa	Mickleover	SK/305342	2.	13.	6	
Aston' super Trentam	Aston upon Trent	SK/414293	1.	14.	9	
Alwaston'	Alvaston	SK/392334		14.	10	
Etewelle	Etwall	SK/269320	1.	2.	0	
Barowe	Barrow upon Trent	SK/353284	1.	4.	10	
Parva Irton'	Ireton	SK/313416		12.	2	
Egynton'	Egginton	SK/268278	2.	17.	8	
Chelaston'[2]	Chellaston [part of]	SK/381304	1.	9.	2	
Chelaston' [A.D]	Chellaston [part of]	SK/381304	1.	3.	0	[T]
Normanton'[2]	Normanton [part of]	SK/346336		7.	0	
Normanton' [A.D]	Normanton [part of]	SL/346336		6.	0	[T]
Codynton'	Coddington	SK/345548		5.	10	
Fynderne	Findern	SK/309304	1.	2.	5	
Potlok'	Potlock	SK/312288		11.	0	
Swerkeston' [A.D][2]	Swarkestone [part of]	SK/372286		12.	0	[T]
Swerkeston'	Swarkestone [part of]	SK/372286		8.	0	
Wylyngton'	Willington	SK/295282		19.	10	

[1] Not on modern maps.   [2] See also next entry.

Parva Weston'	probably Nether Weston	SK/291424	1.	0.	0	
Parva Overe	Littleover	SK/332343	2.	8.	2	
Sydenfen	Sinfin	SK/346315		14.	8	
Steyneston'	Stenson	SK/328301	1.	5.	8	
Twyford	Twyford	SK/328286	2.	6.	8	
Thurleston'	Thulston	SK/410320	1.	14.	3	
Ketleston'	Kedleston	SK/312402		11.	0	
Clifton'	Clifton	SK/165448	2.	7.	0	
Makworth	Mackworth	SK/320378	1.	12.	0	
Marketon'	Markeaton	SK/331376	1.	13.	0	
Murkaston'	Mercaston	SK/278424	1.	2.	0	
Aylwaston	Elvaston	SK/407330	1.	10.	10	
Ambaston'	Ambaston	SK/429327	3.	1.	4	
Wylne	Wilne[1]	SK/449319	1.	6.	2	
Athelastre	Allestree	SK/348398	1.	13.	0	
Mogynton'	Mugginton	SK/283429		12.	0	
Langeleye	Meynell Langley	SK/301398		12.	6	
Boolton'	Boulton	SK/380330		14.	4	
Osmundeston' iuxta Derb' [A.D][2]	Osmaston by Derby [part of]	SK/373342		3.	4	[T]
Osmundeston'	Osmaston by Derby [part of]	SK/373342		6.	8	
Rodebourne	Radbourne	SK/286360	1.	3.	0	
Lutchirch'	Litchurch [in Derby][3]			11.	0	
Kerkelongeleye	Kirk Langley	SK/287388	1.	3.	6	
Brunaldeston'[4]	Burnaston	SK/289323		19.	6	
			54.	5.	1	

Wap. Wyrekesworth' [WIRKSWORTH WAPENTAKE]

Holand	Hulland	SK/249474	2.	17.	9
Tannesleye	Tansley	SK/322599		18.	9
Tyssyngton' & Lee	Tissington and Lea Hall	SK/177523 SK/196517	1.	3.	3
Fennybenteleye	Fenny Bentley	SK/173502	2.	4.	3
Middelton' & Smerhull'	Middleton and Smerrill	SK/195631 SK/199620	1.	17.	0
Elton'	Elton	SK/222610	2.	4.	2
Ibole	Ible	SK/250570	1.	1.	5
Hokenaston'	Hognaston	SK/235505	1.	0.	6
Irton' superior	Kirk Ireton	SK/269502	2.	19.	8
Bradebourne	Bradbourne	SK/208528		14.	5
Balidene	Ballidon	SK/203543	1.	2.	6
Thorp' & Bredelowe	Thorpe and Broadlowash	SK/157502 SK/159501	1.	2.	6
Lee iutxa Dethek	Lea	SK/327574		10.	4
Allerwasleye	Alderwasley	SK/316536	1.	15.	6
Bondessale	Bonsall	SK/280582	2.	19.	0
Wyrkesworth'	Wirksworth	SK/288540	2.	12.	0
Matlok'	Matlock	SK/299603	2.	4.	2
Caldelowe	Callow	SK/269518		15.	4
Middelton' & Crombforde	Middleton and Cromford	SK/278558 SK/293569	2.	1.	8
Alsop	Alsop en le Dale	SK/160551		16.	6

[1] This entry may refer to both Great and Church Wilne. The grid ref. given is to Church Wilne.

[2] See also next entry.   [3] The name is preserved in Litchurch Lane, Derby.

[4] The entries for the last part of Litchurch wapentake are illegible on E 179/91/7. Details are taken from E 179/91/9.

			£	s.	d.
Coldeyton'	Coldeaton	SK/148567	1.	19.	4
Peuerwich'	Parwich	SK/188543	2.	8.	3
Knyveton'	Kniveton	SK/210503	1.	6.	8
Hertyngdon'	Hartington	SK/130604	5.	5.	8
Brassington' &	Brassington and	SK/230543	3.	11.	8
Aldewerk	Aldwark	SK/229573			
Wendesleye &	Wensley and	SK/261611	1.	9.	4
Snyterton	Snitterton	SK/280603			
Hopton' &	Hopton and	SK/257533		19.	6
Kersyngton'	Carsington	SK/252534			
Assheburn'	Ashbourne	SK/180470	6.	11.	2
Mapelton'	Mapleton	SK/166480	1.	17.	10
Underwode	Underwood	SK/198484		7.	4
			58.	17.	1

Hd. Apeltr' [APPLETREE HUNDRED]

			£	s.	d.
Snelleston'	Snelston	SK/155434	2.	1.	3
Eyton' super Douve	Eaton Dovedale	SK/109373	1.	12.	0
Seggessale	Sedsall	SK/110376		11.	1
Langeford	Longford	SK/214383	1.	4.	0
Hatton'	Hatton	SK/216300		7.	0
Holyngton'	Hollington	SK/231398	1.	0.	2
Westbrokton'	West Broughton	SK/145330		11.	0
Hulton'	Hilton	SK/244307	1.	6.	4
Sutton'	Sutton on the Hill	SK/237342	1.	6.	0
Shirleye	Shirley	SK/219417	1.	6.	0
Mershton'	Marston on Dove	SK/232296	1.	2.	0
Edulston'	Edlaston	SK/181426		12.	8
Braylesford	Brailsford	SK/253415	1.	19.	1½
Ednaston'	Ednaston	SK/235423		9.	10
Wyardeston'	Wyaston	SK/184424		9.	0
Somersale Herbert	Somersal Herbert	SK/136351		11.	0
Osmundeston' iuxta	Osmaston	SK/199440	1.	11.	1
Assheburn'					
Thurvaston'	Thurvaston	SK/243379	1.	2.	1
Erleston'	Arleston	SK/373297	1.	2.	6
Benteleye Hungry	Hungry Bentley	SK/178388		13.	5
Foston'	Foston	SK/189318		19.	3
Alkmundeton'	Alkmonton	SK/196385	1.	2.	6
Saperton'	Sapperton	SK/186345		6.	0
Sudbury	Sudbury	SK/158322	3.	9.	4
Bradeleye	Bradley	SK/222460	1.	9.	8
Attelowe	Atlow	SK/231487		11.	9
Howen	Hoon	SK/222311		11.	0
Barton' Bakepus	Barton Blount	SK/209346	1.	2.	4
Boyleston'	Boyleston	SK/181359	1.	2.	1
Marchington'	Marston Montgomery[1]	SK/133378	2.	11.	6
Mongumbry					
Cubbeleye	Cubley	SK/165377	1.	4.	5
Estbroghton'	Church Broughton	SK/205338	1.	8.	0
Yildresleye	Yeldersley	SK/208440	1.	13.	2
Yeveleye	Yeaveley	SK/186403		9.	8
Magister de	Master of Yeaveley Stydd		1.	0.	0
Yeneleghstede ibid'	[House of the Knights				
	Hospitallers]				

[1] Identified as Marston Montgomery, although there seems to be no other record of this form of the place-name (*E.P.N.S.*, *XXIX*, *Derbyshire*, part 3 (1959), 585).

Oslaston'	Osleston	SK/248370		19.	6
Roddesleye	Rodsley	SK/201404	1.	2.	0
Norbury &	Norbury and	SK/125423	2.	1.	0
Rossyngton'	Roston	SK/136409			
Doubrugge	Doveridge	SK/113341	2.	19.	10
Scropton'	Scropton	SK/192302	1.	0.	0
Asshe	Ashe	SK/262326		19.	0
Dalbury	Dalbury	SK/263343		11.	0
Trusseleye	Trusley	SK/253355		14.	6
			50.	5.	0½

Hd. Repyndon' [REPTON HUNDRED]

Neuton' Solny	Newton Solney	SK/279258	2.	11.	2
Tykenhale	Ticknall	SK/351241	1.	18.	8
Wynshull'	Winshill [in Staffordshire]	SK/268235	2.	4.	0
Appelby	Appleby Magna [in Leicestershire]	SK/315098	2.	0.	6
Childecote	Chilcote [in Leicestershire]	SK/284114	1.	0.	8
Swartlyngcote	Swadlincote	SK/302197	1.	3.	5
Bretteby	Bretby	SK/293233	1.	2.	6
Engelby	Ingleby	SK/348271	2.	4.	4
Stonystannton'	Stanton by Bridge	SK/367272	1.	2.	0
Greseleye	Gresley[1]	SK/293182		12.	2
Rostlaston'	Rosliston	SK/243169	1.	1.	0
Walton' super Trentam	Walton upon Trent	SK/216182	2.	18.	5
Repyndon'	Repton	SK/303271	4.	8.	3
Wyuellesleye	Willesley [in Leicestershire]	SK/341147		12.	0
Durannthorp'	Donisthorpe [in Leicestershire]	SK/314139		14.	1
Drakelowe	Drakelow	SK/c.240200	2.	4.	1
Smethesby	Smisby	SK/348191	1.	2.	0
Meysham	Measham [in Leicestershire]	SK/335123	1.	9.	4
Stannton' Warde	Stanton	SK/270199		19.	8
Lynton'	Linton	SK/275172	1.	1.	2
Stapenhull'	Stapenhill [in Staffordshire]	SK/257220	1.	15.	5
Fornewerk	Foremark	SK/330264	1.	9.	0
Cotone	Coton in the Elms	SK/243153		17.	4
Caldewalle	Caldwell	SK/254172	1.	1.	0
Croxhale &	Croxall and	SK/198137		15.	0
Edynghale	Edingale [both in Staffordshire]	SK/214121			
Pakynton'[2]	Packington [in Leicestershire]	SK/358144		12.	7
Okethorp'	Oakthorpe [in Leicestershire]	SK/321129	1.	2.	1
Lollyngton'	Lullington	SK/250130	2.	18.	11
Catton'	Catton	SK/206154		13.	5
Stretton'	Stretton en le Field [in Leicestershire]	SK/303119		8.	4

---

[1] Grid ref. is to Church Gresley, but the entry probably includes Castle Gresley.
[2] Part of Packington was taxed in Leicestershire (Goscote hundred, p. 160).

Melburn' [A.D]	Melbourne	SK/385251	3.	14.	4	[T]
Raveneston'[1]	Ravenstone [in Leicestershire]	SK/402139		11.	4	
Herteshorn'	Hartshorne	SK/328208	1.	3.	2	
			49.	11.	4	

Wap. Alto Pecco [HIGH PEAK WAPENTAKE]

Yelgreve	Youlgreave	SK/212644	2.	4.	0	
Roland	Rowland	SK/213725		10.	0	
Bukstones	Boxton	SK/060735	1.	10.	3	
Edenesouere	Edensor	SK/250699	1.	7.	0	
Overhaddon' [A.D][2]	Over Haddon [part of]	SK/203664		8.	0	[T]
Overhaddon'	Over Haddon [part of]	SK/203664		10.	2	
Shakelcros	Shallcross	SK/013797		11.	1	
Assheford [A.D]	Ashford	SK/195697	2.	1.	4	[T]
Monyasshe	Monyash	SK/151664	2.	9.	0	
Lutone	Litton	SK/164752	3.	0.	0	
Netherhaddon'	Nether Haddon	SK/232661	2.	6.	0	
Derleye	Darley	SK/278633	2.	9.	6	
Hauersegge	Hathersage	SK/231815	5.	13.	4	
Basselowe	Baslow	SK/251723	2.	17.	6	
Belegh'	Beeley	SK/265676	1.	4.	8	
Eyom & Midelton'	Eyam and Stoney Middleton	SK/218765 SK/231755	2.	0.	0	
Parva Longesdon'	Little Longstone	SK/187717	1.	13.	0	
Herthull' & Wynster	Harthill and Winster	SK/229647 SK/239605	2.	4.	2	
Magna Longesdon' [A.D]	Great Longstone	SK/200720	1.	17.	3	[T]
Bowedon	Bowden[3]	SK/067817	5.	2.	2	
Wormhull'	Wormhill	SK/124742	3.	17.	4	
Haselbache	Hazlebadge	SK/172800	2.	4.	2	
Gloshop'	Glossop[4]	SK/041948	5.	13.	0	
Middelcauel	Middle Cale [now New Mills][5]	SK/002858	5.	11.	9	
Tiddeswell'	Tideswell	SK/152758	6.	4.	8	
Cheylmerdon'	Chelmorton	SK/115703	3.	2.	0	
Hassop'	Hassop	SK/223723	1.	14.	8	
Baukwell'	Bakewell	SK/215685	5.	10.	1	
Hope & Shatton' [A.D][6]	Hope and Shatton [part of]	SK/172834 SK/202825		5.	6	[T]
Hope & Shatton'	Hope and Shatton [part of]	SK/172834 SK/202825	4.	0.	0	
Tadyngton' & Prestclyve [A.D]	Taddington and Priestcliffe	SK/141711 SK/139720	5.	11.	2	[T]
Castelton' & Bradewelle	Castleton and Bradwell	SK/150829 SK/175811	3.	13.	4	
			89.	6.	3	

[1] Part of Ravenstone was taxed in Leicestershire (Goscote hundred, p. 160).

[2] See also next entry.

[3] Quota probably covers the large area of Bowden township (see *E.P.N.S., XXVII, Derbyshire*, part 1 (1959), 150).

[4] Grid ref. is to Old Glossop.

[5] For an explanation of this place-name see *E.P.N.S., XXIX, Derbyshire*, part 1 (1959), 150.

[6] See also next entry.

Wap. Scarthesdale [SCARSDALE WAPENTAKE]

Kynwaldesmersh'	Killamarsh	SK/461810	1.	18.	7	
Norton'	Norton [now in	SK/359822	1.	16.	8	
	Sheffield, Yorks. W.R.]					
Ekynton'	Eckington	SK/432798	2.	5.	8	
Brakenthweyt &	Brackenfield and	SK/373590		12.	10	
Wystanton'	Wessington	SK/371578				
Elmenton'	Elmton	SK/502735		12.	0	
Glapwelle	Glapwell	SK/478661	1.	3.	2	
Oxcroft	Oxcroft	SK/481736		8.	3	
Barleburgh' &	Barlborough and	SK/477772	4.	9.	2	
Whitewelle	Whitwell	SK/525768				
Staveleye	Staveley	SK/433748	1.	12.	6	
Barleye &	Barlow and	SK/343747	1.	18.	6	
Aston'	Coal Aston	SK/361794				
Wyngerworth'	Wingerworth	SK/383674	2.	11.	9	
Skartheclyf	Scarcliffe	SK/495688	2.	0.	7	
Shirlond	Shirland	SK/399584	1.	0.	10	
Esshovere	Ashover	SK/349631	2.	4.	1	
Stretton'	Stretton	SK/392613	1.	5.	7	
Holmesfeld	Holmesfield	SK/321777	2.	4.	1	
Sutton' in Dal	Sutton Scarsdale	SK/442689		17.	6	
Bollesovere [A.D]	Bolsover	SK/475704	5.	10.	3	[T]
Beghton'	Beighton	SK/442833	2.	16.	5	
Plesleye	Pleasley	SK/504646	3.	6.	0	
Tybbeshelf	Tibshelf	SK/437605	1.	18.	1	
Alferton'	Alfreton	SK/409558	2.	10.	7	
Southwynnefeld	South Wingfield	SK/376555	2.	11.	0	
Dronefeld	Dronfield	SK/352783	2.	18.	7	
Normanton' &	South Normanton and	SK/442570	2.	4.	1	
Penkeston'	Pinxton	SK/453550				
Dokemanton'	Duckmanton[1]	SK/443714	1.	2.	4	
Morton'	Morton	SK/407601		6.	10	
Steynesby	Stainsby	SK/450654	3.	1.	3¾	
Cloune[2]	Clowne	SK/492754		3.	4	
Blakwelle	Blackwell	SK/443583	1.	8.	8	
Totenleye &	Totley and Dore [both	SK/304799	2.	14.	0	
Doore	now in Sheffield,	SK/307811				
	Yorks. W.R.]					
Whitynton' &	Whittington and	SK/384753	1.	13.	4	
Brymyngton'	Brimington	SK/405735				
Walton'	Walton	SK/359691	1.	13.	4	
Cestrefeld [B]	Chesterfield	SK/385712	6.	15.	7	[T]
Derby [B]	Derby	SK/352365	30.	0.	0	[T]
			101.	15.	5¾	

Ricardus Curzoun de Ketleston'		4.	0.	0
Robertus de Sallowe		3.	0.	0
Simon de Parva Cestr'		1.	0.	0
		8.	0.	0

TOTAL: £471. 3. 4¼[3]

---

[1] Grid ref. is to Long Duckmanton.

[2] Quota includes a personal payment for Robertus Folville. On some rolls this payment is cancelled.

[3] As on 1334 Account, E 179/91/8.

DEVON

DOCUMENTS

8 Edward III: Account   E 179/95/9
8 Edward III: Particulars not extant
10 Edward III: Indenture E 179/95/10 mm. 1–5*
10 Edward III: Particulars E 179/95/10 mm. 6–9

TAXERS

The abbot of Torre and Geoffrey Gilbert

TAX YIELD

15th £712. 12.   8
10th £241.   2.   4
      ——————————————
      £953. 15.   0

Representing assessed movable wealth of

    £13,100. 13.   4

NOTES

Places taxed at a tenth are listed at the end of the roll of 1336. They include the city of Exeter and nineteen taxation boroughs, the same ones as in 1334. As in Cornwall, many of these were obviously small (see ranking list in the essay by Hoskins on the wealth of medieval Devon, reference below) and were created late; some of them are included in Beresford's list of planted towns in Devon (Maurice Beresford, *New Towns of the Middle Ages*, 1967, 417–26).

An unusual feature of the Devon list is that places taxed at a fifteenth are distinguished as either tithings, hamlets, or manors: all entries on the accompanying list refer to tithings (*decennaria*), unless they are marked as hamlets (h) or manors (man.). Chardstock and Stockland, now in Devon, were taxed in Dorset.

Under a charter of 1305 the tinners of Devon and Cornwall were given a number of privileges, among them exemption from lay subsidies (see Willard (1934), op. cit. 118–20, and L. F. Salzman, 'Mines and stannaries', being chapter III in J. F. Willard, W. A. Morris, and W. H. Dunham, Jr., eds., *The English Government at Work, 1327–1336*, iii (1950), especially 88–92). Consequently, while the movables of the tinners were assessed and the amounts of tax decided they were duly exempted by the Exchequer when it came to payment. Unfortunately there are no details of these tinners on the roll of 1336. We do know, however, that of the total tax yield of £953. 15. 0 in 1337, £47. 8. 0 was the charge against the stannary men; 305 of them were said to be true tinners and thirty-one of them false ones (E 179/95/12). After 1337 the tax charges against the stannary men are listed on a number of lay subsidy rolls and these are a valuable source of information on the main centres of activity, the more so because the tinners moved around from place to place. Despite the variations in the tax charges against the tinners the basic 1334 quotas remain the same.

REFERENCES

O. J. Reichel published a list of fifteenths and tenths for Devon *c.* 1384 in an appendix to *Devon Notes and Queries* (April 1907).

C. L'Estrange Ewen, *Devon Taxation Returns in 1334*, 1939.

F. W. Morgan, 'The Domesday geography of Devon', *Trans. Devon Assn.*, lxxii (1940), 305–31, especially 320–1.

H. P. R. Finberg, 'The boroughs of Devon', *Devon and Cornwall Notes and Queries*, xxiv (1951), 203–9.

W. G. Hoskins, 'The wealth of medieval Devon', in W. G. Hoskins and H. P. R. Finberg, *Devonshire Studies*, 1952, 212–49.

Audrey M. Erskine, ed., 'The Devonshire lay subsidy of 1332', *Devon and Cornwall Rec. Soc.*, new series, 14 (1969).

Hd. Haytorre [HAYTOR HUNDRED]

			£	s.	d.
Hemmyston' Cauntelo	Broadhempston	sx/801662	2.	2.	6
Wille Coffyn &	Coffinswell and	sx/891684		18.	8
Dakcombe	Daccombe	sx/902680			
Torre Bryan &	Torbryan and	sx/820668	1.	17.	0
Deueneburi	Denbury	sx/823689			
Wydecomb'	Widecombe in the Moor	sx/719768		6.	6
Boclaunde Inthemore	Buckland in the Moor	sx/720732		4.	4
Spichewyk'	Spitchwick	sx/708725		13.	6
Combe Fishacre	Combe Fishacre	sx/842650		6.	0
Hemmyston' Arundel	Littlehempston	sx/813627		13.	8
Torremohonn	Tormohan	sx/c.912644	1.	8.	8
Carswill' Abbatis	Abbotskerswell	sx/856687		13.	4
Blakedon' Inthemore	Blackaton	sx/695780		4.	0
Notesworthi'	Natsworthy	sx/723796		2.	6
Batleforde	Battleford	sx/831643		4.	0
Wodehiwysh'	Woodhuish	sx/912529		14.	6
Brixham	Brixham	sx/923562	1.	12.	8
Chercheton'	Churston Ferrers	sx/903564	1.	10.	4
Galmeton'	Galmpton	sx/886563		19.	0
Peyngton'	Paignton	sx/887606	6.	0.	0
Seynt Maricherch'	St. Marychurch	sx/918660		16.	0
Wolleburgh' cum	Wolborough with	sx/854704		15.	0
Nyweton' Abbatis	Newton Abbot	sx/862713			
Iplepenne	Ipplepen	sx/834665	2.	19.	0
Staverton'	Staverton	sx/793639	2.	15.	8
Spearkewill'	Sparkwell	sx/787656		6.	10
Biri Pomeray [man.]	Berry Pomeroy	sx/829610	2.	3.	0
Lovenetorre [h]	Loventor	sx/847628		5.	6
Gotheryngton' &	Goodrington and	sx/891585	1.	8.	2
Brouneston'	Brownstone	sx/901506			
Eggenyswille	Edginswell	sx/887661		15.	0
Boklaunde Baronn	Buckland Barton	sx/881718		6.	0
Haccomb'	Haccombe	sx/898702		6.	4
Kyngeswere [h]	Kingswear	sx/883510	1.	6.	8
Kynges Carswill' [man.]	Kingskerswell	sx/876678	1.	18.	0
Cokyngton'	Cockington	sx/891638		16.	8
de tenentibus Hugonis D'Audele Foreste de Dertemore	Hugh de Audley's tenants in Dartmoor Forest			7.	0
			37.	16.	0

Hd. Stanburgh' [STANBOROUGH HUNDRED]

			£	s	d
Alvyngton'	West Alvington	sx/723438	2.	6.	o
Wolston'	Woolston	sx/716416	1.	3.	o
Badeston' &	Batson and	sx/733397	2.	6.	8
Bolteburi	Bolberry	sx/691392			
Soure &	Sewer and West	sx/709379	1.	8.	o
Portlemouth'	Portlemouth	sx/710391			
Galmeton' &	Galmpton and	sx/693402	1.	6.	9
Hywish'	South Huish	sx/691412			
Thorleston'	Thurleston	sx/673429		19.	o
Skiredon' [h] cum	Skerraton	sx/708646		13.	o
Hokene	?				
Milton'	South Milton	sx/698429	1.	10.	2
Brenta	South Brent	sx/696602	2.	2.	4
Cherstouwe	Churchstow	sx/712459	1.	6.	8
Wercomb'	Warcombe	sx/733474		10.	o
Lodeswill'	Loddiswell	sx/721486	1.	6.	8
Loscome [h]	Luscombe	sx/748637		3.	4
Northhiwish	North Huish	sx/712566		17.	2
Dene Priour	Dean Prior	sx/730635		15.	4
Rattrewe	Rattery	sx/740615	1.	9.	8
Alyngton' cum	East Allington with	sx/770483	2.	2.	8
Harlistone	Harleston	sx/793452			
Wodelegh'	Woodleigh	sx/738488	1.	8.	6
Bokfastlegh'	Buckfastleigh	sx/738661	1.	4.	3
Legh' Omni Sanctorum	Leigh	sx/721467	1.	7.	2
Dupeford	Diptford	sx/727567	1.	8.	o
Holne	Holne	sx/706695		18.	o
Dertyngton'	Dartington	sx/795627	1.	6.	8
De Abbate' Bucfast' pro	From the Abbot of Buck-			6.	8
omnibus alienis euntibus	fast, for all the cattle				
ad fald' suas exfine	folded on his land				
			30.	5.	8

Hd. Plympton' [PLYMPTON HUNDRED]

			£	s	d
Plymhom[1]	Plympton St. Mary	sx/543562	2.	11.	o
Wodeforde	Woodford	sx/531573		11.	4
Shaghe	Shaugh Prior	sx/543631		9.	6
Fernhull'	Fernhill	sx/560607		14.	o
Lughtorre	Loughtor	sx/552576		10.	6
Henmerdon'	Hemerdon	sx/564574		8.	6
Backemore	Baccamoor	sx/584582		13.	o
Hareston'	Hareston	sx/567538		9.	o
Brixton'	Brixton	sx/554522		17.	6
Sprideleston'	Spriddlestone	sx/532516		13.	8
Alfamyston'	Yealmpstone	sx/559554		6.	6
Langedon'	Langdon	sx/513498		13.	o
Doune	Down Thomas	sx/504498		9.	6
Brichricheston'	Brixton Barton	sx/543601		2.	o
Stottescomb'	Staddiscombe	sx/513513		7.	o
Gosewill'	Goosewell	sx/517524		3.	o
Westhoo	West Hooe	sx/502522		2.	o
Plymstok'	Plymstock	sx/518530	1.	5.	o
Yalmpton' cum	Yealmpton with	sx/578517	5.	4.	o
Villa atte Nasse	Noss Mayo	sx/548476			

[1] Plympton Erle, the borough, was taxed at a tenth (p. 66).

De tenentibus Prior' de Plympton' ibidem	Tenants of the Prior of Plympton in Yealmpton and Noss Mayo		1.	10.	0
			18.	0.	0

Hd. Rouburgh' [ROBOROUGH HUNDRED]

Whitcherch'	Whitchurch	sx/493727	1.	2.	4
Petrystavy	Petertavy	sx/513777		6.	0
Sannford	Sampford Spiney	sx/534725		3.	10
Mewy	Meavy	sx/540672		13.	4
Ekke Boklannd	Egg Buckland	sx/498578	1.	2.	0
Tamerton' Folyot	Tamerton Foliot	sx/472608	1.	6.	8
Compton'	Compton	sx/495568	1.	7.	4
Weston'	Weston Peverel	sx/479565	1.	15.	4
Tamerton'	Kings Tamerton	sx/453585		4.	0
Stoke Daumarle	Stoke Damarel	sx/463550	2.	0.	0
Buttokeshide	Budshead	sx/458602		10.	0
Colrugg' [h] & Legham	Coleridge and Leigham	sx/495586 sx/515584		3.	0
Boklannde	Buckland Monachorum	sx/490683	1.	1.	10
Bir'	Bere Ferrers	sx/459634	1.	3.	4
Sutton' Vautort [c.h]	Sutton Vautort[1] [with hamlets]	sx/c.480550	10.	12.	8
			23.	11.	8

Hd. Sheftbere' [SHEBBEAR HUNDRED]

Nyweton'	Newton St. Petrock	ss/411122		15.	0
Patrikestouwe	Petrockstow	ss/513092	1.	0.	0
Shepwaysh'	Sheepwash	ss/487063		9.	0
Hiwysh'	Huish	ss/533111		6.	0
Methe	Meeth	ss/548083		12.	0
Beauford	Beaford	ss/552150		11.	0
Yudeslegh'	Iddesleigh	ss/569082	1.	0.	4
Merton'	Merton	ss/525121		18.	0
Parva Toriton'	Little Torrington	ss/491169	1.	2.	0
Frithelistok'	Frithelstock	ss/463194	1.	6.	0
Heannton Sachevill'	Heanton Satchville	ss/534113		18.	0
Boklannd Fillegh'	Buckland Filleigh	ss/466092		13.	4
Petris Merlannde	Peters Marland	ss/478135		18.	0
Langetriwe	Langtree	ss/451156	3.	10.	0
Parkham	Parkham	ss/389214	2.	18.	8
Abbodesham	Abbotsham	ss/424264	2.	11.	4
Alwyngton'	Alwington	ss/408246	1.	18.	0
Litleham	Littleham	ss/443235	1.	16.	0
Boklannd Bruwere	Buckland Brewer	ss/419209	3.	16.	8
Were Gyffard	Weare Giffard	ss/478221		13.	4
Langcars	Landcross	ss/462238		7.	0
Monkelegh'	Monkleigh	ss/457207		16.	0
Bidyforde[2]	Bideford	ss/453265		16.	8
			29.	12.	4

---

[1] By the early fourteenth century the manor of Sutton (the early name for the area of Plymouth) had been divided into the manors of Sutton Vautort, Sutton Ralf, and Sutton Prior. Sutton Prior was taxed as a borough in 1334 (p. 66).

[2] The borough of Bideford was taxed at a tenth (p. 66).

Hd. Fremyngton' [FREMINGTON HUNDRED]

Fremyngton'	Fremington	ss/512326	2.	13.	6
Toustoke	Tawstock	ss/559299	3.	3.	4
Toryton'[1]	Great Torrington	ss/495192	2.	17.	0
Hele	Hele	ss/548324	2.	3.	4
Westlegh'	Westleigh	ss/472286	1.	9.	0
Yeonstouwe cum	Instow with	ss/480310	1.	0.	0
Wolryngton'	Worlington	ss/481306			
Tappelegh'	Tapeley	ss/478291		10.	0
Horwode	Horwood	ss/502277		12.	2
Rouburgh'	Roborough	ss/577171		12.	0
Alverdiscote	Alverdiscott	ss/520252		15.	0
Honshagh'	Huntshaw	ss/506228		13.	4
			16.	8.	8

Hd. Shirewill' [SHIRWELL HUNDRED]

Wollecomb'	Wollacombe	ss/458438	1.	8.	3
Pidekwill'	Pickwell	ss/457410		16.	6
Alryngton'	Arlington	ss/613405		4.	0
Middelton'	Middleton	ss/656446		11.	4
Parrecomb'	Parracombe	ss/669449		10.	0
Mattyngho	Martinhoe	ss/668486		14.	0
Lyn	Lyn[2]	ss/723482		16.	4
Bremdon'	Brendon	ss/770482		14.	6
Choldecomb'	Challacombe	ss/692407		6.	0
Lynton'	Lynton	ss/719495	1.	11.	4
Gratton'	Gratton	ss/688372		12.	4
Hegh' Bray	High Bray	ss/689343		15.	4
Charles	Charles	ss/688330		13.	0
Stoke	Stoke Rivers	ss/633354	1.	17.	4
Shirewill'	Shirwell	ss/598374		18.	0
			12.	8.	3

Hd. Southmolton' [SOUTH MOLTON HUNDRED]

Tauton'	Bishop's Tawton	ss/566301	4.	18.	0
Neuport [h]	Newport	ss/565324		13.	4
Nywelond	Newland	ss/601309	1.	6.	6
Chitelhampton'	Chittlehampton	ss/635256	1.	18.	4
Est Anstye	East Anstey	ss/868265		13.	4
Whiteston'	Whitestone	ss/664265		3.	0
West Anstye	West Anstey	ss/852275		14.	0
Warkelegh'	Warkleigh	ss/642228		16.	8
Saterlegh'	Satterleigh	ss/668225		9.	0
Blakepole	Blackpool	ss/680247		15.	4
West Bray	probably High Bray	ss/678265		8.	0
Est Bray	probably Knight's Bray	ss/691261		14.	8
Bremelrigge	Bremridge	ss/692291		6.	0
Accote	Accott	ss/642325		12.	0
De tenentibus Decani	Tenants of the Dean of			2.	0
Exon' de Tauton' et	Exeter in Bishop's				
Swynbrigge	Tawton and Swimbridge				

[1] The borough of Great Torrington was taxed at a tenth (p. 66).
[2] Grid ref. is to West Lyn.

Nymet Sancti Georgii'	George Nympton	ss/700230		12.	o
Knoueston'	Knowstone	ss/829231		9.	o
Champeston'	Champson	ss/803284		2.	o
Stouford	Stowford	ss/625265		7.	o
Robbecomb' [h][1]	?			3.	o
La Heade [h]	Head Barton	ss/666182		5.	o
Sheftrugge [h]	Shortridge	ss/632225		2.	o
Frensheton'	Frenchstone	ss/714231		12.	o
Yernesburgh'	Ernsborough	ss/640283		2.	8
			17.	4.	10

Hd. Wytherugg' [WITHERIDGE HUNDRED]

Morchard Cruwes	Cruwys Morchard	ss/873122		16.	o
Rakerneford	Rackenford	ss/851182	1.	2.	o
Bysshopes Nymet	Bishop's Nympton	ss/758237	2.	5.	4
Wytherigge	Witheridge	ss/803146	2.	16.	4
Menshagh'	Meshaw	ss/759197		10.	6
Potyngton'	Puddington	ss/833106		14.	o
Marnelegh'	Mariansleigh	ss/743221		18.	o
Okford	Oakford	ss/911213	1.	7.	4
Stodlegh'	Stoodleigh	ss/922188	1.	6.	4
Wasford	Washford Pyne	ss/812119		10.	o
Wolfardesworthi'	Woolfardisworthy	ss/828086	1.	13.	o
Kynges Nymet	King's Nympton	ss/682194	1.	14.	o
West Wolryngton'	West Worlington	ss/770135	1.	0.	o
Est Wolryngton'	East Worlington	ss/775137		4.	8
Thelbrugg' [P]	Thelbridge	ss/787122		15.	o
Esse Rauf'	Rose Ash	ss/788217	1.	6.	o
Chedeldon'	Cheldon	ss/734134		8.	6
Romandeslegh'	Romansleigh	ss/727205		14.	o
Chulmelegh'	Chulmleigh	ss/687142	2.	1.	o
			22.	2.	o

Hd. Criditon' [CREDITON HUNDRED]

Norton'	Norton	sx/887994	1.	4.	8
Smalbrok'	Smallbrook	sx/866986		15.	2
Forde	Ford	sx/792975		9.	o
Youford	Yeoford	sx/783991		17.	10
Youweton'	Upton	sx/828985		10.	8
Rigge Episcopi	Rudge	ss/745075		7.	4
Criditon'[2]	Crediton	ss/836002		17.	o
De tenentibus feod' Canonicorum ibidem	From the tenants of the fee of the Canons in Crediton			11.	o
Kynewardlegh'	Kennerleigh	ss/819075		6.	8
Rolueston'	Rolstone Barton	ss/798056		16.	8
Wolmereston'	Whelmstone Barton	ss/750006		17.	10
Colbrok'	Colebrooke	ss/770001	1.	15.	8
Southcote	Southcott	ss/758056	1.	17.	6

[1] The same place *Roucumb* appears in the *Nomina Villarum* of 1316 (*F.A.* i. 376) where it is not positively identified but is indexed as a member of George Nympton. It is not named on the roll of 1332.

[2] The borough of Crediton was taxed at a tenth (p. 66).

Rigge Arundel	Rudge	sx/850980		16.	0
Wodelond	Woodland	sx/774971		13.	4
Knolle	Knowle	ss/783014	1.	2.	8
Pideslegh'	Pidsley	ss/811051		10.	0
Doderigge	Doddridge	ss/843051	1.	6.	8
Hengstehill'	Henstill	ss/809038	1.	5.	4
			17.	1.	0

Hd. West Buddelegh' [WEST BUDLEIGH HUNDRED]

Raddon'	West Raddon	ss/893023	1.	8.	0
Stokelegh' Pomeray	Stockleigh Pomeroy	ss/876036		15.	0
Sutton' Sachevill'[1]	?			10.	0
Churiton' Fitzpayn	Cheriton Fitzpaine	ss/867062		14.	4
Stoklegh' Englyssh	Stockleigh English	ss/850063	1.	2.	4
Stoklegh' Letcomb[2]	?		1.	7.	3
Shokbrok'	Shobrooke	ss/863011		18.	4
Langelegh'[3]	?		1.	10.	0
Yadburi'	Yedbury	ss/867102		3.	0
Poghhull'	Poughill	ss/857084		9.	2
Shute [h]	Shute	ss/891003		10.	0
Cridia Peytemyn [h]	Lower Creedy	ss/842027		5.	9
Fenne Chalonns [h]	probably Venn Channing	ss/835087		2.	10
Triwe Sancti Jacobi [h]	Trew	ss/857035		1.	6
Dynscomb' [h]	Lower Dunscombe	ss/888060		4.	0
Werthe	Worth	ss/946146		5.	0
Wayshfeld	Washfield	ss/935154		2.	0
Uppeton' Hilyon	Upton Hellions	ss/842033		6.	0
Emylte [h]	Emlett	ss/809083		3.	4
			10.	17.	10

Hd. Tuverton' [TIVERTON HUNDRED]

Lomene Clauyle	Craze Lowman	ss/985142		3.	4
Tuverton'[4]	Tiverton	ss/955125	3.	1.	7
Bolleham	Bolham	ss/952148		13.	4
West Exe	West Exe	ss/948127		15.	0
Honysham	Huntsham	st/001204		10.	0
Uplomene	Uplowman	st/013155		14.	10
Chillelomene	Chieflowman	st/006156		6.	0
West Chyvethorne	Chevithorne	ss/974154		13.	4
Chetiscomb	Chettiscombe	ss/966148		4.	6
Ivedon'	Ivedon	st/144017		7.	8
Battekeworthi' &	probably Batsworthy and	ss/821198		3.	0
Neteleworthi'	Nettleford	ss/810187			
Nuthecote [h][5]	?			9.	8
			8.	2.	3

[1] Identified in *F.A.* i. as Sutton Sacheville in Cheriton Fitzpaine. Erskine, op. cit. 34 n., equates this place with South Stockleigh (a place not mentioned in *E.P.N.S.*, *Devonshire*).

[2] Equated with Little Stockleigh by Erskine, op. cit. 34 n., but again there is no mention of the place in *E.P.N.S.*, *Devonshire*.

[3] This place was linked with Broadridge in aids of 1303 and 1346 (*F.A.* i. 364 and 526) and with *Stokelegh Locombe* in 1316 (ibid. 381). It is not named on the subsidy roll of 1332.   [4] The borough of Tiverton was taxed at a tenth (p. 66).

[5] Identified by Erskine, op. cit. 36, as Ninchecote but I have been unable to locate this place.

Hd. Hemyok' [HEMYOCK HUNDRED]

Cheris Stannton'	Churchstanton [in Somerset]	ST/195145	2.	10.	0
Hydon'	Clayhidon	ST/161156	2.	0.	0
Hemyok'	Hemyock	ST/135133	2.	10.	0
Colmp Stok'	Culmstock	ST/102135	3.	0.	0
Aulescomb'	Awliscombe	ST/133018		13.	4
Bokerel' & Weryngston'	Buckerell and Waringstone	ST/123003 ST/142003		10.	4
Colmp Davyd	Culm Davy	ST/124151		16.	8
Olde Donkeswill'	Dunkeswell	ST/141078	1.	0.	0
			13.	0.	4

Hd. Halberton' [HALBERTON HUNDRED]

Halberton'	Halberton	ST/006129	2.	6.	2
Sannford	Sampford Peverell	ST/030142	1.	5.	10
Wytenych'	Whitnage	ST/027157		6.	0
Botes Leghe	Canonsleigh	ST/066173		3.	2
Ayshford	Ayshford	ST/049152		18.	0
Mokelesbere	Muxbere	ST/039117		13.	0
Wildelond	Willand	ST/037103		9.	0
Moriston'	Moorstone Barton	ST/017099		3.	0
Lynor	Leonard Moor	ST/048138	2.	10	
Esse	Ash Thomas	ST/005109		3.	0
Selake & Manelegh'	Sellake and Manley	ST/002141 SS/989118		5.	0
Sour Apeldore	Appledore	ST/069145	1.	1.	0
			7.	16.	0

Hd. Clyston' [CLISTON HUNDRED]

Clyston'	Broad Clyst	SX/982973	6.	2.	0
Bricheclyston'[1]	lost			5.	4
Colomp Johan	Culumbjohn	SX/960997		10.	1
Wympel	Whimple	SY/043973	1.	19.	11
Clyst Girard	Clyst Gerred	SY/026985		9.	0
Clyst Laurenz	Clyst St. Lawrence	SY/027999		16.	0
Clyst Hydon'	Clyst Hydon	ST/035016		13.	0
Aunk'	Aunk	ST/045002		10.	0
Cobbeton'	Cobden	SY/035963		6.	8
Aysh Clyst'	Ashclyst	SY/011982		5.	2
			11.	17.	2

Hd. Colyton' [COLYTON HUNDRED]

Colyton'	Colyton	SY/246941	4.	2.	0
Brankescomb'	Branscombe	SY/195884	4.	10.	6
Seeton'	Seaton	SY/247905	2.	3.	4
Beare	Beer	SY/230893	1.	3.	4
Gatcomb'	Gatcombe	SY/228911		5.	3
South Legh'	Southleigh	SY/205934		13.	0

---

[1] A lost place in Clyst Honiton parish, *E.P.N.S., IX, Devonshire*, part 2 (1932), 584.

Forwode	Farwood Barton	SY/205953		14.	0
Farweye	Farway	SY/172964	1.	4.	0
North Legh'	Northleigh	SY/196958		19.	6
Wydaworthi'	Widworthy	SY/214993	1.	3.	4
Cottelegh'	Cotleigh	ST/206022		18.	0
Woberneford[1]		lost		6.	6
Whiteford	Whitford	SY/260956	2.	7.	0
Colyford [v]	Colyford	SY/250925	1.	5.	0
			21.	14.	9

Hd. Axeminstr' [AXMINSTER HUNDRED]

Yartecomb'	Yarcombe	ST/246082	2.	12.	0
Mosbiri[2]	Musbury	SY/276945		18.	10
Rouerigg'	Rawridge	ST/202065	1.	7.	8
Combe	Combe Raleigh	ST/158023		16.	8
Kilmeton'	Kilmington	SY/273980	1.	8.	0
Thornecomb'	Thorncombe [in Dorset]	ST/376033	1.	10.	0
Uplym [v]	Uplyme	SY/325935	1.	7.	0
Otery Mohon	Mohun's Ottery	ST/189055	2.	3.	4
Tril [h]	Trill	SY/291956		4.	0
Wycroft	Weycroft	SY/308998		13.	4
Smalrigge &	Smallridge and	ST/303012			
Estmembiri'[3]	Membury	ST/276030			
Churleton'	Charton	ST/301910		3.	4
Honeton' [man.][4]	Honiton	ST/163007		13.	4
			13.	17.	6

Hd. Axemuth' [AXMOUTH HUNDRED]

Axemuth'	Axmouth	SY/256910	2.	13.	4
Mosburi[5]	Musbury	SY/276945		6.	0
Brokland Tril	Bruckland	SY/283933		2.	0
Comb Pyn cum	Combpyne	SY/290923		18.	0
Doune Umframvill'[6]	?				
Doune Rauf'	Rousdon	SY/296913		15.	4
			4.	14.	8

Hd. Wonford [WONFORD HUNDRED]

Combe Intynhide	Combeinteignhead	SX/901716	1.	11.	6
Rocombe Hughe[7]	Rocombe	SX/910701		2.	4
Stok' Intynhide	Stokeinteignhead	SX/916704	1.	6.	8

---

[1] A lost place in Cotleigh parish, *E.P.N.S.*, *IX*, *Devonshire*, part 2 (1932), 625.

[2] Part of Musbury was taxed in Axmouth hundred.

[3] Part of Membury was taxed with Axminster at a tenth (p. 66).

[4] The borough of Honiton was taxed at a tenth (p. 66).

[5] See also Axmouth hundred, above.

[6] Identified as Charton, alias Down Umfraville, in *F.A.* i. 592, but there is no confirmation of this in *E.P.N.S.*, *IX*, *Devonshire*, part 2 (1932), 636. The identification is unlikely as Charton was separately taxed in Axminster hundred, above. The place is not named on the roll of 1332.

[7] Rocombe Hugh was one of two manors in Rocombe: the other, Rocombe Cadiho, was separately taxed and is named later in the hundred.

Rydmor	Ringmore	sx/923722	1.	6.	o
Alfyngton'	Alphington	sx/919899	1.	18.	o
Couwyk' cum	Cowick with	sx/909911	3.	o.	o
Cristouwe	Christow	sx/836851			
Sprayton'	Spreyton	sx/698969		3.	o
Ryshford	Rushford Barton	sx/708891		3.	6
Pynne	Upton Pyne	sx/910977	1.	8.	o
Holebeme	Holbeam	sx/821711		3.	o
Donsford	Dunsford	sx/813892		16.	3
Braunford Spek'	Brampford Speke	sx/927982		6.	8
Couelegh'	Cowley	sx/904957		5.	8
Eggebere	Eggbeer	sx/768926		6.	o
Rewe	Rewe	sx/945992		10.	6
Hutteneslegh'	Hittisleigh	sx/733954		5.	o
Hoxham	Huxham	sx/946978		4.	o
Westwogwill'	West Ogwell	sx/819701		3.	o
Wonford &	Wonford and	sx/940918	1.	o.	o
Halsford	Halsfordwood	sx/876937			
Lamforde	Lambert	sx/751928		8.	o
Poltymor cum	Poltimore with	sx/966968		19.	o
Clyst Moys	West Clyst	sx/975951			
Polslo	Polsloe	sx/935936	1.	1.	6
Stok' Canonicorum	Stoke Canon	sx/939980		17.	10
Clyst Fomyzon	Sowton	sx/977925		6.	8
Ryngeswill'	Ringwell	sx/c.954924		5.	o
Hevetru'	Heavitree	sx/937922		7.	o
Hethe	Heath Barton	sx/846940		5.	6
Whyteston'	Whitestone	sx/868944		7.	o
Holecomb'	Holcombe Burnell	sx/858917		14.	o
Brideford	Bridford	sx/815864		14.	o
Toppesham [man.]	Topsham	sx/965882	1.	7.	o
Foleford [h]	Great Fulford	sx/790917		3.	4
Churiton'	Cheriton Bishop	sx/773936		3.	o
Est Clyfford[1]	Clifford Barton	sx/c.781901		4.	8
West Clyfford[1]	Clifford Barton	sx/c.781901		7.	4
Fursham	Fursham	sx/714934		2.	6
Chageford	Chagford	sx/701875		2.	o
Throulegh'	Throwleigh	sx/669908		13.	2
Fairewode	Great Fairwood	sx/817948		13.	4
Teyngton' Daubernon	Drewsteignton	sx/736908		7.	8
Droscomb' [h] cum	Drascombe with	sx/701920		3.	6
Boggebrok' [h]	Lower Budbrook	sx/755921			
Tetteborn'	Tedburn St. Mary	sx/817942		5.	o
Hakeworthi'	Hackworthy	sx/803932		2.	o
Hiwysh'	Great Huish	sx/828935		5.	6
Melhiwysh'	Melhuish Barton	sx/793925		5.	o
Middelonde	Medland	sx/780951		7.	o
Teyng' Hervy	Teignharvey	sx/915721		6.	o
Estwogwill'	East Ogwell	sx/838701		16.	o
Shilston' [h]	Shilstone	sx/702907			6
Siggeford [h]	Sigford	sx/778740		3.	o
Horigge	Horridge	sx/761742		1.	6
Rocomb' Cadiho[2] [h]	Rocombe	sx/910701		3.	10
Burgh'[3]	probably Burrow	sx/939991		4.	o

[1] East and West Clifford were separate tithings which do not seem to be distinguishable now.

[2] For Rocombe Hugh, see above.

[3] Probably Burrow in Stoke Canon, but perhaps Burrough in Drewsteignton (sx/748910).

Baggetorre	Bagtor	sx/766752	2.	6
Braunford Pyn	Brampford Pyne[1]	sx/927982	7.	o
Heghes	Hayes[2]	sx/913923	3.	o
Stephneston'	Stevenstone	sx/910995	14.	o
Stapilhille [h]	Staplehill	sx/821739	3.	o
			30.	o.	11

Hd. Exemynstr' [EXMINSTER HUNDRED]

Exemynstr'	Exminster	sx/945876	1.	12.	o
Ken	Kenn	sx/922857	1.	18.	o
Toucerston' cum	Towsington with	sx/940873	1.	o.	o
Shillyngford	Shillingford				
Rauf & Abbatis	St. George and	sx/904878			
	Shillingford Abbot	sx/911888			
Pouderham	Powderham	sx/972843		16.	o
Ayshcomb'	Ashcombe	sx/912795	1.	6.	8
Mammeheade	Mamhead	sx/931808		13.	4
Doulysh' cum	Dawlish with	sx/956768	2.	18.	o
Est Teyngmouth'	Teignmouth [East]	sx/c.943740			
Holecomb'	Holcombe	sx/953747		12.	o
Teyngemuth Episcopi [v]	Teignmouth	sx/940730	5.	10.	o
Teyngton' Episcopi	Bishopsteignton	sx/910737	1.	o.	o
Chuddelegh'	Chudleigh	sx/867794	1.	6.	8
Teyng' Sancti Georgii	George Teign Barton	sx/851835		1.	8
Moulysh'	Mowlish	sx/951810		2.	o
Shaplegh' cum	Shapley with	sx/683847		13.	4
Fenne &	Venn and	sx/690845			
Jordanyston'	Jurston	sx/697845			
Trysme	Trusham	sx/856822		10.	o
Aysherston'	Ashton	sx/856846		13.	o
Legh Dodescomb'	Doddiscombsleigh	sx/858865		7.	6
Ide	Ide	sx/897903		11.	8
Denshidiok'	Dunchideock	sx/876876		4.	o
Matford Botir [h] &	Matford [two manors]	sx/930890		7.	2
Matford Joyngnour [h]					
			22.	3.	o

Hd. Teyngbrugg' [TEIGNBRIDGE HUNDRED]

Teyngwyk'	Highweek	sx/847720	2.	o.	4
Lustelegh'	Lustleigh	sx/785813	1.	o.	o
North Bovy	North Bovey	sx/739839	1.	o	o
Aysshperton'[3]	Ashburton	sx/755698	1.	6.	8
Teyng' Bruwere	Teigngrace	sx/849739		14.	4
Bovy Tray'	Bovey Tracey	sx/816785	2.	o.	o
Yuddeford	Ideford	sx/893773	1.	11.	8
Teyngton' Regis	Kingsteignton	sx/871730	1.	12.	o
Ilstyngton'	Ilsington	sx/785762	2.	1.	4
Morton'	Moretonhampstead	sx/756861	1.	18.	6
Maneton'	Manaton	sx/749813	1.	1.	6
Hugheton'	Howton	sx/743871		13.	o

[1] A manor within Brampford Speke (*E.P.N.S., IX, Devonshire*, part 2 (1932), 423).
[2] The site of Hayes is on the west side of the Exe at sx/913923.
[3] The borough of Ashburton was taxed at a tenth (p. 66).

Heanek'	Hennock	sx/830810		8.	o
Teyng' Canonicorum	Canonteign	sx/836827	1.	3.	o
Wrey'	Wray Barton	sx/770745		12.	6
Lolkecomb'	possibly Luscombe	sx/842793		1.	6
			19.	4.	4

Hd. Lyfton' [LIFTON HUNDRED]

Dounterton'	Dunterton	sx/376793		10.	o
Sydenham Danmarle	Sydenham Damarel	sx/409760		13.	o
Bradeston'	Bradstone	sx/382810		12.	6
Stouwe Sancte Marie	Marystow	sx/435829		10.	6
Thrischelton'	Thrushelton	sx/447876		18.	o
Kelly'	Kelly	sx/395814		5.	6
Stouford	Stowford	sx/433871		5.	6
Okhampton'[1]	Okehampton	sx/587951	1.	6.	9
Sourton'	Sourton	sx/536903	1.	13.	4
Bridestouwe	Bridestowe	sx/513894	1.	13.	4
Lyen Trenchard	Lewtrenchard	sx/457861		12.	o
Coriton'	Coryton	sx/457835		6.	o
Tavy Sancte Marie	Marytavy	sx/509787		15.	o
Lamerton'	Lamerton	sx/451771	2.	o.	o
Brodwode Wyger	Broadwoodwidger	sx/412892	1.	o.	o
Virgenstouwe cum Tolyslo	Virginstow with Tilleslow	sx/376927 sx/385932		6.	8
Wyke Langeford	Germansweek	sx/439942		12.	o
Bratton'	Bratton Clovelly	sx/463918	2.	o.	o
			16.	o.	1

Hd. Blaketoriton' [BLACK TORRINGTON HUNDRED]

Blaketoriton'	Black Torrington	ss/464057	2.	3.	o
Heannton'	Highampton	ss/489046		18.	o
Hatherlegh'	Hatherleigh	ss/541046	3.	3.	4
Jacobstouwe	Jacobstowe	ss/587016		15.	o
Ikesborn'	Exbourne	ss/602019		12.	o
Brodwode Kelly cum Honychurch'	Broadwood-Kelly with Honeychurch	ss/617059 ss/629028		18.	o
Cadekbere	Kigbeare	sx/540962		12.	o
Inwardlegh'	Inwardleigh	sx/560995	1.	5.	o
Ayshbury'	Ashbury	sx/508979		9.	o
Lyw	Northlew	sx/505991	1.	18.	o
Beuworthi'	Beaworthy	sx/461994		14.	o
Halghewill'	Halwill	sx/427994		18.	o
Essewaut'	Ashwater	sx/387953	3.	3.	4
Lughyngcote	Luffincott	sx/332947		5.	o
Worryngton'	Werrington	sx/329876	7.	5.	o
Tetecote	Tetcott	sx/332965		13.	o
Clauton'	Clawton	sx/353993	2.	3.	4
Holescomb'	Hollacombe	ss/377031		5.	8
Haldesworthi'	Holsworthy	ss/342037	2.	3.	4
Chelysworthi'	Chilsworthy	ss/327067		4.	o
Pyworthi'	Pyworthy	ss/313029	2.	o.	o

---

[1] The borough of Okehampton was taxed at a tenth (p. 66).

Brugge Rouwel[1]	Bridgerule	ss/282032		19.	0
Bradeworthi' cum	Bradworthy with	ss/324140	4.	19.	0
Wyke	Pancrasweek	ss/296058			
Sottecomb'	Sutcombe	ss/347117	1.	12.	4
Potleforde [h]	West Putford	ss/359156	1.	6.	8
Bukyngton' [h]	Abbots Bickington	ss/384133		4.	0
Milton' cum	Milton Damarel with	ss/384107	2.	3.	4
Cokburi	Cookbury	ss/407060			
Thornbure	Thornbury	ss/401084		19.	0
Sannford cum	Sampford Courtenay	ss/632013	1.	5.	6
Belston'	with Belstone	sx/619935			
Bradeford	Bradford	ss/421072	1.	1.	0
Northcote [h][2]	?			3.	4
Monek' Okhamton'	Monkokehampton	ss/581055		13.	4
			47.	14.	6

Hd. Hertilannd [HARTLAND HUNDRED]

Ayshmandesworthi'	Ashmansworthy	ss/339180	1.	18.	4
Clovely	Clovelly	ss/317247	3.	5.	0
Yernescomb'	Yarnscombe	ss/561236	1.	11.	2
Stoke Netani	Stoke	ss/234247	1.	1.	0
Welcomb'	Welcombe	ss/228184		16.	0
Hole &	Hole[3] and	ss/220200		10.	7
Herdisworthi'	Hardisworthy	ss/230204			
Hertilannde	Hartland	ss/259243	3.	5.	3
			12.	7.	4

Hd. Wynkelegh' [WINKLEIGH HUNDRED]

Wynkelegh'	Winkleigh	ss/633081	4.	4.	11

Hd. Mollond' [MOLLOND HUNDRED]

Mollonde	Molland	ss/807284	4.	0.	0

Hd. Tavystok' [TAVISTOCK HUNDRED]

Tavystok'[4]	Tavistock	sx/481744	5.	15.	4

Hd. Northtauton' [NORTH TAWTON HUNDRED]

Womberlegh' [man.]	Umberleigh	ss/593246	4.	4.	0
Borryngton'	Burrington	ss/638166	1.	13.	0
Idrichescote	Iddlecott	ss/567125		11.	4
Ridelcomb'	Riddlecombe	ss/610140	1.	0.	0
Aysh' Reigny'	Ashreigney	ss/629136	1.	0.	0
Eggenysford	Eggesford	ss/687112		10.	0

[1] Part of Bridgerule, probably West, was assessed in Cornwall (Stratton hundred, p. 33).
[2] Either Northcott (sx/337925) or Northcott in Sutcombe (ss/335131).
[3] Grid ref. is to South Hole.
[4] The borough of Tavistock was taxed at a tenth (p. 66).

Churibeare	Cherubeer	ss/593123		12.	0
Duwelond	Dowland	ss/568103		13.	4
Rayshlegh'	Rashleigh Barton	ss/672128		18.	0
Hoke [h] cum	Hook with Hansford	ss/641142		5.	0
Litelhanntesford [h]	Barton	ss/660154			
Duwelton'	Dolton	ss/570120		18.	0
Chaluelegh'	Chawleigh	ss/712127	2.	0.	0
Wemmeworthi'	Wembworthy	ss/662099		16.	0
Cruk Burnel	Crooke	ss/683009		9.	0
North Tauton'	North Tawton	ss/663017	1.	18.	0
Nymet Rolannd	Nymet Rowland	ss/711082	1.	3.	8
Nymet Tracy'	Nymet Tracey	ss/728007	2.	0.	0
Affeton'	Affeton Barton	ss/756137		12.	0
Sele & Doune	Zeal Monachorum and	ss/720040	1.	12.	0
	Down St. Mary	ss/743044			
Nymet Nichole	Nichols Nymett	ss/691021		8.	0
Nymet Bardevyle	Burston[1]	ss/712023	1.	0.	0
Cloueneburgh' [h]	Clannaborough	ss/747025		9.	0
Walston' [h] &	Walson Barton	ss/734008			
Thorne [h]	Thorne	ss/737002			
Colrigge	Coldridge	ss/698077		13.	4
Lappeford	Lapford	ss/732083		18.	0
Bonelegh'	Bondleigh	ss/651048	1.	1.	0
			27.	4.	8

Hd. Braunton' [BRAUNTON HUNDRED]

Biri'	Berrynarbor	ss/560467	1.	11.	0
Esthagynton'	East Hagginton	ss/552471		14.	8
Churchill	Churchill	ss/595408		11.	2
Merwode	Marwood	ss/544375		13.	4
Bratton'	Bratton Fleming	ss/643377	1.	14.	0
Boklannde Dyneham	North Buckland	ss/479402	1.	2.	0
Ilfardicomb'	Ilfracombe	ss/513473	2.	0.	0
Bradeforde	Bradiford	ss/550343	1.	4.	2
Combe Martyn	Combe Martin	ss/586463	1.	11.	1
Ralegh'	Raleigh	ss/569349	1.	5.	0
Beare[2]	?	ss/523384		12.	0
Estboklannde	East Buckland	ss/677313		12.	0
West Boklannde	West Buckland	ss/657313		12.	0
Lyncomb'	Lincombe	ss/500458	1.	7.	8
West Doune	West Down	ss/517420	1.	8.	8
Bradewill'	Bradwell	ss/499427	1.	18.	0
Est Doune	East Down	ss/602418		18.	0
Morteho	Mortehoe	ss/458452		11.	0
Burghbryton'	Borough	ss/487445		7.	0
Westhagyngton'	West Hagginton	ss/542467		13.	0
Crideho	Croyde	ss/445392	2.	2.	0
Kentesburi'	Kentisbury	ss/623438		11.	0
Saunton'	Saunton	ss/465376	2.	4.	0
Ayshford	Ashford	ss/533353	1.	1.	0
Lobbe	Lobb	ss/472379		18.	8
Godelegh'	Goodleigh	ss/598342		17.	0
Fillegh'	Filleigh	ss/662280		11.	8

[1] For this identification see *E.P.N.S.*, *IX, Devonshire*, part 2 (1932), 375.

[2] I am inclined to identify this as Beer Charter Barton in Braunton (ss/523384) rather than Beara in Bratton (Erskine, op. cit. 80).

Pillannde	Pilland	ss/542350		19.	o
Heannton'	Heanton Punchardon	ss/503356	2.	15.	o
Whitefeld	Whitefield	ss/557394		18.	o
Pilton' [h]	Pilton	ss/556341		13.	4
Wyddedon' [h]	Whiddon	ss/551386		4.	o
Mollecote [h]	Mullacott	ss/513444		3.	o
Furse [h]	Furze	ss/648332		2.	o
Ellewell' [h]	Elwell	ss/663318			6
Snyddelegh' [h]	probably Stoodleigh	ss/657323			6
Medecomb' [h]	Metcombe	ss/537398		4.	o
Brounelond' [h]	South Burland	ss/539412			6
Estschillefenne [h]	Shelfin	ss/508445		2.	o
			35.	12.	11

Hd. Bannton' [BAMPTON HUNDRED]

Bannton'	Bampton	ss/957223	3.	16.	7
Peatton'	Petton	st/007246	1.	o.	o
Cleyhangre cum	Clayhanger with	st/022230	1.	12.	5
Donnyngston'	Donningstone	st/008237			
Hockeworthi'	Hockworthy	st/040195	1.	6.	8
Holecomb'	Holcombe Rogus	st/056190	4.	10.	o
Burdlescomb'	Burlescombe	st/076176		6.	o
Morbathe	Morebath	ss/953251	1.	3.	5
			13.	15.	1

Hd. Harrugge [HAYRIDGE HUNDRED]

Thurverton'	Thorverton	ss/924022	1.	16.	8
Cadeburi'	Cadbury	ss/911049		8.	o
Cadelegh'	Cadeleigh	ss/913079		9.	8
Alre Peverel	Aller	st/050067	1.	8.	2
Bykelegh'	Bickleigh	ss/943072		10.	o
Upexe &	Up Exe and	ss/943025	1.	o.	o
Nitherexe	Nether Exe	ss/935001			
Silferton'	Silverton	ss/957028	1.	2.	8
Colompton'	Cullompton	st/022072	2.	13.	4
Pontisford	Ponsford	st/001073		12.	o
Plymtreu	Plymtree	st/051029		6.	8
Wodebeare	Woodbeer	st/058044		12.	o
Carswill'	Kerswell	st/080060		7.	o
Kentelysbeare	Kentisbeare	st/068081	1.	o.	o
Taleton'	Talaton	sy/068997	1.	15.	o
Payehemburi'	Payhembury	st/088018	1.	3.	o
Shildon'	Sheldon	st/120086	1.	6.	8
Fynaton'	Feniton	sy/108993	1.	1.	o
Brodehemburi'	Broadhembury	st/102047	2.	1.	4
Monke Colmp'[1]	lost		1.	9.	o
Bradenech' [man.][2]	Bradninch	ss/999042	2.	6.	o
Luttokesheghs' [h]	Lockshallis[3]	st/028126		3.	4
Uppeton' [h] &	Upton and	st/030064		6.	8
Weure [h]	Weaver	st/040039			
			23.	18.	2

[1] Monk Culm, a lost place in Silverton parish (*E.P.N.S.*, *IX*, *Devonshire*, part 2 (1932), 570).   [2] The borough of Bradninch was taxed at a tenth (p. 66).
[3] For this identification see *E.P.N.S.*, *IX*, *Devonshire*, part 2 (1932), xiv.

Hd. Colrugg' [COLERIDGE HUNDRED]

Hurberton'	Harberton	sx/778587	5.	14.	1
Ayspryngton'	Ashprington	sx/818572	1.	5.	0
Corneworthi'	Cornworthy	sx/829555	1.	16.	0
Didesham	Dittisham	sx/861551	1.	10.	0
Blakaueton'	Blackawton	sx/805510	4.	0.	0
Stoke Flemyng'	Stoke Fleming	sx/862483	2.	0.	7
Slapton'	Slapton	ss/821450	1.	16.	0
Malston' cum	Malston with	sx/772451		15.	4
Kynedon'	Keynedon	sx/775433			
Dodebrok'[1]	Dodbrooke	sx/738441	1.	5.	0
Churleton'	Charleton	sx/750426	3.	3.	4
North Pole	North Pool	sx/773411	1.	8.	4
South Pole cum	South Pool with	sx/776404	1.	6.	8
Chevelston'	Chivelstone	sx/783388			
Portelemouth'	East Portlemouth	sx/743884		9.	2
Pral &	East Prawle and	sx/780365	1.	5.	6
Godeshaltre	Goodshelter	sx/763388			
Stok' Inhamme [man.]	Stokenham	sx/808428	5.	3.	4
Shirreford	Sherford	sx/779443	1.	0.	0
Wodemanston' [h]	Bearscombe	sx/753447		5.	0
Grymeston' [h] cum	Grimpstonleigh[2]	sx/749491		8.	6
Legh' [h]					
Norton Danne	Norton	sx/853511		18.	4
Sutton' Dertemouth' [v][3]	Dartmouth	sx/878513	5.	0.	0
			40.	10.	2

Hd. Ermyngton' [ERMINGTON HUNDRED]

Ermyngton' [man.]	Ermington	sx/638532	2.	10.	0
Worthihele	Worthele[4]	sx/622543	2.	1.	0
Cornwode	Cornwood	sx/604594		19.	1
Boterford	Butterford	sx/707562		15.	1
Holboghton'	Holbeton	sx/613502	2.	10.	0
Battekesburgh'	Battisborough	sx/601472	1.	6.	8
Lamshide	Lambside	sx/577473	1.	13.	4
Nyweton' Ferers	Newton Ferrers	sx/550482	2.	5.	8
Uggeburgh'	Ugborough	sx/678558	2.	16.	8
Donstanston'	Dunstone	sx/593515		13.	4
Furdel	Fardel	sx/612574	1.	11.	8
Herford	Harford	sx/638595	1.	0.	0
Loudebrok'	Ludbrook	sx/660543	2.	10.	0
Esse Abbatis	Ashford	sx/688486	1.	11.	0
Loperigge	Lupridge	sx/715534		14.	0
Hethfelde	Heathfielde	sx/689509	2.	13.	4
Aveton' Gyffard	Aveton Gifford	sx/693478	2.	13.	4
Stodbury [h]	Stadbury	sx/684460		8.	0
Modbury[5]	Modbury	sx/656516	4.	18.	2
Rydmore	Ringmore	sx/652460	1.	14.	0
Kyngeston'	Kingston	sx/637478	2.	0.	0

---

[1] The borough of Dodbrooke was taxed at a tenth (p. 65).
[2] The wording on the document suggests that Grimpstonleigh consisted of two distinct hamlets in 1334.
[3] The borough of Dartmouth was taxed at a tenth (p. 65).
[4] Grid ref. is to West Worthele.
[5] The borough of Modbury was taxed at a tenth (p. 66).

			£	s.	d.
Bykeburi	Bigbury	sx/668467	2.	0.	0
Langeford	Landford Barton	sx/699569	3.	10.	0
Payneston'	Penson	sx/724543		4.	0
Killeburi	Kilbury	sx/748660		10.	0
Flute Danmarle	Flete	sx/628513		13.	4
			46.	1.	8

Hd. Buddelegh' [EAST BUDLEIGH HUNDRED]

			£	s.	d.
Notewill'	Nutwell	sx/987852		14.	0
Strete	Strete Raleigh	sy/051955		6.	4
Rokebeare	Rockbeare	sy/020953		16.	0
Sydeburi'	Sidbury	sy/140917	5.	3.	4
Lytleham	Littleham	sy/029813	2.	12.	0
Harpeford	Harpford	sy/090903	1.	6.	8
Holbrok'	Holbrook	sx/993919	1.	8.	8
Wodeburi'	Woodbury	sy/009872	2.	10.	0
Limeneston'	Lympstone	sx/993842	1.	0.	0
Daledich'	Dalditch	sy/047835		13.	0
Aylesbeare	Aylesbeare	sy/038920	1.	3.	0
Heghes	Hayes Barton	sy/051852		8.	0
Wythicomb'	Withycombe Raleigh	sy/015822		16.	6
Mershe	Marsh Barton	sx/978882		16.	0
Clyst Sancti Georgii'	Clyst St. George	sx/983889		19.	0
Clyst Sancte Marie	Clyst St. Mary	sx/979903		9.	4
Gydesham	Gittisham	sy/133984	1.	4.	0
Clyst Episcopi	Bishop's Clyst	sx/973910		16.	0
Clyst Hyneton'	Clyst Honiton	sx/989935		8.	6
Saltcomb	Salcombe Regis	sy/148888	2.	6.	8
Coleton'	Colaton Raleigh	sy/082872	1.	3.	0
Oteryngton' [man.]	Otterton	sy/080852	9.	13.	4
Radeueye Abbatis [h]	Radway	sy/c.095860		3.	0
			36.	16.	4

Ufcolmp in hundred' de Baunton'

			£	s.	d.
Ufcolmp'	Uffculme	st/068127	6.	2.	4

Hd. Northmolton' [NORTH MOLTON HUNDRED]

			£	s.	d.
Northmolton'	North Molton	ss/736299	4.	10.	0

[BOROUGHS]

			£	s.	d.	
Exon [civitas]	Exeter	sx/916924	36.	12.	4	[T]
Totton' [B]	Totnes	sx/802604	8.	7.	8	[T]
Clyfton' Dertemouth' [B][1]	Dartmouth	sx/878513	11.	0.	0	[T]
Dodebrok' [B][2]	Dodbrooke	sx/738441	2.	3.	4	[T]
Kyngesbrugge [B]	Kingsbridge	sx/733444	3.	10.	0	[T]

[1] Part of Dartmouth was taxed at a fifteenth (p. 64).
[2] Part of Dodbrooke was taxed at a fifteenth (p. 64).

Ayshperton' [B][1]	Ashburton	sx/755698	3.	6.	11	[T]
Plympton' [B][2]	Plympton Erle	sx/545557	4.	6.	8	[T]
Sutton' Priour [B][3]	Plymouth	sx/480550	24.	o.	o	[T]
Tavystok' [B][4]	Tavistock	sx/481744	9.	o.	o	[T]
Lydeforde [B]	Lydford	sx/509847	1.	3.	4	[T]
Okhampton' [B][5]	Okehampton	sx/587951	1.	12.	8	[T]
Bydiforde [B][6]	Bideford	ss/453265	6.	o.	o	[T]
Toriton' [B][7]	Great Torrington	ss/495192	7.	17.	2	[T]
Barnestapl' [B]	Barnstaple	ss/560334	18.	14.	o	[T]
Southmolton' [B]	South Molton	ss/713260	6.	5.	5	[T]
Criditon' [B][8]	Crediton	ss/836002	4.	1.	1	[T]
Tuverton' [B][9]	Tiverton	ss/955125	2.	o.	o	[T]
Bradenech' [B][10]	Bradninch	ss/999042	2.	16.	8	[T]
Honeton' [B][11]	Honiton	st/163007	2.	16.	8	[T]
Modburi [B][12]	Modbury	sx/656516	3.	10.	o	[T]
			159.	3.	11	[T]

[ANCIENT DEMESNES]

South Tauton' [A.D]	South Tawton	sx/653945	8.	18.	o	[T]
Sheftbere' [A.D]	Shebbear	ss/438092	5.	16.	o	[T]
Kenton' [A.D]	Kenton	sx/958833	9.	3.	4	[T]
Otery Sancte Marie' [A.D]	Ottery St. Mary	sy/098956	20.	o.	o	[T]
South Teyng' [A.D]	Teigncombe	sx/672872	2.	o.	o	[T]
Buddelegh' Fenotery & Brodeham [A.D]	East Budleigh Venn Ottery and Bradham	sy/066849 sy/079912 sy/017816	11.	7.	8	[T]
Axeminstr' & Memburi [A.D][13]	Axminster and Membury	sy/297985 st/276030	5.	o.	o	[T]
Lyfton' [A.D]	Lifton	sx/386851	2.	o.	o	[T]
Exilond [A.D]	Exe Island	sx/914922	4.	o.	o	[T]
Braunton' [A.D]	Braunton	ss/485366	8.	13.	4	[T]
Northam [A.D]	Northam	ss/448291	5.	o.	1	[T]
			81.	18.	5	[T]

TOTAL: £953. 15. o[14]

[1] Part of Ashburton was taxed at a fifteenth (p. 59).
[2] The borough of Plympton Erle was created out of the older settlement of Plympton St. Mary in the late twelfth century. Plympton St. Mary was taxed at a fifteenth (p. 51).
[3] See also Sutton Vautort (p. 52).
[4] Part of Tavistock was taxed at a fifteenth (p. 61).
[5] Part of Okehampton was taxed at a fifteenth (p. 60).
[6] Part of Bideford was taxed at a fifteenth (p. 52).
[7] Part of Great Torrington was taxed at a fifteenth (p. 53).
[8] Part of Crediton was taxed at a fifteenth (p. 54).
[9] Part of Tiverton was taxed at a fifteenth (p. 55).
[10] The manor of Bradninch was taxed at a fifteenth (p. 63).
[11] The manor of Honiton was taxed at a fifteeenth (p. 57).
[12] Part of Modbury was taxed at a fifteenth (p. 64).
[13] Part of Membury was taxed at a fifteenth (p. 57).
[14] As on Account, E 179/95/9.

DORSET

DOCUMENTS

8 Edward III: Account	E 179/103/9
8 Edward III: Particulars	not extant
10 Edward III: Indenture of 1334	E 179/103/7 m. 1*
10 Edward III: Particulars	E 179/103/7 mm. 2–3

TAXERS

The abbot of Cerne and John Maugre

TAX YIELD

15th	£744.	19.	5½
10th	£106.	9.	7
	£851.	9.	0½

Representing assessed movable wealth of

£12,239. 7. 8½

NOTES

Places taxed at a tenth are listed in two blocks, one of them at the end. They include the boroughs of Shaftesbury, Dorchester, Bridport, and Lyme Regis. Blandford, Corfe, Melcombe, and Wareham were all taxed at a tenth but were not considered boroughs as they had been in 1332 (Willard (1933), op. cit. 431).

Since 1334 there have been slight changes along the boundary with Somerset and Devon. Chardstock and Stockland, now in Devon, were then taxed in Dorset; Thorncombe, then taxed in Devon, is now in Dorset. Six places in modern Dorset were taxed in Somerset in 1334, viz. Poyntington, Trent, Holwell, Seaborough, Sandford Orcas, and Goathill.

REFERENCES

E. A. Fry has transcribed the Dorset rolls of 1327 (E 197/103/4) and F. J. Pope that of 1332 (E 179/103/5); I understand that both transcriptions are deposited in the Dorset County Museum.

B. Reynolds, 'Late medieval Dorset; three essays in historical geography', unpublished M.A. thesis, University of London, 1958 (especially essay II).

ACKNOWLEDGEMENT

I am indebted to Mr. David Mills for help in the identification of a number of place-names.

Hd. Sancti Georgii [HUNDRED OF ST. GEORGE]

Mayne Martel	Broadmayne	sy/729866	2.	0.	10
Frome Everard	Frome Belet	sy/715895	1.	8.	9
Bochamptone	Bockhampton[1]	sy/721908	1.	7.	10
Kyngestone	Kingston Maurward	sy/719910	1.	2.	0
Stintesforde	Stinsford	sy/715914	2.	16.	4
Frome Whitefelde	Frome Whitfield	sy/692917	1.	18.	4
Polaynestone &	Pulston and	sy/667953	2.	5.	5
Foradestone	Forston	sy/666956			
Herynggestone	Herringston	sy/689881	1.	2.	4
Wolvetone	Wolfeton	sy/679921		8.	8
Bradeforde &	Bradford Peverell and	sy/659930	3.	7.	0
Mokelford	Muckleford	sy/639935			
Strattone	Stratton	sy/651938	4.	1.	8
Grymstone	Grimstone	sy/639942	3.	6.	0
Wynterborne Martin'	Winterborne St. Martin	sy/647890	4.	7.	4
Cermynstr'	Charminster	sy/679927	1.	4.	8
			30.	17.	2

Hd. Wynifred [WINFRITH HUNDRED]

Estlulleworthe	East Lulworth	sy/853821	2.	5.	5
Gaultone	Galton	sy/777851	1.	2.	3
Holeworthe	Holworth	sy/767833		18.	9
Oure	Owermoigne	sy/769853	1.	15.	7
Combe	Watercombe	sy/756849	2.	19.	4
Ryngstede	Ringstead	sy/747815	1.	5.	6
Burtone	Burton[2]	sy/833870	1.	16.	6
Pockswelle	Poxwell	sy/741841	3.	1.	6
Knytthetone	East Knighton	sy/811855	2.	0.	6
Wymfred	Winfrith Newburgh	sy/805843	4.	17.	7
Warmwelle	Warmwell	sy/752858	2.	0.	3
Wirdesforde	Woodsford	sy/761905		16.	4
Mourtone	Moreton	sy/806892	2.	2.	4
Chaluedone	Chaldon[3]	sy/790831		18.	4
			28.	0.	1

Lib. Bynedone [BINDON LIBERTY]

Welle	Wool	sy/848864	7.	0.	0

Hd. Byre [BERE REGIS HUNDRED]

Byre	Bere Regis	sy/848948	8.	4.	0
Muleborne	Milborne Stileham	sy/803974	2.	3.	6
Kyngestone	Winterborne Kingston	sy/861976	3.	16.	6
			14.	4.	0

[1] Grid ref. is to Lower Bockhampton.   [2] Grid ref. is to East Burton.
[3] Grid ref. is to East Chaldon.

Hd. Hundredsberg' [BARROW HUNDRED]

Affepudele	Affpuddle	sy/805936	5.	8.	7
Tonerpudele	Turners Puddle	sy/830935	2.	7.	8
Shytertone	Shitterton	sy/840950	2.	9.	4
Wyrghrode	Worgret	sy/908869	2.	9.	0
Turbervylepudele	Briantspuddle	sy/817933	2.	7.	10
Stretforde[1]	?		1.	0.	0
			16.	2.	5

Hd. Louseberg' [LOOSEBARROW HUNDRED]

Lousebergh'[2]	[Tarrant Crawford]	st/922035	4.	15.	8
Mapelertone	Mapperton	sy/906986	2.	19.	4
Cherbergh'	Charborough	sy/925978	1.	4.	10
Mordone	East Morden	sy/915950	2.	14.	9
			11.	14.	7

Hd. Pudeletone [PUDDLETOWN HUNDRED]

Hynepudele	Piddlehinton	sy/716972	3.	6.	6½
Loveford	Lovard[3]	lost	1.	9.	6
Litelpudele	Little Puddle	sy/717965	1.	8.	7
Watterestone	Waterston	sy/735952	2.	11.	2
Pudeletone	Puddletown	sy/759943	4.	6.	10
Athelhamptone	Athelhampton	sy/770942		9.	3
Burdolfstone	Burleston	sy/775943	1.	7.	4
Tollepudele	Tolpuddle	sy/791945	3.	18.	4
Elsyngtone	Ilsington	sy/755919		14.	8
Tyncledene	Tincleton	sy/767919	4.	3.	9
Cliue &	Clyff and	sy/779916			
Throp	Throop	sy/827931			
Cheselborneforde	Cheselbourne Ford	sy/c.764994		9.	8
Muleborne	Milborne St. Andrew	sy/803977		11.	4
Bardalfstone	Bardolfeston	sy/766946		18.	4
			25.	15.	3½

Hd. Cocdene [COGDEAN HUNDRED]

Caneforde	Canford	sz/032988	11.	10.	3
La pole [v]	Poole	sz/012908	2.	13.	10
Hamme	Hamworthy	sy/993912	2.	3.	5
Lychet' Munstr'	Lytchett Minster	sy/961931	4.	11.	1
Coumbe Almere	Combe Almer	sy/951973	1.	16.	0
Cherleton	Charlton Marshall	st/901041	3.	2.	4
Corf Molyn	Corfe Mullen	sy/977983	2.	10.	8
Stourmunstr' Mareschal	Sturminster Marshall	st/951004	4.	6.	8
Lychet Mautravers	Lytchett Matravers	st/947955	1.	0.	0
			33.	14.	3

---

[1] Probably the same place as *Strafford*, linked with Hide in the *Nomina Villarum* of 1316 (*F.A.* ii. 42).

[2] This entry must refer to Tarrant Crawford. On later rolls the name *Crauford* is used instead of the hundred name of *Lousebergh*. Tarrant Crawford is also listed within the hundred in 1303 (*F.A.* ii. 28).

[3] A lost place. See A. Fagersten, *The Place-names of Dorset* (1933), 178.

Hd. Whiteweye [WHITEWAY HUNDRED]

Melecombe	Melcombe[1]	ST/750023	4.	2.	o
Heltone	Hilton	ST/781030	5.	3.	o
Edbristone	Ibberton	ST/789076	2.	2.	o
Stoke	Stoke Wake	ST/764064	1.	6.	7
Mideltone	Milton Abbas[2]	ST/799023	7.	3.	o
Cheselborne	Cheselbourne	SY/762996	4.	2.	o
			23.	18.	7
Deuelish' [man.]	Dewlish	SY/775982	2.	14.	7

Hd. Totecumbe [TOTCOMBE HUNDRED]

Pudele Trentehide	Piddletrenthide	ST/702008	5.	0.	1
Minterne	Minterne Magna	ST/659043	1.	5.	o
Godmanstone	Godmanston	SY/666973	2.	3.	7
Cerne Abbatis	Cerne Abbas	ST/666012	5.	1.	5
			13.	10.	1

Hd. Modbergh' [MODBURY HUNDRED]

Sydelyng'	Sydling St. Nicholas	SY/630992	3.	17.	o
Cattestok'	Cattistock	SY/591995	3.	16.	o
Comptone	Compton Abbas = West Compton	SY/562943	1.	8.	o
Hulfelde	Hilfield	ST/635051	1.	6.	o
Uifhide	Fifehead Sydling[3]	ST/c.626014	2.	8.	o
Upsideling'	Up Sydling	ST/626014	1.	17.	8
			14.	12.	8

Hd. Godrenethorne [GODDERTHORN HUNDRED]

Athelington'	Allington	SY/461931	1.	6.	o
Brutton'[4]	Burton Bradstock	SY/489895		16.	6
Sturtel	Sturthill[5]	SY/522917	1.	0.	4
Scheptone	Shipton Gorge	SY/498915	2.	16.	o
Loderes	Loders	SY/491942	6.	4.	11
			12.	3.	9

Hd. Shireborne [SHERBORNE HUNDRED]

Lidelynche	Lydlinch	ST/742133	2.	5.	8
Aultone	Alton Pancras	ST/699023	4.	5.	o

---

[1] Grid ref. is to Higher Melcombe. The quota probably includes amounts for the villages of Melcombe Horsey and Melcombe Binham, both now deserted.

[2] Grid ref. is to the site of the old village of Milton Abbas.

[3] Fagersten, op. cit. 202; a tithing in Sydling St. Nicholas.

[4] Part of Burton Bradstock was taxed in Frampton hundred.

[5] Grid ref. is to Lower Sturthill Farm.

Upcerne	Up Cerne	ST/659028	I.	8.	10
Aluestone	Allweston	ST/665143	2.	0.	6
Caundel Episcopi	Bishop's Caundle	ST/696131	I.	3.	6
Caundel purs	Purse Caundle	ST/696176	I.	19.	10
Doune	Bishop's Down	ST/672121	2.	7.	0
Pyneforde	Pinford	ST/664173		18.	4
Woborne	Oborne	ST/654185	I.	I.	0
Bradeforde	Bradford Abbas	ST/588142	3.	4.	4
Thorneford	Thornford	ST/602132	2.	3.	5
Overcompton'	Over Compton	ST/594169	I.	15.	4
Nithercompton'	Nether Compton	ST/598172	I.	13.	10
Wottone	North Wootton	ST/655148	I.	11.	5
Burtone	Longburton	ST/649128	2.	12.	0
Holnest'	Holnest	ST/656098	3.	5.	9
Haydone	Haydon	ST/670157	2.	3.	10
Lyllyngtone	Lillington	ST/629128	I.	5.	8
Overcombe	Coombe	ST/620183	2.	3.	6
Nithercombe	Nethercombe	ST/633172	I.	14.	10
Hundrestret'	Hound Street	ST/639167	2.	I.	0
Estebury	Eastbury[1]	ST/642166	I.	11.	0
Westbury	Westbury	ST/637163	2.	2.	6
Feod' Abb'	Abbot's Fee[2]	ST/638164	4.	0.	0
Newelond	Newland	ST/640169	4.	10.	0
Casteltone	Castleton	ST/645168		12.	9
			56.	0.	10

Hd. Yatemunstre [YETMINSTER HUNDRED]

Cliftone	Clifton Maybank	ST/577138	2.	I.	2
Yatemunstre	Yetminster	ST/593106	4.	3.	4
Ryme	Ryme Intrinseca	ST/581109	I.	I.	0
Legh'	Leigh	ST/618087	4.	5.	0
Chetiknolle	Chetnole	ST/602082	2.	10.	0
Melebury osmond	Melbury Osmond	ST/573079	I.	11.	0
Melebury bebbe	Melbury Bubb	ST/596065	I.	18.	0
Niwelond	Newland	ST/617052		4.	6
Wolcombe	Woolcombe	ST/600051		8.	0
			18	2	0

Hd. Beymunstre [BEYMINSTER HUNDRED]

Meleplasch'	Melplash	SY/486983	3.	17.	2
Bemunstre	Beaminster	ST/479012	3.	6.	0
Cherdestok'	Chardstock [in Devon]	ST/309045	6.	3.	6
Stoke Abbatis	Stoke Abbott	ST/453006	4.	2.	8
Langedone	Langdon	ST/502014	2.	16.	8
Corscombe	Corscombe	ST/522049	2.	0.	4
Netherbury	Netherbury	SY/473992	3.	17.	4
Assche	Ash	SY/455965	I.	10.	2
			27.	13.	10

[1] Name survives only in the Eastbury Hotel in Long Street, Sherborne.
[2] Grid ref. is to the abbey in Sherborne.

Hd. Halghestok' [HALSTOCK HUNDRED]

Halstock[1]	ST/536083	3.	12.	9

Hd. Ekerdone [EGGARDON HUNDRED]

Wynterborne	Winterbourne Abbas	SY/619904	2.	1.	0
Langebridie	Long Bredy	SY/588890	3.	5.	2
Estareswell'	Askerswell	SY/529926		16.	4
Mapercombe &	Mappercombe and	SY/513952		18.	0
Netelcombe	Nettlecombe	SY/518956			
Miltone	West Milton	SY/499963	4.	15.	6
Hok' &	Hooke and	ST/535002		12.	8
Stapelford	Stapleford	lost			
Kentecumbe	Kingcombe[2]	SY/549998	1.	1.	8
Wroxale	Wraxall[3]	ST/567011	1.	3.	7
			14.	13.	11

Hd. Knoltone [KNOWLTON HUNDRED]

Langekirchol	Long Crichel	ST/978102	3.	15.	0
Gussich'	Gussage All Saints	ST/999108	3.	4.	0
Knolton'	Knowlton	SU/024103	3.	6.	0
Upwymborne	Wimborne St. Giles	SU/032120	3.	18.	1
			14.	3.	1

Hd. La Ridehoue & Beymynistre' for'
[REDHOVE HUNDRED AND BEAMINSTER FOREIGN]

Bradepole	Bradpole	ST/480943	3.	8.	3
Portone	Poorton[4]	ST/519981		18.	0
Mapertone	Mapperton	ST/502998	2.	9.	0
Southpered	South Perrott	ST/471067	1.	4.	4
Mortesthorne	Mosterton	ST/458056	1.	5.	2
			9.	4.	9

Hd. Culfardestre [CULLIFORDTREE HUNDRED]

Osmyngtone	Osmington	SY/724830	2.	5.	5
Souttone	Sutton Poyntz	SY/706836	3.	10.	$7\frac{1}{2}$
Rappole	Radipole	SY/667814		18.	$8\frac{1}{2}$
Chikrel	Chickerell	SY/643806		9.	$4\frac{1}{2}$
Brodewaye	Broadwey	SY/667835	2.	11.	2
Hellewell'	Holwell	SY/654831		19.	$4\frac{1}{2}$
Upwaye	Upwey	SY/664849	1.	5.	3
Aschtone	Ashton	SY/663877		16.	10
Moneketone	Winterborne Monkton	SY/676878		12.	11
Wynterborn Heryng'	Winterborne Herringston	SY/690881	1.	0.	$4\frac{1}{2}$
Wynterborn Belet	Winterborne Belet	lost		11.	$9\frac{1}{2}$

---

[1] Only the hundred is named on the documents, but it is presumed that the entry refers to Halstock village. [2] Grid ref. is to Higher Kingcombe.
[3] Grid ref. is to Higher Wraxall. [4] Grid ref. is to North Poorton.

			£	s.	d.
Wydecombe	Whitcombe	SY/717883		14.	6
Weststaford	West Stafford	SY/726896		14.	9½
Knyttetone	West Knighton	SY/732876	1.	2.	9
Mayne &	Fryer Mayne and	SY/738865	1.	19.	5½
Eststaford	East Stafford	SY/732884			
	[= Lewell?][1]				
			19.	13.	4

Maner' de Brodewyndelsore [BROADWINDSOR]

	£	s.	d.
Summa totius manerii	8.	o.	o

Hd. Whitechurche [WHITCHURCH CANONICORUM HUNDRED]

			£	s.	d.
Stoclonde	Stockland [in Devon]	ST/244045	7.	o.	o
Mershwode	Marshwood	SY/382996	7.	4.	8
Symondesberg'	Symondsbury	SY/444936	4.	8.	4
Calewehagh'	Colway	SY/338928	4.	7.	4
			23.	o.	4

			£	s.	d.	
Gillingham [man.] [A.D]	Gillingham	ST/809265	10.	6.	8	[T]
Fordyngton' [man.] [A.D]	Fordington	SY/699706	7.	10.	4	[T]
Schafton' [B]	Shaftesbury	ST/862230	20.	o.	o	[T]
Dorcestr' [B]	Dorchester	SY/692908	9.	4.	4	[T]
Porstok' [man.] [A.D]	Powerstock	SY/518961	2.	2.	o	[T]
			49.	3.	4	[T]

Hd. Conekesdich' [COMBSDITCH HUNDRED]

			£	s.	d.
Blaneford	Blandford St. Mary	ST/892053	2.	11.	8
Blockesworthe	Bloxworth	SY/881947	3.	11.	o
Fifhasch'	Anderson	SY/880976	2.	2.	4
Turbervylestone	Winterborne Muston	SY/871976	1.	1.	4
Watecomb	Whatcombe[2]	ST/840012	1.	1.	10
Clenchestone	Winterborne Clenston	ST/840028	1.	1.	4
Whitechurch'	Winterborne Whitechurch	ST/866001	3.	13.	8
			15.	3.	2

Hd. La Ridelane [REDLANE HUNDRED]

			£	s.	d.
Hamford	Hanford	ST/845112		16.	4
Ocforde	Child Okeford	ST/835127	3.	5.	8
Manstone	Manston	ST/817150	3.	o.	8¼
Ywerne Courtenay	Iwerne Courtney	ST/860124	2.	17.	3
Suttone	Sutton Waldron	ST/862157	2.	o.	2
Thorntone cum	Thorton with	ST/804180	1.	10.	2¼
Todebere	Todber	ST/800201			

[1] Lost according to Fagersten, op. cit. 159, but according to John Hutchins, *The History and Antiquities of the County of Dorset*, 3rd edition (1861–73), ii. 499, another name for Lewell.   [2] Grid ref. is to Lower Whatcombe.

Stoure prewes	Stour Provost	ST/793216	2.	14.	4¼
Stoure Wak'	East Stour	ST/799228	1.	10.	6
Uifhide	Fifehead Magdalen	ST/782216	1.	0.	6
Westouere	West Stour	ST/785229	1.	10.	3
Kyngtone	Kington Magna	ST/768231	3.	2.	6
Westone	Buckhorn Weston	ST/757247	2.	3.	0
Miltone	Milton on Stour	ST/802246	1.	5.	0
Siltone	Silton	ST/782293	1.	6.	9¼
Libera decenna	Free tithing [or Gillingham Manor] [in Gillingham]	lost	1.	11.	0
			29.	14.	2

Hd. Niwetone & Bouclonde [STURMINSTER NEWTON AND BUCKLAND NEWTON HUNDREDS]

Niwetone	Newton	ST/782134		16.	3¾
Colbere	Colber	ST/780147	1.	4.	8¼
Marnhulle	Marnhull	ST/781188	4.	5.	2
Hentone	Hinton St. Mary	ST/788161	3.	1.	10¼
Acforde	Okeford Fitzpaine	ST/808108	4.	1.	7½
Boucland	Buckland Newton	ST/688052		13.	0¾
Brouchampton'	Brockhampton Green	ST/715061		18.	1½
Plish'	Plush	ST/714021	1.	9.	2¾
Minterne	Minterne Parva	ST/664034	1.	9.	2
Cnolle	Knoll	ST/702048		17.	4
Wottone	Glanvilles Wootton	ST/680082	2.	4.	9
Dountisch'	Duntish	ST/694063	1.	14.	3½
Westpulham	West Pulham	ST/712085	2.	1.	2½
Estpulham	East Pulham	ST/725095	1.	4.	9
Mapoudre	Mappowder	ST/735060	3.	11.	6½
			29.	13.	1¼

Hd. Sexpenne et Henle [SIXPENNY HANDLEY HUNDRED]

Henlegh'	Sixpenny Handley	ST/996173	8.	7.	4¾
Melebury & Comptone	Melbury Abbas and Compton Abbas	ST/882201 ST/869183	7.	8.	3¾
Fontemel	Fontmell Magna	ST/865170	5.	17.	0¼
Ywerne	Iwerne Minster	ST/868145	6.	7.	4¼
			28.	0.	1

Hd. Broneshulle [BROWNSHALL HUNDRED]

Stapelbrigg'	Stalbridge	ST/736176	2.	10.	0
Westone	Stalbridge Weston	ST/720166	1.	15.	0
Caundel Haddone	Stourton Caundle	ST/714152	1.	18.	0
Candel Wak	Caundle Wake	ST/700126		18.	0
Woderewe	Woodrow[1]	ST/698142		18.	7
Thornhulle	Thornhill	ST/740149		19.	0
Gomeresheie	Gummershay	ST/759180	1.	3.	0
Stok'	Stoke Gaylard	ST/722130		15.	0
			10.	16.	7

[1] Grid ref. is to Higher Woodrow Farm.

Hd. Roubergh' [ROWBARROW HUNDRED]

Stondlond	Studland	SZ/034824		12.	0
Whiteclive	Whitecliff	SZ/030807		6.	0
Swanewich'	Swanage	SZ/028788		15.	0
Herstone	Herston	SZ/018788		14.	0
Worthe	Worth Matravers	SY/973774	1.	2.	0
Remmescumbe	Renscombe	SY/965776	1.	10.	3
Kyngestone	Kingston	SY/956795		4.	0
Alfryngtone	Afflington	SY/970801		13.	0
Ore	Ower	SY/998855		3.	0
Rodlyngtone	Rollington	SY/969827	1.	7.	5
			7.	6.	8

Hd. Craneborne [CRANBORNE HUNDRED]

Craneborn'	Cranborne	SU/054132	3.	8.	3
Holewell	Holewell[1]	SU/061131			
Alreholte	Alderholt	SU/122126			
Penterch'	Pentridge	SU/033178	2.	3.	4
Russcheton'	Tarrant Rushton	ST/938059	1.	13.	4
Edmundesham	Edmondsham	SU/061116	1.	10.	4
Boveryng'	Boveridge	SU/064150	2.	5.	6
Perle	West Parley	SZ/087968	2.	0.	8
Wymborne Abbatis	Monkton Up Wimborne	SU/018136	1.	0.	4
Aschemere	Ashmore	ST/912178	1.	19.	10
Wychamptone	Witchampton	ST/989064	1.	18.	8
Tarente Goundevile	Tarrant Gunville	ST/925127	3.	17.	8
Piterichsham	Petersham	SU/021043	1.	11.	0
Tarente Moneketone	Tarrant Monkton	ST/943088	1.	12.	0
Bakebere	Bagber[2]	ST/767157	1.	8.	0
Hamme prestone	Hampreston	SZ/055988	3.	11.	2
Chotul	Chettle	ST/952133	1.	11.	0
Fernham	Farnham	ST/958151	2.	1.	4
Ocford Skilling'	Shillingstone	ST/824114	2.	18.	7
Fifhide	Fifehead St. Quintin	ST/773104	2.	17.	7
			39.	8.	7

Hd. Pymperne [PIMPERNE HUNDRED]

Haselbere	Hazelbury Bryan	ST/743084	4.	1.	5
Fifhude	Fifehead Neville	ST/769110	3.	14.	0
Hamme Mohun	Hammoon	ST/816151	2.	19.	4
Hoghetone	Winterborne Houghton	ST/820043	3.	4.	0
Stikelane	Winterborne Stickland	ST/834046	1.	6.	2
Quarelestone	Quarleston	ST/859057		14.	10
Turneworthe	Turnworth	ST/821075	1.	6.	10
Brianestone	Bryanstone	ST/874070	1.	10.	6
Knyttghetone	Knighton	ST/859081	1.	8.	4
Durewynestone	Durweston	ST/859085	1.	0.	8
Langetone Guldene[3]	Langton Long Blandford	ST/898059		10.	8
Langetone Boteler[3]	Langton Long Blandford	ST/898059	1.	9.	10

---

[1] Grid ref. is to Little Holwell Farm.   [2] Grid ref. is to Lower Bagber Farm.
[3] Separate manors within Langton Long Blandford.

Stoure payn	Stourpaine	ST/861093	1.	4.	2
Assh' &	Ash and	ST/863102	1.	6.	8
Laston'	Lazerton	ST/864106			
Stupeltone	Steepleton Iwerne	ST/862112	1.	10.	4
Prestone	Preston	ST/938050		5.	2
Caynestone	Tarrant Keyneston	ST/924041	1.	12.	8
Antioch'	Tarrant Rawston	ST/939067		5.	8
Lowynston'	Tarrant Launceston	ST/942096	1.	13.	8
Hyneton' Goundevile	Tarrant Hinton	ST/937112	2.	18.	1
Pymperne	Pimperne	ST/903093	3.	17.	10
			38.	0.	10

Hd. Tolreforde [TOLLERFORD HUNDRED]

Wymfred	Wynford Eagle	SY/584959	3.	0.	0
Crockestone	Cruxton	SY/603964	1.	3.	3
Frome Voghechurch'	Frome Vauchurch	SY/596969		17.	4
Litelfrome	Frome St. Quintin	ST/598026	1.	16.	4
Melebury	Melbury Sampford	ST/577060		17.	6
Childefrome	Chilfrome	SY/590988		16.	10
Tolre	Toller Porcorum	SY/561980	3.	5.	4
Ramesham	Rampisham	ST/561022	2.	2.	8
Chaubergh'	Chelborough[1]	ST/542054	1.	16.	3
Niwetone	Maiden Newton	SY/596978	6.	11.	5
			22.	6.	10[2]

Lib. Frompton' [FRAMPTON LIBERTY][3]

Fromptone	Frampton	SY/627950	3.	4.	9
Bruttone[4]	Burton Bradstock	SY/489895	1.	6.	10
Compton'	Compton Valence	SY/592932	3.	9.	9
Byncomb'	Bincombe	SY/686845	1.	19.	5¼
Bettescomb'	Bettiscombe	SY/399999	1.	7.	6
			11.	8.	3¼

Hd. Haselore & Russhmor
[HASLER AND RUSHMORE HUNDREDS]

Povyntone	Povington	SY/883821	1.	1.	0
Enecomb'	Encombe	SY/944786		4.	8
Bradele	Bradle	SY/930806		11.	4
Knolle	Church Knowle	SY/941819	1.	7.	0
Eglynstone	Egliston[5]	SY/893808		14.	4
Langgetone	Langton Matravers	SY/998789	1.	16.	4
Estynham	Tyneham [East][6]	SY/889801		9.	4
Westynham	Tyneham [West][6]	SY/881803		10.	8

---

[1] Grid ref. is to West Chelborough.

[2] The quotas for this hundred in fact add up to £22. 6. 11.

[3] Frampton was a liberty with scattered parts (Fagersten, op. cit. 187).

[4] Part of Burton Bradstock was taxed in Godderthorn hundred.

[5] Grid ref. is to North Egliston.

[6] East and West Tyneham do not appear on modern maps. The grid ref. given for East Tyneham is Tyneham House, and for West Tyneham, Church Tyneham.

Crich'	Creech	SY/911824		9.	4
Blachenwell'	Blashenwell	SY/951803		15.	8
Arn'	Arne	SY/973881		11.	0
Holne	Holme[1]	SY/898860		14.	8
Kymerich'	Kimmeridge	SY/918799		19.	4
Wynterborne	Winterborne Zelston	SY/899978	1.	0.	8
Mordone	Morden [West]	SU/903954	1.	11.	2
			12.	16.	6

Hd. Uggescomb' [UGGESCOMBE HUNDRED]

Abbodesbury	Abbotsbury	SY/578852	4.	8.	$6\frac{1}{4}$
Fynle[2]	?		1.	16.	$5\frac{1}{2}$
Portesham	Portesham	SY/602858	5.	3.	
Raddone	Rodden	SY/611840		19.	4
Shulfhampton'	Shilvinghampton[3]	SY/629844		13.	5
Litelbridie	Littlebredy	SY/588890	2.	10.	$10\frac{1}{4}$
Wynterborne Stupeltone	Winterbourne Steepleton	SY/629898	3.	12.	1
Langgetone	Langton Herring	SY/614824		15.	5
Flete	Fleet[4]	SY/636802	1.	1.	$4\frac{1}{2}$
Corstone	Corton	SY/636854	1.	5.	$9\frac{1}{2}$
Luttone	Litton Cheney	SY/551908	2.	14.	$4\frac{3}{4}$
Pomeknolle	Puncknowle	SY/535886		13.	$2\frac{1}{2}$
Swere	Swyre	SY/528882	1.	3.	$11\frac{1}{4}$
			26.	18.	$5\frac{1}{2}$

Hd. Baddebury [BADBURY HUNDRED]

Kyngestone[5]	Kingston Lacy	ST/978013	10.	8.	10
Bernardesle	Barnsley	ST/996036	1.	14.	10
Prestone	?		2.	0.	10
Kirchel	Moor Crichel	ST/993086	2.	3.	4
Shapewyk'	Shapwick	ST/936017	7.	0.	4
Legh'	Leigh	SZ/024998	4.	19.	9
Dudelyngton'	Didlington	SU/006077	1.	5.	6
Hortone	Horton	SU/030074	2.	14.	0
Gussich'	Gussage St. Michael	ST/986113	5.	5.	4
Wymborne	Wimborne Minster	SZ/009999	4.	9.	8
Hynetone	Hinton[6]	SU/014062	2.	11.	6
			44.	13.	11

Insula de Portlonde [A.D]	Isle of Portland		5.	19.	0	[T]
Wyke &	Wyke Regis and	SY/661779	6.	4.	10	[T]
Helewell' [A.D]	Elwell	SY/669849				
Waymuth' [A.D]	Weymouth	SY/680795	6.	10.	0	[T]

---

[1] Grid ref. is to East Holme.

[2] Identified as a member of Abbotsbury in *F.A.* ii. 5, but not located. Another possible identification is Phillyholme in Hawkchurch, now in Devon.

[3] Grid ref. is to West Shilvinghampton.

[4] Grid ref. is to East Fleet.

[5] It is probable that this entry covers part of Blandford, as Blandford appears with Kingston in aids of 1303 and 1346, *F.A.* ii. 32 and 51.

[6] Grid ref. is to Hinton Martell.

Warham [A.D]	Wareham	SY/923875	6.	7.	0	[T]
Brudeport [B]	Bridport	SY/466928	9.	19.	5	[T]
Melecombe [A.D]	Melcombe Regis	SY/682802	9.	10.	0	[T]
Lym [B]	Lyme Regis	SY/343922	8.	10.	0	[T]
Blaneford [A.D]	Blandford Forum	ST/886063	2.	3.	0	[T]
Corfe Castel [A.D]	Corfe Castle	SY/961820	2.	3.	0	[T]
			57.	6.	3	[T]

TOTAL: £851. 9. 0½[1]

[1] As on 1334 Account, E 179/103/9.

ESSEX

DOCUMENTS

8 Edward III: Account   E 179/107/19
8 Edward III: Particulars E 179/107/18 (imperfect)
11 Edward III: Particulars E 179/107/26*
22 Edward III: Particulars E 179/107/38
22 Edward III: Particulars E 179/107/39

TAXERS

The abbot of Walden and John de Marton

TAX YIELD

15th	£1,185.	17.	0¼
10th	£ 48.	17.	7½
	£1,234.	14.	7¾

Representing assessed movable wealth of

£18,276. 11. 6¾

NOTES

The Essex taxers seem to have been more meticulous than most in that very few of the tax quotas are rounded off; a large number even end in farthings. They were also careful to distinguish many places which have the same second place-name, for example, the nine Rodings, the three Tolleshunts, and the four Colnes. Fourteen places are specifically described as hamlets.

The tax yielded at a tenth is surprisingly low for a county of this size, but this is partly because only three places were taxed at the higher rate. They are Colchester, the only town regarded as a taxation borough consistently throughout the early fourteenth century, and the ancient demesnes of Newport (which was considered a borough in the subsidy of 1306) and Havering atte Bower.

Only in the north does the outline of the 1334 county differ from that of the nineteenth century. Six places that were taxed in Essex have since been transferred to adjacent counties; Great and Little Chishill, and Heydon to Cambridgeshire; Ballingdon, Brundon, and part of Sudbury to Suffolk. Bures, which straddles the Essex–Suffolk boundary, was partly taxed in both counties.

REFERENCE

M. W. Beresford, 'Analysis of some medieval tax assessments, Ongar hundred', in *V.C.H., Essex*, iv (1956), 296–302.

Hd. Hengford [HINCKFORD HUNDRED]

Fynchyngfeld	Finchingfield	TL/686327	9.	11.	4¾
Wetheresfeld	Wethersfield	TL/712312	6.	3.	5½
Stepilbumstede	Steeple Bumpstead	TL/679411	6.	3.	7¾
Stamburne	Stambourne	TL/721389	3.	4.	3¾
Sturmere	Sturmer	TL/690439	3.	17.	0½
Hengham Sibille	Sible Hedingham	TL/776343	7.	12.	0
Topesfeld	Toppesfield	TL/779374	5.	12.	6
Foxhorde	Foxearth	TL/836447	2.	19.	3¾
Pentelowe	Pentlow	TL/813462	3.	2.	2
Listone	Liston	TL/853448	1.	11.	9¼
Beauchamp William	Belchamp Walter	TL/828408	3.	3.	1¾
Beauchamp Otes	Belchamp Otten	TL/803417	2.	19.	5
Borle	Borley	TL/848431		16.	0¾
Beauchamp Pauli'	Belchamp St. Paul	TL/798435	3.	15.	0
Tillebury	Tilbury juxta Clare	TL/759403	1.	13.	9¾
Ovytone	Ovington	TL/763426	1.	2.	6
Asshe	Ashen	TL/747422	2.	4.	6
Rediswelle	Ridgewell	TL/740409	3.	6.	4½
Briddebrok	Birdbrook	TL/707412	4.	13.	11
Gelham Magna	Great Yeldham	TL/758387	4.	0.	4½
Gelham Parva	Little Yeldham	TL/779395	2.	4.	1½
Hegham ad Castru'	Castle Hedingham	TL/785355	4.	8.	2
Bulmer	Bulmer	TL/843401	6.	9.	8½
Broumdon' &	Brundon and	TL/864421	2.	19.	3
Balidon' &	Ballingdon and	TL/863407			
Sudby' int'	Sudbury [between the	TL/871412			
pontes[1]	bridges] [all in Suffolk]				
Henye Magna	Great Henny and	TL/868378	2.	4.	8¼
& Parva	Little Henny	TL/859385			
Bockyngg'	Bocking	TL/761242	5.	3.	11¼
Mapeldestede Magna	Great Maplestead	TL/808345	3.	17.	3½
Mapeldestede Parva	Little Maplestead	TL/822340	1.	17.	1¼
Stistede	Stisted	TL/798246	3.	5.	5¾
Felstede	Felsted	TL/676203	5.	7.	1¼
Reynes Magna	Braintree	TL/756232	6.	3.	1
Reynes Parva	Rayne	TL/732229	1.	14.	10½
Cosfeld	Gosfield	TL/778294	3.	14.	11½
Pantfeld	Panfield	TL/738254	1.	6.	10
Salyng'	Great Saling	TL/699259	1.	2.	5
Schaldeford	Shalford	TL/723292	2.	14.	9
Stebbyngg'	Stebbing	TL/664240	7.	8.	7
Gestnyngthorp'	Gestingthorpe	TL/812385	4.	19.	9¾
Wykham Pauli'	Wickham St. Paul's	TL/827371	2.	7.	8¼
Pebennerssh'	Pebmarsh	TL/854335	3.	7.	8½
Lammersh'	Lamarsh	TL/890361	1.	18.	7¾
Alfamston' &	Alphamstone and	TL/879354	3.	8.	2½
Bures	Bures[2]	TL/905340			
Twynsted	Twinstead	TL/861366	1.	4.	1
Halsted	Halstead	TL/815306	9.	8.	5
Middelton'	Middleton	TL/871397	1.	0.	9¾
			167.	10.	5¼

[1] Most of Sudbury was taxed in Suffolk (Babergh hundred, p. 291).

[2] Bures straddles the county boundary. The part of Bures east of the Stour was taxed in Suffolk (Babergh hundred, p. 290).

Hd. Rochesford [ROCHFORD HUNDRED]

Wakeryngg' Magna & Parva	Great Wakering and Little Wakering	TQ/950875 TQ/934883	8.	1.	10½
Rochesford	Rochford	TQ/872903	3.	15.	2
Canewedon'	Canewdon	TQ/896945	6.	15.	6½
Hakewelle	Hawkwell	TQ/860919	2.	18.	10½
Fambreg' & Assyngdone	South Fambridge and Ashingdon	TQ/862950 TQ/866936			
Hockele	Hockley	TQ/826933	4.	8.	2¾
Schopelond	Shopland	TQ/899883	3.	6.	7¼
Barlyng'	Barling	TQ/932898	2.	0.	0
Pakelesham	Paglesham	TQ/926931	2.	16.	6½
Suthcherch' & Thorp'	Southchurch and Littlethorpe	TQ/902861 TQ/916851	3.	0.	6¼
Schobury' Parva	North Shoebury	TQ/929861	3.	9.	2¾
Schobury' Magna	South Shoebury	TQ/931849	3.	7.	11¾
Stanbregg' Magna	Great Stambridge	TQ/899918	4.	7.	4
Pritelwelle & Middelton'	Prittlewell and Milton[1]	TQ/877867 TQ/874859	10.	11.	9¾
Sutton'	Sutton	TQ/888892	2.	4.	9¾
Stambregg' Parva	Little Stambridge	TQ/888920	1.	6.	8½
Reyleghe	Rayleigh	TQ/809909	4.	17.	9
Raurethe	Rawreth	TQ/781934	3.	3.	11¾
Estwode	Eastwood	TQ/862889	2.	11.	1½
Leghe	Leigh	TQ/843861	2.	0.	3¾
Hadleghe cum tertia parte de Thunderle[2]	Hadleigh with Thundersley [a third part]	TQ/810870 TQ/782886	2.	8.	1
			77.	12.	5¾

Hd. Benkentre [BECONTREE HUNDRED]

Berkyngg'	Barking	TQ/442844	22.	15.	0¾	
Esthamme	East Ham	TQ/425835	9.	4.	10¼	
Westhamme	West Ham	TQ/394839	11.	1.	1¾	
Dakenham	Dagenham	TQ/500846	6.	9.	1¾	
Wodeford	Woodford	TQ/402918	1.	4.	2½	
Weltomstowe	Walthamstow	TQ/371892	3.	11.	11½	
Wansted & Illeford Parva	Wanstead and Little Ilford	TQ/404884 TQ/423844	1.	8.	11¼	
Leytone	Leyton	TQ/377868	1.	14.	11¾	
Haveryng' [A.D]	Havering atte Bower	TQ/512930	15.	19.	4	[T]
			73.	9.	7½	

Hd. Wensetre [WINSTREE HUNDRED]

Estmerseye	East Mersea	TM/051141	2.	6.	4¾
Westmerseye cum Fyngryngho	West Mersea with Fingringhoe	TM/009125 TM/030204	4.	8.	11¾
Peldon' & Adburghton'	Peldon and Abberton	TL/989168 TL/997194	2.	4.	7½
Wyggeberwe Magna & Parva	Great Wigborough and Little Wigborough	TL/968157 TL/981145	3.	2.	2

[1] The name Milton survives only in Milton Road and House in Southend.
[2] Most of Thundersley was taxed in Barstable hundred.

Leyre delhaye	Layer de la Haye	TL/965192	1.	12.	9¾
Leyre Bretonn cum	Layer Breton with	TL/945185	2.	6.	6
Saltecote	Salcott	TL/952136			
Virly[1]	Virley	TL/948138			
Leyre Marny	Layer Marny	TL/928174	1.	8.	7¼
Langenho	Langenhoe	TM/014174	2.	0.	1
			19.	10.	2

Hd. Dounmawe [DUNMOW HUNDRED]

Dounmawe Magna	Great Dunmow	TL/629230	7.	1.	9¾
Alta Estre	High Easter	TL/620148	3.	5.	4½
Plesset'	Pleshey	TL/663143		17.	7¾
Rothyngg' Berners	Berners Roding	TL/602099	2.	0.	1
Masshebury'	Mashbury	TL/652118	1.	1.	5¼
Berneston'	Barnston	TL/652196	1.	12.	0
Dunmawe Parva	Little Dunmow	TL/656212	1.	12.	2
Eystanes Magna	Great Easton	TL/607254	3.	4.	8¾
Lyndesele	Lindsell	TL/643271	1.	16.	0½
Rothyng' Aytrop	Aythorpe Roding	TL/584153	1.	14.	0¼
Rothyng' Margrete cum	Margaret Roding with	TL/599120	1.	9.	11½
feodo Marcy	the fee of Marcy (Marks Hall)	TL/600113			
Rothyng' Alba	White Roding	TL/562133	1.	12.	5
Rothyng' Plumbi'	Leaden Roding	TL/590132	1.	0.	5¼
Brockesheued	Broxted	TL/578274	2.	19.	6¾
Chaurethe	Chaureth	TL/580281	1.	17.	4¾
Thaxstede	Thaxted	TL/610310	8.	7.	11¾
Chegeneye	Chickney	TL/574280	1.	5.	6
Canefeld Magna	Great Canfield	TL/594180	2.	7.	4½
Canefeld Parva	Little Canfield	TL/587209	2.	14.	10
Schelewe Jocelyn &	Shellow Jocelyn	TL/600083	2.	3.	9½
Boweles	[Torrells Hall][2] and Shellow Bowells	TL/607079			
Willynghale Spaygne	Willingale Spain	TL/596073	4.	6.	3½
Rokele cum	Willingale Doe with	TL/596074			
Plessyngho [h]	Plesingho[3]	lost			
Alta Rothyng'	High Roding	TL/603173	2.	4.	2
Godythestre	Good Easter	TL/626120	1.	15.	7¾
Eystanes Parva	Little Easton	TL/604235	2.	0.	2
			60.	10.	10

Hd. Angre [ONGAR HUNDRED][4]

Nastoke	Navestock	TQ/541984	6.	12.	3¼
Lamburne	Lambourne	TQ/479961	2.	17.	0¼
Theydene Boys	Theydon Bois	TQ/448992	1.	19.	4
Theydene ad Monte'	Theydon Mount	TQ/492992	1.	13.	11

[1] It is probable that the entry refers to the separate settlements of Salcott and Virley although Virley alone was once called *Salcote Verly* (*E.P.N.S., XII, Essex* (1935), 323).

[2] For identification see J. H. Round, 'Shellow Bowells and Torrells Hall', *Essex Arch. Trans.*, n.s., xxi (1937), 25–8.

[3] For suggestions as to possible location see *E.P.N.S., XII, Essex* (1935), 501.

[4] 1334 figures for Ongar hundred are printed in *V.C.H., Essex*, iv (1956), 296–302; (M. W. Beresford, 'Analysis of some medieval tax assessments').

Theydene Gernonn	Theydon Garnon	TQ/472994	2.	15.	3¼
Loketon'	Loughton	TQ/429970	1.	11.	10½
Stapelford Tany	Stapleford Tawney	TQ/502991	1.	16.	0¾
Stapelford Abbatis'	Stapleford Abbotts	TQ/501961	2.	4.	2
Chigewelle cum Wlfamton [h]	Chigwell with Woolston	TQ/441938 TQ/449957	4.	17.	0
Laufare Alta	High Laver	TL/528087	3.	12.	11½
Laufare Maddaleyne	Magdalen Laver	TL/513083	2.	1.	10
Rothyng' Beauchamp'	Beauchamp Roding	TL/578097	1.	11.	3¾
Bobbyngworth'	Bobbingworth	TL/534056	2.	4.	5½
Stanford Ryvers	Stanford Rivers	TL/534009	7.	1.	11
Alta Anngre & Passefeld	High Ongar and Paslow	TL/565038	2.	13.	7
Rothyng' Abbesse & Morel	Abbess Roding & Morell Roding[1]	TL/572114 lost	1.	16.	10¼
Laufaure Parva	Little Laver	TL/545096	2.	8.	8¾
Staundon'	Stondon Massey	TL/572017		17.	3
Welde Basset	North Weald Bassett	TL/497041	2.	2.	7¼
Morton'	Moreton	TL/538070	2.	13.	9
Schelleghe	Shelley	TL/554051		16.	10¾
Fyfhiddes	Fyfield	TL/572068	4.	6.	1½
Northtone Mandeville & Parva Northton'[2]	Norton Mandeville ?	TL/579046	1.	12.	6
Kellewedon'	Kelvedon Hatch	TQ/569990	1.	8.	4
Anngre ad Castru'	Chipping Ongar	TL/553029	2.	10.	2¾
			66.	6.	3

Hd. Thurstapl' [THURSTABLE HUNDRED]

Hebregg'	Heybridge	TL/859079	2.	3.	9
Wykham Epi'	Wickham Bishops	TL/837121	1.	8.	8
Langeford	Langford	TL/837090	1.	9.	0
Totham Magna	Great Totham	TL/862110	3.	5.	6½
Tollesby'	Tollesbury	TL/956103	3.	0.	2¼
Toleshunte Mauger	Tolleshunt Major	TL/909111	1.	0.	9
Toleshunte Chyvaller	Tolleshunt Knights	TL/920144		16.	7¾
Toleshunte Tregorz'	Tolleshunt D'Arcy	TL/929117	2.	6.	11¾
Totham Parva	Little Totham	TL/884103	2.	19.	5½
			18.	10.	11¾

Hd. Waltham [WALTHAM HUNDRED]

Waltham Sancte Crucis	Waltham Holy Cross	TL/381006	17.	9.	8¾
Eppynge	Epping	TL/459021	4.	6.	9¾
Nasyngg'	Nazeing	TL/413070	2.	19.	8¼
Chynggeford	Chingford	TQ/385944	2.	19.	10
Reydon'	Reydon Hamlet	TL/423071	1.	18.	4
			29.	14.	4¾

[1] The nearest grid ref. would be Cammass Hall (TL/565153) which was in Morrell Roding.

[2] This may refer to either Forest Hall or Newarks Norton; see V.C.H., Essex, iv (1956), 150 f.

Hd. Danseye [DENGIE HUNDRED]

Danseye	Dengie	TL/989016	3.	17.	9
Suthmenstre[1]	Southminster	TQ/958996	6.	1.	6
Maldone Magna & Parva	Maldon Magna and Parva	TL/856067 TL/840076	9.	6.	11¼
Burnham	Burnham on Crouch	TQ/949970	3.	5.	2¾
Wodeham Water	Woodham Walter	TL/809068	1.	14.	8
Middelmad [h]	Bassetts	TL/787087		18.	5¼
Steple	Steeple	TL/934030	2.	5.	5¾
Purle	Purleigh	TL/842020	4.	8.	0
Mounden'	Mundon	TL/880026	1.	10.	1½
Lallyng'	Lawling	TL/900014	4.	7.	11
Lachedon' cum	Latchingdon	TL/886004			
Dawenerys [h][2]	?				
& Hoo [h][3]	?				
Bradewelle	Bradwell on Sea	TM/004069	4.	1.	5¾
Tillyngham	Tillingham	TL/993038	4.	19.	1½
Asschildham	Asheldham	TL/979013	2.	7.	1
Sancto' Laurencio	St. Lawrence	TL/967043	2.	12.	3¼
Stowe	Stow Maries	TQ/833993	2.	7.	4½
Northtone	Cold Norton	TL/845004	2.	5.	8½
Wodeham Mortymer	Woodham Mortimer	TL/823052	2.	10.	8¾
Fambrege Parva cum Stodleghe [h]	North Fambridge ?	TQ/850971	1.	19.	4
			60.	19.	1¾

Hd. Wyham [WITHAM HUNDRED]

Wytham	Witham	TL/822144	7.	17.	7½
Terlyng'	Terling	TL/773148	3.	10.	4½
Rewenhale	Rivenhall	TL/828178	4.	19.	1¾
Kersyngge	Cressing	TL/795203	3.	4.	7¼
Nottele Alba	White Notley	TL/786183	3.	7.	7¾
Nottele Nigra	Black Notley	TL/761207	4.	3.	3½
Fairstede	Fairstead	TL/768167	3.	16.	9
Chateleghe	Chatley	TL/730176	2.	13.	1¼
Kellevedene	Kelvedon	TL/856185	3.	6.	10
Braxstede Magna	Great Braxted	TL/851154	2.	10.	4
Braxstede Parva	Little Braxted	TL/835147		14.	3¾
Bradewelle	Bradwell	TL/818231	2.	5.	6½
Coggeshale Parva	Coggeshall Hamlet	TL/851216	1.	1.	1
Falkeburne	Faulkbourne	TL/800165	1.	12.	7¾
Ultyngge	Ulting	TL/802088		12.	8
Hatfeld Peverel	Hatfield Peverel	TL/789117	5.	3.	6¾
			50.	19.	6¼

Hd. Claveryngge [CLAVERING HUNDRED]

Claveryng'	Clavering	TL/471319	5.	6.	7¼
Berdene	Berden	TL/468296	2.	10.	5
Bentfeld & Plecheden	Bentfield and Pledgdon	TL/502256 TL/552273	2.	3.	2¾

[1] Mayland, Althorne, and Creeksea are included in this entry on E 179/107/39.

[2] *Dawenerys* seems to refer to the forest of Danegris: *E.P.N.S., XII, Essex* (1935), 249.

[3] Probably Howe Green in Purleigh parish, ibid. 223.

Uggelee	Ugley	TL/519288	2.	4.	0
Farnham	Farnham	TL/482248	2.	4.	0¾
Manewedene	Manuden	TL/491266	3.	9.	9¾
			17.	18.	1½

Hd. Chelmersford [CHELMSFORD HUNDRED]

Retyngdone	Rettendon	TQ/764982	3.	4.	0¾
Gynge Mounteny	Mountnessing	TQ/648966	6.	11.	9
Bromfeld	Broomfield	TL/705105	3.	9.	7
Borham	Boreham	TL/756096	4.	5.	5
Waltham Magna	Great Waltham	TL/695135	9.	18.	2¼
Gynge Joyberd & Laundri'[1]	Gyng Joyberd (Great Blunts) and Gyng Laundri (Little Blunts)	TQ/683971 TQ/671971	4.	0.	2½
Wodeham Ferrers	Woodham Ferrers	TQ/798994	4.	7.	4
Gynge Abbesse	Ingatestone	TQ/651996	3.	1.	9½
Gynge Hospital	Fryerning	TL/639001	3.	10.	7¾
Leghes Magna & Parva	Great Leighs and Little Leighs	TL/739155 TL/719168	3.	6.	9½
Fyngrethe	Fingreth	TL/609036	4.	14.	2
Gynge Margrete	Margaretting	TL/671017	2.	5.	1
Coppefold	Coptfold	TL/659030	1.	12.	2½
Waltham Parva	Little Waltham	TL/712127	2.	12.	8¼
Spryngefeld	Springfield	TL/719080	3.	11.	4¼
Writele	Writtle	TL/677062	17.	15.	6
Wydeford	Widford	TL/693051	1.	16.	9¾
Mulsham [h]	Moulsham	TL/703048	4.	11.	10½
Sandone	Sandon	TL/742048	3.	3.	6½
Hanyngfeld Est West & Suth	East Hanningfield West Hanningfield South Hanningfield	TL/771012 TQ/734998 TQ/744980	11.	7.	0
Badewe Parva	Little Baddow	TL/764081	2.	15.	4
Chelmersford	Chelmsford	TL/708069	4.	12.	1½
Danyngbury	Danbury	TL/779051	2.	18.	9½
Ronewelle	Runwell	TQ/764944	1.	18.	3
Newelonde [h]	Newland	TL/635096	1.	3.	6¼
Badewe Magna	Great Baddow	TL/729049	4.	1.	4¼
Chygenhale Seyn Tany Trenchefoil	Chignall St. James Chignall Smealy	TL/669097 TL/668116	3.	10.	5½
			120.	5.	10

Hd. Berdestaple [BARSTABLE HUNDRED]

Dountone	Dunton	TQ/653883	2.	15.	0
Bures Giffard	Bowers Gifford	TQ/756873	2.	1.	7¾
Langedone	Langdon	TQ/673864	1.	11.	3½
Estle & Westle	East Lee and West Lee	lost TQ/693876			
Horndone	Horndon on the Hill	TQ/669833	4.	14.	4¾
Coryngham	Corringham	TQ/710833	1.	11.	3¾

[1] These two manors, later called Great and Little Blunts (both held by the Le Blound family), now seem to be represented by Buttsbury. For identification see note by J. H. Round in *Essex Arch. Trans.*, n.s., xix (1930), 51.

[Est][1] Horndone Magna	East Horndon	TQ/636894		15.	2
Dounham	Downham	TQ/730953	2.	7.	10
Stanford	Stanford le Hope	TQ/684823	3.	7.	10
Burstede Magna	Great Burstead	TQ/681923	2.	13.	2
[West][2] Horndene Parva	West Horndon	TQ/618918	2.	1.	11¾
Ramesdene Belhus	Ramsden Bellhouse	TQ/719943	2.	14.	8¾
Pytheseye	Pitsea	TQ/738877		19.	7¾
Muckyng'	Mucking	TQ/685812	3.	10.	0¾
Esttillebury	East Tilbury	TQ/689769	4.	0.	9¾
Westillebury	West Tilbury	TQ/662776	2.	4.	5¾
Orsete	Orsett	TQ/644820	5.	1.	0¼
Bemflete Parva	North Benfleet	TQ/762900		14.	11¼
Chaldewelle	Chadwell St. Mary	TQ/646785	4.	18.	5¾
Thurrok' Parva	Little Thurrock	TQ/626778			
Wykford	Wickford	TQ/746931	2.	11.	3¾
Thunderle[3]	Thundersley	TQ/782886	1.	8.	1
Bolefanne	Bulphan	TQ/636859	2.	13.	2½
Schenefeld	Shenfield	TQ/605951	3.	2.	8¾
Dodyngherst	Doddinghurst	TQ/589990	2.	12.	11¾
Ramesdene Creye	Ramsden Crays	TQ/708933	1.	6.	5
Leyndon' & Bartlesdone	Laindon and Basildon	TQ/688895 TQ/714899	2.	9.	6
Fobbyngg'	Fobbing	TQ/718839	4.	5.	0½
Nevendene	Nevendon	TQ/733907		17.	9
Gynge Rauf'	Ingrave	TQ/623920	1.	14.	2¾
Burstede Parva	Little Burstead	TQ/668916	1.	11.	3½
Fange	Vange	TQ/715867	1.	14.	7¼
Hotone	Hutton	TQ/635943	1.	4.	3¾
Bemflete Magna	South Benfleet	TQ/778862	4.	9.	10
			80.	5.	1

Hd. Huddelesford & Froyshwelle

[UTTLESFORD AND FRESHWELL HUNDRED]

Takeleghe	Takeley	TL/555216	4.	8.	8¾
Stanstede Mounfichet	Stansted Mountfitchet	TL/512250	2.	13.	6¼
Bilchangre	Birchanger	TL/507227		11.	2¾
Elsenham	Elsenham	TL/542259	2.	18.	1¾
Henham	Henham	TL/544285	3.	1.	11¾
Wyditone	Widdington	TL/540318	3.	9.	10½
Wymbyssh	Wimbish	TL/590367	3.	8.	10¾
Thunderle	Thunderley	TL/561361		12.	3¾
Waldene	Saffron Walden	TL/537386	4.	14.	8¼
Chestreford Magna	Great Chesterford	TL/505427	2.	18.	1½
Chestreford Parva	Little Chesterford	TL/515417	1.	14.	2
Samford Magna	Great Sampford	TL/642353	3.	8.	9½
Sampford Parva	Little Sampford	TL/653337	2.	15.	5¾
Depedene & Amberdene	Debden and Amberden	TL/551332 TL/555306	3.	13.	6
Litlebury & Strathale	Littlebury and Strethall	TL/517395 TL/485398	2.	7.	0
Haddestoke	Hadstock	TL/558448	2.	0.	9
Bumstede Helionn	Helions Bumpstead	TL/652416	3.	4.	3½

1 Added later to distinguish from West Horndon.

2 Added later to distinguish from East Horndon, above. Grid ref. is to Thorndon Hall.

3 See also Rochford hundred.

Wendene Magna & Parva	Wenden Magna and Parva [now Wendens Ambo][1]	TL/513363	3.	13.	8
Hamstede	Hempstead	TL/634380	2.	19.	0¾
Quendene	Quendon	TL/516306		15.	1
Ryklyng'	Rickling	TL/498315	2.	0.	6¾
Arkisdene	Arkesden	TL/482346	2.	6.	1¾
Crishale	Chrishall	TL/452386	2.	15.	4½
Elmedone	Elmdon	TL/462397	2.	13.	7½
Wykes	Wicken Bonhunt	TL/499333	1.	13.	6¼
Wendene Louth	Wenden Lofts	TL/464387	1.	12.	7
Asshedone	Ashdon	TL/581415	4.	5.	2¼
Heydene	Heydon [in Cambs.]	TL/433400	1.	19.	7¼
Radewyntir'	Radwinter	TL/606372	2.	17.	5½
Berdefeld Magna	Great Bardfield	TL/678303	4.	14.	3
Berdefeld Parva	Little Bardfield	TL/655308	2.	1.	5¾
Chyshulle Magna	Great Chishill [in Cambs.]	TL/422388	3.	14.	3¼
Chyshelle Parva	Little Chishill [in Cambs.]	TL/418373	3.	4.	11¼
Neuport [A.D]	Newport	TL/521341	6.	15.	6½ [T]
			98.	3.	10½

Hd. Chafford [CHAFFORD HUNDRED]

Aluythele	Aveley	TQ/568802	6.	5.	2
Suthwelde cum bosco arso	Southweald with Brentwood	TQ/571939 TQ/597937	7.	16.	3½
Wokyngdon' Epi'	Cranham	TQ/572862	2.	4.	5¼
Thurrok' Grey	Grays Thurrock	TQ/613777	4.	10.	0
Thurrock' West	West Thurrock	TQ/593773	6.	4.	0
Stifford	Stifford	TQ/604803	2.	5.	0
Reynham	Rainham	TQ/521822	9.	3.	0
Wokyndone Septfontayene	North Ockendon	TQ/588848	4.	17.	11¾
Wokyndone Rokele	South Ockendon	TQ/595829	4.	15.	11¾
Wenytone	Wennington	TQ/540810	1.	11.	4¾
Warle Abbesse & Semely	Great Warley and Little Warley	TQ/597884 TQ/604887	3.	5.	3
Chilterdych'	Childerditch	TQ/613893	1.	1.	4
Upmenstre	Upminster	TQ/559865	4.	3.	0
			58.	2.	10

Hd. Lexedene [LEXDEN HUNDRED]

Dedham	Dedham	TM/059332	4.	6.	7
Langham	Langham	TM/034336	4.	3.	9
Boxsted	Boxted	TL/998332	3.	12.	11½
Wyvenho	Wivenhoe	TM/039215	1.	6.	8
Estdonylond	East Donyland	TM/028209		15.	0
Horkesleghe Magna	Great Horkesley	TL/972324	3.	5.	3¾
Horkesleghe Parva	Little Horkesley	TL/961320	1.	16.	2¾
Bergholte	West Bergholt	TL/953281	1.	15.	10
Estthorp	Easthorpe	TL/912215	2.	16.	8
Briche Magna & Parva	Birch and Little Birch	TL/944199 TL/951209			

[1] *E.P.N.S., XII, Essex* (1935), 542. Wendens Ambo from the union of the two parishes of Magna and Parva in 1662.

Messyng' &	Messing and	TL/897189	3.	8.	11¼
Ineworth	Inworth	TL/879179			
Aldham	Aldham	TL/918258	2.	13.	9
Teye Mandeville	Marks Tey	TL/911239	2.	12.	6
Coggeshale cum	Coggeshall with	TL/850226	5.	17.	4¾
Marskeshale	Markshall	TL/840254			
Feryngg' cum	Ferring with	TL/872204	5.	13.	7¾
Patyswyk'	Pattiswick	TL/816240			
Colne Comitis	Earls Colne	TL/861289	4.	5.	5¼
Wythermondeford	Wormingford	TL/932323	2.	2.	5
Colne Parva	Colne Engaine	TL/850304	2.	10.	0¼
Colne Wake Qncy cum	Wakes Colne with	TL/889286	4.	0.	8¼
Creppyng' [h]	Crepping	TL/909284			
Staneweye	Stanway	TL/940243	3.	4.	8¾
Teye Magna	Great Tey	TL/892258	5.	11.	3¼
Fordham	Fordham	TL/928281	2.	15.	7
Bures ad monte'	Mount Bures	TL/905325	1.	4.	1½
Colne Alba	White Colne	TL/880299	1.	15.	1¼
Coppeford	Copford	TL/935337	2.	11.	6¾
Colecestre [B] cum	Colchester with	TL/998252	26.	2.	9 [T]
quatuor hamelettis	Lexden	TL/971251			
Lexedene Mileand	Mile End	TL/990275			
Grenstede &	Greenstead	TM/019250			
Westdonylond	Berechurch	TL/992219			
			100.	8.	11

Hd. Tendryng' [TENDRING HUNDRED]

Sancta' Ositha	St. Osyth	TM/122156	6.	13.	4¼
Holonde Parva	Little Holland	TM/208168	1.	9.	0¾
Ardeleghe	Ardleigh	TM/054295	4.	9.	11½
Claketon' Magna &	Great Clacton and	TM/177165	6.	10.	10¾
Parva	Little Clacton	TM/165188			
Okle Magna	Great Oakley	TM/188274	3.	5.	10½
Thorp'	Thorpe le Soken	TM/179223	2.	11.	4
Kirkeby	Kirby le Soken	TM/219220	2.	5.	8
Waltone	Walton on the Naze	TM/252216	1.	18.	0½
Misteleghe &	Mistley and	TM/114317	4.	1.	2
Manytre	Manningtree	TM/105318			
Tendryng'	Tendring	TM/143242	2.	6.	1
Fryntone	Frinton	TM/238197	1.	9.	2
Beaumond	Beaumont	TM/180246	1.	4.	7
Brithlyngseye	Brightlingsea	TM/087168	5.	6.	6¼
Fratyng'	Frating	TM/082223		12.	6¼
Bentleghe Parva	Little Bentley	TM/122250	2.	0.	0
Alesford	Alresford	TM/065206	1.	7.	8½
Wykes	Wix	TM/163290	2.	8.	0
Oklee Parva	Little Oakley	TM/218292	2.	10.	7
Thorytone	Thorrington	TM/098196	2.	4.	2¼
Bradefeld	Bradfield	TM/143308	2.	4.	3¾
Wrabenase	Wrabness	TM/181314	1.	6.	10½
Rameseye	Ramsey	TM/218304	3.	3.	1¾
Bromleghe Parva	Little Bromley	TM/091279	1.	19.	0¼
Bromleghe Magna	Great Bromley	TM/083263	3.	3.	5
Holonde Magna	Great Holland	TM/219193	2.	5.	10½
Moese	Moze	TM/200261	1.	19.	10¼
Lalleford	Lawford	TM/089315	2.	14.	6¾
Bentleghe Magna	Great Bentley	TM/109216	2.	10.	10½

Wyleghe	Weeley	TM/146223	1.	13.	0
Elmestede	Elmstead	TM/065260	3.	6.	0¾
Herewyk'	Harwich	TM/261326	4.	16.	8
Dovercourt	Dovercourt	TM/239311	3.	2.	3
			89.	0.	7½

Hd. Herlawe [HARLOW HUNDRED]

Hatfeld Regis	Hatfield Broad Oak	TL/547166	10.	12.	4¾
Herlawe	Harlow	TL/471115	5.	18.	6
Hallyngbury' Magna	Great Hallingbury	TL/511195	3.	12.	10
Hallyngbury' Parva	Little Hallingbury	TL/503174	2.	9.	9
Scherynge	Sheering	TL/508136	2.	18.	11½
Matchyngge	Matching	TL/525119	3.	13.	4¼
Lattone	Latton	TL/468095	2.	2.	6
Netleswelle	Netteswell	TL/457094	1.	9.	5
Parndon Magna &	Great Parndon and	TL/432089	2.	15.	4¼
Parva	Little Parndon	TL/439110			
Northwelde cum	North Weald[1]	TL/487048	3.	5.	1
Eppyng' [h][2]	with Epping				
Reyndone	Roydon	TL/408103	3.	0.	8
			41.	18.	9¾

TOTAL: £1,234. 14. 7¾[3]

[1] As Weald Bassett was taxed in Ongar hundred and North Weald in Harlow hundred, the two places seem to have been considered as separate. The modern map shows North Weald Bassett as one place.

[2] This is probably part of Epping (taxed in Waltham hundred) as Epping was partly in Waltham and partly in Harlow hundreds in Domesday Book (V.C.H., Essex, i (1903), 446, 472). Alternatively it could refer to either the original settlement of Epping, near Epping Upland church (E.P.N.S., XII, Essex (1935), 22), or to a separate hamlet.

[3] As on 1334 Account, E 179/107/19. The figures for the hundreds add up to £1234. 14. 7¼.

GLOUCESTERSHIRE

DOCUMENTS

8 Edward III: Account   E 179/113/6
8 Edward III: Particulars E 179/113/7 (imperfect)
10 Edward III: Particulars E 179/113/8 (imperfect)
18 Edward III: Particulars E 179/113/15*
24 Edward III: Account   E 179/113/20 (Bristol)

TAXERS

The abbot of Tewkesbury and Thomas de Evesham

TAX YIELD

15th £1,239. 1.   8
10th £ 181. 18. 10
      ───────────────
      £1,421. 0.   6

Representing assessed movable wealth of

£20,405. 13.   4

Bristol, £220. 0.   0 (in lieu of tenth),

Representing movable wealth of

£2,200. 0.   0

NOTES

The Gloucestershire rolls follow the usual pattern, with the places taxed at a tenth listed separately, in this case at the beginning. Only Gloucester was taxed as a borough; Cheltenham, Cirencester, Newnham, and Winchcombe, each of which had been considered a taxation borough on at least one occasion in the early fourteenth century (see Willard's list (1933), op. cit.), were still taxed at the higher rate but as ancient demesnes. Newent, a tax borough in 1313, was taxed at a fifteenth. Bristol fined for a sum of £220 in 1334 in lieu of the tenth (*C.C.R., 1333–1337*, 689) and is separately documented.

It was not until after the administrative reorganization of the nineteenth century that Gloucestershire took on its modern outline. Throughout the medieval period its boundary in the north-east was intermingled in a most complicated way with Warwickshire and Worcestershire (see C. S. Taylor, 'The northern boundary of Gloucestershire', *Trans. Bristol and Glos. Arch. Soc.* 32 (1909), 109–39). Consequently the Gloucestershire list includes twenty-nine places that have since been transferred to other counties, while twenty-seven places in the modern county are listed on the rolls of adjacent counties in 1334 (summarized in Glasscock, thesis, 1963, op. cit., table 5, 126). While the greatest changes have been in the north-east there have also been minor adjustments along the boundaries with Oxfordshire, Wiltshire, Somerset, and Herefordshire.

REFERENCE

Ralph Bigland, *Historical, Monumental, and Genealogical Collections Relative to the County of Gloucester*, 2 vols., 1786 (includes the subsidy of 1 Edward III (1327): one of the first lay subsidies to be published and used in the study of local history).

[BOROUGHS AND ANCIENT DEMESNES]

Glouc' [B]	Gloucester	SO/832187	54.	1.	6	[T][1]
Cirencestr' [A.D]	Cirencester	SP/023021	25.	0.	0	[T]
Wynchecombe [A.D]	Winchcombe	SP/023282	10.	13.	4	[T]
Mynty [A.D]	Minety [in Wilts.][2]	SU/009912	5.	19.	2	[T]

[LIBERTY OF BARTON REGIS, NEAR BRISTOL]

Libertas de Berton' Regis iuxta Bristoll' [A.D]			17.	0.	0 [T]

Maggodesfeld'	Mangotsfield	ST/665762
Stapelton'	Stapleton	ST/616760
Eston'	Easton[3]	ST/605735
Clifton'	Clifton	ST/572739

[LIBERTY OF KING'S BARTON, NEAR GLOUCESTER]

Libertas Berton' Regis iuxta Glouc' [A.D][4]			8.	5.	1 [T]

Pychenecombe [A.D]	Pitchcombe	SO/852083		13.	4 [T]
Dymmok' [A.D][5]	Dymock	SO/701312	8.	16.	6 [T]

[LIBERTY OF ST. BRIAVELS]

Libertas de Sancto Briavell' [A.D][6]			4.	13.	4 [T]

La Newelond [h] [A.D]	Newland	SO/553095	3.	16.	8 [T]
Aure [v] [p] [A.D][7]	Awre [part of]	SO/709081	7.	0.	0 [T]
Chiltenham [Lib.] [p] [A.D][8]	Liberty of Cheltenham [part of]		7.	2.	10¾ [T]
Arle [A.D]	Arle	SO/927237	2.	17.	6 [T]

---

[1] Includes an unspecified amount for subtaxers.

[2] The whole of Minety parish was transferred to Wiltshire *c.* 1890; before this the greater part had been in Gloucestershire.

[3] Easton was the former name of the parish of St. Philip and St. James.

[4] Thirteen places were taxed in this liberty in 1327 (E 179/113/5); Barton Street, Harescomb, Twigworth, Kingsholm, Upton St. Leonards, Pitchcombe, Wotton, Matson, Langford, Sandhurst, Up Hatherley, Wolstrop, and Bruerne. As Pitchcombe was separately taxed in 1334 (next entry) the figure given is presumed to be the quota for the remaining twelve.

[5] Part of Dymock was taxed at a fifteenth (Botloe hundred).

[6] Three places, St. Briavels, Hewelsfield, and Newland, were taxed in this liberty in 1327 (E 179/113/5). As Newland was separately taxed in 1334 (next entry), the figure given is presumed to be the quota for the other two.

[7] Part of Awre was taxed at a fifteenth (Bledisloe hundred).

[8] This entry almost certainly refers to the town of Cheltenham. On the 1327 roll (E 179/113/5) the heading is *Villata de Chiltenham*.

Alneston' [A.D]	Alstone	SO/932228	1.	10.	0½ [T]
Westhale [A.D]	Westall	SO/934213	2.	13.	1 [T]
Newenton' [A.D]	Naunton	SO/952204			
Stanford [A.D]	Sandford	SO/957213			
Cherleton' [A.D]	Charlton Kings	SO/965204	5.	1.	0¾ [T]
Homme [A.D]	Ham	SO/975212			
Northfeld [A.D]	Northfield	SO/983222			
Rodeleye [A.D]	Rodley	SO/745115	7.	5.	4 [T]
Newenham [A.D]	Newnham	SO/691115	3.	3.	4 [T]
Munstreworth' [A.D]	Minsterworth	SO/773170	6.	6.	8 [T]
			181.	18.	10 [T]

Hd. Respegate [RAPSGATE HUNDRED]

Colesbourn'	Colesbourne	SP/004134	2.	13.	7¾
Cheddeworth'	Chedworth	SP/052122	5.	1.	7¼
Rendecumbe[1]	Rendcomb	SP/018098	2.	2.	0¾
Wodemancote	Woodmancote	SP/004088	1.	13.	6½
Calmundesden'	Calmsden	SP/046087	1.	8.	10¼
Northcerneye	North Cerney	SP/018077	1.	2.	2
Dondesbourn'[2]	Duntisbourne Leer	SO/975075	1.	0.	4
Elkeston'	Elkstone	SO/967123	2.	11.	10¼
Syde	Syde	SO/949108	1.	0.	5
Coberleye	Coberley	SO/966159	2.	4.	6
Coule cum	Cowley with	SO/966146	2.	0.	8¾
Stokwell'	Stockwell	SO/940143			
Brymesfeld'	Brimpsfield	SO/942128	1.	13.	2¼
Cronham	Cranham	SO/891123	2.	6.	0½
			26.	18.	11¼

Hd. Teukesbury [TEWKESBURY HUNDRED]

Teukesbury	Tewkesbury	SO/893327	16.	3.	4
Kenemerton'	Kemerton [in Worcs.]	SO/946368	5.	18.	0
Aston' super Carente	Aston on Carrant	SO/946346	2.	16.	8
Shenyndon	Shenington [in Oxon.]	SP/373428	2.	13.	4
Bourton' [p][3]	Bourton on the Hill [part of]	SP/175325		14.	0
Lemynton'	Lower Lemington	SP/219345	1.	0.	0
Clifford'	Clifford Chambers [in Warwicks.]	SP/198522	2.	5.	0
Tadynton'	Taddington	SP/087311	1.	13.	4
Staneweye	Stanway	SP/061324	1.	13.	4
Aldrynton'	Alderton	SP/002332	2.	4.	0
Dudycote	Didcot	SP/002356	2.	5.	2
Wassebourne	Washbourne[4]	SO/987344	1.	8.	4
Prestecot'	Prescott	SO/983292		10.	6

---

[1] Taxed with a member in 1327 (E 179/113/5).

[2] Identified as Duntisbourne Leer as specified in the 1327 entry (E 179/113/5). Duntisbourne Rouse was taxed elsewhere (Crowthorne hundred); Duntisbourne Abbots is not specifically named in 1334 although listed in Crowthorne hundred in 1327.

[3] Part of Bourton was taxed in Westminster hundred.

[4] Grid ref. is to Great Washbourne. Little Washbourne was in Worcs. (Oswaldslow hundred, p. 350).

Ayston'[1]	Ashton under Hill [in Worcs.]	SO/997377	1.	6.	0
Dyclesden'	Dixton	SO/982306		18.	0
Oxindon'	Oxenton	SO/958314	3.	4.	0
Botynton' [p][2]	Boddington [part of]	SO/894252	1.	4.	6
Northeie	Northway	SO/926343	4.	10.	0
Stoke [p][3]	Stoke Orchard [part of]	SO/922283	1.	5.	0
Muthehok	Mythe Hook[4]	SO/885343	1.	11.	6
Pamynton'	Pamington	SO/939332	3.	1.	0
Natton'	Natton	SO/929327		16.	0
Fydenton'	Fiddington	SO/921309	2.	6.	0
Suthewyk'	Southwick	SO/887303	1.	1.	6
Walton'	Walton Cardiff	SO/907323	1.	5.	0
Tredynton'	Tredington	SO/905295	2.	14.	0
Forthampton'	Forthampton	SO/858326	3.	13.	0
			70.	0.	6

Hd. Clyve [CLEEVE HUNDRED]

Clyve	Bishop's Cleeve	SO/961277	5.	10.	6¾
Wodemancote	Woodmancote	SO/974273	4.	14.	8
Southam	Southam	SO/969255	3.	16.	8
Brokhampton'	Brockhampton	SO/941261	3.	0.	0
Stoke[5]	Stoke Orchard	SO/922283	3.	8.	0
Godrynton'	Gotherington	SO/964296	6.	10.	0
Tenentes Rectore de Clyve	Tenants of the rector of Bishop's Cleeve		1.	4.	10
			28.	4.	8¾

Hd. Byseleye [BISLEY HUNDRED]

Byseleye	Bisley	SO/903059	4.	19.	0½
Pagunhull'	Paganhill	SO/837056	1.	7.	8¼
Lupeghate Inferior	Lower Lypiatt	SO/873038		19.	3
Bydefeld'	Bidfield	SO/909105	2.	0.	1
Lupeyate Superior & Tunleye	Over Lypiatt and Tunley	SO/886058 SO/932044	1.	9.	1½
Saperton'	Sapperton	SO/927034	2.	13.	6
Frompton'	Frampton Mansell	SO/921026	1.	3.	9
Throcham	Througham	SO/920080	1.	19.	9¼
Wyneston'	Winstone	SO/959095		12.	7¾
Eggesworth'	Edgeworth	SO/948060	2.	1.	11
Musarder & Wyshunger'	Miserden and Wishanger	SO/936089 SO/920094	2.	13.	1¼
Payneswywyk	Painswick	SO/867096	12.	7.	9¼[6]
			34.	7.	7¾

[1] Part of Ashton under Hill was taxed in Tibaldstone hundred.

[2] Within the parish of Boddington, the hamlets of Boddington and Barrow were in Tewkesbury hundred, and Hayden and Withybridge were in Westminster hundred.

[3] Part of Stoke Orchard was taxed in Cleeve hundred.

[4] Mythe Hook is the name for an area of marshland between the Severn and Mythe Brook. Its first mention appears to be in the 1327 lay subsidy (*E.P.N.S.*, *XXXIX*, *Glos.*, part 2 (1964), 65).

[5] See also Tewkesbury hundred, above.

[6] E 179/113/15 (1344) has £12. 8. 9¼, in error.

Hd. Langeleie & Swyneshed' [LANGLEY AND SWINESHEAD HUNDREDS]¹

			£	s	d
Rokhampton'	Rockhampton	ST/655933	3.	0.	0
Luteleton'	Littleton upon Severn	ST/596899	1.	6.	8
Overe	Over	ST/588825	1.	0.	0
Frompton' Cotel	Frampton Cotterell	ST/668820	2.	13.	4
Alveston'	Alveston	ST/635883		16.	8
Tokynton'	Tockington	ST/609865	2.	3.	4
Olwuston'	Olveston	ST/601873	1.	8.	0
Button' & Esthanan²	Bitton and Hanham Court	ST/682693 ST/649703	6.	3.	4
Upton' & Beche in Button'	Upton Cheyney and Beach	ST/692701 ST/704708	2.	6.	0
Westhanan & Oldeland in Button'	Hanham and Oldland	ST/646722 ST/669711	2.	4.	0
Doyngton'	Doynton	ST/721741	2.	0.	0
Wynterbourne	Winterbourne	ST/641810	2.	4.	4
Hambrok	Hambrook	ST/641788	1.	3.	0
Hampton' Wodeland Peshale in Wynterbourn'	Hempton Woodlands Patchway	ST/605825 ST/616835 ST/607817	2.	16.	8
			31.	5.	4

Hd. Kyftesgate [KIFTSGATE HUNDRED]

			£	s	d
Campeden'	Campden³	SP/155395	17.	0.	0
Bokeland	Buckland	SP/082360	6.	6.	8
Weston' sub Egge	Weston Subedge	SP/128406	4.	8.	8
Norton' sub Egge	Norton	SP/138430	3.	13.	4
Honybourn'⁴	Cow Honeybourne [in Worcs.]	SP/113436	3.	10.	10
Aston sub Egge	Aston Subedge	SP/138416	2.	16.	8
Mukelton'	Mickleton	SP/162435	9.	6.	8
Clopton'	Clopton [in Warwicks.]⁵	SP/168455	1.	15.	0
Pebbesworth & Merston' Boys	Pebworth [in Worcs.] & Broad Marston [in Worcs.]	SP/128469 SP/139463	10.	0.	0
Ullynton'	Ullington [in Worcs.]	SP/108472	1.	3.	4
Merston'	Long Marston [in Warwicks.]	SP/153481	3.	17.	8
Dersynton'⁶	Dorsington [in Warwicks.]	SP/132497	2.	13.	4
Weston Mauduth	Weston Mauduth [in Warwicks.]⁷	SP/159519	1.	3.	8
Willecote	Willicote [in Warwicks.]	SP/179497	2.	10.	4
Quenton'	Quinton [in Warwicks.]	SP/183470	5.	8.	11

¹ Langley and Swineshead hundreds are listed separately on the 1327 roll (E 179/113/5).

² *Westhanan* on E 179/113/15 is an error. All other documents show this to be East Hanham.

³ Grid ref. is to Chipping Campden, but the entry probably includes Broad Campden and Westington; the three were separately taxed in 1327 (E 179/113/5).

⁴ Church Honeybourne was taxed in Worcestershire (Blackenhurst hundred, p. 355).

⁵ Grid ref. is to Lower Clopton.

⁶ Part of Dorsington was taxed with Milcote in Warwickshire (Barlichway hundred, p. 326).   ⁷ A manor in Weston on Avon held by the Mauduth family.

Adelmynton'	Admington [in Warwicks.]	SP/198457	3.	2.	0
Muno	Meon [in Warwicks.]	SP/183454	3.	3.	10
Hudecote & Barton'[1]	Hidcote Bartrim	SP/177428	1.	3.	0
Larkestoke	Lark Stoke [in Warwicks.][2]	SP/197438	1.	0.	4
Ebrihton' & Hudecote Boys	Ebrington and Hidcote Boyce	SP/183400 SP/173420	8.	0.	0
Charyngworth'	Charingworth	SP/201395	1.	18.	8
Bachesore	Batsford	SP/187339	2.	3.	0
Shemescote	Sezincote	SP/173310		9.	0
Langebergh'	Longborough	SP/179298	4.	8.	6
Swele Superior	Upper Swell	SP/176269	1.	13.	4
Cundycote[3]	Condicote	SP/152283		7.	0
Willarlseye	Willersey	SP/107397	4.	13.	8[4]
Seynebury	Saintbury	SP/117395	4.	13.	4
			112.	10.	9[5]

Hd. Bottelowe [BOTLOE HUNDRED]

Leden'	Upleadon	SO/769270	1.	13.	6
Rodeford'	Rudford	SO/779217		12.	6
Tyberton'	Tibberton	SO/757219	3.	3.	4
Hunteleye	Huntley	SO/713196	1.	16.	8
Magna Teynton'	Taynton	SO/730216	2.	16.	8
Parva Teynton'	Little Taynton[6]	SO/c.749229	1.	12.	0
Newent	Newent	SO/723259	9.	17.	0
Oxenhale	Oxenhall	SO/711266	3.	2.	0
Kempeleye	Kempley	SO/671296	2.	8.	0
Bromesbergh'	Bromsberrow	SO/742337	3.	8.	0
Paunteleye	Pauntley	SO/749290	3.	10.	4
Dymmok'[7]	Dymock	SO/701312	3.	15.	0
			37.	15.	0[8]

Hd. Berkel' [BERKELEY HUNDRED]

Homme	Ham	ST/681983	9.	10.	1
Alkynton' & Hynton'	Alkington and Hinton	ST/693982 SO/683031	9.	15.	6
Wotton' for'	Wotton under Edge [foreign]		13.	11.	4
Wotton' int'	Wotton under Edge	ST/760934	4.	0.	0½
Cromhale	Cromhall	ST/692905	3.	10.	5¾
Hull' & Numdesfeld'	Hill and Nympsfield	ST/649952 SO/801003	8.	7.	2¼

[1] The inclusion of & here is an error. The entry refers to one place only.
[2] Grid ref. is to Upper Lark Stoke.
[3] Part of Condicote was taxed in Salmonsbury hundred.
[4] E 179/113/15 has £4. 13. 4, in error.
[5] A later addition at the end of the 1334 roll (E 179/113/7) is Weston on Avon (in Warwicks.) taxed at 20s. 1d. On some later documents, e.g. E 179/113/15 (1344), it is included within this hundred with a quota of 23s. 4d. but the hundred total remains unchanged. The hundred total on the 1334 roll is a later insertion.
[6] Exactly which part of Taynton was known as Little Taynton is uncertain.
[7] Part of Dymock was taxed at a tenth, above.
[8] E 179/113/15 has £37. 16. 0, in error.

Camme	Cam	ST/758993	11.	9.	11
Coueleye	Coaley	SO/772017	5.	14.	6
Newenton' Baggepathe & Oseleworth'	Newington Bagpath and Ozleworth	ST/816948 ST/794933	4.	2.	0
Iweleie & Wodemancote	Uley and Woodmancote	ST/791985 ST/759977	3.	14.	7
Durseleye	Dursley	ST/757981	3.	15.	5
Beverston	Beverston	ST/862940	5.	2.	9
Kyngescote & Oulepenne	Kingscote and Owlpen	ST/818962 ST/799984	4.	0.	2½
Kyngesweston' & Ailbrighton'	Kings Weston and Elberton	ST/539779 ST/603882	10.	13.	4¾
Horefeld & Filton'	Horfield and Filton	ST/599779 ST/601789	3.	10.	6¼
Almundesbury	Almondsbury	ST/603841	3.	2.	0
Erlyngham	Arlingham	SO/707106	9.	0.	0
Asthelworth'[1]			4.	0.	0
Slymbrugge	Slimbridge	SO/741036	11.	8.	5¾
Berkeleye	Berkeley	ST/683993	3.	11.	8¼
			132.	0.	1

Hd. Langetr' [LONGTREE HUNDRED]

Tettebury	Tetbury	ST/890930	8.	11.	6¾
Aylmundestre	Elmestree	ST/870917	1.	13.	0½
Doughton'	Doughton	ST/878913	2.	5.	5½
Cherlton'	Charlton	ST/882933	1.	14.	8
Upton'	Tetbury Upton	ST/881950	1.	10.	0
Rodemerton'	Rodmarton	ST/942981	1.	5.	0
Colkerton'	Culkerton	ST/930959	1.	18.	0
Chirynton'	Cherington	ST/903985	2.	12.	10
Shipton' Moigne	Shipton Moyne	ST/892896	4.	9.	6½
Weston'	Weston Birt	ST/863895	2.	5.	0
Lasseberewe	Lasborough	ST/822941	1.	5.	0½
Hampton'	Minchinhampton	SO/872008	4.	16.	3
Avenyng'	Avening	ST/879980	2.	9.	11½
Aston'	Aston	ST/901991	1.	5.	1
Rodbergh'	Rodborough	SO/843044	2.	6.	6½
Wodecestr'	Woodchester	SO/840026	1.	17.	1
Horslegh'	Horsley	ST/838980	3.	11.	10½
Ludesmor	Lowsmoor	ST/923997	2.	19.	2
			48.	16.	1¼

Hd. Dudeston' [DUDSTONE HUNDRED]

Hardeperye	Hartpury	SO/781237	2.	12.	0
Marwent	Morwent[2]	lost	1.	13.	4

[1] This is a difficult identification. The two possibilities are: (*a*) Ashleworth, a detached part of the hundred and a member of Berkeley lordship, (*b*) Ashworthy Farm, in Cromhall. The 1327 entry for *Ashelworth Cromhale* (E 179/113/5, m. 16) suggests that Ashworthy Farm is meant, but I am inclined to think that the 1334 entry refers to Ashleworth, as firstly, it is unlikely that two places in the same parish would be taxed at such relatively high amounts, and secondly, if Ashworthy Farm was meant one might expect to find it listed nearer to Cromhall on the roll. For a discussion of the problem of this place-name identification see *E.P.N.S., XL, Glos.*, part 3 (1964), 4 and 152.

[2] For an explanation of this lost place-name see *E.P.N.S., XL, Glos.*, part 3 (1964), 156.

Preston'	Preston	so/679346		18.	6
Marsemor	Maisemore	so/813216	2.	8.	6
Hynhame	Highnam	so/797195	1.	12.	0
Lilton'	Linton	so/800192		12.	8
Hyneleden'	Highleadon	so/770236		16.	8
Lassyndon'	Lassington	so/796212	1.	1.	0
Overe	Over	so/808196	1.	2.	6
Elmor	Elmore	so/767149	4.	3.	4
Heyhampstede	Hempsted	so/813170	2.	0.	0
Tuffeleye	Tuffley	so/833148	1.	6.	8
Whaddon'	Whaddon	so/833137		18.	0
Brokthrop'	Brookthorpe	so/835123	1.	3.	4
Upton'	Upton St. Leonards	so/862150	1.	10.	0
Sandebrugge	Saintbridge	so/848165		16.	8
Snedham	Sneedham's Green	so/849143		6.	8
Langefarde	Longford	so/839209	1.	10.	0
Sandhurste	Sandhurst	so/822233	1.	16.	0
Abbelode	Abload's Court	so/828213		16.	0
Norton' Episcopi	Bishop's Norton	so/849245	1.	14.	0
Norton' Prioris	Prior's Norton	so/870241		15.	6
Brighthampton'	Brickhampton	so/870220		13.	4
Parton'	Parton	so/878208	1.	1.	6
Beggeworth'[1]	Badgeworth	so/903193	1.	10.	0
Parva Benham	part of Bentham[2]	so/912167		10.	0
Magna Benham	Bentham	so/912167	1.	18.	8
Magna Shurdynton'	Shurdington	so/921189	1.	2.	0
Parva Shurdynton'	Little Shurdington	so/918173	1.	8.	0
Parva Wydecombe	Little Witcombe	so/912156	1.	0.	0
Crikeleye	Crickley	so/924160		6.	8
Donnhatherleye	Down Hatherley	so/868225	1.	15.	4
Brokworth'	Brockworth	so/891170	2.	12.	0
Wotton'	Wotton	so/845187	1.	11.	4
Bernewode	Barnwood	so/858177	1.	10.	0
Chirchesdon'	Churchdown	so/884196	1.	3.	4
Piryton'	Pirton Court	so/875203		11.	6
Oke	Noke Court	so/881179		12.	0
Hokelecote	Hucclecote	so/872176	1.	3.	4
Magna Wydecombe	Great Witcombe	so/911148	1.	3.	4
Elbrugge cum Brokstret'	Elmbridge with Brook Street in Gloucester[3]	so/863196		15.	6
			54.	1.	2

Hd. Holeford & Greston [HOLFORD AND GRESTON HUNDRED]

Wykewone[4]	Childswickham [in Worcs.]	sp/075384	10.	3.	4
Dumbelton'	Dumbleton	sp/018357	6.	6.	8
Aston' Somervill'	Aston Somerville [in Worcs.]	sp/047379	4.	0.	0
Twynyng	Twyning	so/893361	4.	17.	6½

[1] *Twyggeworth* on E 179/113/15 (1344) is an error.

[2] Bentham is now a single hamlet; it is uncertain which part was called *Magna* and which *Parva*.

[3] Samuel Rudder, *A New History of Gloucestershire*, 1779, 205: '. . . Brook Street, just without the postern gate, extended to Morin's mill, . . .'.

[4] Murcot was taxed with Childswickham in 1327 (E 179/113/5).

			£	s	d
Froulynton' & Newenton'	Frampton and Naunton	SP/015334 SP/019338	1.	11.	5
Staunton'	Stanton	SP/069343	2.	4.	10
Snoweshull'	Snowshill	SP/097337		11.	8½
Hallyng cum Rowell'	Hawling with Roel	SP/063229 SP/074249	1.	0.	0
Cherlton'	Charlton Abbots	SP/034243		15.	6
Cotesthrop'	Coates	SP/018276	1.	0.	0
Poteslep'	Postlip	SO/999268		16.	8
Sudleye	Sudeley	SP/032277	1.	13.	4
Grette	Greet	SP/025303	1.	7.	8
Grettone	Gretton	SP/006305	1.	0.	8
Stanleye	Stanley Pontlarge	SO/999302	2.	8.	6
Newenton' Baunton'	Naunton ?	SP/019338		10.	0
Todynton'	Toddington	SP/035331	2.	2.	0
Wormynton' Parva	Wormington Grange	SP/046346	1.	3.	0
Wormynton' Dastyn cum Lutleton'	Wormington Daston[1] with Littleton[2]	lost		19.	0
Didebrok	Dudbrook	SP/054314	1.	16.	4
Wormynton' Magna	Wormington	SP/038363	2.	19.	8
Costecombe	Coscombe[3]	SP/075301		3.	8
Pynnokesford & Hide	Pinnock Ford and Hide	SP/075280 SP/088293 SP/089285	1.	8.	10
Francote	Farmcote	SP/062291	1.	5.	10
Catesfalde	Castlett	SP/091258		15.	6
Guytynge Power	Guiting Power	SP/096245	1.	14.	4
Guytynge Templer	Temple Guiting	SP/091279	2.	19.	0
Kyngton'	Kineton	SP/097265		19.	0
Berton'	Barton	SP/100254		10.	3
			59.	4.	3

Hd. Bradeleye [BRADLEY HUNDRED]

			£	s	d
Northlegh' for' cum Cuberl' Parva[4]	Northleach [foreign] with Upper Coberley	SP/112145 SO/979157	4.	16.	8
Northlegh' int'	Northleach [within]	SP/112145	2.	18.	7¾
Brokhampton' cum Sevenhampton'	Brockhampton with Sevenhampton	SP/036223 SP/033218	2.	16.	8
Swytynton'	Whittington	SP/013206	1.	2.	2¾
Wyneston'	Winson	SP/090089	2.	15.	1
Culne Reg'	Coln Rogers	SP/088097	2.	11.	5¼
Yanesworth'	Yanworth	SP/079139	2.	11.	4
Haselton'	Hazleton	SP/080182	1.	4.	2¾
Whithyndon'	Withington	SP/032156	2.	11.	5
Oldeswell'	Owdeswell	SP/025190		6.	4
Hildecote	Hilcot	SO/997162		8.	1¾

[1] A manor in Wormington held by the Daston family. The place does not appear on the 1327 roll, but Robert Dastyn paid in Wormington Parva. *E.P.N.S.*, *XXXIX*, *Glos.*, part 2 (1964), 40, implies that Wormington Magna and Wormington Daston are the same place but their separate mention in this subsidy does not bear this out.

[2] For an explanation of this lost place-name see *E.P.N.S.*, *XXXIX*, *Glos.*, part 2 (1964), 11.

[3] Grid ref. is to Upper Coscombe.

[4] Upper Coberley, although distant from Northleach, was a member of that manor; it was separately taxed in 1327 (E 179/113/5).

Foxcote	Foxcote	SP/012182	1.	17.	5¾
Doudeswell'	Dowdeswell	SP/001199	1.	17.	9½
Peclesworth'	Pegglesworth	SO/990179	1.	6.	10
Shipton' cum	Shipton[1] with	SP/037185	2.	10.	4
Hanenepenne	Hampen	SP/055197			
Aston'	Aston Blank	SP/128199	3.	2.	10½
Natagrave	Notgrove	SP/109199	3.	0.	0¼
Turkedene Superior[2]	Turkdean [part of]	SP/107174	3.	6.	11¼
Salperton'	Salperton	SP/078198	1.	19.	9
Turkedene Inferior[2]	Turkdean [part of]	SP/107174	1.	17.	2¼
Hampton'	Hampnett	SP/100157	1.	12.	6½
Cumpton'	Compton Abdale	SP/059165	2.	3.	0¾
Tormarton'	Farmington	SP/136152	3.	5.	2¼
Stowell'	Stowell	SP/088131	3.	17.	9½
			55.	19.	11¾

Hd. Westm' [WESTMINSTER HUNDRED]

Bourhton'[3]	Bourton on the Hill	SP/175325	15.	10.	0
Todenham	Todenham	SP/243363			
Sutton'	Sutton under Brailes [in Warwicks.]	SP/299274			
Lemynton'	Lemington	SP/222339			
Marton'	Moreton in Marsh	SP/206322			
Caldecote	Coldicote	SP/217311			
Derh'[4]	Deerhurst	SO/870300	18.	13.	4
Walton'	Deerhurst Walton	SO/883282			
Apperleye	Apperley	SO/862281			
Wyghtfeld'	Wightfield	SO/870287			
Herdewyk'	Hardwicke	SO/911275			
Heidon	Hayden	SO/904235			
Botynton'	Boddington	SO/894252			
Yevynton'	Evington	SO/870258			
Trynleye[5]	Tirley	SO/840285	10.	2.	0
Hasfeld'	Hasfield	SO/826275			
Corhs	Corse	SO/789264			
			44.	5.	4

Hd. Crouthorn [CROWTHORNE HUNDRED]

Hampton' Meisy	Meysey Hampton	SP/117001	4.	0.	6¾
Dounameneie	Down Ampney	SU/098965	6.	0.	5¾
Southcerneye	South Cerney	SU/050973	9.	16.	3
Harehull' &	Harnhill and	SP/069004	5.	11.	8½
Driffeld'	Driffield	SU/073998			
Upanmeneye	Ampney[6]	SP/065019	10.	11.	4¼
Preston'	Preston	SP/043009	2.	12.	3
Sothynton'	Siddington	SP/035002	8.	2.	6

---

[1] Grid ref. is to Shipton Oliffe.
[2] Rudder, op. cit. 778, was unable to locate these two manors.
[3] Part of Bourton was taxed in Tewkesbury hundred.
[4] Part of Deerhurst was taxed in Deerhurst hundred.
[5] Part of Tirley was taxed in Deerhurst hundred.
[6] Grid ref. is to Ampney Crucis.

			£	s.	d.
Cotes c.m[1]	Coates [with members]	SO/973010	5.	5.	2¾
Donntesbourn'[2] & Pyndeleye	Duntisbourne Rouse and Pinbury	SO/985060 SO/956049	3.	15.	3¾
Stretton' & Daglyngworth'	Stratton and Daglingworth	SP/010039 SO/993050	6.	3.	11¾
Bagynden'	Bagendon	SP/011067	1.	14.	6
Badynton & Wygewolde	Baunton and Wiggold	SP/022047 SP/046050	2.	5.	4
			65.	19.	5½

Hd. Derherst' [DEERHURST HUNDRED]

			£	s.	d.
Derherste[3]	Deerhurst	SO/870300	1.	4.	0
Leie	Leigh	SO/866258	1.	6.	0
Staverton'	Staverton	SO/890235		19.	4
Hawe & Trilleie[3]	Haw and Tirley	SO/844279 SO/840285	2.	6.	8
Colne	Coln St. Dennis	SP/086109	2.	13.	4
Okynton'	Uckington	SO/917252	2.	4.	8
Preston'	Preston on Stour [in Warwicks.]	SP/203500	3.	13.	0
Welneford'	Welford on Avon [in Warwicks.]	SP/145522	3.	16.	8
Compton'	Little Compton [in Warwicks.]	SP/259302	2.	13.	4
Wolston'	Woolstone	SO/961302	2.	4.	0
Prestebur'	Prestbury	SO/970238	5.	14.	8
			28.	15.	8

Hd. Brytwoldesberwe [BRIGHTWELLS-BARROW HUNDRED]

			£	s.	d.
Lecchelade	Lechlade	SU/215995	10.	7.	6¼
Faireford'	Fairford	SP/152012	11.	12.	8
Kynemasford'	Kempsford	SU/161964	11.	7.	8
Lech Torvile	Eastleach Turville	SP/202054	3.	8.	4½
Estlech	Eastleach Martin	SP/202052	2.	16.	11½
Eycote[4]	Eycotfield	SP/006103		18.	8
Quenton'	Quenington	SP/148039	2.	9.	9¾
Adesworth	Aldsworth	SP/153099	3.	4.	10¼
Southrop'	Southrop	SP/202034	3.	7.	11
Barndesleye	Barnsley	SP/078051	3.	16.	7
Colne Sancti Aylwyni'	Coln St. Aldwyn	SP/143052	2.	9.	3
Hatherthrop	Hatherop	SP/154051	2.	6.	10½
Bybury	Bibury	SP/118065	2.	11.	6
Alurynton'	Arlington	SP/112067	2.	17.	0
Ablynton'	Ablington	SP/105076	2.	3.	2
			65.	18.	9¾

---

[1] Members of Coates in 1327 included Tarlton, Trewsbury, and Hullasey (E 179/113/5).
[2] See footnote to Rapsgate hundred, p. 92.
[3] See also Westminster hundred, above.
[4] A member of the manor of Bibury.

Hd. Tebaldeston' [TIBALDSTONE HUNDRED]

Beckeford'	Beckford [in Worcs.]	SO/976358	25.	11.	7
Grafton'	Grafton [in Worcs.]	SO/986373			
Aishton'[1]	Ashton under Hill [in Worcs.]	SO/997377			
Bayngrove	Bengrove	SO/972326			
Hynton'	Hinton on the Green [in Worcs.]	SP/024400	7.	6.	8
			32.	18.	3

Hd. Thornbur' [THORNBURY HUNDRED]

Thornbury	Thornbury	ST/634905	5.	0.	0
Hope & Bokevor'	Hope and Buckover	ST/676898 ST/664902		10.	0
Kyngton'	Kington	ST/620905	2.	2.	0
Morton'	Morton	ST/644907	2.	13.	4
Wolford'	Woolford's Mill [in Thornbury]	ST/c.644907		3.	0
Oldebur' cum marisco	Oldbury upon Severn with marsh	ST/609919	2.	10.	0
Couhull'	Cowhill	ST/606915		10.	0
Falefeld'	Falfield	ST/683933	1.	6.	0
Sibelond & Oldelond[2]	Sibland ?	ST/648898		16.	8
Tyderynton'	Tytherington	ST/668884	2.	13.	0
Ryngworth'	Rangeworthy	ST/689863		18.	0
Erdecote & La Lee	Gaunts Earthcott and The Lee[3]	ST/635842	1.	3.	4
Acton'	Iron Acton	ST/677837	4.	18.	0
Cote	Cote	ST/581897		13.	4
Marsfeld'	Marshfield	ST/782737	18.	0.	0
			43.	16.	8

Hd. Pokelchirch' [PUCKLECHURCH HUNDRED]

Pokelchirch'	Pucklechurch	ST/700764	2.	8.	0
Westerleie	Westerleigh	ST/699796	5.	6.	8
Wike	Wick	ST/697727	4.	0.	0
Alboteston'	Abson	ST/705749	1.	1.	0
Ciston'	Siston	ST/688752	2.	8.	0
Ayshton'	Cold Ashton	ST/751727	4.	3.	4
			19.	7.	0

Hd. Grimbaldesaysh' [GRUMBALDS ASH HUNDRED]

Derham & Henton'	Dyrham and Hinton	ST/742758 ST/732765	3.	6.	8
Dodynton'	Dodington	ST/752799	1.	5.	0

[1] See also Tewkesbury hundred, above.

[2] *Oldeland* is mentioned in R. Bigland, *Historical, Monumental and Genealogical Collections Relative to the County of Gloucester*, 1786, but it is not identified. Possibly part of Oldland (ST/669711)?

[3] Mentioned in Bigland, op. cit. 1, 41: '... a separate manor called Gaunts-Urcott and The Lee division'.

Acton' Ilger	Acton Ilger	ST/676831		8.	4
Thormarton' &	Tormarton and	ST/769788	5.	0.	0
Lutteton'	West Littleton	ST/761755			
Sobbury Parva	Little Sodbury	ST/758832	1.	10.	0
Badmynton' Magna	Great Badminton	ST/807829	2.	4.	0
Acton' Turvill'	Acton Turville	ST/809809	1.	10.	0
Codrynton'	Codrington	ST/723790	1.	16.	8
Wappeleie	Wapley	ST/714797		15.	0
Torteworth'	Tortworth	ST/704933	1.	16.	8
Charfeld'	Charfield	ST/719911	1.	10.	0
Boxwell'	Boxwell	ST/812927		14.	0
Lentrinton'	Leighterton	ST/823911	1.	6.	8
Wikeware	Wickwar	ST/724885	3.	10.	0
Hildesleye	Hillsley	ST/769897		13.	0
Horton'	Horton	ST1766851	2.	0.	0
Haukesbury	Hawkesbury	ST/768869		18.	4
Badmynton' [h]	Little Badminton	ST/802843	1.	3.	3
Upton [h]	Hawkesbury Upton	ST/781869	2.	4.	3
Selewold' &	Saddlewood	ST/811898	1.	0.	4¾
Ingraston'[1]	?				
Tresham &	Tresham and	ST/792912	1.	10.	4
Kylecote	Kilcott	ST/794884			
Dudemarton' &	Didmarton and	ST/823874	2.	12.	0
Oldbury	Oldbury on the Hill	ST/819882			
Arleie	Alderley	ST/768908	1.	8.	8
Sobbury Magna	Old Sodbury	ST/756818	4.	0.	0
Wykewyk'	Wick Wick	ST/661785		8.	0
			44.	11.	2¾

Hd. Hembury [HENBURY HUNDRED]

Hembur' cum	Henbury with	ST/563788	7.	15.	4¾
Cherlton' [h]	Charlton	ST/583804			
Weston' [h] &	Lawrence Weston and	ST/547784			
Stowyk' [h]	Stowick	ST/540827			
Stoke Giffard &	Stoke Gifford and	ST/622797	6.	17.	10½
Compton'	Compton Greenfield	ST/571822			
Auste cum	Aust with	ST/573891	5.	10.	4
Radewyke [h]	Redwick	ST/549859			
Yate &	Yate and	ST/713828	9.	11.	5
Igynton'	Itchington	ST/660868			
Westbur' cum	Westbury on Trym with	ST/573773	6.	13.	7½
Stoke [h] &	Stoke Bishop and	ST/565755			
Hampton' [h]	Shirehampton	ST/532769			
			36.	8.	7¾

Hd. Salmansbur' [SALMONSBURY HUNDRED]

Odynton'	Oddington	SP/235255	3.	18.	9
Northwell'	Lower Swell	SP/174257	1.	1.	8
Sloughere Superior	Upper Slaughter	SP/155232	1.	15.	3½
Cundicote[2]	Condicote	SP/152283		17.	8½

[1] Probably Inglestone in Hawkesbury (ST/750886). The place was separately taxed in 1327 as Saddlewood was coupled with Hawkesbury Upton (E 179/113/5).

[2] See also Kiftsgate hundred, above.

			£	s.	d.
Iccumbe	Icomb	SP/214226		16.	2
Wedeford	Widford [in Oxon.]	SP/279120		8.	7
Wenrich	Windrush	SP/193130	2.	1.	2½
Wyke	Wick Rissington	SP/192215	1.	13.	8
Rysyndon' Parva	Little Rissington	SP/189199	2.	16.	0
Berynton' Parva	Little Barrington	SP/209128		16.	10½
Berynton' Magna[1]	Great Barrington	SP/205134	3.	13.	6
Shirbourne	Sherborne	SP/169148	5.	4.	5
Coumbe Westcote[2]	Westcote	SP/220206	3.	2.	9½
Newenton'	Naunton	SP/112234	1.	14.	10
Hertford	Harford[3]	SP/130226		8.	7
Eyleworth'	Aylworth	SP/110220		5.	3
Sloughtre Inferior	Lower Slaughter	SP/166226	1.	6.	2½
Bladynton'	Bledington	SP/245225	1.	11.	11
Eyford'	Eyford	SP/146246		9.	6½
Rysyndon' Magna	Great Rissington	SP/195172	5.	0.	4
Stowe	Stow on the Wold	SP/191258	6.	15.	0
Bradewell'	Broadwell	SP/201277	2.	2.	4
Burton'	Bourton on the Water	SP/167209	2.	10.	8
Clopton'	Clapton	SP/163178	1.	1.	8
Tattlesthrop'	Adlestrop	SP/243269	2.	16.	9
Malgarisbur'	Maugersbury	SP/200252	2.	2.	8½
Donynton'	Donnington	SP/192279	1.	10.	7
			58.	3.	0

Hd. Wyston' [WHITSTONE HUNDRED]

			£	s.	d.
Longeneye	Longney	SO/763124	4.	16.	8
Herdewyk'	Hardwicke	SO/793123	3.	3.	0
Quedesleye	Quedgeley	SO/807142	1.	15.	0
Harsefeld'	Haresfield	SO/810104	3.	0.	6
Oxlyng'	Oxlinch	SO/821077	2.	6.	8
Morton'	Moreton Valence	SO/780098	1.	13.	4
Salle	Saul	SO/749094	2.	8.	0
Stonhous'	Stonehouse	SO/808051	4.	3.	4
Stanlegh' Sancti Leonardi	Leonard Stanley	SO/802032	1.	4.	0
Stal' Reg'	King's Stanley	SO/810041	2.	3.	4
Froucestr'	Frocester	SO/771033	2.	13.	4
Alanton'	Alkerton	SO/774053	1.	2.	6
Estynton'	Eastington	SO/781053	1.	6.	8
Whitenhurste	Wheatenhurst	SO/761091	1.	10.	0
Frompton'	Frampton on Severn	SO/743069	1.	16.	0
			35.	2.	4

Hd. Sancto Briavell' [ST. BRIAVELS HUNDRED]

			£	s.	d.
Staunton'	Staunton	SO/551126	1.	3.	4
Bykenore	English Bicknor	SO/581158	2.	5.	0
Ruardyn	Ruardean	SO/621176	2.	4.	0

[1] Part of Barrington was taxed as ancient demesne in Berkshire (Faringdon hundred, p. 11).

[2] Rudder, op. cit. 805, states that the place was formerly called Combe Baskerville to distinguish it from adjacent Icomb. The *Coumbe* element may refer to the settlement of Gawcombe.

[3] Grid ref. is to Lower Harford.

Magna Den' cum Abothe [h]	Mitcheldean with Abenhall	SO/663185 SO/671173	2.	6.	8
Parva Den' [h]	Little Dean	SO/672135	1.	16.	8
Northwode [h]	Northwood	SO/726160		6.	8
Blakeneye [h]	Blakeney	SO/671069		6.	8
Laei [h]	Lea [in Herefordshire]	SO/658217		11.	0
			11.	0.	0

Hd. Bliddeslowe [BLEDISLOE HUNDRED]

Aure[1]	Awre	SO/709081	4.	5.	0
Lydeneie c.m	Lydney [with members]	SO/633025	5.	12.	0
Aylberton'	Aylburton	SO/618020	4.	17.	0
Alvynton'	Alvington	SO/603007	5.	0.	0
			19.	14.	0

Hd. Chiltenham [CHELTENHAM HUNDRED]

Swyndon'	Swindon	SO/935249	2.	15.	$2\frac{3}{4}$
Lechampton'	Leckhampton	SO/943194	2.	13.	$6\frac{3}{4}$
			5.	8.	$9\frac{1}{2}$

Hd. Westbur' [WESTBURY HUNDRED][2]

Westbur'	Westbury on Severn	SO/718139	5.	5.	6
Churchame	Churcham	SO/769182	4.	10.	0
Longehope	Longhope	SO/689189	4.	17.	0
			14.	12.	6

[List of Chief Taxers and Subtaxers]			21.	15.	6

TOTAL: £1,421. 0. 6[3]

Bristoll[4]	Bristol	[in lieu of tenth]	220.	0.	0

[1] Part of Awre was taxed at a tenth, above.

[2] The three places in this hundred were taxed with various members in 1327 (E 179/113/5).

[3] As on 1334 Account, E 179/113/6.

[4] Not included on the Gloucestershire rolls: figure from E 164/7 fol. xxxix.

HAMPSHIRE

DOCUMENTS

8 Edward III: Account   E 179/173/7
8 Edward III: Particulars not extant
11 Edward III: Particulars E 179/173/8 (imperfect)
22 Edward III: Particulars E 179/173/20 (imperfect)
25 Edward III: Particulars E 179/173/21* (incomplete)
25 Edward III: Particulars E 179/173/22

TAXERS

The prior of St. Swithin, Winchester, and Gilbert de Wyggeton

TAX YIELD

15th	£1,103.	6.	7½
10th	£ 237.	9.	8
	£1,340.	16.	3½

Representing assessed movable wealth of

£18,924. 16. 0½

NOTES

Places taxed at a tenth, including six taxation boroughs, are listed at the end of the rolls. Although there were at least twenty boroughs in medieval Hampshire (see list in M. W. Beresford, 'The six new towns of the bishops of Winchester', *Medieval Archaeology*, 3 (1959), 213, appendix II) only six were considered taxation boroughs in 1334, viz. the city of Winchester, the Soke of Winchester, Southampton, Portsmouth, Portchester, and New Alresford. Four others were taxed at the higher rate but not named as boroughs. The choice of the taxation boroughs of Hampshire is puzzling; whatever the criteria of selection they seem to have been unevenly applied (discussed in more detail in Glasscock, thesis, 1963, op. cit. 141–3).

Only on the western boundary was the outline of the county in 1334 substantially different from that of the modern county. A group of places that were in Wiltshire until 1895—Martin, Damerham, Plaitford, and Whitsbury—are listed on the Wiltshire rolls, as are also Bramshaw, West Wellow, and part of Tytherley. Part of Stratfield Saye, now in Hampshire, was taxed in Berkshire in 1334, but as against this, parts of Stratfield Mortimer and Combe, transferred to Berkshire in 1894 and 1895 respectively, were then taxed in Hampshire. Ambersham, now in Sussex, was taxed in Hampshire of which it was formerly a detached part. Kinson, in Dorset until 1930, was probably taxed there in 1334; although not named on the Dorset rolls it was almost certainly included in the large tax quota for Canford.

REFERENCE

Sir Frederick Madden, 'Taxation of the tenth and fifteenth in Hampshire in 1334', *Collectanea Topographica et Genealogica*, 1 (1834), 175–83 (of limited value as the place-names are not identified and there are many inaccuracies).

Hd. Thorngate [THORNGATE HUNDRED]

Hipton' [v][1]	Shipton Bellinger	SU/233453	5.	4.	0¼
Snodynton'	Snoddington	SU/238446	1.	17.	11¾
Tudeworth'[2]	South Tidworth	SU/236477		8.	2
Wollop' Buklond	Over Wallop	SU/283382	11.	19.	4½
Burghton'	Broughton	SU/309329	10.	1.	5¾
Wollop Priorisse	Nether Wallop	SU/304363	12.	1.	8¾
Bosynton'	Bossington	SU/336309	1.	2.	0
Puteleworth'	Pittleworth	SU/328296	1.	9.	0
Bentelegh'	Bentley	SU/310295		12.	5
Motesfonte	Mottisfont	SU/326267	2.	7.	0
Hyda	Hyde	SU/320248		10.	6
Welowe[3]	East Wellow	SU/302203		12.	1
Empnele	Embley	SU/322208		6.	0
Shirfelde	Sherfield English	SU/291222	2.	17.	2¾
Lokerlegh'	Lockerley	SU/298267	1.	12.	0
Estdoene	East Dean	SU/273267	1.	9.	0
Westdoene	West Dean[4]	SU/257273		5.	0
Esttuderlegh'	East Tytherley	SU/292290	2.	5.	0
Westtuderlegh'[5]	West Tytherley	SU/273298	1.	18.	11½
Wyggele	Wigley	SU/326170	3.	1.	1¼
			62.	0.	0½

Hd. Christi Ecclesie [CHRISTCHURCH HUNDRED]

Christi Ecclesia	Christchurch	SZ/158928	2.	13.	0
Westoure	Westover	SU/139044	3.	2.	8
Buryton'	Burton	SZ/162942	2.	16.	8
Nova Lemynton'	Lymington [New]	SZ/326956	6.	3.	0
Vetera Lemynton'	Lymington [Old]		4.	1.	8
Bolre	Boldre	SZ/324992	2.	9.	0
Sweye	Sway	SZ/279983	1.	19.	8
Arnewode	Arnewood	SZ/272973	1.	0.	8
Efford	Efford	SZ/299946	3.	6.	0
Kyhavene	Keyhaven	SZ/304916		19.	0
Mulleforde	Milford on Sea	SZ/291921	1.	15.	0
Hordehulle	Hordle	SZ/273952	1.	14.	4

[1] Later documents show that *Hipton* is a scribal error for *Shipton*.

[2] Most of South Tidworth was taxed in Andover hundred.

[3] The entry refers to East Wellow. West Wellow was in Wiltshire until 1895; the quota for Wellow (£2. 16. 8) in the Wiltshire subsidy (published in *V.C.H., Wilts.* iv (1959)), probably refers to West Wellow only and not to Wellow in Hampshire as there suggested.

[4] West Dean All Saints was a separate Hampshire parish until 1474. The Hampshire portion of the parish of West Dean was amalgamated with West Tytherley in 1883. At this time the county boundary underwent a slight change and, as a result, the site of All Saints Church, West Dean is now in Wiltshire (*V.C.H., Hants.* iv (1911), 519).

[5] Part of Tytherley was taxed in Wiltshire (Amesbury hundred, p. 345).

Asshelegh'	Ashley	SZ/262944	3.	17.	0
Chiueton'	Chewton	SZ/226941	5.	10.	4
Henton'	Hinton	SZ/217956	2.	15.	4
Avene	Avon	SZ/147987	3.	12.	8
Soppelegh'	Sopley	SZ/156967	1.	4.	0
Wyngeton'	Winkton	SZ/162960	1.	13.	8
Boure	Bure	SZ/184928	2.	18.	4
Strete	Street[1]	SZ/169929	1.	2.	8
Hurne	Hurn	SZ/128970	3.	8.	0
Northasshelegh'	North Ashley[2]	SU/136063	2.	0.	1
			60.	2.	9

Hd. Selebourne [SELBORNE HUNDRED]

Selebourne	Selborne	SU/741338	1.	1.	2
Faryndon'	Farringdon	SU/712354	2.	5.	1
Norton'	Norton	SU/739350	1.	15.	6
Sothynton'	Sotherington	SU/754331	1.	2.	11
Imbeshete	Empshott	SU/753313		15.	6
Tystede	East Tisted	SU/701322	1.	19.	3
Nyweton' &	Newton Valence and	SU/723328	4.	10.	6
Haukele	Hawkley	SU/746292			
			13.	9.	11

Hd. Somburne [KING'S SOMBORNE HUNDRED]

Romesey extra ponte'	Romsey Extra	SU/c.350200	3.	3.	8
Cupernam	Cupernham	SU/360219	3.	16.	3
Wolebury[3]	?		3.	19.	4
Lee	Lee	SU/360179	4.	10.	10
Welles	Wells[4]	SU/356180	4.	9.	0
Pershute	Spursholt	SU/335210	1.	4.	0
Mayheweston'	Pauncefoot	SU/343201		12.	0
Oke &	Roke and	SU/338223	1.	14.	0
Stanbrigge	Stanbridge	SU/338232			
Tymberbury	Timsbury	SU/346245	2.	5.	8
Farlegh'	Farley Chamberlaine	SU/395275	1.	1.	8
Elleden' &	Eldon and	SU/364278	2.	3.	2
Compton'	Compton	SU/349291			
Somburn' Regis	King's Somborne	SU/360310	7.	8.	2
Asshelegh'	Ashley	SU/385309	1.	1.	8
Parva Somborn'[5]	Little Somborne	SU/381326	2.	3.	4
Upsomborn'	Upper Somborne	SU/397324	1.	12.	10
Houghton'[6]	Houghton	SU/341327	1.	14.	0
Langestok'	Longstock	SU/359371	3.	3.	6
Lecford[7]	Leckford	SU/373377	2.	0.	0
			48.	3.	1

[1] Street is a tithing name only. [2] Grid ref. is to Ashley Farm.
[3] Probably Woodley in Romsey Infra (SU/370222).
[4] Grid ref. is to Skidmore Farm within the tithing of Wells.
[5] See also footnote 4, p. 108.
[6] Part of Houghton was taxed in Buddlesgate hundred.
[7] On a number of later rolls the component manors of Leckford are listed: Leckford Abbess, Leckford Abbots, and Leckford Richards.

Hd. Butlesgate [BUDDLESGATE HUNDRED]

Mulebrok	Millbrook	su/385131	2.	2.	6
Nhuchshulling'	Nursling	su/359164	2.	7.	0
Muchelmers &	Michelmersh and	su/348260	2.	1.	11
Abrigg'	Awbridge	su/334233			
Westputte Mareschal	West Pitt[1]	lost		19.	4
Compton'	Compton	su/468257	1.	4.	0
Sperkeford &	Sparkford and	su/c.478268		18.	2
Drayton'	Houghton Drayton	su/343320			
Oterburne	Otterbourne	su/457228		16.	4
Houghton'[2]	Houghton	su/341327		8.	10
Chilbolton' &	Chilbolton and	su/394402		11.	11
Grandesbury[3]	Bransbury	su/421423			
Wonsynton' &	Wonston and	su/477395	2.	0.	10
Honton'	Hunton	su/481396			
Eldestok'	Stoke Charity	su/489393	1.	0.	0
Spersholte	Sparsholt	su/435312	3.	3.	3
Dane &	Dean and	su/443310			
Layneston'	Lainston	su/442316			
Luttelton'	Littleton	su/453329	2.	3.	2
Wyk &	Weeke and	su/467308			
Fulflede	Fulflood	su/473300			
Crawele &	Crawley and probably	su/424348	4.	7.	0
Somburne[4]	part of Little	su/381326			
	Somborne				
Merdon'	Merdon	su/420264	4.	19.	11
Putte &	Pitt and	su/451281			
Sulksted	Silkstead	su/445243			
Aumfeld &	Ampfield and	su/407235	5.	4.	1½
Pokenhal	Pucknall	su/384250			
Hurselegh'	Hursley	su/428253	1.	7.	0
			35.	15.	3½

Hd. Andevere [ANDOVER HUNDRED]

Clatford	Upper Clatford	su/357435	3.	4.	10½
Anne Abbatis	Abbotts Ann	su/331436	6.	10.	6½
Anne de Beek'	Monxton	su/312445	2.	2.	0
Anne Savage	Sarson	su/307446	1.	4.	0
Anne de Pourt	Amport	su/299442	1.	19.	6
Gratele	Grateley	su/276420	2.	12.	10
Querle	Quarley	su/272440	1.	15.	10
Tudeworth'[5]	South Tidworth	su/236477	3.	18.	10
Cumenton' &	Kimpton and	su/281467	3.	3.	2½
Littelton'	Littleton	su/290467			
Fifhide	Fyfield	su/295463	1.	14.	10
Chilwarton'[6]	Cholderton	su/240425	3.	6.	0

---

[1] West Pitt, now lost, was one of the Bishop of Winchester's possessions in 1316 (*F.A.* ii. 309).

[2] See also King's Somborne hundred, above.

[3] *Grandesbury* on E 179/173/21 (1352) appears to be a clerical error for *Brandesbury*.

[4] Probably part of Little Somborne, the neighbouring parish to Crawley.

[5] See also Thorngate hundred, above.

[6] This entry refers only to that part of Cholderton in modern Hampshire: the village was taxed in Wiltshire (Amesbury hundred, p. 345).

Trokeleston'	Thruxton	SU/289457	2.	4.	0
Penyton' Crefteyn	Penton Grafton	SU/328475	3.	1.	4
Penyton' Meysy	Penton Mewsey	SU/330473	1.	8.	1
Foxcote	Foxcotte	SU/344474	1.	17.	1
Enham	Knights Enham	SU/368490	1.	6.	0
			41.	8.	11½

Hd. Evyngare [EVINGAR HUNDRED]

Hussebourne Prioris'	Hurstbourne Priors	SU/439467	2.	3.	11
Burne	St. Mary Bourne	SU/422502	2.	0.	8
Swampton'	Swampton	SU/418508		13.	2
Stok'	Stoke	SU/403519	2.	6.	0
Wyke	Wyke[1]	SU/408493	2.	10.	2
Eghebury	Egbury	SU/439526	1.	13.	0
Benele	Binley	SU/420533		19.	11
Henlee	Cole Henley	SU/470510	1.	12.	8
Whitchirch'	Whitchurch	SU/463482	1.	19.	6
Frifolk'	Freefolk	SU/490482	1.	13.	10
Bagehurst	Baughurst	SU/581600		15.	7
Asshemeresworth'	Ashmansworth	SU/411566		14.	10
Wy de Hay	East Woodhay	SU/405613	1.	16.	8
Burghclere	Burghclere	SU/469579	2.	6.	2
Echeneswell'	Ecchinswell	SU/501599	1.	9.	0
Nova Villa	Newtown	SU/477637		17.	0
			25.	12.	1

Hd. Crondal [CRONDALL HUNDRED]

Yatele	Yateley	SU/818609	3.	12.	2
Suthwode	Southwood	SU/852551	1.	18.	6
Farneburgh'	Farnborough	SU/868535		11.	10
Cove	Cove	SU/856557	1.	15.	6
Crondal	Crondall	SU/795485		13.	2
Croukham	Crookham Village	SU/793524	2.	10.	5
Depenhale	Dippenhall	SU/809468	1.	2.	1
Swandroup'	Swanthorpe	SU/784467	1.	11.	6
Ichulle	Itchel	SU/785493	2.	14.	9
Alreshute	Aldershot	SU/859506	2.	15.	2
Sutton'	Long Sutton	SU/739473	2.	9.	2
			21.	14.	3

Hd. Mannesbrugge [MAINSBRIDGE HUNDRED]

Lettele	Netley	SU/454089	2.	11.	10
Badesle	North Baddesley	SU/402209	1.	14.	7
Chalworth	Chilworth	SU/407187	1.	7.	3
Buneyate	Boyatt	SU/451209		12.	3
Estele	Eastleigh	SU/456193	1.	17.	10
Berton'	Barton	SU/459193	1.	2.	0
Tounhelle	Townhill	SU/452150	2.	19.	8
Bottele	Botley	SU/511130	2.	11.	9

[1] Grid ref. is to Middle Wyke Farm.

Aldyngton'	Allington	SU/480172	3.	5.	3
Stonham'	South Stoneham	SU/440156	7.	14.	4
Shirle	Shirley	SU/392142	5.	0.	3
			30.	17.	0

Hd. Tytchefelde [TITCHFIELD HUNDRED]

Tychefelde	Titchfield	SU/541058	7.	7.	11
Swanewyk'	Swanwick	SU/515095	1.	16.	0
Prallyngworth'	Prallingworth[1]	lost	1.	4.	4
Bonewode	Bonewood[2]		2.	0.	4
Fontelegh'	Funtley	SU/563081	1.	13.	4
Houke	Hook	SU/509053	1.	19.	0
Crofton'	Crofton	SU/543046	3.	15.	6
Stubynton'	Stubbington	SU/556030	2.	3.	2
Rowenore	Rowner	SU/584037	3.	16.	6
Wykham	Wickham	SU/576114	6.	8.	6
			32.	4.	7

Hd. Sutton Episcopi [BISHOP'S SUTTON HUNDRED]

Hedligh'	Headley	SU/821362	3.	3.	10
Sutton'	Bishops Sutton	SU/606320	1.	9.	5½
Tystede	West Tisted	SU/650292	1.	2.	11½
Wiketon'[3]	Bighton	SU/610344	1.	11.	4
Brompden'	Bramdean	SU/610278	1.	5.	9½
Roppelegh'	Ropley	SU/646320	2.	13.	4
			11.	6.	8½

Hd. Portesdoune [PORTSDOWN HUNDRED]

Bedhampton'	Bedhampton	SU/703064	4.	8.	10
Farlington'	Farlington	SU/684054	2.	8.	6
Drayton'	Drayton	SU/673035	1.	10.	6
Wydelegh'	Widley	SU/663070		12.	2
Walesworth'	Wellsworth	SU/733114	2.	2.	10
Suthewyk'	Southwick	SU/626086	2.	17.	10
Westbonhonte	West Boarhunt[4]	SU/c.603083	2.	14.	11
Porteseye	Portsea	SU/628003	2.	9.	10
Bourhontherberd	Boarhunt Herbelyn[4]	SU/c.603083	1.	9.	2
Wymeryng &	Wymering and	SU/650055	4.	7.	6
Hulsey	Hilsea	SU/658038			
Midelton'	Milton	SU/664001	3.	10.	8
Esteneye	Eastney	SU/672993	2.	13.	2
Estborhonte	East Boarhunt[4]	SU/c.603083	1.	10.	10
Frodynton'	Fratton	SU/655005	3.	11.	5
			36.	8.	2

[1] Site unknown, but presumably within Fareham Parish (*V.C.H., Hants.* iii (1908), 209).

[2] No evidence for the whereabouts of this place has been found.

[3] *Wiketon* is an error for *Biketon* on E 179/173/21 (1352).

[4] It is not possible to distinguish the three manors of Boarhunt on the ground. An approximate grid ref. is given.

Hd. Estmoenes [EAST MEON HUNDRED]

Estmoenes	East Meon	su/681222	1.	12.	o
Froxefeld	Froxfield	su/703256	4.	17.	o
Stupe	Steep	su/746253	3.	14.	7
Langeryssh	Langrish	su/703238	2.	4.	5
Rammesdon'	Ramsdean	su/705223	3.	5.	5
Oxeneborn'	Oxenbourne	su/691213	3.	1.	o
Coumbe	Coombe	su/661206	1.	7.	o
Rypplynton'	Riplington	su/664237	2.	8.	3
Borden'	Bordean	su/692247	2.	9.	2
Aumbresham	Ambersham [in Sussex][1]	su/916206	2.	2.	o
			27.	o.	10

Hd. Werewelle [WHERWELL HUNDRED]

Wherewell'	Wherwell	su/391408	2.	14.	2
Clatford	Clatford [Lower][2]	su/366426	2.	16.	8
Godeworth' & Anne	Goodworth Clatford and Little Ann	su/366426 su/338437	1.	6.	9
Midelton' & Forton'	Middleton and Forton	su/426439 su/420435	1.	7.	4
Eston'	East Aston	su/436450	2.	11.	6
Bolyndon' & Tokynton'	Bullington and Tufton	su/455412 su/458468	2.	15.	1
			13.	11.	6
Romes' [v][3]	Romsey	su/351212	8.	o.	4
Stokbrigg'	Stockbridge	su/355351	2.	10.	o
			10.	10.	4
Porcestr' for'[4]	Portchester [foreign]		2.	8.	6

Hd. Maynesburgh' [MAINSBOROUGH HUNDRED]

Candevere Abbatis	Brown Candover	su/578392	1.	7.	6
Wodemannecote[5]	Woodmancott	su/562425		8.	5
Chilton'	Chilton Candover	su/592403	1.	11.	11½
			3.	7.	10½
Petrusfeld	Petersfield	su/748232	1.	14.	o
Bentelegh' [Lib.]	Bentley	su/784446	2.	o.	4
Cadelond & Staneswod	Cadland and Stanswood	su/450047 su/465007	1.	12.	8
			5.	7.	o

[1] Grid ref. is to South Ambersham.
[2] As Upper Clatford was taxed in Andover hundred it seems that this entry must refer to Lower Clatford. It seems certain that Goodworth and Lower Clatford were separate places before they merged into the settlement of Goodworth Clatford. All three were listed separately in 1316 (*F.A.* ii. 311–12).
[3] Romsey Extra was taxed in King's Somborne hundred.
[4] Portchester was taxed at a tenth (p. 121).
[5] Part of Woodmancott was taxed in Micheldever hundred.

Hd. Mucheldevere [MICHELDEVER HUNDRED]

Mucheldevere	Micheldever	su/512391	4.	8.	8
Northbrouk' in Much'	Northbrook	su/510395	1.	16.	2
Weston'	Weston Colley	su/502391	2.	11.	0
Slakstede	Slackstead	su/394254	2.	5.	2
Wordi Abbatis	Abbots Worthy	su/498327	1.	19.	6
Barre	Abbots Barton	su/483308		1.	6
Eststratton'	East Stratton	su/512391	2.	8.	1
Weststratton'	West Stratton	su/529404	1.	16.	9
Popham	Popham	su/558438	1.	13.	0
Wodemanecote[1]	Woodmancott	su/562425		9.	2½
Neuhampton'[2]	Northington	su/564373		9.	0
Swareweton'[3]	Swarraton	su/569372		7.	0
Northampton'[2]	Northington	su/564373	1.	1.	3
Drayton'	Drayton	su/427432		17.	10
Crambern'	Cranbourne	su/475406	1.	19.	5½
			24.	3.	7

Hd. Pachestrowe [PASTROW HUNDRED]

Fernham	Vernham Dean	su/340566	3.	10.	10¼
Faccombe	Faccombe	su/390581	2.	17.	10¼
Couenholte[4]	Conholt	su/335550	1.	5.	8½
Tangelegh'	Tangley	su/333524	2.	1.	8½
Linkenholt	Linkenholt	su/363581		18.	10¼
Eston' Crouk'	Crux Easton	su/425562	1.	7.	8¾
Wodecote	Woodcott	su/432549	1.	9.	4¼
Coumbe	Combe [in Berkshire]	su/368607	2.	4.	4¼
Husseborn'	Hurstbourne Tarrant	su/386530	2.	18.	0¾
			18.	14.	5¾

Hd. Overton' [OVERTON HUNDRED]

Larkestok'	Laverstoke	su/488489	1.	9.	4
Suthamton' &	Southington and	su/507495	4.	0.	10
Northampton'	Northington	su/501495			
Polhampton'	Polhampton	su/529506	2.	0.	2
Quidhampton'	Quidhampton	su/519504		18.	8
Assh' &	Ashe and	su/535500	1.	16.	8
Tadelegh'	Tadley	su/598600			
Hauekele	East Oakley[5]	su/573501		19.	8
Bradelegh'	Bradley	su/635417	1.	4.	10
Waltham	North Waltham	su/561463	1.	15.	0
Dene	Deane	su/546502		13.	0
Overton'	Overton	su/514500	3.	12.	8
			18.	10.	10

---

[1] See also Mainsborough hundred, above.
[2] Separate manors in Northington?
[3] Part of Swarraton was taxed in Bountisborough hundred.
[4] The entry refers to Lower Conholt as Conholt village was taxed in 1334 with Chute in Kindwardstone hundred, Wiltshire, p. 348.
[5] Church Oakley was part of Chuteley hundred.

Hd. Munestoke [MEONSTOKE HUNDRED]

Munestoke	Meonstoke	su/614198	4.	11.	0
Flexlonde	Flexland[1]	su/612144	1.	13.	6
Soberton'	Soberton	su/609168	3.	17.	7
Cornhampton'	Corhampton	su/612202		18.	2
Borewelle'	Burwell[2]	su/641137	1.	2.	5
Laumere	Lomer	su/590237	1.	2.	2
Warneford	Warnford	su/622226	3.	13.	0
Hoo	Easthoe	su/636159	2.	4.	5
Lys	Liss Abbas[3]	su/775284	2.	4.	9
Westbury & Stoke	Westbury and Stock	su/657239 su/666266	2.	2.	4
			23.	9.	4

Hd. Boutesburgh' [BOUNTISBOROUGH HUNDRED]

Ichenestok'	Itchen Stoke	su/559323	2.	10.	3½
Abboteston'	Abbotstone	su/565347	1.	16.	4
Ichene	Itchen Abbas	su/534327	3.	0.	4½
Swarweton'[4]	Swarraton	su/569372	1.	10.	7
			8.	17.	7

Hd. Hameldon' [HAMBLEDON HUNDRED]

Hameldon'	Hambledon	su/646152	1.	3.	1¾
Chidden'	Chidden	su/660179	1.	11.	3
Gludden'	Gludden	su/663153	1.	0.	3¼
Denemede	Denmead	su/659121	1.	12.	0
			5.	6.	8

Hd. Edyham [ODIHAM HUNDRED]

Lys[5]	Liss	su/775279	3.	19.	1
Weston'	Weston Patrick	su/691469	1.	12.	11
Lasham	Lasham	su/676425	1.	12.	2
Bynteworth'	Bentworth	su/666402	2.	19.	6¼
Dokemerefeld	Dogmersfield	su/775515	3.	6.	9
Wynchefelde	Winchfield	su/768536		18.	2¼
Shalden'	Shalden	su/693417	1.	15.	2
Mourhale	Murrell Green	su/743550		13.	0
Shirfeld	Sherfield on Loddon	su/671569	1.	14.	1¼
Elvetham	Elvetham	su/782564		16.	5
Hertlegh'	Hartley Wintney	su/769570	1.	8.	10¾
			20.	16.	2½

---

[1] Grid ref. is to Ingoldfield Farm, on the site of the former manor of Flexland.
[2] Grid ref. is to Bittles, on the site of the manor of Burwell.
[3] This is a tithing in Liss: the remainder of Liss was taxed in Odiham hundred.
[4] See also Micheldever hundred, above.
[5] See also Meonstoke hundred, above.

Hd. Aulton' Forinsecus [ALTON FOREIGN HUNDRED]

Aulton' Abbatis	Alton Eastbrook	su/c.720390	2.	4.	7
Anstigh'	Anstey	su/720402	1.	6.	4
Haliborne Estebrouk'[1]	Holybourne [Eastbrook]	su/734413	1.	13.	2
Hurtele Mauduyt'	Hartley Mauditt	su/743361	1.	11.	6
Westworldham	West Worldham	su/741370	1.	11.	0
Estworldham	East Worldham	su/751381	1.	5.	3
Brockesheuede	Broxhead	su/799369	1.	0.	6
Lydeshute	Ludshott	su/842341	1.	2.	10
Brambelshute	Bramshott	su/842329	1.	9.	9
Chiltelegh'	Chiltlee	su/844317		15.	6
Grutham	Greatham	su/773304	1.	7.	0
Okhangre	Oakhanger	su/769357	1.	2.	2
Wynhale	Will Hall	su/706392		11.	0
Chauton'	Chawton	su/708370	1.	10.	2
Froylle	Froyle	su/756429	3.	15.	3
			22.	6.	0

Hd. Fynchesdon' [FINCHDEAN HUNDRED]

Shute	Sheet	su/758246	1.	17.	3
Buryton'	Buriton	su/740200	1.	15.	6
Westyton'	Weston	su/729218	1.	0.	2
Nutstede	Nursted	su/758212	1.	0.	5
Chalghton'	Chalton	su/732160	3.	12.	3
Henton'	Hinton	su/689153	2.	17.	7
Clanefeld	Clanfield	su/698168	2.	15.	0
Idesworth'	Idsworth	su/743141	1.	8.	8
Caterynton'	Catherington	su/696145	4.	1.	11
Blendeworth'	Blendworth	su/711135	5.	11.	6
			26.	0.	3

Hd. Fourde [FORDINGBRIDGE HUNDRED]

Fourde	Fordingbridge	su/145139	2.	0.	11
Hale &	Hale and	su/179187	4.	5.	5
Chardeforde	Charford[2]	su/198196			
Brommere	Breamore	su/153189	3.	13.	$2\frac{1}{2}$
Rokeburne	Rockbourne	su/116183	7.	4.	4
Mygham	Midgham	su/137127	1.	17.	8
Burghate	Burgate	su/143157	4.	7.	0
Wyketon'[3]	Bickton	su/148127	1.	18.	3
Ibbesle	Ibsley	su/149094	2.	14.	0
Elyngham	Ellingham	su/143083	3.	2.	4
			31.	3.	$1\frac{1}{2}$

---

[1] Holybourne Eastbrook, as the name suggests, was the name given to that part of Holybourne parish on the east side of the Holybourne stream; the rest of Holybourne was taxed at a tenth, p. 120.

[2] Grid ref. is to North Charford.

[3] *Wyketon* is an error for *Byketon* on E 179/173/21 (1352).

Hd. Berton' Sacy [BARTON STACEY HUNDRED]

Berton' Sacy	Barton Stacey	SU/434412	4.	17.	2
Nyweton'	Newton Stacey	SU/411404	2.	1.	8
Sutton'	Sutton Scotney	SU/463395	4.	11.	7
Wordy Regis	Kings Worthy	SU/493323	3.	3.	8
Wordy Mortimer	Headbourne Worthy	SU/488320	1.	6.	8
Colemere &	Colemore and	SU/706307	2.	0.	6
Dene	Priors Dean	SU/728296			
Pambre	Bamber	SU/621587	1.	9.	4
Iwerst &	Inhurst and	SU/575613			
Hamme	Ham	SU/578600			
			19.	10.	7

Hd. Rudbrugg' [REDBRIDGE HUNDRED]

Stone	Stone	SZ/458994	1.	5.	4
Brightmanneston'	? Badminstone	SU/466023	1.	0.	2
Depedene	Dibden	SU/398085	4.	9.	7
Burches	?			13.	10
Merchewode	Marchwood	SU/386102	4.	3.	0
Nyweton'	? Newtown Bury	SU/379113	1.	9.	4
Langle	Langley	SU/349105	1.	0.	4
Elynge &	Eling and	SU/367125	1.	1.	0
Colebury	Colbury	SU/349109			
Rombrugg'	Rum Bridge	SU/359128	1.	4.	8
Oure	Ower	SU/325164	1.	15.	10
Totynton'	Totton	SU/360129	2.	6.	4
Terstewode	Testwood	SU/351146	2.	15.	6
Wyndlesore	Winsor	SU/316142	3.	12.	6
Burkle	Bartley	SU/306129			
Natele &	Netley Marsh and	SU/332131			
Tachebury	Tatchbury	SU/328141			
			26.	17.	5

Hd. Kyngesclere [KINGSCLERE HUNDRED]

Kyngesclere [v]	Kingsclere	SU/525586	6.	10.	1½
Wolferton'	Wolverton	SU/442585	2.	11.	0
Iwerst &	Ewhurst and	SU/570569	1.	6.	0
Fynlegh	Finley[1]	SU/c.575573			
Okle &	North Oakley and	SU/538541		18.	8
Tydegrove	Tidgrove	SU/522544			
Hanyton'	Hannington	SU/539554		17.	0
Lidershulue	Litchfield	SU/462540	3.	16.	8
Sydemanton'	Sydmonton	SU/485579	3.	6.	2
Urleston'	Earlstone	SU/480599	2.	16.	10
Edmondesthorp Benham	Edmundsthorpe Benham[2]	SU/517614	1.	13.	8
& Launceleneye	and Hannington	SU/540558			
	Launcelneye				
Stanford	Sandford	SU/541587	3.	10.	2
Frollebury &	Frobury and	SU/512594	1.	19.	11
Clerwodecote	Clere Woodcott[3]	SU/c.531600			
			29.	6.	2½

[1] The name Finley survives in Finley's Row on the north side of Ewhurst Park.
[2] Grid ref. is Benham Court.
[3] The grid ref. is to the area of Clere Woodcott tithing; the name itself does not survive.

Hd. Bosseburgh' cum Insula de Haylyngg'
[BOSMERE HUNDRED WITH HAYLING ISLAND]

Sstok' [v]	Stoke	su/720024	3.	17.	10¾
Estok'	Eastoke	sz/730987	2.	2.	0
Northewode	North Hayling	su/731032	4.	5.	6
Myngham	Mengham	sz/730991	4.	12.	9¾
Southwod	South Hayling	su/722001	2.	7.	11
Westynton'	West Town	sz/713994	2.	8.	1
Wade	Wade	su/721053	2.	10.	3½
Warblynton'	Warblington	su/729054	3.	4.	8
Empnesworth'	Emsworth	su/748061	4.	7.	0
Haylyngg'[1]	Hayling Island			11.	8
			30.	7.	10

Hd. Chutle [CHUTELEY HUNDRED]

Okle	Oakley	su/568503	2.	3.	0
Wotton'	Wootton St. Lawrence	su/592533	1.	0.	3
Wortyngge	Worting	su/601518		12.	9
			3.	16.	0

Hd. Farham [FAREHAM HUNDRED]

Crokereshull'	Crockerhill	su/578095		17.	8¼
Northfarham	North Fareham	su/583078	1.	10.	7¼
Walyngton'	Wallington	su/580068		19.	4½
Cartesfeld	Catisfield	su/548062	1.	4.	4
Farham	Fareham	su/576061		16.	5½
Cammes	Cams	su/589058		19.	10¼
Bronewych'	Brownwich	su/520037		16.	3¼
			7.	4.	7¼

Hd. Nove Foreste [NEW FOREST HUNDRED]

Lyndhurst	Lyndhurst	su/300083	1.	4.	7½
Brokenhurst &	Brockenhurst and	su/300023	2.	19.	0
Brouklegh'	Brookley	su/296023			
Ippelegh' &	Ipley and	lost	4.	17.	0¾
Botesassh'	Buttsash	su/421059			
Hardelegh'	Hardley	su/430050	1.	15.	8
Holebury &	Holebury and	su/430037	1.	13.	4
Langelegh'	Langley	su/445012			
Ecresbury &	Exbury and	su/428002	3.	7.	4
Lupe	Lepe	sz/448987			
Badelegh'	South Baddesley	sz/352967	3.	5.	8
Westburne &	Warborne and	sz/330975	1.	17.	8
Pullee	Pilley	sz/326981			
Batramesle &	Battramsley and	sz/306991		11.	8
Wodyton'	Wootton	sz/231992			

---

[1] Hayling Island is listed in Bosmere hundred on E 179/173/21 (1352). On many other documents it appears in Fawley hundred—as it did in 1332 (E 179/242/15, m. 5). The total tax for these hundreds changes accordingly.

Berlegh'	Burley	SU/211031	I.	9.	4
Lyndwode &	Linwood and	SU/192100	I.	17.	5½
Codeshull'	Codshill	SU/175151			
Frytham	Fritham	SU/232140		9.	0
Canterton'	Canterton	SU/273135		13.	10
Mynstede	Minstead	SU/281109		13.	0
Berkelegh'	Bartley Regis	SU/305124		14.	7
			27.	9.	2¾

Hd. Falelee [FAWLEY HUNDRED]

Havonte [v]	Havant	SU/718064	2.	18.	9
Goseporte	Gosport	SU/607003		10.	8
Burseldon'[1]	Bursledon	SU/484092		4.	10
Exton'	Exton	SU/613211	I.	2.	0
Alwarestok'	Alverstoke	SZ/601988	I.	17.	2
Westmoene	West Meon	SU/640241	I.	13.	6
Kelmeston	Kilmeston	SU/591263	I.	7.	3
Henton'	Hinton Ampner	SU/598275		13.	2
Beoworth'	Beauworth	SU/577261		16.	6
Alresford[2]	Old Alresford	SU/588336	I.	9.	8
Medestede	Medstead	SU/654372		12.	5
Wylda	Wield	SU/629388		19.	1
Chiltecombe	Chilcomb	SU/508284		6.	6
Chireton'	Cheriton	SU/582285	I.	19.	11
Tychebourn'	Tichborne	SU/569302	I.	2.	8
Ovynton'	Ovington	SU/561317		11.	7
Moursted	Morestead	SU/510254		17.	6
Avynton'	Avington	SU/533323		13.	3
Wordy	Martyr Worthy	SU/515328		9.	9
Eston'	Easton	SU/509322		19.	0
Wynhale	Winnall	SU/494299		6.	10
Twyford	Twyford	SU/481251	I.	17.	1
Horton'	Horton Heath	SU/496173	2.	1.	2
Ouslebury	Owslebury	SU/515233	2.	17.	10
			28.	8.	1

Hd. Hosshute [HOLDSHOT HUNDRED]

Holeshute	Holdshott	SU/740603	5.	2.	2
Heghfeld	Heckfield	SU/723604	3.	10.	6
Hurtelee	Hartley Wespall	SU/698583	I.	8.	6
Stratfelde Turgys	Stratfield Turgis	SU/690600	I.	3.	10
Bromeshull'	Bramshill	SU/742612	I.	5.	10
Shilchestr'	Silchester	SU/643623	2.	12.	10
Stratfeld Say[3]	Stratfield Saye	SU/695614	3.	16.	6
Stratfeld Mortimer[4]	Stratfield Mortimer [in Berks.]	SU/669641	I.	2.	6
Everesle	Eversley	SU/779610	2.	5.	0
			22.	7.	8

---

[1] Most of Burseldon was taxed in Bishop's Waltham hundred.
[2] New Alresford borough was taxed at a tenth, p. 121.
[3] Part of Stratfield Saye was taxed in Berkshire (Reading hundred, p. 8).
[4] Most of Stratfield Mortimer was taxed in Berkshire (Theale hundred, p. 8).

Hd. Waltham [BISHOP'S WALTHAM HUNDRED]

Waltham	Bishop's Waltham	su/556176	2.	0.	8
Assheton'	Ashton	su/552193	1.	14.	0
Upham	Upham	su/539206	1.	10.	0
Derlegh'	Durley	su/505170	2.	11.	8
Courderygg'	Curdridge	su/529139	1.	19.	1
Burseldon'[1]	Bursledon	su/484092	1.	5.	4
Fallelee	Fawley	su/458035	1.	13.	0
Byterne	Bitterne	su/453130	1.	11.	3
Swanemere	Swanmore	su/576163	1.	3.	0
Drokeneforde	Droxford	su/608182	1.	11.	0
Shidefeld	Shedfield	su/562133	1.	14.	0
			18.	13.	0

Hd. Bermundesputte [BERMONDSPIT HUNDRED]

Warneburne	South Warnborough	su/721472	5.	14.	0
Hodeketon'	Hoddington	su/702477	1.	9.	11
Upton'	Upton Grey	su/697485	1.	16.	0
Weston' Corbet	Weston Corbett	su/688470		17.	6
Heryerd	Herriard	su/663460	1.	2.	0
Elesefeld	Ellisfield	su/639459		19.	7
Farlegh'	Farleigh Wallop	su/625475	2.	16.	4
Nutlegh'	Nutley	su/610444	1.	10.	0
Dommere	Dummer	su/589460	4.	12.	10
Candevere Preston'	Preston Candover	su/607415	6.	3.	8
			27.	1.	10

Hd. Basyngestok' Forinsecus [BASINGSTOKE FOREIGN HUNDRED]

Basynges	Basing	su/666529	4.	14.	2
Shirborne Sancti Johannis	Sherborne St. John	su/623555	3.	9.	4
Shirborne Coudray	The Vyne	su/637567		18.	4
Bromlegh'	Bramley	su/645590	3.	4.	6
Chinham	Chineham	su/655548	1.	1.	0
Estroup cum Lykeput	Eastrop with Lychpit	su/641521 su/658533	1.	1.	10
Toneworth'	Tunworth	su/672484	2.	2.	6
Wynesflode	Winslade	su/654481	2.	0.	0
Kempeshute	Kempshott	su/605507		10.	3
Cludesden'	Cliddesden	su/632491	1.	10.	5
Hacche	Hatch Warren	su/616488		8.	0
Styvynton'	Steventon	su/551472		18.	0
Niwenham	Newnham	su/703540		17.	6
Natele Scures	Nately Scures	su/697530	1.	5.	0
Somereshull'	Somershill[2]	lost		4.	0
Upnatel	Up Nately	su/701519		11.	10
Mapelderwelle	Mapledurwell	su/688510		18.	2
Wodegarston'	Woodgarston	sp/583550		12.	4
			26.	7.	2

---

[1] See also Fawley hundred, above.
[2] See *V.C.H., Hants.* iv (1911), 114, for suggestions of locality.

Insula Vecta [ISLE OF WIGHT]
Hd. Eastmedeme [EAST MEDINE HUNDRED]

Sancti Elena [v]	St. Helens	sz/629890	5.	2.	4
Estaunden' &	East Standen and	sz/528877	2.	0.	2
Merston'	Merstone	sz/527851			
Westaunden	West Standen	sz/506874	1.	2.	8
Wyppyngham	Whippingham	sz/511936	1.	2.	0
Penne &	Pan[1] and	sz/506886	2.	10.	8
Faierle	Fairlee	sz/507904			
Wodynton'	Wootton	sz/542926	1.	14.	10
Nyweton'	Niton	sz/506768	6.	2.	7
Godeshull' &	Godshill and	sz/527818	3.	10.	0
Stenesbury	Stenbury	sz/525790			
Wytewelle	Whitwell	sz/521777	4.	0.	2
Wroxhale	Wroxall	sz/551800	6.	3.	0
Whathe &	St. Lawrence and	sz/538766	3.	2.	8
Natelcombe	Nettlecombe	sz/527783			
Sandham &	Sandown and	sz/596843	8.	10.	0
Wik'	Week	sz/537779			
Acheston' &	Adgestone and	sz/592861	3.	10.	0
Curne	Kern	sz/579867			
Ardele &	Hardley and	sz/632866	5.	1.	0
Everlond'	Yaverland	sz/614859			
Knyghteton' &	Knighton and	sz/566866	3.	1.	0
Arreton'	Arreton	sz/534867			
Bermardeslee	Barnsley	sz/608902	2.	0.	0
Brerdyngg'	Brading	sz/606873	1.	16.	0
Rouda &	Roud and	sz/516803	7.	18.	0
Roukele	Rockley	sz/507843			
Shenlynch'	Shanklin	sz/582814	1.	10.	2
			69.	17.	3[2]

Hd. Westmedeme [WEST MEDINE HUNDRED]

Chale [v]	Chale	sz/483775	4.	8.	4
Kyngeston'	Kingston	sz/479813	1.	10.	2
Suthshorewell'	South Shorwell [West Court]	sz/452827	1.	11.	8
Agherfeld	Atherfield[3]	sz/470793		18.	6
Broke	Brook	sz/390837	2.	2.	8
Modeston'	Mottistone	sz/405837	6.	6.	2
Afton	Afton	sz/349862	1.	14.	4
Shyde	Shide	sz/503882		17.	8
Gatecombe	Gatcombe	sz/492851	6.	9.	1
Chuliarton' [&	Chillerton and	sz/487837	5.	6.	4
Billyngham][4]	Billingham	sz/485818			
Park'	Park[5]	sz/457882		7.	6
Bouecombe	Bowcombe	sz/470866	5.	9.	6

[1] Grid ref. is to Great Pan Farm.

[2] An entry of £3. 10. 0 for Ashey is sometimes included in East Medine hundred, making the total £73. 7. 3. On E 179/173/21 Ashey is inserted in a later hand, but the original entry for it under the liberty of the Isle of Wight has not been struck through. I have therefore included it under the Isle of Wight liberty in this list, p. 120.

[3] Grid ref. is to Atherfield Farm.

[4] Billingham is omitted from E 179/173/21 (1352) but is listed on 173/22 (1354).

[5] Grid ref. is to Great Park.

Karesbrok'	Carisbrooke	sz/486882	1.	2.	2
Thorle [&	Thorley and	sz/367892	3.	6.	10
Welgh']¹	Wellow	sz/389880			
Northwode	Northwood	sz/493930	7.	5.	0
Nyngwode	Ningwood	sz/401887		19.	4
Shaldeflute	Shalfleet	sz/413892	1.	5.	11
Wtryngwell'	Watchingwell²	sz/445894		18.	2
Compton'	Compton	sz/376851		7.	6
Northorwelle	North Shorwell	sz/457832		17.	10
	[=North Court]				
			53.	4.	8

Lib. Insula Vecta [ISLE OF WIGHT LIBERTY]

Fresshewatere	Freshwater	sz/347873	6.	13.	4
Assheshegh'³	Ashey	sz/584883	3.	10.	0
Ermuth	Yarmouth	sz/355896		19.	0
Neuporte	Newport	sz/499891	7.	5.	0
Sweyneston'	Swainston	sz/442878	11.	13.	0
			30.	0.	4

Basyngstok'⁴ [A.D]	Basingstoke	su/637522	12.	6.	0	[T]

Odiham [A.D] [ODIHAM]

Odiham [A.D]	Odiham	su/740509	4.	2.	8	[T]
Warnebourn' [A.D]	North Warnborough	su/731516	2.	17.	6	[T]
Grewelle [A.D]	Greywell	su/718510	3.	13.	6	[T]
			10.	13.	8	[T]

Aulton' [A.D] [ALTON]

Aulton' [A.D]	Alton	su/714390	5.	10.	0	[T]
Halibourn' [A.D]⁵	Holybourne	su/732412	1.	5.	6	[T]
Suthheghes [A.D]	South Hay	su/773398	1.	13.	0	[T]
Wyke [A.D]	Wyck	su/756395	1.	5.	10	[T]
Westcote [A.D]	West Court	su/765411	1.	4.	0	[T]
Isynton' [A.D]	Isington	su/773429	2.	3.	9	[T]
Whatele [A.D]	Wheatley	su/784401		17.	6	[T]
Bienstied [A.D]	Binsted	su/771409	3.	1.	11	[T]
Kyngesle [A.D]	Kingsley	su/789382	3.	1.	6	[T]
Thudden' [A.D]	Thedden	su/683390		13.	10	[T]
Holtham [A.D] &	Holtham⁶ and	su/c.722318	1.	0.	8	[T]
Rutherfield [A.D]	Rotherfield	su/694323				
			21.	17.	6	[T]

---

¹ Wellow is omitted from E 179/173/21 but is listed on 173/22.

² Grid ref. is to Lower Watchingwell.

³ See note at end of East Medine hundred, above.

⁴ As E 179/173/21 is incomplete, details of the tenth are taken from E 179/173/22 (1354).

⁵ This presumably refers to that part of Holybourne west of the brook as the remainder was taxed in Alton Foreign hundred, above.

⁶ Holtham is marked on old maps one mile south of Newton Valence, but the name is not now used.

Ryngwod' [A.D]	Ringwood	SU/145053	22.	2.	6	[T]
Hardebrigge [A.D]	Harbridge	SU/144101	3.	3.	0	[T]
Penyton' [A.D]	Pennington	SZ/310951	3.	9.	6	[T]
Butesthorn' [A.D]	Bisterne	SU/149012	4.	8.	0	[T]
			33.	3.	0	[T]
Andevere [A.D]	Andover	SU/365458	19.	19.	11	[T]

[BOROUGHS][1]

Suthampton' [V]	Southampton	SU/420113	51.	2.	4	[T]
Alresford [B][2]	New Alresford	SU/589327	4.	19.	6	[T]
Portesmuth' [B]	Portsmouth	SZ/648993	12.	12.	2	[T]
Porcestre int'[3]	Portchester [within]	SU/619054	8.	5.	3	[T]
Civitas Wynton'	Winchester	SU/480295	51.	10.	4	[T]
Soka Wynton'[4]	Soke of Winchester	SU/488293	11.	0.	0	[T]
			139.	9.	7	[T]

TOTAL: £1,340. 16. 3½[5]

[1] The six places below were the taxation boroughs of 1334 (as named on the 1334 Account, E 179/173/7) but some were not considered as boroughs on this later roll of the subsidy, 25 Edward III (1352).

[2] For Old Alresford see Fawley hundred, above.

[3] Portchester foreign was taxed at a fifteenth (p. 111).

[4] The Soke of Winchester, a liberty in the eastern part of the city, was treated as a borough in 1332 and 1334.

[5] As on 1334 Account, E 179/173/7. The figures for the hundreds in the Particulars in fact add up to £1340. 18. 5¾.

HEREFORDSHIRE

DOCUMENTS

8 Edward III: Account   E 179/117/5
8 Edward III: Indenture   E 179/117/4 and 117/19* (continuous)
10 Edward III: Particulars E 179/117/6

TAXERS

Master Stephen de Ledbury, dean of Hereford, and Walter Joce

TAX YIELD

15th	£355.	18.	8
10th	£ 81.	7.	3
	£437.	5.	11

Representing assessed movable wealth of

£6,152.   12.   6

NOTES

The Herefordshire list is distinctive on account of the large number of entries which refer to more than one place-name; of the seventy-three quotas only twenty-nine refer to a single place-name. Furthermore many of the place-names are difficult to identify and there are more than the usual number of uncertainties in the accompanying list.

Places taxed at a tenth are listed at the beginning; they comprise the city of Hereford, the boroughs of Leominster and Weobley, and the ancient demesnes of Lugwardine and Marden.

For reasons unknown many settlements now in the west of the county are not named in 1334 and it is therefore not clear where the western boundary of the county lay at that time. The eastern boundary has changed slightly since 1334. Four places then taxed in Herefordshire have since been transferred to Worcestershire, viz. Stoke Bliss, Perry, Hyde, and Rochford. Five places in the modern county were then taxed in adjacent counties, viz. Acton Beauchamp, Edvin Loach, and Mathon in Worcestershire, Lea in Gloucestershire, and Jay in Shropshire.

ACKNOWLEDGEMENT

I am indebted to Dr. B. G. Charles for help in the identification of a number of place-names.

[BOROUGHS AND ANCIENT DEMESNES]

Civitas Hereford	Hereford	SO/510400	60.	9.	1	[T]
Lugwardyn [A.D][1]	Lugwardine	SO/551410	3.	15.	1	[T]

[1] Part of Lugwardine was taxed at a fifteenth (Radlow hundred).

Maurdyn [A.D][1]	Marden	so/512471	2.	12.	8	[T]
Leominstr [B]	Leominster	so/496591	4.	10.	4	[T]
Webbeley [B]	Weobley	so/402519	5.	0.	1	[T]
Ricardus filius Johannis Monyword			5.	0.	0	[T]
			81.	7.	3	[T]

Hd. Brokkesayssh' [BROXASH HUNDRED]

Magna Cowerne	Much Cowarne	so/619471	6.	15.	11
Avenebur'	Avenebury	so/662532	2.	5.	10
Stokelacy	Stoke Lacy	so/621494	2.	10.	2
Pencombe	Pencombe	so/600528	2.	17.	3
Grenden'	Grendon Warren	so/601547	3.	1.	2
Marshton'	Marston Stannett	so/571552			
Stanford	?				
Stanford Regis	Stanford Regis				
Brydenbury	Bredenbury	so/609564			
Hopton' Solers	Hopton Sollers	so/636496			
Bodenham	Bodenham	so/530509	5.	0.	8
Burghope	Burghope	so/503503			
Boley	Bowley	so/540527			
Bradefeld	Broadfield	so/545531			
Wode	Wood	so/550519			
Brokhamton'	Brockhampton	so/688560			
Mora	Bodenham Moor	so/545501			
Houton'	Houghton	so/559510			
Hope[2]	Dudale's Hope	so/560516			
Dodydale					
Hethe	Heath Corner	so/554538	1.	5.	1
Mawene	Maund Bryan	so/561504			
Wytechirch'	Whitechurch Maund	so/563491			
Mawene	Rosemaund	so/564480			
Grenden' Episcopi	Grendon Bishop	so/598563	9.	15.	7
Waketon'	Wacton	so/615573			
Colynton'[3]	Collington	so/649601			
Colynton'[3]	Little Collington	so/c.657598			
Herton'	Horton	so/635582			
Wolferlowe	Wolferlow	so/669617			
Underlythe	Underley[4]	so/657613			
Roudon'	Rowden	so/631563			
Stokeblees	Stoke Bliss [in Worcs.][5]	so/651629			
Tedesterne Waffre	Tedstone Wafer	so/677590			
Sapy	Upper Sapey[6]	so/683636			
Pirie	Perry Farm [in Stoke Bliss, in Worcs.]	so/629625			

[1] Part of Marden was taxed at a fifteenth (Broxash hundred).

[2] The names of *Hope* and *Dodydale* seem to be represented on modern maps by the settlement of Dudale's Hope; they may have been separate places in 1334.

[3] Great and Little Collington were united as one parish in 1352, following the reduction of the population by the plague (J. Duncombe, *Collections towards the History and Antiquities of the County of Hereford*, ii, pt. 1 (1812), 92). The site of All Saints, the former parish church of Little Collington, is east of the present village.

[4] Grid ref. is to Lower Underley.

[5] Stoke Bliss parish, now in Worcestershire, was formerly chiefly in Broxash hundred, Herefordshire.

[6] Lower Sapey was taxed in Worcestershire.

Hide	Hyde [in Stoke Bliss, in Worcs.]	SO/629619			
Hampton'	Hampton Wafer	SO/577570			
Thornbury	Thornbury	SO/622597			
Tedesterne la Mare	Tedstone Delamere	SO/694587			
Churchwythynton'	Withington	SO/566435	9.	17.	4
Neuynton'	Nunnington	SO/551431			
Ewythynton'	Eau Withington	SO/545429			
Parva 'Thunghull'	Thing-hill Court	SO/568448			
Ocle Pychard	Ocle Pychard	SO/596462			
Ocle Lyre	Livers Ocle	SO/577464			
Felton'	Felton	SO/579485			
Thunghull'	Thing-hill	SO/553449			
Hope	Hope[1]	SO/582503			
Ilyngwyk'	Ullingswick	SO/597499			
Preston'[2]	Preston Wynne	SO/559466			
Preston'	Preston [Lower Town]	SO/555465			
Bromyerd for'	Bromyard [foreign]		4.	9.	7
Bromyerd Denzeyn	Bromyard	SO/656548	3.	8.	3
Wytebourne	Whitbourne	SO/725569	2.	10.	3
Stanford Episcopi	Stanford Bishop	SO/682515	1.	12.	2
Sutton' Frene	Sutton St. Nicholas	SO/534453	8.	1.	7
Maurdyn[3]	Marden	SO/512471			
			63.	10.	10

Hd. Grymeswrosne [GRIMSWORTH HUNDRED]

Hompton'	Hampton Bishop	SO/559380	4.	13.	10
Holemare	Holmer	SO/506423			
Shellewyk'	Shelwick	SO/521430			
Burcote	The Burcott	SO/521421			
Tulynton'	Tillington	SO/468452	7.	9.	8
Burghull'	Burghill	SO/479445			
Burghelton'	Burlton[4]	SO/481425			
Hulle	Hill	SO/452454			
Stretton'	Stretton Sugwas	SO/460420			
Breynton'	Breinton	SO/473395			
Werham	Warham	SO/483396			
Malmeshull' Lacy	Mansell Lacy	SO/426456	5.	13.	5
Brynshope	Brinsop	SO/442448			
Credenhull'	Credenhill	SO/451439			
Wormesley	Wormsley	SO/428478			
Staundon'	Staunton on Wye	SO/376448	10.	8.	6
Malmeshull' Gamage	Mansell Gamage	SO/393445			
Byford'	Byford	SO/398429			
Bruggesolers	Bridge Sollers	SO/415426			
Bysshopeston'	Bishopstone	SO/416439			
Kennestre	Kenchester	SO/433422			
Bunshull'	Bunshill	SO/431425			
Norton'	Norton Canon	SO/382478	3.	16.	8
Yasoure	Yazor	SO/406466			

[1] Grid ref. is to Lower Hope.
[2] Preston Superior and Inferior appear in the *Nomina Villarum* of 1316 (*F.A.* ii. 390). I have identified one of the two Prestons in 1334 as that part of Preston Wynne marked as Lower Town on the O.S. 6″ map, but it might refer to Preston Marsh.
[3] Part of Marden was taxed at a tenth, above.
[4] Grid ref. is to Lower Burlton.

Monyton'	Monnington on Wye	so/373433	2.	o.	2
Brocbury	Brobury	so/346442			
Ludes	Lyde	so/515443	2.	o.	1
Pionia Canonicorum	Canon Pyon	so/450491	6.	19.	10
Welynton'	Wellington	so/497483			
Morton'	Moreton on Lugg	so/505457			
			43.	2.	2

Hd. Wormelowe in Irchenfeld' [WORMELOW HUNDRED]

Garewy	Garway	so/455224	5.	5.	1
Capell' c.h	King's Caple [with hamlets]	so/559289			
Lanhadok' c.h	?				
Caneros	Corras[1]	so/419249			
Orcoppe	Orcop	so/473262			
Treget	Tregate	so/480171			
Seint Wolstan	St. Wolstan's	so/519173			
Neweton'	Welsh Newton	so/499180			
Seint Waynard c.h	St. Weonards [with hamlets]	so/497243			
Sholle[2]	Showle	so/611437	9.	16.	2
Ballyngham c.h	Ballingham [with hamlets]	so/576316			
Bolston'	Bolstone	so/552328			
Acornebury	Aconbury	so/517335			
Byrches Sancti Marie	Little Birch	so/512312			
Hulle	identification uncertain[3]				
Combe c.h	?				
Lanwaran	Llanwarne	so/506282			
Lecheston'	possibly Lyston[4]	so/495287			
Wormeton'	Wormeton[5]	lost			
Foye c.h	Foy [with hamlets]	so/598283			
Deweswell'	Dewsall	so/486335			
Treissak'	Treseck	so/542296			
Athelgwynt	Altwint	so/528308			
Landinabou	Llandinabo	so/518284			
Yuoreston	?				
Byrches Sancti Thom'	Much Birch[6]	so/504305			
Moneketon'	Monkton	so/490267			
Brompley	Bromley	so/532299			

[1] Grid ref. is to Great Corras.

[2] Showle in Yarkhill was a liberty of Wormelow hundred but part was taxed in Radlow hundred.

[3] Four possible identifications for Hulle are: Hills Farm in Llanwarne (so/490276); Hill Gate in Llanwarne (so/496274); Little Hill on the boundary between Llanwarne and Orcop (so/479273); Underhill in Much Birch (so/509304).

[4] Alternatively Lenastone, now in Pencoyd parish, but formerly a chapelry on Llanwarne parish.

[5] It is known that Wormeton was part of the manor of Kilpeck (Revd. A. T. Bannister, *The Place Names of Herefordshire* (1916), 214).

[6] According to the O.S. 6″ map, the church of Much Birch, built in 1837, is dedicated to St. Mary; in fact, the dedication is to both St. Mary and St. Thomas and it seems that the earlier church possessed an alternative dedication.

Kylpek'[1]	Kilpeck	so/445305	8.	14.	6
Deweschirch'	Dewchurch[2]	so/483311			
Rydeby	Ridby	so/467311			
Llanheythok	Llanithog	so/431270			
Wylton' c.m	Wilton [with members]	so/587242			
Brydestowe	Bridstow	so/585249			
Petrestowe	Peterstow	so/563249			
Clyve	Cleeve	so/591237			
Nicheleston'	?				
Meredicheston'	identification uncertain[3]				
Yevaneston'	Everstone	so/552250			
Hendre	Hendre	so/551234			
Penkreid	Pencraig	so/563209			
Blakenorl	Blacknorle				
Martinestowe	Marstow	so/553192			
Brokhaleston'	probably Brelston	so/559201			
Wytefeld'	Whitfield	so/551212			
Landeuenok'	?				
Pencoyt	Pencoyd	so/516265	2.	19.	1
Treberyn	Treberon	so/509259			
Trevays	Trevase	so/511255			
Ritir'	Tretire	so/520239			
Kylbrest'	Kilbreece	so/526235			
Mycheleschyrch'	Michaelchurch	so/521255			
Treradou	Treaddow	so/541242			
Aberhale	Aberhall	so/529241			
Hentlan	Hentland	so/543264			
Damston'	identification uncertain[4]				
Kynyoceston'	Kynaston	so/542271			
Hendresroudre	?				
Kaercradok'	Caradoc	so/559274			
Penketli'	Pengethly	so/543257			
Gyllough	Gillow	so/531253			
Elvareston'	Elvastone	so/524283			
Harewode	Harewood	so/530280			
Langaran	Llangarron	so/531212	3.	2.	8
Kylrek	Kilreague	so/512212			
Lancloudy	Llancloudy	so/498208			
Treosseth	probably Tre-essay	so/505218			
Langhenok'	Llangunnock	so/510233			
Trezevan	Tre-even	so/522223			
Lankeston'	Langstone	so/533220			
Brenythyn	Bernitham	so/540212			
			29.	18.	4

Hd. Greytr' [GREYTREE HUNDRED]

Eton' Tregoz	Hill of Eaton	so/606277	7.	0.	8
Weston'	Weston under Penyard	so/632232			
Kyngeston'	Kingstone	so/631246			

---

[1] On a later roll, E 179/117/18 (7 Ric. II), Wormelow hundred is split into two parts;
the first part of the hundred is named Wormelow in Archenfield, and the second, starting
at the entry for Kilpeck, is headed Wormelow.
[2] Grid ref. is to Much Dewchurch.
[3] Possibly Moraston in Bridstow (so/568255).
[4] Probably Dason Farm in Hentland (so/538267).

Hopemaloysel	Hope Mansel	SO/625196			
Brompton'	Brampton Abbotts	SO/601264			
Aston'	Aston Ingham	SO/683235			
Fonehope	Fownhope	SO/581343	14.	5.	1
Hugh Caple	How Capel	SO/612305			
Falley	Fawley	SO/577301			
Putteley	Putley	SO/646376			
Hope Solers	Sollers Hope	SO/612331			
Hope Woluine	Woolhope	SO/612358			
Frome &	Priors' Frome and	SO/576392			
Dormyton'	Dormington	SO/583402			
Lynton'	Linton	SO/661243	6.	0.	4
Ekcleswall'	Eccleswall	SO/652232			
Magna Markley	Much Marcle	SO/658328	3.	6.	8
Ros Denzeyn	Ross on Wye	SO/598241	3.	8.	4
Ros for'	Ross on Wye [foreign]		8.	4.	1
Walford &	Walford and	SO/587204			
Hule	Howle Hill	SO/598207			
Upton' Episcopi	Upton Bishop	SO/651272			
			42.	5.	2

Hd. Webbetr' [WEBTREE HUNDRED]

Preston'	Preston on Wye	SO/383424	6.	12.	0
Blakemere	Blakemere	SO/362411			
Tyberton'	Tyberton	SO/380399			
Carewardyn	Carwardine Green	SO/402409			
Lulham	Lulham	SO/409413			
Brugge	Canon Bridge	SO/431412			
Wormele	Wormhill	SO/431394			
Bache	Batchy	SO/397367			
Maddeleye	Madley	SO/420387			
Coblynton'	Cublington	SO/400386			
Cobewall'	Cobhall	SO/451360	4.	14.	4
Hongarston'	Hungerstone	SO/445353			
Malfeld	Mawfield	SO/452365			
More Alayn	Allensmore	SO/467359			
Clehungre	Clehonger	SO/465380			
Hommelacy	Holme Lacy	SO/568348	8.	9.	9
Dunre	Dinedor	SO/534367			
Grafton'	Grafton	SO/496370			
Bollynghop' superior	Bullinghope	SO/510371			
Bollynghop' inferior	Lower Bullingham	SO/519383			
Rotherwas	Rotherwas	SO/536382			
Bredwardyn	Bredwardine	SO/335445	2.	0.	6
Mokkas	Moccas	SO/358432			
Eton' Episcopi	Eaton Bishop	SO/443391	6.	0.	5
Chyldeston'	Chilstone	SO/398395			
Bellymare	Bellimoor	SO/394407			
Kyngeston'	Kingstone	SO/424357			
Arcleston'	Arkstone	SO/435361			
Webbeton'	Webton	SO/421365			
Brompton'	Brampton	SO/410367			
Thurcleston'	Thruxton	SO/437347			
Wormbrugg'	Wormbridge	SO/428306	2.	8.	9
Houton'	Howton	SO/414292			
Duddeley	Didley	SO/452322			
Calewe	Callow	SO/494344			
Twyford	Twyford	SO/507344			

Caluhull	?		8.	o.	6
Dorston'	Dorstone	SO/315418			
Snodhull'	Snodhill	SO/320403			
Wylmeston'	Wilmastone	SO/340401			
Maubache	Mowbach	SO/346393			
Wyrkebrok'	Wellbrook	SO/352384			
Petreschyrch'	Peterchurch	SO/345385			
Hayuiry	Urishay	SO/323376			
Thorlokeshop'[1]		lost			
Hynton'	Hinton	SO/340389			
Puston'	Poston	SO/352372			
Turneston'	Turnastone	SO/358365			
Lynhales	Lyonshall	SO/355391			
Fowechyrch'	Vowchurch	SO/362365			
Cheyneston'	Chanstone	SO/363356			
Waltereston'	Walterstone	SO/341250			
Monyton'	Monnington	SO/383368			
Baketon'	Bacton	SO/371323			
			38.	6.	3

Hd. Radelowe [RADLOW HUNDRED]

Froma Episcopi	Bishops Frome	SO/663483	7.	19.	11
Morton'	Moreton Jeffreys	SO/603485			
Egleton'	Eggleton[2]	SO/638450			
Upledene	Upleadon	SO/665421			
Catteley	Catley	SO/682443			
Stoke Edith'	Stoke Edith	SO/604406	20.	6.	2
Pyriton'	Perton	SO/598404			
Sholle[3]	Showle	SO/611437			
Magna Tatynton'	Tarrington	SO/619407			
Yarchull'	Yarkhill	SO/609427			
Weston'	Weston Beggard	SO/583412			
Stretton'	Stretton Grandison	SO/633441			
Asperton'	Ashperton	SO/643415			
Froma Castri	Castle Frome	SO/668459			
Froma Haymond	Halmond's Frome	SO/671479			
Ledene	Leadon	SO/684467			
Esebache	Evesbatch	SO/687482			
Froma Canonicorum	Canon Frome	SO/645435			
Bykerton'	Bickerton	SO/656306	7.	15.	2
Parva Marcley	Little Marcle	SO/671365			
Aylmeton'	Aylton	SO/658377			
Park' &	Court-y-Park and	SO/650396			
Pykesle	Pixley	SO/661388			
Walsopethorn'	Walsopthorne	SO/651423			
Mayneston'	Mainstone	SO/657399			
Monesleye	Munsley	SO/665409			
Westhide	Westhide	SO/586442	4.	13.	4
Whytewyk'	Whitwick	SO/611457			
Hyda Monacorum	Monkhide	SO/615439			
Parva Hida[4]	?				

[1] Named in 1243 and 1403 with Wilmaston in Peterchurch (Bannister, op. cit. 185).
[2] Grid ref. is to Upper Eggleton.
[3] See also Wormelow hundred, above.
[4] Parva Hyde was a holding of the Abbot of Gloucester (*F.A.* ii. 389); the index to the volume places it in Woolhope.

Ledebury foreyn	Ledbury Foreign		8.	6.	7
Ledebury Denzein	Ledbury	SO/713377			
Donynton'	Donnington	SO/709342			
Colewall'	Colwall	SO/739423	2.	12.	0
Cotynton'	Coddington	SO/718427			
Credeley	Cradley	SO/736471	3.	12.	6
Bosebury	Bosbury	SO/695435	1.	7.	0
Estenore	Eastnor	SO/732372	1.	6.	8
Lugwardyn[1]	Lugwardine	SO/551410	1.	14.	10
			59.	14.	2

Hd. Stretford' [STRETFORD HUNDRED]

Stretford'	Stretford	SO/443558	2.	18.	2
Munkleone	Monkland	SO/461577			
Strete &	Street and	SO/425603			
Lauton'[2]	Lawton	SO/446594			
Burley	Birley	SO/453533		18.	10
Sweyneston'	Swanstone	SO/442530			
Dylewe	Dilwyn	SO/415547	1.	17.	4
Kyngesleone	Kingsland	SO/447613	6.	13.	3
Longeuorde	Longford				
Lauton'[2]	Lawton	SO/446594			
Aston'	Aston	SO/462624			
Ersleone	Eardisland	SO/421585	6.	2.	2
Borton'	Burton	SO/423566			
Twyford	Twyford	SO/396591			
Herdynch'	Hardwick[3]	SO/403566			
Brockeswade	Broxwood	SO/363543			
Byrches	The Birches[4]	SO/375525			
Penebrugg'	Pembridge	SO/391581	6.	17.	4
Weston' &	Weston and	SO/365564			
Bury	Barewood	SO/382562			
Akes &	Noke and	SO/372595			
Leone	Leen	SO/383591			
Morcote &	Moorcot and	SO/359558			
Helde	The Yeld	SO/351561			
Shobbedon'	Shobdon	SO/401629	2.	15.	6
Staunton'	Staunton on Arrow	SO/370601	3.	17.	0
Stokkelowe	Stocklow	SO/371616			
Comenhop' &	Covenhope and	SO/408642			
Leye	Lye	SO/406668			
Marshton'	Marston	SO/362576			
Myddelton'	Milton	SO/387609			
Leonhales	Lyonshall	SO/331562	2.	11.	6
Lecton'	Letton	SO/335465	5.	3.	7
Kynardesley	Kinnersley	SO/346496			
Almaly	Almeley	SO/333515			

[1] Part of Lugwardine was taxed at a tenth, above.
[2] Part taxed with Stretford, part with Kingsland.
[3] Grid ref. is to Lower Hardwick.
[4] The Birches is a sixteenth-century house about 1¼ miles south of Broxwood. A reference of 1539 to 'Broxwood Byrches' (Bannister, op. cit. 32) suggests that the 1334 names may refer to one settlement only.

Pionia Regis	King's Pyon	SO/439507	3.	2.	9
Chabbenore	Chadnor[1]	SO/424525			
Webbeley foreyn	Weobley [foreign]		2.	6.	11
			45.	4.	4

Hd. Wolfheye [WOLPHY HUNDRED]

Parva Hereford'	Little Hereford	SO/554680	11.	8.	0
Castru' Ricardi	Richards Castle	SO/484702			
Orleton'	Orleton	SO/494672			
Crofte	Croft	SO/450654			
Pudlesdon'	Pudlestone	SO/566597			
Wyncton'	Woonton	SO/550622			
Whyle	Whyle	SO/559607			
Lastres	Laysters	SO/569632			
Rachesford'	Rochford [in Worcs.]	SO/629685			
			11.	8.	0

Lib. Leom' Hundredum Intrinsecus [LEOMINSTER]

Yvynton'	Ivington	SO/475566	2.	18.	11
Stokton'	Stockton	SO/522612	3.	0.	11
Luston'	Luston	SO/486630	4.	6.	11
Stoke c.h	Stoke Prior [with hamlets]	SO/520564	2.	5.	7
			12.	12.	4

Lib. Leom' Hundredum Forinsecus [LEOMINSTER FOREIGN]

Hompton'	Hampton	SO/521524	9.	16.	9
Neuton'	Newton	SO/507538			
Wauerton'	Wharton	SO/509556			
Bradeford	identification uncertain[2]				
Humbre	Humber	SO/536563			
Rysebury	Risbury	SO/549551			
Eton'	Eaton	SO/509583			
Henore	Hennor	SO/539585			
Yeddefenne	Edwyn Ralph	SO/646574			
Brokmanton'	Brockmanton	SO/550594			
Asshton'	Ashton	SO/517644			
Brymfeld'	Brimfield	SO/527675			
Sarnesfeld'	Sarnesfield	SO/375510			
			9.	16.	9

TOTAL: £437. 5. 11[3]

---

[1] Grid ref. is to Lower Chadnor.

[2] Bannister, op. cit. 24, suggests that *Bradeford* represents Bradward in Stoke Prior.

[3] As on 1334 Account, E 179/117/5. The figures for the hundreds in the Particulars in fact add up to £437. 5. 7.

HERTFORDSHIRE

DOCUMENTS

8 Edward III: Account	E 179/120/13
8 Edward III: Particulars	not extant
10 Edward III: Particulars	E 179/120/14*
10 Edward III: Particulars	E 179/120/16

TAXERS

The abbot of Waltham and Master John de Langetoft

TOTALS

15th	£588.	15.	8¾
10th	£ 23.	16.	9
	£612.	12.	5¾

Representing assessed movable wealth of

£9,070.   3.   5¼

NOTES

The tax returns are listed under the headings of seven hundreds and the liberty of St. Alban. Tax at a tenth yielded only a small sum and was levied on the boroughs of Hertford and Bishop's Stortford and the ancient demesnes of Essendon and Bayford. Fifteen places are specifically described as hamlets.

The boundary of the county in 1334 differed only slightly from that of the modern county. Few settlements are recorded along the southern edge and it is possible that the boundary with Middlesex was still indeterminate in wooded areas. In the north-west four places since transferred to Bedfordshire (Caddington, Kensworth, Barwythe, and part of Meppershall) were taxed in Hertfordshire. On the other hand, Holwell, now in Hertfordshire, was then taxed in Bedfordshire, and part of Royston in Cambridgeshire.

Hd. Hertford [HERTFORD HUNDRED]

Hertford [B]	Hertford	TL/324126	5.	13.	7¾ [T]
Esingdon' [A.D]	Essendon	TL/273088	4.	3.	2¼ [T]
Beyford [A.D]	Bayford	TL/309089	4.	7.	5¼ [T]
Chesthunte	Cheshunt	TL/359022	10.	12.	0
Hedesdone	Hoddesdon	TL/373090	4.	12.	11½
Brokesbourn'	Broxbourne	TL/371069	2.	1.	1½
Wormele	Wormley	TL/365053	1.	9.	5¾
Tewyngg'	Tewin	TL/268143	3.	12.	0¾
Quenhawe	Queen Hoo	TL/278162		19.	7¼
Stapelford	Stapleford	TL/312169		13.	0¾
Benyngeho	Bengeo	TL/325136	6.	0.	8

Berkhamsted Parva	Little Berkhamsted	TL/292079	2.	13.	5½
Brikendon'	Brickendon Bury	TL/330104	3.	11.	4
Amwell'	Amwell[1]	TL/372125	6.	13.	1¾
Hertfordingburi	Hertfordingbury	TL/309120	6.	3.	11½
			63.	7.	1½

Hd. Braugh' [BRAUGHING HUNDRED]

Storteford [B]	Bishop's Stortford	TL/486213	9.	12.	5¾ [T]
Braugh'	Braughing	TL/396252	5.	7.	2¼
Thorle	Thorley	TL/477189	3.	10.	3¼
Wicham	Wickham	TL/474230	1.	19.	8¾
Westmeln'	Westmill	TL/369272	2.	12.	1¼
Stanndon'	Standon	TL/397223	9.	13.	8
Waree	Ware	TL/357145	12.	17.	4½
Stanstede Abbatis	Stanstead Abbots	TL/386122	3.	7.	10
Honesdon'	Hunsdon	TL/418127	4.	3.	8
Wydeford	Widford	TL/413158	1.	8.	7
Estwyk'	Eastwick	TL/434116	1.	12.	6
Sabrichesworth'	Sawbridgeworth	TL/480146	9.	9.	10½
Gedelestone	Gilston	TL/440135	1.	16.	0
			67.	11.	3¼

Hd. Oddeseles [ODSEY HUNDRED]

Asshewell'	Ashwell	TL/268398	9.	19.	9½
Therfeld	Therfield	TL/334371	10.	0.	10½
Reed	Reed	TL/361356	3.	6.	3¼
Roiston' [h][2]	Royston	TL/358407	1.	4.	11
Erdeleye	Ardeley	TL/308271	3.	11.	4½
Coddreth'	Cottered	TL/318292	4.	4.	10½
Russheden'	Rushden	TL/305318	3.	1.	5¼
Henxteworth'	Hinxworth	TL/237403	3.	3.	7¾
Caldecote [h]	Caldecote	TL/237383	2.	2.	4½
Radewell'	Radwell	TL/232358	1.	16.	0¾
Clothale	Clothall	TL/271321	4.	6.	4½
Wanlington'	Wallington	TL/292336	4.	13.	6½
Bigrave	Bygrave	TL/267362	2.	16.	10½
Keleshull'	Kelshall	TL/329362	4.	3.	6¼
Horwell [h]	Orwellbury	TL/329363	1.	8.	6½
Sandon'	Sandon	TL/322346	7.	18.	5½
Bradefeld [h]	Broadfield	TL/325310	1.	6.	3½
			69.	5.	2¾

Hd. Edwynistr' [EDWINSTREE HUNDRED]

Aldeberi	Albury	TL/436247	4.	11.	3
Pelhamfurneys	Furneux Pelham	TL/431280	4.	5.	1¼
Pelham Arsa	Brent Pelham	TL/433308	2.	2.	11½
Stokkene Pelham	Stocking Pelham	TL/448293		13.	9½
Alswyk' [h]	Alswick	TL/370300	2.	3.	9¾
Anesty	Anstey	TL/403329	3.	4.	8½

[1] Grid ref. is to Great Amwell.
[2] Part of Royston was taxed in Cambridgeshire (Armingford hundred, p. 26).

Hormed Magna	Great Hormead	TL/402299	4.	7.	3¼
Hormed Parva	Little Hormead	TL/404290	2.	4.	7
Boklond	Buckland	TL/359338	2.	11.	6¾
Aspeden'	Aspenden	TL/353283	2.	17.	10½
Wydihale	Wyddial	TL/373317	1.	8.	0
Throkkyngg'	Throcking	TL/339301		15.	7¼
Berlai	Barley	TL/402384	4.	10.	6
Berkwey	Barkway	TL/382356	8.	17.	3
Mesdon'	Meesden	TL/439325	1.	2.	2
Hadham Magna	Much Hadham	TL/430197	6.	5.	9
Hadham Parva	Little Hadham	TL/447228	4.	9.	2½
			56.	11.	4¾

Hd. Bradewat' [BROADWATER HUNDRED]

Hatfeld	Hatfield	TL/235088	13.	6.	3
Mundene Furnival	Great Munden	TL/355242	4.	7.	10¼
Munden' Parva	Little Munden	TL/335219	2.	9.	1¼
Baldok'	Baldock	TL/243339	8.	16.	9¼
Ayete Laur'	Ayot St. Lawrence	TL/194169	2.	4.	2¾
Ayetemosichet	Ayot St. Peter	TL/219149	1.	3.	1¾
Dygoneswell'	Digswell	TL/238149	2.	6.	2
Daccheworth'	Datchworth	TL/268193	2.	16.	9¼
Watton'	Watton at Stone	TL/302189	5.	7.	7½
Sauecompe	Sacombe	TL/335194	3.	17.	0¾
Beniton'	Benington	TL/297236	5.	13.	2¾
Aston'	Aston	TL/272226	2.	12.	0¼
Knebbeworth'	Knebworth	TL/231210	3.	4.	5
Welwes	Welwyn	TL/231163	5.	9.	2¼
Stivenach'	Stevenage	TL/241262	5.	19.	4¾
Walkern'	Walkern	TL/293266	4.	11.	8¾
Wilmondele Magna & Parva	Great Wymondley and Little Wymondley	TL/215286 TL/217273	4.	15.	5¼
Wylie	Willian	TL/224307	2.	17.	0¼
Gravel' cum Cheuesfeld [h]	Graveley with Chesfield	TL/235281 TL/248280	2.	17.	6½
Leccheworth'	Letchworth	TL/221323	1.	12.	7
Weston'	Weston	TL/266299	4.	0.	10
			90.	8.	4½

Hd. Hicch' [HITCHIN HUNDRED]

Hicch' [Va]	Hitchin	TL/185292	7.	19.	0
Walden' Regis	King's Walden	TL/161235	6.	7.	11
Kymiton'	Kimpton	TL/178186	4.	14.	8¼
Piriton'	Pirton	TL/147316	8.	8.	9
Mepeshal' [h][1]	Meppershall [in Beds.]	TL/135359		9.	10
Ykelford [h]	Ickleford	TL/182317	2.	11.	3½
Lynleye	Lilley	TL/118264	4.	5.	4
Offeleye	Offley[2]	TL/145268	6.	3.	4¾
Stagenho [h]	Stagenhoe	TL/186227	1.	0.	0

[1] Most of Meppershall was taxed in Bedfordshire (Clifton hundred, p. 4).
[2] Grid ref. is to Great Offley.

Dynesle Temple & Dynesle Furnival	Temple Dinsley and Furnival Dinsley[1]	TL/182248 TL/182274	8.	5.	7¾
Hicch' for'	Hitchin [foreign]		8.	12.	4¾
			58.	18.	3

Lib. Sancti Albani [LIBERTY OF ST. ALBAN][2]

Sancto Albano [v]	St. Albans	TL/146073	17.	13.	11
Redborn'	Redbourn	TL/100116	5.	10.	8
Sandregg'	Sandridge	TL/171105	3.	8.	2½
Westwyk'	Westwick	TL/104067	2.	13.	6½
Briston' [h]	Burston	TL/135037		11.	1½
Wendregg'	Windridge	TL/125057	1.	19.	4¼
Kyngesberi	Kingsbery	TL/142075		18.	5
Childwyk' [h]	Childwick	TL/141107	1.	0.	7¼
Stoka de Parco	Park Street	TL/149039	12.	19.	6
Tytenhangr'	Tyttenhanger	TL/180059	4.	15.	6
Northawe	Northaw	TL/279024	2.	18.	9½
Barnet	Barnet[3]	TQ/243964	5.	19.	6½
Aldenham	Aldenham	TQ/139985	5.	17.	11½
Langeleye Abbatis	Abbots Langley	TL/095022	3.	2.	0
Watford	Watford	TQ/112968	6.	15.	3¾
Rikemersworth'	Rickmansworth	TQ/061942	6.	15.	0
Kayse	Cassio	TQ/105970	7.	1.	8
Henxtoneston	Hexton	TL/103303	3.	9.	3¾
Norton'	Norton	TL/231343	2.	3.	2½
Newenham	Newnham	TL/243376	2.	14.	10¼
Walden' Abbatis	St. Paul's Walden	TL/192223	3.	17.	5¾
Codicote	Codicote	TL/219188	4.	7.	0½
Brantefeld	Bramfield	TL/291156	1.	18.	10
Shepehale	Shephall	TL/256229	1.	15.	1¼
			110.	6.	11¼

Hd. Dacorum [DACORUM HUNDRED]

Trenge	Tring	SP/924114	8.	10.	1¼
Puttenham	Puttenham	SP/885149	1.	17.	11
Stokk'	Stocks	SP/962133	1.	9.	4
Gatesdene Magna	Great Gaddesden	TL/028112	4.	9.	0
Bareworth' [h]	Barwythe [in Beds.]	TL/023148		18.	8
Tyscotte [h]	Tiscott	SP/885178	2.	16.	6½
Flamstede	Flamstead	TL/079146	8.	5.	8½
Whethamsted cum Tyteburst [h]	Wheathampstead with Titburst[4]	TL/177140 TQ/*c.*180995	7.	11.	0
Catindon'[5]	Caddington [in Beds.]	TL/063198	3.	14.	2½
Kenesworth'	Kensworth [in Beds.]	TL/031191	2.	13.	2

[1] Furnival Dinsley (or Maidecroft) was part of the manor of Dinsley (*V.C.H., Herts.* iii. (1912), 10–11). As the name has gone out of use the grid ref. given is to Maydencroft Farm.

[2] The liberty of St. Alban is named as the hundred of Cashio (*Kaysford*) in E 179/120/17 (? 1339).

[3] Grid ref. is to Chipping Barnet.

[4] *V.C.H., Herts.* ii (1908), 149. Titburst, a detached tithing of Wheathampstead, was located on the east side of Watling Street in the parish of Aldenham. It is not clear whether the name referred to a specific settlement or to a part of Aldenham parish.

[5] Part of Caddington was taxed in Bedfordshire (Flitt hundred, p. 3).

Shenele	Shenley	TL/190005	5.	7.	2
Northmynnes	North Mymms	TL/221044	4.	18.	7¼
Bissheye	Bushey	TQ/130952	4.	5.	8¼
Berkhamsted	Berkhamsted	SP/996076	10.	6.	6¼
Berkhamsted for'	Berkhamsted [foreign]		11.	3.	3¼
Hemelhamstede[1] cum	Hemel Hempstead with	TL/078071	14.	17.	0
Gatesden' [h]	Little Gaddesden	SP/998138			
			93.	3.	10¾

TOTAL: £612. 12. 5¾[2]

---

[1] Ashridge appears in place of Hemel Hempstead on E 179/120/17 (? 1339).
[2] As on 1334 Account, E 179/120/13.

HUNTINGDONSHIRE

DOCUMENTS

8 Edward III: Account   E 179/122/8
8 Edward III: Particulars   E 179/122/9 (imperfect)
10 Edward III: Particulars   E 179/122/10*

TAXERS

The abbot of Ramsey and Edmund de Grymesby

TAX YIELD

15th   £394.   7. $7\frac{3}{4}$
10th   £ 50.   0.   3

£444.   7. $10\frac{3}{4}$

Representing assessed movable wealth of

£6,415.   17. $2\frac{1}{4}$

NOTES

Places taxed at a tenth are listed at the beginning and comprise the borough of Huntingdon and the ancient demesnes of Brampton, Godmanchester, Alconbury, Offord Cluny, Hartford, and Kings Ripton.

The outline of the county in 1334 differed only slightly from that of the modern county. Thurning and Hargrave, then taxed in Huntingdonshire, are now in Northamptonshire, and part of Papworth St. Agnes is now in Cambridgeshire. Tilbrook, now in Huntingdonshire, was then taxed in Bedfordshire.

Dominica Regis [DEMESNES OF THE KING]

Hunt' [B]	Huntingdon	TL/240717	12.	0.	0	[T]
Brampton' [A.D]	Brampton	TL/215707	8.	13.	$2\frac{1}{2}$	[T]
Gurmincestr' [A.D]	Godmanchester	TL/245707	14.	5.	4	[T]
Alkemondesbury [A.D]	Alconbury	TL/184762	7.	1.	4	[T]
Offord Cluny [A.D]	Offord Cluny	TL/219670	3.	11.	3	[T]
Hereford [A.D]	Hartford	TL/256725	2.	10.	0	[T]
Ripton' Reg' [A.D]	Kings Ripton	TL/261765	1.	19.	$1\frac{1}{2}$	[T]
			50.	0.	3	[T]

Hd. Toul' [TOSELAND HUNDRED]

Dodington'	Diddington	TL/191659	2.	0.	8
Pappeworth Anneys[1]	Papworth St. Agnes [in Cambs.]	TL/269644	1.	2.	4
Grantisden' Magna	Great Gransden	TL/271556	14.	0.	0

[1] Most of Papworth St. Agnes was taxed in Cambridgeshire (Papworth hundred, p. 25).

Magna Paxton'	Great Paxton	TL/210642	4.	0.	0
Everton'	Everton	TL/203513	2.	5.	0
Wintringham	Wintringham	TL/219598	12.	18.	4
Herdewyk	Eynesbury Hardwick	TL/208565			
Sancto Neoto [v]	St. Neots	TL/183603			
Eynesbury	Eynesbury	TL/183598	9.	0.	5
Southo Lovetot'[1]	Southoe [Lovetot]	TL/183644	4.	5.	10
Southo Winchestr'[1]	Southoe [Winchester]		3.	8.	4
Offord Daneys	Offord D'Arcy	TL/216664	3.	5.	6
Abbeltisle	Abbotsley	TL/228565	6.	11.	0½
Gilling'	Yelling	TL/262623	5.	2.	0
Stanton' cum	Fenstanton with	TL/321688	10.	15.	8
Hilton'	Hilton	TL/291661			
Bokeden'	Buckden	TL/193676	5.	9.	8
Touleslond	Toseland	TL/240625	2.	2.	0
Dilington' cum	Dillington with	TL/136656	4.	14.	5
Bechamsted	Beachampstead[2]	lost			
Werisle	Waresley	TL/249545	4.	16.	3
Hemingford Abbatis	Hemingford Abbots	TL/282712	4.	19.	8
Hemingford Grey	Hemingford Grey	TL/292708	4.	0.	0
Stokton' Magna	Great Staughton	TL/124646	6.	1.	3
Paxton' Parva	Little Paxton	TL/189627	3.	10.	10
			114.	9.	2½

Hd. Hirstingston' [HURSTINGSTONE HUNDRED]

Somersham cum soka	Somersham [with soke][3]	TL/360779	8.	12.	11½
Rameseye	Ramsey	TL/291852	6.	2.	0
Hertmangrave	Hepmangrove[4]	TL/284839			
& Bury	and Bury	TL/287838			
Upwode cum	Upwood with	TL/260826	5.	14.	2½
Ravele &	Great Raveley and	TL/256809			
Wistowe	Wistowe	TL/279810			
Hoghton'	Houghton	TL/281721	4.	15.	10¾
Witton'	Wyton	TL/278722			
Nydyngworth'	Needingworth	TL/343721	5.	14.	10½
Haliwell	Holywell	TL/337708			
Styuecle Magna	Great Stukeley	TL/217746	6.	15.	9¼
Ravele Parva	Little Raveley	TL/256799	1.	19.	4
Wardeboys	Warboys	TL/302799	5.	10.	4
Brughton'	Broughton	TL/281779	3.	14.	0
Ripton' Abbatis	Abbots Ripton	TL/231780	5.	3.	0
Slepe cum Soka	Slepe [St. Ives] [with soke][5]	TL/314712	9.	2.	6
Styuecle Parva	Little Stukeley	TL/209757	3.	8.	4
De Vico Sancti' Ivonis[6]	From the Street of St. Ives	TL/311715	7.	2.	0
			73.	15.	2½

[1] Southoe Lovetot and Southoe Winchester (or Southoe Ferrers) were manors within Southoe.

[2] *V.C.H., Hants.* ii (1932), 359, suggests that the settlement was just north of Great Staughton village.

[3] The soke of Somersham included Colne, Bluntisham, Earith, Pidley, and Fenton.

[4] Hepmangrove is that part of Bury village north-west of the stream; the name is now little used.

[5] The present settlement of St. Ives represents the former township of Slepe. The soke of Slepe included Wood Hurst and Old Hurst.

[6] The entry refers to the manor held by the Prior of St. Ives.

Hd. Normancros [NORMANCROSS HUNDRED]

Overton' Longvile	Orton Longueville	TL/168966	4.	14.	0½
De Vico Canonicorum	identification uncertain[1]		1.	0.	0
Neweton'	Water Newton	TL/108973	6.	13.	3
Overton' Watervill	Orton Waterville	TL/157961	6.	14.	2¾
Aylyngton'	Elton	TL/089936	8.	7.	8
Wassyngl'	Washingley	TL/135890	3.	0.	0
Morburn'	Morborne	TL/139915	3.	7.	8
Folkesworth'	Folksworth	TL/146902	2.	1.	2
Wodeston'	Woodston	TL/186977	2.	18.	9
Haddon'	Haddon	TL/133925	2.	10.	4
Alwalton'	Alwalton	TL/133959	2.	8.	10
Chesterton'	Chesterton	TL/127954	3.	17.	8
Fletton'	Fletton	TL/198971	4.	5.	4
Jakele	Yaxley	TL/177919	15.	2.	0½
Faresheued	Farcet	TL/202946	7.	0.	0
Stanground	Stanground	TL/200975	5.	5.	4½
Sautre	Sawtry	TL/168836	5.	0.	0
Conyngton'	Conington	TL/181859	7.	7.	3
Denton' &	Denton and	TL/150878	3.	15.	3¼
Caldecote	Caldecote	TL/142884			
Stilton'	Stilton	TL/159893	3.	2.	3
Glatton'	Glatton	TL/153861	9.	12.	4
Wodewalton'	Wood Walton	TL/209822	3.	2.	6
			111.	5.	11¼

Hd. Leghtonston' [LEIGHTONSTONE HUNDRED]

Woldweston'	Old Weston	TL/093772	8.	13.	4
Brynton'	Brington	TL/082760			
Bythrn'	Bythorn	TL/057759			
Molesworth'	Molesworth	TL/070758	2.	0.	0
Bukworth'	Buckworth	TL/148768	7.	10.	0
Gyddyng' Magna	Great Gidding	TL/116832	6.	13.	5½
Wolle	Woolley	TL/149745	2.	16.	0
Stepilgyddyng'	Steeple Gidding	TL/132813	2.	13.	1½
Catteworth'	Catworth	TL/089733		14.	8
Spaldewyk' cum soka	Spaldwick [with soke][2]	TL/128728	7.	2.	6
Wenewyk' cum Thirnyng'	Winwick with Thurning [in Northants.]	TL/105807 TL/086828	4.	10.	2
Covynton' cum Hargrave	Covington with Hargrave [in Northants.]	TL/053708 TL/036706	1.	18.	7¼
Elyngton'	Ellington	TL/160718	5.	9.	9¼
Kynbauton' cum soka	Kimbolton [with soke][3]	TL/099679	10.	0.	0
Leghton'	Leighton Bromswold	TL/115752	9.	2.	8

[1] The entry probably refers to that part of the manor of Wood Walton held by the Abbot of Ramsey, which included the Isle of Higney. An entry in the *Nomina Villarum*, 1316 (*F.A.* ii. 473), reads *Waletone cum vico canonicorum est una villa*.

[2] In 1086 Spaldwick, Upthorpe, Barham, Easton, Stow Longa, and the greater part of Little Catworth were included in the soke of Spaldwick.

[3] In 1086 the soke of Kimbolton extended into Swineshead, Great and Little Catworth in Hunts., and Keysoe and *Homefield* in Beds. Before 1334 Kimbolton had become an honor and comprised land in Tilbrook, Dean, Pertenhall, and Little Staughton (*V.C.H., Hunts.* iii (1936), 79).

Gyddyng' Parva	Little Gidding	TL/127816	2.	6.	0
Companford	Coppingford	TL/165800	2.	14.	0
Grafham	Grafham	TL/159691	2.	2.	0
Upton'	Upton	TL/174785	3.	2.	4
Hamerton'	Hamerton	TL/137796	5.	0.	0
Keston'	Keyston	TL/043754	6.	0.	0
			90.	8.	7½

TOTAL: £444. 7. 10¾[1]

---

[1] As on 1334 Account, E 179/122/8.

KENT

DOCUMENTS

   8 Edward III: Account   E 179/123/13
   8 Edward III: Particulars E 179/123/12*

TAXERS

The abbot of St. Augustine, Canterbury, and Thomas Bacoun

TAX YIELD

15th	£1,706.	2.	7¼
10th	£ 221.	3.	6
	£1,927.	6.	1¼

Representing assessed movable wealth of

    £27,803.   14.   0¾

NOTES

The Kent roll of 1334 is unlike those of other counties for two reasons. First, the tax unit in Kent was the hundred not the township and therefore no place-names are given; secondly, the roll retains the long lists of taxpayers and individual tax charges that are characteristic of the rolls of 1327 and 1332. Kent maintained the previous system of the assessment and taxation of the goods of individuals, perhaps because it was better suited to deal with the complications which arose through the exemption from the subsidy of the moneyers of Canterbury and the men of the liberty of the Cinque Ports (see Willard (1934), op. cit. 114–18). Although there seems to have been no intention of collecting money from these men, their movable goods were assessed in 1334 and the appropriate tax charges listed at the end of each hundred on the roll. The boroughs of Dover, Sandwich, Hythe, and New Romney, wholly within the Cinque Ports liberty, thus do not appear on the roll.

    The 1334 roll consists of twenty-six membranes. In the accompanying list only the numbers of taxpayers are given, since the names have already been published (Hanley and Chalklin, 1964, reference below). Places taxed at a fifteenth are listed under the headings of the five lathes, each subdivided into hundreds; only five townships, Brasted, Dartford, Lesnes, Malling, and Newenden served as tax units. Places taxed at a tenth, viz. the cities of Canterbury and Rochester and seven ancient demesnes, are listed at the end of the roll. For a detailed introduction to the county and a transcription of the roll see Hanley and Chalklin.

REFERENCES

H. A. Hanley and C. W. Chalklin, eds., 'The Kent lay-subsidy roll of 1334–5', *Kent Records*, xviii (1964), 58–172.

R. E. Glasscock, 'The distribution of lay wealth in Kent, Surrey, and Sussex, in the early fourteenth century', *Archaeologia Cantiana*, lxxx (1965), 61–8.

Lastus Sancti Augustini [LATHE OF ST. AUGUSTINE]

Hd. Ryngeslo [RINGSLOW HUNDRED]

	£	s	d		£	s	d
377 Persons	62.	3.	10½				
288 Men of Cinque Ports	48.	9.	2				
1 Moneyer		4.	6½				
					110.	17.	7

Hd. Cornylo [CORNILO HUNDRED]

70 Persons	11.	17.	10				
182 Men of Cinque Ports	31.	11.	6				
					43.	9.	4

Hd. Bleengate [BLEANGATE HUNDRED]

103 Persons	44.	1.	11				
19 Men of Cinque Ports	7.	9.	5½				
7 Moneyers	4.	7.	9¾				
					55.	19.	2¼

Hd. Eastri [EASTRY HUNDRED]

129 Persons	24.	16.	8½				
41 Men of Cinque Ports	18.	3.	7				
					43.	0.	3½ [1]

Hd. Dounhampford [DOWNHAMFORD HUNDRED]

124 Persons	27.	15.	2				
8 Men of Cinque Ports	2.	6.	4				
5 Moneyers	2.	17.	0				
1 John de Pulteneye 1 Master of Ospringe	4.	7.	8				
					37.	6.	2

Hd. Petham [PETHAM HUNDRED]

85 Persons	14.	2.	6½				
					14.	2.	6½

Hd. Whytstaple [WHITSTABLE HUNDRED]

106 Persons	14.	13.	8				
1 Man of Cinque Ports	2.	0.	0				
2 Moneyers	1.	0.	0				
					17.	13.	8

Hd. Westgate [WESTGATE HUNDRED]

89 Persons	22.	15.	6				
1 Man of Cinque Ports		2.	6				
23 Moneyers	9.	11.	4				
1 Master of Eastbridge		5.	0				
					32.	14.	4

Hd. Prestone [PRESTON HUNDRED]

63 Persons	7.	13.	1				
3 Men of Cinque Ports	1.	3.	4				
1 Moneyer		10.	0				
					9.	6.	5

---

[1] £43. 0. 5½ on E 179/123/12 is an error.

Hd. Kynhampford [KINGHAMFORD HUNDRED]

105	Persons	15.	17.	9¾			
2	Men of Cinque Ports		6.	0			
1	Moneyer		10.	0			
					16.	13.	9¾

Hd. Beawesberghe [BEWSBOROUGH HUNDRED]

107	Persons	16.	4.	10			
62	Men of Cinque Ports	19.	0.	0¼			
					35.	4.	10¼

Hd. Wyngeham [WINGHAM HUNDRED]

191	Persons	33.	8.	6			
26	Men of Cinque Ports	16.	12.	10			
2	Moneyers		9.	0½			
					50.	10.	4½

Hd. Bregge [BRIDGE HUNDRED]

61	Persons	14.	1.	10			
2	Men of Cinque Ports	1.	0.	0			
3	Moneyers		16.	9½			
1	Master of Eastbridge		3.	4			
					16.	1.	11½
					483.	0.	6¼[1]

Lastus de Scra [LATHE OF SCRAY]

Hd. Wy [WYE HUNDRED]

158	Persons	33.	12.	1½			
					33.	12.	1½

Hd. Chert [CHART HUNDRED]

80	Persons	16.	2.	6¼			
					16.	2.	6¼

Hd. Longhebregge [LONGBRIDGE HUNDRED]

98	Persons	15.	8.	11½			
					15.	8.	11½

Hd. Tenham [TEYNHAM HUNDRED]

150	Persons	25.	18.	3¾			
6	Men of Cinque Ports	3.	3.	4			
2	Moneyers	2.	0.	0			
					31.	1.	7¾

Hd. Faversham [FAVERSHAM HUNDRED]

209	Persons	39.	9.	3			
56	Men of Cinque Ports	17.	12.	1½			
4	Moneyers	1.	6.	4½			
1	Master of Ospringe	2.	6.	0			
					60.	13.	9

---

[1] £483. 0. 6¾ on E 179/123/12 is an error.

Hd. Boctone [BOUGHTON HUNDRED]

132 Persons	27.	10.	11½			
6 Men of Cinque Ports	2.	5.	6½			
1 Moneyer		12.	2¼			
1 John de Sellyngg'	1.	1.	0¾			
				31.	9.	9

Hd. Calhelle [CALEHILL HUNDRED]

281 Persons	31.	4.	4½			
2 Men of Cinque Ports	1.	19.	0			
				33.	3.	4½

Hd. Felbergh' [FELBOROUGH HUNDRED]

92 Persons	17.	10.	2¼			
19 Moneyers	5.	4.	10½			
				22.	15.	0¾

Hd. Bircholt' [BIRCHOLT HUNDRED]

39 Persons	7.	5.	0½			
				7.	5.	0½

Balliva de Kay in Middeltone[1]
[KEY BAILEY IN MILTON]

42 Persons	8.	16.	6			
1 Moneyer		10.	0			
				9.	6.	6

Hd. Badekelegh' [BARCLAY HUNDRED]

75 Persons	13.	0.	9			
				13.	0.	9

Hd. Tenterdenne [TENTERDEN HUNDRED]

86 Persons	13.	4.	11			
1 Man of Cinque Ports	1.	0.	0			
				14.	4.	11

Hd. Rolvyndenne [ROLVENDEN HUNDRED]

50 Persons	7.	2.	5¾			
				7.	2.	5¾

Hd. Blakebourne [BLACKBOURNE HUNDRED]

201 Persons	21.	10.	4			
				21.	10.	4

Hd. Cranebroke [CRANBROOK HUNDRED]

93 Persons	13.	13.	0			
				13.	13.	0

Dm. hd. Bernefeld
[BARNFIELD HALF-HUNDRED]

33 Persons	6.	0.	6			
				6.	0.	6

Hd. Selbritthindenne
[SELBRITTENDEN HUNDRED]

32 Persons	3.	10.	7½			
				3.	10.	7½

----

[1] Partly taxed at a tenth (p. 148).

Va. Newendenne [NEWENDEN]
    11 Persons   1.   14.   11

                                         1.   14.   11

Dm. hd. Merdenne [MARDEN HALF-HUNDRED]
    25 Persons   3.   14.   8

                                         3.   14.   8

                                   345.   10.   11[1]

Lastus de Eyllesford [LATHE OF AYLESFORD]

Hd. Hoo [HOO HUNDRED]
    216 Persons   31.   2.   10

                                     31.   2.   10

Hd. Lauerkefeld [LARKFIELD HUNDRED]
    297 Persons   39.   9.   2¼

                                   39.   9.   2¼

Leucata de Tonebregg' [LOWY OF TONBRIDGE]
    84 Persons   18.   19.   4¾

                                   18.   19.   4¾

Hd. Maydenestane [MAIDSTONE HUNDRED]
    359 Persons   50.   0.   1

                                   50.   0.   1

Hd. Eyhorne [EYHORNE HUNDRED]
    280 Persons   49.   12.   3

                                   49.   12.   3

Hd. Twyford [TWYFORD HUNDRED]
    137 Persons   14.   4.   4½

                                   14.   4.   4½

Hd. Brenchesle [BRENCHLEY HUNDRED]
    132 Persons   16.   1.   4¼

                                   16.   1.   4¼

Hd. Wrotham [WROTHAM HUNDRED]
    102 Persons   20.   15.   0

                                   20.   15.   0

Va. Mallyng' [MALLING]
    32 Persons   5.   5.   0

                                   5.   5.   0

Hd. Wacchelston'
[WASHLINGSTONE HUNDRED]
    82 Persons   12.   16.   6½

                                   12.   16.   6½

Hd. Litelfeld' [LITTLEFIELD HUNDRED]
    61 Persons   10.   0.   9¼

                                   10.   0.   9¼

[1] Total on E 179/123/12 is £345. 10. 9¾.

Hd. Westbernefeld [WEST BARNFIELD HUNDRED]
    19 Persons   2.   0. $1\frac{1}{4}$
                                               2.   0. $1\frac{1}{4}$

Hd. Chetham & Gilyngham [CHATHAM AND
    GILLINGHAM HUNDRED]
        138 Persons   23.   2. $8\frac{1}{2}$
        2 Men of Cinque Ports   2. 13.   1
                                          25. 15. $9\frac{1}{2}$

Hd. Toltyntrowe [TOLTINGTROUGH HUNDRED]
    136 Persons   22. 13. $11\frac{1}{4}$
                                          22. 13. $11\frac{1}{4}$

Hd. Forinc' Roff' [ROCHESTER FOREIGN
    HUNDRED]
        68 Persons   10.   2.   2
        1 Man of Cinque Ports   2.   0
                                          10.   4.   2

Hd. Schamele [SHAMWELL HUNDRED]
    253 Persons   45. 17. $6\frac{3}{4}$
        1 Master of Strode   10.   0
                                          46.   7. $6\frac{3}{4}$
                                       375.   8. $4\frac{1}{4}$

Lastus de Suttone [LATHE OF SUTTON]

Hd. Rokesle [RUXLEY HUNDRED]
    321 Persons   47.   0. $2\frac{1}{2}$
                                          47.   0. $2\frac{1}{2}$

Va. Lesnes [LESNES]
    76 Persons   16.   2.   11
    1 John de Pulteneye   1.   8.   0
                                          17. 10.   11

Hd. Blakeheth' [BLACKHEATH HUNDRED]
    322 Persons   45.   0.   0
    1 John de Pulteneye   2.   0.   0
                                          47.   0.   0

Hd. Littlele [LITTLE HUNDRED]
    63 Persons   15.   8.   2
    1 John de Pulteneye   1. 15.   0
                                          17.   3.   2

Hd. Bromleg' [BROMLEY HUNDRED]
    57 Persons   10. 13.   4
                                          10. 13.   4

Hd. Beghenham [BECKENHAM HUNDRED]
    24 Persons   7.   6. $2\frac{1}{4}$
                                          7.   6. $2\frac{1}{4}$

Hd. Codesheth' [CODSHEATH HUNDRED]

	£	s.	d.	£	s.	d.
164 Persons	26.	11.	4½			
				26.	11.	4½

Hd. Somerdeme [SOMERDEN HUNDRED][1]

	£	s.	d.	£	s.	d.
55 Persons	7.	0.	8½			
				7.	0.	8½

Va. Bradestede [BRASTED]

	£	s.	d.	£	s.	d.
27 Persons	2.	17.	5½			
				2.	17.	5½

Va. Dertford' [DARTFORD]

	£	s.	d.	£	s.	d.
133 Persons	14.	3.	7½			
				14.	3.	7½

Hd. Westerham [WESTERHAM HUNDRED]

	£	s.	d.	£	s.	d.
46 Persons	7.	17.	11½			
				7.	17.	11½

Hd. Akystane [AXTON HUNDRED]

	£	s.	d.	£	s.	d.
151 Persons	50.	3.	10			
				50.	3.	10
				255.	8.	9¼

Lastus de Schipweye [LATHE OF SHIPWAY]

Hd. Sancti Martini [ST. MARTIN'S HUNDRED]

	£	s.	d.	£	s.	d.
58 Persons	11.	1.	0			
25 Men of Cinque Ports	14.	5.	4			
				25.	6.	4

Hd. Langeport' [LANGPORT HUNDRED]

	£	s.	d.	£	s.	d.
80 Men of Cinque Ports	10.	19.	4			
8 Persons	1.	1.	3½			
				12.	0.	7½

Hd. Alowesbregg' [ALOESBRIDGE HUNDRED]

	£	s.	d.	£	s.	d.
142 Persons	17.	0.	9¾			
4 Men of Cinque Ports	1.	0.	0			
				18.	0.	9¾

Hd. Newecherch' [NEWCHURCH HUNDRED]

	£	s.	d.	£	s.	d.
73 Persons	16.	0.	10½			
4 Men of the Cinque Ports		10.	8			
				16.	11.	6½[2]

Hd. Oxene [OXNEY HUNDRED]

	£	s.	d.	£	s.	d.
67 Persons	16.	8.	3			
				16.	8.	3

[1] Personal names are not listed for this hundred; spaces for the names are left on the roll and from these the number has been calculated.

[2] Slightly higher figures were inserted later for this hundred on E 179/123/12, but the total as given here represents the original assessment of 1334.

Hd. Stoutyng' [STOWTING HUNDRED]

	£	s.	d.
65 Persons	11.	16.	3¾
2 Men of Cinque Ports		15.	0
	12.	11.	3¾

Hd. Lonibergh' [LONINGBOROUGH HUNDRED]

197 Persons	29.	9.	11½
4 Men of Cinque Ports	2.	4.	0
	31.	13.	11½

Hd. Strete [STREET HUNDRED]

54 Persons	14.	13.	5¾
10 Men of Cinque Ports	3.	19.	0
	18.	12.	5¾

Hd. Hean [HEANE HUNDRED]

65 Persons	9.	17.	2¼
35 Men of Cinque Ports	4.	7.	2½
	14.	4.	4¾

Hd. Bircholt' [BIRCHOLT HUNDRED]

45 Persons	5.	14.	0¼
3 Men of Cinque Ports		4.	10
	5.	18.	10¼

Hd. Hamme [HAM HUNDRED]

31 Persons	8.	1.	2
1 Man of Cinque Ports		8.	0
	8.	9.	2

Hd. Worthe [WORTH HUNDRED]

71 Persons	15.	9.	3¼
9 Men of Cinque Ports	3.	10.	0
	18.	19.	3¼

Hd. Folkestane [FOLKESTONE HUNDRED]

234 Persons	39.	3.	3¼
30 Men of Cinque Ports	8.	13.	10
	47.	17.	1¼
	246.	14.	1¼

Cantuaria [CANTERBURY]

250 Persons	47.	18.	11¼
18 Moneyers	12.	0.	0
	59.	18.	11¼ [T]

Roff' [ROCHESTER]

61 Persons	11.	12.	10
	11.	12.	10 [T]

Sesaltre [SEASALTER]

21 Persons	3.	6.	8
	3.	6.	8 [T]

Osprenge in Scra' [OSPRINGE]

40 Persons	5.	2.	2¾
	5.	2.	2¾ [T]

Bordenne in Middeltone [BORDEN IN MILTON]

193 Persons	29.	13.	7¼
1 Man of Cinque Ports		5.	0

	29.	18.	7¼ [T]

Balliva de Scapeya [SHEPPEY BAILEY]

184 Persons	26.	6.	8¼
1 Moneyer		3.	0
2 Men of Cinque Ports	5.	0.	0
1 Master of Dover ⎫			
1 Prioress of Sheppey ⎬	4.	0.	0
1 Master of Ospringe ⎭			

	35.	9.	8¼ [T]

Balliva de West in Middelton'
[WEST BAILEY IN MILTON]

300 Persons	34.	10.	5

	34.	10.	5 [T]

Merdenne Baronia [MARDEN BARONY]

73 Persons	11.	15.	6¼

	11.	15.	6¼ [T]

Balliva de Kay in Middilton'[1] [KEY BAILEY IN
MILTON]

164 Persons	28.	8.	0¾
2 Men of Cinque Ports		6.	0
1 Master of Dover		14.	6½

	29.	8.	7¼ [T]

	221.	3.	6 [T]

TOTAL: £1,927. 6. 1¼[2]

---

[1] Partly taxed at a fifteenth (p. 143).
[2] As on 1334 Account, E 179/123/13. The figures for the hundreds in the Particulars in fact add up to £1,927. 6. 2.

LANCASHIRE

DOCUMENTS

8 Edward III: Account   E 179/130/8
8 Edward III: Indenture   E 179/130/7 (imperfect)
11 Edward III: Particulars E 179/130/11*
11 Edward III: Particulars E 179/130/9

TAXERS

The abbot of Whalley and Thomas de Capenhurst

TAX YIELD

15th	£362.	19.	5½
10th	£ 14.	10.	0

£377. 9. 5½

Representing assessed movable wealth of

£5,589. 11. 10½

NOTES

The returns are listed under the headings of six wapentakes. The four taxation boroughs—Wigan, Liverpool, Preston, and Lancaster—account for the total tax yield at a tenth, there being no ancient demesnes.

REFERENCES

J. A. C. Vincent, *Lancashire Lay Subsidies: an Examination of the Lay Subsidy Rolls Henry III–Charles II. Vol. I, 1216–1307* (Record Society for Lancs. and Cheshire), 1893.
J. P. Rylands, *Lancashire Subsidy Roll for 1332* (Record Society for Lancs. and Cheshire), 1896.

ACKNOWLEDGEMENT

I am indebted to Mrs. Wendy Gilding for locating a number of places named on this roll.

Wap. Derbyshire [WEST DERBY WAPENTAKE]

Wygan [B]	Wigan	SD/585055	4.	0.	0	[T]
Leverpull' [B]	Liverpool	SJ/340905	3.	0.	0	[T]
Crosseby Magna	Crosby	SJ/320999	1.	5.	0	
Knouseley	Knowsley	SJ/435958	2.	8.	0	
Hagh'	Haigh	SD/606090		9.	0	
Hyndeley	Hindley	SD/616043	1.	0.	0	
Everton'	Everton	SJ/354923		17.	4	
Kylcheth'	Culcheth	SJ/659960	1.	13.	4	
Allerton'	Allerton	SJ/400874		9.	0	

Skelmerisdale	Skelmersdale	SD/467062	1.	17.	8
Scharisbrek' cum Hurdilton'	Scarisbrick with Hurlston	SD/379134 SD/399115	4.	0.	0
Ines Makerfeld	Ince in Makerfield	SD/593041		11.	0
Burtonwod'	Burtonwood	SJ/564929	1.	2.	0
Croynton'	Cronton	SJ/497883	1.	10.	0
Huyton' cum Raby	Huyton with Roby	SJ/444900 SJ/432909	1.	19.	0
Terbok'	Tarbock	SJ/460876	2.	6.	8
Aghton'	Aughton	SD/391054	3.	2.	0
Dalton'	Dalton	SD/495081	1.	1.	0
Ines Blundel	Ince Blundell	SD/326038	1.	4.	0
Wolueton' Magna	Much Woolton	SJ/423869		17.	0
Derby	West Derby	SJ/397933	2.	16.	8
Speek'	Speke	SJ/430835	2.	4.	0
Wolueton' Parva	Little Woolton	SJ/416855		16.	0
Asteley	Astley	SD/700007		19.	0
Tyldesleygh'	Tyldesley	SD/689020	1.	4.	0
Atherton	Atherton	SD/676032	1.	12.	4
Whistan	Whiston	SJ/477917	1.	2.	0
Sothewrthe cum Croft'	Southworth with Croft	SJ/622934 SJ/633938		12.	6
Newton'	Newton le Willows	SJ/593956	1.	18.	0
Ryxton'	Rixton	SJ/683894	1.	6.	0
Wolton'	Woolston	SJ/646895	1.	6.	0
Lawton' cum Kenyan	Lowton with Kenyon	SJ/616978 SJ/629956	1.	1.	0
Medilton' cum Erbur'	Myddleton with Arbury	SJ/620930 SJ/614928		9.	0
Adburghham	Abram	SD/607015		15.	0
Haydok'	Haydock	SJ/563970		13.	0
Glasebrok'	Glazebrook	SJ/693927		10.	0
Dutton'	Ditton	SJ/498863	2.	6.	0
Boulde	Bold	SJ/533893	3.	10.	0
Dounholand	Downholland	SD/364068	1.	16.	0
Northmelis	North Meols[1]	SD/365183	1.	6.	8
Gerstan	Garston	SJ/405843	1.	4.	0
Bekerstath'	Bickerstaffe	SD/445042	1.	17.	0
Sutton'	Sutton	SJ/522927	2.	4.	0
Werynton'	Warrington	SJ/605881	3.	0.	0
Raynhull'	Rainhill	SJ/493912	1.	11.	0
Goldeburn'	Golborne	SJ/604980		16.	0
Schildewalle	Childwall	SJ/415891		13.	4[2]
Apelton'	Appleton	SJ/514862	2.	16.	0
Letherland	Litherland	SJ/341976		19.	0
Holand	Up Holland	SD/523051	1.	11.	0
Asseheton'	Ashton in Makerfield	SJ/579992	2.	13.	4
Wavertree	Wavertree	SJ/390894		12.	0
Bedeford	Bedford	SJ/663999	1.	13.	0
Maghel	Maghull	SD/374030		13.	4
Thornton'	Thornton	SD/335010	1.	0.	0
Ravenesmeles	Raven Meols	SD/285058		14.	0
Eccliston'	Eccleston	SJ/484955	1.	13.	0
Keerdley	Cuerdley	SJ/544865	1.	19.	0
Crosseby Parva	Little Crosby	SD/319017	1.	12.	0
Seffeton'	Sefton	SD/357012	2.	6.	0½

[1] Grid ref. is to Meols Hall in the modern parish of Southport.
[2] E 179/130/11 has 14s. 4d., in error.

Lydyate	Lydiate	SD/365052	1.	12.	0
Rainford	Rainford	SD/478007	1.	10.	0
Krkeby	Kirkby	SJ/403994	2.	3.	0
Pembirton'	Pemberton	SD/555038	1.	1.	0
Forneby	Formby	SD/300070	1.	5.	0
Sonky cum	Great Sankey with	SJ/568885	1.	19.	0
Penkett	Penketh	SJ/559875			
Botehull'	Bootle	SJ/337950		18.	0
Kyrkedale	Kirkdale	SJ/351934		18.	0
Wyndehull'	Windle	SJ/499976	1.	10.	0
Mellyngh'	Melling	SD/389003	2.	0.	0
Lathu'	Lathom	SD/460091	3.	10.	0
Halsehale	Halsall	SD/371103	2.	13.	0
Bullyngh' cum	Billinge with	SJ/529999		19.	0
Wynstanleygh'	Winstanley	SD/545031			
Par	Parr	SJ/530951	1.	1.	0
Pynynton'	Pennington	SJ/654995		15.	9
Horell	Orrell	SD/535051		8.	0
Hale	Hale	SJ/471820	3.	6.	0
Ayntree	Aintree	SJ/380985		15.	0
Walton'	Walton	SJ/366945	2.	0.	0
Westeleygh'	Westleigh	SD/650018		13.	4
			124.	19.	3½

Wap. Anmoundernesse [AMOUNDERNESS WAPENTAKE]

Preston' [B]	Preston	SD/538297	3.	10.	0	[T]
Gayrstange	Garstang	SD/491450	6.	13.	4	
Stalmyn cum	Stalmine with	SD/374454	1.	6.	8	
Staynolf'	Staynall	SD/361439				
Grenolf' cum	Greenhalgh with	SD/403359	1.	6.	0	
Thessillton'	Thistleton	SD/407378				
Alston' cum	Alston with	SD/612336		17.	4	
Hodersale	Hothersall	SD/631347				
Barton'	Barton	SD/517372	1.	8.	0	
Echeleswyk'	Elswick	SD/423383	1.	6.	0	
Parva Eccliston' cum	Little Eccleston with	SD/413398		16.	0	
Layrbrok'	Larbreck	SD/409405				
Grymeresargh' cum	Grimsargh with	SD/582338		13.	4	
Brokholes	Brockholes[1]	SD/576302				
Lee	Lea	SD/478311		13.	4	
Caterhale	Catterall	SD/495426	1.	5.	0	
Clagton'	Claughton	SD/528423		15.	0	
Horderne cum	Hardhorn with	SD/352373	1.	11.	4	
Newton'	Newton	SD/344368				
Ethelleston'	Elston	SD/600324		18.	8	
Gosenargh'	Goosnargh	SD/560369	2.	9.	8	
Rigebi cum	Ribby with	SD/408318		18.	0	
le Wrae[2]	Wrae	SD/398316				
Syngulton' Magna &	Singleton and	SD/385383	1.	6.	8	
Parva	Little Singleton	SD/376394				
Westeby cum	Westby with	SD/383319		16.	0	
Plumpton'	Plumpton[3]	SD/384333				
Warton'	Warton	SD/412287	1.	6.	0	

[1] Grid ref. is to Lower Brockholes.
[2] Omitted on E 179/130/7 (1334), but included on E 179/130/11 (1337).
[3] Grid ref. is to Great Plumpton.

			£	s.	d.
Eccleston' Magna	Great Eccleston	SD/427402	1.	3.	0
Assheton	Ashton	SD/510307		12.	4
Woddeplumton'	Woodplumpton	SD/500344	2.	6.	8
Inchippe cum	Inskip with	SD/463379	1.	6.	8
Sowreby	Sowerby	SD/475385			
Carleton'	Carleton	SD/329394	1.	4.	0
Newton'	Newton	SD/446306	1.	3.	0
Billisburgh'	Bilsborrow[1]	SD/523401		19.	0
Frekylton'	Freckleton	SD/430290	1.	13.	2
Peshowe cum	Preesall with	SD/367473	1.	10.	0
Haconnshowe	Hackensall	SD/348476			
Ribbilton'	Ribbleton	SD/567313		15.	0
Hamelton'	Hambleton	SD/378424		19.	0
Lyghum	Lytham	SD/370272	1.	9.	0
Merton'	Marton[2]	SD/323346	1.	14.	8
Whytyngham	Whittingham	SD/567362	1.	10.	0
Broghton'	Broughton	SD/529343	1.	10.	0
Laton' cum	Layton with	SD/325365	1.	11.	8
Warchebrek'	Warbreck	SD/322383			
Pulton'	Poulton le Fylde	SD/353398	1.	14.	0
Treuelles	Treales	SD/442329	1.	7.	0
Clifton'	Clifton	SD/467303	1.	5.	4
Wetheton' cum	Weeton with	SD/383347	1.	8.	0
Prees	Preese	SD/378361			
Outroutheclef'	Out Rawcliffe	SD/400420	1.	13.	4
Newsum	Newsham	SD/512360		6.	8
Thornton'	Thornton	SD/340422	1.	7.	0
Fyschewyk'	Fishwick	SD/561293		12.	0
Kyrkaym	Kirkham	SD/425321	1.	3.	0
Byspam cum	Bispham with	SD/316401	1.	8.	0
Northebrek'	Norbreck	SD/313415			
Brynyg' cum	Bryning with	SD/401300	1.	4.	0
Kelgrymesargh'	Kellamergh	SD/403293			
Upperowtheclif'	Upper Rawcliffe[3]	SD/435415		16.	0
Halghton'	Haighton	SD/567346		14.	0
Mithelargh cum	Medlar with	SD/418355	1.	4.	0
Westsu'[4]	Wesham	SD/418330			
			67.	5.	10

Wap. Blakeburneschir' [BLACKBURN WAPENTAKE]

			£	s.	d.
Merley	Mearley	SD/769409		7.	0
Donum	Downham	SD/783443	1.	0.	0
Chatteburn'	Chatburn	SD/769442		12.	0
Schirche	Church	SD/741291		10.	0
Haselynden'	Haslingden	SD/785234		12.	0
Balderston'	Balderstone	SD/631323		9.	0
Symonndestone	Simonstone	SD/777343		12.	0
Penhulton' Magna cum	Pendleton, Great and	SD/759395		10.	0
Parva	Little[5]				
Brounleygh'	Burnley	SD/839327	1.	6.	0
Plesyngton'	Pleasington	SD/642260		14.	0
Lyvessey	Livesey	SD/649248	1.	4.	0

---

[1] Grid ref. is to Bilsborough Hall.   [2] Grid ref. is to Great Marton.
[3] As there is no settlement of Upper Rawcliffe the grid ref. is a general one to the parish.
[4] This entry is omitted from E 179/130/11.   [5] Manors within Pendleton.

			£	s.	d.
Osewaldistwesil	Oswaldtwistle	SD/736273		15.	0
Salebur'	Salesbury	SD/681329		8.	0
Schepyn	Chipping	SD/622433	1.	16.	0
Harewod Magna	Great Harwood	SD/737322	1.	10.	0
Clayton' super Moras	Clayton le Moors	SD/745309		8.	0
Thorneley cum	Thornley with	SD/633411	1.	3.	6
Wheteley	Wheatley	SD/620399			
Rischeton'	Rishton	SD/725302		17.	0
Meluer cum	Mellor with	SD/655310		15.	0
Eccleshull'	Eccleshill	SD/700235			
Overderwend	Darwen [Over]	SD/694222		19.	0
Clayton' in le Dale	Clayton le Dale[1]	SD/657337		14.	0
Colne	Colne	SD/889401	1.	6.	8
Dutton'	Dutton[2]	SD/654386		19.	0
Reued	Read	SD/766347		9.	6
Witton'	Witton	SD/666276		7.	6
Whalley	Whalley	SD/733362		6.	0
Aluetann	Altham	SD/771331		12.	6
Clydirhowe	Clitheroe	SD/744422	2.	7.	0
Worston'	Worston	SD/768428		11.	6
Clevacher	Cliviger	SD/885275	1.	0.	0
Osbaldiston'	Osbaldeston	SD/648318		6.	8
Keuerdale	Cuerdale	SD/576293		15.	6
Parva Harewod	Little Harwood	SD/690290		9.	0
Happeton'	Hapton	SD/792318	1.	0.	0
Padyham	Padiham	SD/793340		13.	4
Samelesbur'	Samlesbury	SD/590303	2.	8.	0
Walton' in Ye Dale	Walton le Dale	SD/562279	2.	14.	0
Aghton'	Aighton[3]	SD/690400	2.	10.	0
Huncote	Huncoat	SD/778304		11.	2
Bretherclif' cum	Briercliffe with	SD/883341	1.	0.	0
Extwesel	Extwistle	SD/876338			
Belyngton'	Billington	SD/728358	1.	6.	0
Netherderwent'	Lower Darwen	SD/688251		13.	4
Blakeburn'	Blackburn	SD/683280	1.	10.	0
Folerygge	Foulridge	SD/890420	1.	3.	0
Merkellesden	Marsden	SD/879381	1.	6.	8
Wissewalle	Wiswell	SD/746374		12.	0
Withesthorne	Worsthorne	SD/876324		12.	0
Mitton'	Little Mitton	SD/718382		11.	0
Henthorne	Henthorn	SD/726404			
Koldecotes	Cold Coats	SD/754384			
Wlipeshir' cum	Wilpshire with	SD/686325		12.	0
Dynkedleygh'	Dinckley[4]	SD/689365			
Ribbelcestr'	Ribchester	SD/650350	2.	5.	0
Twesilton'	Twiston	SD/813439		6.	8
			48.	6.	6

Wap. Salfort' [SALFORD WAPENTAKE]

			£	s.	d.
Salfort'	Salford	SJ/827986	1.	6.	0
Blakerode	Blackrod	SD/612111		10.	0
Radeclefe	Radcliffe	SD/785073		15.	0

[1] Parish name only; grid ref. is to Showley Hall.
[2] Grid ref. is to Dutton Manor.
[3] Grid ref. is to Aighton, Bailey, and Chaigley parish.
[4] Grid ref. is to Dinckley Hall (*Wynkedleygh'* in error on E 179/130/11).

Schatherton'	Chadderton	SD/903055	1.	5.	8
Stretford	Stretford	SJ/798943	1.	6.	8
Botterworth'	Butterworth	SD/934123	1.	5.	0
Ruyton'	Royton	SD/918076		13.	4
Crompeton'	Crompton	SD/946100		15.	0
Holdhum	Oldham	SD/936051	1.	0.	0
Roynton'	Rivington	SD/627145		13.	0
Rediche	Reddish	SJ/897930	1.	5.	0
Asscheton'	Ashton under Lyne	SJ/941990	3.	0.	0
Lostok' cum	Lostock with	SD/656092		16.	0
Rummeworth'	Rumworth	SD/673081			
Spotlond	Spotland	SD/883139	2.	2.	0
Bur'	Bury	SD/805109	2.	10.	0
Hunnerfeld	Hundersfield	SD/948168	1.	18.	4
Castelton'	Castleton	SD/884102		18.	0
Wethynton'	Withington	SJ/849929	4.	5.	0
Mamcestr' cum Roberto de Bulhalgh'	Manchester	SJ/837987	3.	7.	0
Barton'	Barton upon Irwell	SJ/765978	1.	16.	0
Heton' cum Haliwalle	Heaton with Halliwell	SD/685093 SD/700107		15.	0
Medilton'	Middleton	SD/872063	2.	6.	8
Pilkyton'	Pilkington	SD/c.800060	1.	7.	0
Totynton'	Tottington	SD/776131		19.	0
Chetham	Cheetham	SD/841014		5.	6
Penhulleton'	Pendleton	SJ/808990		16.	0
Boulton'	Bolton	SD/718093	1.	5.	0
Halghton'	Westhoughton	SD/652060		17.	1
Cliffton'	Clifton	SD/776035		8.	0
Harewod	Harwood	SD/748110		14.	1
Flixton'	Flixton	SJ/747940		15.	0
Penhulbur'	Pendlebury	SD/782022		6.	0
Hulton'	Hulton[1]	SD/719039		13.	0
Wrkesleygh'	Worsley	SD/749002	1.	5.	0
Prestewyche	Prestwich	SD/822045	1.	0.	0
Tyrton'	Turton	SD/734157		17.	0
Heton' Norreys	Heaton Norris	SJ/880905		15.	6
Heggeworth'	Edgworth	SD/739169		14.	6
Urmeston'	Urmston	SJ/773945		10.	0
Aspelhull'	Aspull	SD/612080		9.	0
Chorleton'	probably Chorlton upon Medlock	SJ/858964		4.	0
			48.	9.	4

Wap. Laylonschir' [LEYLAND WAPENTAKE]

Chernok' Richard	Charnock Richard	SD/553158	1.	3.	0
Parva Hole	Little Hoole	SD/485236		12.	0
Becanshowgh cum Heskert	Becconsall with Hesketh	SD/447232 SD/439236		14.	0
Andirton'	Anderton	SD/628117		14.	0
Breyerton'	Bretherton	SD/476204	1.	10.	0
Hoghwyk' cum Farynton'	Howick with Farington	SD/505280 SD/538250	1.	9.	0
Heghchernok'	Heath Charnock	SD/611146	1.	0.	0
Clayton'	Clayton le Woods	SD/565226	1.	4.	0

Grid ref. is to Little Hulton.

			£	s.	d.
Wethenhull' cum Rothellesworth'	Withnell with Roddlesworth	SD/631223 SD/665215		9.	0
Hoton'	Hutton	SD/499268		16.	0
Hoghton'	Hoghton	SD/614259		9.	0
Mowdesleygh'	Mawdesley	SD/493150	1.	0.	0
Croston	Croston	SD/486186	1.	0.	0
Longeton'	Longton	SD/478257	1.	13.	4
Penwurthham	Penwortham	SD/516293		11.	0
Whelton' cum Hepay	Wheelton with Heapey	SD/602212 SD/601205		13.	0
Tarleton'	Tarleton	SD/452203	1.	6.	8
Perbald	Parbold	SD/495108		15.	0
Rughford	Rufford	SD/463156	1.	5.	8
Chorley cum Bispham	Chorley with Bispham	SD/582175 SD/489134	1.	9.	0
Standische cum Longetree	Standish with Langtree	SD/563103 SD/561111	1.	7.	2
Coppehull' cum Wurthynton'	Coppull with Worthington	SD/568135 SD/580110	1.	15.	0
Eccliston' cum Heskyn	Eccleston with Heskin	SD/517178 SD/532153	1.	13.	4
Sheventon'	Shevington	SD/545105	1.	1.	9
Hole Magna	Much Hoole	SD/463223		18.	0
Wryttynton'	Wrightington	SD/527136	1.	18.	0
Kerden	Cuerden	SD/562238		19.	0
Wlneswalton'	Ulnes Walton	SD/c.510203	1.	6.	8
Burnehill'	Brindle	SD/599243		15.	0
Whetill' in Bosco	Whittle le Woods	SD/579215	1.	0.	0
Leylond	Leyland	SD/540215	1.	3.	6
Dekisbur' cum Adelynton'	Duxbury with Adlington	SD/589151 SD/598128	1.	0.	0
Eukiston'	Euxton	SD/555192	1.	10.	0
Whetill' Waleys	Welch Whittle	SD/535150		9.	3
			36.	10.	4

Wap. Lonesdale Kerteml' & Fourneys
[LONSDALE, CARTMEL, AND FURNESS WAPENTAKE]

			£	s.	d.	
Lanc' [B]	Lancaster	SD/478619	4.	0.	0	[T]
Caton' cum Claghton'	Caton with Claughton	SD/532646 SD/567665	3.	2.	0	
Midilton'	Middleton	SD/422587		7.	0	
Tatham cum Ireby	Tatham with Ireby	SD/606693 SD/654754		11.	0	
Leek	Leck	SD/643766		12.	0	
Skerton'	Skerton	SD/477630		4.	0	
Whitynton'	Whittington	SD/600762		15.	4	
Ellale	Ellel	SD/486559	2.	0.	0	
Ursewyk'	Urswick	SD/268742	1.	14.	0	
Burgh'	Burrow with Burrow	SD/615758		14.	0	
Slyne cum Heyste	Slyne with Hest	SD/478660 SD/469663		13.	0	
Kerkeby Irelet'	Kirkby Ireleth[1]	SD/236840	1.	12.	0	
Penynton'	Pennington	SD/263774		10.	0	
Lees	Leece	SD/243694	1.	14.	0	

[1] Grid ref. is to the church at Beckside.

			£	s	d
Pulton'	Poulton le Sands	SD/440648	1.	6.	8
Bare cum	Bare with	SD/453648			
Torsholme	Torrisholme	SD/454637			
Scotford	Scotforth	SD/481594	1.	3.	4
Ulveriston'	Ulverston	SD/286785	5.	6.	8
Halton'	Halton	SD/499647		19.	0
Kerneford cum	Carnforth with	SD/499705	1.	4.	0
Berewyk	Borwick	SD/525730			
Haldyngham	Aldingham	SD/283711	1.	12.	0
Hulker	Holker	SD/361772	1.	13.	4
Netherkellet	Nether Kellet	SD/505682		6.	0
Bulker cum	Bulk with	SD/503644	1.	0.	0
Aldeclif'	Aldcliffe	SD/466601			
Warton'	Warton	SD/499723	1.	0.	0
Caunsfeld	Cantsfield	SD/620730		4.	0
Tunstalle	Tunstall	SF/614739		4.	0
Mellyng cum	Melling with	SD/599711		9.	0
Wraton'	Wrayton	SD/611722			
Wraa	Wray	SD/602676		10.	0
Wenynton'	Wennington	SD/617701		6.	0
Erghum	Arkholme	SD/589718		12.	0
Horneby	Hornby	SD/585686		6.	8
Heegton' cum	Heaton with	SD/443603		8.	0
Oxclif'	Oxcliffe	SD/450619			
Boulton'	Bolton le Sands	SD/483677	1.	18.	8
Dalton cum	Dalton [in Westmorland]	SD/537757		17.	0
Hoton'	with Priest Hutton	SD/530737			
Overton'	Overton	SD/438580		13.	0
Yelond	Yealand	SD/507748		14.	0
Gersyngham	Gressingham	SD/572699		11.	0
Escheton'	Ashton	SD/461572		16.	0
Thernum	Thurnham	SD/465543		5.	6
Farleton'	Farleton	SD/573671		4.	0
Dalton in Fourneys	Dalton in Furness	SD/232741	3.	0.	0
Heesham	Heysham	SD/415612	1.	3.	0
Alyuthayth	Allithwaite	SD/385768	1.	0.	0
Overkelet	Over Kellet	SD/522696		17.	0
Kokerham	Cockerham	SD/462518	1.	6.	8
Broghton'	Broughton [East]	SD/387817	1.	13.	4
			51.	18.	2

TOTAL: £377. 9. 5½[1]

---

[1] As on Account, E 179/130/8.

LEICESTERSHIRE

DOCUMENTS

8 Edward III: Account   E 179/133/3
8 Edward III: Particulars   not extant
10 Edward III: Particulars   E 179/133/4 (imperfect)
11 Edward III: Particulars   E 179/133/5*

TAXERS

The abbot of Leicester and John de Tiddeswell

TAX YIELD

15th   £680.   5.   1½
10th   £ 77.   7.   9
      £757.   12.   10½

Representing assessed wealth of

    £10,977.   14.   4½

NOTES

As the Particulars for 1334 do not survive and the boroughs are not named on the 1334 Account we must presume that the taxation boroughs were the same as in 1332 and in 1336, namely Leicester, Hinckley, and Mountsorrel. The remainder of the tax at a tenth was on ancient demesnes, principally in Gartree and Goscote hundreds.

The only important difference between the outline of the modern county and that of 1334 was in the west on the border with Derbyshire. While Over and Nether Seal, now in Derbyshire, were taxed in Leicestershire, nine places in modern Leicestershire are named on the Derbyshire rolls. Two other Leicestershire places were taxed elsewhere in 1334: Little Bowden in Northamptonshire, and Belvoir in Lincolnshire.

As there are a large number of extant subsidy rolls for the county, including those for 1327 (E 179/133/1, published by Fletcher) and 1332 (E 179/133/2), it is not surprising that much use has already been made of them in the study of Leicestershire history.

REFERENCES

J. Nichols, *The History and Antiquities of the County of Leicester*, 4 vols., 1795–1815. (This includes a version of the fifteenths and tenths based upon the fifteenth-century book of same, E 164/7.)
Mary Bateson, ed., *Records of the Borough of Leicester*, vol. ii (1901), 34 f.
W. G. D. Fletcher, 'The earliest Leicestershire lay subsidy roll, 1327', *Reports and Papers of the Assoc. Architectural Societies*, 19 (1887–8) and 20 (1889–90).
R. H. Hilton, *The Economic Development of some Leicestershire Estates in the Fourteenth and Fifteenth Centuries*, 1947.

W. G. Hoskins, 'The deserted villages of Leicestershire', *Trans. Leics. Arch. Soc.* 22 (1944–5), 242–64. Reprinted with additions in W. G. Hoskins, *Essays in Leicestershire History*, 1950.

C. T. Smith, 'Population. III. The thirteenth and fourteenth centuries', in *V.C.H., Leics.* iii (1955), 132–6.

| Leycestr' [v][1] [B] | Leicester | SK/585044 | 26. | 13. | 4 [T] |

Hd. Guthlaxton' [GUTHLAXTON HUNDRED]

Burbach &	Burbage and	SP/442926	4.	12.	0
Sketesclif'	Sketchley	SP/424922			
Appelby Parva	Appleby Parva	SK/308088	1.	11.	0
Broughton' Astele	Broughton Astley	SP/526926	4.	0.	0
Sutton' &	Sutton in the Elms	SP/521938			
Thorp'	and Primethorpe	SP/523933			
Wytherdele	Witherley	SP/324973	2.	10.	0
Whytington'	Whittington	SK/486082		10.	0
Barton'	Barton in the Beans	SK/396063	1.	15.	4
Oseberston'	Osbaston	SK/425043	1.	6.	6
Dadelyngton'	Dadlington	SP/403981	1.	4.	2
Hethere	Heather	SK/390109	1.	13.	0
Pottere Merston'	Potters Marston	SP/498964		17.	6
Nailleston'	Nailstone	SK/418071	2.	15.	5½
Neubold &	Newbold Verdon and	SK/446037	1.	17.	6
Brocardescote	Brascote	SK/443025			
Leyre	Leire	SP/526900	1.	13.	0
Oselesthorp'	Ullesthorpe	SP/505876	1.	15.	0
Stanton' iuxta Sapcote	Stoney Stanton	SP/489948	1.	10.	0
Wheston'	Whetstone	SP/558976	3.	14.	0
Foston'	Foston	SP/604950	3.	5.	0
Barwell'	Barwell	SP/443965	3.	6.	8
Cotesbeche	Cotesbach	SP/539824	2.	6.	0
Naneby	Naneby	SK/434025		5.	6
Shatwell'	Shawell	SP/542797	2.	0.	8
Kilby	Kilby	SP/620954	2.	11.	0
Misterton'	Misterton	SP/557840	2.	2.	6
Bitlesby	Bittesby	SP/500860	1.	14.	6
Thornton'	Thornton	SK/468076	1.	1.	0
Bagworth'	Bagworth	SK/449080	1.	7.	0
Eissheby Magna	Ashby Magna	SP/563904	2.	13.	0
Petlyng' Parva	Peatling Parva	SP/589897	1.	10.	6
Lynlee	Lindley	SP/365958	1.	18.	0
Stormesworth'	Stormsworth	SP/580808	1.	11.	0
Cosseby &	Cosby and	SP/548949	2.	9.	0
Thorp	Little Thorpe	SP/542970			
Kirkeby Mallore	Kirkby Mallory	SK/453003	1.	14.	0
Walcote	Walcote	SP/568837	1.	3.	0
Peiccilton'	Peckleton	SK/470009		18.	6

---

[1] Although the 1334 Account (E 179/133/3) refers to boroughs they are not named. There is little doubt that they were the same as in 1332 and 1336, namely Leicester, Hinckley, and Mountsorrel. There is a discussion of the subsidies paid by the borough of Leicester in M. Bateson, op. cit. ii, p. xxix, and an incomplete transcript (pp. 34–40) of a roll of 1336 showing the value of the goods of individuals who contributed to the tenth of that year.

			£	s.	d.
Clenfeld	Glenfield	SK/538060	1.	3.	0
Ibbestoke	Ibstock	SK/404096	3.	0.	0
Gilden Morton'	Gilmorton	SP/570879	2.	4.	0
Swynford	Swinford	SP/569794	1.	19.	0
Petlyng' Magna	Peatling Magna	SP/594925	2.	15.	0
Fenny Drayton'	Fenny Drayton	SP/350971	2.	0.	8
Brantyngthorp'	Bruntingthorpe	SP/601898		17.	0
Sharnford	Sharnford	SP/483919	2.	4.	0
Claybrok' &	Claybrooke Magna &	SP/492887	2.	14.	0
Claybrok'	Claybrooke Parva	SP/496879			
Bitmeswell'	Bitteswell	SP/537859	1.	17.	0
Dunton'	Dunton Bassett	SP/547904	1.	18.	0
Northburgh'	Narborough	SP/541976	3.	5.	0
Outheby	Oadby	SK/624003	3.	2.	0
Whenlesbergh'	Wellsborough	SK/365024	1.	3.	0
Hegham	Higham on the Hill	SP/382956	2.	1.	0
Stoke	Stoke Golding	SP/398973	1.	5.	0
Stannton' sub Berndon'	Stanton under Bardon	SK/466103		15.	0
Wygeston'	Wigston Parva	SP/466898	1.	5.	0
Sapcote	Sapcote	SP/488932	2.	10.	0
Snarkeston'	Snarestone	SK/341094	2.	0.	0
Twyqos	Twycross	SK/339049	1.	10.	0
Gopsull'	Gopsall	SK/353064		18.	0
Cunston'	Congerstone	SK/367054	1.	14.	8
Coton' iuxta Bosworth'	Coton[1]	SK/393023	1.	14.	6
Enderby	Enderby	SP/538995	3.	0.	0
Bildeston'	Bilstone	SK/363052		18.	0
Shepey Parva	Sheepy Parva	SK/333013		14.	6
Templu'	Temple	SK/362025		5.	6
Ouerton' sub Ardern'	Orton on the Hill	SK/304039	2.	9.	0
Assheby Parva	Ashby Parva	SP/525886	2.	0.	6
Aston'	Aston Flamville	SP/462928	1.	7.	0
Norton'	Norton iuxta Twycross	SK/323070	1.	13.	6
Blaby	Blaby	SP/570979	2.	16.	4
Sheuesby	Shearsby	SP/623910	2.	6.	0
Erndesby	Arnesby	SP/618922	3.	6.	8
Lobbesthorp'	Lubbesthorpe	SK/541010	1.	1.	0
Thurleston'	Thurlaston	SP/502991	1.	15.	0
Merkyngfeld	Markfield	SK/487100		13.	6
Shelton'	Earl Shilton	SP/471983	1.	17.	6
Normanton' Turvill'	Normanton Turville	SP/495985	1.	4.	0
Upton'	Upton	SP/363996	1.	18.	6
Cuntasthorp'	Countesthorpe	SP/585954	1.	10.	0
Craft'	Croft	SP/511961	1.	13.	0
Sibbesdon'	Sibson	SK/354009	2.	3.	0
Frollesworth'	Frolesworth	SP/503906	2.	12.	0
Luttreworth'	Lutterworth	SP/543844	4.	13.	2
Kereby	Kirby Muxloe	SK/521046		15.	6
Glen Parva	Glen Parva	SP/580983	1.	13.	0
Cnaptoft'	Knaptoft	SP/625985	2.	12.	0
Borleyston'	Barlestone	SK/428059	1.	10.	0
Normanton' super le Heth'	Normanton le Heath	SK/377127	1.	19.	4
Cateby	Cadeby	SK/426023		14.	3
Carleton' iuxta Bosworth'	Carlton	SK/397050		14.	6
Shakerston'	Shackerstone	SK/374067	1.	8.	0
Stapelton'	Stapleton	SP/435984	1.	15.	0
North Keuelingworth'	North Kilworth	SP/616832	1.	5.	0

[1] Grid ref. is to Near Coton.

Shepey Magna	Sheepy Magna	SK/326013	2.	1.	0
Sutton' iuxta Bosworth'	Sutton Cheney	SK/416005	2.	15.	0
Shengeton'	Shenton	SK/387003	2.	5.	6
Brunkyngthorp'	Bromkinsthorpe[1]	SK/585020		15.	0
Braundeston'	Braunstone	SK/555029	1.	3.	0
Radeclive	Ratcliffe Culey	SP/327994	1.	5.	0
Honecote	Huncote	SP/518974		16.	0
Bochardeston' &	Botcheston and	SK/482049		15.	6
Nueton'	Newton Unthank	SK/490043			
Hucclescote &	Hugglescote and	SK/427127	2.	8.	0
Donygton'	Donington le Heath	SK/420125			
Thorp' iuxta Lilleburn'	Catthorpe	SP/552782	1.	2.	0
Suthkeuelingworth'	South Kilworth	SP/604819	1.	3.	0
Ailmesthorp'	Elmesthorpe	SP/461965	1.	19.	0
Roteby	Ratby	SK/512059	1.	5.	0
Wykene	Wykin	SP/406953		17.	0
Hynkele Bondes	Hinckley Bond[2]		1.	12.	1
Wylughby	Willoughby Waterless	SP/575925	1.	7.	4
Ailleston'	Aylestone	SK/572010	2.	12.	0
Knythton'	Knighton	SK/600013	3.	2.	4
Kilmundcote &	Kimcote and	SP/586866	3.	3.	0
Walton'[3]	Walton	SP/595872			
Dersford'	Desford	SK/479034	1.	1.	6
Oddeston'	Odstone	SK/393079	1.	12.	0
Bosworth'	Market Bosworth	SK/408033	2.	17.	0
Hynkele [B][4]	Hinckley	SP/427938	2.	8.	0 [T]
Pulteneye	Poultney	SP/580850		15.	4[5]
Groby	Groby	SK/523076		15.	6
Neuton' Harecourt	Newton Harcourt	SP/640968	2.	5.	0
Wykyngeston'	Wigston Magna	SP/609992	8.	8.	0
			249.	2.	9½[6]

Hd. Gosecote [GOSCOTE HUNDRED]

Sheile cum Hyda	Seal [in Derbyshire][7]	SK/289129	5.	17.	0
Assheby la zouche	Ashby de la Zouch	SK/361168	7.	5.	0
Pakynton'[8]	Packington	SK/358144	3.	1.	10
Wodecote	Woodcote	SK/354187		10.	0
Overton' Sauce	Coleorton [Saucey]	SK/403176	1.	9.	0
Overton' Quatremars	Coleorton [Quatermarsh[9]]	SK/403176	1.	5.	0
Snypston'	Snibston	SK/416145	1.	5.	0
Raveneston'[10]	Ravenstone	SK/402139		9.	0
Wytewyk'	Whitwick	SK/436163		17.	6

---

[1] Bromkinsthorpe, not marked on modern maps, was a liberty in St. Mary Leicester.

[2] Hinckley Bond was a part of the town outside the borough of Hinckley.

[3] Cotes de Val, now a deserted village, is included in this entry on later documents, e.g. on E 164/7, f. 148 d (fifteenth century).

[4] See footnote to Leicester (p. 158).

[5] Excludes sum of £1 for William Owyn, taxer. See footnote to hundred total.

[6] This total includes £1 for William Owyn, taxer, despite the fact that he was excused payment by writ. The sum of £1 was not included in the figure for Poultney, the vill in which he was taxed.

[7] Grid ref. is to Nether Seal, formerly Seal Magna.

[8] Part of Packington was taxed in Derbyshire (Repton hundred, p. 46).

[9] Coleorton was divided into the two lordships of Overton Saucey and Overton Quatermarsh.

[10] Part of Ravenstone was taxed in Derbyshire (Repton hundred, p. 47).

Swepston'	Swepstone	SK/368105	2.	11.	0	
Neuton' Botiler'	Newton Burgoland	SK/370090	1.	2.	6	
Swanyngton'	Swannington	SK/414162	2.	2.	0	
Threngeston' &	Thringstone and	SK/427173	2.	12.	0	
Osegarthorp'	Osgathorpe	SK/431195				
Belton'	Belton	SK/448208	1.	19.	0	
Staunton' Harold	Staunton Harold	SK/380209		15.	0	
Retherby	Rotherby	SK/675165		13.	0	
Shepesheued	Shepshed	SK/481197	3.	14.	0	
Worthington' &	Worthington and	SK/409205	2.	8.	0	
Neubold	Newbold	SK/402191				
Bredon'	Breedon on the Hill	SK/406233	7.	3.	0	
Underchirche	Anderchurch	SK/392222				
Tungge &	Tonge and	SK/419233				
Weueleston'	Wilson	SK/404247				
Walton' Isly	Isley Walton	SK/424250	1.	8.	6	
Dyseworth'	Diseworth	SK/454245	3.	0.	0	
Hemyngton'	Hemington	SK/457278	1.	19.	6	
Lokyngton'	Lockington	SK/468279	2.	11.	6½	
Castel Donyngton'	Castle Donington	SK/447273	3.	10.	0	
Keggeworth'	Kegworth	SK/488267	5.	2.	0	
Whatton'	Long Whatton	SK/483233	3.	12.	6	
Dalby Chaucomb'	Great Dalby	SK/742144	2.	9.	0	
Assheby Folvill'	Ashby Folville	SK/707120	3.	3.	0	
Barnesby	Barsby	SK/700113	2.	8.	0	
[p] [A.D]	Barsby, ancient demesne		1.	1.	4	[T]
Thorp' Secchevill'	Thorpe Satchville	SK/733117	1.	7.	6	
Reresby	Rearsby	SK/651146	1.	12.	0	
Brokesby	Brocksby	SK/671160	1.	1.	0	
Cayham	Keyham	SK/670066	1.	14.	0	
[p] [A.D]	Keyham, ancient demesne			14.	8	[T]
Barkeby	Barkby	SK/637098	3.	5.	0	
Beby	Beeby	SK/664083	3.	12.	4	
Gaddesby	Gaddesby	SK/690130	3.	18.	0	
[p] [A.D]	Gaddesby, ancient demesne		2.	9.	8	[T]
Friseby	Frisby on the Wreak	SK/696178	2.	19.	6	
[p] [A.D]	Frisby, ancient demesne		1.	8.	4	[T]
Hungerton'	Hungarton	SK/691073		19.	0	
Quenyburgh'	Queniborough	SK/651120	2.	14.	0	
Sitheston'	Syston	SK/626116	2.	16.	0	
Thurmeston'	Thurmaston	SK/610094	2.	5.	0	
Humberston'	Humberstone	SK/626060	4.	9.	6	
Hamelton'	Hamilton	SK/645075		12.	6	
Thorp' iuxta Barkeby	Barkby Thorpe	SK/635091	1.	3.	0	
Grymmeston'	Grimston	SK/686219	1.	14.	0	
[p] [A.D]	Grimston, ancient demesne			8.	8	[T]
Asfordeby [A.D]	Asfordby	SK/708190	3.	15.	0	[T]
Warkeneby [A.D]	Wartnaby	SK/712232	2.	4.	0	[T]
Caldewell' [A.D] &	Chadwell and	SK/782246	1.	15.	0	[T]
Wykeham [A.D]	Wycombe	SK/775248				
Rothelee [A.D]	Rothley	SK/586126	4.	11.	5	[T]
Swythelond	Swithland	SK/544128		17.	0	
Cropston' &	Cropston and	SK/554109	1.	11.	0	
Bradegate	Bradgate	SK/533102				
Thurkeston'	Thurcaston	SK/565106	1.	6.	8	
Ansty	Anstey	SK/549086	1.	7.	0	
Onlep'	Wanlip	SK/602110	1.	10.	6	

Burstall'	Birstall	SK/597089	1.	14.	0	
Abbeygate	Abbey-Gate[1]	SK/583063		4.	0	
Adlokeston'	Allexton	SK/818004	1.	9.	0	
Belgrave	Belgrave	SK/598070	2.	2.	6[2]	
Knyththorp'	Knight Thorpe	SK/509190		15.	0	
South Croxton'	South Croxton	SK/692103	1.	6.	0	
[p] [A.D]	South Croxton, ancient demesne			6.	0	[T]
Tokeby	Tugby	SK/762010	2.	2.	0	
Colde Neuton'	Cold Newton	SK/715064	1.	9.	3½	
Tilton'	Tilton	SK/743056	3.	3.	0	
[p] [A.D]	Tilton, ancient demesne		1.	1.	4	[T]
Whatebergh'	Whatborough	SK/767060		5.	6	
Est Norton'	East Norton	SK/782004	1.	8.	0	
Lodyngton' cum Landa	Loddington with Launde	SK/787020 SK/798043	2.	13.	4	
Queneby	Quenby	SK/702065		18.	6	
Louseby	Lowesby	SK/723074	1.	15.	0	
Hallestede	Halstead	SK/750057	1.	12.	0	
[p] [A.D]	Halstead, ancient demesne			14.	4	[T]
Skeftyngton'	Skeffington	SK/742026	1.	12.	6	
Twyford	Twyford	SK/730101	2.	11.	0	
[p] [A.D]	Twyford, ancient demesne			12.	4	[T]
Saxilby	Saxelby	SK/701210	1.	5.	0	
[p] [A.D]	Saxelby, ancient demesne			8.	6	[T]
Hatherne	Hathern	SK/503224	4.	17.	0	
Loutburgh'	Loughborough	SK/535195	6.	7.	0	
Serlethorp' & Wodethorp'	Skelthorpe and Woodthorpe	SK/545815 SK/543173	1.	1.	6	
Thorp' Haukere	Thorpe Acre	SK/516200		15.	6	
Wymundewold	Wymeswold	SK/603234	4.	5.	0	
Houton'	Hoton	SK/574226	1.	17.	0	
Cotes	Cotes	SK/555208	1.	18.	0	
Prestwold	Prestwold	SK/578214	1.	3.	0	
Burton'	Burton on the Wolds	SK/590213	2.	1.	0	
Walton Super Wald	Walton on the Wolds	SK/592197	1.	16.	0	
Barwe	Barrow upon Soar	SK/577176	6.	16.	0	
Beaumond de prior' Sancti Johannis hospit' Jerusalem in Angl'	Beaumont	SK/568090		6.	8	
Templu' de Rothelegh' de eodem prior'	The Temple[3]	SK/581123		10.	6	
Querendon'	Quorndon	SK/561165	2.	0.	0	
Wodehowes	Woodhouse	SK/538151	2.	0.	0	
Mounserell' [B][4]	Mountsorrel	SK/581151	3.	0.	0	[T]
Sileby	Sileby	SK/601152	2.	15.	0	

---

[1] Abbey-Gate, a street outside the borough of Leicester, and in St. Leonard's parish, led from North Bridge to the abbey.

[2] The quota excludes 10s. for Roger de Belegrave, taxer, who was excused payment by writ.

[3] The present mansion of The Temple stands on the site of a preceptory of the Knights Templars, the lands of which were transferred to the Hospitallers following the seizure by the Crown in 1308. For details see *V.C.H., Leics.* ii (1954), 32.

[4] See footnote to Leicester (p. 158).

Cosyngton'[1]	Cossington	SK/603136	1.	11.	0
Segrave	Seagrave	SK/620176	2.	6.	0
Radeclif'	Ratcliffe on the Wreake	SK/630145	1.	2.	0
Rakedale	Ragdale	SK/662200		19.	6
Wylughes	Willowes	SK/660180			
Houby	Hoby	SK/668173	2.	5.	10
Thurstyngton'	Thrussington	SK/650158	1.	1.	0
Dalby super Wald	Old Dalby	SK/674235	2.	10.	0
Siwoldeby	Shoby	SK/683203		19.	0
Lyndenesforth'	Newtown Linford	SK/522098		8.	0
			225.	5.	1[2]

Hd. Framlond [FRAMLAND HUNDRED]

Melton' Moubray	Melton Mowbray	SK/752192	14.	0.	0	
Howes	Hose	SK/739296	2.	4.	0	
Bokeminster &	Buckminster and	SK/879231	3.	14.	0	
Seusterne	Sewstern	SK/889218				
Normanton'	Normanton	SK/812408	1.	14.	0	
Muston'	Muston	SK/829379	2.	13.	4	
Rademilde	Redmile	SK/797355	2.	14.	0	
Statherne	Stathern	SK/772309	1.	18.	0	
Herdeby	Harby	SK/744310	2.	0.	6	
Coston'	Coston	SK/848222	2.	6.	6	
Croxton' Kiriel	Croxton Kerrial	SK/838291	3.	12.	0	
Barkston'	Barkestone	SK/778349	1.	16.	0	
Botleford	Bottesford	SK/808391	8.	5.	0	
Hareston	Harston	SK/838317	1.	10.	6	
Gnypton'	Knipton	SK/823311	1.	6.	0	
Burton' Sancti Lazari'	Burton Lazars	SK/768169	2.	1.	0	
Dalby Parva	Little Dalby	SK/775136	1.	19.	6	
Somerdeby	Somerby	SK/779105	2.	9.	0	
Saxeby	Saxby	SK/819201	2.	9.	0	
Colde Overton'	Cold Overton	SK/810102	1.	11.	10	
Wythecok' [A.D]	Withcote	SK/796058		17.	0	[T]
Kirkeby Beler	Kirby Bellars	SK/718183	5.	11.	4	
Wymundeham &	Wymondham and	SK/852186	9.	6.	0	
Thorp	Edmondthorpe	SK/858176				
Thorp' Ernald	Thorpe Arnold	SK/770201	3.	4.	0	
Stapelford	Stapleford	SK/813183	3.	16.	0	
Estwell'	Eastwell	SK/775285	2.	8.	0	
Wyvordeby	Wyfordby	SK/793189	1.	3.	0	
Brentyngby	Brentingby	SK/784188	1.	12.	0	
Scaldeford	Scalford	SK/763241	4.	15.	0	
Sixtanby	Sysonby	SK/739190	2.	12.	0	
Oleby	Welby	SK/725210	1.	6.	8	
Fretheby	Freeby	SK/803201	2.	11.	0	

---

[1] Cossington is described as a borough on E 164/7. f. 152 d (fifteenth century) but continued to pay at a fifteenth.

[2] The total given on E 179/133/5 (1337) and many other rolls is as follows: Hundred total £216. 9. 11, of which £24. 10. 2 is a tenth. Both figures are incorrect. The tenth totals £24. 10. 7 (a correction made on some later documents, including E 164/7), and the hundred total should be £225. 5. 1. The error in the total is explained by the omission of the ten quotas at a tenth that referred to parts of places that were ancient demesne (amounting to £9. 5. 2) and the accidental inclusion of the 10s. of Roger de Belegrave, taxer (see footnote, 2 p. 162).

Broughton' in the Vale	Nether Broughton	SK/696262	1.	14.	6
Gouteby	Goadby Marwood	SK/779263	1.	16.	6
Garthorp'	Garthorpe	SK/832209	2.	12.	0
Kettilby	Eye Kettleby	SK/734167	1.	5.	0
Eyton'	Eaton	SK/798291	2.	14.	4
Plungarth'	Plungar	SK/769341	1.	3.	0
Abbekettilby	Ab Kettleby	SK/724229	1.	8.	0
Holwell'	Holwell	SK/736236	1.	14.	0
Stonesby	Stonesby	SK/823244	1.	10.	0
Saltby	Saltby	SK/851266	1.	9.	0
Claxton' in the Vale	Long Clawson	SK/722272	4.	6.	0
Braunston' iuxta Croxton'	Branston	SK/810295	1.	10.	0
Waltham	Waltham on the Wold	SK/802250	3.	8.	0
Bescoldeby	Bescaby	SK/823263	1.	0.	0
Sproxton'	Sproxton	SK/857249	2.	0.	6
Burton Gronge[1]	?		2.	13.	4
			131.	10.	4

Hd. Gertr' [GARTREE HUNDRED]

Stokton'	Stoughton	SK/641021	2.	10.	0	
Houghton'	Houghton on the Hill	SK/677033	1.	17.	0[2]	
Billesdon'	Billesdon	SK/720025	2.	17.	0	
Evyngton'	Evington	SK/628027	5.	16.	0	
Ilneston'	Illston on the Hill	SP/707993	1.	10.	0	
Slauston' & Outhorp'	Slawston and Othorpe	SP/781945 SP/771955	2.	16.	0	
Burton' Noveray	Burton Overy	SP/678983	2.	13.	0	
Frisby	Frisby	SK/704020		13.	0	
Boresworth'	Husbands Bosworth	SP/644844	3.	18.	0	
Hornyngwold	Horninghold	SP/807971	2.	15.	0	
Norton' iuxta Galby	King's Norton	SK/689004		16.	0	
[p] [A.D]	King's Norton, ancient demesne			11.	0	[T]
Stonton' Wyvill	Stonton Wyville	SP/736951	1.	18.	0	
Stratton' Parva	Little Stretton	SK/668003	1.	18.	0	
[p] [A.D]	Little Stretton, ancient demesne		1.	8.	8	[T]
Wistowe	Wistow	SP/643960	1.	11.	6	
Flekeneye	Fleckney	SP/648934	1.	18.	6	
Haliok'	Holyoake	SP/845957	1.	8.	6	
Langhton'	Church Langton	SP/723923	2.	5.	0	
Eston cum Soka	Great Easton [with soke]	SP/849932	6.	14.	0	
Thirneby & Busteby	Thurnby and Bushby	SK/649039 SK/651041	4.	3.	0	
Kibbeworth' Beauchamp'	Kibworth Beauchamp	SP/681938	2.	8.	0	
Thedyngworth'	Theddingworth	SP/668858	3.	0.	0	
Halughton'	Hallaton	SP/786965	7.	2.	0	
Medburn'	Medbourne	SP/800931	5.	7.	0	
[p] [A.D]	Medbourne, ancient demesne		1.	17.	0	[T]

[1] The entry probably refers to a possession of the Hospital of St. Lazarus at Burton Lazars.

[2] The quota excludes 10s. for Roger de Belegrave, taxer, who was excused payment by writ.

			£	s.	d.	
Cnossyngton'	Knossington	SK/801087	1.	4.	6	
Neubold' Sauce	Newbold	SK/765090		19.	6	
Oselueston'	Owston	SK/774080	1.	13.	0	
Mousele	Mowsley	SP/647891	2.	13.	0	
Kibbeworth' Harecourt'	Kibworth Harcourt	SP/684942	2.	12.	0	
Holt'	Nevill Holt	SP/816938	2.	8.	0	
Glorston'	Glooston	SP/749959	1.	6.	0	
Sadyngton'	Saddington	SP/658918	2.	7.	0	
Sangeton'[1]	Shangton	SP/715960	1.	19.	0	
Carleton' Curly	Carlton Curlieu	SP/694973	2.	4.	6	
Smetheton' & Westerby	Smeeton and Westerby (now Smeeton Westerby)[2]	SP/680929	2.	12.	0	
[p] [A.D]	Smeeton and Westerby ancient demesne			11.	0	[T]
Gouteby	Goadby	SP/750989	1.	17.	6	
Foxton'	Foxton	SP/701901	4.	1.	0	
[p] [A.D]	Foxton, ancient demesne		1.	6.	0	[T]
Rolleston'	Rolleston	SK/732004	2.	18.	0	
Thorp iuxta Langeton'	Thorpe Langton	SP/740924	2.	0.	0	
Welham	Welham	SP/766925	2.	2.	0	
Glen Martel	Great Glen	SP/652977	4.	2.	0	
Blaston'	Blaston	SP/805955	2.	2.	6	
Galby	Galby	SK/695010	2.	8.	0	
[p] [A.D]	Galby, ancient demesne			15.	6	[T]
Estlangeton'	East Langton	SP/726926	2.	0.	0	
Erdeburgh'	Burrough on the Hill	SK/758108	2.	6.	0	
Suburbium Leyc'	Suburb of Leicester		1.	16.	0	
Nouesle	Noseley	SP/738985	3.	3.	0	
Gudmundele	Gumley	SP/680902	2.	5	0	
Stratton' Magna	Great Stretton	SK/657005	1.	9.	0	
Keythorp'	Keythorpe	SK/767003	1.	10.	0	
Lobynham	Lubenham	SP/706873	4.	14.	0	
Picwell' & Leuesthorp'	Pickwell and Leesthorpe	SK/786114 SK/791135	2.	2.	0	
West Langeton'	West Langton	SP/715931	1.	19.	0	
Ingwardeby	Ingarsby	SK/685054		9.	0	
Balbegrave	Baggrave	SK/699090	1.	12.	0	
[p] [A.D]	Baggrave, ancient demesne		1.	1.	4	[T]
Mardefeld South & Mardefeld North'	Marefield and North Marefield	SK/746079 SK/752088	2.	14.	0	
[p] [A.D]	Marefield and North Marefield, ancient demesne		1.	4.	6	[T]
Boudon'[3]	Great Bowden	SP/747829	7.	13.	4	
[p] [A.D]	Great Bowden, ancient demesne		7.	5.	0	[T]
Hauebergh' [A.D]	Market Harborough	SP/733872	6.	8.	0	[T]
Scraptoft'	Scraptoft	SK/648056	2.	12.	0	
Stokfaston'	Stockerston	SP/833975	1.	4.	0	
Tirlyngton'	Tur Langton	SP/713945	1.	12.	0	

[1] Hardwick is included in this entry at a later date (E 164/7 f. cliii d).

[2] Modern Smeeton Westerby comprises the two adjacent settlements of Smeeton and Westerby.

[3] Little Bowden was taxed in Northamptonshire (Rothwell hundred, p. 213).

Carnenhowe	Cranoe	SP/762953	I.	7.	6
[p] [A.D]	Cranoe, ancient demesne		II.		3 [T]
			[176.	II.	I][1]

TOTAL: £757. 12. 10½[2]

---

[1] The hundred total as given on E 179/133/5 (1337) of £160. 9. 10 is incorrect. The error arises because the ten quotas at a tenth that referred to parts of places which were ancient demesne (amounting to £16. 11. 3) were omitted from the total, and the 10s. of Roger de Belegrave, taxer, was included (see footnote, p. 164). The same kind of error occurred in Goscote hundred (see footnote, p. 163).

[2] As on 1334 Account, E 179/133/3 (fifteenth £680. 5. 1½; tenth £77. 7. 9). The figures for the hundreds add up to £782. 9. 3½; explanations for the discrepancy in the total may be found by referring to footnotes on p. 163 and above.

LINCOLNSHIRE

DOCUMENTS

8 Edward III: Account	E 179/135/19 (Holland)
8 Edward III: Account	E 179/135/20 (Kesteven and Lindsey)
8 Edward III: Indenture	E 179/135/18* (Holland)
8 Edward III: Particulars	(Kesteven and Lindsey): not extant
12 Edward III: Particulars	E 179/135/24* (Kesteven and Lindsey)

TAXERS

Holland: The abbot of Crowland and Robert de Scardeburgh
Kesteven and Lindsey: The abbot of Bardney and Thomas de Sibethorpe

TAX YIELD

	Holland			Kesteven			Lindsey		
15th	£665.	11.	8	£918.	2.	7¼	£1324.	0.	6
10th				£ 39.	14.	10½	£ 204.	18.	5¼
	£665.	11.	8	£957.	17.	5¾	£1528.	18.	11¼

Total for Lincolnshire £3,152. 8. 1

Representing assessed movable wealth of £46,062. 14. 8¼

NOTES

In Lincolnshire, as in Yorkshire, the size of the county made it difficult for a single pair of taxers to be responsible for the whole area. (In 1334 the abbot of Bardney supervised the taxation of Kesteven and Lindsey, and the abbot of Crowland that of Holland. Only for Holland does a roll of 1334 survive.)

The tax quotas are listed under the headings of the various wapentakes. Of these Holland had three and Kesteven eleven while Lindsey was divided into West Riding (five), North Riding (five), and South Riding (six plus the Liberty of Horncastle and the Soke of Bolingbroke). In all there are 685 quotas on the Lincolnshire rolls; of these, eighty-seven refer to more than one place-name and nineteen places, all in Lindsey, are taxed *cum membris*.

Most of the places taxed at a tenth were in Lindsey where the list is dominated by the city of Lincoln (£100); Grimsby, the only other taxation borough in Lindsey, had a very small quota only slightly larger than some of the forty-three ancient demesnes also taxed at a tenth. Outside Lindsey the only other taxation borough was Stamford, in Kesteven (taxed with its suburb of Bredecroft at £35. 17. 8).

Special mention may be made here of Boston, the outport for Lincoln, not a taxation borough and taxed at the lower rate of a fifteenth but at the considerable sum of £73. 6. 8. Many of the Fenland townships also had large quotas but in most cases these should not be regarded as urban quotas for much of the assessed wealth must have been on the surrounding rural areas. The quotas have been mapped in detail by Glasscock (1964).

The boundary of the county in 1334 seems to have been almost identical to that of the modern county. The rolls include two places that have since been transferred to other counties, Belvoir to Leicestershire and Misson to Nottinghamshire; no places in modern Lincolnshire were taxed elsewhere in 1334.

REFERENCES

C. W. Foster and T. Longley, eds., 'The Lincolnshire Domesday and the Lindsey Survey', *Lincs. Rec. Soc.* 19 (1924).

H. C. Darby, *The Medieval Fenland*, 1940.

W. S. Thompson, 'A Lincolnshire assize roll for 1298', *Lincs. Rec. Soc.* 36 (1944).

H. E. Hallam, 'Some thirteenth century censuses', *Ec.H.R.*, 2nd series, 10 (1958), 340–61.

H. E. Hallam, 'Population density in medieval Fenland', *Ec.H.R.*, 2nd series, 14 (1961), 71–81.

R. E. Glasscock, 'The lay subsidy of 1334 for Lincolnshire', *Lincs. Architectural and Archaeological Soc., Reports and Papers*, 10, part 2 (1964), 115–33.

HOLLAND

Wap. Kyreketon' [KIRTON WAPENTAKE]

Wyberton'	Wyberton	TF/329409	16.	0.	0
Frampton'	Frampton	TF/326392	17.	0.	0
Kyrketon'	Kirton	TF/305385	27.	10.	0
Algerkyrk'	Algarkirk	TF/291353	14.	0.	0
Swynisheuid	Swineshead	TF/237402	19.	0.	0
Byker	Bicker	TF/225377	11.	10.	0
Donyngton'	Donington	TF/208359	16.	13.	4
Quadheryng'	Quadring	TF/224341	15.	0.	0
Wygetoft'	Wigtoft	TF/262362	13.	6.	8
Surflet'	Surfleet	TF/251283	21.	0.	0
Goseberekyrk'	Gosberton	TF/238318	30.	0.	0
Sutterton'	Sutterton	TF/285356	21.	6.	8
			222.	6.	8

Wap. Ellowe [ELLOE WAPENTAKE]

Pincebek'	Pinchbeck	TF/242255	45.	0.	0
Spalding'	Spalding	TF/247224	42.	0.	0
Weston'	Weston	TF/293252	14.	0.	0
Crouland	Crowland	TF/241103	3.	6.	8
Multon'	Moulton	TF/307241	31.	0.	0
Holbeche	Holbeach	TF/359248	33.	0.	0
Quappelade	Whaplode	TF/324240	32.	0.	0
Flet'	Fleet	TF/389237	18.	0.	0
Gedeneye	Gedney	TF/403243	15.	10.	0
Sutton'	Sutton St. James	TF/397184	25.	0.	0
Tydd'	Tydd St. Mary	TF/446186	8.	6.	8
			267.	3.	4

Wap. Skyrbek' [SKIRBECK WAPENTAKE]

Wrangel	Wrangle	TF/424508	15.	13.	4
Leek'	Old Leake	TF/408502	21.	0.	0
Benyngton'	Benington	TF/397465	14.	0.	0
Leverton'	Leverton	TF/400479	13.	6.	8
Butterwyk'	Butterwick	TF/388449	6.	0.	0
Freston'	Freiston	TF/378438	11.	15.	0
Toft'	Fishtoft	TF/364424	10.	0.	0
Skyrbek'	Skirbeck [in Boston]	TF/338431	11.	0.	0
Sancto Botho' [Va]	Boston	TF/326442	73.	6.	8
			176.	1.	8

HOLLAND TOTAL: £665. 11. 8[1]

KESTEVEN

Stannford [B] cum Bradecroft'	Stamford with Bredecroft[2]	TF/031072	35.	17.	8	[T]
Eykle [A.D]	Eagle	TF/876672	3.	6.	2½	[T]
Prior Sancti Johannis Jerusalem in Anglia apud Eykle[3]	Prior of the Hospital of St. John of Jerusalem in Eagle			11.	0	[T]
			39.	14.	10½	[T]

Wap. Nesse [NESS WAPENTAKE]

Stanford de Baronia	Stamford Baron	TF/031068	10.	0.	0
Bergham	Barholm	TF/090110	3.	8.	4
Stowe	Stowe	TF/107110	1.	6.	10½
Estdepyng'	Market Deeping	TF/137103	13.	0.	4
Westdepyng'	West Deeping	TF/109087	2.	18.	4
Uffyngton' cum Casewyk'	Uffington with Casewick	TF/062078 TF/078090	11.	10.	6
Thurleby cum Obethorp'	Thurlby with Obthorpe	TF/105168 TF/095152	10.	19.	11
Gretford	Greatford	TF/086119	5.	9.	2
Langtoft'	Longtoft	TF/123125	11.	14.	10¼
Talyngton'	Tallington	TF/091078	9.	0.	4
Brassyngburn' cum Barnethorp'	Braceborough with Banthorpe	TF/081131 TF/062110	4.	16.	6
Wilsthorp'	Wilsthorpe	TF/092136	4.	0.	3¼
Baston'	Baston	TF/124140	8.	16.	4½
Carleby	Carlby	TF/049139	4.	3.	8
			101.	5.	5½

---

[1] As on 1334 Account, E 179/135/19.

[2] Bredecroft was a western suburb of Stamford; its location is described in Francis Peck, *Antiquarian Annals of Stanford* (1727), 11–12.

[3] There was a preceptory at Eagle. The Hospital of St. John had fined for the subsidy in 1290, after which the property had been taxed consistently for lay subsidies. Willard (1934), op. cit. 96, 108.

Wap. Avelound [AVELAND WAPENTAKE]

Swaton'	Swaton	TF/133376	11.	3.	8
Spanneby	Spanby	TF/094381	2.	7.	8½
Osberneby	Osbournby	TF/069381	6.	0.	2
Horblyng'	Horbling	TF/118352	7.	7.	6
Stokwilughby	Scott Willoughby	TF/054376	2.	5.	6
Dembleby	Dembleby	TF/042377	2.	14.	0¼
Asseby	Haceby	TF/031361	2.	10.	3
Pikworth'	Pickworth	TF/044337	4.	3.	1
Neuton'	Newton	TF/047362	2.	18.	9
Thrychingham	Threekingham	TF/089362	5.	12.	4
Walcote	Walcot	TF/060352	3.	4.	3
Westloghton'	West Laughton	TF/075313	2.	10.	1
Estloghton'	East Laughton	TF/081321	1.	19.	7
Folkyngham	Folkingham	TF/071337	7.	4.	6
Sempyngham	Sempringham	TF/106329	1.	8.	0
Calcetum ad pontem Holand	Bridge End	TF/143363		15.	8
Stowe	Stow	TF/098350	2.	0.	1
Birthorp' cum Useby	Birthorpe with Ouseby	TF/104339 TF/104343	3.	0.	4
Bilingburgh'	Billingborough	TF/118342	7.	8.	11½
Poynton'	Pointon	TF/117319	5.	17.	10
Milnethorp'	Millthorpe	TF/117309	3.	14.	0
Haughthorp'	Avethorpe	TF/068296		19.	4
Greyby	Graby	TF/099295	3.	17.	7¾
Aslakby	Aslackby	TF/085304	6.	18.	0
Douseby	Dowsby	TF/113293	7.	14.	2¼
Kirkeby	Kirkby Underwood	TF/070271	4.	8.	5¼
Ryngesdon'	Ringstone	TF/094269	2.	14.	0½
Reppynghale	Rippingale	TF/098278	11.	10.	6
Dunnesby	Dunsby	TF/105268	6.	4.	4
Haccunby	Hacconby	TF/107253	5.	9.	8
Staynewhayt'	Stainfield	TF/080251	1.	16.	8
Moyton'	Morton	TF/098240	11.	3.	5
Hermethorp'	Hanthorpe	TF/085239	3.	6.	0
Dyk'	Dyke	TF/105225	2.	16.	8
Calthorp'	Cawthorpe	TF/091222	2.	0.	8
Brunne	Bourne	TF/096200	11.	4.	4
			168.	10.	2

Wap. Belteslowe [BELTISLOE WAPENTAKE]

Lauyngton'	Lenton	TF/025303	2.	1.	4
Kyseby	Keisby	TF/038285	3.	9.	6
Billesfeld	Bitchfield	SK/983284	3.	0.	1½
Osgodby	Osgodby	TF/018285	2.	17.	6
Irnham	Irnham	TF/023267	4.	3.	4½
Boleby	Bulby	TF/052262	2.	15.	11
Southorp'	Southorpe	TF/060220	2.	2.	2
Eylesthorp'	Elsthorpe	TF/059238	1.	10.	8½
Edenham	Edenham	TF/062218	3.	19.	8
Toft	Toft	TF/069172	4.	14.	10
Lound	Lound	TF/069182			
Wytham	Witham on the Hill	TF/053166	5.	3.	3¾
Careby	Careby	TF/025164	2.	14.	3¼
Onneby	Aunby	TF/022147	2.	6.	9¼

Southwythme cum Loppyngthorp'	Sough Witham with Lobthorpe	SK/927194 SK/954207	4.	13.	4
Westbitham	Castle Bytham	SK/989183	3.	19.	9
Counthorp'	Counthorpe	TF/004201	1.	6.	8
Northwythme cum Twyford	North Witham with Twyford	SK/928219 SK/930237	2.	12.	10
Styandeby	Stainby	SK/905228	3.	10.	9
Gunneby	Gunby	SK/913216	1.	9.	6¼
Colsterworth'	Colsterworth	SK/931242	3.	14.	2½
Wolsthorp'	Woolsthorpe	SK/923243	1.	14.	8
Skilyngton'	Skillington	SK/896259	2.	15.	9¾
Eston'	Easton	SK/930268	2.	15.	2¾
Basyngthorp' cum Westby	Bassingthorpe with Westby	SK/966285 SK/972283	4.	0.	1½
Birton'	Burton Coggles	SK/979258	4.	1.	6
Corby	Corby	TF/002250	7.	2.	11¾
Swafeld	Swayfield	SK/993226	3.	14.	1
Swynstede	Swinstead	TF/018224	2.	15.	0
Creton'	Creeton	TF/014199	2.	17.	0
Scotilthorp'	Scottlethorpe	TF/054209	2.	14.	4
Grympthorp'	Grimsthorpe	TF/047230	1.	15.	4
Bourthorp' cum Manthorp'	Bowthorpe with Manthorpe	TF/066153 TF/072161	2.	14.	8½
Houerthorp'	Hawthorpe	TF/046275	1.	3.	0
Helewell'	Holywell	TF/001160	3.	10.	6½
Estbitham	Little Bytham	TF/012181	2.	5.	7½
Rectoria de Corby ad firmam dimissam				6.	8
			108.	13.	2¼

Wap. Wynyerbrigg' [WINNIBRIGGS WAPENTAKE]

Berughby	Barrowby	SK/878365	3.	13.	6
Segbrok'	Sedgebrook	SK/857380	2.	18.	0¾
Athelyngton'	Allington	SK/856403	5.	15.	4¼
Denton'	Denton	SK/865325	3.	9.	8
Gunwardeby cum Manthorp'	Great Gonerby with Manthorpe	SK/898382 SK/920379	3.	6.	8
Magna Paunton'	Great Ponton	SK/925305	3.	14.	10
Belverus cum Wolsthorp'	Belvoir [in Leics.] with Woolsthorpe	SK/820339 SK/837339	2.	18.	0
Parva Paunton'	Little Ponton	SK/925323	1.	17.	4
Strouston[1]	Stroxton	SK/902311	1.	8.	7½
Hungerton' cum Wywell'	Hungerton with Wyville	SK/878298 SK/883292	2.	2.	3
Casthorp' cum Staynewath'	Casthorpe with Stenwith	SK/862355 SK/836363	1.	6.	10
Spitelgate Walton' cum Hoghton'	Spittlegate Walton with Houghton	SK/916348 SK/910360 SK/927342	1.	16.	8

[1] The 1334 Account (E 179/135/20) states that the villeins of Stroxton and of Great and Little Ponton were exempt from the subsidy as their lands were held of Thomas de Baumburgh who was exempt from payment because of the King's affection for him, *C.P.R. 1330–1334*, 368. The county roll of 1337 (E 179/135/24) has *nihil* for Stroxton, but Great and Little Ponton have quotas. The quota for Stroxton has been taken from a later document, E 179/135/46 (1348). The case is most unusual in that exemption granted to an individual seems to have extended to the villeins on his lands.

Northstok' cum	Stoke Rochford with	SK/913285	2.	12.	8
Southstok'	South Stoke	SK/921273			
Herlaston'	Harlaxton	SK/883327	2.	16.	4
Grantham	Grantham	SK/915358	19.	10.	0
			59.	6.	9½

Wap. Threhowes [THREO WAPENTAKE]

Honyngton'	Honington	SK/943434	2.	10.	11¼
Barkeston' cum	Barkston with	SK/933415	3.	0.	2
Ryngesthorp'	Ringsthorpe	SK/927415			
Systan	Syston	SK/930409	3.	5.	6
Belton'	Belton	SK/930395	2.	15.	3
Lunderthorp' cum	Londonthorpe with	SK/952380	2.	8.	0
Touthorp'	Towthorpe	SK/925385			
Welleby	Welby	SK/975382	2.	18.	5
Haydour	Heydour	TF/009397	6.	7.	6
Aseby and	Aisby and	TF/012388			
Oseby	Oseby	TF/003390			
Wilsford cum	Wilsford with	TF/006430	4.	2.	4¾
Anecastr' [p][1]	Ancaster [part of]	SK/983437			
Dunsthorp' cum	Dunsthorpe with	SK/c.925358	1.	16.	0
Herierdby &	Harrowby and	SK/937358			
Westhorp'	Westhorpe	SK/c.930340			
Brayceby	Braceby	TF/015354	2.	8.	1½
Saperton'	Sapperton	TF/019340	2.	3.	2¾
Roppeslee cum	Ropsley with	SK/993342	5.	1.	2½
Humby &	Humby and	TF/007323			
Ogarth	Osgarth	SK/990340			
Botheby	Boothby Pagnell	SK/972308	4.	0.	5
Somerby	Old Somerby	SK/964340	1.	18.	9½
			44.	15.	11¼

Wap. Aswardhirn' [ASWARDHURN WAPENTAKE]

Skredyngton'	Scredington	TF/096404	4.	7.	7¾
Hekyngton'	Heckington	TF/143442	9.	18.	4
Vetus Lafford	Old Sleaford	TF/069459	5.	12.	8
Magna Hale	Great Hale	TF/148429	8.	19.	0¼
Iwardeby cum	Ewerby with	TF/122473	6.	3.	11
Ousthorp'	Ewerby Thorpe	TF/132477			
Parva Hale	Little Hale	TF/146416	5.	10.	3¼
Burton'	Burton Pedwardine	TF/119421	7.	16.	5½
Southkyme	South Kyme	TF/175497	3.	2.	6
Howell'	Howell	TF/135463	3.	6.	8
Asgardeby cum	Asgarby with	TF/116454	4.	0.	5
Bakton'	Broughton	TF/123455			
Queringdon' cum	Quarrington with	TF/053444	4.	10.	4½
Milnethorp'	Millthorpe	TF/050440			
Ounesby cum	Aunsby with	TF/044388	3.	1.	11
Crokton'	Crofton	TF/055401			
Evedon'	Evedon	TF/092476	3.	8.	0¾
Swarreby	Swarby	TF/047405	2.	11.	6½
Kelleby	Kelby	TF/003414	2.	4.	0

[1] Part of Ancaster was taxed in Loveden wapentake.

Calwarthorp'	Culverthorpe	TF/024404	2.	12.	9
Aswardeby	Aswarby	TF/068399	3.	8.	7¾
Wilughby & Silkeby	Willoughby and Silkby [now Silk Willoughby][1]	TF/057430 TF/053430	6.	10.	2¾
Ingoldesby	Ingoldsby	TF/011301	5.	9.	4
Kirkby Laylthorp'	Kirkby La Thorpe	TF/099461	5.	9.	6
Helperingham cum Thorp'	Helpringham with Thorpe Latimer	TF/138408 TF/132398	15.	5.	1
			113.	9.	4

Wap. Flaxwell' [FLAXWELL WAPENTAKE]

Nova Lafford	New Sleaford	TF/069459	16.	0.	8¼
Northrouceby	North Rauceby	TF/021464	9.	3.	8
Southrouceby	South Rauceby	TF/023456	5.	17.	7
Handebek'	Handbeck	TF/005432	1.	4.	0¼
Cranewell'	Cranwell	TF/032499	2.	6.	0
Dunnesby	Dunsby	TF/040513	1.	4.	7
Haldyngham	Holdingham	TF/059471	2.	16.	3¼
Riskyngton'	Ruskington	TF/083511	5.	9.	3
Amewyk'	Anwick	TF/114506	3.	7.	4¼
Lesyngham	Lessingham	TF/057486	5.	11.	4½
Roxham	Roxholm	TF/062498	3.	4.	7¾
Templu' Bruer	Temple Bruer	TF/008536	2.	2.	9½
Dirington'	Dorrington	TF/076534	3.	15.	0
Bloxham	Bloxham	TF/064538	4.	0.	0
Brauncewell'	Brauncewell	TF/045524	2.	13.	5¾
Askeby	Ashby de la Launde	TF/055548	3.	3.	0
Diggeby	Digby	TF/081548	4.	0.	5½
Rouston'	Rowston	TF/084564	5.	6.	0
Prior Sancti Johannis Jerusalem in Angl' apud Rouston' et Bruer'	Prior of the Hospital of St. John of Jerusalem in Rowston and Temple Bruer			8.	0
			81.	14.	2

Wap. Langhowe [LANGOE WAPENTAKE]

Nocton'	Nocton	TF/061642	1.	4.	11¼
Dunston'	Dunston	TF/063630	1.	10.	0¾
Metheringham	Metheringham	TF/070613	7.	1.	3
Blannkeney	Blankney	TF/068600	7.	5.	1¼
Marton'	Martin	TF/122599	3.	17.	8¼
Tymberlound	Timberland	TF/122584	2.	12.	8½
Thorp'	Thorpe Tilney	TF/118574	3.	2.	7¼
Walcote	Walcot	TF/131565	3.	14.	3½
Bilinghay	Billinghay	TF/157549	3.	6.	6¾
Northkyme	North Kyme	TF/152527	1.	9.	3
Mere	Mere	TF/008652	2.	11.	0
Kirkeby	Kirkby Green	TF/085578	2.	3.	8¼
Scoupewyk'	Scopwick	TF/070581	7.	11.	11¼
Haneworth'	Potter Hanworth	TF/054661	3.	13.	10

1 The hamlet of Silkby, one-third of a mile west of the church, has become merged with the village of Willoughby.

Braunston'	Branston	TF/021673	5.	0.	0
Wassyngburgh cum Highyngton'	Washingborough with Heighington	TF/018707 TF/030694	6.	10.	0
Canewyk'	Canwick	SK/988696	2.	0.	9¾
Bracebrigg'	Bracebridge	SK/968679	3.	13.	9
Prior Sancti Johannis Jerusalem in Angl' apud Kirkeby	Prior of the Hospital of St. John of Jerusalem in Kirkby Green			4.	0
			68.	13.	5¾

Wap. Lovedon' [LOVEDEN WAPENTAKE]

Ledenham	Leadenham	SK/951518	6.	17.	0½
Broughton'	Brant Broughton	SK/915539	8.	3.	0
Carleton'	Carlton Scroop	SK/948451	2.	19.	0
Fulbek'	Fulbeck	SK/947504	4.	11.	6¾
Haugham	Hougham	SK/887442	4.	18.	3½
Cathorp' cum Freston'	Caythorpe with Frieston	SK/939486 SK/939476	6.	0.	0
Haugh'	Hough on the Hill	SK/923464	4.	13.	4¼
Geuelston'	Gelston	SK/913452	2.	12.	4¾
Stubton'	Stubton	SK/874488	3.	0.	11¾
Claypole	Claypole	SK/845490	7.	12.	4¼
Brandon'	Brandon	SK/903482	3.	5.	5¾
Sudbrok'	Sudbrook	SK/972447	2.	10.	9¾
Wilughby cum Ancastre [p][1]	Willoughby with Ancaster [part of]	SK/967438 SK/983437			
Normanton'	Normanton	SK/949463	2.	10.	4
Merston'	Marston	SK/893437	3.	10.	0
Bekyngham	Beckingham	SK/875538	2.	13.	0
Sutton'	Sutton	SK/876522	2.	6.	3½
Fenton'	Fenton	SK/878507	3.	5.	4
Stragelthorp'	Stragglethorpe	SK/913524	1.	19.	6½
Westburgh' cum Thorp'	Westborough with Thorpe Parva	SK/850443 SK/850440	4.	1.	1¾
Dodyngton' cum Stokkyng'	Dry Doddington with Stocking	SK/849466 SK/c.850465	5.	2.	7½
Benyngton' cum Foston'	Long Bennington with Foston	SK/843439 SK/858429	8.	0.	5½
			90.	13.	0

Wap. Boby [BOOTHBY WAPENTAKE]

Welburn'	Welbourn	SK/968545	6.	7.	9
Welyngoure	Wellingore	SK/982565	6.	0.	0
Skynnand	Skinnand	SK/940575	1.	16.	0
Navenby	Navenby	SK/987579	7.	7.	0
Boby cum Somerton'	Boothby Graffoe with Somerton	SK/987589 SK/954586	3.	14.	0
Colby	Coleby	SK/975606	6.	0.	0
Hermeston'	Harmston	SK/972623	5.	6.	0
Wadyngton'	Waddington	SK/976642	6.	0.	0
			42.	10.	9

[1] See also Threo wapentake, above, p. 172.

Wap. Grafhowe [GRAFFOE WAPENTAKE]

Norton'	Norton Disney	SK/890590	1.	10.	8½
Stapelford'	Stapleford	SK/886576	1.	6.	9¼
Carleton'	Carlton le Moorland	SK/908579	2.	15.	6
Auburn'	Aubourn	SK/919625	2.	0.	0
Dodyngton'	Doddington	SK/901701	1.	13.	11½
Basyngham	Bassingham	SK/908597	2.	11.	6¼
Southicham	South Hykeham	SK/936645	1.	2.	10
Thurleby	Thurlby	SK/908617	1.	13.	9
Northicham	North Hykeham	SK/945659	2.	10.	0
Skeldynghop'	Skellingthorpe	SK/925721	2.	10.	1½
Wisseby	Whisby	SK/903675		9.	0
Thorp' Pigot	Thorpe on the Hill	SK/908655	2.	10.	0
Bultham	Boultham	SK/958693	1.	1.	0
Hadyngton'	Haddington	SK/915630	2.	2.	0
Morton'	Morton	SK/885638	1.	4.	0
Northscarle cum	North Scarle with	SK/848668	3.	7.	8
Swaynthorp'	Swinethorpe	SK/875695			
Swynderby	Swinderby	SK/869632	2.	16.	9½
			33.	5.	7½

KESTEVEN TOTAL: £957. 17. 5¾[1]

LINDSEY

WEST RIDING

Wap. Manle [MANLEY WAPENTAKE]

Haxai	Haxey	SK/764998	11.	13.	7
Belton' c.m	Belton [with members]	SE/783064	8.	12.	3
Epworth' c.m	Epworth [with members]	SE/783040	9.	16.	2
Crulle c.m²	Crowle [with members]	SE/774130	5.	0.	11
Luddington' &	Luddington and	SE/830167	2.	11.	0¼
Watterton'	Waterton	SE/853180			
Gerlethorp'	Garthorpe	SE/849193	3.	9.	8
Amcotes	Amcotts	SE/855141	2.	13.	4
Whytton'	Whitton	SE/903245	4.	0.	6
Wynteringham	Winteringham	SE/925224	4.	16.	11
Alkebarow	Alkborough	SE/882218	3.	10.	6
Walcote	Walcot	SE/878211	2.	2.	0
Colby	Coleby	SE/898197	2.	2.	9
Theulby	Thealby	SE/894180			
Haytheby	Haythby	SE/890190			
Derby	Darby	SE/876180			
Burton' stather³	Burton upon Stather	SE/870179	2.	3.	11
Wynterington'⁴	Winterton	SE/928185	3.	15.	8½
Roxby	Roxby	SE/920170	1.	19.	11¾
Magna Risby &	Great Risby and	SE/920148	2.	4.	0½
Parva	Little Risby	SE/930150			
Appelby	Appleby	SE/952149	5.	2.	0
Flekesburgh'	Flixborough	SE/872151	2.	19.	4¼
Normanby	Normanby	SE/882168	3.	12.	10

[1] As on 1334 Account, E 179/135/20.
[2] Members of Crowle in 1316 included Eastoft, Ealand, and Tetley (*F.A.* iii. 185).
[3] Part of Burton upon Stather was taxed at a tenth (p. 186).
[4] Part of Winterton was taxed at a tenth (p. 186).

Croxeby	Crosby	SE/893122	4.	4.	5
Coningby	Conesby[1]	SE/894138			
Guneys	Gunness	SE/847117			
Salcliff'	Sawcliffe	SE/912145	2.	6.	o½
Santon'	Santon[2]	SE/940129	2.	9.	4
Berghton' c.m[3]	Broughton [with members]	SE/960085	5.	3.	9
Messingham	Messingham	SE/893045	5.	o.	6½
Reddeburn'[4]	Redbourne	SK/973999	2.	15.	o
Holm' c.m[5]	Holme [with members]	SE/920069	1.	10.	8
Hybaldstou[6]	Hibaldstow	SE/977026	1.	10.	6
Botenesford[7]	Bottesford	SE/899070	2.	4.	1
Malmeton'	Manton	SE/934027	1.	3.	10
Stainton' cum Wadingham[8]	Stainton with Waddingham	SK/988963 SK/983962	4.	9.	5¼
Halton' sup Trenta	West Walton	SE/905208	3.	3.	2
Boringham [Ba][9]	Burringham	SE/835094		14.	o
Skalby cum Stretton'	Scawby with Sturton	SE/968056 SE/969046	2.	7.	9½

		121.	10.	o

Wap. Aslakhow [ASLACOE WAPENTAKE]

Glenteworth[10]	Glentworth	SK/945882	2.	12.	4
Filingham	Fillingham	SK/948859	4.	o.	o
Glentham	Glentham	TF/003904	9.	o.	9
Ouneby	Owmby	TF/001873	2.	18.	3
Wylughton'	Willoughton	SK/932934	7.	o.	7½
Cauenby	Caenby	SK/999893	1.	17.	4
Norton' cum parte hospit'[11]	Bishop Norton with part of Spital in the Street	SK/984926 SK/966900	3.	18.	9¼
Helmeswell [Ba][12]	Hemswell	SK/931909	1.	10.	o
Ingham	Ingham	SK/950835	2.	14.	4
Bliburgh'	Blyborough	SK/934946	5.	2.	5
Spridelington'	Spridlington	TF/008845	5.	10.	o¾
Haneworth'	Cold Hanworth	TF/035832	2.	o.	11
Snyterby[13]	Snitterby	SK/985948		12.	o¼
Cotes	Coates	SK/914835	1.	9.	11
Cameringham	Cammeringham	SK/948822	2.	14.	o½

[1] Grid ref. is to Great Conesby. Both Great and Little Conesby are now deserted villages.
[2] Grid ref. is to Low Santon.
[3] Members of Broughton in 1316 included Mausby and Castlethorpe (*F.A.* iii. 184).
[4] Part of Redbourne was taxed at a tenth (p. 186).
[5] Ravensthorpe was listed with Holme in 1316 (*F.A.* iii. 185).
[6] Part of Hibaldstow was taxed at a tenth (p. 186).
[7] Part of Bottesford was taxed at a tenth (p. 186).
[8] Parts of Stainton and Waddingham were taxed at a tenth (p. 186).
[9] Part of Burringham was taxed at a tenth (p. 186).
[10] Part of Glentworth was taxed at a tenth (p. 186).
[11] The inclusion of Spital in the Street (Hospital on Ermine Street) both in the *Nomina Villarum* (1316) and in 1334, confirms the suggestion (*V.C.H., Lincs.* ii (1906), 235) that there was a hospital on this site before the formation of the chantry in 1343, or of the later hospital of 1396. The rest of Spital in the Street was probably assessed in the Soke of Kirton where it was assessed in 1316 (*F.A.* iii. 185).
[12] Part of Hemswell was taxed at a tenth (p. 186).
[13] Part of Snitterby was taxed at a tenth (p. 186).

Frissby	Firsby[1]	SK/988851	2.	10.	10¾
Normanby	Normanby	TF/002881	1.	8.	9
Hakthorn'	Hackthorn	SK/992823	2.	5.	7
Herpeswell[2]	Harpswell	SK/936900	2.	6.	1¼
			61.	13.	1¼

Wap. Coringham [CORINGHAM WAPENTAKE]

Magna Coringham[3]	Corringham	SK/872915		16.	0
Lagchton' &	Laughton and	SK/848973	5.	5.	6
Welesworth'	Wildsworth	SK/808976			
Gaynesburgh'	Gainsborough	SK/817894	8.	1.	9½
Tonhayk' cum	Thonock with	SK/828927	1.	0.	0
Havercroft'	Havercroft	SK/c.830930			
Scotton' &	Scotton and	SK/891991	5.	1.	11
Fer'	East Ferry	SK/815997			
Bliton'[4]	Blyton	SK/853948		13.	0
Tunstall'	Donstall	SK/890936	1.	9.	5
Lee	Lea	SK/831866	1.	10.	1½
Scoter &	Scotter and	SE/888008	5.	11.	0
Stalthorp'	Scotterthorpe	SE/875020			
Greyngham[5]	Grayingham	SK/935962	1.	2.	1
Yolthorp'	Yawthorpe	SK/897920	1.	6.	0
Hepham[6]	Heapham	SK/878885		4.	0
Southhthorp'	Southorpe	SK/885953	1.	17.	3¾
Cletham	Cleatham	SE/933017	2.	0.	10
Norththorp'[7]	Northorpe	SK/895972	1.	12.	5¼
			37.	11.	5

Wap. Laureys [LAWRESS WAPENTAKE]

Asthrop'	Aisthorp	SK/947802	1.	12.	10
Thorkesey	Torksey	SK/837789	4.	11.	0
Fiskerton'	Fiskerton	TF/048720	4.	7.	5
Borotelby	Brattleby	SK/948808	1.	8.	2
Faldingwor:h'	Faldingworth	TF/067847	3.	4.	0
Saxelby c.m[8]	Saxilby [with members]	SK/895762	7.	15.	10
Carleton' Paynel cum	North Carlton with	SK/945776	4.	11.	6½
Parva Carleton'[9]	Middle Carlton	SK/950770			
Repham	Reepham	TF/039739	5.	0.	0½
Boselingthorp'	Boslingthorpe	TF/079852	1.	8.	3¾
Suddebrok &	Sudbrooke and	TF/031761	2.	19.	10
Holm'	Holme	TF/043762			
Donham	Dunholme	TF/024794	2.	4.	0

[1] Grid ref. is to West Firsby.
[2] Part of Harpswell was taxed at a tenth (p. 186).
[3] Part of Corringham was taxed at a tenth (p. 186).
[4] Part of Blyton was taxed at a tenth (p. 186).
[5] Part of Grayingham was taxed at a tenth (p. 186).
[6] Part of Heapham was taxed at a tenth (p. 186).
[7] Part of Northorpe was taxed at a tenth (p. 186).
[8] Members of Saxilby in 1316 included North and South Ingleby (*F.A.* iii. 186).
[9] Middle Carlton is a deserted village, the site of which is in the modern parish of North Carlton. It was taxed with South Carlton in 1327 (E 179/135/11, 26 d) but with North in 1332.

Thorp'	Thorpe in the Fallows	SK/913806	1.	11.	7
Carleton' Wylaker	South Carlton	SK/951766		17.	8
Rysom	Riseholme	SK/983757	1.	6.	2
Gretwell'	Greetwell	TF/014715	2.	19.	1¾
Snartford	Snarford	TF/051825	1.	10.	0
Burton iuxta Linc'	Burton	SK/962746	3.	18.	2
Netilham	Nettleham	TF/008753	4.	11.	11¼
Scothorn'	Scothern	TF/034774	4.	3.	7
Scampton'	Scampton	SK/948785	1.	13.	2
Broxholm'	Broxholme	SK/911781	3.	12.	0
Wolingham	Cherry Willingham	TF/032724	1.	12.	3¼
			66.	18.	8

Wap. Welle [WELL WAPENTAKE]

Stowe cum	Stow with	SK/882820	6.	13.	7¾
parco	Stow Park	SK/866809			
Fenton'	Fenton	SK/847765	3.	13.	0
Kesteby	Kexby	SK/872859	2.	10.	11
Brampton'	Brampton	SK/846795	2.	16.	4
Braunceby	Bransby	SK/899793	2.	0.	7
Gayteburton'	Gate Burton	SK/839829	3.	5.	9¾
Stretton' iuxta Stowe	Sturton by Stow	SK/890805	2.	17.	2
Marton'	Marton	SK/840818	4.	6.	1
Lagchterton' c.m	Laughterton [with members]	SK/837760	3.	9.	5½
Upton'	Upton	SK/868868	3.	11.	9½
Wyuelyngham	Willingham	SK/873845	3.	15.	6
Neuton'	Newton on Trent	SK/833743	4.	13.	3½
Normanby	Normanby	SK/882830	1.	14.	6
Knayth'	Knaith	SK/828846	1.	12.	11
			47.	1.	0

NORTH RIDING

Wap. Yerdeburgh' [YARBOROUGH WAPENTAKE]

Barton'	Barton upon Humber	TA/032220	16.	7.	8
Bekeby c.m[1]	Bigby [with members]	TA/060075	5.	14.	11
Somerby	Somerby	TA/062066	2.	12.	0
Bondeby	Bonby	TA/004155	2.	10.	3
Melton'	Melton Ross	TA/072108	3.	1.	2
Ulseby	Ulceby	TA/103146	5.	0.	2¼
Wotton'	Wootton	TA/088161	3.	13.	6½
Netilton' c.m[2]	Nettleton [with members]	TA/111002	4.	0.	10
Keleby	Keelby	TA/165099	4.	0.	0
Imyngham	Immingham	TA/188150	6.	7.	2
Cadenay &	Cadney and	TA/017033	3.	16.	2
Housom[3]	Howsham	TA/045043			
Clisseby	Clixby	TA/102043	2.	11.	8
Bernetby	Barnetby le Wold	TA/062091	2.	19.	4¾

[1] Members of Bigby in 1316 included Kettleby and Kettleby Thorpe (*F.A.* iii. 181).
[2] Members of Nettleton in 1316 included *Herwyk*, *Wykeham*, and *Draycote*, all lost places in Nettleton parish (*F.A.* iii. 182).
[3] Parts of Cadney and Howsham were taxed at a tenth (p. 186).

Saxeby	Saxby All Saints	SE/992168	5.	3.	7¼
Seuerby	Searby	TA/072059	2.	1.	8
Aldelby &	Audleby and	TA/110040	1.	3.	4½
Hundon'	Hundon	TA/115025			
Halton'	East Halton	TA/141184	7.	15.	5½
Goushull'	Goxhill	TA/102212	9.	2.	2
Ryby	Riby	TA/185074	4.	15.	2½
Northkelsey[1]	North Kelsey	TA/044015	1.	11.	2¼
Stalingburgh'	Stallingborough	TA/195118	8.	8.	1
Brokelesby	Brocklesby	TA/140113	5.	13.	5
Elsham	Elsham	TA/034123	4.	14.	9¼
Wrauby cum Ponte	Wrawby and	TA/020085	4.	7.	1
de Glaumford	[Glandford] Brigg	TA/001072			
Kirnyngton'	Kirmington	TA/105112	3.	10.	0
Outhenby	Owmby	TA/077050	1.	17.	0
Wolrikby	Worlaby	TA/015140	4.	3.	8
Croxton'	Croxton	TA/094123	4.	9.	3
Haburgh'	Habrough	TA/145138	4.	7.	5¼
Magna Limbergh'	Great Limber	TA/135086	5.	10.	0
Kelingholm'	Killingholme[2]	TA/144173	8.	16.	0
Gresseby[3]	Grasby	TA/087049	1.	10.	4
Feriby	South Ferriby	SE/988208	6.	3.	3
Barow	Barrow upon Humber	TA/071214	9.	10.	7
Thornton'	Thornton Curtis	TA/088178	5.	16.	11
Brunham	Burnham	TA/059172			
Horkestow	Horkstow	SE/985185	3.	2.	4
			176.	7.	9

Wap. Walchecroft' [WALSHCROFT WAPENTAKE]

Teuilby	Tealby	TF/157909	4.	8.	6
Thorgamby	Thorganby	TF/208976	1.	7.	0
Normanby	Normanby le Wold	TF/123947	3.	1.	4
Claxby	Claxby	TF/111946			
Walesby	Walesby	TF/133923	4.	0.	10
Ouresby	Owersby[4]	TF/062947	6.	9.	7½
Kynerdby	Kingerby	TF/057929	3.	6.	6
Thoresway	Thoresway	TF/166966	2.	14.	1¼
Bynnebrok'	Binbrook	TF/212939	5.	8.	3
Wylingham	North Willingham	TF/164184	3.	9.	0
Lyndewode	Linwood	TF/113857	2.	2.	4
Toft &	Toft next Newton and	TF/043883	3.	1.	10
Neuton'	Newton by Toft	TF/051873			
Houton' in Mora [Ba][5]	Holton le Moor	TF/082978	1.	2.	3
Westrasen	West Rasen	TF/065894	5.	0.	5
Stainton'	Stainton le Vale	TF/176944	2.	4.	10
Irford	Orford	TF/203948		17.	8
Media Rasen	Middle Rasen	TF/086895	5.	8.	5¼
Thornton' in Mora	Thornton le Moor	TF/049963	4.	10.	0
Estrasen	Market Rasen	TF/106892	2.	7.	2

---

1 Part of North Kelsey was taxed at a tenth (p. 186).
2 Grid ref. is to North Killingholme.
3 Part of Grasby was taxed at a tenth (p. 186).
4 Grid ref. is to North Owersby.
5 Part of Holton le Moor was taxed at a tenth (p. 186).

Kirkeby & Osgodby	Kirkby and Osgodby	TF/063927 TF/071926	3.	14.	8
Croxby	Croxby	TF/192983	1.	10.	7
Southkelsey[1]	South Kelsey	TF/042982	2.	0.	11
			68.	6.	3

Wap. Hawardeshou [HAVERSTOE WAPENTAKE]

Foulestowe	Fulstow	TF/328972	7.	5.	2
Waldneuton'	Wold Newton	TF/242968	4.	7.	9
Briggesley	Brigsley	TA/254017	2.	16.	2
Hawardby	Hawarby	TF/260975	1.	6.	6
Askby & Fenneby	Ashby cum Fenby and Fenby	TA/255010 TF/260992	4.	4.	2
Northcotes	North Coates	TA/350006	3.	10.	8
Greynesby	Grainsby	TF/278995	1.	16.	4
Belesby	Beelsby	TA/208021	2.	16.	1
Bernolby	Barnoldby le Beck	TA/235033	3.	3.	2
Caburn'	Cabourne	TA/140019	1.	13.	2
Estravendale	East Ravendale	TF/236955		19.	10
Westravendale	West Ravendale	TF/228998		15.	4
Rothewell'	Rothwell	TF/151994	2.	8.	0
Wathe	Waithe	TA/283007	3.	2.	10¾
Waltham	Waltham	TA/262039	4.	17.	4
Beseby	Beesby	TF/266966	1.	6.	4
Alwaldby	Autby	TF/281971		13.	8¼
Cokewald	Cuxwold	TA/172012	2.	0.	2
Haddecliff' Gunerby	Hatcliffe Gunnerby	TA/213007 TF/216990	2.	10.	0
Swynop'	Swinhope	TF/216963		17.	1
Thoresby	North Thoresby	TF/290987	3.	3.	8
Cateby	North Cadeby	TF/270960		5.	6
			55.	19.	0

Wap. Loutheburgh' [LUDBOROUGH WAPENTAKE]

Covenham & Calthorp'	Covenham[2] and Cawthorpe	TF/340944 TF/c.350960	6.	0.	2
Foterby c.m	Fotherby [with members]	TF/316916	5.	1.	0½
Utterby & Ormesby	Utterby and North Ormsby	TF/305933 TF/289933	3.	6.	3
Loutheburgh'	Ludborough	TF/295955	3.	4.	7
Wyhom'	Wyham	TF/276951	1.	16.	11
			19.	8.	11½

Wap. Bradley [BRADLEY WAPENTAKE]

Magna Cotes	Great Coates	TA/233097	4.	6.	4
Alesby	Aylesby	TA/203076	5.	4.	0
Swalou	Swallow	TA/176030	2.	12.	2
Clee c.m	Clee [with members]	TA/290084	6.	13.	11

[1] Part of South Kelsey was taxed at a tenth (p. 186).
[2] Grid ref. is to Covenham St. Mary.

Heghling'	Healing	TA/214101	2.	10.	4
Parva Cotes	Little Coates	TA/242090	1.	18.	4¾
Bradlee	Bradley	TA/242067	2.	7.	4
Irby	Irby upon Humber	TA/197050	2.	13.	7
Layseby	Laceby	TA/215065	4.	16.	2
Scarthou	Scartho	TA/267064	3.	1.	2
Tetonai	Tetney	TA/317009	5.	0.	8
Humberstan	Humberston	TA/311052	6.	0.	4
Houton'	Holton le Clay	TA/286028	2.	9.	3¼
			49.	13.	8

SOUTH RIDING

Wap. Wraghow [WRAGGOE WAPENTAKE]

Benyngworth'	Benniworth	TF/209818	3.	4.	0
Loutheford	Ludford[1]	TF/201892	2.	19.	8½
Wolingham	South Willingham	TF/195834	3.	8.	0
Burgh' c.m[2]	Burgh on Bain [with members]	TF/223864	4.	7.	9
Stenifeld	Stainfield	TF/112732	3.	5.	6
Wraggeby	Wragby	TF/134780	3.	12.	8
Kenermond	Kirmond le Mire	TF/186926	2.	3.	9
Haynton'	Hainton	TF/180845	3.	14.	6
Paunton' & Herchewyk'	Panton and Hardwick by Wragby	TF/175789 TF/c.175790	4.	9.	0
Hatton'	Hatton	TF/178768	2.	11.	2
Houton' & Bekering'	Holton and Beckering	TF/116813 TF/121806	5.	0.	11
Westyrington'	West Torrington	TF/135821	1.	14.	2
Esttyrington'	East Torrington	TF/147834	2.	7.	3
Bolington'	Bullington	TF/092779	2.	4.	0
Langton' c.m[3]	Langton by Wragby [with members]	TF/149769	3.	8.	3¾
Stainton' c.m[4]	Stainton by Langworth [with members]	TF/062776	2.	15.	4
Wykyngby	Wickenby	TF/088820	2.	0.	0¾
Snelneslound	Snelland	TF/079806		10.	7¼
Leggesby c.m	Legsby [with members]	TF/137857	3.	12.	2
Rande c.m	Rand [with members]	TF/107791	5.	5.	3
Westbarkeworth'	West Barkwith	TF/159805	2.	5.	3
Sixill'	Sixhills	TF/170872	3.	5.	2
Sotteby	Sotby	TF/205787	2.	19.	8
Estbarkeworth'	East Barkwith	TF/166815	3.	4.	0
Bardenay	Bardney	TF/118694	8.	0.	5
Lyssington'	Lissington	TF/109835	1.	16.	4
			84.	4.	11¼

Wap. Candeleshou [CANDLESHOE WAPENTAKE]

| Weynflet' | Wainfleet[5] | TF/497590 | 15. | 10. | 6 |
| Croft' | Croft | TF/509618 | 5. | 3. | 8 |

[1] Grid ref. is to Ludford Magna.
[2] Girsby was taxed with Burgh on Bain in 1316 (*F.A.* iii. 179).
[3] Strubby was returned with Langton in 1316 (ibid.).
[4] Members of Stainton in 1316 included Newball, Reasby, and Langworth, ibid.
[5] Grid ref. is to Wainfleet All Saints.

Wynthorp'	Winthorpe	TF/560659	5.	12.	5
Freskenay	Friskney	TF/461554	9.	8.	2
Skeggenesse	Skegness	TF/559639	3.	8.	5
Candelesby &	Candlesby and	TF/456673	3.	6.	9¾
Guneby	Gunby	TF/468668			
Dryby	Driby	TF/390745	1.	7.	4
Northolm'	Northolme	TF/499593	3.	8.	11½
Soterby	Sutterby	TF/385724		12.	6
Skendelby	Skendleby	TF/433698	3.	19.	2½
Ingoldmels	Ingoldmells	TF/560689	10.	8.	6
Burgh'	Burgh le Marsh	TF/501651	7.	7.	8½
Orreby	Orby	TF/490673	3.	0.	0
Magna Steping'	Great Steeping	TF/435640	4.	16.	10
Dalby	Dalby	TF/409701	2.	7.	3¼
Drexthorp'	Dexthorpe	TF/406716			
Scremby	Scremby	TF/443676	2.	10.	2¾
Frisby	Firsby	TF/455626	2.	15.	4
Forthington'	Fordington	TF/419716		15.	4¼
Braytoft'	Bratoft	TF/474650	3.	1.	8
Irreby	Irby in the Marsh	TF/468637	1.	12.	5¾
Partenay	Partney	TF/411683	2.	17.	0
Askeby	Ashby by Partney	TF/428668	2.	6.	8
Welton'	Welton le Marsh	TF/470688	2.	17.	6
			98.	14.	6¾

Wap. Geyrtre [GARTREE WAPENTAKE]

Baumburgh'	Baumber	TF/222745	6.	15.	6
Horsington'	Horsington	TF/192687	3.	13.	11¼
Beltesford	Belchford	TF/294754	3.	0.	0
Bokenhale	Bucknall	TF/169688	3.	7.	6
Randeby	Ranby	TF/227791	2.	16.	8
Wyspington'	Wispington	TF/205717	1.	18.	8
Aysterby	Asterby	TF/264796	3.	0.	0
Golkesby	Goulceby	TF/254795			
Wadingworth'	Waddingworth	TF/185713	2.	15.	0
Edelington'	Edlington	TF/234714	6.	13.	4
Burrete	Burreth	TF/152697	1.	3.	0
Stikkeswold	Stixwould	TF/177659	2.	6.	2¾
Langeton'	Langton	TF/237690	2.	0.	10
Donyngton'	Donington on Bain	TF/236830	2.	12.	10
Tumby	Tumby	TF/238598	2.	16.	4¼
Tateressale	Tattershall	TF/212575	3.	17.	4
Conyngesby	Coningsby	TF/223580	7.	19.	8
Strutton'	Great Sturton	TF/214766	2.	0.	0
Mynting' &	Minting and	TF/187735	4.	14.	8
Gauteby	Gautby	TF/174724			
Kirkeby	Kirkby on Bain	TF/242625	2.	0.	10¾
Wylkesby	Wilkeby	TF/283634	1.	1.	1
Thornton'	Thornton	TF/243678	2.	10.	0
Thimelby	Thimbleby	TF/241700	3.	6.	1½
Stainton'	Market Stainton	TF/228799	1.	13.	8
Calkewell	Cawkwell	TF/282800	1.	2.	3½
Scaneldsby	Scamblesby	TF/276785	2.	9.	0¼
Hemmyngby	Hemingby	TF/237744	3.	16.	8
Staynygote	Stenigot	TF/252809	1.	3.	0
Dalderby	Dalderby	TF/249661	1.	10.	10¾

Scrivelby	Scrivelsby	TF/265657	3.	15.	4
Roughton' &	Roughton and	TF/241647	1.	6.	3
Marton'	Martin	TF/239669			
			89.	6.	9

Wap. Louthesk' [LOUTHESK WAPENTAKE]

Salfletby	Saltfleetby[1]	TF/456904	7.	6.	6
Alvyngham	Alvingham	TF/368913	2.	14.	4
Cokerington'	Cockerington[2]	TF/383887	6.	3.	0
Somercotes	Somercotes[3]	TF/422958	8.	9.	3
Northriston'	North Reston	TF/383837	1.	5.	0
Welton'	Welton le Wold	TF/273873	2.	5.	6
Germethorp'	Grainthorpe	TF/388966	5.	7.	9
Luda	Louth	TF/327873	15.	3.	1¾
Halington'	Hallington	TF/304855	3.	1.	11
Whitkale	Withcall	TF/283841	2.	14.	9
Skiddebrok'	Skidbrooke	TF/439932	12.	15.	10
Tathewell'	Tathwell	TF/320829	4.	18.	6
Kelsterne &	Kelstern and	TF/252899	2.	10.	2
Cailesthorp'	Calcethorpe	TF/248885			
Elkyngton'	Elkington[4]	TF/294883	2.	12.	6
Yerdeburgh'	Yarburgh	TF/351931	3.	0.	0½
Grimoldby &	Grimoldby and	TF/392880	2.	15.	4
Steueton'	Stewton	TF/362872			
Manneby	Manby	TF/399867	3.	9.	6
Parva Carleton'	Little Carlton	TF/403854	1.	3.	0
Brakenbergh'	Brackenborough	TF/330906	1.	5.	8
Kedington'	Keddington	TF/345886		15.	2
Rokelound	Ruckland	TF/334781		18.	0
Est Wykham &	East Wykeham and	TF/228884	1.	15.	0
West Wyk'	West Wyckham	TF/213888			
Moketon'	Muckton	TF/375814		5.	0
Conyngesholm'	Conisholme	TF/403955	2.	0.	8½
Hagham	Haugham	TF/335814	1.	11.	4
Malteby &	Maltby and	TF/312842	1.	15.	1
Raytheby	Raithby	TF/311847			
Gayton' &	Gayton le Wold and	TF/236860		15.	0
Grimelthorp'	Grimblethorpe	TF/237865			
Farford	Farforth	TF/319785	1.	0.	6
Maydenwell'	Maidenwell	TF/322794	1.	7.	2
Burwell'[5]	Burwell	TF/356797	1.	1.	10
Carleton' Magna &	Great Carlton and	TF/408856	3.	13.	4
Castelcarleton'	Castle Carlton	TF/398837			
			105.	19.	9¾

Wap. Calsewath' [CALCEWATH WAPENTAKE]

| Sutton | Sutton le Marsh | TF/522808 | 6. | 3. | 10 |
| Mumby | Mumby | TF/515744 | 8. | 14. | 3 |

[1] Grid ref. is to Saltfleetby All Saints.   [2] Grid ref. is to South Cockerington.
[3] Grid ref. is to North Somercotes.   [4] Grid ref. is to South Elkington.
[5] In a fifteenth-century book of fifteenths and tenths (E 164/7, fol. xxxv), Authorp (TF/401808) is included with Burwell and the tax quota is the same.

Old name	Modern name	Grid ref.	£	s.	d.
Thedelthorp'	Theddlethorpe[1]	TF/464882	10.	0.	10
Malberthorp'	Mablethorpe	TF/498846	6.	14.	5¾
Alforth' c.m[2]	Alford [with members]	TF/455761	3.	17.	8
Billesby c.m[3]	Bilsby [with members]	TF/467767	3.	8.	2
Strubby & Wodethorp'	Strubby and Woodthorpe	TF/453825 TF/437804	3.	8.	2
Hotoft	Huttoft	TF/512764	6.	0.	0
Slotheby	Sloothby	TF/495707	6.	0.	8
Anderby	Anderby	TF/523754	5.	6.	8
Ulseby	Ulceby	TF/422726	1.	13.	10
Claxeby	Claxby	TF/453714	2.	3.	7
Foulesthorp' & Trussethorp'	Thorpe and Trusthorpe	TF/498820 TF/514836	2.	12.	4
Swaby	Swaby	TF/387771	2.	3.	0
Calseby	Calceby	TF/387756	1.	4.	9
Malteby	Maltby le Marsh	TF/462814	3.	8.	0
Cumberworth'	Cumberworth	TF/506737	2.	3.	1
Riggesby & Aleby	Rigsby and Ailby	TF/431754 TF/438770	1.	14.	8
Farlestorp'	Farlesthorpe	TF/476740	1.	16.	10
Saleby & Thorestorp'	Saleby and Thoresthorpe	TF/457784 TF/460776	3.	7.	2
Hagh'	Haugh	TF/415759		17.	7¼
Lekeburn'	Legbourne	TF/368844	2.	2.	4
Markeby c.m	Markby [with members]	TF/487788	2.	13.	0
Wilughby & Bronthorp'	Willoughby and Bonthorpe	TF/473719 TF/483728	5.	2.	6
Hoggesthorp'	Hogsthorpe	TF/535722	6.	13.	4
Beseby	Beesby	TF/464802	3.	2.	3
Wythern & Stayn	Withern and Stain	TF/432822 TF/468847	5.	0.	0
Gayton'	Gayton le Marsh	TF/425842	3.	0.	2
Thoresby	South Thoresby	TF/401771	1.	16.	7¾
Clathorp'	Claythorpe	TF/413792	1.	5.	6
Totil & Ryston'	Totill and South Reston	TF/418814 TF/404832	1.	11.	8
Ellowe & Aby	Belleau and Aby	TF/401786 TF/411785	1.	18.	0
			117.	4.	11¾

Lib. Hornecastr' [LIBERTY OF HORNCASTLE]

Old name	Modern name	Grid ref.	£	s.	d.
Marum	Mareham on the Hill	TF/287678	5.	8.	9
Maring'	Mareham le Fen	TF/278613	4.	16.	0
Holtham	Haltham	TF/246635	3.	17.	11¼
Woddenderby	Wood Enderby	TF/273642	2.	3.	11¼
Moreby	Moorby	TF/292641	2.	7.	8
Askeby	West Ashby	TF/266725	3.	3.	0
Tynton' Superior	High Toynton	TF/283698	2.	5.	10
Tynton' Inferior	Low Toynton	TF/275705	2.	2.	10¾
Hornecastre	Horncastle	TF/258695	7.	17.	4
			34.	3.	4¼

[1] Grid ref. is to Theddlethorpe All Saints.
[2] Members of Alford in 1316 included Well, Tothby, and Mawthorpe (*F.A.* iii. 178).
[3] Members of Bilsby in 1316 included Thurlby and Asserby, ibid.

Soka de Bolingbrok' [SOKE OF BOLINGBROKE]

Bolingbrok'	Old Bolingbroke	TF/349652	1.	4.	0
Cybesay	Sibsey	TF/354507	8.	10.	10
Halton'	Halton Holegate	TF/418651	4.	12.	11
Tointon'	Toynton[1]	TF/394636	3.	7.	4
Westkele	West Keal	TF/367637	2.	17.	8
Estkele	East Keal	TF/383639	2.	3.	4
Raytheby	Raithby	TF/373671	1.	5.	10
Stikesford	Stickford	TF/352601	3.	15.	9
Stykenay	Stickney	TF/343571	5.	3.	2
Lusteby	Lusby	TF/340679	1.	6.	0
Spillesby	Spilsby	TF/400661	2.	10.	8
Hundelby	Hundleby	TF/388665		18.	0
Parva Steping'	Little Steeping	TF/433636	2.	15.	11¼
Minyggesby	Miningsby	TF/322642	1.	15.	1
Enderby Malbys	Mavis Enderby	TF/363666	1.	9.	0
Hareby	Hareby	TF/338656		13.	0
Thorp'	Thorpe St. Peter	TF/485607	5.	0.	4
Kirkeby	East Kirkby	TF/333630	3.	4.	1
			52.	12.	11¼

Wap. Hille [HILL WAPENTAKE]

Tetesford	Tetford	TF/334747	3.	0.	6
Foletby	Fulletby	TF/298734	2.	1.	8
Harington' &	Harrington and	TF/367718	1.	15.	4¾
Aswardby	Aswardby	TF/376703			
Ormesby	South Ormsby	TF/369752	3.	10.	3¾
Ketelesby	Ketsby	TF/370768		19.	0
Hagworthingham	Hagworthingham	TF/344693	2.	17.	7½
Wynceby	Winceby	TF/320684		15.	7¼
Bagenderby	Bag Enderby	TF/349721	1.	10.	2
Sauchethorp'	Sausthorpe	TF/382691	1.	9.	8
Claxeby	Claxby Pluckacre	TF/306651		11.	0
Gretham	Greetham	TF/308708		14.	0
Screyfeld	Scrafield	TF/304688		11.	6¾
Hameringham	Hameringham	TF/309672	1.	9.	0
Askeby	Ashby Puerorum	TF/328714	1.	15.	4
Stanesby &	Stainsby and	TF/337715			
Parva Gretham	Little Greetham	TF/308708			
Brinkil	Brinkhill	TF/373736	1.	13.	8
Walmesgare	Walmsgate	TF/362775		14.	0
Salmanby	Salmonby	TF/325735		15.	1
Langeton'	Langton	TF/389704	2.	12.	7½
Oxecombe	Oxcombe	TF/312771	1.	3.	10
Someresby	Somersby	TF/343726	1.	12.	0
Wolrikby	Worlaby	TF/340768	1.	11.	4
			33.	3.	4½

Civitas Lincoln'	Lincoln	SK/977717	100.	0.	0 [T]
Grimesby [B]	Grimsby	TA/272093	9.	14.	5½ [T]
Kirketon' [A.D]	Kirton in Lindsey	SK/934985	7.	17.	7¼ [T]
Misen [A.D][2]	Misson [in Notts.]	SK/691949	2.	8.	9 [T]

[1] Grid ref. is to Toynton All Saints.
[2] The rest of Misson was taxed at a fifteenth in Nottinghamshire, p. 229.

Magna Coringham [A.D][1]	Corringham	SK/872915	1.	12.	10	[T]
Parva Coringham [A.D]	Little Corringham	SK/685903	2.	6.	1	[T]
Aseby [A.D]	Aisby	SK/872929	1.	12.	4	[T]
Pillam [A.D] &	Pilham and	SK/862938	1.	19.	0	[T]
Gilleby [A.D]	Gilby	SK/863933				
Bliton' [A.D][1]	Blyton	SK/853948	1.	16.	6	[T]
Hepham [A.D][1]	Heapham	SK/878885	2.	3.	2¼	[T]
Springthorp' [A.D]	Springthorpe	SK/876898	3.	6.	8	[T]
Warton' [A.D]	Wharton	SK/843935	1.	12.	6	[T]
Northorp' [A.D][1]	Northorpe	SK/895972	1.	5.	3¼	[T]
Stokheth [A.D]	East Stockwith	SK/787945	4.	2.	9¾	[T]
Walcreth' [A.D] &	Walkerith and	SK/788931				
Morton' [A.D]	Morton	SK/810915				
Somerby [A.D]	Somerby	SK/846897	1.	13.	8	[T]
Hibaldstowe [A.D][2]	Hibaldstow	SE/977026	2.	5.	11	[T]
Snyterby [A.D][3]	Snitterby	SK/985948	2.	10.	6	[T]
Atherby [A.D.]	Atterby	SK/982930	1.	11.	7½	[T]
Saxby [A.D]	Saxby	TF/005862	1.	10.	0	[T]
Grehingham [A.D][1]	Grayingham	SK/935962	2.	13.	8½	[T]
Herpeswell' [A.D][3]	Harpswell	SK/936900	4.	1.	3¾	[T]
Helmeswell' [A.D][3]	Hemswell	SK/931909	4.	1.	4	[T]
Glenteworth' [A.D][3]	Glentworth	SK/945882	4.	10.	1½	[T]
Scumthorp' [A.D]	Scunthorpe	SE/897115	1.	9.	10	[T]
Wynterton' [A.D][2]	Winterton	SE/928185	1.	18.	3	[T]
Frothingham [A.D]	Frodingham	SE/891109	1.	11.	0	[T]
Burton [A.D][2]	Burton upon Stather	SE/870179		9.	0	[T]
Brunby [A.D]	Brumby	SE/892096	2.	11.	2	[T]
Askeby [A.D]	Ashby	SE/898086	2.	12.	4	[T]
Boringham [A.D][2]	Burringham	SE/835094	2.	6.	2	[T]
Yatelthorp' [A.D]	Yaddlethorpe	SE/887070		6.	0	[T]
Botenesford [A.D][2]	Bottesford	SE/899070		4.	0	[T]
Stainton' [A.D]	Stainton	SE/988963		9.	6¼	[T]
Wadingham [A.D][2]	Waddingham	SE/983962				
Reddeburn' [A.D][2]	Redbourne	SK/973999	2.	0.	0	[T]
Castre [A.D]	Caistor	TA/117013	3.	18.	2	[T]
Southkelsey [A.D][4]	South Kelsey	TF/042982	5.	7.	2¼	[T]
Northkelsey [A.D][5]	North Kelsey	TA/044015	4.	12.	6½	[T]
Cadenay [A.D] &	Cadney and	TA/017033	5.	12.	10	[T]
Housom [A.D][5]	Howsham	TA/045043				
Gresseby [A.D][5]	Grasby	TA/087049	1.	11.	1	[T]
Houton' in Mora [A.D][4]	Holton le Moor	TF/082978	1.	3.	2	[T]
			204.	18.	5¼	[T]

LINDSEY TOTAL: £1,528. 18. 11¼[6]

LINCOLNSHIRE TOTAL: £3,152. 8. 1

---

[1] See also Corringham wapentake.   [2] See also Manley wapentake.
[3] See also Aslacoe wapentake.   [4] See also Walshcroft wapentake.
[5] See also Yarborough wapentake.
[6] As on 1334 Account, E 179/135/20. The figures for the Lindsey wapentakes add up to £1,528. 18. 11½ which is the total given on E 179/135/24.

LONDON

DOCUMENTS

As no Particulars of the 1334 lay subsidy survive for the city, amounts for the individual wards have been taken from a fifteenth-century book of fifteenths and tenths, E 164/7, fol. xxviii (see Editorial Notes, p. xxxiii, note).

TAXERS

John de Stonore, William de Shareshull, and William de Cossale (later, William de Trussel and Thomas de Blaston, *C.P.R., 1334–1338*, 128–9)

TAX YIELD

The city granted 1,100 marks (£733. 6. 8) for the fifteenth (E 359/8 mm. 4–5)

Representing movable wealth of £11,000. 0. 0

NOTES

London had won the privilege of being taxed at the lower rate of the fifteenth from Edward III in 1327. By fining for 1,100 marks there is little doubt that the city escaped lightly in the 1334 lay subsidy, and although Edward may subsequently have regretted his generosity (see letter quoted in Curtis (1918), 36–7) he could not afford to alienate a community from which the Crown regularly borrowed money. Even so, the fine of 1,100 marks was over three times that of Bristol, probably the most prosperous of the provincial towns. The population of London at this time is a matter of speculation; most estimates are between 30,000 and 40,000 (Gwyn A. Williams, *Medieval London*, 1963, Appendix A). The size of the tax quota relative to those of other towns suggests that London's pre-eminence, so evident in the thirteenth century, certainly had not waned by 1334, and may even have been greater.

The London roll for 1332 (E 179/144/4) survives and its transcription and a discussion of the distribution of wealth within the city were the subjects of a valuable paper by Margaret Curtis in 1918. Her map of the figures for the wards shows that the wealth of the city was concentrated in the south, both in the mercantile wards along the river and in the shop-keeping area of the south-west.

REFERENCES

J. C. L. Stahlschmidt, 'The London lay subsidy, 1411–12', *Archaeological Jnl.* 4 (1887), 56–82.

Margaret Curtis, 'The London lay subsidy of 1332', in G. Unwin, ed., *Finance and Trade under Edward III*, 1918, 35–60.

E. Ekwall, *Two Early London Subsidy Rolls*, Lund, 1951.

[WARDS]

Turris	Tower	45.	10.	0
Byllyngesgate	Billingsgate	31.	10.	0
Pontis	Bridge	49.	10.	0
Douegate	Dowgate	34.	10.	0
Walbrok	Walbrook	39.	0.	0
Candelwykstrete	Candlewick Street	16.	0.	0
Langborne	Langbourn	20.	10.	0
Lymestrete	Lime Street	2.	0.	0
Aldegate	Aldgate	5.	0.	0
Portesogene	Portsoken	9.	0.	0
Byschopesgate	Bishopsgate	21.	10.	0
Cornhull'	Cornhill	16.	0.	0
Bradestrete	Broad Street	25.	0.	0
Vynetria	Vintry	35.	10.	0
Quenhith'	Queenhithe	20.	0.	0
Castri Baynard	Castle Baynard	12.	0.	0
Chepe	Cheap	72.	0.	0
Cordewanerstrete	Cordwainer Street	72.	0.	0
Bredestrete	Bread Street	36.	10.	0
Farndon Infra	Farringdon Within	53.	6.	8
Farndon Extra	Farringdon Without	34.	10.	0
Aldrychegate	Aldersgate	7.	0.	0
Crepulgate Infra	Cripplegate Within	39.	10.	0
Crepulgate Extra	Cripplegate Without	10.	0.	0
Bassyngschawe	Bassishaw	7.	0.	0
Colmanstrete	Coleman Street	19.	0.	0
		£733.	6.	8[1]

[1] As on 1334 Enrolled Account, E 359/8, mm. 4–5.

MIDDLESEX

DOCUMENTS

8 Edward III: Account   E 179/141/6
8 Edward III: Particulars   E 179/141/4*
10 Edward III: Particulars E 179/141/7

TAXERS

The abbot of Westminster and Thomas de Stowe

TAX YIELD

15th   £348. 10.   1¼
10th   £ 2.   3.   11
       ───────────────
       £350. 14.   0¼

Representing assessed movable wealth of

£5,249. 10.   8¾

NOTES

An unusual feature of the 1334 roll for Middlesex is the inclusion of the names of the sub-taxers in each township.

There were no taxation boroughs in 1334, nor had there been at any time in the early fourteenth century. The ancient demesne of Kempton was the only place taxed at a tenth.

The outline of the county in 1334 was much the same as that of the mid-nineteenth century before several parishes were detached to form part of the administrative county of London.

Hd. Spelethorne [SPELTHORNE HUNDRED]

Estbedefont'	East Bedfont	TQ/085736	2.	16.	4¾
Feltham	Feltham	TQ/107732	4.	4.	1¾
Kenytone [A.D]	Kempton	TQ/117695	2.	3.	11 [T]
Stanewell' &	Stanwell and	TQ/057742	8.	16.	3½
Westbedefont	West Bedfont	TQ/068739			
Hamptone	Hampton	TQ/141695	3.	18.	8¼
Sonebury	Sunbury	TQ/107685	1.	8.	3¼
Cherdygton'	Charlton	TQ/083688	2.	1.	3
Lalham	Laleham	TQ/051689	6.	3.	3¾
Echelesford	Ashford	TQ/072714			
Stanes &	Staines and	TQ/034715	8.	6.	7¼
Yeueneye	Yeoveney	TQ/026736			
Lytlinton'	Littleton	TQ/071686	2.	17.	3
Tedynton'	Teddington	TQ/165713	1.	17.	5½
Uphaghford	Upper Halliford	TQ/092683	1.	0.	2¼

Netherhageford	Lower Halliford	TQ/086668	1.	2.	1¼
Shipertone	Shepperton	TQ/078666	3.	14.	11
Haneworth'	Hanworth	TQ/112719	2.	1.	2
			52.	12.	0

Hd. Elethorne [ELTHORNE HUNDRED]

Colham	Colham Green	TQ/071818	18.	13.	1
Couele	Cowley	TQ/054825			
Woxebrugg'	Uxbridge	TQ/055841			
Peche	Cowley Peachey	TQ/055814			
Herefeld	Harefield	TQ/053896	6.	8.	9¼
Magna Greneford	Greenford	TQ/141824	1.	2.	8¼
Russlepe	Ruislip	TQ/101871	12.	6.	0
Northalle	Northolt	TQ/132840	7.	7.	4
Ikenham	Ickenham	TQ/079862			
Parva Greneford	Perivale	TQ/171829			
Southall'	Southall	TQ/132804	11.	9.	11
Hese &	Hayes and	TQ/097811			
Crannford	Cranford	TQ/102769			
Draytone	West Drayton	TQ/061795	3.	9.	4
Harmondesworth'	Harmondsworth	TQ/057778	6.	1.	4
Braynford	Brentford	TQ/173781	2.	9.	8¾
Hanewell'	Hanwell	TQ/156802			
Hardygton'	Harlington	TQ/102782	4.	1.	5½
			73.	9.	7¾

Hd. Oselueston' [OSSULSTONE HUNDRED]

Hakeneye	Hackney	TQ/350845	13.	18.	8½
Folham	Fulham	TQ/243759	11.	7.	5
Westsmethfeld	Smithfield	TQ/315816	18.	9.	0¼
Schordich'	Shoreditch	TQ/333823			
Stoke Newenton'	Stoke Newington	TQ/336864			
Isyldene &	Islington and	TQ/313849			
Finesbury	Finsbury	TQ/325825			
Padynton'	Paddington	TQ/260820	3.	16.	10
Lylleston'	Lisson	TQ/270820			
Tybourn' &	St. Marylebone[1] and	TQ/284821			
Westebourne	Westbourne	TQ/251811			
Knyghttbrugg' &	Knightsbridge and	TQ/280797	3.	15.	0¾
Eye	Ebury	TQ/285784			
Chelchurch'	Chelsea	TQ/272783	1	15	4¾
Wyllesdon'	Willesden	TQ/227846	8	6	8¾
Kensynton'	Kensington	TQ/256797	7.	11.	2½
Chesewyk'	Chiswick	TQ/205785	3.	5.	2½
Suttone	Sutton	TQ/200777			
Finchesle	Finchley	TQ/269905	8.	14.	4
Barnet &	Friern Barnet and	TQ/272929			
Haregey	Hornsey[2]	TQ/307893			
Kenysshetoun	Kentish Town	TQ/292853	4.	17.	2½
Yellyngg'	Ealing	TQ/179808	7.	12.	11

[1] *E.P.N.S., XVIII, Middlesex* (1942), 137. *Marybourne* is a fifteenth-century name: the place was originally *Tybourn* after the river of that name.

[2] Ibid. 121: the modern Harringay is a revival of the early name for Hornsey.

			£	s	d
Actone	Acton	TQ/200802	4.	9.	7
Westm' cum parochiis	Westminster with	TQ/301796	10.	13.	7½
Beate Marie atte Strande	St. Mary in the Strand	TQ/308809			
Martini' in Campis	St. Martin in the Fields	TQ/301805			
Clem' Dacorum	St. Clement Danes	TQ/309811			
Brambeleye &	Bromley and	TQ/375825	5.	7.	3½
Estsmethfeld	East Smithfield	TQ/339805			
Stebbenhuth'	Stepney	TQ/355814	19.	5.	11
Stratford	Bow	TQ/370830			
Soka Sancti Egidii	St. Giles	TQ/301812	5.	17.	0¾
Pourtepol &	Gray's Inn and	TQ/309819			
Blemond'	Bloomsbury	TQ/299822			
Hampstede	Hampstead	TQ/262856	3.	9.	1
			142.	12.	7¼

Hd. Iselworth' [ISLEWORTH HUNDRED]

			£	s	d
Iselworth'	Isleworth	TQ/162758	4.	3.	0½
Hestone	Heston	TQ/131774	5.	0.	1
Twekenham	Twickenham	TQ/161733	4.	1.	0½
			13.	4.	2

Hd. Gore [GORE HUNDRED]

			£	s	d
Hendone	Hendon	TQ/228895	7.	14.	2
Harwe	Harrow	TQ/148871	17.	2.	10½
Eggeswere	Edgware	TQ/204921	9.	0.	1
Magna Stanmer'	Stanmore	TQ/167922			
Parva Stanmer' &	Little Stanmore and	TQ/185913			
Kyngesbury	Kingsbury	TQ/198887			
			33.	17.	1½

Hd. Edelmetone [EDMONTON HUNDRED]

			£	s	d
Edelmetone	Edmonton	TQ/343934	10.	17.	2
Totenham	Tottenham	TQ/333908	7.	3.	11
Enefeld	Enfield	TQ/328967	12.	6.	8¾
Mymmes	South Mimms	TL/222012	4.	10.	8
			34.	18.	5¾

TOTAL: £350. 14. 0¼[1]

---

[1] As on 1334 Account, E 179/141/6.

NORFOLK

DOCUMENTS

8 Edward III: Account   E 179/149/12
8 Edward III: Particulars   E 179/149/11 (incomplete)
10 Edward III: Particulars   E 179/149/13*
11 Edward III: Particulars   E 179/149/15

TAXERS

The prior of Norwich and Thomas de Blaston

TAX YIELD

15th   £3,191.   0.   7
10th   £ 296.   4.   0

    £3,487.   4.   7

Representing assessed movable wealth of

    £50,827.   8.   9

NOTES

The townships are listed under the headings of thirty-two hundreds with additional entries for Norwich and Great Yarmouth. Almost every Norfolk entry refers to a single place-name; only twenty-four out of the 658 refer to more than one.

Most of the tax at a tenth was on the city of Norwich (£94) and the three taxation boroughs of Great Yarmouth (£100), Lynn (£50), and Thetford (£16). The Yarmouth and Lynn figures have the look of conventional payments, whereas that for Norwich is perhaps the result of a more real assessment of movable wealth. It is surprising that the quota for Yarmouth exceeded that of Norwich but it was obviously then very prosperous as a centre of the North Sea herring fisheries and as an outport for Norwich, as Boston was for Lincoln.

As a result of Hudson's early published version of the fifteenths and tenths the 1334 figures have already been used in studies of various aspects of the history of the county.

REFERENCES

W. Hudson, 'The assessment of the townships of the county of Norfolk for the King's Tenths and Fifteenths, as settled in 1334', *Norfolk Archaeology*, 12 (1895), 243–97.
W. E. Lunt, *The Valuation of Norwich*, 1926.
H. C. Darby, *The Medieval Fenland*, 1940.
J. B. Mitchell, *Historical Geography*, 1954, especially 192 and 244–5.
K. J. Allison, 'The lost villages of Norfolk', *Norfolk Archaeology*, 31 (1955), 116–62.
R. E. Glasscock, 'The distribution of wealth in East Anglia in the early fourteenth century', *Trans. Institute British Geographers*, 32 (1963), 113–23.

Hd. Estfleg' [EAST FLEGG HUNDRED]

Harringby	Herringby	TG/446103	2.	0.	0
Thirkeby	Thrigby	TG/461123	2.	10.	0
Skrouteby	Scratby	TG/506154	5.	0.	0
Mauteby	Mautby	TG/481124	6.	13.	4
Stokesby	Stokesby	TG/436106	5.	10.	0
Filby	Filby	TG/469133	9.	0.	0
Ormesby	Ormesby[1]	TG/499146	10.	10.	0
Castre	Caistor on Sea	TG/520123	8.	0.	0
Runham	Runham	TG/460108	4.	4.	0
			53.	7.	4

Hd. Westfleg' [WEST FLEGG HUNDRED]

Hemesby	Hemsby	TG/495174	9.	0.	0
Estsomertone	East Somerton	TG/475196	5.	4.	0
Clepisby	Clippesby	TG/428146	5.	0.	0
Ouby	Oby	TG/415144	1.	10.	0
Bastwik	Bastwick	TG/423177	1.	14.	0
Billokby	Billockby	TG/430135	2.	4.	0
Martham	Martham	TG/455185	9.	14.	0
Burgh'	Burgh St. Margaret	TG/445140	5.	6.	8
Westsomerton'	West Somerton	TG/469199	8.	0.	8
Rollesby	Rollesby	TG/446158	7.	9.	0
Reppes	Repps	TG/422169	4.	5.	0
Askeby	Ashby	TG/419158	1.	10.	0
Thirne	Thurne	TG/405156	1.	8.	0
Wyntertone	Winterton on Sea	TG/492195	6.	15.	0
			69.	0.	4

Hd. Happing' [HAPPING HUNDRED]

Suttone	Sutton	TG/388240	3.	8.	0
Lessingham	Lessingham	TG/392285	2.	8.	0
Ristone	East Ruston	TG/344277	12.	6.	0
Wastenesham	Waxham	TG/441263	4.	12.	0
Pallingg'	Sea Palling	TG/430269	2.	4.	0
Eccles	Eccles	TG/415288	3.	12.	0
Hempstede	Hempstead	TG/403284	4.	3.	0
Brunstede	Brumstead	TG/370268	3.	9.	0
Hekelyngge	Hickling	TG/415243	8.	18.	0
Walcote	Walcott	TG/361318	6.	0.	0
Ingham	Ingham	TG/391260	3.	14.	0
Stalham	Stalham	TG/373263	9.	0.	0
Catefeld	Catfield	TG/382213	6.	14.	0
Happisburgh'	Happisburgh	TG/380312	9.	10.	0
Horseye	Horsey	TG/458231	2.	8.	4
Ludham	Ludham	TG/388183	7.	15.	0
Potterehegham	Potter Heigham	TG/420199	5.	5.	0
			95.	6.	4

[1] Grid ref. is to Ormesby St. Margaret.

Hd. Taverham [TAVERHAM HUNDRED]

Taverham	Taverham	TG/161139	1.	13.	4
Heymforde	Hainford	TG/229196	4.	0.	0
Wroxham	Wroxham	TG/296175	4.	0.	6
Draytone	Drayton	TG/181138	2.	0.	0
Crosthewyt	Crostwick	TG/258158	1.	4.	0
Rakheyth	Rackheath	TG/270150	2.	6.	8
Bestone	Beeston St. Andrew	TG/258139	2.	4.	6
Felthorp'	Felthorpe	TG/170173	1.	0.	0
Neutone iuxta Horsham	Newton St. Faith	TG/218168	1.	18.	0
Horsham Sancte Fid'	Horsham St. Faith	TG/216151	2.	5.	0
Horsforde	Horsford	TG/196154	2.	5.	0
Spikeswrth'	Spixworth	TG/240158	1.	13.	2
Heylesdone	Hellesdon	TG/200106	1.	10.	0
Attlebrigg'	Attlebridge	TG/129169	1.	7.	0
Fretenham	Frettenham	TG/245185	3.	10.	0
Horstede	Horstead	TG/263199	4.	18.	0
Sproustone	Sprowston	TG/249126	6.	0.	0
Cattone	Catton	TG/231123	2.	0.	0
			45.	15.	2

Hd. Blofeld [BLOFIELD HUNDRED]

Suthbirlingham	South Burlingham	TG/372083	4.	13.	4
Wyttone	Witton	TG/314096	1.	14.	0
Lympinhowe &	Limpenhoe and	TG/396040	3.	0.	0
Suthwod	Southwood	TG/392054			
Possewyk'	Postwick	TG/296078	3.	13.	4
Thorp &	Thorpe next Norwich	TG/261084	2.	7.	0
Pokethorp'	and Pockthorpe[1]	TG/239093			
Lyngwode	Lingwood	TG/361091	3.	3.	0
Northbirlingham	North Burlingham	TG/365101	3.	15.	0
Frethorp'	Freethorpe	TG/409055	3.	19.	0[2]
Bukenham Ferie cum	Buckenham with	TG/356058	3.	16.	0
Bassingham[3]	Hassingham	TG/369055			
Cantele	Cantley	TG/382042	6.	0.	0
Brundale	Brundall	TG/337087	2.	18.	0
Plumstede Parva	Little Plumstead	TG/314121	1.	2.	0
Plumstede Magna	Great Plumstead	TG/302100	2.	14.	0
Breidiston' &	Braydeston and	TG/341089	5.	2.	0
Strupshagh'	Strumpshaw	TG/349078			
Blofeld	Blofield	TG/335092	5.	3.	0
			52.	19.	8

Hd. Walsham [WALSHAM HUNDRED]

Hemlington'	Hemblington	TG/353116	2.	0.	0
Walsham	South Walsham	TG/366133	6.	10.	0
Wykhamton'	Wickhampton	TG/427055	3.	0.	0

---

[1] Grid ref. is to the site of Hassetts House, the manor house of Pockthorpe, near the Nelson Barracks in Norwich.

[2] Figure wrongly given as £3. 9. 0 in Hudson, op. cit. 268.

[3] *Bassingham* is a scribal error on E 179/149/13 (1336). Later rolls confirm it is *Hassingham*.

Moutone	Moulton St. Mary	TG/402067	3.	0.	0
Beghetone	Beighton	TG/386083	2.	14.	0
Tunstale	Tunstall	TG/417080	5.	0.	0
Fischele	Fishley	TG/398115	1.	8.	0
Halveryate	Halvergate	TG/418067	3.	6.	0
Randewrth'[1]	Ranworth	TG/356148	4.	5.	0
Ocle	Acle	TG/402103	7.	16.	0
Rudham	Reedham	TG/428025	4.	15.	0
Uptone	Upton	TG/393122	4.	13.	11
Wodebastwyk'	Woodbastwick	TG/332152	2.	4.	0
			50.	11.	11

Hd. Lodene [LODDON HUNDRED]

Loden'	Loddon	TM/363987	10.	9.	9
Hardele	Hardley	TG/386007	3.	0.	0
Langele	Langley	TG/355010	5.	10.	2
Mundham	Mundham	TM/325981	5.	10.	6
Hedenham	Hedenham	TM/312934	4.	0.	0
Thewyt	Thwaite	TM/333949	1.	10.	0
Helgheton'	Hellington	TG/314031	1.	6.	8
Ayscheby	Ashby St. Mary	TG/329022	1.	8.	0
Chategrave	Chedgrave	TM/362994	2.	0.	1
Sitthingg'	Seething	TM/319980	4.	13.	0
Carleton'	Carleton St. Peter	TG/339024	3.	7.	10
Brom'	Broome	TM/350916	2.	17.	0
Langhale	Langhale	TM/302968	3.	11.	0
Claxtone	Claxton	TG/328032	3.	10.	0
Thurtone	Thurton	TG/328007	2.	0.	0
Alpingtone	Alpington	TG/292012	1.	16.	0
Bedingham	Bedingham	TM/285934	3.	13.	2
Thopecroft	Topcroft	TM/266929	4.	12.	0
Dechingham	Ditchingham	TM/330922	4.	2.	0
Wodetone	Woodton	TM/286946	3.	16.	0
			72.	13.	2

Hd. Knaveringg' [CLAVERING HUNDRED]

Elingham	Ellingham	TM/367919	4.	14.	0
Brok'	Brooke	TM/294995	3.	17.	6
Hekyngham	Heckingham	TM/384989	2.	15.	0
Wynston'	Winston	TM/401930	1.	6.	0
Nortone	Norton Subcourse	TM/408988	4.	4.	4
Hales	Hales	TM/383962	2.	10.	0
Aldeby	Aldeby	TM/451934	7.	4.	0
Wyndele	Windle	TM/426936	1.	7.	4
Stoktone	Stockton	TM/388942	6.	5.	0
Gelingham	Gillingham	TM/412923	3.	0.	4
Thoft Monacorum	Toft Monks	TM/426953	5.	12.	0
Bergh' &	Bergh Apton and	TG/306010	5.	13.	4
Apeton'	Apton	TM/311999			
Haddisko	Haddiscoe and	TM/439969	3.	14.	0
Thorp'	Thorpe	TM/436981			
Kirkeby	Kirby Cane	TM/373942	5.	8.	0

[1] It seems certain that the quota for Ranworth included an amount for Panxworth, which is included in E 179/149/15 and by Hudson, op. cit. 268.

Thurton'	Thurlton	TM/417983	3.	11.	0
Ravenigham	Raveningham	TM/398964	5.	8.	11
Qwieteacre	Wheatacre	TM/461940	3.	10.	0
Geldistone	Geldeston	TM/394923	3.	10.	0
Howe	Howe	TG/275000	3.	2.	0
			76.	12.	9

Hd. Depwade [DEPWADE HUNDRED]

Bonewell	Bunwell	TM/125927	6.	0.	0
Multon'	Moulton St. Michael	TM/165908	5.	14.	0
Waketon'	Wacton	TM/179918	2.	6.	8
Aslactone	Aslacton	TM/156912	1.	16.	0
Strattone	Stratton[1]	TM/198923	6.	10.	0
Herdwyk'	Hardwick	TM/222901	1.	8.	0
Tasburgh'	Tasburgh	TM/201959	3.	5.	0
Fretone	Fritton	TM/227933	4.	0.	0
Sheltone	Shelton	TM/221911	3.	5.	0
Hemenhale	Hampnall	TM/241944	7.	2.	0
Fundenhale	Fundenhall	TM/153969	2.	6.	0
Rodekarleton'	Carleton Rode	TM/115925	6.	14.	0
Takeleston'	Tacolneston	TM/139956	3.	0.	0
Fornessete	Forncett	TM/165928	4.	10.	0
Mornigthorp'	Morning Thorpe	TM/218926	2.	13.	0
Eysthewell'	Ashwellthorpe	TM/147977	1.	14.	0
Therstone	Tharston	TM/190943	6.	2.	0
Habeton'	Hapton	TM/176967	2.	10.	0
Tybenham	Tibenham	TM/134899	5.	15.	11
			76.	11.	7

Hd. Hensted [HENSTEAD HUNDRED]

Neuton'[2]	Newton	TG/254078	2.	8.	0
Framlingham Picot	Framingham Pigot	TG/278036	2.	10.	0
Castre	Caistor St. Edmunds	TG/233034	2.	16.	0
Kirkeby Bidon'	Kirby Bedon	TG/278054	6.	13.	4
Rokelounde	Rockland St. Mary	TG/312040	5.	4.	0
Biskele	Bixley	TG/258050	1.	2.	2
Framlingham Comitis	Framingham Earl	TG/277028	1.	14.	0
Yelverton'	Yelverton	TG/292022	2.	0.	0
Wytlingham	Wytlingham	TG/275077	2.	16.	0
Surlingham	Surlingham	TG/306065	6.	4.	0
Ameringhale	Arminghall	TG/253043	1.	6.	8
Saxlingham	Saxlingham Nethergate	TM/232972	7.	6.	8
Holveston'	Holverston	TG/304031	1.	18.	0
Crouchestok'	Stoke Holy Cross	TG/235008	3.	13.	0
Shotisham	Shotesham	TM/246990	12.	0.	0
Poringlond	Poringland	TG/271017	3.	0.	0
Bramerton'	Bramerton	TG/296047	3.	8.	0
			65.	19.	10

---

[1] Grid ref. is to Long Stratton.

[2] Both E 179/149/13 and 149/15 have *Neuton* as a single entry, but E 164/7 f. 213 d and Hudson, op. cit. 271 have *Newton cum Trouse*. Trowse was probably taxed, but whether with Newton or with Brackendale in Humbleyard hundred (see note in Hudson, 275), is uncertain; it may have been partly taxed with both.

Hd. Frethebr' [FREEBRIDGE HUNDRED]

Hillington'	Hillington	TF/723252	7.	10.	o
Bauseye	Bawsey	TF/663207	1.	15.	o
Grimeston'	Grimston	TF/721219	10.	2.	o
Castelrising'	Castle Rising	TF/667248	6.	0.	o
Penteneye	Pentney	TF/721139	2.	8.	o
Tilneye	Tilney[1]	TF/568180	30.	0.	o
Anemere	Anmer	TF/738295	3.	5.	o
Suthwtton'	South Wootton	TF/641226	3.	13.	o
Walpul	Walpole[2]	TF/502175	35.	10.	o
Enemethe	Emneth	TF/489074	13.	0.	o
Congham	Congham	TF/713237	5.	3.	o
Lenne [B]	King's Lynn	TF/617198	50.	0.	o [T]
Wygenhale	Wiggenhall[3]	TF/597140	37.	0.	o
Westacre	West Acre	TF/781152	4.	7.	o
Harpele	Harpley	TF/788261	6.	6.	o
Massingham Parva	Little Massingham	TF/793242	4.	0.	o
Northrungetone	North Runcton	TF/646159	12.	0.	o
Westwalton'	West Walton	TF/472133	23.	0.	o
Bilneye	West Bilney	TF/716153	2.	13.	4
Walsokne	Walsoken	TF/476106	26.	8.	o
Geywode cum	Gaywood with	TF/636204	7.	0.	o
Muntele	Mintlyn	TF/652192			
Castelacre	Castle Acre	TF/816150	12.	0.	o
Geytone	Gayton	TF/731193	15.	0.	o
Massingham Magna	Great Massingham	TF/799230	12.	0.	o
Estwynch'	East Winch	TF/692163	4.	0.	o
Middiltone	Middleton	TF/662160	7.	0.	o
Tyringtone	Terrington[4]	TF/552204	40.	9.	o
Suth' Lenn'	South Lynn	TF/617183	18.	0.	o
Westneuton'	West Newton	TF/696276	2.	9.	o
Aylesthorp'	Gayton Thorpe	TF/745185	2.	6.	8
Flicham	Flitcham	TF/725266	13.	0.	o
Dersingham	Dersingham	TF/693303	7.	7.	o
Babbyngle	Babingley	TF/666261	14.	0.	o
Estwalton'	East Walton	TF/743162	8.	0.	o
			446.	12.	o

Hd. Smeth' [SMETHDEN HUNDRED]

Holm	Holme next the Sea	TF/708435	13.	10.	o
Thornham	Thornham	TF/734434	6.	14.	o
Sharneburne	Shernbourne	TF/713324	4.	10.	o
Branncestre	Brancaster	TF/773439	8.	4.	o
Thoftes	Bircham Tofts	TF/778325	4.	13.	o
Ringisted Parva	Little Ringstead	TF/688399	2.	3.	o
Stanhowe	Stanhoe	TF/802369	9.	10.	o
Suthmere	Summerfield	TF/750384	2.	16.	o
Chosle	Choseley	TF/755408	1.	16.	o
Snetisham	Snettisham	TF/691343	19.	0.	o
Ingaldisthorp'	Ingoldisthorpe	TF/691327	2.	16.	o
Dockynge	Docking	TF/765370	13.	0.	o
Brecham	Great Bircham	TF/770326	11.	10.	o

[1] Grid ref. is to Tilney All Saints. [2] Grid ref. is to Walpole St. Andrew.
[3] Grid ref. is to Wiggenhall St. Germans.
[4] Grid ref. is to Terrington St. Clement.

Hecham	Heacham	TF/681380	16.	10.	o
Hunstanston'	Hunstanton	TF/689420	8.	12.	o
Ringistede Magna	Ringstead	TF/705406	10.	o.	o
Neuton'	Bircham Newton	TF/769339	4.	8.	o
Frenge	Fring	TF/736239	7.	o.	o
Berwyk	Barwick	TF/805352	3.	10.	o
Secheforde	Sedgeford	TF/707365	15.	10.	o
Tichewelle	Titchwell	TF/762439	7.	o.	o
			172.	12.	o

Hd. Broth' [BROTHERCROSS HUNDRED]

Sidstern'	Syderstone	TF/833326	6.	13.	4
Shirforde	Shereford	TF/886296	3.	o.	o
Brunham Westgate	Burnham Westgate	TF/830421	12.	10.	o
Testerton'	Testerton	TF/939267	2.	4.	o
Thoftes	Toftrees	TF/898275	6.	o.	o
Bermere	Barmer	TF/809336	2.	13.	o
Brunham Norton'	Burnham Norton	TF/834428	8.	4.	o
Depedale	Burnham Deepdale	TF/804443	2.	5.	o
Pudingnorton'	Pudding Norton	TF/924277	1.	2.	o
Taterford	Tatterford	TF/865283	2.	2.	o
Estreinham	East Raynham	TF/879255	6.	o.	o
Houton'	Houghton	TF/794284	6.	o.	o
Hemtone	Hempton	TF/916292	2.	o.	o
Westrudham	West Rudham	TF/819276	7.	13.	4
Suthreinham	South Raynham	TF/882243	3.	5.	o
Riburgh' Magna	Great Ryburgh	TF/962273	5.	6.	o
Westreinham	West Raynham	TF/873253	5.	10.	o
Estrudham	East Rudham	TF/826283	6.	10.	o
Dunton' &	Dunton and	TF/879304	4.	2.	o
Doketon'	Doughton	TF/881293			
Bagethorp'	Bagthorpe	TF/796322	2.	2.	o
Helghetone	Helhoughton	TF/869265	3.	7.	8
Brunham Sancti	Burnham Overy	TF/843429	10.	o.	o
Clementis					
			108.	9.	4

Civitas Norwyci' [CITY OF NORWICH]

Leta de Wymer	Wimer's Great Ward	⎫				
Leta de Mancroft	Mancroft Great Ward	⎪	90.	12.	o	[T]
Leta ultra aquam	The Northern Ward	⎬				
Leta de Conesford	Conisford Great Ward	⎭				
Feodum Castr'	The Fee of the Castle		1.	13.	4	[T]
Spitellond	Spitalland		1.	o.	o	[T]
Holmstrete	Holmestrete		1.	6.	8	[T]
			94.	12.	o	[T]

[GREAT YARMOUTH] [B]

North Leta	North Leet	⎫				
Magna Jernem'	Great Yarmouth	⎪				
Northmiddilleta	North-middle leet	⎬	100.	o.	o	[T]
Suthleta	South leet	⎪				
Suthmiddileta	South-middle leet	⎭				

Hd. Galh' [GALLOW HUNDRED]

Suthkreik	South Creake	TF/855363	11.	12.	0
Brunham Sutton'	Burnham Sutton	TF/836417	4.	0.	0
Tatersete	Tattersett	TF/852292	6.	10.	0
Estbarsham	East Barsham	TF/916337	3.	2.	0
Riburgh' Parva	Little Ryburgh	TF/969278	2.	15.	0
Waterdene	Waterden	TF/885358	3.	4.	0
Pensthorp'	Pensthorpe	TF/948291	1.	10.	0
Northkreik'	North Creake	TF/854377	9.	10.	0
Althorp' [A.D]	Alethorpe	TF/950313	1.	0.	0 [T]
Fulmodiston' &	Fulmodestone and	TF/993300	4.	0.	0
Croxstone	Croxton	TF/984310			
Westbarsham	West Barsham	TF/905337	5.	14.	0
Snoring' Parva	Little Snoring	TF/953326	3.	12.	0
Brunham Thorp'	Burnham Thorpe	TF/852418	3.	10.	0
Northbarsham	North Barsham	TF/915350	5.	4.	0
Stiberde	Stibbard	TF/983284	2.	10.	0
Fakenham dam [A.D]	Fakenham	TF/919297	9.	2.	0 [T]
Kettlistone[1]	Kettlestone	TF/968317	3.	5.	0
Sculthorp'	Sculthorpe	TF/899319	4.	7.	0
			84.	7.	0

Hd. Holt [HOLT HUNDRED]

Waburn'	Weybourne	TG/112431	1.	12.	0
Egefeld	Edgefield	TG/093342	2.	0.	0
Gunthorp'	Gunthorpe	TG/012352	2.	12.	0
Brinigham	Briningham	TG/039344	3.	10.	0
Bodham	Bodham	TG/126390	2.	4.	0
Holt	Holt	TG/081388	5.	4.	0
Brintone	Brinton	TG/038357	1.	15.	0
Hemstede	Hempstead	TG/105371	3.	0.	0
Merston'	Morston	TG/008438	5.	4.	0
Thornegge	Thornage	TG/050463	2.	6.	0
Burgh'	Burgh	TG/043335	1.	13.	0
Saxlingham	Saxlingham	TG/026396	4.	0.	0
Stodeye cum	Stody with	TG/056350	4.	12.	0
Honewrth'	Hunworth	TG/064355			
Birstone	Briston	TG/062325	5.	13.	4
Swantone	Swanton Novers	TG/015323	1.	12.	0
Sharingtone	Sharrington	TG/031366	3.	15.	0
Bathele	Bale	TG/011366	2.	12.	0
Meltone	Melton Constable	TG/038319	2.	3.	0
Kellingg'	Kelling	TG/089418	2.	8.	0
Langham	Langham	TG/007412	3.	16.	0
Leringsete	Leatheringsett	TG/061389	3.	12.	0
Snyterle	Blakeney	TG/032436	12.	0.	0
Salthus	Salthouse	TG/076436	7.	0.	0
Glannforde	Glandford	TG/043415	2.	0.	0
Bayfeld	Bayfield	TG/052405	2.	0.	0
Cleye	Cley next the Sea	TG/046437	10.	0.	0
Wyvetone	Wiveton	TG/043428	13.	0.	0
			111.	3.	4

---

[1] According to Hudson, op. cit. 280, Clipstone (*Clifton*) in Fulmodeston is included in this entry.

Hd. Northgr' [NORTH GREENHOE HUNDRED]

Houtone	Houghton St. Giles	TF/923354	2.	6.	o
Bynham	Binham	TF/983396	4.	18.	o
Egemere cum Quarles	Egmere with Quarles	TF/897374 TF/884385	6.	13.	4
Wythtone	Wighton	TF/941400	9.	9.	4
Berneye	Barney	TF/994327	2.	4.	o
Warham	Warham[1]	TF/943416	8.	o.	o
Walsingham Magna	Great Walsingham	TF/938376	8.	o.	o
Thirforde	Thursford	TF/984338	2.	7.	4
Styuekeye	Stiffkey	TF/975430	8.	o.	o
Snoring' Magna	Great Snoring	TF/946345	5.	o.	o
Dallingg'	Field Dalling	TG/006390	6.	7.	o
Welles	Wells	TF/918432	8.	7.	o
Holcham	Holkham	TF/878436	9.	10.	o
Hindringham	Hindringham	TF/984364	7.	o.	o
Walsingham Parva	Little Walsingham	TF/934365	6.	14.	o
			94.	16.	o

Hd. Eynesford [EYNESFORD HUNDRED]

Foxle	Foxley	TG/039218	3.	15.	8
Thimelthorp'	Themelthorpe	TG/058241	1.	8.	2
Alderford	Alderford	TG/123188	1.	15.	8
Kerdistone	Kerdiston	TG/085243	7.	o.	o
Folsham	Foulsham	TG/033250	9.	2.	o
Quitewell	Whitwell	TG/100222	4.	10.	6
Baldiswelle	Bawdeswell	TG/047209	3.	16.	o
Elsingg'	Elsing	TG/052165	3.	19.	4
Ringlonde & Helmigham	Ringland and Helmingham[2]	TG/134141	3.	15.	8
Westone	Weston Longville	TG/113159	4.	14.	2
Brandeston'	Brandiston	TG/142214	3.	11.	o
Lyng	Lyng	TG/069178	3.	6.	o
Swenigton'	Swannington	TG/134193	4.	2.	2
Belaghe	Bylaugh	TG/036183	4.	4.	o
Thirnigg'	Thurning	TG/080295	5.	o.	o
Geysthewyt	Guestwick	TG/062271	4.	5.	o
Salle	Sall	TG/110249	7.	o.	o
Hakeforde	Hackford	TG/079221	2.	7.	3
Wodenortone	Wood Norton	TG/010278	2.	13.	10
Heveringlond	Haveringland	TG/152209	3.	19.	o
Dallingg'	Wood Dalling	TG/090269	8.	1.	2
Geyste	Guist	TG/001255	4.	5.	o
Byntre	Bintree	TG/018235	7.	14.	4
Billingford	Billingford	TG/013204	5.	2.	6
Wechingham	Great Witchingham	TG/103200	7.	16.	o
Sparham	Sparham	TG/072196	7.	5.	o
Hindolveston'	Hindolveston	TG/029291	1.	18.	4
Wechingham Sancte Fid'	Little Witchingham	TG/115202	2.	15.	10
			129.	3.	7

[1] Grid ref. is to Warham St. Mary.
[2] Allison, op. cit. 149, suggests site is c. TG/126157.

Hd. Northerpingham [NORTH ERPINGHAM HUNDRED]

Aylmerton'	Aylmerton	TG/182401	2.	13.	o
Gresham	Gresham	TG/168386	2.	o.	o
Thorp' Market	Thorpe Market	TG/241359	4.	o.	1
Mettone	Metton	TG/198373	1.	8.	o
Felbrigg'	Felbrigg	TG/198390	2.	o.	o
Northwodeberingham	North Barningham	TG/151372	2.	4.	o
Roughtone	Roughton	TG/220365	3.	6.	8
Plumstede	Plumstead	TG/132349	2.	2.	o
Rungetone	Runton[1]	TG/180428	3.	6.	2
Gymigham	Gimingham	TG/287366	4.	2.	o
Sidstronde	Sidestrand	TG/260398	4.	o	o
Monesle	Mundesley	TG/312368	2.	15.	o
Northreppes	Northrepps	TG/245391	7.	4.	2
Bassingham	Bessingham	TG/167370	1.	18.	8
Matelaske	Matlaske	TG/151349	1.	10.	o
Overstronde	Overstrand	TG/241409	2.	15.	8
Sutfeld	Suffield	TG/233313	5.	2.	o
Hanewrth'	Hanworth	TG/203349	3.	13.	4
Shipeden'	Shipden[2]	lost	2.	18.	o
Tunbernigham	Barningham Winter[3]	TG/146356	2.	14.	o
Thurgerton'	Thurgarton	TG/179348	2.	8.	8
Sustede	Sustead	TG/182370	1.	16.	o
Bestone	Beeston Regis	TG/174432	2.	10.	o
Knaptone	Knapton	TG/307342	7.	17.	5
Shiringham	Sheringham	TG/156433	3.	14.	o
Estbekham	East Beckham	TG/157398	2.	o.	o
Trunch'	Trunch	TG/288349	4.	10.	o
Aldeburgh'	Aldborough	TG/179338	2.	16.	o
Suthreppes	Southrepps	TG/257368	6.	13.	4
Trimingham	Trimingham	TG/279388	4.	4.	o
Guntone	Gunton	TG/229342	2.	o.	6
Antingham	Antingham	TG/252328	2.	14.	o
			104.	16.	8

Hd. Sutherp' [SOUTH ERPINGHAM HUNDRED]

Marsham	Marsham	TG/196236	4.	o.	o	
Totyngton'	Tuttington	TG/227272	3.	o.	o	
Saxthorp'	Saxthorpe	TG/116305	3.	10.	o	
Bernigham Parva	Little Barningham	TG/142333	1.	15.	o	
Hevigham	Hevingham	TG/202223	4.	8.	o	
Thewyt	Thwaite	TG/202336	2.	3.	o	
Skeytone	Skeyton	TG/246257	3.	16.	o	
Strattone	Stratton Strawless	TG/222208	2.	10.	o	
Aylesham [A.D]	Aylsham	TG/192270	13.	10.	o	[T]
Bliclinghe	Blickling	TG/179285	4.	10.	o	
Westbecham	West Beckham	TG/143396	1.	3.	o	
Botone	Booton	TG/123224	2.	12.	o	
Colby	Colby	TG/221312	2.	15.	8	
Hauboys Parva	Little Hautbois	TG/251218	1.	o.	o	

---

[1] Grid ref. is to West Runton.

[2] Shipden appears to have been destroyed by the sea sometime during the fifteenth century (Blomefield, viii (1808), 106).

[3] The name Barningham Winter does not appear on modern maps; the grid ref. given is to Barningham Hall.

Oultone	Oulton	TG/136285	4.	10.	o
Irminglond	Irmingland	TG/123294	2.	12.	o
Swanton'	Swanton Abbot	TG/266263	1.	15.	o
Hauboys Magna	Great Hautbois	TG/262204	1.	14.	o
Couteshale	Coltishall	TG/272198	2.	18.	o
Heydene	Heydon	TG/113274	4.	3.	o
Wolterton'	Wolterton	TG/165318	1.	6.	o
Iteringham	Itteringham	TG/145310	2.	7.	o
Erpingham	Erpingham	TG/199313	4.	10.	o
Belhagh'	Belaugh	TG/289184	2.	18.	o
Skothowe	Scottow	TG/265237	8.	13.	4
Calthorp'	Calthorpe	TG/182318	2.	10.	o
Corpesty	Corpusty	TG/115295	1.	19.	o
Banigham	Banningham	TG/216295	3.	10.	o
Wykemere	Wickmere	TG/166338	2.	6.	o
Alby	Alby	TG/193334	2.	10.	4
Baconesthorp'	Baconsthorpe	TG/127368	2.	16.	o
Ingwrth'	Ingworth	TG/191296	1.	6.	o
Lammesse	Lamas	TG/245232	2.	6.	o
Brampton'	Brampton	TG/220246	3.	2.	o
Caustone [A.D]	Cawston	TG/133238	12.	0.	o [T]
Buxtone	Buxton	TG/233227	5.	6.	8
Manigtone	Mannington	TG/143320	1.	6.	o
Burgh'	Burgh next Aylsham	TG/218251	2.	12.	o
Oxenedys	Oxnead	TG/229241	1.	8.	o
			132.	17.	o

Hd. Tunstede [TUNSTEAD HUNDRED]

Wittone	Witton	TG/331315	3.	10.	8
Dilham	Dilham	TG/325248	5.	15.	5
Westwyk'	Westwick	TG/286259	2.	16.	9
Sloleye	Sloley	TG/298242	5.	0.	o
Bestone	Beeston St. Lawrence	TG/328220	1.	15.	o
Honigg'	Honing	TG/326280	5.	0.	o
Bradefeld	Bradfield	TG/268335	3.	14.	o
Tunstede	Tunstead	TG/309227	6.	18.	o
Smalbergh'	Smallburgh	TG/331245	5.	0.	o
Berton'	Barton Turf	TG/323219	4.	5.	6
Northwalsham	North Walsham	TG/283303	15.	0.	o
Swathefeld	Swafield	TG/286331	2.	12.	6
Edyenesthorp'	Edingthorpe	TG/323332	2.	7.	o
Aysmanhagh'	Ashmanhaugh	TG/315212	1.	4.	o
Felmigham	Felmingham	TG/252293	8.	0.	o
Redelingtone	Ridlington	TG/345311	3.	10.	o
Wrstede	Worstead	TG/302261	14.	10.	1¾
Crosthewyt	Crostwight	TG/333300	2.	10.	o
Baketon'	Bacton	TG/336336	8.	17.	8
Bromholm &	Broomholm and	TG/346333			
Caswik'	Keswick	TG/351334			
Hirstede	Irstead	TG/365205	2.	8.	2
Paston'	Paston	TG/323344	5.	19.	o
Houtone Sancti Johnis	Hoveton St. John	TG/309182	3.	6.	8
Houtone Sancti Petri	Hoveton St. Peter	TG/314195	2.	10.	5
Hornigg'	Horning	TG/355166	2.	12.	o
Netishirde	Neatishead	TG/343210	5.	13.	8
			124.	16.	6¾

Hd. Clak' [CLACKCLOSE HUNDRED]

Thorp'	Shouldham Thorpe	TF/661080	2.	16.	o
Fostone	Foston	TF/654088	1.	10.	o
Fincham	Fincham	TF/688065	14.	0.	o
Suthereye	Southery	TL/622946	5.	0.	o
Denevere	Denver	TF/614017	7.	4.	o
Wirham	Wereham	TF/683014	5.	16.	o
Cremplisham	Crimplesham	TF/655038	5.	14.	o
Marham	Marham	TF/708097	10.	10.	o
Dunham Hith'	Downham Market	TF/613033	6.	14.	o
Wallington' &	Wallington and	TF/626076	1.	13.	o
Thorplonde	Thorpland	TF/615084			
Bucktone	Boughton	TF/700023	4.	10.	o
Helgeye	Hilgay	TL/623982	8.	0.	o
Shuldham	Shouldham	TF/682089	8.	10.	o
Wynbotesham &	Wimbotsham and	TF/622049	7.	1.	o
Stowe	Stow Bardolph	TF/629057			
Westderham	West Dereham	TF/668022	10.	0.	o
Waterwell[1]	Upwell and/or Outwell		13.	0.	o
Bertone bendysch'	Barton Bendish	TF/712057	10.	7.	o
Fordham	Fordham	TL/617995	8.	0.	o
Rungeton' Holm	Runcton Holme	TF/618095	7.	4.	o
Stradessete	Stradsett	TF/668057	5.	0.	o
Stokeferie cum	Stoke Ferry with	TL/705998	5.	11.	o
Wrottone	Wretton	TL/691999			
Bekiswell cum	Bexwell with	TF/631034	7.	0.	o
Ristone	Ryston	TF/625012			
Bychamwell	Beechamwell	TF/751054	10.	0.	o
Watlingtone	Watlington	TF/621112	10.	14.	o
Wyrmegeye	Wormegay	TF/674120	4.	12.	o
			180.	6.	o

Hd. Southgr' [SOUTH GREENHOE HUNDRED]

Neuton' cum	Newton with	TF/831155	3.	12.	o
Suthacre	South Acre	TF/810143			
Noketon' cum	Necton with	TF/878098	8.	18.	o
Sparham	Sparham	TF/876112			
Sporle	Sporle	TF/850115	12.	10.	10
Cleye iuxta Swafham	Cockley Cley	TF/792042	8.	0.	o
Cressingham	Great Cressingham	TF/853018	4.	10.	o
Magna					
Dodelington'	Didlington	TL/779970	5.	7.	o
Estbradenham	East Bradenham	TF/931084	7.	0.	o
Houtone	Houghton on the Hill	TF/869053	3.	13.	o
Oxeburgh'	Oxborough	TF/742013	8.	0.	o
Nerforde	Narford	TF/764138	3.	12.	o
Northpikenham	North Pickenham	TF/865069	4.	0.	o
Hilberwrth'	Hilborough	TF/825001	3.	16.	o
Halholm	Holme Hale	TF/887075	7.	8.	o
Westbradenham	West Bradenham	TF/918092	3.	6.	o
Bodeneye	Bodney	TL/832989	5.	8.	o
Goderiston'	Gooderstone	TF/762022	6.	16.	2

[1] Hudson, op. cit. 286 identifies this as Upwell and Outwell; *E.P.N.S.*, *XIX*, *Cambs.* (1943), 288, implies that it could be either place. Similar uncertainty exists over the Cambridgeshire entry of *Welle* (Cambs., Wisbech hundred, p. 28).

Langstede	Langford	TL/838965	1.	18.	0
Cressingham Parva	Little Cressingham	TF/870002	5.	10.	0
Fouldone	Fouldon	TL/766990	8.	19.	0
Swafham	Swaffham	TF/821090	20.	0.	0
Suthpikenham	South Pickenham	TF/856042	3.	10.	0
Narburgh'	Narborough	TF/747130	6.	0.	0
			141.	14.	0

Hd. Wailond [WAYLAND HUNDRED]

Tomestone	Thompson	TL/930970	6.	14.	4
Gristone	Griston	TL/943993	6.	19.	3
Aisle	Ashill	TF/884042	8.	1.	0
Castone	Caston	TL/959976	6.	0.	0
Elingham	Little Ellingham	TM/005992	4.	16.	8
Wattone	Watton	TF/922009	6.	10.	0
Breccles	Breccles	TL/958946	4.	4.	8
Mertone	Merton	TL/912981	4.	10.	6
Kerbrok'	Carbrooke	TF/949023	6.	12.	7
Totingtone	Tottington	TL/893955	6.	7.	6
Skulton'	Scoulton	TF/973010	3.	10.	0
Threkeston'	Threxton	TF/885002	3.	0.	0
Ovytone	Ovington	TF/925026	4.	10.	0
Saham	Saham Toney	TF/899020	10.	7.	4
Stowebidonn	Stow Bedon	TL/962956	3.	7.	0
			85.	10.	10

Hd. Grimeshowe [GRIMSHOE HUNDRED]

Wilton'	Wilton	TL/735880	9.	12.	6
Wetyngg'	Weeting	TL/777892	7.	10.	0
Santone	Santon	TL/829873	3.	2.	4
Linforde	Lynford	TL/819934	2.	10.	0
Colveston'	Colveston	TL/794955	2.	5.	4½
Stanforde	Stanford	TL/858948	6.	10.	6
Croxtone	Croxton	TL/873866	4.	6.	5
Mundeford	Mundford	TL/801938	3.	17.	10
Bokenham Parva	Buckenham Tofts	TL/838947	1.	8.	0
Methelwold	Methwold	TL/732948	10.	12.	10
Ikeburgh	Ickburgh	TL/817951	2.	15.	3¼
Northwolde	Northwold	TL/756970	14.	14.	0¼
Westoft	West Tofts	TL/836929	3.	14.	8¾
Sterston'	Sturston	TL/875949	2.	12.	7
Cranewyz	Cranwich	TL/783949	2.	16.	8
Feltewell	Feltwell	TL/715908	12.	6.	5½
			90.	15.	6¼

Hd. Mitforde [MIDFORD HUNDRED]

Hardingham	Hardingham	TG/035051	5.	6.	0
Hokeringge	Hockering	TG/072132	1.	14.	0
Iaxham	Yaxham	TG/006106	3.	10.	0
Lettone	Letton	TF/970060	3.	10.	0
Suthbergh'	Southburgh	TG/003048	2.	6.	0
Thurston'	Thuxton	TG/032071	4.	0.	0
Qwynebergh'	Whinburgh	TG/006089	3.	4.	0

Northtudenham	North Tuddenham	TG/056130	7.	10.	0
Estderham	East Dereham	TF/989133	14.	10.	0
Shipedham	Shipdham	TF/958073	10.	0.	0
Woderising'	Woodrising	TF/988034	3.	0.	0
Mateshale	Mattishall	TG/053111	8.	4.	0
Gerveston'	Garveston	TG/023073	3.	10.	0
Reymerston'	Reymerston	TG/020060	3.	16.	0
Esttudenham	East Tuddenham	TG/085114	5.	0.	0
Cranewrth'	Cranworth	TF/983045	2.	10.	0
Westfeld	Westfield	TF/993099	2.	2.	0
			83.	12.	0

Hd. Shroppham [SHROPHAM HUNDRED]

Wilby	Wilby	TM/031899	4.	0.	0	
Estwrottham	East Wretham	TL/915906	2.	15.	0	
Kylverdeston'	Kilverstone	TL/894840	2.	10.	0	
Hocham	Hockham	TL/951921	4.	4.	0	
Besthorp'	Besthorpe	TM/065956	3.	14.	0	
Bokenham Vet'	Old Buckenham	TM/068915	6.	16.	0	
Snyterton'	Snetterton	TL/993910	5.	10.	0	
Hargham	Hargham	TM/020913	1.	15.	0	
Eccles	Eccles	TM/019893	1.	10.	0	
Brigham	Bridgham	TL/958858	4.	0.	0	
Rokelunde	Rockland[1]	TL/994960	4.	10.	0	
Illington'	Illington	TL/948900	2.	13.	0	
Westwretham	West Wretham	TL/900915	3.	4.	0	
Attleburg	Attleborough	TM/049953	8.	0.	0	
Brethenham	Brettenham	TL/932834	2.	15.	0	
Theforde [B]	Thetford	TL/870832	16.	0.	0	[T]
Shropham	Shropham	TL/984928	7.	13.	4	
Lirling'	Larling	TL/982898	3.	4.	0	
Roudham	Roudham	TL/956872	3.	14.	0	
Nova Bokenham	New Buckenham	TM/088906	6.	3.	0	
Elingham	Great Ellingham	TM/020972	6.	4.	0	
			100.	14.	4	

Hd. Gildecros [GUILTCROSS HUNDRED]

Garboldesham	Garboldisham	TM/003816	8.	0.	0
Snareshill	Snarehill	TL/892835	2.	0.	0
Kenynghale	Kenninghall	TM/040861	3.	10.	0
Estherlingg'	East Harling	TL/990867	7.	0.	0
Redeliswrth'	Riddlesworth	TL/967813	4.	0.	0
Lopham	Lopham	TM/036825	5.	12.	0
Gasthorp'	Gasthorpe	TL/982812	2.	10.	0
Westherlingg'	West Harling	TL/975852	3.	10.	0
Blonortone	Blo Norton	TM/013797	2.	10.	0
Ruschewrth'	Rushford[2]	TL/923813	4.	0.	0
Quidenham	Quidenham	TM/028877	4.	0.	0
Banham	Banham	TM/063882	4.	0.	0
Media Herling'	Middle Harling	TL/984855	2.	0.	0
			52.	12.	0

---

[1] Grid ref. is to Rockland All Saints.
[2] Rushford straddled the Norfolk/Suffolk boundary until recently; a part was taxed in Suffolk (Blackbourne hundred, p. 293).

Hd. Fourh' [FOREHOE HUNDRED]

Morle	Morley[1]	TG/069002	5.	0.	0
Carletone	Carleton Forehoe	TG/089059	2.	12.	0
Eston'	Easton	TG/135109	2.	6.	0
Wycclewode	Wicklewood	TG/070024	3.	14.	0
Bauburgh'	Bawburgh	TG/152086	2.	2.	0
Corston' & hamlet'	Coston [and hamlets]	TG/062062	1.	0.	0
Costesseye	Costessey	TG/178124	2.	17.	0
Wramplingham	Wramplingham	TG/113060	2.	10.	0
Hengham	Hingham	TG/022021	9.	0.	0
Depham	Deopham	TG/050005	7.	0.	0
Honyngham	Honingham	TG/114113	5.	0.	0
Bykeriston'	Bickerston	TG/086087		18.	0
Bernham	Barnham Broom	TG/083078	2.	0.	0
Bouththorp'	Bowthorpe	TG/177091	2.	0.	0
Marlingford	Marlingford	TG/127083	1.	18.	0
Hakeforde	Hackford	TG/059023	1.	0.	0
Welburne	Welborne	TG/068102	1.	18.	0
Brandon'	Brandon Parva	TG/070081	1.	16.	0
Berforde	Barford	TG/108080	2.	8.	0
Runhale	Runhall	TG/058068	4.	2.	0
Crungethorp'	Crownthorpe	TG/083032	1.	11.	0
Kimbirle	Kimberley	TG/072042	4.	4.	0
Colton' & Thorp'	Colton and Honingham Thorpe	TG/104093 TG/109099	4.	6.	8
Wymundham	Wymondham	TG/107015	13.	0.	0
			84.	2.	8

Hd. Humill' [HUMBLEYARD HUNDRED]

Hedersete	Hethersett	TG/161049	5.	9.	0
Merkishale	Markshall	TG/228047	1.	2.	0
Estkarleton'	East Carleton	TG/180021	2.	14.	0
Dunston'	Dunston	TG/228023	1.	10.	0
Magna Melton'	Great Melton	TG/141062	4.	10.	0
Etone	Eaton	TG/203059	1.	5.	0
Neuton' Flotema' & Kenigham	Newton Flotman and Keningham	TM/213984 TM/206999	4.	0.	0
Erlham	Earlham	TG/190083	2.	2.	0
Hethill	Hethel	TG/171004	2.	10.	0
Colneye	Colney	TG/181080	1.	13.	0
Lakenham	Lakenham	TG/233062	1.	13.	0
Keteryngham	Ketteringham	TG/164026	4.	4.	0
Cringilford	Cringleford	TG/198058	1.	10.	0
Swerdiston'	Swardeston	TG/199023	3.	0.	0
Wreningham & Nelonde	Wreningham and Nayland[2]	TM/163988	4.	0.	0
Mulkebertone	Mulbarton	TG/194012	2.	16.	0
Brakne	Bracon Ash	TG/171003	1.	15.	0
Sweynesthorp'	Swainsthorpe	TG/219009	2.	9.	0
Flordon'	Flordon	TM/189973	2.	15.	0
Intewode	Intwood	TG/196042	2.	5.	0
Braknedele	Brackendale	TG/240074	1.	0.	0

[1] Grid ref. is to Morley St. Botolph.

[2] Nayland was a member of Great Wreningham manor, to which the village was annexed in 1414 (Blomefield, v (1806), 116).

Kessewyk'	Keswick	TG/213047	1.	17.	0
Melton' Parva	Little Melton	TG/153069	1.	17.	0
Hegham	Heigham	TG/220085	2.	5.	0
			60.	1.	0

Hd. Disce [DISS HUNDRED]

Frense	Frenze	TM/136804	1.	5.	0
Ferfeld	Fersfield	TM/066828	1.	14.	0
Diccleburgh'	Dickleburgh	TM/168824	3.	16.	0
Osmudiston'	Scole	TM/151791	1.	17.	0
Tiveteshale	Tivetshall	TM/163871	3.	0.	0
Parva Thorp'	Thorpe Parva	TM/160795	1.	4.	0
Disce	Diss	TM/118800	7.	8.	0
Reydone	Roydon	TM/096803	2.	10.	0
Burston'	Burston	TM/137832	2.	12.	0
Thelveton'	Thelveton	TM/153813	2.	0.	0
Wynferying'	Winfarthing	TM/109857	1.	16.	0
Gissingg'	Gissing	TM/146853	3.	8.	0
Bresingham	Bressingham	TM/078808	3.	14.	0
Shelfangel	Shelfanger	TM/108837	1.	7.	0
Shimpling'	Shimpling	TM/156827	1.	15.	0
			39.	6.	0

Hd. Ersham [EARSHAM HUNDRED]

Brokedysch'	Brockdish	TM/213797	4.	0.	0
Reueshale	Rushall	TM/198827	3.	16.	0
Denton'	Denton	TM/286874	6.	10.	0
Redenhale	Redenhall	TM/264844	13.	0.	0
Prilliston'	Billingford	TM/168791	2.	18.	0
Ersham	Earsham	TM/326888	5.	2.	0
Pulham	Pulham[1]	TM/212853	12.	4.	0
Thorp'	Thorpe Abbots	TM/204795	2.	4.	0
Sterston'	Starston	TM/234843	4.	13.	0
Aldebergh'	Alburgh	TM/271873	5.	0.	0
			59.	7.	0

Hd. Laundz [LAUNDITCH HUNDRED]

Rougham	Rougham	TF/830205	8.	5.	0
Patesle	Patesley	TF/899241	1.	12.	0
Dunham Magna	Great Dunham	TF/873146	7.	18.	0
Milham	Mileham	TF/923196	3.	16.	0
Stanfeld	Stanfield	TF/939208	3.	10.	0
Gatele	Gateley	TF/960245	2.	13.	4
Godwyk	Godwick	TF/904222	1.	4.	0
Kemston'	Kempstone	TF/886160	2.	12.	0
Oxewyk	Oxwick	TF/911253	2.	6.	8
Brisle	Brisley	TF/951215	6.	4.	0
Wendlingg'	Wendling	TF/932132	1.	19.	0
Wyssingsete	Whissonsett	TF/919233	3.	2.	0
Swanton'	Swanton Morley	TG/019172	12.	0.	0

[1] Grid ref. is to Pulham St. Mary.

Hornigtoft	Horningtoft	TF/932235	2.	14.	o
Wesenham	Weasenham[1]	TF/851216	8.	o.	o
Skernigge	Scarning	TF/954122	10.	14.	o
Welyngham	Willingham	TF/872223	2.	o.	o
Lucham	Litcham	TF/886176	3.	7.	o
Westlexham	West Lexham	TF/843172	1.	14.	o
Fransham Magna	Great Fransham	TF/899131	5.	10.	o
Dunham Parva	Little Dunham	TF/863129	3.	16.	11
Fransham Parva	Little Fransham	TF/902122	3.	8.	o
Betele de libertate de Northelmham	Beetley	TF/974185	3.	12.	o
Tyteleshale	Tittleshall	TF/895212	5.	4.	o
Longham	Longham	TF/932162	2.	15.	o
Colkirke	Colkirk	TF/918265	2.	6.	8
Cressenhale & Beterynge Magna	Cressenhall and Great Bittering	TF/959155 TF/940174	6.	o.	o
Hoo	Hoe	TF/997164	6.	10.	o
Estbilneye	East Bilney	TF/955196	2.	14.	o
Estlexham	East Lexham	TF/860172	2.	2.	o
Northelmham	North Elmham	TF/988215	7.	10.	o
Bestone & Beteringg' Parva	Beeston and Little Bittering	TF/908158 TF/960169	9.	o.	o
			145.	19.	7

TOTAL: £3,487. 4. 7[2]

[1] Grid ref. is to Weasenham All Saints.
[2] As on 1334 Account, E 179/149/12. The figures for the hundreds add up to £3,487. 4. 6 as on E 179/149/13 (1336).

NORTHAMPTONSHIRE

DOCUMENTS

8 Edward III: Account   E 179/155/4
8 Edward III: Indenture   E 179/155/3*
           (to this Indenture is attached a *Nomina Villarum* of the 1332
           subsidy)
22 Edward III: Particulars, also E 179/155/3

TAXERS

The prior of Daventry and Robert de Foxton

TAX YIELD

15th   £1,059.   17.   7½
10th   £ 101.   7.   10¾

     £1,161.   5.   6¼

Representing assessed movable wealth of

    £16,912.   3.   4

NOTES

The only taxation borough was Northampton. Rockingham and Rothwell had been considered boroughs on one previous occasion, in 1307, but in 1334 both were taxed at a fifteenth; their curious position at the end of the list is probably a legacy of their former status. Most of the tax at a tenth was on twenty ancient demesnes concentrated for the most part in Willybrook hundred and in the Kettering area.

A feature of the Northamptonshire rolls is the large number of places taxed *cum membris*; there are twenty-eight entries of this type on the 1334 roll, and additional ones on later rolls suggest that other places should have been similarly described in 1334.

To judge from the places listed in 1334, Northamptonshire had largely assumed its modern outline by 1334, in contrast to the much larger county of 1086 (H. C. Darby and I. B. Terrett, eds., *The Domesday Geography of Midland England*, 1954, 379–81). Three places taxed in the county in 1334 (Little Bowden, Grimsbury, and Stoneton) have since been transferred to neighbouring counties. Only two places in the modern county were taxed elsewhere in 1334—Thurning and Hargrave, both in Huntingdonshire.

Hd. Suttone [KING'S SUTTON HUNDRED][1]

Suttone [A.D]	King's Sutton	SP/497361	6.	3.	5 [T]
Chacombe	Chacombe	SP/491440	2.	17.	2
Grymmesbury	Grimsbury [in Oxfordshire]	SP/463408	2.	4.	4
Croultone	Croughton	SP/546335	2.	17.	2
Thenford'	Thenford	SP/519415	2.	3.	8
Stene	Steane	SP/554390	2.	0.	4
Faryngho	Farthinghoe	SP/536398	3.	15.	7½
Hynton'	Hinton in the Hedges	SP/558369	1.	19.	11
Syresham	Syresham	SP/631420	2.	14.	0
Coleworth'	Culworth	SP/544470	3.	10.	9
Helmedene	Helmdon	SP/590432	3.	10.	0
Neubotle[2]	Newbottle	SP/524369	4.	12.	0
Middelton' Cheyndut'	Middleton Cheney	SP/499421	4.	16.	4
Hals cum Veteri Brackele	Halse with Old Brackley	SP/566403 SP/592373	3.	13.	11
Stucesbury	Stuchbury	SP/569441	1.	16.	4
Thropmundevyle	Thorpe Mandeville	SP/532450	2.	1.	2
Warworth'	Warkworth	SP/487407	1.	16.	8
Mersshton' Sancti Laur'	Marston St. Lawrence	SP/536421	2.	12.	2
Evenele & Astwyk'	Evenley and Astwick	SP/583351 SP/570342	2.	8.	4
Wapenham	Wappenham	SP/624456	2.	9.	1
Rodeston' & Whitefeld	Radstone and Whitfield	SP/588405 SP/608395	4.	10.	10
Aynho cum Walton'	Aynho with Walton Grounds	SP/514331 SP/506346	4.	9.	9
Astwelle & Faucote	Astwell and Falcutt	SP/609441 SP/594428	3.	0.	9
			72.	3.	8½

Hd. Wardone [CHIPPING WARDEN HUNDRED]

Wardone & Stontone	Chipping Warden and Stoneton [in Warwicks.]	SP/499487 SP/463547	7.	19.	9
Botyngdon'	Boddington[3]	SP/483533	4.	19.	3½
Hochecote	Edgcote	SP/505479	3.	11.	0
Gretteworth'	Greatworth	SP/552423	2.	6.	8
Eydone	Eydon	SP/541500	3.	0.	6
Bifeld & Trafford'	Byfield and Trafford	SP/519530 SP/527486	4.	13.	3½
Sulgrave	Sulgrave	SP/557453	3.	6.	11
Aston' & Appultr'	Aston le Walls and Appletree	SP/496508 SP/483496	2.	14.	9
Wodeford' c.m[4]	Woodford Halse [with members]	SP/543529	4.	1.	10¾
			36.	14.	0¾

[1] On the Northamptonshire roll, E 179/155/3, all places are designated *villata* except those in Nassaburgh hundred and the six at the end of the list.

[2] *cum membris* on E 179/155/20 (1352).   [3] Grid ref. is to Upper Boddington.

[4] Members of Woodford Halse in 1316 included Hinton and Farndon (*F.A.* iv. 20).

Hd. Nortone [GREEN'S NORTON HUNDRED]

Norton' [A.D] & Sulveston' [A.D]	Green's Norton and Silverstone	SP/669499 SP/668442	10.	12.	4½ [T]
Blacoluesle[1]	Blakesley	SP/628504	6.	6.	10
Atneston' & Maydeforde	Adstone and Maidford	SP/596514 SP/610525	3.	14.	0
Wedon' Weston' & Plumpton'	Weedon Lois Weston and Plumpton	SP/602470 SP/589469 SP/598483	3.	9.	4¼
Morton' & Assheby	Moreton Pinkney and Canons Ashby	SP/574491 SP/578505	4.	15.	0
Slapton' & Braddene	Slapton and Bradden	SP/640469 SP/647485	4.	9.	0
			33.	6.	6¾

Hd. Touescestr' [TOWCESTER HUNDRED]

Touecestr'	Towcester	SP/694487	8.	0.	0
Pateshull'	Pattishall	SP/672543	5.	6.	2
Hegham & Foxle	Cold Higham and Foxley	SP/662535 SP/641518	2.	12.	0
Gaytone	Gayton	SP/706548	2.	13.	0
Tiffelde	Tiffield	SP/699516	1.	18.	4
			20.	9.	6

Hd. Cleile [CLELEY HUNDRED]

Hertwelle c.m[2]	Hartwell [with members]	SP/785504	7.	14.	5
Densanger' & Passenham	Deanshanger and Passenham	SP/761396 SP/781394	4.	14.	0
Grafton'	Grafton Regis	SP/759469	3.	19.	3
Estneston' & Hulcote	Easton Neston and Hulcote	SP/702492 SP/704500	4.	8.	6
Wyke Dyue & Wike Hamod'	Wicken[3]	SP/745395	4.	4.	10
Couesgrave & Fortho	Cosgrove and Furtho	SP/791424 SP/773431	5.	10.	0
Stokebruer' c.m[4]	Stoke Bruerne [with members]	SP/741499	5.	14.	4
Estpiree c.m[5]	Potterspury [with members]	SP/762433	7.	13.	2
Westpirie c.m[6]	Paulerspury [with members]	SP/716455	7.	0.	0
			50.	18.	6

[1] *cum membris* on E 179/155/20 (1352). Members in 1316 included Kirby Grounds, Woodend, and Seawell (*F.A.* iv. 20).

[2] Members in 1316 included Roade and Ashton (*F.A.* iv. 22).

[3] Wicken takes its name from the two *Wic* manors (*E.P.N.S.*, X, *Northants.* (1933), 107–8).

[4] Members in 1316 included Shutlanger and Alderton (*F.A.* iv. 22).

[5] A member in 1316 was Yardley Gobion, ibid.

[6] A member in 1316 was Heathencote, ibid.

Hd. Hegham [HIGHAM FERRERS HUNDRED]

Hegham c.m[1]	Higham Ferrers [with members]	SP/961685	8.	10.	0
Irencestr' c.m	Irchester [with members]	SP/925660	6.	0.	0
Raundes c.m	Raunds [with members]	TL/001731	12.	19.	0
Stanewygge	Stanwick	SP/980715	5.	17.	2
Risshendene	Rushden	SP/958665	6.	17.	0
Eston' c.m[2]	Easton Maudit [with members]	SP/889589	8.	6.	8
Wolaston' cum medietate Strixton'[3]	Wollaston with Strixton [half of]	SP/909631 SP/903616	8.	3.	6
			56.	13.	4

Hd. Orlingber [ORLINGBURY HUNDRED]

Brikkelesworth'	Brixworth	SP/747712	3.	15.	3
Faxton' & Malesle	Faxton & Mawsley	SP/785751 SP/808768	1.	18.	8
Wolde	Old	SP/786731	3.	3.	9
Harewedon' Magna & Parva	Great Harrowden and Little Harrowden	SP/880708 SP/871717	3.	13.	11
Hanygtone	Hannington	SP/812709	1.	19.	0
Isham	Isham	SP/885739	2.	7.	6
Langeport' & Hoghton'	Lamport and Hanging Houghton	SP/758745 SP/753737	3.	7.	10
Orlingb' & Wythemal	Orlingbury and Wythemail	SP/859726 SP/841719	2.	10.	0
Scaldewell'	Scaldwell	SP/768725	2.	10.	7
Waldegrave	Walgrave	SP/802720	3.	7.	0
Broghton'	Broughton	SP/837757	2.	17.	5
Cranesle	Cransley	SP/828765	1.	10.	0
Et de decima eiusdem vill' [A.D][4]	Cransley [ancient demesne]			17.	3¼ [T]
Pigteslegh'	Pytchley	SP/860748	4.	18.	0
			38.	16.	2¼

Hd. Rothewell' [ROTHWELL HUNDRED]

Ouerton'	Orton	SP/806794	1.	15.	8
Suleby	Sulby	SP/666817	1.	11.	0
Sibertoft'	Sibbertoft	SP/682828	3.	5.	2
Hothorp'	Hothorpe	SP/669852	1.	16.	4
Mersshton' Trussel	Marston Trussell	SP/693859	2.	5.	6
Braybrok'	Braybrooke	SP/765846	3.	17.	0
Heryngton'	Harrington	SP/773800	5.	4.	0
Rysshton'	Rushton	SP/841829	3.	11.	7¼

---

[1] Returned with Rushden in 1316 (*F.A.* iv. 29).
[2] Returned with Bozeat and half of Strixton in 1316 (*F.A.* iv. 30).
[3] *V.C.H., Northants.* iv (1937), 55. Part of Strixton was held with Wollaston and part with Easton Maudit. It is likely that the other half of Strixton was taxed as a member of Easton Maudit, above.
[4] Part of Cransley had been held by the royal manor of Rothwell before 1334.

Thorp iuxta Lobenham	Thorpe Lubbenham	SP/705866		12.	o
Clipston' &	Clipston and	SP/713815	4.	5.	o
Neubolt	Nobold	SP/698821			
Keylmerssh'	Kelmarsh	SP/735792	4.	12.	8
Arnyngworth'	Arthingworth	SP/755814	3.	7.	o
Desburgh'	Desborough	SP/803831	4.	12.	8
Bereford [A.D][1]	Barford	SP/851827	3.	19.	o [T]
Farndon'	East Farndon	SP/717851	3.	5.	2
Boudon' Parva	Little Bowden [in Leics.]	SP/740870	3.	9.	o
Oxendon' Magna	Great Oxendon	SP/732833	3.	7.	o
Oxendon' Parva	Little Oxendon	SP/728840	1.	12.	o
Aselbech'	Haselbech	SP/712773	2.	12.	o
Maydewell'	Maidwell	SP/749769	2.	16.	8¾
Draughton'	Draughton	SP/762768	3.	2.	o
Lodyngton'	Loddington	SP/815783	2.	3.	o
Thorp' Maleseures	Thorpe Malsor	SP/833790	1.	9.	o
			68.	10.	6

Hd. Nasso Burgh [NASSABURGH HUNDRED]

Burgo Sancti Petri c.m[2]	Peterborough [with members]	TL/193987	25.	10.	6
Makeseye	Maxey	TF/120080	14.	16.	o
Bernak' c.m	Barnack [with members]	TF/079051	17.	19.	o
Castre c.m	Castor [with members]	TL/125985	18.	8.	o
Glynton' c.m	Glinton [with members]	TF/154060	11.	16.	o
Paston c.m	Paston [with members]	TF/181022	16.	15.	o
Thornhawe c.m	Thornhaugh [with members]	TF/069006	8.	9.	o
			113.	13.	6

Hd. Willibrok' [WILLYBROOK HUNDRED]

Ludington c.m[3]	Lutton [with members]	TL/112878	3.	12.	11
Glapethorn &	Glapthorn and	TL/024902	5.	11.	o½
Cotherstok'	Cotterstock	TL/049905			
Fodryngeye	Fotheringhay	TL/060932	4.	10.	o
Nassyngton' [A.D] &	Nassington and	TL/063962	6.	16.	5 [T]
Yarewell' [A.D]	Yarwell	TL/071978			
Dodyngton' [A.D]	Duddington	SK/988009	3.	4.	o [T]
Clyve [A.D] &	King's Cliffe and	TL/007971	5.	17.	o [T]
Hale [A.D]	Halefield	TL/028933			
Tansouere c.m[4]	Tansor [with members]	TL/053909	4.	15.	4
Eston' c.m[5]	Easton on the Hill [with members]	TF/011047	2.	18.	o
Suthewyk' &	Southwick and	TL/021921	3.	4.	11½
Piriho	Perio	TL/041918			

[1] On some later documents, e.g. E 179/155/20 (1352), Glendon (SP/846814) is linked with Barford (as is was in 1316).

[2] All places named in this hundred were returned *cum membris* in 1316; the names of the members are not stated (*F.A.* iv. 27–8).

[3] Members in 1316 included Warmington and Luddington in the Brook (*F.A.* iv. 23).

[4] Returned with Elmington in 1316, ibid.

[5] Returned with Collyweston in 1316, ibid.

Apethorp [A.D] &	Apethorpe and	TL/025957	5.	2.	6 [T]
Neuton' [A.D]	Woodnewton	TL/032945			
Weston'	Collyweston	SK/996028		17.	0
			46.	9.	2

Hd. Pokebrok' [POLEBROOK HUNDRED]

Clopton'	Clapton	TL/066800	5.	16.	0
Undele c.m	Oundle [with members]	TL/023876	9.	9.	9
Thrapston' c.m	Thrapston [with members]	SP/997787	5.	10.	10¼
Wadenho	Wadenhoe	TL/008833	2.	18.	11½
Bernewell'	Barnwell[1]	TL/049849	5.	17.	11
Pokebrok' c.m	Polebrook [with members]	TL/068870	5.	7.	0
Wermyngton' c.m	Warmington [with members]	TL/078910	3.	19.	0
Tichemerssh'	Titchmarsh	TL/022798	8.	7.	9
Thorp' &	Thorpe Waterville and	TL/023816	4.	3.	0
Achirche	Achurch	TL/021831			
Stokedoyly	Stoke Doyle	TL/027863	4.	19.	0
Pilketon' cum	Pilton with	TL/024845	2.	8.	6
Parva Liveden' [p]	Little Lyveden [part of][2]	SP/982859			
Hemyngton' c.m	Hemington [with members]	TL/092850	5.	8.	6½
Benyfeld' c.m	Benefield [with members]	SP/988885	6.	5.	0
			70.	11.	3¼

Hd. Hokeslowe [HUXLOE HUNDRED]

Lilleford c.m	Lilford [with members]	TL/038832	6.	15.	0
Irtlyngburgh'	Irthlingborough	SP/948706	7.	11.	9½
Adyngton' Maior	Great Addington	SP/958752	3.	9.	0
Adyngton' Parva	Little Addington	SP/959736	3.	0.	0
Grafton'	Grafton Underwood	SP/922802	2.	3.	2
Slipton'	Slipton	SP/951792	1.	10.	10
Twywell'	Twywell	SP/952782	2.	5.	2
Lufwyk'	Lowick	SP/977810	2.	13.	0
Islep	Islip	SP/986789	2.	8.	8
Wodeford'	Woodford	SP/969768	4.	17.	10
Keteryngg'	Kettering	SP/868784	6.	3.	0
Burton'	Burton Latimer	SP/903750	6.	12.	8
Barton'	Barton Seagrave	SP/887773	3.	6.	0
Craneford'	Cranford[3]	SP/927771	2.	7.	7
Aldewynch'	Aldwincle	TL/006818	3.	13.	4
Suthborgh'	Sudborough	SP/968821	2.	10.	0
Deneford'	Denford	SP/991766	4.	7.	0
Werketon'	Warkton	SP/893798	2.	1.	10
			67.	15.	10½

[1] Grid ref. is to Barnwell St. Andrew.
[2] Lyveden was a lordship, parts of which were in Pilton, Oundle, Brigstock, and Aldwincle.
[3] Grid ref. is to Cranford St. John.

Hd. Corby [CORBY HUNDRED]

Corby	Corby	SP/898888	2.	2.	4	
Bolewyk'	Bulwick	SP/962942	5.	12.	3½	
Deen c.m¹	Deene [with members]	SP/952928	4.	14.	7	
Bramton' iuxta Dyngele	Brampton Ash	SP/788874	3.	0.	0	
Stokedaubeney	Stoke Albany	SP/805883	5.	4.	11½	
Neuton Parva &	Little Newton and	SP/883833	2.	19.	11½	
Okle Magna	Great Oakley	SP/871859				
Haryngworth'	Harringworth	SP/917974	6.	6.	0	
Weldon' Magna &	Great Weldon and	SP/928893	5.	8.	11	
Parva	Little Weldon	SP/923897				
Wykle	Weekley	SP/888810	2.	17.	10	
Geytyngton' [A.D]	Geddington	SP/895830	4.	16.	5	[T]
Boughton'	Boughton	SP/900815		9.	3½	
Grettone [A.D] &	Gretton and	SP/898944	6.	14.	4	[T]
Coten' [A.D]	Coten²					
Cotyngham &	Cottingham and	SP/846899	5.	5.	0	
Middelton'	Middleton	SP/841900				
Wakerle	Wakerley	SP/957992	3.	0.	0	
Dyngele	Dingley	SP/770877	2.	4.	0	
Brixtoke [A.D] &	Brigstock and	SP/946852	9.	0.	0	[T]
Stanerne [A.D]	Stanion	SP/915868				
Magna Neuton	Great Newton	SP/884834	1.	19.	0	
Acle Parva	Little Oakley	SP/892856	1.	19.	0	
Asshele	Ashley	SP/793911	5.	8.	0.	
Carlton'	East Carlton	SP/831893	3.	10.	10	
Blatherwyk' &	Blatherwycke and	SP/974957	5.	18.	0½	
Laxton'	Laxton	SP/951960				
Sutton' &	Sutton Bassett and	SP/771903	4.	11.	0	
Weston	Weston by Welland	SP/778914				
			93.	1.	9½³	

Hd. Fallewesle [FAWSLEY HUNDRED]

Daventr'	Daventry	SP/572623	6.	13.	6¾	
Thorp' &	Thrupp Grounds and	SP/603653	6.	4.	0	
Norton'	Norton	SP/603637				
Brandeston'	Braunston	SP/537662	4.	7.	10	
Lychesbarwe	Litchborough	SP/633543	2.	13.	4	
Stavertone	Staverton	SP/541611	2.	17.	4	
Wedene Bek'	Weedon Bec	SP/633593	4.	0.	10	
Berughby	Barby	SP/543703	2.	19.	1	
Catesby	Catesby	SP/526594	4.	11.	4	
Fallewesle [A.D]	Fawsley	SP/566568	2.	16.	8	[T]
Assheby Liger	Ashby St. Ledgers	SP/573682	5.	7.	0	
Welton'	Welton	SP/581660	3.	17.	0	
Charwelton'	Charwelton	SP/544555	2.	2.	8	
Farthyngston'	Farthingstone	SP/613550	1.	15.	0	
Everdon'	Everdon	SP/595574	3.	8.	11	

¹ Members in 1316 included Kirby and Deenethorpe (*F.A.* iv. 25).

² Last recorded mention is 1355 (*E.P.N.S.*, X, *Northants.* (1933), 166). Site is suggested as SP/?890926 in K. J. Allison *et al.*, *The Deserted Villages of Northamptonshire*, Leicester Occasional Papers, No. 18 (1966), 37.

³ The hundred total is £93. 1. 9 on E 179/155/20 (1352), although the vill totals are the same as above. The slight difference may be a clue to the slight discrepancy in the final total for the county (see note, p. 218).

Stowe	Church Stowe	SP/639577	1.	9.	8
Preston' Capes	Preston Capes	SP/574549	3.	6.	10
Baddeby &	Badby and	SP/560587	4.	9.	4
Newenham	Newnham	SP/581597			
Doddeford'	Dodford	SP/612605	3.	0.	6
Kildesby	Kilsby	SP/563711	1.	10.	0
			67.	10.	10$\frac{3}{4}$

Hd. Gildesburgh' [GUILSBOROUGH HUNDRED]

Nauesby	Naseby	SP/689781	4.	0.	4[1]
Thurneby	Thornby	SP/669756	3.	0.	2
Coldassheby	Cold Ashby	SP/656762	2.	3.	10
Gildesburgh' c.m	Guilsborough [with members]	SP/676727	5.	2.	9$\frac{3}{4}$
Yelvertoft	Yelvertoft	SP/602752	3.	8.	0
Welleford'	Welford	SP/641803	4.	2.	5
Crek'	Crick	SP/588725	6.	13.	10
Buckeby	Long Buckby	SP/627677	6.	16.	8
Stanford' &	Stanford on Avon &	SP/589789	3.	13.	4
Doune	Downtown	SP/614800			
Wynewyk'	Winwick	SP/626739	3.	3.	5$\frac{1}{2}$
Creton' Magna	Great Creaton	SP/707719	2.	0.	4
Creton' Parva	Little Creaton	SP/713717		18.	0
Watford'	Watford	SP/602687	4.	2.	5
Lilleburne	Lilbourne	SP/560774	4.	18.	2
Westhaddon'	West Haddon	SP/632719	2.	10.	2
Cotesbrok'	Cottesbrooke	SP/710735	3.	6.	0
			59.	19.	11$\frac{1}{4}$

Hd. Neubotlegrave [NOBOTTLE-GROVE HUNDRED]

Flore	Flore	SP/642598	5.	16.	0
Kiselyngburi'	Kislingbury	SP/698597	3.	19.	9
Heyford'	Heyford[2]	SP/659587	3.	12.	2
Brampton' Maior &	Church Brampton and	SP/718657	4.	2.	2
Minor	Chapel Brampton	SP/728662			
Whelton'	Whilton	SP/636648	2.	14.	6
Duston'	Duston	SP/725611	3.	16.	6$\frac{3}{4}$
Brochole	Brockhall	SP/632626	2.	13.	6$\frac{1}{2}$
Ravenesthorp	Ravensthorpe	SP/671703	3.	1.	1
Brynton' c.m	Brington[3] [with members]	SP/666650	7.	17.	4
Daylyngton'	Dallington	SP/738617	3.	13.	4
Horepol	Harpole	SP/691609	3.	19.	8
Esthaddon'	East Haddon	SP/667682	3.	6.	8
Upton' [A.D]	Upton	SP/718602	3.	12.	6 [T]
Buckebrok'	Bugbrooke	SP/673573	3.	7.	0$\frac{1}{2}$
Herleston'	Harlestone	SP/701646	3.	11.	0
Haldenby	Holdenby	SP/692675	3.	2.	10
			$\overline{62}$.	6.	1$\frac{3}{4}$

[1] The Naseby quota drops to £3. 15. 4 in later years (as on the roll of 1344, E 179/155/3 (c)). The hundred total changes accordingly.
[2] Grid ref. is to Nether Heyford.   [3] Grid ref. is to Great Brington.

Hd. Spelho [SPELHOE HUNDRED]

Oveston'	Overstone	SP/806661	3.	3.	4
Multon'	Moulton	SP/783663	5.	0.	0
Abyndon'	Abingdon	SP/775615	2.	11.	3½
Weston' Fauvel	Weston Favell	SP/789619	3.	0.	6½
Pisseford'	Pitsford	SP/754682	2.	4.	8
Sprotton'	Spratton	SP/718701	3.	15.	0
Boketon'	Boughton	SP/753659	2.	3.	8
Billyng Parva	Little Billing	SP/804618	2.	17.	3
Billyng Magna	Great Billing	SP/808629	4.	0.	6
			28.	16.	3

Hd. Wymersle [WYMERSLEY HUNDRED]

Yerdele	Yardley Hastings	SP/866571	5.	10.	8
Blyseworth'	Blisworth	SP/725534	2.	10.	8
Cortenhale	Courteenhall	SP/764529	2.	10.	8
Middelton' &	Milton and	SP/737555	5.	16.	0¾
Colentr'	Collingtree	SP/751557			
Hougton' Magna	Great Houghton	SP/792590	4.	18.	4½
Cogenho	Cogenhoe	SP/830610	2.	16.	2
Hardyngsthorn &	Hardingstone and	SP/763578	4.	13.	4
Cotes	Cotton	SP/750592			
Preston' &	Preston Deanery and	SP/789557	4.	11.	0
Quenton'	Quinton	SP/777543			
Grendon'	Grendon	SP/879604	6.	18.	0
Rytheresthrop	Rothersthorpe	SP/714566	3.	0.	0
Pidyngton' &	Piddington and	SP/801546	4.	12.	9¾
Hacklynton'	Hackleton	SP/806550			
Whesshton' cum	Whiston with	SP/852605	2.	14.	10
Dodyngton' (p)[1]	Denton [part of]	SP/839580			
Assheby Davyd	Castle Ashby	SP/864592	4.	10.	0
Chaddeston'	Chadstone	SP/854586			
Braunfeld' &	Brafield on the Green	SP/822591	7.	11.	2
Parva Houghton'	and Little Houghton	SP/803596			
Wottone	Wootton	SP/762565	5.	10.	6
Horton'	Horton	SP/819543	2.	14.	10
			70.	19.	1

Hd. Aunfordesho [HAMFORDSHOE HUNDRED]

Eketon'	Ecton	SP/829635	4.	4.	4½
Magna Dodyngton'	Great Doddington	SP/881648	4.	17.	8½
Assheby Mars	Mears Ashby	SP/838667	3.	11.	1
Herdwyk'	Hardwick	SP/851698	1.	15.	6
Sywoll'	Sywell	SP/822672	3.	0.	0
Barton' Comitis	Earls Barton	SP/852638	7.	3.	4½
Wenlyngburgh'	Wellingborough	SP/892680	9.	6.	2
Holcote	Holcot	SP/792698	2.	8.	8
Wileby	Wilby	SP/867662	2.	13.	1
			38.	19.	11½

[1] The rest of Denton was probably taxed with Yardley Hastings, with which it was listed in 1316 (*F.A.* iv. 26).

Norht' [B]	Northampton	SP/753605	27.	0.	0	[T]
Brackele	New Brackley	SP/586370	11.	0.	4	
Kyngesthorp' [A.D]	Kingsthorpe	SP/754632	4.	16.	0	[T]
Rothewell'	Rothwell	SP/816812	9.	0.	0	
Rokyngham	Rockingham	SP/867914	2.	9.	0	
Thyngdene	Finedon	SP/912719	4.	16.	0	
			59.	1.	4	

TOTAL: £1,161. 5. 6¼[1]

---

[1] As on 1334 Account, E 179/155/4. The figures for the hundreds in the Particulars in fact add up to £1,161. 5. 6¾.

NORTHUMBERLAND (1336)

DOCUMENTS

8 Edward III: Not taxed
10 Edward III: Particulars   E 179/158/7
10 Edward III: Particulars   E 179/158/8*
10 Edward III: Particulars   E 179/158/9

TAXERS

1334 The prior of Tynemouth and William de Emeldon (vacated)
1336 John de Insula and Nicholas de Punchardon
        Richard de Acton and John de Denton (for Newcastle)

TAX YIELD

15th	£315.	13.	8½
10th	£ 17.	14.	0
	£333.	7.	8½

Representing assessed movable wealth of

£4,912.   5.   7½

Newcastle, £133. 6. 8 (200 marks in lieu of tenth)

Representing wealth of £1,333. 6. 8

NOTES

Northumberland, like the north-western counties of Cumberland and Westmorland, was excused the 1334 tax on account of recent devastation by the Scots.
It was taxed, however, in 1336 and one of the surviving rolls of that year (E 179/
158/7), as yet unpublished, includes the names of the taxpayers. (While these
are not included in the accompanying list they should be used in any detailed
work on the county.) The names of the taxpayers in the liberty of Redesdale
are published as Appendix A in C. M. Fraser's recent study of the lay subsidy of
1296, an invaluable work on the county.

Places taxed at a tenth comprise the boroughs of Corbridge and Bamburgh
and the ancient demesnes of Shoreston and North Sunderland. Newcastle, one
of the most prosperous provincial towns of England, settled for exemption from
the tenth by a payment of 200 marks (C.P.R., 1334–1338, 397). It should be
borne in mind that the tax quotas for this county may be unduly low owing to
the unsettled conditions prevailing at the time.

REFERENCES

F. Bradshaw, 'The Lay subsidy roll of 1296: Northumberland at the end of the
    13th century', Archaeologia Aeliana, 3rd series, xiii (1916).
C. M. Fraser, The Northumberland Lay Subsidy Roll of 1296, Society of
    Antiquaries, Newcastle upon Tyne, Record Series, No. 1, 1968.

Ward de Tyndal' [TYNEDALE WARD]

Byrtleye	Birtley	NT/878780	1.	0.	7
Colwell'	Colwell	NY/950755		18.	1¼
Baronsford	Barrasford	NY/916734	1.	0.	4
Gunwarton'	Gunnerton	NY/905750		17.	3
Swynburnest'	Little Swinburn	NY/949776		17.	1
Chipchese	Chipchase	NY/883757		15.	2
Sholuerton'	Chollerton	NY/931720		12.	4
Foustanes	Fourstones	NY/888679	2.	6.	8
Hayden	Haydon	NY/843654	1.	15.	0
Langleye	Langley	NY/828612	2.	10.	0
Allerwashe	Allerwash	NY/866664	3.	7.	2¾
Weydon'	Wydon	NY/691631		16.	8
Blencanhop'	Blenkinsopp	NY/665644	1.	2.	6
Fertanhalgh'	Featherstone	NY/673610	1.	6.	8
Thokryngton'	Thockrington	NY/959790	1.	10.	0
Babbyngton' Magna	Great Bavington	NY/983804	2.	0.	0
Babbyngton' Parva	Little Bavington	NY/988787	1.	3.	4
Wardon'	Warden	NY/913665		10.	0
Kircheton'	Kirkheaton	NZ/018773	2.	2.	4
Rihill'	Ryal	NZ/015742	1.	6.	8
Kirkherll'	Kirkharle	NZ/011825	1.	9.	6
Westherll'	West Harle	NY/990820		8.	5
Whelpyngdon'	Kirkwhelpington	NY/996844	1.	11.	10
Hauwyk'	Hawick	NY/963826		10.	0
Blacheddon'	Blackheddon	NZ/080760		18.	8
Blechefeld	Bitchfield	NZ/090770		10.	0
Bradford	Bradford	NZ/067796	1.	5.	1
Denum	Deanham	NZ/033834		17.	4
Shafthou	Shafthoe[1]	NZ/045814		15.	0
Heton' Magna	Capheaton	NZ/032803	1.	3.	6
Stanfordham	Stamfordham	NZ/077720	1.	15.	0
Haucwell'	Hawkwell	NZ/078717		13.	4
Echelwyk'	Eachwick	NZ/117711		16.	0
Dalton'	Dalton	NZ/112720		7.	0
Matfen[2]	Matfen [East]	NZ/040713		19.	3
Hirlau	Harlow Hill	NZ/079683	1.	13.	4
Horsleye	Horsley	NZ/094660	1.	6.	8
Eltryngham	Eltringham	NZ/073627		9.	11
Whittill'	Whittle	NZ/075654		3.	8
Naffreton'	Nafferton	NZ/056654		9.	9
Berhill'	Bearl	NZ/055641		8.	8
Acom	Acomb	NY/932664		9.	4
Bywell'	Bywell	NZ/048614	1.	12.	11
Thornburgh'	Thornbrough	NZ/009644	1.	3.	7
Micleye	Mickley	NZ/075621		10.	6
Neuton'	Newton	NZ/033644	1.	0.	3
Whittynton' Magna	Great Whittington	NZ/004708		13.	5
Halton'	Halton	NY/998678	1.	6.	6
Whittynton' Parva	Little Whittington	NY/990695		5.	7
Whitchestr'	Whitchester	NZ/100683		12.	10½
Hidwyn	West Heddon	NZ/125688		11.	5¼
Hedon' super Murum'	Heddon on the Wall	NZ/134669	1.	2.	3¼

[1] Grid ref. is to West Shafthoe.

[2] This entry refers to East Matfen, as West Matfen is specifically named and separately taxed (p. 221).

			£	s.	d.	
Aydene	Aydon	NZ/008660	1.	1.	4	
Hedleye	Hedley on the Hill	NZ/080592		19.	5	
Hyndley	Hindley	NZ/050591		11.	9	
Bromley	Broomley	NZ/038600		12.	5	
Bromhalgh'	Broomhaugh	NZ/018613	2.	1.	7¼	
Rouchestr'	Rudchester	NZ/113674		7.	7	
Dyuelston'	Dilston	NY/976633	1.	16.	11	
Ovyngham	Ovingham	NZ/085637		8.	0	
Ovyngton'	Ovington	NZ/063639		19.	8	
Shotley	Shotley	NZ/088527		18.	4	
Stauley	Slaley	NY/973577	1.	10.	0	
Cromclyf'	Cronkley	NZ/020524		10.	0	
Stifford	Styford	NZ/018621		13.	4	
Youhou	Ingoe	NZ/038748	1.	6.	10	
Belsshou	Belsay	NZ/085785	1.	1.	3	
Faldreley	Fotherley	NZ/020572		3.	9	
Swynburn' West'	Great Swinburn	NY/935754		10.	0	
Fenwyk'	Fenwick	NZ/057730	1.	0.	0	
Whittonstall'	Whittonstall	NZ/072572		11.	3	
Matfen West	Matfen	NZ/031717	2.	0.	3	
Correbrigg' [B]	Corbridge	NY/988644	9.	0.	0	[T]
Hirbotill'	Harbottle	NT/933046	1.	6.	2	
Lynsheles	Linsheeles	NT/892062		12.	10	
Ellesden'	Elsdon	NY/937934		13.	8	
Oterburn'	Otterburn	NY/885931	6.	4.	0	
Chesterhop'	Chesterhope	NY/900852	1.	2.	6	
Wodeburn'	Woodburn[1]	NY/893868	2.	6.	6	
Trouwhen	Troughend	NY/866924	1.	0.	8	
			97.	8.	6¼	

Warda de Int' ['INTER' WARD]

			£	s.	d.
Morpath'	Morpeth	NZ/198860	3.	0.	3¾
Mitford	Mitford	NZ/169856	1.	4.	1½
Mollesdon'	Molesden	NZ/149843		6.	8
Schilynton'	Shilvington	NZ/158809	1.	7.	0
Twisill'	Twizzle	NZ/159788		16.	2
Oggle	Ogle	NZ/140790		13.	7
Caluerton' Valence	High Callerton	NZ/161705		12.	4
Pont Eland	Ponteland	NZ/166730	1.	0.	9
Creclau	Kirkley	NZ/150772	{	16.	5
			1.	7.	0
Berwyk'	Berwick Hill	NZ/175755	1.	7.	11
Distington' de Lavall'	South Dissington	NZ/122701		12.	0
Neuham	Newham	NZ/110764		9.	0
Meldon'	Meldon	NZ/119838		13.	4
Merdesfen'	Mason	NZ/209735	1.	6.	8
Bruclau	Brenkley	NZ/219751	1.	0.	0
Neuburn'	Newburn	NZ/167654	4.	15.	0
Blackauerdon'	Black Callerton	NZ/174698		13.	0
Prestwyk'	Prestwick	NZ/183724	1.	3.	5
Caliddon Parva	probably Little Callerton	NZ/158722		13.	4
Milburn'	Milbourne	NZ/118751		10.	7
Heton'	Heaton	NZ/268654		13.	4
Benton' Parva	Little Benton	NZ/280676		8.	8

[1] Grid ref. is to West Woodburn.

Benton' Magna	Longbenton	NZ/277690	1.	6.	8
Byker	Byker	NZ/273639		15.	8
Walker	Walker	NZ/292643		6.	8
Killyngworth'	Killingworth	NZ/283708		17.	0
Burnton' West'	West Brunton	NZ/219709		7.	8
Clyfton'	Clifton	NZ/203827		13.	4
Gosford	Gosforth	NZ/243681		16.	0
Cramlynton'	Cramlington	NZ/267769		19.	2½
Wetslad	Weetslade	NZ/260725	1.	3.	0
Shotton'	Shotton	NZ/223780		13.	4
Blacden'	Blagdon	NZ/215772		13.	4
Stanynton'	Stannington	NZ/210794		16.	0
Dudden'	Duddo	NZ/185797		11.	8
Saltwyk'	Saltwick	NZ/172800		10.	1
Middilton' South'	South Middleton	NZ/050834	1.	8.	3
Angreton'	Angerton	NZ/094851	2.	0.	3
Wotton'	Longwitton	NZ/080886	1.	0.	0
Middelton' North'	Middleton	NZ/060850	1.	13.	4
Rotheley	Rothley	NZ/044880		13.	6
Camhou	Cambo	NZ/027857		18.	7
Walyngton'	Wallington	NZ/028842		11.	0
Neuton' Undrewod	Newton Underwood	NZ/148860		11.	6
Stanton'	Stanton	NZ/131899	1.	3.	0
Horsley North'	Longhorsley	NZ/146946	2.	0.	0
Hertwayton'	Hartington	NZ/025885	1.	7.	0
Thornton'	Thornton	NZ/097866		11.	9
Bolom	Bolam	NZ/092827		17.	2
Wyndgatis	Wingates	NZ/099951		17.	0
Lythdon'	Greenleighton	NZ/025920		14.	1
Werkworth'	Warkworth	NU/247062		16.	10
Aclynton'	Acklington	NU/227018	1.	8.	1
Haddiston'	Hadston	NU/257003	1.	10.	4
Thrastreston'	Thirston	NU/185002	1.	10.	0
Morwyk'	Morwick	NU/233040		10.	0
Chevynton' Est	East Chevington	NZ/250998	1.	11.	0
Chevynton' West	West Chevington	NZ/228973	1.	0.	0
Wydryngton'	Widdrington	NZ/253955	1.	6.	8
Bokenfeld	Bockenfield	NZ/179978	1.	1.	0
Whalton'	Whalton	NZ/131813		17.	0
Tyrtlynton'	Tritlington	NZ/205925	1.	3.	1
Whitworth'[1]	lost		1.	5.	0
Hepscot'	Hepscott	NZ/223842		13.	4
Heburn'	Hebron	NZ/194898		18.	4
Peggesworth'	Pegswood	NZ/226875		15.	0
Thorppill'	Throphill	NZ/130858	1.	5.	0
Fenrother	Fenrother	NZ/177920		13.	4
Langhirst'	Longhirst	NZ/225888		17.	0
Wodhorn	Woodhorn	NZ/301888	1.	17.	3
Elynton'	Ellington	NZ/275917	1.	7.	0
Thogeden'	Togston	NU/250027		10.	0
Seton' Wodhorn	probably North Seaton	NZ/296866	1.	10.	0
Aldmore	Old Moor	NZ/246897		11.	1
Wytton'	Nether Witton	NZ/100904	1.	13.	4
Neubigg'	Newbiggin by the Sea	NZ/310876	5.	16.	3
Haliwell'	Holywell	NZ/315744		17.	4
Burton Est'	East Brunton	NZ/235705		15.	9

[1] A lost member of Bothal. The quota may include an amount for Bothal (NZ/240866) which is not mentioned in the subsidy.

Esshenden'	Ashington	NZ/270876		3.	4
Kynton'	Kenton	NZ/219676	1.	1.	7
Denton'	Denton	NZ/200654		19.	8
Benwell'	Benwell	NZ/218640		19.	0
Horton'	Horton[1]	NZ/279797		17.	8
Gosford South'	South Gosforth	NZ/256682		5.	2
Pycden'	Pigdon	NZ/155882		10.	0
Benrygg'	Benridge	NZ/166872		10.	0
Ulgham	Ulgham	NZ/234924	1.	7.	8
Hertlau	Hartley	NZ/342757	2.	11.	2
Seton' de Lavall'	Seaton Delaval	NZ/320763	1.	13.	4
Copton'	probably Cowpen	NZ/290818		5.	10
Neusom	Newsham	NZ/305790		5.	5½
Donyngton'	Dinnington	NZ/208732		8.	0
De libertate de Tynmouth'	Tynemouth [liberty]		16.	0.	0
			114.	3.	6¼

Ward de Cocdall' [COQUETDALE WARD]

Alnwyk'	Alnwick	NU/184135	3.	0.	0
Felton'	Felton	NU/178001	1.	0.	0
Framlynton'	Longframlington	NU/130010	1.	6.	4
Swarland	Swarland	NU/162018		11.	0
Acton'	Acton	NU/190028		5.	0
Haysand	Hazon	NU/193045		16.	5
Gysens	Guyzance	NU/211039		8.	7
Botleston' Superior	High Buston	NU/231087		6.	4
Botleston' Inferior	Low Buston	NU/224074		7.	8
Shilbotill'	Shilbottle	NU/196087		16.	4
Bilton'	Bilton	NU/227108		10.	0
Woldon'	Wooden	NU/235096		8.	0
Alenham	Alnham	NT/991110	1.	0.	3
Whittincham	Whittingham	NU/066120	1.	6.	8
Tronnton'	Thrunton	NU/089109		17.	4
Glanton'	Glanton	NU/071144		14.	5
Shauden'	Shawdon	NU/095144		6.	6
Tytlingt'	Titlington	NU/100152	1.	2.	0
Albrewyk'	Abberwick	NU/128132		13.	4
Lemocton'	Lemmington	NU/120110		12.	0
Edlyngcham	Edlingham	NU/114092	1.	2.	9
Esslyngton'	Eslington	NU/040120	1.	0.	0
Calouley	Callaly	NU/052095	2.	0.	2
Lourbotill'	Lorbottle	NU/041080	1.	0.	0
Yetlynton'	Yetlington	NU/024099	1.	12.	8
Ryhill Parva	Little Ryle	NU/020111		7.	10
Ryhill Magna	Great Ryle	NU/020126		10.	1
Prendwyk'	Prendwick	NU/003123		8.	0
Scranwod	Scrainwood	NT/990096		16.	0
Neddreton'	Netherton	NT/988076		12.	4
Boroudon'	Burradon	NT/983062		6.	8
Bidlesden'	Biddlestone	NT/955083		13.	0
Clenhill'	Clennell	NT/929071		13.	4
Alwenton'	Alwinton	NT/920064	1.	7.	4
Sharbreton'	Sharperton	NT/958040		10.	0

---

[1] Grid ref. is to Low Horton.

			£	s.	d.
Thirnam	Farnham	NT/967026		14.	0
Heppall'	Hepple	NT/985006		16.	5
Bykerton'	Bickerton	NT/996002		7.	10
Tossan	Tosson	NU/029005	1.	0.	0
Fletwayton'	Flotterton	NU/001024		13.	5
Warton'	Warton	NU/007028		10.	8
Tirwhit'	Trewhitt	NU/003065		13.	
Cartington'[1]	Cartington	NU/038045		4.	9
Routhbr'	Rothbury	NU/058016	1.	0.	0
Neuton'	Newton	NU/035010		10.	0
Tropton'	Thropton	NU/028022		10.	0
Snittir	Snitter	NU/024035	1.	0.	0
Catton'	Chatton	NU/056284	1.	10.	0
Cheuelyngham	Chillingham	NU/062259	1.	10.	0
Higley	Hedgeley	NU/061177		12.	10
Benley	Beanley	NU/080183		6.	9
Bremton'	Branton	NU/046163	1.	2.	0
Bromdon'	Brandon	NU/041171		12.	0
Angreham	Ingram	NU/019163		16.	8
Rosseden'	Roseden	NU/030125		16.	0
Weperden'	Wooperton	NU/040203		6.	8
Ildreton'	Ilderton	NU/017218	1.	1.	0
Middelton'	South Middleton	NT/998233		5.	1
Folbiry	Fowberry	NU/038293		10.	0
Glantley	Glantlees	NU/140054		5.	0
Overgares	Overgrass	NU/150038		6.	8
Lilburn'	Lilburn	NU/022243	1.	10.	0
Henry de Percy			3.	3.	4
			52.	2.	5

Ward de Glend' [GLENDALE WARD]

			£	s.	d.
Wollou'	Wooler	NT/993280	2.	10.	0
Eworth'	Ewart	NT/964315	1.	15.	5
Homyldon'	Humbleton	NT/976284	1.	4.	8
Ackyld	Akeld	NT/958296	1.	1.	8
Ford	Ford	NT/945374		12.	9
Croucom	Crookham	NT/917382		7.	3
Hedreslawe	Heatherslaw	NT/933381		19.	0
Middelton'	probably North Middleton	NT/990255		10.	0
Doddyngton'	Doddington	NT/997322	2.	2.	4
Wetwod	Weetwood	NU/017297		10.	0
Horton'	Horton	NU/028308	1.	0.	0
Hetpoll'	Hethpool	NT/895285		16.	0
Lyham	Lyham	NU/069310		10.	8
Heselrygg'	Hazlerigg[2]	NU/050336		10.	0
Houburn'	Holburn	NU/041361		10.	4
Bydnall'	Beadnell	NU/230293		15.	0
Ulcestr'	Outchester	NU/140333		12.	8
Loucre	Lucker	NU/152302		16.	4
Belford	Belford	NU/108340	1.	10.	0
Middelton'	Middleton	NU/094355		13.	4
Ellewyk'	Elwick	NU/115369		8.	0

---

[1] Part of Cartington was taxed in Embleton liberty (p. 226).
[2] Grid ref. is to South Hazlerigg.

			£	s.	d.
Faloudon'	Fallodon	NU/205235		6.	8
Mulsen'	Mousen	NU/117314		8.	0
Alemouth'	Alnmouth	NU/247105		5.	0
Hoghton' Magna	Longhoughton	NU/243151	1.	0.	1
Houghton' Parva	Little Houghton	NU/231164		12.	0
Lestebiry	Lesbury	NU/236116	1.	0.	0
Houwyk'	Howick	NU/248174	1.	2.	8
Denwyk'	Denwick	NU/205143		15.	2
Renyngton'	Rennington	NU/213185		15.	4
Rok'	Rock	NU/202203		15.	0
Hauchill'	Hawkhill	NU/224126		12.	8
Charleton' South'	South Charlton	NU/164203		15.	8
Charleton' North'	North Charlton	NU/169229	1.	0.	8
Dycheburn'	Ditchburn	NU/140213		14.	4
Burnton'	Brunton	NU/208248		13.	4
Doxford	Doxford	NU/182233		10.	4
Ellyncham	Ellingham	NU/175256		11.	4
Preston'	Preston	NU/185254		9.	0
Neuham	Newham	NU/174284		14.	0
Botill'	Budle	NU/156350		10.	0
Spindelstan'	Spindlestone	NU/151332		19.	0
Unthank'	?			6.	8
Bollesdon'	Bowsden	NT/992417		16.	0
Lowyk	Lowick	NU/012397	1.	6.	4
Bairmor'	Barrmoor	NT/997398		10.	0
Yeuer	Yeavering[1]	NT/923304		5.	0
Werk'	Wark	NT/826385	1.	0.	0
Leuermouth'	Learmouth[2]	NT/862375	1.	8.	0
Coupland	Coupland	NT/936310		10.	4
Heddon'[3]	identification uncertain			5.	0
Shotton'	Shotton	NT/842303		9.	8
Langton'	Lanton	NT/926312	1.	0.	8
Neuton'	Kirknewton	NT/913302		6.	8
Dennom	Downham	NT/865340		8.	8
Killom	Kilham	NT/884324	1.	2.	8
Holtall'	Howtel	NT/898340		12.	0
Myndrom	Mindrum	NT/841327	1.	2.	0
Presfen'	Pressen	NT/835358		10.	0
Etall'	Etal	NT/929394		17.	0
Heddon'[3]	identification uncertain			6.	8
Palxton'	Pawston	NT/854327		10.	0
Branston'	Branxton	NT/894376		16.	4
			48.	15.	4

Ward de Baumburgh' [BAMBURGH WARD]

			£	s.	d.	
Baumburgh' [B]	Bamburgh	NU/178350	5.	0.	0	[T]
Shoston' [A.D]	Shoreston	NU/203324	1.	14.	0	[T]
Sondreland [A.D]	North Sunderland	NU/212314	2.	0.	0	[T]
Neuton'	Newton	NU/231249		4.	0	
Eddreston'	Adderstone	NU/135302		10.	0	
Dychand	Detchant	NU/087364		10.	4	

[1] Grid ref. is to Old Yeavering.
[2] Grid ref. is to East Learmouth.
[3] As there are two entries for *Heddon* in this ward it is not certain to which places they refer. Both quotas are small. They probably refer to the Hettons (NU/c.040334).

Tuggall'	Tughall	NU/217167	1.	0.	0
Swynhou	Swinhoe	NU/210283		15.	1
Osbrewyk'	Osburwick [=Newstead]	NU/152272		4.	10
			11.	18.	3

Lib. Emeldon' [EMBLETON LIBERTY]

Emeldon'	Embleton	NU/230224	1.	13.	4
Stanford	Stamford	NU/223193	1.	5.	8
Donstan	Dunstan	NU/248197		7.	0
Neuton' super Mare	Newton by the Sea	NU/234250	1.	7.	4
Hilburn'	probably Hepburn (Hebburn)	NU/068245		6.	8
Yerdle	Earle	NT/987262		6.	0
Crancestr'	Craster	NU/258198		13.	0
Neton' super Mora	Newton on the Moor	NU/170053		3.	4
Burton'	Burton	NU/180330		16.	4
Shepley	Shipley	NU/148169		12.	0
Med' Cartyngton'[1]	Cartington [half of]	NU/038045		3.	0
Warnham	Warenton	NU/107304		6.	8
Fenton'	Fenton	NT/970337	1.	0.	4
			9.	0.	8

TOTAL: £333. 7. 8½[2]

NEWCASTLE: £133. 6. 8[3]

---

[1] Partly taxed in Coquetdale ward (p. 224).

[2] As the 1336 Particulars of Account, E 179/158/8. The figures for the wards add up to £333. 8. 8½.

[3] Newcastle fined for 200 marks for the tenth instead of reassessment at every grant (*C.P.R., 1334–1338*, 397). See also Willard (1934), op. cit. 136.

NOTTINGHAMSHIRE

DOCUMENTS

8 Edward III: Account   E 179/159/6
8 Edward III: Particulars not extant
10 Edward III: Particulars E 179/159/7
10 Edward III: Particulars E 179/159/8*

TAXERS

The prior of Shelford and William de Lound

TAX YIELD

15th	£607.	9.	11¾
10th	£ 98.	12.	3½
	£706.	2.	3¼

Representing assessed movable wealth of

£10,098. 12.   7¼

NOTES

Places taxed at a tenth (the boroughs of Nottingham and Retford and twenty ancient demesnes) are listed at the end of the rolls. Newark on Trent was not considered a taxation borough and was taxed at a fifteenth.

The outline of the county in 1334 seems to have been much the same as that of the modern county. Part of Misson was taxed at a tenth in Lincolnshire. Part of Auckley, now in the West Riding, was taxed with Finningley in Nottinghamshire.

Wap. Bersetlowe [BASSETLAW WAPENTAKE]

Claworth'	Clayworth	SK/726884	5.	8.	7¾
Wiston'	Wiseton	SK/717897	2.	5.	0¼
Bole super Trent	Bole	SK/792871	3.	8.	7½
Hapelstorp'	Habblesthorpe	SK/785820	1.	16.	10¼
Suth' Leverton cum	South Leverton with	SK/783811	5.	19.	10
Cotu'¹	Cottam	SK/819801			
Clareburgh'	Clarborough	SK/735833	1.	14.	4
Herewell'	Harwell	SK/685915		7.	1½
Walkringham	Walkeringham	SK/770923	6.	13.	4½
Misterton' cum	Misterton with	SK/764948	6.	18.	9
Stokheth	West Stockwith	SK/790948			
Bekyngham	Beckingham	SK/779903	4.	6.	8
Hayton' cum	Hayton with	SK/727842	2.	12.	0
Tylne	Tiln	SK/703842			
Wellu' cum	Welham with	SK/727919	3.	11.	1
Mora &	Moorgate and	SK/710824			
Bola'	Bolham	SK/705825			

¹ Part of Cottam was taxed with Ragnall, below.

Stretton' cum	Sturton Le Steeple with	SK/789839	6.	1.	10
Fenton'	Fenton	SK/793830			
North' Leverton' cum	North Leverton with	SK/787822	2.	4.	6
Cotes	Coates	SK/820813			
Lyttelburgh'	Littleborough	SK/824826		17.	3¾
Grenley	Little Gringley	SK/733811		17.	0
Everton'	Everton	SK/691913	2.	15.	8¼
Scafteworth'	Scaftworth	SK/664917	2.	1.	6
Lanu'	Laneham	SK/807763	4.	8.	9
Egmanton'	Egmanton	SK/736689	1.	18.	8½
Grove	Grove	SK/738795	1.	14.	1
Dunham	Dunham	SK/815745	4.	15.	10
Estmarkham	East Markham	SK/743727	4.	7.	1¾
Estdrayton'	East Drayton	SK/776753	2.	15.	0
Wympton'	Whimpton	SK/795740	2.	5.	0
Stocum	Stokeham	SK/782769	1.	8.	0
Ragenhill[1] &	Ragnall and	SK/802737	1.	8.	0
Cotu'[2]	Cottam	SK/819801			
Gamelston'	Gamston	SK/709760	2.	3.	11
Askham	Askham	SK/740750	2.	5.	0
Rampton'	Rampton	SK/799786	5.	7.	5
Tyreswell'	Treswell	SK/782793	4.	6.	10
Ordesale cum	Ordsall with	SK/704796	1.	11.	0
Thurmeton'	Thrumpton	SK/702800			
Westdrayton'	West Drayton	SK/711747		10.	9
Tuxford	Tuxford	SK/737711	5.	2.	0
Parva Marckham &	West Markham and	SK/722727			
Milneton'	Milton	SK/715730			
Kyrketon'	Kirton	SK/692693	1.	8.	3¼
Byldesthorp'	Bilsthorpe	SK/654603		10.	6
Hedon'	Headon	SK/748771	2.	5.	6¾
Laxton' cum	Laxton with	SK/722670	5.	1.	4½
Morehous	Moorhouse	SK/753667			
Upton'	Upton	SK/745763	2.	2.	9
Eykering'	Eakring	SK/675622	2.	16.	10
Welhagh'	Wellow	SK/671661	2.	12.	8
Almeton'	Ompton	SK/688653		11.	10
Bughton'	Boughton	SK/678685		14.	4
Clumber[3]	Clumber	SK/627747		9.	3½
Walesby	Walesby	SK/685708	1.	9.	11½
Blyd	Blyth	SK/623872	6.	11.	3¼
Styrop' &	Styrrup with	SK/609906	2.	3.	6
Oulecotes	Oldcoates	SK/587887			
Harworth'	Harworth	SK/613916	3.	12.	7
Hesele	Hesley	SK/618957			
Marton' &	Martin and	SK/635941			
Plumtr'	Plumtree	SK/632922			
Rauenskelf'	Ranskill	SK/657878	1.	12.	11¼
Fynnygley &	Finningley and	SK/669991		13.	8½
Alkeley[4]	Auckley [in	SE/650012			
	Yorkshire W.R.]				
Scroby	Scrooby	SK/652908	2.	2.	7
Mathersay &	Mattersey and	SK/690893	2.	4.	4
Thorp'	Mattersey Thorpe	SK/683898			

[1] Part of Ragnall was taxed at a tenth (p. 233).

[2] Part of Cottam was taxed with South Leverton, above.

[3] Part of Clumber was taxed at a tenth (p. 233).

[4] Part of Auckley was taxed with Blaxton in Yorkshire, West Riding (Strafforth wapentake, p. 392).

Bylby	Bilby	SK/638831	1.	5.	6
Peuerlethorp'	Perlethorpe	SK/645710		16.	9¾
Allerton'	Ollerton	SK/654674	2.	3.	4¼
Raneby	Ranby	SK/651807	1.	2.	4
Eton'	Eaton	SK/710780	3.	0.	9
Carleton' in Lyndrick'	Carlton in Lindrick	SK/589839	3.	7.	7¼
Warsop'[1]	Warsop	SK/568678	5.	12.	0¼
Hodesak' cum soca	Hodsock [with soke]	SK/612853	4.	6.	5¼
Serleby cum	Serlby with	SK/635895	1.	15.	10
Torworth'	Torworth	SK/658867			
Barneby	Barnby Moor	SK/663844	1.	2.	1
Bothumsell' cum	Bothamsall with	SK/675733	1.	12.	8
Normanton'	Normanton	SK/650747			
Bevercotes	Bevercotes	SK/700725	1.	3.	9½
Elkesley	Elkesley	SK/689755	1.	16.	0
Osberton'	Osberton	SK/624800	1.	11.	8
Cokenay c.m	Cuckney [with members]	SK/566714	4.	7.	3
Hoghton'	Haughton	SK/692730		17.	0½
Westretford	West Retford	SK/702813	2.	2.	7
Babworth' cum	Babworth with	SK/686808	2.	1.	0
Morton'	Morton	SK/676801			
Sutton'	Sutton	SK/681850	3.	9.	1
Lounde	Lound	SK/691859	2.	3.	0
Saundeby	Saundby	SK/785880	2.	4.	8
Burton' super Trent	West Burton	SK/798855	3.	2.	6
North' Wettelay	North Wheatley	SK/762859	5.	6.	9
Suth Wettelay	South Wheatley	SK/766855	2.	9.	10¾
Grymeston'	Grimston	SK/682658	1.	0.	6
Misen[2]	Misson	SK/691949		18.	9¼
Wyrsop' c.m	Worksop [with members]	SK/585794	7.	14.	7¾
			214.	6.	5

Wap. Brokestowe [BROXTOW WAPENTAKE]

Sutton' Passeis	Sutton Passeys[3]	lost		14.	0
Kymmerlay	Kimberley	SK/500447		11.	2
Cossale	Cossall	SK/484423		12.	6
Toueton'	Toton	SK/504343	1.	15.	6¼
Esttwayt	Eastwood	SK/466470	1.	0.	6
Bramcot'	Bramcote	SK/508378	1.	0.	6
Aldesworth'	Awsworth	SK/482441		9.	8
Wolaton'	Wollaton	SK/525398	2.	5.	0
Gresley	Greasley	SK/489472	2.	11.	2
Teveresholt	Teversal	SK/483619	1.	11.	4½
Lenton'	Lenton	SK/555393	3.	7.	0
Radeford &	Radford and	SK/545405			
Kyketon'	Keighton	SK/542382			
Chilwell'	Chilwell	SK/520358	5.	4.	8
Selston'	Selston	SK/459533	2.	18.	0

[1] Part of Warsop was taxed at a tenth (p. 233).

[2] Part of Misson was taxed at a tenth in Lincolnshire (p. 185).

[3] According to *E.P.N.S., XVII, Notts.* (1940), 154, Sutton Passeys was in the present Wollaton Park, south-east of Wollaton village (SK/*c.*530390).

Bylburgh'	Bilborough	SK/520419		19.	9½
Strelley	Strelley	SK/507422	2.	1.	8
Kyrkeby in Assheffeld	Kirkby in Ashfield	SK/490562	3.	8.	3
Baseford cum Algarthorp'	Basford with Algarthorpe	SK/539435 SK/555425	3.	6.	0
Brynnesley	Brinsley	SK/461492		13.	6
Neuthorp'	Newthorpe	SK/482463		15.	0
Watenowe	Watnall[1]	SK/500461	1.	10.	0
Nothale	Nuthall	SK/514445		10.	8½
Papelwyk'	Papplewick	SK/546515		12.	0
Stapilford	Stapleford	SK/488373	1.	5.	8
Brokestowe	Broxtow	SK/527427		9.	3¼
Annesley	Annesley	SK/504524	1.	8.	3¾
Trowell'	Trowell	SK/483397	3.	6.	4
Hokenal Torkard	Hucknall Torkard	SK/533494	1.	6.	0
Beston'	Beeston	SK/527366	5.	5.	5¼
			50.	19.	0

Wap. Rysclif' [RUSHCLIFFE WAPENTAKE]

Rotington'	Ruddington	SK/573332	3.	5.	0
Barton'	Barton in Fabis	SK/522328	3.	15.	0
Radcleve super sora	Ratcliffe on Soar	SK/495289	1.	13.	0
Thurmeton'	Thrumpton	SK/510312	1.	19.	4
Gotham	Gotham	SK/536301	1.	12.	0¼
Brademere	Bradmore	SK/583312	1.	17.	10
Sutton' cum Bonyngton'	now Sutton Bonington[2]	SK/504254	1.	12.	8
Stanford	Stanford on Soar	SK/543221	2.	4.	8
Normanton' super sora	Normanton on Soar	SK/519229	4.	1.	2
Cortelyngestok	Costock	SK/575264	1.	4.	0
Clifton' iuxta Notingh'	Clifton	SK/541349	2.	15.	4
Wydmerpoll'	Widmerpool	SK/629282	2.	4.	2
Wysowe	Wysall	SK/604272	1.	14.	0
Esterleyk	East Leake	SK/552262	3.	11.	8
Thorp in Glebus	Thorpe in the Glebe	SK/607258	1.	6.	6
Westerleyk	West Leake	SK/527264	2.	1.	4
Remeston'	Rempstone	SK/575245	1.	18.	4
Boneye	Bunny	SK/583296	2.	5.	7
Wylleford	Wilford	SK/567378	1.	5.	0
Kynston'	Kingston on Soar	SK/501278	2.	7.	6
Stannston' super le Wold	Stanton on the Wolds	SK/632306	1.	11.	4¾
Keworth'	Keyworth	SK/613308	2.	7.	0
Normanton' iuxta Plumtre	Normanton on the Wolds	SK/621331		7.	0
Plumtre	Plumtree	SK/615331	1.	8.	4
Edwalton'	Edwalton	SK/599350	1.	14.	10
Briggeford ad pontem	West Bridgford	SK/582376	1.	10.	8
Wylghby	Willoughby on the Wolds	SK/633254	3.	1.	5¼
			56.	14.	9¼

---

[1] Grid ref. is to Watnall Chaworth.
[2] Sutton Bonington has been formed from the union of the two separate vills of Bonington and Sutton which lay to the south of Bonington (*E.P.N.S.*, *XVII*, *Notts.* (1940), 256).

Wap. Thurgarton' & Lyth' [THURGARTON AND LYTHE WAPENTAKE]

Hoveringham	Hoveringham	SK/699466	1.	9.	4
Epirston'	Epperstone	SK/651485	1.	13.	4
Suth' Muskham	South Muskham	SK/793573	1.	15.	2
Thurgarton'	Thurgarton	SK/692492	3.	17.	4
Horspoll' &	Horsepool and	SK/706478			
Fyskerton'	Fiskerton	SK/735510			
Halghton'	Halloughton	SK/691518		11.	2½
Wodburgh'	Woodborough	SK/632477	2.	5.	4
North' Carleton'	Carlton on Trent	SK/799640	1.	18.	2
Ossyngton'	Ossington	SK/759652	2.	13.	5
Sutton' super Trenta	Sutton on Trent	SK/798659	2.	12.	1
Gresthorp'	Grassthorpe	SK/795677	3.	4.	4
Marnham	Marnham[1]	SK/807694	3.	3.	4
Averham	Averham	SK/768543	2.	1.	0
Crumbwell'	Cromwell	SK/799615	2.	0.	3½
North' Muskham	North Muskham	SK/798586	2.	12.	5
Kelm	Kelham	SK/773554	1.	10.	11¼
Knesale	Kneesall	SK/704642	1.	3.	0
Fletburgh' cum	Fledborough with	SK/812712	3.	9.	4
Wodcotes	Woodcoates	SK/780715			
Weston' cum	Weston with	SK/773680	2.	9.	0
Skegby [p]	Skegby [part of]	SK/785700			
Wynkburne cum	Winkburn with	SK/712583	3.	15.	8
Hokerton'	Hockerton	SK/716564			
Suthwell'	Southwell	SK/697535	5.	9.	6½
Westhorp'	Westhorpe	SK/687535	3.	17.	1¾
Wodhous &	Holbeck Woodhouse and				
Holbek'	Holbeck				
Blytheworth'	Blidworth	SK/586556	1.	6.	7½
Roldeston' cum	Rolleston with	SK/742525	4.	4.	2
Starthorp'	Staythorpe	SK/753540			
Loudam cum soca	Lowdham [with soke]	SK/662468	5.	19.	0
Byrton'	Burton Joyce	SK/648437	1.	5.	9
Nethercolewyk' &	Colwick and	SK/613401	1.	11.	4
Overcolwyk'	Over Colwick	SK/602390			
Normanton' iuxta	Normanton	SK/708548	1.	2.	0
Suthwell'					
Mapelbek	Maplebeck	SK/711608	2.	13.	7½
Northwell'	Norwell	SK/775618	3.	15.	0
Morton'	Morton	SK/727514	1.	17.	6
Kyrnesale	Kersall	SK/714620	1.	5.	8
Blesby	Bleasby	SK/718495	3.	19.	10
Govirton' &	Goverton and	SK/705500			
Gippesmere	Gibsmere	SK/720489			
Lamlay	Lambley	SK/632454	2.	3.	6¾
Oxton'	Oxton	SK/630514	3.	4.	6
Calneton' cum	Caunton with	SK/745600	1.	11.	8
Knapethorp'	Knapthorpe	SK/741587			
Bulcot'	Bulcote	SK/657447	1.	11.	0¼
Gedlyng'	Gedling	SK/618425	4.	0.	6
Carleton'	Carlton	SK/612415	2.	0.	9¾
Stokbardolf	Stoke Bardolph	SK/647416	1.	16.	10½
Gonaldeston'	Gonalston	SK/682474	1.	5.	7¾
Upton' iuxta Suthwell'	Upton	SK/737543	2.	3.	3½
Snayntton'	Sneinton	SK/581401	1.	1.	5

[1] Grid ref. is to Low Marnham.

Kyrtlyngton'	Kirklington	SK/679576	3.	1.	5¼
Farnesfeld	Farnsfield	SK/646565	1.	19.	5
Calvirton'	Calverton	SK/618492	1.	13.	10¾
Edyngley cum Halum	Edingley with Halam	SK/665558 SK/678543	3.	4.	5¼
			113.	10.	4¼

Wap. Byngham [BINGHAM WAPENTAKE]

Estbriggeford	East Bridgford	SK/691431	3.	3.	11
Screveton'	Screveton	SK/729434	2.	12.	0
Whatton'	Whatton	SK/744397	1.	18.	5¼
Hickelyng'	Hickling	SK/691293	3.	4.	9
Holme	Holme Pierrepont	SK/624393		17.	3
Orston'	Orston	SK/770411	1.	19.	2
Thuruerton'	Thoroton	SK/764425	1.	5.	8½
Kercolton'	Car Colston	SK/721430	2.	19.	10
Neweton'	Newton	SK/685419	1.	5.	6
Elton'	Elton	SK/768388	1.	9.	0
Houkesworth'	Hawksworth	SK/753434	1.	0.	0
Thitheby	Tithby	SK/699369	1.	2.	0½
Knyueton'	Kneeton	SK/710461	1.	12.	10
Clipeston' super le hille	Clipston	SK/635341	1.	10.	0
Colstonbasset	Colston Bassett	SK/695338	4.	4.	8½
Radeclif' super Trent'	Radcliffe on Trent	SK/645393	4.	5.	8
Kynalton'	Kinoulton[1]	SK/662304	1.	14.	0
Adbolton'	Adbolton	SK/600384		8.	6
Gamelston'	Gamston	SK/603372	1.	1.	0
Codgrave	Cotgrave	SK/644353	4.	15.	0
Torlaton'	Tollerton	SK/616347	2.	15.	0
Basyngfeld'	Bassingfield	SK/620373	1.	7.	6
Byngham	Bingham[2]	SK/715398	4.	16.	8
Boghton'	?			7.	6
Skeryngton'	Scarrington	SK/735415		16.	0
Saxendale	Saxondale	SK/683397		18.	6
Langar & Berneston'	Langar and Barnstone	SK/722346 SK/736356	4.	1.	5
Aslakton'	Aslockton	SK/743402	1.	11.	11½
Crophill Botiler	Cropwell Butler	SK/685370	1.	18.	0½
Crophill Bisshop'	Cropwell Bishop	SK/685355	1.	8.	8
Flyntham	Flintham	SK/739461	3.	0.	8¼
Wyverton'	Wiverton	SK/715365	1.	6.	8
Granby cum Sutton'	Granby with Sutton	SK/752361 SK/762374	2.	13.	0
Broghton'	Upper Broughton	SK/683263	1.	4.	8
Shelford	Shelford	SK/662423	4.	5.	3
Outhorp'	Owthorpe	SK/672334	1.	11.	4
			76.	12.	2

[1] Grid ref. is to the site of Old Kinoulton. The present Kinoulton village is one mile to the east at 676306.

[2] Grid ref. is to the early site of Bingham.

Wap. Newerk' [NEWARK WAPENTAKE]

Stok' iuxta Neuwerk'	East Stoke	SK/748500	3.	2.	7
Averton'	Alverton	SK/793422	1.	2.	0
Kylvyngton'	Kilvington	SK/801429	1.	6.	0
Staunton'	Staunton in the Vale	SK/805433	1.	12.	0
Flaubergh'	Flawborough	SK/782429	1.	12.	0
Cotington'	Coddington	SK/834545	2.	6.	0
Suthcolyngham	South Collingham	SK/826613	4.	3.	4
Dornthorp'	Danethorpe	SK/842577	1.	9.	6
Landeford	Langford	SK/822591	3.	8.	8
Syreston'	Syerston	SK/746475	1.	9.	4
Spaldeford	Spalford	SK/837692	1.	8.	0
Barneby	Barnby in the Willows	SK/860522	2.	19.	10
Suthscarle	South Scarle	SK/848641	1.	9.	0
Northcolyngham	North Collingham	SK/830620	5.	11.	1
Thornhagh'	Thorney	SK/859728	1.	19.	2
Hertheby	Harby	SK/878705	1.	10.	0
Wiggesley	Wigsley	SK/860702	1.	1.	7
Meryngg' cum	Meering with	SK/812655	1.	0.	7½
Gretton'	Girton	SK/825662			
Northclyfton'	North Clifton	SK/823722	2.	6.	6
Thorp'	Thorpe	SK/768502	1.	3.	0¼
Wynthorp'	Winthorpe	SK/812563	2.	0.	4
Besthorp'	Besthorpe	SK/825647	1.	3.	2
Suthclifton'	South Clifton	SK/822704	3.	1.	4
Northgate	Northgate	SK/c.798541	2.	8.	0¼
Farnedon'	Farndon	SK/768518	3.	5.	10
Balderton'	Balderton	SK/817515	3.	15.	5¼
Newerk'	Newark on Trent	SK/797540	26.	0.	2
Eyleston'	Elston	SK/759480	3.	4.	0
Sybthorp'	Sibthorpe	SK/764454	1.	8.	0
Cotum	Cotham	SK/795476	2.	0.	10
Shelton'	Shelton	SK/781446	1.	12.	0
Houton'	Hawton	SK/788511	3.	7.	11
			95.	7.	3¼

[BOROUGHS AND ANCIENT DEMESNES]

Notingh' [B]	Nottingham	SK/572395	37.	1.	0	[T]
Retford [B]¹	East Retford	SK/709805	10.	13.	10	[T]
Thouresby [A.D]	Thoresby	SK/638712	1.	12.	7	[T]
Scofton' [A.D] &	Scofton and	SK/628803	1.	19.	6	[T]
Reueton' [A.D]	Rayton	SK/613792				
Boteby [A.D]	Budby	SK/619701	1.	4.	1	[T]
Clumber [A.D]²	Clumber	SK/627747		18.	2	[T]
Warsop' [A.D]³ cum	Warsop with	SK/568678	1.	6.	0	[T]
Nettelworth' [A.D]	Nettleworth	SK/549658				
Edenstowe [A.D]	Edwinstowe	SK/625670	4.	3.	7¼	[T]
Carberton' [A.D]	Carburton	SK/611733	2.	15.	4	[T]
Clyppeston' [A.D]	Clipstone	SK/602648	2.	15.	2¾	[T]
Ragenhill' [A.D]²	Ragnall	SK/802737	1.	14.	1	[T]
Derleton' [A.D]	Darlton	SK/779737	2.	15.	4¾	[T]

¹ East Retford was listed as a borough in 1334 (E 179/159/6), but is not described as such on the roll of 1336.

² Partly taxed at a fifteenth (p. 228).

³ Partly taxed at a fifteenth (p. 229).

Grynggeley [A.D]	Gringley on the Hill	SK/736907	4.	5.	0	[T]
Mamesfeld [A.D]	Mansfield	SK/538610	7.	0.	0	[T]
Mamesfeld Wodehouse [A.D]	Mansfield Woodhouse	SK/538632	3.	2.	0	[T]
Lyndeby [A.D]	Linby	SK/534509	2.	15.	11¾	[T]
Bulwell' [A.D]	Bulwell	SK/542450	1.	14.	0	[T]
Arnal [A.D]	Arnold	SK/579459	4.	1.	6	[T]
Sutton' super Asshefeld [A.D]	Sutton in Ashfield	SK/493590	5.	4.	0	[T]
Skekby [A.D]	Skegby	SK/499609	1.	11.	0	[T]
			98.	12.	3½	[T]

TOTAL: £706. 2. 3¼[1]

---

[1] As on 1334 Account, E 179/159/6.

OXFORDSHIRE

DOCUMENTS

8 Edward III: Account   E 179/161/11
9 Edward III: Particulars   not extant
10 Edward III: Particulars   E 179/161/12 (imperfect)
12 Edward III: Particulars   E 179/161/13*
18 Edward III: Particulars   E 179/161/17

TAXERS

The abbot of Osney and Thomas de Londeleye

TAX YIELD

15th	£1,217.	2.	5
10th	£ 186.	6.	1
	£1,403.	8.	6

Representing assessed movable wealth of

£20,119.   17.   1

NOTES

Of the 315 entries on the Oxfordshire list, 276 refer to one place-name, thirty-three to more than one, and six are *cum membris*. Twenty hamlets are specified.

Places taxed at a tenth are listed at the end; they include the three taxation boroughs of Oxford, Henley, and Woodstock. The remainder of the tenth was tax on ancient demesnes, of which Headington and Bloxham had the highest tax quotas. In terms of lay wealth per square mile as recorded in 1334 Oxfordshire was the richest county in England (see map I).

Since 1334 Oxfordshire has lost some territories and gained others. Boycott, Tythrop, Stokenchurch, and Lillingstone Lovell are now in Buckinghamshire. Shenington and Widford have been gained from Gloucestershire, Caversfield and Towersey from Buckinghamshire, Grimsbury from Northamptonshire, and Langford, Shilton, Little Faringdon, and Grandpont from Berkshire.

REFERENCES

W. G. Hoskins and E. M. Jope, 'The medieval period', being chapter 11 in A. F. Martin and R. W. Steel, eds., *The Oxford Region*, 1954.
R. F. Walker, 'Tax assessments of the villages and hamlets of Bullingdon hundred, 1306–1523', in *V.C.H., Oxon.* v (1957), 318–19.
M. D. Lobel, *et al.* Statistical table of village tax assessments, 1306–1523, for Ploughley hundred, in *V.C.H., Oxon.* vi (1959), 358–9.

Hd. Chad' [CHADLINGTON HUNDRED]

Chepyngnorton' (va)	Chipping Norton	SP/312273	14.	14.	4
Hogenorton' (va)	Hook Norton	SP/355331	8.	13.	9
Swereford &	Swerford and	SP/372311	6.	4.	6
Soutcrop'	Southrop	SP/357329			
Enstan	Enstone	SP/379250	1.	4.	2
Nethenstan	Neat Enstone	SP/376244	2.	5.	0
Clevele	Cleveley	SP/392239	1.	13.	0
Radeford	Radford	SP/410239	1.	11.	8
Gadelyngwell'	Gagingwell	SP/408251	2.	7.	8
Shipton'	Shipton under	SP/279180	3.	7.	2
	Wychwood				
Middelton'	Milton under	SP/263182	5.	4.	2
	Wychwood				
Escot' comitis	Ascott Earl	SP/296183	1.	12.	3
Ramusden'	Ramsden	SP/357152	2.	6.	0
Walcote	Walcot	SP/347198		18.	0
Shorthampton'	Shorthampton	SP/329201	2.	4.	6
Swynbroke	Swinbrook	SP/280122	3.	10.	0
Teynton'	Taynton	SP/233135	7.	14.	4
Podelicote c.m[1]	Pudlicote [with members]	SP/313204	4.	5.	5
Cherchehull'	Churchill	SP/283241	10.	13.	5
Asterle &	Asterleigh and	SP/400224	1.	19.	0
Overcudynton'	Over Kiddington	SP/410221			
Idebury c.m[2]	Idbury [with members]	SP/236201	6.	3.	8
Sercheden'	Sarsden	SP/291233	2.	14.	8
La More	Northmoor	SP/422028	6.	16.	11
Munstre'	Minster Lovell	SP/324114	4.	4.	6
Spellesbur'	Spelsbury	SP/349215	7.	7.	2
Turstan	Taston	SP/360220			
Dychele	Ditchley	SP/390211			
Folewell'	Fulwell	SP/378232			
Chadelyngton'	Chadlington Eastend	SP/333220	9.	3.	8
Estend' & Chad	and Westend	SP/326217			
Wahull'					
Lynham	Lyneham	SP/278203	5.	1.	11
Rollendrith' Magna &	Great Rollright and	SP/327315	7.	10.	5
Bradeneston'	Broadstonehill	SP/356264			
La Felde	Leafield	SP/318153	4.	11.	7
Felebroke	Fulbrook	SP/258130	6.	4.	5
Rollendrith' Parva	Little Rollright	SP/293301	1.	5.	11
Cornewell'	Cornwell	SP/274271	1.	12.	4
Kengham	Kingham	SP/258237	5.	14.	4
Astecote Doyly	Ascott D'Oyley	SP/306188	4.	8.	2
Castelton'	Chastleton	SP/249291	4.	9.	4
Dene	Dean	SP/342225	4.	15.	6
Chalford	Chalford	SP/343257			
Lydenestan	Lidstone	SP/356247			
Etthrop'	Heythrop	SP/351277			
Fifehide	Fifield	SP/239188	3.	3.	7
Saltford	Salford	SP/286281	2.	18.	1
			170.	14.	6

---

[1] Sarsden, separately taxed in 1334, was returned with Pudlicote in 1316 (*F.A.* iv. 165).
[2] Foscot was returned with Idbury in 1316, ibid.

Hd. Bampton' [BAMPTON HUNDRED]

			£	s	d
Norton' Brune & Astrop'	Brize Norton and Astrop	SP/300075 SP/306081	5.	14.	0
Bradewell'	Broadwell	SP/251041	4.	7.	9
Kelmescot'	Kelmscott	SU/249992	4.	7.	10
Halewell'	Holwell	SP/232091	4.	10.	0
Fylkyng'	Filkins	SP/238042	4.	8.	7
Westwell'	Westwell	SP/223101	3.	6.	7
Kenecote	Kencott	SP/254048	3.	18.	8
Opton' & Seynat'	Upton and Signet	SP/243125 SP/247102	4.	5.	2
Brughton'	Broughton Poggs	SP/236038	2.	17.	6
Astalle	Asthall	SP/287114	3.	13.	10
Astallynglegh'	Asthall Leigh	SP/307126	1.	6.	2
Craule	Crawley	SP/341120	1.	19.	4
Crutebrugg'	Curbridge	SP/333087	3.	13.	0
Alvecote	Alvescot	SP/273046	7.	4.	2
Roccote & Grafton'	Radcot and Grafton	SP/278000 SP/269007	4.	16.	4
Dokelyngton'	Ducklington	SP/359076	5.	15.	3
Stanlake	Standlake	SP/398036	10.	15.	6
Shiford	Shifford	SP/372019	4.	0.	0
Bourghton'	Black Bourton	SP/287042	8.	6.	2
Bereford	Burford	SP/253124	9.	16.	2
Wytteney	Witney	SP/356092	11.	18.	6
Herdewyk' c.m	Hardwick [with members]	SP/380060	7.	5.	0
Glanefeld	Clanfield	SP/283021	8.	7.	8
Bampton' c.m[1]	Bampton [with members]	SP/312033	64.	12.	1
Hayle	Hailey	SP/354126	5.	11.	5
			196.	16.	8

Hd. Pogh' [PLOUGHLEY HUNDRED][2]

			£	s	d
Lyllyngston'	Lillingstone Lovell [in Bucks.]	SP/712405	3.	13.	5[3]
Boycote	Boycott [in Bucks.]	SP/662372	1.	12.	4
Fynemere	Finmere	SP/636332	5.	3.	0
Myxebur'	Mixbury	SP/609340	1.	13.	8
Wyllaston'	Willaston	SP/602298		15.	0
Ferryngford	Fringford	SP/606292	3.	5.	4
Etthe	Hethe	SP/593294	3.	6.	0
Newenton' Purcel	Newton Purcell	SP/625307	1.	14.	10
Shaldeswell'	Shelswell	SP/605306	1.	9.	8
Cottesford	Cottisford	SP/587311	1.	16.	0
Sulthorn'	Souldern	SP/523317	5.	2.	7
Somerton'	Somerton	SP/497286	5.	12.	0
Fretewell'	Fritwell	SP/524293	5.	6.	6

[1] Members of Bampton in 1316 included Lew, Weald, Aston, Chimney, and Haddon (*F.A.* iv. 162).

[2] Fourteenth-century tax assessments for this hundred are printed in *V.C.H., Oxon.* vi (1959), 358–9.

[3] Assessment wrongly given as £3. 3. 5 on E 179/161/13 (1338/9).

Heyford Waryn	Upper Heyford	SP/495259	4.	15.	4
Heyford ad pontem &	Lower Heyford and	SP/485249	5.	17.	4
Caldecote	Caulcott	SP/508241			
Tosmere	Tusmore	SP/564306	1.	1.	6
Herdwyk'	Hardwick	SP/576296	2.	9.	10
Bockenhull'	Bucknell	SP/561256	5.	0.	6
Medelyngton'	Middleton Stoney	SP/531233	4.	15.	8
Godyngdon'	Godington	SP/642278	2.	17.	4
Wendelebury	Wendlebury	SP/561196	5.	2.	8
Stoke	Stoke Lyne	SP/567283	3.	16.	1
Feucote	Fewcott	SP/539280	1.	0.	6
Baynton'	Bainton	SP/578269	2.	15.	9
Ardele	Ardley	SP/542274	2.	12.	5
Curthynton'	Kirtlington	SP/501195	5.	19.	8
Belgenhull'	Bignell	SP/559221	2.	3.	11
Bircestr' Kyngeshynd	Bicester, King's End	SP/583222	5.	5.	2
Bircestr' Buryend	Bicester, Market End	SP/588223	10.	19.	10
Cherleton'	Charlton on Otmoor	SP/562158	6.	10.	7
Chesterton'	Chesterton	SP/562213	6.	6.	2
Weston'	Weston on the Green	SP/531186	3.	10.	10
Hampton ad pontem	Hampton Poyle	SP/499155	5.	2.	8
medietatis de Oke[1]	and Noke [half of]	SP/544132			
Blechesdon'	Bletchingdon	SP/507181	6.	7.	8
Hampton' Gay	Hampton Gay	SP/486165			
Islep'	Islip	SP/527141	6.	2.	8
Langton'	Launton	SP/604228	6.	2.	1
Mercote &	Murcott and	SP/585157	5.	7.	2
Fencote	Fencott	SP/572160			
Otyngdon'	Oddington	SP/552148	3.	10.	0
Oke[2]	Noke	SP/544132	1.	19.	9
Nothbroke	Northbrook	SP/493220	1.	4.	2
			159.	7.	7[3]

Hd. Piriton' [PYRTON HUNDRED]

Schirebourne	Shirburn	SU/697959	4.	4.	3
Weston' &	South Weston and	SU/701987	2.	17.	3
Waremotescombe	Warmscombe[4]	SU/727873			
Wytefeld	Wheatfield	SU/688993	2.	18.	6
Stok' Thalemache	Stoke Talmage	SU/678992	1.	19.	10
Watelynton'	Watlington	SU/685947	5.	6.	0
Wattecombe [h]	Watcombe Manor	SU/689941	2.	0.	2
Pushull' [h]	Pishill	SU/726898	1.	4.	6
Pyriton'	Pyrton	SU/688957	5.	8.	6
Claiore	Clare	SU/675984	4.	14.	10
Staindelue	Standhill[5]	SP/652003	4.	6.	9
Goldore [h]	Golder	SU/665977	1.	0.	11
			36.	1.	6

[1] For the remainder of Noke see below. [2] above.
[3] On E 179/161/13 (1338/9) the figure of £158. 14. 6 has been inserted in place of £159. 7. 7. The difference of 13s. 1d. is the tax on the Hospital of St. John in Oddington, which, although listed after Oddington and included in the 1334 total, was deleted from later taxations.
[4] The name Warmscombe survives only in Warmscombe Firs and Warmscombe Lane.
[5] Grid ref. is to the site of the deserted village.

Hd. Bolynden' [BULLINGDON HUNDRED][1]

			£	s.	d.
Newenham	Nuneham Courtenay	SU/542981	6.	16.	11
Chibenhurst	Chippinghurst	SP/601012	2.	0.	2
Bruggeset'	Brugeset[2]	lost		8.	8
Yeftele	Iffley	SP/527035	4.	19.	4
Stannton' Sancti Johannis	Stanton St. John	SP/577093	6.	18.	0
Halegton'	Holton	SP/605063	5.	10.	6
Cheleworth' Musard	Chilworth Musard[3]	SP/634038		18.	6
Combe	Coombe[3]	lost	1.	9.	6
Cheleworth' Warlery	Chilworth Valery[3]	SP/615051	1.	15.	2
Forsthulle	Forest Hill	SP/582075	2.	12.	4
Whatele	Wheatley	SP/597058	7.	14.	11
Codeston'	Cuddesdon	SP/601031	4.	10.	2
Denton'	Denton	SP/595025	5.	1.	10
Gersindon'	Garsington	SP/581020	9.	2.	5
Pedyngton'	Piddington	SP/640170	5.	16.	11
Blakethern'	Blackthorn	SP/621194	8.	0.	4
Aumbresdon'	Ambrosden	SP/603194	1.	14.	10
Meriton'	Merton	SP/578178	9.	6.	4
Wodepyrye	Woodperry	SP/575103	2.	4.	6
Arnecote Abbatis & Arnecote Prioris	Lower Arncott and Upper Arncott	SP/610180 SP/612173	2.	13.	6
Wodeton'	Woodeaton	SP/535119	1.	16.	4
Bekeleye	Beckley	SP/562112	1.	6.	7
Horton'	Horton	SP/588127	3.	1.	6
Stodleye	Studley	SP/594124		10.	2
Templecoueleye	Temple Cowley	SP/540045	5.	3.	10
Chirchecouele	Cowley	SP/539038	8.	9.	10
Litelmor	Littlemore	SP/538028	6.	9.	7
Santford	Sandford on Thames	SP/534018	3.	15.	2
Waterpirie	Waterperry	SP/629063	2.	12.	8
Ledhale	Ledall	SP/618080	2.	13.	4
Thomele	Thomley	SP/631090	1.	2.	0
Elsefeld	Elsfield	SP/541101	3.	1.	4
Tedynton'	Tiddington	SP/650052	1.	16.	4
Aldebury	Albury	SP/655051	1.	5.	4
Horspath' Inferior	Horspath	SP/571049	4.	3.	8
Horspath' Superior	Old Horspath	SP/589048	3.	1.	11
Parva Baldon'	Little Baldon	SU/565986	1.	16.	4
Mershbaldon'	Marsh Baldon	SU/561991	2.	18.	8
Baldonlaurence'	Baldon St. Lawrence[4]	SP/568002	1.	1.	6
Totbaldon'	Toot Baldon	SP/567007	1.	0.	4
			147.	1.	3

[1] Fourteenth-century tax assessments for this hundred are printed in *V.C.H., Oxon.* v (1957), 318–19.

[2] Was near Magdalen Bridge in Oxford (*E.P.N.S., XXIII, Oxon.*, part 1 (1953), 20).

[3] All three places are now deserted, probably depopulated by later enclosure. Exact identification of places with sites is difficult. See discussion of the three in K. J. Allison, *et al., The Deserted Villages of Oxfordshire*, Leicester Occasional Papers, No. 17 (1965), 34–5.

[4] Baldon St. Lawrence was a part of Toot Baldon. It is now Baldon Row, where the church is dedicated to St. Lawrence.

Hd. Ewelme [EWELME HUNDRED]

Haseley Magna	Great Haseley	SP/645017	2.	11.	0
Haseley Parva	Little Haseley	SP/642006	3.	2.	2
Lacheford	Latchford	SP/660015	1.	13.	10
Magna Rycote	Rycote	SP/668045	3.	3.	6
Parva Rycote	Rycotelane	SP/662038	1.	19.	6
Draycote [h]	Draycot	SP/648059	1.	6.	0
Brightwell'	Brightwell Baldwin	SU/652950	7.	3.	8
Cadewell'	Cadwell	SU/644957		13.	4
Esyndon'	Easington	SU/662971	1.	1.	10
Werpesgrave	Warpsgrove	SU/651982	1.	14.	4
Coxham [h]	Cuxham	SU/666952	2.	15.	4
Brokhampton'	Brookhampton	SU/603982	2.	1.	10
Holecombe [h]	Holcombe[1]	SU/610968	1.	16.	6
Newynton'	Newington	SU/609965	1.	19.	6
Brutewell' Prioris	Britwell Priory	SU/674934		10.	0
Berewyk'	Berrick Salome	SU/623942	5.	16.	4
Rofford [h]	Rofford	SU/627985	2.	3.	2
Ewelme	Ewelme	SU/647914	6.	7.	2
Chalgrave	Chalgrove	SU/637965	13.	1.	4
Swynecombe [h]	Swyncombe	SU/683902	1.	2.	0
Croumersh Bataill'	Crowmarsh Battle	SU/616902	1.	5.	2
Huntercombe Abbatis	Huntercombe	SU/688877		12.	6
			64.	0.	0

Hd. Benefeld [BINFIELD HUNDRED]

Dunesden'	Dunsden	SU/740771	4.	16.	7
Sheppelake	Shiplake	SU/768783	2.	7.	7
Lachebrok'	Lashbrook	SU/778797	1.	5.	9
Bolehught'	Bolney	SU/777805		18.	6
Harpeden[1]	Harpsden	SU/763809	1.	11.	0
Retherfeld Pypard	Rotherfield Peppard	SU/713815	1.	0.	9
Retherfeld Gay &	Rotherfield Greys and	SU/726823	2.	9.	11
Baggerugg'	Badgemore	SU/747831			
Mapeldorham	Mapledurham (manor of	SU/670767	2.	6.	2
Gornay[2]	Gurney)				
Bixegibewyn &	Bix-Gibwen and	lost	1.	17.	0
Bixebrond	Bix-Brand [parts of	SU/729851			
	Bix][3]				
Caversham	Caversham [in Berkshire]	SU/721746	6.	17.	3
			25.	10.	6

Hd. Lyugnore [LEWKNOR HUNDRED]

Chynnore c.m[4]	Chinnor [with members]	SP/758009	7.	1.	5
Aston'	Aston Rowant	SU/728990	2.	14.	4
Stockenchirch	Stokenchurch [in Bucks.]	SU/761963	3.	16.	4
Chalford	Chalford	SP/719008		18.	11

[1] Grid ref. is to Great Holcombe.
[2] Chazey, the second manor in Mapledurham, was taxed in Langtree hundred.
[3] These separate places in Bix were referred to as late as 1797 (*E.P.N.S.*, *XXIII*, *Oxon.*, part 1 (1953), 66–7).
[4] Members of Chinnor in 1316 included Sydenham, Oakley, and Tythrop (*F.A.* iv. 171).

Copcote [h]	Cop Court	SP/708010	1.	2.	9
Nethercote [h]	Nethercote	SU/710984		9.	9
Kyngeston'	Kingston Blount	SU/740995	2.	16.	7
Leukenore	Lewknor	SU/716976	10.	6.	0
Brutwell'	Britwell	SU/671930	1.	6.	4
Hemmyngton'	Emmington	SP/742024	2.	16.	3
Crouwell'	Crowell	SU/745997	1.	6.	2
Tythrop'	Tythrop [in Bucks.]	SP/740070	1.	13.	6
Henton'	Henton	SP/763023	2.	16.	0
Adewell' [h]	Adwell	SU/696996	1.	10.	6
			40.	14.	10

Hd. Bannebury [BANBURY HUNDRED]

Shetteford	Shutford	SP/387402	3.	12.	4
La Lee [h]	Lea	SP/389385	2.	6.	2
Swalclyve	Swalcliffe	SP/378379	3.	11.	7
Wycham	Wykham	SP/441379	2.	19.	7
Wardynton' &	Wardington and	SP/491463	4.	13.	2
Cotes	Coton	SP/490444			
Cropry	Cropredy	SP/469467	4.	18.	6
Cherlebury	Charlbury	SP/355194	3.	4.	6
Cotes [h]	Coat	SP/355214	1.	7.	6
Faulore [h]	Fawler	SP/372170	2.	7.	8
Fynstoke &	Finstock and	SP/361161	4.	11.	8
Tapwell'	Topples Wood	SP/371165			
Cleydon'	Claydon	SP/457501	2.	15.	3
Prestcote	Prescote	SP/473468	1.	3.	5
Willamscote	Williamscot	SP/480455	2.	5.	0
Magna Burghton'	Great Bourton	SP/457455	1.	8.	4
Parva Burton'	Little Bourton	SP/458441		12.	2
Herdwyk'	Hardwick	SP/459430		6.	0
Netrop' &	Neithrop and	SP/449409	1.	12.	3
Cotrop'	Calthorp	SP/454403			
Banbury [va]	Banbury	SP/455403	17.	15.	6
			61.	10.	7

Hd. Wotton' [WOOTTON HUNDRED]

Newenton'	South Newington	SP/407333	2.	7.	2
Bereford Sancti	Barford St. Michael	SP/432326	4.	4.	2
Michaelis					
Parva Tywe	Little Tew	SP/383285	2.	19.	2
Sewell'	Showell	SP/358291	2.	3.	9
Overorton'	Over Worton	SP/430292	2.	12.	6
Netherorton' &	Nether Worton and	SP/426301	1.	16.	0
Selubury	Ilbury	SP/435310			
Dunstwe	Duns Tew	SP/458284	3.	5.	8
Magna Barton'	Steeple Barton	SP/449249	4.	6.	8
Middel Barton'	Middle Barton	SP/437256	2.	14.	8
Sandford	Sandford St. Martin	SP/420267	3.	7.	9
Leddewell'	Ledwell	SP/419281	2.	6.	6
Parva Barton'	Westcott Barton	SP/431256	1.	9.	9
Grave	Grove Ash	SP/412310	2.	8.	6
Barton' Oede	Sesswell's Barton	SP/453250	2.	3.	7
Roulesham	Rousham	SP/480242	4.	14.	4

Tackle	Tackley	SP/476202	5.	10.	9
Wythull'	Whitehill	SP/476189	2.	7.	8
Dernford	Dornford	SP/450205	2.	6.	10
Glympton'	Glympton	SP/423218	2.	6.	3
Lodewell'	Ludwell	SP/433223		15.	4
Nethercudynton'	Kiddington	SP/411229	1.	12.	3
Stannton' Harecourt'	Stanton Harcourt	SP/417056	8.	2.	8
Sutton' [h] &	Sutton and	SP/416063	5.	19.	9
Pyncle [h]	Pinkhill	SP/437072			
Leghhampstalle	South Leigh and	SP/393090	4.	13.	4
	Armstalls[1]	SP/415084			
Eynesham	Eynsham	SP/433092	3.	9.	4
Eylgarsle[2]	Tilgarsley	lost	4.	14.	10
Carsynton'	Cassington	SP/455106	4.	13.	2
Worton'	Worton	SP/463113	3.	6.	0
Cogges &	Cogges and	SP/361096	4.	13.	4
Weuelcote	Wilcote	SP/371153			
Northlegh'	North Leigh	SP/387137	4.	17.	9
Bokebrok'	Begbroke	SP/469139	2.	9.	4
Erdynton'	Yarnton	SP/478117	3.	8.	4
Wolgarcote	Wolvercote	SP/489096	5.	1.	5
Cudlynton'	Kidlington	SP/497148	7.	9.	6
Trop'	Thrupp	SP/481158	3.	8.	4
Goseford	Gosford	SP/498133	1.	18.	10
Watereton'	Water Eaton	SP/515121	2.	11.	6
Codeslowe	Cutteslowe	SP/508112		8.	0
Schipton'	Shipton on Cherwell	SP/480165	4.	10.	8
Hensynton'	Hensington	SP/449169		13.	10
Stepulaston'	Steeple Aston	SP/476261	2.	5.	0
Middelaston'	Middle Aston	SP/475270	2.	5.	0
Northaston'	North Aston	SP/481289	4.	4.	5
Magna Tywe	Great Tew	SP/399289	10.	6.	5
Dadynton'	Deddington	SP/468317	9.	10.	4
Clyfton' &	Clifton and	SP/490318			
Empton'	Hempton	SP/444318			
			163.	0.	4[3]

Hd. Bloxham [BLOXHAM HUNDRED]

Aberbury	Adderbury[4]	SP/471353	10.	12.	2
Middelton'	Milton	SP/451350	2.	18.	3
Bodycote	Bodicote	SP/459376	2.	13.	0
Hornle &	Horley and	SP/417440	10.	1.	11
Hornton'	Hornton	SP/392450			
Broughton' &	Broughton and	SP/419383	5.	4.	4
Newenton'	North Newington	SP/418398			

[1] Armstalls is a farm on or near the site of Hamstall village.

[2] *Eylgarsle* is a clerical error for *Tylgarsle*. Although the site of the village of Tilgarsley is stated to be on the site of Britannia Inn (SP/405106) (*E.P.N.S.*, *XXIV*, *Oxon.*, part 2 (1954), 260) no trace can be seen on the ground. Allison, op. cit. 44, suggests site is SP/*c.*434092.

[3] Tax charges against the Master of the Hospital of St. John, Oxford, are noted after the entries for South Newington, Nether Worton and Ilbury, and Shipton on Cherwell, and although they are not cancelled the amounts are not included in the total for the hundred.

[4] Grid ref. is to East Adderbury.

Tademarton'	Tadmarton	SP/392378	3.	18.	3
Wroxton'	Wroxton	SP/418418	4.	15.	4
Balscote	Balscott	SP/390417	1.	19.	4
Alcrynton'	Alkerton	SP/378429	1.	16.	2
Wygenton'	Wigginton	SP/391333	2.	15.	8
Middelcombe	Milcombe	SP/411346	2.	14.	11
Bereford Sancti Johannis	Barford St. John	SP/438332	2.	0.	8
Hanewell'	Hanwell	SP/436436	3.	1.	1
Drayton'	Drayton	SP/428416	1.	13.	6
Molynton'[1]	Mollington	SP/442474	2.	8.	2
Sibbeford	Sibford[2]	SP/352378	8.	19.	8
			67.	12.	5

Hd. Dorkcestr' [DORCHESTER HUNDRED]

Dorkcestr'	Dorchester	SU/579942	3.	19.	8
Stoke Abbatis & Wodecote	South Stoke and Woodcote	SU/599836 SU/644821	3.	11.	2
Clifton'	Clifton Hampden	SU/547955	2.	17.	2
Brudecote	Burcot	SU/562960	2.	15.	6
Drayton'	Drayton St. Leonard	SU/596964	2.	1.	3
Stodham	Stadhampton	SU/603988	1.	17.	9
Chyselhampton'	Chislehampton	SU/593990	3.	0.	3
Ippewell'	Epwell[3]	SP/352404	3.	10.	1
			23.	12.	10

Hd. Langetr' [LANGTREE HUNDRED]

Stoke Marmyon & Chakenden'	Littlestoke and Checkendon	SU/600850 SU/663831	2.	14.	0
Stoke Basset & Yppesden'	North Stoke and Ipsden	SU/609862 SU/630852	4.	2.	0
Mongewell' [h]	Mongewell	SU/610878		18.	2
Newenham	Newnham Murren	SU/619889	1.	14.	5
Croumersh	Crowmarsh Gifford	SU/615893	1.	11.	6
Garynges & Gethampton'	Goring and Gatehampton	SU/598807 SU/609798	5.	15.	10
Mapuldorham Chause[4]	Mapledurham (manor of Chazey)	SU/670767	2.	5.	10
Whitchirch'	Whitchurch	SU/635770	3.	13.	9
			22.	15.	6

Hd. Thame [THAME HUNDRED]

Nova Thame[5]	New Thame	SP/706058	9.	2.	8
Tetlesworth'	Tetsworth	SP/687016	3.	19.	3

[1] Part of Mollington was taxed in Warwickshire (Kineton hundred, p. 321).
[2] Grid ref. is to Sibford Gower.
[3] Epwell was a detached part of the hundred in north Oxfordshire.
[4] For Gurney, the second manor in Mapledurham, see Binfield hundred, above, p. 240.
[5] Not taxed as a borough, although New Thame had been developed as a borough in the late twelfth century by the bishops of Lincoln on land south of the old village of Thame (M. W. Beresford, *New Towns of the Middle Ages* (1967), 477–8).

Astcote	Ascott	su/613981	2.	15.	8
Milton' Magna &	Great Milton and	sp/628024	8.	2.	10
Parva	Little Milton	sp/617007			
Waterstok'	Waterstock	sp/635056	3.	2.	4
Vet' Thame	Old Thame	sp/704063	3.	7.	9
Morton' &	Moreton and	sp/696046	4.	18.	11
Attyndon'	Attington	sp/690015			
Weston'	North Weston	sp/681059	2.	14.	6
			38.	3.	11

Burgus Oxon cum suburbio eiusdem
OXFORD (SP/511064) and SUBURBS[1]

Parochia Sancte Crucis &	St. Cross and		8.	3.	2	[T]
Sancti Petri in Oriente	St. Peter's in the East					
Pa. Beate Marie	St. Mary the Virgin		7.	19.	11	[T]
Virginis						
Pa. Omnium Sanctorum	All Saints		10.	18.	5	[T]
Pa. Sancti Johannis &	St. John and		4.	12.	0	[T]
Sancti Edwardi cum	St. Edward					
Bunseye	with Binsey	sp/493077				
Pa. Sancte Mildrede	St. Mildred the Virgin		2.	9.	0	[T]
Virginis						
Pa. Sancti Michaelis ad	St. Michael North		8.	19.	8	[T]
Portam Borealem						
Pa. Sancti Martini	St. Martin		14.	11.	1	[T]
Pa. Sancti Petri in	St. Peter le Bailey		10.	8.	10	[T]
Ballio						
Pa. Sancte Ebbe	St. Ebbe		2.	12.	5	[T]
Pa. Sancti Michaelis ad	St. Michael South		3.	1.	2	[T]
Portam Austrum						
Pa. Sancti Thome de	St. Thomas Stockwell		2.	18.	2	[T]
Stokwell' & Twentyakr'	and Twenty Acre					
Pa. Sancte Marie	St. Mary Magdalen		4.	9.	4	[T]
Magdalene						
Pa. Sancti Egidii	St. Giles		3.	15.	6	[T]
Pa. Sancti Aldathi	St. Aldate		6.	9.	2	[T]
			91.	7.	10	[T]

Henlegh' [B]	Henley on Thames	su/763826	6.	0.	6	[T]
Bloxham [A.D]	Bloxham	sp/430357	17.	6.	8	[T]
Hanebergh' [A.D]	Hanborough[2]	sp/426128	7.	11.	0	[T]
Wotton [A.D]	Wootton	sp/439199	6.	17.	8	[T]
Hordele [A.D] &	Hordley and	sp/448192				
Oldewodestok' [A.D]	Old Woodstock	sp/442171				
Bladen' [h] [A.D]	Bladon	sp/449148	3.	1.	8	[T]
Combe [A.D]	Combe	sp/413159	5.	14.	8	[T]

[1] For the locations of the Oxford parishes see: (i) Herbert Hurst, 'Oxford Topography' (*Ox. Hist. Soc.* xxxix, 1899); (ii) Revd. H. E. Salter, 'Medieval Oxford' (*Ox. Hist. Soc.* c, 1936); (iii) Andrew Clark, ed., 'Survey of the antiquities of the city of Oxford (1661)', (*Ox. Hist. Soc.* xv, 1889).
[2] Grid ref. is to Church Hanborough.

Wodestok' [B][1]	Woodstock	SP/443167	3.	16.	7	[T]
Stuntesfeld [h] [A.D]	Stonesfield	SP/393171	2.	10.	6	[T]
Hedyndon' c.m [A.D]	Headington [with members]	SP/544076	21.	18.	8	[T]
Bensynton' [A.D]	Benson	SU/615916	9.	15.	6	[T]
Shillyngford [h] [A.D]	Shillingford	SU/597927	1.	17.	8	[T]
Warebergh' [h] [A.D]	Warborough	SU/599936	8.	7.	2	[T]
			94.	18.		[T]

TOTAL: £1,403. 8. 6[2]

---

[1] The borough was New Woodstock; for Old Woodstock see above.
[2] As on 1334 Account, E 179/161/11.

RUTLAND

DOCUMENTS

  8 Edward III: Account   E 179/165/5
  8 Edward III: Indenture E 179/165/7*
10 Edward III: Particulars E 179/165/7
10 Edward III: Particulars E 179/165/6

TAXERS

The prior of Brooke and William Wade

TAX YIELD

15th	£178.	12.	11¾
10th	£ 37.	5.	6¾
	£215.	18.	6½

Representing assessed movable wealth of

    £3,052. 10. 3¾

NOTES

The tax at a tenth was on five ancient demesnes; there is no mention of any borough. The county seems to have had its modern outline by 1334; no places in modern Rutland were taxed elsewhere and no places outside the county are named on the rolls of Rutland.

Hd. Martinesle [MARTINSLEY HUNDRED]

Ocham [A.D]	Oakham	SK/861089	12.	7.	10 [T]
Langham [A.D]	Langham	SK/843112	14.	0.	1¾ [T]
Egilton' [A.D]	Egleton	SK/877075	3.	5.	10¾ [T]
Braundeston'	Braunston	SK/832066	2.	17.	3¾
Lye	Leighfield	SK/829041	1.	1.	0¼
Wardeleye	Wardley	SK/832002	1.	12.	0½
Brok'	Brook	SK/850057	1.	4.	0
Beltone	Belton	SK/817013	2.	16.	1
Ridelington'	Ridlington	SK/848027	3.	3.	11½
Astone	Ayston	SK/859009	1.	12.	8½
Uppingham	Uppingham	SP/867997	4.	10.	1½
Prestone	Preston	SK/870023	2.	4.	10½
Wenge	Wing	SK/893030	2.	17.	11
Martinesthorp'	Martinsthorpe	SK/868045	2.	0.	8
Mantone	Manton	SK/880046	3.	17.	9
Lyndone [A.D]	Lyndon	SK/907044	2.	6.	2 [T]
Normantone	Normanton	SK/933063	2.	12.	1
Hameldone	Hambleton¹	SK/900075	3.	18.	2

¹ Grid ref. is to Upper Hambleton.

Westone	Edith Weston	SK/928053	4.	3.	0
Gunthorp'	Gunthorpe	SK/869057	1.	3.	2
Pikworth'	Pickworth	SK/992138	5.	0.	5
Kilpesham	Clipsham	SK/970163	4.	5.	9
			83.	1.	1

Hd. Aluestowe [ALSTOE HUNDRED]

Wissindene	Whissendine	SK/825143	11.	4.	2
Assewelle	Ashwell	SK/866138	6.	14.	7
Ty	Teigh	SK/865160	3.	8.	3
Overtone	Market Overton	SK/886164	3.	4.	5¾
Berg' &	Barrow and	SK/890153	1.	16.	3
Wenton	Wenton	SK/899146			
Thisteltone	Thistleton	SK/913180	2.	16.	10¾
Cotesmor	Cottesmore	SK/902136	4.	5.	10
Gretham	Greetham	SK/924146	4.	14.	9¾
Strettone [A.D]	Stretton	SK/949158	5.	5.	6¼ [T]
Extone	Exton	SK/921112	6.	19.	6¾
Witewell'	Whitwell	SK/923088	2.	5.	6¾
Burleie &	Burley &	SK/882102	2.	19.	11½
Alesthorp	Alsthorpe	SK/891123			
			55.	15.	10½

Esthundredum [EAST HUNDRED]

Empingham	Empingham	SK/951085	8.	13.	3½
Ketene	Ketton	SK/981042	7.	8.	2½
Rihale &	Ryhall and	TF/037108	6.	3.	8
Belnesthorp'	Belmesthorpe	TF/043103			
Tynewell' &	Tinwell and	TF/006063	5.	16.	11
Ingethorp'	Ingthorpe	SK/996089			
Magna Castertone	Great Casterton	TF/001087	3.	17.	1
Parva Castertone	Little Casterton	TF/019099	3.	5.	7
Tikyncote	Tickencote	SK/990095	2.	0.	3½
Horn	Horn	SK/953117	1.	13.	5
Esindene	Essendine	TF/049128	1.	19.	4¾
			40.	17.	10¼

Hd. Wrangdik' [WRANDIKE HUNDRED]

Bergdone	Barrowden	SK/948002	3.	5.	2½
Morcote	Morcott	SK/925008	3.	15.	9½
Piltone	Pilton	SK/915029	1.	4.	1
Nortluffenham &	North Luffenham and	SK/934032	5.	6.	9½
Sculthorp'	Sculthorp	SK/930027			
Soutluffenham	South Luffenham	SK/941019	3.	16.	2
Tikesovere	Tixover	SP/971998	3.	3.	1
Seytone	Seaton	SP/903982	4.	3.	0
Thorp'	Thorpe by Water	SP/893964	1.	8.	5
Lidingtone	Lyddington	SP/877970	2.	4.	0
Caldecote &	Caldecott and	SP/868937	1.	9.	6
Snelleston'	Snelston	SP/864953			

Driestoke	Stoke Dry	SP/856968	1.	19.	2¼
Glastone	Glaston	SK/896005	1.	16.	10
Bissebrok'	Bisbrooke	SP/888997	2.	11.	8
			36.	3.	8¾

TOTAL: £215. 18. 6½[1]

_____

[1] As on 1334 Account, E 179/165/5.

SHROPSHIRE

DOCUMENTS

8 Edward III: Account   E 179/166/4
8 Edward III: Particulars E 179/242/32 (incomplete)
10 Edward III: Particulars E 179/166/5*

TAXERS

The abbot of Shrewsbury and Robert de Shareshull

TAX YIELD

15th	£518.	6.	0½
10th	£126.	5.	11¾
	£644.	12.	0¼

Representing assessed movable wealth of

£9,037. 10. 5

NOTES

For Shropshire there is coverage for the first three lay subsidies of Edward III. The 1327 roll (E 179/166/1) was published at the turn of the century by Fletcher and the 1332 roll (E 179/166/2) is extant. The 1334 roll, of three membranes, is incomplete but is of some interest as it shows not only the tax quotas but the system whereby money was handed over in instalments by the collectors. Willard referred to this unique roll as 'the account book' of the 1334 collectors.

The hundreds of Oswestry in the north-west and Clun in the south-west were not included in the subsidy as they were both exempt from English law. Furthermore, some places in modern Shropshire were formerly in Cheshire which, as a palatinate, was also exempt. Sheriff Hales, in the modern county, was taxed in Staffordshire in 1334, while two places then taxed in Shropshire have since been transferred to other counties—Jay to Herefordshire, and Halesowen to Worcestershire.

Although boroughs are mentioned on the 1334 Account they are not specified there. It may, however, be presumed that Shrewsbury and Bridgnorth were meant; both were considered taxation boroughs in 1336 and throughout the early fourteenth century. Newport, which had been a borough in 1306 and 1307, was taxed at a fifteenth. The other places taxed at a tenth were Church Stretton and Claverley and a number of places around Shrewsbury and Bridgnorth.

REFERENCE

W. G. D. Fletcher, 'The Shropshire lay subsidy roll of 1327', *Shropshire Arch. and Nat. Hist. Soc.*, 2nd series, 1 (1887)–11 (1899): 3rd series, 5 (1905)–7 (1907).

Hd. Bradeford [BRADFORD HUNDRED]

			£	s	d
Betton' sub Lyme	Betton	SJ/690366	3.	0.	0
Albo Monasterio	Whitchurch	SJ/541414	8.	18.	0
Wouere	Woore	SJ/731424	3.	6.	4
Gravenhunger &	Gravenhunger and	SJ/738432			
Dorynton'	Dorrington	SJ/731409			
Stoke super Tyrne	Stoke upon Tern	SJ/639280	5.	4.	10
Adderdeleye	Adderley	SJ/661395	2.	16.	1
Quyxhale	Whixall	SJ/519349	2.	0.	5
Hodynet	Hodnet	SJ/612286	6.	17.	8
Drayton' in le Halys	Market Drayton	SJ/676341	2.	13.	6½
Longeford	Longford	SJ/645340	3.	1.	0
Sondford	Sandford	SJ/582340			
Wloncuslowe	Longslow	SJ/654354			
Wemme	Wem	SJ/512289	10.	3.	6
Solton'	Soulton	SJ/543303	4.	7.	5½
Lakene	Lacon[1]	SJ/536304			
Leye sub brochurst'	Lee Brockhurst	SJ/545272			
Moston'	Moston	SJ/560265			
Hopton'	Hopton	SJ/592263			
Espele	Espley	SJ/610267			
Colde Hatton'	Cold Hatton	SJ/619211			
Erkalewe Magna	High Ercall	SJ/594173	2.	0.	0
Morton' corbet	Moreton Corbet	SJ/561232	1.	16.	0
Penynton'	Poynton	SJ/570178			
Hynstoke &	Hinstock and	SJ/693263	7.	6.	8
Clyve	Cliff	SJ/649322			
Ightefeld &	Ightfield and	SJ/592387	2.	3.	0
Calverhale	Calverhall	SJ/602372			
Roulton'	Rowton	SJ/615199	1.	19.	6
Elwardyn	Ellerdine	SJ/609209			
Leghton'	Leighton	SJ/613051	1.	2.	8
Eton'	Eaton Constantine	SJ/598062			
Garmuston'	Garmston	SJ/607061			
Parva Buldewas	Little Buildwas[2]	SJ/c.642043			
Chesewardyn	Cheswardine	SJ/719299	2.	8.	0
Prees	Prees	SJ/557334	2.	6.	8
Eyton' Abbatis	Eyton on Severn	SJ/572062	2.	8.	4
Wythiford Magna	Great Wytheford	SJ/572190	2.	0.	6¼
Atyncham	Atcham	SJ/541091	3.	0.	6¾
Okynton'	Uckington	SJ/578099			
Adbrighteleye	Albrightlee	SJ/523162			
Tyrne	Tern	SJ/621168			
Opynton'	Uppington	SJ/597093			
Ercalewe Parva	Child's Ercall	SJ/666251	2.	13.	4
Rubeo castro	Red Castle	SJ/572294	5.	0.	4
Wythmerton'	Withington	SJ/577130	1.	10.	8
Chetewynde	Chetwynd	SJ/735213	7.	2.	4
Staunton'	Stanton upon Hine Heath	SJ/568238	1.	12.	0
Uffynton'	Uffington	SJ/529139	1.	18.	10
Pymbeleye	Pimley	SJ/521143			
Rodynton'	Rodington	SJ/582141	2.	3.	8
Rodene	Roden	SJ/576165			
Rodenhurst'	Rodenhurst	SJ/589155			
Sogedon'	Sugdon	SJ/603148			

[1] Grid ref. is to Lower Lacon.
[2] Little Buildwas, not on modern maps, was on the opposite bank of the Severn to Buildwas.

Boulwas	Great Bolas	sj/647212	1.	18.	2
Upton'	Upton Magna	sj/552124	1.	17.	0
Hunkynton'	Hunkington	sj/567136			
Haulghton	Haughton	sj/552163			
Lylleshull'	Lilleshall	sj/728153	2.	10.	3
Shawebur'	Shawbury	sj/559211	1.	11.	4
Parva Withiford	Little Wytheford	sj/561195			
Wrocwardyn	Wrockwardine	sj/623121	3.	1.	8
Wroxcestr'	Wroxeter	sj/563082			
Styrchesleye	Stirchley	sj/699707	3.	0.	8
Haddeleye	Hadley	sj/669124			
Wodecote	Woodcote	sj/768153			
Lyndon'	Lynn	sj/784158			
Slepe	Sleap	sj/631176	2.	0.	5
Crugelton'	Crudginton	sj/632181			
Leye combrey	Leegomery	sj/669129	2.	4.	0
Welynton'	Wellington	sj/651118	2.	15.	8
Ardeston'	Arleston	sj/662108			
Neuport	Newport	sj/745192	11.	15.	0
Egemundon'	Edgmond	sj/720193			
Morton'	Moreton Say	sj/630345	3.	0.	0
Bletcheleye	Bletchley	sj/622336			
Woluerton'	Wollerton	sj/621303		16.	0
			139.	12.	1

Hd. Pymenhull' [PIMHILL HUNDRED]

Shrewardyn	Shrawardine	sj/400152	3.	12.	3½
Hadenhale	Hadnall	sj/522200	2.	10.	7
Baschyrche	Baschurch	sj/422219	5.	14.	4½
Clyve	Clive	sj/514240	2.	5.	0
Stanwordyn in bosco	Stanwardine in the	sj/429278	1.	16.	4
Borleton'	Wood				
Mudle	Myddle	sj/468235	3.	11.	3½
Eton'	Eyton	sj/441229			
Roshale	Rossall[1]	sj/466152			
Nesse Extranea	Great Ness	sj/398190	2.	14.	3
Fyttes	Fitz	sj/448178	1.	17.	3¼
Preston'	Preston Brockhurst	sj/538247	1.	17.	0
Besseford	Besford	sj/551250			
Harlascote	Harlescott	sj/501163	1.	17.	0
Adbrighton'	Albrighton	sj/498180			
Monachorum					
Bourghton'	Broughton	sj/498242	1.	15.	0
Yorton'	Yorton	sj/503234			
Astleye	Astley	sj/530189	1.	2.	0
Bykedon'	Bicton	sj/448148	3.	9.	0
Roshale	Rossall[2]	sj/466152			
Berewyc'	Berwick	sj/472148			
Lopynton'	Loppington	sj/471293	2.	13.	1
Preston' Gobald	Preston Gubbals	sj/491196	1.	11.	0
Sontsawe	Sansaw	sj/509232	2.	13.	1¼
Acton' Reyn'	Acton Reynald	sj/534233			
Greneshull'	Grinshill	sj/520234			

[1] Part of Rossall was taxed with Bicton, below.
[2] Part of Rossall was taxed with Myddle, above.

Balderton'	Balderton	SJ/481239	I.	16.	10½
Murydon'	Merrington	SJ/472209			
Hampton'	Welshampton	SJ/433349	2.	13.	8½
Weston'	Weston Lullingfields	SJ/425249			
Petton'	Petton	SJ/438266			
Stanwordyn in the feld	Stanwardine in the Fields	SJ/413240	2.	10.	6½
Colmere	Colemere	SJ/438329	I.	17.	0
Franketon'	English Frankton	SJ/452298			
Okleye[1]	?		2.	4.	11½
Leton'	Leaton	SJ/469183			
Felton' Botiler	Felton Butler	SJ/393175			
			52.	I.	8

Hd. Conedovere [CONDOVER HUNDRED]

Emustre	Emstrey	SJ/526104	2.	4.	4
Byryton'	Berrington	SJ/529069	2.	6.	9
Eton Mascot'	Eaton Mascott	SJ/536058			
Cantelhope	Cantlop	SJ/522058			
Crissegge	Cressage	SJ/592040	2.	2.	I
Harleye	Harley	SJ/597014	I.	14.	0
Kenleye	Kenley	SJ/562008			
Acton' Burnell'	Acton Burnell	SJ/532019	2.	4.	7
Pychford	Pitchford	SJ/530038			
Acton' Pygot	Acton Pigott	SJ/541028			
Longenolr	Longnor	SJ/489005	I.	13.	6
Wolstanston'	Woolstaston	SO/452984	I.	6.	2
Preone	Church Preen	SO/542981			
Smethecote	Smethcott	SO/449993	2.	18.	I
Wilderdeleye	Wilderley	SJ/433018			
Leye in Bottewode	Leebotwood	SO/471986			
Condovere	Condover	SJ/494058	2.	11.	6
Pulrebache	Church Pulverbatch	SJ/430029	2.	10.	1½
Longeleye	Langley	SJ/538001	2.	13.	11
Stepulton'	Stapleton	SJ/471045			
Berton'	Boreton	SJ/512066	I.	3.	11
Norton'	Norton	SJ/493071			
Beystan	Bayston	SJ/491081			
Foresta Monachorum[2]	?		I.	19.	0
Conede	Cound	SJ/558050	2.	11.	3¾
			29.	19.	3¼

Hd. Forde [FORD HUNDRED]

Forde [man.]	Ford	SJ/412138	10.	10.	3¾
Watlesborugh'	Wattlesborough	SJ/357117	I.	17.	8½
Pontesbury	Pontesbury	SJ/400061	I.	16.	5
Munsterleye	Minsterley	SJ/373050	2.	16.	4¼
Wortham	Worthen	SJ/329047	3.	2.	I
Longedon'	Longden	SJ/441064	I.	11.	4

[1] Possibly Oteley in Ellesmere (SJ/415346) although this is a considerable distance from the two places with which it is linked.

[2] As most of the hundred of Condover had been within the jurisdiction of the Forest in 1086, it is presumed that this entry refers to a specific part of the Long Forest.

Haberleye	Habberley	SJ/399035	I.	0.	6
Alburbur'	Alberbury	SJ/359144	I.	5.	5¼
Routon'	Rowton	SJ/363123	2.	17.	4
Eyton'	Eyton	SJ/376140			
Horton'	Hortonlane	SJ/440115	2.	6.	2
Mersh'	Marsh	SJ/333110			
Preston'	Preston Montford	SJ/432143	I.	12.	11
Asterleye	Asterley	SJ/374071			
Yokenhulle	Yockleton	SJ/395101	3.	2.	11
Wylaston'	Wollaston	SJ/329122			
Kaus	Cause	SJ/337078	3.	7.	8¼
Wonanton'	Winnington[1]	SJ/311104			
Westbury	Westbury	SJ/355094	I.	16.	4
			39.	3.	6½

Hd. Pusselowe [PURSLOW HUNDRED]

Jay	Jay [in Herefordshire]	SO/390749	I.	16.	0
Rotlinchope	Ratlinghope	SO/402969	2.	14.	2
Sybeton'	Sibdon Carwood	SO/412831			
Lee &	Lea and	SO/351891	I.	15.	4
Okeleye	Oakeley	SO/339881			
Colebach'	Colebatch	SO/319870			
Brocton'	Brockton	SO/328859			
Lydebury	Lydbury North	SO/352860	2.	4.	4
More	More	SO/342915			
Castre Episcopi	Bishop's Castle	SO/323883	2.	5.	7
Eyton'	Eyton	SO/371876			
Wontenore	Wentnor	SO/383927	I.	9.	6
Stowe	Stow	SO/311737	2.	3.	8
Lydom	Lydham	SO/335910			
Coston'	Coston	SO/385803	I.	16.	0
Clongeneford	Clungunford	SO/395788			
Eggedon'	Edgton	SO/387859	I.	12.	6
Linleye	Linley	SO/350928			
Toderton'	Totterton	SO/360874	I.	13.	0½
Northbury	Norbury	SO/363928			
Bokenhull'	Bucknell	SO/354739	I.	10.	3
Clonebury	Clunbury	SO/371806			
Hopton'	Hopton Castle	SO/363782	3.	0.	0
Astamton'	Asterton	SO/399913			
Munede	Myndtown	SO/391895			
Hopesay	Hopesay	SO/389832	4.	16.	0
Clonton'	Clunton	SO/335813			
Aston'	Aston on Clun	SO/393818			
			28.	16.	4½

Hd. Overes [OVERS HUNDRED]

Neensolers	Neen Sollars	SO/660722	2.	16.	3
Marbroc'	Marlbrook	SO/661703			
Cleaton'	Cleeton St. Mary	SO/611787	I.	10.	8
Silveton'	Silvington	SO/621799			
Boreford	Burford	SO/583680	2.	4.	8

[1] Grid ref. is to Upper Winnington.

Asshe	Nash	so/603717	2.	18.	8
Tilsop	Tilsop	so/611726			
Mulston'	Milson	so/640728			
Greote	Greete	so/578708	4.	3.	3¼
Wytton'	Whitton	so/577728			
Buterleye	Bitterley ♦	so/571773			
			13.	13.	6¼

Hd. Munselowe [MUNSLOW HUNDRED]

Lodelowe	Ludlow	so/512746	16.	0.	0
Stannton' Lacy	Stanton Lacy	so/496789	5.	18.	2½
Corfham maner'	Corfham	so/525850	5.	15.	4½
Myddelton'	Middleton	so/540773	1.	14.	6¼
Magna Bromfeld	Bromfield	so/482768	3.	12.	10¼
Lauton'	Lawton	so/513838	1.	18.	10
Corfton'	Corfton	so/498846			
Parva Sutton'	Little Sutton	so/512824			
Acton' rounde	Acton Round	so/634956	1.	10.	11
Tuggeford	Tugford	so/558870	2.	19.	3½
Thongelond	Thonglands	so/549891			
Cardyton'	Cardington	so/507952	1.	10.	0
Lydeleye	Lydley Heys	so/488963			
Esthop'	Easthope	so/566952	3.	16.	6
Euldon'	Aldon	so/436795			
Felthampton'	Felhampton	so/445873			
Munselowe	Munslow	so/521877	2.	0.	1
Aston'	Aston	so/509866			
Stokesay	Stokesay	so/436817	2.	0.	0
Hope boulers	Hope Bowdler	so/476924	3.	19.	0
Millynchope	Millichope	so/528883			
Skottesacton'	Acton Scott	so/453894			
Castro Ricardi	Richard's Castle [Salop]	so/494706	4.	14.	10
Stokemilborugh'	Stoke St. Milborough	so/567822	1.	17.	9½
Eton'	Eaton	so/500900	2.	4.	10
Dodyton'	Ditton Priors	so/609891	1.	14.	7½
Shipton'	Shipton	so/561919	3.	13.	5
Caulghton'	Callaughton	so/618974			
Hopton'	Monkhopton	so/626934			
Bourghton'	Bourton	so/598963	2.	0.	2
Corve	Corve	so/595937			
Bradeleye	Bradeley	so/596948			
Atturleye	Atterley	so/642978	4.	0.	7
Walton'	Wenlock Walton	so/638989			
Parva Wenloc'	Little Wenlock	sj/647068			
Madeleye	Madeley	sj/697041			
Magna Wenloc'	Much Wenlock	so/623999	2.	10.	3
Hughleye	Hughley	so/564980	2.	8.	0
Presthop'	Presthope	so/582973			
Grotynton'	Gretton	so/514952			
Borewardesleye	Broseley	sj/672018	4.	8.	11
Wyhleye	Willey	so/672992			
Lynleye	Linley	so/687986			
Longefeld	Cheney Longville	so/420849	3.	0.	5
Westhop'	Westhope	so/470862			
Middelhop'	Middlehope	so/498884			
Wyttyngesluwe	Whittingslow	so/432890			
Assheford carbonell'	Ashford Carbonel	so/525710			
Sheldreton'	Shelderton	so/406777			

			£.	s.	d.
Onybury	Onibury	so/456792	1.	13.	8
Russhebury	Rushbury	so/514919	1.	13.	6
Holgod	Holdgate	so/561896	4.	9.	8
Bolledon'	Bouldon	so/546852			
Longestannton'	Stanton Long	so/571907			
Clee Sancti Margarete	Clee St. Margaret	so/564843			
Styvynton'	Steventon	so/522733			
Parva Bromfeld	Little Bromfield[1]	lost	1.	0.	3¾
Beckebur'	Beckbury	sj/766015	1.	0.	9
Baggesouere	Badger	so/768996			
Pykethorn'	Pickthorn	so/669842			
			95.	7.	3¾

Hd. Stottesdon' [STOTTESDON HUNDRED]

			£.	s.	d.
Stottesdon'	Stottesdon	so/672829	2.	18.	3½
Aluycheleye	Alveley	so/759845	3.	6.	0
Nordeleye	Kingsnordley	so/773877	2.	7.	9
Erdyton'	Eardington	so/722905	3.	9.	1
Aston Boterell'	Aston Botterell	so/632841			
Hopton' Wafre	Hopton Wafers	so/637765	2.	13.	8
Dodynton'[2] &	?				
Chetynton'	Chetton	so/663903			
Astleye Abbatis	Astley Abbots	so/709962	2.	0.	6
Aston' Ayer	Aston Eyre	so/652941	4.	19.	0
Hagurcote	Harcourt	so/690828			
Glaseleye	Glazeley	so/702882			
Eudon' Burnell	Eudon Burnell	so/700893			
Byllynggesleye	Billingsley	so/703853			
Oldebur'	Oldbury	so/711921	4.	8.	0
Tasseleye	Tasley	so/697942			
Cleburynorth	Cleobury North	so/622870			
Bolde	The Bold	so/641848			
Myddelton'	Middleton Scriven	so/681875			
Duddlewyc'	Duddlewick	so/656833	3.	11.	0½
Upton'	Upton Cressett	so/656924			
Momerfeld	Morville	so/669939			
Neen Sauvage	Neen Savage	so/674773	3.	17.	0
Overton'	Overton	so/665868			
Eudon'	Eudon George	so/689890			
Walton'	Walton	so/676812			
Borewarton'	Burwarton	so/618849			
Clebury Mortym'	Cleobury Mortimer	so/673758	3.	0.	1
Asshford	Ashford[3]	so/529719	2.	5.	0
Huntyndon'	Huntington	so/538710			
Cheylmersh'	Chelmarsh	so/721879	3.	10.	0
Dodyton'[4]	?		1.	19.	0
Huggeleye	Highley	so/741832	1.	16.	2½
Ernewod	Earnwood	so/737805			

---

[1] R. W. Eyton, *Antiquities of Shropshire* (1854), v. 220, states that the distinction between Bromfield and Little Bromfield had disappeared by the Dissolution and that its site cannot now be traced.

[2] The identification of this place is uncertain. It could be Doddington (so/615761) in Hopton Wafers, Earlsditton (so/629756) in Hopton Wafers, or Detton (so/667796) in Neen Savage. See also *Dodyton'*, below.

[3] The entry probably refers to Upper Ashford.

[4] The problem of identification is the same as that for *Dodynton'*, above.

Hyntes	Hints	so/611750	2.	0.	2
Corleye	Coreley	so/612739			
Kaynham	Caynham	so/553732	2.	7.	8½
Snytton'	Snitton	so/557753			
Nenton'	Neenton	so/638877			
Sudbur'	Sidbury	so/683858			
Rugge	Rudge	so/812974	1.	10.	0
Shippleye	Shipley	so/810958			
Cynlet	Kinlet	so/719803	1.	11.	0
			53.	9.	6

Hd. Brimestr' [BRIMSTREE HUNDRED]

Halysoweyn	Halesowen [in Worcestershire][1]	sj/968835	9.	0.	0
Sutton' Madoc'	Sutton Maddock	sj/719013	2.	10.	6
Albrighton'	Albrighton	sj/813041	3.	0.	0
Tonge	Tong	sj/795074	4.	13.	2
Donyton'	Donington	sj/809046			
Kembrighton'	Kemberton	sj/729045	4.	4.	0
Bolynghal'	Boningale	sj/812026			
Huggeford	Higford	sj/753007			
Worvelde	Worfield	so/758958	8.	0.	7
Bebrugge	Beobridge	so/783911	2.	16.	10¾
Gataker	Gatacre	so/791903			
Borton'	probably Broughton	so/806915			
Luddesdon'	Ludstone	so/801945			
Wytemere	Whittimere	so/821926			
Ideshale	Shifnal	sj/748077	10.	9.	9
Grenehull'	Grindle	sj/750030			
Hemme	The Hem	sj/730059			
Leye	Priorslee	sj/713098			
Stonton'	Stanton	sj/771075			
Opton'	Upton	sj/756064			
Hatton'	Hatton	sj/759043			
Wyke	The Wyke	sj/730068			
Wodehous	The Woodhouse	sj/722100			
Haughton'	Haughton	sj/744086			
			44.	14.	10¾

Hd. Chyrebur' [CHIRBURY HUNDRED]

Aston' Rog'	Aston Rogers	sj/341063	2.	2.	4
Hope	Hope	sj/341014			
Woderton'	Wotherton	sj/282005	1.	2.	2
Dodeston'	Dudston	so/243974	3.	1.	10½
Walton'	Walton[2]	sj/292054			
Brompton'	Brompton	so/251933			
Chyrebur'	Chirbury	so/261985	2.	3.	4
Wynnesbury	Winsbury	so/247983			
Walcote	Walcot	so/264994	2.	11.	0
Rorynton'	Rorrington	sj/301005			
Middelton'	Middleton	so/297990			

[1] Halesowen, part of which had been in Shropshire since the late eleventh century, was finally transferred to Worcestershire in 1844.
[2] Grid ref. is to Middle Walton.

Maryton'	Marrington	SO/272970	4.	17.	10
Bromlowe	Bromlow	SJ/319018			
Weston Prestes	Priestweston	SO/291973			
Wilmynton'	Wilmington	SJ/297019			
Ruston	Rhiston	SO/260951			
Timyburth	Timberth	SO/252965	2.	0.	2
Mokelwyc'	Mucklewick	SO/332967			
Munton'	Munton[1]	lost			
Rytton'	Ritton	SO/345977			
Beenweston'	Binweston	SJ/301042	1.	1.	8
Shelve	Shelve	SO/336990	1.	0.	0
Aston' Pygot	Aston Pigott	SJ/338060		10.	6
Hoculton'	Hockleton	SJ/273001		17.	0
Stocton'	Stockton	SJ/267011			
			21.	7.	10½

Salop'[2]	Shrewsbury	SJ/492125	80.	0.	0 [T]
Sholton' [A.D]	Shelton	SJ/459132			
Hennecote [A.D]	Hencott	SJ/493150			
Sutton' [A.D]	Sutton	SJ/502100			
Moele Bracy [A.D]	Meole Brace	SJ/486106	14.	0.	6¼ [T]
Neuton' [A.D]	Newton	SJ/461106			
Egebaldenham [A.D]	Edgebold[3]	SJ/452102			
Monkemoel[4] [A.D]	Meole	SJ/c.486106			
Stretton' [A.D]	Church Stretton	SO/452936	4.	2.	1½ [T]
Claverleye [A.D]	Claverley	SO/792934	3.	15.	1¼ [T]
Brugenorth[5]	Bridgnorth	SO/718929	24.	8.	2¾ [T]
Remesleye [A.D]	Romsley	SO/781832			
Quatte [A.D]	Quatt	SO/756882			
Dodemaston' [A.D]	Dudmaston	SO/747887			
			126.	5.	11¾ [T]

TOTAL: £644. 12. 0¼[6]

---

[1] Eyton, op. cit. xi. 78–80, gives various documentary references to Munton but the site is not known.

[2] The 1334 Account does not specifically state the boroughs but it is reasonable to assume that they were Shrewsbury and Bridgnorth as in 1332 and 1336.

[3] Grid ref. is to Lower Edgebold.

[4] Monkemoel was that part of the manor of Meole held by Buildwas abbey.

[5] See footnote to Shrewsbury, above.   [6] As on 1334 Account, E 179/166/4.

SOMERSET

DOCUMENTS

   8 Edward III: Account   E 179/169/8
   8 Edward III: Particulars not extant
  10 Edward III: Particulars E 179/169/9*
  10 Edward III: Particulars E 179/169/10

TAXERS

The abbot of Forde and John Inge

TAX YIELD

15th £1,218. 9. 0½
10th £ 139. 10. 2
              ────────────
     £1,357. 19. 2½

Representing assessed movable wealth of

    £19,671. 17. 3½

NOTES

The Somerset subsidy rolls follow the usual pattern. While some places taxed at a tenth are listed within the hundreds others are listed separately. Somerset had seventeen taxation boroughs in 1334; many of them had extremely small quotas and could hardly have been truly urban in function.

Since 1334 there have been slight changes in the boundary of the county, mainly along the border with Dorset. The Somerset list includes six places now in Dorset, two in Wiltshire, and one in Gloucestershire. Churchstanton, in the modern county, was taxed in Devon in 1334.

REFERENCE

F. H. Dickinson, 'Lay subsidy, 1327 ($\frac{1}{20}$, 1 Edward III)', *Somerset Rec. Soc.* 3 (1889), 79–284 (mapped in M. Williams, *The Draining of the Somerset Levels*, 1970, 77–81).

ACKNOWLEDGEMENT

I am indebted to Mr. D. M. M. Shorrocks, Assistant County Archivist, and to Miss Ann Hamlin and Mr. David Mills for suggestions for some place-name identifications, and to Dr. M. Williams for correspondence concerning the subsidies of 1327 and 1334.

Hd. Wynterstok' [WINTERSTOKE HUNDRED]

			£	s.	d.	
Yattone[1]	Yatton	ST/431655	1.	15.	6	
Churchulle	Churchill	ST/437602	1.	13.	5	
Blakedone	Blagdon	ST/503590	1.	15.	4	
Harpetre	East Harptree	ST/565560	1.	13.	9	
Ken	Kenn	ST/415690	1.	18.	2	
Wyke	Wick St. Lawrence	ST/366654		8.	1	
Clyve	Cleeve	ST/460661	1.	3.	3	
Stoke	Rodney Stoke	ST/482498		13.	2	
Roubergh' &	Rowberrow and	ST/449587		19.	10	
Shopham	Shipham	ST/443574				
Compton'	Compton Bishop	ST/396554	2.	16.	10	
Lokeston'	Loxton	ST/376558	3.	18.	4	
Personat' de Yattone	?		1.	11.	4	
Lokkynge	Locking	ST/363597	1.	2.	8	
Huttone	Hutton	ST/352585	1.	4.	8	
Wynescombe	Winscombe	ST/412567	5.	1.	7	
Banewelle	Banwell	ST/399592	4.	9.	5	
Wolfareshulle	Woolvershill	ST/381607	4.	11.	1	
Westone	Weston super Mare	ST/318620	2.	1.	1	
Worle	Worle	ST/353629	4.	5.	1	
Ceddre [A.D]	Cheddar	ST/460530	4.	0.	11	[T]
Congeresbury [A.D]	Congresbury	ST/435638	9.	16.	2	[T]
			56.	19.	8	

Hd. Cattesassh' [CATSASH HUNDRED]

			£	s.	d.
Castelcarilond	Castle Cary	ST/639321	9.	0.	0
Northcadebury	North Cadbury	ST/635271	6.	0.	0
Lovyngton'	Lovington	ST/597308	2.	0.	0
Maperton'	Maperton	ST/672262		10.	0
Ludeford	West Lydford	ST/565319	2.	0.	0
Westone	Weston Bampfylde	ST/611250	1.	0.	0
Sparkeford	Sparkford	ST/603263	2.	6.	0
Barewe[2]	Barrow	ST/608293	1.	0.	0
Kynewardeston'	Kingweston	ST/525313	3.	0.	0
Babbecary	Babcary	ST/562288	1.	12.	2
Barton'	Barton St. David	ST/540317		10.	0
			28.	18.	2

Maner' de Puttenye Lortyey [PITNEY MANOR]

			£	s.	d.
Puttenye	Pitney	ST/444285	1.	10.	0
Bere	Beer	ST/407312		10.	0
Knolle	Knole	ST/483251	1.	5.	11
Donehefde	possibly Downhead	ST/566254		8.	0
			3.	13.	11

[1] See also *Personat' de Yattone* below.

[2] This entry possibly refers to both North and South Barrow as they are linked together in the *Nomina Villarum* of 1316 (*F.A.* iv. 319). In the tax of 1327 only North Barrow is listed (Dickinson, op. cit. 207).

Sterte [man.]	Steart	ST/562277		10.	0
Combe Episcopi [man.]	Combe	ST/421280	3.	8.	0
Northovere	Northover	ST/523232	2.	0.	0
			5.	18.	0

Hd. Forinsecus de Mulverton' [MILVERTON FOREIGN HUNDRED]

Saumford	Sampford Arundel	ST/108189	2.	0.	0
Gryndenham	Greenham	ST/078202	1.	10.	0
Ronyngton'	Runnington	ST/119219		13.	4
Asshebrutel	Ashbrittle	ST/052213	1.	13.	4
Wellesford	Wellisford	ST/094221		13.	4
Staulegh'	Stawley	ST/061227	1.	6.	8
Kydesford	Kittisford	ST/078223	2.	0.	0
Badialtone	Bathealton	ST/079241	2.	10.	0
			12.	6.	8

Hd. Andredesfeld [ANDREWSFIELD HUNDRED][1]

Merrygge	Merridge	ST/208343	1.	2.	0
Bromfeld	Broomfield	ST/224320	1.	10.	0
Herecombe	Heathcombe	ST/229346	2.	1.	5
Enemere	Enmore	ST/240352	1.	14.	0
Lekesworth'	Lexworthy	ST/259358	1.	0.	0
Gothurst	Goathurst	ST/257343	2.	11.	0
			9.	18.	5

Hd. Northpedertone [NORTH PETHERTON HUNDRED]

Northpederton'	North Petherton	ST/290331	2.	0.	0
Chedesye	Chedzoy	ST/341377	5.	0.	0
Donewere	Dunwear	ST/323361	3.	10.	0
Horsy	Horsey	ST/321393	2.	13.	4
Baudrip	Bawdrip	ST/341396	2.	0.	0
Stretcholte	Stretcholt	ST/295440	2.	10.	0
Poulet	Pawlett	ST/301427		16.	0
Purye	Perry	ST/280392	2.	2.	0
Saumford	Sandford	ST/271381	1.	4.	3
Pegenesse	Horsey-Pignes	ST/c.310393	1.	2.	0
Chiltone[2]	Chilton Trinity	ST/297392		6.	8
Hamme	Hamp	ST/301362	1.	16.	0
Honteworth'	Huntworth	ST/312344		18.	0
Wolmereston'	Woolmersdon	ST/283341		16.	0
Syrerdeston'	Shearston	ST/282307	1.	0.	0
Horlokeston'	Thurloxton	ST/274304		13.	4
Nywton'	North Newton	ST/301311	2.	0.	0
Tokerton'	Tuckerton	ST/298299	1.	6.	8
Durston'	Durston	ST/291281		7.	2
			32.	1.	5

Langeford [man.]	Langford Budville	ST/112230	2.	14.	3

[1] In the 1327 subsidy for this hundred (Dickinson, op. cit. 162–4) there are five places apparently not mentioned in 1334, viz., *Oggesole*, *Castrum*, *Blakesle*, *Honestyele*, and *Dorleghe*.   [2] Most of Chilton was taxed in Cannington hundred.

Hd. Chiwtone [CHEWTON HUNDRED]

Chiwtone	Chewton Mendip	ST/597532	6.	0.	0
Paltone	Paulton	ST/650565	1.	6.	0
Weleweton'	Welton	ST/669548	2.	0.	0
Midsomeresnorton'	Midsomer Norton	ST/662542	1.	10.	0
Clopton'	Clapton	ST/641533		16.	0
Doune	Downside	ST/624449	1.	0.	0
Childecompton'	Chilcompton	ST/647524	1.	14.	6
Empnebergh'	Emborough	ST/614513	1.	13.	4
Stonyeston'	Ston Easton	ST/623534	1.	12.	0
Farnton'	Farrington Gurney	ST/635557	1.	13.	4
Lutleton' &	High Littleton and	ST/645580	1.	12.	4
Halghetre	Hallatrow	ST/639571			
Cloude	Temple Cloud	ST/623576		10.	0
Henton' &	Hinton Blewett and	ST/594570	1.	10.	0
Camelegh'	Cameley	ST/610575			
Westarpetre	West Harptree	ST/560569	6.	0.	0
Compton' &	Compton Martin and	ST/545570	1.	6.	8
Morton'	Moreton[1]	ST/562592			
Obbelegh'	Ubley	ST/529582	2.	0.	0
Brokkelegh'	Brockley	ST/466670	1.	10.	0
Kyngeston' Seymor	Kingston Seymour	ST/401669	5.	0.	0
			38.	14.	2

Hd. Forinsecus Bathon' [BATH FOREIGN HUNDRED]

Claverton'	Claverton	ST/788641	5.	5.	0
Hampton'	Bathampton	ST/777665	4.	0.	0
Aumarle Chaumpflur	Amoril	ST/690780	4.	10.	0
Calueston'	Kelston	ST/699669	4.	0.	0
Northstok'	North Stoke	ST/704691	1.	13.	0
Langerigge	Langridge	ST/740695	2.	10.	4
Swayneswyk &	Swainswick and	ST/757684	2.	0.	10
Fersshford	Freshford	ST/790601			
Southstok'	Southstoke	ST/747612	1.	10.	0
Wyke Abbatisse	Bathwick	ST/757651	1.	6.	8
Estone	Batheaston	ST/778676	4.	0.	0
Walecote	Walcot	ST/752657	1.	4.	0
Westone	Weston	ST/731663	2.	10.	0
Lynecombe	Lyncombe	ST/751643	3.	2.	0
Cherlecombe	Charlcombe	ST/749673	2.	6.	0
Forde	Bathford	ST/788667	3.	2.	0
Wollegh'	Woolley	ST/750685	1.	6.	8
Coumbe	Monkton Combe	ST/772619	1.	10.	10
			45.	17.	4

Hd. Kynemeresdone [KILMERSDON HUNDRED]

Kynemeresdone cum	Kilmersdon with	ST/697523	4.	0.	0
Asshwik'	Ashwick	ST/637484			
Hemyngton'	Hemington	ST/728530	4.	0.	0
Hardyngton'	Hardington	ST/742526	1.	6.	8
Boklonde Dynham	Buckland Dinham	ST/755512	3.	0.	8

[1] Village now submerged beneath Chew Valley Lake.

Babyngton'	Babington	ST/705510	3.	6.	8
Lokyngton' &	Luckington and	ST/692501	2.	6.	8
Walton'	Walton	ST/692519			
Radestok'	Radstock	ST/688548		16.	0
Stratton'	Stratton on the Fosse	ST/659508	1.	6.	8
Holecoumbe	Holcombe	ST/670497		12.	0
Tenentes, Templar' et				16.	8
Priorisse					
Wrytelyngtone	Writhlington	ST/704551	1.	6.	8
Melles [man.]	Mells	ST/728492	4.	6.	8
Bedmynstre [man.]	Bedminster [in	ST/575710	7.	9.	3
	Bristol]				
Legh'	Abbots Leigh	ST/544741	4.	10.	9
			39.	5.	4

Hd. Bemston' [BEMPSTONE HUNDRED][1]

Wedmor[2]	Wedmore	ST/435479	6.	0.	0
More[2]	?		4.	10.	0
Bydesham	Biddisham	ST/381535	1.	6.	8
Wedmor[2]	Wedmore	ST/435479		16.	0
Wedmor [Lib.][2]	Wedmore [liberty]	ST/435479		6.	8
Blakeford	Blackford	ST/409478	2.	4.	4
Were[3] &	Weare and	ST/414526	2.	6.	8
Alwarton'	Chapel Allerton	ST/409502			
Tornok'	Tarnock	ST/376525	1.	12.	4
Breene	Brean	ST/296561	1.	4.	0
Burnham	Burnham on Sea	ST/305494	3.	0.	0
Alstone	Alstone	ST/314468	2.	0.	0
Aston' Sutton'	Alston Sutton	ST/415515		10.	0
			25.	16.	8

Hd. Stone [STONE HUNDRED][4]

Chilterne	Chilthorne Domer	ST/525194	1.	11.	0
Brompton'	Brympton	ST/519154		19.	6
Hynesforde	Hendford	ST/554156	1.	6.	8
Kyngeston'	Kingston	ST/554165	2.	10.	4
Preston' Plokenet[5]	Preston Plucknett	ST/535165		18.	0
Astyngton'	Ashington	ST/561214	1.	0.	0
Merssh'	lost	ST/c.542164		13.	4
Yevele	Yeovil	ST/557161	3.	5.	0

[1] In the 1327 subsidy for this hundred (Dickinson, op. cit. 169–73), there are five places apparently not mentioned in 1334, viz., *Modesleghe, Merke, Alnestone, Baggeworth,* and *Alwryntone.* Some of these are no doubt included within the quotas for other places in 1334.

[2] It is impossible to say exactly to which parts of Wedmore these quotas refer. The four quotas presumably include amounts for Mark, Mudgley, Churchland, Theale, and Sand, all named in the *Nomina Villarum* of 1316 (*F.A.* iv. 322).

[3] Part of Weare was taxed at a tenth (p. 272).

[4] In the 1327 subsidy for Stone Hundred (Dickinson, op. cit. 210–15) there are thirteen places apparently not mentioned in 1334, viz., *Chyltone, Attebere, Hynton, Thorne, Chilternfage, Lokestone, Hundestone, Lwyngtone, Sokmalherbe, Ocle, Bruttone, Berewyk,* and *Stannarde.* Some of these are no doubt included within the quotas for other places in 1334.

[5] See below also (*Preston' Beremondeseye*).

Modeford	Mudford	ST/573199	2.	12.	2
Lymyngton'	Limington	ST/541223	4.	6.	8
Preston' Beremondeseye	part of Preston Plucknett	ST/535165		13.	4
Stone	Stone	ST/558183		18.	0
			20.	14.	0

Berewyk' [man.]	Barwick	ST/558138	2.	0.	0
Chiltone	Chilton Cantelo	ST/570222	2.	11.	0
Stoford [B]	Stoford	ST/567135		16.	10 [T]
			5.	7.	10

Hd. Somertone Forinsecus [SOMERTON FOREIGN HUNDRED]

Bryghamton'	Bridgehampton	ST/562241	1.	0.	0
Jevelton'	Yeovilton	ST/547230	1.	6.	8
Kyngesdone	Kingsdon	ST/515263	4.	0.	0
Cherleton'	Charlton Mackrell	ST/528283	2.	2.	0
Ludeford	East Lydford	ST/572313		4.	0
Lutleton'	Littleton	ST/491305	1.	6.	8
Suttone	Long Sutton	ST/469253	3.	9.	0
Alre	Aller	ST/397289	3.	3.	2
Cammel Abbatis	West Camel	ST/580246	1.	6.	4
Somertone Erlegh'	Somerton Erleigh	ST/500285		13.	4
			18.	11.	2[1]

Camel Regis [man.] [A.D]	Queen Camel	ST/597249	3.	1.	4 [T]
Langfort [B]	Langport	ST/422267	4.	0.	0 [T]
Tauntone [B]	Taunton	ST/225244	10.	3.	4 [T]
			17.	4.	8 [T]

Hd. Northcory [NORTH CURRY HUNDRED]

Thurlebere	Thurlbear	ST/265211	1.	6.	8
Westhacche	West Hatch	ST/285210	1.	13.	2
Thorne	Thornfalcon	ST/283239	1.	10.	0
Wrentych'[2]	Wrantage	ST/306223	1.	2.	6
Lillesdone	Lillesdon	ST/302235	2.	15.	6
Knap'[2]	Knapp	ST/301254	1.	4.	2
Niwport	Newport	ST/317234		8.	4
Northcory[2]	North Curry	ST/319256	3.	0.	0
Byestcory[2]	East Curry	ST/374292	1.	4.	10
Corylode[2]	Curload	ST/340279	2.	0.	0
Stath'[2][3]	Stathe	ST/374290	1.	11.	2
Wrentich' [A.D][4]	Wrantage	ST/306223	1.	2.	6 [T]
Knap' [A.D][4]	Knapp	ST/301254		13.	4 [T]

[1] Total of £18. 11. 4 on E 179/169/9 is an error.
[2] Part taxed at a tenth, below.
[3] *Stath'* substituted for *Hacche* on E 179/169/9; despite cancellation *Hacche* continues to appear in later documents, e.g. E 164/7, f. cccix (fifteenth-century book of fifteenths and tenths).
Part taxed at a fifteenth, above.

Northcory [A.D][1]	North Curry	ST/319256	1.	0.	0 [T]
Byestcory [A.D][1]	East Curry	ST/374292	2.	11.	0 [T]
Corylode [A.D][1]	Curload	ST/340279		18.	0 [T]
Stathe [A.D][1]	Stathe	ST/374290	2.	1.	0 [T]
			26.	2.	2

Hd. Brente [BRENT HUNDRED]

Suthbrente	Brent Knoll	ST/335508	4.	17.	8
Burghes	Berrow	ST/294524	9.	2.	2
Lympelesham	Lympsham	ST/336542	5.	18.	11
Estbrente	East Brent	ST/343519	10.	7.	11
Wryngton' [man.]	Wrington	ST/468627	10.	0.	0
Insula de Muchelnye	Muchelney	ST/429249	4.	0.	0
			44.	6.	8

Hd. Taunton' [TAUNTON HUNDRED]

Helfnaked	probably Henlade	ST/273230	3.	10.	0
Ruystone	Ruishton	ST/263251	1.	11.	0
Oterford	Otterford	ST/222143		18.	6
Holeweye	Holway	ST/245237	1.	6.	0
Galmynton'	Galmington	ST/211239	3.	8.	10
Wedelonde	?		2.	1.	6
Stoke	Stoke St. Mary	ST/266223	3.	6.	2
Decenna extra portam	Extra portam	ST/233249		5.	0
Blakedone[2]	Blagdon	ST/211188	1.	18.	0
Pyppemynstre	Pitminster	ST/220191	1.	5.	0
Fulford	Fulwood	ST/210204	2.	19.	0
Suthtrendle	South Trendle	ST/225210	1.	16.	0
Crof	Corfe	ST/232197	1.	13.	0
Cothelestone[3]	Cothelstone	ST/181319	4.	7.	0
Leghe	Leigh	ST/198192	2.	14.	0
Trendle	Trull	ST/217222	1.	8.	0
Romwelle	Rumwell	ST/192233		12.	0
Dypforde	Dipford	ST/204219		13.	0
Hulle	Bishop's Hull	ST/203246		11.	0
Burlond	Burlands	ST/207273		13.	0
Stapelgrave	Staplegrove	ST/211264	1.	6.	0
Holeford[4]	Holford	ST/145337	1.	1.	0
Tonbrigge	Obridge[5]	ST/235255		16.	0
Illebare	Illbeare	ST/193280		10.	0
Pyrlonde	Pyrland	ST/228276		15.	0
Mullane	Mill Lane	ST/225248		15.	0
Grascrofte	Grass Croft	ST/227249		8.	0
Cossewyssh'	Coshuish	ST/197306		8.	0
Kyngeston'	Kingston St. Mary	ST/223297		15.	2
Fulford	Fulford	ST/211293	1.	1.	0
Nailesburne	Nailsbourne	ST/216285		10.	2
Norton'	Norton Fitzwarren	ST/197260	1.	8.	2
Fenhamton'	Vennhampton	ST/187267		10.	0

[1] Part taxed at a fifteenth, above.
[2] See also *Blakedone Prioris*, below.
[3] There is an entry for another part of Cothelstone later in this hundred.
[4] Possibly one of the Holfords in Lydeard St. Lawrence.
[5] See also *Thoubrigge Prioris*, below.

Langeford	Langford	ST/201270		6.	2
Hethfelde	Heathfield	ST/160265		9.	2
Bradeforde	Bradford on Tone	ST/173230	1.	9.	3
Hele	Hele	ST/187246		8.	0
Hulle Feronn	Hillfarance	ST/168247		10.	0
Ake	Oake	ST/152252		13.	4
Pykstone	Pixton Barton	ST/135238		6.	0
Nyghenhyde Flory	Nynehead	ST/138228		17.	0
Nighenhyde Monachorum	East Nynehead	ST/154229		9.	4
Ocharde	Orchard Portman	ST/243216		6.	8
Blakedone Prioris[1]	Blagdon	ST/211186		7.	0
Fonte Prioris	probably Fons George	ST/224238		6.	8
Villa extra portam prioris	Extra portam	ST/233249		4.	0
Thoubrigge Prioris[1]	part of Obridge	ST/235255		3.	2
Legh' Militis	Angersleigh	ST/198190		3.	6
Bageburgh'	West Bagborough	ST/169337		8.	6
Toulonde	Tolland	ST/101323		5.	0
Chapellegh'	Chapel Leigh	ST/128296		5.	6
Occombe	Hoccombe	ST/113298		4.	6
Coumbe Flory	Combe Florey	ST/151312		13.	8
Lydyard Sancti Laurenc'	Lydeard St. Lawrence	ST/128321		6.	8
Cotheleston'[2]	Cothelstone	ST/181319		7.	0
Chedene	Cheddon Fitzpaine	ST/243276		13.	8
Wythele	Withiel Florey	SS/987333		8.	0
Hestercombe	Hestercombe	ST/208298		16.	0
Fydok'	Fideock	ST/192250		15.	6
Holeford	probably Holford Corseley	ST/140330		4.	0
Churchelegh'					
Lydyard Ponchardon'	Lydeard Punchardon	ST/177298		8.	0
			59.	14.	9

Libera Maneria [FREE MANORS]

Bromptone Regis	Brompton Regis	SS/951314	2.	12.	0
Dulverton'	Dulverton	SS/914280	2.	2.	0
Exton'	Exton	SS/926336	2.	18.	0
Craucombe[3]	Crowcombe	ST/141367	1.	18.	10
Wynesford	Winsford	SS/904350	2.	1.	0
Preston'[3] &	Preston and	ST/101358	1.	2.	6
Selver	Monksilver	ST/073374			
Brisshford	Brushford	SS/919258	1.	12.	0
Clyve	Old Cleeve	ST/041419	2.	1.	0
Wylytone	Williton	ST/077410	3.	0.	0
Halse	Halse	ST/140278	2.	14.	10
Brompton' Rauf'	Brompton Ralph	ST/084323		16.	8
Lenge	Lyng	ST/333288	2.	1.	0
Crych'	Creech St. Michael	ST/274253	11.	0.	0
			35.	19.	10

[1] See also above.
[2] There is an entry for another part of Cothelstone earlier in this hundred.
[3] Partly taxed in Williton hundred, below.

Hd. Abbedyk' [ABDICK HUNDRED]

Stapele[1]	Staple Fitzpaine	ST/263183	3.	0.	0
Bykenhull'	Bickenhall	ST/283187		6.	8
Hacche	Hatch Beauchamp	ST/306212	2.	5.	0
Capelond[2]	Capland	ST/303188		5.	2
Stiflegh'	Stewley	ST/315185		6.	8
Bere	Beercrocombe	ST/326204	1.	2.	4
Cory Malet	Curry Mallet	ST/333209	3.	0.	0
Iltone[3]	Ilton	ST/351175	2.	6.	8
Stokelynch'	Stocklinch	ST/386171		10.	0
Athelardeston'	Atherstone	ST/383164		7.	10
Wyghtlakyngton'[4]	Whitelackington	ST/379153	1.	15.	8
Illemynstre[5]	Ilminster	ST/361146	1.	0.	0
Doneyate	Donyatt	ST/339141		13.	6
Asshulle	Ashill	ST/321173	1.	4.	0
Ilemynstre[5]	Ilminster	ST/361146	2.	11.	10
Ile Abbatis	Isle Abbotts	ST/352209	1.	11.	0
			22.	6.	4

Hd. Wylytone [WILLITON HUNDRED]

Benicombe	Bincombe	ST/184392		12.	10
Honybere	Honibere	ST/182435	1.	0.	6
Culuetone	Kilton	ST/166422	1.	0.	0
Kylve	Kilve	ST/149429	1.	1.	0
Estcauntokeshefd	East Quantoxhead	ST/137437		15.	6
Westcauntokeshefde	West Quantoxhead	ST/113420		16.	0
Bykenalre	Bicknoller	ST/111395	1.	2.	0
Halsweye	Halsway	ST/130378		12.	10
Craucombe[6]	Crowcombe	ST/141367	1.	0.	0
Westowe	Westowe	ST/124328		10.	0
Elleworth'	Elworthy	ST/082350		18.	0
Preston[6] &	Preston and	ST/101358		13.	4
Stok' Gommer'	Stogumber	ST/098373			
Saumford Brutel	Sampford Brett	ST/090402		13.	4
Netelcombe	Nettlecombe	ST/057378	1.	4.	0
Lodehiwyssh'	Lodhuish	ST/c.045396		6.	0
Wode	Woodadvent	ST/037373		4.	0
Toru](eston'	Torweston	ST/093408		5.	0
Cloteworthy	Clatworthy	ST/052309		14.	0
Syndercombe	Syndercombe	ST/038308		8.	0
Hiwissh' Chaumpflur	Huish Champflower	ST/049293	1.	0.	0
Radyngton'	Raddington	ST/020260		8.	6
Chypstapele	Chipstable	ST/043271		16.	0
Skylegate	Skilgate	ST/987273		15.	6
			16.	16.	4

---

[1] *cum Corilond* in 1327 (Dickinson, op. cit. 187).
[2] Partly taxed in Bulstone hundred (p. 272).
[3] *cum Bradene et Murifeld* in 1327 (Dickinson, op. cit. 187–90).
[4] *cum Athelarstone et Stoklinche* in 1327, ibid.
[5] Presumably a different part of Ilminster to the other entry.
[6] See also p. 265.

Hd. Whitston' [WHITESTONE HUNDRED]

Corscombe	Croscombe	ST/591444	3.	10.	0
Shepton' Malet	Shepton Mallet	ST/620436	10.	11.	4
Doultynge	Doulting	ST/646432	5.	5.	10
Cherltone	Charlton	ST/630433	2.	8.	10
Batecombe	Batcombe	ST/690390	4.	14.	6
Lameyete	Lamyatt	ST/661362	1.	4.	4
Dychesyete	Ditcheat	ST/626363	3.	0.	0
Alapton'	Alhampton	ST/628346	2.	0.	4
Hornbloutone	Hornblotton	ST/591341		9.	4
Pennard	East Pennard	ST/597374	5.	9.	8
Pulle	Pylle	ST/607383	2.	1.	0
Bradelegh'	West Bradley	ST/558369	1.	3.	8
Lottesham	Lottisham	ST/570351	1.	5.	0
Baltonesbergh'	Baltonsborough	ST/542348	2.	13.	0
Pultone	Pilton	ST/589408	4.	0.	0
Comptone	Compton[1]	ST/593422	3.	14.	8
Wottone	North Wootton	ST/563418	3.	8.	8
Dunheued	Downhead	ST/692462		13.	4
			57.	13.	6

Hd. Chiw [CHEW HUNDRED]

Clutton'	Clutton	ST/623589		17.	4
Tymysbergh'	Timsbury	ST/667586	2.	8.	0
Staweye	Stowey	ST/599594	1.	2.	2
Suttone Militis	Knighton Sutton	ST/599608		12.	10
Stok' Abbatis[2]	Stoke Abbot		1.	2.	8
Stoke Militis[2]	Knighton Stoke		1.	15.	5
Northton' Hautevill'	Norton Hawkfield	ST/593646	1.	8.	1
Northton' Marleward	Norton Malreward	ST/603650	1.	14.	6
Lutleton'	Littleton	ST/556636		9.	4
Dondray	Dundry	ST/558669	1.	18.	8
Northwyk'	North Wick	ST/585654	1.	4.	8
Northelme	North Elm	ST/577636		11.	8
Stone	West Chew			5.	0
Knolle	Knowle Hill	ST/582611	2.	0.	0
Suttone Episcopi	Bishop Sutton	ST/590594	1.	9.	8
			19.	0.	0

Hd. Canyngton' [CANNINGTON HUNDRED]

Corypole	Currypool	ST/227384	1.	0.	2
Canyngton'	Cannington	ST/258395	1.	6.	0
Addescombe	Adscombe	ST/182378		6.	8
Pleynesfeld	Plainsfield	ST/195366	1.	6.	0
Spaxton'	Spaxton	ST/225371	1.	5.	0
Shireueton'	Shurton	ST/201442	1.	4.	8
Stoklond Gaunt	Stockland Bristol	ST/240436	1.	6.	8
Strengeston'	Stringston	ST/177424		12.	0
Fytyngton'	Fiddington	ST/216406	1.	10.	0
Radeweye	Rodway	ST/256402	1.	12.	0
Assholte	Aisholt	ST/193356	2.	18.	0

[1] Grid ref. is to West Compton. [2] Manors of Chew Stoke (ST/557619).

Ichestok'	Edstock	ST/233409		13.	4
Wyke	Wick	ST/216445	3.	10.	8
Oterhampton'	Otterhampton	ST/246432	1.	0.	0
Coumbwych'	Combwich	ST/259423		10.	0
Chiltone[1]	Chilton Trinity	ST/297392	3.	10.	0
			23.	11.	2

Hd. Welewe [WELLOW HUNDRED]

Welewe	Wellow	ST/742584	5.	10.	0
Telesford &	Tellisford and	ST/801557	2.	0.	0
Farlegh'	Farleigh Hungerford	ST/800573			
Lutleton' &	Stony Littleton and	ST/730566	2.	0.	0
Foxton'	Foxcote	ST/716556			
Wyttokesmede	White Ox Mead	ST/720583	1.	0.	0
Henton' &	Hinton Charterhouse	ST/777583	1.	0.	0
Bagerigge	and Baggridge	ST/748568			
Norton'	Norton St. Philip	ST/772557	1.	0.	0
Donkerton'	Dunkerton	ST/711593	2.	0.	0
Camelerton'	Camerton	ST/687575	1.	0.	8
Coumelehaweye	Combe Hay	ST/735599	1.	2.	10
Corston'	Corston	ST/695653	2.	1.	2
Niwton'	Newton St. Loe	ST/701649	4.	0.	4
Inglescombe	English Combe	ST/717629	3.	6.	8
Tyuerton'	Twerton	ST/723647	1.	16.	0
			27.	17.	8

Hd. Frome [FROME HUNDRED]

Frome	Frome	ST/777479	8.	13.	3[2]
Clouord	Cloford	ST/727440	2.	6.	8
Mershton'	Marston Bigot	ST/755450	1.	10.	0
Elme	Elm	ST/747493	1.	4.	0
Wondestre[3]	Wanstrow	ST/710417	2.	18.	0
Whattelegh'	Whatley	ST/734476	3.	1.	0
Rode	Rode	ST/803538	4.	2.	0
Lullyngton'	Lullington	ST/783519		12.	4
Laurton'	Laverton	ST/775534	1.	1.	0
Orchardlegh'	Orchardleigh	ST/772510		13.	4
Radene	Rodden	ST/799477		10.	0
Staurewyk'	Standerwick	ST/820507	2.	10.	0
Nony	Nunney	ST/738457	4.	0.	0
Bekyngton'	Beckington	ST/802516		14.	0
			33.	15.	7

Hd. Briwtone [BRUTON HUNDRED]

| Yerdlyngton' | Yarlington | ST/655293 | 2. | 9. | 0 |
| Miltone | Milton Clevedon | ST/665378 | 1. | 16. | 8 |

[1] Part of Chilton was taxed in North Petherton hundred, above.
[2] £8. 13. 4 on E 179/169/9 is an error.
[3] Part of Wanstrow was taxed with Upton Noble in Bruton hundred (p. 269).

Wyke	Wyke Champflower	ST/662344	2.	12.	0
Colle &	Cole and	ST/672335			
Pydecombe	Pitcombe	ST/672327			
Honywyk'	Honeywick	ST/653325	3.	6.	0
Briwham[1]	Brewham	ST/720362	5.	3.	0
Redlissh'	Redlynch	ST/700333	1.	12.	0
Briwtone	Bruton	ST/685348	6.	6.	8
Uptone &	Upton Noble and	ST/712393	1.	10.	0
Wondestr'[2]	Wanstrow	ST/710417			
			24.	15.	4

Hd. Nortone [NORTON FERRIS HUNDRED]

Norton'	Norton Ferris [in Wiltshire]	ST/790366	2.	12.	0
Culmeton'	Kilmington [in Wiltshire]	ST/780359	2.	10.	0
Penne	Penselwood	ST/756314	1.	16.	0
Cherlton'	Charlton Musgrove	ST/720299	2.	2.	0
Sheptone	Shepton Montague	ST/682318	3.	6.	4
Cokelyngton'	Cucklington	ST/755277	4.	0.	0
Wyncaultone	Wincanton	ST/712285	6.	0.	0
			22.	6.	4

Hd. Horethurne [HORETHORNE HUNDRED]

Stawelle	Stowell	ST/687223	1.	10.	0
Cherlton'	Charlton Horethorne	ST/665231	5.	0.	0
Hengstrigge	Henstridge	ST/723197	4.	10.	0
Poyntynton'	Poyntington [in Dorset]	ST/650199	2.	10.	4
Chyryton'[3]	Cheriton	ST/687258	1.	2.	8
Trente	Trent [in Dorset]	ST/589185	2.	16.	8
Holewale	Holwell [in Dorset]	ST/699120	2.	16.	8
Horsyngton'	Horsington	ST/703238	2.	11.	0
Coumbe Abbatisse &	Combe Abbas and	ST/709227	1.	11.	0
Temple	Temple Combe	ST/709221			
Sandford	Sandford Orcas	ST/622211	1.	6.	8
Gothulle	Goathill [both in Dorset]	ST/675172			
Rympton'	Rimpton	ST/610219	3.	0.	0
Mershton'	Marston Magna	ST/593223	2.	0.	0
Corfton'	Corton Denham	ST/636226	2.	16.	0
			33.	11.	0

Hd. Hundesbergh' [HOUNDSBOROUGH HUNDRED]

Perret	North Perrott	ST/472095	1.	12.	0
Haselbere	Haselbury Plucknett	ST/471110	1.	11.	4
Westchynnok'	West Chinnock	ST/467133	1.	12.	0
Chuselbergh'	Chiselborough	ST/468149	2.	16.	8

---

[1] The entry probably covers North and South Brewham; the grid ref. given is to South.
[2] Most of Wanstrow was taxed in Frome hundred (p. 268).
[3] The entry probably covers North and South Cheriton; the grid ref. given is to North.

Nortone	Norton Sub Hamdon	ST/470160	5.	0.	0
Odecombe	Odcombe	ST/507155	2.	10.	0
Estchynnok'	East Chinnock	ST/499132	3.	0.	8
			18.	2.	8

Hd. Kyngesbury [KINGSBURY HUNDRED]

Kyngesbury	Kingsbury Episcopi	ST/437211	11.	4.	8
Hywissh[1]	Huish Episcopi	ST/427266	3.	5.	11
Wynesham	Winsham	ST/374063	1.	4.	10
Cherde[2]	Chard	ST/322085	2.	15.	7
Welyngton'	Wellington	ST/141209	1.	8.	8
Purye[3]	probably Perry Elm	ST/118195	5.	15.	9
Boklond	West Buckland	ST/173205	3.	2.	9
Wyvelescombe	Wiveliscombe	ST/083277	6.	0.	0
Lydyard	Bishop's Lydeard	ST/168298	1.	10.	8
			36.	8.	10

Hd. Coker' [COKER HUNDRED]

Estcoker	East Coker	ST/539122	4.	2.	0
Clonesworth'	Closworth	ST/563101	4.	4.	0
Westcoker	West Coker	ST/516136	3.	10.	0
Hardyngton'	Hardington Mandeville	ST/512120	1.	14.	8
Merssh'	Hardington Marsh	ST/506097	1.	6.	8
Penne	Pendomer	ST/521104		16.	0
Sutton'	Sutton Bingham	ST/548111	2.	1.	0
			17.	14.	4

Hd. Kaynesham [KEYNSHAM HUNDRED]

Kaynesham	Keynsham	ST/654688	3.	10.	4½
Chiwton'	Chewton Keynsham	ST/652664	3.	0.	11
Filtone	Whitchurch	ST/612675	2.	6.	5
Bristolton'	Brislington	ST/621708	3.	0.	8
Staunton' Dru	Stanton Drew	ST/598632	1.	10.	0
Throbbewelle	Nempnett Thrubwell	ST/533603	1.	17.	1
Belgheton'	Belluton	ST/613644		8.	0
Pobbelewe	Publow	ST/623642	1.	4.	6½
Compton' Daundo	Compton Dando	ST/646647	1.	0.	6½
Saltford	Saltford	ST/686675		11.	0
Burnet	Burnett	ST/664653		6.	2
Merkesbury	Marksbury	ST/667623		12.	1
Staunton' Prior	Stanton Prior	ST/678627	1.	5.	2½
Prisshton'	Priston	ST/693604	1.	15.	6
Cheleworthy	Chelwood	ST/635619		18.	2
Farnbergh'	Farmborough	ST/661605	1.	0.	6
			24.	7.	2

[1] Part of Huish Episcopi was taxed at a tenth (p. 273).
[2] Chard borough was taxed at a tenth (p. 273).
[3] Identification uncertain. The quota is large for what is now a small place and it may represent a number of settlements in this area. *Payton* is included with *Purye* in 1327, Dickinson, op. cit. 258–9.

Hd. Forinsecus de Welles [WELLS FOREIGN HUNDRED]

Evercrych'	Evercreech	ST/649387	1.	18.	8
Chesterblade	Chesterblade	ST/661413		13.	10
Cranemere[1]	Cranmore	ST/682435	2.	12.	4
Whitcherche	Whitchurch	ST/635535	2.	6.	0
Doulcecote &	Dulcote and	ST/564445	1.	1.	2
Chelecote	Chilcote	ST/585462			
Milton' &	Milton and	ST/546474	1.	13.	0
Woky	Wookey Hole	ST/532478			
Burecote	Burcott	ST/526452		9.	4
Dynre	Dinder	ST/575445		15.	8
Wormesterre	Worminster	ST/572429		7.	0
Hornyngdon'	Horrington[2]	ST/581467	1.	12.	10
Yurdlogh'	Yarley	ST/502452	4.	13.	4
Woky	Wookey	ST/518458		17.	0
Eston'	Easton	ST/513477		16.	6
Prydye	Priddy	ST/528514	1.	6.	2
Luttone	Litton	ST/593547		12.	2
Cokeslegh'	Coxley	ST/531438	1.	12.	8
Westbury	Westbury sub Mendip	ST/500487	1.	15.	8
			25.	3.	4
Honespulle [man.]	Huntspill	ST/305454	11.	6.	8
Moneketon' [man.]	West Monkton	ST/263284	4.	0.	4
			15.	7.	0

Hd. Hareclyve [HARTCLIFFE HUNDRED]

Asshton'	Long Ashton	ST/553710	4.	13.	1½
Barewe	Barrow Gurney	ST/528681	1.	8.	8
Bakwelle	Backwell	ST/492684	5.	0.	7½
Chelvy	Chelvey	ST/466683		18.	4
Wyndfred &	Winford and	ST/543650	4.	6.	7
Felton'	Felton	ST/515656			
Bodycombe &	Butcombe and	ST/515619	2.	2.	4
Raggelbury	Regilbury	ST/528628			
			18.	9.	8

Hd. Portbury [PORTBURY HUNDRED]

Eston'	Easton in Gordano	ST/513757	1.	19.	8
Portbury	Portbury	ST/503754	5.	19.	3½
Wrexhale	Wraxall	ST/490720	7.	17.	10
Clopton'	Clapton in Gordano	ST/468736	1.	5.	4
Tykenham	Tickenham	ST/458715	2.	17.	9
Porteshefd'	Portishead	ST/466760	3.	19.	9½
Walton'	Walton in Gordano	ST/426732		15.	8½
Clyvedone	Clevedon	ST/407713	2.	11.	3½
			27.	6.	8

[1] The manor of Cranmore was taxed separately (p. 273).
[2] Grid ref. is to East Horrington.

Hd. Carampton' [CARHAMPTON HUNDRED]

			£	s.	d.
Carampton'	Carhampton	ST/009427	2.	10.	0
Mynnehefde	Minehead	SS/968462	2.	10.	0
Wottone	Wootton Courtney	SS/938434	2.	0.	0
Loccombe	Luccombe	SS/911445	1.	6.	0
Alresford	Allerford	SS/904470	1.	2.	4
Bosyngton'	Bossington	SS/898478		16.	0
Porloc	Porlock	SS/887467	1.	10.	4
Codicombe	Cutcombe	SS/931393	1.	0.	0
Lokerbergh'	Luxborough	SS/973380	1.	3.	4
Wythycombe	Withycombe	ST/015413	1.	8.	10
Tymbercombe	Timberscombe	SS/957420		18.	0
Avele	Avill	SS/977431		10.	0
Broune[1]	?			15.	0
Almannesworth'	Almsworthy	SS/c.840420	1.	10.	4
Exeford	Exford	SS/858385		11.	4
Ore	Oare	SS/802473		12.	6
Yarnere	Yearnor	SS/848477	1.	13.	3
			21.	17.	3

Hd. Bulston [BULSTONE HUNDRED]

			£	s.	d.
Cory Ryvel	Curry Rivel	ST/391254	4.	10.	0
Hambrigge	Hambridge	ST/392210	2.	4.	4
Radeweye	Broadway	ST/320154	2.	6.	6
Capelonde[2]	Capland	ST/303188		11.	0
Wyke	Wick	ST/400268		6.	2
Langeford	Langford	ST/359229		3.	0
Staweye	Stowey	ST/343223		2.	6
Cryket	Cricket Malherbie	ST/361115		12.	0
Deuelissh'	West Dowlish	ST/362132		14.	0
Pokyngton'	Puckington	ST/377183		14.	10
Baryngton'[3]	Barrington	ST/389181		3.	0
Bradene	South Bradon	ST/366187		6.	8
Ilebruere	Isle Brewers	ST/369211	1.	0.	10
Erneshulle	Earnshill	ST/386217		2.	6
Swelle	Swell	ST/369235		10.	0
More	West Moor	ST/415216		3.	0
Gosebradene	Goosebradon	ST/388207		3.	6
Bokelonde	Buckland St. Mary	ST/271134		3.	6
Westovere	Westover	ST/421247	1.	1.	0
Fifhyde	Fivehead	ST/353229		13.	4
Draytone	Drayton	ST/405247	1.	9.	10½
			18.	1.	6½

			£	s.	d.	
Axebrigge [B]	Axbridge	ST/432546	4.	10.	0	[T]
Were [B][4]	Weare	ST/414526	1.	8.	0	[T]
Stok' Curcy [B]	Stogursey	ST/204428	2.	0.	2	[T]
Nitherstoweye [B]	Nether Stowey	ST/197396		13.	4	[T]
Briggewater [B]	Bridgwater	ST/298370	26.	0.	0	[T]

[1] A manor in Treborough: perhaps the name survives in Brown Cottages, SS/998368 (six-inch map)?   [2] Partly taxed in Abdick hundred (p. 266).
[3] Most of Barrington was taxed in South Petherton hundred (p. 275).
[4] Part of Weare was taxed with Chapel Allerton at a fifteenth (p. 262).

			£	s.	d.	
Mulverton' [B] cum hundred' intrinsec' [A.D]	Milverton [with hundred]	ST/121259	2.	5.	0	[T]
Mulverton' [B]	Milverton	ST/121259	3.	10.	0	[T]
			40.	6.	6	[T]
Bageworth' [man.] [A.D]	Badgworth	ST/395526	1.	16.	0	[T]
Hiwissh' [man.] [A.D][1]	Huish Episcopi	ST/427266	1.	4.	0	[T]
Densterre [B]	Dunster	SS/990435	3.	2.	4	[T]
Cherde [B][2]	Chard	ST/322085	1.	6.	0	[T]
Mulebornepourt [B]	Milborne Port	ST/677189	3.	0.	0	[T]
Somerton' [v]	Somerton	ST/490286	5.	19.	9	[T]
Hurdecote	Hurcot	ST/506296	1.	3.	2	
			17.	11.	3	
Civitas Bathon'	Bath City	ST/751648	13.	6.	8	[T]
Welles [B]	Wells	ST/550458	19.	0.	0	[T]
Heghehamme [man.]	High Ham	ST/425311	3.	0.	10	
Puttenye Plokenet [man.]	Wearne	ST/426281	1.	10.	8	
Bleedone [man.]	Bleadon	ST/341569	3.	10.	0	
Cranemere [man.][3]	Cranmore	ST/682435	1.	2.	2	
Kyngesbury Reg' [A.D]	Kingsbury Regis	ST/676194	2.	2.	0	[T]
Westcomelonde	Westcombland	ST/c.250145	1.	17.	0	
Glaston' cum xii hidis	Glastonbury	ST/500390	12.	6.	8	
			57.	16.	0	

Hd. Crukerne [CREWKERNE HUNDRED]

			£	s.	d.
Crukerne	Crewkerne	ST/441097	9.	3.	10
Hiwissh'	Hewish	ST/421083		18.	0
Clopton'	Clapton	ST/414065		7.	10
Estham	Lower Eastham	ST/457105		10.	4
Henton'	Hinton St. George	ST/418127	1.	16.	2
Othulle	Oathill	ST/405055	1.	7.	8
Wayforde	Wayford	ST/409068	1.	3.	0
Seuebergh'	Seaborough [in Dorset]	ST/430060		10.	6
Wolmereston'	Woolminstone	ST/410080		13.	4
Coumbe	Coombe	ST/410094		8.	7
Craft	Croft	ST/412113		6.	8
Mynsterton'	Misterton	ST/452082	1.	12.	8
Forlonde	Furland	ST/429117		10.	2
Meryet	Merriott	ST/442129	5.	6.	8
			24.	15.	5

Hd. Whitelegh' [WHITLEY HUNDRED]

			£	s.	d.
Weston'	Westonzoyland	ST/352348	9.	0.	1
Middelsowy	Middlezoy	ST/375331	8.	2.	4
Othery	Othery	ST/382316	8.	14.	3
Murlynch'	Moorlinch	ST/398369	1.	1.	2
Grynton'	Greinton	ST/412363	1.	10.	0
Schapewyk'	Shapwick	ST/418382	1.	9.	4

---

[1] Part of Huish Episcopi was taxed at a fifteenth (p. 270).
[2] Part of Chard was taxed at a fifteenth (p. 270).
[3] See also p. 271.

			£	s.	d.
Asshcote	Ashcott	ST/437372	2.	11.	4
Waltone	Walton	ST/462363	1.	5.	4
Stret'	Street	ST/488372	1.	12.	8
Buddecleye	Butleigh	ST/520339	1.	14.	4
Middelton'	Podimore	ST/545250		19.	8
Cary	Cary Fitzpaine	ST/550270		10.	0
Dondene	Dundon	ST/479326	2.	16.	0
Cadecote	Catcott	ST/394393	1.	0.	0
Edyngton'	Edington	ST/388398	1.	1.	2
Cheleton'	Chilton Polden	ST/373400		13.	8
Cosyngton'	Cossington	ST/357403	1.	7.	4
Stawelle	Stawell	ST/368383		16.	2
Sutton'	Sutton Mallet	ST/372369		16.	4
Woolavington'	Woolavington	ST/348417	2.	0.	0
Blakeford	Blackford	ST/658261		14.	4
Whethull'	Wheathill	ST/582308		6.	8
Middelton'[1]	?			9.	0
			50.	11.	2
Puryton' [man.]	Puriton	ST/321417	2.	15.	0

Hd. Mertok' [MARTOCK HUNDRED]

			£	s.	d.
Mertok'	Martock	ST/462192	3.	8.	0
Henton'	Bower Hinton	ST/457182	4.	11.	0
Hurste	Hurst	ST/457188	3.	4.	0
Cote	Coat	ST/453204	3.	14.	4
Stapelton'	Stapleton	ST/463210	3.	5.	0
Miltone	Milton	ST/468219	2.	2.	0
Lade	Long Load	ST/465233	1.	12.	0
Asshe	Ash	ST/472207	3.	0.	4
Wydecoumbe	Witcombe	ST/476216	3.	17.	8
			28.	14.	4
Wachet [B]	Watchet	ST/072433	1.	2.	4 [T]
Monteacute [B]	Montacute	ST/497169	3.	4.	0 [T]
			4.	6.	4 [T]

Hd. Tyntenhulle [TINTINHULL HUNDRED]

			£	s.	d.
Kyngeston'	Kingstone	ST/379137	3.	2.	8
Stoke	Stoke sub Hamdon	ST/473176	4.	10.	0
Stoket	East Stoke	ST/487175	1.	8.	8
Hestecombe	Hescombe		1.	12.	6
Draycote	Draycott	ST/549217	1.	11.	7
Tyntenhull'	Tintinhull	ST/498197	2.	3.	8
Bisshopeston'	Bishopstone	ST/497170	2.	16.	7
			17.	5.	8
Iuelcestre [B] cum	Ilchester with	ST/522226	2.	0.	0 [T]
Stok' Deneys [A.D]	Sock Dennis	ST/516213			
Sok' Deneys [A.D][2]	Sock Dennis	ST/516213	1.	16.	2 [T]
			3.	16.	2 [T]

---

[1] Possibly the same Middleton as above.   [2] See also previous entry.

Hd. Suthpederton' [SOUTH PETHERTON HUNDRED]

Stauntone	Whitestaunton	ST/281105	1.	4.	3
Leghe	Leigh	ST/355062		10.	0
Strete &	Street and	ST/352071			
Libenersh'	Lidmarsh	ST/357089			
Chastcombe &	Chaffcombe and	ST/353102	1.	6.	8
Knolle	Knowle St. Giles	ST/345114			
Codeworth'	Cudworth	ST/380105		15.	0
Cryket Thomas	Cricket St. Thomas	ST/373087		16.	6
Dynyngton'	Dinnington	ST/402128	1.	2.	0
Shepton' Beauchamp	Shepton Beauchamp	ST/403172	1.	10.	0
Sevenhampton' Abbatis	Seavington Abbots	ST/407153		10.	4
Sevenhampton' Vaux	Seavington St. Mary	ST/403150	1.	11.	4
Sevenhampton' Deneys	Seavington St. Michael	ST/410150		16.	2
Lepene	Lopen	ST/427145	1.	16.	4
Baryngton'[1]	Barrington	ST/389181	1.	10.	0
Cheleton'	Chillington	ST/389111		18.	10
Deuelissh Wake	Dowlish Wake	ST/376130	1.	0.	8
Suttharpe	South Harp	ST/435150	1.	14.	0
Stratton'	Over Stratton	ST/434152	1.	0.	2
Suthpederton'	South Petherton	ST/431171	4.	2.	4
			22.	4.	7

[Additional Payments][2]   53.   0.   0

TOTAL: £1,357. 19. 2½[3]

---

[1] See also p. 272.

[2] These comprise increments additional to the payments made in 1332 against:

  (i) the bishop of Bath (£20, for possessions in the hundreds of Winterstoke, Chew, Kingsbury and Wells Foreign, the manor of Combe, and the borough of Axbridge).

  (ii) the abbot of Glastonbury (£20, for possessions in the hundreds of Whitestone and Whitley, the manors of Mells, Leigh, Wrington, West Monkton, and Marksbury in Keynsham hundred).

  (iii) Maurice de Berkeley (£3, for possessions in the hundreds of Hartcliffe and Portbury, and the manor of Bedminster).

  (iv) the bishop of Winchester (£5, for possessions in Taunton hundred and the borough of Taunton).

  (v) Martock hundred (£5).

While the places concerned are denoted by marginal abbreviations on the roll there is no means of allocating specific tax amounts to particular places. Nor is it clear from the roll (E 179/169/9) why these payments are listed separately in this way.

[3] As on 1334 Account, E 179/169/8.

STAFFORDSHIRE

DOCUMENTS

    8 Edward III: Account   E 179/177/3
    8 Edward III: Particulars   not extant
   12 Edward III: Particulars   E 179/177/6*
   13 Edward III: Particulars   E 179/177/7

TAXERS

The abbot of Burton on Trent and William de Bromleye

TAX YIELD

15th	£485.	16.	$1\frac{1}{4}$
10th	£ 92.	14.	$4\frac{1}{2}$
	£578.	10.	$5\frac{3}{4}$

Representing assessed movable wealth of

    £8,214.   5. $3\frac{3}{4}$

NOTES

Places taxed at a tenth are listed at the beginning of the roll of 12 Edward III. They include the four taxation boroughs of Stafford, Lichfield, Newcastle under Lyme, and Tamworth (part of which was taxed in Warwickshire). Burton on Trent and Eccleshall, which had been considered boroughs in 1313, were taxed at a fifteenth. Over half of the tax at a tenth was that on ancient demesnes scattered throughout the county.

In Staffordshire many places were linked together for taxation purposes. Twelve entries are *cum membris* and there are no details of these members either in the rolls of 1327 and 1332 or in the *Nomina Villarum* of 1316.

Mainly as a result of the administrative reorganization of the nineteenth century the outline of the modern county differs from that of 1334. The Staffordshire list includes eight places which have since been transferred to other counties, viz. Clent, Broom, and Upper Arley to Worcestershire, Sheriff Hales to Shropshire, and Harborne, Handsworth, Perry Barr, and Little Barr to Warwickshire. On the other hand, Staffordshire has gained that part of Tamworth which was taxed in Warwickshire in 1334, and also four places then taxed in Derbyhire: Croxall, Edingale, Stapenhill, and Winshill.

REFERENCES

G. Wrottesley, 'The Exchequer subsidy roll of A.D. 1327', *William Salt Arch. Soc.* 7 (1886), part 1, 195–255.

G. Wrottesley, 'The subsidy roll of 6 Edward III, A.D. 1332–3', *William Salt Arch. Soc.* 10 (1889), part 1, 79–132.

E. M. Yates, 'A contribution to the historical geography of north-west Staffordshire', *Geographical Studies*, 2 (1955), 39–52.

[BOROUGHS AND ANCIENT DEMESNES]

Staff [B]	Stafford	SJ/922232	14.	8.	0	[T]
Novi' Castri' [B]	Newcastle under Lyme	SJ/847461	10.	16.	8	[T]
Penghull' [A.D]	Penkhull	SJ/869448	5.	2.	4	[T]
Shelton' [A.D]	Shelton	SJ/873480				
Clatton' [A.D]	Clayton	SJ/852432				
Sheperugg' [A.D]	Seabridge	SJ/837434				
Wolstanton' [A.D]	Wolstanton	SJ/857481				
Keel [A.D]	Keele	SJ/810452	1.	9.	0	[T]
Lychefeld [B]	Lichfield	SK/118095	13.	6.	8	[T]
Tamworth [B] [p]¹	Tamworth [part of]	SK/208041	3.	13.	6	[T]
Wygynton' [A.D]	Wigginton	SK/209068	5.	4.	0	[T]
Hopewas [A.D]	Hopwas	SK/176051				
Coton' [A.D]	Coton	SK/185051				
Comberford [A.D]	Comberford	SK/191072				
Allerwas [A.D]	Alrewas	SK/167153	3.	10.	0	[T]
Bromleye Reg' [A.D]	King's Bromley	SK/122170	2.	18.	0	[T]
Walshale c.m [A.D]²	Walsall [with members]	SP/013986	6.	6.	1½	[T]
Wednesbury [A.D]	Wednesbury	SO/986947				
Mere [A.D] &	Meretown and	SJ/756204	3.	15.	0	[T]
Forton' [A.D]	Forton	SJ/754212				
Tetenhale [A.D]³	Tettenhall	SO/878992	5.	14.	10	[T]
Kynfare [A.D]	Kinver	SO/847831	7.	10.	0	[T]
Haffecote [A.D]	Halfcot	SO/866854				
Compton' [A.D]	Compton	SO/822846				
Clent [A.D] &	Clent and	SO/929794	2.	10.	9	[T]
Brome [A.D]	Broom [both in Worcestershire]	SO/902785				
Swynford Reg' [A.D]	Kingswinford	SO/894893	2.	17.	3	[T]
Roweley [A.D]	Rowley Regis	SO/971874	3.	12.	3	[T]
			92.	14.	4½	[T]

Hd. Pirhull' [PIREHILL HUNDRED]

Heiwode	Haywood⁴	SJ/998227	7.	4.	9¼
Morton'	Moreton	SK/026227			
Bisshopeston'	Bishton	SK/022207			
Wolseleye	Wolseley	SK/023203			
Frodeswall'	Fradswell	SJ/992312			
Colton'	Colton	SK/048203	3.	16.	8
Bromley Bagot	Bagot's Bromley	SK/066260	2.	0.	0¾
Bromley Abbatis	Abbot's Bromley	SK/079245	5.	7.	8
Neuton' &	Newton and	SK/039255	2.	10.	0
Blithefeld	Blithfield	SK/044240			
Charteleye	Chartley	SK/007284	5.	6.	8
Weston'	Weston upon Trent	SJ/973271			
Ingestre	Ingestre	SJ/978247	1.	0.	1
Tixale	Tixall	SJ/979228	1.	18.	0

¹ The rest of the borough of Tamworth, which straddled the county boundary, was taxed in Warwickshire (p. 320).

² For this county it is not possible to suggest from other documents which places were included in entries *cum membris*. Neither in the rolls of 1327 and 1332, nor in the aid of 1316, are any of these members named.

³ Part of Tettenhall was taxed in Seisdon hundred at a fifteenth (p. 283).

⁴ Grid ref. is to Great Haywood.

Old name	Modern name	Grid ref			
Hopton' &	Hopton and	SJ/943261	2.	0.	7½
Coton'	Coton	SJ/930240			
Sondon'	Sandon	SJ/954294	3.	3.	4
Salt' &	Salt and	SJ/953279	1.	6.	8
Enston'	Enson	SJ/941288			
Mereston'	Marston	SJ/921277	3.	10.	0
Tylynton'	Tillington	SJ/913258		12.	6
Cressewall'	Creswell	SJ/898260	1.	6.	0
Whitegreve	Whitgreave	SJ/898282		8.	0
Aston' &	Aston and	SJ/914318	1.	15.	8
Burneston'	Burston	SJ/935300			
Walton' iuxta Stone	Walton	SJ/900333	2.	5.	6
Stone &	Stone and	SJ/900341	4.	2.	0
Stalynton'	Stallington	SJ/944393			
Cubbleston'	Kibblestone	SJ/913362	4.	10.	0
Derlaston'	Darlaston	SJ/884356	1.	4.	8
Mulewich'	Milwich	SJ/971320	2.	0.	0
Hildreston'	Hilderstone	SJ/950347	2.	6.	8
Fulford &	Fulford and	SJ/952383	2.	10.	2¼
Severleye	Saverley	SJ/966386			
Draycote	Draycott in the Moors	SJ/981402	2.	17.	0
Fenton' Vivian	Fenton [Vivian][1]	SJ/899451	1.	8.	2
Longeton' &	Longton and	SJ/910437			
Hanley	Hanley	SJ/882476			
Fenton' Culvart	Fenton [Culvert]	SJ/899451	3.	2.	3
Buckenhale	Bucknall	SJ/905478			
Bidulf'	Biddulph	SJ/890591	2.	6.	0
Norton' othe mores	Norton in the Moors	SJ/894515	3.	0.	0
Chesterton'	Chesterton	SJ/831494	1.	8.	0¼
Tunstal iuxta Castru'	Tunstall	SJ/864513	2.	16.	8
Knotton' c.m	Knutton [with members]	SJ/833471	2.	8.	10
Whitemore &	Whitmore and	SJ/810410	1.	4.	6
Hamchirche	Hanchurch	SJ/848414			
Trentham	Trentham	SJ/865409	2.	11.	4
Titeneshore	Tittensor	SJ/873382	1.	2.	0
Standon'	Standon	SJ/819349	2.	13.	4
Swynerton'	Swynnerton	SJ/852355	3.	2.	0
Eccleshale	Eccleshall	SJ/828291	7.	18.	7¼
Walton'	Walton	SJ/860279			
Elynhale	Ellenhall	SJ/841265			
Sosteford	Seighford	SJ/882250			
Charnes	Charnes	SJ/785340			
Burghton'	Broughton	SJ/767337	9.	3.	2¼
Bromlegh'	Gerrard's Bromley	SJ/775348			
Chatculne	Chatcull	SJ/795345			
Podemor	Podmore	SJ/782358			
Slyndon' &	Slindon and	SJ/828322			
Aspeleye	Aspley	SJ/816331			
Sogunhull' Magna	Sugnall	SJ/798309			
Offeley	Bishop's Offley	SJ/781297			
Mulnemes	Millmeece	SJ/834332			
Brocton'	Brockton	SJ/818318	10.	10.	2¼
Bedenhale &	Baden Hall and	SJ/849313			
Emkerdon'	Ankerton	SJ/836317			
Knytton'	Knighton	SJ/748271			
Flossebrok'	Flashbrook	SJ/746253			
Cherleton'	Chorlton[2]	SJ/813377			

[1] Fenton was divided into the two liberties of Vivian and Culvert (next entry).
[2] Grid ref. is to Chapel Chorlton.

Chaueldon'[1]	Shelton under Harley	SJ/818395			
Radwode	Radwood	SJ/773412			
Pesshale	Pershall	SJ/818298			
Coldemes	Coldmeece	SJ/853326			
Croxton'	Croxton	SJ/787320			
Bruggeford Magna &	Great Bridgeford and	SJ/884270			
Parva	Little Bridgeford	SJ/878274			
Tunstal &	Tunstall and	SJ/773274			
Adbaston'	Adbaston	SJ/762279			
Chebeseye	Chebsey	SJ/860286	2.	13.	11
Colde Norton'	Cold Norton	SJ/878322	1.	14.	0
Dodynton'	Derrington	SJ/891229		13.	4½
Ronton' &	Ranton and	SJ/855242	2.	14.	0
Coton'	Coton	SJ/872233			
Leuynton	Loynton	SJ/779243		8.	0
Alta Offeleye	High Offley	SJ/783262	2.	13.	4½
Algunnton'[1]	Almington	SJ/702344	2.	15.	10
Mere &	Maer and	SJ/793383	3.	15.	8
Aston[1]	Aston	SJ/752411			
Onyleye[1]	Onneley	SJ/750431		17.	0
Merkeleston'	Mucklestone	SJ/725374	2.	4.	4
Maddeleye subter Lyma'	Madeley	SJ/772443	3.	0.	0
Assheleye	Ashley	SJ/763364	2.	12.	8
Betteleye	Betley	SJ/756484	1.	8.	0
Audeleye	Audley	SJ/799509	3.	18.	0
Gayton'[1]	Gayton	SJ/978283	2.	0.	0
Balterdeleye[1]	Balterley	SJ/761503	1.	11.	4
Berleston'	Barlaston	SJ/894392		15.	0
			155.	12.	4

Hd. Offelowe [OFFLOW HUNDRED]

Horborn' &	Harborne [in Warwicks.]	SP/018848	2.	11.	5¼
Smithewik'	and Smethwick	SP/021885			
Honnesworth'	Handsworth [in Warwicks.]	SP/047896	2.	11.	2
Pirye &	Perry and	SP/068920	2.	3.	0
Parva Barre	Little Barr [in Warwicks.]	lost			
Barre &	Great Barr and	SP/049959	4.	10.	0
Allerwich'	Aldridge	SK/060007			
Bromwich'	West Bromwich	SP/002914	1.	16.	10
Tybynton'	Tipton	SO/954923	1.	8.	4
Russhale	Rushall	SK/028011	1.	18.	11
Sheneston'	Shenstone	SK/110043	5.	1.	1
Drayton' Basset	Drayton Bassett	SK/193002	2.	10.	7½
Hyntes	Hints	SK/158028	1.	1.	6
Clyfton'	Clifton Campville	SK/252108	3.	0.	0
Derleston' &	Darlaston and	SO/978968		14.	6
Benteleye	Bentley[2]	SO/984994			
Elleford	Elford	SK/185106	2.	9.	0
Herton' &	Horton and	lost	1.	2.	0
Thomenhorn'	Tamhorn	SK/180071			
Pakynton'	Packington	SK/169048	1.	3.	6

[1] Place-name illegible on E 179/177/6; spelling is taken from E 179/177/7.

[2] Bentley, a settlement removed by colliery workings, appears only on the first edition, O.S. six-inch map.

Corburgh' &	Curborough and	SK/130122	2.	0.	0
Elmhurst'	Elmhurst	SK/113122			
Wyford &	Weeford and	SK/141039	2.	2.	2¼
Tikkebrom	Thickbroom	SK/131038			
Thorp' Constantyn	Thorpe Constantine	SK/259087	1.	0.	0
Herlaston'	Harlaston	SK/214109	2.	4.	3
Sirescote	Syerscote	SK/223076	1.	7.	1¼
Wychenore	Wychnor	SK/177161		18.	0
Barton'	Barton under Needwood	SK/188185	4.	10.	0½
Burton'	Burton on Trent	SK/248230	4.	0.	0
Stretton'	Stretton	SK/253263	1.	3.	0¾
Hurnyglowe	Horninglow	SK/241252	1.	6.	0¾
Brontesdon'	Branston	SK/222211		16.	0
Okeleye	Oakley	SK/193133		18.	4
Marchynton' c.m	Marchington [with members]	SK/138307	4.	10.	11¾
Falde &	Fauld and	SK/181286			
Hambury	Hanbury	SK/171279			
Tuttebury	Tutbury	SK/211291	1.	16.	3
Rolleston'	Rolleston	SK/236277	2.	2.	0
Anzedeleye	Anslow	SK/211253		15.	4
Neweburgh'	Newborough	SK/135253	1.	3.	0
Hoxhale	Yoxall	SK/142190	2.	4.	0
Rydeware Mauuesyn	Mavesyn Ridware	SK/081169	2.	4.	1½
Rydeware Hampstal'	Hamstall Ridware	SK/106193	2.	3.	10½
Parva Rideware	Pipe Ridware	SK/097177		9.	5
Hondesacre	Handsacre	SK/090160	1.	7.	10
Fisshereswik'	Fisherwick	SK/174098		9.	0
Morghale &	?[1]		2.	6.	7
Strethay	and Streethay	SK/141103			
Freford	Freeford	SK/135076	1.	0.	0
Whitington'	Whittington	SK/159083	2.	8.	8
Pipe c.m	Pipe Green (with members)	SK/102097	4.	13.	10
Longedon'	Longdon	SK/082141	4.	13.	6
Homerwich'	Hammerwich	SK/070073	2.	4.	6
Norton' &	Norton Canes and	SK/010078	1.	9.	0½
Wirleye[2]	Little Wyrley	SK/011059			
Stotford &	Statfold and	SK/238071	1.	6.	0
Hasele	Haselour	SK/207107			
			95.	14.	10½

Hd. Tatemoneslowe [TOTMANSLOW HUNDRED]

Gretewich'	Gratwich	SK/029317		14.	6
Kyngeston'	Kingston	SK/061295	2.	5.	3
Felde	Field	SK/027334	1.	0.	7½
Leye	Leigh[3]	SK/023358	4.	1.	4
Maddeleye Alfegh'	Madeley Holme[4]	SK/064383	2.	3.	4
Bromshulf'	Bramshall	SK/061332	1.	3.	5
Tene	Tean[5]	SK/011397	1.	18.	4

[1] Perhaps Ogley Hay?
[2] This must refer to Little Wyrley as Great Wyrley was taxed in Cuttlestone hundred.
[3] Grid ref. is to Church Leigh.
[4] The manor was long known as Madeley Ulfac or Alfac.
[5] Grid ref. is to Upper Tean.

Uttoxsith' c.m	Uttoxeter [with members]	SK/093334	6.	18.	0
Roucestr'	Rocester	SK/112393	2.	10.	0
Eclaston'	Ellastone	SK/117434	2.	5.	0
Wotton'	Wootton	SK/106451	1.	0.	5
Caldon'	Cauldon	SK/078494		16.	0
Alueton' c.m	Alton [with members]	SK/073423	4.	10.	4
Okevere	Okeover	SK/159481	1.	5.	0
Matherfeld	Mayfield	SK/154461	2.	3.	6
Grendon'	Grindon	SK/086545	3.	3.	2
Wetton' &	Wetton and	SK/109553	2.	16.	8
Troulay	Throwley	SK/110526			
Shene	Sheen	SK/113615		10.	0
Rodeyerd	Rudyard	SJ/952579		17.	7
Bradenop'	Bradnop	SK/011552	1.	15.	0
Leek c.m &	Leek [with members]	SJ/985565	6.	6.	8
Rouston'	and Rushton	SJ/940625			
Astonesfelde	Alstonfield	SK/132553	8.	0.	0
Worselowe	Warslow	SK/087587			
Longenore	Longnor	SK/089650			
Stanope	Stanshope	SK/128542			
Endon' c.m	Endon [with members]	SJ/925532	2.	12.	0
Chetelton'	Cheddleton	SJ/971524	2.	18.	2
Elkesdon'	Elkstone[1]	SK/056591		19.	4
Ipstones	Ipstones	SK/018502	1.	4.	0
Buturdon'	Butterton	SK/076566	1.	14.	0
Waterfall'	Waterfall	SK/082517	1.	8.	4
Kengesleye	Kingsley	SK/009471	1.	4.	0
Chedle	Cheadle	SK/008432	4.	13.	4
Duluerne &	Dilhorne and	SJ/971433	2.	2.	0
Fossebrok'	Forsbrook	SJ/965415			
Caverswall'	Caverswall	SJ/952428	2.	16.	0
			79.	15.	3½

Hd. Cothelston' [CUTTLESTONE HUNDRED]

Acton'	Acton Trussell	SJ/938174	6.	17.	6¼
Bedenhale	Bednall	SJ/954178			
Brocton'	Brocton	SJ/968194			
Walton' Super le Kanoc	Walton on the Hill	SJ/958210			
Dunston'	Dunston	SJ/928177	1.	16.	4
Penkerigg' c.m	Penkridge [with members]	SJ/921141	5.	0.	0
Canok c.m	Cannock [with members]	SJ/981101	4.	13.	8
Magna Wirley	Great Wyrley	SJ/993073			
Huntyndon'	Huntington	SJ/973134			
Ruggeley	Rugeley	SK/046179	4.	13.	11½
Sharschuf'	Shareshill	SJ/943066	1.	4.	6¼
Magna Sardon'	Great Saredon	SJ/951085	1.	11.	7¼
Otherton' &	Otherton and	SJ/930124		14.	6
Rodbaston'	Rodbaston	SJ/925120			
Pilatonhale	Pillaton Old Hall	SJ/940128	1.	10.	0
Esynton'	Essington	SJ/961033		8.	10
Covene	Coven	SJ/912067	1.	6.	0

[1] Grid ref. is to Upper Elkstone.

Brewode	Brewood	SJ/883086	7.	13.	8
Chilinton'	Chillington	SJ/860070			
Horsebrok'	Horsebrook	SJ/883103			
Sonterford	Somerford	SJ/900088			
Engleton'	Engleton	SJ/898101			
Atton'	Hatton	SJ/888046			
Gunston'	Gunstone	SJ/872046			
Stretton'	Stretton	SJ/884114	2.	4.	0
Eton'	Water Eaton	SJ/902110	2.	12.	2
Wiston' &	Whiston and	SJ/891141	1.	3.	4
Bikeford	Bickford	SJ/886143			
Levedale[1]	Levedale	SJ/899168	1.	3.	0
Mutton'[1]	Mitton	SJ/883151	1.	10.	8
Longenhore	Longnor	SJ/865140		14.	6
Lappeley &	Lapley and	SJ/872129	4.	13.	4
Aston'	Wheaton Aston	SJ/851125			
Merston'	Marston	SJ/835140	1.	2.	0
Parva Onne	Little Onn	SJ/839161	1.	0.	0
Wolaston' &	Woollaston[2] and	SJ/859163	1.	0.	0
Sharadecot	Shredicote	SJ/872162			
Eyton'	Church Eaton	SJ/849176	2.	12.	2
Magna Onne	High Onn	SJ/828161	1.	15.	0
Blymecchull' &	Blymhill and	SJ/808122	2.	10.	0
Brinton'	Brineton	SJ/809136			
Morton' &	Moreton and	SJ/798172	1.	15.	4
Wilbrighton'	Wilbrighton	SJ/795186			
Hales c.m	Sheriff Hales [in Shropshire] [with members]	SJ/758120	4.	10.	0
Northbury	Norbury	SJ/787234	1.	15.	0
Weston' Jones	Weston Jones	SJ/761240	1.	3.	10
Knychteleye	Knightley	SJ/811251	2.	15.	6
Couleye	Cowley	SJ/830197	2.	13.	8
Berchton' &	Barton and	SJ/872181	1.	1.	4
Apeton'	Apeton	SJ/851182			
Alureston' &	Alstone and	SJ/860188	1.	0.	0
Rewell'	Reule[3]	SJ/845196			
Halghton'	Haughton	SJ/866204	1.	19.	0
Bradeleye	Bradley	SJ/880180	1.	6.	3½
Bilynton'	Billington	SJ/889206	2.	0.	8
Coppenhale	Coppenhall	SJ/908194		11.	0
Borton'	Burton	SJ/914205		16.	4
Gnoushale	Gnosall	SJ/830208	2.	5.	8
Weston' Hwes	Weston under Lizard	SJ/806106	1.	19.	0
			89.	3.	4¾

Hd. Seysedon' [SEISDON HUNDRED]

Pendeford	Pendeford	SJ/895038	1.	3.	4
Bisshebury	Bushbury	SJ/923024	2.	6.	8
Mollesleye	Moseley	SJ/930040		10.	0

[1] Place-name illegible on E 179/177/6; spelling is taken from E 179/177/7.
[2] Grid ref. is to Lower Woollaston where the original manor house may have been situated (*V.C.H., Staffs.* iv (1958), 84).
[3] Grid ref. is to Lower Reule.

			£	s	d
Wolvernehampton c.m	Wolverhampton [with members]	SO/916986	13.	13.	4
Pelleshale	Pelsall	SK/021031			
Wodnesfeld	Wednesfield	SJ/945002			
Wilston'[1]	Bilston	SO/950966			
Welenhale	Willenhall	SO/968984			
Hatherdon'	Hatherton[2]	SJ/958103			
Fetherston'	Featherstone	SJ/935055			
Kenwaston'	Kinvaston	SJ/908123			
Hulton'	Hilton	SJ/951051			
Oddeshale	Codsall	SJ/867040			
Seggesleye	Sedgley	SO/918938	4.	9.	5
Bradeleye	Bradley	SO/953956		17.	8
Amulcote	Amblecoat	SO/898858		7.	8
Arleye	Upper Arley [in Worcs.]	SO/763805	3.	6.	0
Euenefeld	Enville	SO/823868	2.	19.	0
Morf'	Morfe	SO/829877	3.	1.	7
Bobynton'	Bobbington	SO/808905	3.	15.	0
Lutteleye	Lutley	SO/817890	1.	17.	4
Himeleye	Himley	SO/882911	2.	5.	0
Wombourn &	Wombourn and	SO/877932	3.	11.	0
Oxeleye	Oxley	SJ/905025			
Ouerton'	Orton	SO/869953	1.	15.	8
Overpenne	Upper Penn	SO/895953	1.	3.	2
Netherpenne	Lower Penn	SO/870960	1.	15.	4
Tresele &	Trysull and	SO/852943	2.	19.	6
Seisedon	Seisdon	SO/840948			
Patleshull'	Patshull	SJ/801006	1.	2.	6
Wrottesleye	Wrottesley	SJ/852017	1.	3.	0
Oke	Oaken	SJ/857027	1.	17.	6½
Perton'	Perton	SO/858987	2.	1.	0
Tetenhale decen' clericorum[3]	Tettenhall	SO/878992	1.	19.	3
Patyngham	Pattingham	SO/821992	2.	10.	3
			62.	10.	2½
Personal payments			3.	0.	0

TOTAL: £578. 10. 5¾[4]

[1] *Wilston* is a clerical error for *Bilston* on E 179/177/6 and 7.
[2] Hatherton was a detached part of Wolverhampton manor, nine miles to the north.
[3] Most of Tettenhall was taxed as ancient demesne at a tenth (p. 277).
[4] As on 1334 Account, E 179/177/3.

SUFFOLK

DOCUMENTS

8 Edward III: Account	E 179/180/7
8 Edward III: Particulars	not extant
10 Edward III: Particulars	E 179/180/8 (imperfect)
10 Edward III: Particulars	E 179/180/9*
18 Edward III: Particulars	E 179/180/14

TAXERS

The prior of Butley and William de Scothowe

TAX YIELD

15th £1,306. 14. 6¾
10th £ 132. 10. 6
      ─────────────────
      £1,439.   5. 0¾

Representing assessed movable wealth of

£20,926.   3.   5¼

NOTES

The 1334 tax quotas can be calculated from the roll of 1336 (E 179/180/9) which shows the total for each township in 1332 plus the *incrementum* which raised the sum to the agreed amount of 1334. The 1327 roll (E 179/180/6), one of the finest subsidy rolls of the period, includes personal names and is already available in print.

The three taxation boroughs of Ipswich, Orford, and Dunwich appear together towards the end of the list. Eye, although taxed at a tenth, was not considered a borough in 1334, yet it had been one in 1332 and was again in 1336 (see Willard's list (1933), op. cit. 434). Bury St Edmunds, although listed with the boroughs, owed this placing to its extra-hundredal position; the town was never considered a taxation borough in the early fourteenth century and was always taxed at the lower rate of the fifteenth. The remainder of the tax raised at a tenth was that on ancient demesnes, all of them in east Suffolk.

The outline of modern Suffolk differs slightly from that of 1334. Four places south of the Waveney and then taxed in Suffolk are now in Norfolk, viz. Gorleston with the lost Reston, and two parts of Yarmouth—Southtown and *Northvilla*. Part of Rushford, then also taxed in Suffolk, is now in Norfolk. In the south Suffolk has now gained Ballingdon, Brundon, and parts of Sudbury from Essex. In the west, the half-hundred of Exning had become part of Suffolk by 1334 (it was in Cambridgeshire in 1086), but its late insertion in different writing on the roll of 1336 suggests that some uncertainty about its exact status still existed. The comparatively new settlement of Newmarket (*Saxston' cum novo mercato*) and part of Kentford, both now in Suffolk, were then taxed in Cambridgeshire.

REFERENCES

S. H. A. Hervey, 'Suffolk in 1327', *Suffolk Green Books*, 9 (1906) (being the lay
  subsidy of 1 Edward III, 1327 (E 179/180/6)).

E. Powell, *A Suffolk Hundred in 1283*, 1910 (a detailed and useful work on the
  hundred of Blackbourne).

Hd. Sannford' [SAMFORD HUNDRED]

Kyrketon'	Shotley	TM/238358	3.	6.	2	
Freston'	Freston	TM/171395	1.	1.	4	
Stratford	Stratford St. Mary	TM/052346	2.	7.	4	
Berghholt	East Bergholt	TM/071343	5.	16.	9¼	
Herkested	Harkstead	TM/194353	1.	12.	8	
Capele	Capel St. Mary	TM/085382	3.	5.	o	
Tatyngston'	Tattingstone	TM/136372	1.	10.	4	
Qwersted	Wherstead	TM/162407	1.	11.	o½	
Coppedok'	Copdock	TM/120415	2.	1.	6	
Wenham Magna &	Great Wenham and	TM/071381	2.	10.	6	
Parva	Little Wenham	TM/081391				
Holton'	Holton St. Mary	TM/059368	1.	17.	6	
Benteleye	Bentley	TM/118382	2.	0.	o	
Holbrok'	Holbrook	TM/171361	2.	1.	10	
Sprouton'	Sproughton	TM/125450	3.	14.	o	
Hegham	Higham	TM/036352	1.	17.	6	
Hyntlesham	Hintlesham	TM/088434	2.	13.	2¼	
Burstall'[1]	Burstall	TM/097446	1.	5.	7¼	
Shelleye	Shelley	TM/031384	2.	7.	8	
Reydon'	Raydon	TM/049386	3.	7.	2	
Brantham	Brantham	TM/112342	2.	16.	o	
Belsted Parva[2]	Belstead	TM/127411	1.	16.	4	
Stutton'	Stutton	TM/162344	2.	0.	6	
Euerwardton'	Erwarton	TM/221347	2.	4.	8	
Belsted Magna[2]	Great Belstead	TM/110426	2.	10.	6	
	(Washbrook)					
Chelmyngton' [A.D] &	Chelmondiston and	TM/205373	3.	0.	o	[T]
Wulfirston' [A.D]	Woolverstone	TM/190386				
			60.	15.	1¼	

Hd. Bosmer' [BOSMERE HUNDRED]

Berkyngg' cum	Barking with	TM/076536	5.	16.	4
Needham	Needham Market	TM/088552			
Ofton' cum	Offton with	TM/066496	3.	10.	o
Wylasham	Willisham	TM/070506			
Somersham cum	Somersham with	TM/091484	3.	0.	o
Floketon'	Flowton	TM/082468			
Blakenham Parva	Little Blakenham	TM/105488	1.	18.	6
Hemyngston'	Hemingstone	TM/145536	2.	6.	6
Beylham	Baylham	TM/103515	2.	13.	10

[1] Part of Burstall was taxed in Bosmere hundred.

[2] Belstead on the modern map appears to represent Belstead Parva. Great Belstead may
be identified with the manor of Washbrook. See W. A. Copinger, *The Manors of Suffolk*,
vi (1910), 3.

Blakenham Magna	Great Blakenham	TM/118508	1.	13.	6
Nettlested	Nettlestead	TM/088493	1.	8.	6
Rynggeshere	Ringshall	TM/043529	4.	4.	6
Assch'	Ashbocking	TM/169545	2.	4.	0
Eston' Gosbek'	Gosbeck	TM/151556	1.	10.	6
Stonham Antegan cum	Stoneham Aspal with	TM/133595	4.	13.	10
Miklefeld	Mickfield	TM/135617			
Stonham Gernegan	Little Stonham	TM/112602	2.	6.	0
Stonham Comitis	Earl Stonham	TM/108588	2.	19.	8
Cretyng' Sancti Olavi'[1]	Creeting St. Olave	TM/094567	4.	0.	6
Cretyng' Omnium	Creeting All Saints				
Sanctorum &	and				
Sancte Marie	Creeting St. Mary				
Batesford cum	Battisford with	TM/055543	4.	1.	8
Baddele	Badley	TM/062559			
Codenham cum	Coddenham with	TM/133542	5.	13.	8
Croffeld	Crowfield	TM/143578			
Braunford cum	Bramford with	TM/126463	6.	17.	8
Burstall'[2]	Burstall	TM/097446			
Bresete &	Great Bricett and	TM/038507	2.	10.	2
Bresete Parva	Little Bricett	TM/048500			
			63.	9.	4

Hd. Cleydon' [CLAYDON HUNDRED]

Helmynghugham	Helmingham	TM/191576	3.	9.	8½
Cleydon'	Claydon	TM/136499	2.	3.	10
Akenham	Akenham	TM/148488	1.	14.	6
Thorleston' cum	Thurleston with	TM/158482	2.	13.	6
Whityngton'	Whitton	TM/150477			
Henleye	Henley	TM/158513	2.	5.	6
Berwham	Barham	TM/136509	1.	14.	6
Westerfeld cum	Westerfield with	TM/175476	2.	7.	6
Swynelond	Swilland	TM/188529			
			16.	9.	0½

Hd. Mutford [MUTFORD HUNDRED]

Kessynglond	Kessingland	TM/528863	5.	8.	6¾
Pakefeld cum	Pakefield with	TM/538903	3.	0.	2½
Kyrkele	Kirkley	TM/537909			
Gyslyngham cum	Gisleham with	TM/514886	3.	4.	4
Rysshmer' [p][3]	Rushmere [part of]	TM/495880			
Mutford cum	Mutford with	TM/486886	3.	2.	0
Barneby &	Barnby and	TM/481900			
Rysshmer' [p]	Rushmere [part of]	TM/495880			
Carleton'	Carlton Colville	TM/510902	2.	12.	0
			17.	7.	1¼

---

[1] William White, *History, Gazetteer and Directory of Suffolk* (1844), 257. The three Creetings, All Saints, St. Olave's, and St. Mary's, although originally separate parishes, formed one village in which the houses were intermixed. St. Mary's Church now serves the three (Creeting St. Peter is in Stow hundred).

[2] Most of Burstall was separately taxed in Samford hundred, above.

[3] See also next entry.

Hd. Hertesmer' [HARTISMERE HUNDRED]

Eye[1]	Eye	TM/149737	7.	1.	8 [T]
Mendlisham	Mendlesham	TM/106658	6.	0.	2
Redgrave	Redgrave	TM/057782	5.	12.	4
Broom	Broome	TM/145765	2.	1.	2
Palegrave	Palgrave	TM/115784	2.	0.	9
West Thorp'	Westhorpe	TM/044692	3.	0.	0
Risshangles	Rishangles	TM/160686	1.	15.	4
Oclee	Oakley	TM/157773	3.	0.	10
Cranel [A.D]	Cranley	TM/152729	5.	15.	6 [T]
Cokynle [A.D][2]	?				
Langgeton' [A.D] cum	Langton	TM/144747			
Suddon' [A.D]	?				
Gyslyngham	Gislingham	TM/077718	3.	13.	9½
Stustone	Stuston	TM/135778	1.	17.	0
Briseword	Braiseworth	TM/138712	1.	12.	2
Redelyngfeld	Redlingfield	TM/186707	1.	7.	7½
Yakesle	Yaxley	TM/119743	2.	12.	3
Rykynghale Parva	Rickinghall Inferior	TM/038752	1.	18.	8
Thorndon' [A.D]	Thorndon	TM/142697	4.	4.	4 [T]
Wycham	Wickham Skeith	TM/099692	2.	14.	0
Baketon'	Bacton	TM/053672	3.	2.	8
Thrandeston'	Thrandeston	TM/116764	3.	14.	4
Wortham	Wortham	TM/083772	5.	10.	7
Burgate	Burgate	TM/082756	2.	15.	10
Thornham Parva	Thornham Parva	TM/109726		18.	0
Aspale	Aspall	TM/168650	2.	1.	0
Okholt [A.D] cum	Occold with	TM/156709	2.	13.	3 [T]
Benyngham [A.D]	Benningham	TM/168709			
Stoke	Stoke Ash	TM/115704	2.	6.	8
Wyverston'	Wyverstone	TM/042679	2.	2.	3
Melles	Mellis	TM/100744	2.	5.	6
Fynyngham	Finningham	TM/066694	3.	1.	7
Wetheringset'	Wetheringsett with	TM/128668	4.	10.	10
cum Brocford	Brockford	TM/122655			
Cottone	Cotton	TM/070669	3.	10.	0
Thornham Magna	Thornham Magna	TM/103714	2.	18.	2
Tweyt	Thwaite	TM/113682	1.	10.	0
			99.	8.	3

Hd. Stowe [STOW HUNDRED]

Westretingge	Creeting St. Peter	TM/081577	2.	5.	0
Wetherdene	Wetherden	TM/008628	3.	6.	11
Gyppingge Neutone	Gipping	TM/072636	1.	10.	0
Onhous cum	Onehouse with	TM/017594	2.	13.	0
Herleston' &	Harleston and	TM/018604			
Shenlonde	Shelland	TM/004603			
Fynbergh' Magna	Great Finborough	TM/014579	2.	13.	4
Buxhale	Buxhall	TM/003576	3.	4.	4
Dagword	Dagworth	TM/041615	1.	5.	0
Neutone Vet'	Old Newton	TM/059624	2.	1.	3

---

[1] Eye was considered a borough in both 1332 and 1336 but not in 1334.

[2] Possibly Cookley in Eye (TM/166742). All four places are mentioned as hamlets within the manor of Netherhall (Copinger, op. cit. iii. 260).

Combus cum	Combs with	TM/043565	6.	10.	6¼
Fynbergh' Parva	Little Finborough	TM/018550			
Thorneie[1]	Thorney [now	TM/049587	6.	10.	0
	Stowmarket]				
Stowemarket	Stowmarket	TM/049587	3.	19.	0
Haule [A.D]	Haughley	TM/026623	7.	8.	0 [T]

| | | | 43. | 6. | 4¼ |

Hd. Hoxne [HOXNE HUNDRED]

Horham cum	Horham with	TM/210724	4.	6.	4
Alyngton'	Athelington	TM/210710			
Keleshale cum	Kelsale with	TM/388652	2.	6.	0
Carleton'	Carlton	TM/382640			
Silham cum	Syleham with	TM/204790	3.	13.	0
Esham[2]	Esham				
Laxfeld	Laxfield	TM/296724	5.	0.	0
Badingham	Badingham	TM/305683	5.	1.	6
Tatington' cum	Tannington with	TM/243675	3.	14.	4
Burnedich'	Brundish	TM/266696			
Dynytone	Dennington	TM/282670	4.	0.	0
Wilbegh'	Wilby	TM/242721	2.	18.	4
Bedingfeld cum	Bedingfield with	TM/180688	4.	4.	2
Southolt	Southolt	TM/193688			
Stradebrok' cum	Stradbroke with	TM/232740	9.	0.	0
Wynggefeld	Wingfield	TM/230769			
Bedefeld cum	Bedfield with	TM/227663	2.	13.	4
Sachsted	Saxtead	TM/262657			
Weibred cum	Weybread with	TM/241801	4.	13.	4
Wytheresdale	Withersdale	TM/284808			
Fresingfeld cum	Fressingfield with	TM/261775	8.	10.	4
Witingham [h] &	Whittingham and	TM/279782			
Chebenhale [h]	Chippenhall	TM/287760			
Wirlingword cum	Worlingworth with	TM/234687	5.	0.	0
Saham	Monk Soham	TM/213651			
Mendham cum	Mendham with	TM/269829	7.	0.	0½
Medefeld	Metfield	TM/294803			
Hoxne cum	Hoxne with	TM/181775	11.	0.	8
Denham	Denham	TM/188748			

| | | | 83. | 1. | 4½ |

Hd. Blythyngge [BLYTHING HUNDRED]

Braunfeld	Bramfield	TM/399738	4.	19.	10¾
Pesenhale &	Peasenhall and	TM/355692			
Mellis	Mells	TM/405768			
Walpol	Walpole	TM/366746	4.	5.	9
Sybtone cum	Sibton with	TM/368695			
Cokeleye	Cookley	TM/349753			
Upston' cum	Ubbeston with	TM/323726	2.	7.	10
Hevenyngham	Heveningham	TM/333726			

[1] Thorney was the manor in which the market for Stow hundred (i.e. Stowmarket) was sited. For its extent see Revd. A. G. H. Hollingsworth, *The History of Stowmarket* (Ipswich, 1844), 45.

[2] I have not located Esham on any maps. For details of the manor up to the sixteenth century see Copinger, op. cit. iv. 93.

Bramptone cum Stovene[1]	Brampton with Steven	TM/435815 TM/448816	4.	0.	0
Middilton' cum Fordele	Middleton with Fordley	TM/430678 TM/428668	2.	3.	5
Hensted	Henstead	TM/489861	1.	16.	1
Huntingfeld cum Lynsted Magna & Parva	Huntingfield with Linstead Magna and Linstead Parva	TM/336743 TM/318763 TM/336777	3.	4.	4
Henham	Henham	TM/452782	1.	8.	0
Soterton	Sotherton	TM/442796	1.	2.	0
Eston'	Easton Bavents	TM/515780	1.	16.	8
Souhtcove	South Cove	TM/500809	1.	9.	6
Southweld	Southwold	TM/508764	3.	12.	2
Thoriton' cum Wennaston'	Thorington with Wenhaston	TM/423742 TM/425755	2.	9.	4
Westhale	Westhall	TM/423804	2.	14.	0
Chedestan cum Bliford	Chediston with Blyford	TM/358778 TM/424768	5.	0.	0
Bennacr' Bulcampe & Bregg'[2]	Benacre Bulcamp and ?	TM/512844 TM/436765	5.	6.	8
Halesword	Halesworth	TM/386774	4.	0.	2
Huggenhale cum Frostenton'	Uggeshall with Frostenden	TM/455803 TM/479817	3.	11.	0
Blyburgh' cum Walberswik'	Blythburgh with Walberswick	TM/451753 TM/490748	6.	14.	10
Wrentham	Wrentham	TM/489830	3.	8.	8
Reydon'	Reydon	TM/491782	4.	13.	0¾
Westletone	Westleton	TM/441691	5.	7.	6
Leystone cum Cisewall'	Leiston with Sizewell	TM/445626 TM/475626	8.	1.	4
Northhales	Covehithe	TM/523819	9.	0.	0
Cratfeld	Cratfield	TM/313748	2.	11.	8
Dersham cum Yoxford	Darsham with Yoxford	TM/421699 TM/395690	5.	1.	1
Whysete cum Rumburgh' Specceshale & Holtone	Wissett with Rumburgh Spexhall and Holton	TM/366793 TM/347818 TM/378802 TM/402779	6.	0.	0
			106.	4.	11½

Hd. Wayneforth' [WANGFORD HUNDRED]

Weilingham cum Cove	Worlingham with North Cove	TM/445898 TM/462894	4.	4.	9
Rynggefeld cum Redesham	Ringsfield with Little Redisham	TM/403884 TM/402864	2.	2.	7
Soterle cum Shanefeld & Wilingham	Sotterley with Shadingfield and Willingham	TM/458853 TM/435838 TM/446864	5.	16.	0
Bungeye	Bungay	TM/336898	6.	6.	6
Beccles	Beccles	TM/422905	14.	4.	3
Barsham cum Shipmedwe	Barsham with Shipmeadow	TM/396897 TM/382900	3.	14.	0
Metingham	Mettingham	TM/363900	2.	9.	9
Ilketelishale	Ilketshall	TM/378873	7.	13.	7

---

[1] Entry omitted from E 179/180/9 (1336).   [2] Perhaps Bridge Farm (TM/473707).

Weston' [A.D]	Weston	TM/428872	4.	15.	0	[T]
Elgh [A.D] &	Ellough and	TM/443867				
Upredesham [A.D]	Redisham	TM/408843				
Souhtelmham	South Elmham	TM/338847	14.	13.	3½	
			65.	19.	8½	

Hd. Ludynglond' [LOTHINGLAND HUNDRED]

Blundeston'	Blundeston	TM/513973	2.	15.	11	
Holton' cum	Oulton with	TM/509936	2.	7.	8½	
Flixton'	Flixton	TM/518955				
Herlyngflot	Herringfleet	TM/477978	1.	10.	0	
Askeby	Ashby	TM/489990	1.	2.	0	
Bradewell'	Bradwell	TG/503038	2.	3.	3¼	
Belton'	Belton	TG/486029	3.	14.	3¼	
Lound	Lound	TM/506990	2.	0.	8¾	
Burgh'	Burgh Castle	TG/476050		15.	7	
Hopeton'	Hopton	TG/524001	1.	13.	8	
Freton'	Fritton	TG/473002	2.	0.	0	
Guntone	Gunton	TM/542958	1.	9.	0	
Corton'	Corton	TM/538981	3.	1.	4	
Somerleton'	Somerleyton	TM/493972	2.	13.	8	
Louwystoft [A.D]	Lowestoft	TM/550932	3.	15.	2¼	[T]
Gorleston' [A.D]	Gorleston [in Norfolk]	TG/524044	2.	15.	9¾	[T]
Reston' cum	Reston [in Gorleston] with	lost	6.	4.	4	
Gorleston'	Gorleston [in Norfolk]	TG/524044				
Parva Jernem'	Southtown [in Gorleston,	TG/523065	3.	16.	8	
	in Norfolk] with					
cum Northvilla	Northtown	?				
			43.	19.	1¾	

Lib. Sancti Edmundi [THE LIBERTY OF ST. EDMUND]

Hd. Babberg' [BABERGH HUNDRED]

Stoke	Stoke by Nayland	TL/986363	4.	15.	6	
Cavendich'	Cavendish	TL/805465	5.	9.	8½	
Waldyngfeld Magna	Great Waldingfield	TL/912439	4.	6.	8¾	
Neylond	Nayland	TL/976342	3.	0.	0	
Cornerde Magna	Great Cornard	TL/883404	2.	8.	6	
Cornerde Parva	Little Cornard	TL/902391	2.	1.	2	
Neuton'	Newton	TL/919413	3.	7.	2	
Lausill'	Lawshall	TL/864542	3.	17.	8	
Illeye Combust'	Brent Eleigh	TL/942483	2.	17.	3	
Bures[1]	Bures	TL/907340	3.	4.	0	
Hertherst	Hartest	TL/835524	1.	18.	8	
Somerton'	Somerton	TL/812530	1.	13.	0	
Alfeton'	Alpheton	TL/873505	1.	3.	9	
Asyngton'	Assington	TL/936388	3.	0.	5	
Shymplyngg'	Shimpling	TL/859513	3.	3.	4½	
Boxsted	Boxted	TL/825505	1.	16.	0	
Polstede	Polstead	TL/989381	3.	6.	8	
Weston'	Wissington	TL/951347	2.	3.	4	
Preston'	Preston	TL/946503	2.	13.	0	

[1] That part of Bures west of the Stour, in Essex, was taxed there (Hinckford hundred, p. 80).

Waldyngfeld Parva	Little Waldingfield	TL/924452	2.	10.	o
Boxford	Boxford	TL/963405	2.	9.	9½
Cokefeld	Cockfield	TL/904550	4.	16.	o
Aketon'	Acton	TL/892452	3.	14.	2¾
Brotene[1]	Groton	TL/960417	2.	1.	8½
Stanstede	Stanstead	TL/843493	2.	3.	8¼
Illeye Monachorum	Monks Eleigh	TL/966477	2.	13.	3½
Meldyngg'	Milden	TL/958465	2.	12.	4½
Edwardeston'	Edwardstone	TL/940421	3.	13.	o
Lavenham	Lavenham	TL/913491	7.	4.	o
Glemesford	Glemsford	TL/834484	3.	15.	6
Melford	Long Melford	TL/865468	7.	6.	5
Sudbir'[2]	Sudbury	TL/874413	18.	14.	o
			119.	19.	10¾

Hd. Cosford [COSFORD HUNDRED]

Aldham	Aldham	TM/041443	2.	8.	o½
Elmesete	Elmsett	TM/059472	2.	6.	4
Hecham	Hitcham	TL/984511	5.	8.	3
Ketilberston'	Kettlebaston	TL/965503	1.	14.	2
Kerseye	Kersey	TM/003439	2.	16.	9
Neddyngg'	Nedging	TL/998482	1.	14.	10
Chelesword	Chelsworth	TL/981479	1.	6.	o¾
Whatefeld	Whatfield	TM/025465	3.	14.	4
Bildeston'	Bildeston	TL/985492	2.	18.	o
Bretthenham	Brettenham	TL/968542	2.	10.	o
Wachesham	Wattisham	TM/010514	1.	17.	4
Semere	Semer	TL/999468	1.	1.	o
Lelesheye	Lindsay	TL/978449	1.	17.	2
Leyham	Layham	TM/031403	2.	5.	8½
Thorpmurieux	Thorpe Morieux	TL/943533	2.	16.	o
Hadleye	Hadleigh	TM/026425	8.	10.	o
			45.	3.	11¾

Hd. Thyngh' [THINGOE HUNDRED]

Fornham Omnium Sanctorum	Fornham All Saints	TL/838677	1.	16.	o
Thelvyngton'[3]	Chevington	TL/789601	4.	10.	o
Ikeword	Ickworth	TL/813611	2.	9.	o
Brockeleye cum Reede	Brockley with Rede	TL/827556 TL/804559	2.	18.	8
Lackford	Lackford	TL/798703	3.	15.	8
Saxham Magna	Great Saxham	TL/789628	1.	16.	4
Hemgrave	Hengrave	TL/825686	1.	8.	9
Hornyngesher' Magna	Horringer	TL/825620	2.	13.	4
Hargrave	Hargrave	TL/767608	2.	11.	8
Neuton'	Nowton	TL/864605	1.	10.	4½
Saxham Parva	Little Saxham	TL/799638	2.	10.	2
Hausted	Hawstead	TL/856593	2.	15.	8
Risby	Risby	TL/803663	3.	13.	4
Westle	Westley	TL/824645	2.	4.	o

[1] *Brotene* is a clerical error for *Grotene*.
[2] Part of Sudbury was taxed in Essex (Hinckford hundred, p. 80).
[3] *Thelvyngton'* on E 179/180/9 is a clerical error for *Chelvyngton'*.

Hornynggeshere Parva	Little Horringer	TL/818628		19.	1
Barwe	Barrow	TL/761646	4.	0.	0
Flempton'	Flempton	TL/813699	1.	17.	2
Whepsted	Whepstead	TL/832582	3.	0.	1
			46.	9.	3½

Hd. Thedwardistre [THEDWARDISTRE HUNDRED]

Berton'	Great Barton	TL/890661	8.	11.	5
Heggessete cum Beketon'	Hessett with Beyton	TL/937619 TL/933628	4.	3.	8
Lyverude Magna	Great Livermere	TL/885713	3.	19.	5¼
Wulpit	Woolpit	TL/973625	2.	3.	4
Drenggeston'	Drinkstone	TL/959616	3.	17.	5
Rattlisden'	Rattlesden	TL/978591	2.	9.	8
Rougham	Rougham	TL/912626	4.	2.	3
Testoke	Tostock	TL/960636	2.	0.	0
Fornham Sancte Genouese & Sancti Martini	Fornham St. Genevieve and Fornham St. Martin	TL/840683 TL/853670	2.	6.	6
Whelnetham Magna & Whelnetham Parva	Great Welnetham Little Welnetham	TL/878593 TL/889600	2.	12.	4¾
Geddyng' cum Falsham	Gedding with Felsham	TL/952582 TL/947570	4.	3.	3½
Tymeword cum Ampton'	Timworth with Ampton	TL/861697 TL/866713	4.	11.	4
Thurston'	Thurston	TL/929653	2.	17.	8
Stanefeld cum Bradefeld Parva	Stanningfield with Bradfield Combust	TL/877564 TL/892573	4.	0.	0
Pakenham	Pakenham	TL/930671	5.	13.	6
Bradefeld Monachorum	Bradfield St. George	TL/907600	2.	5.	0
Bradefeld Seint Cler'	Bradfield St. Clare	TL/910578	1.	2.	0
Risshbrok'	Rushbrooke	TL/893615	1.	8.	4
			62.	7.	2½

Hd. Blakeburn' [BLACKBOURNE HUNDRED]

Ixword	Ixworth	TL/931703	2.	15.	4
Hopeton'	Hopton	TL/994790	4.	3.	6
Hildercle	Hinderclay	TM/027768	1.	14.	0
Fakenham Parva	Little Fakenham[1]		1.	19.	0
Stanton'	Stanton	TL/967734	4.	16.	8
Lyvermere Parva	Little Livermere	TL/882719	2.	12.	3
Euston'	Euston	TL/901785	2.	13.	0
Ingham	Ingham	TL/855706	2.	5.	0
Weston'	Market Weston	TL/990782	2.	14.	0
Bernham	Barnham	TL/872792	3.	6.	0
Asshfeld Magna	Great Ashfield	TL/995678	2.	2.	0
Hepword	Hepworth	TL/988749	4.	3.	4
Rykynghall'	Rickinghall Superior	TM/045755	2.	8.	1
Elmeswell'	Elmswell	TL/982636	2.	13.	6
Norton'	Norton	TL/962663	3.	5.	4
Berdewell'	Bardwell	TL/942736	7.	0.	2

---

[1] Nothing now remains of Little Fakenham, enclosed within Euston Park in the seventeenth century.

Asshfeld Parva	Badwell Ash	TL/989690	2.	13.	4
Coneweston'	Coney Weston	TL/963782	3.	9.	6
Sapeston'	Sapiston	TL/921742	2.	0.	8
Bernyngham	Barningham	TL/968769	3.	12.	11
Rissheword[1]	Rushford [in Norfolk]	TL/923813		16.	0
Granteshall'	Knettishall	TL/972804	2.	13.	9
Croston'[2]	Troston	TL/901723	3.	8.	4
Fakenham Magna	Fakenham	TL/911766	2.	2.	6
Thelnetham	Thelnetham	TM/018783	2.	4.	11
Langham	Langham	TL/981691	1.	11.	0
Stowelangtot	Stowlangtoft	TL/958682	1.	16.	10½
Huntereston'	Hunston	TL/976681	1.	17.	0
Culforth'	Culford	TL/833703	1.	14.	8
Ixworththorp'	Ixworth Thorpe	TL/918725	1.	16.	4
Honton'	Honington	TL/913746	2.	13.	6
Wattlesfeld	Wattisfield	TM/010742	2.	14.	6
Walsham	Walsham le Willows	TL/999712	2.	15.	8
Westowe	West Stow	TL/819706	3.	0.	0
Wridewell'	Wordwell	TL/828720	2.	2.	6
			95.	15.	1½

Hd. Lackford [LACKFORD HUNDRED]

Mildenhal'	Mildenhall	TL/711747	11.	10.	0¾
Brandon'	Brandon	TL/777862	5.	17.	4
Iklyngham	Icklingham	TL/775726	6.	2.	6
Lakynghith'	Lakenheath	TL/714828	6.	19.	9¼
Heringeswell'	Herringswell	TL/718700	3.	14.	0
Ereswell'	Eriswell	TL/723781	7.	0.	9
Elveden'	Elveden	TL/823799	4.	0.	0
Hegham	Higham	TL/746656	2.	1.	3¾
Cavenham	Cavenham	TL/764697	3.	3.	0
Dounham	Santon Downham	TL/816876	2.	13.	4
Wridelingtone	Worlington	TL/692738	5.	10.	0
Frekenham	Freckenham	TL/616717	4.	14.	4½
Wangford	Wangford	TL/751835	2.	16.	5
Todenham	Tuddenham	TL/738713	4.	3.	1¼
Berton' Parva	Barton Mills	TL/717738	3.	10.	4
			73.	16.	3½

Dm. hd. Ixnyngg' [EXNING HALF-HUNDRED]

			14.	4.	1¾

Hd. Rysbregge [RISBRIDGE HUNDRED]

Denham	Denham	TL/756619	2.	5.	5
Hverille	Haverhill	TL/672455	6.	15.	8½
Gediton'	Kedington	TL/705470	3.	8.	8
Depeden' cum	Depden with	TL/778567	3.	13.	4
Cheteber'	Chedburgh	TL/796575			
Bradeleie' Parva	Little Bradley	TL/682522	1.	10.	0
Honeden'	Hundon	TL/739488	4.	1.	11½
Ouisdene	Ousden	TL/736596	1.	12.	4
Bernardeston'	Barnardiston	TL/712488	2.	3.	0

---

[1] Rushford straddled the Norfolk/Suffolk boundary until recently. Most of Rushford was taxed in Norfolk (Guiltcross hundred, p. 205).

[2] *Croston'* on E 179/180/9 is a clerical error for *Troston'*.

			£.	s.	d.	
Thrillowe Magna	Great Thurlow	TL/681504	2.	18.	4¼	
Wichambrook'	Wickhambrook	TL/754545	8.	3.	4	
Stradishill' cum	Stradishall with	TL/748526	3.	14.	0	
Denardeston'	Denston	TL/760529				
Haketen' cum	Hawkedon with	TL/798530	2.	2.	4	
Thurstenten'	Thurston End	TL/797514				
Clare	Clare	TL/769455	5.	0.	0	
Wrottingg' Magna	Great Wratting	TL/688482	3.	0.	5	
Stanesfeld	Stansfield	TL/783525	2.	2.	4	
Widekissho	Wixoe	TL/718430	1.	9.	9	
Multon'	Moulton	TL/700642	4.	6.	8	
Poselingword cum	Poslingford with	TL/770482	2.	12.	2	
Chippeleie'	Chipley	TL/762498				
Thrillowe Parva	Little Thurlow	TL/680512	2.	15.	4½	
Dalham cum	Dalham with	TL/725625	2.	17.	4	
Tunstall'	Dunstall Green	TL/746611				
Stoke	Stoke by Clare	TL/741433	5.	2.	9¾	
Chilton' &	Chilton Street and	TL/754470				
Boytone	Boyton End	TL/720445				
Wrottingg' Parva	Little Wratting	TL/691476	3.	3.	10	
Bradeleye Magna	Great Bradley	TL/674532	3.	10.	11½	
Withresfeld	Withersfield	TL/652477	4.	6.	8¼	
Lydgate	Lidgate	TL/721582	5.	1.	3	
Gaisle cum	Gazeley with	TL/719642	5.	3.	4	
Nedham &	Needham and	TL/721656				
Kentford[1]	Kentford	TL/707668				
Coulyngge	Cowlinge	TL/718549	4.	14.	0¼	
			97.	15.	4½	
Sancte Edmunde	Bury St. Edmunds	TL/856640	24.	0.	0	
Gyppewico [B]	Ipswich	TM/165445	64.	10.	6	[T]
Orfford [B]	Orford	TM/422500	10.	0.	0	[T]
Donewico [B]	Dunwich	TM/475705	12.	0.	0	[T]
			110.	10.	6	

Lib. Sancte Etheldrede [LIBERTY OF ST. ETHELDREDA]

Hd. Plomesgat' [PLOMESGATE HUNDRED]

			£.	s.	d.	
Aldeburgh' cum	Aldeburgh with	TM/463566	2.	16.	8	
Haselwod	Hazlewood	TM/434588				
Ikene	Iken	TM/413567	2.	7.	0	
Chiselford &	Chillesford and	TM/383523				
Donyngword	Dunningworth	TM/386573				
Sternefeld	Sternfield	TM/391616	1.	16.	2	
Glemham Parva cum	Little Glemham with	TM/346587	2.	8.	0	
Stratford	Stratford St. Andrew	TM/358602				
Glemham Magna	Great Glemham	TM/340616	2.	3.	10	
Southbourne	Sudbourne	TM/421520	2.	14.	0	
Rendham	Rendham	TM/350644	4.	4.	10	
Bursierd	Bruisyard	TM/325662				
Blaxhale cum	Blaxhall with	TM/356569	2.	14.	10	
Tunstall' [p][2]	Tunstall [part of]	TM/363551				
Benhale	Benhall	TM/372618	4.	14.	5	
Saxmundham &	Saxmundham and	TM/388630				
Farnham	Farnham	TM/362600				

---

[1] See also part taxed in Cambridgeshire, p. 24.
[2] See also part taxed with Wantisden, below.

Wantesdene cum Tunstall' [p] & Lenacr'	Wantisden with Tunstall [part of] and ?	TM/362533 TM/363551	2.	12.	9
Snape cum Frestone	Snape with Friston	TM/395593 TM/413605	2.	14.	0
Cranesford cum Swiftlingg'	Cransford with Swefling	TM/316647 TM/348638	3.	11.	5
Perham	Parham	TM/309605	2.	4.	0
			37.	1.	11

Hd. Wilford [WILFORD HUNDRED]

Aldertone	Alderton	TM/343417	2.	14.	8
Sutton'	Sutton	TM/306464	3.	6.	8
Boytone cum Capell'	Boyton with Capel St. Andrew	TM/372471 TM/375482	1.	17.	6
Ramisholt cum Bromeswell'	Ramsholt with Bromeswell	TM/306421 TM/303507	2.	0.	0
Holesle cum Chatesham	Hollesley with Shottisham	TM/353443 TM/321447	2.	3.	4
Wicham Peterstre cum Ludham	Wickham Market Pettistree with Loudham	TM/302558 TM/298549 TM/309542	3.	11.	3
Baudeseie'	Bawdsey	TM/346401	7.	1.	0
Bulche Debach' & Dalingho[1]	Boulge Debach and Dallinghoo	TM/254528 TM/242543 TM/265550	2.	4.	4
Melton' cum Ufford	Melton with Ufford	TM/283506 TM/298522	3.	4.	4
Bredefeld [A.D]	Bredfield	TM/269530		16.	5 [T]
			28.	19.	6

Hd. Lose [LOES HUNDRED]

Hachiston'	Hacheston	TM/312585	2.	6.	0
Letheringham cum Chasfeld	Letheringham with Charsfield	TM/268586 TM/254565	3.	4.	6
Eston' cum Ketlebergh'	Eston with Kettleburgh	TM/283587 TM/265606	2.	12.	7
Gretingham cum Brandeston' & Monewedene	Cretingham with Brandeston and Monewden	TM/227605 TM/248603 TM/239586	5.	11.	8
Ayssh	Campsey Ash	TM/329559	2.	1.	4
Rendlesham	Rendlesham	TM/325528	3.	6.	8
Saham cum Kentone	Earl Soham with Kenton	TM/237633 TM/191659	3.	7.	0
Framlyngham	Framlingham	TM/285635	3.	13.	4
Eyk'	Eyke	TM/318518	2.	6.	8
Hoo cum Dalyngho[2] & Wodebrigg'	Hoo with Dallinghoo and Woodbridge	TM/256593 TM/265550 TM/271491	4.	15.	10
Marlesford cum Buttele [p][3]	Marlesford with Butley [part of]	TM/323583 TM/373502	2.	7.	0
			35.	12.	7

[1] Part of Dallinghoo was taxed in Loes hundred, below.
[2] Part of Dallinghoo was taxed in Wilford hundred, above.
[3] It is not clear where the remainder of Butley was taxed.

Hd. Carleford [CARLFORD HUNDRED]

Wytnesham	Witnesham	TM/180509	3.	7.	4
Rischemere cum	Rushmere St. Andrew	TM/196461	2.	4.	9¼
Alnesburne	with Alnesbourne	TM/192404			
Plaiford cum	Playford with	TM/218482	2.	17.	0
Brightwell'	Brightwell	TM/249435			
Tudenham cum	Tuddenham with	TM/192484	3.	0.	0
Culpho	Culpho	TM/211492			
Groundesburg' cum	Grundisburgh with	TM/223511	3.	17.	0¼
Burgh'	Burgh	TM/223522			
Belyng' Magna &	Great Bealings and	TM/231489	4.	6.	0
Parva	Little Bealings	TM/229480			
Hasketon'	Hasketon	TM/251504	2.	16.	0
Clopton'	Clopton	TM/221526	4.	5.	0
Martlesham	Martlesham	TM/262469	2.	18.	0
Foxhol' cum	Foxhall with	TM/230436	1.	11.	6
Kessegrave	Kesgrave	TM/219457			
Oteleye	Otley	TM/204549	4.	0.	10
			35.	3.	5½

Hd. Colneise [COLNEIS HUNDRED]

Tremeleye &	Trimley and	TM/278371	7.	6.	10
Altenston'	Alston	TM/263368			
Naketon'	Naston	TM/218397	3.	13.	0
Levyngton' &	Levington and	TM/234390			
Stratton'	Stratton	TM/244388			
Kirketon' &	Kirton and	TM/282397	7.	6.	0
Falcenham	Falkenham	TM/293391			
Bucklesham &	Bucklesham and	TM/244421			
Elmesle	Hemley	TM/286423			
Walton' &	Walton and	TM/296356	6.	4.	8
Flichesstowe	Felixstowe	TM/299344			
			24.	10.	6

Hd. Tridlyngg' [THREDLING HUNDRED]

Asshfeld cum	Ashfield with	TM/210626	2.	6.	4
Thorp	Thorpe	TM/201623			
Framesden' cum	Framsden with	TM/201597	2.	4.	4
Pethagh'	Pettaugh	TM/168596			
Debenham cum	Debenham with	TM/174632	5.	10.	2
Wynston'	Winston	TM/180616			
			10.	0.	10

TOTAL: £1,439. 5. 0¾[1]

---

[1] Although the county total agrees with that given on the 1334 Account, E 179/180/7, the totals at a fifteenth and at a tenth differ. According to the 1334 Account the tenth amounted to £132. 10. 6 (in the above list it is £128. 15. 8), and the fifteenth to £1,306. 14. 6¾ (in the above list it is £1,310. 9. 4¾). This means that in the above list some quotas which are shown as a fifteenth should be at a tenth; I have been unable to trace these.

SURREY

DOCUMENTS

8 Edward III: Account   E 179/184/5
8 Edward III: Particulars not extant
10 Edward III: Particulars E 179/184/6*
11 Edward III: Particulars E 179/184/8

TAXERS

The prior of Merton and John de Bampton

TAX YIELD

15th   £499. 18.   1¼
10th   £ 88.   o.   6¾
      ─────────────────
      £587. 18.   8

Representing assessed movable wealth of

    £8,378. 17.   2¼

NOTES

The two volumes on the Surrey taxation returns with introductions by J. F. Willard and H. C. Johnson are standard works on the lay subsidies. The second volume contains transcriptions of E 179/184/5 and 6 referred to above, and also a list of all surviving documents (numbering 210) relating to the fifteenth and tenth for Surrey between 1322 and 1623.

There were three taxation boroughs in Surrey in 1334: Guildford, Southwark, and Bletchingley. Why Reigate had lost the burghal status that it had held in all taxations between 1295 and 1332 is puzzling, as is the status of Kingston upon Thames, the town with the highest tax quota in the county. Both were taxed at a tenth as ancient demesnes.

The Surrey list is unusual in two respects. First, the tax on the sub-taxers in each hundred is stated, and secondly special mention is made of the tax on villeins of certain ecclesiastics, as in 1332 (see pp. xviii–xix).

To judge from the places listed in the subsidy the outline of the county was practically the same in 1334 as in 1889 when several parishes were detached to form part of the administrative county of London.

REFERENCES

H. E. Malden, 'The ship money assessment of Surrey in 1636', in *V.C.H., Surrey,* 1 (1902), 441–4 (this includes the 1334 quotas).

J. F. Willard, H. C. Johnson *et al., Surrey Taxation Returns,* Surrey Rec. Soc. xviii (1922) and xxxiii (1932).

R. E. Glasscock, 'The distribution of lay wealth in Kent, Surrey, and Sussex, in the early fourteenth century', *Archaeologia Cantiana,* lxxx (1965), 61–8.

Dominica Domini Regis [DEMESNES OF THE KING]

Guldeford' [B]	Guildford	su/996496	15.	2.	9½ [T]
Kyngeston' [A.D]	Kingston upon Thames	TQ/179693	21.	2.	1 [T]
Reygate [A.D][1]	Reigate	TQ/256509	4.	0.	7¾ [T]
Suthwerk' [B]	Southwark	TQ/325803	17.	2.	11¾ [T]
Blecchyngelegh' [B][2]	Bletchingley	TQ/328508	2.	5.	0 [T]
Shene [A.D]	Sheen [Richmond][3]	TQ/180749	3.	0.	9½ [T]
Banstede [A.D]	Banstead	TQ/255596	3.	18.	5½ [T]
Byfflete [A.D]	Byfleet	TQ/063604	2.	11.	1¼ [T]
Gatton' [A.D]	Gatton	TQ/276529	3.	0.	2 [T]
Wytle [A.D]	Witley	su/947397	15.	16.	6½ [T]
			88.	0.	6¾ [T]

Hd. Farnham [FARNHAM HUNDRED]

Farnham	Farnham	su/842468	5.	16.	3¼
Wreclesham	Wrecclesham	su/827452	2.	1.	1½
Fermesham	Frensham	su/842414	2.	8.	4
Ronewyk'	Runwick	su/821457	2.	0.	3¼
Churt	Churt	su/853385	3.	9.	0¼
Elstede	Elstead	su/903434	2.	10.	6
Tilleforde	Tilford	su/873432	1.	15.	6½
Roneualle	Runfold	su/870476	1.	17.	1
Twongham	Tongham	su/887490	3.	8.	5¼
Batesshate	Badshot	su/866486	2.	0.	8½
Compton'	Compton	su/853464		15.	4
Taxatores	Taxers			14.	8
			28.	17.	3½

Hd. Godalmyngg' [GODALMING HUNDRED]

Godalmyngg'	Godalming	su/968440	16.	9.	10¾
Catteshulle	Catteshall	su/982444	1.	0.	4½
Farncombe	Farncombe	su/978450	2.	0.	7¼
Piperharghe	Peper Harow	su/934441	2.	3.	8¾
Hurtmere	Hurtmore	su/965450		10.	0¼
Putenham	Puttenham	su/932479	2.	10.	1¾
Compton'	Compton	su/954471	3.	5.	2½
Herdyndon'	Artington	su/992477	3.	10.	3¼
Hameldon'	Hambledon	su/970390	1.	3.	5¼
Taxatores	Taxers			19.	0
			33.	12.	8¼

Hd. Blakehethe [BLACKHEATH HUNDRED]

Bromlegh'	Bramley	TQ/009449	19.	16.	10
Shaldeford	Shalford	su/999478	6.	17.	7
Shyre	Shere	TQ/075478	5.	7.	8

---

[1] Reigate foreign was taxed at a fifteenth (Reigate hundred).
[2] Bletchingley foreign was taxed at a fifteenth (Tandridge hundred).
[3] Sheen was renamed Richmond by Henry VII, about 1500, *E.P.N.S.*, *XI*, *Surrey* (1934), 66.

Aldebury	Albury[1]	TQ/065479	3.	3.	0
Gomeshulue	Gomshall	TQ/087478	8.	6.	8
Taxatores	Taxers			13.	8
			44.	5.	5

Hd. Wodeton' [WOTTON HUNDRED]

Dorkyngg'	Dorking	TQ/165495	7.	8.	5½
Becheswortthe	Betchworth [West]	TQ/175495	1.	13.	7¼
Midilton'	Milton	TQ/151493	1.	14.	9
Westcote	Westcott	TQ/139484	2.	10.	4
Wodeton'	Wotton	TQ/126480	2.	2.	3¼
Abyngeworth' & Padynden'	Abinger and Paddington	TQ/115459 TQ/101471	3.	4.	2¾
Ockelegh'	Ockley	TQ/157407	3.	16.	9½
Taxatores	Taxers			11.	2
			23.	1.	7¼

Hd. Reygate [REIGATE HUNDRED]

Chepstede & Kyngeswode	Chipstead and Kingswood	TQ/283564 TQ/242555	4.	10.	8
Merstham	Merstham	TQ/291538	4.	7.	0½
Nutfeld	Nutfield	TQ/309509	4.	12.	3½
Boclonde	Buckland	TQ/221509	3.	14.	6
Becheswortthe & Brocham	Betchworth [East] and Brockham	TQ/211498 TQ/198494	5.	15.	0¼
Reygate for'[2]	Reigate [foreign]	TQ/254500	5.	12.	1½
Leghe	Leigh	TQ/224470	3.	8.	2¼
Cherlewode	Charlwood	TQ/241412	5.	12.	7
Horle	Horley	TQ/277428	7.	1.	3¾
Taxatores	Taxers			15.	8
Bourstouwe	Burstow	TQ/312412	5.	2.	11
			50.	12.	3¾

Hd. Wockyngg' [WOKING HUNDRED]

Asshe	Ash	SU/898508	2.	1.	5
Villani Abbatis de Certes' ibidem	Villeins of the Abbot of Chertsey in Ash			7.	6½
Wanebergh'	Wanborough	SU/934489		2.	11
Werplesdon'	Worplesdon	SU/972535	4.	9.	10¾
Burgham	Burpham	TQ/017523	1.	11.	5¾
Wockyngge	Woking [Old]	TQ/021569	10.	13.	7
Pirisright	Pirbright	SU/942559	3.	5.	8¾
Wyndlesham	Windlesham	SU/930637	3.	14.	3
Ocham & Wysshele	Ockham and Wisley	TQ/067565 TQ/057596	2.	18.	10
Sende	Send	TQ/018543	2.	17.	7¾
Westhorslegh'	West Horsley	TQ/078530	2.	19.	7¼
Esthorslegh'	East Horsley	TQ/094528	2.	14.	7½
Estclendon'	East Clandon	TQ/059516		4.	10½

[1] Grid ref. is to the deserted medieval village, not to modern Albury.
[2] Reigate borough was taxed at a tenth, above.

Villani Abbatis de Certes' ibidem	Villeins of the Abbot of Chertsey in East Clandon		'	7.	1½
Westclendon'	West Clandon	TQ/043512	1.	2.	8¾
Merwe	Merrow	TQ/029507	2.	11.	11¼
Stokes	Stoke	SU/998508	2.	15.	7¼
Tytyngg'	Tyting	TQ/022487		2.	10
Taxatores	Taxers			11.	2
			45.	13.	9½[1]

Hd. Godele [GODLEY HUNDRED]

Pirford	Pyrford	TQ/040583	2.	12.	0½
Villani Abbatis Westmonasterii in Pirford'	Villeins of the Abbot of Westminster in Pyrford		2.	5.	5½
Taxatores de Pirford'	Taxers			3.	6
Certes'	Chertsey	TQ/043670	2.	13.	7½
Villani Abbatis de Certes' ibidem	Villeins of the Abbot of Chertsey in Chertsey			6.	11
Chabeham	Chobham	SU/973618	1.	0.	0½
Villani Abbatis de Certes' ibidem	Villeins of the Abbot of Chertsey in Chobham		2.	6.	8
Egeham	Egham	TQ/011713	1.	13.	11¾
Villani Abbatis de Certes' ibidem	Villeins of the Abbot of Chertsey in Egham			14.	10¾
Thorp'	Thorpe	TQ/023687		19.	9½
Villani Abbatis de Certes' ibidem	Villeins of the Abbot of Chertsey in Thorpe			17.	1
Taxatores	Taxers			10.	6
			16.	4.	6

Hd. Waleton' [WALLINGTON HUNDRED]

Waleton'	Wallington	TQ/288644	1.	8.	0
Bedyngton'	Beddington	TQ/296652	1.	15.	3
Wodecote	Woodcote	TQ/300618	1.	14.	6¾
Bandon'	Bandonhill	TQ/298640	2.	17.	7½[2]
Waddon'	Waddon	TQ/310652	2.	14.	2½
Adynton'	Addington	TQ/371640	3.	4.	7¾
Sanderstede	Sanderstead	TQ/341614	2.	15.	9½
Colesdon' & Watindon'	Coulsdon and Waddington	TQ/312582 TQ/324582	1.	12.	1¾
Villani Abbatis de Certes' ibidem	Villeins of the Abbot of Chertsey in Coulsdon and Waddington			18.	9¾
Wodemerstorn'	Woodmansterne	TQ/277599	1.	8.	2¼
Sutton'	Sutton	TQ/259641	1.	18.	3½
Villani Abbatis de Certes' ibidem	Villeins of the Abbot of Chertsey in Sutton			15.	9¼
Kersalton'	Carshalton	TQ/278642	5.	0.	0
Mordone	Morden	TQ/251674		9.	9

[1] The hundred total on E 179/184/6 (1336) was later changed to £45. 13. 10.
[2] The £2. 17. 8½ on E 179/184/6 is in error.

Villani Abbatis Westmonasterii ibidem	Villeins of the Abbot of Westminster in Morden			13.	11¼
Micham	Mitcham	TQ/277685	5.	0.	11
Westcheyham	West Cheam	TQ/242639		15.	1¾
Eastcheyham	East Cheam	TQ/250639	2.	5.	10½
Selesdon'	Selsdon	TQ/351624		17.	3½
Bunchesham	Bensham	TQ/318675	1.	14.	8¾
Croydon'	Croydon	TQ/319654	9.	2.	9½
Adescompe	Addiscombe	TQ/344662	4.	2.	3½
Taxatores	Taxers		1.	7.	8
			54.	13.	8¼

Hd. Emelbrygg' [ELMBRIDGE HUNDRED]

Waybrygg'	Weybridge	TQ/072648	1.	13.	4¾
Waleton'	Walton upon Thames	TQ/102665	7.	0.	0
Moleseye	Molesey[1]	TQ/134684	2.	10.	7¼
Weston'	Weston	TQ/150662	3.	0.	4¾
Esshere	Esher	TQ/138647	2.	9.	9½
Stok'	Stoke D'Abernon	TQ/129584		18.	2
Coveham	Cobham	TQ/108597	2.	11.	6½
Villani Abbatis de Certes' ibidem	Villeins of the Abbot of Chertsey in Cobham		2.	2.	8
Taxatores	Taxers			19.	8
			23.	6.	2¾

Hd. Kyngeston' [KINGSTON HUNDRED]

Hamme & Petrichesham	Ham and Petersham	TQ/181718 TQ/182733	1.	18.	2
Villani Abbatis de Certes' ibidem	Villeins of the Abbot of Chertsey in Ham and Petersham		1.	1.	6¼
Tameseditton' & Longeditton'	Thames Ditton and Long Ditton	TQ/161672 TQ/169669	4.	15.	6
Hertyndon' & Combe	Hartington and Coombe	lost TQ/211719	2.	11.	11
Maldon' & Taleworth'	Malden and Tolworth	TQ/211662 TQ/195660	5.	6.	1
			15.	13.	2¼

Dm. Hd. Effyngham [HALF-HUNDRED OF EFFINGHAM]

Effyngham	Effingham	TQ/118539	7.	1.	5
Bocham	Bookham[2]	TQ/135546	2.	17.	4
Villani Abbatis de Certes' ibidem	Villeins of the Abbot of Chertsey in Bookham			17.	7¼
Taxatores	Taxers			12.	4
			11.	8.	8¼

[1] Grid ref. is to West Molesey.   [2] Grid ref. is to Great Bookham.

Hd. Coppedethorne [COPTHORNE HUNDRED]

Mikelham	Mickleham	TQ/170533	4.	13.	9
Fecham	Fetcham	TQ/150556	3.	5.	8½
Wauton'	Walton on the Hill	TQ/223551	3.	9.	9½
Hedlegh'	Headley	TQ/204549	1.	12.	8
Nywedegate	Newdigate	TQ/198421	1.	3.	4
Leddrede	Leatherhead	TQ/167562	9.	11.	7
Ebesham	Epsom	TQ/212607	2.	8.	3½
Villani Abbatis de Certes' ibidem	Villeins of the Abbot of Chertsey in Epsom				7¼
Asshestede	Ashtead	TQ/192580	3.	10.	0¼
Codynton'	Cuddington[1]	TQ/228632	4.	0.	2¼
Taddeworth'	Tadworth	TQ/240563	3.	19.	0½
Preston' &	Preston and	TQ/240576			
Berghe	Burgh	TQ/238585			
Ewelle	Ewell	TQ/221629	6.	12.	8¾
Taxatores	Taxers			15.	6
			45.	3.	2½

Hd. Brixistone [BRIXTON HUNDRED]

Pecham & Camerwell'	Peckham and Camberwell	TQ/343763 TQ/329766	5.	0.	0
Hacchesham Rutherhuth' & Bermundeseye	Hatcham Rotherhithe and Bermondsey	TQ/358770 TQ/359804 TQ/343794	2.	7.	2
Nywenton' & Waleworth'	Newington and Walworth	TQ/323790 TQ/325782	2.	0.	0
Mariscum Epi'	Lambeth Marsh	TQ/c.306795		4.	6
Lamhuthe Keneton'	Lambeth Kennington	TQ/307790 TQ/312775		16.	8
Stokwell' & Southlamhuth'	Stockwell and South Lambeth	TQ/306760 TQ/304768	1.	1.	0
Lamhuthe & Dene	Lambeth and Lambeth Dean	TQ/307790 TQ/c.320750	2.	11.	2
Dylewyssh	Dulwich	TQ/334733		15.	8
Legham & Stretham	Leigham and Streatham	TQ/303728 TQ/299716	2.	8.	8
Clopham	Clapham	TQ/293760	1.	2.	2
Totyngg' gravenel & Totyngge Bek'	Tooting Graveney and Tooting Bec	TQ/279711 TQ/293724	1.	10.	0
Merton'	Merton	TQ/258698		11.	8
Wandlesworth'	Wandsworth	TQ/255746	4.	11.	5
Wymbeldon'	Wimbledon	TQ/245714	2.	19.	4
Puttenhuth' & Hampton'	Putney and Roehampton	TQ/236752 TQ/226737	2.	19.	10
Shene	East Sheen	TQ/203750	4.	15.	0
Batricheseye	Battersea	TQ/268768	2.	7.	8
Wassyngham & Rudon'	Wassingham and Roydon[2]	lost lost			

[1] Grid ref. is to the church of the medieval village of Cuddington, discovered during the excavation of Nonsuch Palace in 1959.

[2] Wassingham and Roydon were both in Battersea.

Villani Abbatis Westmonasterii in Batricheseye	Villeins of the Abbot of Westminster in Battersea		11.		9½
Taxatores	Taxers		13.		10
			39.	7.	6½

Hd. Tanregge [TANDRIDGE HUNDRED]

Lyngefeld'	Lingfield	TQ/389438	14.	0.	1¼
Horne	Horne	TQ/337443	3.	6.	10
Bletchyngelegh for'[1]	Bletchingley [foreign]	TQ/328508	3.	18.	6½
Caterham	Caterham	TQ/336553	2.	14.	5¾
Warlyngham	Warlingham	TQ/357586	2.	14.	4½
Chelesham	Chelsham	TQ/389591	2.	8.	0½
Farlegh'	Farleigh	TQ/372601	1.	16.	0
Tatlesfeld'	Tatsfield	TQ/417562		19.	7¼
Waldyngham	Woldingham	TQ/371557	1.	1.	2
Tycheseye	Titsey	TQ/409550	1.	12.	8½
Ocstede	Oxted	TQ/390530	4.	15.	1
Crawhurst	Crowhurst	TQ/390474	2.	8.	4
Tanregge	Tandridge	TQ/374512	2.	19.	8
Waknestede	Godstone	TQ/357515	6.	2.	8
Taxatores	Taxers		1.	11.	8
			52.	9.	3¼

Lib. Abbatis de Bello de Lymenesfeld	Liberty of the Abbot of Battle in Limpsfield	TQ/405532	6.	18.	3¼
Villani Abbatis de Bello ibidem	Villeins of the Abbot of Battle in Limpsfield		2.	0.	3
Taxatores	Taxers			3.	6
			9.	2.	0¼

Taxatores	Taxers (Chief)		3.	13.	4

TOTAL: £587. 18. 8[2]

---

[1] Bletchingley borough was taxed at a tenth, above.

[2] The 1334 Account, E 179/184/5, although giving the total of the fifteenth as £499. 18. 1¼ and the tenth as £88. o. 6¾, makes the total £587. 18. 7¼.

SUSSEX

DOCUMENTS

8 Edward III: Account   E 179/189/8
8 Edward III: Particulars   E 179/189/7*
10 Edward III: Particulars   E 179/189/9

TAXERS

The abbot of Battle and James de Kyngeston

TAX YIELD

15th	£1,027.	19.	4½
10th	£ 76.	8.	4
	£1,104.	7.	8½

Representing assessed movable wealth of

£16,183.   13.   11½

NOTES

As will be apparent from the list of references below much work has already been done on the Sussex subsidy rolls and among those already published are those of 1296, 1327, 1332, and 1334. The data have been used in studies of various aspects of medieval Sussex.

W. Hudson's transcription of the 1334 roll (E 179/189/7) is very accurate, but place-names are seldom identified there since he saved this aspect of the work for his introduction to the three earlier subsidy rolls published three years later in 1910. The following list duplicates Hudson's with some amendments. Places taxed at a tenth are listed at the beginning; they include the city of Chichester, eight boroughs, and six ancient demesnes. Apart from that for Chichester the quotas for the boroughs were very small and the tax yield at a tenth in the county was surprisingly small. Hastings, Pevensey, Rye, and Winchelsea, as places within the liberty of the Cinque Ports, were excluded (see p. xxi).

The outline of the county in 1334 was much the same as that of modern Sussex. The coastline has of course changed slightly and there were minor alterations in the border with Kent in the nineteenth century. Ambersham, in modern Sussex, was taxed in Hampshire as it was a detached part of Steep parish until 1832.

REFERENCES

W. Hudson, 'The assessment of the hundreds of Sussex to the King's tax in 1334', *Sussex Arch. Coll.* 50 (1907), 153–75.

W. Hudson, 'The three earliest subsidies for the county of Sussex in the years 1296, 1327, 1332', *Sussex Rec. Soc.* 10 (1910).

R. A. Pelham, 'Studies in the historical geography of medieval Sussex', *Sussex Arch. Coll.* 72 (1931), 157–84.

R. A. Pelham, 'Some medieval sources for the study of historical geography', *Geography* 17 (1932), 32–8.

E. M. Yates, 'Medieval assessments in north-west Sussex', *Trans. Institute British Geographers*, 20 (1954), 75–92.

L. F. Salzman, 'Early taxation in Sussex', *Sussex Arch. Coll.* 98 (1960), 29–43, and 99 (1961), 1–19.

J. L. M. Gulley, 'The Wealden landscape in the early seventeenth century and its antecedents', unpublished Ph.D. thesis, University of London, 1960.

R. E. Glasscock, 'The distribution of lay wealth in Kent, Surrey, and Sussex, in the early fourteenth century', *Archaeologia Cantiana*, lxxx (1965), 61–8.

[BOROUGHS]

Civitas Cicestr'	Chichester	su/861049	22.	0.	0	[T]
Midhurst [B]	Midhurst	su/887215	5.	10.	0	[T]
Arundell' [B]	Arundel	TQ/016072	6.	7.	4½	[T]
Shoreham [B]	New Shoreham	TQ/216052	12.	0.	0	[T]
Stenyng' [B]	Steyning	TQ/178111	4.	19.	0	[T]
Brembre [B]	Bramber	TQ/186106	1.	10.	0	[T]
Horsham [B]	Horsham	TQ/170306	3.	13.	4	[T]
Lewes [B]	Lewes	TQ/416102	4.	1.	0	[T]
Estgrenestede [B]	East Grinstead	TQ/397380	3.	15.	3	[T]
			63.	15.	11½	[T]

[ANCIENT DEMESNES]

Est Asshelyng'	East Ashling	su/821077	1.	2.	6	[T]
West Asshelyng'	West Ashling	su/812073	1.	18.	8¼	[T]
Fontiton'	Funtington	su/801082	2.	8.	0½	[T]
Southwode	Southwood	su/806032	6.	3.	1¾	[T]
Woderyng' in Hundredo de Pageham	Withering[1]	lost		10.	0	[T]
Boseham[2]	Bosham	su/803039		10.	0	[T]
			12.	12.	4½	[T]
			76.	8.	4	[T]

Rapus de Cicestr' [RAPE OF CHICHESTER]

Hd. Westbourn' [WESTBOURNE HUNDRED]

Westbourn'	Westbourne	su/755073	3.	2.	8
Pernested	Prinsted	su/766053	3.	2.	7
Aldesworth' & Wodemancot'	Aldsworth and Woodmancote	su/765087 su/772076	3.	6.	0
Nutbourn'	Nutbourne	su/778054	2.	4.	8
Raketon'	Racton	su/779092	2.	9.	8
Walderton'	Walderton	su/789106	3.	6.	8

[1] *E.P.N.S.*, *VI*, *Sussex*, part 1 (1929), 96; a lost port at the entry to Pagham harbour.
[2] Most of Bosham was taxed at a fifteenth (Bosham hundred).

Stoghton'	Stoughton	su/801116	5.	6.	9
Northmeredon'	North Marden	su/807162	2.	10.	4¼
Estmeredon'	East Marden	su/807146	2.	19.	8
Compton'	Compton	su/778148	1.	8.	6
Westmeredon'	West Marden	su/772136	1.	2.	11
Upmeredon'	Up Marden	su/796141	1.	6.	8
			32.	7.	1¼

Hd. Boseham [BOSHAM HUNDRED]

Boseham[1]	Bosham	su/803039	2.	4.	4¼
Chudeham	Chidham	su/788039	2.	6.	11
Thornye	West Thorney	su/770023	1.	2.	0½
Stok'	West Stoke	su/826087	2.	8.	3¾
			8.	1.	7½

Hd. Dempford [DUMPFORD HUNDRED]

Southertyng'	South Harting	su/786195	2.	8.	10½
Westhertyng'	West Harting	su/783208	5.	15.	8¼
Dudelyng'	Didling	su/837186	2.	5.	6
Elnestede	Elsted	su/816196	2.	10.	0
Esthertyng'	East Harting	su/800197	3.	14.	2½
Stratiton'	Trotton	su/836225	2.	10.	0
Chitehurst	Chithurst	su/842230		8.	7½
Treford	Treyford	su/822190	1.	6.	8
Rogate	Rogate	su/807237	3.	2.	0½
			24.	1.	7¼

Hd. Esebourn' [EASEBOURNE HUNDRED]

Esebourn'	Easebourne	su/895225	5.	0.	0
Budyton'	Buddington	su/882234	1.	2.	0
Wolbedyng'	Woolbeding	su/872226	2.	6.	0
Stedeham	Stedham	su/863225	3.	0.	0
Ippyng'	Iping	su/852230	1.	18.	0
Cokkyng'	Cocking	su/879175	2.	15.	0
Bebiton'	Bepton	su/855182	2.	0.	0
Lynche	Lynch	su/849184	1.	15.	0
Lodesworth'	Lodsworth	su/931227	2.	6.	8
Suleham	Selham	su/933207	1.	6.	8
Heshite	Heyshott	su/898181	2.	13.	8
Grofham	Graffham	su/928167	2.	0.	0
			28.	3.	0

Hd. Sengelton' [SINGLETON HUNDRED]

Sengelton'	Singleton	su/878130	1.	13.	6
Cherleton'	Charlton	su/888129	1.	16.	6
Estden'	East Dean	su/905132	2.	18.	6
Westden'	West Dean	su/862126	3.	3.	10

[1] Part of Bosham was taxed at a tenth, above.

Chulegrave	Chilgrove	SU/835144	1.	11.	7½
Bunderton'	Binderton	SU/850108	2.	2.	6½
Lovent[1]	Mid Lavant	SU/855086	1.	16.	5
			15.	2.	11

Hd. Pageham [PAGHAM HUNDRED]

Mundeham	South Mundham	SU/878003	3.	11.	8¾
Pageham	Pagham	SZ/883975	1.	9.	5½
Cherleton'	Charlton[2]	lost	1.	11.	6
Shryppeux	Shripney	SU/936022	1.	0.	8
Northberghstede	North Bersted	SU/926013	2.	9.	8
Southberghstede	South Bersted	SU/934002	4.	6.	1¾
Bogenore	Bognor	SZ/935995	1.	13.	0¾
Aldewyk'	Aldwick	SZ/910990	1.	12.	10½
Cremesham	Crimsham	SU/898010	1.	3.	9¾
Lovent	Lavant[3]	SU/862084	3.	17.	6¾
Thedacre	Headacre[4]	lost		9.	0
Tangmere	Tangmere	SU/901061	2.	2.	6
Slyndon'	Slindon	SU/961083	4.	2.	0¼
			29.	10.	0

Hd. Manewood [MANHOOD HUNDRED]

Wyghtryng'	Wittering[5]	SZ/777984	9.	11.	0
Bridham	Birdham	SU/823003	5.	2.	0
Sidlesham	Sidlesham	SZ/855990	13.	7.	0
Seleseye	Selsey	SZ/856937	8.	0.	0
			36.	0.	0

Hd. Boxe & Stokebrugge [BOX AND STOCKBRIDGE HUNDRED]

Halnaked	Halnaker	SU/907081	3.	6.	0¼
Boxgrave	Boxgrove	SU/907075	1.	6.	9
Esthampton'	East Hampnett	SU/915068	1.	4.	0
Strethampton'	Strettington	SU/893074	1.	11.	0
Westerton'	Westerton	SU/886073	1.	0.	0
Fisshebourn'	[New] Fishbourne	SU/843046	1.	3.	8¾
Suburbium Civitatis Cicestr'	Suburb of Chichester		2.	0.	0
Wodecote	Woodcote	SU/880077	3.	0.	11
Ovyng'	Oving	SU/901051	2.	13.	4
Coleworth'	Colworth	SU/916028	2.	0.	0
Drayton'	Drayton	SU/882047	2.	15.	0
Mundeham	North Mundham	SU/875021	5.	0.	0
Rungeton'	Runcton	SU/885021	2.	6.	8
Mershston'	Merston	SU/893026	2.	6.	8
Rumbaldeswyk'	Rumboldswhyke	SU/869036	2.	15.	0[6]

[1] Lavant was taxed in Pagham hundred.

[2] A lost tithing of Pagham.

[3] Grid ref. is to East Lavant although the entry may refer to both East and West. Mid Lavant was taxed in Singleton hundred, above.

[4] *E.P.N.S.*, *VI*, *Sussex*, part 1 (1929), 12; an area in the suburbs of Chichester.

[5] Grid ref. is to West Wittering.

[6] Incorrectly given as £3. 0. 0 by Hudson (1907), op. cit. 166.

Hunston'	Hunston	su/864014	2.	5.	o
Waltham &	Up Waltham and	su/942138	3.	2.	o
Ertham	Eartham	su/938093			
Aldyngbourn'	Aldingbourne	su/923055	3.	14.	o
Donegheton'	Donnington	su/852023	1.	10.	o
			45.	0.	1

[Total of Rape of Chichester]		218.	6.	4

Rapus de Arundell' [RAPE OF ARUNDEL]

Hd. Avesford [AVISFORD HUNDRED]

Forde (va)	Ford	TQ/002037	7.	8.	o
Codelawe	Cudlow[1]	su/997007	2.	16.	o
Stok' &	South Stoke and	TQ/026101	2.	1.	o
Offam	Offham	TQ/028088			
Bulesham &	Bilsham and	su/974020	4.	0.	o
Madhurst	Madehurst	su/984100			
Felgham	Felpham	sz/949999	3.	6.	8
Walberton' &	Walberton and	su/972058	7.	16.	4
Bernham	Barnham	su/961043			
Atheryngton' &	Atherington and	TQ/006008	2.	5.	o
Gate	Eastergate	su/945051			
Middelton'	Middleton	su/976003	2.	6.	8
Toriton' &	Tortington and	TQ/003050	2.	2.	o
Bienstede	Binsted	su/982060			
Yabeton'	Yapton	su/981035	3.	6.	8
			37.	8.	4

Hd. Rutherbrugg' [ROTHERBRIDGE HUNDRED]

Peteworth'	Petworth	su/977218	11.	5.	o
Treue	River	su/940228	5.	0.	o
Tuliton'	Tillington	su/963220	2.	10·	o
Iburnehou	Ebernoe	su/973280	1.	3·	1¼
Stopeham	Stopham	TQ/026189	3.	6.	8
Sutton'	Sutton	su/979155	4.	0.	o
Wollaviton'	Woolavington [= East Lavington]	su/946163		19.	4¼
Berlaviton'	Barlavington	su/972161	4.	0.	2
Duneketon'	Duncton	su/961175	4.	13.	8
			36.	17.	11½

Hd. Westesewrith' [WEST EASEWRITHE HUNDRED]

Storghton'	Storrington	TQ/086141	6.	5.	o
Wykenholte	Wiggonholt	TQ/060167	4.	0.	o
Pulbergh'	Pulborough	TQ/048188	2.	18.	o
Nutbourne &	Nutbourne and	TQ/074188	3.	0.	o
Nytymbre	Nyetimber	TQ/084194			
Billyngeshurst	Billingshurst	TQ/088259	2.	16.	8

[1] Grid ref. is to Cudlow Barn, the last trace of a parish eroded away by the sea.

Dunhurst & Howyk'	Dounhurst and Howick	TQ/036279 TQ/079316	1.	17.	9
Amberle & Rekham	Amberley and Rackham	TQ/029132 TQ/048140	4.	0.	4
Perham & Gretham	Parham and Greatham	TQ/060141 TQ/043160	3.	10.	0
			28.	7.	9

Hd. Palyng' [POLING HUNDRED]

Eklesdon'	Ecclesden	TQ/078043	5.	6.	0
Estangermeryng'[1]	East Angmering	TQ/071043	2.	16.	8
Hamme cum Bargham	Ham Manor with Barpham	TQ/058036 TQ/068088	2.	2.	0
Rustyngton'	Rustington	TQ/055028	7.	0.	0
Ferryng'	Ferring	TQ/095025	3.	0.	0
Garyng'	Goring	TQ/111027	4.	0.	0
Estpreston'	East Preston	TQ/072023	2.	6.	8
Kyngeston'	Kingston	TQ/080021	5.	10.	0
Todyngton'	Toddington	TQ/038032	2.	6.	0
Hampton'	Littlehampton	TQ/031021	2.	15.	0
Lenemenstre	Lyminster	TQ/022048	2.	5.	1½
Warnecamp'	Warningcamp	TQ/033072	3.	8.	0
Burgham	Burpham	TQ/039090	2.	6.	0
Wapham	Wepham	TQ/043084	2.	8.	0
Northstok'	North Stoke	TQ/020108	2.	7.	5¼
Palyng'	Poling	TQ/047046	1.	18.	0
Slyndefold	Slinfold	TQ/118315		17.	0
			52.	11.	10¾

Dm. hd. Bury [BURY HALF-HUNDRED]

Hoghton'	Houghton	TQ/021116	2.	5.	0
Bury	Bury	TQ/017031	1.	12.	0
Westburton'	West Burton	TQ/001139	2.	5.	0
Bygeneuere	Bignor	SU/982146	1.	8.	0
Waltham	Coldwaltham	TQ/023166	2.	0.	0
Fitelworth' & Sonde	Fittleworth and Sond	TQ/009193 lost	2.	4.	0
Wysbergh'	Wisborough Green	TQ/052258	1.	0.	0
			12.	14.	0
[Total of Rape of Arundel]			167.	19.	11¼

Rapus de Brembre [RAPE OF BRAMBER]

Hd. Stenyng' [STEYNING HUNDRED]

Warnham[2]	Warnham	TQ/159336	4.	14.	4
Wassyngton'	Washington	TQ/119129	4.	15.	0

[1] One of the two manors of Angmering. West Angmering is probably represented by Ecclesden, above.

[2] It is likely that Rusper and Nuthurst are covered by this entry; both places were listed with Warnham in 1327, Hudson (1910), op. cit. 154–5.

Cherleton' & Shrottesfeld	Charlton and Shortsfield	TQ/169119 lost	5.	0.	0
Wistneston'	Wiston	TQ/155123	2.	3.	0
Coumbes	Coombes	TQ/191082	4.	0.	0
Annyngedon'	Annington	TQ/188094	1.	8.	0
Bydelyngton'	Bidlington [now Maudlin House]	TQ/178103	3.	10.	5
			25.	10.	9

Dm. hd. Estesewrith' [EAST EASEWRITHE HALF-HUNDRED]

Thackham	Thakeham	TQ/111173	6.	6.	8[1]
Wormynghurst	Warminghurst	TQ/118169	1.	5.	0
Sullyngton'	Sullington	TQ/098131	3.	3.	4[1]
Chiltyngton'	West Chiltington	TQ/090183	1.	15.	0
Disshenhurst	Dishenhurst	lost	1.	16.	0
			14.	6.	0[1]

Hd. West Grenstede [WEST GRINSTEAD HUNDRED]

Grenstede	West Grinstead	TQ/171207	4.	13.	4
Byne	Byne[2]		4.	6.	8
Wycham	Wyckham	TQ/190131	3.	8.	0
Eshurst	Ashurst	TQ/176163	4.	11.	9
Epsle	Apsley	TQ/116195	4.	3.	0
			21.	2.	9

Hd. Brutford [BRIGHTFORD HUNDRED]

Fyndon'	Findon	TQ/116085	4.	0.	0
Clopham	Clapham	TQ/096067	2.	17.	0
Hyen & Offyngton'	Heene and Offington	TQ/138028 TQ/134052	3.	3.	0
Launcyng'	Lancing[3]	TQ/182055	5.	8.	0
Somityng'	Sompting	TQ/161056	4.	10.	0
Bradewater	Broadwater	TQ/147043	4.	0.	0
Duryngton'	Durrington	TQ/118052	2.	15.	0
Segewyk'	Sedgewick	TQ/181270	2.	1.	0
			28.	14.	0

Hd. Burghbech [BURBEACH HUNDRED]

Shoreham	Old Shoreham	TQ/208060	2.	15.	0
Iryngham	Erringham	TQ/206077	2.	10.	0
Bydyng'[4]	Beeding	TQ/198103	4.	6.	8

---

[1] Minor error in this figure in Hudson's version (1907), op. cit. 168. E 179/189/7 is illegible at this point.

[2] Bines Farm (TQ/c.192176) is the probable location for this lost vill.

[3] Grid ref. is to North Lancing.

[4] This entry probably refers to both Upper and Lower Beeding, although the two places are several miles apart. The two settlements are discussed in *E.P.N.S.*, *VI*, *Sussex*, part 1 (1929), 205. Grid ref. is to Upper Beeding.

Horton'	Horton	TQ/209115	2.	6.	0
Edburghton'	Edburton	TQ/232115	2.	7.	0
Ifeud	Ifield	TQ/247376	2.	10.	0
			16.	14.	8

Dm. hd. Typenok' [TIPNOAK HALF-HUNDRED]

Alebourn'	Albourne	TQ/266163	3.	8.	0
Hanefeld	Henfield	TQ/212162	3.	0.	0
			6.	8.	0

Dm. hd. Wyndeham [WYNDHAM HALF-HUNDRED][1]

Wyndeham	Wyndham	TQ/236203	5.	7.	0½
Iwehurst	Ewhurst	TQ/211190	4.	11.	3½
			9.	18.	4

Dm. hd. Fissheresgate [FISHERSGATE HALF-HUNDRED]

Kyngeston'	Kingston by Sea	TQ/235052	5.	10.	0
Southwyk'	Southwick	TQ/239054	5.	1.	0
			10.	11.	0
	[Total of Rape of Bramber]		133.	5.	6

Rapus de Lewes [RAPE OF LEWES]

Hd. Swambergh' [SWANBOROUGH HUNDRED]

Iford	Iford	TQ/408073	4.	15.	5¼
Kyngeston'	Kingston [near Lewes]	TQ/392082	2.	16.	8
Villani Prioris de Lewes de Kyngeston'	Villeins of the Prior of Lewes in Kingston		1.	1.	0
Westout'	Westout	TQ/413100	3.	9.	1
			12.	2.	2¼

Hd. Holmestrowe [HOLMESTROW HUNDRED]

Radmeld	Rodmell	TQ/422063	10.	0.	0
Southese	Southease	TQ/423052	5.	0.	0
Mechyng'	Newhaven	TQ/443012	5.	12.	0
			20.	12.	0

[1] Half of Wyndham hundred was separately taxed, below.

Hd. Yenesmere [YOUNSMERE HUNDRED]

Rottyngdene	Rottingdean	TQ/370026	6.	10.	0
Ovyngdene	Ovingdean	TQ/356036	1.	14.	2¾
Baldesdenne	Balsdean	TQ/379059	2.	1.	2¾
Falmere cum	Falmer with	TQ/354088	1.	0.	0
Burghmere	Balmer	TQ/359099			
			11.	5.	5½

Hd. Whalesbone [WHALESBORNE HUNDRED]

Pecham cum	Patcham with	TQ/302091	8.	4.	5¾
Blechyngton'	West Blatchington	TQ/273065			
Preston &	Preston and	TQ/307067	4.	0.	0
Hove	Hove	TQ/288051			
Brightelmston'	Brighton	TQ/307045	6.	16.	8
			19.	1.	1¾

Dm. hd. Fissheresgate [FISHERSGATE HALF-HUNDRED]

Aldryngton'	Aldrington	TQ/266053	3.	3.	4
Porteslad	Portslade	TQ/255063	3.	3.	0
Hangelton'	Hangleton	TQ/268074	2.	18.	8
			9.	5.	0

Hd. Ponynges [POYNINGS HUNDRED]

Perchyng'	Perching	TQ/245114	4.	0.	0
Ponyng'	Poynings	TQ/264120	3.	0.	9½
Nytymbre	Newtimber	TQ/271134	4.	2.	0
Pycombe	Pyecombe	TQ/292125	2.	16.	8
			13.	19.	5½

Hd. Buttynghull' [BUTTINGHILL HUNDRED]

Clayton'	Clayton	TQ/299139	7.	4.	1¼
Kymere &	Keymer and	TQ/314153			
Hurst	Hurstpierpoint	TQ/279164			
Cokesfeld &	Cuckfield and	TQ/303244	4.	8.	4
Slagham	Slaugham	TQ/257280			
Werth'	Worth	TQ/302362	3.	5.	9
Burle[1]	Burleigh	TQ/355372	3.	5.	7
			18.	3.	9¼

Dm. hd. Wyndeham [WYNDHAM HALF-HUNDRED][2]

6.	3.	5

[1] In 1332 Burleigh was taxed in two hundreds, in error; see footnote to Lindfield, p. 313.
[2] Although it is not clear from the 1334 roll this entry probably refers to one place, Wyndham, as it did in 1332 (Hudson (1910), op. cit. 292). In 1334 part of Wyndham was taxed in the other half-hundred (p. 311).

Hd. Strete [STREAT HUNDRED]

Strete	Streat	TQ/351152	13.	1.	10¾
Lofeld	Lovel Barn	TQ/383196	3.	1.	5¾
Lyndefeld & Lyndefeld[1]	Lindfield	TQ/349258	10.	9.	2
			26.	12.	6½

Hd. Bercompe [BARCOMBE HUNDRED]

Northborgh'	Newick	TQ/421208	2.	12.	3
Middelborgh'	Barcombe	TQ/418142	4.	0.	2
Southborgh'	Hamsey	TQ/413121	6.	10.	4¼
			13.	2.	9¼

Dm. hd. Southnore [SOUTHOVER HALF-HUNDRED]

Southover	TQ/c.413096	3.	8.	0

[Total of Rape of Lewes]	153.	15.	9½[2]

Rapus de Pevenes' [RAPE OF PEVENSEY]

Hd. Shepelak' [SHIPLAKE HUNDRED]

Laughton'	Laughton	TQ/501126	3.	0.	5¾
Hodlegh'	East Hoathly	TQ/520162	6.	3.	9
Chyntyngleye	Chiddingly	TQ/544141	3.	8.	9½[3]
Ripp'	Ripe	TQ/513099	4.	15.	4¾
			17.	8.	5

Hd. Hertfeld [HARTFIELD HUNDRED]

Parrok'	Parrock	TQ/451348	3.	8.	0½
Folkenehurst	Faulkner's Farm	TQ/480385	2.	10.	10¼
Blakehamme	Blackham	TQ/501379	2.	13.	5¼
Burchyndenne	Birchden	TQ/535365	2.	12.	8
			11.	5.	0

---

[1] Described as Lindfield Bardolf and Archbishops Lindfield on the roll of 1327 (E 179/189/3).
  Some confusion had arisen over Lindfield in 1332, when it was taxed twice, once in Streat hundred and once in Loxfield hundred. An inquisition held on 1 Jan. 1335, and attached to the 1334 roll makes it clear that there was only the one Lindfield, in Streat hundred. It also makes clear that there was only one Burleigh, in Buttinghill hundred, another place where people had been taxed twice in 1332. (Hudson (1910), op. cit. xxxiii.)
[2] This is the total stated on the documents; in fact the figures add up to £153. 15. 10.
[3] Incorrectly given as £3. 8. 10½ by Hudson (1907), op. cit. 171.

Hd. Rutherfeld [ROTHERFIELD HUNDRED]

Rutherfeld	Rotherfield	TQ/556297	6.	3.	1¾
Northborgh'	The north 'borgh' of Rotherfield		2.	13.	0¼
Ferthe	Frant	TQ/591356	2.	6.	1¼
			11.	2.	3¼

Hd. Wylyngdon' [WILLINGDON HUNDRED]

Excete	Exceat	TV/519995	7.	9.	0
Berlyng'	Birling	TV/557970	4.	7.	0¼
Jevyngeton'	Jevington	TQ/561015	3.	1.	4½
Wylyngdon'	Willingdon	TQ/588025	6.	3.	1¾
			21.	0.	6½

Hd. Estbourne [EASTBOURNE HUNDRED]

Operton'	Upperton	TV/605998	6.	2.	2
Esthalle	Easthall[1]	lost	3.	14.	10
Lamport'	Lamport	lost	3.	13.	0
			13.	10.	0

Hd. Flaxbergh' [FLEXBOROUGH HUNDRED]

Chyntyng'	Chyngton	TV/504987	2.	18.	6
Blachyngton'[2]	East Blatchington	TV/483998	1.	16.	8
Sutheghton'	South Heighton	TQ/451027	1.	16.	0
Sutton'	Sutton	TV/493996	2.	10.	0
Norton'	Norton	TQ/471018	3.	0.	0
Denton'	Denton	TQ/454025	1.	11.	0
Bisshopeston'	Bishopstone	TQ/472010	1.	2.	0
			14.	14.	2

Hd. Middelton' [MIDDLETON HUNDRED][3]

		3.	16.	0

Hd. Ristonedenne [RUSHMONDEN HUNDRED]

Shiffeld	Sheffield	TQ/412245	8.	10.	0
Horstedekeynes	Horsted Keynes	TQ/383286	8.	0.	0
Marsefeud & Nutly	Maresfield and Nutley	TQ/466240 TQ/444278	5.	10.	0
			22.	0.	0

[1] East Hale Bottom, a valley in the chalk, preserves the name of the lost tithing of Easthall (TV/c.579972).

[2] Also taxed in Alciston hundred with Alfriston (p. 315).

[3] There being no indication on the 1334 roll, it is not clear to how many places this entry refers. It may be just to Milton in Arlington (as in 1332) or to Milton and the lost Werlington in Heddingly (as in 1327). For these entries see Hudson (1910), op. cit. 194 and 305. On these earlier rolls the heading is Middleton half-hundred.

Hd. Lokkesfeld [LOXFIELD HUNDRED]

Fremfeld	Framfield	TQ/495202	11.	6.	1½
Ryngmere	Ringmer	TQ/446125	11.	5.	0
Wadhurst & Maghefeld[1]	Wadhurst and Mayfield	TQ/641319 TQ/586270	12.	0.	0
			34.	11.	1½

Hd. Tottenore [TOTNORE HUNDRED]

Bedynghamme	Beddingham	TQ/445079	5.	3.	11¾
Preston'[2]	Preston [in Beddingham]	TQ/459076	2.	5.	0½
Preston'	Preston [in West Firle]	TQ/465079	2.	6.	8½
Heghton'	Heighton	TQ/479073	3.	4.	6½[3]
			13.	0.	3¼

Hd. Estgrenstede [EAST GRINSTEAD HUNDRED]

Imberhorne	Imberhorne	TQ/378383	4.	3.	6¼
Brembeltye	Brambletye	TQ/414365	2.	7.	2½
Asshehurst	Ashhurstwood	TQ/419365	2.	9.	5½
Shelverstrod	Shovelstrode	TQ/420379		16.	3
			9.	16.	5¼

Dm. hd. Alssiston' [ALCISTON HALF-HUNDRED]

Blachyngton'[4] & Alfricheston'	East Blatchington and Alfriston	TV/483998 TQ/521030	2.	12.	0
Alston'	Alciston	TQ/506055		11.	8
			3.	3.	8

Hd. Thille [DILL HUNDRED]

Haillesham	Hailsham	TQ/592094	6.	10.	4¼
Hellynglegh'	Hellingly	TQ/581123	3.	16.	8¼
Isenehurst	Isenhurst	TQ/566231	4.	9.	7½
			14.	16.	8

Hd. Langebrugg' [LONGBRIDGE HUNDRED]

Wylmyngton'	Wilmington	TQ/543043	5.	4.	0
Berewyk'	Berwick	TQ/519050	5.	9.	4
			10.	13.	4

[1] After this entry there is a note on Lindfield and Burleigh, saying that the Inquisition attached to the roll makes it clear that Lindfield is to be taxed in Streat hundred and Burleigh in Buttinghill. Confusion had arisen over these in 1332 (see footnote 1, p. 313).

[2] For identification of the two Prestons in earlier taxations see Hudson (1910), op. cit. xxxvi.

[3] Incorrectly given as £3. 14. 6½ by Hudson (1907), op. cit. 173.

[4] Blatchington was also taxed in Flexborough hundred, above. The part taxed with Alfriston was that belonging to Battle Abbey.

Seford [va]	Seaford	TV/482990	7.	10.	0
Appelderham [va]	Appledram	SU/842033	1.	1.	9¼
			8.	11.	9¼

| [Total of Rape of Pevensey] | 209. | 9. | 8 |

Rapus de Hastyng' [RAPE OF HASTINGS]

Dm. hd. Bello [BATTLE HUNDRED]

Middelburgh'[1]	Middleborough		1.	9.	6
Sandlak'	Sandlake		2.	11.	8
Monioye	Mountjoy		2.	4.	4
Telham	Telham	TQ/756149	1.	9.	3
			7.	14.	9

Dm. hd. Naddrefeld [NETHERFIELD HALF-HUNDRED]

Mundefeld	Mountfield	TQ/734203	2.	4.	4
Neddrefeld &	Netherfield and	TQ/722185	1.	11.	0
Penhurst	Penhurst	TQ/695165			
Brightlyng'	Brightling	TQ/683210	2.	9.	0
			6.	4.	4

Hd. Foxherle [FOXEARLE HUNDRED]

Worthyng'	Wartling	TQ/658092	4.	17.	1¾
Herst	Herstmonceux	TQ/642102	2.	14.	7
Esshbournham	Ashburnham	TQ/689145	2.	18.	0¼
Coppedebech'	Cowbeech	TQ/619146	2.	10.	3
			13.	0.	0

Hd. Nenenesfeld [NINFIELD HUNDRED]

Nenenesfeld	Ninfield	TQ/704123	2.	18.	0¼
Catesfeld	Catsfield	TQ/724136	1.	11.	3¼
Codyng'	Cooden	TQ/715071	1.	2.	8
Hou	Hooe	TV/689092	3.	5.	6½
			8.	17.	6

Hd. Gosetrowe [GOSTROW HUNDRED]

Brede	Brede	TQ/825182	6.	18.	5½
Udymere	Udimore	TQ/875188	5.	12.	6¼
			12.	10.	11¾

---

[1] Middleborough, Sandlake, and Mountjoy were the ancient divisions of the borough of Battle (TQ/748158).

Hd. Baldeslowe [BALDSLOW HUNDRED]

Ore	Ore	TQ/820121	4.	12.	4¼
Inlegh'	Inlegh[1]	lost	1.	15.	9¾
Crouhurst	Cowhurst	TQ/758123	2.	7.	8
Wyltyng'	Wilting	TQ/772109	3.	4.	2
			12.	0.	0

Hd. Gestlyng' [GUESTLING HUNDRED]

Gestlyng'	Guestling	TQ/855144	4.	13.	4
Iklesham	Icklesham	TQ/880164	5.	2.	0
Putte	Pett	TQ/872139	1.	11·	0
Farlegh'	Fairlight	TQ/860119	3.	5.	0
			14.	11.	4

Dm. hd. Buxle [BEXHILL HALF-HUNDRED]

| Buxle | Bexhill | TQ/739075 | 5. | 12. | 0½ |

Hd. Colspure [GOLDSPUR HUNDRED]

Knelle	Great Knelle	TQ/853257	3.	8.	0
Wyvelrugg'	Wivelridge[2]	lost	4.	15.	0
Hope	Hope	TQ/869257	3.	18.	0
Helghton'	Heighton	lost	1.	19.	0
			14.	0.	0

Hd. Staple [STAPLE HUNDRED]

Iwhurst	Ewhurst	TQ/795246	5.	3.	2
Sedelescombe	Sedlescombe	TQ/777188	3.	6.	8
Chitecombe	Chitcombe	TQ/815203	3.	16.	8
Northihamme	Northiam	TQ/830245	2.	11.	0
			14.	17.	6

Hd. Haukesbergh' [HAWKSBOROUGH HUNDRED]

Warbelton'	Warbleton	TQ/609182	2.	16.	3¾
Todyngwerth'	Tottingworth	TQ/615219	2.	14.	0¼
Burghersh	Burwash	TQ/677247	2.	9.	4¾
Byvelhamme	Bivelham	TQ/631263	3.	2.	3¾
			11.	2.	0½

Hd. Showeswell' [SHOYSWELL HUNDRED]

Passelegh'	Pashley	TQ/706291	2.	15.	4¼
Hodlegh'	Hoadley[3]	lost	2.	14.	10¼
Tycheshurst'	Ticehurst	TQ/689301	3.	16.	5½
			9.	6.	8

---

[1] One of the borghs of Baldslow hundred. *E.P.N.S., VI, Sussex,* part 2 (1930), 506.
[2] One of the borghs of Goldspur hundred, ibid. 532.
[3] Hoadley Wood (TQ/c.660280) preserves the name of Hoadley vill.

Hd. Henhurst [HENHURST HUNDRED]

Funterugg'	Frontridge	TQ/703246	5.	10.	0
Glottyngham	Glottenham	TQ/729222	3.	10.	0
Salhurst	Salehurst	TQ/749242	2.	15.	0
Irugg'	Iridge	TQ/737269	3.	10.	0
			15.	5.	0

[Total of Rape of Hastings]   145.   2.   1¾

TOTAL: £1,104. 7. 8½¹

---

¹ As on 1334 Account, E 179/189/8.

WARWICKSHIRE

DOCUMENTS

8 Edward III: Account   E 179/192/6a
8 Edward III: Particulars   E 179/192/6* (with *Nomina Villarum* of 1332
                             attached)
10 Edward III: Particulars   E 179/192/7

TAXERS

The prior of Kenilworth and Roger de Guldesbergh

TAX YIELD

15th	£763.	0.	9¾
10th	£ 79.	17.	3
	£842.	18.	0¾

Representing assessed movable wealth of

£12,244.   4.   8¼

NOTES

The list begins with two boroughs, Warwick and Tamworth (now in Stafford-shire), and the ancient demesnes taxed at a tenth. These include Alcester, Brinklow, Henley in Arden, and Stratford upon Avon, all of which were considered taxation boroughs in 1332 and again in 1336 but which curiously are not specified as such in 1334. Coventry, having protested during the reign of Edward I that it was not a borough (Willard (1933), op. cit. 420), escaped taxation at the higher rate and paid a conventional sum of £50 at a fifteenth.

It was not until after the administrative reorganization of the nineteenth century that Warwickshire took on its modern outline. In 1334 its territory was still intermingled in a complicated way with Gloucestershire and Worcestershire. Consequently thirty-four places in modern Warwickshire are to be found on the tax rolls of other counties in 1334 (summarized in Glasscock, thesis, 1963, op. cit., Table 9, 285), and the Warwickshire list includes five places that have since been transferred to adjacent counties.

REFERENCES

Midland Record Society, 'The lay subsidy roll for Warwickshire of 1327', supplement to *Trans. Midland Rec. Soc.* 3–6 (1899–1902).
W. F. Carter, ed., 'The lay subsidy roll for Warwickshire of 6 Edward III (1332)', *Dugdale Soc. Publications*, 6 (1926).

[BOROUGHS AND ANCIENT DEMESNES]

			£	s.	d.	
Tamworth' [B]¹	Tamworth [in Staffs.]	SK/208041	6.	15.	8	[T]
Henley [A.D]	Henley in Arden	SP/151659	4.	3.	8	[T]
Stoneley c.m	Stoneleigh [with members]	SP/330726	8.	13.	4	[T]
Hulle [A.D]	King's Hill *olim* Helenhull	SP/331743				
Crulefeld [A.D]	Cryfield	SP/299747				
Hurst' [A.D]	Hurst	SP/285754				
Warr' infra [B]	Warwick [within]	SP/282650	8.	9.	4	[T]
Warr' extra [A.D]	Warwick [without]		11.	o.	4	[T]
Kynton' [A.D]	Kineton	SP/336511	7.	18.	o	[T]
Budyford [A.D]	Bidford on Avon	SP/101519	7.	14.	o	[T]
Brynkelowe [A.D]	Brinklow	SP/437797	2.	13.	8	[T]
Stretford super Aven' [A.D]	Stratford upon Avon	SP/201547	13.	2.	o	[T]
Alycestr' [A.D]	Alcester	SP/091574	9.	7.	3	[T]
			79.	17.	3	[T]

Hd. Kynton' [KINETON HUNDRED]

			£	s.	d.	
Walton' Deyvill²	Walton [Deyville]	SP/285524	2.	1.	o	
Walton' Mauduyt	Walton [Mauduit]		1.	15.	o	
Wellesburn' Hastang'	Wellesbourne Hastings	SP/277556	3.	o.	o	
Wellesburn' Montfort	Wellesbourne Mountford	SP/277553	4.	o.	o	
Hunstancote	Hunscote	SP/250550		19.	o	
Cherlecote	Charlecote	SP/262565	3.	1.	o	
Wasperton'	Wasperton	SP/266588	1.	14.	6	
Hethecote	Heathcote	SP/294589				
Bereford	Barford	SP/272609	3.	6.	6	
Neubold Pacy	Newbold Pacey	SP/299573		16.	1	
Asshorn'	Ashorne	SP/304577	1.	8.	o	
Tachebrok Episcopi	Bishop's Tachbrook	SP/313613	3.	8.	o	
Tachebrok Mallore	Tachbrook Mallory	SP/320618	1.	15.	o	
Toneworth'	Tanworth	SP/113704	6.	4.	8	
Lapworth'	Lapworth	SP/163712	3.	5.	2	
Pacwode	Packwood	SP/171728	2.	2.	11	
Halford	Halford	SP/258456	2.	3.	o	
Etyndon' c.m³	Ettington [with members]	SP/248474	5.	18.	o	
Aylaston'	Ailstone	SP/209511	2.	o.	o	
Athereston'	Atherstone on Stour	SP/206510	2.	11.	o	
Whytchirch'	Whitchurch	SP/227487	3.	4.	o	
Compton' Scorfen	Compton Scorpion	SP/213406		19.	o	
Ilmendon'	Ilmington	SP/209435	7.	1.	8	
Foxcote	Foxcote	SP/199419				
Stretton' super Fosse	Stretton on Fosse	SP/223383	1.	6.	2	
Ditcheford	Ditchford	SK/239391	1.	1.	o	
Utlicote	Idlicote	SP/283442	2.	10.	4	
Bercheston'	Barcheston	SP/265399		17.	o	
Wolauynton'	Willington	SP/268390	1.	8.	8	
Honynton'	Honington	SP/261426	4.	11.	11	
Wolford Parva	Little Wolford	SP/263352	1.	19.	o	

¹ Part of the borough of Tamworth, which straddled the county boundary, was taxed in Staffordshire (p. 277).

² Walton was divided into the two manors of Deyville and Mauduit (next entry).

³ Members of Ettington in 1316 included Fullready and Thornton (*F.A.* v. 175).

Wolford Magna	Great Wolford	SP/250345	3.	15.	0
Barton'	Barton on the Heath	SP/256324	1.	9.	0
Compton' Magna	Long Compton	SP/287331	6.	15.	5
Burmynton'	Burmington	SP/263379	2.	8.	8
Weston iuxta Chiriton'	Weston	SP/280357	1.	19.	8
Wynterton'	Winderton	SP/325404	1.	13.	2
Stourton'	Stourton	SP/296368	2.	3.	4
Chiriton'	Cherington	SP/292366	2.	16.	5½
Wyccheford	Whichford	SP/312346	4.	4.	0
Brayles	Brailes	SP/315393	9.	10.	4
Chelmescote	Chelmscote	SP/315426		18.	0
Compton' atte Wynyate	Compton Wynyates	SP/323430	1.	9.	0
Whatcote	Whatcote	SP/298445	3.	2.	0½
Pilardynton' superior	Pillerton Priors	SP/293476	2.	2.	10
Pilardynton' Hercy	Pillerton Hersey	SP/298489	2.	17.	0
Oxhullue	Oxhill	SP/317455	3.	7.	0
Tysso c.m	Tysoe [with members]	SP/341443	8.	14.	8
Merston' Botiller	Butlers Marston	SP/321500	3.	8.	0
Compton' Murdak	Compton Verney	SP/310529	4.	10.	8
Lythethirn'	Lighthorne	SP/335560	2.	18.	10
Morton' Merhull	Moreton Morrell	SP/311555	4.	17.	0
Kyngeston'	Kingston	SP/361575	2.	11.	0
Chesterton'	Chesterton	SP/358582	4.	1.	2
Geydon'	Gaydon	SP/364539	3.	5.	0
Chadleshunte	Chadshunt	SP/349530	2.	9.	0
Mollynton'[1]	Mollington [in Oxon.]	SP/442474	1.	8.	6
Shoteswell	Shotteswell	SP/426455	2.	6.	2
Warmynton'	Warmington	SP/410474	2.	7.	0
Rotteley	Ratley	SP/383473	2.	2.	6
Upton' super Egge	Upton	SP/368456	1.	4.	6
Radewey[2]	Radway	SP/386481	1.	12.	8
Orlascote	Arlescote	SP/390486	2.	0.	2
Farneburgh'	Farnborough	SP/434495	3.	13.	10
Avene Derset	Avon Dassett	SP/410500	2.	9.	2
Derset c.m	Dassett [with members]	SP/398512	13.	12.	2
Buryton'	Burton [now Burton Dassett][3]				
Southende	South End	SP/390520			
Radewey	Radway[4]	SP/368481			
Herdwyk'	Hardwick	SP/370515			
Knyttecote	Knightcote	SP/399545			
Northende	North End	SP/393526			
Fennycompton'	Fenny Compton	SP/416522	3.	11.	0
Wylmeletton'	Wormleighton	SP/448539	3.	12.	5
Shuckburgh Inferior	Lower Shuckburgh	SP/489627		13.	4
Herdwyk' Prioris	Priors Hardwick	SP/471562	2.	3.	0
Merston' Prioris	Priors Marston	SP/489576	5.	0.	4
Broghton'	Broughton	SP/204462		5.	4
			211.	15.	11

[1] Part of Mollington was taxed in Oxfordshire (Bloxham hundred, p. 243).
[2] Part of Radway was taxed with Burton Dassett, below.
[3] The modern settlement of Burton Dassett was formerly two distinct places.
[4] Part of Radway was separately taxed, above.

Hd. Knytlowe [KNIGHTLOW HUNDRED][1]
[LEET OF MERTON]

Hodenhull	Hodnell	SP/424574	1.	14.	0
Lodebrok	Ladbroke	SP/413589	3.	10.	8
Rodburn'	Radbourn[2]	SP/440570		13.	0
Southam	Southam	SP/418618	4.	9.	5
Napton'	Napton on the Hill	SP/462612	6.	10.	10
Shuckeburgh superior	Upper Shuckburgh	SP/497617	1.	10.	9½
Fleckenho	Flecknoe	SP/515634	3.	10.	4
Wolfhamcote	Wolfhampcote	SP/530653	3.	1.	0
Nethircote	Nethercote	SP/517641			
Greneburgh c.m	Grandborough [with members]	SP/492670	7.	10.	8
Wolscote	Woolscott	SP/498679			
Caldecote	Calcutt	SP/471650			
Salebrigg'	Sawbridge	SP/506659	2.	9.	4
Wyleby	Willoughby	SP/515673	3.	4.	8
Lemynton'	Leamington Hastings	SP/443676	7.	5.	0
Hastang' c.m	[with members]				
Hulle	Hill	SP/452670			
Bradewell	Broadwell	SP/456657			
Herdwyk'	Kites Hardwick	SP/469682			
Burthingbury	Birdingbury	SP/432685	1.	18.	0
Stocton'	Stockton	SP/437635	3.	0.	0
Stonythorp'	Stoney Thorpe	SP/405621		12.	0
Bascote	Bascote	SP/404636	1.	11.	0
Arleye &	Arley and	SP/283906	2.	5.	4
Sloleye	Slowley	SP/270888			
Ichynton' longa	Long Itchington	SP/412651	6.	0.	0
Merton'	Marton	SP/407689	2.	14.	2
Ethorp'	Eathorpe	SP/392692	2.	0.	0
Honyngham	Hunningham	SP/372680	2.	10.	4
Whappenburi'	Wappenbury	SP/378692	2.	6.	8
Stretton' super donnesmor	Stretton on Dunsmore	SP/406725	2.	8.	0
Franketon'	Frankton	SP/423701	2.	14.	2
Bourton' &	Bourton on Dunsmore	SP/436703	2.	8.	11
Draycote	and Draycote	SP/445699			
Thurlaston'	Thurlaston	SP/469709	3.	7.	0
Dunchirch cum	Dunchurch with	SP/486712	2.	13.	0
Toft'	Toft	SP/478706			
Hulle Morton'	Hillmorton	SP/534739	1.	14.	3
Clifton'	Clifton upon Dunsmore	SP/531764	2.	2.	0
Rokeby	Rugby	SP/504752	2.	10.	0
Beulton'	Bilton	SP/488739	2.	1.	4
Chirch Lalleford	Church Lawford	SP/452763	2.	11.	1
Wolricheston'	Wolston	SP/409758	4.	16.	0
			99.	12.	11½

Leta de Stoneley in Hd. Knytlowe
[LEET OF STONELEIGH IN KNIGHTLOW HUNDRED]

Herburbury	Harbury	SP/373600	3.	16.	8
Stivechale	Stivichall	SP/330768	1.	6.	4

[1] Knightlow hundred was subdivided into three leets; for details see *E.P.N.S.*, *XIII*, *Warwicks.* (1936), 95.

[2] Grid ref. is to the site of Radbourn village in the modern parish of Lower Radbourn.

Ichinton' Episcopi	Bishop's Itchington	SP/388577	5.	11.	2
Whytenassh	Whitnash	SP/328636	1.	16.	4
Olughton'	Ufton	SP/379621	2.	8.	0
Offchirch'	Offchurch	SP/358656	2.	5.	0
Radeford Symeli'	Radford Semele	SP/342647	2.	6.	2
Lemynton' Prior'	Leamington	SP/317657	2.	3.	10
Neubold Comyn	Newbold Comyn	SP/c.330660	1.	16.	0
Mulverton &	Old Milverton and	SP/297674	2.	13.	0
Edulmescote	Emscote	SP/304657			
Lillynton'	Lillington	SP/324673	2.	10.	0
Cobynton'	Cubbington	SP/343683	2.	4.	0
Weston' iuxta Wethele	Weston under Wetherley	SP/360692	1.	5.	0
Bobenhull	Bubbenhall	SP/360725	2.	6.	8
Ruton' super Donnesmor	Ryton on Dunsmore	SP/386745	1.	12.	0
Braundon	Brandon	SP/409765	3.	10.	0
Bretford	Bretford	SP/429771	2.	1.	6
Sowe &	Walsgrave on Sowe and	SP/379809	2.	12.	4
Caludon'	Caludon	SP/375802			
Wykene	Wyken	SP/367807	1.	9.	0
Wylnhale	Willenhall	SP/364759	1.	0.	0
Stokebigging'	Stoke and	SP/358794	1.	11.	9
	Bigging	SP/355786			
Pinnele	Pinley	SP/357777			
Whytele	Whitley	SP/348768			
Bilney	Binley	SP/377785	1.	2.	0
Coventre ex parte	Coventry	SP/333793	50.	0.	0
comitis et prioris					
Coundulme	Coundon	SP/311813	1.	15.	0
Radeford	Radford	SP/324804			
Allesley	Allesley	SP/302806	4.	16.	8
Bathekynton'	Baginton	SP/343747	2.	9.	0
Kenylworth'	Kenilworth	SP/288721	2.	9.	0
Assho	Ashow	SP/312702	1.	1.	0
Wodecote	Woodcote	SP/283692	1.	7.	0
Lecwotton' &	Leek Wootton and	SP/288687	1.	15.	0
Hull	Hill Wootton	SP/303687			
			114.	19.	5

Leta De Brynkelowe in Eodem Hundredum
[LEET OF BRINKLOW IN KNIGHTLOW HUNDRED]

Newenham Regis	Kings Newnham	SP/448772	3.	0.	0
Herdburgh Magna	Harborough Magna	SP/476793	1.	18.	0
Herdburgh Parva	Harborough Parva	SP/480788		13.	6
Longa Lalleford	Long Lawford	SP/472762	4.	16.	0
Neubold Paunton'	Newbold on Avon	SP/486771	1.	16.	0
Cosford	Cosford	SP/499791	2.	7.	0
Parva Lalleford	Little Lawford	SP/469772		18.	6
Brouneswavere	Brownsover	SP/507773	2.	3.	4
Neuton' iuxta Clifton'	Newton	SP/530781	2.	16.	6
Chirchwavere	Churchover	SP/510809	2.	6.	0
Thesterwavere	Cesters Over	SP/504820	1.	10.	0
Walton' iuxta Kirkeby	Little Walton	SP/492831		19.	0
Newenham Parva	Newnham Paddox	SP/480837	1.	10.	0
Paillinton'	Pailton	SP/471819	2.	14.	0
Neubold Stretton'	Newbold Revel	SP/456809	1.	10.	0
Esenhull	Easenhall	SP/464794	2.	15.	0
Wilye	Willey	SP/496848	1.	17.	10

Wybetoft	Wibtoft	SP/479878	1.	13.	0
Kirkeby Monachorum	Monks Kirby	SP/462831	1.	8.	0
Brochurst	Brockhurst	SP/469835	1.	11.	0
Copston' Maior	Copston Magna	SP/453884	2.	3.	0
Strotardeston'	Street Ashton	SP/458823		18.	0
Whytbrok'	Withybrook	SP/436841	4.	3.	0
Happesforde	Hopsford	SP/425838			
Ansty	Ansty	SP/399837	2.	15.	6
Bernangel	Barnacle	SP/384847	1.	12.	0
Shulton'	Shilton	SP/403844	2.	1.	0
Copston' Parva	Copston Parva	SP/c.445890		15.	9
Wolfey	Wolvey	SP/430880	2.	12.	0
Bourton' &	Burton Hastings and	SP/411899	1.	16.	0
Shirford	Shelford	SP/426886			
Stretton' Baskervill	Stretton Baskerville	SP/420910		19.	0
Hyde	Hydes Pastures	SP/c.396923		9.	7¼
Bromcote	Bramcote	SP/412883	1.	19.	0
Ruton' iuxta Bulkynton'	Ryton	SP/396866		17.	0
Bulkynton' iuxta Ruton'	Bulkington	SP/391868	1.	10.	0
Weston'	Weston in Arden	SP/386872	2.	1.	0
Merston' Jabet	Marston Jabbett	SP/377884	2.	6.	6
Bedeworth'	Bedworth	SP/359869	2.	2.	0
Eccleshale	Exhall [juxta Coventry]	SP/341851	2.	1.	0
Folshull	Foleshill	SP/353825	2.	6.	8
Kersleye	Keresley	SP/317825	1.	9.	2
Asteleye	Astley	SP/311893	3.	4.	0
Prensthorp'	Princethorpe	SP/399708	2.	8.	0
			82.	11.	10¼

Total for Knightlow Hundred [three leets]	297.	4.	2¾

Hd. Humelyngford [HEMLINGFORD HUNDRED]

Greyve &	Griff and	SP/358885	4.	10.	10
Chelvercote	Chilvers Coton	SP/355911			
Eton'	Nuneaton	SP/361919	6.	11.	2
Grendon'	Grendon	SK/287009	4.	2.	2
Pollesworth'	Polesworth	SK/263023	6.	11.	0
Kyngesneuton'	Newton Regis	SK/279074	1.	16.	0
Wylmundecote	Wilncote	SK/226013	1.	6.	8
Aldelnestr'	Austrey	SK/296062	2.	18.	9
Mancestr'	Mancetter	SP/320967		18.	0
Baddesle Endesouere	Baddesley Ensor	SP/271986	1.	8.	6
Caldecote	Caldecote	SP/349951		17.	7
Bromcote	Bramcote	SK/273043	1.	5.	0
Filongley &	Fillongley and	SP/282873	4.	17.	6
Corleye	Corley	SP/301851			
Maxstoke	Maxstoke	SP/235869	2.	0.	0
Alspathe	Alspath	SP/266825	2.	16.	7
Pakynton' Prior'	Great Packington	SP/230840	2.	12.	0
Pakynton' Pigot	Little Packington	SP/212843	1.	0.	0
Hampton' in Ardena	Hampton in Arden	SP/202808	1.	14.	0
Baddesle Clynton'	Baddesley Clinton	SP/202713		7.	0
Bykenhull c.m	Bickenhill [with members]	SP/188823	4.	8.	5
Kynton'	Kineton	SP/123814			
Lyndon'	Lyndon End	SP/143843			

			£	s	d
Elmedon'	Elmdon	SP/163827		13.	0
Coleshull	Coleshill	SP/202890	4.	8.	4
Whytacre Inferior	Nether Whitacre	SP/231929	3.	4.	0
Shustok'	Shustoke	SP/243910	1.	15.	9
Whytacr' Superior	Over Whitacre	SP/254910	2.	7.	10
Baxterleye	Baxterley	SP/257971		19.	0
Athereston'	Atherstone	SP/308980	2.	12.	0
Wedynton'	Weddington	SP/359936	1.	18.	3
Hardeshull	Hartshill	SP/326944	4.	12.	0
Anstele	Ansley	SP/290926			
Sekyndon'	Seckington	SK/260074	1.	4.	7
Dersthull	Dosthill	SP/212998		15.	
Amynton'	Amington	SK/235044	3.	4.	0
La Lee iuxta Kynnesburi'	Lea Marston	SP/204927	1.	10.	0
Kynnesbury	Kingsbury	SP/215963	4.	18.	0
Cruddeworth' &	Curdworth and	SP/178928	2.	7.	6
Myneworth'	Minworth	SP/159920			
Middelton'	Middleton	SP/177983	4.	2.	7
Sutton' in Colfeld	Sutton Coldfield	SP/122963	6.	8.	0
Aston' c.m	Aston [with members]	SP/082899	12.	16.	8
Wytton'	Witton	SP/087907			
Erdynton'	Erdington	SP/110917			
Echeles	Nechells	SP/091891			
Dodeston'	Vauxhall [olim Duddeston Hall]	SP/090880			
Bordesle	Bordesley	SP/098864			
Salteleye	Saltley	SP/097876			
Parva Bromwych'	Ward end [olim Little Bromwich]	SP/114886			
Overton'	Water Orton	SP/178911			
Castel Bromwych'	Castle Bromwich	SP/143898			
Egebaston'	Edgbaston	SP/057847	1.	15.	6
Byrmyngham	Birmingham	SP/069862	9.	8.	0
Sheldon'	Sheldon	SP/153846	1.	8.	6
Solyhull	Solihull	SP/153793	6.	9.	0
Borstaston'	Barston	SP/208780	1.	3.	10
Baleshale	Balsall	SP/239763	3.	19.	5
Berkeswell	Berkswell	SP/244792	3.	17.	8
Wysshawe	Wishaw	SP/177945		8.	6
			140.	8.	1

Hd. Barlychwey [BARLICHWAY HUNDRED]

			£	s	d
Aspaley	Aspley	SP/088537		14.	6
Wroxhale	Wroxall	SP/222708	1.	2.	0
Bodebrok' c.m¹	Budbrooke [with members]	SP/259656	3.	13.	6
Haseleye	Haseley	SP/240685	1.	17.	0
Honyley	Honiley	SP/245722			
Hatton'	Hatton	SP/236673	2.	7.	0
Beausale	Beausale	SP/241707			
Shreweley	Shrewley	SP/217673		14.	6
Rowynton'	Rowington	SP/204693	4.	11.	11
Pynnele	Pinley	SP/211663			

¹ Members of Budbrooke in 1316 included Hampton on the Hill, Norton Curlieu, and *Wodeford* (F.A. v. 179).

Whyteleye	Whitley	SP/162660	2.	8.	9
Preston'	Preston Bagot	SP/175660			
Claverdon'	Claverdon	SP/198646	2.	2.	8
Longeley	Langley	SP/192628	1.	8.	1
Norton' Lyndeseye	Norton Lindsey	SP/228631		16.	0
Shirburn'	Sherborne	SP/262614	1.	7.	6
Fulbrok'	Fulbrook[1]	SP/253607	1.	1.	0
Wolvardynton'	Wolverton	SP/207623	1.	13.	7
Snytenfeld	Snitterfield	SP/219601	4.	6.	11
Burleye	Bearley	SP/182604		18.	6
Edryston'	Edstone	SP/175618	1.	0.	0
Billeleye	Billesley	SP/147568	2.	14.	10
Aston Cantelowe c.m[2]	Aston Cantlow [with members]	SP/138598	5.	5.	2
Rowenhale	Great Alne	SP/117595	2.	5.	9
Morton' Bagot	Morton Bagot	SP/112647	2.	2.	0
Offord	Offord	SP/c.150620	1.	5.	2
Spernouere	Spernall	SP/085622	1.	5.	0
Stodeleye	Studley	SP/074634	2.	12.	11
Ippesleye	Ipsley [in Worcs.]	SP/065665	3.	5.	0
Terdebigg'[3]	Tardebigge [in Worcs.]	SO/996692	1.	6.	0
Sombourn'	Sambourne	SP/059618	1.	8.	0
Cokton'	Coughton	SP/084604	2.	7.	4
Kynwarton'	Kinwarton	SP/105583		12.	0
Whyteley	Weethley	SP/055555		10.	2
Haselouere	Haselor	SP/123579	1.	13.	3
Upton'	Upton	SP/121578	2.	12.	0
Overesley	Oversley	SP/094569	2.	13.	0
Bynyngton'	Binton	SP/146540	3.	5.	0
Eccleshale	Exhall [juxta Alcester]	SP/103551		18.	0
Kyngesbrome	King's Broom	SP/088530		16.	8
Grafton'	Temple Grafton	SP/124548	1.	6.	2
Hilberworth'	Hillborough	SP/123520	1.	9.	0
Whytlaxford	Wixford	SP/089549		15.	6
Arwe	Arrow	SP/082565	1.	13.	8
Saltford Abbatis	Abbot's Salford	SP/067501	1.	16.	5
Saltford Prior' c.m[4]	Salford Priors [with members]	SP/078510	1.	1.	5
Coppebevynton'	Cock Bevington	SP/054527	1.	1.	5
Donynton'	Dunnington	SP/067535	1.	11.	4
Wodebevynton'	Wood Bevington	SP/057538	1.	0.	8
Mulcote &	Milcote and	SP/172513	2.	6.	6
Dersynton'[5]	Dorsington	SP/132497			
Bykemersh	Bickmarsh [in Worcs.]	SP/109495	1.	16.	6
			86.	19.	3

Lib. Pathelowe [PATHLOW LIBERTY]

Wotton &	Wooton Wawen and	SP/153633	3.	17.	0
Ulnhale	Ullenhall	SP/121672			

[1] Grid ref. is to Lower Fulbrook.

[2] Members of Aston Cantlow in 1316 included Wilmcote, Newnham, and Little Alne (*F.A.* v. 178).

[3] Part of Tardebigge was taxed in Worcestershire (Halfshire hundred, p. 352).

[4] Members of Salford Priors in 1316 included Cock and Wood Bevington, here separately taxed (*F.A.* v. 178).

[5] Most of Dorsington was taxed in Gloucestershire (Kiftsgate hundred, p. 94).

Wylmecote Parva	Little Wilmcote	SP/167577		15.	6
Drayton'	Drayton	SP/164549	1.	10.	0
Lodynton'	Luddington	SP/167524	2.	11.	9
Hampton' Episcopi c.m	Hampton Lucy [with members]	SP/256570	1.	12.	4
Hatton'	Hatton	SP/c.240565	1.	14.	0
Clopton'	Clopton	SP/201568		10.	0
Oldestretford	Old Stratford	SP/200550		16.	0
Shotreth'	Shottery	SP/186546	2.	2.	0
Welcumbe	Welcombe	SP/208567	1.	5.	0
Bysshopesdon'	Bishopton	SP/188565	1.	9.	0
Lockesley	Loxley	SP/258531	2.	10.	10
Alveston'	Alveston	SP/232563	1.	13.	5
Tydington'	Tiddington	SP/223559	1.	17.	4
Clifford	Ruin Clifford	SP/c.204526	1.	17.	8
Inge	Ingon	SP/215574		11.	6
			26.	13.	4

TOTAL: £842. 18. 0¾[1]

---

[1] As on 1334 Account, E 179/192/6a.

WESTMORLAND (1336)

DOCUMENTS

10 Edward III: Enrolled Account	E 359/8a, m. 11d.
10 Edward III: Particulars	E 179/195/2*
11 Edward III: Particulars	E 179/195/4

TAXERS

1334: Richard de Pykeryng and Thomas de Gergrave (vacated)
1336: John de Stirkeland and Roger de Bromholmesheued

TAX YIELD

15th	£187.	15.	1
10th	£ 3.	0.	5½
	£190.	15.	6½

Representing assessed movable wealth of

£2,846. 10. 10

NOTES

Westmorland, like Cumberland and Northumberland, was excused the 1334 tax on account of recent devastation by the Scots. The subsidy list here is therefore that of 1336. The tax quotas may be unduly low because of the prevailing conditions in the north. Appleby, the single taxation borough in the county, is the only place taxed at a tenth.

REFERENCE

C. M. Fraser, 'The Cumberland and Westmorland lay subsidies for 1332', *Trans. Cumberland and Westmorland Antiq. and Arch. Soc.*, new series, 66 (1966), 131–58.

Bourgh' sub Staynemore [v]	Brough	NY/796145	4.	0.	0
Hellebek' [v]	Hillbeck	NY/795155	1.	0.	0
Soureby iuxta Bourgh'	Brough Sowerby	NY/793127	1.	0.	0
Cabergh'	Kaber	NY/798114		13.	4
Wynton'	Winton	NY/785105	2.	6.	8
Kirkeby Stephan cum Allerstang	Kirkby Stephen with Mallerstang	NY/775088 NY/783015	3.	6.	8

General footnote: There are a number of instances in this county where the medieval place-name is identifiable as a modern parish name but not as a specific settlement. It is probable that the assessments referred to areas and not to villages. Where this is the case the grid reference given is a general one to the parish.

Querton'	Wharton	NY/771062	1.	0.	0
Smerdale	Smardale	NY/739080		10.	0
Nateby	Nateby	NY/773068	1.	0.	0
Watteby	Waitby	NY/751082		15.	0
Souleby	Soulby	NY/749110	2.	10.	0
Hartecla	Hartley	NY/782086	1.	0.	0
Crosseby Jerard	Crosby Garrett	NY/729097	2.	0.	0
Musegreve Magna	Great Musgrave	NY/768132	1.	13.	4
Musegreve Parva	Little Musgrave	NY/760132		13.	8
Warthecoppe	Warcop	NY/746153	3.	0.	0
Sandforth'	Sandford	NY/729162	2.	10.	0
Helton sub Lith'	Hilton	NY/733206	1.	3.	0
Morton'	Murton	NY/728217	1.	2.	0
Langeton'	Langton	NY/710201		18.	0
Knok'	Knock	NY/681270		10.	0
Dufton'	Dufton	NY/692250	4.	0.	4
Merton'	Long Marton	NY/666240	1.	2.	0
Millingburn	Milburn	NY/654293	1.	10.	4
Neubigging'	Newbiggin	NY/629284	1.	0.	0
Soureby Tempil	Temple Sowerby	NY/612272	1.	6.	8
Kirkeby Thore	Kirkby Thore	NY/639259	3.	10.	0
Crakanthorp'	Crackenthorpe	NY/662220	1.	8.	0
Appelby cum	Appleby with	NY/685204	1.	18.	0¾
Bondgath' [BA]	Bongate barony[1]	NY/690198			
Appelby [B]	Appleby	NY/683204	3.	0.	5½ [T]
Drybeck'	Drybeck	NY/666153	1.	15.	0
Ouerton'	Orton	NY/622083	5.	13.	4
Tebay	Tebay	NY/616044	4.	0.	0
Raunskeldale	Ravenstonedale	NY/723039	2.	0.	0
Ormesheued Magna &	Great Ormside	NY/702177	1.	19.	4
Parva	Little Ormside	NY/708167			
Askeby Magna	Great Asby	NY/681132	2.	16.	8
Askeby Parva	Little Asby	NY/699096	2.	0.	0
Brampton'	Brampton	NY/680233		14.	6
Hepp'	Shap	NY/564153	6.	0.	0
Rossogill'	Rosgill	NY/537167	1.	4.	0
Bampton' Condale[2]	Bampton [Cundale]	NY/515182	1.	14.	0
Bampton' Paterik'	Bampton [Patrick]	NY/515182	2.	0.	0
Helton' Flechan	Helton	NY/510221		10.	0
Askton'	Askham	NY/518238	1.	6.	8
Louthre	Lowther	NY/536236		13.	4
Louthrequale	Whale	NY/522215		17.	0
Barton' c.h	Barton [with hamlets]	NY/488263	12.	0.	0
Yawenwith'	Yanwath	NY/511279	1.	6.	8
Clifton'	Clifton	NY/534266	1.	0.	0
Melcamthroph'	Melkinthorpe	NY/557251		15.	0
Wynanderwath'	Winderwath	NY/598293		13.	4
Burgham cum	Brougham with	NY/529283	1.	10.	0
Clauso	Close	?			
Cleborn	Cliburn	NY/588245	1.	4.	0
Morlond	Morland	NY/598225	2.	0.	0
Neuby	Newby	NY/590213	2.	10.	0
Stirkeland Magna	Great Strickland	NY/555229	1.	13.	4
Stirkeland Parva	Little Strickland	NY/562198	1.	0.	2
Hacthorp'	Hackthorpe	NY/543232		18.	0
Thirneby	Thrimby	NY/553202		10.	0

[1] Grid ref. is to that part of Appleby east of the Eden.
[2] Bampton was divided into the moieties of Cundale and Patrick.

Slegil	Sleagill	NY/597192	1.	10.	0
Meburn Regis	King's Meaburn	NY/620213		15.	0
Bolton'	Bolton	NY/636233	3.	0.	4
Meburn Malde cum Reuegile	Maulds Meaburn with Reagill	NY/624163 NY/603176	5.	0.	0
Crosseby Ravenswart	Crosby Ravensworth	NY/621149	3.	6.	8
Colleby	Colby	NY/665205		13.	4
Stirkeland Ketel	Strickland Ketel	SD/504958		13.	4
Staveleygodemond	Nether Staveley	SD/470980		16.	0
Kirkeby in Kendale	Kendal [formerly Kirkby Kendal]	SD/520930	2.	7.	10
Heverisham	Heversham	SD/497834	2.	0.	0
Haverbreck'	Haverbrack	SD/488803		13.	4
Bethom	Beetham	SD/496795	1.	5.	0
Farlton'	Farleton	SD/535810		13.	4
Witherslack'	Witherslack	SD/431842		13.	4
Hencastr'	Hincaster	SD/509847		12.	0
Skelmerbergh'	Skelsmergh	SD/529954		16.	0
Selsacht	Selside	SD/535992	1.	0.	0
Whitewelle	Whitwell	SD/534985		9.	0
Appeltwait'	Applethwaite	SD/413988	1.	7.	1¼
Gresmere	Grasmere	NY/337074	3.	12.	8
Langedon'	Langdale	NY/300065			
Louherig &	Loughrigg and	NY/365056			
Rydale	Rydal	NY/364063			
Stirkeland Randolf	Strickland Randolph[1]	lost		17.	0
Burton'	Burton	SD/531770		13.	4
Clerthorp'	Clawthorpe	SD/532775		10.	0
Troutebek' &	Troutbeck and	NY/413029	2.	8.	0
Amelsath'	Ambleside	NY/376045			
Sleddale	Sleddale	NY/500029	1.	0.	0
Hoton Rof'	Hutton Roof	SD/569787		15.	0
Nateland	Natland	SD/521892		13.	4
Grenerigg'	Greenriggs	SD/470912	1.	17.	4
Preston' Thomas	Preston Patrick	SD/544837	1.	13.	4
Veteri Hoton'	Old Hutton	SD/560887	1.	11.	2¼
Crosthayt	Crosthwaite	SD/445912	1.	7.	0
Hilsyngton'	Helsington	SD/489889	2.	0.	0
Levenes	Levens	SD/485857		17.	5
Staynton'	Stainton	SD/526860	1.	6.	8
Crok' in Kendale	Crook	SD/465952		13.	4
Preston' Richard	Preston Richard	SD/533845	1.	4.	0
Grarig'	Grayrigg	SD/579972	1.	0.	0
Lambrig'	Lambrigg	SD/599947		10.	0
Respeton' &	Reston and	SD/457986		17.	0
Hogayl	Hugill	SD/450996			
Staveley Gamel	Over Staveley	SD/470984		16.	2
Nova Hoton'	New Hutton	SD/562912	2.	5.	9
Kentmere	Kentmere	NY/457042	2.	7.	4
Lupton'	Lupton	SD/553813	1.	0.	0
Quynfeld	Whinfell	SD/565985	2.	0.	0
Holm	Holme	SD/523788	1.	4.	0
Patton'	Patton	SD/548960		10.	0
Killyngton'	Killington	SD/613890	2.	7.	10½
Bereburn	Barbon	SD/628825	1.	15.	5
Casterton'	Casterton	SD/625797	1.	7.	4

[1] Now lost; probably part of the manor of Strickland Ketel, *E.P.N.S.*, *XLII*, *Westmorland*, part 1 (1964–5), 154–5.

Freland	Firbank	sd/627941		10.	0
Manserg'	Mansergh	sd/602827	1.	6.	11½
Kirkeby Lonesdale	Kirkby Lonsdale	sd/611788	2.	0.	0
Skalethwayt Rigg'	Scalthwaiterigg	sd/549956		18.	0
Middelton'	Middleton	sd/623862	2.	10.	0
[Personal Payments]	[Two Taxers]		1.	6.	8
			190.	15.	6½

TOTAL: £190. 15. 6½[1]

---

[1] As on E 179/195/2 (1336). The total is ½d. more than on the Enrolled Account for 1336, E 359/8a, m. 11d. The assessments as listed above in fact add up to £190. 15. 6¾.

WILTSHIRE

DOCUMENTS

8 Edward III: Account   E 179/196/9
8 Edward III: Indenture   E 179/196/10* (imperfect)
10 Edward III: Particulars E 179/196/12 (incomplete)
12 Edward III: Particulars E 179/196/14

TAXERS

The abbot of Malmesbury and Master Robert de Brok

TAX YIELD

15th	£1,421.	6.	1
10th	£ 174.	7.	6¾
	£1,595.	13.	7¾

Representing assessed movable wealth of

£23,063.   6.   10½

NOTES

The Wiltshire roll of 1334 is unusual in that, following the pattern of 1332, personal names are given for Salisbury, Ludgershall, and Hindon, the first three entries on the roll. The roll then takes on the usual format. Most of the places taxed at a tenth are listed at the beginning, and the number of boroughs (twelve including Salisbury) exceeds the number of ancient demesnes.

There has been considerable change in the outline of the county since 1334 when the county had detached parts. The Wiltshire list includes twenty-seven places that have since been transferred to other counties: twelve to Berkshire, seven to Hampshire and eight to Gloucestershire. On the other hand Wiltshire has gained a few places from adjacent counties: Minety was taxed in Gloucestershire in 1334, Norton Ferris and Kilmington in Somerset, and Shalbourne, Bagshot, and Inglesham in Berkshire.

REFERENCE

M. W. Beresford, 'Fifteenths and tenths: quotas of 1334', in *V.C.H. Wilts.* iv (1959), 294–303.

ACKNOWLEDGEMENT

I am indebted to Mr. K. Rogers for help in the identification and location of some place-names.

				£	s	d	
Nove Sarum¹	Salisbury		SU/143300				
[Aldermanries]							
Foro	Market	[76]		26.	5.	0	[T]
Sancto Martino	St. Martin's	[65]		23.	17.	8	[T]
Prato	Meadow	[15]		4.	6.	0	[T]
Novo Vico	New Street	[65]		19.	2.	9	[T]
	Tax on the collectors	[4]		1.	8.	9	[T]
		[225]		75.	0.	2	[T]
Lutegarshale [B]	Ludgershall (24 named and 60 at 5d. per head not named)		SU/263509	3.	8.	4¾	[T]²
Hynedon' [va]	Hindon	[12]	ST/910330	1.	8.	9²	
Wilton' [B]³	Wilton		SU/095313	8.	10.	0	[T]
Dounton' [B]	Downton		SU/182216	5.	10.	0	[T]
Chippenham [B] cum Roudon' [A.D]	Chippenham with Rowden		ST/919739 ST/918721	17.	6.	8	[T]
Devises [B]	Devizes		SU/007614	6.	0.	0	[T]
Malmesbury [B]	Malmesbury		ST/933873	11.	10.	0	[T]
Calne [B]	Calne		ST/998710	5.	10.	0	[T]
Crekelade [B]	Cricklade		SU/099935	5.	10.	0	[T]
Bedewynde [B]	Bedwyn⁴		SU/278643	2.	6.	8	[T]
Marlebergh' [B]	Marlborough		SU/189692	8.	0.	0	[T]⁵
Veteris Sarum [B]	Old Sarum		SU/140327		17.	4	[T]
Roudes [Lib.]	Rowde Liberty		ST/978627	5.	6.	8	[T]
Bertona de Marlebergh'	Marlborough, Barton		SU/185688	3.	10.	0	[T]⁵
				79.	17.	4	[T]

Hd. Stapele [STAPLE HUNDRED]

			£	s	d	
Pyriton'	Purton	SU/097872	7.	0.	0	
Eton' Monial'	Water Eaton	SU/127937	1.	0.	0	
Chelesworth [A.D]	Chelworth	SU/085924	2.	16.	8	[T]
			10.	16.	8	

¹ As was the standard procedure for all places in 1327 and 1332, the names of the taxpayers for the first three Wiltshire entries, Salisbury, Ludgershall, and Hindon, are listed on the roll, a most unusual feature for a roll of 1334. The number of taxpayers is shown above in brackets after the place-name.

² Includes a tax charge of 2s. on two collectors.

³ As the names of some of the boroughs are illegible on E 179/196/10 these place-name spellings have been taken from E 179/196/14 (1338).

⁴ Grid ref. is to Great Bedwyn.

⁵ Includes a tax on the goods of John Godhyne, merchant.

Hd. Domerham [DAMERHAM HUNDRED]

Domerham	Damerham [in Hampshire]	SU/108158	6.	10.	o
Compton'	Compton Chamberlayne	SU/029301	6.	6.	8
Merton'	Martin [in Hampshire]	SU/070195	8.	6.	8
			21.	3.	4

Hd. Mere [MERE HUNDRED]

Mere	Mere	ST/812323	10.	10.	o
Knoel	West Knoyle	ST/860327	3.	10.	o
Chadenwych'	Charnage	ST/833320	1.	18.	o
Bradelegh'	Maiden Bradley	ST/803387	3.	5.	o
Kyngeston'[1]	Kingston Deverill	ST/846371	1.	18.	o
Storton'	Stourton	ST/776340	4.	18.	o
Sceles	Zeals	ST/781318	5.	0.	o
			30.	19.	o

Hd. Caudon' [CAWDON HUNDRED]

Brutford'	Britford	SU/163284	6.	6.	8
Bremelschawe	Bramshaw [in Hampshire]	SU/270154	1.	5.	o
Langeford	Longford	SU/170268	1.	12.	o
Odestoke	Odstock	SU/152261	1.	10.	o
Coumbe	Coombe Bissett	SU/108263	3.	10.	o
Stratford Tony	Stratford Tony	SU/092263	3.	0.	o
Harnham	Harnham	SU/145288	3.	10.	o[2]
Whychebury	Whitsbury [in Hampshire]	SU/129192	2.	0.	o
Homynton'	Homington	SU/123260	2.	10.	o
			25.	3.	8

Hd. Dounton' [DOWNTON HUNDRED]

Cherleton'	Charlton	SU/176241	10.	0.	o
Bottenham	Bodenham	SU/167260	1.	13.	4
Hampteworth'	Hamptworth	SU/242193	2.	0.	o
Dounton' for.	Downton foreign	SU/c.182216	2.	6.	8
Pendelesworth'	Pensworth	SU/208220	2.	13.	4
Nounton'	Nunton	SU/159260	1.	18.	o
Berford	Barford	SU/182225	1.	18.	o
Bissopiston'	Bishopstone	SU/073262	1.	12.	o
Netton'	Netton	SU/071258	1.	14.	o
Flamberdeston'	Flamston	SU/064257	1.	5.	o
Croucheston'	Croucheston	SU/067254	2.	16.	8
Throup'	Throope	SU/088263		16.	o
Fallardeston'	Faulston	SU/075256		18.	o
Wyke	Wick	SU/171213	2.	5.	o

---

[1] Part of Kingston Deverill was taxed in Amesbury hundred (p. 346).
[2] Includes an amount for John de Harnham, taxer.

Waleton'	Walton	su/165215	1.	13.	4
Wytheton'	Witherington	su/182248	1.	16.	0
Stanlynch'	Standlynch	su/191240	1.	13.	4
			38.	18.	8

Hd. Cadeworth' [CADWORTH HUNDRED]

Sutton' Maundevyle	Sutton Mandeville	st/986288	2.	15.	0
Foffunte	Fovant	su/004288	3.	8.	0
Hurdecote	Hurdcott	su/041310	1.	5.	0
Babestok'	Baverstock	su/029315		18.	0
Bereford	Barford St. Martin	su/057314	3.	3.	4
Netherhampton'	Netherhampton	su/108298	2.	12.	0
Brudecombe[1]	Burcombe [South]	su/071309	1.	2.	0
Oggeford[2]	Ugford [South]	su/083303		13.	4
			15.	16.	8[3]

| Bromham [Lib.] | Bromham | st/963652 | 7. | 0. | 0 |

| Deverel Langebrigg' [Lib.] | Longbridge Deverill | st/867413 | 5. | 10. | 0 |

Hd. Thornhull' [THORNHILL HUNDRED]

Brome [A.D]	Broome	su/164822	2.	15.	0	[T]
Draycote	Draycot Foliat	su/180777	2.	10.	0	
Baddebury	Badbury	su/195804	4.	6.	8	
Ludynton'	Liddington	su/206812	6.	6.	8	
Chuseldene	Chiseldon	su/187800	6.	6.	8	
Wambergh'	Wanborough	su/207826	14.	0.	0	
			36.	5.	0	

Hd. Swanebergh' [SWANBOROUGH HUNDRED]

Uphavene	Upavon	su/136551	4.	13.	4
Rusteshale	Rushall	su/129559	2.	18.	0
Cherleton'	Charlton	su/118560	1.	16.	0
Wyuelysford	Wilsford	su/103573	2.	14.	0
Merwedene	Marden	su/086579	1.	15.	0
Stoke	Beechingstoke	su/086593	1.	18.	0
Wodebergh'[4]	Woodborough	su/114601	1.	8.	0
Staunton'	Stanton St. Bernard	su/092624	2.	2.	0
Aulton' Bern'	Alton Barnes	su/105620	2.	0.	0
Draycote	Draycot Fitz Payne	su/143628	1.	5.	0
Ore	Oare	su/159631	2.	5.	0
Wylecote	Wilcot	su/140608	1.	17.	0

[1] For North Burcombe see Branch hundred (p. 342).
[2] For North Ugford see Branch hundred (p. 342).
[3] E 179/196/10 (1334) has £16. 6. 8 in error.
[4] In some later documents, e.g. in E 164/7, Stowell in Wilcot is included in this entry.
In 1334 Stowell was taxed in Elstub hundred.

Nywenton'	North Newnton	su/131577	2.	13.	4
Manyngford Bohun	Manningford Bohune	su/138577	2.	16.	o
Manyngford Brewes[1]	Manningford Bruce	su/138589	4.	6.	8
			36.	7.	4

Hd. Stodfold [STUDFOLD HUNDRED]

Wedhampton'	Wedhampton	su/060577	3.	2.	o
Erchesfonte	Urchfont	su/041573	3.	10.	o
Estcote	Eastcott	su/023556	2.	2.	o
Conek'	Conock	su/067573	1.	13.	4
Churghton'	Chirton	su/073577	2.	5.	o
Sterte	Stert	su/030594	1.	10.	o
Canyng'	All Cannings	su/070616	6.	6.	8
Alyngton'	Allington	su/068630	3.	0.	o
Echelhampton'	Etchilhampton	su/045602	2.	8.	o
			25.	17.	o

Hd. Wonderdych' [UNDERDITCH HUNDRED]

Wyueleford	Wilsford	su/135398	2.	5.	o
Lake	Lake	su/133390	4.	0.	o
Wodeford maior	Woodford[2]	su/120361	4.	10.	o
Hyle	Heale	su/123368	1.	15.	o
Wodeford minor	Woodford [Little]	su/126352	2.	18.	o
Stratford	Stratford Sub Castle	su/131324	2.	12.	4
Muleford[3]	Milford	su/157298	3.	18.	o
			21.	18.	4

Hd. Furstefeld [FRUSTFIELD HUNDRED]

Laneford	Landford	su/261201	3.	6.	8
Abbodeston'	Abbotstone	su/244235	2.	10.	o
Aldredeston'	Alderstone	su/245244		13.	4
Whelpelegh'	Whelpley	su/231240	2.	4.	o
Couelesfeld	Cowesfield	su/260244	5.	0	o
			13.	14.	o

Hd. Westbury [WESTBURY HUNDRED]

Westbury	Westbury	st/874514	6.	10.	o
Brok'	Brook	st/856516	1.	0.	o
Lye	Westbury Leigh	st/863502	1.	13.	4
Chepmanslade	Chapmanslade	st/827478	1.	5.	o
Penlegh'	Penleigh	st/856508		15.	o
Hauekryg'	Hawkeridge	st/863536		16.	o
Hewode	Heywood	st/872536	1.	14.	o
Bratton'	Bratton	st/914519	2.	13.	4
Mulebourne	Melbourne	st/910526		9.	o
Stoke	Stoke	st/913520		10.	o

[1] Manningford Abbots is included in this entry in E 164/7.
[2] Grid ref. is to Lower Woodford.
[3] Part of Milford was taxed in Alderbury hundred (p. 345).

Merssh'	Dilton Marsh	ST/850498		18.	0
Bremelrigg'	Bremeridge	ST/849508	1.	15.	0
			19.	18.	8

Hd. Cheggelewe [CHEDGLOW HUNDRED]

Wockeseye	Oaksey	ST/991936	3.	13.	4
Asschelegh' Pole	Ashley	ST/931947	3.	6.	8
	Poole Keynes [both in Gloucestershire]	ST/999954			
Kemele	Kemble	ST/989970	3.	6.	8
Ewelme	Ewen [both in Gloucestershire]	SP/004975			
Sutton'	Sutton Benger	ST/947787	1.	10.	0
Rodbourn'	Rodbourne	ST/933834	2.	16.	0
Corston'	Corston	ST/926839			
Bourton'	Burton Hill	ST/934864	2.	16.	0
Brokenbergh'	Brokenborough	ST/918892			
Mulebourn'	Milbourne	ST/943876	2.	10.	0
Lega	Lea	ST/957863			
Cherleton'	Charlton	ST/959889	3.	10.	0
Garesdon	Garsdon	ST/967878			
Cleverdon'	Cleverton	ST/978857		18.	0
Nywenton'	Long Newnton [in Glos.]	ST/909924	2.	8.	0
Cheggelewe	Chedglow	ST/943930			
Cruddewell'	Crudwell	ST/956929	2.	5.	0
Cheleworth'	Chelworth	ST/970942			
Escote	Eastcourt	ST/976925	3.	10.	0
Hanekynton'	Hankerton	ST/972907			
			32.	9.	8

Hd. Calne [CALNE HUNDRED]

Calstone	Calstone Wellington	SU/027682	3.	0.	0
Stockelegh'	Stockley	ST/997676	1.	16.	8
Quemerford	Quemerford	SU/005698	3.	4.	0
Estmanestrete	Eastmanstreet	lost	1.	2.	0
Churyel	Cherhill	SU/038703	4.	16.	8
Whytelegh'	Whitley	ST/993736	1.	5.	0
Beveresbrok'	Beversbrook	SU/009735	1.	8.	0
Stodlegh'	Studley	ST/963710	1.	18.	0
Compton'	Compton Bassett	SU/031716	8.	0.	0
Blakelond	Blackland	SU/012685	1.	15.	0
Hedynton'	Heddington	ST/999662	5.	6.	8
Stokke	Stock Street	ST/996695	2.	0.	0
Wetham	Whetham	ST/979681	1.	2.	0
Berewyk'	Berwick Bassett	SU/098735	3.	10.	0
Iatesbury	Yatesbury	SU/063715	5.	8.	0
			45.	12.	0

Hd. Doneworth' [DUNWORTH HUNDRED]

Dounheued c.h	Donhead [with hamlets][1]	ST/914248	13.	0.	0
Tyssebury	Tisbury	ST/944292	9.	0.	0

[1] Grid ref. is to Donhead St. Andrew but the entry probably refers to St. Andrew and St. Mary, with hamlets.

Hacche	Hatch	ST/908282	3.	10.	o
Chilmerk'	Chilmark	ST/970328	2.	6.	8
Berewyk' cum Chyclad [h]	Berwick St. Leonard with Chicklade	ST/923332 ST/912345	1.	13.	4
Fontel	Fonthill Gifford	ST/930312	1.	14.	o
Anestegh'	Ansty	ST/956266	4.	10.	o
Swalweclive	Swallowcliffe	ST/963271	1.	13.	4
Teffonte	Teffont Evias	ST/992312	1.	o.	o
			38.	7.	4

Hd. Melkesham [MELKSHAM HUNDRED]

Troubrigge	Trowbridge	ST/857581	6.	10.	o
Stodlegh'	Studley	ST/852572	2.	15.	o
Troll'[1]	Trowle	ST/c.839584		5.	o
Staverton' & Wyke	Staverton and Wyke	ST/855608 ST/862597	2.	18.	o
Hulprynton'	Hilperton	ST/872592	3.	o.	o
Whaddon'	Whaddon	ST/880613	2.	6.	o
Bulkynton'	Bulkington	ST/940583	5.	6.	8
Paulesholte	Poulshot	ST/970597	2.	16.	8
Erlestok'	Erlestoke	ST/965540	5.	10.	o
Sende	Seend	ST/944609	3.	13.	4
Melkesham [A.D]	Melksham	ST/903637	10.	10.	o [T]
			45.	10.	8

Hd. Remmesbur' [RAMSBURY HUNDRED]

Remmesbur'	Ramsbury	SU/273715	2.	10.	o[2]
Asscherigge[3]	?		1.	16.	8[3]
Estrigge	Eastridge	SU/303731	1.	13.	4
Beydon'	Baydon	SU/279779	2.	10.	o
Bissopeston'[4]	Bishopstone	SU/243837	5.	o.	o
			13.	10.	o

Hd. Werewellisdon' [WHORWELLSDOWN HUNDRED]

Stepulaston'	Steeple Ashton	ST/907571	7.	6.	8
Westasston'	West Ashton	ST/879559	3.	16.	8
Kyvele	Keevil	ST/918580	5.	6.	8
Tydelueshyde[5]	Tilshead	SU/035480	1.	4.	o
Coueleston'	Coulston[6]	ST/952540	2.	16.	8
Beynton'	Baynton[7]	ST/943537	1.	10.	o
Tynhyde	Tinhead	ST/933533	2.	16.	8
Edyndon'	Edington	ST/926533	3.	2.	o

---

[1] Most of Trowle was taxed in Bradford hundred (p. 347).

[2] Includes a tax charge on Hildebrand of London.

[3] Includes a tax charge on Hildebrand of London. The identification of this place is uncertain. Marridge Hill (SU/287744) is a possibility if the initial M was omitted from the documents in error. For the forms of this name see *E.P.N.S., XVI, Wilts.* (1939), 288.

[4] Part of Bishopstone was taxed in Elstub hundred (p. 340).

[5] Part of Tilshead was taxed in Dole hundred (p. 341).

[6] Grid ref. is to East Coulston.   [7] Grid ref. is to Upper Baynton Farm.

Henton'	Great Hinton	ST/909592	1.	16.	o
Lytelton'	Littleton	ST/908602	1.	8.	o
Sembleton'	Semington	ST/898606	1.	13.	4
Bradelegh'	North Bradley	ST/854549	2.	12.	o
Suthwyke	Southwick	ST/838552	3.	o.	o
			38.	8.	8

Hd. Selkele [SELKLEY HUNDRED]

Aldebourn'	Aldbourne	SU/263759	10.	6.	8
Snappe	Snap	SU/225762		8.	o
Upham	Upham[1]	SU/226772	1.	10.	o
Okebourn' Sancti Georgii	Ogbourne St. George	SU/196746	4.	o.	o
Okebourn' Sancti Andr'	Ogbourne St. Andrew	SU/188723	3.	6.	8
Ricardeston'	Richardson	SU/097742		12.	o
Roucle	Rockley	SU/161718	5.	o.	o[2]
Berbury	Barbury	SU/151758		11.	o
Mildehale	Mildenhall	SU/210695	1.	12.	o
Stotescombe	Stitchcombe	SU/228694	1.	10.	o
Manton' Honor'	Manton [Honor]	SU/172684	1.	4.	o[2]
Polton'	Poulton	SU/197697		16.	o
Clatford	Clatford	SU/159685		18.	o
Avebury	Avebury	SU/099700	5.	16.	8
Wynterbourn' Monachorum	Winterbourne Monkton	SU/098720	2.	o.	o
Schawe	Shaw	SU/131653		8.	o
Rabbedeston'	Rabson	SU/099745		10.	o
Wynterbourn' Basset	Winterbourne Bassett	SU/101749		13.	4
Henton'	Broad Hinton	SU/106763	3.	13.	4
Okebourn' Moysy	Ogbourne Maizey	SU/186716	1.	14.	o
Lokerig'	Lockeridge	SU/148678	1.	o.	o
Overtone Abbatisse	West Overton	SU/133682	1.	3.	o
Estkynet	East Kennett	SU/117674	2.	o.	o
Westkynet	West Kennett	SU/111683	1.	10.	o
Bachampton'	Beckhampton	SU/090690	1.	19.	o
			54.	1.	8

Hd. Sterkele [STARTLEY HUNDRED]

Brenkworth' & Grittenham	Brinkworth and Grittenham	SU/013846 SU/029827	3.	13.	4
Foxle	Foxley	ST/898860	1.	o.	o
Cristemaleford	Christian Malford	ST/960783	6.	o.	o
Daunteseye & Smythecote	Dauntsey and Smithcot	ST/980824 SU/002830	4.	o.	o
Segre	Seagry[3]	ST/958808	2.	6.	8
Hundlavynton' & Bradefeld	Hullavington and Bradfield	ST/894820 ST/895830	2.	o.	o
Norton' & Brumelham	Norton and Bremilham	ST/885843 ST/903863	2.	6.	8
Draycote & Eston'	Draycot Cerne and probably Easton Piercy	ST/935786 ST/886777	1.	15.	o

[1] Grid ref. is to Upper Upham.
[2] Includes a tax charge on John Godhyne, merchant.
[3] Grid ref. is to Lower Seagry.

Somerford Maudyt' &	Little Somerford and	ST/967844	4.	0.	0
Somerford Mautravers	Great Somerford	ST/964831			
Stanton'	Stanton St. Quintin	ST/906798	2.	10.	0
			29.	11.	8

Hd. Elestubbe [ELSTUB HUNDRED]

Hyneton'	Little Hinton	SU/232832	3.	16.	8
Hamme	Ham	SU/329630	1.	15.	0
Pateneye	Patney	SU/072584	2.	8.	0
Worfton'	Wroughton	SU/146805	5.	6.	8
Overton' &	East Overton and	SU/c.133682	4.	0.	0
Fyfhyde	Fyfield	SU/148687			
Bissopeston'[1]	Bishopstone	SU/243837	1.	14.	0
Westwode	Westwood	ST/810591	6.	0.	0
Stocton'	Stockton	ST/982382	3.	0.	0
Netherhaven'	Netheravon	SU/148483	3.	10.	0
Eneford	Enford	SU/141516	3.	6.	8
Lytlecote &	Littlecott and	SU/143517			
Fifhyde	Fifield	SU/146503			
Fytelton' &	Fittleton and	SU/146495	1.	6.	8[2]
Combe	Coombe	SU/150504			
Aulton &	Alton Priors and	SU/109622	4.	2.	0
Stowell'	Stowell	SU/146620			
Chesyngbury	Chisenbury[3]	SU/141527	2.	3.	4
			42.	9.	0

Hd. Roughbergh' Episcopi [BISHOP'S ROWBOROUGH HUNDRED]

Poterne	Potterne	ST/995585	8.	13.	4
Lavynton' Episcopi	West Lavington	SU/006530	12.	0.	0
Mersshton'	Marston	ST/967567	5.	12.	0
Worton'	Worton	ST/971574	5.	13.	4
			31.	18.	8

Hd. Heghtredebury [HEYTESBURY HUNDRED]

Heighterbury	Heytesbury	ST/925425	5.	6.	8
Tuderynton'	Tytherington	ST/917411	1.	18.	0
Knok'	Knook	ST/938418	2.	0.	0
Ubeton'	Upton Lovell	ST/945409	2.	5.	0
Immere[4]	Imber	ST/965484	3.	0.	0
Boyton'	Boyton	ST/950395	1.	18.	0
Cortyngton'	Corton	ST/935405	3.	13.	4
Codeford	Codford[5]	ST/975397	4.	10.	0
Depeford	Deptford	SU/012383	1.	4.	0
Batthampton'	Bathampton[6]	SU/017380	2.	13.	4

[1] Most of Bishopstone was taxed in Ramsbury hundred (p. 338).
[2] Includes a tax charge on Hildebrand of London.
[3] Grid ref. is to East Chisenbury.
[4] Part of Imber was taxed in King's Rowborough hundred (p. 343).
[5] Grid ref. is to Codford St. Mary.
[6] Grid ref. is to Great Bathampton. The quota probably covers Great and Little Bathampton, both now depopulated.

Orcheston'	Orcheston St. George	su/060450	3.	4.	0
Chyttern'	Chitterne	st/992441	5.	10.	0
Asshton'	Ashton Giffard	st/959400	1.	16.	0
Bailleclyve	Baycliff	st/813397		12.	0
Anestygh'[1]	Ansty	st/c.842402		8.	0
Hulle	Hill Deverill	st/866402	2.	5.	0
Hornyngesham	Horningsham	st/821414	2.	18.	0
Bryghteston'	Brixton Deverill	st/863387	2.	10.	0
Whyteclyve	Whitecliff	st/859383		6.	8
			47.	18.	0

Hd. Blakegrove [BLACKGROVE HUNDRED]

Fasterne	Vastern	su/049814	4.	6.	8
Migghale	Midgehall	su/080840		12.	0
Benknolle	Bincknoll	su/108792	2.	3.	4
Saltharpe	Salthrop	su/118802		19.	0
Lydyard tregoz	Lydiard Tregoze	su/103848	4.	0.	0
Meyhyndone	Mannington	su/128842		18.	0
Westswyndon' &	West Swindon and	su/c.142848	1.	13.	4
Weklyscote	Westlecott	su/145827			
Estcote	Eastcott[2]	su/c.142848	2.	18.	0
Westcote &	Westcott and	su/c.142848			
Walecote	Walcot	su/173843			
Alta Swyndon'	High Swindon	su/158839	6.	13.	4
Overworston'	Overtown	su/153796	3.	10.	0
Ofcote	Uffcott	su/126775	1.	13.	4
Elecombe	Elcombe	su/133801	3.	12.	0
			32.	19.	0

Hd. Dollesfeld [DOLE HUNDRED]

Gore	St. Joan à Gore	su/010510	1.	0.	0
Tydolueshyde[3]	Tilshead	su/035480	3.	10.	0
Orcheston'	Orcheston St. Mary	su/060449	1.	13.	4
Eleston'	Elston	su/069448	3.	2.	0
Schirreneton'	Shrewton	su/067438	1.	16.	8
Abbedeston'	Addestone	su/066430		5.	0
Madynton'	Maddington	su/070444	3.	4.	0
Burton'	Bourton	su/064435	1.	13.	4
Netton'	Net Down	su/093453		18.	0
Homanton'	Homanton	su/069430	1.	0.	0
Wynterbournestoke	Winterbourne Stoke	su/077407	2.	10.	0
Assherton'	Asserton	su/075394		13.	4
Berewyk'	Berwick St. James	su/072392	4.	10.	0
			25.	15.	8

---

[1] Identified as Ansty in Knook by Beresford in *V.C.H., Wilts.* iv (1959), 299. Having regard to where it comes in the list I think it far more likely to be Ansty in Horningsham, now surviving only as a field name (*E.P.N.S., XVI, Wiltshire* (1939), 482).

[2] Eastcott and Westcott appear on Greenwood's map of 1820; the sites are now covered by the railway works.

[3] Part of Tilshead was taxed in Whorwellsdown hundred (p. 338).

Hd. Knoel Episcopi [BISHOP'S KNOYLE HUNDRED]

Knoel Episcopi	East Knoyle	ST/880305	5.	0.	0
Upton'	Upton	ST/871320	1.	12.	0
Fontel	Bishop's Fonthill	ST/934330	3.	16.	0
Hynedon'[1]	Hindon	ST/910330			
			10.	8.	0

Hd. Crekkelade [CRICKLADE HUNDRED]

Latton'	Latton	SU/093958	8.	0.	0
Pulton'	Poulton [in Gloucestershire]	SP/099007	4.	16.	8
Cernecote	Shorncote [in Gloucestershire]	SU/025967	2.	6.	8
Aishton'	Ashton Keynes	SU/042944	5.	16.	8
Somerford	Somerford Keynes [in Gloucestershire]	SU/016955	5.	0.	0
			26.	0.	0

Hd. Brenchesbergh' [BRANCH HUNDRED]

Shernton'	Sherrington	ST/961392	2.	12.	0
Wyly	Wylye	SU/008378	3.	5.	0
Hangynglangford	Hanging Langford	SU/031371	2.	0.	0
Litellangeford	Little Langford	SU/048366	1.	10.	0
Stupellangeford	Steeple Langford	SU/037375	2.	8.	0
Lytelwychford	Little Wishford	SU/077361		15.	0
Stapelford	Stapleford	SU/071374	4.	0.	0
Muchelwychford	Great Wishford	SU/081355	3.	0.	0
Stoford	Stoford	SU/084353	1.	6.	0
Nyweton'	South Newton	SU/088343	1.	13.	4
Childhampton'	Chilhampton	SU/094331	1.	3.	4
Fogheleston'	Fugglestone	SU/102313		15.	0
Dychhampton'	Ditchampton	SU/093316	1.	12.	0
Uggeford[2]	Ugford [North]	SU/083312	3.	10.	0
Brudecombe[3]	Burcombe [North]	SU/073311	1.	0.	0
Avene	Avon	SU/126331	1.	2.	0
Qwedhampton'	Quidhampton	SU/108310	3.	4.	0
Bymerton'	Bemerton	SU/121306	1.	13.	4
Fissherton'	Fisherton Anger	SU/139301	1.	5.	0
			37.	14.	0

Hd. Chalk' [CHALKE HUNDRED]

Stokeuerdon	Stoke Farthing	SU/057254	3.	4.	0
Knyghteton'	Knighton	SU/052253	3.	0.	0
Chalk' Magna	Broad Chalke	SU/041253	4.	6.	8
Fifhyde	Fifield Bavent	SU/018251	1.	10.	0
Bourchalk'	Bowerchalke	SU/019230	4.	10.	0

[1] Listed separately at the beginning of the roll.
[2] For South Ugford see Cadworth hundred (p. 335).
[3] For South Burcombe see Cadworth hundred (p. 335).

Eblesbourn'	Ebbesbourne Wake	ST/991242	3.	4.	0
Alvedeston'	Alvediston	ST/977240	4.	0.	0
Berewyk' &	Berwick St. John and	ST/946223	3.	10.	0
Brudemer'	Bridmore	ST/960220			
Semelegh'	Semley	ST/892269	2.	18.	0
Tollard	Tollard Royal	ST/943177	3.	4.	0
			33.	6.	8

Hd. Heigheworth' [HIGHWORTH HUNDRED]

Lydyard &	Lydiard Millicent and	SU/093860	3.	10.	0
Schawe	Shaw	SU/120853			
Swyndon'	Swindon	SU/154844	1.	2.	0
Rodbourne	Rodbourne Cheney	SU/140867	1.	0.	0
Mordone	Moredon	SU/131873	1.	0.	0
Haydon' &	Haydon and	SU/127885	2.	13.	4
Wyke	Haydon Wick	SU/133878			
Grondewell'	Groundwell	SU/151890	1.	10.	0
Bluntesdon Sancti Andr'	Blunsdon St. Andrew	SU/136897		12.	0
Bluntesdon' Gay	Blunsdon Gay	SU/c.152908	1.	2.	0
Westwydyhull' &	Widhill (Upper and	SU/137906	1.	8.	0
Northwydyhull'	Lower)	SU/127912			
Nortmerston'	Marston Meysey	SU/128971	3.	0.	0
Etone Meysy	Castle Eaton	SU/147960	3.	12.	0
Lusteshull'	Lus Hill	SU/160942	1.	13.	4
Hanyndon'	Hannington	SU/182928	9.	6.	8
Inglesham[1]	Inglesham	SU/205984	1.	10.	0
Hampton'	Hampton	SU/190922	1.	8.	0
Westthrop'	Westrop	SU/202930	1.	13.	4
Heigheworth'	Highworth	SU/201924	1.	16.	0
Estthrop'	Eastrop	SU/207924	4.	3.	4
Fershedon'	Fresden	SU/228921		11.	0
Sevenhampton'	Sevenhampton	SU/209903	3.	18.	0
Southmerston'	South Marston	SU/195880	5.	16.	0
Brodebluntesdon'	Broad Blunsdon	SU/153907	3.	6.	8
Burybluntesdon'	Burytown	SU/161916	2.	0.	0
Stannton'[2]	Stanton Fitzwarren	SU/178902	2.	12.	0
Stratton' Inferior	Stratton St. Margaret	SU/179871	3.	18.	0
Stratton' Superior	Upper Stratton	SU/162877	2.	0.	0
			66.	1.	8

Hd. Roughbergh' Reg' [KING'S ROWBOROUGH HUNDRED]

Lutleton'	Littleton Pannell	ST/999541	4.	5.	0
Chiverel Parva	Little Cheverell	ST/991535	2.	13.	0
Chiverel Magna	Great Cheverell	ST/981543	5.	0.	0
Immer'[3]	Imber	ST/965484	2.	10.	0
Stupellavynton'	Market Lavington	SU/014541	8.	10.	0
			22.	18.	0

[1] Part of Inglesham was taxed in Berkshire (Faringdon hundred, p. 11).
[2] This and the next two entries are obliterated on E 179/196/10; spellings are from E 179/196/14.
[3] Part of Imber was taxed in Heytesbury hundred (p. 340).

Hd. Kyngbrugg' [KINGSBRIDGE HUNDRED]

Helmerton'	Hilmarton	SU/020753	6.	10.	0
Lutlecote	Littlecott	SU/033770	1.	6.	8
Wydecombe	Witcomb	SU/026755	1.	15.	0
Lynham	Lyneham	SU/023787	3.	16.	8
Westokham	West Tockenham	SU/037792	1.	0.	0
Estokham	East Tockenham	SU/040794	2.	8.	0
Clyvewauncy	Clevancy	SU/050752	2.	3.	4
Corfton'	Corton	SU/052757	1.	16.	0
Wodhull'	Woodhill	SU/062769	1.	2.	0
Clive Pipard	Clyffe Pypard	SU/074770	1.	14.	0
Thornhull'	Thornhill	SU/080785	2.	2.	0
Brodetoun	Broad Town	SU/090780	2.	0.	0
			27.	13.	8

Hd. Chipenham [CHIPPENHAM HUNDRED]

Bremel	Bremhill	ST/980730	15.	10.	0
Tuderynton'	Tytherton Lucas	ST/950741	3.	7.	0
Stanlegh'	Stanley	ST/960730	2.	12.	0
Langelegh Burel	Langley Burrell	ST/928758	2.	8.	0
Cokelbergh'	Cocklebury	ST/928739		12.	0
Hardenehewish'	Hardenhuish	ST/910747		18.	0
Cosham	Corsham	ST/874705	15.	0.	0
Lacok'	Lacock	ST/917685	8.	0.	0
Hertham	Hartham	ST/864715		13.	4
Slaghtenford	Slaughterford	ST/840740	1.	0.	0
Boxe	Box	ST/823684	3.	12.	0
Colerne	Colerne	ST/819710	5.	0.	0
Wroxhale	North Wraxall	ST/818751	1.	18.	0
Alyngton'	Allington	ST/895752	2.	6.	8
Budeston'	Biddestone	ST/862735	2.	5.	0
Yattone	Yatton Keynell	ST/866763		16.	0
Coumbe	Castle Combe	ST/842772	3.	0.	0
Westkyngton'[1]	West Kington	ST/813775	3.	5.	0
Legh'	Leigh Delamere	ST/884792	2.	10.	0
Lyttleton' Dreu	Littleton Drew	ST/832802	1.	0.	0
Aldryngton'	Alderton	ST/841830	1.	16.	8
Lokyngton'	Luckington	ST/838840	1.	12.	0
Sopworth	Sopworth	ST/828863	1.	0.	0
Sherston' Magna	Sherston	ST/852858	4.	6.	8
Sherston Parva	Sherston Parva [or Pinkney]	ST/862866		17.	0
Eston' Gray	Easton Grey	ST/881877		18.	0
Syrendene	Surrendell	ST/874821	1.	2.	0
Netelynton'	Nettleton	ST/818783	6.	10.	0
Grutelynton'	Grittleton	ST/860800	4.	0.	0
Kyngton Mich'	Kington St. Michael	ST/903772	7.	6.	8
			105.	2.	0[2]

---

[1] As the 1334 roll is illegible at this point the place-name spellings of the next six entries are taken from E 179/196/14 (1338).

[2] Total incorrect in *V.C.H., Wilts.* iv (1959), 298.

Hd. Alwardbury [ALDERBURY HUNDRED]

			£	s	d
Alwardbury	Alderbury	SU/182270	2.	18.	o
Muleford[1]	Milford	SU/157298	1.	o.	o
Laverkestoke	Laverstock	SU/159309	2.	15.	o
Hurdecote	Hurdcott	SU/170337		18.	o
Wynterbourn' Comitis	Winterbourne Earls	SU/170340	2.	10.	o
Wynterbourn' Daunteseye	Winterbourne Dauntsey	SU/175345	2.	o.	o
Wynterbourne Cherborgh'	Winterbourne Gunner	SU/181353	2.	5.	o
Gomeldon'	Gomeldon	SU/182356	2.	18.	o
Pourton'	Porton	SU/190364	3.	4.	o
Edemeston'	Idmiston	SU/197373	3.	o.	o
Wynterslowe[2]	Winterslow [West]	SU/235321	3.	o.	o
Farlegh'	Farley	SU/225296	1.	2.	o
Putton'	Pitton	SU/212316	2.	10.	o
Deone	West Dean	SU/257272	2.	10.	o
Estgrymstede	East Grimstead	SU/226280	2.	o.	o
Westgrymstude	West Grimstead	SU/212266	2.	10.	o
Whaddene	Whaddon	SU/196263	1.	8.	o
Playtford	Plaitford [in Hampshire]	SU/277193	2.	3.	4
			40.	11.	4

Hd. Aumbresbury [AMESBURY HUNDRED]

			£	s	d
Aumbresbury	Amesbury	SU/153415	9.	13.	4
Westaumbresbury	West Amesbury	SU/141414	1.	8.	o
Aumbresbury Priorisse	Amesbury Priors		1.	6.	8
Normanton'	Normanton	SU/137403		12.	o
Rotheven	Ratfyn	SU/162424		5.	6
Bultford	Bulford	SU/168434	2.	3.	4
Hyndurynton'	[in Durrington]	lost	1.	16.	o
Bryghtmerston'	Brigmerston	SU/162456	2.	16.	8
Mildeston'	Milston	SU/162452	1.	o.	o
Durynton'	Durrington	SU/157448	7.	4.	o
Knyghteton'	Knighton	SU/154454	3.	o.	o
Sexhamcote	Syrencot	SU/160461	2.	o.	o
Ablynton'	Ablington	SU/159469	4.	10.	o
Fyghildene	Figheldean	SU/153474	3.	16.	8
Durneford Magna	Great Durnford	SU/137383	2.	3.	4
Durneford Parva	Little Durnford	SU/125342	1.	2.	o
Salterton'	Salterton	SU/127360	1.	5.	o
Netton'	Netton	SU/130366	1.	10.	o
Nyweton	Newtown	SU/129357		18.	o
Borscombe	Boscombe	SU/201386	3.	16.	8
Aldynton'	Allington	SU/204394	1.	10.	o
Nyweton' Tony	Newton Toney	SU/218402	3.	3.	4
Cheldrynton'[3]	Cholderton	SU/228425	2.	16.	8
Tuderlegh'[4]	Tytherley [in Hampshire]	SU/273298		3.	o

---

[1] Most of Milford was taxed in Underditch hundred (p. 336).

[2] For East Winterslow see Amesbury hundred (p. 346).

[3] Part of Cholderton was taxed in Hampshire (Andover hundred, p. 108).

[4] Most of Tytherley, East and West, was taxed in Hampshire (Thorngate hundred, p. 106).

Wynterslewe[1]	Winterslow [East]	su/246326	4.	0.	0
Tudeworth'	North Tidworth	su/234490	2.	0.	0
Berghfeld[2]	?		9.		0
Buddesdene	Biddesden	su/295510		16.	0
Kyngeston' Deverel[3]	Kingston Deverill	st/846371	2.	18.	0
Welwe	West Wellow [in Hampshire]	su/292189	2.	16.	8
Compton'[4]	Compton	su/132520		13.	4
Aleton'	Alton	su/153466		11.	4
Cholleston'	Choulston	su/151485		4.	0
Bydenham	Diddenham [in Berkshire]	su/698665	1.	10.	0
Farlegh'	Farley Hill [in Berkshire]	su/750646	1.	4.	0
Twyford	Twyford [in Berkshire]	su/789759		6.	8
Scheprugg' Magna	Great Sheepbridge [in Berkshire]	su/c.721653	3.	0.	0
Scheprugg' Parva	Little Sheepbridge [in Berkshire]	su/c.721653	1.	6.	8
Bech' [d]	Beaches [in Berkshire]	su/807691	1.	10.	0
Boukhurste [d]	Buckhurst [in Berkshire]	su/836686	1.	8.	0
Henton' Ode	Odes [in Berkshire]	su/812741	1.	2.	0
Henton' Pippard	Hinton Pipard [in Berkshire]	su/800752		16.	0
Hacche [d]	Hinton Hatch [in Berkshire]	su/804747		4.	0
Henton'	Hinton [in Berkshire]	su/803747	1.	0.	0
			87.	15.	10

Lib. Everle [EVERLEIGH LIBERTY]

Everle	Everleigh	su/199542	5.	10.	0
Colyngbourn' Comitis	Collingbourne Ducis	su/242536	4.	10.	0
Compton'[5]	Compton	su/132520	1.	3.	4
Hakeneston'	Haxton	su/149494	4.	10.	0
			15.	13.	4

Hd. Weremunstr' [WARMINSTER HUNDRED]

Corselegh'	Corsley	st/829467	6.	10.	0
Whytebourne	Whitbourne[6]	st/825448	1.	6.	8
Tholueston'	Thoulstone	st/838481	1.	10.	0
Bisshopestrowe	Bishopstrow	st/895437	1.	13.	4
Middeldon'	Middleton	st/907444	1.	15.	0
Norton'	Norton Bavent	st/907433	6.	0.	0
Crokerton'	Crockerton	st/860426		14.	0
Sutton' Magna	Great Sutton [? Sutton Veny]	st/902418	4.	0.	0

[1] For West Winterslow see Alderbury hundred (p. 345).

[2] Beresford in *V.C.H.*, *Wilts.* iv (1959), 297, notes that *Berghfeld* was probably in or near Chute; it was linked with Biddesden in the poll tax of 1377.

[3] Part of Kingston Deverill was taxed in Mere hundred (p. 334).

[4] Partly taxed in Everleigh Liberty, below.

[5] Partly taxed in Amesbury hundred, above.

[6] Grid ref. is to Middle Whitbourne.

Sutton' Parva	Little Sutton		2.	10.	0
Porteworth'	Pertwood	ST/890358	1.	8.	0
Fishton'	Fisherton de la Mere	SU/001385	4.	0.	0
Babeton'	Bapton	ST/992382	5.	0.	0
Teffunte	Teffont Magna	ST/989324	5.	0.	0
Donynton'	Dinton	SU/009317	5.	6.	8
Nywenham	Newnham	ST/908415		16.	0
Norrigge	Norridge	ST/853470	2.	0.	0
Upton'	Upton Scudamore	ST/865476	5.	8.	0
Bogelegh'	Bugley	ST/855448		12.	0
Weremunstr'	Warminster	ST/874451	7.	10.	0
Smalebrok'	Smallbrook	ST/881444		18.	0
Buryton'	Boreham	ST/890443	1.	8.	0
			65.	5.	8[1]

Hd. Bradeford [BRADFORD HUNDRED]

Bradeford	Bradford on Avon	ST/824609	4.	16.	8
Wyneslegh'	Winsley	ST/799610	4.	3.	4
Roughle	Rowley		2.	13.	4
Trol[2]	Trowle	ST/c.839584	1.	6.	0
Atteworth'	Atworth	ST/859657	1.	18.	0
Farlegh'	Monkton Farleigh	ST/806653	1.	16.	8
Wroxhale	South Wraxall	ST/833648	2.	8.	0
Holte	Holt	ST/861615	5.	6.	8
Chaldefeld	Chalfield	ST/861631	1.	4.	0
Broughton'	Broughton Gifford	ST/878632	3.	10.	0
			29.	2.	8

Hd. Kynewardeston [KINWARDSTONE HUNDRED]

Fyfhyde	Fyfield	SU/176605		12.	0
Middelton'	Milton Lilbourne	SU/190605		18.	0
Eston'	Easton	SU/207604	1.	6.	8
Wotton' &	Wootton Rivers and	SU/198630	1.	0.	0
Wyk'	Wick	SU/189639			
Burbach' &	Burbage and	SU/230615	2.	2.	0
Durlegh'	Durley	SU/238641			
Wolfhale	Wolf Hall	SU/242619	1.	0.	0
Westgrafton' &	West Grafton and	SU/246602	2.	0.	0
Estgrafton'	East Grafton	SU/258604			
Wolton'	Wilton	SU/267615	2.	0.	0
Crofton' &	Crofton and possibly	SU/263623	1.	6.	8
Berlegh'	Bewley [in Great Bedwyn]				
Stoke &	Stokke and	SU/266648		8.	6
Fourd'	Forde	SU/275638			
Chussebury	Chisbury	SU/277663	5.	8.	0
Hynsete &	Henset and	SU/c.240680		13.	4
Puthale	Puthall	SU/239681			
Wexcombe	Wexcombe	SU/272590	2.	13.	4
Tytecombe &	Tidcombe and	SU/290583	2.	13.	4
Merton'	Marten	SU/284602			

[1] Total incorrect in V.C.H., Wilts. iv (1959), 302.
[2] Part of Trowle was taxed in Melksham hundred (p. 338).

Chut' &	Chute and	su/300540	2.	10.	0
Couenholt	Conholt	su/323550			
Forstebury &	Fosbury and	su/314586	1.	13.	4
Butermere	Buttermere	su/343610			
Shaldebourne¹ &	Shalbourne and	su/315635	3.	0.	0
Hardene cum	Harding with	su/296626			
Estbedewynde	Little Bedwyn	su/291662			
Chilton' &	Chilton Foliat	su/319705	1.	10.	0
Cherleton'²	?				
Staundene &	North Standen [in Berks.]	su/313672	2.	0.	0
Staundene cum	Standen with	su/309539			
Froxfeld	Froxfield	su/300680			
Peuesy	Pewsey	su/164599	7.	0.	0
Colyngbourne	Collingbourne Kingston	su/239558	5.	6.	8
			47.	1.	10

Hd. Canynges [CANNINGS HUNDRED]

Bourton' &	Bourton and	su/043646	2.	3.	4
Eston'	Easton	su/049645			
Horton'	Horton	su/050633	3.	13.	4
Canyng'	Bishops Cannings	su/038642	8.	0.	0
Cotes	Coate	su/040619	7.	10.	0
Ryndeweye	Roundway	su/013634	3.	6.	8
Chiteue	Chittoe	st/957666	1.	10.	0
Betteberwe	Bedborough	su/c.025630	2.	0.	0
Wyke &	Wick Green and	su/008605	3.	6.	8
Noustede	Nursteed	su/022605			
Hyghweye	Highway	su/043745	1.	14.	0
			33.	4.	0

TOTAL: £1,595. 13. 7¾³

¹ Part of Shalbourne was taxed in Berkshire (Kintbury hundred, p. 10). Bagshot, in Shalbourne, was also taxed in Kintbury hundred.

² Beresford identifies this place as Charnham Street in Hungerford, Berkshire (*V.C.H.*, *Wilts.* iv (1959), 300) but this seems doubtful.

³ As on 1334 Account, E 179/196/9.

WORCESTERSHIRE

DOCUMENTS

8 Edward III: Account	E 179/200/4
8 Edward III: Particulars	E 179/200/3*
10 Edward III: Particulars	E 179/200/3
10 Edward III: Particulars	E 179/200/5

TAXERS

The prior of Great Malvern (who replaced the abbot of Evesham who was too infirm to act) and Henry de Stratford

TAX YIELD

15th	£436.	6.	8½
10th	£ 65.	11.	2
	£501.	17.	10½

Representing assessed movable wealth of

£7,200. 12. 3½

NOTES

The list begins with the city of Worcester, the only town considered a borough for taxation purposes. Droitwich, a borough in the three taxations of 1313–16 and again in 1332, continued to be taxed at the higher rate of the tenth but as ancient demesne. Five other places, widely scattered, were taxed as ancient demesne.

The outline of the county in 1334 was very different from that of today, especially in the south and east where parts of the county were intermingled with parts of Gloucestershire and Warwickshire. The Worcestershire list includes thirty-six places since transferred to other counties, while twenty-two places now in Worcestershire were taxed in adjacent counties in 1334 (summarized in Glasscock, thesis, 1963, op. cit., Table 10, 295).

REFERENCES

J. W. Willis Bund and J. Amphlett, 'Lay subsidy roll for the county of Worcester, circa 1280', *Worcs. Hist. Soc.* (1893).

F. J. Eld, 'Lay subsidy roll for the county of Worcester, 1 Edward I' (*recte* III), *Worcs. Hist. Soc.* (1895).

J. Amphlett, 'Lay subsidy roll, A.D. 1332–3, and Nonarum Inquisitiones, 1340, for the county of Worcester', *Worcs. Hist. Soc.* (1899).

K. M. Buchanan, 'Worcestershire', being part 68 of L. Dudley Stamp, ed., *The Land of Britain*, 1944 (includes a reconstruction of the agricultural geography of the early fourteenth century based on contemporary sources, including lay subsidies).

Hd. Oswulduslowe [OSWALDSLOW HUNDRED]

Wygorn' [B]	Worcester	so/849548	20.	0.	0	[T]
Stoke Prioris	Stoke Prior	so/949677	2.	19.	4	
Grymeleye	Grimley	so/837606	4.	11.	3	
Hallowe	Hallow	so/829579	1.	17.	6	
Bedewardyn	Bedwardine	so/823535		16.	10	
Holte &	Holt and	so/829625	3.	11.	3	
Wyteleye	Little Witley	so/783635				
Elmeley Beuchamp	Elmley Castle	so/982410	3.	2.	8	
Codeston'	Cutsdean [in Glos.]	sp/088301		17.	6	
Wassebourn'¹	Little Washbourne [in Glos.]	so/989333	1.	14.	9	
Lyndrugg'	Lindridge	so/675690	5.	11.	0	
North' Wyk'	Northwick	so/843580	4.	18.	4	
Warmedon'	Warndon	so/888569		12.	0	
Hyndelep'	Hindlip	so/880586		7.	8	
Oddyngleye	Oddingley	so/915591		6.	6	
Kemes c.m²	Kempsey [with members]	so/848491	5.	7.	4	
Bredon'	Bredon	so/920370	2.	3.	8	
Herdewyk'	Bredon's Hardwick	so/913355	2.	5.	8	
Kelmesham	Kinsham	so/934356		7.	7	
Norton'	Bredon's Norton	so/931390	3.	11.	1	
Westmuncote	Westmancote	so/938376		13.	5	
Wenlond	Welland	so/798399		11.	11	
Parva Malverne	Little Malvern	so/771404		8.	4	
Wyk Episcopi c.m³	Wick Episcopi [with members]	so/828531	6.	7.	5	
Bradewas	Broadwas	so/754551	1.	4.	0	
Rippel	Ripple	so/875377	8.	6.	8	
Crombe Adam cum	Earl's Croome with	so/871420				
Bocton'	Baughton	so/879420				
Berewe	Berrow	so/793342	1.	7.	8	
Pendok'	Pendock	so/818337	1.	2.	9	
Rydmarl' Dabetoft'	Redmarley D'Abitot [in Glos.]	so/752315	3.	2.	6	
Overbury	Overbury	so/957373	1.	10.	6½	
Conterton'	Conderton	so/964370	1.	8.	9½	
Tedynton'	Teddington [in Glos.]	so/964329	1.	14.	6½	
Alston'	Alstone [in Glos.]	so/982324	1.	0.	11½	
Mutton'	Mitton	so/903339	1.	18.	10	
Croule	Crowle	so/922559		17.	0	
Hodynton'	Huddington	so/943572		14.	4	
Hambury	Hanbury	so/954644	3.	5.	4	
Clyve Prioris	Cleeve Prior	sp/088493	2.	9.	10	
Hereforton'	Harvington	sp/057488	1.	12.	9	
Upton'	Upton upon Severn	so/852402	5.	4.	11	
Holefast cum	Holdfast with	so/852378	1.	8.	10	
Estynton'	Eastington	so/831381				
Wolfardeleye	Wolverley	so/829793	3.	3.	6	
Humelton' &	Himbleton and	so/948588	4.	0.	3	
Tyberton'	Tibberton	so/902570				

---

¹ Great Washbourne was taxed in Gloucestershire (Tewkesbury hundred, p. 92).

² Members of Kempsey in 1275 included Broomhall, Draycott, Hatfield, Kerswell Green, Mucknell, Norton, Stonehall, Upper Wolverton, Lower Wolverton, and *Yeuenhale* (?) (Eld, op. cit. xviii).

³ Members of Wick Episcopi in 1275 included Crowneast and Upper Wick (Eld, op. cit. xx).

			£	s.	d.
Alvechirche	Alvechurch	SP/026723	4.	6.	11
Batenhale	Battenhall[1]	SO/867531	1.	0.	0
Spechesl' & Codel'	Spetchley and Cudleigh	SO/896539 SO/891545		10.	0
Chirchehull' & Bradecote	Churchill and Bredicot	SO/922535 SO/906549	1.	4.	6
Aston' Episcopi	White Ladies Aston	SO/922527		5.	8
Tredynton'	Tredington [in Warwicks.]	SP/259435		16.	0
Tydelmynton'	Tidmington [in Warwicks.]	SP/261385	2.	16.	10
Longedon'	Longdon [in Warwicks.]	SP/221416	1.	0.	2
Derlyngescote	Darlingscott [in Warwicks.]	SP/229421	1.	1.	4
Edmundescote	Armscote [in Warwicks.]	SP/246448	1.	16.	0
Taclinton'	Talton [in Warwicks.]	SP/239470	1.	1.	0
Neubolde	Newbold on Stour [in Warwicks.]	SP/247462	2.	5.	0
Fladebury	Fladbury	SO/995463	1.	6.	0
Craucombe	Craycombe	SO/999473		19.	0
Pydele	Wyre Piddle	SO/962473	1.	1.	4
More	Moor[2]	SO/978472		17.	0
Hulle	Hill	SO/983481		15.	10
Throkemerton'	Throckmorton	SO/981499	2.	4.	9
Byshampton'	Bishampton	SO/990519	2.	1.	0
Habbelench'	Abbots Lench	SP/012518		17.	0
Bradeley & Stock	Bradley and Stock Green	SO/987602 SO/980587		12.	10
Hertelbury c.m	Hartlebury [with members]	SO/841709	5.	19.	10
Blacwelle	Blackwell [in Warwicks.]	SP/242434	2.	15.	8
Shypeston'	Shipston on Stour [in Warwicks.]	SP/260406	3.	8.	9
Croppethorne	Cropthorne	SO/999452	1.	16.	3
Segesberewe	Sedgeberrow	SP/024385	2.	10.	6
Chorleton'	Charlton	SP/009457	2.	2.	0
Netherton'	Netherton	SO/991416	1.	11.	8
Incebargh'	Inkberrow	SP/016572	4.	19.	5
Lench' Rondulf'	Rous Lench	SP/015533	1.	1.	8
Iccombe	Hill Croome	SO/888403	1.	3.	0
Blockel' & Upton'	Blockley [in Glos.] and Upton [in Glos.]	SP/164350 SP/148348	2.	17.	0
Northwyk'	Northwick [in Glos.]	SP/168364	1.	4.	0
Draycote	Draycott [in Glos.]	SP/181358	1.	6.	11
Dychford Superior	Upper Ditchford [in Glos.]	SP/202368	1.	10.	0
Dychford Media	Middle Ditchford [in Glos.]	SP/213374	1.	0.	1
Paxford	Paxford [in Glos.]	SP/183379	2.	8.	0
Dorne	Dorn [in Glos.]	SP/203339	1.	16.	0
Aston'	Aston Magna [in Glos.]	SP/202357	2.	10.	0
Daylesford	Daylesford [in Glos.]	SP/242259	1.	0.	1
Evenelod'	Evenlode [in Glos.]	SP/221291	2.	1.	0
			192.	17.	0

---

[1] Grid ref. is to Middle Battenhall Farm.
[2] Grid ref. is to Lower Moor.

Hd. Dodyntre [DODDINGTREE HUNDRED]

Marteleye [A.D]	Martley	so/756599	7.	6.	8	[T]
Dodenham	Doddenham	so/754562		16.	4	
More	Rock Moor	so/727714		14.	0	
Colyngwyk'	Conningswick	sp/738712				
Sned &	Snead and	so/732697	1.	4.	8	
Ribbesford	Ribbesford	so/786740				
Estham	Eastham	so/658689	1.	9.	11	
Childrenhanleye	Hanley Child	so/650652		11.	9	
Hanleye Wiliam	Hanley William	so/673660		9.	3	
Stanford	Stanford on Teme	so/702657	1.	10.	2	
Olerton'	Orleton	so/699671				
Sheldesl' Waleys	Shelsley Walsh	so/722629		12.	2	
Homme	Hamcastle	so/733618		12.	1	
Astleye	Astley	so/787676	2.	11.	6	
Glashampton'	Glasshampton	so/799669		9.	4	
Abbedeleye	Abberley	so/752680	2.	13.	4	
Sheldesleye	Shelsley Beauchamp	so/731629	2.	4.	6	
Bayton'	Bayton	so/691732	1.	11.	6	
Ridmarl' Olyver	Redmarley	so/760663		16.	2	
Lynden'	Lindon[1]	lost		18.	6	
Coderugge	Cotheridge	so/784546	1.	11.	0	
Curewyard	Kyre Magna [al. Kyre Wyard]	so/626635	1.	12.	0	
Sockeleye [A.D]	Suckley	so/721516	3.	18.	10	[T]
Shraueleye	Shrawley	so/806648	1.	14.	0	
Momele &	Mamble and	so/689716	2.	2.	11	
Sodynton'	Sodington	so/693710				
Carkedon'	Carton	so/712734		13.	2	
Holyne &	Hollin and	so/722702		14.	4	
Stilledon'	Stildon	so/711698				
Stokton'	Stockton on Teme	so/716674		16.	6	
Temdebury	Tenbury	so/594684	7.	3.	3	
Beryton' &	Berrington and	so/571675				
Bokelynton'	Bockleton	so/593614				
Clyfton'	Clifton upon Teme	so/715616	1.	9.	4	
Parva Sapy[2]	Lower Sapey	so/699602	1.	2.	6	
Yedeffen	Edvin Loach [in Herefordshire]	so/662584		6.	6	
Acton'	Acton Beauchamp [in Herefordshire]	so/679503	1.	6.	2	
			51.	2.	4	

Hd. Dimidii Comitatus [HALFSHIRE HUNDRED]

Wych' [A.D]	Droitwich	so/900633	10.	13.	4	[T]
Benteleye	Bentley	so/998653	1.	15.	1	
Tardebigg'[3]	Tardebigge	so/996692	1.	14.	3	
Wychebaud	Wychbold	so/930659	5.	15.	5	
Elmeleye Lovet	Elmley Lovett	so/865696	3.	3.	0	
Hampton' Lovet	Hampton Lovett	so/888656	2.	3.	6	
Salwarp'	Walwarpe	so/874621	3.	6.	2	

---

[1] *E.P.N.S., IV, Worcs.* (1927), 73, fn. 1, suggests that the site of Lindon was in the north-west of Rock parish.

[2] Upper Sapey was taxed in Herefordshire (Broxash hundred, p. 123).

[3] Part of Tardebigge was taxed in Warwickshire (Barlichway hundred, p. 326).

Frankeleye	Frankley	SO/999804	I.	O.	10	
Chadleswych' & Wylyngwyk'	Chadwich and Willingwick[1]	SO/976760 lost	I.	3.	2	
Bremesgrave [A.D]	Bromsgrove	SO/960705	10.	2.	6	[T]
Kyngesnorton' [A.D]	King's Norton [in Warwicks.]	SP/049790	8.	3.	10	[T]
Forfeld	Fairfield	SO/948752	2.	7.	10	
Belne	Belbroughton	SO/919769	I.	4.	10	
Pebmor	Pedmore	SO/911821	I.	8.	4	
Chirchull'	Churchill	SO/879794	I.	7.	6	
Swyneford	Old Swinford	SO/905834	2.	5.	8	
Haggeleye	Hagley	SO/921808	I.	4.	2	
Chirch' Lench'	Church Lench	SP/024513		12.	4	
Kynton'	Kington	SO/990559		16.	8	
Upton' Waren	Upton Warren	SO/931674	I.	5.	6	
Grafton'	Grafton	SO/939691	I.	4.	0	
Wodecote	Woodcote Green	SO/913727	I.	2.	6	
Cokeseye	Cooksey Green	SO/908696	I.	7.	4	
Russhok'	Rushock	SO/884712	I.	8.	8	
Hadesore & Whytton'	Hadzor and Witton	SO/916625 SO/894623	I.	4.	0	
Doverdale	Doverdale	SO/861660	I.	6.	4	
Northfeld	Northfield [in Warwicks.]	SP/025793	2.	2.	6	
Worueleye	Warley Wigorn	SO/995870		12.	3	
Cradeleye	Cradley	SO/932851		14.	0	
Lodeleye	Lutley	SO/941831		11.	8	
Cofton'	Cofton Hackett	SP/012753		10.	6	
Duddeleye	Dudley	SO/946904	5.	1.	9	
Feckenham [A.D]	Feckenham	SP/009616	5.	6.	0	[T]
Kydermunstre	Kidderminster	SO/831769	5.	15.	0	
Stone	Stone	SO/862749	2.	11.	9	
Dunclent & Hetheye	Dunclent and Heathy Mill	SO/860756 SO/848754		14.	8	
Kyngesford	Kingsford	SO/819814		7.	0	
Mutton'	Mitton	SO/813718	I.	1.	2	
Chaddesleye Corbet	Chaddesley Corbett	SO/891736	9.	2.	2	
			103.	17.	2	

Hd. Pershore [PERSHORE HUNDRED]

Pershore	Pershore	SO/949458	4.	4.	4	
Beoleye	Beoley	SP/065696	2.	4.	4	
Dormeston'	Dormston	SO/988576	I.	17.	6	
Yerdeleye	Yardley Wood [in Warwicks.]	SP/092796	3.	3.	10½	
Stregesham	Strensham	SP/911406	2.	8.	0	
Besford	Besford	SO/911448	I.	15.	I	
Hanleye	Hanley Castle	SO/839419	4.	6.	0	
Eldresfeld	Eldersfield	SO/800312	6.	6.	8	
Pyryton'	Pirton	SO/886468	2.	10.	0	
Morton'	Castlemorton	SO/795372	8.	6.	8	
Longedon' & Chaddesleye	Longdon and Chaceley [in Glos.]	SO/838362 SO/855306				

---

[1] *E.P.N.S.*, IV, *Worcs.* (1927), 345, fn. 2, states that Willingwick lay contiguous to Chadwick. The last recorded mention seems to be sixteenth century (*V.C.H.*, *Worcs.* iii (1913), 24).

Aldremonston'	Alderminster [in Warwicks.]	SP/230486	2.	12.	0
Goldecote	Goldicote [in Warwicks.]	SP/240518		19.	0
Byrlyngham	Birlingham	SO/932432	4.	11.	0
Ekynton' &	Eckington and	SO/922413	9.	3.	0
Defford	Defford	SO/917432			
Bussheleye	Bushley	SO/875343	2.	17.	4
Pull' &	Pull and	SO/863361			
Quenhull'	Queenhill	SO/861367			
Severnestok'	Severn Stoke	SO/856440	2.	14.	11[1]
Newynton'	Naunton Beauchamp	SO/962524	1.	0.	6
Pydele	North Piddle	SO/968545		18.	0
Flavel	Flyford Flavell	SO/979549		13.	10
Wyk' iuxta Pershore	Wick	SO/963453	2.	13.	7
Brighlampton'	Bricklehampton	SO/982423	1.	19.	6
Pendesham	Pensham	SO/940442	1.	5.	4
Cumberton' Parva	Little Comberton	SO/967427	1.	8.	2
Cumberton' Magna	Great Comberton	SO/954421	2.	2.	2
Upton' Snodesbury	Upton Snodsbury	SO/943543	2.	18.	0
Grafton Subtus Flavel	Grafton Flyford	SO/962558	2.	2.	1
Staunton' &	Staunton [in Glos.]	SO/782293	2.	4.	6
Morton' Brut	and Birtsmorton	SO/801355			
Baldenhale	Baldenhall[2]	lost	3.	19.	5
Matresfeld	Madresfield	SO/805475			
Neulond	Newland	SO/796485			
Poywyk	Powick	SO/832516	6.	5.	9
Clivelode &	Clevelode and	SO/836470			
Braunseford	Bransford	SO/795527			
Legh &	Leigh and	SO/784532	6.	3.	7
Mathme	Mathon [in Herefordshire]	SO/733459			
Walcote c.m[3]	Walcot [with members]	SO/942482	3.	15.	9
Bradeweye	Broadway	SP/095373	4.	6.	0
Brokcoton' Haket	Broughton Hackett	SO/924545	1.	1.	0
Pupplynton'	Peopleton and	SO/938503	2.	12.	0
Pendefen	Pinvin	SO/958489			
Merton' Hosyntre	Martin Hussingtree	SO/882602	1.	3.	7
			108.	12.	5½

Hd. Blakenhurst' [BLACKENHURST HUNDRED]

Evesham	Evesham	SP/037437	8.	5.	6
Lenchwyk'	Lenchwick	SP/034473	3.	2.	3
Uffenham	Offenham	SP/053463	1.	16.	4
Luttelton'	Littleton[4]	SP/076462	3.	2.	8
Aldynton'	Aldington	SP/064441	3.	2.	10

[1] By 1336, the quota for Severn Stoke had changed to £3. 14. 11 because of a tax of 20 shillings levied on Walter de Newynton, a taxer. In consequence the total for the hundred and the county rose by the same amount.

[2] The possible location of Baldenhall is discussed in *E.P.N.S.*, IV, *Worcs.* (1927), 210, fn. 2.

[3] Members of Walcote in 1275 included Drake's Broughton, Caldewell, and Abberton (Eld, op. cit. xx).

[4] Although the grid ref. given is to South Littleton, it is not clear whether this entry refers to both North and South Littleton, or only to one of these. In 1327 South Littleton was jointly taxed with Offenham, and North Littleton with Church Honeybourne (Eld, op. cit. 55 and 70).

Wykewane	Wickhamford	SP/068422	2.	2.	0
Morton	Abbots Morton	SP/028549	1.	5.	6
Atchelench'	Atch Lench	SP/033508			
Ombresleye	Ombersley	SO/844635	7.	17.	5
Lench' Uic'[1]	?		1.	2.	0
Benyngworth'	Bengeworth	SP/044436	3.	2.	8
Hampton'	Great Hampton	SP/029431	3.	3.	3
Bretforton'	Bretforton	SP/092438	4.	14.	0
Honyborne[2]	Church Honeybourne	SP/120441	2.	2.	0
Ulbergh'	Oldberrow [in Warwicks.]	SP/121660		10.	6
			45.	8.	11

TOTAL: £501. 17. 10½[3]

[1] Possibly a part of Lenchwick.
[2] Cow Honeybourne was taxed in Gloucestershire (Kiftsgate hundred, p. 94).
[3] As on 1334 Account, E 179/200/4.

YORKSHIRE

DOCUMENTS

East Riding
  8 Edward III: Account   E 179/202/36
  8 Edward III: Particulars   not extant
 19 Edward III: Particulars   E 179/202/43*
 20 Edward III: Particulars   E 179/202/45

North Riding
  8 Edward III: Account   E 179/211/9
  8 Edward III: Particulars   E 179/211/8 (imperfect)
 11 Edward III: Particulars   E 179/211/10*

West Riding
  8 Edward III: Account   E 179/206/16
  8 Edward III: Particulars   not extant
 18 Edward III: Particulars   E 179/206/20 (imperfect)
 20 Edward III: Particulars   E 179/206/22*

TAXERS

East Riding: the prior of Warter and Thomas de Brayton

North Riding: the abbot of St. Mary, York, Nicholas de Hugate, provost of the church of St. John, Beverley, and Robert de Scorburgh

West Riding: the abbot of Selby and Thomas de Blaston

TAX YIELD

East Riding:	15th	£924.	5.	8
	10th	£ 55.	0.	4
		£979.	6.	0
Hull		£ 33.	6.	8 (50 marks in lieu of tenth)

Representing assessed movable wealth of
    £14,747. 15. 0

North Riding:	15th	£570.	3.	9
	10th	£ 12.	12.	4
		£582.	16.	1
Scarborough		£ 33.	6.	8 (50 marks in lieu of tenth)

Representing assessed movable wealth of
    £9,012. 6. 3

West Riding: 15th   £712.   2.   4½
          10th   £ 26.   8.   4

£738.   10.   8½

Representing assessed movable wealth of

£10,945.   18.   11½

City of York: 10th   £162.   0.   0

Representing assessed movable wealth of

£1,620.   0.   0

Total for Yorkshire: £2,529.   6.   1½

Representing assessed movable wealth of

£36,326.   0.   2½

NOTES

East Riding: Places taxed at a tenth are at the end of the list. They include two boroughs: Hedon and Ravenser Odd (lost to the sea shortly afterwards), and three ancient demesnes: Pocklington, Kilham, and Great Driffield. Hull compounded for 50 marks in lieu of the tenth. Many places in the East Riding appear in the returns both in the Wapentakes and in the liberties to which parts of them belonged.

North Riding: Like Hull, Scarborough compounded for 50 marks in lieu of the tenth. Other than this there was very little tax at the higher rate of a tenth; the rate was levied on the four ancient demesnes of the Soke of Pickering: Scalby, Easingwold with Huby, and Cold Kirby. Richmond, Thirsk, and Northallerton were taxed at a fifteenth despite the fact that they had all been considered boroughs on at least one occasion earlier in the century.

West Riding: The higher rate of a tenth was levied on twenty places in the liberty of Knaresborough, including Boroughbridge and Knaresborough; both of these had been considered boroughs in the taxations of 1313 and 1316, but they were not taxed as such in 1334.

YORKSHIRE: EAST RIDING

Holdernesse [HOLDERNESS]

Suttun[1]	Sutton on Hull	TA/118330	4.	0.	0
Merflete	Marfleet	TA/139297	3.	6.	0
Skeflyng'	Skeffling	TA/371191	2.	13.	4
Berneston' cum	Barmston with	TA/156589	1.	10.	0
Wylton'	Winkton	TA/150590			
Fitling'	Fitling	TA/252338		18.	0
Eske	Eske	TA/057431	1.	6.	8

[1] Also listed in the Liberty of the Chapter of Beverley, p. 368.

			£.	s.	d.
Outneuton'	Out Newton	TA/382216	1.	13.	4
Brustwyk &	Burstwick and	TA/228277	1.	14.	0
Skeftling'	Skeckling	TA/220280			
Rymeswelle	Rimswell	TA/311287	1.	14.	8
Patrington'[1]	Patrington	TA/316225	7.	0.	0
Halsham	Halsham	TA/268278	2.	17.	0
Pidse Burton	Burton Pidsea	TA/251311	2.	17.	10
Aldburgh'	Aldbrough	TA/243387	2.	10.	0
Outhorn'	Owthorne	TA/338281	1.	8.	4
Wythornse	Withernsea	TA/341280	1.	16.	8
Gauenstede	Ganstead	TA/150342	2.	0.	0
Holmeton' cum	Holmpton with	TA/367233	3.	0.	0
Rysum	Rysome	TA/361220			
Kayngham	Keyingham	TA/245255	4.	0.	0
Thorp' cum	Welwick Thorpe with	TA/330218	2.	13.	4
Penithorp'	Pensthorpe	TA/c.345210			
Frismersk	Frismarsh[2]	lost	1.	6.	8
Hombelton'	Humbleton	TA/227349	1.	6.	0
Oustwyk &	Owstwick and	TA/270325	3.	4.	0
Hildeston'	Hilston	TA/284335			
Otringham[3]	Ottringham	TA/268243	5.	7.	0
Southkyrlagh'	South Skirlaugh	TA/141398		19.	0
Garton'	Garton	TA/271353	2.	0.	0
Esington' cum	Easington with	TA/399192	5.	0.	0
Dymbelton'	Dimlington	TA/398208			
Reston'[4]	Long Riston	TA/122427	1.	10.	0
Kylnese	Kilnsea	TA/411159	5.	6.	4
Tykton'	Tickton	TA/064419	2.	14.	0
Wele	Weel	TA/064394			
Ruda[5]	Routh	TA/091424		16.	8
Wythornwyk[6]	Withernwick	TA/194406	1.	15.	0
Rihill' cum	Ryhill with	TA/222258	3.	14.	8
Camerington'	Camerton	TA/217261			
Pagula	Paull	TA/166265	2.	0.	0
Holm'	Paull Holme	TA/183248	1.	10.	0
Paghelfiete	Paull Fleet[7]	lost	3.	0.	0
Hattfield	Hatfield	TA/183429	1.	10.	0
North Skirlagh &	North Skirlaugh and	TA/142400	1.	10.	0
Arnal[8]	Arnold	TA/126414			
Routon'	Rowton	TA/134400			
Attyngwyk	Atwick	TA/190508	1.	6.	0
Hornese Burton'	Hornsea Burton	TA/207461	1.	8.	0
Skypse cum	Skipsea with	TA/166550	2.	0.	0
Hyda	The Hithe	TA/c.162554			
Goushill'	Goxhill	TA/185448		18.	0
Mapelton'	Mappleton	TA/225439	1.	13.	4

[1] Also listed in the Liberty of the Provost of Beverley, p. 369.

[2] A lost Humber town (*E.P.N.S.*, *XIV*, *Yorks. E.R.* (1937), 24); the town was suffering inundation by the sea in the early fourteenth century and there is a marginal note concerning its destruction on E 179/202/43 where the figure of £1. 6. 8 is struck through and £5. 10. 0 substituted.

[3] Also listed in the Liberty of the Provost of Beverley, p. 369.

[4] Also listed in the liberties of the Chapter of Beverley and the Provost of Beverley, pp. 368, 369.

[5] Also listed in the Liberty of the Provost of Beverley, p. 369.

[6] Ditto, p. 369.

[7] A lost place in Paull parish. (*E.P.N.S.*, *XIV*, *Yorks. E.R.* (1937), 37.)

[8] Also listed in the Liberty of the Chapter of Beverley, p. 368.

Catwyk[1] &	Catwick and	TA/131454	1.	17.	10
Catfosse	Catfoss	TA/142470			
Rolleston	Rolston	TA/213453	1.	6.	8
Brandesburton'[2]	Brandesburton	TA/119476	3.	6.	8
Coldon Magna &	Great and	TA/230427	1.	10.	0
Parva	Little Cowden[3]	TA/242420			
Dringhowe	Dringhoe	TA/150550	1.	13.	0
Grimeston'	Grimston	TA/290350	1.	6.	8
Estandwyk &	Elstronwick and	TA/233323	1.	16.	0
Danthorp'	Danthorpe	TA/243326			
Wineton'[2]	Wyton	TA/179334	1.	4.	4
Sprotteley	Sproatley	TA/194343	2.	6.	8
Elwardby	Ellerby	TA/169376	1.	16.	8
Turkelby &	Thirtleby and	TA/177347			
Douthorp'	Dowthorpe	TA/154381			
Kylling'	Nunkeeling	TA/142496		12.	0
Ryngburgh'	Ringbrough	TA/272372		12.	0
Neuton'[4]	East Newton	TA/266379			
Beghum &	Bewholme and	TA/166500		18.	0
Erghum	Arram	TA/165492			
Tharlethorp'	Tharlesthorpe[5]	lost	3.	3.	0
Preston'[6]	Preston	TA/187306	10.	10.	0
Constable Burton' &	Burton Constable and	TA/190368	1.	10.	0
Neuton	West Newton	TA/199379			
Rosse	Roos	TA/291304	2.	0.	0
Tunstall'	Tunstall	TA/305320	2.	0.	0
Lelle &	Lelley and	TA/209325	1.	4.	0
Dyk	Lelley Dyke	TA/212333			
Risse	Rise	TA/149419	1.	0.	0
North Frothingham	North Frodingham	TA/100532	4.	0.	0
Beford	Beeford	TA/129544	2.	4.	0
Flinton'[7]	Flinton	TA/220361	1.	8.	0
Etherwyk	Etherdwick	TA/231373			
Holem	Hollym	TA/343252	2.	16.	4
Merton	Marton	TA/180392	1.	13.	4
Fosham &	Fosham and	TA/209389			
Carleton'	Carlton	TA/229390			
Waughen'[8]	Wawne	TA/091368	2.	6.	8
Benyngholm'	Benningholme[9]	TA/128390		19.	0
Neusom	Newsome	TA/309266	1.	10.	0
Frothingham	Frodingham	TA/312263			
Ullerham	Ulrome	TA/162568	3.	0.	0
Swyn &	Swine and	TA/134359	4.	0.	0
Coniston	Coniston	TA/155351			
Dodyngton'	Dunnington	TA/152521		18.	0
Bilton[10]	Bilton	TA/156326		14.	0

[1] Also listed in the Liberty of the Provost of Beverley, p. 369.
[2] Ditto, p. 369.
[3] Grid ref. is to the medieval village now eroded by the sea.
[4] Identified as two places, although it is possible that *Ryngburgh' Neuton'* was the name used for East Newton to distinguish it from West Newton. Some examples of this use are given in *E.P.N.S., XIV, Yorks. E.R.* (1937), 60–1.
[5] A lost place on the Humber. See note in *E.P.N.S., XIV, Yorks. E.R.* (1937), 25.
[6] Also listed in the Liberty of St. Peter, p. 367.
[7] Also listed in the Liberty of the Provost of Beverley, p. 369.
[8] ? Also listed in the Liberty of St. Peter, p. 367.
[9] Grid ref. is to the deserted village of East Benningholme.
[10] Also listed in the Liberty of the Provost of Beverley, p. 369.

Waxham	Waxholme	TA/327296	1.	19.	0
Lesek cum	Lisset with	TA/144580	1.	0.	0
Parva Kelk	Little Kelk	TA/101606			
Bonnewyk	Bonwick[1]	TA/168534		18.	0
Thorngombald	Thorngumbald	TA/208263	2.	1.	0
Wynestede	Winestead	TA/299238	2.	5.	0
			175.	19.	8[2]

Herthill' [HARTHILL WAPENTAKE]

South Burton'[3]	Bishop Burton	SE/991397	7.	10.	0
Scorburgh'[4]	Scorborough	TA/015455	1.	2.	0
Bubwyth[5]	Bubwith	SE/712362	2.	10.	0
Kelyngwyk iuxta Watton'	Kilnwick	SE/997495	3.	10.	0
Spaldyngton'	Spaldington	SE/760334	2.	16.	8
Wylardby	Willerby	TA/025303	3.	0.	0
Northe Feribi'	North Ferriby	SE/989258	2.	16.	8
Benteley	Bentley	TA/019359	3.	2.	0
Houeton'	Houghton	SE/888391	1.	12.	0
Skyrne	Skerne	TA/046551	1.	14.	0
Braken	Bracken	SE/983503	4.	18.	0
Hothom[6]	Hotham	SE/894346	1.	1.	0
Santon'[7]	Sancton	SE/900395	1.	14.	0
Wolferton'	Wolfreton	TA/036304	1.	0.	0
South Brun	Southburn	SE/989544	3.	7.	0
Brantingham[8]	Brantingham	SE/943301	1.	14.	0
Tybthorp'	Tibthorpe	SE/961555	6.	0.	0
Northeclif'	North Cliffe	SE/873370	1.	4.	0
Mideltone[9]	Middleton on the Wolds	SE/947496	4.	13.	4
Andlagby[10]	Anlaby	TA/036288	3.	16.	0
Wyleghtoft'	Willitoft	SE/744350		14.	0
Skitby	Skidby	TA/015336	6.	10.	0
Ripplingham	Riplingham	SE/960320	1.	18.	0
Hesill'	Hessle	TA/032263	8.	13.	4
Shupton'	Shipton Thorpe	SE/852432	3.	11.	2
Folkerthorp'[11]	Foggathorpe	SE/755376		18.	0
Waldeby	Wauldby	SE/974297	2.	0.	0
Southeclift'	South Cliffe	SE/873361	1.	7.	0
Erghes	Arras[12]	SE/923417	1.	8.	0
Hundeslay	Hunsley	SE/950350	1.	13.	0
Nessingwyk	Neswick	SE/974528	4.	8.	0
Elgheton'	Elloughton	SE/943282	6.	9.	0

[1] Grid ref. is to the deserted village.

[2] The quotas for this hundred are $\frac{1}{4}d$. short of the total of £175. 19. 8¼ as given on E 179/202/43. The figure of £175. 19. 8 is likely to be the correct one, since after the increase of £4. 3. 4 in the quota for Frismarsh (p. 358), the total was changed to £180. 3. 0.

[3] Also listed in the Liberty of St. Peter, p. 368.

[4] Part of Scorborough was taxed in Howdenshire liberty, p. 363.

[5] Also listed in the Liberty of St. Peter, p. 367.

[6] Also listed in the liberties of Howdenshire, p. 363, and the Chapter of Beverley, p. 368.

[7] Also listed in the Liberty of the Chapter of Beverley, p. 368.

[8] Also listed in Howdenshire liberty, p. 363.

[9] Also listed in the Liberty of the Provost of Beverley, p. 369.

[10] Also listed in the liberties of the Blessed Mary of York, p. 366, and the Chapter of Beverley, p. 368.

[11] Also listed in the Liberty of the Blessed Mary of York, p. 366.

[12] Grid ref. is to the deserted village.

Swannesland	Swanland	SE/997280	5.	10.	o
Brighton'	Breighton	SE/709337	2.	o.	o
Herlethorp'	Harlthorpe	SE/741373	1.	o.	o
Besewyk	Beswick	TA/012481	2.	10.	o
Hoton	Hutton	TA/023533	5.	o.	o
Crauncewyk[1]	Cranswick	TA/025522			
Sutton' super Derwent	Sutton upon Derwent	SE/708467	1.	15.	o
North Cave[2]	North Cave	SE/897328	4.	o.	o
Skulcote[3]	Sculcoates	TA/115305	1.	14.	o
Kylingwyk Percy	Kilnwick Percy	SE/824495	1.	10.	o
Lokynton'[4]	Lockington	SE/993475	4.	14.	o
Estthorp'	Easthorpe	SE/882453	2.	10.	o
Wilberfosse	Wilberfoss	SE/733510	1.	6.	8
Ellerton'	Ellerton	SE/702399	2.	10.	o
South Cave[5]	South Cave	SE/917311	4.	o.	o
Gripthorp'	Gribthorpe	SE/760356	1.	4.	o
Wyghton'	Market Weighton	SE/878418	8.	o.	o
Lathum	Laytham	SE/749396	1.	o.	o
Lofthousom	Loftsome	SE/708302		15.	o
Melburne cum	Melbourne with	SE/752440	2.	2.	o
Storwath	Storwood	SE/712440			
Brunby	Burnby	SE/836463	3.	o.	o
Gouthmundham[6]	Goodmanham	SE/890432	1.	10.	o
Ullesthorp'	Ousethorpe	SE/812515		6.	8
Hatton'	Hayton	SE/821460	4.	13.	4
Lounesburgh'	Londesborough	SE/869454	3.	17.	11
Alwarthorp'	Allerthorpe	SE/786474	2.	13.	4
Wapplington'	Waplington	SE/775465	1.	8.	4
Everthorp'	Everthorpe	SE/909320	2.	10.	o
Sunderlandwyk[7]	Sunderlandwick	TA/010550		12.	o
Yapum	Yapham	SE/789520	1.	16.	o
Aghton'	Aughton	SE/701386	1.	10.	o
Foulsutton'	Full Sutton	SE/746554	1.	13.	o
Beleby	Bielby	SE/789436	2.	13.	4
Wartre	Warter	SE/870504	4.	13.	4
Seton'	Seaton Ross	SE/781412	2.	3.	o
Catton'	Catton	SE/705540	1.	11.	o
Boulton'	Bolton	SE/771522	1.	13.	4
Thorneton'	Thornton	SE/760452	2.	10.	o
Fangfosse	Fangfoss	SE/766532	3.	o.	o
Hundburton'[8]	lost		1.	14.	3
Pons Belli'[9]	Stamford Bridge	SE/712554			
Wylton'[10]	Bishop Wilton	SE/798552	3.	18.	o
Etton'[11]	Etton	SE/981436	2.	13.	o

---

[1] Both listed in the Liberty of the Provost of Beverley, p. 369.

[2] Also listed in the liberties of St. Peter, p. 367, St. Leonard, p. 368, and the Chapter of Beverley, p. 368.

[3] Also listed in the Liberty of the Provost of Beverley, p. 369.

[4] Also listed in the liberties of Howdenshire, p. 363, St. Leonard, p. 368, and the Provost of Beverley, p. 369.

[5] Also listed in the liberties of St. Peter, p. 367, and St. Leonard, p. 368.

[6] Also listed in the Liberty of St. Peter, p. 368.

[7] Also listed in additional payments for this wapentake, p. 370.

[8] A lost place; c. SE/725557.

[9] Part of Stamford Bridge was taxed with Scoreby, p. 364.

[10] Also listed in the Liberty of St. Peter, p. 367.

[11] Also listed in the liberties of the Chapter of Beverley, p. 368, and the Provost of Beverley, p. 369.

Hugate[1]	Huggate	SE/882556	3.	10.	0
Estbrun	Eastburn	SE/991556	3.	10.	0
Rotse	Rotsea	TA/065516	1.	8.	10
Wycheton'	Little Weighton	SE/988339	3.	10.	0
Eluelay[2]	Kirk Ella	TA/020298	5.	0.	0
Holm in Spaldyngmore	Holme upon Spalding Moor	SE/821390	5.	0.	0
Bainton'	Bainton	SE/965523	7.	13.	4
Everingham	Everingham	SE/803423	3.	0.	0
Neuton' super Derwent	Newton upon Derwent	SE/720494	1.	6.	8
Lund	Lund	SE/971481	4.	10.	0
Molthorp'	Youlthorpe	SE/766555		17.	0
Meltenby	Meltonby	SE/796524		12.	0
Brounhom'	Nunburnholme	SE/848478	1.	15.	2
Neusom & Brende	Newsholme and Brind	SE/720296 SE/743310	3.	3.	0
North Geveldale	Great Givendale	SE/813539		18.	0
West Brun	Kirkburn	SE/980551	3.	0.	0
Thorp'	Thorpe le Street	SE/837440	1.	6.	8
Ersewelle	Harswell	SE/820408			
Gouthorp'	Gowthorpe	SE/763546		9.	0
Wresill	Wressle	SE/708312	1.	8.	0
Molcroft[3]	Molescroft	TA/019408	1.	0.	0
North Dalton'[4]	North Dalton	SE/934522	4.	10.	0
Lekynfeld	Leconfield	TA/015438	1.	3.	0
Faxflete	Faxfleet	SE/862241	1.	1.	0
Dreuton'	Drewton	SE/925334	1.	0.	0
Watton'	Watton	TA/022498		18.	0
Cotyngham	Cottingham	TA/048330	22.	0.	0
			287.	0.	4

Lib. Houden' [HOWDENSHIRE LIBERTY]

North Duffeld	North Duffield	SE/685369	3.	5.	0
Barthelby	Barlby	SE/632340	3.	6.	8
Menthorp'[5]	Menthorpe	SE/701344		9.	0
Beleassise	Bellasize	SE/826279	1.	0.	0
Skelton'	Skelton	SE/766259	4.	0.	0
South Duffeld	South Duffield	SE/681334	1.	13.	4
Grenayk	Greenoak	SE/813280		19.	0
Cayvill	Cavil	SE/770305	1.	2.	5[6]
Balkholm'	Balkholme	SE/785281	1.	8.	0
Linton'	Linton[7]	SE/801283	1.	3.	0
Askelby	Asselby	SE/720280	2.	8.	9
Barneby	Barmby on the Marsh	SE/690285	3.	3.	0
Brakenholm'	Brackenholm	SE/700300	1.	15.	7
Cotnesse	Cotness	SE/800240	1.	13.	9
Metham	Metham	SE/810248		12.	0
Yukflete	Yokefleet	SE/822242	5.	12.	0

---

[1] Also listed in the liberties of St. Peter, p. 367, St. Leonard, p. 368, and the Chapter of Beverley, p. 368.

[2] Also listed in the Liberty of the Chapter of Beverley, p. 368.

[3] Also listed in the liberties of the Chapter of Beverley, p. 368, and the Provost of Beverley, p. 369.

[4] Ditto, pp. 368, 369.

[5] Partly taxed in wapentake between Ouse and Derwent, p. 364.

[6] £1. 3. 5 on E 179/202/43 is an error.　　　　[7] Grid ref. is to East Linton.

Saltmerche	Saltmarshe	SE/787241	4.	6.	8
Hemyngburgh'	Hemingbrough	SE/673305	2.	10.	0
Cliff'	Cliffe	SE/662317	2.	18.	0
Sandholm'	Sandholme	SE/825306		13.	4
Wodhalle	Wood Hall	SE/696318		17.	0
Howeden'	Howden	SE/748282	8.	0.	0
Estrington'	Eastrington	SE/797300	3.	0.	0
Laxton'	Laxton	SE/792255	2.	12.	0
Hithe	Hive	SE/821310		18.	0
Ousthorp'	Owsthorpe	SE/810310		17.	0
Skalleby	Scalby	SE/840295	1.	18.	6
Bolthorp'	Bowthorpe	SE/698330	1.	13.	4
Blactoft'	Blacktoft	SE/841243	4.	6.	6
Knetlington'	Knedlington	SE/734280	1.	13.	4
Kilpin	Kilpin	SE/772267	1.	10.	0
Dyk	Gilberdyke	SE/832293	1.	10.	0
Ricale[1]	Riccall	SE/620378	1.	7.	11
Belby	Belby	SE/771290	1.	12.	4
Skipwith[2]	Skipwith	SE/657385	1.	0.	0
Hothum[3]	Hotham	SE/894346		17.	0
Thorp'	Thorpe	SE/760299	1.	2.	0
Ellerker'	Ellerker	SE/922294	7.	13.	4
Walkinton'[4]	Walkington	SE/997371	7.	4.	11
Gerthum	Gardham[5]	SE/945415	1.	0.	0
Melton'	Melton	SE/972264	2.	10.	4
Welton'	Welton	SE/959272	6.	8.	5
Brantyngham[6]	Brantingham	SE/943301	2.	15.	1
Osgodby	Osgodby	SE/644339	2.	10.	0
Neuland	Newland	SE/802291		15.	0
Benetland	Bennetland	SE/826287		15.	0
Lokinton'[7]	Lockington	SE/993475		8.	6
Skorburgh'[8]	Scorborough	TA/015455		18.	0
Portyngton'	Portington	SE/788308		18.	0
Birland	Burland	SE/775303		13.	4
Howome[9]	Holme on the Wolds	SE/968463	2.	13.	0[10]
			115.	17.	4

Inter Ouse et Derwent [WAPENTAKE between OUSE and DERWENT]

Kexby	Kexby	SE/701510	1.	6.	8
Thorgramby	Thornganby	SE/689416	1.	10.	0
Hemelsay	probably Gate Helmsley [in Yorkshire N.R.]	SE/691552		16.	0
Grimeston'[11]	Grimston	SE/646515		12.	0
Skipwith[12]	Skipwith	SE/657385		10.	0
Cottyngwith[13] & Cressome	West Cottingwith ?	SE/691420		13.	4

[1] Also listed in the Liberty of St. Peter, p. 367.
[2] Partly taxed in wapentake between Ouse and Derwent, below.
[3] See also p. 360, and the Liberty of the Chapter of Beverley, p. 368.
[4] Also listed in the Liberty of the Provost of Beverley, p. 369.
[5] Grid ref. is to the deserted village. [6] See also p. 360.
[7] See also p. 361, and the liberties of St. Leonard, p. 368, and the Provost of Beverley, p. 369. [8] See also p. 360.
[9] See also p. 368. [10] Quota later changed to £3. 3. 0 (E 179/202/43).
[11] Also listed in the Liberty of St. Peter, p. 367. [12] See also above.
[13] Part of Cottingwith was taxed in the Liberty of St. Peter, p. 367.

Stillingflete &	Stillingfleet and	SE/593410	3.	15.	0
Morby	Moreby	SE/595433			
Naburne	Naburn	SE/599453	3.	0.	0
Queldrik	Wheldrake	SE/683450	5.	10.	0
Kelfeld	Kelfield	SE/595384	2.	18.	0
Skorby &	Scoreby and	SE/698529	2.	15.	0
Pons Belli'[1]	Stamford Bridge	SE/712554			
Menthorp'[2]	Menthorpe	SE/701344		11.	6
Elvington'	Elvington	SE/701475	1.	10.	0
Heslington'[3]	Heslington	SE/628505		6.	8
			25.	14.	2

Bukcrosse [BUCKROSE WAPENTAKE]

Estheslarton'	East Heslerton	SE/926766	1.	13.	0
Melthorp'	Mowthorpe[4]	SE/895670	1.	10.	0
Kyrkeby	Kirby Grindalythe	SE/903675	1.	18.	0
Dugelby	Duggleby	SE/879670	1.	14.	0
Neuton' iuxta	Newton	SE/887725	1.	12.	6
Wynteringham					
Norton'	Norton	SE/793713	1.	14.	0
Helperthorp'	Helperthorpe	SE/952703	1.	8.	0
Wellome	Welham	SE/783697		12.	4
Skyrkenbek'[5] &	Skirpenbeck and	SE/749573	1.	18.	0
Thoraldby	Thoralby	SE/771585			
Thorlkelby	Thirkleby	SE/920687	1.	10.	0
Thorp Basset'	Thorpe Basset	SE/885733		16.	0
Skakelthorp'	Scagglethorpe	SE/835724		12.	0
Yedyngham	Yedingham	SE/893793		17.	0
West Lutton'	West Lutton	SE/930692	1.	8.	6
Est Lutton'	East Lutton	SE/942696		12.	4
West Heslarton'	West Heslerton	SE/911758	1.	17.	0
Crohome	Croom	SE/934658	1.	10.	0
Menyngthorp'	Menethorpe	SE/770677	1.	6.	8
Sledmere	Sledmere	SE/930646	7.	6.	8
Wynestowe	Westow	SE/753652	1.	8.	0
Sixendale[6]	Thixendale	SE/842611	1.	10.	0
Raisthorp'[7]	Raisthorpe	SE/855617		17.	0
Winteringham	Wintringham	SE/888732	1.	16.	8
Knapton'	Knapton	SE/880756	1.	6.	8
Shirburne	Sherburn	SE/959774	2.	16.	8
Collome	Cowlam	SE/966656		17.	0
Fridaithorp'[8]	Fridaythorpe	SE/875593		13.	0
Lepinton	Leppington	SE/763612	1.	7.	0
Bergthorp'	Burythorpe	SE/789651		11.	0
Touthorp'[9]	Towthorpe	SE/901630	1.	4.	0
Levenyng'	Leavening	SE/785630	1.	2.	0
Bridale	Burdale	SE/871623	1.	2.	6
Wharrum Percy	Wharram Percy	SE/858642		18.	0
Seterington'	Settrington	SE/839703	5.	13.	4

[1] See also p. 361.   [2] See also p. 362.
[3] Also listed in the liberties of St. Peter, p. 367, and St. Leonard, p. 368.
[4] Grid ref. is to Low Mowthorpe.
[5] Also listed in the Liberty of St. Peter, p. 367.
[6] Also listed in the Liberty of the Blessed Mary of York, p. 366.
[7] Ditto, p. 366.   [8] Also listed in the Liberty of St. Peter, p. 367.
[9] Also listed in the Liberty of the Provost of Beverley, p. 369.

Gerwardby	Garrowby	SE/795573	1.	3.	0
Bridsale	Birdsall	SE/818654	4.	18.	0
Wyverthorp'	Weaverthorpe	SE/967711	3.	6.	8
Bugthorp'[1]	Bugthorpe	SE/772579		18.	0
Est Wharrum	Wharram le Street	SE/863659		16.	0
Barkthorp'	Barthorpe	SE/770595		13.	0
Housome	Howsham	SE/738629	1.	10.	0
Kenerthorp'	Kennythorpe	SE/789659		12.	0
Wetewang'[2]	Wetwang	SE/932591	5.	0.	0
Skrayngham	Scrayingham	SE/733603	2.	0.	0
Acclome	Acklam	SE/784617	1.	3.	0
Langeton'	Langton	SE/797671	3.	0.	0
Grimeston'[3]	North Grimston	SE/841678		15.	0
Edilthorp' &	Eddlethorpe[4] and	SE/773661			
Fritheby	Firby	SE/745664			
Rillington'	Rillington	SE/852743		17.	0
Skameston'	Scampston	SE/861754		12.	4
Thornthorp'	Thornthorpe	SE/782672		10.	0
			82.	12.	10

Dykeryng' [DICKERING WAPENTAKE]

Wylareby	Willerby	TA/008792	1.	8.	0
Kernetby[5]	Carnaby	TA/144656	4.	15.	0
Muston'	Muston	TA/099798	2.	6.	8
Thorp'	Thorpe	TA/110678		12.	0
Foston'[6]	Foston on the Wolds	TA/100558	1.	5.	0
Bynington'	Binnington	SE/996787	1.	12.	0
Bridlington'	Bridlington	TA/189671	6.	6.	8
Bugton' &	Buckton and	TA/183726	2.	6.	8
Bampton'	Bempton	TA/191721			
Boythorp'	Boythorpe	SE/998720		12.	0
Hundmanbi'	Hunmanby	TA/096775	6.	16.	0
Grauncemore	Gransmoor	TA/123595	1.	0.	0
Twenge	Thwing	TA/049702	4.	3.	0
Nafferton'	Nafferton	TA/055590	3.	0.	0
Galmeton'	Ganton	SE/990776	2.	10.	0
Okton'	Octon	TA/032700		14.	0
Harpham	Harpham	TA/092616	3.	0.	0
Swathorp'	Swaythorpe	TA/037690	1.	1.	0
Neuton'	Wold Newton	TA/045732	4.	6.	8
Burton' Annays	Burton Agnes	TA/102633	3.	6.	8
Brompton'	Potter Brompton	SE/979770		19.	0
Eston'	Easton	TA/153680	1.	13.	0
Foxholes	Foxholes	TA/010732	1.	13.	4
Erghome	Argam	TA/112713	2.	12.	0
Berkendale	Bartindale	TA/109730			
Flixton'	Flixton	TA/041795	2.	14.	0
Flokton'	Folkton	TA/053797	1.	13.	4
Besingby	Bessingby	TA/159660	1.	16.	0
Rudstan[7]	Rudston	TA/098678	3.	12.	0

---

[1] Also listed in the Liberty of St. Peter, p. 367.   [2] Ditto, p. 367.
[3] Ditto, p. 367.
[4] Grid ref. is to the deserted village.
[5] Also listed in the Liberty of St. Leonard, p. 368.
[6] Also listed in the Liberty of the Chapter of Beverley, p. 368.
[7] Also listed in the Liberty of the Blessed Mary of York, p. 367.

Staxton'	Staxton	TA/019792	2.	5.	0
Brigham	Brigham	TA/079538	1.	11.	0
Louthorp[1]	Lowthorpe	TA/079608	1.	5.	0
Flotmanby	Flotmanby	TA/073796		11.	0
Fordon'	Fordon	TA/049752	1.	16.	8
Butterwyk	Butterwick	SE/991714	2.	0.	0
Burton' Flemyng'	Burton Fleming	TA/083723	5.	0.	0
Hilderthorp'	Hilderthorpe	TA/175655		16.	0
Welesthorp'	Wilsthorpe	TA/170640	1.	2.	0
Suardby[2]	Sewerby	TA/202691	2.	13.	4
Alburne	Auburn	TA/167627	1.	0.	0
Fiueley	Filey	TA/116806	4.	0.	0
Grendale[3]	Grindale	TA/132712	1.	12.	0
Flamburgh'	Flamborough	TA/226702	3.	6.	8
Speton'	Speeton	TA/150746	1.	10.	0
Fraisthorp'	Fraisthorpe	TA/154617	1.	4.	0
Boynton'	Boynton	TA/136680	3.	3.	4
Garton'[4]	Garton on the Wolds	SE/982593	4.	10.	0
Wandesford	Wansford	TA/062566	1.	18.	0
Thirnu'	Thornholme	TA/115638	1.	16.	8
Carethorp'[5]	Caythorpe	TA/120678		15.	0
Pokthorp'	Pockthorpe	TA/040634		11.	0
Ryghton'[6]	Reighton	TA/131752	2.	6.	8
			114.	7.	4

Lib. Beate Marie [LIBERTY OF THE BLESSED MARY OF YORK]

Grimeston'	Hanging Grimston	SE/800607	5.	10.	0
Hunkelby	Uncleby	SE/811591			
Panesthorp'	Painsthorpe	SE/812583			
Sixendale[7]	Thixendale	SE/842611			
Kirkeby Hundhold	Kirby Underdale	SE/809586			
Raysthorp'[8]	Raisthorpe	SE/855617			
Anelaghby[9]	possibly Anlaby	TA/036288			
Folkerthorp'[10]	Foggathorpe	SE/755376		18.	0
Hornese	Hornsea	TA/201476	3.	6.	8
Northorp'	Northorpe	TA/196491		13.	4
Suththorp'	Southorpe	TA/196464	1.	6.	8
Cottyngwyth'[11]	East Cottingwith	SE/703424	2.	0.	0
Fulford[12]	Fulford	SE/610495	3.	6.	8
Estkrik'	Escrick	SE/629431	3.	10.	0
Elmeswelle	Elmswell	SE/997583	1.	16.	0
Fymmere[13]	Fimber	SE/894606	2.	6.	8

---

[1] Also listed in the Liberty of the Provost of Beverley, p. 369.
[2] Also listed in the Liberty of St. Peter, p. 367.   [3] Ditto, p. 367.
[4] Also listed in the Liberty of the Chapter of Beverley, p. 368.
[5] Also listed in the Liberty of St. Peter, p. 367.
[6] Also listed in the Liberty of the Provost of Beverley, p. 369.
[7] See also p. 364.   [8] See also p. 364.
[9] See also p. 360 and the Liberty of the Chapter of Beverley, p. 368.
[10] See also p. 360.
[11] Part of Cottingwith was taxed in the Liberty of St. Peter, p. 367.
[12] This may refer to either Gate Fulford or Water Fulford: see also the Liberty of St. Peter, p. 367.
[13] Also listed in the Liberty of the Provost of Beverley, p. 369.

			£	s.	d.
Rudstan[1]	Rudston	TA/098678	2.	13.	4
Dyghton'	Deighton	SE/627441	2.	6.	8
			29.	14.	0

Lib. Beati Petri [LIBERTY OF ST. PETER]

			£	s.	d.
Langtoft	Langtoft	TA/008670	2.	0.	0
Cotome	Cottam	SE/993648	1.	14.	0
Holm'	?		1.	5.	0
Donyngton' cum Grimeston'[2]	Dunnington with Grimston	SE/668528 SE/646515	3.	6.	0
Heslyngton'[3]	Heslington probably Water	SE/628505	1.	15.	0
Fulford	Fulford[4]	SE/610495			
Cottyngwyth	Cottingwith (East or West ?)[5]			6.	6
Ruall[6]	Riccall	SE/620378	2.	10.	0
Poklinton'[7] cum Barneby	Pocklington with Barmby Moor	SE/803490 SE/777489	3.	18.	0
South Cave[8]	South Cave	SE/917311		15.	0
Preston'[9]	Preston	TA/187306		8.	0
Suwardby[10] cum Merton'	Sewerby with Marton	TA/202691 TA/201697		17.	0
Belkthorp'	Belthorpe	SE/780541	1.	3.	4
Grendale[11]	Grindale	TA/132712	1.	4.	0
Driffeld[12]	Great Driffield	TA/022580		18.	0
Wetwang'[13]	Wetwang	SE/932591	1.	2.	0
Grimeston'[14]	North Grimston	SE/841678		10.	0
Fridaithorp'[15]	Fridaythorpe	SE/875593	1.	0.	0
Wylton'[16]	Bishop Wilton	SE/798552		10.	0
Milington'[17] & Geveldale	Millington and Little Givendale	SE/830519 SE/823530	1.	8.	0
Bugthorp'[18]	Bugthorpe	SE/772579	1.	3.	4
Skyrkenbek[19]	Skirpenbeck	SE/749573		6.	0
Hugate[20]	Huggate	SE/882556	1.	0.	0
Carethorp'[21]	Caythorpe	TA/120678		8.	0
Waghon	? part of Wawne			6.	6
Bubwith'[22]	Bubwith	SE/712362		6.	6
North Cave[23]	North Cave	SE/897328	1.	6.	0

[1] See also p. 365.　　[2] See also p. 363.

[3] See also p. 364 and the Liberty of St. Leonard, p. 368.

[4] Water Fulford is listed in this liberty in the poll tax of 1377; information, M. W. Beresford. See also p. 366.

[5] I am uncertain whether this entry refers to East or West Cottingwith; both were taxed elsewhere, pp. 363 and 368.

[6] See also p. 363.　　[7] Part of Pocklington was taxed at a tenth, p. 369.

[8] See also p. 361, and the Liberty of St. Leonard, p. 368.　　[9] See also p. 359.

[10] See also p. 366.　　[11] See also p. 366.

[12] Most of Great Driffield was assessed at a tenth, p. 369.　　[13] See also p. 365.

[14] See also p. 365.　　[15] See also p. 364.　　[16] See also p. 361.

[17] See also Millington barony, p. 370.　　[18] See also p. 365.

[19] See also p. 364.

[20] See also p. 362 and the liberties of St. Leonard, p. 368, and the Chapter of Beverley, p. 368.

[21] See also p. 366.　　[22] See also p. 360.

[23] See also p. 361 and the liberties of St. Leonard, p. 368, and the Chapter of Beverley, p. 368.

Gouthmundham[1]	Goodmanham	SE/890432	6.	0
South Burton'[2]	Bishop Burton	SE/991397	2.	6
Neubold	Newbald[3]	SE/912367	8. 6.	8

| | | 40. 1. | 4 |

Lib. Sancti Leonardi [LIBERTY OF ST. LEONARD]

Hugate[4]	Huggate	SE/882556
Kernetby[5]	Carnaby	TA/144656
Lokynton'[6]	Lockington	SE/993475
North Cave[7]	North Cave	SE/897328
South Cave[8]	South Cave	SE/917311
Broumflete	Broomfleet	SE/882272
Heslington'[9]	Heslington	SE/628505

| | | 5. 3. 4 |

Lib. Capituli Beverlaci' [LIBERTY OF THE CHAPTER OF BEVERLEY]

Anlaghby[10]	Anlaby	TA/036288
Eluelay[11]	Kirk Ella	TA/020298
North Cave[12]	North Cave	SE/897328
Santon'[13]	Sancton	SE/900395
Molecroft'[14]	Molescroft	TA/019408
Rosseby[15]	probably Risby	TA/006349
Arnal'[16]	Arnold	TA/126414
Riston'[17]	Long Riston	TA/122427
Sutton[18]	Sutton on Hull	TA/118330
Foston'[19]	Foston on the Wolds	TA/100558
Holm'[20]	probably Holme on the Wolds	SE/968463
Garton'[21]	Garton on the Wolds	SE/982593
North Burton'[22]	Cherry Burton	SE/993420
North Dalton'[23]	North Dalton	SE/934522
Etton'[24]	Etton	SE/981436
Hothum[25]	Hotham	SE/894346
Hugate[26]	Huggate	SE/882556

| | | 8. 10. 0 |

---

[1] See also p. 361.   [2] See also p. 360.   [3] Grid ref. is to North Newbald.
[4] See also pp. 362, 367, and the Liberty of the Chapter of Beverley, below.
[5] See also p. 365.
[6] See also pp. 361, 363, and the Liberty of the Provost of Beverley, p. 369.
[7] See also pp. 361, 367, and the Liberty of the Chapter of Beverley, below.
[8] See also pp. 361, 367.   [9] See also pp. 364, 367.   [10] See also pp. 360, 366.
[11] See also p. 362.   [12] See also pp. 361, 367, and above.   [13] See also p. 360.
[14] See also p. 362, and the Liberty of the Chapter of Beverley, p. 369.
[15] See also the Liberty of the Provost of Beverley, p. 369.
[16] See also p. 358.
[17] See also p. 358 and the Liberty of the Provost of Beverley, p. 369.
[18] See also p. 357.   [19] See also p. 365.   [20] See also p. 363.   [21] See also p. 366.
[22] See also the Liberty of the Provost of Beverley, p. 369.
[23] See also p. 362 and the Liberty of the Provost of Beverley, p. 369.
[24] See also p. 361 and the Liberty of the Provost of Beverley, p. 369.
[25] See also pp. 360, 363.   [26] See also pp. 362, 367, and above.

Lib. Prepositur' Beverlaci' [LIBERTY OF THE PROVOST OF BEVERLEY]

Bverlac'	Beverley	TA/033396	7.	0.	0
Flinton'[1]	Flinton	TA/220361	26.	0.	0
Patrington'[2]	Patrington	TA/316225			
Brandesburton'[3]	Brandesburton	TA/119476			
Sighelsthorn'	Sigglesthorne	TA/153456			
Skulcote[4]	Sculcoates	TA/115305			
Dripol	Drypool	TA/106289			
Seton	Seaton	TA/162469			
Welwyk'	Welwick	TA/341211			
Bilton'[5]	Bilton	TA/156326			
Wighton[5]	Wyton	TA/179334			
Wythenwyk'[6]	Withernwick	TA/194406			
Catwik'[7]	Catwick	TA/131454			
Otringham[8]	Ottringham	TA/268243			
Walkurton'[9]	Walkington	SE/997371			
Resseby[10]	Risby	TA/006349			
Genelyng'	Gembling	TA/110570			
North Dalton'[11]	North Dalton	SE/934522			
Kelk Magna	Great Kelk	TA/103581			
Lokinton'[12]	Lockington	SE/993475			
Etton'[13]	Etton	SE/981436			
North Burton'[14]	Cherry Burton	SE/993420			
Molscroft'[15]	Molescroft	TA/019408			
Louthorp'[16]	Lowthorpe	TA/079608			
Midelton'[17]	Middleton on the Wolds	SE/947496			
Ryghton'[18]	Reighton	TA/131752			
Fymmere[19] cum Touthorp'[20]	Fimber with Towthorpe	SE/894606 SE/901630			
South Dalton'	South Dalton	SE/968455			
Hasthorp'	Haisthorpe	TA/128647			
Leven	Leven	TA/106453			
Ruda[21]	Routh	TA/091424			
Hoton'[22]	Hutton	TA/023533			
Crauncewyk[23]	Cranswick	TA/025522			
Reston'[24]	Long Riston	TA/122427			
			33.	0.	0

[ANCIENT DEMESNES]

Poklinton'[25]	Pocklington	SE/803490	8.	12.	0	[T]
Killum[26]	Kilham	TA/063643	10.	15.	0	[T]
Driffeld[27]	Great Driffield	TA/022580	10.	0.	0	[T]
			29.	7.	0	[T]

[1] See also p. 359.   [2] See also p. 358.   [3] See also p. 359.
[4] See also p. 361.   [5] See also p. 359.   [6] See also p. 358.
[7] See also p. 359.   [8] See also p. 358.   [9] See also p. 363.
[10] See also p. 368.   [11] See also pp. 362, 368.   [12] See also pp. 361, 363, 368.
[13] See also pp. 361, 368.   [14] See also p. 368.   [15] See also pp. 362, 368.
[16] See also p. 366.   [17] See also p. 360.   [18] See also p. 366.
[19] See also p. 366.   [20] See also p. 364.   [21] See also p. 358.
[22] See also p. 361.   [23] See also p. 361.   [24] See also pp. 358, 368.
[25] Part of Pocklington was taxed at a fifteenth, p. 367.   [26] Ditto, p. 370.
[27] Ditto, p. 367.

[BOROUGHS]

Ravenesrode	Ravenser Odd[1]	lost	15.	0.	0	[T]
Kyngeston' super Hull'	Kingston upon Hull	TA/100292	33.	6.	8	[T][2]
Hedon'	Hedon	TA/188287	10.	13.	4	[T]

Adhuc Herthill' [HARTHILL WAPENTAKE]

Sidse	Sicey	TA/084362	2.	6.	0
Wodmanse &	Woodmansey and	TA/062375			
Thorn'	Thearne	TA/073367			

Adhuc Herthill' [HARTHILL WAPENTAKE]

Millyngton' de Baronia[3]	Millington	SE/830519		9.	0
Raventhorp'	Raventhorpe	TA/004425		10.	0
Witheley	Weedley	SE/954330	1.	6.	8
Sunderlandwyk[4]	Sunderlandwick	TA/010550		10.	0
Kelingthorp'	Kelleythorpe	TA/012564		9.	0
			5.	10.	8

Houden' [HOWDENSHIRE LIBERTY]

Ake	Aike	TA/049459		15.	0

Dykering' [DICKERING WAPENTAKE]

Killum [man.][5]	Kilham	TA/063643	1.	0.	0

EAST RIDING TOTAL: £979. 6. 0[6]

HULL: £ 33. 6. 8

---

[1] For the site of this port see G. de Boer, 'Spurn Head: its history and evolution', *Trans. Inst. British Geographers*, 34 (1964), 82.

[2] Quota given as 50 marks. Hull fined for 50 marks in 1334 and its quota does not appear on the 1334 Account for the East Riding, E 179/202/36.

[3] See also p. 367.　　　　　　　　　　　　　　　　　　　　　　　[4] See also p. 361.

[5] Kilham was mostly taxed at a tenth, p. 369. There is a note on E 179/202/43 to the effect that Rysome is not included here because it was taxed with Holmpton in Holderness, p. 358.

[6] As on 1334 Account, E 179/202/36. Of this total £924. 5. 8 is the fifteenth and £55. 0. 4 the tenth. The quotas at a fifteenth on E 179/202/43 add up to £925. 6. 0 and I have been unable to locate the discrepancy of £1. 0. 4 from 1334. On most documents there is an additional charge against the Archbishop of York for rents in Beverley but the amount varies from one tax to another and the sum is not included in the total for the East Riding.

YORKSHIRE: NORTH RIDING

Richem' [RICHMONDSHIRE]

Halikeld [HALIKELD WAPENTAKE]

Thornton'	Thornton Bridge	SE/430714	1.	13.	4
Cundal' &	Cundall and	SE/422731			
Letteby	Leckby	SE/415745			
Mildeby cum	Milby with	SE/402678		12.	0
Hundburton'[1]	Humburton	SE/421686			
Kirkeby super Moram	Kirby Hill	SE/393686	1.	6.	0
Diceford	Dishforth	SE/382731	1.	13.	4
Aystenby	Asenby	SE/398752	1.	6.	0
Ranyngton' cum	Rainton with	SE/370752	1.	0.	0
Neuby	Newby	SE/380760			
Melmorby	Melmerby	SE/334768	1.	0.	0
Midelton' Qwerenhow	Middleton Quernhow	SE/333783	1.	0.	0
Wath'	Wath	SE/325771	1.	3.	4
Estanfeld	East Tanfield	SE/289779	1.	18.	0
Westanfeld	West Tanfield	SE/268788	1.	13.	4
Kyrtlyngton'	Kirklington	SE/319811	1.	6.	0
Sutton'	Sutton Howgrave	SE/317791		8.	6
Carthorp'	Carthorpe	SE/307837	2.	0.	0
Aynderby Qwerenhowe	Ainderby Quernhow	SE/350809		16.	0
Synderby	Sinderby	SE/346821		18.	0
Pykhall'	Pickhill	SE/347837	1.	16.	0
Swaynby	Swainby	SE/337855		18.	0
Gaytanby	Gatenby	SE/324879		16.	0
Thexton'	Theakston	SE/301856	2.	2.	0
Eskelby	Exelby	SE/295870	2.	10.	0
Norton in Luto	Norton le Clay	SE/407712		16.	0

Hang' [HANG WAPENTAKE]

Scorueton'	Scruton	SE/300925		15.	0
Fencots	Fencote[2]	SE/283936	1.	4.	0
Kyrkeby Fletham	Kirkby Fleetham	SE/284944	1.	15.	8
Caterygg'	Catterick	SE/240980	2.	3.	0
Burgh'	Brough	SE/215980		13.	4
Colburn	Colburn	SE/198991	1.	3.	0
Hippeswell'	Hipswell	SE/188983		17.	0
Tunstall'	Tunstall	SE/217958	1.	4.	0
Apeltons'	East and West	SE/236957	1.	2.	0
	Appleton[3]				
Crakhall'	Crakehall[4]	SE/240902	1.	14.	0
Bedal'	Bedale	SE/266884	1.	6.	8
Aykescogh'	Aiskew	SE/271884	2.	3.	4
Borel' cum	Burrill with	SE/239872	1.	2.	0
Collyng'	Cowling	SE/237876			
Patrikbrumpton'	Patrick Brompton	SE/219907	1.	16.	0

---

[1] Part of Humburton was taxed at a tenth in the West Riding (Knaresborough liberty, p. 395).

[2] Grid ref. is to Great Fencote but the entry probably refers to both Great and Little.

[3] Grid ref. is to East Appleton; both are deserted villages.

[4] Grid ref. is to Great Crakehall.

Hakford	Hackforth	SE/243932	I.	4.	o
Neuton' cum	Newton le Willows	SE/214895	I.	14.	o
Ryswyk'	with Ruswick	SE/195895			
Aynderby cum	Ainderby Mires with	SE/257927	I.	2.	o
Holtby	Holtby	SE/268922			
Thornton' Watlous	Thornton Watlass	SE/232853	I.	4.	o
Snap cum	Snape with	SE/266843		18.	o
Thorppirrowe	Thorp Perrow	SE/262855			
Well' cum	Well with	SE/268820		18.	o
Nosterfeld	Nosterfield	SE/278804			
Hunton'	Hunton	SE/190926	I.	2.	o
Heselton'	Hessleton	SE/199917		12.	o
Burton super Yore	Burton on Ure	SE/227827	I.	6.	8
Massham	Masham	SE/227807	I.	14.	o
Thyrn cum	Thirn with	SE/216859		6.	o
Clifton'	Clifton on Ure	SE/218844			
Swynton'	Swinton	SE/213798		13.	4
Ilketon'	Ilton	SE/187782		15.	4
Helagh'	Healey	SE/183806		15.	4
Fegherby	Fearby	SE/193810		15.	4
Ellyngtons'	Ellington[1]	SE/198833	I.	8.	8
Ellyngstryng'	Ellingstring	SE/174838		6.	8
Baynbrigg' cum	Bainbridge	SD/933901	4.	o.	o
Uall'	?				
Askrygg'	Askrigg	SD/948910	I.	17.	o
Thornton' Rust'	Thornton Rust	SD/972889	I.	2.	o
Kerperby	Carperby	SE/005898	2.	o.	o
Aykesgarth'	Aysgarth	SE/003884	I.	5.	o
Thoraldby	Thoralby	SE/001867	2.	13.	o
Estboulton'	East Bolton	SE/041909	I.	2.	o
Westboulton'	West Bolton	SE/020910		13.	4
Thoresby	Thoresby	SE/030900		6.	o
Ridmer'	Redmire	SE/045912	I.	8.	4
Preston'	Preston under Scar	SE/071911		16.	o
Westwytton'	West Witton	SE/061885		15.	o
Ellerton' cum	Ellerton with	SE/078972	I.	10.	o
Staynton'	Stainton	SE/103965			
Walburn'	Walburn	SE/119959		15.	o
Dunun'	Downholme	SE/113978		15.	4
Hudeswell'	Hudswell	NZ/141004		14.	o
Bellerby	Bellerby	SE/115928		15.	o
Berden'	Barden	SE/147937	I.	2.	o
Westhaukeswell'	West Hauxwell	SE/165930	I.	2.	o
Esthaukeswell'	East Hauxwell	SE/168938	I.	10.	o
Layborn'	Leyburn	SE/113904	I.	16.	o
Hernby	Harmby	SE/128896		8.	o
Spenythorn	Spennithorne	SE/138890	2.	1.	o
Danby super Yhore	Danby on Ure	SE/171869	I.	10.	o
Thornton' Steuard	Thornton Steward	SE/179871	I.	15.	o
Burton' Conestable	Constable Burton	SE/169908		13.	o
Huton' Hang'	Hutton Hang	SE/170888		8.	6
Fynghall'	Finghall	SE/181897		12.	o
Estwytton'	East Witton	SE/147860	2.	16.	8
Wencelaw'	Wensley	SE/092895	I.	2.	o
Grynton'	Grinton	SE/046984	I.	14.	o
Midelham	Middleham	SE/127879		15.	o
Coverham	Coverham	SE/104863		13.	o

[1] Grid ref. is to High Ellington but the entry probably refers to both High and Low.

Carlton' in Coverdale	Carlton	SE/064846	1.	12.	8
Caldbergh'	Caldbergh	SE/093850		16.	0
Westscrafton'	West Scrafton	SE/073836		11.	0
Melmorby	Melmerby	SE/076853		11.	0
Burton' in Bisshopedale	West Burton	SE/017865	2.	12.	0
Scotton'	Scotton	SE/190959		6.	8
Hornby	Hornby	SE/222937	1.	0.	0

Gyllyng' [GILLING WAPENTAKE]

Mikkelton'	Mickleton	NY/969237		14.	0
Hunderthwayt'	Hunderthwaite	NY/985211		15.	0
Cotherston'	Cotherstone	NZ/012193		15.	0
Lyrtyngton'	Lartington	NZ/015176		17.	6
Boghes	Bowes	NY/993136	2.	0.	0
Stretford'	Startforth	NZ/048159	1.	4.	0
Brygenhale	Brignall	NZ/072123	1.	0.	0
Rokeby	Rokeby	NZ/084144		16.	0
Thorpmortham	Thorpe and	NZ/104142	1.	2.	0
	Mortham	NZ/086142			
Wyclif' cum	Wycliffe with	NZ/117143		10.	0
Gryllyngton'	Girlington	NZ/128138			
Ulvyngton'	Ovington	NZ/132147		12.	0
Huton' Longuilers	Hutton Magna	NZ/127124	1.	0.	0
Berford[1]	Barforth	NZ/162167		13.	6
Cliff'	Cliffe	NZ/205152	1.	0.	0
Appelby super Tese	Eppleby	NZ/179133	1.	10.	0
Caldwell'	Caldwell	NZ/162134	1.	3.	4
Forset	Forcett	NZ/176123		18.	0
Staynwegges	Stanwick	NZ/185120		13.	4
Westlaton'	West Layton	NZ/142100		10.	0
Estlaton'	East Layton	NZ/163098	1.	0.	0
Aldburgh'	Aldbrough	NZ/202113	1.	10.	0
Melsamby	Melsonby	NZ/201084	1.	0.	0
Gyllyng' cum	Gilling West with	NZ/182051	1.	10.	0
Hertford'	Hartforth	NZ/171062			
Skytheby	Skeeby	NZ/201026	1.	0.	0
Eseby	Easby	NZ/185003		16.	0
Ask'	Aske	NZ/178034		5.	0
Ravenswath'[2]	Ravensworth	NZ/141078	1.	10.	0
Daltons'[3]	Dalton	NZ/115083	1.	6.	8
Neusom cum	Newsham with	NZ/107100		18.	0
Broghtonlyth'	Broughton Lythe	lost			
Bernyngham	Barningham	NZ/085104	1.	0.	0
Skargill' cum	Scargill with	NZ/051106	1.	0.	0
Rotherford	Rutherford	NZ/032118			
Mersk'	Marske	NZ/104005	1.	6.	8
Marrygg'	Marrick	SE/075981	1.	0.	0
Rych' c.h	Richmond [with hamlets]	NZ/173010	8.	0.	0
Richem'[4]	Richmond	NZ/173010	5.	0.	0

[1] *Hertford* on E 179/211/10 is an error. Hartforth is listed with Gilling, below.

[2] Part of Ravensworth was taxed in the Liberty of St. Mary and St. Leonard, p. 380.

[3] This entry probably refers to three Daltons already distinguished by 1334 (*E.P.N.S.*, V, *Yorks. N.R.* (1928), 290).

[4] This entry probably refers to the town of Richmond (curiously not a taxation borough in the early fourteenth century and therefore not taxed at the higher rate of the tenth), whereas the preceding entry is for Richmond *extra* and outlying hamlets.

Arkylgarth'[1]	Arkengarthdale	NZ/009020	1.	10.	0
Manfeld	Manfield	NZ/222133	1.	4.	8
Clesebi	Cleasby	NZ/251130		18.	0
Stapilton'	Stapleton	NZ/263122		18.	0
Croft'[2]	Croft	NZ/288098	1.	9.	4
Northcouton'	North Cowton	NZ/283039		12.	0
Southcouton'	South Cowton	NZ/293026		16.	0
Templecouton'	East Cowton	NZ/307032	1.	6.	8
Barton'	Barton	NZ/230090		15.	0
Midelton'	Middleton Tyas	NZ/235056	1.	4.	0
Multon'	Moulton	NZ/236037	1.	0.	0
Scorton'	Scorton	NZ/252002	1.	3.	0
Ellerton'	Ellerton on Swale	SE/256979		19.	0
Kyplyng'	Kiplin	SE/272977		14.	0
Magna Langton'	Great Langton	SE/294964		18.	0
Parva Langton'	Little Langton	SE/303955		18.	0
Danby super Wysk'	Danby Wiske	SE/338983	1.	8.	0
Yafford	Yafforth	SE/343945		16.	0
Warlaudby	Warlaby	SE/350914		13.	4
Neuby	Newby Wiske	SE/367877		10.	0
Morton'	Morton on Swale	SE/326920	1.	10.	0
Mauneby	Maunby	SE/352864	1.	4.	0
Brumpton' super Swale	Brompton on Swale	SE/216997		18.	0
Aynderby Wythesteple	Ainderby Steeple	SE/334921		14.	0
Kyrkeby Wysk'	Kirby Wiske	SE/377848		8.	0
Solbergh'	Solberge	SE/355891		8.	0
Thyrntoft'	Thrintoft	SE/323933	1.	0.	0
Eryum	Eryholme	NZ/320090	1.	8.	8
Neuton' Morel'	Newton Morrell	NZ/240095		11.	9
			187.	12.	1

Langbergh' [LANGBARGH WAPENTAKE]

Yarum	Yarm	NZ/417129	9.	0.	0
Ingelby sub Erenclif'	Ingleby Arncliffe	NZ/452002	1.	9.	0
Rungeton'	Rounton[3]	NZ/422033	1.	4.	0
Wyrksale	Low Worsall	NZ/392100		17.	0
Kyrklevyngton'	Kirk Leavington	NZ/431099		16.	4
Castellevyngton'	Castle Leavington	NZ/461103		8.	0
Thwerlton'	Whorlton	NZ/484025	1.	4.	0
Pothow	Potto	NZ/473037		15.	0
Huton' iuxta Rudby	Hutton Rudby	NZ/468064	1.	6.	8
Scotherskelf'	Skutterskelfe	NZ/483071		6.	8
Midelton'	Middleton on Leven	NZ/465099		18.	0
Hilton'	Hilton	NZ/465113	1.	5.	4
Semer'	Seamer	NZ/498103	1.	0.	0
Neuby	Newby	NZ/508122	1.	4.	0
Stokesley	Stokesley	NZ/526085	1.	4.	0
Nunthorp'	Nunthorpe	NZ/541133		18.	0
Magna Upsale cum Morton'	Upsall with Morton	NZ/563160 NZ/555145		16.	0
Tunstall'	Tunstall	NZ/531124		10.	0

---

[1] This entry probably refers to scattered settlements in Arkengarthdale. The grid ref. is to Arkle Town.

[2] Part of Croft was taxed with Smeaton in the Liberty of St. Mary and St. Leonard, p. 380.

[3] Grid ref. is to East Rounton.

Neuton' sub Osenbergh'	Newton	NZ/569133		13.	4
Pynchunthorp'	Pinchinthorpe	NZ/578142	1.	0.	0
Hoton' iuxta Gysborn'	Hutton Lowcross	NZ/601139	1.	0.	0
Carlton'	Carlton	NZ/507045		6.	8
Buskby	Busby[1]	NZ/523057		13.	4
Magna Broughton'	Broughton	NZ/547063		16.	0
Parva Broughton'	Little Broughton	NZ/560068		6.	8
Eseby	Easby	NZ/578088	1.	0.	0
Aton'	Ayton	NZ/558109	2.	7.	0
Grenhow	Greenhow	NZ/c.595035	1.	4.	0
Ingelby sub Grenhow	Ingleby Greenhow	NZ/581063	1.	6.	8
Bathersby	Battersby	NZ/595075	1.	0.	0
Gysborn'	Guisborough	NZ/613160	4.	0.	0
Toucots	Tocketts	NZ/619175		10.	0
Ingelby cum Berewyk'	Ingleby with Barwick	NZ/432132 NZ/432146		16.	0
Thormotby	Thornaby on Tees	NZ/450183		13.	4
Leuenthorp'	Linthorpe	NZ/490190	1.	4.	0
Aclom	Acklam	NZ/485173	2.	0.	0
Staynton' cum Thornton'	Stainton with Thornton	NZ/481141 NZ/479138	1.	6.	8
Maltby	Maltby	NZ/466133		13.	4
Hemelyngton'	Hemlington	NZ/501143		16.	0
Marton'	Marton	NZ/516158	2.	10.	0
Ormesby	Ormesby	NZ/531167	2.	10.	0
Normanby	Normanby	NZ/547182	1.	6.	0
Eston'	Eston	NZ/548188	1.	12.	0
Lackenby	Lackenby	NZ/564194		18.	0
Laysyngby	Lazenby	NZ/572198		16.	0
Wylton'	Wilton	NZ/582198	1.	6.	8
Lythom cum Estcotom	Kirkleatham with Coatham	NZ/593218 NZ/595251	3.	13.	4
Mersk'	Marske by the Sea	NZ/633223	2.	0.	0
Skelton'	Skelton	NZ/660190	2.	0.	0
Brotton'	Brotton	NZ/692198	1.	0.	0
Kylton' cum Thorp'	Kilton with Kilton Thorpe	NZ/700183 NZ/693177		13.	4
Eggeton'	Egton	NZ/810058	2.	15.	0
Lyth'	Lythe	NZ/850132	1.	10.	0
Ugthorp'	Ugthorpe	NZ/799111		13.	0
Mikelby	Mickleby	NZ/802130		13.	4
Aselby	Aislaby	NZ/857086		6.	8
Hoton' iuxta Molgreve	Hutton Mulgrave	NZ/835100		14.	0
Ellerdeby	Ellerby	NZ/799147	1.	3.	0
Hilderswell'	Hinderwell	NZ/793166	1.	10.	0
Neuton' in Whytebystrand'	Newton Mulgrave	NZ/789156		13.	0
Rouceby	Roxby	NZ/761163		16.	0
Berghby	Borrowby	NZ/770156		12.	0
Esyngton'	Easington	NZ/743180	1.	2.	0
Lofthous	Loftus	NZ/722183	2.	10.	0
Lyverton'	Liverton	NZ/712158		16.	0
Barnby cum Pyckton'	Barnby with Picton	NZ/827125 NZ/416075	1.	10.	0
Fayceby cum Sexhowe	Faceby with Sexhow	NZ/495031 NZ/477062		13.	4
Kyrkeby cum Dromondby	Kirkby with Dromonby	NZ/539061 NZ/534057		10.	0

---

[1] Grid ref. is to Great Busby.

			£.	s.	d.
Kildale	Kildale	NZ/603095	1.	0.	0
Danby cum Glasdale & Staynesby[1]	Danby with Glaisdale and ?	NZ/708085 NZ/774053	3.	18.	8
Crathorn'	Crathorne	NZ/442075	1.	4.	0
Westerdale	Westerdale	NZ/664058	1.	10.	0
			95.	0.	4

Bulmer' [BULMER WAPENTAKE]

			£.	s.	d.
Huntyngton' c.h	Huntington [with hamlets]	SE/618562		18.	0
Stocton'	Stockton on the Forest	SE/657560		14.	0
Holtby	Holtby	SE/675542		14.	0
Sandhuton'	Sand Hutton	SE/695585	1.	0.	0
Buttercramb'	Buttercrambe	SE/734581	1.	10.	0
Barnby cum Boscal'	Barnby with Bossall	SE/726610 SE/718608		18.	0
Flaxton'	Flaxton	SE/679623		15.	0
Barton'	Barton le Willows	SE/713633		18.	0
Huton' super Derwent	Hutton[2]	SE/762677		16.	0
Conysthorp'	Coneysthorpe	SE/712714		13.	4
Hilderskelf' cum Gamelthorp'	Hinderskelfe with Ganthorpe	SE/719700 SE/689703		16.	0
Bulmer	Bulmer	SE/699676		16.	0
Stittenum	Stittenham	SE/679676		17.	0
Hoton' Shirreff'	Sheriff Hutton	SE/657663	1.	0.	2
Cornburgh'	Cornbrough	SE/630670	1.	2.	3½
Ferlyngton' cum Westlyllyng'	Farlington with West Lilling	SE/614675 SE/648650		15.	0
Tyueryngton'	Terrington	SE/671708	2.	0.	0
Wygynthorp'	Wiganthorpe	SE/663724		12.	0
Brandesby cum Steresby	Brandsby[3] cum Stearsby	SE/589719 SE/610715	1.	8.	0
Sutton' in Galtres	Sutton on the Forest	SE/582647	1.	10.	0
Aldwerk'	Aldwark	SE/467633		14.	2
Thorlthorp' cum Flathwath'	Tholthorpe with Flawith	SE/475670 SE/482653	1.	2.	0
Brafferton'	Brafferton	SE/436702		16.	8
Thormotby	Thormanby	SE/496750		15.	0
Scouesby	Skewsby	SE/628710		16.	8
Welborn'	Welburn	SE/721678		14.	2
Lynton' cum Yholton'	Linton on Ouse with Youlton	SE/496606 SE/491635	1.	13.	4
Quenby	Whenby	SE/631699		6.	8
Raskelf'	Raskelf	SE/490708		8.	0
			26.	19.	5½

Rydale [RYEDALE WAPENTAKE]

			£.	s.	d.
Bildesdale	Bilsdale[4]	NZ/566004	1.	2.	0
Skalton'	Scawton	SE/549836		13.	0

[1] Possibly Stainsby in Stainton (NZ/463158) but this is a long way from the other two places.

[2] Grid ref. is to Low Hutton.   [3] Grid ref. is to the deserted village.

[4] The townships of Bilsdale cover a large area; the entry probably includes many small places within the dale.

			£	s.	d.
Pokley	Pockley	SE/638859		16.	0
Nalton'[1] cum	Nawton with	SE/656847		13.	4
Bodelom	Beadlam	SE/652846			
Wymbelton'[2]	Wombleton	SE/669839		15.	0
Kyrkebymoresheued	Kirkbymoorside	SE/696866	7.	3.	4
Edeston'	Edstone	SE/705840		18.	0
Mouscots	Muscoates	SE/690802	1.	0.	0
Berghes	Barugh	SE/747790		12.	0
Habtons'	Habton	SE/758763		15.	0
Ryton'	Ryton	SE/793755	1.	4.	0
Oswaldkyrk' cum	Oswaldkirk with	SE/621789	1.	10.	0
Ampelford[3]	Ampleforth	SE/583787			
Helmesley	Helmsley	SE/612838	3.	16.	0
Sproxton'	Sproxton	SE/613815	1.	8.	0
Nonyngton'[4]	Nunnington	SE/666791	2.	8.	0
Nesse	Ness[5]	SE/688792	2.	0.	0
Harum	Harome	SE/647821	1.	6.	0
Southolm'	South Holme	SE/701774	1.	0.	0
Calueton'	Cawton	SE/642767	1.	0.	0
Hovyngham	Hovingham	SE/666757	2.	2.	0
Slengesby	Slingsby	SE/697750	2.	0.	0
Barton'	Barton le Street	SE/721742		10.	0
Butterwyk' cum	Butterwick with	SE/731774	1.	0.	0
Neusom	Newsham	SE/c.740760			
Apelton'	Appleton le Street	SE/734736		8.	0
Aymonderby	Amotherby	SE/751734	1.	0.	0
Swynton'	Swinton	SE/758732		6.	8
Stayngrif' cum	Stonegrave with	SE/656779	1.	0.	0
Rycolf'	Riccal	SE/678806			
Vet' Malton'	Old Malton	SE/799725	2.	3.	4
How &	Howe and	SE/806753			
Wycomb'	Wykeham	SE/816752			
Nova Malton'	[New] Malton	SE/786717	3.	6.	8
Fryton'	Fryton	SE/688750		10.	0
Colton'	Coulton	SE/636742		8.	0
De grang' & cot'			2.	15.	4
Abbatis Ryenall' ad					
firmam dimissis					
			47.	9.	8

Brudford [BIRDFORTH WAPENTAKE]

			£	s.	d.
Welbergh'	Welbury	NZ/400022	1.	4.	0
Estherlsay	East Harlsey	SE/424998	1.	6.	8
Parva Sylton'	Over Silton	SE/451933		17.	0
Sylton' Paynell'	Nether Silton	SE/457923	1.	0.	0
Kepwyk'[6]	Kepwick	SE/468908	1.	8.	0
Couesby	Cowesby	SE/464900		18.	0
Kyrkebyknoll'	Kirby Knowle	SE/468873		13.	0
Boltby	Boltby	SE/491866	1.	10.	0

[1] Part of Nawton was taxed with Wombleton in the Liberty of St. Peter, p. 379.
[2] Part of Wombleton was taxed with Nawton in the Liberty of St. Peter, p. 379.
[3] Parts of Ampleforth were taxed in the liberties of St. Peter, p. 379, and Whitby and Byland, p. 381.
[4] Part of Nunnington was taxed in the Liberty of St. Mary and St. Leonard, p. 380.
[5] Grid ref. is to West Ness.
[6] Part of Kepwick was taxed in Allerton liberty, p. 379.

			£	s.	d.
Thirlby	Thirlby	SE/487840	1.	0.	0
Halmby	Hawnby	SE/542898		18.	0
Dale	Dale Town	SE/535885	1.	10.	0
Kilborn'	Kilburn	SE/513796	1.	2.	0
Cokewald	Coxwold	SE/533772	1.	10.	0
Ulueston'	Oulston	SE/547745	1.	6.	0
Yheuersley	Yearsley	SE/585744	1.	9.	0
Brudford	Birdforth	SE/487758	1.	8.	0
Crakhale cum	Crakehill with	SE/430735		16.	0
Elmetmer'	Eldmire	SE/421747			
Dalton'	Dalton	SE/435763	1.	0.	0
Topclif' cum	Topcliffe with	SE/400760	1.	4.	10
Grysthwayt	Gristhwaite	SE/425785			
Catton'	Catton	SE/370780	1.	6.	8
Skypton'	Skipton on Swale	SE/368798	1.	10.	0
Neusom cum	Newsham with	SE/379848	1.	6.	0
Brakenbergh'	Breckenbrough	SE/383833			
Thornton' in Mora	Thornton le Moor	SE/393883	1.	12.	0
Southkylvyngton'	South Kilvington	SE/426840		18.	0
Upsale cum	Upsall with	SE/453872	1.	4.	0
Thornbergh'	Thornbrough	SE/427847			
Thurkelby	Thirkleby	SE/473787	1.	10.	0
Carlton' cum	Carlton Miniott with	SE/395810		17.	0
Iselbeck'	Islebeck[1]	SE/447775			
Sourby	Sowerby	SE/432814	1.	10.	0
Thresk'	Thirsk	SE/430820	6.	0.	0
Sandhoton'	Sandhutton	SE/382820	1.	0.	0
Thornton' cum	Thornton on the Hill	SE/532741		14.	0
Baxby	with Baxby	SE/512752			
De grang' & cot'			1.	14.	8
Abbatis Ryenall' ad					
firmam dimissis					
			43.	2.	10

Lib. Aluerton' [ALLERTON LIBERTY]

			£	s.	d.
Didensale	Over Dinsale	NZ/349116		16.	0
Grysby	Girsby	NZ/354083		12.	0
Wyrksale	High Worsall	NZ/387093		14.	0
Hornby	Hornby	NZ/362054		8.	8
Thorprowe	Thorpe Row	NZ/355045			
Westrongton' cum	West Rounton with	NZ/413034		16.	8
Irby	Irby	NZ/410030			
Dyghton'	Deighton	NZ/381018		14.	0
Bretteby	Birkby	NZ/331024		5.	0
Hoton' super Wysk'	Hutton Bonville	NZ/336002		12.	0
Brumpton'	Brompton	SE/373963	1.	0.	0
Wynton'	Winton	SE/410966	1.	4.	0
Westherlsay	West Harlsey	SE/415981		13.	4
Ellerbeck'	Ellerbeck	SE/433967		18.	0
Osmunderle	Osmotherley	SE/456972		12.	0
Thimbelby cum	Thimbleby with	SE/450954	1.	0.	0
Foxton'	Foxton	SE/422962			
Siggeston'	Sigston	SE/426947		18.	0
Hoton' Coygners	Hutton Conyers	SE/323733		18.	0

[1] Grid ref. is to the deserted village.

Norton' Coygners	Norton Conyers	SE/319763	1.	5.	0
Holm cum	Holme with	SE/356823		15.	0
Hougrave	Howgrave	SE/314793			
Heton' Ceszay[1]	Hutton Sessay	SE/475762	1.	10.	0
	Sessay	SE/456754			
Thornton' in Strata	Thornton le Street	SE/414862	2.	2.	0
Knayngton'	Knayton	SE/433880	2.	18.	0
Berouby	Borrowby	SE/428893	1.	8.	4
Kepwyk'[2]	Kepwick	SE/468908		8.	0
Landmot	Landmoth	SE/425927		15.	0
Sourby	Sowerby under	SE/412936		17.	0
	Cotcliffe				
Northkylvyngton'	North Kilvington	SE/423855	1.	10.	0
Romondby	Romanby	SE/360933		14.	4
Thornton' in Viuar'	Thornton le Beans	SE/399905	1.	4.	0
Northaluerton'	Northallerton	SE/368942	4.	0.	0
Northotryngton'	North Otterington	SE/363897		16.	4
			32.	4.	8

Lib. Sancti Petri' [LIBERTY OF ST. PETER]

Osbaldwyk'	Osbaldwick	SE/635519		18.	4
Warthill'	Warthill	SE/674553		10.	0
Hemelsay cum Brygg'[3]	Helmsley with the	SE/691552		18.	0
	bridge				
Haxby	Haxby	SE/607583	1.	13.	4
Wygyngton'	Wigginton	SE/601584		10.	0
Strensale	Strensall	SE/630607	1.	16.	0
Styuelyngton'	Stillington	SE/583678		17.	6
Husthwayt	Husthwaite	SE/518751		15.	10
Carlton'	Carlton Husthwaite	SE/499767		10.	0
Ampelford[4]	Ampleforth	SE/583787		16.	0
Saleton' &	Salton and	SE/717799	2.	4.	7
Brawby	Brawby	SE/738782			
Nalton' cum	Nawton with	SE/656847		12.	0
Wymbelton'[5]	Wombleton	SE/669839			
Dalton' super Tese	Dalton on Tees	NZ/297080		11.	0
Helperby	Helperby	SE/439698		12.	0
Alne	Alne	SE/495653		18.	0
Tollerton'	Tollerton	SE/509640	1.	10.	0
Skelton' cum	Skelton with	SE/568565		18.	0
Rouclif'[6]	Rawcliffe	SE/582552			
Clifton'[7]	Clifton	SE/593532		13.	4
Bouthom[8]	Bootham	SE/600524	1.	4.	0
Moreton'	Murton	SE/649527		18.	0
			19.	5.	11

---

[1] Identified as two places; the name appears as *Hoton et Cessay* in the *Nomina Villarum* of 1316 (*F.A.* vi. 187).

[2] See also p. 377.

[3] It is likely that this entry refers to Gate and Upper Helmsley; the bridge was that across the Derwent to Stamford Bridge in the East Riding.

[4] See also pp. 377, 381.   [5] See also p. 377.

[6] Partly taxed in the Liberty of St. Mary and St. Leonard, p. 380.

[7] Ditto, p. 380.   [8] Ditto, p. 380.

Lib. Sancte Marie & Sancti Leonardi
[LIBERTY OF ST. MARY AND ST. LEONARD]

Clifton'[1]	Clifton	SE/593532		10.	0
Rouclif'[2]	Rawcliffe	SE/582552		10.	0
Overton'	Overton	SE/553557	1.	16.	8
Schupton'	Shipton	SE/553590	1.	6.	8
Myton'	Myton on Swale	SE/439666	1.	8.	0
Spaunton'	Spaunton	SE/724899	1.	6.	8
Hoton'	Hutton le Hole	SE/704900	1.	10.	0
Apelton'	Appleton le Moors	SE/734881	1.	6.	8
Normanby cum	Normanby with	SE/734816		13.	4
Kyrkebymysperton'	Kirby Misperton	SE/779795			
Gyllyng'	Gilling East	SE/616769		18.	4
Nonyngton'[3]	Nunnington	SE/666791		3.	0
Foston'	Foston	SE/699652		12.	0
Thornton'	Thornton le Clay	SE/683652		15.	0
Estlyllyng'	East Lilling	SE/664645		13.	0
Brynyston'	Burneston	SE/309849	1.	16.	0
Gilmanby	Gilmonby	NY/995130		12.	0
Smetheton'[4] cum	Smeaton with	NZ/348044		15.	0
Croft'[5]	Croft	NZ/288098			
Kyrkeby Ravenswath'	Kirby Ravensworth	NZ/140065		10.	0
Langthorn	Langthorne	SE/250917		16.	0
Harton' cum	Harton with	SE/680622	2.	10.	0
Claxton'	Claxton	SE/694602			
Dalby	Dalby	SE/638712		8.	8
Heworth'	Heworth	SE/618527		5.	0
Bouthom[6]	Bootham	SE/600524	1.	0.	0
Neuton super Usam cum	Newton on Ouse with	SE/511600	3.	6.	8
Benyngburgh'	Beningbrough	SE/530577			
How	Howe	SE/359803		12.	0
			26.	0.	8

Lib. Whyteby & Bellalanda [LIBERTY OF WHITBY AND BYLAND]

Hakenesse	Hackness	SE/969905	2.	0.	0
Southfeld cum	Suffield cum	SE/984906	1.	10.	0
Everle	Everley	SE/974889			
Silfhow	Silpho	SE/965921	1.	16.	0
Stoup cum	Stoupe Brow with	NZ/953024	1.	0.	1
Thirnaugh'	Thorny Brow	NZ/947017			
Fyghelyng'	Fyling	NZ/940033	1.	10.	0
Haukesgarth' cum	Hawsker with	NZ/925077	1.	0.	0
Staynesker'	Stainsacre	NZ/922084			
Sneton'	Sneaton	NZ/893079	1.	6.	8
Ugilbardby	Ugglebarnby	NZ/880072	1.	10.	0
Sleghtes	Sleights	NZ/867069	1.	13.	4
Rysewerp'	Ruswarp	NZ/889092	1.	0.	0
Dunsley cum	Dunsley with	NZ/858111	1.	6.	8
Neuham	Newholm	NZ/867105			

[1] See also p. 379.   [2] See also p. 379.   [3] See also p. 377.
[4] This entry probably refers to both Great and Little Smeaton; the grid ref. is to Great Smeaton.
[5] See also p. 374.   [6] See also p. 379.

Mildesburgh' cum Neuham	Middlesbrough with Newham	NZ/495205 NZ/517133	1.	0.	0
Brokesay	Broxa	NZ/945915		13.	4
Whyteby	Whitby	NZ/902113	13.	0.	0
Ampelford[1]	Ampleforth	SE/583787		10.	0
Skakelden'	Scackleton	SE/648729		12.	0
Faldyngton' cum Baxby[2]	Fawdington with Bagby	SE/435729 SE/463806		12.	0
Southotrington'	South Otterington	SE/371875	1.	16.	0
Sutton' cum Whytstanclif'	Sutton under Whitestonecliffe	SE/485825	2.	0.	0
Felycekyrk' cum Mathersby	Felixkirk with Marderby	SE/468848 SE/468839		18.	0
			36.	14.	1

Lib. Pykeryng' [PICKERING LIBERTY]

Cropton' cum Hartoft'	Cropton with Hartoft End	SE/758891 SE/750930	1.	16.	0
Synelyngton' cum Marton'	Sinnington with Marton	SE/744857 SE/734832		12.	0
Wrelton'	Wrelton	SE/768861	1.	3.	4
Aslagby	Aislaby	SE/774857	1.	6.	8
Midelton'	Middleton	SE/782854	1.	10.	0
Neuton'	Newton	SE/812904	1.	0.	0
Levesham	Levisham	SE/833905	1.	8.	0
Lokton'	Lockton	SE/843900	1.	12.	0
Kynthorp'	Kingthorpe[3]	SE/835858		15.	0
Thornton'	Thornton Dale	SE/833830	3.	0.	0
Farmanby	Farmanby	SE/840832	2.	0.	0
Wilton'	Wilton	SE/861828	1.	2.	0
Aluestan	Allerston	SE/879829	2.	10.	0
Ebreston'	Ebberston	SE/892833	5.	0.	0
Sneyngton'	Snainton	SE/920823	2.	10.	0
Brumpton' cum Salden'	Brompton with Sawdon	SE/942822 SE/943849	5.	10.	0
Ruston' cum Wykham	Ruston with Wykeham	SE/958832 SE/964834	2.	6.	8
Huton' Bussell'	Hutton Buscel	SE/973840	1.	14.	0
Aton'[4]	Ayton	SE/991850	4.	10.	0
Semer cum Irton'	Seamer with Irton	TA/015834 TA/010842	4.	6.	7
Leberston'	Lebberston	TA/078826	2.	0.	0
Cayton' cum Osgodby	Cayton with Osgodby	TA/056833 TA/055846	1.	12.	9½
Pykeryng' cum Godland	Pickering with Goathland	SE/799840 NZ/832012	6.	0.	0
			55.	5.	0½

[1] See also pp. 377, 379.   [2] Baxby is omitted from E 179/211/10.
[3] Grid ref. is to the deserted village.
[4] This entry probably refers to both East and West Ayton; the grid ref. is to East Ayton.

[ANCIENT DEMESNES]

Soca de Pykeryng'	Soke of Pickering		1.	9.	0	[T]
Scalby	Scalby	TA/009903	5.	0.	0	[T]
Esyngwald cum Hoby	Easingwold with Huby	SE/525700 SE/566654	4.	13.	4	[T]
Kerby	Cold Kirby	SE/533844	1.	10.	0	[T]
Scardeburgh'[1] & Whallesgrave	Scarborough and Falsgrave	TA/046892 TA/033875	33.	6.	8	[T]
			45.	19.	0	[T]

TOTAL: £582. 16. 1[2]

YORKSHIRE: WEST RIDING

Wap. Steynclyf' [STAINCLIFFE WAPENTAKE]

Braycewell' [va]	Bracewell	SD/863484	1.	0.	0
Hebbeden' [va]	Hebden	SE/026630		16.	0
Thorneton' [va]	Thornton in Craven	SE/901483	1.	9.	0
Neusom' [va]	Newsholme	SD/840515		7.	0
Rymyngton' [va]	Rimington	SD/812459		15.	0
Midhop' [va]	Middop	SD/834453		13.	4
Gysburn' [va]	Gisburn	SD/829489	1.	0.	0
Otreburn' [va]	Otterburn	SD/883577		6.	8
Stretton' [va]	Stirton	SD/972528		12.	0
Hertlyngton' [va]	Hartlington	SE/037611		16.	0
Farnhill' [va]	Farnhill	SE/005466		13.	0
Skypton' [va]	Skipton	SD/989513		8.	0
Halton' West' [va]	Halton West	SD/846545		11.	0
Brynishale [va]	Burnsall	SE/033613	1.	0.	0
Sighelsden' [va]	Silsden	SE/042465	1.	0.	0
Adygham [va]	Addingham	SE/076499		15.	0
Glusburn' [va]	Glusburn	SE/001449		13.	0
Coldconyston' [va]	Coniston Cold	SD/903554		11.	0
Pathorn'	Paythorne	SD/830518		13.	4
Haukeswyk'	Hawkswick	SD/956705		16.	0
Essheton'	Eshton	SD/935562		8.	0
Rylleston'	Rylstone	SD/972588		14.	0
Langeclyf'	Langcliffe	SD/823650		13.	0
Litton'	Litton	SD/905741	1.	2.	0
Swynden'	Swinden	SD/861543		19.	0
Malghom	Malham	SD/900627	1.	7.	0
Gykleswyk'	Giggleswick	SD/811640	1.	9.	0
Arneclyf'	Arncliffe	SD/933720	1.	0.	0

[1] Although fining for 50 marks in lieu of the tenth Scarborough was not a taxation borough in 1334, but it was considered one and described as a borough on the roll of 1336, E 179/211/10. Although assessed at £33. 6. 8 it was excused payment and the quota is omitted from the total on the 1334 Account, E 179/211/9.

[2] As on 1334 Account, E 179/211/9. This total comprised £570. 3. 9 at a fifteenth and £12. 12. 4 at a tenth (Scarborough excluded). The figures for the fifteenth for the wapentakes and liberties in the Particulars add up to £569. 14. 9 and £569. 14. 9 is in fact the figure stated for the fifteenth in 1336 and subsequent years (e.g. on E 179/211/10, 11, and 20), when, with the inclusion of Scarborough, the total for the North Riding became £615. 13. 9.

Crakhawe	Cracoe	SD/977600		13.	4
Boulton' in Boghland	Bolton by Bowland	SD/787493	1.	3.	0
Routhemel	Rathmell	SD/804599		12.	0
Setyl	Settle	SD/820637	1.	6.	8
Flasceby	Flasby	SD/946567		10.	0
Marton'	Martons Both[1]	SD/908507	1.	0.	0
Pathenal	Painley	SD/842500		15.	0
Preston'	Long Preston	SD/833583	1.	0.	0
Scothorp'	Scosthorp	SD/902596		9.	0
Ketelwell'	Kettlewell	SD/971723	1.	9.	0
Haghenlyth'	Hanlith	SD/901612		6.	0
Lynton'	Linton	SD/998627		19.	0
Broghton'	Broughton	SD/941514	1.	6.	8
Slaytburn'	Slaidburn	SD/710522	1.	5.	0
Esyngton'	Easington	SD/707507		12.	0
Hamerton'	Hammerton	SD/720537		12.	0
Conyston' in Ketelweldale	Conistone	SD/981674		17.	0
Helghfeld	Hellifield	SD/857565		18.	0
Gairegrave	Gargrave	SD/932539	1.	10.	0
Kirkeby	Kirkby Malham	SD/894610		7.	6
Calton'	Calton	SD/909592		12.	0
Ayreton'	Airton	SD/902593		15.	0
Heton' [va]	Hetton	SD/961588		16.	0
Neuton'	Bank Newton	SD/909531		10.	0
Horton' [va]	Horton	SD/857503		11.	0
Carleton'	Carleton	SD/972497	1.	3.	0
Wyclesworth'	Wigglesworth	SD/809569		13.	4
Staynford	Stainforth	SD/821673		18.	0
Bradeley	Bradleys Both	SE/003484		13.	4
Gersyngton'	Grassington	SE/003641	1.	3.	0
Thresfeld	Threshfield	SD/990637	1.	1.	0
Skibdon'	Skibeden	SE/016526		8.	0
Apeltrewyk'	Appletreewick	SE/054601	1.	3.	0
Emesey	Embsay	SE/011541		15.	0
Halton' super le Hill'	Halton East	SE/043539		11.	0
Kyldwyk'	Kildwick	SE/011459		13.	4
Collyng'	Cowling	SD/968431		14.	0
Sutton'	Sutton	SE/007442		12.	0
Styueton'	Steeton	SE/034445		19.	0
Kyghley	Keighley	SE/060410		15.	0
Draghton'	Draughton	SE/039524		12.	0
Bukeden' cum Langetrothe	Buckden with Langstrothdale	SD/942772 SD/926783		10.	0
Neuton' in Boghland	Newton	SD/697504	1.	2.	0
Grenlyngton'	Grindleton	SD/759457	1.	7.	0
Bradford	West Bradford	SD/744444	1.	3.	0
Wadyngton'	Waddington	SD/729439	1.	2.	0
Mitton'	Great Mitton	SD/715389		12.	0
Bakshelf'	Bashall Eaves	SD/696433		12.	0
			62.	4.	6

Wap. Yuccros [EWCROSS WAPENTAKE]

Horton'	Horton in Ribblesdale	SD/810721		13.	4
Burton' in Lonesdale	Burton in Lonsdale	SD/652722		14.	0

[1] Grid ref. is to East Marton.

Austwyk'	Austwick	SD/767684	1.	2.	0
Sedbergh'	Sedbergh	SD/656921	1.	2.	0
Dent'	Dent	SD/705870	1.	8.	0
Bentham	Bentham	SD/668688		19.	0
Thorneton'	Thornton in Lonsdale	SD/686736		9.	0
Clapham	Clapham	SD/746694	1.	0.	0
Ingleton'	Ingleton	SD/695733	1.	3.	0
			8.	10.	4

Wap. Clarowe [CLARO WAPENTAKE]

Newall	Newall	SE/200463		19.	0
Weston'	Weston	SE/178467		9.	0
Nesfeld	Nesfield	SE/093495		10.	0
Farnelay	Farnley	SE/213481		19.	0
Denton'	Denton	SE/144489		18.	0
Colthorp	Cowthorpe	SE/428527		11.	0
Middelton'[1]	Middleton	SE/123492		8.	0
Ryppelay	Ripley	SE/282605		15.	0
Nunmunketon'	Nun Monkton	SE/512580	1.	1.	0
Plumpton'	Plompton	SE/357540	1.	1.	0
Askwyth'	Askwith	SE/170484	1.	2.	0
Spofforth'	Spofforth	SE/364511		11.	0
Lynton'	Linton	SE/390468		19.	0
Letheley[2]	Leathley	SE/231470		12.	0
Wethreby cum hospitilar'	Wetherby	SE/404483		18.	0
Syclynghale	Sicklinghall	SE/362483		19.	0
Parva Usburn'	Little Ouseburn	SE/452612		10.	0
Parva Rybstan'[3]	Little Ribston	SE/385533		10.	0
Dunsford	Dunsforth	SE/443649		6.	0
Rybstan' cum hospitilar'	Ribston	SE/392536	1.	0.	0
Casteley	Castley	SE/266458		9.	0
Wytheton'[4]	Weeton	SE/284465		7.	0
Staynburn'	Stainburn	SE/249484		16.	0
Kirkeby Malessart'	Kirkby Malzeard	SE/235745	3.	6.	4
Rygton'	Rigton	SE/280491		18.	0
Parva Tymbel	Little Timble	SE/c.190525		6.	0
Aterlawe	Azerley	SE/259743	2.	4.	0
Grenhamerton'	Green Hammerton	SE/460567		11.	0
Kirkehamerton'	Kirk Hammerton	SE/465555	1.	1.	0
Wyxlay	Whixley	SE/442583	1.	0.	2
Southdyghton'	Kirk Deighton	SE/399505	1.	13.	0
Aldefeld	Aldfield	SE/263693	1.	0.	0
Hunsynghoure	Hunsingore	SE/429535		16.	0
Goldesburgh'	Goldsborough	SE/384561	1.	13.	4
Gruelthorp'	Grewelthorpe	SE/231761	2.	10.	0
Bemesley	Beamsley	SE/078524		16.	0
Wyckersley	Winksley	SE/252712		18.	0
Flasceby	Flaxby	SE/394579		11.	0
Lyndeley	Lindley	SE/223490		3.	4
Allerton' Mauleverer	Allerton Mauleverer	SE/415580		13.	0
Dunkesewyk'	Dunkeswick	SE/307469		5.	0

[1] See also the Liberty of St. Leonard, p. 386.
[2] Ditto, p. 386.
[3] Ditto, p. 385.
[4] Ditto, p. 386.

Kereby	Kearby	SE/347470		13.	4
Kirkeby Orblawer	Kirkby Overblow	SE/324492		10.	0
Folyfayt'	Follifoot	SE/343526		8.	0
Magna Cathall'	Cattal	SE/449542	1.	7.	0
Coppegrave	Copgrove	SE/346632		9.	0
Northdyghton'	North Deighton	SE/391516		17.	0
			40.	19.	6

Wap. Aynesty [AINSTY WAPENTAKE]

Askham Brian	Askham Bryan	SE/553484	1.	10.	0
Acastre Selby[1]	Acaster Selby	SE/575414	1.	5.	0
Acastre Malby	Acaster Malbis	SE/595458	1.	0.	0
Bysshopthorp'	Bishopthorpe	SE/595479		13.	4
Helagh'	Healaugh	SE/498479		15.	0
Wyghale	Wighill	SE/473465		16.	0
Colton'	Colton	SE/542447		18.	0
Thorparches	Thorp Arch	SE/438461	1.	8.	0
Wylsthorp'	Wilstrop	SE/484553		17.	0
Askham Richard	Askham Richard	SE/537480		15.	0
Bykerton'	Bickerton	SE/451505		14.	0
Folyfayt'	Follifoot	SE/457463		10.	6
Apelton'[2]	Appleton Roebuck	SE/554423	1.	3.	0
Bylburgh'	Bilbrough	SE/530464	1.	0.	0
Rughford cum ten' Sancti Leonardi	Rufforth [with tenants of the hospital of St. Leonard]	SE/528514		18.	0
Munketon'[3]	Moor Monkton	SE/508569		10.	0
Styueton'	Steeton	SE/532441	1.	4.	0
Coupmanthorp[4]	Copmanthorpe	SE/565468	1.	13.	4
Waulton'	Walton	SE/441479		15.	0
Boulton' Percy	Bolton Percy	SE/532413	1.	6.	8
Bylton'	Bilton	SE/476501		8.	0
Merston'	Long Marston	SE/502512	1.	2.	0
Tokwyth'	Tockwith	SE/466523		8.	0
Hoton'	Hutton Wandesley	SE/505508	1.	0.	0
Oxton'	Oxton	SE/504430		8.	0
Katherton' cum ten' Sancti Leonardi	Catterton [with tenants of the hospital of St. Leonard]	SE/510460		7.	0
Drynghous	Dringhouses	SE/588497		6.	8
Skakylthorp'	Scagglethorpe	SE/c.540550		3.	0
			23.	14.	6

Lib. Sancti Leonardi [LIBERTY OF ST. LEONARD]

De tenent' libertat' hospital Sancti Leonard in vill' de		
Bramphop'	Bramhope	SE/250433
Parva Rybstan'[5]	Little Ribston	SE/385533

[1] See also the Liberty of St. Mary, York, p. 387.
[2] Ditto, p. 387.
[3] Ditto, p. 387.
[4] See also the Liberty of St. Leonard, p. 386.
[5] See also Claro wapentake, p. 384.

Nappay	Nappa	SD/856533
Coupmanthorp'[1]	Copmanthorpe	SE/565468
Halgh'	?	
Ulthwayt'	?	
Letheley[2]	Leathley	SE/231470
Stokyld	Stockeld	SE/372492
Middelton'[3]	? Middleton	SE/123492
Wytheton[4]	? Weeton and	SE/284465
Donecastre [p][5]	Doncaster [part of]	SE/578032

3.	13.	4

Wap. Barkeston' [BARKSTON ASH WAPENTAKE]

Esthathelsey	Goose Haddesley	SE/589259		14.	o
Birne	Burn	SE/594285	1.	5.	o
Gaitford	Gateforth	SE/562286	1.	8.	o
Bretton'	Burton Salmon	SE/492274	1.	3.	o
Hamelton'	Hambleton	SE/553308	2.	7.	o
Carleton'	Carlton	SE/648240	3.	15.	o
Saxton'	Saxton	SE/476369	3.	o.	o
Rithre	Ryther	SE/555393	1.	6.	8
Toueton'	Towton	SE/485395	3.	o.	7
Clyfford	Clifford	SE/430443	1.	12.	o
Wystowe	Wistow	SE/592357	5.	6.	8
Sutton'	Sutton	SE/494252	1.	15.	o
Stutton'	Stutton	SE/479414	1.	6.	8
Berley	Barlow	SE/642287	2.	o.	o
Fenton'	Church Fenton	SE/515367	2.	2.	o
Southmilford	South Milford	SE/497317	2.	6.	o
Lutryngton'	Lotherton	SE/440360	1.	2.	10
Heselwod	Hazlewood	SE/449398	1.	o.	o
Bramham[6] cum	Bramham with	SE/428430	1.	5.	o
Oklesthorp'	Oglethorpe	SE/448441			
Shirburn'	Sherburn in Elmet	SE/488334	6.	o.	o
Tolleston'	Toulston	SE/452440		18.	o
Cawode	Cawood	SE/578378	4.	10.	o
Birkyn	Birkin	SE/531265	1.	4.	o
Mikelfeld	Micklefield	SE/442336	1.	6.	o
Kirkeby	Kirkby Wharfe	SE/506411		15.	o
Neuton' Kyme	Newton Kyme	SE/466449		17.	o
Barkeston'	Barkston	SE/492360	1.	2.	o
Thorpwilghby	Thorpe Willoughby	SE/579313		8.	o
Hudleston' cum	Huddleston with	SE/467339	1.	6.	8
Lumby	Lumby	SE/486303			
Grymston'	Grimston	SE/499413		4.	o
Ledesham [p][7]	Ledsham [part of]	SE/456298		6.	o
Tadcastre	Tadcaster	SE/485433	2.	o.	o
Brayton'	Brayton	SE/601305	1.	5.	o
Hirst'	Hirst Courtney	SE/613244	1.	o.	o
Westhathelsay	West Haddesley	SE/564267	1.	10.	o
Farburn'	Fairburn	SE/471279	2.	o.	4½
Drax'	Drax	SE/676263	2.	18.	8
Fryston'	Monk Fryston	SE/504297	1.	2.	o
Neuton' Waleys	Newton Waleys	SE/446279		14.	o

[1] See also Ainsty wapentake, p. 385.
[3] Ditto, p. 384.
[5] For Doncaster see Strafforth wapentake, p. 393.
[6] See also the Liberty of St. Mary, York, p. 387.

[2] See also Claro wapentake, p. 384.
[4] Ditto, p. 384.
[7] Ditto, p. 387.

Hillom	Hillam	SE/509289	I.	10.	0
Byrom'	Byram	SE/497262		17.	0
Brotherton' [parte Archepiscopi][1]	Brotherton [part belonging to the Archbishop of York]	SE/482257		3.	4
Selby	Selby	SE/616324	8.	0.	0
			79.	12.	5½

Lib. Beate Marie [LIBERTY OF ST. MARY, YORK]

Eadem libertat' in					
Hessay	Hessay	SE/522533	I.	10.	0
Munketon'[2]	Moor Monkton	SE/508569			
Knapton'	Knapton	SE/561521			
Apelton'[3] &	Appleton Roebuck and	SE/554423			
Acastre[4]	Acaster Selby	SE/575414			
Popelton' superiore	Upper Poppleton	SE/555540	2.	8.	0
Popelton' inferiore	Nether Poppleton	SE/564550	2.	3.	0
Eadem libertat' in Bramham[5]	Bramham	SE/428430	I.	5.	0
Acome cum Holgate	Acomb with Holgate	SE/572514 SE/583514	3.	8.	0
Eadem libertat' in Hewyk'[6]	Copt Hewick	SE/340712		7.	0
Ulskelf'	Ulleskelf	SE/520400	I.	6.	0
Gaitehill'	Gate Hill	SE/420586		8.	0
Neuthorp cum Ledesham[7]	Newthorpe with Ledsham	SE/472322 SE/456298		16.	0
Morton' cum Grafton'	Marton cum Grafton	SE/418628 SE/416631	I.	0.	0
Eadem libertat' in Brotherton'[8]	Brotherton	SE/482257		12.	0
			15.	3.	0

Wap. Skyreyk' [SKYRACK WAPENTAKE]

Otteley	Otley	SE/202454	I.	10.	0
Hewkesworth'	Hawksworth	SE/163419		9.	0
Carleton'	Carlton	SE/217430		10.	0
Preston'	Great Preston	SE/402294	I.	13.	0
Rygton'	East Rigton	SE/370438	2.	8.	0
Baildon'	Baildon	SE/156397		12.	0
Gyselay	Guiseley	SE/192422		10.	0
Woudousom	Wothersome	SE/c.404425		13.	4
Swylyngton'	Swillington	SE/385305	3.	2.	0
Ledeston'	Ledston	SE/436289	I.	8.	0
Horsford	Horsforth	SE/237380		17.	0
Allerton' Gledhou	Allerton Gledhow [obsolete name, in Leeds]	SE/310372	I.	5.	0
Pouel	Pool	SE/244452		13.	4

---

[1] For the rest of Brotherton, see below. [2] See also Ainsty wapentake, p. 385.
[3] Ditto, p. 385. [4] Ditto, p. 385.
[5] See also Barkston Ash wapentake, p. 386.
[6] For Bridge Hewick see the Liberty of Ripon, p. 394.
[7] See also Barkston Ash wapentake, p. 386.
[8] See also above.

Kypask'	Kippax	SE/417303	2.	13.	4
Yedon'	Yeadon	SE/209412		14.	0
Secroft'	Seacroft	SE/358360	1.	7.	0
Thornoure	Thorner	SE/380405	1.	8.	0
Estkesewyk'	East Keswick	SE/361444	1.	0.	0
Alwaldley	Alwoodley	SE/c.301413		16.	0
Ousthorp'	Austhorpe	SE/370336	1.	4.	0
Neusom	Temple Newsam	SE/358323	3.	2.	0
Mensyngton'	Menston	SE/168439		14.	0
Wyk'	Wike	SE/337421		18.	0
Wordelay	Weardley	SE/297446		10.	0
Potter Neuton'	Potter Newton	SE/315359	1.	10.	0
Berewyk'	Barwick in Elmet	SE/401374	3.	0.	0
Heddyngley	Headingley	SE/280360	1.	0.	0
Colyngham	Collingham	SE/390461	1.	4.	0
Parlyngton'	Parlington	SE/421363	1.	0.	0
Allerton' iuxta aquam	Allerton Bywater	SE/418279	1.	4.	0
Abreford	Aberford	SE/432372		13.	0
Ilkeley	Ilkley	SE/116476		15.	0
Wygdon'	Wigton	SE/c.320410		18.	0
Byngley	Bingley	SE/108393	2.	15.	0
Morton'	Morton	SE/100423		13.	0
Raudon'	Rawdon	SE/209398		12.	0
Harewode	Harewood	SE/314450	1.	12.	0
Arthyngton'	Arthington	SE/276446		15.	0
Adel	Adel	SE/277403	1.	1.	0
Shadewell'	Shadwell	SE/342398	1.	7.	0
Ledes	Leeds	SE/302337	3.	13.	0
Burlay	Burley in Wharfedale	SE/165464		13.	0
Thorpstapelton'	Thorpe Stapleton	SE/352309		10.	0
Skarthecroft'	Scarcroft	SE/361409		7.	0
Gerford de libertat' beate Marie	Garforth [liberty of St. Mary, York]	SE/404330	1.	7.	0
			56.	6.	0

Wap. Morley [MORLEY WAPENTAKE]

Mirfeld	Mirfield	SE/202196	1.	2.	0
Shypley	Shipley	SE/146375		9.	0
Wyk'	Wyke	SE/151267		7.	0
Calverley	Calverley	SE/208372		16.	0
Northbirle	North Bierley	SE/160290		8.	2
Lofthous	Lofthouse	SE/333260		8.	0
Skyrcotes	Skircoat	SE/093228		5.	0
Heton' Clak'	Cleckheaton	SE/192253		16.	0
Hauworth'	Haworth	SE/030372		8.	0
Bateley	Batley	SE/242245		9.	0
Shelf'	Shelf	SE/124289		13.	0
Eland	Elland	SE/108212		9.	0
Manyngham	Manningham	SE/155345		6.	8
Ovenden'	Ovenden	SE/081273		13.	0
Boulton'	Bolton	SE/155363		6.	0
Clayton'	Clayton	SE/119320		13.	4
Barkesland	Barkisland	SE/054199		10.	0
Heckmondwyk'	Heckmondwike	SE/218234		6.	8
Gomersale	Gomersal	SE/206260		17.	0
Steynland	Stainland	SE/081196		15.	0
Bollyng'	Bowling	SE/174312		6.	0

Leversegge	Liversedge	SE/207237		10.	0
Horton'	Horton	SE/142317		10.	0
Middelton'	Middleton	SE/302284		17.	0
Tonge	Tong	SE/219305		9.	0
Southouram	Southowram	SE/120236		10.	0
Rysseworth'	Rishworth	SE/032179		11.	0
Warlullay	Warley	SE/057247		16.	0
Waddesworth'	Wadsworth[1]	SD/c.995285		16.	0
Eccleshill'	Eccleshill	SE/175355		13.	0
Miggelay	Midgley	SE/027263		13.	0
Fekesby	Fixby	SE/131195		5.	0
Halifax'	Halifax	SE/093253		11.	0
Staynsfeld'	Stansfield[2]	SD/c.940247		16.	0
Langefeld	Langfield[2]	SD/c.936238		14.	0
Rastrik'	Rastrick	SE/139216		13.	0
Quyk'	?			15.	0
Bradford	Bradford	SE/163330	1.	0.	0
Farnelay	Farnley	SE/251325		15.	0
Brameley	Bramley	SE/245351	1.	3.	0
Wirkeley	Wortley	SE/263321		10.	0
Farsley	Farsley	SE/217350		7.	0
Beston'	Beeston	SE/282307		14.	0
Podesey	Pudsey	SE/222335	1.	0.	0
Dryghtlyngton'	Drighlington	SE/224292		16.	0
Heton'	Heaton	SE/145351		11.	0
Sothill'	Soothill	SE/261243		12.	0
Northouram	Northowram	SE/113270		17.	0
Hyperum	Hipperholme	SE/131256	1.	0.	0
Allerton'	Chapel Allerton	SE/305371		15.	0
Sourby	Sowerby	SE/043232		16.	0
Thornton'	Thornton	SE/105327		16.	0
Hundesworth'	Hunsworth	SE/190268		8.	0
Hunsflet'	Hunslet	SE/309308	1.	0.	0
Clyfton'	Clifton	SE/161228		13.	0
Rothewell &	Rothewell and	SE/343283	1.	12.	0
Carleton'	Carlton	SE/337272			
Dewesbiry	Dewsbury	SE/248219		13.	4
Idel	Idle	SE/178376		15.	0
Morlay	Morley	SE/265274	1.	3.	0
Erdeslowe	Ardsley	SE/309258	1.	6.	0
Hertesheued	Hartshead	SE/182225		9.	0
			40.	14.	2

Wap. Agbrigg' [AGBRIGG WAPENTAKE]

Wakefeld'	Wakefield	SE/333208	6.	0.	0
Heton'	probably Kirkheaton	SE/254212		16.	0
Dalton'	Dalton	SE/171168		11.	6
Farnele Tyeis	Farnley Tyas	SE/163128		15.	0
Holmefryth'	Holmfirth	SE/143082	1.	3.	0
Slaghtwayt'	Slaithwaite	SE/082139		10.	0
Combreworth'	Cumberworth	SE/211088		10.	0
Hodresfeld'	Huddersfield	SE/146168		13.	4
Lepton'	Lepton	SE/200151		19.	0

[1] There is no village of Wadsworth and the site of the original settlement in the parish of this name is not known (E.P.N.S., XXXIII, Yorks., West Riding, part III (1961), 199).
[2] Stansfield and Langfield are both ancient townships now included in Todmorden.

			£.	s.	d.
Querneby	Quarmby	SE/112167		19.	0
Northtcrosseland	North Crosland[1]	lost		12.	0
Crosseland Fosse	South Crosland	SE/114127		7.	6
Floketon'	Flockton	SE/239149	1.	2.	0
Ayketon'	Ackton	SE/412220		12.	0
Whitwode	Whitwood	SE/403244		11.	0
Shitlyngton'	Sitlington	SE/265172		16.	0
Warnefeld	Warmfield	SE/373211		19.	0
Whitley	Whitley	SE/222177		18.	0
Normanton' cum hospitil'	Normanton	SE/383227	1.	0.	0
Syntale	Snydale	SE/403214		17.	0
Almanbiry	Almondbury	SE/168151		16.	0
Shellay	Shelley	SE/212114		14.	6
Shepelay	Shepley	SE/192098		14.	0
Meltham	Meltham	SE/099107		12.	0
Thornhill'	Thornhill	SE/253189	1.	5.	0
Osset	Ossett	SE/278205	1.	0.	0
Staineley	Stanley	SE/347230	1.	11.	0
Altoftes	Altofts	SE/378238	1.	5.	0
Walton'	Walton	SE/353170	1.	6.	0
Thurstaneland	Thurstonland	SE/166108		12.	0
Sandale	Sandal Magna	SE/338182	1.	0.	0
Bretton'	probably Monk Bretton	SE/363076		12.	0
Birton'	Kirkburton	SE/198125		12.	0
Metheley	Methley	SE/391267	2.	0.	0
Horbiry	Horbury	SE/296184		17.	0
Crigleston'	Crigglestone	SE/316163		17.	0
Emelay	Emley	SE/244133		13.	4
Crofton'	Crofton	SE/378182	1.	9.	0
Sharneston'	Sharlston	SE/392187	1.	6.	8
Honelay	Honley	SE/138121		11.	0
			40.	4.	10

Wap. Osgodcrosse [OSGOLDCROSS WAPENTAKE]

			£.	s.	d.
Castilford	Castleford	SE/425258	1.	0.	0
Polyngton'	Pollington	SE/611192	3.	0.	0
Hoghton'	Glass Houghton	SE/437246	1.	0.	0
Baddesworth'	Badsworth	SE/463150	1.	0.	0
Skelbrok'	Skelbrooke	SE/511121	1.	12.	0
Knottyngley	Knottingley	SE/500241	2.	2.	0
Fryston'	Ferry Fryston [now Ferrybridge]	SE/480241	1.	12.	0
Thorpaudelyn	Thorpe Audlin	SE/479160	1.	4.	0
Pontefracte	Pontefract	SE/462224	18.	0.	0
Redenesse extra lib' beate Marie[2]	Reednesse [the part outside the Liberty of St. Mary]	SE/798231	3.	16.	9
Hethensale	Hensall	SE/590233	1.	6.	8
Athelyngflet'	Adlingfleet	SE/843210	3.	0.	0
Whitgift'	Whitgift	SE/809226	1.	12.	0
Folkwardby	Fockerby	SE/848193	2.	0.	0
Heck'	Heck	SE/591210	1.	16.	0
Goldale	Gowdall	SE/625222	1.	10.	0

---

[1] A lost place, *E.P.N.S.*, *XXXII*, *Yorks.*, *West Riding*, part II (1961), 265.
[2] For the rest of Reednesse see p. 391.

Snayth'	Snaith	SE/641222	6.	0.	0
Rouclyf'	Rawcliffe	SE/685230	3.	0.	0
Skelale	Skellow	SE/522104	2.	4.	0
Bramwyth'	Kirk Bramwith	SE/620118	1.	4.	0
Darthyngton'	Darrington	SE/485202	2.	10.	0
Cridelyng'	Cridling Stubbs	SE/520213	1.	10.	0
Kirkesmecheton'	Kirk Smeaton	SE/520167	1.	10.	0
Preston'	Purston Jaglin	SE/423199	1.	11.	0
Houk'	Hook	SE/759254	3.	4.	0
Haldanby	Haldenby	SE/c.820170	1.	18.	0
Carleton'	Carleton	SE/468202	1.	0.	0
Egburgh'	Eggborough	SE/562234	1.	5.	0
Beghale	Beal	SE/535253	1.	12.	0
Fetherstan	Featherstone	SE/428210	1.	0.	0
Kelyngton'	Kellington	SE/551249	1.	6.	8
Queldale	Wheldale	SE/452266		10.	0
Stapelton'	Stapleton	SE/508192	1.	5.	0
Parva Smetheton'	Little Smeaton	SE/525168	1.	6.	8
Southelmesale	South Elmsall	SE/475114	1.	6.	8
Rouhale	Roall	SE/570251		15.	0
Acworth'	Ackworth	SE/440180	1.	5.	0
Wrangbrok'	Wrangbrook	SE/493132		19.	0
Stubbeswaldyng'	Walden Stubbs	SE/550169	1.	4.	0
Upton'	Upton	SE/476132	1.	4.	0
Norton'	Norton	SE/549153	2.	12.	4
Northelmesale	North Elmsall	SE/477127	1.	11.	0
Burghwaleys	Burghwallis	SE/537120	2.	5.	0
Wilmersley	Womersley	SE/532190	4.	15.	0
Ouston'	Owston	SE/551112	4.	6.	8
Campsale	Campsall	SE/544141	7.	2.	0
Whitley	Whitley	SE/562210		19.	0
Southkirkeby	South Kirkby	SE/453111	1.	15.	0
Redenesse de lib' beate Marie[1]	Reedness [the part in the liberty of St. Mary]	SE/798231	1.	10.	0
Ayremyn	Airmyn	SE/726252	1.	13.	4
Ouseflet'	Ousefleet	SE/830231	2.	1.	0
			116.	11.	9

Wap. Steyncrosse [STAINCROSS WAPENTAKE]

Hunsshelf'	Hunshelf	SK/274996	1.	1.	0
Gunnylthwayt'	Gunthwaite	SE/238065		13.	4
Silkeston'	Silkstone	SE/291059	1.	5.	0
Langeside	Langsett	SE/212004	1.	3.	0
Worteley	Wortley	SK/307994	1.	8.	0
Welueley	Woolley	SE/320130		16.	0
Bircheworth'	Ingbirchworth	SE/223060		7.	0
Dodworth'	Dodworth	SE/314052	1.	0.	0
Ospryng'	Oxspring	SE/273022		16.	0
Ryhill	Ryhill	SE/386143		18.	0
Thurgerland	Thurgoland	SE/290010		16.	0
Clayton'	Clayton West	SE/259110		16.	0
Holandswan [va]	Hoyland Swaine	SE/260053		14.	0
Denby	Denby Dale	SE/228085	1.	0.	0
Notton'	Notton	SE/342130		13.	0
Westbretton'	West Bretton	SE/287136		9.	0

[1] See also p. 390.

Roston'	Royston	SE/364113		16.	0
Hegholand	High Hoyland	SE/274106		16.	0
Tankersley	Tankersley	SK/350996		18.	0
Cotheworth'	Cudworth	SE/387085		19.	0
Shafton'	Shafton	SE/392111		13.	4
Bernesley	Barnsley	SE/345064	1.	11.	0
Skelmerthorp'	Skelmanthorpe	SE/249104		12.	0
Erdesley	Ardsley	SE/381056		9.	0
Chevet'	Chevet	SE/345153		8.	0
Brereley	Brierley	SE/410110		19.	0
Penyston'	Penistone	SE/246033		14.	0
Hymelesworth'	Hemsworth	SE/429133	1.	11.	0
Kesseburgh'	Kexbrough	SE/303096	1.	2.	0
Wyntersete	Wintersett	SE/382157		12.	0
Derton'	Darton	SE/311100	1.	10.	0
Bergh'	Barugh	SE/312084		17.	0
Thurleston'	Thurlstone	SE/232038	2.	16.	0
Havercroft'	Havercroft	SE/396144		13.	0
Calthorn'	Cawthorne	SE/285080	2.	7.	0
Wirkesburgh'	Worsborough	SE/350026	2.	10.	0
Hyndlay[1]	Hiendley	SE/398124		16.	0
Steynburgh'	Stainborough	SE/314030		14.	0
			37.	18.	8

Wap. Strafford [STRAFFORTH WAPENTAKE]

Rosyngton'	Rossington	SK/625984	1.	0.	0
Braythewell'	Braithwell	SK/530947	1.	4.	0
Wambewell'	Wombwell	SE/395031	3.	16.	0
Halghton'	Houghton	SE/432065	1.	5.	0
Thribergh'	Thrybergh	SK/467955		12.	0
Conyngesbergh'	Conisbrough	SK/512985	1.	2.	0
Bautre	Bawtry	SK/653930	3.	0.	0
Herthill'	Harthill	SK/493810	2.	13.	4
Bilham	Bilham	SE/485069		16.	0
Balby &	Balby and	SE/563014	1.	6.	0
Exthorp'	Hexthorpe	SE/565025			
Brynsford	Brinsworth	SK/422903		13.	0
Brampton iuxta Wath'[2]	Brampton Bierlow	SE/413013		18.	0
Wath'[3]	Wath upon Dearne	SE/440009		16.	0
Wermisworth' [va][4]	Warmsworth	SE/552006		12.	0
Brameley	Bramley	SK/490923		11.	0
Ousterfeld	Austerfield	SK/661945		12.	0
Bramcroft'	probably Brancroft	SK/668971		11.	0
Dalton'	Dalton	SK/465930		16.	0
Ullay	Ulley	SK/465876		16.	0
Ecclesfeld	Ecclesfield	SK/353942	2.	6.	0
Arnethorp'	Armthorpe	SE/621049		14.	0
Derfeld	Darfield	SE/418043	1.	6.	8
Pikeburn' [p]	Pickburn [part of]	SE/517074		16.	0
Loversale	Loversall	SK/576987	1.	0.	0
Blakeston' &	Blaxton and	SE/670003	1.	10.	0
Alkeley[5]	Auckley	SE/650012			

[1] It is uncertain whether this entry refers to Cold Hiendley or South Hiendley, or both; the grid ref. given is to South Hiendley.
[2] See also Tickhill Liberty, p. 393.   [3] Ditto, p. 393.   [4] See also p. 393.
[5] Part of Auckley was taxed with Finningley in Nottinghamshire (Bassetlaw wapentake, p. 228).

			£	s.	d.
Raumersshe	Rawmarsh	SK/436961	1.	8.	0
Edlyngton'	Edlington	SK/532973	1.	10.	0
Sandale Waitlowe	Long Sandall	SE/604069	1.	10.	0
Bradfeld	Bradfield	SK/267925	6.	0.	0
Haitefeld	Hatfield	SE/663096	1.	16.	0
Totewyk'	Todwick	SK/498842		16.	0
Kirkesandale	Kirk Sandall	SE/610081	1.	6.	8
Clayton'	Clayton	SE/454078		13.	4
Barneby	Barnby Dun	SE/618092	2.	13.	4[1]
Fysshelak'	Fishlake	SE/656132	1.	12.	0
Thorne	Thorne	SE/689132		18.	0
Cateby	Cadeby	SE/514005	1.	6.	8
Stubbes	Stubbs	SE/496112		13.	4
Hoton' Paynel	Hooton Pagnell	SE/485080	2.	6.	0
Whitstan'	Whiston	SK/451900	1.	10.	0
Canteley	Cantley	SE/619015	1.	10.	0
Treton'	Treeton	SK/432877		18.	0
Langethwayt'	Langthwaite	SE/c.555063	1.	11.	0
Thyrnscogh'	Thurnscoe	SE/450056		18.	0
Staynford'	Stainforth	SE/642119	1.	4.	0
Hikelton'	Hickleton	SE/483053	1.	13.	0
Brampton' in Morthyng'	Brampton en le Morthen	SK/485882		15.	0
Frykeley	Frickley	SE/468079		16.	0
Ravenfeld	Ravenfield	SK/485954		12.	0
Donecastre[2]	Doncaster	SE/578032	17.	0.	0
Handesworth'	Handsworth	SK/410862	2.	5.	0
Aston' in Morthyng'	Aston	SK/468854	1.	13.	4
Anstane	Anston	SK/520844		8.	0
Hoton' Lyvet'	Hooton Levitt	SK/520914		11.	0
Roderham	Rotherham	SK/429929	4.	0.	0
Sheffeld'	Sheffield	SK/355873	7.	3.	4
Wermisworthe[3] & Kerhous de lib' beate Marie	Warmsworth and Carr House [the parts in the Liberty of St. Mary]	SE/552006 SK/579999		13.	4
			100.	2.	4

Lib. Tykhill' [TICKHILL LIBERTY]

			£	s.	d.
Barneburgh'	Barnburgh	SE/484033	1.	10.	0
Bentlay	Bentley	SE/566056	3.	16.	0
Kymberworth'	Kimberworth	SK/410927	1.	15.	0
Thorp' Rekenyld	Thorpe Salvin	SK/520812	1.	1.	0
Di' Brampton'[4]	Brampton Bierlow [half of]	SE/413013	1.	0.	0
Di' Wath'[5]	Wath upon Dearne [half of]	SE/440009		13.	4
Holand	Hoyland Nether	SE/369005	1.	1.	0
Wales	Wales	SK/478827		13.	4
Wyntworth'	Wentworth	SK/384983	1.	14.	8
Wykersley	Wickersley	SK/478917		11.	0
Sprotburgh'	Sprotbrough	SE/540020	2.	0.	0

[1] Erroneously given as 3 marks on many rolls.
[2] A small part of Doncaster was taxed in the Liberty of St. Leonard, p. 386.
[3] See also p. 392.   [4] Ditto, p. 392.   [5] Ditto, p. 392.

Billyngley	Billingley	SE/436046		11.	0
Mekesburgh'	Mexborough	SK/475998	1.	13.	0
Stansale	Stancil	SK/608959	1.	2.	0
Waddesworth'	Wadworth	SK/569971	1.	5.	0
Swynton'	Swinton	SK/452993	1.	6.	8
Broddesworth'	Brodsworth	SE/507073	1.	5.	0
Mar	Marr	SE/514053	2.	0.	0
Boulton'	Bolton upon Dearne	SE/455025	1.	0.	0
Addewyk'	Adwick upon Dearne	SE/470014	1.	0.	0
Athewyk'	Adwick le Street	SE/541086	2.	6.	0
Staynton'	Stainton	SK/554936	1.	13.	0
Denyngby	Denaby	SK/483992		13.	4
Stodefould	Stotfold	SE/472063		6.	0
Hoton' Robert	Hooton Roberts	SK/483970		19.	0
Maltby	Maltby	SK/528919	1.	14.	0
Halghton' in Morthyng'[1]	Laughton en le Morthen	SK/516882	1.	6.	8
Scauceby	Scawsby	SE/539052		19.	0
Tynneslowe	Tinsley	SK/399909	2.	11.	0
Hegh' Melton'	High Melton	SE/509019	1.	13.	4
Gresbrok'	Greasbrough	SK/418957	1.	16.	0
Tykhill'	Tickhill	SK/591931	12.	10.	0
Parva Halghton'	Little Houghton	SE/423056		13.	0
			55.	18.	4

Lib. Rypon' [RIPON LIBERTY]

Weswyk'	Westwick	SE/355664		5.	0
Nunewyk'	Nunwick	SE/322745	1.	8.	0
Northstaynley	North Stainley	SE/286770		13.	4
Syuendale[2]	Givendale	SE/338692		13.	0
Bondegate & Asmondreby	Bondgate and Aismunderby	SE/315707 SE/305686	1.	0.	0
Sallay	Sawley	SE/249677	1.	5.	0
Ingerthorp'	Ingerthorpe	SE/290660		15.	0
Merkyngton'	Markington	SE/286649	1.	1.	0
Stodeley	probably Studley Royal	SE/278702	1.	5.	0
Nidde	Nidd	SE/301608	1.	5.	0
Eveston'	Eavestone	SE/224683	1.	5.	0
Skelton'	Skelton	SE/360680	1.	6.	0
Thorp'	Littlethorpe	SE/323693		17.	0
Neuby	Newby	SE/347675		12.	0
Hewyk'	Bridge Hewick	SE/338703	1.	0.	0
Thorneton'	Bishop Thornton	SE/263636	1.	14.	0
Sharhow	Sharow	SE/328721	1.	0.	0
Clutherom & Bysshopton'	Clotherholme and Bishopton	SE/287722 SE/301711		11.	0
Muncketon'	Bishop Monkton	SE/329660	1.	6.	8
Rypon'	Ripon	SE/312713	11.	6.	8
			30.	8.	8

---

[1] *Halghton'* is a clerical error; *Laughton'* is the usual version on later documents.
[2] *Syuendale* seems to be a clerical error for *Gyuendale*.

Lib. Knaresburgh' [KNARESBOROUGH LIBERTY]

Tymbel [A.D]	Timble	SE/180530	1.	0.	0	[T]
Thorescrosse [A.D]	Thruscross	SE/149585	1.	3.	0	[T]
Clynt' [A.D]	Clint	SE/260598	1.	7.	0	[T]
Kelynghale [A.D]	Killinghall	SE/286584	1.	8.	6	[T]
Brereton' [A.D]	Brearton	SE/321608		19.	0	[T]
Burton' [A.D]	Burton Leonard	SE/327638	1.	7.	0	[T]
Erkenden' [A.D]	Arkendale	SE/389610	1.	1.	0	[T]
Farnham [A.D]	Farnham	SE/348605		19.	0	[T]
Southstaneley [A.D]	South Stainley	SE/307632	1.	0.	0	[T]
Staveley [A.D]	probably Staveley	SE/362626	1.	7.	0	[T]
Skrevyn [A.D]	Scriven	SE/348585	1.	10.	0	[T]
Scotton' [A.D]	Scotton	SE/326593	1.	1.	0	[T]
Knaresburgh' [A.D]	Knaresborough	SE/351568	2.	13.	0	[T]
Ponteburgo [A.D]	Boroughbridge	SE/398665	3.	0.	0	[T]
Aldeburgh' [A.D]	Aldborough	SE/406664	1.	13.	4	[T]
Mynskyp' [A.D]	Minskip	SE/389648	1.	4.	0	[T]
Magna Usburn' [A.D]	Great Ouseburn	SE/449618		16.	0	[T]
Rauclyf' [A.D]	Roecliffe	SE/375660	1.	3.	0	[T]
Hundburton' [A.D]	probably Humberton [in Yorks., North Riding]	SE/421686	1.	2.	0	[T]
Kirkeby Catall [A.D]	Kirkby Ouseburn [now Kirby Hall]	SE/465610		14.	6	[T]
			26.	8.	4	[T]

TOTAL: £738. 10. 8½[1]

Civitas Ebor' [CITY OF YORK] 162. 0. 0 [T][2]

---

[1] As on 1334 Account, E 179/206/16.
[2] As on 1334 Enrolled Account, E 359/8a, m. 6, no. 6.

INDEX OF PLACE-NAMES

Almost all the places named in the lay subsidy are here indexed under their modern identifications, even if these are, in a few cases, problematical. Where a name has not been identified it is listed (in italics) as it appears on the documents.

If a place is not named in 1334 it does not necessarily mean that it did not contribute to the lay subsidy; it may have been included, unnamed, within the return for a nearby place. If, therefore, a place which is known from other sources to have been in existence in 1334 does not appear in the Index readers are advised to look at the returns for the hundred or wapentake concerned, from which it may be possible to speculate whether or not it was included within another entry.

Where identical modern place-names occur within the same county they are differentiated in this Index by the hundred or wapentake in which they are listed in 1334; if this is not clear from the documents or if there are identical place-names within the same hundred then they are differentiated by reference to a nearby place.

ABBREVIATIONS FOR COUNTIES

Bd	Bedfordshire	Nf	Norfolk
Brk	Berkshire	Np	Northamptonshire
Bk	Buckinghamshire	Nb	Northumberland
Ca	Cambridgeshire	Nt	Nottinghamshire
Co	Cornwall	Ox	Oxfordshire
Cu	Cumberland	Ru	Rutland
Db	Derbyshire	Sa	Shropshire
Dev	Devon	So	Somerset
Do	Dorset	St	Staffordshire
Ess	Essex	Sf	Suffolk
Gl	Gloucestershire	Sr	Surrey
Ha	Hampshire	Sx	Sussex
He	Herefordshire	Wa	Warwickshire
Hrt	Hertfordshire	We	Westmorland
Hu	Huntingdonshire	Wlt	Wiltshire
K	Kent	Wo	Worcestershire
La	Lancashire	YE	Yorkshire: East Riding
Lei	Leicestershire	YN	Yorkshire: North Riding
Li	Lincolnshire	YW	Yorkshire: West Riding
Mx	Middlesex		

Abberley, Wo, 352
Abberton, Ess, 81
Abberton, Wo, 354 n.
Abberwick, Nb, 223
Abbey-Gate, Lei, 162
Abbotsbury, Do, 77
Abbotsham, Dev, 52
Abbotskerswell, Dev, 50
Abbotsley, Hu, 137
Abbotstone, Ha, 113
Abbotstone, Wlt, 336
Abdick, hundred, So, 266
Abenhall, Gl, 104
Aberford, YW, 388

Aberhall, He, 126
Abingdon, Brk, 12
Abingdon, Np, 217
Abinger, Sr, 299
Abington, Great, Ca, 27
Abington, Little, Ca, 27
Abington Pigotts, Ca, 26
Ablington, Gl, 100
Ablington, Wlt, 345
Abload's Court, Gl, 97
Abram, La, 150
Abson, Gl, 101
Aby, Li, 184
Acaster Malbis, YW, 385

Acaster Selby, YW, 385, 387
Accott, Dev, 53
Achurch, Np, 214
Acklam, YE, 365
Acklam, YN, 375
Acklington, Nb, 222
Ackton, YW, 390
Ackworth, YW, 391
Acle, Nf, 195
Acomb, Nb, 220
Acomb, YW, 387
Aconbury, He, 125
Acre, Castle, Nf, 197
Acre, South, Nf, 203
Acre, West, Nf, 197
Acton, Mx, 191
Acton, Nb, 223
Acton, Sf, 291
Acton Beauchamp, He, 122, 352
Acton Burnell, Sa, 252
Acton Ilger, Gl, 102
Acton Iron, Gl, 101
Acton Pigott, Sa, 252
Acton Reynald, Sa, 251
Acton Round, Sa, 254
Acton Scott, Sa, 254
Acton Trussell, St, 281
Acton Turville, Gl, 102
Adbaston, St, 279
Adbolton, Nt, 232
Adderbury, Ox, 242
Adderley, Sa, 250
Adderstone, Nb, 225
Addestone, Wlt, 341
Addingham, YW, 382
Addington, Bk, 16
Addington, Sr, 300
Addington, Great, Np, 214
Addington, Little, Np, 214
Addiscombe, Sr, 301
Adel, YW, 388
Adgestone, Ha, 119
Adlestrop, Gl, 103
Adlingfleet, YW, 390
Adlington, La, 155
Admington, Wa, 95
Adscombe, So, 267
Adstock, Bk, 16
Adstone, Np, 211
Advent, Co, 33
Adwell, Ox, 241
Adwick le Street, YW, 394
Adwick upon Dearne, YW, 394
Affeton Barton, Dev, 62
Afflington, Do, 75
Affpuddle, Do, 69
Afton, Ha, 119
Agbrigg, wapentake, YW, 389
Aighton, La, 153
Aike, YE, 370

Aikton, Cu, 38
Ailby, Li, 184
Ailstone, Wa, 320
Ainderby Mires, YN, 372
Ainderby Quernhow, YN, 371
Ainderby Steeple, YN, 374
Ainstable, Cu, 37
Ainsty, wapentake, YW, 385
Aintree, La, 151
Airmyn, YW, 391
Airton, YW, 383
Aisby [in Threo wap.], Li, 172
Aisby, Li, 186
Aisholt, So, 267
Aiskew, YN, 371
Aislaby [in Langbargh wap.], YN, 375
Aislaby [in Pickering lib.], YN, 381
Aismunderby, YW, 394
Aisthorp, Li, 177
Akeld, Nb, 224
Akeley, Bk, 16
Akenham, Sf, 286
Alberbury, Sa, 253
Albourne, Sx, 311
Albrightlee, Sa, 250
Albrighton [in Brimstree lib.], Sa, 256
Albrighton [in Pimhill hd.], Sa, 251
Alburgh, Nf, 207
Albury, Hrt, 132
Albury, Ox, 239
Albury, Sr, 299
Alby, Nf, 202
Alcester, Wa, 319, 320
Alciston, Sx, 315
Alciston, half-hundred, Sx, 315
Alconbury, Hu, 136
Aldborough, Nf, 201
Aldborough, YW, 395
Aldbourne, Wlt, 339
Aldbrough, YE, 358
Aldbrough, YN, 373
Aldcliffe, La, 156
Aldeburgh, Sf, 294
Aldeby, Nf, 195
Aldenham, Hrt, 134
Alderbury, Wlt, 345
Alderbury, hundred, Wlt, 345
Alderford, Nf, 200
Alderholt, Do, 75
Alderley, Gl, 102
Aldermaston, Brk, 8
Alderminster, Wa, 354
Aldershot, Ha, 109
Alderstone, Wlt, 336
Alderton, Gl, 92
Alderton, Np, 211 n.
Alderton, Sf, 295
Alderton, Wlt, 344
Alderwasley, Db, 44
Aldfield, YW, 384

Aldham, Ess, 88
Aldham, Sf, 291
Aldingbourne, Sx, 308
Aldingham, La, 156
Aldington, Wo, 354
Aldon, Sa, 254
Aldridge, St, 279
Aldrington, Sx, 312
Aldsworth, Gl, 100
Aldsworth, Sx, 305
Aldwark, Db, 45
Aldwark, YN, 376
Aldwick, Sx, 307
Aldwincle, Np, 214 and n.
Aldworth, Brk, 13
Alethorpe, Nf, 199
Alford, Li, 184
Alfreton, Db, 48
Alfriston, Sx, 315
Algarkirk, Li, 168
Algarthorpe, Nt, 230
Alhampton, So, 267
Alkborough, Li, 175
Alkerton, Gl, 103
Alkerton, Ox, 243
Alkington, Gl, 95
Alkmonton, Db, 45
Allensmore, He, 127
Aller, Dev, 63
Aller, So, 263
Allerdale, wapentake, Cu, 39
Allerford, So, 272
Allerston, YN, 381
Allerthorpe, YE, 361
Allerton, La, 149
Allerton Bywater, YW, 388
Allerton, Chapel, So, 262
Allerton, Chapel, YW, 389
Allerton Gledhow, YW, 387
Allerton, liberty, YN, 378
Allerton Mauleverer, YW, 384
Allerwash, Nb, 220
Allesley, Wa, 323
Allestree, Db, 44
Allexton, Lei, 162
Allington, Do, 70
Allington, Ha, 110
Allington, Li, 171
Allington [in Studfold hd.], Wlt, 336
Allington [in Chippenham hd.], Wlt, 344
Allington [in Amesbury hd.], Wlt, 345
Allington, East, Dev, 51
Allithwaite, La, 156
Allweston, Do, 71
Almeley, He, 129
Almington, St, 279
Almondbury, YW, 390
Almondsbury, Gl, 96
Almsworthy, So, 272
Alne, YN, 379

Alne, Great, Wa, 326
Alne, Little, Wa, 326 n.
Alnesbourne, Sf, 296
Alnestone, So, 262 n.
Alnham, Nb, 223
Alnmouth, Nb, 225
Alnwick, Nb, 223
Aloesbridge, hundred, K, 146
Alphamstone, Ess, 80
Alpheton, Sf, 290
Alphington, Dev, 58
Alpington, Nf, 195
Alresford, Ess, 88
Alresford, New, Ha, 105, 121
Alresford, Old, Ha, 117
Alrewas, St, 277
Alsop en le Dale, Db, 44
Alspath, Wa, 324
Alsthorpe, Ru, 247
Alstoe, hundred, Ru, 247
Alston, La, 151
Alston, Sf, 296
Alstone [near Cheltenham], Gl, 92
Alstone [near Teddington], Gl, 350
Alstone, So, 262
Alstone, St, 282
Alstonfield, St, 281
Alston Sutton, So, 262
Alswick, Hrt, 132
Altarnun, Co, 33
Altham, La, 153
Althorne, Ess, 84 n.
Altofts, YW, 390
Alton, Ha, 120
Alton, St, 281
Alton, Wlt, 346
Alton Barnes, Wlt, 335
Alton Eastbrook, Ha, 114
Alton Foreign, hundred, Ha, 114
Alton Pancras, Do, 70
Alton Priors, Wlt, 340
Altwint, He, 125
Alvaston, Db, 43
Alvechurch, Wo, 351
Alvediston, Wlt, 343
Alveley, Sa, 255
Alverdiscott, Dev, 53
Alverstoke, Ha, 117
Alverton, Nt, 233
Alvescot, Ox, 237
Alveston, Gl, 94
Alveston, Wa, 327
Alvingham, Li, 183
Alvington, Gl, 104
Alvington, West, Dev, 51
Alwalton, Hu, 138
Alwington, Dev, 52
Alwinton, Nb, 223
Alwoodley, YW, 388
Alwrynstone, So, 262 n.

Ambaston, Db, 44
Amberden, Ess, 86
Amberley, Sx, 309
Ambersham, Sx, 105, 111, 304
Amblecoat, St, 283
Ambleside, We, 330
Ambrosden, Ox, 239
Amcotts, Li, 175
Amersham, Bk, 15, 22
Amesbury, Wlt, 345
Amesbury, hundred, Wlt, 345
Amesbury Priors, Wlt, 345
Amesbury, West, Wlt, 345
Amington, Wa, 325
Amoril, So, 261
Amotherby, YN, 377
Amounderness, wapentake, La, 151
Ampfield, Ha, 108
Ampleforth, YN, 371, 379, 381
Ampney, Gl, 99
Ampney, Down, Gl, 99
Amport, Ha, 108
Ampthill, Bd, 3
Ampton, Sf, 292
Amwell, Hrt, 26, 132
Ancaster, Li, 172, 174
Anderby, Li, 184
Anderchurch, Lei, 161
Anderson, Do, 73
Anderton, La, 154
Andover, Ha, 121
Andover, hundred, Ha, 108
Andrewsfield, hundred, So, 260
Angersleigh, So, 265
Angerton, Nb, 222
Angmering, East, Sx, 309
Ankerton, St, 278
Anlaby, YE, 360, 366, 368
Anmer, Nf, 197
Ann, Abbotts, Ha, 108
Ann, Little, Ha, 111
Annesley, Nt, 230
Annington, Sx, 310
Ansley, Wa, 325
Anslow, St, 280
Anstey, Ha, 114
Anstey, Hrt, 132
Anstey, Lei, 161
Anstey, East, Dev, 53
Anstey, West, Dev, 53
Anston, YW, 393
Ansty, Wa, 324
Ansty [in Dunworth hd.], Wlt, 338
Ansty [in Heytesbury hd.], Wlt, 341
Antingham, Nf, 201
Antony, Co, 34
Anville's Farm, Brk, 10
Anwick, Li, 173
Apethorpe, Np, 214
Apeton, St, 282

Apperley, Gl, 99
Appleby, Li, 175
Appleby, We, 328, 329
Appleby Magna, Lei, 46
Appleby Parva, Lei, 158
Appledore, Dev, 56
Appledram, Sx, 316
Appleford, Brk, 13
Applethwaite, We, 330
Appleton, Brk, 12
Appleton, La, 150
Appleton, East, YN, 371
Appleton le Moors, YN, 380
Appleton le Street, YN, 377
Appleton Roebuck, YW, 385, 387
Appleton, West, YN, 371
Appletree, Np, 210
Appletree, hundred, Db, 45
Appletreewick, YW, 383
Apsley, Sx, 310
Apton, Nf, 195
Arallas, Co, 31
Arborfield, Brk, 7
Arbury, La, 150
Ardeley, Hrt, 132
Ardington, Brk, 11
Ardleigh, Ess, 88
Ardley, Ox, 238
Ardsley [in Morley wap.], YW, 389
Ardsley [in Staincross wap.], YW, 392
Argam, YE, 365
Arkendale, YW, 395
Arkengarthdale, YN, 374
Arkesden, Ess, 87
Arkholme, La, 156
Arkstone, He, 127
Arle, Gl, 91
Arlescote, Wa, 321
Arlesey, Bd, 4
Arleston, Db, 45
Arleston, Sa, 251
Arley, Wa, 322
Arley, Upper, Wo, 276, 283
Arlingham, Gl, 96
Arlington, Dev, 53
Arlington, Gl, 100
Armathwaite, Cu, 38
Armingford, hundred, Ca, 25
Arminghall, Nf, 196
Armscote, Wa, 351
Armstalls, Ox, 242
Armthorpe, YW, 392
Arncliffe, YW, 382
Arncott, Lower, Ox, 239
Arncott, Upper, Ox, 239
Arne, Do, 77
Arnesby, Lei, 159
Arnewood, Ha, 106
Arnold, Nt, 234
Arnold, YE, 358, 368

Arram, YE, 359
Arras, YE, 360
Arreton, Ha, 119
Arrington, Ca, 26
Arrow, Wa, 326
Arthington, YW, 388
Arthingworth, Np, 213
Arthuret, Cu, 38 and n.
Artington, Sr, 298
Arundel, Sx, 305
Arundel, rape, Sx, 308
Asby, Great, We, 329
Asby, Little, We, 329
Ascott, Ox, 244
Ascott D'Oyley, Ox, 236
Ascott Earl, Ox, 236
Asenby, YN, 371
Asfordby, Lei, 161
Asgarby, Li, 172
Ash [in Beyminster hd.], Do, 71
Ash [in Pimperne hd.], Do, 76
Ash, So, 274
Ash, Sr, 299
Ash, Rose, Dev, 54
Ash Thomas, Dev, 56
Ashbocking, Sf, 286
Ashbourne, Db, 45
Ashbrittle, So, 260
Ashburnham, Sx, 316
Ashburton, Dev, 59, 66
Ashbury, Brk, 11
Ashbury, Dev, 60
Ashby, Li, 186
Ashby, Nf, 193
Ashby, Sf, 290
Ashby, Canons, Np, 211
Ashby, Castle, Np, 217
Ashby, Cold, Np, 216
Ashby cum Fenby, Li, 180
Ashby de la Launde, Li, 173
Ashby de la Zouch, Lei, 160
Ashby Folville, Lei, 161
Ashby Magna, Lei, 158
Ashby Mears, Np, 217
Ashby Parva, Lei, 159
Ashby Puerorum, Li, 185
Ashby St. Ledgers, Np, 215
Ashby St. Mary, Nf, 195
Ashby, West, Li, 184
Ashclyst, Dev, 56
Ashcombe, Dev, 59
Ashcott, So, 274
Ashdon, Ess, 87
Ashe, Db, 46
Ashe, Ha, 112
Asheby by Partney, Li, 182
Asheldham, Ess, 84
Ashen, Ess, 80
Ashendon, Bk, 19
Ashendon, hundred, Bk, 19

Ashey, Ha, 120
Ashfield, Sf, 296
Ashfield, Great, Sf, 292
Ashford, Db, 47
Ashford [in Braunton hd.], Dev, 62
Ashford [in Ermington hd.], Dev, 64
Ashford, Mx, 189
Ashford, Sa, 255
Ashford Carbonel, Sa, 254
Ashhurstwood, Sx, 315
Ashill, Nf, 204
Ashill, So, 266
Ashingdon, Ess, 81
Ashington, Nb, 223
Ashington, So, 262
Ashley, Ca, 27
Ashley, Gl, 337
Ashley, Ha, 107
Ashley, Np, 215
Ashley, St, 279
Ashley, North, Ha, 107
Ashling, East, Sx, 305
Ashling, West, Sx, 305
Ashmanhaugh, Nf, 202
Ashmansworth, Ha, 109
Ashmansworthy, Dev, 61
Ashmore, Do, 75
Ashorne, Wa, 320
Ashover, Db, 48
Ashow, Wa, 323
Ashperton, He, 128
Ashprington, Dev, 64
Ashreigney, Dev, 61
Ashridge, Hrt, 135 n.
Ashtead, Sr, 302
Ashton, Dev, 59
Ashton, Do, 72
Ashton, Ha, 118
Ashton, He, 130
Ashton [in Amounderness wap.], La, 152
Ashton [in Lonsdale, Cartmel, and Furness wap.], La, 156
Ashton, Np, 211 n.
Ashton, Cold, Gl, 101
Ashton Giffard, Wlt, 341
Ashton in Makerfield, La, 150
Ashton Keynes, Wlt, 342
Ashton, Steeple, Wlt, 338
Ashton, Street, Wa, 324
Ashton under Hill, Wo, 93, 101
Ashton under Lyne, La, 154
Ashton, West, Wlt, 338
Ashurst, Sx, 310
Ashwater, Dev, 60
Ashwell, Hrt, 132
Ashwell, Ru, 247
Ashwellthorpe, Nf, 196
Ashwick, So, 261
Aske, YN, 373
Askerton, Cu, 38

Askerwell, Do, 72
Askham, Nt, 228
Askham, We, 329
Askham Bryan, YW, 385
Askham Richard, YW, 385
Askrigg, YN, 372
Askwith, YW, 384
Aslackby, Li, 170
Aslacoe, wapentake, Li, 176
Aslacton, Nf, 196
Aslockton, Nt, 232
Aspall, Sf, 287
Aspatria, Cu, 39
Aspenden, Hrt, 133
Aspley, St, 278
Aspley, Wa, 325
Aspley Guise, Bd, 4
Aspull, La, 154
Asscherigge, Wlt, 338
Asselby, YE, 362
Asserby, Li, 184 n.
Asserton, Wlt, 341
Assington, Sf, 290
Asterby, Li, 182
Asterleigh, Ox, 236
Asterley, Sa, 253
Asterton, Sa, 253
Asthall, Ox, 237
Asthall Leigh, Ox, 237
Asthelworth', Gl, 96
Astley, La, 150
Astley, Sa, 251
Astley, Wa, 324
Astley, Wo, 352
Astley Abbots, Sa, 255
Aston, Brk, 13
Aston, Gl, 96
Aston, He, 129
Aston, Hrt, 133
Aston, Ox, 237 n.
Aston, Sa, 254
Aston [near Stone], St, 278
Aston [near Madeley], St, 279
Aston, Wa, 325
Aston, YW, 393
Aston Abbots, Bk, 18
Aston Blank, Gl, 99
Aston Botterell, Sa, 255
Aston Cantlow, Wa, 326
Aston Clinton, Bk, 20
Aston, Coal, Db, 48
Aston, East, Ha, 111
Aston Eyre, Sa, 255
Aston Flamville, Lei, 159
Aston Ingham, He, 127
Aston le Walls, Np, 210
Aston, Long, So, 271
Aston Magna, Gl, 351
Aston, Middle, Ox, 242
Aston Mullins, Bk, 20

Aston, North, Ox, 242
Aston on Carrant, Gl, 92
Aston on Clun, Sa, 253
Aston Pigott, Sa, 257
Aston Rogers, Sa, 256
Aston Rowant, Ox, 240
Aston Sandford, Bk, 20
Aston Somerville, Wo, 97
Aston, Steeple, Ox, 242
Aston Subedge, Gl, 94
Aston Tirrold, Brk, 13 n.
Aston upon Trent, Db, 43
Aston, Wheaton, St, 282
Aston, White Ladies, Wo, 351
Astrop, Ox, 237
Astwell, Np, 210
Astwick, Bd, 2
Astwick, Np, 210
Astwood, Bk, 17
Aswarby, Li, 173
Aswardby, Li, 185
Aswardhurn, wapentake, Li, 172
Atch Lench, Wo, 355
Atcham, Sa, 250
Athelarstone, So, 266 n.
Athelhampton, Do, 69
Athelington, Sf, 288
Atherfield, Ha, 119
Atherington, Sx, 308
Atherstone, So, 266
Atherstone, Wa, 325
Atherstone on Stour, Wa, 320
Atherton, La, 150
Atlow, Db, 45
Attebere, So, 262 n.
Atterby, Li, 186
Atterley, Sa, 254
Attington, Ox, 244
Attleborough, Nf, 205
Attlebridge, Nf, 194
Atwick, YE, 358
Atworth, Wlt, 347
Aubourn, Li, 175
Auburn, YE, 366
Auckley, YW, 227, 228, 392
Audleby, Li, 179
Audley, St, 279
Aughton, La, 150
Aughton, YE, 361
Aunby, Li, 170
Aunk, Dev, 56
Aunsby, Li, 172
Aust, Gl, 102
Austerfield, YW, 392
Austhorpe, YW, 388
Austrey, Wa, 324
Austwick, YW, 384
Autby, Li, 180
Authorpe, Li, 183 n.
Avebury, Wlt, 339

Aveland, wapentake, Li, 170
Aveley, Ess, 87
Avenbury, He, 123
Avening, Gl, 96
Averham, Nt, 231
Avethorpe, Li, 170
Aveton Gifford, Dev, 64
Avill, So, 272
Avington, Brk, 10
Avington, Ha, 117
Avisford, hundred, Sx, 308
Avon, Ha, 107
Avon, Wlt, 342
Avon Dassett, Wa, 321
Awbridge, Ha, 108
Awliscombe, Dev, 56
Awre, Gl, 91, 104
Awsworth, Nt, 229
Axbridge, So, 272
Axminster, Dev, 66
Axminster, hundred, Dev, 57
Axmouth, Dev, 57
Axmouth, hundred, Dev, 57
Axton, hundred, K, 146
Aydon, Nb, 221
Aylburton, Gl, 104
Aylesbeare, Dev, 65
Aylesbury, Bk, 15, 22
Aylesbury, hundred, Bk, 20
Aylesby, Li, 180
Aylesford, lathe, K, 144
Aylestone, Lei, 160
Aylmerton, Nf, 201
Aylsham, Nf, 201
Aylton, He, 128
Aylworth, Gl, 103
Aynho, Np, 210
Ayot St. Lawrence, Hrt, 133
Ayot St. Peter, Hrt, 133
Aysgarth, YN, 372
Ayshford, Dev, 56
Ayston, Ru, 246
Ayton [in Langbargh wap.], YN, 375
Ayton [in Pickering lib.], YN, 381
Azerley, YW, 384

Babcary, So, 259
Babergh, hundred, Sf, 290
Babingley, Nf, 197
Babington, So, 262
Babraham, Ca, 27
Babworth, Nt, 229
Baccamoor, Dev, 51
Backwell, So, 271
Baconsthorpe, Nf, 202
Bacton, He, 128
Bacton, Nf, 202
Bacton, Sf, 287
Badbury, Wlt, 335

Badbury, hundred, Do, 77
Badby, Np, 216
Baddesley Clinton, Wa, 324
Baddesley Ensor, Wa, 324
Baddesley, North, Ha, 109
Baddesley, South, Ha, 116
Baddow, Great, Ess, 85
Baddow, Little, Ess, 85
Baden Hall, St, 278
Badgemore, Ox, 240
Badger, Sa, 255
Badgeworth, Gl, 97
Badgworth, So, 273
Badingham, Sf, 288
Badley, Sf, 286
Badlingham, Ca, 24
Badminstone, Ha, 115
Badminton, Great, Gl, 102
Badminton, Little, Gl, 102
Badshot, Sr, 298
Badsworth, YW, 390
Badwell Ash, Sf, 293
Bagber, Do, 75
Bagborough, West, So, 265
Bagby, YN, 381
Bagendon, Gl, 100
Baggeworth, So, 262 n.
Baggrave, Lei, 165
Baggridge, So, 268
Baginton, Wa, 323
Bagnor, Brk, 9
Bagshot, Wlt, 6, 10, 332
Bagthorpe, Nf, 198
Bagtor, Dev, 59
Bagworth, Lei, 158
Baildon, YW, 387
Bainbridge, YN, 372
Bainton, Ox, 238
Bainton, YE, 362
Bakewell, Db, 47
Balby, YW, 392
Baldenhall, Wo, 354
Balderstone, La, 152
Balderton, Nt, 233
Balderton, Sa, 252
Baldock, Hrt, 133
Baldon, Little, Ox, 239
Baldon, Marsh, Ox, 239
Baldon, St. Lawrence, Ox, 239
Baldon, Toot, Ox, 239
Baldslow, hundred, Sx, 317
Bale, Nf, 199
Balkholme, YE, 362
Ballidon, Db, 44
Ballingdon, Sf, 79, 80, 284
Ballingham, He, 125
Balmer, Sx, 312
Balsall, Wa, 325
Balscott, Ox, 243
Balsdean, Sx, 312

Balsham, Ca, 27
Balterley, St, 279
Baltonsborough, So, 267
Bamber, Ha, 115
Bamburgh, Nb, 219, 225
Bamburgh, ward, Nb, 225
Bampton, Dev, 63
Bampton, Ox, 237
Bampton (Cundale), We, 329
Bampton, hundred, Dev, 63
Bampton, hundred, Ox, 237
Bampton (Patrick), We, 329
Banbury, Ox, 241
Banbury, hundred, Ox, 241
Bandonhill, Sr, 300
Banham, Nf, 205
Banningham, Nf, 202
Banstead, Sr, 298
Banthorpe, Li, 169
Banwell, So, 259
Bapton, Wlt, 347
Barbon, We, 330
Barbury, Wlt, 339
Barby, Np, 215
Barcheston, Wa, 320
Barclay, hundred, K, 143
Barcombe, Sx, 313
Barcombe, hundred, Sx, 313
Barden, YN, 372
Bardfield, Great, Ess, 87
Bardfield, Little, Ess, 87
Bardney, Li, 181
Bardolfeston, Do, 69
Bardwell, Sf, 292
Bare, La, 156
Barewood, He, 129
Barford, Nf, 206
Barford, Np, 213
Barford, Wa, 320
Barford, Wlt, 334
Barford, Great, Bd, 2
Barford, hundred, Bd, 2
Barford, Little, Bd, 2
Barford St. John, Ox, 243
Barford St. Martin, Wlt, 335
Barford St. Michael, Ox, 241
Barforth, YN, 373, 380
Barham, Ca, 27
Barham, Hu, 138 n.
Barham, Sf, 286
Barholm, Li, 169
Barkby, Lei, 161
Barkby Thorpe, Lei, 161
Barkestone, Lei, 163
Barkham, Brk, 7
Barking, Ess, 81
Barking, Sf, 285
Barkisland, YW, 388
Barkston, Li, 172
Barkston, YW, 386

Barkston Ash, wapentake, YW, 386
Barkway, Hrt, 133
Barkwith, East, Li, 181
Barkwith, West, Li, 181
Barlaston, St, 279
Barlavington, Sx, 308
Barlborough, Db, 48
Barlby, YE, 362
Barlestone, Lei, 159
Barley, Hrt, 133
Barlichway, hundred, Wa, 325
Barling, Ess, 81
Barlow, Db, 48
Barlow, YW, 386
Barmby Moor, YE, 367
Barmby on the Marsh, YE, 362
Barmer, Nf, 198
Barmston, YE, 357
Barnack, Np, 213
Barnacle, Wa, 324
Barnardiston, Sf, 293
Barnburgh, YW, 393
Barnby, Sf, 286
Barnby [in Bulmer wap.], YN, 376
Barnby [in Langbargh wap.], YN, 375
Barnby Dun, YW, 393
Barnby in the Willows, Nt, 233
Barnby Moor, Nt, 229
Barnet, Hrt, 134
Barnet, Friern, Mx, 190
Barnetby le Wold, Li, 178
Barney, Nf, 200
Barnfield, half-hundred, K, 143
Barnfield, West, hundred, K, 145
Barnham, Sf, 292
Barnham, Sx, 308
Barnham Broom, Nf, 206
Barningham, Sf, 293
Barningham, YN, 373
Barningham, Little, Nf, 201
Barningham, North, Nf, 201
Barningham Winter, Nf, 201
Barnoldby le Beck, Li, 180
Barnsley, Do, 77
Barnsley, Gl, 100
Barnsley, Ha, 119
Barnsley, YW, 392
Barnstaple, Dev, 66
Barnston, Ess, 82
Barnstone, Nt, 232
Barnwell, Np, 214
Barnwood, Gl, 97
Barpham, Sx, 309
Barr, Great, St, 279
Barr, Little, Wa, 276, 279
Barr, Perry, Wa, 276, 279
Barrasford, Nb, 220
Barrington, Ca, 26
Barrington, So, 272, 275
Barrington, Great, Gl, 6, 11, 103

Barrington, Little, Gl, 103
Barrmoor, Nb, 225
Barrow, Ru, 247
Barrow, Sf, 292
Barrow, So, 259
Barrow Gurney, So, 271
Barrow, hundred, Do, 69
Barrow upon Humber, Li, 179
Barrow upon Soar, Lei, 162
Barrow upon Trent, Db, 43
Barrowby, Li, 171
Barrowden, Ru, 247
Barsby, Lei, 161
Barsham, Sf, 289
Barsham, East, Nf, 199
Barsham, North, Nf, 199
Barsham, West, Nf, 199
Barstable, hundred, Ess, 85
Barston, Wa, 325
Barthorpe, YE, 365
Bartindale, YE, 365
Bartley, Ha, 115
Bartley Regis, Ha, 117
Bartlow, Ca, 27
Barton, Ca, 26
Barton, Gl, 98
Barton, Ha, 109
Barton, La, 151
Barton, St, 282
Barton, We, 329
Barton, YN, 374
Barton, Abbots, Ha, 112
Barton Bendish, Nf, 203
Barton Blount, Db, 45
Barton, Earls, Np, 217
Barton, Great, Sf, 292
Barton Hartshorn, Bk, 16
Barton in Fabis, Nt, 230
Barton in the Beans, Lei, 158
Barton, King's, liberty, Gl, 91
Barton le Clay, Bd, 3
Barton le Street, YN, 377
Barton le Willows, YN, 376
Barton, Middle, Ox, 241
Barton Mills, Sf, 293
Barton on the Heath, Wa, 321
Barton Regis, liberty, Gl, 91
Barton St. David, So, 259
Barton Seagrave, Np, 214
Barton, Sesswell's, Ox, 241
Barton Stacey, Ha, 115
Barton Stacey, hundred, Ha, 115
Barton Steeple, Ox, 241
Barton Street, Gl, 91 n.
Barton Turf, Nf, 202
Barton under Needwood, St, 280
Barton upon Humber, Li, 178
Barton upon Irwell, La, 154
Barton, Westcott, Ox, 241
Barugh, YN, 377

Barugh, YW, 392
Barwell, Lei, 158
Barwick, Nf, 198
Barwick, So, 263
Barwick, YN, 375
Barwick in Elmet, YW, 388
Barwythe, Bd, 1, 131, 134
Baschurch, Sa, 251
Bascote, Wa, 322
Basford, Nt, 230
Bashall Eaves, YW, 383
Basildon, Brk, 13
Basildon, Ess, 86
Basing, Ha, 118
Basingstoke, Ha, 120
Basingstoke Foreign, hundred, Ha, 118
Baslow, Db, 47
Bassenthwaite, Cu, 39
Bassetlaw, wapentake, Nt, 227
Bassetts, Ess, 84
Bassingbourn, Ca, 25
Bassingfield, Nt, 232
Bassingham, Li, 175
Bassingthorpe, Li, 171
Baston, Li, 169
Bastwick, Nf, 193
Batchy, He, 127
Batcombe, So, 267
Bath, So, 273
Bathampton, So, 261
Bathampton, Wlt, 340
Bathealton, So, 260
Batheaston, So, 261
Bathford, So, 261
Bath Foreign, hundred, So, 260
Bathwick, So, 261
Batley, YW, 388
Batsford, Gl, 95
Batson, Dev, 51
Batsworthy, Dev, 55
Battenhall, Wo, 351
Battersby, YN, 375
Battersea, Sr, 302
Battisborough, Dev, 64
Battisford, Sf, 286
Battle, hundred, Sx, 316
Battleford, Dev, 50
Battlesden, Bd, 4
Battramsley, Ha, 116
Baughton, Wo, 350
Baughurst, Ha, 109
Baulking, Brk, 10
Baumber, Li, 182
Baunton, Gl, 100
Baunton', Gl, 98
Baverstock, Wlt, 335
Bavington, Great, Nb, 220
Bavington, Little, Nb, 220
Bawburgh, Nf, 206
Bawdeswell, Nf, 200

Bawdrip, So, 260
Bawdsey, Sf, 295
Bawsey, Nf, 197
Bawtry, YW, 392
Baxby, YN, 378
Baxterley, Wa, 325
Baycliff, Wlt, 341
Baydon, Wlt, 338
Bayfield, Nf, 199
Bayford, Hrt, 131
Baylham, Sf, 285
Baynton, Wlt, 338
Bayston, Sa, 252
Bayton, Wo, 352
Beach, Gl, 94
Beachampstead, Hu, 137
Beachampton, Bk, 16
Beachendon, Bk, 19
Beaches, Brk, 346
Beaconsfield, Bk, 22
Beadlam, YN, 377
Beadnell, Nb, 224
Beaford, Dev, 52
Beal, YW, 391
Bealings, Great, Sf, 296
Bealings, Little, Sf, 296
Beaminster, Do, 71
Beaminster Foreign, Do, 72
Beamsley, YW, 384
Beanley, Nb, 224
Beara, Dev, 62 n.
Beare, Dev, 62
Bearl, Nb, 220
Bearley, Wa, 326
Bearscombe, Dev, 64
Beaumont, Cu, 37
Beaumont, Ess, 88
Beaumont, Lei, 162
Beausale, Wa, 325
Beauworth, Ha, 117
Beaworthy, Dev, 60
Beccles, Sf, 289
Becconsall, La, 154
Beckbury, Sa, 255
Beckenham, hundred, K, 145
Beckering, Li, 181
Beckett, Brk, 10
Beckford, Wo, 101
Beckham, East, Nf, 201
Beckham, West, Nf, 201
Beckhampton, Wlt, 339
Beckingham, Li, 174
Beckingham, Nt, 227
Beckington, So, 268
Beckley, Ox, 239
Beckside, La, 155 n.
Becontree, hundred, Ess, 81
Bedale, YN, 371
Bedborough, Wlt, 348
Beddingham, Sx, 315

Beddington, Sr, 300
Bedfield, Sf, 288
Bedfont, East, Mx, 189
Bedfont, West, Mx, 189
Bedford, Bd, 1, 5
Bedford, La, 150
Bedfordshire, 1–5
Bedhampton, Ha, 110
Bedingfield, Sf, 288
Bedingham, Nf, 195
Bedminster, Bristol, 262
Bednall, St, 281
Bedwardine, Wo, 350
Bedworth, Wa, 324
Bedwyn, Wlt, 333
Bedwyn, Little, Wlt, 348
Beeby, Lei, 161
Beechamwell, Nf, 203
Beech Hill, Brk, 8
Beechingstoke, Wlt, 335
Beeding, Sx, 310
Beedon, Brk, 9
Beeford, YE, 359
Beeley, Db, 47
Beelsby, Li, 180
Beenham, Brk, 7
Beer, Dev, 56
Beer, So, 259
Beer Charter Barton, Dev, 62 n.
Beercrocombe, So, 266
Beesby [in Calcewath wap.], Li, 184
Beesby [in Haverstoe wap.], Li, 180
Beeston, Bd, 3
Beeston, Nf, 208
Beeston, Nt, 230
Beeston, YW, 389
Beeston Regis, Nf, 201
Beeston St. Andrew, Nf, 194
Beeston St. Lawrence, Nf, 202
Beetham, We, 330
Beetley, Nf, 208
Begbroke, Ox, 242
Beighton, Db, 48
Beighton, Nf, 195
Belaugh, Nf, 202
Belbroughton, Wo, 353
Belby, YE, 363
Belchamp Otten, Ess, 80
Belchamp St. Paul, Ess, 80
Belchamp Walter, Ess, 80
Belchford, Li, 182
Belford, Nb, 224
Belgrave, Lei, 162
Bellasize, YE, 362
Belleau, Li, 184
Bellerby, YN, 372
Bellimoor, He, 127
Belluton, So, 270
Belmesthorpe, Ru, 247
Belper, Db, 43

Belsay, Nb, 221
Belstead, Sf, 285
Belstead, Great, Sf, 285
Belstone, Dev, 61
Belthorpe, YE, 367
Beltisloe, wapentake, Li, 170
Belton, Lei, 161
Belton [in Manley wap.], Li, 175
Belton [in Threo wap.], Li, 172
Belton, Ru, 246
Belton, Sf, 290
Belvoir, Lei, 157, 168, 171
Bemerton, Wlt, 342
Bempstone, hundred, So, 262
Bempton, YE, 365
Benacre, Sf, 289
Benefield, Np, 214
Benfleet, North, Ess, 86
Benfleet, South, Ess, 86
Bengeo, Hrt, 131
Bengeworth, Wo, 355
Bengrove, Gl, 101
Benhall, Sf, 294
Benham, Hoe, Brk, 9
Benham, Marsh, Brk, 10
Beningbrough, YN, 380
Benington, Hrt, 133
Benington, Li, 168
Bennetland, YE, 363
Benningham, Sf, 287
Benningholme, YE, 359
Bennington, Long, Li, 174
Benniworth, Li, 181
Benridge, Nb, 223
Bensham, Sr, 301
Benson, Ox, 245
Bentfield, Ess, 84
Bentham, Gl, 97
Bentham, YW, 384
Bentley [in Thorngate hd.], Ha, 106
Bentley, liberty, Ha, 111
Bentley, Sf, 285
Bentley, St, 279
Bentley, Wo, 352
Bentley, YE, 360
Bentley, YW, 393
Bentley, Fenny, Db, 44
Bentley, Great, Ess, 88
Bentley, Hungry, Db, 45
Bentley, Little, Ess, 88
Benton, Little, Nb, 221
Bentworth, Ha, 113
Benwell, Nb, 223
Beobridge, Sa, 256
Beoley, Wo, 353
Bepton, Sx, 306
Berden, Ess, 84
Berechurch, Ess, 88
Bere Ferrers, Dev, 52
Bere Regis, Do, 68

Bere Regis, hundred, Do, 68
Berewyk, So, 262 n.
Bergh Apton, Nf, 195
Berghfeld, Wlt, 346
Bergholt, East, Sf, 285
Bergholt, West, Ess, 87
Berkeley, Gl, 96
Berkeley, hundred, Gl, 95
Berkhamsted, Hrt, 135
Berkhamsted (foreign), Hrt, 135
Berkhamsted, honor, Bk, 22
Berkhamsted, Little, Hrt, 132
Berkshire, 6–14
Berkswell, Wa, 325
Bermondsey, Sr, 302
Bermondspit, hundred, Ha, 118
Bernitham, He, 126
Berrick Salome, Ox, 240
Berrier, Cu, 37
Berrington, Sa, 252
Berrington, Wo, 352
Berrow, So, 264
Berrow, Wo, 350
Berrynarbor, Dev, 62
Berry Pomeroy, Dev, 50
Bersted, North, Sx, 307
Bersted, South, Sx, 307
Berwick, Sa, 251
Berwick, Sx, 315
Berwick Bassett, Wlt, 337
Berwick Hill, Nb, 221
Berwick St. James, Wlt, 341
Berwick St. John, Wlt, 343
Berwick St. Leonard, Wlt, 338
Bescaby, Lei, 164
Besford, Sa, 251
Besford, Wo, 353
Bessels Leigh, Brk, 12
Bessingby, YE, 365
Bessingham, Nf, 201
Besthorpe, Nf, 205
Besthorpe, Nt, 233
Beswick, YE, 361
Betchworth [East], Sr, 299
Betchworth [West], Sr, 299
Beterton, Brk, 11
Betley, St, 279
Bettiscombe, Do, 76
Betton, Sa, 250
Bevercotes, Nt, 229
Beverley, YE, 369
Beverley, Chapter of, liberty, YE, 368
Beverley, Provost of, liberty, YE, 369
Beversbrook, Wlt, 337
Beverston, Gl, 96
Bevington, Cock, Wa, 326 and n.
Bevington, Wood, Wa, 326 and n.
Bewaldeth, Cu, 39

Bewcastle, Cu, 38
Bewholme, YE, 359
Bewley, Wlt, 347
Bewsborough, hundred, K, 142
Bexhill, Sx, 317
Bexhill, half-hundred, Sx, 317
Bexwell, Nf, 203
Beyminster, hundred, Do, 71
Beynhurst, hundred, Brk, 6
Beyton, Sf, 292
Bibury, Gl, 100 and n.
Bicester, King's End, Ox, 238
Bicester, Market End, Ox, 238
Bickenhall, So, 266
Bickenhill, Wa, 324
Bicker, Li, 168
Bickerstaffe, La, 150
Bickerston, Nf, 206
Bickerton, He, 128
Bickerton, Nb, 224
Bickerton, YW, 385
Bickford, St, 282
Bickington, Abbots, Dev, 61
Bickleigh, Dev, 63
Bickmarsh, Wo, 326
Bicknoller, So, 266
Bicknor, English, Gl, 103
Bickton, Ha, 114
Bicton, Sa, 251
Biddenham, Bd, 2
Biddesden, Wlt, 346
Biddestone, Wlt, 344
Biddisham, So, 262
Biddlestone, Nb, 223
Biddulph, St, 278
Bideford, Dev, 52, 66
Bidfield, Gl, 93
Bidford on Avon, Wa, 320
Bidlington, Sx, 310
Bielby, YE, 361
Bierley, North, YW, 388
Bigbury, Dev, 65
Bigby, Li, 178
Bigging, Wa, 323
Biggleswade, Bd, 1
Biggleswade, hundred, Bd, 1
Bighton, Ha, 110
Bignell, Ox, 238
Bignor, Sx, 309
Bilborough, Nt, 230
Bilbrough, YW, 385
Bilby, Nt, 229
Bildeston, Sf, 291
Bilham, YW, 392
Billesdon, Lei, 164
Billesley, Wa, 326
Billing, Great, Np, 217
Billing, Little, Np, 217
Billingborough, Li, 170
Billinge, La, 151

Billingford [in Earsham hd.], Nf, 207
Billingford [in Eynesford hd.], Nf, 200
Billingham, Ha, 119
Billinghay, Li, 173
Billingley, YW, 394
Billingshurst, Sx, 308
Billingsley, Sa, 255
Billington, La, 153
Billington, St, 282
Billockby, Nf, 193
Bilney, East, Nf, 208
Bilney, West, Nf, 197
Bilsborrow, La, 152
Bilsby, Li, 184
Bilsdale, YN, 376
Bilsham, Sx, 308
Bilsthorpe, Nt, 228
Bilston, St, 283
Bilstone, Lei, 159
Bilton, Nb, 223
Bilton, Wa, 322
Bilton, YE, 359, 369
Bilton, YW, 385
Binbrook, Li, 179
Bincknoll, Wlt, 341
Bincombe, Do, 76
Bincombe, So, 266
Binderton, Sx, 307
Bindon, liberty, Do, 68
Binfield, Brk, 14
Binfield, hundred, Ox, 240
Bingham, Nt, 232
Bingham, wapentake, Nt, 232
Bingley, YW, 388
Binham, Nf, 200
Binley, Ha, 109
Binley, Wa, 323
Binnington, YE, 365
Binstead, Sx, 308
Binsted, Ha, 120
Binton, Wa, 326
Bintree, Nf, 200
Binweston, Sa, 257
Birch, Ess, 87
Birch, Little, Ess, 87
Birch, Little, He, 125
Birch, Much, He, 125
Bircham, Great, Nf, 197
Bircham Newton, Nf, 198
Bircham Tofts, Nf, 197
Birchanger, Ess, 86
Birchden, Sx, 313
Birches, The, He, 129
Birchmoor, Bd, 4
Bircholt, hundred [in Lathe of Scray], K, 143
Bircholt, hundred [in Lathe of Shipway], K, 147
Birdbrook, Ess, 80
Birdforth, YN, 378

Birdforth, wapentake, YN, 377
Birdham, Sx, 307
Birdingbury, Wa, 322
Birdsall, YE, 365
Birkby, Cu, 40
Birkby, YN, 378
Birkin, YW, 386
Birley, He, 129
Birling, Sx, 314
Birlingham, Wo, 354
Birmingham, Wa, 325
Birstall, Lei, 162
Birthorpe, Li, 170
Birtley, Nb, 220
Birtsmorton, Wo, 354
Bisbrooke, Ru, 248
Bisham, Brk, 6
Bishampton, Wo, 351
Bishops, Brk, 12
Bishop's Castle, Sa, 253
Bishopsteignton, Dev, 59
Bishopstone, He, 124
Bishopstone, So, 274
Bishopstone, Sx, 314
Bishopstone [in Downton hd.], Wlt, 334
Bishopstone [in Ramsbury hd.], Wlt, 338, 340
Bishopstrow, Wlt, 346
Bishopthorpe, YW, 385
Bishopton, Wa, 327
Bishopton, YW, 394
Bishton, St, 277
Bisley, Gl, 93
Bisley, hundred, Gl, 93
Bispham [in Amounderness wap.], La, 152
Bispham [in Leyland wap.], La, 155
Bisterne, Ha, 121
Bitchfield, Li, 170
Bitchfield, Nb, 220
Bittering, Great, Nf, 208
Bittering, Little, Nf, 208
Bitterley, Sa, 254
Bitterne, Ha, 118
Bittesby, Lei, 158
Bitteswell, Lei, 159
Bittles, Ha, 113 n.
Bitton, Gl, 94
Bivelham, Sx, 317
Bix-Brand, Ox, 240
Bix-Gibwen, Ox, 240
Bixley, Nf, 196
Blaby, Lei, 159
Blackaton, Dev, 50
Blackawton, Dev, 64
Blackbourne, hundred, K, 143
Blackbourne, hundred, Sf, 292
Blackburn, La, 153
Blackburn, wapentake, La, 152
Blackenhurst, hundred, Wo, 354
Blackford [in Bempstone hd.], So, 262

Blackford [in Whitley hd.], So, 274
Blackgrove, Bk, 19 n.
Blackgrove, hundred, Wlt, 341
Blackham, Sx, 313
Blackheath, hundred, K, 145
Blackheath, hundred, Sr, 298
Blackheddon, Nb, 220
Blackland, Wlt, 337
Blacknorle, He, 126
Blackpool, Dev, 53
Blackrod, La, 153
Blackthorn, Ox, 239
Blacktoft, YE, 363
Blackwell, Cu, 38
Blackwell, Db, 48
Blackwell, Wa, 351
Bladon, Ox, 244
Blagdon, Nb, 222
Blagdon [in Taunton hd.], So, 264, 265
Blagdon [in Winterstoke hd.], So, 259
Blagrave, Brk, 10
Blakemere, He, 127
Blakeney, Gl, 104
Blakeney, Nf, 199
Blakenham, Great, Sf, 286
Blakenham, Little, Sf, 285
Blakesle, So, 260 n.
Blakesley, Np, 211
Blandford, Do, 67, 77 n.
Blandford Forum, Do, 78
Blandford St. Mary, Do, 73
Blankney, Li, 173
Blashenwell, Do, 77
Blaston, Lei, 165
Blatchington, East, Sx, 314, 315
Blatchington, West, Sx, 312
Blatherwycke, Np, 215
Blaxhall, Sf, 294
Blaxton, YW, 392
Bleadon, So, 273
Bleangate, hundred, K, 141
Bleasby, Nt, 231
Bledington, Gl, 103
Bledisloe, hundred, Gl, 104
Bledlow, Bk, 21
Blencarn, Cu, 37
Blencogo, Cu, 37
Blencow, Cu, 37
Blendworth, Ha, 114
Blenkinsopp, Nb, 220
Blennerhasset, Cu, 39
Bletchingdon, Ox, 238
Bletchingley, Sr, 297, 298
Bletchingley (foreign), Sr, 303
Bletchley, Sa, 251
Bletsoe, Bd, 2
Blewbury, Brk, 8, 13
Blickling, Nf, 201
Blidworth, Nt, 231
Blindcrake, Cu, 39

Blisland, Co, 33
Blisworth, Np, 217
Blithfield, St, 277
Blockley, Gl, 351
Blofield, Nf, 194
Blofield, hundred, Nf, 194
Bloomsbury, Mx, 191
Bloxham, Ox, 235, 244
Bloxham, hundred, Ox, 242
Bloxholm, Li, 173
Bloxworth, Do, 73
Blundeston, Sf, 290
Blunham, Bd, 2
Blunsdon, Broad, Wlt, 343
Blunsdon Gay, Wlt, 343
Blunsdon St. Andrew, Wlt, 343
Bluntisham, Hu, 137 n.
Blunts, Great, Ess, 85
Blunts, Little, Ess, 85
Blyborough, Li, 176
Blyford, Sf, 289
Blymhill, St, 282
Blyth, Nt, 228
Blythburgh, Sf, 289
Blything, hundred, Sf, 288
Blyton, Li, 177, 186
Boarhunt, East, Ha, 110
Boarhunt Herbelyn, Ha, 110
Boarhunt, West, Ha, 110
Boarstall, Bk, 22 n.
Bobbington, St, 283
Bobbingworth, Ess, 83
Bockenfield, Nb, 222
Bockhampton, Brk, 10
Bockhampton, Do, 68
Bocking, Ess, 80
Bockleton, Wo, 352
Boconnoc, Co, 34
Boddington, Gl, 93, 99
Boddington, Np, 210
Boddington, Sx, 306
Bodenham, He, 123
Bodenham, Wlt, 334
Bodenham Moor, He, 123
Bodham, Nf, 199
Bodicote, Ox, 242
Bodmin, Co, 33
Bodmin Extra, Co, 32
Bodney, Nf, 203
Boghton', Nt, 232
Bognor, Sx, 307
Bolam, Nb, 222
Bolas, Great, Sa, 251
Bolberry, Dev, 51
Bold, La, 150
Bold, The, Sa, 255
Boldre, Ha, 106
Bole, Nt, 227
Bolham, Dev, 55
Bolham, Nt, 228

Bolingbroke, Old, Li, 185
Bolingbroke, Soke, Li, 167, 185
Bolney, Ox, 240
Bolnhurst, Bd, 5
Bolsover, Db, 48
Bolstone, He, 125
Boltby, YN, 377
Bolton [in Allerdale wap.], Cu, 39
Bolton [in Egremont lib.], Cu, 40
Bolton', Cu, 40
Bolton, La, 154
Bolton, We, 330
Bolton, YE, 361
Bolton, YW, 388
Bolton by Bowland, YW, 383
Bolton, East, YN, 372
Bolton le Sands, La, 156
Bolton Percy, YW, 385
Bolton upon Dearne, YW, 394
Bolton, West, YN, 372
Bonby, Li, 178
Bondgate, YW, 394
Bondleigh, Dev, 62
Bonewood, Ha, 110
Bongate, We, 329
Boningale, Sa, 256
Bonsall, Db, 44
Bonthorpe, Li, 184
Bonwick, YE, 360
Bookham, Sr, 301
Bootham, YN, 379, 380
Boothby Graffoe, Li, 174
Boothby Pagnell, Li, 172
Boothby, wapentake, Li, 174
Bootle, La, 151
Booton, Nf, 201
Bordean, Ha, 111
Borden [in Milton], K, 147
Bordesley, Wa, 325
Boreham, Ess, 85
Boreham, Wlt, 347
Boreton, Sa, 252
Borley, Ess, 80
Borough, Dev, 62
Boroughbridge, YW, 357, 395
Borrowby [in Allerton lib.], YN, 379
Borrowby [in Langbargh wap.], YN, 375
Borwick, La, 156
Bosbury, He, 129
Boscastle, Co, 33
Boscombe, Wlt, 345
Bosham, Sx, 305, 306
Bosham, hundred, Sx, 306
Boslingthorpe, Li, 177
Bosmere, hundred, Ha, 116
Bosmere, hundred, Sf, 285
Bossall, YN, 376
Bossington, Ha, 106
Bossington, So, 272
Boston, Li, 167, 169, 192

Bosworth, Husbands, Lei, 164
Bosworth, Market, Lei, 160
Botcherby, Cu, 38
Botchergate, Cu, 40
Botcheston, Lei, 160
Bothal, Nb, 222 n.
Bothamsall, Nt, 229
Bothel, Cu, 39
Botley, Brk, 12
Botley, Ha, 109
Botloe, hundred, Gl, 95
Bottesford, Lei, 163
Bottesford, Li, 176, 186
Bottisham, Ca, 24
Botus Fleming, Co, 35
Boughton, Nf, 203
Boughton [in Corby hd.], Np, 215
Boughton [in Spelhoe hd.], Np, 217
Boughton, Nt, 228
Boughton, hundred, K, 143
Bouldon, Sa, 255
Boulge, Sf, 295
Boultham, Li, 175
Boulton, Db, 44
Bountisborough, hundred, Ha, 113
Bourn, Ca, 26
Bourne, Li, 170
Bourton [in Rowley hd.], Bk, 16
Bourton [in Shrivenham hd.], Brk, 10
Bourton, Sa, 254
Bourton [in Cannings hd.], Wlt, 348
Bourton [in Dole hd.], Wlt, 341
Bourton, Black, Ox, 237
Bourton, Great, Ox, 241
Bourton, Little, Ox, 241
Bourton on Dunsmore, Wa, 322
Bourton on the Hill, Gl, 92, 99
Bourton on the Water, Gl, 103
Boveridge, Do, 75
Bovey, North, Dev, 59
Bovey Tracey, Dev, 59
Bow, Mx, 191
Bowcombe, Ha, 119
Bowden, Db, 47
Bowden, Great, Lei, 165
Bowden, Little, Lei, 157, 209, 213
Bowerchalke, Wlt, 342
Bowers Gifford, Ess, 85
Bowes, YN, 373
Bowley, He, 123
Bowling, YW, 388
Bowness on Solway, Cu, 37
Bowsden, Nb, 225
Bowthorpe, Li, 171
Bowthorpe, Nf, 206
Bowthorpe, YE, 363
Box, Wlt, 344
Box and Stockbridge, hundred, Sx, 307
Boxford, Brk, 9
Boxford, Sf, 291

Boxgrove, Sx, 307
Boxted, Ess, 87
Boxted, Sf, 290
Boxton, Db, 47
Boxwell, Gl, 102
Boxworth, Ca, 25
Boyatt, Ha, 109
Boycott, Bk, 15, 235, 237
Boyleston, Db, 45
Boynton, YE, 366
Boythorpe, YE, 365
Boyton, Co, 33
Boyton, Sf, 295
Boyton, Wlt, 340
Boyton End, Sf, 294
Bozeat, Np, 212 n.
Braceborough, Li, 169
Bracebridge, Li, 174
Braceby, Li, 172
Bracewell, YW, 382
Bracken, YE, 360
Brackenborough, Li, 183
Brackendale, Nf, 206
Brackenfield, Db, 48
Brackenholm, YE, 362
Brackley, New, Np, 218
Brackley, Old, Np, 210
Bracon Ash, Nf, 206
Bradbourne, Db, 44
Bradden, Np, 211
Braddock, Co, 34
Bradeford, He, 130
Bradeley, Sa, 254
Bradene, So, 266 n.
Bradenham, Bk, 21
Bradenham, East, Nf, 203
Bradenham, West, Nf, 203
Bradfield, Brk, 8
Bradfield, Ess, 88
Bradfield, Nf, 202
Bradfield, Wlt, 339
Bradfield, YW, 393
Bradfield Combust, Sf, 292
Bradfield St. Clare, Sf, 292
Bradfield St. George, Sf, 292
Bradford, Dev, 61
Bradford, Nb, 220
Bradford, YW, 389
Bradford Abbas, Do, 71
Bradford, hundred, Sa, 250
Bradford, hundred, Wlt, 347
Bradford on Avon, Wlt, 347
Bradford on Tone, So, 265
Bradford Peverell, Do, 68
Bradford, West, YW, 383
Bradgate, Lei, 161
Bradham, Dev, 66
Bradiford, Dev, 62
Brading, Ha, 119
Bradle, Do, 76

Bradley, Db, 45
Bradley, Ha, 112
Bradley, Li, 181
Bradley [in Cuttlestone hd.], St, 282
Bradley [in Seisdon hd.], St, 283
Bradley, Wo, 351
Bradley, Great, Sf, 294
Bradley, hundred, Gl, 98
Bradley, Little, Sf, 293
Bradley, Maiden, Wlt, 334
Bradley, North, Wlt, 339
Bradley, wapentake, Li, 180
Bradley, West, So, 267
Bradleys Both, YW, 383
Bradmore, Nt, 230
Bradninch, Dev, 63, 66
Bradnop, St, 281
Bradon, South, So, 272
Bradpole, Do, 72
Bradstone, Dev, 60
Bradwell, Bk, 17
Bradwell, Db, 47
Bradwell, Dev, 62
Bradwell, Ess, 84
Bradwell, Sf, 290
Bradwell on Sea, Ess, 84
Bradworthy, Dev, 61
Brafferton, YN, 376
Brafield on the Green, Np, 217
Brailes, Wa, 321
Brailsford, Db, 45
Braintree, Ess, 80
Braiseworth, Sf, 287
Braithwaite, Cu, 39 n., 40
Braithwell, YW, 392
Bramber, Sx, 305
Bramber, rape, Sx, 309
Brambletye, Sx, 315
Bramcote, Nt, 229
Bramcote, Wa, 324
Bramdean, Ha, 110
Bramerton, Nf, 196
Bramfield, Hrt, 134
Bramfield, Sf, 288
Bramford, Sf, 286
Bramham, YW, 386, 387
Bramhope, YW, 385
Bramley, Ha, 118
Bramley, Sr, 298
Bramley [in Morley wap.], YW, 389
Bramley [in Strafforth wap.], YW, 392
Brampford Pyne, Dev, 59
Brampford Speke, Dev, 58
Brampton, Cu, 38
Brampton, He, 127
Brampton, Hu, 136
Brampton, Li, 178
Brampton, Nf, 202
Brampton, Sf, 289
Brampton, We, 329

Brampton Abbotts, He, 127
Brampton Ash, Np, 215
Brampton Bierlow, YW, 329, 393
Brampton, Chapel, Np, 216
Brampton, Church, Np, 216
Brampton en le Morthen, YW, 393
Bramshall, St, 280
Bramshaw, Ha, 105, 334
Bramshill, Ha, 117
Bramshott, Ha, 114
Bramworth, Kirk, YW, 391
Brancaster, Nf, 197
Branch, hundred, Wlt, 342
Brancroft, YW, 392
Brandesburton, YW, 359, 369
Brandeston, Sf, 295
Brandiston, Nf, 200
Brandon, Li, 174
Brandon, Nb, 224
Brandon, Sf, 293
Brandon, Wa, 323
Brandon Parva, Nf, 206
Brandsby, YN, 376
Bransbury, Ha, 108
Bransby, Li, 178
Branscombe, Dev, 56
Bransford, Wo, 354
Branston, Lei, 164
Branston, Li, 174
Branston, St, 280
Brantham, Sf, 285
Brantingham, YE, 360, 363
Branton, Nb, 224
Branxton, Nb, 225
Brascote, Lei, 158
Brassington, Db, 45
Brasted, K, 140, 146
Bratoft, Li, 182
Brattleby, Li, 177
Bratton, Wlt, 336
Bratton Clovelly, Dev, 60
Bratton Fleming, Dev, 62
Braughing, Hrt, 132
Braughing, hundred, Hrt, 132
Brauncewell, Li, 173
Braunston, Np, 215
Braunston, Ru, 246
Braunstone, Lei, 160
Braunton, Dev, 66
Braunton, hundred, Dev, 62
Brawby, YN, 379
Braxted, Great, Ess, 84
Braxted, Little, Ess, 84
Bray, Brk, 14
Bray, High, Dev, 53
Bray, hundred, Brk, 14
Bray, Knight's, Dev, 53
Braybrooke, Np, 212
Braydeston, Nf, 194
Brayton, YW, 386

Breadsall, Db, 42
Breage, Co, 30
Breamore, Ha, 114
Brean, So, 262
Brearton, YW, 395
Breaston, Db, 43
Breckenbrough, YN, 378
Breckles, Nf, 204
Brede, Sx, 316
Bredecroft, Li, 167, 169
Bredenbury, He, 123
Bredfield, Sf, 295
Bredicot, Wo, 351
Bredon, Wo, 350
Bredwardine, He, 127
Bredy, Long, Do, 72
Breedon on the Hill, Lei, 161
Bregg, Sf, 289
Breighton, YE, 361
Breinton, He, 124
Brelston, He, 126
Bremeridge, Wlt, 337
Bremhill, Wlt, 344
Bremilham, Wlt, 339
Bremridge, Dev, 53
Brenchley, hundred, K, 144
Brendon, Dev, 53
Brenkley, Nb, 221
Brent, East, So, 264
Brent Eleigh, Sf, 290
Brent, hundred, So, 264
Brent Knoll, So, 264
Brent, South, Dev, 51
Brentford, Mx, 190
Brentingby, Lei, 163
Brentwood, Ess, 87
Bressingham, Nf, 207
Bretby, Db, 46
Bretford, Wa, 323
Bretforton, Wo, 355
Bretherton, La, 154
Brettenham, Nf, 205
Brettenham, Sf, 291
Bretton, Monk, YW, 390
Bretton, West, YW, 392
Brewham, So, 269
Brewood, St, 282
Briantspuddle, Do, 69
Bricett, Great, Sf, 286
Bricett, Little, Sf, 286
Bricheclyston', Dev, 56
Brickendon Bury, Hrt, 132
Brickhampton, Gl, 97
Brickhill, Bow, Bk, 17
Brickhill, Great, Bk, 17
Brickhill, Little, Bk, 17
Bricklehampton, Wo, 354
Bridekirk, Cu, 39
Bridestowe, Dev, 60
Bridford, Dev, 58

Bridge, Canon, He, 127
Bridge End, Li, 170
Bridge Farm, Sf, 289 n.
Bridge, hundred, K, 142
Bridge Sollers, He, 124
Bridgeford, Great, St, 279
Bridgeford, Little, St, 279
Bridgehampton, So, 263
Bridgerule, Dev, 33, 61
Bridgford, East, Nt, 232
Bridgford, West, Nt, 230
Bridgham, Nf, 205
Bridgnorth, Sa, 249, 257
Bridgwater, So, 272
Bridlington, YE, 365
Bridmore, Wlt, 343
Bridport, Do, 67, 78
Bridstow, He, 126
Briercliffe, La, 153
Brierley, YW, 392
Brigg, Li, 179
Brigham, Cu, 39
Brigham, YE, 366
Brightford, hundred, Sx, 310
Brightling, Sx, 316
Brightlingsea, Ess, 88
Brighton, Sx, 312
Brightwalton, Brk, 13
Brightwell, Brk, 13
Brightwell, Sf, 296
Brightwell Baldwin, Ox, 240
Brightwells-Barrow, hundred, Gl, 100
Brigmerston, Wlt, 345
Brignall, YN, 373
Brigsley, Li, 180
Brigstock, Np, 214 n., 215
Brill, Bk, 15, 22
Brimfield, He, 130
Brimington, Db, 48
Brimpsfield, Gl, 92
Brimpton, Brk, 9
Brimstree, hundred, Sa, 256
Brind, YE, 362
Brindle, La, 155
Brineton, St, 282
Brington, Hu, 138
Brington, Np, 216
Briningham, Nf, 199
Brinkhill, Li, 185
Brinkley, Ca, 27
Brinklow, Wa, 319, 320
Brinklow, leet, Wa, 323
Brinkworth, Wlt, 339
Brinsley, Nt, 230
Brinsop, He, 124
Brinsworth, YW, 392
Brinton, Nf, 199
Brisco, Cu, 40
Brisley, Nf, 207
Brislington, So, 270

Bristol, 90
Briston, Nf, 199
Britford, Wlt, 334
Britwell, Ox, 241
Britwell Priory, Ox, 240
Brixham, Dev, 50
Brixton, Dev, 51
Brixton Barton, Dev, 51
Brixton Deverill, Wlt, 341
Brixton, hundred, Sr, 302
Brixworth, Np, 212
Broadfield, He, 123
Broadfield, Hrt, 132
Broadhembury, Dev, 63
Broadhempston, Dev, 50
Broadlowash, Db, 44
Broadmayne, Do, 68
Broadridge, Dev, 55 n.
Broadstonehill, Ox, 236
Broadwas, Wo, 350
Broadwater, Sx, 310
Broadwater, hundred, Hrt, 133
Broadway, Do, 72
Broadway, So, 272
Broadway, Wo, 354
Broadwell, Gl, 103
Broadwell, Ox, 237
Broadwell, Wa, 322
Broadwindsor, Do, 73
Broadwood-Kelly, Dev, 60
Broadwoodwidger, Dev, 60
Broad Town, Wlt, 344
Brobury, He, 125
Brockdish, Nf, 297
Brockenhurst, Ha, 116
Brockford, Sf, 287
Brockhall, Np, 216
Brockham, Sr, 299
Brockhampton [in Bradley hd.], Gl, 98
Brockhampton [in Cleeve hd.], Gl, 93
Brockhampton, He, 123
Brockhampton Green, Do, 74
Brockholes, La, 151
Brockhurst, Wa, 324
Brocklesby, Li, 179
Brockley, Sf, 291
Brockley, So, 260
Brockmanton, He, 130
Brocksby, Lei, 161
Brockton, Sa, 253
Brockton, St, 278
Brockworth, Gl, 97
Brocton, St, 281
Brodsworth, YW, 394
Brokenborough, Wlt, 337
Bromeswell, Sf, 295
Bromfield, Cu, 39
Bromfield, Sa, 254
Bromfield, Little, Sa, 255
Bromham, Bd, 2

Bromham, Wlt, 335
Bromkinsthorpe, Lei, 160
Bromley, He, 125
Bromley, Mx, 191
Bromley, Abbott's, St, 277
Bromley, Bagot's, St, 277
Bromley, Gerrard's, St, 278
Bromley, Great, Ess, 88
Bromley, hundred, K, 145
Bromley, King's, St, 277
Bromley, Little, Ess, 88
Bromlow, Sa, 257
Brompton, Sa, 256
Brompton [in Allerton lib.], YN, 378
Brompton [in Pickering lib.], YN, 381
Brompton on Swale, YN, 374
Brompton, Patrick, YN, 371
Brompton, Potter, YE, 365
Brompton Ralph, So, 265
Brompton Regis, So, 265
Bromsberrow, Gl, 95
Bromsgrove, Wo, 353
Bromwich, Castle, Wa, 325
Bromwich, Little, Wa, 325
Bromwich, West, St, 279
Bromyard, He, 124
Bromyard (foreign), He, 124
Brook, Ha, 119
Brook, Ru, 246
Brook, Wlt, 336
Brook Street, Gl, 97
Brooke, Nf, 195
Brookethorpe, Gl, 97
Brookhampton, Ox, 240
Brookley, Ha, 116
Broom, Wo, 276, 277
Broom, King's, Wa, 326
Broome, Nf, 195
Broome, Sf, 287
Broome, Wlt, 335
Broomfield, Ess, 85
Broomfield, So, 260
Broomfleet, YE, 368
Broomhall, Wo, 350 n.
Broomhaugh, Nb, 221
Broomholm, Nf, 202
Broomley, Nb, 221
Broseley, Sa, 254
Brothercross, hundred, Nf, 198
Brotherton, YW, 387
Brotton, YN, 375
Brough, We, 328
Brough, YN, 371
Brough Sowerby, We, 328
Brougham, We, 329
Broughton [in Aylesbury hd.], Bk, 20
Broughton [in Moulsoe hd.], Bk, 17
Broughton, Cu, 39
Broughton, Ha, 106
Broughton, Hu, 137

Broughton, La, 152
Broughton [in Aswardhurn wap.], Li, 172
Broughton [in Manley wap.], Li, 176
Broughton, Np, 212
Broughton, Ox, 242
Broughton [in Brimstree hd.], Sa, 256
Broughton [in Pimhill hd.], Sa, 251
Broughton, St, 278
Broughton, Wa, 321
Broughton, YN, 375
Broughton, YW, 383
Broughton Astley, Lei, 158
Broughton, Brant, Li, 174
Broughton, Church, Db, 45
Broughton, Drake's, Wo, 354 n.
Broughton (East), La, 156
Broughton Gifford, Wlt, 347
Broughton Hackett, Wo, 354
Broughton, Little, YN, 375
Broughton Lythe, YN, 373
Broughton, Nether, Lei, 164
Broughton Poggs, Ox, 237
Broughton, Upper, Nt, 232
Broughton, West, Db, 45
Broune', So, 272
Brownshall, hundred, Do, 74
Brownsover, Wa, 323
Brownstone, Dev, 50
Brownwich, Ha, 116
Broxa, YN, 381
Broxash, hundred, He, 123
Broxbourne, Hrt, 131
Broxhead, Ha, 114
Broxholme, Li, 178
Broxted, Ess, 82
Broxtow, Nt, 230
Broxtow, wapentake, Nt, 229
Broxwood, He, 129
Bruckland, Dev, 57
Bruer, Temple, Li, 173
Bruerne, Gl, 91 n.
Brugeset, Ox, 239
Bruisyard, Sf, 294
Brumby, Li, 186
Brumstead, Nf, 193
Brundall, Nf, 194
Brundish, Sf, 288
Brundon, Sf, 79, 80, 284
Bruntingthorpe, Lei, 159
Brunton, Nb, 225
Brunton, East, Nb, 222
Brunton, West, Nb, 222
Brushford, So, 265
Bruton, So, 269
Bruton, hundred, So, 268
Bruttone, So, 262 n.
Bryanstone, Do, 75
Brympton, So, 262
Bryning, La, 152
Bubbenhall, Wa, 323

Bubwith, YE, 360, 367
Buckby, Long, Np, 216
Buckden, Hu, 137
Buckden, YW, 383
Buckenham, Nf, 194
Buckenham, New, Nf, 205
Buckenham, Old, Nf, 205
Buckenham Tofts, Nf, 204
Buckerell, Dev, 56
Buckfastleigh, Dev, 51
Buckhurst, Brk, 346
Buckingham, Bk, 16
Buckingham, hundred, Bk, 16
Buckinghamshire, 15–22
Buckland, Brk, 12
Buckland, Bk, 20
Buckland, Gl, 94
Buckland, Hrt, 133
Buckland, Sr, 299
Buckland Barton, Dev, 50
Buckland Brewer, Dev, 52
Buckland Dinham, So, 261
Buckland, East, Dev, 62
Buckland Filleigh, Dev, 52
Buckland in the Moor, Dev, 50
Buckland Monachorum, Dev, 52
Buckland Newton, Do, 74
Buckland Newton, hundred, Do, 74
Buckland, North, Dev, 62
Buckland St. Mary, So, 272
Buckland, West, Dev, 62
Buckland, West, So, 270
Bucklebury, Brk, 7
Bucklebury, hundred, Brk, 8
Bucklesham, Sf, 296
Buckminster, Lei, 163
Bucknall, Li, 182
Bucknall, St, 278
Bucknell, Ox, 238
Bucknell, Sa, 253
Buckover, Gl, 101
Buckrose, wapentake, YE, 364
Buckton, YE, 365
Buckworth, Hu, 138
Budbrook, Lower, Dev, 58
Budbrooke, Wa, 325
Budby, Nt, 233
Buddlesgate, hundred, Ha, 108
Budle, Nb, 225
Budleigh, East, Dev, 66
Budleigh, East, hundred, Dev, 65
Budleigh, West, hundred, Dev, 55
Budock, Co, 30
Budshead, Dev, 52
Bugbrooke, Np, 216
Bugley, Wlt, 347
Bugthorpe, YE, 365, 367
Bulby, Li, 170
Bulcamp, Sf, 289
Bulcote, Nt, 231

Bulford, Wlt, 345
Bulk, La, 156
Bulkington, Wa, 324
Bulkington, Wlt, 338
Bullingdon, hundred, Ox, 239
Bullingham, Lower, He, 127
Bullinghope, He, 127
Bullington, Ha, 111
Bullington, Li, 181
Bulmer, Ess, 80
Bulmer, YN, 376
Bulmer, wapentake, YN, 376
Bulphan, Ess, 86
Bulstone, hundred, So, 272
Bulwell, Nt, 234
Bulwick, Np, 215
Bumpstead, Helions, Ess, 86
Bumpstead, Steeple, Ess, 80
Bungay, Sf, 289
Bunny, Nt, 230
Bunshill, He, 124
Bunsty, hundred, Bk, 17
Bunwell, Nf, 196
Burbage, Lei, 158
Burbage, Wlt, 347
Burbeach, hundred, Sx, 310
Burches, Ha, 115
Burcombe (North), Wlt, 335, 342
Burcombe (South), Wlt, 335, 342
Burcot, Ox, 243
Burcott, So, 271
Burcott, The, He, 124
Burdale, YE, 364
Bure, Ha, 107
Bures, Ess & Sf, 79, 80, 290
Bures, Mount, Ess, 88
Burford, Ox, 237
Burford, Sa, 253
Burgate, Ha, 114
Burgate, Sf, 287
Burgh, Nf, 199
Burgh, Sf, 296
Burgh, Sr, 302
Burgh by Sands, Cu, 37
Burgh Castle, Sf, 290
Burgh le Marsh, Li, 182
Burgh next Aylsham, Nf, 202
Burgh on Bain, Li, 181
Burgh St. Margaret, Nf, 193
Burghclere, Ha, 109
Burghfield, Brk, 8
Burghfield Regis, Brk, 8
Burghill, He, 124
Burghope, He, 123
Burghwallis, YW, 391
Buriton, Ha, 114
Burland, YE, 363
Burland, South, Dev, 63
Burlands, So, 264
Burleigh, Sx, 312, 313

Burlescombe, Dev, 63
Burleston, Do, 69
Burley, Ha, 117
Burley, Ru, 247
Burley in Wharfedale, YW, 388
Burlingham, North, Nf, 194
Burlingham, South, Nf, 194
Burlton, He, 124
Burmington, Wa, 321
Burn, YW, 386
Burnaston, Db, 44
Burnby, YE, 361
Burneston, YN, 380
Burnett, So, 270
Burnham, Bk, 21
Burnham, Li, 179
Burnham Deepdale, Nf, 198
Burnham, hundred, Bk, 21
Burnham Norton, Nf, 198
Burnham on Crouch, Ess, 84
Burnham on Sea, So, 262
Burnham Overy, Nf, 198
Burnham Sutton, Nf, 199
Burnham Thorpe, Nf, 199
Burnham Westgate, Nf, 198
Burnley, La, 152
Burnsall, YW, 382
Burpham, Sr, 299
Burpham, Sx, 309
Burradon, Nb, 223
Burreth, Li, 182
Burrill, YN, 371
Burringham, Li, 176, 186
Burrington, Dev, 61
Burrough, Dev, 58 n.
Burrough Green, Ca, 27
Burrough on the Hill, Lei, 165
Burrow, Dev, 58
Burrow with Burrow, La, 155
Bursledon, Ha, 117, 118
Burstall, Sf, 285, 286
Burstead, Great, Ess, 86
Burstead, Little, Ess, 86
Burston, Bk, 18
Burston, Dev, 62
Burston, Hrt, 134
Burston, Nf, 207
Burston, St, 278
Burston, Lower, Bk, 18 n.
Burstow, Sr, 299
Burstwick, YE, 358
Burton, Do, 68
Burton, Ha, 106
Burton, He, 129
Burton, Li, 178
Burton, Nb, 226
Burton, St, 282
Burton, Wa, 321
Burton, We, 330
Burton Agnes, YE, 365

Burton, Bishop, YE, 360, 368
Burton Bradstock, Do, 70, 76
Burton, Cherry, YE, 368, 369
Burton Coggles, Li, 171
Burton Constable, YE, 359
Burton, Constable, YN, 372
Burton Dassett, Wa, 321
Burton Fleming, YE, 366
Burton, Gate, Li, 178
Burton Gronge, Lei, 164
Burton Hastings, Wa, 324
Burton Hill, Wlt, 337
Burton in Lonsdale, YW, 383
Burton Joyce, Nt, 231
Burton Latimer, Np, 214
Burton Lazars, Lei, 163
Burton Leonard, YW, 395
Burton on the Wolds, Lei, 162
Burton on Trent, St, 276
Burton on Ure, YN, 372
Burton Overy, Lei, 164
Burton Pedwardine, Li, 172
Burton Pidsea, YE, 358
Burton Salmon, YW, 386
Burton upon Stather, Li, 175, 186
Burton upon Trent, St, 280
Burton, West, Nt, 229
Burton, West, Sx, 309
Burton, West, YN, 373
Burtonwood, La, 150
Burwarton, Sa, 255
Burwash, Sx, 317
Burwell, Ca, 24
Burwell, Ha, 113
Burwell, Li, 183
Bury, Hu, 137
Bury, La, 154
Bury, Sx, 309
Bury, half-hundred, Sx, 309
Bury St. Edmunds, Sf, 284, 294
Burythorpe, YE, 364
Burytown, Wlt, 343
Busby, YN, 375
Buscot, Brk, 11
Bushbury, St, 282
Bushby, Lei, 164
Bushey, Hrt, 135
Bushley, Wo, 354
Buston, High, Nb, 223
Buston, Low, Nb, 223
Butcombe, So, 271
Butleigh, So, 274
Butley, Sf, 295
Buttercrambe, YN, 376
Butterford, Dev, 64
Buttermere, Wlt, 348
Butterton, St, 281
Butterwick, Li, 169
Butterwick, YE, 366
Butterwick, YN, 377

Butterworth, La, 154
Buttinghill, hundred, Sx, 312
Buttsash, Ha, 116
Buildwas, Little, Sa, 250
Buxhall, Sf, 287
Buxton, Nf, 202
Byfield, Np, 210
Byfleet, Sr, 298
Byford, He, 124
Bygrave, Hrt, 132
Byker, Nb, 222
Bylaugh, Nf, 200
Byne, Sx, 310
Byram, YW, 387
Bytham, Castle, Li, 171
Bytham, Little, Li, 171
Bythorn, Hu, 138
Bywell, Nb, 220

Cabourne, Li, 180
Cadbury, Dev, 63
Cadbury, North, So, 259
Caddington, Bd, 1, 3, 131, 134
Cadeby, Lei, 159
Cadeby, YW, 393
Cadeby, North, Li, 180
Cadeleigh, Dev, 63
Cadland, Ha, 111
Cadney, Li, 178, 186
Cadwell, Ox, 240
Cadworth, hundred, Wlt, 335
Caenby, Li, 176
Caerhays, Co, 31
Cainhoe, Bd, 3
Caistor, Li, 186
Caistor on Sea, Nf, 193
Caistor St. Edmunds, Nf, 196
Calceby, Li, 184
Calcethorpe, Li, 183
Calcewath, wapentake, Li, 183
Calcot, Brk, 10
Calcutt, Wa, 322
Caldbeck, Cu, 39
Caldbergh, YN, 373
Caldecote, Bk, 17
Caldecote, Ca, 26
Caldecote, Hrt, 132
Caldecote, Hu, 138
Caldecote, Wa, 324
Caldecotes, Cu, 40
Caldecott, Ru, 247
Calder, Cu, 40
Caldewell, Wo, 354 n.
Caldwell, Db, 46
Caldwell, YN, 373
Cale, Middle, Db, 47
Calehill, hundred, K, 143
Callaly, Nb, 223
Callaughton, Sa, 254
Callerton, Black, Nb, 221

E e

Callerton, High, Nb, 221
Callerton, Little, Nb, 221
Callow, Db, 44
Callow, He, 127
Calmsden, Gl, 92
Calne, Wlt, 333
Calne, hundred, Wlt, 337
Calstock, Co, 35
Calstone Wellington, Wlt, 337
Calthorp, Ox, 241
Calthorpe, Nf, 202
Calton, YW, 383
Caludon, Wa, 323
Caluhull, He, 128
Calverhall, Sa, 250
Calverley, YW, 388
Calverton, Bk, 17
Calverton, Nt, 232
Cam, Gl, 96
Camberwell, Sr, 302
Cambo, Nb, 222
Camborne, Co, 30
Cambridge and wards, Ca, 23-4
Cambridgeshire, 23-8
Camel, Queen, So, 263
Camel, West, So, 263
Cameley, So, 260
Camelford, Co, 33
Camerton, Cu, 39
Camerton, So, 268
Camerton, YE, 358
Cammas Hall, Ess, 83 n.
Cammeringham, Li, 176
Camois, Ca, 28
Campden, Gl, 94
Campden, Broad, Gl, 94 n.
Campden, Chipping, Gl, 94 n.
Camps, Castle, Ca, 27
Camps, Shudy, Ca, 27
Campsall, YW, 391
Campsey Ash, Sf, 295
Campton, Bd, 4
Cams, Ha, 116
Candlesby, Li, 182
Candleshoe, wapentake, Li, 181
Candover, Brown, Ha, 111
Candover, Chilton, Ha, 111
Canewdon, Ess, 81
Canfield, Great, Ess, 82
Canfield, Little, Ess, 82
Canford, Do, 69
Cannings, All, Wlt, 336
Cannings, Bishops, Wlt, 348
Cannings, hundred, Wlt, 348
Cannington, So, 267
Cannington, hundred, So, 267
Cannock, St, 281
Canonsleigh, Dev, 56
Canonteign, Dev, 60
Canterbury, K, 140, 147

Canterton, Ha, 117
Cantley, Nf, 194
Cantley, YW, 393
Cantlop, Sa, 252
Cantsfield, La, 156
Canwick, Li, 174
Capel St. Andrew, Sf, 295
Capel St. Mary, Sf, 285
Capheaton, Nb, 220
Capland, So, 266, 272
Caple, King's, He, 125
Caradoc, He, 126
Carbrooke, Nf, 204
Carburton, Nt, 233
Cardington, Bd, 3
Cardington, Sa, 254
Cardinham, Co, 34
Careby, Li, 170
Carhampton, So, 272
Carhampton, hundred, So, 272
Carisbrooke, Ha, 120
Carlatton, Cu, 41
Carlby, Li, 169
Carleton [near Carlisle], Cu, 40
Carleton [near Penrith], Cu, 41
Carleton, La, 152
Carleton [in Osgoldcross wap.], YW, 391
Carleton [in Staincliffe, wap.], YW, 383
Carleton, East, Nf, 206
Carleton Forehoe, Nf, 206
Carleton Rode, Nf, 196
Carleton St. Peter, Nf, 195
Carlford, hundred, Sf, 296
Carlisle, Cu, 36, 41
Carlisle, Bishop of, liberty, Cu, 40
Carlisle, Prior of, liberty, Cu, 40
Carlton, Bd, 2
Carlton, Ca, 27
Carlton, Lei, 159
Carlton, Nt, 231
Carlton, Sf, 288
Carlton, YE, 359
Carlton [in Hang wap.], YN, 373
Carlton [in Langbargh wap.], YN, 375
Carlton [in Barkston Ash wap.], YW, 386
Carlton [in Morley wap.], YW, 389
Carlton [in Skyrack wap.], YW, 387
Carlton, Castle, Li, 183
Carlton Colville, Sf, 286
Carlton Curlieu, Lei, 165
Carlton, East, Np, 215
Carlton, Great, Li, 183
Carlton Husthwaite, YN, 379
Carlton in Lindrick, Nt, 229
Carlton le Moorland, Li, 175
Carlton, Little, Li, 183
Carlton, Middle, Li, 177
Carlton Miniott, YN, 378
Carlton, North, Li, 177
Carlton on Trent, Nt, 231

Carlton Scroop, Li, 174
Carlton, South, Li, 178
Carnaby, YE, 365, 368
Carnforth, La, 156
Carperby, YN, 372
Carr House, YW, 393
Carrock, Castle, Cu, 38
Carshalton, Sr, 300
Carsington, Db, 45
Carswell, Brk, 12
Carthorpe, YN, 371
Cartington, Nb, 224, 226
Carton, Wo, 352
Cary, Castle, So, 259
Cary Fitzpaine, So, 274
Casewick, Li, 169
Cassington, Ox, 242
Cassio, Hrt, 134
Casterton, We, 330
Casterton, Great, Ru, 247
Casterton, Little, Ru, 247
Casthorpe, Li, 171
Castleford, YW, 390
Castlemorton, Wo, 353
Castlerigg, Cu, 39
Castlethorpe, Li, 176 n.
Castleton, Db, 47
Castleton, Do, 71
Castleton, La, 154
Castlett, Gl, 98
Castley, YW, 384
Caston, Nf, 204
Castor, Np, 213
Castrum, So, 260 n.
Catcott, So, 274
Caterham, Sr, 303
Catesby, Np, 215
Catfield, Nf, 193
Catfoss, YE, 359
Catherington, Ha, 114
Catisfield, Ha, 116
Catley, He, 128
Catmore, Brk, 13
Caton, La, 155
Catsash, hundred, So, 259
Catsfield, Sx, 316
Cattal, YW, 385
Catterall, La, 151
Catterick, YN, 371
Catterlen, Cu, 37
Catterton, YW, 385
Catteshall, Sr, 298
Catthorpe, Lei, 160
Cattistock, Do, 70
Catton, Db, 46
Catton, Nf, 194
Catton, YE, 361
Catton, YN, 378
Catwick, YE, 359, 369
Catworth, Hu, 138

Catworth, Little, Hu, 138 n.
Caulcott, Ox, 238
Cauldon, St, 281
Caundle, Bishop's, Do, 71
Caundle, Purse, Do, 71
Caundle, Stourton, Do, 74
Caundle Wake, Do, 74
Caunton, Nt, 231
Cause, Sa, 253
Cave, North, YE, 361, 367, 368
Cave, South, YE, 361, 367, 368
Cavendish, Sf, 290
Cavenham, Sf, 293
Caversfield, Ox, 15, 16, 235
Caversham, Brk, 6, 240
Caverswall, St, 281
Cavil, YE, 362
Cawardine Green, He, 127
Cawdon, hundred, Wlt, 334
Cawkwell, Li, 182
Cawood, YW, 386
Cawston, Nf, 202
Cawthorne, YW, 392
Cawthorpe [in Aveland wap.], Li, 170
Cawthorpe [in Ludborough wap.], Li, 180
Cawton, YN, 377
Caxton, Ca, 26
Caynham, Sa, 256
Caythorpe, Li, 174
Caythorpe, YE, 366, 367
Cayton, YN, 381
Cerne Abbas, Do, 70
Cerne, Up, Do, 71
Cerney, North, Gl, 92
Cerney, South, Gl, 99
Cesters Over, Wa, 323
Chaceley, Gl, 353
Chackmore, Bk, 16
Chacombe, Np, 210
Chadderton, La, 154
Chaddesden, Db, 43
Chaddesley Corbett, Wo, 353
Chaddleworth, Brk, 9
Chadlington, Eastend, Ox, 236
Chadlington, hundred, Ox, 236
Chadlington, Westend, Ox, 236
Chadnor, He, 130
Chadshunt, Wa, 321
Chadstone, Np, 217
Chadwell, Lei, 161
Chadwell St. Mary, Ess, 86
Chadwich, Wo, 353
Chaffcombe, So, 275
Chafford, hundred, Ess, 87
Chagford, Dev, 58
Chaldon, Do, 68
Chale, Ha, 119
Chalfield, Wlt, 347
Chalfont St. Giles, Bk, 21
Chalfont St. Peter, Bk, 21

Chalford [in Chadlington hd.], Ox, 236
Chalford [in Lewknor hd.], Ox, 240
Chalgrave, Bd, 4
Chalgrove, Ox, 240
Chalke, Broad, Wlt, 342
Chalke, hundred, Wlt, 342
Challacombe, Dev, 53
Challow, Brk, 9
Chalton, Ha, 114
Champson, Dev, 54
Chanstone, He, 128
Chapmanslade, Wlt, 336
Charborough, Do, 69
Chard, So, 270, 273
Chardstock, Dev, 49, 67, 71
Charfield, Gl, 102
Charford, Ha, 114
Charingworth, Gl, 95
Charlbury, Ox, 241
Charlcombe, So, 261
Charlecote, Wa, 320
Charles, Dev, 53
Charleton, Dev, 64
Charlton, Brk, 11
Charlton [in Henbury hd.], Gl, 102
Charlton [in Longtree hd.], Gl, 96
Charlton, Mx, 189
Charlton, So, 267
Charlton [in Pagham hd.], Sx, 307
Charlton [in Singleton hd.], Sx, 306
Charlton [in Steyning hd.], Sx, 310
Charlton [in Chedglow hd.], Wlt, 337
Charlton [in Downton hd.], Wlt, 334
Charlton [in Swanborough hd.], Wlt, 335
Charlton, Wo, 351
Charlton Abbotts, Gl, 98
Charlton Horethorne, So, 269
Charlton, hundred, Brk, 7
Charlton Kings, Gl, 92
Charlton Mackrell, So, 263
Charlton Marshall, Do, 69
Charlton Musgrove, So, 269
Charlton, North, Nb, 225
Charlton on Otmoor, Ox, 238
Charlton, South, Nb, 225
Charlwood, Sr, 299
Charminster, Do, 68
Charnage, Wlt, 334
Charnes, St, 278
Charney Bassett, Brk, 12
Charnham Street, Brk, 10 n., 348 n.
Charnock Richard, La, 154
Charsfield, Sf, 295
Chart, hundred, K, 142
Chartley, St, 277
Charton, Dev, 57
Charwelton, Np, 215
Chastleton, Ox, 236
Chatburn, La, 152
Chatcull, St, 278

Chatham and Gillingham, hundred, K, 145
Chatley, Ess, 84
Chatteris, Ca, 28
Chatton, Nb, 224
Chaureth, Ess, 82
Chawleigh, Dev, 62
Chawley, Brk, 12
Chawston, Bd, 2
Chawton, Ha, 114
Chazey, Ox, 240 n.
Cheadle, St, 281
Cheam, East, Sr, 301
Cheam, West, Sr, 301
Chearsley, Bk, 19
Chebsey, St, 279
Checkendon, Ox, 243
Chedburgh, Sf, 293
Cheddar, So, 259
Cheddington, Bk, 18
Cheddleton, St, 281
Cheddon Fitzpaine, So, 265
Chedglow, Wlt, 337
Chedglow, hundred, Wlt, 337
Chedgrave, Nf, 195
Chediston, Sf, 289
Chedworth, Gl, 92
Chedzoy, So, 260
Cheetham, La, 154
Chelborough, Do, 76
Cheldon, Dev, 54
Chellaston, Db, 43
Chellington, Bd, 2
Chelmarsh, Sa, 255
Chelmondiston, Sf, 285
Chelmorton, Db, 47
Chelmscote, Wa, 321
Chelmsford, Ess, 85
Chelmsford, hundred, Ess, 85
Chelsea, Mx, 190
Chelsham, Sr, 303
Chelsworth, Sf, 291
Cheltenham, Gl, 90
Cheltenham, hundred, Gl, 104
Cheltenham, liberty, Gl, 91
Chelvey, So, 271
Chelwood, So, 270
Chelworth [in Chedglow hd.], Wlt, 337
Chelworth [in Staple hd.], Wlt, 333
Cheney Longville, Sa, 254
Cherington, Gl, 96
Cherington, Wa, 321
Cheriton, Ha, 117
Cheriton, So, 269
Cheriton Bishop, Dev, 58
Cheriton Fitzpaine, Dev, 55
Cherleton', Wlt, 348
Chertsey, Sr, 300
Cherubeer, Dev, 62
Cherwill, Wlt, 337
Cheselbourne, Do, 70

Cheselbourne Ford, Do, 69
Chesfield, Hrt, 133
Chesham, Bk, 21
Cheshunt, Hrt, 131
Chester, Little, Db, 43
Chesterblade, So, 271
Chesterfield, Db, 42, 48
Chesterford, Great, Ess, 86
Chesterford, Little, Ess, 86
Chesterhope, Nb, 221
Chesterton, Ca, 24
Chesterton, Hu, 138
Chesterton, Ox, 238
Chesterton, St, 278
Chesterton, Wa, 321
Chesterton, hundred, Ca, 25
Cheswardine, Sa, 250
Chetnole, Do, 71
Chettiscombe, Dev, 55
Chettle, Do, 75
Chetton, Sa, 255
Chetwode, Bk, 16
Chetwynd, Sa, 250
Cheveley, Ca, 27
Cheveley, hundred, Ca, 27
Cheverell, Great, Wlt, 343
Cheverell, Little, Wlt, 343
Chevet, YW, 392
Chevington, Sf, 291
Chevington, East, Nb, 222
Chevington, West, Nb, 222
Chevithorne, Dev, 55
Chew, hundred, So, 267
Chew Stoke, So, 267 n.
Chew, West, So, 267
Chewton, Ha, 107
Chewton, hundred, So, 261
Chewton Keynsham, So, 270
Chewton Mendip, So, 261
Chicheley, Bk, 17
Chichester, Sx, 304, 305
Chichester, rape, Sx, 305
Chichester, suburb, Sx, 307
Chickerell, Do, 72
Chicklade, Wlt, 338
Chickney, Ess, 82
Chidden, Ha, 113
Chiddingly, Sx, 313
Chidham, Sx, 306
Chieflowman, Dev, 55
Chieveley, Brk, 9
Chignall St. James, Ess, 85
Chignall Smealy, Ess, 85
Chigwell, Ess, 83
Chilbolton, Ha, 108
Chilcomb, Ha, 117
Chilcompton, So, 261
Chilcote, Lei, 46
Chilcote, So, 271
Childerditch, Ess, 87

Childerley, Great, Ca, 25
Childerley, Little, Ca, 25
Childrey, Brk, 11
Childswickham, Wo, 97
Childwall, La, 150
Childwick, Hrt, 134
Chilford, hundred, Ca, 27
Chilfrome, Do, 76
Chilgrove, Sx, 307
Chilhampton, Wlt, 342
Chillerton, Ha, 119
Chillesford, Sf, 294
Chillingham, Nb, 224
Chillington, So, 275
Chillington, St, 282
Chilmark, Wlt, 338
Chilstone, He, 127
Chilsworthy, Dev, 60
Chilternfage, So, 262 n.
Chilthorne Domer, So, 262
Chiltington, West, Sx, 310
Chiltlee, Ha, 114
Chilton, Brk, 13
Chilton, Bk, 20
Chilton Cantelo, So, 263
Chilton Foliat, Wlt, 348
Chilton Polden, So, 274
Chilton Street, Sf, 294
Chilton Trinity, So, 260, 268
Chilvers Coton, Wa, 324
Chilwell, Nt, 229
Chilworth, Ha, 109
Chilworth Musard, Ox, 239
Chilworth Valery, Ox, 239
Chimney, Ox, 237 n.
Chineham, Ha, 118
Chingford, Ess, 83
Chinnock, East, So, 270
Chinnock, West, So, 269
Chinnor, Ox, 240
Chipchase, Nb, 220
Chipley, Sf, 294
Chippenhall, Sf, 288
Chippenham, Ca, 24
Chippenham, Wlt, 333
Chippenham, hundred, Wlt, 344
Chipping, La, 153
Chippinghurst, Ox, 239
Chipstable, So, 266
Chipstead, Sr, 299
Chirbury, Sa, 256
Chirbury, hundred, Sa, 256
Chirton, Wlt, 336
Chisbury, Wlt, 347
Chiselborough, So, 269
Chisenbury, Wlt, 340
Chishill, Great, Ca, 23, 79, 87
Chishill, Little, Ca, 23, 79, 87
Chisledon, Wlt, 335
Chislehampton, Ox, 243

Chiswick, Mx, 190
Chitcombe, Sx, 317
Chithurst, Sx, 306
Chitterne, Wlt, 341
Chittlehampton, Dev, 53
Chittoe, Wlt, 348
Chivelstone, Dev, 64
Chobham, Sr, 300
Cholderton, Ha, 108
Cholderton, Wlt, 108 n., 345
Chollerton, Nb, 220
Cholsey, Brk, 8
Chorley, La, 155
Chorlton, St, 278
Chorlton upon Medlock, La, 154
Choseley, Nf, 197
Choulston, Wlt, 346
Chrishall, Ess, 87
Christchurch, Ha, 106
Christchurch, hundred, Ha, 106
Christian Malford, Wlt, 339
Christow, Dev, 58
Chudleigh, Dev, 59
Chulmleigh, Dev, 54
Church, La, 152
Churcham, Gl, 104
Churchdown, Gl, 97
Churchill, Dev, 62
Churchill, Ox, 236
Churchill, So, 259
Churchill [in Halfshire hd.], Wo, 353
Churchill [in Oswaldslow hd.], Wo, 351
Churchover, Wa, 323
Churchstanton, So, 56, 258
Churchstow, Dev, 51
Churston Ferrers, Dev, 50
Churt, Sr, 298
Chute, Wlt, 348
Chuteley, hundred, Ha, 116
Chyltone, So, 262 n.
Chyngton, Sx, 314
Cinque Ports, liberty, K, 140
Cippenham, Bk, 21
Circourt, Brk, 12
Cirencester, Gl, 90, 91
Clackclose, hundred, Nf, 203
Clacton, Great, Ess, 88
Clacton, Little, Ess, 88
Clandon, East, Sr, 299
Clandon, West, Sr, 300
Clanfield, Ha, 114
Clanfield, Ox, 237
Clannaborough, Dev, 62
Clapcot, Brk, 13
Clapham, Bd, 5
Clapham, Sr, 302
Clapham, Sx, 310
Clapham, YW, 384
Clapton, Gl, 103
Clapton, Np, 214

Clapton [in Chewton hd.], So, 261
Clapton [in Crewkerne hd.], So, 273
Clapton in Gordano, So, 271
Clarborough, Nt, 227
Clare, Ox, 238
Clare, Sf, 294
Claro, wapentake, YW, 384
Clatford, Wlt, 339
Clatford (Lower), Ha, 111
Clatford, Upper, Ha, 108
Clatworthy, So, 266
Claughton [in Amounderness wap.], La, 151
Claughton [in Lonsdale, Cartmel, and Furness wap.], La, 155
Claverdon, Wa, 326
Clavering, Ess, 84
Clavering, hundred, Ess, 84
Clavering, hundred, Nf, 195
Claverley, Sa, 249, 257
Claverton, So, 261
Clawson, Long, Lei, 164
Clawthorpe, We, 330
Clawton, Dev, 60
Claxby [in Calcewath wap.], Li, 184
Claxby [in Walshcroft wap.], Li, 179
Claxby Pluckacre, Li, 185
Claxton, Nf, 195
Claxton, YN, 380
Claybrooke Magna, Lei, 159
Claybrooke Parva, Lei, 159
Claydon, Ox, 241
Claydon, Sf, 286
Claydon, Botolph, Bk, 19
Claydon, East, Bk, 19
Claydon, hundred, Sf, 286
Claydon, Middle, Bk, 19
Claydon, Steeple, Bk, 16
Clayhanger, Dev, 63
Clayhidon, Dev, 56
Claypole, Li, 174
Claythorpe, Li, 184
Clayton, St, 277
Clayton, Sx, 312
Clayton [in Morley wap.], YW, 388
Clayton [in Strafforth wap.], YW, 393
Clayton le Dale, La, 153
Clayton le Moors, La, 153
Clayton le Woods, La, 154
Clayton, West, YW, 391
Clayworth, Nt, 227
Cleasby, YN, 374
Cleatham, Li, 177
Cleator, Cu, 40
Cleckheaton, YW, 388
Clee, Li, 180
Clee St. Margaret, Sa, 255
Cleeton St. Mary, Sa, 253
Cleeve, He, 126
Cleeve, So, 259
Cleeve, Bishop's, Gl, 93

Cleeve, hundred, Gl, 93
Cleeve, Old, So, 265
Cleeve Prior, Wo, 350
Clehonger, He, 127
Cleley, hundred, Np, 211
Clennell, Nb, 223
Clent, Wo, 276, 277
Cleobury Mortimer, Sa, 255
Cleobury North, Sa, 255
Clere Woodcott, Ha, 115
Clevancy, Wlt, 344
Clevedon, So, 271
Cleveley, Ox, 236
Clevelode, Wo, 354
Cleverton, Wlt, 337
Clewer, Brk, 7
Cley, Cockley, Nf, 203
Cley next the Sea, Nf, 199
Cliburn, We, 329
Cliddesden, Ha, 118
Cliff, Sa, 250
Cliffe, YE, 363
Cliffe, YN, 373
Cliffe, King's, Np, 213
Cliffe, North, YE, 360
Cliffe, South, YE, 360
Clifford, YW, 386
Clifford Barton, Dev, 58
Clifford Chambers, Wa, 92
Clifford, Ruin, Wa, 327
Clifton, Bd, 4
Clifton, Cu, 39
Clifton, Db, 44
Clifton, Gl, 91
Clifton [in Amounderness wap.], La, 152
Clifton [in Salford wap.], La, 154
Clifton, Nb, 222
Clifton, Nt, 230
Clifton, Ox, 242
Clifton, We, 329
Clifton, YN, 379, 380
Clifton, YW, 389
Clifton Campville, St, 279
Clifton Hampden, Ox, 243
Clifton, hundred, Bd, 4
Clifton Maybank, Do, 71
Clifton, North, Nt, 233
Clifton on Ure, YN, 372
Clifton Reynes, Bk, 17
Clifton, South, Nt, 233
Clifton upon Dunsmore, Wa, 322
Clifton upon Teme, Wo, 352
Clint, YW, 395
Clippesby, Nf, 193
Clipsham, Ru, 247
Clipston, Np, 213
Clipston, Nt, 232
Clipstone, Nf, 199 n.
Clipstone, Nt, 233
Cliston, hundred, Dev, 56

Clitheroe, La, 153
Clive, Sa, 251
Cliviger, La, 153
Clixby, Li, 178
Cloford, So, 268
Clophill, Bd, 3
Clopton, Ca, 25
Clopton, Sf, 296
Clopton [near Mickleton], Wa, 94
Clopton [near Stratford upon Avon], Wa, 327
Close, We, 329
Closworth, So, 270
Clothall, Hrt, 132
Clotherholme, YW, 394
Cloud, Temple, So, 260
Clovelly, Dev, 61
Clowne, Db, 48
Clumber, Nt, 228, 233
Clun, hundred, Sa, 249
Clunbury, Sa, 253
Clungunford, Sa, 253
Clunton, Sa, 253
Clutton, So, 267
Clyff, Do, 69
Clyffe Pypard, Wlt, 344
Clyst, Bishop's, Dev, 65
Clyst Broad, Dev, 56
Clyst Gerred, Dev, 56
Clyst Honiton, Dev, 65
Clyst Hydon, Dev, 56
Clyst St. George, Dev, 65
Clyst St. Lawrence, Dev, 56
Clyst St. Mary, Dev, 65
Clyst, West, Dev, 58
Coaley, Gl, 96
Coat, Ox, 241
Coat, So, 274
Coate, Wlt, 348
Coates [in Crowthorne hd.], Gl, 100
Coates [in Holford and Greston hd.], Gl, 98
Coates, Li, 176
Coates, Nt, 228
Coates, Great, Li, 180
Coates, Little, Li, 181
Coates, North, Li, 180
Coatham, YN, 375
Cobden, Dev, 56
Coberley, Gl, 92
Coberley, Upper, Gl, 98
Cobhall, He, 127
Cobham, Sr, 301
Cock, Wa, 326 n.
Cockerham, La, 156
Cockerington, Li, 183
Cockermouth, Cu, 39
Cockermouth, liberty, Cu, 40 n.
Cockfield, Sf, 291
Cocking, Sx, 306
Cockington, Dev, 50

Cocklebury, Wlt, 344
Coddenham, Sf, 286
Coddington, Db, 43
Coddington, He, 129
Coddington, Nt, 233
Codford, Wlt, 340
Codicote, Hrt, 134
Codnor, Db, 43
Codrington, Gl, 102
Codsall, St, 283
Codsheath, hundred, K, 146
Codshill, Ha, 117
Coffinswell, Dev, 50
Cofton Hackett, Wo, 353
Cogdean, hundred, Do, 69
Cogenhoe, Np, 217
Cogges, Ox, 242
Coggeshall, Ess, 88
Coggeshall Hamlet, Ess, 84
Coker, East, So, 270
Coker, hundred, So, 270
Coker, West, So, 270
Cokynle, Sf, 287
Colan, Co, 32
Colaton Raleigh, Dev, 65
Colber, Do, 74
Colburn, YN, 371
Colbury, Ha, 115
Colby, Nf, 201
Colby, We, 330
Colchester, Ess, 79, 88
Cold Coats, La, 153
Coldeaton, Db, 45
Coldecotte, Bk, 17 n.
Coldicote, Gl, 99
Coldmeece, St, 279
Coldridge, Dev, 62
Coldwaltham, Sx, 309
Cole, So, 269
Colebatch, Sa, 253
Colebrooke, Dev, 54
Coleby [in Boothby wap.], Li, 174
Coleby [in Manley wap.], Li, 175
Colemere, Sa, 252
Colemore, Ha, 115
Coleorton (Quartermarsh), Lei, 160
Coleorton (Saucey), Lei, 160
Coleridge, Dev, 52
Coleridge, hundred, Dev, 64
Colerne, Wlt, 344
Colesbourne, Gl, 92
Coleshill, Brk, 11
Coleshill, Wa, 325
Coley, Brk, 7
Colham Green, Mx, 190
Colkirk, Nf, 208
Collingbourne Ducis, Wlt, 346
Collingbourne Kingston, Wlt, 348
Collingham, YW, 388
Collingham, North, Nt, 233

Collingham, South, Nt, 233
Collington, He, 123
Collington, Little, He, 123
Collingtree, Np, 217
Collyweston, Np, 213 n., 214
Colmworth, Bd, 2
Coln Rogers, Gl, 98
Coln St. Aldwyn, Gl, 100
Coln St. Dennis, Gl, 100
Colne, Hu, 137 n.
Colne, La, 153
Colne, Earls, Ess, 88
Colne Engaine, Ess, 88
Colne, Wakes, Ess, 88
Colne, White, Ess, 88
Colneis, hundred, Sf, 296
Colney, Nf, 206
Colsterworth, Li, 171
Colston Bassett, Nt, 232
Colston, Car, Nt, 232
Colthrop, Brk, 9
Coltishall, Nf, 202
Colton, Nf, 206
Colton, St, 277
Colton, YW, 385
Columbjohn, Dev, 56
Colveston, Nf, 204
Colwall, He, 129
Colway, Do, 73
Colwell, Nb, 220
Colwick, Nt, 231
Colwick, Over, Nt, 231
Colworth, Sx, 307
Colyford, Dev, 57
Colyton, Dev, 56
Colyton, hundred, Dev, 56
Combe, Brk, 6, 105, 112
Combe, He, 125
Combe, Ox, 244
Combe, So, 260
Combe Abbas, So, 269
Combe Almer, Do, 69
Combe Baskerville, Gl, 103 n.
Combe, Castle, Wlt, 344
Combe Fishacre, Dev, 50
Combe Florey, So, 265
Combe Hay, So, 268
Combe Martin, Dev, 62
Combe Raleigh, Dev, 57
Combe, Temple, So, 269
Combeinteignhead, Dev, 57
Comberford, St, 277
Comberton, Ca, 26
Comberton, Great, Wo, 354
Comberton, Little, Wo, 354
Combpyne, Dev, 57
Combs, Sf, 288
Combsditch, hundred, Do, 73
Combwich, So, 268
Compton, Brk, 13

Compton, Dev, 52
Compton [in Buddlesgate hd.], Ha, 108
Compton [in King's Somborne hd.], Ha, 107
Compton [in West Medine hd.], Ha, 120
Compton, So, 267
Compton [in Farnham hd.], Sr, 298
Compton [in Godalming hd.], Sr, 298
Compton, St, 277
Compton, Sx, 306
Compton, Wlt, 346
Compton Abbas, Do, 74
Compton Abdale, Gl, 99
Compton Bassett, Wlt, 337
Compton Beauchamp, Brk, 10
Compton Bishop, So, 259
Compton Chamberlayne, Wlt, 334
Compton Dando, So, 270
Compton, Fenny, Wa, 321
Compton Greenfield, Gl, 102
Compton, hundred, Brk, 13
Compton, Little, Wa, 100
Compton, Long, Wa, 321
Compton Martin, So, 260
Compton, Nether, Do, 71
Compton, Over, Do, 71
Compton Scorpion, Wa, 320
Compton Valence, Do, 76
Compton Verney, Wa, 321
Compton, West, Brk, 13
Compton, West, Do, 70
Compton Wynyates, Wa, 321
Conderton, Wo, 350
Condicote, Gl, 95, 102
Condover, Sa, 252
Condover, hundred, Sa, 252
Conesby, Li, 176
Coneysthorpe, YN, 376
Congerstone, Lei, 159
Congham, Nf, 197
Congresbury, So, 259
Conholt, Ha, 112
Conholt, Wlt, 348
Coningsby, Li, 182
Conington, Ca, 25
Conington, Hu, 138
Conisbrough, YW, 392
Conisholme, Li, 183
Coniston, YE, 359
Coniston Cold, YW, 382
Conistone, YW, 383
Conningswick, Wo, 352
Conock, Wlt, 336
Constantine, Co, 30
Cooden, Sx, 316
Cookbury, Dev, 61
Cookham, Brk, 14
Cookham, hundred, Brk, 14
Cookley, Sf, 288
Cooksey Green, Wo, 353
Coombe, Do, 71

Coombe, Ha, 111
Coombe, Ox, 239
Coombe, So, 273
Coombe, Sr, 301
Coombe, Wlt, 340
Coombe Bissett, Wlt, 334
Coombes, Sx, 310
Cop Court, Ox, 241
Copdock, Sf, 285
Copford, Ess, 88
Copgrove, YW, 385
Cople, Bd, 2
Copmanthorpe, YW, 385, 386
Coppenhall, St, 282
Coppingford, Hu, 139
Coppull, La, 155
Copston Magna, Wa, 324
Copston Parva, Wa, 324
Coptfold, Ess, 85
Copthorne, hundred, Sr, 302
Coquetdale, ward, Nb, 223
Corbridge, Nb, 219, 221
Corby, Li, 171
Corby, Np, 215
Corby, Great, Cu, 38
Corby, hundred, Np, 215
Corby, Little, Cu, 38
Coreley, Sa, 256
Corfe, So, 264
Corfe Castle, Do, 67, 78
Corfe Mullen, Do, 69
Corfham, Sa, 254
Corfton, Sa, 254
Corhampton, Ha, 113
Corilond, So, 266 n.
Corley, Wa, 324
Cornard, Great, Sf, 290
Cornard, Little, Sf, 290
Cornbrough, YN, 376
Cornilo, hundred, K, 141
Cornwall, 30–5
Cornwell, Ox, 236
Cornwood, Dev, 64
Cornworthy, Dev, 64
Corpusty, Nf, 202
Corras, He, 125
Corringham, Ess, 85
Corringham, Li, 177, 186
Corringham, Little, Li, 186
Corringham, wapentake, Li, 177
Corscombe, Do, 71
Corse, Gl, 99
Corsham, Wlt, 344
Corsley, Wlt, 346
Corston, So, 268
Corston, Wlt, 337
Corton, Do, 77
Corton, Sf, 290
Corton [in Heytesbury hd.], Wlt, 340
Corton [in Kingsbridge hd.], Wlt, 344

Corton Denham, So, 269
Corve, Sa, 254
Coryton, Dev, 60
Cosby, Lei, 158
Coscombe, Gl, 98
Cosford, Wa, 323
Cosford, hundred, Sf, 291
Cosgrove, Np, 211
Coshuish, So, 264
Cossall, Nt, 229
Cossington, Lei, 163
Cossington, So, 274
Costessey, Nf, 206
Costock, Nt, 230
Coston, Lei, 163
Coston, Nf, 206
Coston, Sa, 253
Cote, Gl, 101
Coten, Np, 215
Cotes, Lei, 162
Cotesbach, Lei, 158
Cotes de Val, Lei, 160 n.
Cotgrave, Nt, 232
Cotham, Nt, 233
Cothelstone, So, 264, 265
Cotheridge, Wo, 352
Cotherstone, YN, 373
Cotleigh, Dev, 57
Cotness, YE, 362
Coton, Ca, 26
Coton, Lei, 159
Coton, Ox, 241
Coton [east of Stafford], St, 278
Coton [west of Stafford], St, 279
Coton [near Tamworth], St, 277
Coton in the Elms, Db, 46
Cottam, Nt, 227, 228
Cottam, YE, 367
Cottenham, Ca, 25
Cottered, Hrt, 132
Cotterstock, Np, 213
Cottesbrooke, Np, 216
Cottesloe, hundred, Bk, 18
Cottesmore, Ru, 247
Cottingham, Np, 215
Cottingham, YE, 362
Cottingwith, YE, 363, 366, 367
Cottingwith, East, YE, 366, 367
Cottingwith, West, YE, 363, 367
Cottisford, Ox, 237
Cotton, Np, 217
Cotton, Sf, 287
Cotton End, Bd, 3 n.
Cottsettlesford, hundred, Brk, 9
Coughton, Wa, 326
Coulsdon, Sr, 300
Coulston, Wlt, 338
Coulton, YN, 377
Cound, Sa, 252
Coundon, Wa, 323

Countesthorpe, Lei, 159
Counthorpe, Li, 171
Coupland, Nb, 225
Court, North, Ha, 120
Court, West [near Alton], Ha, 120
Court, West [Isle of Wight], Ha, 119
Courteenhall, Np, 217
Court-y-Park, He, 128
Cove, Ha, 109
Cove, North, Sf, 289
Cove, South, Sf, 289
Covehithe, Sf, 289
Coven, St, 281
Coveney, Ca, 28
Covenham, Li, 180
Covenhope, He, 129
Coventry, Wa, 319, 323
Coverham, YN, 372
Covington, Np, 138
Cowarne, Much, He, 123
Cowbeech, Sx, 316
Cowden, Great, YE, 359
Cowden, Little, YE, 359
Cowesby, YN, 377
Cowesfield, Wlt, 336
Cowhill, Gl, 101
Cowhurst, Sx, 317
Cowick, Dev, 58
Cowlam, YE, 364
Cowley, Bk, 16
Cowley, Dev, 58
Cowley, Gl, 92
Cowley, Mx, 190
Cowley, Ox, 239
Cowley, St, 282
Cowley Peachey, Mx, 190
Cowley, Temple, Ox, 239
Cowling, YN, 371
Cowling, YW, 383
Cowlinge, Sf, 294
Cowpen, Nb, 223
Cowthorpe, YW, 384
Cowton, East, YN, 374
Cowton, North, YN, 374
Cowton, South, YN, 374
Coxley, So, 271
Coxwell, Great, Brk, 11
Coxwell, Little, Brk, 11
Coxwold, YN, 378
Crackenthorpe, We, 329
Cracoe, YW, 383
Cradley, He, 129
Cradley, Wo, 353
Crakehall, YN, 371
Crakehill, YN, 378
Cramlington, Nb, 222
Cranborne, Do, 75
Cranborne, hundred, Do, 75
Cranbourne, Ha, 112
Cranbrook, hundred, K, 143

Cranfield, Bd, 3
Cranford, Mx, 190
Cranford, Np, 214
Cranham, Ess, 87
Cranham, Gl, 92
Cranley, Sf, 287
Cranmore, So, 271, 273
Cranoe, Lei, 166
Cransford, Sf, 295
Cransley, Np, 212
Cranswick, YE, 361, 369
Crantock, Co, 32
Cranwell, Bk, 19 n.
Cranwell, Li, 173
Cranwich, Nf, 204
Cranworth, Nf, 205
Craster, Nb, 226
Cratfield, Sf, 289
Crathorne, YN, 376
Crawley, Ha, 108
Crawley, Ox, 237
Crawley, Little, Bk, 17
Crawley, North, Bk, 17
Craycombe, Wo, 351
Creake, North, Nf, 199
Creake, South, Nf, 199
Creaton, Great, Np, 216
Creaton, Little, Np, 216
Credenhill, He, 124
Crediton, Dev, 54, 66
Crediton, hundred, Dev, 54
Creech, Do, 77
Creech St. Michael, So, 265
Creed, Co, 31
Creedy, Lower, Dev, 55
Creeksea, Ess, 84 n.
Creeting All Saints, Sf, 286
Creeting St. Mary, Sf, 286
Creeting St. Olave, Sf, 286
Creeting St. Peter, Sf, 287
Creeton, Li, 171
Crendon, Long, Bk, 20
Crepping, Ess, 88
Creslow, Bk, 18
Cressage, Sa, 252
Cressenhall, Nf, 208
Cressing, Ess, 84
Cressingham, Great, Nf, 203
Cressingham, Little, Nf, 204
Cressome, YE, 363
Cresswells, Brk, 7
Creswell, St, 278
Cretingham, Sf, 295
Crewkerne, So, 273
Crewkerne, hundred, So, 273
Crich, Db, 42
Crichel, Long, Do, 72
Crichel, Moor, Do, 77
Crick, Np, 216
Cricket Malherbie, So, 272

Cricket St. Thomas, So, 275
Cricklade, Wlt, 333
Cricklade, hundred, Wlt, 342
Crickley, Gl, 97
Cridling Stubbs, YW, 391
Crigglestone, YW, 390
Crimplesham, Nf, 203
Crimsham, Sx, 307
Cringleford, Nf, 206
Crockerhill, Ha, 116
Crockerton, Wlt, 346
Croft, He, 130
Croft, La, 150
Croft, Lei, 159
Croft, Li, 181
Croft, So, 273
Croft, YN, 374, 380
Crofton, Ha, 110
Crofton, Li, 172
Crofton, Wlt, 342
Crofton, YW, 390
Croglin, Cu, 37
Cromford, Db, 44
Cromhall, Gl, 95
Crompton, La, 154
Cromwell, Nt, 231
Crondall, Ha, 109
Crondall, hundred, Ha, 109
Cronkley, Nb, 221
Cronton, La, 150
Crook, We, 330
Crooke, Dev, 62
Crookham, Brk, 7
Crookham, Nb, 224
Crookham Village, Ha, 109
Croom, YE, 364
Croome, Earl's, Wo, 350
Cropredy, Ox, 241
Cropston, Lei, 161
Cropthorne, Wo, 351
Cropton, YN, 381
Cropwell Bishop, Nt, 232
Cropwell Butler, Nt, 232
Crosby, La, 149
Crosby, Li, 176
Crosby Garrett, We, 329
Crosby, Little, La, 150
Crosby Ravensworth, We, 330
Croscombe, So, 267
Crosland, North, YW, 390
Crosland, South, YW, 390
Crosscanonby, Cu, 39
Crosthwaite, We, 330
Croston, La, 155
Crostwick, Nf, 194
Crostwight, Nf, 202
Croucheston, Wlt, 334
Croughton, Np, 210
Crowan, Co, 30, 31
Crowcombe, So, 265, 266

Crowell, Ox, 241
Crowfield, Sf, 286
Crowhurst, Sr, 303
Crowland, Li, 168
Crowle, Li, 175
Crowle, Wo, 350
Crowmarsh Battle, Ox, 240
Crowmarsh Gifford, Ox, 243
Crowneast, Wo, 350 n.
Crownthorpe, Nf, 206
Crowthorne, hundred, Gl, 99
Croxall, St, 46, 276
Croxby, Li, 180
Croxton, Ca, 26
Croxton, Li, 179
Croxton [in Gallow hd.], Nf, 199
Croxton [in Grimshoe hd.], Nf, 204
Croxton, St, 279
Croxton Kerrial, Lei, 163
Croxton, South, Lei, 162
Croyde, Dev, 62
Croydon, Ca, 25
Croydon, Sr, 301
Cruchfield, Brk, 7
Crudgington, Sa, 251
Crudwell, Wlt, 337
Cruwys Morchard, Dev, 54
Crux Easton, Ha, 112
Cruxton, Do, 76
Cryfield, Wa, 320
Cubbington, Wa, 323
Cubert, Co, 32
Cubley, Db, 45
Cublington, Bk, 18
Cublington, He, 127
Cuby, Co, 31
Cuckfield, Sx, 312
Cucklington, So, 269
Cuckney, Nt, 229
Cuddesdon, Ox, 239
Cuddington, Bk, 20
Cuddington, Sr, 302
Cudleigh, Wo, 351
Cudlow, Sx, 308
Cudworth, So, 275
Cudworth, YW, 392
Cuerdale, La, 153
Cuerden, La, 155
Cuerdley, La, 150
Culcheth, La, 149
Culford, Sf, 293
Culgaith, Cu, 37
Culkerton, Gl, 96
Cullifordtree, hundred, Do, 72
Cullompton, Dev, 63
Culm Davy, Dev, 56
Culmstock, Dev, 56
Culpho, Sf, 296
Culverthorpe, Li, 173
Culworth, Np, 210

Cumberland, 36–41
Cumberland, wapentake, Cu, 37
Cumberworth, Li, 184
Cumberworth, YW, 389
Cumcrew, Cu, 38
Cumnor, Brk, 12
Cumwhinton, Cu, 38
Cumwhitton, Cu, 38
Cundall, YN, 371
Cupernham, Ha, 107
Curborough, St, 280
Curbridge, Ox, 237
Curdridge, Ha, 118
Curdworth, Wa, 325
Curload, So, 264
Curridge, Brk, 9
Curry, East, So, 264
Curry Mallet, So, 266
Curry, North, So, 264
Curry, North, hundred, So, 263
Curry Rivel, So, 272
Currypool, So, 267
Curthwaite, East, Cu, 38
Curthwaite, West, Cu, 38
Cury, Co, 31
Cutcombe, So, 272
Cutsdean, Gl, 350
Cutteslowe, Ox, 242
Cuttlestone, hundred, St, 281
Cuxham, Ox, 240
Cuxwold, Li, 180

Daccombe, Dev, 50
Dacorum, hundred, Hrt, 134
Dacre, Cu, 37
Dadlington, Lei, 158
Dagenham, Ess, 81
Daglingworth, Gl, 100
Dagworth, Sf, 287
Dalbury, Db, 46
Dalby, Li, 182
Dalby, YN, 380
Dalby, Great, Lei, 161
Dalby, Little, Lei, 163
Dalby, Old, Lei, 163
Dalderby, Li, 182
Dalditch, Dev, 65
Dale Town, YN, 378
Dalham, Sf, 294
Dalling, Field, Nf, 200
Dalling, Wood, Nf, 200
Dallinghoo, Sf, 295
Dallington, Np, 216
Dalston, Cu, 40
Dalton, La, 150
Dalton, Nb, 220
Dalton, We, 156
Dalton [in Birdforth wap.], YN, 378
Dalton [in Gilling wap.], YN, 373
Dalton [in Agbrigg wap.], YW, 389

Dalton [in Strafforth wap.], YW, 392
Dalton in Furness, La, 156
Dalton, North, YE, 362, 368, 369
Dalton on Tees, YN, 379
Dalton, South, YE, 369
Damerham, Ha, 105, 334
Damerham, hundred, Wlt, 334
Damston', He, 126
Danbury, Ess, 85
Danby, YN, 376
Danby on Ure, YN, 372
Danby Wiske, YN, 374
Danegris, forest, Ess, 84 n.
Danethorpe, Nt, 233
Danthorpe, YE, 359
Darby, Li, 175
Darfield, YW, 392
Darlaston [in Pirehill hd.], St, 278
Darlaston [in Offlow hd.], St, 279
Darley, Db, 47
Darlingscott, Wa, 351
Darlton, Nt, 233
Darrington, YW, 391
Darsham, Sf, 289
Dartford, K, 140, 146
Dartington, Dev, 51
Dartmouth, Dev, 64, 65
Darton, YW, 392
Darwen, Lower, La, 153
Darwen (Over), La, 153
Dassett, Wa, 321
Datchet, Bk, 21
Datchworth, Hrt, 133
Dauntsey, Wlt, 339
Daventry, Np, 215
Davidstow, Co, 33
Dawenerys, Ess, 84
Dawlish, Dev, 59
Daylesford, Gl, 351
Dean, Bd, 5
Dean, Cu, 39
Dean, Ha, 108
Dean, Ox, 236
Dean, East, Ha, 106
Dean, East, Sx, 306
Dean, Little, Gl, 104
Dean Prior, Dev, 51
Dean, Priors, Ha, 115
Dean, West, Ha, 106
Dean, West, Sx, 306
Dean, West, Wlt, 345
Deane, Ha, 112
Deanham, Nb, 220
Deanshanger, Np, 211
Dearham, Cu, 39
Debach, Sf, 295
Debden, Ess, 86
Debenham, Sf, 296
Deddington, Ox, 242
Dedham, Ess, 87

Dedworth, Brk, 7
Deene, Np, 215
Deenethorpe, Np, 215 n.
Deeping, Market, Li, 169
Deeping, West, Li, 169
Deerhurst, Gl, 99, 100
Deerhurst, hundred, Gl, 100
Deerhurst Walton, Gl, 99
Defford, Wo, 354
Deighton, YE, 367
Deighton, YN, 378
Deighton, Kirk, YW, 384
Deighton, North, YW, 385
Dembleby, Li, 170
Denaby, YW, 394
Denbury, Dev, 50
Denby, Db, 43
Denby Dale, YW, 391
Denchworth, Brk, 11
Denford, Brk, 10
Denford, Np, 214
Dengie, Ess, 84
Dengie, hundred, Ess, 84
Denham, Bk, 21
Denham [in Hoxne hd.], Sf, 288
Denham [in Risbridge hd.], Sf, 293
Denmead, Ha, 113
Dennington, Sf, 288
Denston, Sf, 294
Dent, YW, 384
Denton, Cu, 38
Denton, Hu, 138
Denton, Li, 171
Denton, Nb, 223
Denton, Nf, 207
Denton, Np, 217
Denton, Ox, 239
Denton, Sx, 314
Denton, YW, 384
Denver, Nf, 203
Denwick, Nb, 225
Deopham, Nf, 206
Depden, Sf, 293
Deptford, Wlt, 340
Depwade, hundred, Nf, 196
Derby, Db, 42, 48
Derby, West, La, 150
Derby, West, wapentake, La, 149
Derbyshire, 42–8
Dereham, East, Nf, 205
Dereham, West, Nf, 203
Derrington, St, 279
Dersingham, Nf, 197
Desborough, Np, 213
Desborough, hundred, Bk, 21
Desford, Lei, 160
Detchant, Nb, 225
Devizes, Wlt, 333
Devon, 49–66
Dewchurch, He, 126

Dewlish, Do, 70
Dewsall, He, 125
Dewsbury, YW, 389
Dexthorpe, Li, 182
Dibden, Ha, 115
Dickering, wapentake, YE, 365
Dickleburgh, Nf, 207
Didcot, Brk, 13
Didcot, Gl, 92
Diddenham, Brk, 346
Diddington, Hu, 136
Didley, He, 127
Didling, Sx, 306
Didlington, Do, 77
Didlington, Nf, 203
Didmarton, Gl, 102
Digby, Li, 173
Digswell, Hrt, 133
Dilham, Nf, 202
Dilhorne, St, 281
Dill, hundred, Sx, 315
Dillington, Hu, 137
Dilston, Nb, 221
Dilton Marsh, Wlt, 337
Dilwyn, He, 129
Dimlington, YE, 358
Dinckley, La, 153
Dinder, So, 271
Dinedor, He, 127
Dingley, Np, 215
Dinnington, Nb, 223
Dinnington, So, 275
Dinsdale, Over, YN, 378
Dinsley, Furnival, Hrt, 134
Dinsley, Temple, Hrt, 134
Dinton, Bk, 20
Dinton, Wlt, 347
Dipford, So, 264
Dippenhall, Ha, 109
Diptford, Dev, 51
Diseworth, Lei, 161
Dishenhurst, Sx, 310
Dishforth, YN, 371
Diss, Nf, 207
Diss, hundred, Nf, 207
Dissington, South, Nb, 221
Distington, Cu, 40
Ditchampton, Wlt, 342
Ditchburn, Nb, 225
Ditcheat, So, 267
Ditchford, Wa, 320
Ditchford, Middle, Gl, 351
Ditchford, Upper, Gl, 351
Ditchingham, Nf, 195
Ditchley, Ox, 236
Dittisham, Dev, 64
Ditton, La, 150
Ditton, Fen, Ca, 24
Ditton, Long, Sr, 301
Ditton Priors, Sa, 254

Ditton, Thames, Sr, 301
Dixton, Gl, 93
Docking, Nf, 197
Dodbrooke, Dev, 64, 65
Doddenham, Wo, 352
Doddershall, Bk, 19
Doddinghurst, Ess, 86
Doddington, Ca, 28
Doddington, Li, 175
Doddington, Nb, 224
Doddington, Dry, Li, 174
Doddington, Great, Np, 217
Doddingtree, hundred, Wo, 352
Doddiscombsleigh, Dev, 59
Doddridge, Dev, 55
Dodford, Np, 216
Dodington, Gl, 101
Dodworth, YW, 391
Dodynton', Sa, 255
Dogmersfield, Ha, 113
Dole, hundred, Wlt, 341
Dolton, Dev, 62
Doncaster, YW, 386, 393
Donhead, Wlt, 337
Donington, Li, 168
Donington, Sa, 256
Donington, Castle, Lei, 161
Donington le Heath, Lei, 160
Donington on Bain, Li, 182
Donisthorpe, Lei, 46
Donningstone, Dev, 63
Donnington, Brk, 9
Donnington, Gl, 103
Donnington, He, 129
Donnington, Sx, 308
Donstall, Li, 177
Donyatt, So, 266
Donyland, East, Ess, 87
Dorchester, Do, 67, 73
Dorchester, Ox, 243
Dorchester, hundred, Ox, 243
Dore, YW, 48
Dorking, Sr, 299
Dorleghe, So, 260 n.
Dormington, He, 127
Dormston, Wo, 353
Dorn, Gl, 351
Dorney, Bk, 22
Dornford, Ox, 242
Dorrington, Li, 173
Dorrington, Sa, 250
Dorset, 67–78
Dorsington, Wa, 94, 326
Dorstone, He, 128
Dorton, Bk, 20
Dosthill, Wa, 325
Doughton, Gl, 96
Doughton, Nf, 198
Doulting, So, 267
Doune Umfraville, Dev, 57

Dounhurst, Sx, 309
Dover, K, 140
Dovercourt, Ess, 89
Doverdale, Wo, 353
Doveridge, Db, 46
Dowdeswell, Gl, 99
Dowland, Dev, 62
Dowlish Wake, So, 275
Dowlish, West, So, 272
Down, Bishop's, Do, 71
Down, East, Dev, 62
Down St. Mary, Dev, 62
Down Thomas, Dev, 51
Down, West, Dev, 62
Downham, Ca, 28
Downham, Ess, 86
Downham, La, 152
Downham, Nb, 225
Downham Market, Nf, 203
Downhamford, hundred, K, 141
Downhead [in Pitney manor], So, 259
Downhead [in Whitestone hd.], So, 267
Downholland, La, 150
Downholme, YN, 372
Downside, So, 261
Downton, Wlt, 333
Downton, foreign, Wlt, 334
Downton, hundred, Wlt, 334
Downtown, Np, 216
Dowsby, Li, 170
Dowthorpe, YE, 359
Doynton, Gl, 94
Doxford, Nb, 225
Drakelow, Db, 46
Drascombe, Dev, 58
Draughton, Np, 213
Draughton, YW, 383
Drax, YW, 386
Draycot, Ox, 240
Draycot Cerne, Wlt, 339
Draycot Fitz Payne, Wlt, 335
Draycot Foliat, Wlt, 335
Draycote, Li, 178 n.
Draycote, Wa, 322
Draycott, Db, 43
Draycott, Gl, 351
Draycott, So, 274
Draycott, Wo, 350 n.
Draycott in the Moors, St, 278
Draycott Moor, Brk, 12
Drayton, Brk, 13
Drayton [in Micheldever hd.], Ha, 112
Drayton [in Portsdown hd.], Ha, 110
Drayton, Nf, 194
Drayton, Ox, 243
Drayton, So, 272
Drayton, Sx, 307
Drayton, Wa, 327
Drayton Bassett, St, 279
Drayton Beauchamp, Bk, 18

Drayton, Dry, Ca, 25
Drayton, East, Nt, 228
Drayton, Fen, Ca, 25
Drayton, Fenny, Lei, 159
Drayton, Market, Sa, 250
Drayton Parslow, Bk, 19
Drayton St. Leonard, Ox, 243
Drayton, West, Mx, 190
Drayton, West, Nt, 228
Drewsteignton, Dev, 58
Drewton, YE, 362
Driby, Li, 182
Driffield, Gl, 99
Driffield, Great, YE, 357, 367, 369
Drigg, Cu, 40
Drighlington, YW, 389
Dringhoe, YE, 359
Dringhouses, YW, 385
Drinkstone, Sf, 292
Droitwich, Wo, 349, 352
Dromonby, YN, 375
Dronfield, Db, 48
Droxford, Ha, 118
Drybeck, We, 329
Drypool, YE, 369
Ducklington, Ox, 237
Duckmanton, Db, 48
Dudbrook, Gl, 98
Duddeston Hall, Wa, 325
Duddington, Np, 213
Duddlewick, Sa, 255
Duddo, Nb, 222
Dudley, Wo, 353
Dudmaston, Sa, 257
Dudston, Sa, 256
Dudstone, hundred, Gl, 96
Duffield, Db, 43
Duffield, North, YE, 362
Duffield, South, YE, 362
Dufton, We, 329
Duggleby, YE, 364
Dulcote, So, 271
Dullingham, Ca, 27
Duloe, Co, 34
Dulverton, So, 265
Dulwich, Sr, 302
Dumbleton, Gl, 97
Dummer, Ha, 118
Dumpford, hundred, Sx, 306
Dunchideock, Dev, 59
Dunchurch, Wa, 322
Dunclent, Wo, 353
Duncton, Sx, 308
Dundon, So, 274
Dundraw, Cu, 37
Dundry, So, 267
Dunham, Nt, 228
Dunham, Great, Nf, 207
Dunham, Little, Nf, 208
Dunholme, Li, 177

Dunkerton, So, 268
Dunkeswell, Dev, 56
Dunkeswick, YW, 384
Dunmow, Great, Ess, 82
Dunmow, hundred, Ess, 82
Dunmow, Little, Ess, 82
Dunnington, Wa, 326
Dunnington [in Holderness wap.], YE, 359
Dunnington [in Liberty of St. Peter], YE, 367
Dunningworth, Sf, 294
Dunsby [in Aveland wap.], Li, 170
Dunsby [in Flaxwell wap.], Li, 173
Dunscombe, Lower, Dev, 55
Dunsden, Ox, 240
Dunsford, Dev, 58
Dunsforth, YW, 384
Dunsley, YN, 380
Dunstable, Bd, 4
Dunstall Green, Sf, 294
Dunstan, Nb, 226
Dunster, So, 273
Dunsthorpe, Li, 172
Dunston, Li, 173
Dunston, Nf, 206
Dunston, St, 281
Dunstone, Dev, 64
Dunterton, Dev, 60
Duntisbourne Leer, Gl, 92
Duntisbourne Rouse, Gl, 92, 100
Duntish, Do, 74
Dunton, Bd, 1
Dunton, Bk, 19
Dunton, Ess, 85
Dunton, Nf, 198
Dunton Bassett, Lei, 159
Dunwear, So, 260
Dunwich, Sf, 284, 294
Dunworth, hundred, Wlt, 337
Durley, Ha, 118
Durley, Wlt, 347
Durnford, Great, Wlt, 345
Durnford, Little, Wlt, 345
Durrington, Sx, 310
Durrington, Wlt, 345
Dursley, Gl, 96
Durston, So, 260
Durweston, Do, 75
Duston, Np, 216
Dutton, La, 153
Duxbury, La, 155
Duxford, Ca, 27
Dyke, Li, 170
Dymock, Gl, 91, 95
Dyrah, Cu, 37
Dyrham, Gl, 101

Eachwick, Nb, 220
Eagle, Li, 169
Eagle, hundred, Brk, 9

Eaglesfield, Cu, 39
Eakley, Bk, 18
Eakring, Nt, 228
Ealand, Li, 175 n.
Ealing, Mx, 190
Eardington, Sa, 255
Eardisland, He, 129
Earith, Hu, 137 n.
Earle, Nb, 226
Earley, Brk, 7
Earlham, Nf, 206
Earlstone, Ha, 115
Earnshill, So, 272
Earnwood, Sa, 255
Earsham, Nf, 207
Earsham, hundred, Nf, 207
Eartham, Sx, 308
Earthcott, Gaunts, Gl, 101
Easby [in Gilling wap.], YN, 373
Easby [in Langbargh wap.], YN, 375
Easebourne, Sx, 306
Easebourne, hundred, Sx, 306
Easenhall, Wa, 323
Easewrithe, East, half-hundred, Sx, 310
Easewrithe, West, hundred, Sx, 308
Easington, Bk, 20
Easington, Ox, 240
Easington, YE, 358
Easington, YN, 375
Easington, YW, 383
Easingwold, YN, 357, 382
East, hundred, Co, 34
East, hundred, Ru, 247
Eastbourne, hundred, Sx, 314
Eastburn, YE, 362
Eastbury, Brk, 10
Eastbury, Do, 71
Eastcott [in Blackgrove hd.], Wlt, 341
Eastcott [in Studfold hd.], Wlt, 336
Eastcotts, Bd, 3
Eastcourt, Wlt, 337
Easter, Good, Ess, 82
Easter, High, Ess, 82
Eastergate, Sx, 308
Easthall, Sx, 314
Eastham, Wo, 352
Eastham, Lower, So, 273
Easthamstead, Brk, 7
Easthoe, Ha, 113
Easthope, Sa, 254
Easthorpe, Ess, 87
Easthorpe, YE, 361
Eastington, Gl, 103
Eastington, Wo, 350
Eastleach Martin, Gl, 100
Eastleigh, Ha, 109
Eastleigh Turville, Gl, 100
Eastmanstreet, Wlt, 337
Eastney, Ha, 110
Eastnor, He, 129

Eastoft, Li, 175 n.
Eastoke, Ha, 116
Easton, Brk, 9
Easton, Cu, 39
Easton, Gl, 91
Easton, Ha, 117
Easton, Hu, 138 n.
Easton, Li, 171
Easton, Nf, 206
Easton, So, 271
Easton [in Cannings hd.], Wlt, 348
Easton [in Kinwardstone hd.], Wlt, 347
Easton, YE, 365
Easton Bavents, Sf, 289
Easton, Great, Ess, 82
Easton, Great, Lei, 164
Easton Grey, Wlt, 344
Easton in Gordano, So, 271
Easton, Little, Ess, 82
Easton Maudit, Np, 212
Easton Neston, Np, 211
Easton on the Hill, Np, 213
Easton Piercy, Wlt, 339
Eastridge, Wlt, 338
Eastrington, YE, 363
Eastrop, Ha, 118
Eastrop, Wlt, 343
Eastry, hundred, K, 141
Eastwell, Lei, 163
Eastwick, Hrt, 132
Eastwood, Ess, 81
Eastwood, Nt, 229
Eathorpe, Wa, 322
Eaton, He, 130
Eaton, Lei, 164
Eaton, Nf, 206
Eaton, Nt, 229
Eaton, Sa, 254
Eaton Bishop, He, 127
Eaton Bray, Bd, 4
Eaton, Castle, Wlt, 343
Eaton, Church, St, 282
Eaton Constantine, Sa, 250
Eaton Dovedale, Db, 45
Eaton Hastings, Brk, 11
Eaton, Hill of, He, 126
Eaton, Little, Db, 42
Eaton, Long, Db, 43
Eaton Mascott, Sa, 252
Eaton Socon, Bd, 2
Eaton, Water, Bk, 17
Eaton, Water, Ox, 242
Eaton, Water, St, 282
Eaton, Water, Wlt, 333
Eavestone, YW, 394
Ebberston, YN, 381
Ebbesbourne Wake, Wlt, 343
Ebernoe, Sx, 308
Ebrington, Gl, 95
Ebury, Mx, 190

Ecchinswell, Ha, 109
Eccles [in Shropham hd.], Nf, 205
Eccles [in West Flegg hd.], Nf, 193
Ecclesden, Sx, 309
Ecclesfield, YW, 392
Eccleshall, St, 276, 278
Eccleshill, La, 153
Eccleshill, YW, 389
Eccleston [in Leyland wap.], La, 155
Eccleston [in West Derby wap.], La, 150
Eccleston, Great, La, 152
Eccleston, Little, La, 151
Eccleswall, He, 127
Eckington, Db, 48
Eckington, Wo, 354
Ecton, Np, 217
Edburton, Sx, 311
Eddlethorpe, YE, 365
Edenhall, Cu, 37
Edenham, Li, 170
Edensor, Db, 47
Edgbaston, Wa, 325
Edgcote, Np, 210
Edgcott, Bk, 16
Edgebold, Sa, 257
Edgefield, Nf, 199
Edgeworth, Gl, 93
Edgmond, Sa, 251
Edgton, Sa, 253
Edgware, Mx, 191
Edgworth, La, 154
Edingale, St, 46, 276
Edingley, Nt, 232
Edingswell, Dev, 50
Edingthorpe, Nf, 202
Edington, So, 274
Edington, Wlt, 338
Edlaston, Db, 45
Edlesborough, Bk, 18
Edlingham, Nb, 223
Edlington, Li, 182
Edlington, YW, 393
Edmondsham, Do, 75
Edmondthorpe, Lei, 163
Edmonton, Mx, 191
Edmonton, hundred, Mx, 191
Edmundsthorpe Benham, Ha, 115
Ednaston, Db, 45
Edstock, So, 268
Edstone, Wa, 326
Edstone, YN, 377
Edvin Loach, He, 122, 352
Edwalton, Nt, 230
Edwardstone, Sf, 291
Edwinstowe, Nt, 233
Edwinstree, hundred, Hrt, 132
Edworth, Bd, 1
Edwyn Ralph, He, 130
Effingham, Sr, 301
Effingham, half-hundred, Sr, 301

F f

Efford, Ha, 106
Egbury, Ha, 109
Egg Buckland, Dev, 52
Eggardon, hundred, Do, 72
Eggbeer, Dev, 58
Eggborough, YW, 391
Eggesford, Dev, 61
Egginton, Db, 43
Eggleton, He, 128
Egham, Sr, 300
Egleton, Ru, 246
Egliston, Do, 76
Egloshayle, Co, 33
Egloskerry, Co, 35
Egmanton, Nt, 228
Egmere, Nf, 200
Egremont, Cu, 40
Egremont, liberty, Cu, 40
Egton, YN, 375
Elberton, Gl, 96
Elcombe, Wlt, 341
Eldersfield, Wo, 353
Eldmire, YN, 378
Eldon, Ha, 107
Eleigh, Monks, Sf, 291
Eletesford, hundred, Brk, 13
Elford, St, 279
Eling, Brk, 8
Eling, Ha, 115
Elington, Brk, 7
Elkesley, Nt, 229
Elkington, Li, 183
Elkstone, Gl, 92
Elkstone, St, 281
Ella, Kirk, YE, 362, 368
Elland, YW, 388
Ellastone, St, 281
Ellel, La, 155
Ellenborough, Cu, 39
Ellenhall, St, 278
Ellerbeck, YN, 378
Ellerby, YE, 359
Ellerby, YN, 375
Ellerdine, Sa, 250
Ellerker, YE, 363
Ellerton, YE, 361
Ellerton, YN, 372
Ellerton on Swale, YN, 374
Ellesborough, Bk, 20
Ellingham, Ha, 114
Ellingham, Nb, 225
Ellingham, Nf, 195
Ellingham, Great, Nf, 205
Ellingham, Little, Nf, 204
Ellingstring, YN, 372
Ellington, Hu, 138
Ellington, Nb, 222
Ellington, YN, 372
Ellisfield, Ha, 118
Elloe, wapentake, Li, 168

Ellough, Sf, 290
Elloughton, YE, 360
Elm, Ca, 28
Elm, So, 268
Elm, North, So, 267
Elmbridge, Gl, 97
Elmbridge, hundred, Sr, 301
Elmdon, Ess, 87
Elmdon, Wa, 325
Elmesthorpe, Lei, 160
Elmestree, Gl, 96
Elmham, North, Nf, 208
Elmham, South, Sf, 290
Elmhurst, St, 280
Elmington, Np, 213 n.
Elmley Castle, Wo, 350
Elmley Lovett, Wo, 352
Elmore, Gl, 97
Elmsall, North, YW, 391
Elmsall, South, YW, 391
Elmsett, Sf, 291
Elmstead, Ess, 89
Elmswell, Sf, 292
Elmswell, YE, 366
Elmton, Db, 48
Elsdon, Nb, 221
Elsenham, Ess, 86
Elsfield, Ox, 239
Elsham, Li, 179
Elsing, Nf, 200
Elstead, Sr, 298
Elsted, Sx, 306
Elsthorpe, Li, 170
Elston, La, 151
Elston, Nt, 233
Elston, Wlt, 341
Elstow, Bd, 3
Elstronwick, YE, 359
Elstub, hundred, Wlt, 340
Elswick, La, 151
Elsworth, Ca, 25
Elthorne, hundred, Mx, 190
Eltisley, Ca, 26
Elton, Db, 44
Elton, Hu, 138
Elton, Nt, 232
Eltringham, Nb, 220
Elvaston, Db, 44
Elvastone, He, 126
Elveden, Sf, 293
Elvetham, Ha, 113
Elvington, YE, 364
Elwell, Dev, 63
Elwell, Do, 77
Elwick, Nb, 224
Elworthy, So, 266
Ely, Ca, 28
Ely, Isle of, Ca, 28
Emberton, Bk, 17
Embleton, Nb, 226

Embleton, liberty, Nb, 226
Embley, Ha, 106
Emborough, So, 261
Embsay, YW, 383
Emlett, Dev, 55
Emley, YW, 390
Emmington, Ox, 241
Emneth, Nf, 197
Empingham, Ru, 247
Empshott, Ha, 107
Emscote, Wa, 323
Emstrey, Sa, 252
Emsworth, Ha, 116
Enborne, Brk, 10
Encombe, Do, 76
End, North, Wa, 321
End, South, Wa, 321
Enderby, Lei, 159
Enderby, Bag, Li, 185
Enderby, Mavis, Li, 185
Endon, St, 281
Enfield, Mx, 191
Enford, Wlt, 340
Englefield, Brk, 8
Engleton, St, 282
English Combe, So, 268
Enham, Knights, Ha, 109
Enmore, So, 260
Enson, St, 278
Enstone, Ox, 236
Enstone, Neat, Ox, 236
Enville, St, 283
Epperstone, Nt, 231
Epping, Ess, 83, 89
Eppleby, YN, 373
Epsom, Sr, 302
Epwell, Ox, 243
Epworth, Li, 175
Ercall, Child's, Sa, 250
Ercall, High, Sa, 250
Erdington, Wa, 325
Eriswell, Sf, 293
Erlestoke, Wlt, 338
Ermington, Dev, 64
Ermington, hundred, Dev, 64
Ernsborough, Dev, 54
Erpingham, Nf, 202
Erpingham, North, hundred, Nf, 201
Erpingham, South, hundred, Nf, 201
Erringham, Sx, 310
Erwarton, Sf, 285
Eryholme, YN, 374
Escrick, YE, 366
Esham, Sf, 288
Esher, Sr, 301
Eshton, YW, 382
Eskdale, wapentake, Cu, 38
Eske, YE, 357
Eslington, Nb, 223
Espley, Sa, 250

Essendine, Ru, 247
Essendon, Hrt, 131
Essex, 79–89
Essington, St, 281
Eston, Sf, 295
Eston, YN, 375
Etal, Nb, 225
Etchilhampton, Wlt, 336
Etherdwick, YE, 359
Eton, Bk, 21
Ettington, Wa, 320
Etton, YE, 361, 368, 369
Etwall, Db, 43
Eudon Burnell, Sa, 255
Eudon George, Sa, 255
Euston, Sf, 292
Euxton, La, 155
Evedon, Li, 172
Evenley, Np, 210
Evenlode, Gl, 351
Evercreech, So, 271
Everdon, Np, 215
Everingham, YE, 362
Everleigh, Wlt, 346
Everleigh, liberty, Wlt, 346
Everley, YN, 380
Eversden, Ca, 26
Evershaw, Bk, 16
Eversholt, Bd, 4
Eversley, Ha, 117
Everstone, He, 126
Everthorpe, YE, 361
Everton, Bd, 2
Everton, Hu, 137
Everton, La, 149
Everton, Nt, 228
Evesbatch, He, 128
Evesham, Wo, 354
Evingar, hundred, Ha, 109
Evington, Gl, 99
Evington, Lei, 164
Ewart, Nb, 224
Ewcross, wapentake, YW, 383
Ewell, Sr, 302
Ewelme, Ox, 240
Ewelme, hundred, Ox, 240
Ewen, Gl, 337
Ewerby, Li, 172
Ewerby Thorpe, Li, 172
Ewhurst, Ha, 115
Ewhurst [in Staple hd.], Sx, 317
Ewhurst [in Wyndham half-hd], Sx, 311
Exbourne, Dev, 60
Exbury, Ha, 116
Exceat, Sx, 314
Exe Island, Dev, 66
Exe, Nether, Dev, 63
Exe, Up, Dev, 63
Exe, West, Dev, 55
Exelby, YN, 371

Exeter, Dev, 49, 65
Exford, So, 272
Exhall [juxta Alcester], Wa, 326
Exhall [juxta Coventry], Wa, 324
Exminster, Dev, 59
Exminster, hundred, Dev, 59
Exning, Sf, 284
Exning, half-hundred, Sf, 293
Exton, Ha, 117
Exton, Ru, 247
Exton, So, 265
Extra Portan, So, 264, 265
Extwistle, La, 153
Eyam, Db, 47
Eycotfield, Gl, 100
Eydon, Np, 210
Eye, Sf, 284, 287
Eye, Little, Ox, 15, 20
Eyeworth, Bd, 2
Eyford, Gl, 103
Eyhorne, hundred, K, 144
Eyke, Sf, 295
Eynesbury, Hu, 137
Eynesbury Hardwick, Hu, 137
Eynesford, hundred, Nf, 200
Eynsham, Ox, 242
Eythrope, Bk, 19
Eyton [in Ford hd.], Sa, 253
Eyton [in Pimhill hd.], Sa, 251
Eyton [in Purslow hd.], Sa, 253
Eyton on Severn, Sa, 250

Faccombe, Ha, 112
Faceby, YN, 375
Fairburn, YW, 386
Fairfield, Wo, 353
Fairford, Gl, 100
Fairlee, Ha, 119
Fairlight, Sx, 317
Fairstead, Ess, 84
Fairwood, Great, Dev, 58
Fakenham, Nf, 199
Fakenham, Sf, 293
Fakenham, Little, Sf, 292
Falcutt, Np, 210
Faldingworth, Li, 177
Faldo, Bd, 3
Falfield, Gl, 101
Falkenham, Sf, 296
Fallodon, Nb, 225
Falmer, Sx, 312
Falsgrave, YN, 382
Fambridge, North, Ess, 84
Fambridge, South, Ess, 81
Fangfoss, YE, 361
Farcet, Hu, 138
Fardel, Dev, 64
Fareham, Ha, 116
Fareham, hundred, Ha, 116

Fareham, North, Ha, 116
Farforth, Li, 183
Faringdon, Brk, 11
Faringdon, hundred, Brk, 11
Faringdon, Little, Ox, 6, 11, 235
Farington, La, 154
Farlam, Cu, 38
Farleigh, Sr, 303
Farleigh Hungerford, So, 268
Farleigh Wallop, Ha, 118
Farlesthorpe, Li, 184
Farleton, La, 156
Farleton, We, 330
Farley, Wlt, 345
Farley Chamberlaine, Ha, 107
Farley Hill, Brk, 346
Farlington, Ha, 110
Farlington, YN, 376
Farmanby, YN, 381
Farmborough, So, 270
Farmcote, Gl, 98
Farmington, Gl, 99
Farnborough, Brk, 13
Farnborough, Ha, 109
Farnborough, Wa, 321
Farncombe, Sr, 298
Farndon, Np, 210 n.
Farndon, Nt, 233
Farndon, East, Np, 213
Farnham, Do, 75
Farnham, Ess, 85
Farnham, Nb, 224
Farnham, Sf, 294
Farnham, Sr, 298
Farnham, YW, 395
Farnham, hundred, Sr, 298
Farnham Royal, Bk, 21
Farnhill, YW, 382
Farnley [in Claro wap.], YW, 384
Farnley [in Morley wap.], YW, 389
Farnley Tyas, YW, 389
Farnsfield, Nt, 232
Farringdon, Ha, 107
Farrington Gurney, So, 261
Farsley, YW, 389
Farthinghoe, Np, 210
Farthingstone, Np, 215
Farway, Dev, 57
Farwood Barton, Dev, 57
Fauld, St, 280
Faulkbourne, Ess, 84
Faulkner's Farm, Sx, 313
Faulston, Wlt, 334
Faversham, hundred, K, 142
Fawdington, YN, 381
Fawler, Brk, 10
Fawler, Ox, 241
Fawley, Brk, 9
Fawley, Bk, 21
Fawley, Ha, 118

Fawley, He, 127
Fawley, hundred, Ha, 117
Fawley, South, Brk, 9
Fawsley, Np, 215
Fawsley, hundred, Np, 215
Faxfleet, YE, 362
Faxton, Np, 212
Fearby, YN, 372
Featherstone, Nb, 220
Featherstone, St, 283
Featherstone, YW, 391
Feckenham, Wo, 353
Felborough, hundred, K, 143
Felbrigg, Nf, 201
Felhampton, Sa, 254
Felixkirk, YN, 381
Felixstowe, Sf, 296
Felmersham, Bd, 2
Felmingham, Nf, 202
Felpham, Sx, 308
Felsham, Sf, 292
Felsted, Ess, 80
Feltham, Mx, 189
Felthorpe, Nf, 194
Felton, He, 124
Felton, Nb, 223
Felton, So, 271
Felton Butler, Sa, 252
Feltwell, Nf, 204
Fenby, Li, 180
Fencote, YN, 371
Fencott, Ox, 238
Feniton, Dev, 63
Fenrother, Nb, 222
Fenstanton, Hu, 137
Fenton, Cu, 39
Fenton, Hu, 137 n.
Fenton [in Loveden wap.], Li, 174
Fenton [in Well wap.], Li, 178
Fenton, Nb, 226
Fenton, Nt, 228
Fenton, Church, YW, 386
Fenton [Culvert], St, 278
Fenton [Vivian], St, 278
Fenwick, Nb, 221
Feock, Co, 31
Fernham, Brk, 11
Fernhill, Dev, 51
Ferriby, North, YE, 360
Ferriby, South, Li, 179
Ferring, Ess, 88
Ferring, Sx, 309
Ferry, East, Li, 177
Ferrybridge, YW, 390
Fersfield, Nf, 207
Fetcham, Sr, 302
Fewcott, Ox, 238
Fiddington, Gl, 93
Fiddington, So, 267
Fideock, So, 265

Field, St, 280
Fifehead Magdalen, Do, 74
Fifehead Neville, Do, 75
Fifehead St. Quentin, Do, 75
Fifield, Ox, 236
Fifield, Wlt, 340
Fifield Bavent, Wlt, 342
Figheldean, Wlt, 345
Filby, Nf, 193
Filey, YE, 366
Filgrave, Bk, 17
Filkins, Ox, 237
Filleigh, Dev, 62
Fillingham, Li, 176
Fillongley, Wa, 324
Filton, Gl, 96
Fimber, YE, 366, 369
Finborough, Great, Sf, 287
Finborough, Little, Sf, 288
Fincham, Nf, 203
Finchampstead, Brk, 7
Finchdean, hundred, Ha, 114
Finchingfield, Ess, 80
Finchley, Mx, 190
Findern, Db, 43
Findon, Sx, 310
Finedon, Np, 218
Fingest, Bk, 21
Finghall, YN, 372
Fingreth, Ess, 85
Fingringhoe, Ess, 81
Finley, Ha, 115
Finmere, Ox, 237
Finningham, Sf, 287
Finningley, Nt, 227, 228
Finsbury, Mx, 190
Finstock, Ox, 241
Firbank, We, 331
Firby, YE, 365
Firsby [in Aslacoe wap.], Li, 177
Firsby [in Candleshoe wap.], Li, 182
Fishbourne [New], Sx, 307
Fishergate, half-hundreds, Sx, 311, 312
Fisherton Anger, Wlt, 342
Fisherton de la Mere, Wlt, 347
Fisherwick, St, 280
Fishlake, YW, 393
Fishley, Nf, 195
Fishtoft, Li, 169
Fishwick, La, 152
Fiskerton, Li, 177
Fiskerton, Nt, 231
Fitling, YE, 357
Fittleton, Wlt, 340
Fittleworth, Sx, 309
Fitz, Sa, 251
Fivehead, So, 272
Fixby, YW, 389
Fladbury, Wo, 351
Flamborough, YE, 366

Flamstead, Hrt, 134
Flamston, Wlt, 334
Flasby, YW, 383
Flashbrook, St, 278
Flawborough, Nt, 233
Flawith, YN, 376
Flaxby, YW, 384
Flaxton, YN, 376
Flaxwell, wapentake, Li, 173
Fleckney, Lei, 164
Flecknoe, Wa, 322
Fledborough, Nt, 231
Fleet, Do, 77
Fleet, Li, 168
Flegg, East, hundred, Nf, 193
Flegg, West, hundred, Nf, 193
Flemdish, hundred, Ca, 24
Flempton, Sf, 292
Flete, Dev, 65
Fletton, Hu, 138
Flexborough, hundred, Sx, 314
Flexland, Ha, 113
Flintham, Nt, 232
Flinton, YE, 359, 369
Flitcham, Nf, 197
Flitt, hundred, Bd, 3
Flitwick, Bd, 3
Flixborough, Li, 175
Flixton, La, 154
Flixton, Sf, 290
Flixton, YE, 365
Flockton, YW, 390
Flordon, Nf, 206
Flore, Np, 216
Flotmanby, YE, 366
Flotterton, Nb, 224
Flowton, Sf, 285
Flyford Flavell, Wo, 354
Fobbing, Ess, 86
Fockerby, YW, 390
Foggathorpe, YE, 360, 366
Foleshill, Wa, 324
Folkestone, hundred, K, 147
Folkingham, Li, 170
Folksworth, Hu, 138
Folkton, YE, 365
Follifoot [in Ainsty wap.], YW, 385
Follifoot [in Claro wap.], YW, 385
Fons George, So, 265
Fonthill, Bishop's, Wlt, 342
Fonthill Gifford, Wlt, 338
Fontmell Magna, Do, 74
Forcett, YN, 373
Ford, Dev, 54
Ford, Gl, 98
Ford, Nb, 224
Ford, Sa, 252
Ford, Sx, 308
Ford, hundred, Sa, 252
Forde, Wlt, 347

Fordham, Ca, 24
Fordham, Ess, 88
Fordham, Nf, 203
Fordingbridge, Ha, 114
Fordingbridge, hundred, Ha, 114
Fordington, Do, 73
Fordington, Li, 182
Fordley, Sf, 289
Fordon, YE, 366
Forehoe, hundred, Nf, 206
Foremark, Db, 46
Forest Hall, Ess, 83 n.
Forest Hill, Ox, 239
Foresta Monarchorum, Sa, 252
Formby, La, 151
Forncett, Nf, 196
Fornham All Saints, Sf, 291
Fornham St. Genevieve, Sf, 292
Fornham St. Martin, Sf, 292
Forston, Do, 68
Forthampton, Gl, 93
Forton, Ha, 111
Forton, St, 277
Fosbrook, St, 281
Fosbury, Wlt, 348
Fosham, YE, 359
Foston, Db, 45
Foston, Lei, 158
Foston, Li, 174
Foston, Nf, 203
Foston, YN, 380
Foston on the Wolds, YE, 365, 368
Fotherby, Li, 180
Fotheringay, Np, 213
Fotherley, Nb, 221
Foukholm', Cu, 41
Fouldon, Nf, 204
Foulridge, La, 153
Foulsham, Nf, 200
Foulwod, Cu, 38
Fourstones, Nb, 220
Fovant, Wlt, 335
Fowberry, Nb, 224
Fowey, Co, 31
Fowey Extra, Co, 31
Fowlmere, Ca, 27
Fownhope, He, 127
Foxcote, Bk, 16
Foxcote, Gl, 99
Foxcote, So, 268
Foxcote, Wa, 320
Foxcotte, Ha, 109
Foxearle, hundred, Sx, 316
Foxearth, Ess, 80
Foxhall, Sf, 296
Foxholes, YE, 365
Foxley, Nf, 200
Foxley, Np, 211
Foxley, Wlt, 339
Foxton, Ca, 26

Foxton, Lei, 165
Foxton, YN, 378
Foy, He, 125
Fradswell, St, 277
Fraisthorpe, YE, 366
Framfield, Sx, 315
Framingham Earl, Nf, 196
Framingham Pigot, Nf, 196
Framland, hundred, Lei, 163
Framlingham, Sf, 295
Frampton, Do, 76
Frampton, Gl, 98
Frampton, Li, 168
Frampton Cotterell, Gl, 94
Frampton, liberty, Do, 76
Frampton Mansell, Gl, 93
Frampton on Severn, Gl, 103
Framsden, Sf, 296
Frankley, Wo, 353
Frankton, Wa, 322
Frankton, English, Sa, 252
Fransham, Great, Nf, 208
Fransham, Little, Nf, 208
Frant, Sx, 314
Frating, Ess, 88
Fratton, Ha, 110
Freckenham, Sf, 293
Freckleton, La, 152
Freebridge, hundred, Nf, 197
Freeby, Lei, 163
Freefolk, Ha, 109
Freeford, St, 280
Freethorpe, Nf, 194
Freiston, Li, 169
Fremington, Dev, 53
Fremington, hundred, Dev, 53
Frenchstone, Dev, 54
Frensham, Sr, 298
Frenze, Nf, 207
Fresden, Wlt, 343
Freshford, So, 261
Freshwater, Ha, 120
Fressingfield, Sf, 288
Freston, Sf, 285
Frettenham, Nf, 194
Frickley, YW, 393
Fridaythorpe, YE, 364, 367
Frieston, Li, 174
Frilford, Brk, 12
Frilsham, Brk, 8
Fring, Nf, 198
Fringford, Ox, 237
Frinton, Ess, 88
Frisby, Lei, 164
Frisby on the Wreak, Lei, 161
Friskney, Li, 182
Frismarsh, YE, 358
Friston, Sf, 295
Fritham, Ha, 117
Frithelstock, Dev, 52

Fritton, Nf, 196
Fritton, Sf, 290
Fritwell, Ox, 237
Frizington, Cu, 40
Frobury, Ha, 115
Frocester, Gl, 103
Frodingham, Li, 186
Frodingham, YE, 359
Frodingham, North, YE, 359
Frolesworth, Lei, 159
Frome, So, 268
Frome Belet, Do, 68
Frome, Bishops, He, 128
Frome, Canon, He, 128
Frome, Castle, He, 128
Frome, Halmond's, He, 128
Frome, hundred, So, 268
Frome, Prior's, He, 127
Frome St. Quentin, Do, 76
Frome Vauchurch, Do, 76
Frome Whitfield, Do, 68
Frontridge, Sx, 318
Frostenden, Sf, 289
Froxfield, Ha, 111
Froxfield, Wlt, 348
Froyle, Ha, 114
Frustfield, hundred, Wlt, 336
Fryerning, Ess, 85
Fryston, Ferry, YW, 390
Fryston, Monk, YW, 386
Fryton, YN, 377
Fugglestone, Wlt, 342
Fulbeck, Li, 174
Fulbourn, Ca, 24
Fulbrook, Bk, 19
Fulbrook, Ox, 236
Fulbrook, Wa, 326
Fulflood, Ha, 108
Fulford, So, 264
Fulford, St, 278
Fulford, YE, 366, 367
Fulford, Great, Dev, 58
Fulford, Water, YE, 366, 367
Fulham, Mx, 190
Fulletby, Li, 185
Fullready, Wa, 320 n.
Fulmer, Bk, 21
Fulmodestone, Nf, 199
Fulscot, Brk, 13
Fulstow, Li, 180
Fulwell, Ox, 236
Fulwood, So, 264
Fundenhall, Nf, 196
Funtington, Sx, 305
Funtley, Ha, 110
Furland, So, 273
Fursham, Dev, 58
Furtho, Np, 211
Furze, Dev, 63
Fyfield, Brk, 12

Fyfield, Ess, 83
Fyfield, Ha, 108
Fyfield [in Elstub hd.], Wlt, 340
Fyfield [in Kinwardstone hd.], Wlt, 347
Fyling, YN, 380
Fynle, Do, 77

Gaddesby, Lei, 161
Gaddesden, Great, Hrt, 134
Gaddesden, Little, Hrt, 135
Gagingwell, Ox, 236
Gainsborough, Li, 177
Galby, Lei, 165
Gallow, hundred, Nf, 199
Galmington, So, 264
Galmpton [in Haytor hd.], Dev, 50
Galmpton [in Stanborough hd.], Dev, 51
Galton, Do, 68
Gamblesby, Cu, 36
Gamlingay, Ca, 26
Gamston [in Bassetlaw wap.], Nt, 228
Gamston [in Bingham wap.], Nt, 232
Ganfield, hundred, Brk, 11
Ganstead, YE, 358
Ganthorpe, YN, 376
Ganton, YE, 365
Garboldisham, Nf, 205
Gardham, YE, 363
Garford, Brk, 12
Garforth, YW, 388
Gargrave, YW, 383
Garmston, Sa, 250
Garrowby, YE, 365
Garsdon, Wlt, 337
Garsington, Ox, 239
Garstang, La, 151
Garston, La, 150
Garston, East, Brk, 10
Garthorpe, Lei, 164
Garthorpe, Li, 175
Garton, YE, 358
Garton on the Wolds, YE, 366, 368
Gartree, hundred, Lei, 157, 164
Gartree, wapentake, Li, 182
Garveston, Nf, 205
Garway, He, 125
Gasthorpe, Nf, 205
Gatacre, Sa, 256
Gatcombe, Dev, 56
Gatcombe, Ha, 119
Gate Hill, YW, 387
Gateforth, YW, 386
Gatehampton, Ox, 243
Gateley, Nf, 207
Gatenby, YN, 371
Gatton, Sr, 298
Gautby, Li, 182
Gawcott, Bk, 22
Gaydon, Wa, 321
Gayhurst, Bk, 18

Gayton, Nf, 197
Gayton, Np, 211
Gayton, St, 279
Gayton le Marsh, Li, 184
Gayton le Wold, Li, 183
Gayton Thorpe, Nf, 197
Gaywood, Nf, 197
Gazeley, Sf, 294
Gedding, Sf, 292
Geddington, Np, 215
Gedling, Nt, 231
Gedney, Li, 168
Geldeston, Nf, 196
Gelston, Li, 174
Gembling, YE, 369
George Teign Barton, Dev, 59
Germansweek, Dev, 60
Gerrans, Co, 31
Gestingthorpe, Ess, 80
Gibsmere, Nt, 231
Gidding, Great, Hu, 138
Gidding, Little, Hu, 139
Gidding, Steeple, Hu, 138
Giggleswick, YW, 382
Gilberdyke, YE, 363
Gilby, Li, 186
Gilcrux, Cu, 39
Gilling East, YN, 380
Gilling, wapentake, YN, 373
Gilling West, YN, 373
Gillingham, Do, 73
Gillingham, Nf, 195
Gillingham Manor, Do, 74
Gillow, He, 126
Gilmonby, YN, 380
Gilmorton, Lei, 159
Gilston, Hrt, 132
Gimingham, Nf, 201
Ginge, East, Brk, 11
Ginge, West, Brk, 11
Gipping, Sf, 287
Girlington, YN, 373
Girsby, YN, 378
Girton, Ca, 25
Girton, Nt, 233
Gisburn, YW, 382
Gisleham, Sf, 286
Gislingham, Sf, 287
Gissing, Nf, 207
Gittisham, Dev, 65
Givendale, YW, 394
Givendale, Great, YE, 362
Givendale, Little, YE, 367
Glaisdale, YN, 376
Glanford, Nf, 199
Glantlees, Nb, 224
Glanton, Nb, 223
Glapthorn, Np, 213
Glapwell, Db, 48
Glasshampton, Wo, 352

Glassonby, Cu, 37
Glaston, Ru, 248
Glastonbury, So, 273
Glatton, Hu, 138
Glazebrook, La, 150
Glazeley, Sa, 255
Glemham, Great, Sf, 294
Glemham, Little, Sf, 294
Glemsford, Sf, 291
Glen, Great, Lei, 165
Glen Parva, Lei, 159
Glendale, ward, Nb, 224
Glendon, Np, 213 n.
Glenfield, Lei, 159
Glentham, Li, 176
Glentworth, Li, 176, 186
Glinton, Np, 213
Glooston, Lei, 165
Glossop, Db, 47
Glottenham, Sx, 318
Gloucester, Gl, 90, 91
Gloucestershire, 90–104
Gludden, Ha, 113
Glusburn, YW, 382
Glympton, Ox, 242
Gnosall, St, 282
Goadby, Lei, 165
Goadby Marwood, Lei, 164
Goathill, Do, 67, 269
Goathland, YN, 381
Goathurst, So, 260
Godalming, Sr, 298
Godalming, hundred, Sr, 298
Godderthorn, hundred, Do, 70
Godington, Ox, 238
Godley, hundred, Sr, 300
Godmanchester, Hu, 136
Godmanston, Do, 70
Godshill, Ha, 119
Godstone, Sr, 303
Godwick, Nf, 207
Godyngflod, Brk, 10 n.
Golborne, La, 150
Golder, Ox, 238
Goldicote, Wa, 354
Goldington, Bd, 2
Goldsborough, YW, 384
Goldspur, hundred, Sx, 317
Gomeldon, Wlt, 345
Gomersal, YW, 388
Gomshall, Sr, 299
Gonalston, Nt, 231
Gonerby, Great, Li, 171
Gooderstone, Nf, 203
Goodleigh, Dev, 62
Goodmanham, YE, 361, 368
Goodrington, Dev, 50
Goodshelter, Dev, 64
Goodworth Clatford, Ha, 111
Goosebradon, So, 272

Goosewell, Dev, 51
Goosey, Brk, 12
Goosnargh, La, 151
Gopsall, Lei, 159
Gore, hundred, Mx, 191
Goring, Ox, 243
Goring, Sx, 309
Gorleston, Nf, 284, 290
Gosbeck, Sf, 286
Gosberton, Li, 168
Goscote, hundred, Lei, 157, 160
Gosfield, Ess, 80
Gosford, Ox, 242
Gosforth, Cu, 40
Gosforth, Nb, 222
Gosforth, South, Nb, 223
Gosport, Ha, 117
Gostrow, hundred, Sx, 316
Gotham, Nt, 230
Gotherington, Gl, 93
Goulceby, Li, 182
Goverton, Nt, 231
Gowdall, YW, 390
Gowthorpe, YE, 362
Goxhill, Li, 179
Goxhill, YE, 358
Graby, Li, 170
Grade, Co, 30
Graffham, Sx, 306
Graffoe, wapentake, Li, 175
Grafham, Hu, 139
Grafton, He, 127
Grafton, Ox, 237
Grafton [near Bromsgrove], Wo, 353
Grafton [near Ashton under Hill], Wo, 101
Grafton, YW, 387
Grafton, East, Wlt, 347
Grafton Flyford, Wo, 354
Grafton Regis, Np, 211
Grafton, Temple, Wa, 326
Grafton Underwood, Np, 214
Grafton, West, Wlt, 347
Grainsby, Li, 180
Grainthorpe, Li, 183
Graistokskales, Cu, 36
Grampound, Co, 31
Granborough, Bk, 19
Granby, Nt, 232
Grandborough, Wa, 322
Grandpont, Ox, 6, 12, 235
Gransden, Great, Hu, 136
Gransden, Little, Ca, 26
Gransmoor, YE, 365
Grantchester, Ca, 26
Grantham, Li, 172
Grasby, Li, 179, 186
Grasmere, We, 330
Grass Croft, So, 264
Grassington, YW, 383
Grassthorpe, Nt, 231

Grateley, Ha, 108
Gratton, Dev, 53
Gratwich, St, 280
Graveley, Ca, 25
Graveley, Hrt, 133
Gravenhunger, Sa, 250
Gravenhurst, Bd, 3
Grayingham, Li, 177, 186
Grayrigg, We, 330
Gray's Inn, Mx, 191
Grazeley, Brk, 7
Greasbrough, YW, 394
Greasley, Nt, 229
Greatford, Li, 169
Greatham, Ha, 114
Greatham, Sx, 309
Greatworth, Np, 210
Greenford, Mx, 190
Greenhalgh, La, 151
Greenham, Brk, 9
Greenham, So, 260
Greenhoe, North, hundred, Nf, 200
Greenhoe, South, hundred, Nf, 203
Greenhow, YN, 375
Greenleighton, Nb, 222
Greenoak, YE, 362
Greenriggs, We, 330
Greenstead, Ess, 88
Greet, Gl, 98
Greete, Sa, 254
Greetham, Li, 185
Greetham, Ru, 247
Greetham, Little, Li, 185
Greetwell, Li, 178
Greinton, So, 273
Grendon, Np, 217
Grendon, Wa, 324
Grendon Bishop, He, 123
Grendon Underwood, Bk, 19
Grendon Warren, He, 123
Gresham, Nf, 201
Gresley, Db, 46
Gressingham, La, 156
Gretton, Gl, 98
Gretton, Np, 215
Gretton, Sa, 254
Grewelthorpe, YW, 384
Greysouthen, Cu, 39
Greystoke, Cu, 36
Greytree, hundred, He, 126
Greywell, Ha, 120
Gribthorpe, YE, 361
Griff, Wa, 324
Grimblethorpe, Li, 183
Grimley, Wo, 350
Grimoldby, Li, 183
Grimpstonleigh, Dev, 64
Grimsargh, La, 151
Grimsbury, Ox, 209, 210, 235
Grimsby, Li, 167, 185

Grimshoe, hundred, Nf, 204
Grimstead, East, Wlt, 345
Grimstead, West, Wlt, 345
Grimsthorpe, Li, 171
Grimston, Lei, 161
Grimston, Nf, 197
Grimston, Nt, 229
Grimston [in Holderness], YE, 359
Grimston [in wap. between Ouse and Derwent], YE, 363, 367
Grimston, YW, 386
Grimston, Hanging, YE, 366
Grimston, North, YE, 365, 367
Grimstone, Do, 68
Grimsworth, hundred, He, 124
Grindale, YE, 366, 367
Grindle, Sa, 256
Grindleton, YW, 383
Grindon, St, 281
Gringley, Little, Nt, 228
Gringley on the Hill, Nt, 234
Grinsdale, Cu, 37
Grinshill, Sa, 251
Grinstead, East, Sx, 305
Grinstead, East, hundred, Sx, 315
Grinstead, West, Sx, 310
Grinstead, West, hundred, Sx, 310
Grinton, YN, 372
Gristhwaite, YN, 378
Griston, Nf, 204
Grittenham, Wlt, 339
Grittleton, Wlt, 344
Groby, Lei, 160
Grogoth, Co, 31
Groton, Sf, 291
Groundwell, Wlt, 343
Grove, Brk, 11
Grove, Nt, 228
Grove Ash, Ox, 241
Grumbalds Ash, hundred, Gl, 101
Grundisburgh, Sf, 296
Guestling, Sx, 317
Guestling, hundred, Sx, 317
Guestwick, Nf, 200
Guildford, Sr, 297, 298
Guilsborough, Np, 216
Guilsborough, hundred, Np, 216
Guiltcross, hundred, Nf, 205
Guisborough, YN, 375
Guiseley, YW, 387
Guist, Nf, 200
Guiting Power, Gl, 98
Guiting, Temple, Gl, 98
Gulval, Co, 30
Gumley, Lei, 165
Gummershay, Do, 74
Gunby [in Beltisloe wap.], Li, 171
Gunby [in Candleshoe wap.], Li, 182
Gunnerby, Li, 180
Gunnerton, Nb, 220

Gunness, Li, 176
Gunstone, St, 282
Gunthorpe, Nf, 199
Gunthorpe, Ru, 247
Gunthwaite, YW, 391
Gunton, Nf, 201
Gunton, Sf, 290
Gussage All Saints, Do, 72
Gussage St. Michael, Do, 77
Guthlaxton, hundred, Lei, 158
Guyzance, Nb, 223
Gwennap, Co, 30
Gwinear, Co, 30
Gwithian, Co, 30
Gyng Joyberd (Great Blunts), Ess, 85
Gyng Laundri (Little Blunts), Ess, 85

Habberley, Sa, 253
Habbesthorpe, Nt, 227
Habrough, Li, 179
Habton, YN, 377
Haccombe, Dev, 50
Hacconby, Li, 170
Haceby, Li, 170
Hacheston, Sf, 295
Hackensall, La, 152
Hackford [in Eynesford hd.], Nf, 200
Hackford [in Forehoe hd.], Nf, 206
Hackforth, YN, 372
Hackleton, Np, 217
Hackness, YN, 380
Hackney, Mx, 190
Hackthorn, Li, 177
Hackthorpe, We, 329
Hackworthy, Dev, 58
Haddenham, Bk, 20
Haddenham, Ca, 28
Haddesley, Goose, YW, 386
Haddesley, West, YW, 386
Haddington, Li, 175
Haddiscoe, Nf, 195
Haddon, Hu, 138
Haddon, Ox, 237 n.
Haddon, East, Np, 216
Haddon, Nether, Db, 47
Haddon, Over, Db, 47
Haddon, West, Np, 216
Hadham, Little, Hrt, 133
Hadham, Much, Hrt, 133
Hadleigh, Ess, 81
Hadleigh, Sf, 291
Hadley, Sa, 251
Hadnall, Sa, 251
Hadstock, Ess, 86
Hadston, Nb, 222
Hadzor, Wo, 353
Hagbourne, East, Brk, 13
Hagbourne, West, Brk, 13
Hagginton, East, Dev, 62
Hagginton, West, Dev, 62

Hagley, Wo, 353
Hagworthingham, Li, 185
Haigh, La, 149
Haighton, La, 152
Haile, Cu, 40
Hailey, Ox, 237
Hailsham, Sx, 315
Hainford, Nf, 194
Hainton, Li, 181
Haisthorpe, YE, 369
Halam, Nt, 232
Halberton, Dev, 56
Halberton, hundred, Dev, 56
Haldenby, YW, 391
Hale, Ha, 114
Hale, La, 151
Hale, Great, Li, 172
Hale, Little, Li, 172
Halefield, Np, 213
Hales, Nf, 195
Halesowen, Wo, 249, 256
Halesworth, Sf, 289
Halfcot, St, 277
Halford, Wa, 320
Halfshire, hundred, Wo, 352
Halgh', YW, 386
Halifax, YW, 389
Halikeld, wapentake, YN, 371
Hallam, Kirk, Db, 42
Hallam, Little, Db, 43
Hallam, West, Db, 42
Hallaton, Lei, 164
Hallatrow, So, 260
Halliford, Lower, Mx, 190
Halliford, Upper, Mx, 189
Hallingbury, Great, Ess, 89
Hallingbury, Little, Ess, 89
Hallington, Li, 183
Halliwell, La, 154
Halloughton, Nt, 231
Hallow, Wo, 350
Halnaker, Sx, 307
Halsall, La, 151
Halse, Np, 210
Halse, So, 265
Halsfordwood, Dev, 58
Halsham, YE, 358
Halstead, Ess, 80
Halstead, Lei, 162
Halstock, Do, 72
Halstock, hundred, Do, 72
Halsway, So, 266
Haltham, Li, 184
Halton, Bk, 20
Halton, La, 156
Halton, Nb, 220
Halton, East, Li, 179
Halton East, YW, 383
Halton Holegate, Li, 185
Halton, West, YW, 382

Halvergate, Nf, 195
Halwill, Dev, 60
Ham [in Berkeley hd.], Gl, 95
Ham [in St. Briavels lib.], Gl, 92
Ham, Ha, 115
Ham, Sr, 301
Ham, Wlt, 340
Ham, East, Ess, 81
Ham, High, So, 273
Ham, hundred, K, 147
Ham Manor, Sx, 309
Ham, West, Ess, 81
Hambleden, Bk, 21
Hambledon, Ha, 113
Hambledon, Sr, 298
Hambledon, hundred, Ha, 113
Hambleton, La, 152
Hambleton, Ru, 246
Hambleton, YW, 386
Hambridge, So, 272
Hambrook, Gl, 94
Hamcastle, Wo, 352
Hameringham, Li, 185
Hamerton, Hu, 139
Hamfordshoe, hundred, Np, 217
Hamilton, Lei, 161
Hammerton, YW, 383
Hammerton, Green, YW, 384
Hammerton, Kirk, YW, 384
Hammerwich, St, 280
Hammoon, Do, 75
Hamp, So, 260
Hampden, Great, Bk, 20
Hampden, Little, Bk, 20
Hampen, Gl, 99
Hampnall, Nf, 196
Hampnett, Gl, 99
Hampnett, East, Sx, 307
Hampreston, Do, 75
Hampshire, 105–21
Hampstead, Mx, 191
Hampstead Norris, Brk, 8
Hampton, He, 130
Hampton, Mx, 189
Hampton, Wlt, 343
Hampton Bishop, He, 124
Hampton Gay, Ox, 238
Hampton, Great, Wo, 355
Hampton in Arden, Wa, 324
Hampton Lovett, Wo, 352
Hampton Lucy, Wa, 327
Hampton, Meysey, Gl, 99
Hampton on the Hill, Wa, 325 n.
Hampton Poyle, Ox, 238
Hampton Wafer, He, 124
Hamptworth, Wlt, 334
Hamsey, Sx, 313
Hamstead Marshall, Brk, 10
Hamworthy, Do, 69
Hanborough, Ox, 244

Hanbury, St, 280
Hanbury, Wo, 350
Hanchurch, St, 278
Handbeck, Li, 173
Handsacre, St, 280
Handsworth, Wa, 276, 279
Handsworth, YW, 393
Hanford, Do, 73
Hang, wapentake, YN, 371
Hangleton, Sx, 312
Hanham, Gl, 94
Hanham Court, Gl, 94
Hankerton, Wlt, 337
Hanley, St, 278
Hanley Castle, Wo, 353
Hanley Child, Wo, 352
Hanley William, Wo, 352
Hanlith, YW, 383
Hanney, East, Brk, 11, 12
Hanney, West, Brk, 11
Hanningfield, East, Ess, 85
Hanningfield, South, Ess, 85
Hanningfield, West, Ess, 85
Hannington, Ha, 115
Hannington, Np, 212
Hannington, Wlt, 343
Hannington Launcelneye, Ha, 115
Hansford Barton, Dev, 62
Hanslope, Bk, 17
Hanthorpe, Li, 170
Hanwell, Mx, 190
Hanwell, Ox, 243
Hanworth, Mx, 190
Hanworth, Nf, 201
Hanworth, Cold, Li, 176
Hanworth, Potter, Li, 173
Happing, hundred, Nf, 193
Happisburgh, Nf, 193
Hapton, La, 153
Hapton, Nf, 196
Harberton, Dev, 64
Harborne, Wa, 276, 279
Harborough Magna, Wa, 323
Harborough, Market, Lei, 165
Harborough Parva, Wa, 323
Harbottle, Nb, 221
Harbridge, Ha, 121
Harbury, Wa, 322
Harby, Lei, 163
Harby, Nt, 233
Harcourt, Sa, 255
Hardenhuish, Wlt, 344
Hardhorn, La, 151
Harding, Wlt, 348
Hardingham, Nf, 204
Hardingstone, Np, 217
Hardington, So, 261
Hardington Mandeville, So, 270
Hardington Marsh, So, 270
Hardisworthy, Dev, 61

Hardley [in East Medine hd.], Ha, 119
Hardley [in New Forest hd.], Ha, 116
Hardley, Nf, 195
Hardmead, Bk, 17
Hardwick, Bk, 18
Hardwick, Ca, 26
Hardwick, He, 129
Hardwick, Nf, 196
Hardwick, Np, 217
Hardwick [in Bampton hd.], Ox, 237
Hardwick [in Banbury hd.], Ox, 241
Hardwick [in Ploughley hd.], Ox, 238
Hardwick, Wa, 321
Hardwick, Bredon's, Wo, 350
Hardwick by Wragby, Li, 181
Hardwick, Kites, Wa, 322
Hardwick, Priors, Wa, 321
Hardwicke [in Westminster hd.], Gl, 99
Hardwicke [in Whitstone hd.], Gl, 103
Hareby, Li, 185
Harefield, Mx, 190
Harescombe, Gl, 91 n.
Haresfield, Gl, 103
Hareston, Dev, 51
Harewood, He, 126
Harewood, YW, 388
Harford, Dev, 64
Harford, Gl, 103
Hargham, Nf, 205
Hargrave, Np, 136, 138, 209
Hargrave, Sf, 291
Harkstead, Sf, 285
Harlaston, St, 280
Harlaxton, Li, 172
Harle, West, Nb, 220
Harlescott, Sa, 251
Harleston, Dev, 51
Harleston, Sf, 287
Harlestone, Np, 216
Harley, Sa, 252
Harling, East, Nf, 205
Harling, Middle, Nf, 205
Harling, West, Nf, 205
Harlington, Bd, 4
Harlington, Mx, 190
Harlow, Ess, 89
Harlow Hill, Nb, 220
Harlow, hundred, Ess, 89
Harlsey, East, YN, 377
Harlsey, West, YN, 378
Harlthorpe, YE, 361
Harlton, Ca, 26
Harmby, YN, 372
Harmondsworth, Mx, 190
Harmston, Li, 174
Harnham, Wlt, 334
Harnhill, Gl, 99
Harome, YN, 377
Harp, South, So, 275
Harpford, Dev, 65

Harpham, YE, 365
Harpley, Nf, 197
Harpole, Np, 216
Harpsden, Ox, 240
Harpswell, Li, 177, 186
Harptree, East, So, 259
Harptree, West, So, 260
Harringay, Mx, 190 n.
Harrington, Cu, 40
Harrington, Li, 185
Harrington, Np, 212
Harringworth, Np, 215
Harrold, Bd, 2
Harrow, Mx, 191
Harrowby, Li, 172
Harrowden, Great, Np, 212
Harrowden, Little, Np, 212
Harston, Ca, 26
Harston, Lei, 163
Harswell, YE, 362
Hartcliffe, hundred, So, 271
Hartest, Sf, 290
Hartfield, hundred, Sx, 313
Hartford, Hu, 136
Hartforth, YN, 373
Hartham, Wlt, 344
Harthill, Db, 47
Harthill, YW, 392
Harthill, wapentake, YE, 360, 370
Harting, East, Sx, 306
Harting, South, Sx, 306
Harting, West, Sx, 306
Hartington, Db, 45
Hartington, Nb, 222
Hartington, Sr, 301
Hartismere, hundred, Sf, 287
Hartland, Dev, 61
Hartland, hundred, Dev, 61
Hartlebury, Wo, 351
Hartley, Nb, 223
Hartley, We, 329
Hartley Dummer, Brk, 8
Hartley Mauditt, Ha, 114
Hartley Wespall, Ha, 117
Hartley Wintney, Ha, 113
Hartlington, YW, 382
Hartoft End, YN, 381
Harton, YN, 380
Hartpury, Gl, 96
Hartridge, Brk, 8
Hartshead, YW, 389
Hartshill, Wa, 325
Hartshorne, Db, 47
Hartwell, Bk, 20
Hartwell, Np, 211
Harvington, Wo, 350
Harwell, Brk, 13
Harwell, Nt, 227
Harwich, Ess, 89
Harwood, La, 154

Harwood, Great, La, 153
Harwood, Little, La, 153
Harworth, Nt, 228
Haselbech, Np, 213
Haselbury Plucknett, So, 269
Haseley, Wa, 325
Haseley, Great, Ox, 240
Haseley, Little, Ox, 240
Haselor, Wa, 326
Haselour, St, 280
Hasfield, Gl, 99
Hasketon, Sf, 296
Hasler and Rushmore, hundred, Do, 76
Haslingden, La, 152
Haslingfield, Ca, 26
Hassingham, Nf, 194
Hassop, Db, 47
Hastings, Sx, 304
Hastings, rape, Sx, 316
Hatch, Wlt, 338
Hatch Beauchamp, So, 266
Hatch Warren, Ha, 118
Hatch, West, So, 263
Hatcham, Sr, 302
Hatcliffe, Li, 180
Hatfield, Hrt, 133
Hatfield, Wo, 350 n.
Hatfield, YE, 358
Hatfield, YW, 393
Hatfield Broad Oak, Ess, 89
Hatfield Peverel, Ess, 84
Hatford, Brk, 12
Hatherleigh, Dev, 60
Hatherley, Down, Gl, 97
Hatherley, Up, Gl, 91 n.
Hathern, Lei, 162
Hatherop, Gl, 100
Hathersage, Db, 47
Hatherton, St, 283
Hatley, Cockayne, Bd, 1
Hatley, East, Ca, 25
Hatley St. George, Ca, 26
Hatton, Db, 45
Hatton, Li, 181
Hatton, Sa, 256
Hatton, St, 282
Hatton [in Barlichway hd.], Wa, 325
Hatton [in Pathlow lib.], Wa, 327
Hatton, Cold, Sa, 250
Haugh, Li, 184
Haugham, Li, 183
Haughley, Sf, 288
Haughton, Nt, 229
Haughton [in Bradford hd.], Sa, 251
Haughton [in Brimstree hd.], Sa, 256
Haughton, St, 282
Hautbois, Great, Nf, 202
Hautbois, Little, Nf, 201
Hauxton, Ca, 26
Hauxwell, East, YN, 372

Hauxwell, West, YN, 372
Havant, Ha, 117
Haverbrack, We, 330
Havercroft, Li, 177
Havercroft, YW, 392
Haverhill, Sf, 293
Havering atte Bower, Ess, 79, 81
Haveringland, Nf, 200
Haversham, Bk, 17
Haverstoe, wapentake, Li, 180
Haw, Gl, 100
Hawarby, Li, 180
Hawick, Nb, 220
Hawkedon, Sf, 294
Hawkeridge, Wlt, 336
Hawkesbury, Gl, 102
Hawkesbury Upton, Gl, 102
Hawkhill, Nb, 225
Hawkley, Ha, 107
Hawksborough, hundred, Sx, 317
Hawkswick, YW, 382
Hawksworth, Nt, 232
Hawksworth, YW, 387
Hawkwell, Ess, 81
Hawkwell, Nb, 220
Hawling, Gl, 98
Hawnby, YN, 378
Haworth, YW, 388
Hawsker, YN, 380
Hawstead, Sf, 291
Hawthorpe, Li, 171
Hawton, Nt, 233
Haxby, YN, 379
Haxey, Li, 175
Haxton, Wlt, 346
Hay, South, Ha, 120
Hayden, Gl, 99
Haydock, La, 150
Haydon, Do, 71
Haydon, Nb, 220
Haydon, Wlt, 343
Haydon Wick, Wlt, 343
Hayes, Dev, 59
Hayes, Mx, 190
Hayes Barton, Dev, 65
Hayling Island, Ha, 116
Hayling, North, Ha, 116
Hayling, South, Ha, 116
Haynes, Bd, 3
Hayridge, hundred, Dev, 63
Haythby, Li, 175
Hayton, Cu, 38
Hayton, Nt, 227
Hayton, YE, 361
Haytor, hundred, Dev, 50
Haywood, St, 277
Hazelbury Bryan, Do, 75
Hazlebadge, Db, 47
Hazlerigg, Nb, 224
Hazleton, Gl, 98

Hazlewood, Sf, 294
Hazlewood, YW, 386
Hazon, Nb, 223
Heacham, Nf, 198
Head Barton, Dev, 54
Head, High, Cu, 38
Headacre, Sx, 307
Headingley, YW, 388
Headington, Ox, 235, 245
Headley, Ha, 110
Headley, Sr, 302
Headon, Nt, 228
Heage, Db, 43
Healaugh, YW, 385
Heale, Wlt, 336
Healey, YN, 372
Healing, Li, 181
Heane, hundred, K, 147
Heanor, Db, 43
Heanton Punchardon, Dev, 63
Heanton Satchville, Dev, 52
Heapey, La, 155
Heapham, Li, 177, 186
Heath, Barton, Dev, 58
Heath Charnock, La, 154
Heath Corner, He, 123
Heathcombe, So, 260
Heathcote, Wa, 320
Heathencote, Np, 211 n.
Heather, Lei, 158
Heatherslaw, Nb, 224
Heathfield, Dev, 64
Heathfield, So, 265
Heathy Mill, Wo, 353
Heaton [in Lonsdale, Cartmel, and Furness wap.], La, 156
Heaton [in Salford wap.], La, 154
Heaton, Nb, 221
Heaton, YW, 389
Heaton Norris, La, 154
Heavitree, Dev, 58
Hebburn, Nb, 226
Hebden, YW, 382
Hebron, Nb, 222
Heck, YW, 390
Heckfield, Ha, 117
Heckingham, Nf, 195
Heckington, Li, 172
Heckmondwike, YW, 388
Heddington, Wlt, 337
Heddon', Nb, 225
Heddon on the Wall, Nb, 220
Heddon, West, Nb, 220
Hedenham, Nf, 195
Hederesford, Cu, 38
Hedgeley, Nb, 224
Hedgerley, Bk, 21 n.
Hedingham, Castle, Ess, 80
Hedingham, Sible, Ess, 80
Hedley on the Hill, Nb, 221

Hedon, YE, 357, 370
Hedsor, Bk, 21
Heene, Sx, 310
Heigham, Nf, 207
Heigham, Potter, Nf, 193
Heighington, Li, 174
Heighton [in Goldspur hd.], Sx, 317
Heighton [in Totnore hd.], Sx, 315
Heighton, South, Sx, 314
Hele, Dev, 53
Hele, So, 265
Helenhull, Wa, 320
Helhoughton, Nf, 198
Helland, Co, 33
Hellesdon, Nf, 194
Hellifield, YW, 383
Hellingly, Sx, 315
Hellington, Nf, 195
Helmdon, Np, 210
Helmingham, Nf, 200
Helmingham, Sf, 286
Helmsley [in Liberty of St. Peter], YN, 379
Helmsley [in Ryedale wap.], YN, 377
Helmsley, Gate, YN, 363, 379 n.
Helmsley, Upper, YN, 379 n.
Helperby, YN, 379
Helperthorpe, YE, 364
Helpringham, Li, 173
Helsington, We, 330
Helsthorpe, Bk, 18
Helston, Co, 31
Helton, We, 329
Hem, The, Sa, 256
Hemblington, Nf, 194
Hemerdon, Dev, 51
Hemingbrough, YE, 363
Hemingby, Li, 182
Hemingford Abbots, Hu, 137
Hemingford Grey, Hu, 137
Hemingstone, Sf, 285
Hemington, Lei, 161
Hemington, Np, 214
Hemington, So, 261
Hemley, Sf, 296
Hemlingford, hundred, Wa, 324
Hemlington, YN, 375
Hempstead, Ess, 87
Hempstead, Gl, 97
Hempstead [in Happing hd.], Nf, 193
Hempstead [in Holt hd.], Nf, 199
Hempstead, Hemel, Hrt, 135
Hempton, Gl, 94
Hempton, Nf, 198
Hempton, Ox, 242
Hemsby, Nf, 193
Hemswell, Li, 176, 186
Hemsworth, YW, 392
Hemyock, Dev, 56
Hemyock, hundred, Dev, 56

Henbury, Gl, 102
Henbury, hundred, Gl, 102
Hencott, Sa, 257
Hendford, So, 262
Hendon, Mx, 191
Hendre, He, 126
Hendred, East, Brk, 8, 11
Hendred, West, Brk, 11
Hendresroudre, He, 126
Henfield, Sx, 311
Hengrave, Sf, 291
Henham, Ess, 86
Henham, Sf, 289
Henhurst, hundred, Sx, 318
Henlade, So, 264
Henley, Sf, 286
Henley, Cole, Ha, 109
Henley in Arden, Wa, 319, 320
Henley on Thames, Ox, 235, 244
Henlow, Bd, 4
Hennock, Dev, 60
Hennor, He, 130
Henny, Great, Ess, 80
Henny, Little, Ess, 80
Hensall, YW, 390
Henset, Wlt, 347
Hensington, Ox, 242
Henstead, Sf, 289
Henstead, hundred, Nf, 196
Henstill, Dev, 55
Henstridge, So, 269
Henthorn, La, 153
Hentland, He, 126
Henton, Ox, 241
Henwick, Brk, 7
Hepburn, Nb, 226
Hepmangrove, Hu, 137
Hepple, Nb, 224
Hepscott, Nb, 222
Hepworth, Sf, 292
Hereford, He, 122
Hereford, Little, He, 130
Herefordshire, 122–30
Herriard, Ha, 118
Herringby, Nf, 193
Herringfleet, Sf, 290
Herringston, Do, 68
Herringswell, Sf, 293
Herstmonceux, Sx, 316
Herston, Do, 75
Hertford, Hrt, 131
Hertford, hundred, Hrt, 131
Hertfordingbury, Hrt, 132
Hertfordshire, 131–5
Herwyk, Li, 178 n.
Hescombe, So, 274
Hesketh, La, 154
Heskin, La, 155
Heslerton, East, YE, 364
Heslerton, West, YE, 364

Hesley, Nt, 228
Heslington, YE, 364, 367, 368
Hessay, YW, 387
Hessett, Sf, 292
Hessle, YE, 360
Hessleton, YN, 372
Hest, La, 155
Hestercombe, So, 265
Heston, Mx, 191
Hethe, Ox, 237
Hethel, Nf, 206
Hethersett, Nf, 206
Hethpool, Nb, 224
Hetton, YW, 383
Hettons, Nb, 225 n.
Heveningham, Sf, 288
Heversham, We, 330
Hevingham, Nf, 201
Hewelsfield, Gl, 91 n.
Hewick, Bridge, YW, 394
Hewick, Copt, YW, 387
Hewish, So, 273
Heworth, YN, 380
Hexthorpe, YW, 392
Hexton, Hrt, 134
Heybridge, Ess, 83
Heydon, Ca, 23, 79, 87
Heydon, Nf, 202
Heydour, Li, 172
Heyford, Np, 216
Heyford, Lower, Ox, 238
Heyford, Upper, Ox, 238
Heysham, La, 156
Heyshott, Sx, 306
Heytesbury, Wlt, 340
Heytesbury, hundred, Wlt, 340
Heythorp, Ox, 236
Heywood, Wlt, 336
Hibaldstow, Li, 176, 186
Hickleton, YW, 393
Hickling, Nf, 193
Hickling, Nt, 232
Hidcote Bartrim, Gl, 95
Hidcote Boyce, Gl, 95
Hidden, Brk, 10
Hide, Gl, 98
Hiendley, YW, 392
Higford, Sa, 256
High Peak, wapentake, Db, 47
Higham [in Lackford hd.], Sf, 293
Higham [in Samford hd.], Sf, 285
Higham, Cold, Np, 211
Higham Ferrers, Np, 212
Higham Ferrers, hundred, Np, 212
Higham Gobion, Bd, 3
Higham on the Hill, Lei, 159
Highamton, Dev, 60
Highleadon, Gl, 97
Highley, Sa, 255
Highnam, Gl, 97

Highway, Wlt, 348
Highweek, Dev, 59
Highworth, Wlt, 343
Highworth, hundred, Wlt, 343
Hilborough, Nf, 203
Hilcot, Gl, 98
Hildersham, Ca, 27
Hilderstone, St, 278
Hilderthorpe, YE, 366
Hilfield, Do, 70
Hilgay, Nf, 203
Hill, Gl, 95
Hill, He, 124
Hill, Wa, 322
Hill, Wo, 351
Hill Croome, Wo, 351
Hill Deverill, Wlt, 341
Hill, King's, Wa, 320
Hill North, Co, 34
Hill, South, Co, 34
Hill, wapentake, Li, 185
Hillam, YW, 387
Hillbeck, We, 328
Hillborough, Wa, 326
Hillend, Brk, 12
Hillesden, Bk, 16
Hillfarance, So, 265
Hillington, Nf, 197
Hillmorton, Wa, 322
Hillsley, Gl, 102
Hilmarton, Wlt, 344
Hilperton, Wlt, 338
Hilsea, Ha, 110
Hilston, YE, 358
Hilton, Db, 45
Hilton, Do, 70
Hilton, Hu, 137
Hilton, St, 283
Hilton, We, 329
Hilton, YN, 374
Himbleton, Wo, 350
Himley, St, 283
Hincaster, We, 330
Hinckford, hundred, Ess, 80
Hinckley, Lei, 157, 160
Hinckley Bond, Lei, 160
Hinderclay, Sf, 292
Hinderskelfe, YN, 376
Hinderwell, YN, 375
Hindley, La, 149
Hindley, Nb, 221
Hindlip, Wo, 350
Hindolveston, Nf, 200
Hindon, Wlt, 332, 333, 342
Hindringham, Nf, 200
Hingham, Nf, 206
Hinksey, North, Brk, 12
Hinksey, South, Brk, 12
Hinstock, Sa, 250
Hintlesham, Sf, 285

Hinton, Brk, 346
Hinton, Do, 77
Hinton [in Berkeley hd.], Gl, 95
Hinton [in Grumbalds Ash hd.], Gl, 101
Hinton [in Christchurch hd.], Ha, 107
Hinton [in Finchdean hd.], Ha, 114
Hinton, He, 128
Hinton, Np, 210 n.
Hinton Ampner, Ha, 117
Hinton Blewett, So, 260
Hinton, Bower, So, 274
Hinton, Broad, Wlt, 339
Hinton Charterhouse, So, 268
Hinton, Cherry, Ca, 24
Hinton, Great, Wlt, 339
Hinton Hatch, Brk, 346
Hinton in the Hedges, Np, 210
Hinton, Little, Wlt, 340
Hinton on the Green, Wo, 101
Hinton Pipard, Brk, 346
Hinton St. George, So, 273
Hinton St. Mary, Do, 74
Hinton Waldrist, Brk, 12
Hints, Sa, 256
Hints, St, 279
Hinxton, Ca, 27
Hinxworth, Hrt, 132
Hipperholme, YW, 389
Hipswell, YE, 371
Hirst Courtney, YW, 386
Histon, Ca, 25
Hitcham, Bk, 22
Hitcham, Sf, 291
Hitchin, Hrt, 133
Hitchin [foreign], Hrt, 134
Hitchin, hundred, Hrt, 133
Hithe, The, YE, 358
Hittisleigh, Dev, 58
Hive, YE, 363
Hoadley, Sx, 317
Hoathly, East, Sx, 313
Hoby, Lei, 163
Hoccombe, So, 265
Hockering, Nf, 204
Hockerton, Nt, 231
Hockham, Nf, 205
Hockleton, Sa, 257
Hockley, Ess, 81
Hockliffe, Bd, 4
Hockworthy, Dev, 63
Hodcott, Brk, 13
Hoddesdon, Hrt, 131
Hoddington, Ha, 118
Hodnell, Wa, 322
Hodnet, Sa, 250
Hodsock, Nt, 229
Hoe, Nf, 208
Hoggeston, Bk, 18
Hoghton, La, 155
Hognaston, Db, 44

G g

Hogshaw, Bk, 19
Hogsthorpe, Li, 184
Hokene, Dev, 51
Holbeach, Li, 168
Holbeam, Dev, 58
Holbeck, Nt, 231
Holbeck Woodhouse, Nt, 231
Holbeton, Dev, 64
Holbrook, Db, 43
Holbrook, Dev, 65
Holbrook, Sf, 285
Holburn, Nb, 224
Holcombe, Dev, 59
Holcombe, Ox, 240
Holcombe, So, 262
Holcombe Burnell, Dev, 58
Holcombe Rogus, Dev, 63
Holcot, Bd, 4
Holcot, Np, 217
Holdenby, Np, 216
Holderness, YE, 357
Holdfast, Wo, 350
Holdgate, Sa, 255
Holdingham, Li, 173
Holdshot, hundred, Ha, 117
Holdshott, Ha, 117
Hole, Dev, 61
Holebury, Ha, 116
Holford, So, 264
Holford and Greston, hundred, Gl, 97
Holford Corseley, So, 265
Holgate, YW, 387
Holker, La, 156
Holkham, Nf, 200
Hollacombe, Dev, 60
Holland, Li, 167, 168–9
Holland, Great, Ess, 88
Holland, Little, Ess, 88
Holland, Up, La, 150
Hollesley, Sf, 295
Hollin, Wo, 352
Hollington, Db, 45
Hollym, YE, 359
Holm, YE, 367
Holm Cultram, Cu, 38
Holme, Bd, 2
Holme, Do, 77
Holme [in Lawress wap.], Li, 177
Holme [in Manley wap.], Li, 176
Holme, We, 330
Holme, YN, 379
Holme Hale, Nf, 203
Holme Lacy, He, 127
Holme next the Sea, Nf, 197
Holme on the Wolds, YE, 363, 368
Holme Pierrepont, Nt, 232
Holme, South, YN, 377
Holme upon Spalding Moor, YE, 362
Holmer, He, 124
Holmesfield, Db, 48

Holmestrow, hundred, Sx, 311
Holmfirth, YW, 389
Holmpton, YE, 358
Holne, Dev, 51
Holnest, Do, 71
Holsworthy, Dev, 60
Holt, Brk, 10
Holt, Nf, 199
Holt, Wlt, 347
Holt, Wo, 350
Holt, hundred, Nf, 199
Holt, Nevill, Lei, 165
Holtby [in Bulmer wap.], YN, 376
Holtby [in Hang wap.], YN, 372
Holtham, Ha, 120
Holton, Li, 181
Holton, Ox, 239
Holton, Sf, 289
Holton le Clay, Li, 181
Holton le Moor, Li, 179, 186
Holton St. Mary, Sf, 285
Holverston, Nf, 196
Holway, So, 264
Holwell, Hrt, 1, 4, 131
Holwell, Lei, 164
Holwell [near Bishop's Caundle], Do, 67, 269
Holwell [near Broadwey], Do, 72
Holwell [near Cranborne], Do, 75
Holwell, Ox, 237
Holworth, Do, 68
Holybourne, Ha, 120
Holybourne [Eastbrook], Ha, 114
Holyoake, Lei, 164
Holywell, Hu, 137
Holywell, Li, 171
Holywell, Nb, 222
Homanton, Wlt, 341
Homington, Wlt, 334
Honestyele, So, 260 n.
Honeybourne, Church, Wo, 355
Honeybourne, Cow, Wo, 94
Honeychurch, Dev, 60
Honeywick, So, 269
Honibere, So, 266
Honiley, Wa, 325
Honing, Nf, 202
Honingham, Nf, 206
Honingham Thorpe, Nf, 206
Honington, Li, 172
Honington, Sf, 293
Honington, Wa, 320
Honiton, Dev, 57, 66
Honley, YW, 390
Hoo, Ess, 84
Hoo, Sf, 295
Hoo, hundred, K, 144
Hoo, Queen, Hrt, 131
Hooe, Sx, 316
Hooe, West, Dev, 51

Hook, Dev, 62
Hook, Ha, 110
Hook, YW, 391
Hooke, Do, 72
Hoole, Little, La, 154
Hoole, Much, La, 155
Hoon, Db, 45
Hooton Levitt, YW, 393
Hooton Pagnell, YW, 393
Hooton Roberts, YW, 394
Hope, Db, 47
Hope, Gl, 101
Hope, He, 124
Hope, Sa, 256
Hope, Sx, 317
Hope Bowdler, Sa, 254
Hope, Dudale's, He, 123
Hope Mansel, He, 127
Hope, Sollers, He, 127
Hopesay, Sa, 253
Hopsford, Wa, 324
Hopton, Db, 45
Hopton, Sa, 250
Hopton [in Blackbourne hd.], Sf, 292
Hopton [in Lothingland hd.], Sf, 290
Hopton, St, 278
Hopton Castle, Sa, 253
Hopton Sollers, He, 123
Hopton Wafers, Sa, 255
Hopwas, St, 277
Hopwell, Db, 43
Horbling, Li, 170
Horbury, YW, 390
Hordle, Ha, 106
Hordley, Ox, 244
Horethorne, hundred, So, 269
Horfield, Gl, 96
Horham, Sf, 288
Horkesley, Great, Ess, 87
Horkesley, Little, Ess, 87
Horkstow, Li, 179
Horley, Ox, 242
Horley, Sr, 299
Hormead, Great, Hrt, 133
Hormead, Little, Hrt, 133
Hormer, hundred, Brk, 12
Horn, Ru, 247
Hornblotton, So, 267
Hornby, La, 156
Hornby [in Allerton lib.], YN, 378
Hornby [in Hang wap.], 373
Horncastle, Li, 184
Horncastle, liberty, Li, 167, 184
Horndon, East, Ess, 86
Horndon on the Hill, Ess, 85
Horndon, West, Ess, 86
Horne, Sr, 303
Horning, Nf, 202
Horninghold, Lei, 164
Horninglow, St, 280

Horningsea, Ca, 24
Horningsham, Wlt, 341
Horningtoft, Nf, 208
Hornsea, YE, 366
Hornsea Burton, YE, 358
Hornsey, Mx, 190
Hornton, Ox, 242
Horridge, Dev, 58
Horringer, Sf, 291
Horringer, Little, Sf, 292
Horrington, So, 271
Horsebrook, St, 282
Horseheath, Ca, 27
Horsenden, Bk, 21
Horsepool, Nt, 231
Horsey, Nf, 193
Horsey, So, 260
Horsey-Pignes, So, 260
Horsford, Nf, 194
Horsforth, YW, 387
Horsham, Sx, 305
Horsham, St. Faith, Nf, 194
Horsington, Li, 182
Horsington, So, 269
Horsley, Db, 43
Horsley, Gl, 96
Horsley, Nb, 220
Horsley Castle, Db, 43
Horsley, East, Sr, 299
Horsley, West, Sr, 299
Horsley Woodhouse, Db, 43
Horspath, Ox, 239
Horspath, Old, Ox, 239
Horstead, Nf, 194
Horstead Keynes, Sx, 314
Horton, Bk, 21
Horton, Do, 77
Horton, Gl, 102
Horton, He, 123
Horton [in Glendale ward], Nb, 224
Horton [in 'Inter' ward], Nb, 223
Horton, Np, 217
Horton, Ox, 239
Horton, St, 279
Horton, Sx, 311
Horton, Wlt, 348
Horton [in Morley wap.], YW, 389
Horton [in Staincliffe wap.], YW, 383
Horton Heath, Ha, 117
Horton in Ribbesdale, YW, 383
Hortonlane, Sa, 253
Horwood, Dev, 53
Horwood, Great, Bk, 19
Horwood, Little, Bk, 18
Hose, Lei, 163
Hotham, YE, 360, 363, 368
Hothersall, La, 151
Hothorpe, Np, 212
Hoton, Lei, 162
Hough on the Hill, Li, 174

Hougham, Li, 174
Houghton, Cu, 38
Houghton, Ha, 107, 108
Houghton, He, 123
Houghton, Hu, 137
Houghton, Li, 171
Houghton, Nf, 198
Houghton, Sx, 309
Houghton, YE, 360
Houghton, YW, 392
Houghton Conquest, Bd, 3
Houghton Drayton, Ha, 108
Houghton, Glass, YW, 390
Houghton, Great, Np, 217
Houghton, Hanging, Np, 212
Houghton, Little, Nb, 225
Houghton, Little, Np, 217
Houghton, Little, YW, 394
Houghton on the Hill, Lei, 164
Houghton on the Hill, Nf, 203
Houghton Regis, Bd, 4
Houghton St. Giles, Nf, 200
Hound Street, Do, 71
Houndsborough, hundred, So, 269
Hove, Sx, 312
Hoveringham, Nt, 231
Hoveton St. John, Nf, 202
Hoveton St. Peter, Nf, 202
Hovingham, YN, 377
How Capel, He, 127
Howden, YE, 363
Howdenshire, liberty, YE, 362, 370
Howe, Nf, 196
Howe [in Liberty of St. Mary and St. Leonard], YN, 380
Howe [in Ryedale wap.], YN, 377
Howe Green, Ess, 84 n.
Howell, Li, 172
Howgrave, YN, 379
Howick, La, 154
Howick, Nb, 225
Howick, Sx, 309
Howle Hill, He, 127
Howsham, 178, 186
Howsham, YE, 365
Howtel, Nb, 225
Howton, Dev, 59
Howton, He, 127
Hoxne, Sf, 288
Hoxne, hundred, Sf, 288
Hoyland, High, YW, 392
Hoyland Nether, YW, 393
Hoyland Swaine, YW, 391
Huby, YN, 357, 382
Hucclecote, Gl, 97
Hucknall Torkard, Nt, 230
Huddersfield, YW, 389
Huddington, Wo, 350
Huddleston, YW, 386
Hudswell, YN, 372

Huggate, YE, 362, 367, 368
Hugglescote, Lei, 160
Hughendon, Bk, 21
Hughley, Sa, 254
Hugill, We, 330
Huish, Dev, 52
Huish Champflower, So, 266
Huish Episcopi, So, 270, 273
Huish, Great, Dev, 58
Huish, North, Dev, 51
Huish, South, Dev, 51
Hulcote, Np, 211
Hulcott, Bk, 20
Hull, YE, 356, 357, 370
Hull, YN, 357
Hull, Bishop's, So, 264
Hulland, Db, 44
Hullasey, Gl, 100 n.
Hullavington, Wlt, 339
Hulle, He, 125
Hulton, La, 154
Humber, He, 130
Humbershoe, Hrt, 4 n.
Humberston, Li, 181
Humberstone, Lei, 161
Humberton, YN, 395
Humbleton, Nb, 224
Humbleton, YE, 358
Humbleyard, hundred, Nf, 206
Humburton, YN, 371, 395
Humby, Li, 172
Huncoat, La, 153
Huncote, Lei, 160
Hundburton', YE, 361
Hundersfield, La, 154
Hunderthwaite, YN, 373
Hundestone, So, 262 n.
Hundleby, Li, 185
Hundon, Li, 179
Hundon, Sf, 293
Hungarton, Lei, 161
Hungerford, Brk, 10
Hungerstone, He, 127
Hungerton, Li, 171
Hunkington, Sa, 251
Hunmanby, YE, 365
Hunningham, Wa, 322
Hunscote, Wa, 320
Hunsdon, Hrt, 132
Hunshelf, YW, 391
Hunsingore, YW, 384
Hunslet, YW, 389
Hunsley, YE, 360
Hunstanton, Nf, 198
Hunston, Sf, 293
Hunston, Sx, 308
Hunsworth, YW, 389
Huntercombe, Ox, 240
Huntingdon, Hu, 136
Huntingdon, Sa, 255

Huntingdonshire, 136–9
Huntingfield, Sf, 289
Huntington, St, 281
Huntington, YN, 376
Huntley, Gl, 95
Hunton, Ha, 108
Hunton, YN, 372
Huntsham, Dev, 55
Huntshaw, Dev, 53
Huntspill, So, 271
Huntworth, So, 260
Hunworth, Nf, 199
Hurcot, So, 273
Hurdcott [in Alderbury hd.], Wlt, 345
Hurdcott [in Cadworth hd.], Wlt, 335
Hurley, Brk, 6
Hurlston, La, 150
Hurn, Ha, 107
Hursley, Ha, 108
Hurst, Brk, 7
Hurst, So, 274
Hurst, Wa, 320
Hurstbourne Priors, Ha, 109
Hurstbourne Tarrant, Ha, 112
Hurstingstone, hundred, Hu, 137
Hurstpierpoint, Sx, 312
Hurtmore, Sr, 298
Husborne Crawley, Bd, 4
Husthwaite, YN, 379
Huttoft, Li, 184
Hutton, Ess, 86
Hutton, La, 155
Hutton, So, 259
Hutton, YE, 361, 369
Hutton, YN, 376
Hutton Bonville, YN, 378
Hutton Buscel, YN, 381
Hutton Conyers, YN, 378
Hutton Hang, YN, 372
Hutton in the Forest, Cu, 37
Hutton John, Cu, 37
Hutton le Hole, YN, 380
Hutton Lowcross, YN, 375
Hutton Magna, YN, 373
Hutton Mulgrave, YN, 375
Hutton, New, We, 330
Hutton, Old, We, 330
Hutton, Priest, La, 156
Hutton Roof, Cu, 37
Hutton Roof, We, 330
Hutton Rudby, YN, 374
Hutton, Sand, YN, 376
Hutton Sessay, YN, 379
Hutton, Sheriff, YN, 376
Hutton Wandesley, YW, 385
Huxham, Dev, 58
Huxloe, hundred, Np, 214
Huyton, La, 150
Hyde, Ha, 106
Hyde, Wo, 122, 124

Hydes Pastures, Wa, 324
Hykeham, North, Li, 175
Hykeham, South, Li, 175
Hyndurynton', Wlt, 345
Hynton, So, 262 n.
Hythe, K, 140

Ibberton, Do, 70
Ible, Db, 44
Ibsley, Ha, 114
Ibstock, Lei, 159
Ibstone, Bk, 21
Ickburgh, Nf, 204
Ickenham, Mx, 190
Ickford, Bk, 20
Ickleford, Hrt, 133
Icklesham, Sx, 317
Ickleton, Ca, 27
Icklingham, Sf, 293
Ickworth, Sf, 291
Icomb, Gl, 103
Idbury, Ox, 236
Iddesleigh, Dev, 52
Iddlecott, Dev, 61
Ide, Dev, 59
Ideford, Dev, 59
Idle, YW, 389
Idlicote, Wa, 320
Idmiston, Wlt, 345
Idstone, Brk, 11
Idsworth, Ha, 114
Iffley, Ox, 239
Ifield, Sx, 311
Iford, Sx, 311
Ightfield, Sa, 250
Iken, Sf, 294
Ilbury, Ox, 241, 242 n.
Ilchester, So, 274
Ilderton, Nb, 224
Ilford, Little, Ess, 81
Ilfracombe, Dev, 62
Ilkeston, Db, 42
Ilketshall, Sf, 289
Ilkley, YW, 388
Illbeare, So, 264
Illington, Nf, 205
Illogan, Co, 30
Illston on the Hill, Lei, 164
Ilmer, Bk, 20
Ilmington, Wa, 320
Ilminster, So, 266
Ilsington, Dev, 59
Ilsington, Do, 69
Ilsley, East, Brk, 13
Ilsley, West, Brk, 13
Ilton, So, 266
Ilton, YN, 372
Imber, Wlt, 340, 343
Imberhorne, Sx, 315
Immingham, Li, 178

Impington, Ca, 25
Ince Blundell, La, 150
Ince in Makerfield, La, 150
Ingarsby, Lei, 165
Ingatestone, Ess, 85
Ingbirchworth, YW, 391
Ingerthorpe, YW, 394
Ingestre, St, 277
Ingham, Li, 176
Ingham, Nf, 193
Ingham, Sf, 292
Ingleby, Db, 46
Ingleby, YN, 375
Ingleby Arncliffe, YN, 374
Ingleby Greenhow, YN, 375
Ingleby, North, Li, 177 n.
Ingleby, South, Li, 177 n.
Inglesham, Wlt, 6, 11, 332, 343
Inglestone, Gl, 102 n.
Ingleton, YW, 384
Inglewood, Brk, 10
Ingoe, Nb, 221
Ingoldfield Farm, Ha, 113 n.
Ingoldisthorpe, Nf, 197
Ingoldmells, Li, 182
Ingoldsby, Li, 173
Ingon, Wa, 327
Ingram, Nb, 224
Ingraston', Gl, 102
Ingrave, Ess, 86
Ingthorpe, Ru, 247
Ingworth, Nf, 202
Inhurst, Ha, 115
Inkberrow, Wo, 351
Inkpen, Brk, 10
Inlegh, Sx, 317
Inskip, La, 152
Instow, Dev, 53
'Inter', Ward, Nb, 221
Intwood, Nf, 206
Inwardleigh, Dev, 60
Inworth, Ess, 88
Ion, Bd, 3
Iping, Sx, 306
Ipley, Ha, 116
Ipplepen, Dev, 50
Ipsden, Ox, 243
Ipsley, Wo, 326
Ipstones, St, 281
Ipswich, Sf, 284, 294
Irby, YN, 378
Irby in the Marsh, Li, 182
Irby upon Humber, Li, 181
Irchester, Np, 212
Ireby, Cu, 39
Ireby, La, 155
Ireton, Db, 43
Ireton, Kirk, Db, 44
Iridge, Sx, 318
Irmingland, Nf, 202

Irnham, Li, 170
Irstead, Nf, 202
Irthington, Cu, 38
Irthlingborough, Np, 214
Irton, YN, 381
Isenhurst, Sx, 315
Isham, Np, 212
Isington, Ha, 120
Isle Abbotts, So, 266
Isle Brewers, So, 272
Isle of Wight, Ha, 119–20
Isle of Wight, liberty, Ha, 120
Islebeck, YN, 378
Isleham, Ca, 24
Isleworth, Mx, 191
Isleworth, hundred, Mx, 191
Islington, Mx, 190
Islip, Np, 214
Islip, Ox, 238
Itchel, Ha, 109
Itchen Abbas, Ha, 113
Itchen Stoke, Ha, 113
Itchington, Gl, 102
Itchington, Bishop's, Wa, 323
Itchington, Long, Wa, 322
Itteringham, Nf, 202
Ivedon, Dev, 55
Iver, Bk, 21
Ivinghoe, Bk, 18
Ivington, He, 130
Iwerne Courtney, Do, 73
Iwerne Minster, Do, 74
Ixhill, hundred, Bk, 20
Ixworth, Sf, 292
Ixworth Thorpe, Sf, 293

Jacobstow, Co, 33
Jacobstowe, Dev, 60
Jay, He, 122, 249, 253
Jevington, Sx, 314
Johnby, Cu, 37
Jurston, Dev, 59

Kaber, We, 328
Kea, Co, 31
Keal, East, Li, 185
Keal, West, Li, 185
Kearby, YW, 385
Keddington, Li, 183
Kedington, Sf, 293
Kedleston, Db, 44
Keelby, Li, 178
Keele, St, 277
Keevil, Wlt, 338
Kegworth, Lei, 161
Keighley, YW, 383
Keighton, Nt, 229
Keisby, Li, 170
Kelby, Li, 172
Kelfield, YE, 364

Kelham, Nt, 231
Kelk, Great, YE, 369
Kelk, Little, YE, 360
Kellamergh, La, 152
Kellet, Nether, La, 156
Kellet, Over, La, 156
Kelleythorpe, YE, 370
Kelling, Nf, 199
Kellington, YW, 391
Kelly, Dev, 60
Kelmarsh, Np, 213
Kelmscott, Ox, 237
Kelsale, Sf, 288
Kelsey, North, Li, 179, 186
Kelsey, South, Li, 180, 186
Kelshall, Hrt, 132
Kelstern, Li, 183
Kelston, So, 261
Kelton, Cu, 40
Kelvedon, Ess, 84
Kelvedon Hatch, Ess, 83
Kemberton, Sa, 256
Kemble, Gl, 337
Kemerton, Wo, 92
Kempley, Gl, 95
Kempsey, Wo, 350
Kempsford, Gl, 100
Kempshott, Ha, 118
Kempston, Bd, 3
Kempstone, Nf, 207
Kempton, Mx, 189
Kenchester, He, 124
Kencott, Ox, 237
Kendal, We, 330
Kenilworth, Wa, 323
Keningham, Nf, 206
Kenley, Sa, 252
Kenn, Dev, 59
Kenn, So, 259
Kennerleigh, Dev, 54
Kennet, Ca, 24
Kennett, East, Wlt, 339
Kennett, West, Wlt, 339
Kenninghall, Nf, 205
Kennington, Brk, 12
Kennington, Sr, 302
Kennythorpe, YE, 365
Kensington, Mx, 190
Kensworth, Bd, 1, 131, 134
Kent, 140–8
Kentford, Sf, 23, 24, 284, 294
Kentisbeare, Dev, 63
Kentisbury, Dev, 62
Kentish Town, Mx, 190
Kentmere, We, 330
Kenton, Dev, 66
Kenton, Nb, 223
Kenton, Sf, 295
Kenwyn, Co, 31
Kenyon, La, 150

Kepwick, YN, 377, 379
Kerdiston, Nf, 200
Keresley, Wa, 324
Kern, Ha, 119
Kerrier, hundred, Co, 30
Kersall, Nt, 231
Kersey, Sf, 291
Kerswell, Dev, 63
Kerswell Green, Wo, 350 n.
Kesgrave, Sf, 296
Kessingland, Sf, 286
Kesteven, Li, 167, 169–75
Keswick, Cu, 39 n.
Keswick [in Humbleyard hd.], Nf, 207
Keswick [in Tunstead hd.], Nf, 202
Keswick, East, YW, 388
Ketsby, Li, 185
Kettering, Np, 214
Ketteringham, Nf, 206
Kettlebaston, Sf, 291
Kettleburgh, Sf, 295
Kettleby, Li, 178 n.
Kettleby, Ab, Lei, 164
Kettleby, Eye, Lei, 164
Kettleby Thorpe, Li, 178 n.
Kettlestone, Nf, 199
Kettlewell, YW, 383
Ketton, Ru, 247
Kexbrough, YW, 392
Kexby, Li, 178
Kexby, YE, 363
Key, Bailey [in Milton], K, 143, 148
Keyham, Lei, 161
Keyhaven, Ha, 106
Keyingham, YE, 358
Keymer, Sx, 312
Keynedon, Dev, 64
Keynsham, So, 270
Keynsham, hundred, So, 270
Keysoe, Bd, 5
Keyston, Hu, 139
Keythorpe, Lei, 165
Keyworth, Nt, 230
Kibblestone, St, 278
Kibworth Beauchamp, Lei, 164
Kibworth Harcourt, Lei, 165
Kidderminster, Wo, 353
Kiddington, Ox, 242
Kiddington, Over, Ox, 236
Kidlington, Ox, 242
Kidsleypark, Db, 42
Kiftsgate, hundred, Gl, 94
Kigbeare, Dev, 60
Kilbreece, He, 126
Kilburn, Db, 43
Kilburn, YN, 378
Kilbury, Dev, 65
Kilby, Lei, 158
Kilcott, Gl, 102
Kildale, YN, 376

Kildwick, YW, 383
Kilham, Nb, 225
Kilham, YE, 357, 369, 370
Kilkhampton, Co, 33
Kilkhampton (Rural), Co, 33
Killamarsh, Db, 48
Killinghall, YW, 395
Killingholme, Li, 179, 186
Killington, We, 330
Killingworth, Nb, 222
Kilmersdon, So, 261
Kilmersdon, hundred, So, 261
Kilmeston, Ha, 117
Kilmington, Dev, 57
Kilmington, Wlt, 269, 332
Kilnsea, YE, 358
Kilnwick, YE, 360
Kilnwick Percy, YE, 361
Kilpeck, He, 126
Kilpin, YE, 363
Kilreague, He, 126
Kilsby, Np, 216
Kilton, So, 266
Kilton, YN, 375
Kilton Thorpe, YN, 375
Kilve, So, 266
Kilverstone, Nf, 205
Kilvington, Nt, 233
Kilvington, North, YN, 379
Kilvington, South, YN, 378
Kilworth, North, Lei, 159
Kilworth, South, Lei, 160
Kimberley, Nf, 206
Kimberley, Nt, 229
Kimberworth, YW, 393
Kimble, Great, Bk, 20
Kimble, Little, Bk, 20
Kimbolton, Hu, 138
Kimcote, Lei, 160
Kimmeridge, Do, 77
Kimpton, Ha, 108
Kimpton, Hrt, 133
Kineton, Gl, 98
Kineton [near Butlers Marston], Wa, 320
Kineton [near Solihull], Wa, 324
Kingcombe, Do, 72
Kingerby, Li, 179
Kingfield, Cu, 38 n.
Kingham, Ox, 236
Kinghamford, hundred, K, 142
Kingsbery, Hrt, 134
Kingsbridge, Dev, 65
Kingsbridge, hundred, Wlt, 344
Kingsbury, Mx, 191
Kingsbury, Wa, 325
Kingsbury Episcopi, So, 270
Kingsbury, hundred, So, 270
Kingsbury Regis, So, 273
Kingsclere, Ha, 115
Kingsclere, hundred, Ha, 115

Kingscote, Gl, 96
Kingsdon, So, 263
Kingsey, Bk, 20
Kingsford, Wo, 353
Kingsholm, Gl, 91 n.
Kingskerswell, Dev, 50
Kingsland, He, 129
Kingsley, Ha, 120
Kingsley, St, 281
Kingsnordley, Sa, 255
Kingsteignton, Dev, 59
Kingsthorpe, Np, 218
Kingston, Ca, 26
Kingston, Dev, 64
Kingston, Do, 75
Kingston, Ha, 119
Kingston, So, 262
Kingston, St, 280
Kingston [in Poling hd.], Sx, 309
Kingston [in Swanborough hd.], Sx, 311
Kingston, Wa, 321
Kingston Bagpuize, Brk, 12
Kingston Blount, Ox, 241
Kingston by Sea, Sx, 311
Kingston Deverill, Wlt, 334, 346
Kingston, hundred, Sr, 301
Kingston Lacy, Do, 77
Kingston Lisle, Brk, 10
Kingston Maurward, Do, 68
Kingston on Soar, Nt, 230
Kingston, St. Mary, So, 264
Kingston Seymour, So, 260
Kingston upon Hull, YE, 356, 357, 370
Kingston upon Thames, Sr, 297, 298
Kingstone [in Greytree hd.], He, 126
Kingstone [in Webtree hd.], He, 127
Kingstone, So, 274
Kingswear, Dev, 50
Kingswinford, St, 277
Kingswood, Sr, 299
Kingthorpe, YN, 381
Kington, Gl, 101
Kington, Wo, 353
Kington Magna, Do, 74
Kington St. Michael, Wlt, 344
Kington, West, Wlt, 344
Kingweston, So, 259
Kinlet, Sa, 256
Kinnersley, He, 129
Kinoulton, Nt, 232
Kinsham, Wo, 350
Kinson, Ha, 105
Kintbury, Brk, 10
Kintbury, hundred, Brk, 10
Kintbury-Amesbury, Brk, 9
Kinvaston, St, 283
Kinver, St, 277
Kinwardstone, hundred, Wlt, 347
Kinwarton, Wa, 326
Kiplin, YN, 374

Kippax, YW, 388
Kirby, Np, 215 n.
Kirby Bedon, Nf, 196
Kirby Bellars, Lei, 163
Kirby Cane, Nf, 195
Kirby, Cold, YN, 357, 382
Kirby Grindalythe, YE, 364
Kirby Grounds, Np, 211 n.
Kirby Hall, YW, 395
Kirby Hill, YN, 371
Kirby Knowle, YN, 377
Kirby le Soken, Ess, 88
Kirby Misperton, YN, 380
Kirby, Monks, Wa, 324
Kirby Muxloe, Lei, 159
Kirby Ravensworth, YN, 380
Kirby Underdale, YE, 366
Kirby Wiske, YN, 374
Kirkandrews upon Eden, Cu, 37
Kirkbampton, Cu, 37
Kirkbride, Cu, 38
Kirkburn, YE, 362
Kirkburton, YW, 390
Kirkby, La, 151
Kirkby, Li, 180
Kirkby, YN, 375
Kirkby, East, Li, 185
Kirkby Fleetham, YN, 371
Kirkby Green, Li, 173
Kirkby in Ashfield, Nt, 230
Kirkby Ireleth, La, 155
Kirkby Kendal, We, 330
Kirkby la Thorpe, Li, 173
Kirkby Lonsdale, We, 331
Kirkby Malham, YW, 383
Kirkby Mallory, Lei, 158
Kirkby Malzeard, YW, 384
Kirkby on Bain, Li, 182
Kirkby Ouseburn, YW, 395
Kirkby Overblow, YW, 385
Kirkby, South, YW, 391
Kirkby Stephen, We, 328
Kirkby Thore, We, 329
Kirkby Underwood, Li, 170
Kirkby Wharfe, YW, 386
Kirkbymoorside, YN, 377
Kirkcambeck, Cu, 38
Kirkdale, La, 151
Kirkeby, Cu, 40
Kirkham, La, 152
Kirkharle, Nb, 220
Kirkheaton, Nb, 220
Kirkheaton, YW, 389
Kirkland [in Allerdale wap.], Cu, 39
Kirkland [in Leath wap.], Cu, 37
Kirkleatham, YN, 375
Kirkley, Nb, 221
Kirkley, Sf, 286
Kirklington, Nt, 232
Kirklington, YN, 371

Kirklinton, Cu, 38
Kirklinton Middle, Cu, 38 n.
Kirknewton, Nb, 225
Kirkoswald, Cu, 36
Kirksanton, Cu, 40
Kirkwhelpington, Nb, 220
Kirmington, Li, 179
Kirmond le Mire, Li, 181
Kirtling, Ca, 27
Kirtlington, Ox, 238
Kirton, Li, 168
Kirton, Nt, 228
Kirton, Sf, 296
Kirton in Lindsey, Li, 185
Kirton, wapentake, Li, 168
Kislingbury, Np, 216
Kittisford, So, 260
Knaith, Li, 178
Knapp, So, 263
Knapthorpe, Nt, 231
Knaptoft, Lei, 159
Knapton, Nf, 201
Knapton, YE, 364
Knapton, YW, 387
Knapwell, Ca, 25
Knaresborough, YW, 357, 395
Knaresborough, liberty, YW, 357, 395
Knayton, YN, 379
Knebworth, Hrt, 133
Knedlington, YE, 363
Kneesall, Nt, 231
Kneesworth, Ca, 26
Kneeton, Nt, 232
Knelle, Great, Sx, 317
Knettishall, Sf, 293
Knight Thorpe, Lei, 162
Knightcote, Wa, 321
Knightley, St, 282
Knightlow, hundred, Wa, 322
Knighton, Do, 75
Knighton, Ha, 119
Knighton, Lei, 160
Knighton, St, 278
Knighton [in Amesbury hd.], Wlt, 345
Knighton [in Chalke hd.], Wlt, 342
Knighton, East, Do, 68
Knighton Stoke, So, 267
Knighton Sutton, So, 267
Knighton, West, Do, 73
Knightsbridge, Mx, 190
Knipton, Lei, 163
Kniveton, Db, 45
Knock, We, 329
Knole, So, 259
Knoll, Do, 74
Knook, Wlt, 340
Knossington, Lei, 165
Knotting, Bd, 5
Knottingley, YW, 390
Knowle, Dev, 55

Knowle, Church, Do, 76
Knowle Hill, So, 267
Knowle St. Giles, So, 275
Knowlton, Do, 72
Knowlton, hundred, Do, 72
Knowsley, La, 149
Knowstone, Dev, 54
Knoyle, Bishop's, hundred, Wlt, 342
Knoyle, East, Wlt, 342
Knoyle, West, Wlt, 334
Knutton, St, 278
Kyme, North, Li, 173
Kyme, South, Li, 172
Kynaston, He, 126
Kyre Magna, Wo, 352
Kyre Wyard, Wo, 352

Laceby, Li, 181
Lackenby, YN, 375
Lackford, Sf, 291
Lackford, hundred, Sf, 293
Lacock, Wlt, 344
Lacon, Sa, 250
Ladbroke, Wa, 322
Ladhuish, So, 266
Ladock, Co, 31
Laindon, Ess, 68
Lainston, Ha, 108
Lake, Wlt, 336
Lakenham, Nf, 206
Lakenheath, Sf, 293
Laleham, Mx, 189
Lamarsh, Ess, 80
Lamas, Nf, 202
Lambert, Dev, 58
Lambeth, Sr, 302
Lambeth Dean, Sr, 302
Lambeth Marsh, Sr, 302
Lambeth, South, Sr, 302
Lambley, Nt, 231
Lambourn, Brk, 10
Lambourn, hundred, Brk, 10
Lambourn, Upper, Brk, 10
Lambourne, Ess, 82
Lambrigg, We, 330
Lambside, Dev, 64
Lamerton, Dev, 60
Lamonby, Cu, 37
Lamorran, Co, 31
Lamplugh, Cu, 40
Lamport, Bk, 16
Lamport, Np, 212
Lamport, Sx, 314
Lamyatt, So, 267
Lancashire, 149–56
Lancaster, La, 149, 155
Lancing, Sx, 310
Landbeach, Ca, 25
Landcross, Dev, 52
Landeuenok', He, 126

Landewednack, Co, 30
Landford, Wlt, 336
Landford Barton, Dev, 65
Landmoth, YN, 379
Landrake, Co, 34
Landulph, Co, 34
Landwade, Ca, 24
Laneham, Nt, 228
Lanercost, Cu, 38
Langar, Nt, 232
Langbargh, wapentake, YN, 374
Langcliffe, YW, 382
Langdale, We, 330
Langdon, Dev, 51
Langdon, Do, 71
Langdon, Ess, 85
Langelegh', Dev, 55
Langenhoe, Ess, 82
Langfield, YW, 389
Langford, Bd, 1
Langford, Ess, 83
Langford, Gl, 91 n.
Langford, Nf, 204
Langford, Nt, 233
Langford, Ox, 6, 11, 235
Langford [in Bulstone hd.], So, 272
Langford [in Taunton hd.], So, 265
Langford Budville, So, 260
Langford, Hanging, Wlt, 342
Langford, Little, Wlt, 342
Langford, Steeple, Wlt, 342
Langhale, Nf, 195
Langham, Ess, 87
Langham, Nf, 199
Langham, Ru, 246
Langham, Sf, 293
Langley, Brk, 9
Langley [in New Forest hd.], Ha, 116
Langley [in Redbridge hd.], Ha, 115
Langley, Nb, 220
Langley, Nf, 195
Langley, Sa, 252
Langley, Wa, 326
Langley, Abbots, Hrt, 134
Langley and Swineshead, hundred, Gl, 94
Langley Burrell, Wlt, 344
Langley, Kirk, Db, 44
Langley Marish, Bk, 21
Langley, Meynell, Db, 44
Langoe, Wapentake, Li, 173
Langport, So, 263
Langport, hundred, K, 146
Langridge, So, 261
Langrish, Ha, 111
Langsett, YW, 391
Langstone, He, 126
Langstrothdale, YW, 383
Langthorne, YN, 380
Langthwaite, YW, 393
Langtoft, YE, 367

Langton [in Gartree wap.], Li, 182
Langton [in Hill wap.], Li, 185
Langton, Sf, 287
Langton, We, 329
Langton, YE, 365
Langton by Wragby, Li, 181
Langton, Church, Lei, 164
Langton, East, Lei, 165
Langton, Great, YN, 374
Langton Herring, Do, 77
Langton Long Blandford, Do, 75
Langton Matravers, Do, 76
Langton, Thorpe, Lei, 165
Langton, Tur, Lei, 165
Langton, West, Lei, 165
Langtree, Dev, 52
Langtree, La, 155
Langtree, hundred, Ox, 243
Langwathby, Cu, 41
Langworth, Li, 181 n.
Lanhadok', He, 125
Lanherne, Co, 32
Lanhydrock, Co, 32
Lanivet, Co, 32
Lanlivery, Co, 32
Lanreath, Co, 34
Lansallos, Co, 34
Lanteglos [in West hd.], Co, 34
Lanteglos by Camelford, Co, 33
Lanton, Nb, 225
Lapford, Dev, 62
Lapley, St, 282
Lapworth, Wa, 320
Larbreck, La, 151
Lark Stoke, Wa, 95
Larkfield, hundred, K, 144
Larling, Nf, 205
Lartington, YN, 373
Lasborough, Gl, 96
Lasham, Ha, 113
Lashbrook, Ox, 240
Lassington, Gl, 97
Latchford, Ox, 240
Latchingdon, Ess, 84
Lathbury, Bk, 18
Lathom, La, 151
Latton, Ess, 89
Latton, Wlt, 342
Laughterton, Li, 178
Laughton, Li, 177
Laughton, Sx, 313
Laughton, East, Li, 170
Laughton en le Morthen, YW, 394
Laughton, West, Li, 170
Launcells, Co, 33
Launceston, Co, 35
Launde, Lei, 162
Launditch, hundred, Nf, 207
Launton, Ox, 238

Lavant, Sx, 307
Lavant, Mid, Sx, 307
Lavendon, Bk, 18
Lavenham, Sf, 291
Laver, High, Ess, 83
Laver, Little, Ess, 83
Laver, Magdalen, Ess, 83
Laverstock, Wlt, 345
Laverstoke, Ha, 112
Laverton, So, 268
Lavington, East, Sx, 308
Lavington, Market, Wlt, 343
Lavington, West, Wlt, 340
Lawford, Ess, 88
Lawford, Church, Wa, 322
Lawford, Little, Wa, 323
Lawford, Long, Wa, 323
Lawhitton, Co, 34
Lawling, Ess, 84
Lawress, wapentake, Li, 177
Lawshall, Sf, 290
Lawton, He, 129
Lawton, Sa, 254
Laxfield, Sf, 288
Laxton, Np, 215
Laxton, Nt, 228
Laxton, YE, 363
Layer Breton, Ess, 82
Layer de la Haye, Ess, 82
Layer Marny, Ess, 82
Layham, Sf, 291
Laysters, He, 130
Laytham, YE, 361
Layton, La, 152
Layton, East, YN, 373
Layton, West, YN, 373
Lazenby, YN, 375
Lazerton, Do, 76
Lazonby, Cu, 37
Lea, Db, 44
Lea, He, 104, 122
Lea, La, 151
Lea, Li, 177
Lea, Ox, 241
Lea, Sa, 253
Lea, Wlt, 337
Lea Hall, Db, 44
Lea Marston, Wa, 325
Leadenham, Li, 174
Leadon, He, 128
Leafield, Ox, 236
Leake, East, Nt, 230
Leake, Old, Li, 169
Leake, West, Nt, 230
Leamington, Wa, 323
Leamington Hastings, Wa, 322
Learmouth, Nb, 225
Leath, wapentake, Cu, 36
Leatherhead, Sr, 302
Leatheringsett, Nf, 199

Leathley, YW, 384, 386
Leaton, Sa, 252
Leavening, YE, 364
Leavington, Castle, YN, 374
Leavington, Kirk, YN, 374
Lebberston, YN, 381
Lechlade, Gl, 100
Leck, La, 155
Leckby, YN, 371
Leckford, Ha, 107
Leckhampstead, Bk, 16
Leckhampstead, Brk, 9
Leckhampton, Gl, 104
Leconfield, YE, 362
Ledall, Ox, 239
Ledbury, He, 129
Ledbury Foreign, He, 129
Ledsham, YW, 386, 387
Ledston, YW, 387
Ledwell, Ox, 241
Lee, Ha, 107
Lee Brockhurst, Sa, 250
Lee, East, Ess, 85
Lee, The, Gl, 101
Lee, West, Ess, 85
Leebotwood, Sa, 252
Leece, La, 155
Leeds, YW, 388
Leegomery, Sa, 251
Leek, St, 281
Leen, He, 129
Leesthorpe, Lei, 165
Legbourne, Li, 184
Legsby, Li, 181
Leicester, Lei, 157, 158
Leicester, suburb of, Lei, 165
Leicestershire, 157–66
Leigh, Dev, 51
Leigh [in Badbury hd.], Do, 77
Leigh [in Yetminster hd.], Do, 71
Leigh, Ess, 81
Leigh, Gl, 100
Leigh [in South Petherton hd.], So, 275
Leigh [in Taunton hd.], So, 264
Leigh, Sr, 299
Leigh, St, 280
Leigh, Wo, 354
Leigh, Abbots, So, 262
Leigh, Chapel, So, 265
Leigh Delamere, Wlt, 344
Leigh, North, Ox, 242
Leigh, South, Ox, 242
Leigham, Dev, 52
Leigham, Sr, 302
Leighfield, Ru, 246
Leighs, Great, Ess, 85
Leighs, Little, Ess, 85
Leighterton, Gl, 102
Leighton, Sa, 250
Leighton Bromswold, Hu, 138

Leighton Buzzard, Bd, 4
Leightonstone, hundred, Hu, 138
Leire, Lei, 158
Leiston, Sf, 289
Lelant, Co, 30
Lelley, YE, 359
Lelley Dyke, YE, 359
Lemington, Gl, 99
Lemington, Lower, Gl, 92
Lemmington, Nb, 223
Lenacr', Sf, 295
Lenborough, Bk, 16
Lench, Abbots, Wo, 351
Lench, Church, Wo, 353
Lench, Rous, Wo, 351
Lench' Uic', Wo, 355
Lenchwick, Wo, 354
Lenton, Li, 170
Lenton, Nt, 229
Leominster, He, 122, 123
Leominster Foreign, He, 130
Leominster, hundred, He, 130
Leonard Moor, Dev, 56
Lepe, Ha, 116
Leppington, YE, 364
Lepton, YW, 389
Lesbury, Nb, 225
Lesnes, K, 140, 145
Lesnewth, Co, 33
Lessingham, Li, 173
Lessingham, Nf, 193
Letchworth, Hrt, 133
Letcombe Bassett, Brk, 9
Letcombe Regis, Brk, 9
Letheringham, Sf, 295
Letton, He, 129
Letton, Nf, 204
Levedale, St, 282
Leven, YE, 369
Levens, We, 330
Leverington, Ca, 28
Leverton, Brk, 10
Leverton, Li, 169
Leverton, North, Nt, 228
Leverton, South, Nt, 227
Levington, Sf, 296
Levisham, YN, 381
Lew, Ox, 237 n.
Lewannick, Co, 34
Lewell, Do, 73
Lewes, Sx, 305
Lewes, rape, Sx, 311
Lewknor, Ox, 241
Lewknor, hundred, Ox, 240
Lewtrenchard, Dev, 60
Lexden, Ess, 88
Lexden, hundred, Ess, 87
Lexham, East, Nf, 208
Lexham, West, Nf, 208
Lexworthy, So, 260

Leyburn, YN, 372
Leyland, La, 155
Leyland, wapentake, La, 154
Leyton, Ess, 81
Lezant, Co, 34
Lichfield, St, 276, 277
Liddel, Cu, 39
Liddington, Wlt, 335
Lidgate, Sf, 294
Lidlington, Bd, 3
Lidmarsh, So, 275
Lidstone, Ox, 236
Lifton, Dev, 66
Lifton, hundred, Dev, 60
Lighthorne, Wa, 321
Lilbourne, Np, 216
Lilburn, Nb, 224
Lilford, Np, 214
Lillesdon, So, 263
Lilleshall, Sa, 251
Lilley, Hrt, 133
Lilling, East, YN, 380
Lilling, West, YN, 376
Lillingstone Dayrell, Bk, 16
Lillingstone Lovell, Bk, 15, 235, 237
Lillington, Do, 71
Lillington, Wa, 323
Limber, Great, Li, 179
Limington, So, 263
Limpenhoe, Nf, 194
Linby, Nt, 234
Lincoln, Li, 167, 185
Lincolnshire, 167–86
Lincombe, Dev, 62
Lindfield, Sx, 313
Lindley, Lei, 158
Lindley, YW, 384
Lindon, Wo, 352
Lindridge, Wo, 350
Lindsay, Sf, 291
Lindsell, Ess, 82
Lindsey, Li, 167, 175–86
Linford, Great, Bk, 17
Linford, Little, Bk, 18
Lingfield, Sr, 303
Lingwood, Nf, 194
Linkenholt, Ha, 112
Linkinhorne, Co, 35
Linley [in Munslow hd.], Sa, 254
Linley [in Purslow hd.], Sa, 253
Linsheeles, Nb, 221
Linslade, Bk, 18
Linstead Magna, Sf, 289
Linstead Parva, Sf, 289
Linstock, Cu, 40
Linthorpe, YN, 375
Linton, Ca, 27
Linton, Db, 46
Linton, Gl, 97
Linton, He, 127

Linton, YE, 362
Linton [in Claro wap.], YW, 384
Linton [in Staincliffe wap.], YW, 383
Linton, Little, Ca, 27
Linton on Ouse, YN, 376
Linwood, Ha, 117
Linwood, Li, 179
Liskeard, Co, 34
Liskeard [Rural], Co, 34
Liss, Ha, 113
Liss Abbas, Ha, 113
Lisset, YE, 360
Lissington, Li, 181
Lisson, Mx, 190
Liston, Ess, 80
Litcham, Nf, 208
Litchborough, Nf, 215
Litchfield, Ha, 115
Litchurch, Db, 44
Litchurch, wapentake, Db, 43
Litherland, La, 150
Litlington, Ca, 26
Little, hundred, K, 145
Littleborough, Nt, 228
Littlebredy, Do, 77
Littlebury, Ess, 86
Littlecote, Bk, 18
Littlecott [in Elstub hd.], Wlt, 340
Littlecott [in Kingsbridge hd.], Wlt, 344
Littlefield, hundred, K, 144
Littleham [in East Budleigh hd.], Dev, 65
Littleham [in Shebbear hd.], Dev, 52
Littlehampton, Sx, 309
Littlehempston, Dev, 50
Littlemore, Ox, 239
Littleover, Db, 44
Littleport, Ca, 28
Littlestoke, Ox, 243
Littlethorpe, Ess, 81
Littlethorpe, YW, 394
Littleton, Gl, 98
Littleton [in Andover hd.], Ha, 108
Littleton [in Buddlesgate hd.], Ha, 108
Littleton, Mx, 189
Littleton [in Chew hd.], So, 267
Littleton [in Somerton Foreign hd.], So, 263
Littleton, Wlt, 339
Littleton, Wo, 354
Littleton Drew, Wlt, 344
Littleton, High, So, 260
Littleton Pannell, Wlt, 343
Littleton, Stoney, So, 268
Littleton upon Severn, Gl, 94
Littleton, West, Gl, 102
Littleworth, Brk, 11
Litton, Db, 47
Litton, So, 271
Litton, YW, 382
Litton Cheney, Do, 77
Livermere, Great, Sf, 292

Livermere, Sf, 292
Liverpool, La, 149
Liversedge, YW, 389
Liverton, YN, 375
Livesey, La, 152
Llancloudy, He, 126
Llandinabo, He, 125
Llangarron, He, 126
Llangunnock, He, 126
Llanithog, He, 126
Llanwarne, He, 125
Load, Long, 274
Lobb, Dev, 62
Lobthorpe, Li, 171
Lockeridge, Wlt, 339
Lockerley, Ha, 106
Locking, So, 259
Lockinge, Brk, 11
Lockington, Lei, 161
Lockington, YE, 361, 363, 368, 369
Lockshallis, Dev, 63
Lockton, YN, 381
Loddington, Lei, 162
Loddington, Np, 213
Loddiswell, Dev, 51
Loddon, Nf, 195
Loddon, hundred, Nf, 195
Loders, Do, 70
Lodsworth, Sx, 306
Loes, hundred, Sf, 295
Lofthouse, YW, 388
Loftsome, YE, 361
Loftus, YN, 375
Lokestone, So, 262 n.
Lolworth, Ca, 25
Lomer, Ha, 113
Londesborough, YE, 361
London, and wards, 187–8
Londonthorpe, Li, 172
Longbenton, Nb, 222
Longborough, Gl, 95
Longbridge Deverill, Wlt, 335
Longbridge, hundred, K, 142
Longbridge, hundred, Sx, 315
Longburton, Do, 71
Longcot, Brk, 11
Longden, Sa, 252
Longdon, St, 280
Longdon, Wa, 351
Longdon, Wo, 353
Longford, Db, 45
Longford, Gl, 97
Longford, He, 129
Longford, Sa, 250
Longford, Wlt, 334
Longframlington, Nb, 223
Longham, Nf, 208
Longhirst, Nb, 222
Longhope, Gl, 104
Longhorsley, Nb, 222

Longhoughton, Nb, 225
Longney, Gl, 103
Longnor, Sa, 252
Longnor [in Cuttlestone hd.], St, 282
Longnor [in Totmanslow hd.], St, 281
Longslow, Sa, 250
Longstanton, Ca, 25
Longstock, Ha, 107
Longstone, Great, Db, 47
Longstone, Little, Db, 47
Longstow, hundred, Ca, 26
Longstowe, Ca, 26
Longtoft, Li, 169
Longton, La, 155
Longton, St, 278
Longtree, hundred, Gl, 96
Longwitton, Nb, 222
Longworth, Brk, 12
Loningborough, hundred, K, 147
Lonsdale, Cartmel, and Furness, wapentake, La, 155
Looe, East, Co, 34
Looe, West, Co, 34
Loosebarrow, hundred, Do, 69
Lopen, So, 275
Lopham, Nf, 205
Loppington, Sa, 251
Lorbottle, Nb, 223
Lostock, La, 154
Lostwithiel, Co, 32
Lotherton, YW, 386
Lothingland, hundred, Sf, 290
Lottisham, So, 267
Loudham, Sf, 295
Loughborough, Lei, 162
Loughrigg, We, 330
Loughton, Bk, 17
Loughton, Ess, 83
Loughtor, Dev, 51
Lound, Li, 170
Lound, Nt, 229
Lound, Sf, 290
Louth, Li, 183
Louthesk, wapentake, Li, 183
Lovard, Do, 69
Loveden, wapentake, Li, 174
Lovel Barn, Sx, 313
Loventor, Dev, 50
Loversall, YW, 392
Lovington, So, 259
Lowdham, Nt, 231
Lowesby, Lei, 162
Lowestoft, Sf, 290
Lowick, Nb, 225
Lowick, Np, 214
Lowman, Craze, Dev, 55
Lowsmoor, Gl, 96
Lowther, We, 329
Lowthorpe, YE, 366, 369
Lowton, La, 150

Loxfield, hundred, Sx, 315
Loxley, Wa, 327
Loxton, So, 259
Loynton, St, 279
Lubbesthorpe, Lei, 159
Lubenham, Lei, 165
Luccombe, So, 272
Lucker, Nb, 224
Luckington, So, 262
Luckington, Wlt, 344
Ludborough, Li, 180
Ludborough, wapentake, Li, 180
Ludbrook, Dev, 64
Luddington, Li, 175
Luddington, Wa, 327
Luddington in the Brook, Np, 213 n.
Ludford, Li, 181
Ludgershall, Bk, 19
Ludgershall, Wlt, 332, 333
Ludgvan, Co, 30
Ludham, Nf, 193
Ludlow, Sa, 254
Ludshott, Ha, 114
Ludstone, Sa, 256
Ludwell, Ox, 242
Luffenham, North, Ru, 247
Luffenham, South, Ru, 247
Luffincott, Dev, 60
Lugwardine, He, 122, 129
Lulham, He, 127
Lullington, Db, 46
Lullington, So, 268
Lulworth, East, Do, 68
Lumby, YW, 386
Lund, YE, 362
Lupridge, Dev, 64
Lupton, We, 330
Lus hill, Wlt, 343
Lusby, Li, 185
Luscombe [in Stanborough hd.], Dev, 51
Luscombe [in Teignbridge, hd.], Dev, 60
Lustleigh, Dev, 59
Luston, He, 130
Lutley, St, 283
Lutley, Wo, 353
Luton, Bd, 3
Lutterworth, Lei, 159
Lutton, Np, 213
Lutton, East, YE, 364
Lutton, West, YE, 364
Luxborough, So, 272
Luxulyan, Co, 31
Lwyngtone, So, 262 n.
Lychpit, Ha, 118
Lydbury North, Sa, 253
Lyddington, Ru, 247
Lyde, He, 125
Lydeard, Bishop's, So, 270
Lydeard Punchardon, So, 265
Lydeard St. Lawrence, So, 265

Lydford, Dev, 66
Lydford, East, So, 263
Lydford, West, So, 259
Lydham, Sa, 253
Lydiard Millicent, Wlt, 343
Lydiard Tregoze, Wlt, 341
Lydiate, La, 151
Lydley Heys, Sa, 254
Lydlinch, Do, 70
Lydney, Gl, 104
Lye, He, 129
Lyford, Brk, 12
Lyham, Nb, 224
Lyme Regis, Do, 67, 78
Lymington [New], Ha, 106
Lymington [Old], Ha, 106
Lyminster, Sx, 309
Lympsham, So, 264
Lympstone, Dev, 65
Lyn, Dev, 53
Lynch, Sx, 306
Lyncombe, So, 261
Lyndhurst, Ha, 116
Lyndon, Ru, 246
Lyndon End, Wa, 324
Lyneham, Ox, 236
Lyneham, Wlt, 344
Lynford, Nf, 204
Lyng, Nf, 200
Lyng, So, 265
Lynn, Sa, 251
Lynn, King's, Nf, 192, 197
Lynn, South, Nf, 197
Lynton, Dev, 53
Lyonshall [in Stretford hd.], He, 129
Lyonshall [in Webtree hd.], He, 128
Lypiatt, Lower, Gl, 93
Lypiatt, Over, Gl, 93
Lyston, He, 125
Lytchett, Matravers, Do, 69
Lytchett Minster, Do, 69
Lytham, La, 152
Lythe, YN, 375
Lyveden, Little, Np, 214

Mabe, Co, 30
Mablethorpe, Li, 184
Mackney, Brk, 13
Mackworth, Db, 44
Maddington, Wlt, 341
Madehurst, Sx, 308
Madeley, Sa, 254
Madeley, St, 279
Madeley Holme, St, 280
Madingley, Ca, 25
Madley, He, 127
Madresfield, Wo, 354
Madron, Co, 30
Maer, St, 279
Maghull, La, 150

Maidencourt, Brk, 10
Maidenhatch, Brk, 7
Maidenhead, Brk, 7 n.
Maidenwell, Li, 183
Maidford, Np, 211
Maidstone, hundred, K, 144
Maidwell, Np, 213
Mainsborough, hundred, Ha, 111
Mainsbridge, hundred, Ha, 109
Mainstone, He, 128
Maisemore, Gl, 97
Maker, Co, 35
Malden, Sr, 301
Maldon Magna, Ess, 84
Maldon Parva, Ess, 84
Malham, YW, 382
Mallerstang, We, 328
Malling, K, 140, 144
Malmesbury, Wlt, 333
Malston, Dev, 64
Maltby, Li, 183
Maltby, YN, 375
Maltby, YW, 394
Maltby le Marsh, Li, 184
Malton, Ca, 26
Malton, New, YN, 377
Malton, Old, YN, 377
Malvern, Little, Wo, 350
Mamble, Wo, 352
Mamhead, Dev, 59
Manaccan, Co, 30
Manaton, Dev, 59
Manby, Li, 183
Mancetter, Wa, 324
Manchester, La, 154
Manea, Ca, 28
Manfield, YN, 374
Mangotsfield, Gl, 91
Manhood, hundred, Sx, 307
Manley, Dev, 56
Manley, wapentake, Li, 175
Manningford Abbots, Wlt, 336 n.
Manningford Bohune, Wlt, 336
Manningford Bruce, Wlt, 336
Manningham, YW, 388
Mannington, Nf, 202
Mannington, Wlt, 341
Manningtree, Ess, 88
Mansell Gamage, He, 124
Mansell Lacy, He, 124
Mansergh, We, 331
Mansfield, Nt, 234
Mansfield Woodhouse, Nt, 234
Manshead, hundred, Bd, 4
Manston, Do, 73
Manthorpe [in Beltisloe wap.], Li, 171
Manthorpe [in Winnibriggs wap.], Li, 171
Manton, Li, 176
Manton, Ru, 246
Manton, Honor, Wlt, 339

Manuden, Ess, 85
Maperton, So, 259
Maplebeck, Nt, 231
Mapledurham (Chazey), Ox, 243
Mapledurham (Gurney), Ox, 240
Mapledurwell, Ha, 118
Maplestead, Great, Ess, 80
Maplestead, Little, Ess, 80
Mapleton, Db, 45
Mappercombe, Do, 72
Mapperton [in Loosebarrow hd.], Do, 69
Mapperton [in Redhove hd.], Do, 72
Mappleton, YE, 358
Mappowder, Do, 74
Marcham, Brk, 12
Marchington, St, 280
Marchwood, Ha, 115
Marcle, Little, He, 128
Marcle, Much, He, 127
Marcy, fee of, Ess, 82
Marden, He, 122, 123, 124
Marden, Wlt, 335
Marden, barony, K, 148
Marden, East, Sx, 306
Marden, half-hundred, K, 144
Marden, North, Sx, 306
Marden, Up, Sx, 306
Marden, West, Sx, 306
Marderby, YN, 381
Marefield, Lei, 165
Marefield, North, Lei, 165
Mareham le Fen, Li, 184
Mareham on the Hill, Li, 184
Maresfield, Sx, 314
Marfleet, YE, 357
Margaretting, Ess, 85
Marham, Nf, 203
Marhamchurch, Co, 33
Mariansleigh, Dev, 54
Markby, Li, 184
Markeaton, Db, 44
Markfield, Lei, 159
Markham, East, Nt, 228
Markham, West, Nt, 228
Markington, YW, 394
Marks Hall, Ess, 82
Marksbury, So, 270
Markshall, Ess, 88
Markshall, Nf, 206
Marland, Peters, Dev, 52
Marlborough, Wlt, 333
Marlborough, Barton, Wlt, 333
Marlbrook, Sa, 253
Marlesford, Sf, 295
Marlingford, Nf, 206
Marlow, Bk, 15, 21, 22
Marlow, Little, Bk, 21
Marlston, Brk, 8
Marnham, Nt, 231
Marnhull, Do, 74

Marr, YW, 394
Marrick, YN, 373
Marrington, Sa, 257
Marsden, La, 153
Marsh, Bk, 16
Marsh, Sa, 253
Marsh Barton, Dev, 65
Marsh Gibbon, Bk, 16
Marsham, Nf, 201
Marshfield, Gl, 101
Marshwood, Do, 73
Marske, YN, 373
Marske by the Sea, YN, 375
Marston, He, 129
Marston, Li, 174
Marston [in Cuttlestone hd.], St, 282
Marston [in Pirehill hd.], St, 278
Marston, Wlt, 340
Marston Bigot, So, 268
Marston, Broad, Wo, 94
Marston, Butlers, Wa, 321
Marston, Fleet, Bk, 19
Marston Jabbett, Wa, 324
Marston, Long, Wa, 94
Marston, Long, YW, 385
Marston Magna, So, 269
Marston Meysey, Wlt, 343
Marston Montgomery, Db, 45
Marston Moretaine, Bd, 3
Marston, North, Bk, 19
Marston on Dove, Db, 45
Marston, Potters, Lei, 158
Marston, Priors, Wa, 321
Marston St. Lawrence, Np, 210
Marston, South, Wlt, 343
Marston Stannett, He, 123
Marston Trussell, Np, 212
Marstow, He, 126
Marsworth, Bk, 18
Marten, Wlt, 347
Martham, Nf, 193
Martin, Ha, 105, 334
Martin [in Gartree wap.], Li, 183
Martin [in Langoe wap.], Li, 173
Martin, Nt, 228
Martin Hussingtree, Wo, 354
Martinhoe, Dev, 53
Martinsley, hundred, Ru, 246
Martinsthorpe, Ru, 246
Martlesham, Sf, 296
Martley, Wo, 352
Martock, So, 274
Martock, hundred, So, 274
Marton, La, 152
Marton, Li, 178
Marton, Wa, 322
Marton [in Holderness], YE, 359
Marton [in Liberty of St. Peter], YE, 367
Marton [in Langbargh wap.], YN, 375
Marton [in Pickering lib.], YN, 381

Marton, YW, 387
Marton, Long, We, 329
Martons Both, YW, 383
Marwood, Dev, 62
Marystow, Dev, 60
Marytavy, Dev, 60
Masham, YN, 372
Mashbury, Ess, 82
Mason, Nb, 221
Massingham, Great, Nf, 197
Massingham, Little, Nf, 197
Matching, Ess, 89
Matfen, Nb, 221
Matfen (East), Nb, 220
Matford, Dev, 59
Mathon, He, 122, 354
Matlaske, Nf, 201
Matlock, Db, 44
Matson, Gl, 91 n.
Matterdale, Cu, 37
Mattersey, Nt, 229
Mattersey Thorpe, Nt, 229
Mattishall, Nf, 205
Maudlin House, Sx, 310
Maugersbury, Gl, 103
Maulden, Bd, 3
Maunby, YN, 374
Maund Bryan, He, 123
Mausby, Li, 176 n.
Mautby, Nf, 193
Mawdesley, La, 155
Mawfield, He, 127
Mawgan, Co, 30
Mawnan, Co, 30
Mawsley, Np, 212
Mawthorpe, Li, 184 n.
Maxey, Np, 213
Maxstoke, Wa, 324
Maydencroft Farm, Hrt, 134 n.
Mayfield, St, 281
Mayfield, Sx, 315
Mayland, Ess, 84 n.
Mayne, Fryer, Do, 73
Meaburn, King's, We, 330
Meaburn, Maulds, We, 330
Mearley, La, 152
Measham, Lei, 46
Meavy, Dev, 52
Medbourne, Lei, 164
Medine, East, hundred, Ha, 119
Medine, West, hundred, Ha, 119
Medland, Dev, 58
Medlar, La, 152
Medmenham, Bk, 21
Medstead, Ha, 117
Meering, Nt, 233
Meesden, Hrt, 133
Meeth, Dev, 52
Melbourn, Ca, 26
Melbourne, Db, 47

Melbourne, Wlt, 336
Melbourne, YE, 361
Melbury Abbas, Do, 74
Melbury Bubb, Do, 71
Melbury Osmond, Do, 71
Melbury Sampford, Do, 76
Melchbourne, Bd, 4
Melcombe, Do, 67, 70
Melcombe Binham, Do, 70 n.
Melcombe Horsey, Do, 70 n.
Melcombe Regis, Do, 78
Meldon, Nb, 221
Meldreth, Ca, 25
Melford, Long, Sf, 291
Melhuish Barton, Dev, 58
Melkinthorpe, We, 329
Melksham, Wlt, 338
Melksham, hundred, Wlt, 338
Melling [in Lonsdale, Cartmel, and Furness wap.], La, 156
Melling [in West Derby wap.], La, 151
Mellis, Sf, 287
Mellor, La, 153
Mells, Sf, 288
Mells, So, 262
Melmerby, Cu, 36
Melmerby [in Halikeld wap.], YN, 371
Melmerby [in Hang wap.], YN, 373
Melplash, Do, 71
Melsonby, YN, 373
Meltham, YW, 390
Melton, Sf, 295
Melton, YE, 363
Melton Constable, Nf, 199
Melton, Great, Nf, 206
Melton, High, YW, 394
Melton, Little, Nf, 207
Melton Mowbray, Lei, 163
Melton Ross, Li, 178
Meltonby, YE, 362
Membury, Dev, 57, 66
Mendham, Sf, 288
Mendlesham, Sf, 287
Menethorpe, YE, 364
Mengham, Ha, 116
Menheniot, Co, 34
Menston, YW, 388
Menthorpe, YE, 362, 364
Mentmore, Bk, 18
Meole, Sa, 257
Meole Brace, Sa, 257
Meols, North, La, 150
Meols, Raven, La, 150
Meon, Wa, 95
Meon, East, Ha, 111
Meon, East, hundred, Ha, 111
Meon, West, Ha, 117
Meonstoke, Ha, 113
Meonstoke, hundred, Ha, 113
Mepal, Ca, 28

Meppershall, Bd, 1, 4, 131, 134
Mercaston, Db, 44
Merdon, Ha, 108
Mere, Li, 173
Mere, Wlt, 334
Mere, hundred, Wlt, 334
Meredicheston', He, 126
Meretown, St, 277
Merke, So, 262 n.
Merridge, So, 260
Merrington, Sa, 252
Merriott, So, 273
Merrow, Sr, 300
Mersea, East, Ess, 81
Mersea, West, Ess, 81
Merssh', So, 262
Merstham, Sr, 299
Merston, Sx, 307
Merstone, Ha, 119
Merther, Co, 31
Merther Uny, Co, 31
Merton, Dev, 52
Merton, Nf, 204
Merton, Ox, 239
Merton, Sr, 302
Merton, leet, Wa, 322
Meshaw, Dev, 54
Messing, Ess, 88
Messingham, Li, 176
Metcombe, Dev, 63
Metfield, Sf, 288
Metham, YE, 362
Metheringham, Li, 173
Methley, YW, 390
Methwold, Nf, 204
Mettingham, Sf, 289
Metton, Nf, 201
Mevagissey, Co, 32
Mexborough, YW, 394
Michaelchurch, He, 126
Michaelstow, Co, 33
Micheldever, Ha, 112
Micheldever, hundred, Ha, 112
Michelmersh, Ha, 108
Mickfield, Sf, 286
Mickleby, YN, 375
Micklefield, YW, 386
Mickleham, Sr, 302
Mickleover, Db, 43
Mickleton, Gl, 94
Mickleton, YN, 373
Mickley, Nb, 220
Middelton', So, 274
Middleborough, Sx, 316
Middleham, YN, 372
Middlehope, Sa, 254
Middlesbrough, YN, 381
Middlesceugh, Cu, 37
Middlesex, 189–91
Middleton [near Wirksworth], Db, 44

Middleton [near Youlgreave], Db, 44
Middleton, Dev, 53
Middleton, Ess, 80
Middleton, Ha, 111
Middleton [in Lonsdale, Cartmel, and Furness wap.], La, 155
Middleton [in Salford wap.], La, 154
Middleton [in Glendale ward], Nb, 224
Middleton [in 'Inter' ward], Nb, 222
Middleton, Nf, 197
Middleton, Np, 215
Middleton [in Chirbury hd.], Sa, 256
Middleton [in Munslow hd.], Sa, 254
Middleton, Sf, 289
Middleton, Sx, 308
Middleton, Wa, 325
Middleton, We, 331
Middleton, Wlt, 346
Middleton, YN, 381
Middleton [in Claro wap.], YW, 384, 386
Middleton [in Morley wap.], YW, 389
Middleton Cheney, Np, 210
Middleton, hundred, Sx, 314
Middleton, North, Nb, 224
Middleton on Leven, YN, 374
Middleton on the Wolds, YE, 360, 369
Middleton Quernhow, YN, 371
Middleton Scriven, Sa, 255
Middleton, South [in Coquetdale ward], Nb, 224
Middleton, South [in 'Inter' ward], Nb, 222
Middleton Stoney, Ox, 238
Middleton, Stoney, Db, 47
Middleton Tyas, YN, 374
Middlezoy, So, 273
Middop, YW, 382
Midford hundred, Nf, 204
Midgehall, Wlt, 341
Midgham, Brk, 9
Midgham, Ha, 114
Midgley, YW, 389
Midhurst, Sx, 305
Milborne Port, So, 273
Milborne St. Andrew, Do, 69
Milborne Stileham, Do, 68
Milbourne, Nb, 221
Milbourne, Wlt, 337
Milburn, We, 329
Milby, YN, 371
Milcombe, Ox, 243
Milcote, Wa, 326
Milden, Sf, 291
Mildenhall, Sf, 293
Mildenhall, Wlt, 339
Mile End, Ess, 88
Mileham, Nf, 207
Milford, Wlt, 336, 345
Milford on Sea, Ha, 106
Milford, South, YW, 386
Mill Lane, So, 264

Millbrook, Bd, 3
Millbrook, Ha, 108
Millichope, Sa, 254
Millington, YE, 367, 370
Millmeece, St, 278
Millom, Cu, 40
Millow, Bd, 1
Millthorpe [in Ashwardhurn wap.], Li, 172
Millthorpe [in Aveland wap.], Li, 170
Milson, Sa, 254
Milston, Wlt, 345
Milton, Brk, 13
Milton, Ca, 25
Milton, Ess, 81
Milton, Ha, 110
Milton, He, 129
Milton, Np, 217
Milton, Nt, 228
Milton, Ox, 242
Milton [in Martock hd.], So, 274
Milton [in Wells Foreign hd.], So, 271
Milton, Sr, 299
Milton Abbas, Do, 70
Milton Bryan, Bd, 4
Milton Clevedon, So, 268
Milton Damarel, Dev, 61
Milton Ernest, Bd, 5
Milton, Great, Ox, 244
Milton Keynes, Bk, 17
Milton Lilbourne, Wlt, 347
Milton, Little, Ox, 244
Milton on Stour, Do, 74
Milton, South, Dev, 51
Milton under Wychwood, Ox, 236
Milton, West, Do, 72
Milverton, So, 273
Milverton Foreign, hundred, So, 260
Milverton, Old, Wa, 323
Milwich, St, 278
Mimms, South, Mx, 191
Minchinhampton, Gl, 96
Mindrum, Nb, 225
Minehead, So, 272
Minety, Wlt, 91, 332
Miningsby, Li, 185
Minskip, YW, 395
Minstead, Ha, 117
Minster, Co, 33
Minster Lovell, Ox, 236
Minsterley, Sa, 252
Minsterworth, Gl, 92
Minterne Magna, Do, 70
Minterne Parva, Do, 74
Minting, Li, 182
Mintlyn, Nf, 197
Minworth, Wa, 325
Mirfield, YW, 388
Miserden, Gl, 93
Missenden, Great, Bk, 20
Missenden, Little, Bk, 20

Misson, Nt, 168, 185, 227, 229
Misterton, Lei, 158
Misterton, Nt, 227
Misterton, So, 273
Mistley, Ess, 88
Mitcham, Sr, 301
Mitcheldean, Gl, 104
Mitchell, Co, 32
Mitford, Nb, 221
Mitton, St, 282
Mitton [in Halfshire hd.], Wo, 353
Mitton [in Oswaldslow hd.], Wo, 350
Mitton, Great, YW, 383
Mitton, Little, La, 153
Mixbury, Ox, 237
Moccas, He, 127
Modbury, Dev, 64, 66
Modbury, hundred, Do, 70
Modesleghe, So, 262 n.
Mogerhanger, Bd, 3
Molescroft, YE, 362, 368, 369
Molesden, Nb, 221
Molesey, Sr, 301
Molesworth, Hu, 138
Molland, Dev, 61
Molland, hundred, Dev, 61
Mollington, Ox, 243, 321
Molton, North, Dev, 65
Molton, North, hundred, Dev, 65
Molton, South, Dev, 66
Molton, South, hundred, Dev, 53
Monewden, Sf, 295
Mongewell, Ox, 243
Monk Culm, Dev, 63 n.
Monkhide, He, 128
Monkhopton, Sa, 254
Monkland, He, 129
Monkleigh, Dev, 52
Monkokehampton, Dev, 61
Monksilver, So, 265
Monkton, He, 125
Monkton, Bishop, YW, 394
Monkton Combe, So, 261
Monkton Farleigh, Wlt, 347
Monkton, Moor, YW, 385, 287
Monkton, Nun, YW, 384
Monkton Up Wimborne, Do, 75
Monkton, West, So, 271
Monnington, He, 128
Monnington on Wye, He, 125
Montacute, So, 274
Monxton, Ha, 108
Monyash, Db, 47
Moor, Wo, 351
Moor, Old, Nb, 222
Moor, West, So, 272
Moorby, Li, 184
Moorcot, He, 129
Moorgate, Nt, 228
Moorhouse, Nt, 228

Moorlinch, So, 273
Moorstone Barton, Dev, 56
Morborne, Hu, 138
Morcott, Ru, 247
Morden, Sr, 300
Morden, East, Do, 69
Morden, Guilden, Ca, 26
Morden, Steeple, Ca, 26
Morden [West], Do, 77
More, Sa, 253
More, So, 262
Morebath, Dev, 63
Moreby, YE, 364
Moredon, Wlt, 343
Morestead, Ha, 117
Moreton, Bk, 21
Moreton, Do, 68
Moreton, Ess, 83
Moreton, Ox, 244
Moreton, So, 260
Moreton [in Cuttlestone hd.], St, 282
Moreton [in Pirehill hd.], St, 277
Moreton Corbet, Sa, 250
Moreton, hundred, Brk, 13
Moreton in Marsh, Gl, 99
Moreton Jeffreys, He, 128
Moreton, Maids', Bk, 16
Moreton Morrell, Wa, 321
Moreton, North, Brk, 13
Moreton on Lugg, He, 125
Moreton Pinkney, Np, 211
Moreton Say, Sa, 251
Moreton, South, Brk, 13
Moreton Valence, Gl, 103
Moretonhampstead, Dev, 59
Morfe, St, 283
Morghale, St, 280
Morland, We, 329
Morley, Db, 43
Morley, Nf, 206
Morley, YW, 389
Morley, wapentake, YW, 388
Morleyston, wapentake, Db, 42
Morning Thorpe, Nf, 196
Morpeth, Nb, 221
Morston, Nf, 199
Mortehoe, Dev, 62
Mortham, YN, 373
Morton, Db, 48
Morton, Gl, 101
Morton [near Bourne], Li, 170
Morton [near Gainsborough], Li, 186
Morton [near Swinderby], Li, 175
Morton [in Bassetlaw wap.], Nt, 229
Morton [in Thurgarton and Lythe wap.], Nt, 231
Morton, YN, 374
Morton, YW, 388
Morton, Abbots, Wo, 355
Morton Bagot, Wa, 326

Morton on Swale, YN, 374
Morvah, Co, 30
Morval, Co, 34
Morville, Sa, 255
Morwenstow, Co, 33
Morwent, Gl, 96
Morwick, Nb, 222
Moseley, St, 282
Mosterton, Do, 72
Moston, Sa, 250
Motherby, Cu, 37
Mottisfont, Ha, 106
Mottistone, Ha, 119
Moulsford, Brk, 13
Moulsham, Ess, 85
Moulsoe, Bk, 17
Moulsoe, hundred, Bk, 17
Moulton, Li, 168
Moulton, Np, 217
Moulton, Sf, 294
Moulton, YN, 374
Moulton St. Mary, Nf, 195
Moulton St. Michael, Nf, 196
Mountfield, Sx, 316
Mountjoy, Sx, 316
Mountnessing, Ess, 85
Mountsorrel, Lei, 157, 162
Mousen, Nb, 225
Mowbach, He, 128
Mowlish, Dev, 59
Mowsley, Lei, 165
Mowthorpe, YE, 364
Moze, Ess, 88
Muchelney, So, 264
Mucking, Ess, 86
Muckleford, Do, 68
Mucklestone, St, 279
Mucklewick, Sa, 257
Mucknell, Wo, 350 n.
Muckton, Li, 183
Mudford, So, 263
Mugginton, Db, 44
Mulbarton, Nf, 206
Mullacott, Dev, 63
Mullion, Co, 30
Mumby, Li, 183
Muncaster, Cu, 40
Munden, Great, Hrt, 133
Munden, Little, Hrt, 133
Mundesley, Nf, 201
Mundford, Nf, 204
Mundham, Nf, 195
Mundham, North, Sx, 307
Mundham, South, Sx, 307
Mundon, Ess, 84
Mungrisdale, Cu, 37
Munsley, He, 128
Munslow, Sa, 254
Munslow, hundred, Sa, 254
Munton, Sa, 257

Murcot, Wo, 97 n.
Murcott, Ox, 238
Murifeld, So, 266 n.
Murrell Green, Ha, 113
Mursley, Bk, 19
Mursley, hundred, Bk, 18
Murton, Cu, 40
Murton, We, 329
Murton, YN, 379
Musbury, Dev, 57
Muscoates, YN, 377
Musgrave, Great, We, 329
Musgrave, Little, We, 329
Muskham, North, Nt, 231
Muskham, South, Nt, 231
Muston, Lei, 163
Muston, YE, 365
Mutford, Sf, 286
Mutford, hundred, Sf, 286
Muxbere, Dev, 56
Myddle, Sa, 251
Myddleton, La, 150
Mylor, Co, 30
Mymms, North, Hrt, 135
Myndtown, Sa, 253
Mythe Hook, Gl, 93
Myton on Swale, YN, 380

Naburn, YE, 364
Nafferton, Nb, 220
Nafferton, YE, 365
Nailsbourne, So, 264
Nailstone, Lei, 158
Naneby, Lei, 158
Nappa, YW, 386
Napton on the Hill, Wa, 322
Narborough, Lei, 159
Narborough, Nf, 204
Narford, Nf, 203
Naseby, Np, 216
Nash, Bk, 19
Nash, Sa, 254
Nassaburgh, hundred, Np, 210 n., 213
Nassington, Np, 213
Naston, 296
Nateby, We, 329
Nately Scures, Ha, 118
Nately, Up, Ha, 118
Natland, We, 330
Natsworthy, Dev, 50
Natton, Gl, 93
Naunton [in Cheltenham hd.], Gl, 92
Naunton [in Holford and Greston hd.], Gl, 98
Naunton [in Salmonsbury hd.], Gl, 103
Naunton Beauchamp, Wo, 354
Navenby, Li, 174
Navestock, Ess, 82
Nawton, YN, 377, 379
Nayland, Nf, 206

Nayland, Sf, 290
Nazeing, Ess, 83
Neatishead, Nf, 202
Nechells, Wa, 325
Necton, Nf, 203
Nedging, Sf, 291
Needham, Sf, 294
Needham Market, Sf, 285
Needingworth, Hu, 137
Neen Savage, Sa, 255
Neen Sollars, Sa, 253
Neenton, Sa, 256
Neithrop, Ox, 241
Nempnett Thrubwell, So, 270
Nesfield, YW, 384
Ness, YN, 377
Ness, Great, Sa, 251
Ness, wapentake, Li, 169
Neswick, YE, 360
Net Down, Wlt, 341
Netheravon, Wlt, 340
Netherbury, Do, 71
Nethercombe, Do, 71
Nethercote, Ox, 241
Nethercote, Wa, 322
Netherfield, Sx, 316
Netherfield, half-hundred, Sx, 316
Netherhampton, Wlt, 335
Netherseal, Lei, 160 n.
Netherton, Nb, 223
Netherton, Wo, 351
Netley, Ha, 109
Netley Marsh, Ha, 115
Netteswell, Ess, 89
Nettlecombe, Do, 72
Nettlecombe, Ha, 119
Nettlecombe, So, 266
Nettleford, Dev, 55
Nettleham, Li, 178
Nettlestead, Sf, 286
Nettleton, Li, 178
Nettleton, Wlt, 344
Nettleworth, Nt, 233
Netton [in Amesbury hd.], Wlt, 345
Netton [in Downton hd.], Wlt, 334
Nevendon, Ess, 86
New Forest, hundred, Ha, 116
New Mills, Db, 47
Newall, YW, 384
Newark on Trent, Nt, 227, 233
Newark, wapentake, Nt, 233
Newbald, YE, 368
Newball, Li, 181 n.
Newbiggin, Cu, 37
Newbiggin, We, 329
Newbiggin by the Sea, Nb, 222
Newbold [in Gartree hd.], Lei, 165
Newbold [in Goscote hd.], Lei, 161
Newbold Comyn, Wa, 323
Newbold on Avon, Wa, 323

Newbold on Stour, Wa, 351
Newbold Pacey, Wa, 320
Newbold Revel, Wa, 323
Newbold Verdon, Lei, 158
Newborough, St, 280
Newbottle, Np, 210
Newburn, Nb, 221
Newbury, Brk, 9
Newby, We, 329
Newby [in Halikeld wap.], YN, 371
Newby [in Langbargh wap.], YN, 374
Newby, YW, 394
Newby Wiske, YN, 374
Newcastle on Tyne, Nb, 219
Newcastle under Lyme, St, 276, 277
Newchurch, hundred, K, 146
Newdigate, Sr, 302
Newenden, K, 140, 144
Newent, Gl, 90, 95
Newham [in Glendale ward], Nb, 225
Newham [in 'Inter' ward], Nb, 221
Newham, Yn, 381
Newhaven, Sx, 311
Newholm, YN, 380
Newick, Sx, 313
Newington, Ox, 240
Newington, Sr, 302
Newington Bagpath, Gl, 96
Newington, North, Ox, 242
Newington, South, Ox, 241, 242 n.
Newland, Dev, 53
Newland [in Sherborne hd.], Do, 71
Newland [in Yetminster hd.], Do, 71
Newland, Ess, 85
Newland, Gl, 91
Newland, Wo, 354
Newland, YE, 363
Newlyn, Co, 32
Newmarket, Sf, 23, 28, 284
Newnham, Ca, 24
Newnham, Gl, 90, 92
Newnham, Ha, 118
Newnham, Hrt, 134
Newnham, Np, 216
Newnham, Wa, 326 n.
Newnham, Wlt, 347
Newnham, Kings, Wa, 323
Newnham Murren, Ox, 243
Newnham Paddox, Wa, 323
Newnton, Long, Gl, 337
Newnton, North, Wlt, 336
Newport, Dev, 53
Newport, Ess, 79, 87
Newport, Ha, 120
Newport, Sa, 249, 251
Newport Pagnell, Bk, 16
Newsam, Temple, YW, 388
Newsham, La, 152
Newsham, Nb, 223
Newsham [in Birdforth wap.], YN, 378

Newsham [in Gilling wap.], YN, 373
Newsham [in Ryedale wap.], YN, 377
Newsholme, YE, 362
Newsholme, YW, 382
Newsome, YE, 359
Newstead, Nb, 226
Newthorpe, Nt, 230
Newthorpe, YW, 387
Newtimber, Sx, 312
Newton [in Thriplow hd.], Ca, 26
Newton [in Wisbech hd.], Ca, 28
Newton, Cu, 40
Newton, Do, 74
Newton, He, 130
Newton [near Clifton], La, 152
Newton [near Staining], La, 151
Newton, Li, 170
Newton [in Bamburgh ward], Nb, 225
Newton [in Coquetdale ward], Nb, 224
Newton [in Tynedale ward], Nb, 220
Newton [in Henstead hd.], Nf, 196
Newton [in South Greenhoe hd.], Nf, 203
Newton, Nt, 232
Newton, Sa, 257
Newton, Sf, 290
Newton, St, 277
Newton, Wa, 323
Newton, YE, 364
Newton [in Langbargh wap.], YN, 375
Newton [in Pickering lib.], YN, 381
Newton, YW, 383
Newton Abbot, Dev, 50
Newton, Bank, YW, 383
Newton Blossomville, Bk, 17
Newton Burgoland, Lei, 161
Newton by the Sea, Nb, 226
Newton by Toft, Li, 179
Newton, Cold, Lei, 162
Newton, East, YE, 359
Newton Ferrers, Dev, 64
Newton Flotman, Nf, 206
Newton, Great, Np, 215
Newton Harcourt, Lei, 160
Newton Kyme, YW, 386
Newton le Willows, La, 150
Newton le Willows, YN, 372
Newton, Little, Np, 215
Newton Longville, Bk, 17
Newton, Maiden, Do, 76
Newton Morrell, YN, 374
Newton Mulgrave, YN, 375
Newton, North, So, 260
Newton, Old, Sf, 287
Newton on Ouse, YN, 380
Newton on the Moor, Nb, 226
Newton on Trent, Li, 178
Newton, Out, YE, 358
Newton, Potter, YW, 388
Newton Purcell, Ox, 237
Newton Regis, Wa, 324

Newton Reigny, Cu, 37
Newton St. Faith, Nf, 194
Newton St. Loe, So, 268
Newton St. Petrock, Dev, 52
Newton Solney, Db, 46
Newton, South, Wlt, 342
Newton Stacey, Ha, 115
Newton Toney, Wlt, 345
Newton Underwood, Nb, 222
Newton Unthank, Lei, 160
Newton upon Derwent, YE, 362
Newton Valence, Ha, 107, 120 n.
Newton Waleys, YW, 386
Newton, Water, Hu, 138
Newton, Welsh, He, 125
Newton, West, Nf, 197
Newton, West, YE, 359
Newton, Wold, Li, 180
Newton, Wold, YE, 365
Newtown, Ha, 109
Newtown, Wlt, 345
Newtown Bury, Ha, 115
Newtown Linford, Lei, 163
Nicheleston', He, 126
Nicholforest, Cu, 38
Nidd, YW, 394
Ninfield, Sx, 316
Ninfield, hundred, Sx, 316
Ningwood, Ha, 120
Niton, Ha, 119
Nobold, Np, 213
Nobottle-Grove, hundred, Np, 216
Nocton, Li, 173
Noke, He, 129
Noke, Ox, 238
Noke Court, Gl, 97
Norbreck, La, 152
Norbury, Db, 46
Norbury, Sa, 253
Norbury, St, 282
Norfolk, 192–208
Normanby [in Aslacoe wap.], Li, 177
Normanby [in Manley wap.], Li, 175
Normanby [in Well wap.], Li, 178
Normanby [in Langbargh wap.], YN, 375
Normanby [in Liberty of St. Mary and St. Leonard], YN, 380
Normanby le Wold, Li, 179
Normancross, hundred, Hu, 138
Normanton, Db, 43
Normanton, Lei, 163
Normanton, Li, 174
Normanton [in Bassetlaw wap.], Nt, 229
Normanton [in Thurgarton and Lythe wap.], Nt, 231
Normanton, Ru, 246
Normanton, Wlt, 345
Normanton, YW, 390
Normanton le Heath, Lei, 159
Normanton on Soar, Nt, 230

Normanton on the Wolds, Nt, 230
Normanton, South, Db, 48
Normanton Turville, Lei, 159
Norridge, Wlt, 347
Northallerton, YN, 357, 379
Northam, Dev, 66
Northampton, Np, 209, 218
Northamptonshire, 209–18
Northaw, Hrt, 134
Northbrook, Ha, 112
Northbrook, Ox, 238
Northcote, Dev, 61
Northcott, Dev, 61 n.
Northcourt, Brk, 12
Northfield, Gl, 92
Northfield, Wa, 353
Northgate, Nt, 233
Northiam, Sx, 317
Northill, Bd, 3
Northington [in Micheldever hd.], Ha, 112
Northington [in Overton hd.], Ha, 112
Northleach [Foreign], Gl, 98
Northleach [Within], Gl, 98
Northleigh, Dev, 57
Northlew, Dev, 60
Northmoor, Ox, 236
Northmore, Cu, 38
Northolme, Li, 182
Northolt, Mx, 190
Northorpe, Li, 177, 186
Northorpe, YE, 366
Northover, So, 260
Northowram, YW, 389
Northrepps, Nf, 201
Northstow, hundred, Ca, 25
Northtown, Sf, 290
Northumberland, 219–26
Northway, Gl, 93
Northwick, Gl, 351
Northwick, Wo, 350
Northwold, Nf, 204
Northwood, Gl, 104
Northwood, Ha, 120
Norton [in Coleridge hd.], Dev, 64
Norton [in Crediton hd.], Dev, 54
Norton, Gl, 94
Norton, Ha, 107
Norton, Hrt, 134
Norton, Np, 215
Norton, Sa, 252
Norton, Sf, 292
Norton, Sx, 314
Norton, Wlt, 339
Norton, Wo, 350 n.
Norton, YE, 364
Norton [in Osgoldcross wap.], YW, 391
Norton [in Sheffield], YW, 48
Norton Bavent, Wlt, 346
Norton, Bishop, Li, 176
Norton, Bishop's, Gl, 97

Norton, Blo, Nf, 205
Norton, Bredon's, Wo, 350
Norton, Brize, Ox, 237
Norton Canes, St, 280
Norton Canon, He, 124
Norton, Chipping, Ox, 236
Norton, Cold, Ess, 84
Norton, Cold, St, 279
Norton Conyers, YN, 379
Norton Curlieu, Wa, 325 n.
Norton Disney, Li, 175
Norton, East, Lei, 162
Norton Ferris, Wlt, 269, 332
Norton Ferris, hundred, So, 269
Norton Fitzwarren, So, 264
Norton, Green's, Np, 211
Norton, Green's, hundred, Np, 211
Norton Hawkfield, So, 267
Norton, Hook, Ox, 236
Norton in the Moors, St, 278
Norton iuxta Twycross, Lei, 159
Norton, King's, Lei, 164
Norton, King's, Wa, 353
Norton le Clay, YN, 371
Norton Lindsey, Wa, 326
Norton Malreward, So, 267
Norton Mandeville, Ess, 83
Norton, Midsomer, So, 261
Norton, Newarks, Ess, 83 n.
Norton, Prior's, Gl, 97
Norton, Pudding, Nf, 198
Norton St. Philip, So, 268
Norton Subcourse, Nf, 195
Norton sub Hamdon, So, 270
Norton, Wood, Nf, 200
Norwell, Nt, 231
Norwich, Nf, 192, 198
Noseley, Lei, 165
Noss Mayo, Dev, 51
Nosterfield, YN, 372
Notgrove, Gl, 99
Notley, Black, Ess, 84
Notley, White, Ess, 84
Nottingham, Nt, 227, 233
Nottinghamshire, 227–34
Notton, YW, 391
Nowton, Sf, 291
Nunburnholme, Ye, 362
Nuneaton, Wa, 324
Nuneham Courtenay, Ox, 239
Nunhide, Brk, 8
Nunkeeling, YE, 359
Nunney, So, 268
Nunnington, He, 124
Nunnington, YN, 377, 380
Nunthorpe, YN, 374
Nunton, Wlt, 334
Nunwick, YW, 394
Nursling, Ha, 108
Nursted, Ha, 114

Nursteed, Wlt, 348
Nutbourne [in Westbourne hd.], Sx, 305
Nutbourne [in West Easewrithe hd.], Sx, 308
Nutfield, Sr, 299
Nuthall, Nt, 230
Nuthecote, Dev, 55
Nuthurst, Sx, 309 n.
Nutley, Ha, 118
Nutley, Sx, 314
Nutwell, Dev, 65
Nyetimber, Sx, 308
Nymet Tracey, Dev, 62
Nymett, Nichols, Dev, 62
Nympsfield, Gl, 95
Nympton, Bishop's, Dev, 54
Nympton, George, Dev, 54
Nympton, King's, Dev, 54
Nynehead, So, 265
Nynehead, East, So, 265

Oadby, Lei, 159
Oake, So, 265
Oakeley, Sa, 253
Oaken, St, 283
Oakford, Dev, 54
Oakham, Ru, 246
Oakhanger, Ha, 114
Oakington, Ca, 25
Oakley, Bd, 5
Oakley, Ha, 116
Oakley, Ox, 240 n.
Oakley, Sf, 287
Oakley, St, 280
Oakley, East, Ha, 112
Oakley, Great, Ess, 88
Oakley, Great, Np, 215
Oakley, Little, Ess, 88
Oakley, Little, Np, 215
Oakley, North, Ha, 115
Oaksey, Wlt, 337
Oakthorpe, Lei, 46
Oare, So, 272
Oare, Wlt, 335
Oathill, So, 273
Oborne, Do, 71
Obridge, So, 264, 265
Obthorpe, Li, 169
Oby, Nf, 193
Occold, Sf, 287
Ock, hundred, Brk, 12
Ockbrook, Db, 43
Ockendon, North, Ess, 87
Ockendon, South, Ess, 87
Ockham, Sr, 299
Ockley, Sr, 299
Ocle, So, 262 n.
Ocle, Livers, He, 124
Ocle Pychard, He, 124
Octon, YE, 365

Odcombe, So, 270
Oddingley, Wo, 350
Oddington, Gl, 102
Oddington, Ox, 238
Odell, Bd, 2
Odes, Brk, 346
Odiham, Ha, 120
Odiham, hundred, Ha, 113
Odsey, hundred, Hrt, 132
Odstock, Wlt, 334
Odstone, Brk, 10
Odstone, Lei, 160
Offchurch, Wa, 323
Offenham, Wo, 354
Offham, Sx, 308
Offington, Sx, 310
Offley, Hrt, 133
Offley, Bishop's, St, 278
Offley, High, St, 279
Offlow, hundred, St, 279
Offord, Wa, 326
Offord Cluny, Hu, 136
Offord D'Arcy, Hu, 137
Offton, Sf, 285
Ogbourne, St. Andrew, Wlt, 339
Ogbourne St. George, Wlt, 339
Ogbourne Maizey, Wlt, 339
Oggesole, So, 260 n.
Ogle, Nb, 221
Oglethorpe, YW, 386
Ogley Hay, St, 280 n.
Ogwell, East, Dev, 58
Ogwell, West, Dev, 58
Okeford, Child, Do, 73
Okeford Fitzpaine, Do, 74
Okehampton, Dev, 60, 66
Okeover, St, 281
Okleye, Sa, 252
Old, Np, 212
Oldberrow, Wa, 355
Oldbury, Sa, 255
Oldbury on the Hill, Gl, 102
Oldbury upon Severn, Gl, 101
Oldcoates, Nt, 228
Oldelond, Gl, 101
Oldham, La, 154
Oldland, Gl, 94
Ollerton, Nt, 229
Olney, Bk, 18
Olveston, Gl, 94
Ombersley, Wo, 355
Ompton, Nt, 228
Onehouse, Sf, 287
Ongar, Chipping, Ess, 83
Ongar, hundred, Ess, 82
Ongar, High, Ess, 83
Onibury, Sa, 255
Onn, High, St, 282
Onn, Little, St, 282
Onneley, St, 279

Orby, Li, 182
Orchard Portman, So, 265
Orchardleigh, So, 268
Orcheston St. George, Wlt, 341
Orcheston St. Mary, Wlt, 341
Orcop, He, 125
Ordsall, Nt, 228
Ore, Sx, 317
Orford, Li, 179
Orford, Sf, 284, 294
Orleton, He, 130
Orleton, Wo, 352
Orlingbury, Np, 212
Orlingbury, hundred, Np, 212
Ormesby, Nf, 193
Ormesby, YN, 375
Ormsby, North, Li, 180
Ormsby, South, Li, 185
Ormside, Great, We, 329
Ormside, Little, We, 329
Orrell, La, 151
Orsett, Ess, 86
Orston, Nt, 232
Orton, Cu, 37
Orton, Np, 212
Orton, St, 283
Orton, We, 329
Orton Longueville, Hu, 138
Orton on the Hill, Lei, 159
Orton, Water, Wa, 325
Orton Waterville, Hu, 138
Orwell, Ca, 26
Orwellbury, Hrt, 132
Osbaldeston, La, 153
Osbaldwick, YN, 379
Osbaston, Lei, 158
Osberton, Nt, 229
Osbournby, Li, 170
Osburwick, Nb, 226
Oseby, Li, 172
Osgarth, Li, 172
Osgathorpe, Lei, 161
Osgodby [in Beltisloe wap.], Li, 170
Osgodby [in Walshcroft wap.], Li, 180
Osgodby, YE, 363
Osgodby, YN, 381
Osgoldcross, wapentake, YW, 390
Osleston, Db, 46
Osmaston, Db, 45
Osmaston by Derby, Db, 44
Osmington, Do, 72
Osmotherley, YN, 378
Ospringe, K, 147
Ossett, YW, 390
Ossington, Nt, 231
Ossulstone, hundred, Mx, 190
Oswaldkirk, YN, 377
Oswaldslow, hundred, Wo, 350
Oswaldtwistle, La, 153
Oswestry, hundred, Sa, 249

Oteley, Sa, 252 n.
Otherton, St, 281
Othery, So, 273
Othorpe, Lei, 164
Otley, Sf, 296
Otley, YW, 387
Otterbourne, Ha, 108
Otterburn, Nb, 221
Otterburn, YW, 382
Otterford, So, 264
Otterham, Co, 33
Otterhampton, So, 268
Otterington, North, YN, 379
Otterington, South, YN, 381
Otterton, Dev, 65
Ottery, Mohun's, Dev, 57
Ottery St. Mary, Dev, 66
Ottringham, YE, 358, 369
Oulston, YN, 378
Oulton, Cu, 38
Oulton, Nf, 202
Oulton, Sf, 290
Oundle, Np, 214, 214 n.
Ousby, Cu, 41
Ousden, Sf, 293
Ouse and Derwent, wapentake between, YE, 363
Ouseburn, Great, YW, 395
Ouseburn, Little, YW, 384
Ouseby, Li, 170
Ousefleet, YW, 391
Ousethorpe, YE, 361
Outchester, Nb, 224
Outwell, Ca, 28 n., 203 n.
Outwell, Nf, 203
Ovenden, YW, 388
Over, Ca, 25
Over [in Dudstone hd.], Gl, 97
Over [in Langley and Swineshead hd.], Gl, 94
Overbury, Wo, 350
Overgrass, Nb, 224
Overs, hundred, Sa, 253
Oversley, Wa, 326
Overstone, Np, 217
Overstrand, Nf, 201
Overton, Ha, 112
Overton, La, 156
Overton, Sa, 255
Overton, YN, 380
Overton, Cold, Lei, 163
Overton, East, Wlt, 340
Overton, hundred, Ha, 112
Overton, Market, Ru, 247
Overton, West, Wlt, 339
Overtown, Wlt, 341
Oving, Sx, 307
Ovingdean, Sx, 312
Ovingham, Nb, 221
Ovington, Ess, 80

Ovington, Ha, 117
Ovington, Nb, 221
Ovington, Nf, 204
Ovington, YN, 373
Owdeswell, Gl, 98
Ower, Do, 75
Ower, Ha, 115
Owermoigne, Do, 68
Owersby, Li, 179
Owlpen, Gl, 96
Owmby [in Aslacoe wap.], Li, 176
Owmby [in Yarborough wap.], Li, 179
Owslebury, Ha, 117
Owsthorpe, YE, 363
Owston, Lei, 165
Owston, YW, 391
Owstwick, YE, 358
Owthorne, YE, 358
Owthorpe, Nt, 232
Oxborough, Nf, 203
Oxcliffe, La, 156
Oxcombe, Li, 185
Oxcroft, Db, 48
Oxenbourne, Ha, 111
Oxendon, Great, Np, 213
Oxendon, Little, Np, 213
Oxenhall, Gl, 95
Oxenton, Gl, 93
Oxford, Ox, 235, 244
Oxfordshire, 235–45
Oxhill, Wa, 321
Oxley, St, 283
Oxlinch, Gl, 103
Oxnead, Nf, 202
Oxney, hundred, K, 146
Oxspring, YW, 391
Oxted, Sr, 303
Oxton, Nt, 231
Oxton, YW, 385
Oxwick, Nf, 207
Ozleworth, Gl, 96

Packington, Lei, 42, 46, 160
Packington, St, 279
Packington, Great, Wa, 324
Packington, Little, Wa, 324
Packwood, Wa, 320
Padbury, Bk, 16
Paddington, Mx, 190
Paddington, Sr, 299
Padiham, La, 153
Padstow, Co, 32
Padworth, Brk, 8
Paganhill, Gl, 93
Pagham, Sx, 307
Pagham, hundred, Sx, 307
Paglesham, Ess, 81
Paignton, Dev, 50
Pailton, Wa, 323
Painley, YW, 383

Painsthorpe, YE, 366
Painswick, Gl, 93
Pakefield, Sf, 286
Pakenham, Sf, 292
Palgrave, Sf, 287
Palling, Sea, Nf, 193
Pamington, Gl, 93
Pampisford, Ca, 27
Pan, Ha, 119
Pancrasweek, Dev, 61
Panfield, Ess, 80
Pangbourne, Brk, 7
Panton, Li, 181
Panxworth, Nf, 195 n.
Papcastle, Cu, 39
Papplewick, Nt, 230
Papworth Everard, Ca, 25
Papworth, hundred, Ca, 25
Papworth St. Agnes, 23, 25, 136
Parbold, La, 155
Parham, Sf, 295
Parham, Sx, 309
Park, Ha, 119
Park Street, Hrt, 134
Parkham, Dev, 52
Parley, West, Do, 75
Parlington, YW, 388
Parndon, Great, Ess, 89
Parndon, Little, Ess, 89
Parr, La, 151
Parracombe, Dev, 53
Parrock, Sx, 313
Parsonby, Cu, 39
Partney, Li, 182
Parton, Cu, 38
Parton, Gl, 97
Parva Hida, He, 128
Parva Northton', Ess, 83
Parva Schenle, Bk, 17
Parwich, Db, 45
Pashley, Sx, 317
Paslow, Ess, 83
Passenham, Np, 211
Paston, Nf, 202
Paston, Np, 213
Pastrow, hundred, Ha, 112
Patcham, Sx, 312
Patchway, Gl, 94
Patesley, Nf, 207
Pathlow, liberty, Wa, 326
Patney, Wlt, 340
Patrington, YE, 358, 369
Patshull, St, 283
Pattingham, St, 283
Pattishall, Np, 211
Pattiswick, Ess, 88
Patton, We, 330
Paul, Co, 30
Paulerspury, Np, 211
Paull, YE, 358

Paull Fleet, YE, 358
Paull Holme, YE, 358
Paulton, So, 261
Pauncefoot, Ha, 107
Pauntley, Gl, 95
Pavenham, Bd, 2
Pawlett, So, 260
Pawston, Nb, 225
Paxford, Gl, 351
Paxton, Great, Hu, 137
Paxton, Little, Hu, 137
Payhembury, Dev, 63
Paythorne, YW, 382
Peasemere, Brk, 9
Peasenhall, Sf, 288
Peatling Magna, Lei, 159
Peatling Parva, Lei, 158
Pebmarsh, Ess, 80
Pebworth, Wo, 94
Peckham, Sr, 302
Peckleton, Lei, 158
Pedmore, Wo, 353
Pegglesworth, Gl, 99
Pegswood, Nb, 222
Peldon, Ess, 81
Pelham, Brent, Hrt, 132
Pelham, Furneux, Hrt, 132
Pelham, Stocking, Hrt, 132
Pelsall, St, 283
Pelynt, Co, 34
Pemberton, La, 151
Pembridge, He, 129
Pencombe, He, 123
Pencoyd, He, 126
Pencraig, He, 126
Pendeford, St, 282
Pendlebury, La, 154
Pendleton, La, 154
Pendleton, Great, La, 152
Pendleton, Little, La, 152
Pendock, Wo, 350
Pendomer, So, 270
Pengethly, He, 126
Penhurst, Sx, 316
Penistone, YW, 392
Penketh, La, 151
Penkhull, St, 277
Penknight, Co, 32
Penkridge, St, 281
Penleigh, Wlt, 336
Penmayne, Co, 32
Penn, Bk, 21
Penn, Lower, St, 283
Penn, Upper, St, 283
Pennard, East, So, 267
Pennington, Ha, 121
Pennington [in Lonsdale, Cartmel, and
    Furness wap.], La, 155
Pennington [in West Derby wap.], La,
    151

Penrith, Cu, 36, 41
Penrith, liberty, Cu, 41
Penryn, Co, 30
Penselwood, So, 269
Pensham, Wo, 354
Penson, Dev, 65
Pensthorpe, Nf, 199
Pensthorpe, YE, 358
Pensworth, Wlt, 334
Pentlow, Ess, 80
Pentney, Nf, 197
Penton Grafton, Ha, 109
Penton Mewsey, Ha, 109
Pentrich, Db, 42
Pentridge, Do, 75
Penwith, hundred, Co, 30
Penwortham, La, 155
Peopleton, Wo, 354
Peper Harow, Sr, 298
Perching, Sx, 312
Perio, Np, 213
Perivale, Mx, 190
Perlethorpe, Nt, 229
Perranarworthal, Co, 30
Perranuthnoe, Co, 30
Perranzabuloe, Co, 32
Perrott, North, So, 269
Perrott, South, Do, 72
Perry, So, 260
Perry, St, 279
Perry, Wo, 122
Perry Elm, So, 270
Perry Farm, Wo, 123
Pershall, St, 279
Pershore, Wo, 353
Pershore, hundred, Wo, 353
Pertenhall, Bd, 4
Perton, He, 128
Perton, St, 283
Pertwood, Wlt, 347
Peterborough, Np, 213
Peterchurch, He, 128
Petersfield, Ha, 111
Petersham, Do, 75
Petersham, Sr, 301
Peterstow, He, 126
Petertavy, Dev, 52
Petham, hundred, K, 141
Petherick, Little, Co, 32
Petherton, North, So, 260
Petherton, North, hundred, So, 260
Petherton, South, So, 275
Petherton, South, hundred, So, 275
Petherwin, South, Co, 34
Petrockstow, Dev, 52
Pett, Sx, 317
Pettaugh, Sf, 296
Pettistree, Sf, 295
Petton, Dev, 63
Petton, Sa, 252

Petworth, Sx, 308
Pevensey, Sx, 304
Pevensey, rape, Sx, 313
Pewsey, Wlt, 348
Phillack, Co, 30
Philleigh, Co, 31
Phillyholme, Dev, 77 n.
Pickburn, YW, 392
Pickenham, North, Nf, 203
Pickenham, South, Nf, 204
Pickering, YN, 381
Pickering, liberty, YN, 381
Pickering, soke, YN, 357, 382
Pickhill, YN, 371
Pickthorn, Sa, 255
Pickwell, Dev, 53
Pickwell, Lei, 165
Pickworth, Li, 170
Pickworth, Ru, 247
Picton, YN, 375
Piddington, Np, 217
Piddington, Ox, 239
Piddle, North, Wo, 354
Piddle, Wyre, Wo, 351
Piddlehinton, Do, 69
Piddletrenthide, Do, 70
Pidley, Hu, 137 n.
Pidsley, Dev, 55
Pigdon, Nb, 223
Pilham, Li, 186
Pilkington, La, 154
Pilland, Dev, 63
Pillaton, Co, 35
Pillaton Old Hall, St, 281
Pillerton Hersey, Wa, 321
Pillerton Priors, Wa, 321
Pilley, Ha, 116
Pilton, Dev, 63
Pilton, Np, 214, 214 n.
Pilton, Ru, 247
Pilton, So, 267
Pimhill, hundred, Sa, 251
Pimley, Sa, 250
Pimperne, Do, 76
Pimperne, hundred, Do, 75
Pinbury, Gl, 100
Pinchbeck, Li, 168
Pinchinthorpe, YN, 375
Pincote, Ca, 25
Pinford, Do, 71
Pinkhill, Ox, 242
Pinkney, Wlt, 344
Pinley [in Barlichway hd.], Wa, 325
Pinley [in Knightlow hd.], Wa, 323
Pinnock, Gl, 98
Pinvin, Wo, 354
Pinxton, Db, 48
Pipe Green, St, 280
Pirbright, Sr, 299
Pirehill, hundred, St, 277

Pirton, Hrt, 133
Pirton, Wo, 353
Pirton Court, Gl, 97
Pishill, Ox, 238
Pitchcombe, Gl, 91, 91 n.
Pitchcott, Bk, 19
Pitchford, Sa, 252
Pitcombe, So, 269
Pitminster, So, 264
Pitney, So, 259
Pitney manor, So, 259
Pitsea, Ess, 86
Pitsford, Np, 217
Pitstone, Bk, 18
Pitt, Ha, 108
Pitt, West, Ha, 108
Pittleworth, Ha, 106
Pitton, Wlt, 345
Pixley, He, 128
Pixton Barton, So, 265
Plainsfield, So, 267
Plaitford, Ha, 105, 345
Playford, Sf, 296
Pleasington, La, 152
Pleasley, Db, 48
Pledgdon, Ess, 84
Pleshey, Ess, 82
Plesingho, Ess, 82
Plomesgate, hundred, Sf, 294
Plompton, YW, 384
Ploughley, hundred, Ox, 237
Plumbland, Cu, 39
Plumpton, La, 151
Plumpton, Np, 211
Plumstead, Nf, 201
Plumstead, Great, Nf, 194
Plumstead, Little, Nf, 194
Plumtree [in Bassetlaw wap.], Nt, 228
Plumtree [in Rushcliffe wap.], Nt, 230
Plungar, Lei, 164
Plush, Do, 74
Plymouth, Dev, 52 n., 66
Plympton Erle, Dev, 51, 66
Plympton, hundred, Dev, 51
Plympton St. Mary, Dev, 51
Plymstock, Dev, 51
Plymtree, Dev, 63
Pockley, YN, 377
Pocklington, YE, 357, 367, 369
Pockthorpe, Nf, 194
Pockthorpe, YE, 366
Podimore, So, 274
Podington, Bd, 2
Podmore, St, 278
Pointon, Li, 170
Polebrook, Np, 214
Polebrook, hundred, Np, 214
Polesworth, Wa, 324
Polhampton, Ha, 112
Poling, Sx, 309

Poling, hundred, Sx, 309
Pollicott, Bk, 19
Pollington, YW, 390
Polsloe, Dev, 58
Polstead, Sf, 290
Poltimore, Dev, 58
Ponsford, Dev, 63
Pontefract, YW, 390
Ponteland, Nb, 221
Pontesbury, Sa, 252
Ponton, Great, Li, 171
Ponton, Little, Li, 171
Pool, YW, 387
Pool, North, Dev, 64
Pool, South, Dev, 64
Poole, Do, 69
Poole Keynes, Gl, 337
Poorton, Do, 72
Popham, Ha, 112
Poppleton, Nether, YW, 387
Poppleton, Upper, YW, 387
Poringland, Nf, 196
Porlock, So, 272
Portbury, So, 271
Portbury, hundred, So, 271
Portchester, Ha, 105, 111, 121
Portesham, Do, 77
Portington, YE, 363
Portishead, So, 271
Portland, Isle of, Do, 77
Portlemouth, East, Dev, 64
Portlemouth, West, Dev, 51
Porton, Wlt, 345
Portsdown, hundred, Ha, 110
Portsea, Ha, 110
Portslade, Sx, 312
Portsmouth, Ha, 105, 121
Poslingford, Sf, 294
Postlip, Gl, 98
Poston, He, 128
Postwick, Nf, 194
Potlock, Db, 43
Potsgrove, Bd, 4
Potterne, Wlt, 340
Potterspury, Np, 211
Potto, YN, 374
Potton, Bd, 1
Poughill, Co, 33
Poughill, Dev, 55
Poulshot, Wlt, 338
Poultney, Lei, 160
Poulton, Gl, 342
Poulton, Wlt, 339
Poulton le Fylde, La, 152
Poulton le Sands, La, 156
Poundstock, Co, 33
Povington, Do, 76
Powder, hundred, Co, 31
Powderham, Dev, 59
Powerstock, Do, 73

Powick, Wo, 354
Poxwell, Do, 68
Poynings, Sx, 312
Poynings, hundred, Sx, 312
Poyntington, Do, 67, 269
Poynton, Sa, 250
Prallingworth, Ha, 110
Prawle, East, Dev, 64
Prebend End, Bk, 22
Preen, Church, Sa, 252
Prees, Sa, 250
Preesall, La, 152
Preese, La, 152
Prendwick, Nb, 223
Prescote, Ox, 241
Prescott, Gl, 92
Pressen, Nb, 225
Prestbury, Gl, 100
Presthope, Sa, 254
Preston, Do, 76
Preston [in Crowthorne hd.], Gl, 99
Preston [in Dudstone hd.], Gl, 97
Preston [Lower Town], He, 124
Preston, La, 149, 151
Preston, Nb, 225
Preston, Ru, 246
Preston, Sf, 290
Preston, So, 265, 266
Preston, Sr, 302
Preston [in Beddingham] [in Totmore hd.], Sx, 315
Preston [in West Firle] [in Totmore hd.], Sx, 315
Preston [in Whalesborne hd.], Sx, 312
Preston, YE, 359, 367
Preston Bagot, Wa, 326
Preston Bisset, Bk, 16
Preston Brockhurst, Sa, 251
Preston Candover, Ha, 118
Preston Capes, Np, 216
Preston Deanery, Np, 217
Preston, East, Sx, 309
Preston, Great, YW, 387
Preston Gubbals, Sa, 251
Preston, hundred, K, 141
Preston, Long, YW, 383
Preston Montford, Sa, 253
Preston on Stour, Wa, 100
Preston on Wye, He, 127
Preston Patrick, We, 330
Preston Plucknett, So, 262, 263
Preston Richard, We, 330
Preston under Scar, YN, 372
Preston Wynne, He, 124
Prestone, Do, 77
Prestwich, La, 154
Prestwick, Nb, 221
Prestwold, Lei, 162
Priddy, So, 271
Priestcliffe, Db, 47

Priestley, Bd, 4
Priestweston, Sa, 257
Primethorpe, Lei, 158
Princethorpe, Wa, 324
Prinstead, Sx, 305
Priorslee, Sa, 256
Priston, So, 270
Prittlewell, Ess, 81
Probus, Co, 31
Publow, So, 270
Puckington, So, 272
Pucklechurch, Gl, 101
Pucklechurch, hundred, Gl, 101
Pucknall, Ha, 108
Puddington, Dev, 54
Puddle, Little, Do, 69
Puddle, Turners, Do, 69
Puddletown, Do, 69
Pudlestone, He, 130
Pudlicote, Ox, 236
Pudsey, YW, 389
Pulborough, Sx, 308
Pulham, Nf, 207
Pulham, East, Do, 74
Pulham, West, Do, 74
Pull, Wo, 354
Pulloxhill, Bd, 3
Pulston, Do, 68
Pulverbatch, Church, Sa, 252
Pucknowle, Do, 77
Puriton, So, 274
Purleigh, Ess, 84
Purley, Brk, 8
Purley Parva, Brk, 8
Purslow, hundred, Sa, 253
Purston Jaglin, YW, 391
Purton, Wlt, 333
Pusey, Brk, 12
Putford, West, Dev, 61
Puthall, Wlt, 347
Putley, He, 127
Putney, Sr, 302
Puttenham, Hrt, 134
Puttenham, Sr, 298
Pyder, hundred, Co, 32
Pyecombe, Sx, 312
Pylle, So, 267
Pyon, Canon, He, 125
Pyon, King's, He, 130
Pyrford, Sr, 300
Pyrland, So, 264
Pyrton, Ox, 238
Pyrton, hundred, Ox, 238
Pytchley, Np, 212
Pyworthy, Dev, 60

Quadring, Li, 168
Quainton, Bk, 19
Quantoxhead, East, So, 266
Quantoxhead, West, So, 266

Quarles, Nf, 200
Quarleston, Do, 75
Quarley, Ha, 108
Quarmby, YW, 390
Quarndon, Db, 43
Quarrendon, Bk, 19
Quarrington, Li, 172
Quatt, Sa, 257
Quedgeley, Gl, 103
Queenhill, Wo, 354
Quemerford, Wlt, 337
Quenby, Lei, 162
Quendon, Ess, 87
Queniborough, Lei, 161
Quenington, Gl, 100
Quethiock, Co, 34
Quidenham, Nf, 205
Quidhampton, Ha, 112
Quidhampton, Wlt, 342
Quinton, Np, 217
Quinton, Wa, 94
Quorndon, Lei, 162
Quyk', YW, 389

Rabson, Wlt, 339
Rackenford, Dev, 54
Rackham, Sx, 309
Rackheath, Nf, 194
Racton, Sx, 305
Radbourn, Wa, 322
Radbourne, Db, 44
Radcliffe, La, 153
Radcliffe on Trent, Nt, 232
Radclive, Bk, 16
Radcot, Ox, 237
Raddington, So, 266
Raddon, West, Dev, 55
Radfield, hundred, Ca, 27
Radford, Nt, 229
Radford, Ox, 236
Radford, Wa, 323
Radford Semele, Wa, 323
Radipole, Do, 72
Radley, Brk, 12
Radlow, hundred, He, 128
Radnage, Bk, 22
Radstock, So, 262
Radstone, Np, 210
Radway, Dev, 65
Radway, Wa, 321
Radwell, Hrt, 132
Radwinter, Ess, 87
Radwood, St, 279
Ragdale, Lei, 163
Ragnall, Nt, 228, 233
Rainford, La, 151
Rainham, Ess, 87
Rainhill, La, 150
Rainton, YN, 371
Raisthorpe, YE, 364, 366

Raithby [in Louthesk wap.], Li, 183
Raithby [in Soke of Bolingbroke], Li, 185
Raleigh, Dev, 62
Rame, Co, 34
Rampisham, Do, 76
Rampton, Ca, 25
Rampton, Nt, 228
Ramsbury, Wlt, 338
Ramsbury, hundred, Wlt, 338
Ramsdean, Ha, 111
Ramsden, Ox, 236
Ramsden Bellhouse, Ess, 86
Ramsden Crays, Ess, 86
Ramsey, Ess, 88
Ramsey, Hu, 137
Ramsholt, Sf, 295
Ranby, Li, 182
Ranby, Nt, 229
Rand, Li, 181
Rangeworthy, Gl, 101
Ranskill, Nt, 228
Ranton, St, 279
Ranworth, Nf, 195
Rapsgate, hundred, Gl, 92
Rasen, Market, Li, 179
Rasen, Middle, Li, 179
Rasen, West, Li, 179
Rashleigh Barton, Dev, 62
Raskelf, YN, 376
Rastrick, YW, 389
Ratby, Lei, 160
Ratcliffe Culey, Lei, 160
Ratcliffe on Soar, Nt, 230
Ratcliffe on the Wreake, Lei, 163
Ratfyn, Wlt, 345
Rathmell, YW, 383
Ratley, Wa, 321
Ratlinghope, Sa, 253
Rattery, Dev, 51
Rattlesden, Sf, 292
Rauceby, North, Li, 173
Rauceby, South, Li, 173
Raughton, Cu, 38
Raunds, Np, 212
Raveley, Great, Hu, 137
Raveley, Little, Hu, 137
Ravendale, East, Li, 180
Ravendale, West, Li, 180
Ravenfield, YW, 393
Raveningham, Nf, 196
Ravensden, Bd, 2
Ravenser Odd, YE, 357, 370
Ravensthorpe, Np, 216
Ravenstone, Bk, 17
Ravenstone, Lei, 42, 47, 160
Ravenstonedale, We, 329
Ravensworth, YN, 373
Raventhorpe, YE, 370
Rawcliffe, YN, 379, 380
Rawcliffe, YW, 391

Rawcliffe, Out, La, 152
Rawcliffe, Upper, La, 152
Rawdon, YW, 388
Rawmarsh, YW, 393
Rawreth, Ess, 81
Rawridge, Dev, 57
Raydon, Sf, 285
Rayleigh, Ess, 81
Rayne, Ess, 80
Raynham, East, Nf, 198
Raynham, South, Nf, 198
Raynham, West, Nf, 198
Rayton, Nt, 233
Read, La, 153
Reading, Brk, 6, 14
Reading, hundred, Brk, 7
Reagill, We, 330
Rearsby, Lei, 161
Reasby, Li, 181 n.
Red Castle, Sa, 250
Redbornstoke, hundred, Bd, 3
Redbourn, Hrt, 134
Redbourne, Li, 176, 186
Redbridge, hundred, Ha, 115
Reddish, La, 154
Rede, Sf, 291
Redenhall, Nf, 207
Redesdale, liberty, Nb, 219
Redgrave, Sf, 287
Redhove, hundred, Do, 72
Redisham, Sf, 290
Redisham, Little, Sf, 289
Redlane, hundred, Do, 73
Redlingfield, Sf, 287
Redlynch, So, 269
Redmarley, Wo, 352
Redmarley D'Abitot, Gl, 350
Redmile, Lei, 163
Redmire, YN, 372
Redruth, Co, 30
Redwick, Gl, 102
Reed, Hrt, 132
Reedham, Nf, 195
Reedness, YW, 390, 391
Reepham, Li, 177
Regilbury, So, 271
Reigate, Sr, 297, 298
Reigate [Foreign], Sr, 299
Reigate, hundred, Sr, 299
Reighton, YE, 366, 369
Remenham, Brk, 6
Rempstone, Nt, 230
Rendcomb, Gl, 92
Rendham, Sf, 294
Rendlesham, Sf, 295
Renhold, Bd, 2
Rennington, Nb, 225
Renscombe, Do, 75
Renwick, Cu, 37
Repps, Nf, 193

Repton, Db, 46
Repton, hundred, Db, 46
Respryn, Co, 34
Reston, Nf, 284, 290
Reston, We, 330
Reston, North, Li, 183
Reston, South, Li, 184
Restormel, Co, 32
Retford, Nt, 227
Retford, East, Nt, 233
Retford, West, Nt, 229
Rettendon, Ess, 85
Reule, St, 282
Rewe, Dev, 58
Reydon, Sf, 289
Reydon Hamlet, Ess, 83
Reymerston, Nf, 205
Rhiston, Sa, 257
Ribbesford, Wo, 352
Ribbleton, La, 152
Ribby, La, 151
Ribchester, La, 153
Ribston, YW, 384
Ribston, Little, YW, 384, 385
Ribton, Cu, 39
Riby, Li, 179
Riccal, YN, 377
Riccall, YE, 363, 367
Richards Castle, He, 130
Richard's Castle, Sa, 254
Richardson, Wlt, 339
Richmond, Sr, 298
Richmond, YN, 357, 373
Richmondshire, YN, 371
Rickergate, Soke beyond, Cu, 41
Rickinghall Inferior, Sf, 287
Rickinghall Superior, Sf, 292
Rickling, Ess, 87
Rickmansworth, Hrt, 134
Ridby, He, 126
Riddlecombe, Dev, 61
Riddlesworth, Nf, 205
Ridgewell, Ess, 80
Ridgmont, Bd, 3
Ridlington, Nf, 202
Ridlington, Ru, 246
Ridware, Hamstall, St, 280
Ridware, Mavesyn, St, 280
Ridware, Pipe, St, 280
Rigsby, Li, 184
Rigton, YW, 384
Rigton, East, YW, 387
Rillington, YE, 365
Rimington, YW, 382
Rimpton, So, 269
Rimswell, YE, 358
Ringbrough, YE, 359
Ringland, Nf, 200
Ringmer, Sx, 315
Ringmore [in Ermington hd.], Dev, 64

Ringmore [in Wonford hd.], Dev, 58
Ringsfield, Sf, 289
Ringshall, Sf, 286
Ringslow, hundred, K, 141
Ringstead, Do, 68
Ringstead, Nf, 198
Ringstead, Little, Nf, 197
Ringsthorpe, Li, 172
Ringstone, Li, 170
Ringwell, Dev, 58
Ringwood, Ha, 121
Ripe, Sx, 313
Ripley, Db, 42
Ripley, YW, 384
Riplingham, YE, 360
Riplington, Ha, 111
Ripon, YW, 394
Ripon, liberty, YW, 394
Rippingale, Li, 170
Ripple, Wo, 350
Ripplesmere, hundred, Brk, 7
Ripton, Abbots, Hu, 137
Ripton, Kings, Hu, 136
Risborough, hundred, Bk, 21
Risborough, Monks, Bk, 21
Risborough, Princes, Bk, 21
Risbridge, hundred, Sf, 293
Risbury, He, 130
Risby, Sf, 291
Risby, YE, 368, 369
Risby, Great, Li, 175
Risby, Little, Li, 175
Rise, YE, 359
Riseholme, Li, 178
Riseley, Bd, 4
Rishangles, Sf, 287
Rishton, La, 153
Rishworth, YW, 389
Rising, Castle, Nf, 197
Risley, Db, 43
Rissington, Great, Gl, 103
Rissington, Little, Gl, 103
Rissington, Wick, Gl, 103
Riston, Long, YE, 358, 368, 369
Ritton, Sa, 257
Rivenhall, Ess, 84
River, Sx, 308
Rivington, La, 154
Rixton, La, 150
Roade, Np, 211 n.
Roall, YW, 391
Robbecomb', Dev, 54
Roborough, Dev, 53
Roborough, hundred, Dev, 52
Roby, La, 150
Rocester, St, 281
Roche, Co, 31
Rochester, K, 140, 147
Rochester Foreign, hundred, K, 145
Rochford, Ess, 81

Rochford, Wo, 122, 130
Rochford, hundred, Ess, 81
Rock, Nb, 225
Rock Moor, Wo, 352
Rockbeare, Dev, 65
Rockbourne, Ha, 114
Rockcliffe, Cu, 37
Rockhampton, Gl, 94
Rockingham, Np, 209, 218
Rockland, Nf, 205
Rockland St. Mary, Nf, 196
Rockley, Ha, 119
Rockley, Wlt, 339
Rocombe, Dev, 57, 58
Rodbaston, St, 281
Rodborough, Gl, 96
Rodbourne, Wlt, 337
Rodbourne Cheney, Wlt, 343
Rodden, Do, 77
Rodden, So, 268
Roddlesworth, La, 155
Rode, So, 268
Roden, Sa, 250
Rodenhurst, Sa, 250
Roding, Abbess, Ess, 83
Roding, Aythorpe, Ess, 82
Roding, Beauchamp, Ess, 83
Roding, Berners, Ess, 82
Roding, High, Ess, 82
Roding, Leaden, Ess, 82
Roding, Margaret, Ess, 82
Roding, Morrell, Ess, 83
Roding, White, Ess, 82
Rodington, Sa, 250
Rodley, Gl, 92
Rodmarton, Gl, 96
Rodmell, Sx, 311
Rodsley, Db, 46
Rodway, So, 267
Roeburg, hundred, Brk, 9
Roecliffe, YW, 395
Roehampton, Sr, 302
Roel, Gl, 98
Rofford, Ox, 240
Rogate, Sx, 306
Roke, Ha, 107
Rokeby, YN, 373
Rollesby, Nf, 193
Rolleston, Lei, 165
Rolleston, Nt, 231
Rolleston, St, 280
Rollington, Do, 75
Rollright, Great, Ox, 236
Rollright, Little, Ox, 236
Rolston, YE, 359
Rolstone Barton, Dev, 54
Rolvenden, hundred, K, 143
Romanby, YN, 379
Romansleigh, Dev, 54
Romney, New, K, 140

Romsey, Ha, 111
Romsey Extra, Ha, 107
Romsley, Sa, 257
Roos, YE, 359
Ropley, Ha, 110
Ropsley, Li, 172
Rorrington, Sa, 256
Roseden, Nb, 224
Rosemaund, He, 123
Rosgill, We, 329
Rosliston, Db, 46
Ross on Wye, He, 127
Rossall, Sa, 251
Rossington, YW, 392
Roston, Db, 46
Rothbury, Nb, 224
Rotherbridge, hundred, Sx, 308
Rotherby, Lei, 161
Rotherfield, Ha, 120
Rotherfield, Sx, 314
Rotherfield Greys, Ox, 240
Rotherfield, hundred, Sx, 314
Rotherfield Peppard, Ox, 240
Rotherham, YW, 393
Rotherhithe, Sr, 302
Rothersthorpe, Np, 217
Rotherwas, He, 127
Rothley, Lei, 161
Rothley, Nb, 222
Rothwell, Li, 180
Rothwell, Np, 209, 218
Rothwell, YW, 389
Rothwell, hundred, Np, 212
Rotsea, YE, 362
Rottingdean, Sx, 312
Roucumb, Dev, 54 n.
Roud, Ha, 119
Roudham, Nf, 205
Rougham, Nf, 207
Rougham, Sf, 292
Roughton, Li, 183
Roughton, Nf, 201
Roundway, Wlt, 348
Rounton, YN, 374
Rounton, West, YN, 378
Rousdon, Dev, 57
Rousham, Ox, 241
Routh, YE, 358, 369
Rowbarrow, hundred, Do, 75
Rowberrow, So, 259
Rowborough, Bishop's, hundred, Wlt, 340
Rowborough, King's, hundred, Wlt, 343
Rowde, liberty, Wlt, 333
Rowden, He, 123
Rowden, Wlt, 333
Rowington, Wa, 325
Rowland, Db, 47
Rowley, Wlt, 347
Rowley, hundred, Bk, 16
Rowley Regis, St, 277

Rowner, Ha, 110
Rowston, Li, 173
Rowton [in Bradford hd.], Sa, 250
Rowton [in Ford hd.], Sa, 253
Rowton, YE, 358
Roxby, Li, 175
Roxby, YN, 375
Roxholm, Li, 173
Roxton, Bd, 2
Roydon, Ess, 89
Roydon, Nf, 207
Roydon, Sr, 302
Royston, Hrt, 23, 26, 131, 132
Royston, YW, 392
Royton, La, 154
Ruan Lanihorne, Co, 32
Ruan Major, Co, 30
Ruan Minor, Co, 31
Ruardean, Gl, 103
Ruckland, Li, 183
Rudchester, Nb, 221
Ruddington, Nt, 230
Rudford, Gl, 95
Rudge [near Crediton], Dev, 53
Rudge [near Lapford], Dev, 54
Rudge, Sa, 256
Rudham, East, Nf, 198
Rudham, West, Nf, 198
Rudston, YE, 365, 367
Rudyard, St, 281
Rufford, La, 155
Rufforth, YW, 385
Rugby, Wa, 322
Rugeley, St, 281
Ruishton, So, 264
Ruislip, Mx, 190
Rum Bridge, Ha, 115
Rumboldswhyke, Sx, 307
Rumburgh, Sf, 289
Rumwell, So, 264
Rumworth, La, 154
Runcton, Sx, 307
Runcton Holme, Nf, 203
Runcton, North, Nf, 197
Runfold, Sr, 298
Runhall, Nf, 206
Runham, Nf, 193
Runnington, So, 260
Runton, Nf, 201
Runwell, Ess, 85
Runwick, Sr, 298
Ruscombe, Brk, 7
Rushall, Nf, 207
Rushall, St, 279
Rushall, Wlt, 335
Rushbrooke, Sf, 292
Rushbury, Sa, 255
Rushcliffe, wapentake, Nt, 230
Rushden, Hrt, 132
Rushden, Np, 212, 212 n.

Rushford, Nf, 205, 293
Rushford Barton, Dev, 58
Rushmere, Sf, 286
Rushmere St. Andrew, Sf, 296
Rushmonden, hundred, Sx, 314
Rushock, Wo, 353
Rushton, Np, 212
Rushton, St, 281
Ruskington, Li, 173
Rusper, Sx, 309 n.
Rustington, Sx, 309
Ruston, YN, 381
Ruston, East, Nf, 193
Ruswarp, YN, 380
Ruswick, YN, 372
Rutherford, YN, 373
Rutland, 246–8
Ruxley, hundred, K, 145
Ryal, Nb, 220
Ryburgh, Great, Nf, 198
Ryburgh, Little, Nf, 199
Rycote, Ox, 240
Rycotelane, Ox, 240
Rydal, We, 330
Rye, Sx, 304
Ryedale, wapentake, YN, 376
Ryhall, Ru, 247
Ryhill, YE, 358
Ryhill, YW, 391
Ryle, Great, Nb, 223
Ryle, Little, Nb, 223
Rylstone, YW, 382
Ryme Intrinseca, Do, 71
Rysome, YE, 358
Ryston, Nf, 203
Ryther, YW, 386
Ryton, Wa, 324
Ryton, YN, 377
Ryton on Dunsmore, Wa, 323

Sacombe, Hrt, 133
Saddington, Lei, 165
Saddlewood, Gl, 102
Saham Toney, Nf, 204
St. Agnes, Co, 32
St. Alban, liberty, Hrt, 134
St. Albans, Hrt, 134
St. Allen, Co, 31
St. Anthony in Meneage, Co, 30
St. Anthony in Roseland, Co, 31
St. Augustine, lathe, K, 141
St. Austell, Co, 31
St. Bees, Cu, 40
St. Blazey, Co, 31
St. Breock, Co, 32
St. Breward, Co, 33
St. Briavels, Gl, 91 n.
St. Briavels, hundred, Gl, 103
St. Briavels, liberty, Gl, 91
St. Buryan, Co, 30

St. Cleer, Co, 34
St. Clement, Co, 31
St. Clement Danes, Mx, 191
St. Clether, Co, 33
St. Columb Major, Co, 32
St. Columb Minor, Co, 32
St. Cuthbert Without, Cu, 41 n.
St. Dennis, Co, 31
St. Dominick, Co, 34
St. Edmund, liberty, Sf, 290
St. Endellion, Co, 32
St. Enoder, Co, 32
St. Erme, Co, 31
St. Erth, Co, 30
St. Ervan, Co, 32
St. Etheldreda, liberty, Sf, 294
St. Eval, Co, 32
St. Ewe, Co, 31
St. Gennys, Co, 33
St. George, hundred, Do, 68
St. Germans, Co, 35
St. Giles, Mx, 191
St. Gluvias, Co, 30
St. Goran, Co, 31
St. Helens, Ha, 119
St. Hilary, Co, 30
St. Issey, Co, 32
St. Ive, Co, 34
St. Ives, Co, 30
St. Ives, Hu, 137
St. Ives, Street of, Hu, 137
St. Joan à Gore, Wlt, 341
St. John, Co, 34
St. Juliot, Co, 33
St. Just, Co, 30
St. Just in Roseland, Co, 31
St. Keverne, Co, 30
St. Kew, Co, 32
St. Keyne, Co, 34
St. Lawrence, Ess, 84
St. Lawrence, Ha, 119
St. Leonard, liberty, YE, 368
St. Leonard, liberty, YW, 385
St. Levan, Co, 30
St. Mabyn, Co, 32
St. Martin, Co, 34
St. Martin in Meneage, Co, 30
St. Martin in the Fields, Mx, 191
St. Martin's, hundred, K, 146
St. Mary and St. Leonard, liberty, YN, 380
St. Mary Bourne, Ha, 109
St. Mary in the Strand, Mx, 191
St. Marychurch, Dev, 50
St. Marylebone, Mx, 190
St. Mawes, Co, 31
St. Mellion, Co, 34
St. Merryn, Co, 32
St. Mewan, Co, 31
St. Michael Penkevil, Co, 31
St. Michaels, Co, 30

St. Minver, Co, 32
St. Neot, Co, 34
St. Neots, Hu, 137
St. Osyth, Ess, 88
St. Paul's Walden, Hrt, 134
St. Peter, liberty, YE, 367
St. Peter, liberty, YN, 379
St. Philip and St. James, Gl, 91 n.
St. Pinnock, Co, 34
St. Sampson, Co, 31
St. Stephen by Launceston, Co, 34
St. Stephen in Brannel, Co, 31
St. Teath, Co, 32
St. Tudy, Co, 33
St. Veep, Co, 34
St. Wenn, Co, 32
St. Weonards, He, 125
St. Winnow, Co, 34
St. Wolstan's, He, 125
Saintbridge, Gl, 97
Saintbury, Gl, 95
Salcombe Regis, Dev, 65
Salcott, Ess, 82
Saleby, Li, 184
Salehurst, Sx, 318
Salesbury, La, 153
Salford, Bd, 4
Salford, La, 153
Salford, Ox, 236
Salford, Abbot's, Wa, 326
Salford Priors, Wa, 326
Salford, wapentake, La, 153
Saling, Great, Ess, 80
Salisbury (and aldermanries), Wlt, 332-3
Salkeld, Great, Cu, 41
Salkeld, Little, Cu, 40
Sall, Nf, 200
Salmonby, Li, 185
Salmonsbury, hundred, Gl, 102
Salperton, Gl, 99
Salt, St, 278
Saltash, Co, 35
Saltby, Lei, 164
Salterton, Wlt, 345
Saltfleetby, Li, 183
Saltford, So, 270
Salthouse, Nf, 199
Salthrop, Wlt, 341
Saltley, Wa, 325
Saltmarshe, YE, 363
Salton, YN, 379
Saltwick, Nb, 222
Sambourne, Wa, 326
Samford, hundred, Sf, 285
Samlesbury, La, 153
Sampford Arundel, So, 260
Sampford Brett, So, 266
Sampford Courtenay, Dev, 61
Sampford, Great, Ess, 86
Sampford, Little, Ess, 86

Sampford Peverell, Dev, 56
Sampford Spiney, Dev, 52
Sancreed, Co, 30
Sancton, YE, 360, 368
Sandal Magna, YW, 390
Sandall, Kirk, YW, 393
Sandall, Long, YW, 393
Sanderstead, Sr, 300
Sandford, Gl, 92
Sandford, Ha, 115
Sandford, Sa, 250
Sandford, So, 260
Sandford, We, 329
Sandford, Dry, Brk, 12
Sandford on Thames, Ox, 239
Sandford Orcas, Do, 67, 269
Sandford St. Martin, Ox, 241
Sandholme, YE, 363
Sandhurst, Brk, 7
Sandhurst [in Dudstone hd.], Gl, 97
Sandhurst [in King's Barton lib.], Gl, 91 n.
Sandhutton, YN, 378
Sandiacre, Db, 43
Sandlake, Sx, 316
Sandon, Ess, 85
Sandon, Hrt, 132
Sandon, St, 278
Sandon Fee, Brk, 10
Sandown, Ha, 119
Sandridge, Hrt, 134
Sandwich, K, 140
Sandy, Bd, 1
Sankey, Great, La, 151
Sansaw, Sa, 251
Santon, Cu, 40
Santon, Li, 176
Santon, Nf, 204
Santon Downham, Sf, 293
Sapcote, Lei, 159
Sapey, Lower, Wo, 352
Sapey, Upper, He, 123
Sapiston, Sf, 293
Sapperton, Db, 45
Sapperton, Gl, 93
Sapperton, Li, 172
Saredon, Great, St, 281
Sarnesfield, He, 130
Sarsden, Ox, 236
Sarson, Ha, 108
Sarum, Old, Wlt, 333
Satterleigh, Dev, 53
Saul, Gl, 103
Saundby, Nt, 229
Saunderton, Bk, 21
Saunton, Dev, 62
Sausthorpe, Li, 185
Saverley, St, 278
Sawbridge, Wa, 322
Sawbridgeworth, Hrt, 132

Sawcliffe, Li, 176
Sawdon, YN, 381
Sawley, Db, 43
Sawley, YW, 394
Sawston, Ca, 27
Sawtry, Hu, 138
Saxby, Lei, 163
Saxby, Li, 186
Saxby All Saints, Li, 179
Saxelby, Lei, 162
Saxham, Great, Sf, 291
Saxham, Little, Sf, 291
Saxilby, Li, 177
Saxlingham, Nf, 199
Saxlingham Nethergate, Nf, 196
Saxmundham, Sf, 294
Saxon, Ca, 28
Saxondale, Nt, 232
Saxtead, Sf, 288
Saxthorpe, Nf, 201
Saxton, YW, 386
Scackleton, YN, 381
Scaftworth, Nt, 228
Scagglethorpe, YE, 364
Scagglethorpe, YW, 385
Scalby, YE, 363
Scalby, YN, 357, 382
Scaldwell, Np, 212
Scaleby, Cu, 38
Scalford, Lei, 163
Scalthwaiterigg, We, 331
Scamblesby, Li, 182
Scampston, YE, 365
Scampton, Li, 178
Scarborough, YN, 356, 357, 382
Scarcliffe, Db, 48
Scarcroft, YW, 388
Scargill, YN, 373
Scarisbrick, La, 150
Scarle, North, Li, 175
Scarle, South, Nt, 233
Scarning, Nf, 208
Scarrington, Nt, 232
Scarsdale, wapentake, Db, 48
Scartho, Li, 181
Scawby, Li, 176
Scawsby, YW, 394
Scawton, YN, 376
Scofton, Nt, 233
Scole, Nf, 207
Scopwick, Li, 173
Scorborough, YE, 360, 363
Scoreby, YE, 364
Scorton, YN, 374
Scosthorp, YW, 383
Scotby, Cu, 41
Scotforth, La, 156
Scothern, Li, 178
Scotter, Li, 177
Scotterthorpe, Li, 177

Scottlethorpe, Li, 171
Scotton, Li, 177
Scotton, YN, 373
Scotton, YW, 395
Scottow, Nf, 202
Scoulton, Nf, 204
Scrafield, Li, 185
Scrafton, West, YN, 373
Scrainwood, Nb, 223
Scraptoft, Lei, 165
Scratby, Nf, 193
Scray, lathe, K, 142
Scrayingham, YE, 365
Scredington, Li, 172
Scremby, Li, 182
Screveton, Nt, 232
Scrivelsby, Li, 183
Scriven, YW, 395
Scrooby, Nt, 228
Scropton, Db, 46
Scruton, YN, 371
Sculcoates, YE, 361, 369
Sculthorp, Ru, 247
Sculthorpe, Nf, 199
Scunthorpe, Li, 186
Seaborough, Do, 67, 273
Seabridge, St, 277
Seacourt, Brk, 12
Seacroft, YW, 388
Seaford, Sx, 316
Seagrave, Lei, 163
Seagry, Wlt, 339
Seal, Db, 160
Seal, Nether, Db, 42, 157
Seal, Over, Db, 42, 157
Seamer [in Langbargh wap.], YN, 374
Seamer [in Pickering lib.], YN, 381
Searby, Li, 179
Seasalter, K, 147
Seaton [in Allerdale wap.], Cu, 39
Seaton [in Egremont lib.], Cu, 40
Seaton, Dev, 56
Seaton, Ru, 247
Seaton, YE, 369
Seaton Delaval, Nb, 223
Seaton, North, Nb, 222
Seaton Ross, YE, 361
Seavington Abbots, So, 275
Seavington St. Mary, So, 275
Seavington St. Michael, So, 275
Seawell, Np, 211 n.
Sebergham, Cu, 38 n., 40
Seckington, Wa, 325
Seckloe, hundred, Bk, 16
Sedbergh, YW, 384
Sedgebarrow, Wo, 351
Sedgebrook, Li, 171
Sedgeford, Nf, 198
Sedgewick, Sx, 310
Sedgley, St, 283

Sedlescombe, Sx, 317
Sedsall, Db, 45
Seend, Wlt, 338
Seething, Nf, 195
Sefton, La, 150
Segenhoe, Bd, 3
Seighford, St, 278
Seisdon, St, 283
Seisdon, hundred, St, 282
Selborne, Ha, 107
Selborne, hundred, Ha, 107
Selbrittenden, hundred, K, 143
Selby, YW, 387
Selham, Sx, 306
Selkley, hundred, Wlt, 339
Sellake, Dev, 56
Selsdon, Sr, 301
Selsey, Sx, 307
Selside, We, 330
Selston, Nt, 229
Semer, Sf, 291
Semington, Wlt, 339
Semley, Wlt, 343
Sempringham, Li, 170
Send, Sr, 299
Sennen, Co, 30
Serlby, Nt, 229
Sessay, YN, 379
Settle, YW, 383
Settrington, YE, 364
Sevenhampton, Gl, 98
Sevenhampton, Wlt, 343
Sewer, Dev, 51
Sewerby, YE, 366, 367
Sewstern, Lei, 163
Sexhow, YN, 375
Sezincote, Gl, 95
Shabbington, Bk, 20
Shackerstone, Lei, 159
Shadingfield, Sf, 289
Shadwell, YW, 388
Shaftesbury, Do, 67, 73
Shafthoe, Nb, 220
Shafton, YW, 392
Shalbourne, Wlt, 6, 10, 332, 348
Shalden, Ha, 113
Shalfleet, Ha, 120
Shalford, Ess, 80
Shalford, Sr, 298
Shallcross, Db, 47
Shalstone, Bk, 16
Shamwell, hundred, K, 145
Shangton, Lei, 165
Shanklin, Ha, 119
Shap, We, 329
Shapley, Dev, 59
Shapwick, Do, 77
Shapwick, So, 273
Shardlow, Db, 43
Shareshill, St, 281

Sharlston, YW, 390
Sharnbrook, Bd, 2
Sharnford, Lei, 159
Sharow, YW, 394
Sharpenhoe, Bd, 3
Sharperton, Nb, 223
Sharrington, Nf, 199
Shatton, Db, 47
Shaugh Prior, Dev, 51
Shaw, Brk, 9
Shaw [in Highworth hd.], Wlt, 343
Shaw [in Selkley hd.], Wlt, 339
Shawbury, Sa, 251
Shawdon, Nb, 223
Shawell, Lei, 158
Shearsby, Lei, 159
Shearston, So, 260
Shebbear, Dev, 66
Shebbear, hundred, Dev, 52
Shedfield, Ha, 118
Sheen, Sr, 298
Sheen, St, 281
Sheen, East, Sr, 302
Sheepbridge, Great, Brk, 346
Sheepbridge, Little, Brk, 346
Sheepwash, Dev, 52
Sheepy Magna, Lei, 160
Sheepy Parva, Lei, 159
Sheering, Ess, 89
Sheet, Ha, 114
Sheffield, Sx, 314
Sheffield, YW, 393
Sheffield Bottom, Brk, 8
Shefford, Bd, 4
Shefford, East, Brk, 9
Shefford, Great, Brk, 9
Shelderton, Sa, 254
Sheldon, Dev, 63
Sheldon, Wa, 325
Shelf, YW, 388
Shelfanger, Nf, 207
Shelfin, Dev, 63
Shelford, Nt, 232
Shelford, Wa, 324
Shelford, Great, Ca, 27
Shelford, Little, Ca, 27
Shelland, Sf, 287
Shelley, Ess, 83
Shelley, Sf, 285
Shelley, YW, 390
Shellingford, Brk, 11
Shellow Bowells, Ess, 82
Shellow Jocelyn, Ess, 82
Shelsley Beauchamp, Wo, 352
Shelsley Walsh, Wo, 352
Shelswell, Ox, 237
Shelton, Bd, 4
Shelton, Nf, 196
Shelton, Nt, 233
Shelton, Sa, 257

Shelton, St, 277
Shelton under Harley, St, 279
Shelve, Sa, 257
Shelwick, He, 124
Shenfield, Ess, 86
Shenington, Ox, 92, 235
Shenley, Bk, 17, 18
Shenley, Hrt, 135
Shenstone, St, 279
Shenton, Lei, 160
Shephall, Hrt, 134
Shepley, YW, 390
Shepperton, Mx, 190
Sheppey, bailey, K, 147
Shepreth, Ca, 26
Shepshed, Lei, 161
Shepton Beauchamp, So, 275
Shepton Mallet, So, 267
Shepton Montague, So, 269
Sherborne, Gl, 103
Sherborne, Wa, 326
Sherborne, hundred, Do, 70
Sherborne St. John, Ha, 118
Sherburn, YE, 364
Sherburn in Elmet, YW, 386
Shere, Sr, 298
Shereford, Nf, 198
Sherfield English, Ha, 106
Sherfield on Loddon, Ha, 113
Sherford, Dev, 64
Sheriff Hales, Sa, 249, 276, 282
Sheringham, Nf, 201
Sherington, Bk, 17
Shernbourne, Nf, 197
Sherrington, Wlt, 342
Sherston, Wlt, 344
Sherston Parva, Wlt, 344
Shevington, La, 155
Sheviock, Co, 35
Shide, Ha, 119
Shifford, Ox, 237
Shifnal, Sa, 256
Shilbottle, Nb, 223
Shillingford, Ox, 245
Shillingford Abbot, Dev, 59
Shillingford St. George, Dev, 59
Shillingstone, Do, 75
Shillington, Bd, 3
Shilstone, Dev, 58
Shilton, Ox, 6, 11, 235
Shilton, Wa, 324
Shilton, Earl, Lei, 159
Shilvinghampton, Do, 77
Shilvington, Nb, 221
Shimpling, Nf, 207
Shimpling, Sf, 290
Shinfield, Brk, 7
Shingay, Ca, 25
Shipden, Nf, 201
Shipdham, Nf, 205

Shipham, So, 259
Shiplake, Ox, 240
Shiplake, hundred, Sx, 313
Shipley, Db, 43
Shipley, Nb, 226
Shipley, Sa, 256
Shipley, YW, 388
Shipmeadow, Sf, 289
Shippon, Brk, 12
Shipston on Stour, Wa, 351
Shipton, Bk, 18
Shipton, Gl, 99
Shipton, Sa, 254
Shipton, YN, 380
Shipton Bellinger, Ha, 106
Shipton Gorge, Do, 70
Shipton Lee, Bk, 19
Shipton Moyne, Gl, 96
Shipton on Cherwell, Ox, 242, 242 n.
Shipton Thorpe, YE, 360
Shipton under Wychwood, Ox, 236
Shipway, lathe, K, 146
Shirburn, Ox, 238
Shirehampton, Gl, 102
Shirland, Db, 48
Shirley, Db, 45
Shirley, Ha, 110
Shirwell, Dev, 53
Shirwell, hundred, Dev, 53
Shitterton, Do, 69
Shobdon, He, 129
Shobrooke, Dev, 55
Shoby, Lei, 163
Shoebury, North, Ess, 81
Shoebury, South, Ess, 81
Shopland, Ess, 81
Shoreditch, Mx, 190
Shoreham, New, Sx, 305
Shoreham, Old, Sx, 310
Shoreston, Nb, 219, 225
Shorncote, Gl, 342
Shorthampton, Ox, 236
Shortridge, Dev, 54
Shortsfield, Sx, 310
Shorwell, North, Ha, 120
Shorwell, South, Ha, 119
Shotesham, Nf, 196
Shotley, Nb, 221
Shotley, Sf, 285
Shottery, Wa, 327
Shottesbrooke, Brk, 6
Shotteswell, Wa, 321
Shottisham, Sf, 295
Shotton [in Glendale ward], Nb, 225
Shotton [in 'Inter' ward], Nb, 222
Shouldham, Nf, 203
Shouldham Thorpe, Nf, 203
Shovelstrode, Sx, 315
Showell, Ox, 241
Showle, He, 125, 128

Showley Hall, La, 153 n.
Shoyswell, hundred, Sx, 317
Shrawardine, Sa, 251
Shrawley, Wo, 352
Shredicote, St, 282
Shrewley, Wa, 325
Shrewsbury, Sa, 249, 257
Shrewton, Wlt, 341
Shripney, Sx, 307
Shrivenham, Brk, 10
Shrivenham, hundred, Brk, 10
Shropham, Nf, 205
Shropham, hundred, Nf, 205
Shropshire, 249–57
Shuckburgh, Lower, Wa, 321
Shuckburgh, Upper, Wa, 322
Shurdington, Gl, 97
Shurdington, Little, Gl, 97
Shurton, So, 267
Shustoke, Wa, 325
Shute, Dev, 55
Shutford, Ox, 241
Shutlanger, Np, 211 n.
Sibbertoft, Np, 212
Sibdon Carwood, Sa, 253
Sibford, Ox, 243
Sibland, Gl, 101
Sibsey, Li, 185
Sibson, Lei, 159
Sibthorpe, Nt, 233
Sibton, Sf, 288
Sicey, YE, 370
Sicklinghall, YW, 384
Sidbury, Dev, 65
Sidbury, Sa, 256
Siddington, Gl, 99
Sidestrand, Nf, 201
Sidlesham, Sx, 307
Sigford, Dev, 58
Sigglesthorne, YE, 369
Signet, Ox, 237
Sigston, YN, 378
Silchester, Ha, 117
Sileby, Lei, 162
Silecroft, Cu, 40
Silkby, Li, 173
Silkstead, Ha, 108
Silkstone, YW, 391
Silpho, YN, 380
Silsden, YW, 382
Silsoe, Bd, 3
Silton, Do, 74
Silton, Nether, YN, 377
Silton, Over, YN, 377
Silverley, Ca, 27
Silverstone, Np, 211
Silverton, Dev, 63
Silvington, Sa, 253
Simonstone, La, 152
Simpson, Bk, 17

Sinderby, YN, 371
Sinfin, Db, 44
Singleborough, Bk, 19
Singleton, La, 151
Singleton, Sx, 306
Singleton, hundred, Sx, 306
Singleton, Little, La, 151
Sinnington, YN, 381
Siston, Gl, 101
Sithney, Co, 31
Sitlington, YW, 390
Sixhills, Li, 181
Sixpenny Handley, Do, 74
Sixpenny Handley, hundred, Do, 74
Sizewell, Sf, 289
Skeckling, YE, 358
Skeeby, YN, 373
Skeffington, Lei, 162
Skeffling, YE, 357
Skegby [near Mansfield], Nt, 234
Skegby [near Normanton on Trent], Nt, 231
Skegness, Li, 182
Skelbrooke, YW, 390
Skellingthorpe, Li, 175
Skellow, YW, 391
Skelmanthorpe, YW, 392
Skelmersdale, La, 150
Skelsmergh, We, 330
Skelthorpe, Lei, 162
Skelton, Cu, 37
Skelton, YE, 362
Skelton [in Langbargh wap.], YN, 375
Skelton [in Liberty of St. Peter], YN, 379
Skelton, YW, 394
Skendleby, Li, 182
Skerne, YE, 360
Skerraton, Dev, 51
Skerton, La, 155
Sketchley, Lei, 158
Skewsby, YN, 376
Skeyton, Nf, 201
Skibeden, YW, 383
Skidbrooke, Li, 183
Skidby, YE, 360
Skilgate, So, 266
Skillington, Li, 171
Skinnand, Li, 174
Skipsea, YE, 358
Skipton, YW, 382
Skipton on Swale, YN, 378
Skipwith, YE, 363
Skirbeck, Li, 169
Skirbeck, wapentake, Li, 169
Skircoat, YW, 388
Skirlaugh, North, YE, 358
Skirlaugh, South, YE, 358
Skirpenbeck, YE, 364, 367
Skirwith, Cu, 37
Skutterskelfe, YN, 374

Skyrack, wapentake, YW, 387
Slackstead, Ha, 112
Slaidburn, YW, 383
Slaithwaite, YW, 389
Slaley, Nb, 221
Slapton, Bk, 18
Slapton, Dev, 64
Slapton, Np, 211
Slaugham, Sx, 312
Slaughter, Lower, Gl, 103
Slaughter, Upper, Gl, 102
Slaughterford, Wlt, 344
Slawston, Lei, 164
Sleaford, New, Li, 173
Sleaford, Old, Li, 172
Sleagill, We, 330
Sleap, Sa, 251
Sleddale, We, 330
Sledmere, YE, 364
Sleights, YN, 380
Slepe, Hu, 137
Slimbridge, Gl, 96
Slindon, St, 278
Slindon, Sx, 307
Slinford, Sx, 309
Slingsby, YN, 377
Slipton, Np, 214
Sloley, Nf, 202
Sloothby, Li, 184
Slowley, Wa, 322
Slyne, La, 155
Smallbrook, Dev, 54
Smallbrook, Wlt, 347
Smallburgh, Nf, 202
Smalley, Db, 42
Smallridge, Dev, 57
Smardale, We, 329
Smeaton, YN, 380
Smeaton, Kirk, YW, 391
Smeaton, Little, YW, 391
Smeeton, Lei, 165
Smeeton Westerby, Lei, 165
Smerrill, Db, 44
Smethcott, Sa, 252
Smethden, hundred, Nf, 197
Smethwick, St, 279
Smisby, Db, 46
Smithcot, Wlt, 339
Smithfield, Mx, 190
Smithfield, East, Mx, 191
Snailwell, Ca, 24
Snainton, YN, 381
Snaith, YW, 391
Snap, Wlt, 339
Snape, Sf, 295
Snape, YN, 372
Snarehill, Nf, 205
Snarestone, Lei, 159
Snarford, Li, 178
Snead, Wo, 352

Sneaton, YN, 380
Sneedham's Green, Gl, 97
Sneinton, Nt, 231
Snelland, Li, 181
Snelson, Bk, 18
Snelston, Db, 45
Snelston, Ru, 247
Snetterton, Nf, 205
Snettisham, Nf, 197
Snibston, Lei, 160
Snitter, Nb, 224
Snitterby, Li, 176, 186
Snitterfield, Wa, 326
Snitterton, Db, 45
Snittlegarth, Cu, 39
Snitton, Sa, 256
Snoddington, Ha, 106
Snodhill, He, 128
Snoring, Great, Nf, 200
Snoring, Little, Nf, 199
Snowshill, Gl, 98
Snydale, YW, 390
Soberton, Ha, 113
Sock Dennis, So, 274
Sodbury, Little, Gl, 102
Sodbury, Old, Gl, 102
Sodington, Wo, 352
Soham, Ca, 24
Soham, Earl, Sf, 295
Soham, Monk, Sf, 288
Sokmalherbe, So, 262 n.
Solberge, YN, 374
Solihull, Wa, 325
Solport, Cu, 39
Somborne, King's, Ha, 107
Somborne, King's, hundred, Ha, 107
Somborne, Little, Ha, 107, 108
Somborne, Upper, Ha, 107
Somerby, Lei, 163
Somerby [near Brigg], Li, 178
Somerby [near Gainsborough], Li, 186
Somerby, Old, Li, 172
Somercotes, Li, 183
Somerden, hundred, K, 146
Somerford, St, 282
Somerford, Great, Wlt, 340
Somerford Keynes, Gl, 342
Somerford, Little, Wlt, 340
Somerleyton, Sf, 290
Somersal Herbert, Db, 45
Somersby, Li, 185
Somerset, 258–75
Somersham, Hu, 137
Somersham, Sf, 285
Somershill, Ha, 118
Somerton, Li, 174
Somerton, Ox, 237
Somerton, Sf, 290
Somerton, So, 273
Somerton, East, Nf, 193

Somerton Erleigh, So, 263
Somerton Foreign, hundred, So, 263
Somerton, West, Nf, 193
Sompting, Sx, 310
Sond, Sx, 309
Sonning, Brk, 7
Sonning, hundred, Brk, 7
Soothill, YW, 389
Sopley, Ha, 107
Sopworth, Wlt, 344
Sotby, Li, 181
Sotherington, Ha, 107
Sotherton, Sf, 289
Sotterley, Sf, 289
Sotwell, Brk, 13
Soulbury, Bk, 18
Soulby, Cu, 37
Soulby, We, 329
Souldern, Ox, 237
Soulton, Sa, 250
Sourton, Dev, 60
Southall, Mx, 190
Southam, Gl, 93
Southam, Wa, 322
Southampton, Ha, 105, 121
Southburgh, Nf, 204
Southburn, YE, 360
Southchurch, Ess, 81
Southcote, Brk, 8
Southcott, Dev, 54
Southease, Sx, 311
Southery, Nf, 203
Southill, Bd, 3
Southington, Ha, 112
Southleigh, Dev, 56
Southminster, Ess, 84
Southoe [Lovetot], Hu, 137
Southoe [Winchester], Hu, 137
Southolt, Sf, 288
Southorpe [in Beltisloe wap.], Li, 170
Southorpe [in Corringham wap.], Li, 177
Southorpe, YE, 366
Southover, Sx, 313
Southover, half-hundred, Sx, 313
Southowram, YW, 389
Southrepps, Nf, 201
Southrop, Gl, 100
Southrop, Ox, 236
Southstoke, So, 261
Southtown, Nf, 290
Southwark, Sr, 297, 298
Southweald, Ess, 87
Southwell, Nt, 231
Southwick, Gl, 93
Southwick, Ha, 110
Southwick, Np, 213
Southwick, Sx, 311
Southwick, Wlt, 339
Southwold, Sf, 289
Southwood, Ha, 109

Southwood, Nf, 194
Southwood, Sx, 305
Southwood Manor, Db, 43
Southworth, La, 150
Sowerby, La, 152
Sowerby, YN, 378
Sowerby, YW, 389
Sowerby, Castle, Cu, 41
Sowerby, Temple, We, 329
Sowerby under Cotcliffe, YN, 379
Sowton, Dev, 58
Spalding, Li, 168
Spaldington, YE, 360
Spaldwick, Hu, 138
Spalford, Nt, 233
Spanby, Li, 170
Sparham [in Eynesford hd.], Nf, 200
Sparham [in South Greenhoe hd.], Nf, 203
Sparket, Cu, 37
Sparkford, Ha, 108
Sparkford, So, 259
Sparkwell, Dev, 50
Sparsholt, Brk, 11
Sparsholt, Ha, 108
Spaunton, YN, 380
Spaxton, So, 267
Speen, Brk, 9
Speenhamland, Brk, 9
Speeton, YE, 366
Speke, La, 150
Spelhoe, hundred, Np, 217
Spelsbury, Ox, 236
Spelthorne, hundred, Mx, 189
Spencers, Brk, 7 n.
Spennithorne, YN, 372
Spernall, Wa, 326
Spetchley, Wo, 351
Spexhall, Sf, 289
Spilsby, Li, 185
Spindlestone, Nb, 225
Spital in the Street, Li, 176
Spitchwick, Dev, 50
Spittlegate, Li, 171
Spixworth, Nf, 194
Spofforth, YW, 384
Spondon, Db, 43
Sporle, Nf, 203
Spotland, La, 154
Spratton, Np, 217
Spreyton, Dev, 58
Spriddlestone, Dev, 51
Spridlington, Li, 176
Springfield, Ess, 85
Springthorpe, Li, 186
Sproatley, YE, 359
Sprotborough, YW, 393
Sproughton, Sf, 285
Sprowston, Nf, 194
Sproxton, Lei, 164
Sproxton, YN, 377

Spursholt, Ha, 107
Stadbury, Dev, 64
Staddiscombe, Dev, 51
Stadhampton, Ox, 243
Stafford, St, 276, 277
Stafford, East, Do, 73
Stafford, West, Do, 73
Staffordshire, 276–83
Stagenhoe, Hrt, 133
Stagsden, Bd, 2
Stain, Li, 184
Stainborough, YW, 392
Stainburn, YW, 384
Stainby, Li, 171
Staincliffe, wapentake, YW, 382
Staincross, wapentake, YW, 391
Staine, hundred, Ca, 24
Staines, Mx, 189
Stainfield [in Aveland wap.], Li, 170
Stainfield [in Wraggoe wap.], Li, 181
Stainforth [in Staincliffe wap.], YW, 383
Stainforth [in Strafforth wap.], YW, 393
Stainland, YW, 388
Stainley, North, YW, 394
Stainley, South, YW, 395
Stainsacre, YN, 380
Stainsby, Db, 48
Stainsby, Li, 185
Stainton [in Cumberland wap.], Cu, 37
Stainton [in Leath wap.], Cu, 37
Stainton, Li, 176, 186
Stainton, We, 330
Stainton [in Hang wap.], YN, 372
Stainton [in Langbargh wap.], YN, 375
Stainton, YW, 394
Stainton by Langworth, Li, 181
Stainton le Vale, Li, 178
Stainton, Market, Li, 182
Stalbridge, Do, 74
Stalbridge Weston, Do, 74
Stalham, Nf, 193
Stallingborough, Li, 179
Stallington, St, 278
Stalmine, La, 151
Stambourne, Ess, 80
Stambridge, Great, Ess, 81
Stambridge, Little, Ess, 81
Stamford, Li, 167, 169
Stamford, Nb, 226
Stamford Baron, Li, 169
Stamford Bridge, YE, 361, 364
Stamfordham, Nb, 220
Stanborough, hundred, Dev, 51
Stanbridge, Bd, 4
Stanbridge, Ha, 107
Stancil, YW, 394
Standen, Wlt, 348
Standen, East, Ha, 119
Standen, North, Brk, 10 n., 348
Standen, West, Ha, 119

Standerwick, So, 268
Standhill, Ox, 238
Standish, La, 155
Standlake, Ox, 237
Standlynch, Wlt, 335
Standon, Hrt, 132
Standon, St, 278
Stanfield, Nf, 207
Stanford, Bd, 3
Stanford, He, 123
Stanford, Nf, 204
Stanford Bishop, He, 124
Stanford Dingley, Brk, 8
Stanford in the Vale, Brk, 11
Stanford le Hope, Ess, 86
Stanford on Avon, Np, 216
Stanford on Soar, Nt, 230
Stanford on Teme, Wo, 352
Stanford Regis, He, 123
Stanford Rivers, Ess, 83
Stanground, Hu, 138
Stanhoe, Nf, 197
Stanion, Np, 215
Stanley, Db, 43
Stanley, Wlt, 344
Stanley, YW, 390
Stanley, King's, Gl, 103
Stanley, Leonard, Gl, 103
Stanley Pontlarge, Gl, 98
Stanmore, Mx, 191
Stanmore, Little, Mx, 191
Stannarde, So, 262 n.
Stanningfield, Sf, 292
Stannington, Nb, 222
Stansfield, Sf, 294
Stansfield, YW, 389
Stanshope, St, 281
Stanstead, Sf, 291
Stanstead Abbots, Hrt, 132
Stansted Mountfitchet, Ess, 86
Stanswood, Ha, 111
Stanton, Db, 46
Stanton, Gl, 98
Stanton, Nb, 222
Stanton, Sa, 256
Stanton, Sf, 292
Stanton by Bridge, Db, 46
Stanton by Dale, Db, 42
Stanton Drew, So, 270
Stanton Fitzwarren, Wlt, 343
Stanton Harcourt, Ox, 242
Stanton Lacy, Sa, 254
Stanton Long, Sa, 255
Stanton on the Wolds, Nt, 230
Stanton Prior, So, 270
Stanton St. Bernard, Wlt, 335
Stanton St. John, Ox, 239
Stanton St. Quintin, Wlt, 340
Stanton, Stoney, Lei, 158
Stanton under Bardon, Lei, 159

Stanton upon Hine Heath, Sa, 250
Stantonbury, Bk, 17
Stanwardine in the Fields, Sa, 252
Stanwardine in the Wood, Sa, 251
Stanway, Ess, 88
Stanway, Gl, 92
Stanwell, Mx, 189
Stanwick, Np, 212
Stanwick, YN, 373
Stanwix, Cu, 41
Stapenhill, St, 46, 276
Staple Fitzpaine, So, 266
Staple, hundred, Sx, 317
Staple, hundred, Wlt, 333
Stapleford, Ca, 27
Stapleford, Do, 72
Stapleford, Hrt, 131
Stapleford, Lei, 163
Stapleford, Li, 175
Stapleford, Nt, 230
Stapleford, Wlt, 342
Stapleford, Abbotts, Ess, 83
Stapleford Tawney, Ess, 83
Staplegrove, So, 264
Staplehill, Dev, 59
Stapleton, Cu, 38
Stapleton, Gl, 91
Stapleton, Lei, 159
Stapleton, Sa, 252
Stapleton, So, 274
Stapleton, YN, 374
Stapleton, YW, 391
Staploe, hundred, Ca, 24
Starston, Nf, 207
Startforth, YN, 373
Startley, hundred, Wlt, 339
Statfold, St, 280
Stathe, So, 264
Stathern, Lei, 163
Staughton, Great, Hu, 137
Staunton [in St. Briavels hd.], Gl, 103
Staunton [in Pershore hd.], Gl, 254
Staunton Harold, Lei, 161
Staunton in the Vale, Nt, 233
Staunton on Arrow, He, 129
Staunton on Wye, He, 124
Staveley, Db, 48
Staveley, YW, 395
Staveley, Nether, We, 330
Staveley, Over, We, 330
Staverton, Dev, 50
Staverton, Gl, 100
Staverton, Np, 215
Staverton, Wlt, 338
Stawell, So, 274
Stawley, So, 260
Staxton, YE, 366
Staynall, La, 151
Staynesby, YN, 376
Staythorpe, Nt, 231

Steane, Np, 210
Stearsby, YN, 376
Steart, So, 260
Stebbing, Ess, 80
Stedham, Sx, 306
Steep, Ha, 111
Steeping, Great, Li, 182
Steeping, Little, Li, 185
Steeple, Ess, 84
Steepleton Iwerne, Do, 76
Steeton [in Ainsty wap.], YW, 385
Steeton [in Staincliffe wap.], YW, 383
Stenbury, Ha, 119
Stenigot, Li, 182
Stenson, Db, 44
Stenwith, Li, 171
Stepney, Mx, 191
Steppingley, Bd, 3
Sternfield, Sf, 294
Stert, Wlt, 336
Steven, Sf, 289
Stevenage, Hrt, 133
Stevenstone, Dev, 59
Steventon, Brk, 13
Steventon, Ha, 118
Steventon, Sa, 255
Stevington, Bd, 2
Stewkley, Bk, 18
Stewley, So, 266
Stewton, Li, 183
Steyning, Sx, 305
Steyning, hundred, Sx, 309
Stibbard, Nf, 199
Stickford, Li, 185
Stickney, Li, 185
Stiffkey, Nf, 200
Stifford, Ess, 87
Stildon, Wo, 352
Stillingfleet, YE, 364
Stillington, YN, 379
Stilton, Hu, 138
Stinsford, Do, 68
Stirchley, Sa, 251
Stirton, YW, 382
Stisted, Ess, 80
Stitchcombe, Wlt, 339
Stithians, Co, 30
Stittenham, YN, 376
Stivichall, Wa, 322
Stixwold, Li, 182
Stock, Ha, 113
Stock Green, Wo, 351
Stock Street, Wlt, 337
Stockbridge, Ha, 111
Stockeld, YW, 380
Stockerston, Lei, 165
Stocking, Li, 174
Stockland, Dev, 49, 67, 73
Stockland Bristol, So, 267
Stockleigh English, Dev, 55

Stockleigh Pomeroy, Dev, 55
Stockleigh, South, Dev, 55 n.
Stockley, Wlt, 337
Stocklinch, So, 266
Stocklow, He, 129
Stocks, Hrt, 134
Stockton, He, 130
Stockton, Nf, 195
Stockton, Sa, 257
Stockton, Wa, 322
Stockton, Wlt, 340
Stockton on Teme, Wo, 352
Stockton on the Forest, YN, 376
Stockwell, Gl, 92
Stockwell, Sr, 302
Stockwith, East, Li, 186
Stockwith, West, Nt, 227
Stodden, hundred, Bd, 4
Stodfold, hundred, Bk, 16
Stodleghe, Ess, 84
Stody, Nf, 199
Stoford, So, 263
Stoford, Wlt, 342
Stogumber, So, 266
Stogursey, So, 272
Stoke, Dev, 61
Stoke [in Bosmere hd.], Ha, 116
Stoke [in Evingar hd.], Ha, 109
Stoke, Sr, 300
Stoke, Wa, 323
Stoke, Wlt, 336
Stoke Abbot, Do, 71
Stoke Abbot, So, 267
Stoke Albany, Np, 214
Stoke Ash, Sf, 287
Stoke Bardolph, Nt, 231
Stoke Bishop, Gl, 102
Stoke Bliss, Wo, 122, 123
Stoke Bruerne, Np, 211
Stoke by Clare, Sf, 294
Stoke by Nayland, Sf, 290
Stoke Canon, Dev, 58
Stoke Charity, Ha, 108
Stoke Climsland, Co, 34
Stoke D'Abernon, Sr, 301
Stoke Damarel, Dev, 52
Stoke Doyle, Np, 214
Stoke Dry, Ru, 248
Stoke, East, Nt, 233
Stoke, East, So, 274
Stoke Edith, He, 128
Stoke Farthing, Wlt, 342
Stoke Ferry, Nf, 203
Stoke Fleming, Dev, 64
Stoke Gaylard, Do, 74
Stoke Gifford, Gl, 102
Stoke Golding, Lei, 159
Stoke Goldington, Bk, 18
Stoke Hammond, Bk, 17
Stoke Holy Cross, Nf, 196

Stoke, hundred, Bk, 21
Stoke Lacy, He, 123
Stoke Lyne, Ox, 238
Stoke Mandeville, Bk, 20
Stoke Newington, Mx, 190
Stoke, North, Ox, 243
Stoke, North, So, 261
Stoke, North, Sx, 309
Stoke Orchard, Gl, 93
Stoke Poges, Bk, 21
Stoke Prior, He, 130
Stoke Prior, Wo, 350
Stoke Rivers, Dev, 53
Stoke Rochford, Li, 172
Stoke, Rodney, So, 259
Stoke St. Mary, So, 264
Stoke St. Milborough, Sa, 254
Stoke, Severn, Wo, 354
Stoke, South, Li, 172
Stoke, South, Ox, 243
Stoke, South, Sx, 308
Stoke sub Hamdon, So, 274
Stoke Talmage, Ox, 238
Stoke upon Tern, Sa, 250
Stoke Wake, Do, 70
Stoke, West, Sx, 306
Stokeham, Nt, 228
Stokeinteignhead, Dev, 57
Stokelegh Locombe, Dev, 55 n.
Stokenchurch, Bk, 15, 235, 240
Stokenham, Dev, 64
Stokesay, Sa, 254
Stokesby, Nf, 193
Stokesley, YN, 374
Stokke, Wlt, 347
Stoklegh' Letcomb, Dev, 55
Stoklinche, So, 266 n.
Ston Easton, So, 261
Stondon Massey, Ess, 83
Stone, Bk, 20
Stone, Ha, 115
Stone, So, 263
Stone, St, 278
Stone, Wo, 353
Stone, hundred, Bk, 20
Stone, hundred, So, 262
Stonegrave, YN, 377
Stonehall, Wo, 350 n.
Stoneham Aspal, Sf, 286
Stoneham, South, Ha, 110
Stonehouse, Gl, 103
Stoneleigh, Wa, 320
Stoneleigh, leet, Wa, 322
Stonesby, Lei, 164
Stonesfield, Ox, 245
Stoneton, Wa, 209, 210
Stoney Thorpe, Wa, 322
Stonham, Earl, Sf, 286
Stonham, Little, Sf, 286
Stonton Wyville, Lei, 164

Stoodleigh [in Braunton hd.], Dev, 63
Stoodleigh [in Witheridge hd.], Dev, 54
Stopham, Sx, 308
Stormsworth, Lei, 158
Storrington, Sx, 308
Stortford, Bishop's, Hrt, 131, 132
Storwood, YE, 361
Stotfold, Bd, 4
Stotfold, YW, 394
Stottesdon, Sa, 255
Stottesdon, hundred, Sa, 255
Stoughton, Lei, 164
Stoughton, Sx, 306
Stoupe Brow, YN, 380
Stour, East, Do, 74
Stour Provost, Do, 74
Stour, West, Do, 74
Stourpaine, Do, 76
Stourton, Wa, 321
Stourton, Wlt, 334
Stow, Bk, 16
Stow [in Aveland wap.], Li, 170
Stow [in Well wap.], Li, 178
Stow, Sa, 253
Stow Bardolph, Nf, 203
Stow Bedon, Nf, 204
Stow cum Quy, Ca, 24
Stow, hundred, Sf, 287
Stow Longa, Hu, 138 n.
Stow Maries, Ess, 84
Stow on the Wold, Gl, 103
Stow Park, Li, 178
Stow, West, Sf, 293
Stowe, Li, 169
Stowe, Church, Np, 216
Stowell, Gl, 99
Stowell, So, 269
Stowell [in Elstub hd.], Wlt, 340
Stowell [in Swanborough hd.], Wlt, 335 n.
Stowey [in Bulstone hd.], So, 272
Stowey [in Chew hd.], So, 267
Stowey, Nether, So, 272
Stowford [in Lifton hd.], Dev, 60
Stowford [in South Molton hd.], Dev, 54
Stowick, Gl, 102
Stowlangtoft, Sf, 293
Stowmarket, Sf, 288
Stowting, hundred, K, 147
Stradbroke, Sf, 288
Stradishall, Sf, 294
Stradsett, Nf, 203
Strafforth, wapentake, YW, 392
Stragglethorpe, Li, 174
Stratfield Mortimer, Brk, 6, 8, 105, 117
Stratfield Saye, Ha, 6, 8, 105, 117
Stratfield Turgis, Ha, 117
Stratford, Old, Wa, 327
Stratford St. Andrew, Sf, 294
Stratford St. Mary, Sf, 285
Stratford, Stony, Bk, 17

Stratford sub Castle, Wlt, 336
Stratford Tony, Wlt, 334
Stratford upon Avon, Wa, 319, 320
Stratford, Water, Bk, 16
Stratton, Bd, 2
Stratton, Co, 33
Stratton, Do, 68
Stratton, Gl, 100
Stratton, Nf, 196
Stratton, Sf, 296
Stratton, East, Ha, 112
Stratton, hundred, Co, 33
Stratton on the Fosse, So, 262
Stratton, Over, So, 275
Stratton St. Margaret, Wlt, 343
Stratton Strawless, Nf, 201
Stratton, Upper, Wlt, 343
Stratton, West, Ha, 112
Streat, Sx, 313
Streat, hundred, Sx, 313
Streatham, Sr, 302
Streatley, Bd, 3
Streatley, Brk, 13
Street, Ha, 107
Street, He, 129
Street [in South Petherton hd.], So, 275
Street [in Whitley hd.], So, 274
Street, hundred, K, 147
Streethay, St, 280
Streetly End, Ca, 27
Strelley, Nt, 230
Strensall, YN, 379
Strensham, Wo, 353
Stretcholt, So, 260
Stretchworth, Ca, 27
Strete Raleigh, Dev, 65
Stretford, He, 129
Stretford, La, 154
Stretford, hundred, He, 129
Stretforde, Do, 69
Strethall, Ess, 86
Stretham, Ca, 28
Strettington, Sx, 307
Stretton, Db, 48
Stretton, Ru, 247
Stretton [in Cuttlestone hd.], St, 282
Stretton [in Offlow hd.], St, 280
Stretton Baskerville, Wa, 324
Stretton, Church, Sa, 249, 257
Stretton en le Field, Lei, 46
Stretton Grandison, He, 128
Stretton, Great, Lei, 165
Stretton, Little, Lei, 164
Stretton on Dunsmore, Wa, 322
Stretton on Fosse, Wa, 320
Stretton Sugwas, He, 124
Strickland, Great, We, 329
Strickland Ketel, We, 330
Strickland, Little, We, 329
Strickland Randolph, We, 330

Stringston, So, 267
Strixton, Np, 212, 212 n.
Stroud, Brk, 12
Stroxton, Li, 171
Strubby [in Calcewath wap.], Li, 184
Strubby [in Wraggoe wap.], Li, 181 n.
Strumpshaw, Nf, 194
Stubbington, Ha, 110
Stubbs, YW, 393
Stubhill, Cu, 38
Stubton, Li, 174
Stuchbury, Np, 210
Studfold, hundred, Wlt, 336
Studham, Bd, 4
Studland, Do, 75
Studley, Ox, 239
Studley, Wa, 326
Studley [in Calne hd.], Wlt, 337
Studley [in Melksham hd.], Wlt, 338
Studley Royal, YW, 394
Stukeley, Great, Hu, 137
Stukeley, Little, Hu, 137
Stuntney, Ca, 28 n.
Sturmer, Ess, 80
Sturminster Marshall, Do, 69
Sturminster Newton, hundred, Do, 74
Sturston, Nf, 204
Sturthill, Do, 70
Sturton, Li, 176
Sturton by Stow, Li, 178
Sturton, Great, Li, 182
Sturton le Steeple, Nt, 228
Stuston, Sf, 287
Stutton, Sf, 285
Stutton, YW, 386
Styford, Nb, 221
Styrrup, Nt, 228
Suckley, Wo, 352
Sudborough, Np, 214
Sudbourne, Sf, 294
Sudbrook, Li, 174
Sudbrooke, Li, 177
Sudbury, Db, 45
Sudbury, Sf, 79, 80, 284, 291
Suddon', Sf, 287
Sudeley, Gl, 98
Suffield, Nf, 201
Suffield, YN, 380
Suffolk, 284–96
Sugdon, Sa, 250
Sugnall, St, 278
Sulby, Np, 212
Sulgrave, Np, 210
Sulham, Brk, 8
Sulhamstead Abbots, Brk, 7
Sulhamstead Bannister, Brk, 8
Sullington, Sx, 310
Summerfield, Nf, 197
Sunbury, Mx, 189
Sunderland, North, Nb, 219, 225

Sunderlandwick, YE, 361, 370
Sundon, Bd, 3
Sunninghill, Brk, 14
Sunningwell, Brk, 12
Surfleet, Li, 168
Surlingham, Nf, 196
Surrendell, Wlt, 344
Surrey, 297–303
Sussex, 304–18
Sustead, Nf, 201
Sutcombe, Dev, 61
Sutterby, Li, 182
Sutterton, Li, 168
Sutton, Bd, 1
Sutton, Ca, 28
Sutton, Ess, 81
Sutton, La, 150
Sutton, Li, 174
Sutton, Mx, 190
Sutton, Nf, 193
Sutton [in Bassetlaw wap.], Nt, 229
Sutton [in Bingham wap.], Nt, 232
Sutton, Ox, 242
Sutton, Sa, 257
Sutton, Sf, 295
Sutton, Sr, 300
Sutton [in Flexborough hd.], Sx, 314
Sutton [in Rotherbridge hd.], Sx, 308
Sutton [in Barkston Ash wap.], YW, 386
Sutton [in Staincliffe wap.], YW, 383
Sutton Bassett, Np, 215
Sutton Benger, Wlt, 337
Sutton Bingham, So, 270
Sutton, Bishop, So, 267
Sutton, Bishop's, Ha, 110
Sutton, Bishop's, hundred, Ha, 110
Sutton Bonnington, Nt, 230
Sutton Cheney, Lei, 160
Sutton Coldfield, Wa, 325
Sutton Courtenay, Brk, 13
Sutton, Full, YE, 361
Sutton, Great, Wlt, 346
Sutton Howgrave, YN, 371
Sutton, hundred, Brk, 13
Sutton in Ashfield, Nt, 234
Sutton in the Elms, Lei, 158
Sutton, King's, Np, 210
Sutton, King's, hundred, Np, 210
Sutton, lathe, K, 145
Sutton le Marsh, Li, 183
Sutton, Little, Sa, 254
Sutton, Little, Wlt, 347
Sutton, Long, Ha, 109
Sutton, Long, So, 263
Sutton Maddock, Sa, 254
Sutton Mallet, So, 274
Sutton Mandeville, Wlt, 335
Sutton on Hull, YE, 357, 368
Sutton on the Forest, YN, 376
Sutton on the Hill, Db, 45

Sutton on Trent, Nt, 231
Sutton Passeys, Nt, 229
Sutton Poyntz, Do, 72
Sutton Sachevill', Dev, 55
Sutton Sacheville, Dev, 55 n.
Sutton St. James, Li, 168
Sutton St. Nicholas, He, 124
Sutton Scarsdale, Db, 48
Sutton Scotney, Ha, 115
Sutton under Brailes, Wa, 99
Sutton under Whitestonecliffe, YN, 381
Sutton upon Derwent, YE, 361
Sutton Vautort, Dev, 52, 66
Sutton Veny, Wlt, 346
Sutton Waldron, Do, 73
Sutton Wick, Brk 13
Swaby, Li, 184
Swadlincote, Db, 46
Swaffham, Nf, 204
Swaffham Bulbeck, Ca, 24
Swaffham Prior, Ca, 24
Swafield, Nf, 202
Swainby, YN, 371
Swainsthorpe, Nf, 206
Swainston, Ha, 120
Swainswick, So, 261
Swalcliffe, Ox, 241
Swallow, Li, 180
Swallowcliffe, Wlt, 338
Swallowfield, Brk, 7
Swampton, Ha, 109
Swanage, Do, 75
Swanborough, hundred, Sx, 311
Swanborough, hundred, Wlt, 335
Swanbourne, Bk, 19
Swanland, YE, 361
Swanmore, Ha, 118
Swannington, Lei, 161
Swannington, Nf, 200
Swanstone, He, 129
Swanthorpe, Ha, 109
Swanton Abbot, Nf, 202
Swanton Morley, Nf, 207
Swanton Novers, Nf, 199
Swanwick, Ha, 110
Swarby, Li, 172
Swardeston, Nf, 206
Swarkestone, Db, 43
Swarland, Nb, 223
Swarraton, Ha, 112, 113
Swaton, Li, 170
Swavesey, Ca, 25
Sway, Ha, 106
Swayfield, Li, 171
Swaythorpe, YE, 365
Swefling, Sf, 295
Swell, So, 272
Swell, Lower, Gl, 102
Swell, Upper, Gl, 95
Swepstone, Lei, 161

Swerford, Ox, 236
Swilland, Sf, 286
Swillington, YW, 387
Swinbrook, Ox, 236
Swinburn, Great, Nb, 221
Swinburn, Little, Nb, 220
Swinden, YW, 382
Swinderby, Li, 175
Swindon, Gl, 104
Swindon, Wlt, 343
Swindon, High, Wlt, 341
Swindon, West, Wlt, 341
Swine, YE, 359
Swineshead, Li, 168
Swinethorpe, Li, 175
Swinford, Brk, 12
Swinford, Lei, 159
Swinford, Old, Wo, 353
Swinhoe, Nb, 226
Swinhope, Li, 180
Swinstead, Li, 171
Swinton [in Hang wap.], YN, 372
Swinton [in Ryedale wap.], YN, 377
Swinton, YW, 394
Swithland, Lei, 161
Swyncombe, Ox, 240
Swynnerton, St, 278
Swyre, Do, 77
Syde, Gl, 92
Sydenham, Ox, 240 n.
Sydenham Damarel, Dev, 60
Syderstone, Nf, 198
Sydling, Fifehead, Do, 70
Sydling St. Nicholas, Do, 70
Sydling, Up, Do, 70
Sydmonton, Ha, 115
Syerscote, St, 280
Syerston, Nt, 233
Syleham, Sf, 288
Symondsbury, Do, 73
Syndercombe, So, 266
Syrencot, Wlt, 345
Syresham, Np, 210
Sysonby, Lei, 163
Syston, Lei, 161
Syston, Li, 172
Sywell, Np, 217

Tachbrook, Bishop's, Wa, 320
Tachbrook Mallory, Wa, 320
Tackley, Ox, 242
Tacolneston, Nf, 196
Tadcaster, YW, 386
Taddington, Db, 47
Taddington, Gl, 92
Tadley, Ha, 112
Tadlow, Ca, 25
Tadmarton, Ox, 343
Tadworth, Sr, 302
Takeley, Ess, 86

Talaton, Dev, 63
Talland, Co, 34
Tallington, Li, 169
Talton, Wa, 351
Tamerton Foliot, Dev, 52
Tamerton, Kings, Dev, 52
Tamerton, North, Co, 33
Tamhorn, St, 279
Tamworth, St, 276, 277, 319, 320
Tandridge, Sr, 303
Tandridge, hundred, Sr, 303
Tanfield, East, YN, 371
Tanfield, West, YN, 371
Tangley, Ha, 112
Tangmere, Sx, 307
Tankersley, YW, 392
Tannington, Sf, 288
Tansley, Db, 44
Tansor, Np, 213
Tanworth, Wa, 320
Tapeley, Dev, 53
Taplow, Bk, 21
Tarbock, La, 150
Tardebigge, Wo, 326, 352
Tarleton, La, 155
Tarlton, Gl, 100 n.
Tarnock, So, 262
Tarrant Crawford, Do, 69
Tarrant Gunville, Do, 75
Tarrant Hinton, Do, 76
Tarrant Keyneston, Do, 76
Tarrant Launceston, Do, 76
Tarrant Monkton, Do, 75
Tarrant Rawston, Do, 76
Tarrant Rushton, Do, 75
Tarrington, He, 128
Tasburgh, Nf, 196
Tasley, Sa, 255
Taston, Ox, 236
Tatchbury, Ha, 115
Tatham, La, 155
Tathwell, Li, 183
Tatsfield, Sr, 303
Tattenhoe, Bk, 18
Tatterford, Nf, 198
Tattersett, Nf, 199
Tattershall, Li, 182
Tattingstone, Sf, 285
Taunton, So, 263
Taunton, hundred, So, 264
Taverham, Nf, 194
Taverham, hundred, Nf, 194
Tavistock, Dev, 61, 66
Tavistock, hundred, Dev, 61
Tawstock, Dev, 53
Tawton, Bishop's, Dev, 53
Tawton, North, Dev, 62
Tawton, North, hundred, Dev, 61
Tawton, South, Dev, 66
Taynton, Gl, 95

Taynton, Ox, 236
Taynton, Little, Gl, 95
Tealby, Li, 179
Tean, St, 280
Tebay, We, 329
Tedburn St. Mary, Dev, 58
Teddington, Gl, 350
Teddington, Mx, 189
Tedstone Delamere, He, 124
Tedstone Wafer, He, 123
Teffont Evias, Wlt, 338
Teffont Magna, Wlt, 347
Teigh, Ru, 247
Teignbridge, hundred, Dev, 59
Teigncombe, Dev, 66
Teigngrace, Dev, 59
Teignharvey, Dev, 58
Teignmouth, Dev, 59
Teignmouth [East], Dev, 59
Telham, Sx, 316
Tellisford, So, 268
Temple, Co, 33
Temple, Lei, 159
Temple, The, Lei, 162
Templeton, Brk, 10
Tempsford, Bd, 2
Tenbury, Wo, 352
Tendring, Ess, 88
Tendring, hundred, Ess, 88
Tenterden, hundred, K, 143
Tercrosset, Cu, 38
Terling, Ess, 84
Tern, Sa, 250
Terrington, Nf, 197
Terrington, YN, 376
Testerton, Nf, 198
Testwood, Ha, 115
Tetbury, Gl, 96
Tetbury Upton, Gl, 96
Tetchwick, Bk, 19
Tetcott, Dev, 60
Tetford, Li, 185
Tetley, Li, 175 n.
Tetney, Li, 181
Tetsworth, Ox, 243
Tettenhall, St, 277, 283
Teversal, Nt, 229
Teversham, Ca, 24
Tew, Duns, Ox, 241
Tew, Great, Ox, 242
Tew, Little, Ox, 241
Tewin, Hrt, 131
Tewington, Co, 31
Tewkesbury, Gl, 92
Tewkesbury, hundred, Gl, 92
Tey, Great, Ess, 88
Tey, Marks, Ess, 88
Teynham, hundred, K, 142
Thakeham, Sx, 310
Thame, hundred, Ox, 243

Thame, New, Ox, 243
Thame, Old, Ox, 244
Tharlesthorpe, YE, 359
Tharston, Nf, 196
Thatcham, Brk, 6, 14
Thaxted, Ess, 82
Theakston, YN, 371
Thealby, Li, 175
Theale, hundred, Brk, 7
Thearne, YE, 370
Thedden, Ha, 120
Theddingworth, Lei, 164
Theddlethorpe, Li, 184
Thedwardistre, hundred, Sf, 292
Thelbridge, Dev, 54
Thelnetham, Sf, 293
Thelveton, Nf, 207
Themelthorpe, Nf, 200
Thenford, Np, 210
Therfield, Hrt, 132
Thetford, Nf, 192, 205
Thetford, Little, Ca, 28
Theydon Bois, Ess, 82
Theydon Garnon, Ess, 83
Theydon Mount, Ess, 82
Thickbroom, St, 280
Thimbleby, Li, 182
Thimbleby, YN, 378
Thing-Hill, He, 124
Thing-Hill Court, He, 124
Thingoe, hundred, Sf, 291
Thirkleby, YE, 364
Thirkleby, YN, 378
Thirlby, YN, 378
Thirn, YN, 372
Thirsk, YN, 357, 378
Thirston, Nb, 222
Thirtleby, YE, 359
Thistleton, La, 151
Thistleton, Ru, 247
Thistlewood, Cu, 37
Thixendale, YE, 364, 366
Tholthorpe, YN, 376
Thomley, Ox, 239
Thompson, Nf, 204
Thonglands, Sa, 254
Thonock, Li, 177
Thoralby, YE, 364
Thoralby, YN, 372
Thoresby, Nt, 233
Thoresby, YN, 372
Thoresby, North, Li, 180
Thoresby, South, Li, 184
Thoresthorpe, Li, 184
Thoresway, Li, 179
Thorganby, Li, 179
Thorganby, YE, 363
Thorington, Sf, 289
Thorley, Ha, 120
Thorley, Hrt, 132

Thorlokeshop', He, 128
Thormanby, YN, 376
Thornaby on Tees, YN, 375
Thornage, Nf, 199
Thornborough, Bk, 16
Thornborough, Nb, 220
Thornborough, YN, 378
Thornbury, Dev, 61
Thornbury, Gl, 101
Thornbury, He, 124
Thornbury, hundred, Gl, 101
Thornby, Np, 216
Thorncombe, Do, 57
Thorndon, Sf, 287
Thorne, Dev, 62
Thorne, So, 262 n.
Thorne, YW, 393
Thornecombe, Do, 67
Thorner, YW, 388
Thorney, Nt, 233
Thorney, Sf, 288
Thorney, West, Sx, 306
Thornfalcon, So, 263
Thornford, Do, 71
Thorngate, hundred, Ha, 106
Thorngumbald, YE, 360
Thornham, Nf, 197
Thornham Magna, Sf, 287
Thornham Parva, Sf, 287
Thornhaugh, Np, 213
Thornhill, Do, 74
Thornhill, Wlt, 344
Thornhill, YW, 390
Thornhill, hundred, Wlt, 335
Thornholme, YE, 366
Thornley, La, 153
Thornthorpe, YE, 365
Thornton, Bk, 16
Thornton [in Amounderness wap.], La, 152
Thornton [in West Derby wap.], La, 150
Thornton, Lei, 158
Thornton, Li, 182
Thornton, Nb, 222
Thornton, Wa, 320 n.
Thornton, YE, 361
Thornton, YN, 375
Thornton, YW, 389
Thornton, Bishop, YW, 394
Thornton Bridge, YN, 371
Thornton Curtis, Li, 179
Thornton Dale, YN, 381
Thornton in Craven, YW, 382
Thornton in Lonsdale, YW, 384
Thornton le Beans, YN, 379
Thornton le Clay, YN, 380
Thornton le Moor, Li, 179
Thornton le Moor, YN, 378
Thornton le Street, YN, 379
Thornton on the Hill, YN, 378
Thornton Rust, YN, 372

Thornton Steward, YN, 372
Thornton Watless, YN, 372
Thorny Brow, YN, 380
Thoroton, Nt, 232
Thorp Arch, YW, 385
Thorp Perrow, YN, 372
Thorpe, Db, 44
Thorpe, Li, 184
Thorpe, Nf, 195
Thorpe, Nt, 233
Thorpe, Sf, 296
Thorpe, Sr, 300
Thorpe [in Dickering wap.], YE, 365
Thorpe [in Howdenshire lib.], YE, 363
Thorpe, YN, 373
Thorpe Abbots, Nf, 207
Thorpe Acre, Lei, 162
Thorpe Arnold, Lei, 163
Thorpe Audlin, YW, 390
Thorpe Basset, YE, 364
Thorpe by Water, Ru, 247
Thorpe Constantine, St, 280
Thorpe in the Fallows, Li, 178
Thorpe in the Glebe, Nt, 230
Thorpe Latimer, Li, 173
Thorpe le Soken, Ess, 88
Thorpe le Street, YE, 362
Thorpe, Little, Lei, 158
Thorpe Lubbenham, Np, 213
Thorpe Malsor, Np, 213
Thorpe Mandeville, Np, 210
Thorpe Market, Nf, 201
Thorpe Morieux, Sf, 291
Thorpe next Norwich, Nf, 194
Thorpe on the Hill, Li, 175
Thorpe Parva, Li, 174
Thorpe Parva, Nf, 207
Thorpe Row, YN, 378
Thorpe St. Peter, Li, 185
Thorpe Salvin, YW, 393
Thorpe Satchville, Lei, 161
Thorpe Stapleton, YW, 388
Thorpe Tilney, Li, 173
Thorpe Waterville, Np, 214
Thorpe Willoughby, YW, 386
Thorpland, Nf, 203
Thorrington, Ess, 88
Thorton, Do, 73
Thorverton, Dev, 63
Thoulstone, Wlt, 346
Thrandeston, Sf, 287
Thrapston, Np, 214
Thredling, hundred, Sf, 296
Threekingham, Li, 170
Threlkeld, Cu, 37
Threo, wapentake, Li, 172
Threshfield, YW, 383
Threxton, Nf, 204
Thrigby, Nf, 193
Thrimby, We, 329

Thringstone, Lei, 161
Thrintoft, YN, 374
Thriplow, Ca, 26
Thriplow, hundred, Ca, 26
Throcking, Hrt, 133
Throckington, Nb, 220
Throckmorton, Wo, 351
Throop, Do, 69
Throope, Wlt, 334
Throphill, Nb, 222
Thropton, Nb, 224
Througham, Gl, 93
Throwleigh, Dev, 58
Throwley, St, 281
Thrumpton [in Bassetlaw wap.], Nt, 228
Thrumpton [in Rushcliffe wap.], Nt, 230
Thrunton, Nb, 223
Thrupp, Brk, 12
Thrupp, Ox, 242
Thrupp Grounds, Np, 215
Thruscross, YW, 395
Thrushelton, Dev, 60
Thrussington, Lei, 163
Thruxton, Ha, 109
Thruxton, He, 127
Thrybergh, YW, 392
Thulston, Db, 44
Thunderley, Ess, 86
Thundersley, Ess, 81, 86
Thurcaston, Lei, 161
Thurgarton, Nf, 201
Thurgarton, Nt, 231
Thurgarton and Lythe, wapentake, Nt, 231
Thurgoland, YW, 391
Thurlaston, Lei, 159
Thurlaston, Wa, 322
Thurlbear, So, 263
Thurlby [in Calcewath wap.], Li, 184 n.
Thurlby [in Graffoe wap.], Li, 175
Thurlby [in Ness wap.], Li, 169
Thurleigh, Bd, 2
Thurleston, Dev, 51
Thurleston, Sf, 286
Thurlow, Great, Sf, 294
Thurlow, Little, Sf, 294
Thurloxton, So, 260
Thurlstone, YW, 392
Thurlton, Nf, 196
Thurmaston, Lei, 161
Thurnby, Lei, 164
Thurne, Nf, 193
Thurnham, La, 156
Thurning, Nf, 200
Thurning, Np, 136, 138, 209
Thurnscoe, YW, 393
Thurrock, Grays, Ess, 87
Thurrock, Little, Ess, 86
Thurrock, West, Ess, 87
Thursby, Cu, 37
Thursford, Nf, 200

Thurstable, hundred, Ess, 83
Thurston, Sf, 292
Thurston End, Sf, 294
Thurstonland, YW, 390
Thurton, Nf, 195
Thurvaston, Db, 45
Thuxton, Nf, 204
Thwaite [in Loddon hd.], Nf, 195
Thwaite [in South Erpingham hd.], Nf, 201
Thwaite, Sf, 287
Thwing, YE, 365
Tibaldstone, hundred, Gl, 101
Tibberton, Gl, 95
Tibberton, Wo, 350
Tibenham, Nf, 196
Tibshelf, Db, 48
Tibthorpe, YE, 360
Ticehurst, Sx, 317
Tichborne, Ha, 117
Tickencote, Ru, 247
Tickenham, So, 271
Tickford End, Bk, 16
Tickhill, YW, 394
Tickhill, liberty, YW, 393
Ticknall, Db, 46
Tickton, YE, 358
Tidcombe, Wlt, 347
Tiddington, Ox, 239
Tiddington, Wa, 327
Tideswell, Db, 47
Tidgrove, Ha, 115
Tidmarsh, Brk, 8
Tidmington, Wa, 351
Tidworth, North, Wlt, 346
Tidworth, South, Ha, 106, 108
Tiffield, Np, 211
Tilbrook, Hu, 1, 4, 136
Tilbury, East, Ess, 86
Tilbury juxta Clare, Ess, 80
Tilbury, West, Ess, 86
Tilehurst, Brk, 7
Tilford, Sr, 298
Tilgarsley, Ox, 242
Tilleslow, Dev, 60
Tillingham, Ess, 84
Tillington, He, 124
Tillington, St, 278
Tillington, Sx, 308
Tiln, Nt, 227
Tilney, Nf, 197
Tilshead, Wlt, 338, 341
Tilsop, Sa, 254
Tilsworth, Bd, 4
Tilton, Lei, 162
Timberland, Li, 173
Timberscombe, So, 272
Timberth, Sa, 257
Timble, YW, 395
Timble, Little, YW, 384
Timsbury, Ha, 107

Timsbury, So, 267
Timworth, Sf, 292
Tincleton, Do, 69
Tingewick, Bk, 16
Tingrith, Bd, 4
Tinhead, Wlt, 338
Tinsley, YW, 394
Tintagel, Co, 33
Tintinhull, So, 274
Tintinhull, hundred, So, 274
Tinwell, Ru, 247
Tipnoak, half-hundred, Sx, 311
Tipton, St, 279
Tirley, Gl, 99, 100
Tisbury, Wlt, 337
Tiscott, Hrt, 134
Tissington, Db, 44
Tisted, East, Ha, 107
Tisted, West, Ha, 110
Titburst, Hrt, 134
Titchfield, Ha, 110
Titchfield, hundred, Ha, 110
Titchmarsh, Np, 214
Titchwell, Nf, 198
Titcomb, Brk, 10
Tithby, Nt, 232
Titlington, Nb, 223
Titsey, Sr, 303
Tittensor, St, 278
Tittleshall, Nf, 208
Tiverton, Dev, 55, 66
Tiverton, hundred, Dev, 55
Tivetshall, Nf, 207
Tixall, St, 277
Tixover, Ru, 247
Tockenham, East, Wlt, 344
Tockenham, West, Wlt, 344
Tocketts, YN, 375
Tockington, Gl, 94
Tockwith, YW, 385
Todber, Do, 73
Toddington, Bd, 4
Toddington, Gl, 98
Toddington, Sx, 309
Todenham, Gl, 99
Todwick, YW, 393
Toft, Ca, 26
Toft, Li, 170
Toft, Wa, 322
Toft Monks, Nf, 195
Toft next Newton, Li, 179
Toftrees, Nf, 198
Tofts, West, Nf, 204
Togston, Nb, 222
Tolland, So, 265
Tollard Royal, Wlt, 343
Toller Porcorum, Do, 76
Tollerford, hundred, Do, 76
Tollerton, Nt, 232
Tollerton, YN, 379

Tollesbury, Ess, 83
Tolleshunt D'Arcy, Ess, 83
Tolleshunt Knights, Ess, 83
Tolleshunt Major, Ess, 83
Tolpuddle, Do, 69
Toltingtrough, hundred, K, 145
Tolworth, Sr, 301
Tonbridge, lowy, K, 144
Tong, Sa, 256
Tong, YW, 389
Tonge, Lei, 161
Tongham, Sr, 298
Tooting Bec, 302
Tooting Graveney, Sr, 302
Topcliffe, YN, 378
Topcroft, Nf, 195
Toppesfield, Ess, 80
Topples Wood, Ox, 241
Topsham, Dev, 58
Torbryan, Dev, 50
Torksey, Li, 177
Tormarton, Gl, 102
Tormohan, Dev, 50
Torpenhow, Cu, 39
Torrells Hall, Ess, 82
Torrington, Black, Dev, 60
Torrington, Black, hundred, Dev, 60
Torrington, East, Li, 181
Torrington, Great, Dev, 53, 66
Torrington, Little, Dev, 52
Torrington, West, Li, 181
Torrisholme, La, 156
Tortington, Sx, 308
Tortworth, Gl, 102
Torweston, So, 266
Torworth, Nt, 229
Toseland, Hu, 137
Toseland, hundred, Hu, 136
Tosson, Nb, 224
Tostock, Sf, 292
Totcombe, hundred, Do, 70
Totham, Great, Ess, 83
Totham, Little, Ess, 83
Tothby, Li, 184 n.
Totill, Li, 184
Totley, YW, 48
Totmanslow, hundred, St, 280
Totnes, Dev, 65
Totnore, hundred, Sx, 315
Toton, Nt, 229
Tottenham, Mx, 191
Totternhoe, Bd, 4
Totterton, Sa, 253
Tottington, La, 154
Tottington, Nf, 204
Tottingworth, Sx, 317
Totton, Ha, 115
Toulston, YW, 386
Towcester, Np, 211
Towcester, hundred, Np, 211

Towednack, Co, 30
Towersey, Ox, 15, 20, 235
Townhill, Ha, 109
Towsington, Dev, 59
Towthorpe, Li, 172
Towthorpe, YE, 364, 369
Towton, YW, 386
Toynton, Li, 185
Toynton, High, Li, 184
Toynton, Low, Li, 184
Trafford, Np, 210
Treaddow, He, 126
Treales, La, 152
Treberon, He, 126
Tredington, Gl, 93
Tredington, Wa, 351
Tre-Essay, He, 126
Treeton, YW, 393
Tre-Even, He, 126
Tregate, He, 125
Tregoney, Co, 31
Trematon, Co, 34
Trendle, South, So, 264
Treneglos, Co, 33
Trent, Do, 67, 269
Trentham, St, 278
Treseck, He, 125
Tresham, Gl, 102
Treswell, Nt, 228
Tretire, He, 126
Trevalga, Co, 33
Trevase, He, 126
Trew, Dev, 55
Trewhitt, Nb, 224
Trewsbury, Gl, 100 n.
Treyford, Sx, 306
Triermain, Cu, 38
Trigg, hundred, Co, 32
Trill, Dev, 57
Trimingham, Nf, 201
Trimley, Sf, 296
Tring, Hrt, 134
Tritlington, Nb, 222
Troston, Sf, 293
Trotton, Sx, 306
Troughend, Nb, 221
Troutbeck, We, 330
Trowbridge, Wlt, 338
Trowell, Nt, 230
Trowle, Wlt, 338, 347
Trull, So, 264
Trumpington, Ca, 26
Trunch, Nf, 201
Truro, Co, 32
Trusham, Dev, 59
Trusley, Db, 46
Trusthorpe, Li, 184
Trysull, St, 283
Tubney, Brk, 12
Tuckerton, So, 260

Tuddenham [in Carlford hd.], Sf, 296
Tuddenham [in Lackford hd.], Sf, 293
Tuddenham, East, Nf, 205
Tuddenham, North, Nf, 205
Tuffley, Gl, 97
Tufton, Ha, 111
Tugby, Lei, 162
Tugford, Sa, 254
Tughall, Nb, 226
Tumby, Li, 182
Tunley, Gl, 93
Tunstall, La, 156
Tunstall, Nf, 195
Tunstall, Sf, 294, 295
Tunstall [near Adbaston], St, 279
Tunstall [near Burslem], St, 278
Tunstall, YE, 359
Tunstall [in Hang wap.], YN, 371
Tunstall [in Langbargh wap.], YN, 374
Tunstead, Nf, 202
Tunstead, hundred, Nf, 202
Tunworth, Ha, 118
Turkdean, Gl, 99
Turnastone, He, 128
Turnworth, Do, 75
Turton, La, 154
Turvey, Bd, 2
Turville, Bk, 21
Turweston, Bk, 16
Tusmore, Ox, 238
Tutbury, St, 280
Tuttington, Nf, 201
Tuxford, Nt, 228
Twerton, So, 268
Twickenham, Mx, 191
Twigworth, Gl, 91 n.
Twinstead, Ess, 80
Twiston, La, 153
Twizzle, Nb, 221
Twycross, Lei, 159
Twyford, Bk, 16
Twyford, Brk, 346
Twyford, Db, 44
Twyford, Ha, 117
Twyford [in Stretford hd.], He, 129
Twyford [in Webtree hd.], He, 127
Twyford, Lei, 162
Twyford, Li, 171
Twyford, hundred, K, 144
Twyning, Gl, 97
Twywell, Np, 214
Tyberton, He, 127
Tybourn, Mx, 190 n.
Tydd St. Giles, Ca, 28
Tydd St. Mary, Li, 168
Tyldesley, La, 150
Tynedale, ward, Nb, 220
Tyneham [East], Do, 76
Tyneham [West], Do, 76
Tynemouth, Nb, 223

Tyringham, Bk, 17
Tysoe, Wa, 321
Tytherington, Gl, 101
Tytherington, Wlt, 340
Tytherley, Ha, 105, 106, 345
Tytherley, East, Ha, 106
Tytherley, West, Ha, 106
Tytherton Lucas, Wlt, 344
Tythrop, Bk, 15, 235, 240 n., 241
Tyting, Sr, 300
Tyttenhanger, Hrt, 134
Tywardreath, Co, 31

Uall', YN, 372
Ubbeston, Sf, 288
Ubley, So, 260
Uckington, Gl, 100
Uckington, Sa, 250
Udimore, Sx, 316
Uffcott, Wlt, 341
Uffculme, Dev, 65
Uffington, Brk, 10
Uffington, Li, 169
Uffington, Sa, 250
Ufford, Sf, 295
Ufton, Wa, 323
Ufton Nervet, Brk, 8
Ufton Robert, Brk, 8
Ugborough, Dev, 64
Ugford [North], Wlt, 342
Ugford [South], Wlt, 335
Uggescombe, hundred, Do, 77
Uggeshall, Sf, 289
Ugglebarnby, YN, 380
Ugley, Ess, 85
Ugthorpe, YN, 375
Ulceby [in Calcewath wap.], Li, 184
Ulceby [in Yarborough wap.], Li, 178
Uldale, Cu, 39
Uley, Gl, 96
Ulgham, Nb, 223
Ullenhall, Wa, 326
Ulleskelf, YW, 387
Ullesthorpe, Lei, 158
Ulley, YW, 392
Ullingswick, He, 124
Ullington, Wo, 94
Ulnes Walton, La, 155
Ulrome, YE, 359
Ulthwayt', YW, 386
Ulting, Ess, 84
Ulverston, La, 156
Umberleigh, Dev, 61
Uncleby, YE, 366
Underditch, hundred, Wlt, 336
Underley, He, 123
Underwood, Db, 45
Unthank, Cu, 37
Unthank', Nb, 225
Upavon, Wlt, 335

Upham, Ha, 118
Upham, Wlt, 339
Upleadon, Gl, 95
Upleadon, He, 128
Uplowman, Dev, 55
Uplyme, Dev, 57
Upmanby, Cu, 39
Upminster, Ess, 87
Upperby, Cu, 41
Upperton, Sx, 314
Uppingham, Ru, 246
Uppington, Sa, 250
Upsall [in Birdforth wap.], YN, 378
Upsall [in Langbargh wap.], YN, 374
Upthorpe, Hu, 138 n.
Upton [in Stoke hd.], Bk, 21
Upton [in Stone hd.], Bk, 20
Upton, Brk, 13
Upton [in Crediton hd.], Dev, 54
Upton [in Hayridge hd.], Dev, 63
Upton, Gl, 351
Upton, Hu, 139
Upton, Lei, 159
Upton, Li, 178
Upton, Nf, 195
Upton, Np, 216
Upton [in Bassetlaw wap.], Nt, 228
Upton [in Thurgarton and Lythe wap.], Nt, 231
Upton, Ox, 237
Upton, Sa, 256
Upton [in Barlichway hd.], Wa, 326
Upton [in Kineton hd.], Wa, 321
Upton, Wlt, 342
Upton, YW, 391
Upton Bishop, He, 127
Upton Cheyney, Gl, 94
Upton Cressett, Sa, 255
Upton Grey, Ha, 118
Upton Hellions, Dev, 55
Upton Lovell, Wlt, 340
Upton Magna, Sa, 251
Upton Noble, So, 269
Upton Pyne, Dev, 58
Upton St. Leonards, Gl, 91 n., 97
Upton Scudamore, Wlt, 347
Upton Snodsbury, Wo, 354
Upton upon Severn, Wo, 350
Upton Warren, Wo, 353
Upwell, Ca, 28, 203 n.
Upwell, Nf, 203
Upwey, Do, 72
Upwood, Hu, 137
Urchfont, Wlt, 336
Urishay, He, 128
Urmston, La, 154
Urswick, La, 155
Utterby, Li, 180
Uttlesford and Freshwell, hundred, Ess, 86
Uttoxeter, St, 281

Uxbridge, Mx, 190

Vange, Ess, 86
Vastern, Wlt, 341
Vauxhall, Wa, 325
Venn, Dev, 59
Venn Channing, Dev, 55
Venn Ottery, Dev, 66
Vennhampton, So, 264
Vernham Dean, Ha, 112
Veryan, Co, 31
Vico Canonicorum, Hu, 138
Vineyards, Brk, 12
Virginstow, Dev, 60
Virley, Ess, 82
Vowchurch, He, 128
Vyne, The, Ha, 118

Wacton, He, 123
Wacton, Nf, 196
Waddesdon, Bk, 19
Waddesdon, hundred, Bk, 19
Waddingham, Li, 176, 186
Waddington, Li, 174
Waddington, Sr, 300
Waddington, YW, 383
Waddingworth, Li, 182
Waddon, Sr, 300
Wade, Ha, 116
Wadenhoe, Np, 214
Wadhurst, Sx, 315
Wadsworth, YW, 389
Wadworth, YW, 394
Wainfleet, Li, 181
Waitby, We, 329
Waithe, Li, 180
Wakefield, YW, 389
Wakering, Great, Ess, 81
Wakering, Little, Ess, 81
Wakerley, Np, 215
Walberswick, Sf, 289
Walberton, Sx, 308
Walburn, YN, 372
Walcot [in Aveland wap.], Li, 170
Walcot [in Langhoe wap.], Li, 173
Walcot [in Manley wap.], Li, 175
Walcot, Ox, 236
Walcot, Sa, 256
Walcot, So, 261
Walcot, Wlt, 341
Walcot, Wo, 354
Walcote, Lei, 158
Walcott, Nf, 193
Walden, King's, Hrt, 133
Walden, Saffron, Ess, 86
Walden Stubbs, YW, 391
Walderton, Sx, 305
Waldingfield, Great, Sf, 290
Waldingfield, Little, Sf, 291
Waldridge, Bk, 20

Wales, YW, 393
Walesby, Li, 179
Walesby, Nt, 228
Walford, He, 127
Walgrave, Np, 212
Walker, Nb, 222
Walkeringham, Nt, 227
Walkerith, Li, 186
Walkern, Hrt, 133
Walkington, YE, 363, 369
Wallingford, Brk, 6, 14
Wallington, Ha, 116
Wallington, Hrt, 132
Wallington, Nb, 222
Wallington, Nf, 203
Wallington, Sr, 300
Wallington, hundred, Sr, 300
Wallop, Nether, Ha, 106
Wallop, Over, Ha, 106
Walmsgate, Li, 185
Walpole, Nf, 197
Walpole, Sf, 288
Walsall, St, 277
Walsgrave on Sowe, Wa, 323
Walsham, hundred, Nf, 194
Walsham, North, Nf, 202
Walsham le Willows, Sf, 293
Walsham, South, Nf, 194
Walshcroft, wapentake, Li, 179
Walsingham, Great, Nf, 200
Walsingham, Little, Nf, 200
Walsoken, Nf, 197
Walson Barton, Dev, 62
Walsopthorne, He, 128
Walterstone, He, 128
Waltham, Li, 180
Waltham, Bishop's, Ha, 118
Waltham, Bishop's, hundred, Ha, 118
Waltham, Great, Ess, 85
Waltham Holy Cross, Ess, 83
Waltham, hundred, Ess, 83
Waltham, Little, Ess, 85
Waltham, North, Ha, 112
Waltham on the Wold, Lei, 164
Waltham St. Lawrence, Brk, 14
Waltham, Up, Sx, 308
Waltham, White, Brk, 6
Walthamstow, Ess, 81
Walton, Bk, 17 n.
Walton, Cu, 38
Walton, Db, 48
Walton, La, 151
Walton, Lei, 160
Walton, Li, 171
Walton [in Chirbury hd.], Sa, 256
Walton [in Stottesdon hd.], Sa, 255
Walton, Sf, 296
Walton [in Kilmersdon hd.], So, 262
Walton [in Whitley hd.], So, 274
Walton [near Eccleshall], St, 278

Walton [near Stone], St, 278
Walton, Wlt, 335
Walton [in Agbrigg wap.], YW, 390
Walton [in Ainsty wap.], YW, 385
Walton Cardiff, Gl, 93
Walton [Deyville], Wa, 320
Walton, East, Nf, 197
Walton Grounds, Np, 210
Walton in Gordano, So, 271
Walton, Isley, Lei, 161
Walton le Dale, La, 153
Walton, Little, Wa, 323
Walton [Mauduit], Wa, 320
Walton on the Hill, Sr, 302
Walton on the Hill, St, 281
Walton on the Naze, Ess, 88
Walton on the Wolds, Lei, 162
Walton upon Thames, Sr, 301
Walton upon Trent, Db, 46
Walton, Wenlock, Sa, 254
Walton, West, Li, 176
Walton, West, Nf, 197
Walton Wood, Cu, 38
Walton, Wood, Hu, 138
Walwarpe, Wo, 352
Walworth, Sr, 302
Wanborough, Sr, 299
Wanborough, Wlt, 335
Wandsworth, Sr, 302
Wangford, Sf, 293
Wangford, hundred, Sf, 289
Wanlip, Lei, 161
Wansford, YE, 366
Wanstead, Ess, 81
Wanstrow, So, 268, 269
Wantage, Brk, 11
Wantage, hundred, Brk, 11
Wantisden, Sf, 295
Wapley, Gl, 102
Waplington, YE, 361
Wappenbury, Wa, 322
Wappenham, Np, 210
Warbleton, Sx, 317
Warblington, Ha, 116
Warborne, Ha, 116
Warborough, Ox, 245
Warboys, Hu, 137
Warbreck, La, 152
Warbstow, Co, 33
Warcombe, Dev, 51
Warcop, We, 329
Ward end, We, 325
Warden, Nb, 220
Warden, Chipping, Wa, 210
Warden, Chipping, hundred, Np, 210
Warden, Old, Bd, 3
Wardington, Ox, 241
Wardley, Ru, 246
Ware, Hrt, 132
Wareham, Do, 67, 78

Warenton, Nb, 226
Waresley, Hu, 137
Warfield, Brk, 14
Wargrave, Brk, 14
Wargrave, hundred, Brk, 6
Warham, He, 124
Warham, Nf, 200
Waringstone, Dev, 56
Wark, Nb, 225
Warkleigh, Dev, 53
Warkton, Np, 214
Warkworth, Nb, 222
Warkworth, Np, 210
Warlaby, YN, 374
Warleggan, Co, 34
Warley, YW, 389
Warley, Great, Ess, 87
Warley, Little, Ess, 87
Warley Wigorn, Wo, 353
Warlingham, Sr, 303
Warmfield, YW, 390
Warminghurst, Sx, 310
Warmington, Np, 213 n., 214
Warmington, Wa, 321
Warminster, Wlt, 347
Warminster, hundred, Wlt, 346
Warmscombe, Ox, 238
Warmsworth, YW, 392, 393
Warmwell, Do, 68
Warnborough, North, Ha, 120
Warnborough, South, Ha, 118
Warndon, Wo, 350
Warnford, Ha, 113
Warnham, Sx, 309
Warningcamp, Sx, 309
Warpsgrove, Ox, 240
Warrington, La, 150
Warslow, St, 281
Warsop, Nt, 229, 233
Warter, YE, 361
Warthill, YN, 379
Wartling, Sx, 316
Wartnaby, Lei, 161
Warton [in Amounderness wap.], La, 151
Warton [in Lonsdale, Cartmel, and Furness wap.], La, 156
Warton, Nb, 224
Warwick, Cu, 38
Warwick, Wa, 319, 320
Warwickshire, 319–27
Washbourne, Gl, 92
Washbourne, Little, Gl, 350
Washbrook, Sf, 285
Washfield, Dev, 55
Washford Pyne, Dev, 54
Washingborough, Li, 174
Washingley, Hu, 138
Washington, Sx, 309
Washlingstone, hundred, K, 144
Wasing, Brk, 9

Wasperton, Wa, 320
Wassingham, Sr, 302
Watchet, So, 274
Watchfield, Brk, 11
Watchingwell, Ha, 120
Watcombe Manor, Ox, 238
Waterbeach, Ca, 25
Watercombe, Do, 68
Waterden, Nf, 199
Waterfall, St, 281
Waterperry, Ox, 239
Waterstock, Ox, 244
Waterston, Do, 69
Waterton, Li, 175
Watford, Hrt, 134
Watford, Np, 216
Wath, YN, 371
Wath upon Dearne, YW, 392, 393
Watlington, Nf, 203
Watlington, Ox, 238
Watnall, Nt, 230
Wattisfield, Sf, 293
Wattisham, Sf, 291
Wattlesborough, Sa, 252
Watton, Nf, 204
Watton, YE, 362
Watton at Stone, Hrt, 133
Wauldby, YE, 360
Wavendon, Bk, 17
Waverton, Cu, 37
Wavertree, La, 150
Wawne, YE, 359, 367
Waxham, Nf, 193
Waxholme, YE, 360
Wayford, So, 273
Wayland, hundred, Nf, 204
Weald, Ox, 237 n.
Weald, North, Ess, 89
Weald, North, Bassett, Ess, 83
Weardley, YW, 388
Weare, So, 262, 272
Weare Giffard, Dev, 52
Wearne, So, 273
Weasenham, Nf, 208
Weaver, Dev, 63
Weaverthorpe, YE, 365
Webton, He, 127
Webtree, hundred, He, 127
Weddington, Wa, 325
Wedelonde, So, 264
Wedhampton, Wlt, 336
Wedmore, So, 262
Wedmore [liberty], So, 262
Wednesbury, St, 277
Wednesfield, St, 283
Weedley, YE, 370
Weedon, Bk, 18
Weedon Bec, Np, 215
Weedon Lois, Np, 211
Weeford, St, 280

Week, Ha, 119
Week St. Mary, Co, 33
Weeke, Ha, 108
Weekley, Np, 215
Weel, YE, 358
Weeley, Ess, 89
Weethley, Wa, 326
Weeting, Nf, 204
Weeton, La, 152
Weeton, YW, 384, 386
Weetslade, Nb, 222
Weetwood, Nb, 224
Weighton, Little, YE, 362
Weighton, Market, YE, 361
Welborne, Nf, 206
Welbourn, Li, 174
Welburn, YN, 376
Welbury, YN, 377
Welby, Lei, 163
Welby, Li, 172
Welcombe, Dev, 61
Welcombe, Wa, 327
Weldon, Great, Np, 215
Weldon, Little, Np, 215
Welford, Brk, 9
Welford, Np, 216
Welford on Avon, Wa, 100
Welham, Lei, 165
Welham, Nt, 228
Welham, YE, 364
Well, Li, 184 n.
Well, YN, 372
Well, wapentake, Li, 178
Welland, Wo, 350
Wellbrook, He, 128
Welle, Ca, 28 n.
Wellesbourne Hastings, Wa, 320
Wellesbourne Mountford, Wa, 320
Wellhouse, Brk, 8
Wellingborough, Np, 217
Wellingore, Li, 174
Wellington, He, 125
Wellington, Sa, 251
Wellington, So, 270
Wellisford, So, 260
Wellow, Ha, 120
Wellow, Nt, 228
Wellow, East, Ha, 106
Wellow, hundred, So, 268
Wellow, West, Ha, 105, 346
Wells, Ha, 107
Wells, Nf, 200
Wells, So, 273
Wells Foreign, hundred, So, 271
Wellsborough, Lei, 159
Wellsworth, Ha, 110
Welnetham, Great, Sf, 292
Welnetham, Little, Sf, 292
Welshampton, Sa, 252
Welton, Np, 215

Welton, So, 261
Welton, YE, 363
Welton le Marsh, Li, 182
Welton le Wold, Li, 183
Welwick, YE, 369
Welwick Thorpe, YE, 358
Welwyn, Hrt, 133
Wem, Sa, 250
Wembworthy, Dev, 62
Wenden Lofts, Ess, 87
Wenden Magna, Ess, 87
Wenden Parva, Ess, 87
Wendens Ambo, Ess, 87
Wendlebury, Ox, 238
Wendling, Nf, 207
Wendover, Bk, 15, 22
Wendron, Co, 31
Wendy, Ca, 25
Wenham, Great, Sf, 285
Wenham, Little, Sf, 285
Wenhaston, Sf, 289
Wenlock, Little, Sa, 254
Wenlock, Much, Sa, 254
Wennington, Ess, 87
Wennington, La, 156
Wensley, Db, 45
Wensley, YN, 372
Wentnor, Sa, 253
Wenton, Ru, 247
Wentworth, Ca, 28
Wentworth, YW, 393
Weobley, He, 122, 123
Weobley [foreign], He, 130
Wepham, Sx, 309
Wereham, Nf, 203
Werrington, Dev, 60
Wesham, La, 152
Wessington, Db, 48
West, bailey, K, 148
West, hundred, Co, 34
West Town, Ha, 116
Westall, Gl, 92
Westborough, Li, 174
Westbourne, Mx, 190
Westbourne, Sx, 305
Westbourne, hundred, Sx, 305
Westbrook, Brk, 11
Westbury, Bk, 16
Westbury, Do, 71
Westbury, Ha, 113
Westbury, Sa, 253
Westbury, Wlt, 336
Westbury, hundred, Gl, 104
Westbury, hundred, Wlt, 336
Westbury Leigh, Wlt, 336
Westbury on Severn, Gl, 104
Westbury on Trym, Gl, 102
Westbury sub Mendip, So, 271
Westby, La, 151
Westby, Li, 171

Westcombland, So, 273
Westcote, Gl, 103
Westcott, Sr, 299
Westcott, Wlt, 341
Westerby, Lei, 165
Westerdale, YN, 376
Westerfield, Sf, 286
Westerham, hundred, K, 146
Westerleigh, Gl, 101
Westerton, Sx, 307
Westfield, Nf, 205
Westgate, hundred, K, 141
Westhall, Sf, 289
Westhide, He, 128
Westhope, Sa, 254
Westhorpe, Li, 172
Westhorpe, Nt, 231
Westhorpe, Sf, 287
Westhoughton, La, 154
Westington, Gl, 94 n.
Westlecott, Wlt, 341
Westleigh, Dev, 53
Westleigh, La, 151
Westleton, Sf, 289
Westley, Sf, 291
Westley Waterless, Ca, 27
Westlinton, Cu, 39
Westmancote, Wo, 350
Westmill, Hrt, 132
Westminster, Mx, 191
Westminster, hundred, Gl, 99
Westmorland, 328–31
Westnewton, Cu, 39
Weston, Brk, 9
Weston, Ha, 114
Weston, He, 129
Weston, Hrt, 133
Weston, Li, 168
Weston, Np, 211
Weston, Nt, 231
Weston, Sf, 290
Weston, So, 261
Weston, Sr, 301
Weston, Wa, 321
Weston, YW, 384
Weston Bampfylde, So, 259
Weston Beggard, He, 128
Weston Birt, Gl, 96
Weston, Buckhorn, Do, 74
Weston by Welland, Np, 215
Weston Colley, Ha, 112
Weston Colville, Ca, 27
Weston, Coney, Sf, 293
Weston Corbett, Ha, 118
Weston, Edith, Ru, 247
Weston Favell, Np, 217
Weston in Arden, Wa, 324
Weston Jones, St, 282
Weston, Kings, Gl, 96
Weston, Lawrence, Gl, 102

Weston Longville, Nf, 200
Weston Lullingfields, Sa, 252
Weston, Market, Sf, 292
Weston Mauduth, Wa, 94
Weston, Nether, Db, 44
Weston, North, Ox, 244
Weston, Old, Hu, 138
Weston on Avon, Wa, 95 n.
Weston on the Green, Ox, 238
Weston Patrick, Ha, 113
Weston Peverel, Dev, 52
Weston, South, Ox, 238
Weston Subedge, Gl, 94
Weston super Mare, So, 259
Weston Turville, Bk, 20
Weston under Lizard, St, 282
Weston under Penyard, He, 126
Weston under Wetherley, Wa, 323
Weston Underwood, Bk, 18
Weston upon Trent, Db, 43
Weston upon Trent, St, 277
Westoning, Bd, 4
Westonzoyland, So, 273
Westout, Sx, 311
Westover, Ha, 106
Westover, So, 272
Westow, YE, 364
Westowe, So, 266
Westrop, Wlt, 343
Westwell, Ox, 237
Westwick, Ca, 25
Westwick, Hrt, 134
Westwick, Nf, 202
Westwick, YW, 394
Westwood, Wlt, 340
Wetheral, Cu, 38
Wetherby, YW, 384
Wetherden, Sf, 287
Wetheringsett, Sf, 287
Wetherley, hundred, Ca, 26
Wethersfield, Ess, 80
Wetton, St, 281
Wetwang, YE, 365, 367
Wexcombe, Wlt, 347
Weybourne, Nf, 199
Weybread, Sf, 288
Weybridge, Sr, 301
Weycroft, Dev, 57
Weymouth, Do, 77
Whaddon, Bk, 19
Whaddon, Ca, 26
Whaddon, Gl, 97
Whaddon [in Alderbury hd.], Wlt, 345
Whaddon [in Melksham hd.], Wlt, 338
Whale, We, 329
Whalesborne, hundred, Sx, 312
Whalley, La, 153
Whalton, Nb, 222
Whaplode, Li, 168
Wharram le Street, YE, 365

Wharram Percy, YE, 364
Wharton, He, 130
Wharton, Li, 186
Wharton, We, 329
Whatborough, Lei, 162
Whatcombe, Brk, 9
Whatcombe, Do, 73
Whatcote, Wa, 321
Whatfield, Sf, 291
Whatley, So, 268
Whatton, Nt, 232
Whatton, Long, Lei, 161
Wheatacre, Nf, 196
Wheatenhurst, Gl, 103
Wheatfield, Ox, 238
Wheathampstead, Hrt, 134
Wheathill, So, 274
Wheatley, Ha, 120
Wheatley, La, 153
Wheatley, Ox, 239
Wheatley, North, Nt, 229
Wheatley, South, Nt, 229
Wheelton, La, 155
Wheldale, YW, 391
Wheldrake, YE, 364
Whelmstone Barton, Dev, 54
Whelpley, Wlt, 336
Whenby, YN, 376
Whepstead, Sf, 292
Wherstead, Sf, 285
Wherwell, Ha, 111
Wherwell, hundred, Ha, 111
Whetham, Wlt, 337
Whetstone, Lei, 158
Whichford, Wa, 321
Whiddon, Dev, 63
Whilton, Np, 216
Whimple, Dev, 56
Whimpton, Nt, 228
Whinburgh, Nf, 204
Whinfell, Cu, 40
Whinfell, We, 330
Whippingham, Ha, 119
Whisby, Li, 175
Whissendine, Ru, 247
Whissonsett, Nf, 207
Whiston, La, 150
Whiston, Np, 217
Whiston, St, 282
Whiston, YW, 393
Whitacre, Nether, Wa, 325
Whitacre, Over, Wa, 325
Whitbourne, He, 124
Whitbourne, Wlt, 346
Whitby, YN, 381
Whitby and Byland, liberty, YN, 380
Whitchester, Nb, 220
Whitchurch, Bk, 18
Whitchurch, Dev, 52
Whitchurch, Ha, 109

Whitchurch, Ox, 243
Whitchurch, Sa, 250
Whitchurch [in Keynsham hd.], So, 270
Whitchurch [in Wells Foreign hd.], So, 271
Whitchurch, Wa, 320
Whitchurch Canonicorum, hundred, Do, 73
Whitcombe, Do, 73
White Ox Mead, So, 268
Whitechurch Maund, He, 123
Whitecliff, Do, 75
Whitecliff, Wlt, 341
Whitefield, Dev, 63
Whitehill, Ox, 242
Whitelackington, So, 266
Whitestaunton, So, 275
Whitestone [in South Molton hd.], Dev, 53
Whitestone [in Wonford hd.], Dev, 58
Whitestone, hundred, So, 267
Whiteway, hundred, Do, 70
Whitfield, He, 126
Whitfield, Np, 210
Whitford, Dev, 57
Whitgift, YW, 390
Whitgreave, St, 278
Whitley [in Hormer hd.], Brk, 12
Whitley [in Reading hd.], Brk, 7
Whitley [in Barlichway hd.], Wa, 326
Whitley [in Knightlow hd.], Wa, 323
Whitley, Wlt, 337
Whitley [in Agbrigg wap.], YW, 390
Whitley [in Osgoldcross wap.], YW, 391
Whitley, hundred, So, 273
Whitmore, St, 278
Whitnage, Dev, 56
Whitnash, Wa, 323
Whitrigg, Cu, 37
Whitsbury, Ha, 105, 334
Whitstable, hundred, K, 141
Whitstone, Co, 33
Whitstone, hundred, Gl, 103
Whittimere, Sa, 256
Whittingham, La, 152
Whittingham, Nb, 223
Whittingham, Sf, 288
Whittingslow, Sa, 254
Whittington, Db, 48
Whittington, Gl, 98
Whittington, La, 155
Whittington, Lei, 158
Whittington, St, 280
Whittington, Great, Nb, 220
Whittington, Little, Nb, 220
Whittle, Nb, 220
Whittle le Woods, La, 155
Whittle, Welch, La, 155
Whittlesey, Ca, 28
Whittlesford, Ca, 27
Whittlesford, hundred, Ca, 27

Whitton, Li, 175
Whitton, Sa, 254
Whitton, Sf, 286
Whittonstall, Nb, 221
Whitwell, Ca, 26
Whitwell, Db, 48
Whitwell, Ha, 119
Whitwell, Nf, 200
Whitwell, Ru, 247
Whitwell, We, 330
Whitwick, He, 128
Whitwick, Lei, 160
Whitwood, YW, 390
Whitworth', Nb, 222
Whixhall, Sa, 250
Whixley, YW, 384
Whorlton, YN, 374
Whorwellsdown, hundred, Wlt, 338
Whyle, He, 130
Wibtoft, Wa, 324
Wick, Gl, 101
Wick [in Bulstone hd.], So, 272
Wick [in Cannington hd.], So, 268
Wick [in Downton hd.], Wlt, 334
Wick [in Kinwardstone hd.], Wlt, 347
Wick, Wo, 354
Wick Episcopi, Wo, 350
Wick Green, Wlt, 348
Wick, North, So, 267
Wick St. Lawrence, So, 259
Wick, Upper, Wo, 350 n.
Wick Wick, Gl, 102
Wicken, Ca, 24
Wicken, Np, 211
Wicken Bonhunt, Ess, 87
Wickenby, Li, 181
Wickersley, YW, 393
Wickford, Ess, 86
Wickham, Brk, 9
Wickham, Ha, 110
Wickham, Hrt, 132
Wickham Bishops, Ess, 83
Wickham Market, Sf, 295
Wickham St. Paul's, Ess, 80
Wickham Skeith, Sf, 287
Wickham, West, Ca, 27
Wickhambrook, Sf, 294
Wickhamford, Wo, 355
Wickhampton, Nf, 194
Wicklewood, Nf, 206
Wickmere, Nf, 202
Wickwar, Gl, 102
Widdington, Ess, 86
Widdrington, Nb, 222
Widecombe in the Moor, Dev, 50
Widford, Ess, 85
Widford, Hrt, 132
Widford, Ox, 103, 235
Widhill, Wlt, 343
Widley, Ha, 110

Widmerpool, Nt, 230
Widworthy, Dev, 57
Wield, Ha, 117
Wigan, La, 149
Wiganthorpe, YN, 376
Wigborough, Great, Ess, 81
Wigborough, Little, Ess, 81
Wiggenhall, Nf, 197
Wigginton, Ox, 243
Wigginton, St, 277
Wigginton, YN, 379
Wigglesworth, YW, 383
Wiggold, Gl, 100
Wiggonholt, Sx, 308
Wighill, YW, 385
Wightfield, Gl, 99
Wighton, Nf, 200
Wigley, Ha, 106
Wigsley, Nt, 233
Wigston Magna, Lei, 160
Wigston Parva, Lei, 159
Wigtoft, Li, 168
Wigton, Cu, 37
Wigton, YW, 388
Wike, YW, 388
Wilberfoss, YE, 361
Wilbraham, Great, Ca, 24
Wilbraham, Little, Ca, 24
Wilbrighton, St, 282
Wilburton, Ca, 28
Wilby, Nf, 205
Wilby, Np, 217
Wilby, Sf, 288
Wilcot, Wlt, 335
Wilcote, Ox, 242
Wilden, Bd, 2
Wilderley, Sa, 252
Wildsworth, Li, 177
Wilford, Nt, 230
Wilford, hundred, Sf, 295
Wilkeby, Li, 182
Will Hall, Ha, 114
Willand, Dev, 56
Willaston, Ox, 237
Willen, Bk, 17
Willenhall, St, 283
Willenhall, Wa, 323
Willerby [in Dickering wap.], YE, 365
Willerby [in Harthill wap.], YE, 360
Willersey, Gl, 95
Willesden, Mx, 190
Willesley, Lei, 46
Willey, Wa, 323
Willey, Sa, 254
Willey, hundred, Bd, 2
Williamscot, Ox, 241
Willian, Hrt, 133
Willicote, Wa, 94
Willingale Doe, Ess, 82
Willingale Spain, Ess, 82

Willingdon, Sx, 314
Willingdon, hundred, Sx, 314
Willingham [in Papworth hd.], Ca, 25
Willingham [in Radfield hd.], Ca, 27
Willingham, Li, 178
Willingham, Nf, 208
Willingham, Sf, 289
Willingham, Cherry, Li, 178
Willingham, North, Li, 179
Willingham, South, Li, 181
Willington, Bd, 2
Willington, Db, 43
Willington, Wa, 320
Willingwick, Wo, 353
Willisham, Sf, 285
Willitoft, YE, 360
Williton, So, 265
Williton, hundred, So, 266
Willoughby [in Aswardhurn wap.], Li, 173
Willoughby [in Calcewath wap.], Li, 184
Willoughby [in Loveden wap.], Li, 174
Willoughby, Wa, 322
Willoughby on the Wolds, Nt, 230
Willoughby, Scott, Li, 170
Willoughby, Silk, Li, 173
Willoughby Waterless, Lei, 160
Willoughton, Li, 176
Willowes, Lei, 163
Willybrook, hundred, Np, 209, 213
Wilmastone, He, 128
Wilmcote, Wa, 326 n.
Wilmcote, Little, Wa, 327
Wilmington, Sa, 257
Wilmington, Sx, 315
Wilncote, Wa, 324
Wilne, Db, 44
Wilpshire, La, 153
Wilsford, Li, 172
Wilsford [in Swanborough hd.], Wlt, 335
Wilsford [in Underditch hd.], Wlt, 336
Wilshamstead, Bd, 3
Wilson, Lei, 161
Wilsthorpe, Db, 43
Wilsthorpe, Li, 169
Wilsthorpe, YE, 366
Wilstrop, YW, 385
Wilting, Sx, 317
Wilton, Cu, 40
Wilton, He, 126
Wilton, Nf, 204
Wilton [in Kinwardstone hd.], Wlt, 347
Wilton [near Salisbury], Wlt, 333
Wilton [in Langbargh wap.], YN, 375
Wilton [in Pickering lib.], YN, 381
Wilton, Bishop, YE, 361, 367
Wiltshire, 332–48
Wimbish, Ess, 86
Wimbledon, Sr, 302

Wimborne Minster, Do, 77
Wimborne St. Giles, Do, 72
Wimbotsham, Nf, 203
Wimpole, Ca, 26
Wincanton, So, 269
Winceby, Li, 185
Winch, East, Nf, 197
Winchcombe, Gl, 90, 91
Winchelsea, Sx, 304
Winchendon, Lower, Bk, 19
Winchendon, Upper, Bk, 19
Winchester, Ha, 105, 121
Winchester, soke, Ha, 105, 121
Winchfield, Ha, 113
Winderton, Wa, 321
Winderwath, We, 329
Windle, La, 151
Windle, Nf, 195
Windlesham, Sr, 299
Windley, Db, 43
Windridge, Hrt, 134
Windrush, Gl, 103
Windsor [New], Brk, 6, 14
Windsor, Old, Brk, 7
Windsor Underoure, Brk, 8
Winestead, YE, 360
Winfarthing, Nf, 207
Winford, So, 271
Winfrith, hundred, Do, 68
Winfrith Newburgh, Do, 68
Wing, Bk, 18
Wing, Ru, 246
Wingates, Nb, 222
Wingerworth, Db, 48
Wingfield, Sf, 288
Wingfield, South, Db, 48
Wingham, hundred, K, 142
Wingrave, Bk, 18
Winkburn, Nt, 231
Winkfield, Brk, 7
Winkleigh, Dev, 61
Winkleigh, hundred, Dev, 61
Winksley, YW, 384
Winkton, Ha, 107
Winkton, YE, 357
Winnall, Ha, 117
Winnersh, Brk, 7
Winnianton, Co, 31
Winnibriggs, wapentake, Li, 171
Winnington, Sa, 253
Winsbury, Sa, 256
Winscombe, So, 259
Winsford, So, 265
Winsham, So, 270
Winshill, St, 46, 276
Winslade, Ha, 118
Winsley, Wlt, 347
Winslow, Bk, 18
Winson, Gl, 98
Winsor, Ha, 115

Winstanley, La, 151
Winster, Db, 47
Winston, Nf, 195
Winston, Sf, 296
Winstone, Gl, 93
Winstree, hundred, Ess, 81
Winterborne Belet, Do, 72
Winterborne Clenston, Do, 73
Winterborne Herringston, Do, 72
Winterborne Houghton, Do, 75
Winterborne Kingston, Do, 68
Winterborne Monkton, Do, 72
Winterborne Muston, Do, 73
Winterborne St. Martin, Do, 68
Winterborne Stickland, Do, 75
Winterborne Whitechurch, Do, 73
Winterborne Zelston, Do, 77
Winterbourne, Brk, 9
Winterbourne, Gl, 94
Winterbourne Abbas, Do, 72
Winterbourne Bassett, Wlt, 339
Winterbourne Dauntsey, Wlt, 345
Winterbourne Earls, Wlt, 345
Winterbourne Gunner, Wlt, 345
Winterbourne Monkton, Wlt, 339
Winterbourne Steepleton, Do, 77
Winterbourne Stoke, Wlt, 341
Winteringham, Li, 175
Wintersett, YW, 392
Winterslow [East], Wlt, 346
Winterslow [West], Wlt, 345
Winterstoke, hundred, So, 259
Winterton, Li, 175, 186
Winterton on Sea, Nf, 193
Winthorpe, Li, 182
Winthorpe, Nt, 233
Winton, We, 328
Winton, YN, 378
Wintringham, Hu, 137
Wintringham, YE, 364
Winwick, Hu, 138
Winwick, Np, 216
Wirksworth, Db, 44
Wirksworth, wapentake, Db, 44
Wisbech, Ca, 28
Wisbech, hundred, Ca, 28
Wisborough, Green, Sx, 309
Wiseton, Nt, 227
Wishanger, Gl, 93
Wishaw, Wa, 325
Wishford, Great, Wlt, 342
Wishford, Little, Wlt, 342
Wisley, Sr, 299
Wispington, Li, 182
Wissett, Sf, 289
Wissington, Sf, 290
Wiston, Sx, 310
Wistow, Hu, 137
Wistow, Lei, 164
Wistow, YW, 386

Wiswell, La, 153
Witcham, Ca, 28
Witchampton, Do, 75
Witchford, Ca, 28
Witchford, hundred, Ca, 28
Witchingham, Great, Nf, 200
Witchingham, Little, Nf, 200
Witcomb, Wlt, 344
Witcombe, So, 274
Witcombe, Great, Gl, 97
Witcombe, Little, Gl, 97
Witham, Ess, 84
Witham, hundred, Ess, 84
Witham, North, Li, 171
Witham on the Hill, 170
Witham, South, Li, 171
Withcall, Li, 183
Withcote, Lei, 163
Witheridge, Dev, 54
Witheridge, hundred, Dev, 54
Withering, Sx, 305
Witherington, Wlt, 335
Witherley, Lei, 158
Withern, Li, 184
Withernsea, YE, 358
Withernwick, YE, 358, 369
Withersdale, Sf, 288
Withersfield, Sf, 294
Witherslack, We, 330
Withiel, Co, 32
Withiel Florey, So, 265
Withington, Gl, 98
Withington, He, 124
Withington, La, 154
Withington, Sa, 250
Withington, Eau, He, 124
Withnell, La, 155
Withybrook, Wa, 324
Withycombe, So, 272
Withycombe Raleigh, Dev, 65
Witley, Sr, 298
Witley, Little, Wo, 350
Witnesham, Sf, 296
Witney, Ox, 237
Wittenham, Little, Brk, 13
Wittenham, Long, Brk, 13
Wittering, Sx, 307
Witton, La, 153
Witton [in Blofield hd.], Nf, 194
Witton [in Tunstead hd.], Nf, 202
Witton, Wa, 325
Witton, Wo, 353
Witton, East, YN, 372
Witton, Nether, Nb, 222
Witton, West, YN, 372
Wiveliscombe, So, 270
Wivelridge, Sx, 317
Wivenhoe, Ess, 87
Wiverton, Nt, 232
Wiveton, Nf, 199

Wix, Ess, 88
Wixamtree, hundred, Bd, 2
Wixford, Wa, 326
Wixoe, Sf, 294
Woberneford, Dev, 57
Wodeford, Wa, 325 n.
Wokefield, Brk, 8
Woking, hundred, Sr, 299
Woking [Old], Sr, 299
Wokingham, Brk, 7
Wolborough, Dev, 50
Woldingham, Sr, 303
Wolebury, Ha, 107
Wolf Hall, Wlt, 347
Wolferlow, He, 123
Wolfeton, Do, 68
Wolf hampcote, Wa, 322
Wolford, Great, Wa, 321
Wolford, Little, Wa, 320
Wolfreton, YE, 360
Wollacombe, Dev, 53
Wollaston, Np, 212
Wollaston, Sa, 253
Wollaton, Nt, 229
Wollerton, Sa, 251
Wolphy, hundred, He, 130
Wolseley, St, 277
Wolstanton, St, 277
Wolston, Wa, 322
Wolstrop, Gl, 91 n.
Wolterton, Nf, 202
Wolvercote, Ox, 242
Wolverhampton, St, 283
Wolverley, Wo, 350
Wolverton, Bk, 17
Wolverton, Ha, 115
Wolverton, Wa, 326
Wolverton, Lower, Wo, 350 n.
Wolverton, Upper, Wo, 350 n.
Wolvey, Wa, 324
Wombleton, YN, 377, 379
Wombourn, St, 283
Wombwell, YW, 392
Womersley, YW, 391
Wonford, Dev, 58
Wonford, hundred, Dev, 57
Wonston, Ha, 108
Wooburn, Bk, 21
Wood, He, 123
Wood Enderby, Li, 184
Wood Hall, YE, 363
Woodadvent, So, 266
Woodbastwick, Nf, 195
Woodbeer, Dev, 63
Woodborough, Nt, 231
Woodborough, Wlt, 335
Woodbridge, Sf, 295
Woodburn, Nb, 221
Woodbury, Dev, 65
Woodchester, Gl, 96

Woodcoates, Nt, 231
Woodcote, Lei, 160
Woodcote, Ox, 243
Woodcote, Sa, 251
Woodcote, Sr, 300
Woodcote, Sx, 307
Woodcote, Wa, 323
Woodcote Green, Wo, 353
Woodcott, Ha, 112
Woodditton, Ca, 28
Woodeaton, Ox, 239
Wooden, Nb, 223
Woodend, Np, 211 n.
Woodford, Dev, 51
Woodford, Ess, 81
Woodford, Np, 214
Woodford, Wlt, 336
Woodford Halse, Np, 210
Woodford [Little], Wlt, 336
Woodgarston, Ha, 118
Woodham Ferrers, Ess, 85
Woodham Mortimer, Ess, 84
Woodham Walter, Ess, 84
Woodhay, East, Ha, 109
Woodhay, West, Brk, 10
Woodhill, Wlt, 344
Woodhorn, Nb, 222
Woodhouse, Lei, 162
Woodhouse, The, Sa, 256
Woodhuish, Dev, 50
Woodland, Dev, 55
Woodlands, Gl, 94
Woodleigh, Dev, 51
Woodley, Ha, 107 n.
Woodmancote [in Berkeley hd.], Gl, 96
Woodmancote [in Cleeve hd.], Gl, 93
Woodmancote [in Rapsgate hd.], Gl, 92
Woodmancote, Sx, 305
Woodmancott, Ha, 111, 112
Woodmansey, YE, 370
Woodmansterne, Sr, 300
Woodnewton, Np, 214
Woodperry, Ox, 239
Woodplumpton, La, 152
Woodrising, Nf, 205
Woodrow, Do, 74
Woodsford, Do, 68
Woodspeen, Brk, 9
Woodstock, Ox, 235, 245
Woodstock, Old, Ox, 244
Woodston, Hu, 138
Woodthorpe, Lei, 162
Woodthorpe, Li, 184
Woodton, Nf, 195
Wookey, So, 271
Wookey Hole, So, 271
Wool, Do, 68
Woolavington, So, 274
Woolavington, Sx, 308
Woolbeding, Sx, 306

Woolcombe, Do, 71
Wooler, Nb, 224
Woolfardisworthy, Dev, 54
Woolford's Mill, Gl, 101
Woolhampton, Brk, 8
Woolhope, He, 127
Woollaston, St, 282
Woolley, Brk, 9
Woolley, Hu, 138
Woolley, So, 261
Woolley, YW, 391
Woolmersdon, So, 260
Woolminstone, So, 273
Woolpit, Sf, 292
Woolscott, Wa, 322
Woolstaston, Sa, 252
Woolsthorpe [in Beltisloe wap.], Li, 171
Woolsthorpe [in Winnibriggs wap.], Li, 171
Woolston, Dev, 51
Woolston, Ess, 83
Woolston, La, 150
Woolstone, Brk, 10
Woolstone, Gl, 100
Woolstone, Great, Bk, 17
Woolstone, Little, Bk, 17
Woolton, Little, La, 150
Woolton, Much, 150
Woolvershill, So, 259
Woolverstone, Sf, 285
Woonton, He, 130
Wooperton, Nb, 224
Woore, Sa, 250
Wooton, Bd, 3
Wooton, hundred, Ox, 241
Wooton Rivers, Wlt, 347
Wooton Wawen, Wa, 326
Wootton, Brk, 12
Wootton [in East Medine hd.], Ha, 119
Wootton [in New Forest hd.], Ha, 116
Wootton, Li, 178
Wootton, Np, 217
Wootton, Ox, 244
Wootton, St, 281
Wootton Courtney, So, 272
Wootton, Glanvilles, Do, 74
Wootton, Hill, Wa, 323
Wootton, Leek, Wa, 323
Wootton, North, Do, 71
Wootton, North, So, 267
Wootton St. Lawrence, Ha, 116
Wootton, South, Nf, 197
Worcester, Wo, 349, 350
Worcestershire, 349–55
Wordwell, Sf, 293
Worfield, Sa, 256
Worgret, Do, 69
Workington, Cu, 40
Worksop, Nt, 229
Worlaby [in Hill wap.], Li, 185

Worlaby [in Yarborough wap.], Li, 179
Worldham, East, Ha, 114
Worldham, West, Ha, 114
Worle, So, 259
Worlingham, Sf, 289
Worlington, Dev, 53
Worlington, Sf, 293
Worlington, East, Dev, 54
Worlington, West, Dev, 54
Worlingworth, Sf, 288
Wormbridge, He, 127
Wormegay, Nf, 203
Wormelow, hundred, He, 125
Wormeton, He, 125
Wormhill, Db, 47
Wormhill, He, 127
Wormingford, Ess, 88
Worminghall, Bk, 20
Wormington, Gl, 98
Wormington Daston, Gl, 98
Wormington Grange, Gl, 98
Worminster, So, 271
Wormleighton, Wa, 321
Wormley, Hrt, 131
Wormsley, He, 124
Worplesdon, Sr, 299
Worsall, High, YN, 378
Worsall, Low, YN, 374
Worsborough, YW, 392
Worsley, La, 154
Worstead, Nf, 202
Worsthorne, La, 153
Worston, La, 153
Worth, Dev, 55
Worth, Sx, 312
Worth, hundred, K, 147
Worth Matravers, Do, 75
Wortham, Sf, 287
Worthele, Dev, 64
Worthen, Sa, 252
Worthington, La, 155
Worthington, Lei, 161
Worthy, Abbots, Ha, 112
Worthy, Headbourne, Ha, 115
Worthy, Kings, Ha, 115
Worthy, Martyr, Ha, 117
Worting, Ha, 116
Wortley [in Morley wap.], YW, 389
Wortley [in Staincross wap.], YW, 391
Worton, Ox, 242
Worton, Wlt, 340
Worton, Nether, Ox, 241, 242 n.
Worton, Over, Ox, 241
Wothersome, YW, 387
Wotherton, Sa, 256
Wotton [in Dudstone hd.], Gl, 97
Wotton [in Liberty of King's Barton], Gl, 91 n.
Wotton, Sr, 299

Wotton, hundred, Sr, 299
Wotton under Edge, Gl, 95
Wotton Underwood, Bk, 19
Woughton on the Green, Bk, 17
Wrabness, Ess, 88
Wrae, La, 151
Wragby, Li, 181
Wraggoe, wapentake, Li, 181
Wramplingham, Nf, 206
Wrandike, hundred, Ru, 247
Wrangbrook, YW, 391
Wrangle, Li, 169
Wrantage, So, 263
Wratting, Great, Sf, 294
Wratting, Little, Sf, 294
Wratting, West, Ca, 27
Wrawby, Li, 179
Wraxall, Do, 72
Wraxall, So, 271
Wraxall, North, Wlt, 344
Wraxall, South, Wlt, 347
Wray, La, 156
Wray Barton, Dev, 60
Wraysbury, Bk, 21
Wrayton, La, 156
Wreay, Cu, 40
Wrecclesham, Sr, 298
Wrelton, YN, 381
Wreningham, Nf, 206
Wrentham, Sf, 289
Wressle, YE, 362
Wrestlingworth, Bd, 2
Wretham, East, Nf, 205
Wretham, West, Nf, 205
Wretton, Nf, 203
Wrightington, La, 155
Wrington, So, 264
Writhlington, So, 262
Writtle, Ess, 85
Wrockwardine, Sa, 251
Wrotham, hundred, K, 144
Wrottesley, St, 283
Wroughton, Wlt, 340
Wroxall, Ha, 119
Wroxall, Wa, 325
Wroxeter, Sa, 251
Wroxham, Nf, 194
Wroxton, Ox, 243
Wyaston, Db, 45
Wyberton, Li, 168
Wyboston, Bd, 2
Wychbold, Wo, 352
Wychnor, St, 280
Wyck, Ha, 120
Wyckham, Sx, 310
Wyckham, West, Li, 183
Wycliffe, YN, 373
Wycombe, Lei, 161
Wycombe, High, Bk, 15, 22
Wycombe, High [Foreign], Bk, 21

Wycombe, West, Bk 21
Wyddial, Hrt, 133
Wydon, Nb, 220
Wye, hundred, K, 142
Wyfordby, Lei, 163
Wyham, Li, 180
Wyke, Ha, 109
Wyke, Wlt, 338
Wyke, YW, 388
Wyke Champflower, So, 269
Wyke Regis, Do, 77
Wyke, The, Sa, 256
Wykeham, Li, 178 n.
Wykeham [in Pickering lib.], YN, 381
Wykeham [in Ryedale wap.], YN, 377
Wykeham, East, Li, 183
Wyken, Wa, 323
Wykham, Ox, 241
Wykin, Lei, 160
Wylye, Wlt, 342
Wymering, Ha, 110
Wymersley, hundred, Np, 217
Wymeswold, Lei, 162
Wymington, Bd, 2
Wymondham, Lei, 163
Wymondham, Nf, 206
Wymondley, Great, Hrt, 133
Wymondley, Little, Hrt, 133
Wyndham, Sx, 311
Wyndham, half-hundred, Sx, 311, 312
Wynford Eagle, Do, 76
Wyrley, Great, St, 281
Wyrley, Little, St, 280
Wysall, Nt, 230
Wytham, Brk, 12
Wytheford, Great, Sa, 250
Wytheford, Little, Sa, 251
Wythemail, Np, 212
Wytlingham, Nf, 196
Wyton, Hu, 137
Wyton, YE, 359, 369
Wyverstone, Sf, 287
Wyville, Li, 171

Yaddlethorpe, Li, 186
Yafforth, YN, 374
Yanwath, We, 329
Yanworth, Gl, 98
Yapham, YE, 361
Yapton, Sx, 308
Yarborough, wapentake, Li, 178
Yarburgh, Li, 183
Yarcombe, Dev, 57
Yardley Gobion, Np, 211 n.
Yardley Hastings, Np, 217
Yardley hundred, Bk, 18
Yardley Wood, Wa, 353
Yarkhill, He, 128
Yarley, So, 271

Yarlington, So, 268
Yarm, YN, 374
Yarmouth, Ha, 120
Yarmouth, Great, Nf, 192, 198, 284
Yarnscombe, Dev, 61
Yarnton, Ox, 242
Yarwell, Np, 213
Yate, Gl, 102
Yateley, Ha, 109
Yatesbury, Wlt, 337
Yattendon, Brk, 8
Yatton, So, 259
Yatton Keynell, Wlt, 344
Yattone, Personat' de, So, 259
Yaverland, Ha, 119
Yawthorpe, Li, 177
Yaxham, Nf, 204
Yaxley, Hu, 138
Yaxley, Sf, 287
Yazor, He, 124
Yeadon, YW, 388
Yealand, La, 156
Yealmpstone, Dev, 51
Yealmpton, Dev, 51
Yearnor, So, 272
Yearsley, YN, 378
Yeaveley, Db, 45
Yeavering, Nb, 225
Yedbury, Dev, 55
Yedingham, YE, 364
Yeld, The, He, 129
Yelden, Bd, 4
Yeldersley, Db, 45
Yeldham, Great, Ess, 80
Yeldham, Little, Ess, 80
Yelling, Hu, 137
Yelvertoft, Np, 216
Yelverton, Nf, 196
Yen Hall, Ca, 27
Yeoford, Dev, 54
Yeoveney, Mx, 189
Yeovil, So, 262
Yeovilton, So, 263
Yetlington, Nb, 223
Yetminster, Do, 71
Yetminster, hundred, Do, 71
Yeuenhale, Wo, 350 n.
Yockleton, Sa, 253
Yokefleet, YE, 362
York, 357, 395
York, Liberty of the Blessed Mary, YE, 366
York, Liberty of St. Mary, YW, 387
Yorkshire, East Riding, 356, 357–70
Yorkshire, North Riding, 356, 357, 371–82
Yorkshire, West Riding, 356, 357, 382–95
Yorton, Sa, 251
Youlgreave, Db, 47

Youlthorpe, YE, 362
Youlton, YN, 376
Younsmere, hundred, Sx, 312
Yoxall, St, 280
Yoxford, Sf, 289

Yuoreston, He, 125

Zeal Monachorum, Dev, 67
Zeals, Wlt, 334
Zennor, Co, 30